'Diverse criminologists critically update readers on "glocal" green harms including climate change, crimes against animals and e-waste. In analyzing new(er) green problems such as medical waste, fracking and food crime, the authors demonstrate how rapidly green criminological boundaries are advancing to attend to the intricate and dynamic complexities of human–environment relationships.'

Meredith Gore, *Michigan State University, USA*

'This is an excellent follow-up to the first edition of the *Handbook* and one that again brings together leading scholars in the field of green criminology. This expanded second edition of the *Handbook* illustrates the rapid growth and importance of the subdiscipline. It provides a broad tour de horizon that does justice to the richness of green criminological thinking and research. The book will help to inspire students and scholars around the world to delve deeper into specific subjects and thereby contribute to understanding and reducing the problems of environmental crimes and harm.'

Toine Spapens, *Tilburg University, the Netherlands*

'This book provides valuable insights and theoretical discussions into the world of environmental crime. Recommended for scholars, students, researchers and anyone interested in understanding crimes against nature and wildlife, this handbook will certainly inspire future work in green criminology.'

Rebecca Wong, *City University of Hong Kong*

Routledge International Handbook of Green Criminology

The *Routledge International Handbook of Green Criminology* was the first comprehensive and international anthology dedicated to green criminology. It presented green criminology to an international audience, described the state of the field, offered a description of a range of environmental issues of regional and global importance, and argued for continued criminological attention to environmental crimes and harms, setting an agenda for further study.

In the six years since its publication, the field has continued to grow and thrive. This revised and expanded second edition of the *Handbook* reflects new methodological orientations, new locations of study, such as Asia, Canada and South America, and new responses to environmental harms. While a number of the original chapters have been revised, the second edition offers a range of fresh chapters covering new and emerging areas of study, such as:

- conservation criminology,
- eco-feminism,
- environmental victimology,
- fracking,
- migration and eco-rights, and
- e-waste.

This handbook continues to define and capture the field of green criminology and is essential reading for students and researchers engaged in green crime and environmental harm.

Avi Brisman (MFA, JD, PhD) is an Associate Professor in the School of Justice Studies at Eastern Kentucky University (Richmond, KY, USA), an Adjunct Associate Professor in the School of Justice at Queensland University of Technology (Brisbane, Queensland, Australia), and a Conjoint Associate Professor at Newcastle Law School at the University of Newcastle (Callaghan, New South Wales, Australia). He is also Editor-in-Chief of *Critical Criminology: An International Journal.*

Nigel South is Professor of Sociology and Director of the Centre for Criminology, University of Essex; Honorary Visiting Professor, School of Law and Social Sciences, University of Suffolk; and a visiting Adjunct Professor at the Crime and Justice Research Centre, Queensland University of Technology. He is a Fellow of the UK Academy of Social Sciences.

Routledge International Handbooks

Routledge International Handbook of Poverty
Edited by Bent Greve

Routledge International Handbook of New Digital Practices in Galleries, Libraries, Archives, Museums and Heritage Sites
Edited by Hannah Lewi, Wally Smith, Dirk vom Lehn and Steven Cooke

Routledge International Handbook of Human Trafficking
A Multi-Disciplinary and Applied Approach
Edited by Rochelle L. Dalla and Donna Sabella

The Routledge Handbook of Comparative Rural Policy
Edited by Matteo Vittuari, John Devlin, Marco Pagani and Thomas Johnson

Routledge International Handbook of Masculinity Studies
Edited by Lucas Gottzén, Ulf Mellström and Tamara Shefer

Routledge Handbook of European Welfare Systems 2e
Edited by Sonja Blum, Johanna Kuhlmann and Klaus Schubert

Routledge International Handbook of Heterosexualities Studies
Edited by James Joseph Dean and Nancy L. Fischer

Routledge Handbook of Contemporary European Social Movements
Protest in Turbulent Times
Edited by Cristina Flesher Fominaya and Ramón A. Feenstra

The Routledge International Handbook of Military Psychology and Mental Health
Edited by Updesh Kumar

Routledge International Handbook of Green Criminology 2e
Edited by Avi Brisman and Nigel South

For more information about this series, please visit: www.routledge.com/Routledge-International-Handbooks/book-series/RIHAND

Routledge International Handbook of Green Criminology

Second Edition

Edited by Avi Brisman and Nigel South

Routledge
Taylor & Francis Group
LONDON AND NEW YORK

First published 2012 by Routledge
Second edition published 2020 by Routledge

2 Park Square, Milton Park, Abingdon, Oxon OX14 4RN
605 Third Avenue, New York, NY 10017

Routledge is an imprint of the Taylor & Francis Group, an informa business

First issued in paperback 2022

Publisher's Note

The publisher has gone to great lengths to ensure the quality of this reprint but points out that some imperfections in the original copies may be apparent.

British Library Cataloguing-in-Publication Data
A catalogue record for this book is available from the British Library

Library of Congress Cataloging-in-Publication Data
A catalog record has been requested for this book

ISBN: 978-1-138-63380-3 (hbk)
ISBN: 978-1-03-233640-4 (pbk)
DOI: 10.4324/9781315207094

Typeset in Bembo
by Swales & Willis, Exeter, Devon, UK

Contents

Figures

Tables

Contributors

Robert Agnew is Samuel Candler Dobbs Professor of Sociology, Emeritus, at Emory University and now resides in Brevard, North Carolina, United States.

Kellie Alexander is a doctoral student in the Department of Sociology at Colorado State University in Fort Collins, Colorado, United States.

Tammy Ayres is a Lecturer in Criminology in the School of Criminology at the University of Leicester in Leicester, United Kingdom.

Kimberly L. Barrett is an Associate Professor in the Department of Sociology, Anthropology and Criminology, and affiliated faculty, Environmental Science and Society program, at Eastern Michigan University in Ypsilanti, Michigan, United States.

Lieselot Bisschop is an Assistant Professor in the Department of Criminology and the Erasmus Initiative on Dynamics of Inclusive Prosperity at Erasmus University Rotterdam in Rotterdam, the Netherlands.

Tim Boekhout van Solinge works as an independent international consultant and criminologist, based in Amsterdam, the Netherlands. He also is research fellow in the Department of Criminology of Erasmus University Rotterdam in Rotterdam, the Netherlands.

Elizabeth A. Bradshaw is an Associate Professor in the Department of Sociology, Anthropology and Social Work at Central Michigan University, Mount Pleasant, Michigan, United States.

Avi Brisman is an Associate Professor in the School of Justice Studies at Eastern Kentucky University in Richmond, Kentucky, United States, an Adjunct Associate Professor in the School of Justice at Queensland University of Technology in Brisbane, Queensland, Australia, and a Conjoint Associate Professor at Newcastle Law School at the University of Newcastle in Callaghan, New South Wales, Australia. He is also Editor-in-Chief of Critical Criminology: An International Journal.

Christina Burton is a doctoral student in the Department of Criminal Justice in the College of Community Innovation and Education at the University of Central Florida in Orlando, Florida, United States.

Sarah Coulthard is a Senior Lecturer in International Development at Northumbria University in Newcastle upon Tyne, United Kingdom.

Devin Cowan is a doctoral student in the Department of Criminal Justice in the College of Community Innovation and Education at the University of Central Florida in Orlando, Florida, United States.

Nikhil Deb is a Lecturer in the Department of Sociology at the University of Tennessee in Knoxville, Tennessee, United States. Previously, he was an Assistant Professor of Sociology at the Shahjalal University of Science and Technology in Sylhet, Bangladesh.

Jacquelynn Doyon-Martin is an Associate Professor in the School of Criminal Justice in the College of Community and Public Service at Grand Valley State University in Grand Rapids, Michigan, United States.

Louise du Toit is a Senior Researcher with the Global Risk Governance Programme at the University of Cape Town in Cape Town, South Africa, and a Postdoctoral Fellow in the Law Faculty at North-West University in Potchefstroom, South Africa.

Katja Eman is an Associate Professor in the Faculty of Criminal Justice and Security at the University of Maribor in Ljubljana, Slovenia.

Johanna Espin is a Professor in the Center of Security and Defense at the Institute of Higher National Studies (IAEN) in Quito, Ecuador.

Jeff Ferrell is a Professor in the Department of Sociology and Anthropology at Texas Christian University in Fort Worth, Texas, United States, and a Visiting Professor in the School of Social Policy, Sociology and Social Research (SSPSSR) at the University of Kent in Canterbury, United Kingdom.

Amy J. Fitzgerald is an Associate Professor in the Department of Sociology, Anthropology & Criminology and cross-appointed to the Great Lakes Institute for Environmental Research (GLIER) at the University of Windsor in Windsor, Ontario, Canada.

David Rodríguez Goyes is a post-doctoral researcher in the Department of Criminology and Sociology of Law at the University of Oslo in Oslo, Norway.

Matthew Hall is a Professor of Law & Criminal Justice at Lincoln Law School in the College of Social Science at the University of Lincoln in Lincoln, United Kingdom.

Diane Heckenberg, formerly of the University of Tasmania, Hobart, Tasmania, Australia, is co-author, with Rob White, of *Green Criminology: An Introduction to the Study of Environmental Harm* (Routledge, 2014).

James Heydon is an Assistant Professor in Criminology at the University of Nottingham in Nottingham, United Kingdom. He is also the Chair of the British Society of Criminology's Green Criminology Research Network.

Cameron Holley is a Professor at UNSW Law at the University of New South Wales in Sydney, New South Wales, Australia.

Melissa L. Jarrell is Dean of the University College and a Professor in the Department of Criminal Justice at Texas A&M University-Corpus Christi in Corpus Christi, Texas, United States.

Kelly Johnson is a Sociology PhD researcher specializing in 3D wellbeing, and social and environmental harms at the School of Arts, Design and Social Science at Northumbria University in Newcastle upon Tyne, United Kingdom.

Ronald C. Kramer is a Professor in the Department of Sociology and a former Director of the Criminal Justice program at Western Michigan University, Kalamazoo, Michigan, United States.

Jack Adam Lampkin received his PhD from Lincoln Law School in the College of Social Science at the University of Lincoln in Lincoln, United Kingdom.

Michael A. Long is an Associate Professor in the Department of Sociology at Oklahoma State University in Stillwater, Oklahoma, United States.

Michael J. Lynch is a Professor in the Department of Criminology in the College of Behavioral and Community Sciences at the University of South Florida in Tampa, Florida, United States.

Jennifer Maher is a Senior Lecturer at the Centre for Criminology in the School of Social Sciences of the Faculty of Business and Society at the University of South Wales in Cardiff, Wales, United Kingdom.

KuoRay Mao is an Assistant Professor in the Department of Sociology in the College of Liberal Arts at Colorado State University in Fort Collins, Colorado, United States.

Jordan E. Mazurek is a doctoral student in the School of Social Policy, Sociology and Social Research (SSPSSR) at the University of Kent in Canterbury, United Kingdom.

Bill McClanahan is an Assistant Professor in the School of Justice Studies of the College of Justice and Safety at Eastern Kentucky University in Richmond, Kentucky, United States.

Gorazd Meško is a Professor in the Faculty of Criminal Justice and Security at the University of Maribor in Ljubljana, Slovenia.

William Moreto is an Associate Professor in the Department of Criminal Justice in the College of Community Innovation and Education at the University of Central Florida in Orlando, Florida, United States.

Lorenzo Natali is a Researcher in Criminology at the School of Law of the University of Milano-Bicocca, Milan, Italy.

Angus Nurse is an Associate Professor and Deputy Head of the Department of Criminology and Sociology at Middlesex University School of Law at Middlesex University in London, United Kingdom.

Cassandra O'Neill was awarded Criminology BSc and MA in Criminology and Criminal Justice from Northumbria University in Newcastle upon Tyne, United Kingdom.

Tara Opsal is an Associate Professor in the Department of Sociology at Colorado State University in Fort Collins, Colorado, United States.

Joshua Ozymy is a Professor in the Department of Political Science and Director of the Honors Program at Texas A&M University-Corpus Christi in Corpus Christi, Texas, United States.

David N. Pellow is Professor and Dehlsen Chair in the Environmental Studies Program at the University of California, Santa Barbara, in Santa Barbara, California, United States.

Liam Phelan is a Senior Lecturer in the School of Environmental and Life Sciences in the Faculty of Science at the University of Newcastle in Callaghan, New South Wales, Australia.

Justin Piché is an Associate Professor in the Department of Criminology and Director of the Carceral Studies Research Collective at the University of Ottawa in Ottawa, Ontario, Canada.

Harriet Pierpoint is an Associate Professor at the Centre for Criminology in the School of Social Sciences of the Faculty of Business and Society at the University of South Wales in Cardiff, Wales, United Kingdom.

Vincenzo Ruggiero is a Professor in the Department of Criminology and Sociology and Director of the Social and Criminological Research Centre at Middlesex University School of Law at Middlesex University in London, United Kingdom.

Siv Rebekka Runhovde is a researcher at the Department of Research at the Norwegian Police University College in Oslo, Norway.

Tameka Samuels-Jones is a Ruth D. Peterson Fellow for the American Society of Criminology. She holds a PhD in Criminology, Law & Society from the University of Florida in Gainesville, Florida, United States.

Judah Schept is an Associate Professor in the School of Justice Studies in the College of Justice and Safety at Eastern Kentucky University in Richmond, Kentucky, United States.

Yan Shan is a PhD candidate in the Department of Sociology in the College of Liberal Arts at Colorado State University in Fort Collins, Colorado, United States.

Clifford Shearing is a Professor in the Department of Public Law at the University of Cape Town in Cape Town, South Africa, a Professor in the School of Criminology and Criminal Justice at Griffith University in Mount Gravatt, Queensland, Australia, an Adjunct Professor in the School of Criminology at the University of Montreal in Montreal, Quebec, Canada, and a Visiting Professorial Fellow at UNSW Law in the University of New South Wales in Sydney, New South Wales, Australia.

Tara O'Connor Shelley is a Professor in the School of Criminology, Criminal Justice and Strategic Studies at Tarleton State University in Fort Worth, Texas, United States.

Damien Short is Director of the Human Rights Consortium (HRC) and a Reader in Human Rights at the School of Advanced Study of the University of London in London, United Kingdom.

Ragnhild Sollund is a Professor in the Department of Criminology and Sociology of Law at the University of Oslo, Norway.

Nigel South is a Professor of Sociology and Director of the Centre for Criminology at the University of Essex in Colchester, Essex, United Kingdom, an Honorary Visiting Professor in the School of Law and Social Sciences, University of Suffolk in Suffolk, United Kingdom, and a visiting Adjunct Professor at the Crime and Justice Research Centre at Queensland University of Technology in Brisbane, Queensland, Australia. He is also a Fellow of the UK Academy of Social Sciences.

Paul B. Stretesky is a Professor and Research Lead in the Department of Social Sciences at Northumbria University, Newcastle upon Tyne, United Kingdom.

Staci Strobl is an Associate Professor and Assistant Dean at the University of Wisconsin-Platteville in Platteville, Wisconsin, United States.

Ryan Thomson is an Assistant Professor in the Department of Agricultural Economics and Rural Sociology at Auburn University in Auburn, Alabama, United States.

Wesley Tourangeau is an Assistant Professor in the Department of Criminology at Saint Mary's University in Halifax, Nova Scotia, Canada.

Wim van Herk received a master's degree from the Willem Pompe Institute for Criminal Law and Criminology in the Faculty of Law, Economics and Governance at Utrecht University in Utrecht, the Netherlands.

Daan van Uhm is Assistant Professor at the Willem Pompe Institute for Criminal Law and Criminology in the Faculty of Law, Economics and Governance at Utrecht University in Utrecht, the Netherlands.

Julie Viollaz is the Wildlife Crime Research Officer for the Crime Research Section of the United Nations Office on Drugs and Crime.

Reece Walters is a Professor in the School of Humanities and Social Sciences in the Faculty of Arts and Education at Deakin University in Waurn Ponds, Victoria, Australia.

Rob White is a Professor in the School of Social Sciences at the University of Tasmania in Hobart, Tasmania, Australia.

Tanya Wyatt is a Professor in the Department of Social Sciences at Northumbria University in Newcastle upon Tyne, United Kingdom.

Zhong Zhao is an LLM candidate in the Faculty of Law at the University of Hong Kong in Hong Kong SAR, China, and the Chairman of the Board of the Gansu "Green Camel Bell" Environment Protection and Development Center in Lanzhou, Gansu, China.

Yiliang Zhu is a Professor and the Biostatistics, Epidemiology, and Research Design Director in the UNM Health Services Center in the School of Medicine at the University of New Mexico in Albuquerque, New Mexico, United States.

The Wrinkled Rhinoceros (2015)

There are two kinds of rhinos,
black and white.
Rhinos charge toward you with
lots of might.
Poachers sell the rhino's horns
for Asian medicine,
Rhinos need their horns
to go with their wrinkled skin.
Yes, rhinos have very wrinkled skin,
It would not hurt if they were stuck by a pin!
There are about 3,000 Black Rhinos
left in the wild,
Did you know that rhino's tempers are really mild?
Several rhinos are called a crash,
They can run past you in a flash!

Sam Quintero, age 7

The Rising Rhino (2019)

Charging with its sharp horns,
Living in the hot savanna,
Winning in a battle,
Growing a new horn
when it falls off in a battle,
Moving really slowly,
Eating leaves every day,
It's tough being an endangered rhino
My horns getting cut off
by poachers for medicine,
Ouch!

Brady Nahra, age 7

Preface to the second edition of the *Routledge International Handbook of Green Criminology*

Avi Brisman and Nigel South

The first edition of the *Routledge International Handbook of Green Criminology* (the '*Handbook*'), published in 2013, was the first comprehensive and international anthology dedicated to green criminology. While a couple of readers (South and Beirne 2006; White 2009), a few short edited volumes (Beirne and South 2007; Sollund 2008; White 2010) and a handful of monographs (Beirne 2009; Burns, Lynch and Stretesky 2008; Walters 2011; White 2008, 2011) had appeared prior to the publication of the *Handbook*, none offered the same breadth and depth with respect to substantive issues, methodological concerns and case studies.

The *Handbook* was divided into six Parts:

I History, theory and methods (5 chapters)
II International and transnational issues for a green criminology (6 chapters)
III Region-specific problems: some case studies (3 chapters)
IV Relationships in green criminology: environment and economy (4 chapters)
V Relationships in green criminology: humans and non-human species (3 chapters)
VI Relationships in green criminology: environment and culture (4 chapters).

The goal of the volume was twofold. First, it intended to present green criminology to an international audience, describe the state of the perspective to date, and offer a description of a range of environmental issues of regional and global importance that had been explored by criminologists of different theoretical orientations. Second, the volume hoped to be prospective—to argue for continued criminological attention to environmental crimes and harms and to set an agenda for further study.

Overall, the volume was prodigiously well-received (see, e.g., Buckle 2015; Eman 2013; Jarrell 2014; Potter 2014; Westerhuis 2014). And in the years since the publication of the *Handbook*, green criminology has exploded. The Economic and Social Research Council (ESRC) Green Criminology Research Seminar Series was held from 2012–2014—a series that consisted of six conferences/seminars at various institutions in the United Kingdom, attended by an international audience. Two new book series have been developed: *Green Criminology* (https://www.routledge.com/Green-Criminology/book-series/GREENCRIM)

and *Palgrave Studies in Green Criminology* (www.palgrave.com/gp/series/14622). Special journal issues on green criminology have been published in *Crime, Law and Social Change* (Volume 59, Issue 3, 2013); *Critical Criminology: An International Journal* (Volume 23, Issue 4, 2015; Volume 25, Issue 1, 2017); the *International Journal of Crime, Justice and Social Democracy* (Volume 3, Issue 2, 2014; Volume 8, Issue 3, 2019); *Revista Crítica Penal y Poder* [*Criminal Criticism and Power*] (Número 16, Marzo-Abril, 2019); and *Theoretical Criminology* (Volume 22, Issue 4, 2018). Research and scholarship in green criminology has continued to blossom with a healthy range of: monographs on both green criminology in general (e.g., Hall 2015; Lynch and Stretesky 2014) and particular environmental issues or approaches (e.g., Beirne 2015; Bisschop 2015; Brisman and South 2014; Cao 2017; Cianchi 2015; Hall 2013; Mol 2017; Natali 2016; Nurse 2013, 2015; Schally 2018; Stretesky, Long and Lynch 2014; Sollund 2018; White 2013; White and Pink 2016; Wong, M. T. 2019; Wong, R. W. Y., 2019; Wyatt 2013); edited volumes on specific issues (e.g., Arroyo-Quiroz and Wyatt 2018; Brisman, South and White 2015; Ellefsen, Sollund and Larsen 2012; Goyes et al. 2017; Lemieux 2014; Lynch and Pires 2019; Maas et al. 2013; Moreto 2018; Sollund, Stefes and Germani 2016; Walters, Westerhuis and Wyatt 2013; White 2012) or from certain conferences (e.g., Hall et al. 2017; Sollund 2015; Potter, Nurse and Hall 2016; Spapens, White and Kluin 2014; Spapens, White and Huisman 2016; Spapens et al. 2018); and textbooks (e.g., Nurse 2016; White and Heckenberg 2014).

In addition, green criminology now has its own 'stream' or 'sub-area' at the Annual Meeting of the American Society of Criminology (ASC), the first one being coordinated by one of the co-editors of this volume (Nigel South), and members of the International Green Criminology Working Group (IGCWG; https://greencriminology.org/) meet at ASC on a yearly basis. In January 2019, the British Society of Criminology launched the Green Criminology Research Network (www.britsoccrim.org/networks/greencrime/), chaired by Dr. James Heydon, one of the contributors to this second edition of the *Handbook*. Finally, green criminology is now offered as an undergraduate, masters or doctoral level course, module or unit in a number of universities in Australia, Europe and the United States, meaning that a new generation of scholars is being trained in the criminological study of environmental crimes and harms.

To date, however, no volume has attempted to mirror or otherwise replicate the range and originality of the first edition of the *Handbook*. While many of the chapters in the first edition have remained highly influential, others have become slightly dated, owing in part to work building on the initial contributions in that first edition of this *Handbook*. In order to ensure the continued relevance of the volume, while at the same time reflecting recent developments in methodology and theory, we have developed this second edition.

Taking into account some of the suggestions offered by reviewers of the first edition (e.g., Jarrell 2014), the goals of this second edition are fourfold:

1 to update those chapters that have been particularly significant for the continued emergence and development of the field;
2 to replace those chapters based on empirical data now several years out of date with new work by emerging scholars;
3 to include new chapters reflecting new methodological orientations (e.g., situational prevention of wildlife crime), new locations of study (e.g., in Asia, in South America), and responses to environmental harms (e.g., activism, resistance); and
4 to offer readers a more sophisticated analysis of ongoing environmental issues of green criminological concern (e.g., animal abuse, climate change).

All in all, the second edition of the *Handbook* contains 31 new chapters, bringing the total number of chapters from 27 (including an Introduction and Conclusion) to 40 (including an Introduction and Conclusion).

References

Arroyo-Quiroz, Ines, and Tanya Wyatt, eds. 2018. *Green Crime in Mexico*. London: Palgrave Macmillan.

Beirne, Piers. 2009. *Confronting Animal Abuse: Law, Criminology, and Human-Animal Relationships*. Lanham, MD: Rowman & Littlefield.

Beirne, Piers. 2015. *Hogarth's Art of Animal Cruelty: Satire, Suffering and Pictorial Propaganda*. Basingstoke, Hampshire, UK: Palgrave Macmillan.

Beirne, Piers, and Nigel South, eds. 2007. *Issues in Green Criminology: Confronting Harms against Environments, Humanity and Other Animals*. Cullompton, Devon, UK: Willan.

Bisschop, Lieselot. 2015. *Governance of the Illegal Trade in E-Waste and Tropical Timber: Case Studies on Transnational Environmental Crime*. Surrey, UK: Ashgate.

Brisman, Avi, and Nigel South. 2014. *Green Cultural Criminology: Constructions of Environmental Harm, Consumerism, and Resistance to Ecocide*. Abingdon, Oxon, UK: Routledge.

Brisman, Avi, Nigel South, and Rob White, eds. 2015. *Environmental Crime and Social Conflict: Contemporary and Emerging Issues*. Surrey, UK: Ashgate.

Buckle, Jo. 2015. Book Reviews: Green Cultural Criminology: Constructions of Environmental Harm, Consumerism, and Resistance to Ecocide Brisman A and South N (2014). Routledge; 162pp. ISBN 979-0415630740 (pbk). Routledge International Handbook of Green Criminology South N and Brisman A (eds) (2014). Routledge; 448pp. ISBN 978-1138846692 (pbk). *Scottish Justice Matters* 3(1) [March]: 39–40. Accessed at: http://scottishjusticematters.com/wp-content/uploads/SJM_3_1_Mar2015_LoRes.pdf AND http://scottishjusticematters.com/wp-content/uploads/Pages-from-SJM_3_1_Mar2015-Book Reviews.pdf.

Burns, Ronald G., Michael J. Lynch, and Paul Stretesky. 2008. *Environmental Law, Crime, and Justice*. New York: LFB.

Cao, Ngoc Ahn. 2017. *Timber Trafficking in Vietnam: Crime, Security and the Environment*. London: Palgrave Macmillan.

Cianchi, John. 2015. *Radical Environmentalism: Nature, Identity and More-than-human Agency*. Basingstoke, Hampshire, UK: Palgrave Macmillan.

Ellefsen, Rune, Ragnhild Sollund, and Guri Larsen, eds. 2012. *Eco-global Crimes: Contemporary Problems and Future Challenges*. Surrey, UK: Ashgate.

Eman, Katja. 2013. Nigel South in Avi Brisman (ur.), Routledge International Handbook of Green Criminology (Mednarodni priročnik o ekološki kriminologiji založbe Routledge). *Revija za kriminalistiko in kriminologijo [Magazine of Criminalistics and Criminology]* 64(2): 204–205. Accessed at: www.policija.si/images/stories/Publikacije/RKK/PDF/2013/02/RKK2013-02_Recenzije.pdf.

Goyes, David Rodríguez, Hanneke Mol, Avi Brisman, and Nigel South, eds. 2017. *Environmental Crime in Latin America: The Theft of Nature and the Poisoning of the Land*. London: Palgrave Macmillan.

Hall, Matthew. 2013. *Victims of Environmental Harm: Rights, Recognition and Redress under National and International Law*. London and New York: Routledge.

Hall, Matthew. 2015. *Exploring Green Crime: Introducing the Legal, Social and Criminological Contexts of Environmental Harm*. Basingstoke, Hampshire, UK: Palgrave Macmillan.

Hall, Matthew, Jennifer Maher, Angus Nurse, Gary Potter, Nigel South, and Tanya Wyatt, eds. 2017. *Greening Criminology in the 21st Century: Contemporary Debates and Future Directions in the Study of Environmental Harm*. Abingdon, Oxon, UK: Routledge.

Jarrell, Melissa. 2014. Book Review: Nigel South and Avi Brisman (eds), Routledge International Handbook of Green Criminology. *Theoretical Criminology* 17(4): 585–588.

Lemieux, AM, ed. 2014. *Situational Prevention of Poaching*. London and New York: Routledge.

Lynch, Michael J., and Stephen F. Pires, eds. 2019. *Quantitative Studies in Green and Conservation Criminology: The Measurement of Environmental Harm and Crime*. Abingdon, Oxon, UK: Routledge.

Lynch, Michael J., and Paul B. Stretesky. 2014. *Exploring Green Criminology: Toward a Green Criminological Revolution*. Surrey, UK: Ashgate.

Maas, Achim, Balázs Bodó, Clementine Burnley, Irina Comardicea, and Roger Roffey, eds. 2013. *Global Environmental Change: New Drivers for Resistance, Crime and Terrorism?* Baden-Baden, Germany: Nomos Verlagsgesellschaft.

Mol, Hanneke. 2017. *The Politics of Palm Oil Harm: A Green Criminological Perspective*. London: Palgrave Macmillan.

Moreto, William D. ed. 2018. *Wildlife Crime: From Theory to Practice*. Philadelphia, PA: Temple University Press.

Natali, Lorenzo. 2016. *A Visual Approach for Green Criminology: Exploring the Social Perception of Environmental Harm*. London: Palgrave Macmillan.

Nurse, Angus. 2013. *Animal Harm: Perspectives on Why People Harm and Kill Animals*. Surrey, UK: Ashgate.

Nurse, Angus. 2015. *Policing Wildlife: Perspectives on the Enforcement of Wildlife Legislation*. Basingstoke, Hampshire, UK: Palgrave Macmillan.

Nurse, Angus. 2016. *An Introduction to Green Criminology & Environmental Justice*. Thousand Oaks, CA: SAGE.

Potter, Gary R. 2014. Book Review: Nigel South & Avi Brisman (eds.), Routledge Handbook of Green Criminology. *Journal of Qualitative Criminal Justice and Criminology* 2(2): 309–311. Accessed at: www.jqcjc.org/documents/v2i2.pdf#page=127.

Potter, Gary R., Angus Nurse, and Matthew Hall, eds. 2016. *The Geography of Environmental Crime: Conservation, Wildlife Crime and Environmental Activism*. Basingstoke, Hampshire, UK: Palgrave Macmillan.

Schally, Jennifer L. 2018. *Legitimizing Corporate Harm: The Discourse of Contemporary Agribusiness*. London: Palgrave Macmillan.

Sollund, Ragnhild, ed. 2008. *Global Harms: Ecological Crime and Speciesism*. New York: Nova Science.

Sollund, Ragnhild Aslaug, ed. 2015. *Green Harms and Crimes: Critical Criminology in a Changing World*. Basingstoke, Hampshire, UK: Palgrave Macmillan.

Sollund, Ragnhild Aslaug. 2018. *The Crimes of Wildlife Trafficking: Issues of Justice, Legality and Morality*. Abingdon, Oxon, UK: Routledge.

Sollund, Ragnhild, Christoph H. Stefes, and Rita Germani, eds. 2016. *Fighting Environmental Crime in Europe and Beyond: The Role of the EU and Its Member States*. London: Palgrave Macmillan.

South, Nigel, and Piers Beirne. 2006. *Green Criminology*. Aldershot, UK: Ashgate.

South, Nigel, and Avi Brisman, eds. 2013. *Routledge International Handbook of Green Criminology*, first edition. Abingdon, Oxon, UK: Routledge.

Spapens, Toine, Rob White, and Wim Huisman, eds. 2016. *Environmental Crime in Transnational Context: Global Issues in Green Enforcement and Criminology*. Abingdon, Oxon, UK: Routledge.

Spapens, Toine, Rob White, and Marieke Kluin, eds. 2014. *Environmental Crime and Its Victims: Perspectives within Green Criminology*. Surrey, UK: Ashgate.

Spapens, Toine, Rob White, Daan van Uhm, and Wim Huisman, eds. 2018. *Green Crimes and Dirty Money*. Abingdon, Oxon, UK: Routledge.

Stretesky, Paul, Michael A. Long, and Michael J. Lynch. 2014. *The Treadmill of Crime: Political Economy and Green Criminology*. London and New York: Routledge.

Walters, Reece. 2011. *Eco Crime and Genetically Modified Food*. Abingdon, Oxon, UK: Routledge.

Walters, Reece, Diane Solomon Westerhuis, and Tanya Wyatt, eds. 2013. *Emerging Issues in Green Criminology: Exploring Power, Justice and Harm*. Basingstoke, Hampshire, UK: Palgrave Macmillan.

Westerhuis, Diane Solomon. 2014. South, Nigel & Avi Brisman (eds): Routledge International Handbook of Green Criminology. *Critical Criminology: An International Journal* 22(1): 159–161.

White, Rob. 2008. *Crimes against Nature: Environmental Criminology and Ecological Justice*. Cullompton, Devon, UK: Willan.

White, Rob, ed. 2009. *Environmental Crime: A Reader*. Cullompton, Devon, UK: Willan.

White, Rob, ed. 2010. *Global Environmental Harm: Criminological Perspectives*. Cullompton, Devon, UK: Willan.

White, Rob. 2011. *Transnational Environmental Crime: Toward an Eco-global Criminology*. Abingdon, Oxon, UK: Routledge.

White, Rob, ed. 2012. *Climate Change from a Criminological Perspective*. New York: Springer.

White, Rob. 2013. *Environmental Harm: An Eco-justice Perspective*. Bristol, UK: Policy Press.

White, Rob, and Diane Heckenberg. 2014. *Green Criminology: An Introduction to the Study of Environmental Harm*. London and New York: Routledge.

White, Rob, and Grant Pink. 2016. *Environmental Crime and Collaborative State Intervention*. Basingstoke, Hampshire, UK: Palgrave Macmillan.

Wong, Marcela Torres. 2019a. *Natural Resources, Extraction and Indigenous Rights in Latin America: Exploring the Boundaries of Environmental and State-Corporate Crime in Bolivia, Peru, and Mexico*. Abingdon, Oxon, UK: Routledge.

Wong, Rebecca W.Y. 2019b. *The Illegal Wildlife Trade in China: Understanding the Distribution Networks*. London: Palgrave.

Wyatt, Tanya. 2013. *Wildlife Trafficking: A Deconstruction of the Crime, the Victims and the Offenders*. Basingstoke, Hampshire, UK: Palgrave Macmillan.

Acknowledgments

The editors would like to thank the contributors for making this project possible and Tom Sutton at Routledge for getting it started and seeing it through to completion. Avi would like to thank Laura, Zeia and Adelaide for their patience and support. Nigel would like to thank Alison and Daniel for being great role models. International Visiting Fellowships at the University of Essex in Spring 2017 and Spring 2019 enabled Avi to travel to Colchester to work side by side with Nigel at the beginning and ending stages of the second edition. The editors are thus grateful to the University of Essex for its financial support in this way. Both would also like to thank Jana Kappeler for the compelling image we have been able to use on the cover.

Every effort has been made to contact copyright holders for their permission to reprint material in this book. The publishers would be grateful to hear from any copyright holder who is not here acknowledged and will undertake to rectify any errors or omissions in future editions of this book.

References to internet websites (URLs) were accurate at the time of writing. Neither the individual authors nor the Editors nor Routledge is responsible for URLs that may have expired or changed since the manuscript was prepared.

Introduction

New horizons, ongoing and emerging issues and relationships in green criminology

Avi Brisman and Nigel South

In our Introduction to the first edition of the *Routledge International Handbook of Green Criminology* (the 'Handbook'), we began with the following observation by Dunne (2009: 46):

> Every age seems to invent a master narrative about its own demise. At the turn of the twentieth century, the fear was of a violent struggle between races and civilisations. In the post-1945 world, the nightmare was of a nuclear holocaust. The narrative of demise that haunts us today is the threat that environmental harm holds for the planet and its ability to support human and other life forms.

We noted that Hollywood had seized this narrative and run with it, mentioning, as an example, that in the beginning of *Waterworld* (1995), the globe in the Universal logo morphs into a world with the continents submerged under water. An ominous voice states: 'The future: the polar ice caps have melted, covering the Earth with water. Those who survive have adapted to a new world'. *The Day After Tomorrow* (2004), we also pointed out, depicts violent catastrophic weather, including a massive snowstorm in New Delhi, a powerful hailstorm striking Tokyo, and a series of devastating tornadoes in Los Angeles. Viewers learn that the build up of greenhouse gases in the atmosphere has increased surface ocean temperatures and reduced salinity, completely shutting down the Atlantic thermohaline circulation, causing temperatures in New York to plummet and the Statue of Liberty to become buried in snow.[1]

While these examples may seem a bit dated, Hollywood still seems enthralled with the narrative of environmental demise. Only now, we have started to see how environmental harm and resource exploitation has permeated the underlying premises for various cinematic scripts. For example, in *Man of Steel* (2013), Kal-El (aka 'Clark Kent', aka 'Superman') is sent to Earth from his native planet, Krypton, right before Krypton's core collapses and the planet breaks apart. Whereas in previous permutations, Krypton is referred to as a 'dying planet' and the planet is destroyed in a 'natural cataclysm', in *Man of Steel*, the planet implodes because its residents had exhausted its energy reserves and began harvesting its core, causing the core to become unstable. In a more recent superhero film, *Aquaman* (2018), Arthur Curry (aka 'Aquaman') seeks to prevent his Atlantean half-brother and King of Atlantis (Orm Marius aka 'Ocean Master') from uniting the seven underwater kingdoms to declare war on the 'surface world' for humanity's pollution of the seas. And in a different vein, *Hotel Artemis* (2018), set in Los Angeles in 2028, follows Jean 'the Nurse' Thomas, who operates a secret, 13-story members-only hospital for criminals. A riot has broken out over the affordability and availability of water after it has become privatised, complicating entrance to and exit from the hospital. None of these films (*Man of Steel*, *Aquaman*, or *Hotel Artemis*) focus on human-induced environmental disaster (as in *The Day After Tomorrow*) or present a post-apocalyptic world where humans struggle to survive (*Waterworld*). Rather, the threat of chaos or war as a result of environmental harm serves simply (or only) as a backdrop—either a minor detail to advance the plot or a realistic feature to make the storyline actually more believable and compelling.

Has it come to the point where we simply expect resource exploitation or pollution to cause *something* spectacular—the arrival of Kal-El/Clark Kent/Superman from resource-depleted Krypton? An attack from Atlantis in response to overfishing and ocean dumping? Riots over water privatisation?

Maybe we are no longer haunted by 'the threat that environmental harm holds for the planet and its ability to support human and other life forms'. Maybe the 'narrative of demise' of today of which Dunne speaks has become the setting, not the story. Maybe we are no longer frightened and preoccupied by the threat of environmental disaster and that, instead, we experience it as boring or some other emotion—useful only insofar as it brings us closer to the 'real action'—the gripping fight scenes for which we purchase our admission tickets. In other words, while the narrative of environmental demise should be *more* haunting now than ten years ago, it seems as if the opposite has transpired.

Unfortunately, environmental degradation and demise is not just the stuff of Hollywood. According to a sweeping assessment by the United Nations in May 2019, more than *one million* species of animals and plants are now at risk of extinction due to humans' dramatic transformations of the Earth's natural landscapes (Plumer 2019; Renkl 2019).[2] Not one million *individual creatures*, but, as Renkl (2019) laments, '[e]very individual creature in a species—*times one million*' (emphasis in original). Over the past 50 years, global biodiversity loss has occurred due to 'direct activities', such as the clearing of forests for farmland, the expansion of cities and roads, hunting and poaching, logging, overfishing, the transport of invasive species around the world, and water pollution. For example, the razing of rain forest in Indonesia for palm oil plantations has destroyed the habitat of orangutans and Sumatran tigers, both critically endangered, while in Mozambique, ivory poachers killed approximately 7,000 elephants between 2009 and 2011 alone (Plumer 2019). Extinction rates are currently tens to hundreds of times higher than they have been in the past ten million years, and since the eighteenth century, humans have altered significantly three-quarters of the world's land area and 85 per cent of the world's wetlands have vanished (Plumer 2019). According to the United Nations' Food and Agriculture Organization, an estimated three-quarters of the world's agricultural biodiversity disappeared in the twentieth century (D'Auria 2019).[3] In October of 2019, the World Wildlife Fund declared that since 1970, populations of thousands of vertebrate species have declined by an average of 60 per cent. 'Plants and animals are disappearing at rates comparable to past mass extinctions', writes Nuwer (2019: 34), 'only this time those losses are driven not by asteroids or super-volcanoes but by us, fellow creatures inhabiting this planet. And things are likely to worsen as climate change cranks up and wreaks havoc on delicately balanced ecosystems'. Unless nations drastically improve their efforts to protect remaining natural habitats, Plumer (2019) reports, we could witness the disappearance of 40 per cent of amphibian species, one-third of marine mammals and one-third of reef-forming corals—shocking figures given that scientists have catalogued only a fraction of living creatures (some 1.3 million of an estimated 8 million animal and plant species).

At the same time, the United Nations assessment finds that 'indirect activity', such as the emission of greenhouse gases that accelerates climate change, compounds the threat:

> [g]lobal warming has become a major driver of wildlife decline … by shifting or shrinking the local climates that many mammals, birds, insects, fish and plants evolved to survive in. When combined with the other ways humans are damaging the environment, climate change is now pushing a growing number of species, such as the Bengal tiger, closer to extinction. … Roughly 5 percent of species worldwide are threatened with climate-related extinction if global average temperatures rise 2 degrees Celsius above preindustrial levels.
>
> *(Plumer 2019)*

Echoing Nuwer's (2019) comment above, Dr Richard Pearson, an ecologist at the University College of London, points out that

> If climate change were the only problem we were facing, a lot of species could probably move and adapt. But when populations are already small and losing genetic diversity, when natural land scapes are already fragmented, when plants and animals can't move to find newly suitable habitats, then we have a real threat on our hands.
>
> *(quoted in Plumer 2019)*

The United Nations report describes in detail how closely human well-being—indeed, *survival*—is intertwined with the fate and future of other species. For example, in the Americas alone, nature provides an estimated $24 trillion of non-monetised benefits to humans each year:

> The Amazon rain forest absorbs immense quantities of carbon dioxide and helps slow the pace of global warming. Wetlands purify drinking water. Coral reefs sustain tourism and fisheries in the Caribbean. Exotic tropical plants form the basis of a variety of medicines.
>
> *(Plumer 2019)*

In other words, a dwindling number of species will not only make the world less verdant, less wondrous, less biologically rich, but it poses risks to humans in terms of food security (as humans continue to rely on significantly fewer varieties of animals and plants to produce food, and the food system becomes less resilient to diseases and pests), availability of and access to clean water, and increased risk of flooding (due to the loss of mangrove forests and coral reefs along coasts).

Almost ten years ago, Reece Walters (2010: 174)—one of the contributors to this volume—pointed out that '[c]ollectively, there are more treaties, protocols, directives and statutes that address environmental issues than any other area of law, including trade, health, security, employment and education (Bodansky et al. 2007)'. Given the United Nations' report on the decline of global biodiversity and dangers that plants, animals and humans face as a result, it might be easy to conclude that international environmental protocols and treaties have failed. To some extent, this is true. While there have been successes—such as the Montreal Protocol on Substances that Deplete the Ozone Layer (an international treaty designed to protect the ozone layer by phasing out the production of ozone-depleting substances)—some countries encounter (or create) difficulties with the implementation of international environmental law. According to Walters (2010: 197), implementation may be frustrated by an 'implementation deficit', which he describes as 'a country's lack of financial and technical resources, limited expertise in international environmental law, inability to keep pace with the rapid expansion in treaties, overstretched and under-resourced ministries and state institutions, and cultural and religious factors (UNEP 2006)'. The solution, then, would seem to be not necessarily *more* international directives and statutes, but better mechanisms to ensure compliance—especially from those countries that lack the expertise or the financial and technical resources necessary.

To be sure, closing the 'implementation deficit'—or preventing any 'implementation deficits' in the first place—should be a concern in the drafting of *any* international environmental treaty. But as Dr Sandra M. Díaz, an ecosystems ecologist at the National University of Córdoba in Argentina and a lead author of the United Nations study maintains, 'It's not enough to focus just on environmental policy' (quoted in Plumer 2019). 'We need to build biodiversity considerations into trade and infrastructure decisions, the way that health or human rights are built into every aspect of social and economic-decision-making.'

In other words, just as biodiversity—and non-human nature, more broadly—should not be conceptualised as 'other' or 'separate from humans', our approach(es) to environmental degradation, harm and loss should not be compartmentalised as 'environmental law' or 'environmental policy', whereby only those statutes labelled as explicitly 'environmental' are conceptualised as having bearing on flora and fauna, and air, soil and water quality. Rather, for the environment to improve, we need to understand 'the environment' as having relevance for all legislation and as permeating all facets of life.

Diaz's mandate is not just an argument for an ecophilosophical, legal or ideological recalibration, but a case for cross-, inter- and multi-disciplinary approaches to addressing environmental despoliation. Over the years, various writers across a range of academic disciplines (and at points of overlap and convergence) have attempted to address environmental issues and problems, exposing political inertia, failures of regulation, and avoidance of corporate, state and personal responsibility regarding environmental harms and threats (such as those noted above), and preservation of the environment. For too long, criminology stood on the sideline, leaving the study of environmental crimes, harms, laws, and regulations to researchers in other fields.[4] But over the past three decades—and even more so in the years since the publication of the first edition of the Handbook—a (now substantial) body of work concerned with risk and harm to the environment has emerged.

As the first chapter of this second edition to the Handbook, 'The growth of a field: A short history of a 'green' criminology', discusses, there is something of a debate about the appropriate name or label for this sub-field or perspective within criminology. And in the years since the first edition, even more terms have been suggested (e.g., 'blue criminology' (Paulson 2018); 'climate change criminology' (White 2018); 'una criminología crítica verde del sur'—a southern green critical criminology (Weis 2019)). Nevertheless, 'green criminology' is the term that criminologists employ most frequently to describe the exploration and examination of causes of and responses to 'ecological', 'environmental', or 'green' crimes, harms and hazards. Moreover, many of these newer appellations focus on a particular kind or approach to the study of environmental harm and position themselves as expanding 'green criminology', rather than offering an alternative or challenge to the 'green criminology' title. As such—and because '[g]reen criminology [still] provides an umbrella under which to theorise and critique the emerging terminology related to environmental and species harm' (Walters 2007: 199)—we refer to our endeavour here and the chapters within this volume as contributing to and serving to enhance 'green criminological' scholarship.

'Problems are not a given', Schön (1993: 144) argues in 'Generative Metaphor: A Perspective on Problem-Setting in Social Policy'. Rather, '[t]hey are constructed by human beings in their attempts to make sense of complex and troubling situations'. Schön may be correct that social policy might be more effective if more attention was devoted to problem *setting* than problem *solving*—to 'ways in which we frame the purposes to be achieved than with the selection of optimal means for achieving them' (1993: 138).[5] But it is unlikely that one would view the harms against the environment, humanity and animals by both powerful institutions (e.g., governments, transnational corporations, military apparatus) and ordinary people as mere constructs. The problems discussed in this Handbook are real and have been or soon will be experienced by humans, non-human species and entire ecosystems. These problems may have been created by us—they may be the result of humans building, erecting, fabricating, industrialising, manufacturing and mass-producing—but they are not imaginary or phantasmagoric.

Nevertheless, some sort of 'framing' or 'circumscribing' needs to occur to organise a volume, such as this one, with so many contributions by scholars whose 'home base' and geographic loci of exploration span the globe. An important point might be made about the amount, degree, or interrelatedness of various environmental problems by simply placing the chapters in alphabetical order by author or by assigning each chapter a random number and inserting them into the volume in ascending order. In keeping with the organisation of the first edition, we have chosen to group the chapters in this Handbook in such a way as to call attention to six particular features and themes within—and sets of relationships between—chapters, but we would certainly encourage instructors, readers and students to craft their own itinerary as they approach this volume. In sum, we envision the Handbook as a *vade mecum*, rather than a rigid set of marching orders.

Part I of the Handbook, 'History, theory and methods', introduces readers to some of the ways in which environmental crimes, harms, hazards and responses thereto have been conceptualised and researched within green criminology. Picking up on some of the points raised in this Introduction, the first chapter, 'The growth of a field: a short history of a "green" criminology', presents readers with some of the substantive themes, topics and orienting typologies of and in 'green criminology'. The approach of this chapter is necessarily broad and is intended as an overview to green criminology, rather than a definitive history or catalogue raisonné.

The second chapter, 'The ordinary acts that contribute to ecocide: A criminological analysis', by Robert Agnew, attempts to situate 'green criminology' within the larger discipline of criminology. Agnew draws on existing social-psychological theories of crime to explain why individuals and small groups engage in a range of 'ordinary' acts that contribute to the destruction of the natural environment, and offers suggestions for their control. With examples such as driving automobiles with poor gas mileage, living in relatively large homes, and consuming large amounts of meat, Agnew breathes new life into and improves the utility of mainstream criminological theory. In so doing, Agnew's chapter serves to broaden the acceptance of green criminology within the field of criminology. At the same time, his work crosses disciplines, lending support to claims, such as that of Egan (2019: A22), who asserts that 'ditching meat for substitutes, faux or otherwise, is the most effective thing an individual can do to fight climate change', while posing a challenge to economists, such as Gernot Wagner (2011), who has argued that the changes necessary to save the tuna, protect the rain forest, or combat climate change are so immense and profound that they are beyond the reach of individual action, and that only certain economic policies will induce noticeable change.

Whereas Agnew's chapter draws on criminological theories that attempt to address root causes of crime, such as psychological or social influences on behavior, the third chapter, 'Wildlife crime: A situational crime prevention perspective' by Christina Burton, Devin Cowan and William Moreto, explores the potential application of situational crime prevention (SCP) measures to prevent and reduce wildlife crime. Whereas traditional crime prevention measures would seek to address underlying problems, such as unemployment and disorderly communities, SCP, on the other hand, targets situational characteristics of the immediate environment in an effort to reduce the potential for criminal opportunities. Burton, Cowan and Moreto argue that such strategies can provide an alternative to—or, at least, can accompany—approaches that rely primarily on law enforcement. Recognising that scholars of green criminology and SCP, as well as crime science and environmental criminology, have tended to work in theoretical silos (see Moreto 2018), Burton, Cowan and Moreto demonstrate how green criminology and SCP can be used in tandem to develop contextually appropriate strategies.

Because the SCP approach, as Burton, Cowan and Moreto explain, is inherently crime- and context-specific, these techniques provide local communities with the ability to address poaching within their area in a manner tailored specifically to the problem. In contrast, the fourth chapter, 'Expanding treadmill of production analysis within green criminology by integrating metabolic rift and ecological unequal exchange theories' by Michael J. Lynch, Paul B. Stretesky, Michael A. Long and Kimberly L. Barrett, draws upon the treadmill of production (ToP) theoretical framework to demonstrate how capitalism produces environmental crimes and harms at both the local and global level (see, e.g., Lynch et al. 2013; Stretesky et al. 2013). Lynch and his colleagues extend the political economic orientation of ToP by connecting it to two other radical political economic theories designed to make the linkage between capitalism and ecological destruction more visible: metabolic rift theory and ecological unequal exchange theory. The authors argue that these views help round out the ToP approach, can be applied to understand any number of environmental crimes and injustices associated with ecological disorganisation, and encourage further application by green criminologists. Doing so, they maintain, can help establish connections to the ecological Marxist and environmental sociology literatures, as well as to the growing number of empirical studies in those fields that support these approaches.

In the fifth chapter, 'The visual dimensions of green criminology', Lorenzo Natali and Bill McClanahan describe some analytical, methodological and theoretical principles for the use of the photographic image as a method for researching environmental crimes and harms. The authors begin by discussing and exploring photo-elicitation methods—one technique for a green criminology *with* images, whereby the interviewer uses images to facilitate responses to questions and to delve deeper into the interviewee/participant's verbal narratives. From here, Natali and McClanahan turn their attention to possible techniques for a green criminology *about* images (e.g., visual archival materials, images from popular visual culture, images taken by satellite or aerial photography), suggesting ways in which a green-visual criminology can contribute to the development of new forms of participatory research and praxis, as well as increased criminological insight into the visual dimensions of environmental *change* and *harm*, environmental *conflict*, and *resistance* to environmental harm. Natali and McClanahan conclude with some thoughts on the broad potential and applicability of a green visual mode of analysis and research.

The first five chapters endeavour to provide readers with some of the history of the emergence of green criminology, to demonstrate the theoretical breadth on which exploration of environmental harms can draw, and to call attention to green criminology's importance for criminology as an academic field and for the sustainability of the environment as a living entity. The sixth chapter takes a slightly different path. Diane Heckenberg and Rob White's 'Innovative approaches to researching environmental crime' explores a variety of methods, tools and routes that can be employed to research environmental harms and crimes, noting that such research tends to be international in scope and politically sensitive, and looking to the future as well as to the present and the past. Key topics in this chapter relate to the practice of horizon scanning, socio-legal analysis, case studies, ethnography and cross-national comparison in the area of green criminological research. Multi-jurisdictional, multi-agency and cross-cultural research all involve a dynamic process that is fraught with ethical and practical issues—but it is a process increasingly necessary in the light of globalisation and the transnational nature of environmental harms. Recognising that ultimately, 'the appropriate method depends on the research objectives', to quote Stubbs (2008: 13), Heckenberg and White open avenues for research by both beginning and seasoned scholars of green criminology, while at the same time lending a lens through which readers might more fully appreciate the range of methodologies employed by authors throughout the Handbook.

One of the key points that Heckenberg and White make is that the dimensions of environmental harm pose challenges for researchers insofar as different types of knowledge are required for dealing with specific kinds of environmental harm. Green criminological analysis, therefore, needs to take into account considerable diversity in terms of who the victim is (human or non-human). As Heckenberg and White maintain, environmental victimisation has been central to dispossession and maltreatment of Indigenous peoples over many continents and over a period of several centuries. The question of 'whose knowledge is privileged?' in interpreting 'the best interests' of a community or region has been vital to dispossession and disregard in relation to Indigenous cultures.

The issue of environmental victimisation, which we were encouraged to explore more directly in this second edition (see Jarrell 2013), is considered in the seventh and eight chapters—the last two in Part I. In Chapter 7, 'Environmental refugees as environmental victims', Matthew Hall charts the development of a distinct current within that field which focusses attention specifically on the human and non-human victims of environmental harms—a so-called 'green victimology'. He then turns to the ongoing debate and controversy around the issue of 'environmental refugees' (which Avi Brisman, Nigel South and Reece Walters contemplate in Chapter 10, 'Global environmental divides and dislocations: Climate apartheid, atmospheric injustice and the blighting of the planet'). By discussing both issues concurrently, Hall demonstrates: (1) how green victimology might assist with the incorporation of environmental refugees within green criminological discourse; and (2) how victimological insights might better aid us in understanding the plight of environmental refugees. Hall describes how criminal justice and other agencies have tended to respond to such refugees, especially in so-called 'receiving countries', and he puts forth the argument that conceiving of 'environmental refugees' as 'environmental victims' helps us move beyond formulistic debates around legal definitions of 'refugees' versus 'migrants' to focus attention instead on such persons' lived experiences. To address the question of how national and international legal orders might address these matters, Hall explores the 1985 UN Declaration of Basic Principles of Justice for Victims of Crime and Abuse of Power (often referred to as the '1985 UN Declaration'). While Chapter 7 focusses on the displacement of *human beings*, and is thus primarily anthropocentric in its orientation, Hall takes pains to point out that this emphasis should not be taken to imply that this is an issue unconnected from disruptions to the wider ecosystem. Indeed, Hall points to considerable evidence that the same environmentally degrading activities and impacts that are compelling human populations to migrate are also having significant effects on animals, disrupting their migration and herding patterns. From an ecocentric perspective, therefore, Hall asserts that there is no cogent reason to exclude such harms from the scope of 'environmental victimisation'—a topic that resurfaces in the chapters in Part V.

Chapter 8, 'How criminologists can help victims of green crimes through scholarship and activism', by Joshua Ozymy, Melissa L. Jarrell and Elizabeth A. Bradshaw, continues Hall's inquiry. In this chapter, Ozymy and his co-authors focus on practical ways to protect victims of state-corporate environmental crimes, examining solutions for reducing victimisation through political, legal and grassroots efforts, and offering suggestions for ways in which green criminologists can aid the plight of victims of state-corporate crimes through scholarship and direct action. The chapter builds on the authors' own work and leverages their experience in community involvement on behalf of environmental justice communities to contemplate how criminologists can play a role in protecting and advocating for victims of green crimes. In so doing, Ozymy, Jarrell and Bradshaw lend support to Nuwer's (2019: 39) reminder that '[i]naction … is never an option for those who believe that protecting the amazing panoply of life is our job in this world'.

With the foundation offered by Part I, Part II ('International and transnational issues for a green criminology') and Part III ('Region-specific problems: Some case studies') raise and address questions regarding spatial and geographic aspects and components of environmental crimes, harms and hazards. As White (2010: 17) has argued, '[a]nalysis of environmental harm from a criminological perspective … must incorporate … a sensitivity to how human action places stress on environments large and small'. 'Scale matters', White (2010: 17) continues, and thus 'it is important to have a sense of the "where" of environmental harm, as well as the "how", "why" and "who"'. Although White (2010: 9) distinguishes between 'the local', 'the national', 'the regional', 'the global' and 'the transnational'—and although he calls for criminologists to be attuned to the physical location of environmental harm within particular geo-political contexts—a suggestion that resonates with Burton, Cowan and Moreto's point that preventing wildlife crime requires attention to specific cultural and socio-political contexts—ultimately, White reminds us, '[w]hat happens in any one place is intrinsically important to what happens worldwide'. In a similar vein, Walters (2010: 200) has advocated that

> [c]riminologists must continue to engage in issues of global significance while being attentive to local and national interests. The various environmental issues broadly defined within green criminology demonstrate that criminology is capable of moving beyond domestic borders and contributing to debates of international significance.

While Part II focusses on the former—issues of global significance—and Part III on the latter—issues of local and national interest—a problem does not lack international importance simply because it is manifested within the borders of a specific nation-state (or generated by and experienced in multiple nation-states in similar but geographically separate nation-states). Nor should the global dimensions of a problem—i.e., the fact that all nations face them (see Lynch and Stretesky 2010: 63)—mean that the problem is experienced, interpreted, understood and responded to equally, proportionately and identically; climate change, for example, is and means different things to Midwestern Americans than to Maldivians and the ability of local and national governmental entities to respond to the real and perceived problems their people face may be vastly dissimilar. As Lynch and Stretesky (2010: 63) explain, some problems represent 'global concerns'. but are 'country-dependent and related to national level politics and priorities' (citation omitted).

It is with these caveats that we place the chapters by Ronald C. Kramer and Elizabeth A. Bradshaw; Avi Brisman, Nigel South and Reece Walters; Wesley Tourangeau and Amy J. Fitzgerald; David Rodríguez Goyes; Tammy Ayres; and Jordan E. Mazurek, Justin Piché and Judah Schept into Part II of the Handbook, 'International and transnational issues for a green criminology'. These chapters discuss, in varying ways, environmental problems that cross international borders (such as air and water pollution), environmental harms to the commons (such as climate change), or environmental issues and responses to these that are or should be present in multiple countries and are not nation-state-specific. The chapters in Part II either address problems of global concern in the sense that action or inaction in one location/nation-state adversely impacts the environment in/of another, or they examine problems occurring in a particular country or region that could occur or have occurred in other geographical areas. While the issues discussed in this Part are far-ranging—and, indeed, entire volumes could be dedicated to the subject of just one of the topics discussed therein—the chapters are united in that they illuminate issues of causation, as well as obstacles that appear in addressing *ex ante* or *ex post* environmental harm (e.g., the drafting and application of law, governmental corruption, the role of corporate lobbying).

Part II begins with two chapters on climate change—which White (2010: 11) refers to as 'the most pressing and important international issue facing humanity today'. In Chapter 9, 'Climate crimes: the case of ExxonMobil', Ronald C. Kramer and Elizabeth A. Bradshaw explain that climate change may create new categories of offenders and victims, as well as new types of crime. After offering an overview of the literature on green criminology and climate change, and defining the concept of *climate crimes*, Kramer and Bradshaw develop a conceptual framework for understanding these types of crime by drawing on Agnew's notion of blameworthy harms. Next, the authors identify four different types of climate crimes: Crimes of Continuing Extraction and Emissions; Crimes of Denial; Crimes of Political Omission; and Crimes of Unjust and Militaristic Adaptation. Finally, to demonstrate some of the theoretical and empirical questions of *climate crimes*, Kramer and Bradshaw provide a case study of the ExxonMobil Corporation's ('ExxonMobil') continuing extraction of fossil fuels and the greenhouse gas (GHG) emissions it produces, particularly as it pertains to the process of hydraulic fracturing (or 'fracking')—the subject of Chapter 19, 'Fracking the Rockies: The production of harm', by Kellie Alexander, Tara O'Connor Shelley and Tara Opsal; Chapter 26, 'Energy harms: 'Extreme energy', fracking and water' by Damien Short; and Chapter 27, 'The uncertainty of community financial incentives for 'fracking': Pursuing ramifications for environmental justice', by Jack Adam Lampkin.

In Chapter 10, 'Global environmental divides and dislocations: Climate apartheid, atmospheric injustice and the blighting of the planet', Avi Brisman, Nigel South and Reece Walters extend Kramer and Bradshaw's description of climate change and crime, while revisiting the issue of environmental victimisation and refugees raised by Hall in Chapter 7. In particular, Brisman, South and Walters examine some of the ways in which global warming and climate change may impact the (im)mobility of those who have contributed the *least* to anthropogenic climate change. In doing so, they engage with the related projects of southern criminology and green criminology as they pertain to, *inter alia*, knowledge production and problems of bias, inequality and injustice—issues that resurface in Chapter 12, 'Monopolising seeds, monopolising society: A guide to contemporary criminological research on biopiracy' by David Rodríguez Goyes. Because the causes and consequences of global warming and climate change are transboundary in nature, Brisman, South and Walters assert that recognition of the shared concerns of southern criminology and green criminology could be helpful in responding to this complexity.

One of the points that Brisman and his co-authors make is that in addition to forced migration, we are witnessing how rising global temperatures and the concomitant loss of biodiversity (discussed at the outset of this Introduction) has resulted in 'cultural extinction'—specifically, Indigenous groups' loss of traditions associated with various habitats, such as food practices. At the same time, Brisman, South and Walters note that economic stress and crop failures could lead to increased competition for dwindling resources, such as food and water, sparking large-scale migrations and, in turn, escalating tensions, upheavals and violence.

Wesley Tourangeau and Amy J. Fitzgerald continue the discussion of food in Chapter 11, 'Food crime and green criminology'. They begin with a survey of food crime typologies, focussing on two broad categories: (1) food crimes defined as such by legal standards (including food adulteration, counterfeiting and poisoning); and (2) food crimes that represent violations of moral standards, but which may not be proscribed by law. This second category challenges the limits of legally defined food crimes, and it includes important systemic issues and individual actions that are harmful but not prohibited by law. Tourangeau and Fitzgerald utilise recent cases from numerous national contexts to illustrate both the categorical distinctions and the applied real consequences of each, offering a brief case study of current efforts to update Canada's 'livestock' transportation regulations in order to demonstrate the complexity and difficulty of defining what constitutes a 'food crime' (or any 'crime' for that matter), and the limitations of restricting the subject of 'food crime' to legalistic definitions. As Tourangeau and Fitzgerald reveal, an examination of the proposed changes to Canada's 'livestock' transportation regulations and the related consultative process helps to illuminate the sites where legal boundaries are drawn, as well as to reveal how these boundaries can be rather arbitrary and yet extremely impactful. This act of drawing boundaries is an inherently complex task, the authors note, involving the ethical and normative dimensions of law formation, in addition to the injection of public and private interests. Overall, Tourangeau and Fitzgerald's case study provides an examination of how these dimensions and interests are weighted in matters of animal welfare and economic profitability—issues that this Handbook contemplates further in Part V.

Tourangeau and Fitzgerald note the significance of biopiracy—the subject of Chapter 12, 'Monopolising seeds, monopolising society: A guide to contemporary criminological research on biopiracy' by David Rodríguez Goyes. In this chapter, Goyes distinguishes between 'biopiracy' and 'bioprospecting', before identifying characteristics, elements and features of biopiracy, and then delineating the harms produced by biopiracy (e.g., distributive, ecological, sociological, symbolic, epistemological). From here, he discusses the 'actors' involved in biopiracy (e.g., 'users', 'suppliers') and the 'target market' or 'market designation' for the different 'source materials'—the basic resource or raw material used. The chapter concludes with some future challenges for green criminologists interested in researching further the processes and impacts of biopiracy.

An overarching theme of Goyes' chapter is that countries in the Global South have been paying a huge ecological and human price for policies and practices developed and driven by affluent nations in the Global North. Tammy Ayres focusses on the environmental impact of drug prohibition, in general, and of the War on Drugs more specifically, in Chapter 13, 'The war on drugs and its invisible collateral damage: Environmental harm and climate change'. Following del Olmo (1993, 1998), Ayres investigates the link between drug prohibition, crop eradication, deforestation and environmental damage (e.g., biodiversity loss, pollution of air, soil, water) and the public health of Indigenous populations. As she reveals, much of this harm is disavowed and official discourse centres on the harm caused by the drugs themselves and their link to organised crime, insurgency and violence, which is used to justify more draconian and harmful drug interdiction strategies. Accordingly, Ayres argues, drug prohibition and the War on Drugs reflect not concern about the human health consequences of illicit substances, but the prioritisation of the exigencies of capitalism, including its territorial and social expansion, and improving the conditions for direct foreign investment and the free-market economy.

One of Ayres' key points is that prohibition often *creates* or *exacerbates* armed conflict and crime (e.g., corruption, organised crime, terrorism, violence), and that the 'War on Drugs' has become a 'War against Certain People'—one which disproportionately affects poor, ethnic minority groups in countries of both the Global South and Global North. In the United States, prison admissions climbed in the years following President Richard M. Nixon's declaration of a 'War on Drugs' and began to soar in the early 1980s under President Ronald Reagan. Skyrocketing incarceration rates[6] generated a need for more physical space to house more people convicted pursuant to federal and state emphasis on drug enforcements (see generally Schept and Mazurek 2017). As Schoenfeld (2018: 4) notes, '[i]n the past forty years, states and the federal government built over 1,500 prisons' (footnote omitted). And each prison that has been or is slated to be built requires land, as well as concrete, steel, water and other building materials and resources.

The last chapter in Part II—Chapter 14, '"Greening" injustice: Penal reform, carceral expansion and greenwashing' by Jordan E. Mazurek, Justin Piché and Judah Schept—examines the emergence of 'green' jails and prisons—new carceral spaces being built using environmentally friendly construction materials and practices, along with infrastructure that (purportedly) reduces energy consumption and waste, while improving the environment in which incarcerated individuals live and work. More specifically, the authors consider how claims concerning the sustainability of facility construction and operations have contributed to the establishment of new and bigger institutions designed to deprive people of their liberty. In addition, by analysing and assessing the marketing materials of the agencies promoting green initiatives in criminal justice, Mazurek, Piché and Schept demonstrate that, in some cases, neither sustainability nor prison reform are primary or even normative goals. Rather, these initiatives are driven by their ability to cut state or municipal costs. Accordingly, the authors urge skepticism of 'greening justice', given such initiatives' role in legitimating carceral expansion and penal reforms that fail to challenge the persistence of 'human caging'. Importantly, the authors also devote attention to organisers and groups protesting the construction of new jails and prisons, in part through campaigns that point to the social and ecological toxicity of such facilities (whether touted as 'green' or not).

Mazurek, Piché and Schept's discussion of the fight against toxic jails and prisons speaks to the activist orientation of Ozymy, Jarrell and Bradshaw's chapter (noted above), as well as to the pursuit of environmental justice, described by David N. Pellow in Chapter 32 (see below). More theoretically, Mazurek, Piché and Schept respond to the call by Jewkes and Moran (2015: 466) 'to address the paradox at the heart of the green prison … that rather than challenging the hegemony of incarceration, advocates of green prisons are arguably perpetuating and legitimizing the expanding penal estate'. Mazurek and his co-authors expose the contradiction between well-intentioned efforts to address environmental degradation caused by correctional institutions and their effect at sustaining, or even growing, a system so violently threatening to the lives of so many. Even as well-meaning scholars may see important opportunities for interventions in the form of 'green' design and meaningful environmental work opportunities for incarcerated individuals, Mazurek, Piché and Schept caution against embracing 'greening justice' as a kind of normative goal. Going beyond the claim that '[t]he greenest prison is an empty one' (Anderson 2015: 1, quoting Matt Clarke, a writer for *Prison Legal News*), Mazurek and his co-authors assert: 'there is no greener approach to incarceration than not having jails and prisons in the first place'.

Part III, 'Region-specific problems: Some case studies', builds on the examples in Part II to discuss certain types of environmental harms or environmental harm-causing behaviours that are peculiar to a given location, region, or nation-state. While the focus of these chapters is nation-state- or region-specific, the issues discussed therein are, to reiterate our point from above, no less 'international' than those in Part II. For example, rain forest depletion, the subject of Chapter 15, 'The Amazon Rainforest: Green criminological perspective' by Tim Boekhout van Solinge, is not just a problem in or for Brazil (see, e.g., Plumer 2017; Tullis 2019). In a somewhat different vein, Katja Eman and Gorazd Meško, in Chapter 16, attempt to identify patterns of environmental crimes in South-Eastern Europe, highlighting how, for instance, the illegal trafficking of wildlife and timber and corporate-state corruption create adverse environmental effects that cross boundaries and present challenges of governance.

We begin Part III with Tim Boekhout van Solinge, who, in his chapter on deforestation, illegal logging and the harmful exploitation of the Amazon in the west of Pará, Brazil, asks, 'Can Brazil's international promises to limit deforestation be fulfilled? How will Brazil deal with the tension between agricultural development and rainforest conservation? To what extent are these entirely Brazilian issues?' Boekhout van Solinge is less than sanguine in his outlook and responses to the first two questions; his answer to the third is in the negative. For Boekhout van Solinge, the Amazonian forest (and its diverse plant and animal species) is both the victim of crime, harm and violence, and the locus of crime, harm and violence against Indigenous peoples. As Boekhout van Solinge tacks back and forth between talking about the environmental harm to the forests (deforestation and the loss of species, as well as water pollution from soy production) and the violence perpetrated on Indigenous peoples by those seeking to exploit the Amazon's natural resources, he demonstrates how land conversion for cattle and soy, which has been the main cause of Amazonian deforestation (often preceded by illegal logging), are the first steps in a global commodity chain. Most of Brazil's soy and an increasing percentage of its beef are exported abroad, Boekhout van Solinge explains. As such, the hamburger or tofu that Westerners consume unreflectively may well have contributed to the loss of plant, animal and human life in Pará, Brazil—a phenomenon that further illustrates the points made by Agnew, and Tourangeau and Fitzgerald, in their respective chapters, about the origins of our food and personal responsibility for 'ordinary' acts that contribute to ecocide. As Brazil—which has one of the highest rates of biodiversity on Earth (see Tullis 2019)—continues to seek to expand its political and economic power in Latin America—efforts that include opening areas of protected forest to large-scale agriculture (Romero 2012), tapping oil from its recent offshore discoveries (Romero 2011b), constructing hydroelectric plants in Ecuador and dams in Peru (Romero 2011a)—Western complicity in these subsequent environmental harms increases.

Whereas Chapter 15 focusses on a handful of environmental problems in a single country—albeit problems inextricably intertwined with international consumer tastes and multinational corporate operations—Katja Eman and Gorazd Meško, in Chapter 16, 'Green issues in South-Eastern Europe', provide an overview of a wide range of environmental problems in Albania, Bosnia and Herzegovina, Bulgaria, Croatia, Hungary, Kosovo, the Republic of North Macedonia, Romania, Serbia, Slovenia and the Ukraine. Despite the difficulty posed by the differences between countries and diversity of languages in the region, Eman and Meško are able to identify some common characteristics of the environmental problems in the area of South-Eastern Europe, such as air, water and soil pollution, caused by corporations and state-owned facilities (especially coal dust, ash, thermal power-plant pollution of air and water in Albania, Bosnia and Herzegovina, Bulgaria, Kosovo, Moldova, Serbia and the Ukraine), as well as waste trafficking and illegal waste disposal, animal and plant species trafficking, and poaching and illegal fishing. Their analysis shows the heavy influence of organised crime in the region, whereby loopholes in environmental protection legislation and gaps in infrastructure and enforcement allow perpetrators of such harms and crimes to avoid prosecution and/or punishment. Although Eman and Meško stress that systematic prosecution of environmental crimes is necessary in order to ensure that much environmental damage is reduced or eliminated (i.e., so that the risk of detection and the threat of serious punishment outweighs financial profit), they recognise that the specific environmental and political nature of each country must not be ignored, and many issues (such as those pertaining to marine and coastal ecosystems pollution in Croatia, hunting tourism in Hungary and Serbia, nuclear and radioactive waste pollution in Moldova and the Ukraine, and timber logging in Albania, Bosnia and Herzegovina, Hungary and the Republic of North Macedonia) will have to be tackled by more focussed cooperation between and within countries, rather than as regional initiatives. Nevertheless, by identifying patterns of environmental crimes in South-Eastern Europe, their work holds the potential to stimulate and enable cooperation between countries in order to protect and preserve the environment of the entire South-Eastern Europe region.

In the article, 'The End of the Line' (2019), Duncan Tarr and Noor Us-Sabah, two Michigan-based organisers, describe how the rusting fossil-fuel industry of the upper Midwestern United States connects the poisoned residents of Flint, Michigan, to the Athabasca Chipewyan First Nations and the fight over Canada's oil sands. In 2014, in Flint, Michigan, the state-appointed Emergency Manager switched Flint's water source from Lake Huron and Detroit River to the Flint River in an effort to save money. State environmental agencies failed to apply corrosion controls to the newly sourced water, however, leading to corrosion of the pipelines and contamination of the water; it took more than a year before city and state government officials acknowledged the complaints of lead poisoning by the predominantly poor African American residents of Flint (see Brisman et al. 2018). Meanwhile—and farther north—the extraction of bitumen from the oil sands (also known as 'tar sands' or 'bituminous sands') of northern Alberta, Canada, has had a substantial impact on its surrounding environment—and on the First Nations who live in and around the deposit. For Tarr and Us-Sabah, 'Mid Michigan', as the area where Flint is located is called, and northeastern Alberta are connected by the exigencies of capital. Whereas in Flint, 'the state and city governments valued a budget cut over the health and safety of … poor, black, and brown people' (Tarr and Us-Sabah 2019: 89), in northern Alberta, oil and gas companies' extractive processes, driven by the demand for more energy necessary for the endless growth of capitalism, are creating a new 'sacrifice zone'—an area of the planet now largely uninhabitable.

We return to the concept of 'sacrifice zones' later in Chapter 34 by Tameka Samuels-Jones, Ryan Thomson and Johanna Espin. For now, the water crisis of Flint and the extraction-as-genocide in and around the Athabasca oil sands serve as the subjects of Chapters 17 and 18, respectively. In Chapter 17, 'The Flint water crisis: A case study of state-sponsored environmental (in)justice', Jacquelynn Doyon-Martin provides an overview of Flint's geography and demography, as well as a description of the processes by which state emergency management laws in the United States permit state officials (such as the governor) to appoint a receiver, state agency, or financial control board to oversee local (city) government—a transfer of decision-making authority that precipitated the switch in Flint's water source. From here, Doyon-Martin offers a timeline of the water crisis, noting failures at the local, state and federal level, while pointing out the lasting impacts of environmental injustice in Flint. As Doyon-Martin explains, the placement of an Emergency Manager, by the governor, into a position of authority, heightened already existing disparities in the lack of political capital among the residents of Flint—a dynamic that, she notes, is often present in cases of environmental justice (a topic explored in greater depth in Chapter 27 by Jack Adam Lampkin, Chapter 32 by David N. Pellow, and Chapter 33 by Angus Nurse). Doyon-Martin concludes by describing how the corrosion of pipes has led to the erosion of public health and public trust in government—and that while the city has returned to its original water source, the economic and social futures of its residents remain murky.

'As conventional oil resources have dwindled', write Tarr and Us-Sabah (2019: 82),

> oil companies have had to turn to more-difficult-to-extract and environmentally-devastating sources. Tar sands oil is extremely energy-intensive to refine, meaning that as it adds more cheap fossil fuels to be consumed it also increases overall consumption. The result is more emissions and habitat destruction.

In Chapter 18, 'Indigenous environmental victimisation in the Canadian oil sands', James Heydon describes the environmental impact of the process of extracting bitumen from the ground. In so doing, he draws out some of the conceptual contours of 'cultural loss'—which Gregory and Trousdale (2009: 2470) define as the 'adverse impacts on the range of traditional activities, emotional well-being or social relations engaged in by an individual and/or an Aboriginal community as a result of changes in the land'. Next, Heydon considers the 'land–culture' relationship maintained by Indigenous peoples, more broadly, and the First Nations of Canada, more specifically, before exploring how contamination of the water, air, and culturally significant species affects the traditional land-based practices of First Nations in and around the oil sands.

'Exploitation of most if not all energy sources poses risks to public health and the environment', caution Michaels and Simon (2013: 15). 'Like the proverbial lunch', they continue, 'ultimately it is not free'. Just as Heydon demonstrates the veracity of this statement—how significant environmental and public health impacts accompany the exploitation of energy sources—so, too, do Kellie Alexander, Tara O'Connor Shelley and Tara Opsal in Chapter 19, 'Fracking the Rockies: The production of harm'. Hydraulic fracturing (or 'fracking') entails the forceful injection of 'fluid'[7] at high levels of pressure into deep underground shale deposits in order to dislodge gas; once the rock formation has been broken up or 'fractured', the gas can flow to a well, where it is pumped out of the ground (Davis and Fisk 2017; Michaels and Simon 2013). In the United States, natural gas production has increased considerably over the last decade because of the oil and gas (O&G) industry's embrace of this technique, but not without controversy. Proponents contend that fracking affords access to an abundant source of domestic energy that helps reduce the United States' dependence on imported oil and gas from countries that are unstable politically (see, e.g., Davis and Fisk 2017). Moreover, supporters of fracking assert that electricity from natural gas is cleaner and emits less carbon dioxide (CO_2) than coal, and they stress the economic benefits of fracking operations, which they claim creates well-paid jobs and generates tax revenue for local governments (see, e.g., Davis and Fisk 2017 for a discussion). Opponents, on the other hand, contend that fracking operations produce noise and traffic congestion, deplete and/or pose risks to groundwater and surface water resources, and present threats to public health from accidents and exposure to harmful substances used at well sites (see, e.g., Davis and Fisk 2017 for a discussion; see also Short, this volume, Chapter 26).

Alexander and her co-authors intercede in this debate over fracking. Noting that there remains a paucity of research focussed on understanding individuals' *direct* experiences and perceptions of risk associated with fracking-related harm and externalities, particularly those associated with spills of fracking fluid and produced water, as well as a dearth of research on regulatory responses after spills or leaks occur on or near citizens' property, Alexander, O'Connor Shelley and Opsal examine a wide range of data, including qualitative interviews with citizens, official COGCC (Colorado Oil & Gas Conservation Commission) data, and survey data from a sample of citizens filing complaints with the COGCC. While their focus is on Colorado, a state in the Rocky Mountain region of the United States, their findings enhance our understanding of who experiences the burdens of resource extraction expansion.

One of the key figures that Alexander and her co-authors provide pertains to the number of leaks or spills reported to the COGCC—the state's O&G permit-granting and regulatory enforcement agency. As Alexander, O'Connor Shelley and Opsal explain, not only has the expansion of O&G development led to the state granting more permits to O&G companies in Colorado, but it has also resulted in increased instances of spills on residents' property: in 2000, there were 274 reported spills to COGCC, while in 2016, this figure increased to 524, representing a 91 per cent increase in spills from 2000–2016. In Chapter 20 by Nikhil Deb, the focus is on just one environmental disaster—the Magurchara gas explosion in Moulvibazar, Bangladesh. The chapter, entitled 'Corporate capitalism, environmental damage, and the rule of law: the Magurchara gas explosion in Bangladesh', offers a political economic analysis of the explosion, which took place during exploration of a well at a site operated by Occidental Petroleum Corporation, the multinational oil and gas exploration and production company. As Deb explains, the gas in the Magurchara Gas Field continued to burn for 17 days, causing harm to the people living nearby, as well as infrastructure loss and extensive environmental destruction, including damage to rain forests, farmlands and tea plantations. Deb illustrates how the Magurchara gas explosion exemplifies the nature of capitalist resource exploitation, lending further support to the claim that the people of poor countries suffer higher social and environmental risks than people living in developed countries.

Deb begins his chapter by providing a brief history of exploration for and extraction of natural resources in Bangladesh, highlighting all major bidding rounds since Bangladesh's independence in 1971. With this background on the relationship between multinational energy corporations and the Bangladeshi state, Deb offers a short account of the Magurchara gas explosion with heightened attention to its socioecological consequences. From here, Deb provides a critical examination of corporate negligence in and after the disaster, explaining why the Bangladeshi government is complicit with corporate interests. This leads Deb to a consideration of what went wrong in the negotiations over compensation, describing how the consequences of the Magurchara gas explosion continue today, and how the demand for justice for socioecological damage remains largely obscured and unresolved. Deb concludes his chapter with a discussion of implications for scholars studying the political economy of environmental harm, urging sensitivity to how law, as it pertains to environmental disasters, is not power-neutral: it favours systematically some groups at the expense of others. By combining an analysis of the role of the state, corporations and the rule of law (or lack thereof), scholars can shed light on the underlying causes of and responses to environmental harm, and the ways in which corporations can use law as a legitimising tool in their efforts to evade responsibilities in the wake of environmental disasters.

In Chapter 21—'Authoritarian environmentalism and environmental regulation enforcement: A case study of medical waste crime in northwestern China'—the last chapter in Part III, KuoRay Mao, Yiliang Zhu, Zhong Zhao and Yan Shan offer one of the first studies to examine critically the connection between deficiencies in China's regulatory apparatus and the criminality associated with illegal dumping and trading of medical waste—specifically as it pertains to waste dumping in rural northwestern China. The authors begin with a brief review of green criminology's approach to waste crime and summarise the literature on top-down environmental regulation enforcement in China. Next, they describe the development of the medical waste regulation framework and highlight the current obstacles to enforcement in China. Mao and his colleagues then introduce a case study to illustrate how institutional incentives in the job performance evaluation system of bureaucrats resulted in the under-enforcement of medical waste regulations at the level of rural governance. Their chapter concludes by suggesting that to study environmental offenses in China, green criminologists must examine how the institutional practices of the fragmented bureaucracy shape the economic, political and social contexts that have structured the complexity of environmental regulation enforcement in this illiberal and restrictive society.

What is particularly compelling about Mao and his colleagues' chapter is that it responds to the call for a more systematic analysis of waste crime by demonstrating how transformations in rural healthcare institutions and conflicts within the regulation enforcement apparatus contribute to an implementation gap in China's medical waste regulatory framework in rural areas. Their study thus reveals how deficiencies related to the authoritarian model of environmental governance in China hinder the enforcement of environmental regulations at the grassroots level, and how without institutionalised public oversight, the implementation of environmental regulations by the centralised regime will remain inefficient and unsatisfactory.

While Mao and his co-authors focus quite clearly on the mismanagement of medical waste in China, their chapter demonstrates how the governance of waste disposal is really a global issue because the interrelations between legal stakeholders and illicit enterprises in different social contexts have a direct impact on the degree of regulation enforcement and compliance in different jurisdictions and at different administrative scales—a point made elsewhere by, for example, Bisschop and Huisman (2018). As such it offers a nice segue to the first chapter in Part IV—'Relationships in green criminology: Environment and economy'—by Wim van Herk and Lieselot Bisschop.

'E-waste'—discarded (broken/non-functioning or obsolete/outdated) electronic devices, such as laptops, refrigerators and televisions—can damage the environment by leaking dangerous chemicals into the soil and groundwater; it can also pose a direct threat to people who scavenge recyclable materials by hand (Yee 2019). In Chapter 22, 'E-waste in the twilight zone between crime and survival', van Herk and Bisschop explore the transport of 'e-waste' from industrialised countries to developing countries—a common practice in the last decades. As the authors explain, discarded but reusable electronics are an important market share of the reusable electronics sold on the global second-hand market. Many other discarded electronics are non-reusable, however; they never make it to the second-hand market and are disassembled immediately for recovery of their raw materials. While the reusable share can be traded legally between OECD (Organization for Economic Cooperation and Development) and non-OECD countries, non-reusable electronics are traded illegally as 'second-hand goods'. The dismantling of this trafficked e-waste happens in precarious circumstances, with toxins leaking into the air, soil and water, causing harm to the environment and human health.

To demonstrate the nature and extent of 'e-waste' trade and trafficking, van Herk and Bisschop draw on the findings of two empirical studies about e-waste. The first focusses on illegal trade in e-waste between the port of Antwerp, Belgium and Accra, Ghana (Bisschop 2012, 2013, 2015). A second study focusses on data from e-waste traders in Hong Kong (van Herk 2016). By comparing e-waste trafficking in these two different locations, van Herk and Bisschop attempt to illustrate both the importance of locality when considering the global dimensions of the e-waste trade, and the economic, political and socio-cultural factors that influence the definitional processes, social organisation and governance of e-waste. Their chapter, thus, explores the wide range of characteristics of e-waste and its effects and uses, and contemplates the implications for control and prevention policy.

Van Herk and Bisschop begin their chapter by examining current international and European legislation for e-waste, including a discussion of the definitional challenges that are inherent to it. Next, they investigate the growing (informal) e-waste economy and illustrate the harm connected to the trafficking and informal recycling of e-waste. This section discusses global estimates of illegal e-waste trade but also considers the changes in consumption of electronics that influence the amount of discarded items. (As for the geographical orientation, the authors focus on the major regions and countries of origin, transit and destination, contemplating both interregional (North–South) trafficking and the emerging intraregional trade among developing nations.) From here, van Herk and Bisschop highlight the social organisation of the trafficking and informal recycling of e-waste by centring on the roles played by formal as well as informal actors in the e-waste economy. This allows the authors to reflect, in the final section, on the complexities in implementing governance policy about e-waste and about the relevance of this topic for the field of green criminology.

In their chapter, van Herk and Bisschop illustrate the legal-illegal interfaces in e-waste flows, stressing how legality, illegality and informality are inextricably intertwined. Accordingly, they urge green criminologists interested in the various dynamics of e-waste to think beyond such dichotomies. Chapter 23, 'The environment and the crimes of the economy', by Vincenzo Ruggiero, falls in line with this thinking—that environmental harm may be produced by both criminal conduct and completely lawful initiatives. Like van Herk and Bisschop, Ruggiero asserts that environmental harm cannot be reduced to a simple legal-illegal binary. Rather, environmental harm exists along a legal-illegal continuum. Ruggiero identifies 'foundational power crime' in the spaces between 'legal' and 'illegal' harm. Crimes are 'foundational', Ruggiero explains, when they occur in a grey area in which various conducts await the outcome of the criminalisation-decriminalisation conflict, in the sense that they may be subject to regulation or become accepted routine. While Ruggiero seeks to identify factors that might influence the outcome—that might affect whether conduct becomes regulated or routinised—his attention is to the novel traits of the crimes of the powerful, which make the causes of environmental harm possible, and to how the very logic of economic development, supported by the 'science' of economics, may be, even if legitimate, equally or more harmful and destructive. Throughout, Ruggiero maintains an international focus, drawing on examples from Europe and North America in order to demonstrate how certain types of environmental harm result from partnerships between members of conventional criminal organisations and official actors operating in the economic and political spheres. In so doing, he exposes and indicts those who participate in 'crimes of the economy'—pervasive and persistent harm caused by the economic initiative itself, aided by the philosophies underpinning and legitimising it.

In the section of his chapter entitled 'Axioms and risk', Ruggiero contends that '[l]ittle attention is given to the growing signs that the use of natural resources implied by an economic model based on infinite development is unsustainable, and that the time left to change it is becoming dramatically brief'. This point resonates with Michael J. Lynch's argument, in Chapter 24, 'Green criminology and the working class: Political ecology and the expanded implications of political economic analysis in green criminology', that labour cannot be exploited unless nature is also exploited. As Lynch explains, the process of industrial capitalist production requires raw material inputs, and those raw materials must first be extracted from nature using working class labour to initiate production. The more nature is exploited for its resources, the more the working class will be exploited in the aggregate—that is, the exploitation of nature allows the exploitation of the worker. As the exploitation of nature expands, the mass of surplus value also expands by increasing the mass of production. Consequently, the more nature is exploited for its resources, the more the working class can be exploited for its labour—through what can be described as a 'non-recursive relationship'. This understanding is integral to conceptualising the political economic analysis of the conjoined green victimisation of the working class and nature.

Lynch begins his chapter by connecting the exploitation of the working class and nature in political economic thought, before turning to a short account of working class responses to ecological destruction under capitalism. This is followed by a discussion of the linkages between workers and environmental movements from a political economic perspective. Lynch then considers working class concerns with exposure to environmental toxins in workplaces and communities, and how these may develop into contested illness struggles. This is followed by a brief consideration of the political economic analysis of environmental conflicts and struggles faced by the working class and poor in less-developed nations. As an example, Lynch describes how the recycling of e-waste has important detrimental ecological and public health effects on working class and poor peoples in less developed nations—a move that recalls van Herk and Bisschop's chapter at the beginning of this Part.

From Lynch's argument for expanding the political economic analysis of working class environmental issues within green criminology, we turn next to Liam Phelan, Cameron Holley, Clifford Shearing and Louise du Toit's exploration of the role of the global insurance industry in creating, adapting to and mitigating climate risk. In Chapter 25, 'Insurance and climate change', Phelan and his colleagues note that since 1988, 100 companies have been responsible for 71 per cent of global industrial greenhouse gas emissions (Griffin 2017: 8). Because fossil-fuel-based economic activity is dependent on the insurance industry, insurers are implicated strongly in the creation of climate change and climate risk (see generally Rauber 2019). Indeed, given the magnitude of the risks that climate change presents to human societies, Phelan and his co-authors contend that the ways in which insurers respond to climate change, including through shaping others' behaviour, becomes important.

Despite green criminology's history of critical narratives against corporate (and state) activities that harm humans and the environment (see, e.g., Short, this volume, Chapter 26, discussed below), Phelan, Holley, Shearing and du Toit suggest looking beyond state visions of governance to other providers of environmental security, and thus premise their chapter on the view that, in addition to creating harms, the private sector (which includes the insurance industry) has a role in addressing environmental harms and delivering public goods, like safety and environmental security. And it is with this backdrop—insurers as shapers of climate risk—that Phelan and his colleagues flesh out the historical and continuing role of insurers in creating climate risks (namely, how, during the period since industrialisation, insurers have facilitated the accelerating fossil-fuel-based economic development and growth that causes climate change (cf. South 2015).

In the third section of their chapter, Phelan, Holley, Shearing and du Toit review insurers' responses over the past decade to increasing climate risk. Responses have been largely adaptive, the authors explain, and aimed at increasing insurers' capacity to accommodate the climate risks faced by their policyholders. Some responses have been 'weakly mitigative', however, meaning that they provide for some mitigation, but on a very limited scale and largely as side effects of initiatives unrelated to climate change. In marked contrast, Phelan and his co-authors clarify, a very limited number of recent 'divest and decline' actions by insurance industry actors can be described as 'strongly mitigative'; these are noted in the fourth section of the chapter. Section five concludes the chapter with some remarks on the prospects for further strong mitigation action from insurers on climate change and their role as governors of security beyond the state.

Broadly, Phelan, Holley, Shearing and du Toit take the stance that criminology has traditionally concentrated its attention on responses to harm by professionals working within the 'criminal justice sub-assemblage (system)'. Within the context of the emerging 'harmscapes' that have begun to characterise the first quarter of the twenty-first century—which Berg and Shearing (2018: 75) define as 'new landscapes of local and global harms … for instance, the hypothesized multifarious harms associated with climate change'—it has become increasingly clear, Phelan and his colleagues submit, that criminology should extend its gaze beyond its established boundaries to include institutions outside of criminal justice. This notion that the management of 'harmscapes' should fall to a wider set of private governors (such as insurers and related financial actors) is called into question by Damien Short in Chapter 26, 'Energy harms: "Extreme energy", fracking and water'. While Short does not engage directly with Phelan and his co-authors, he observes that major international actors, namely nation-states and multi- and transnational corporations, have responded to the downward global trend in oil discovery and supply by taking various actions since the end of the Cold War to secure access to remaining conventional oil supplies. Short provides examples of corporate–state collaboration to further non-renewable energy use, before undertaking a broad holistic inquiry that highlights the causal drivers and the economic, political and social connections between corporate 'externalities', the global capitalist economy, the limits to (or of) a growth economy, political corruption and resource depletion, as well as community collective trauma and the criminalisation of protest.

Central to Short's argument is the claim that as conventional reserves are depleted and demand for energy rises, there is increasing pressure to exploit unconventional energy sources (rather than *renewable* energy sources). Klare (2010; see also Gross 2010) has coined the term, 'extreme energy', to describe a range of relatively new, higher-risk, non-renewable resource extraction processes that have become more attractive to the conventional energy industry as the more easily accessible supplies dwindle. Klare's (2010) notion of 'extreme energy'—and of the 'reckless drive to extract oil and natural gas from extreme environmental locations'—lacks explanatory and predictive power, Short contends. Drawing on earlier work (Short 2016; Short et al. 2015), Short develops a different understanding of 'extreme energy'—one that acknowledges that extraction methods grow more intense (or 'extreme') over time, as resources that are easier to extract become depleted: 'those energy sources which require the least amount of effort to extract will be used first; only once those become more scarce will more effort be exerted to gain similar resources'.

As energy extraction becomes more extreme, Short explains, the rest of the economy is squeezed by decreasing energy availability and rising prices. The energy industry's rising costs are then offset by the rising revenues it receives, and the net result is thus a reallocation—through the market or otherwise—of resources from the rest of society to the energy industry in order to allow the energy industry to target ever more difficult-to-extract resources. Under the process of 'extreme energy', one of the most precious resources that is being reallocated away from society to industry is water and, after a discussion of fracking and fracking harms, Short considers the impact of unconventional energy extraction on water resources (e.g., contaminated water waste disposal, excessive water use, groundwater contamination). Short's outlook is not particularly sanguine and he ends his chapter with the recognition that green criminologists will need to identify and analyse many considerable harms in the coming years, with the expansion of unconventional energy, as our more efficient resources dwindle, and while governments refuse to divorce themselves from the influence of the extractive industries.

Chapter 27, 'The uncertainty of community financial incentives for "fracking": Pursuing ramifications for environmental justice', by Jack Adam Lampkin, rounds out this Handbook's examination of some of the ways in which economic issues and processes affect and contribute to environmental harm. Lampkin's focus, like Short's in the previous chapter, is on the ways in which energy extraction processes contribute to ecological destruction and, in particular, on the emergence of *unconventional hydraulic fracturing* (UHF) in the United Kingdom. Drawing on interviews conducted with 20 key informants, Lampkin explores *community financial incentives* (CFIs) that are provided to communities by companies wishing to undertake UHF, and he analyses the subsequent ramifications that such payments may have for environmental justice in the communities that permit fracking to occur.

Lampkin notes that dwindling supplies of traditional fossil fuel energies, such as gas and oil, combined with increasing energy demand for a growing global population, raises practical and philosophical questions as to how humans can bridge the environment–energy nexus and perform an ecological balancing act. After surveying the evidence that suggests UHF has created multiple instances of both environmental and social harms in the areas where UHF has occurred, Lampkin considers the economic justifications for fracking. In particular, he asks whether CFIs mitigate the negative impacts of UHF or whether they function more as an 'admission of guilt' or 'corporate financial bribery'. Rather than offering a conclusive answer or a one-size-fits-all response, Lampkin urges us to consider issues such as, 'what constitutes *the community* with respect to CFIs?' As Lampkin explains, how *the community* is defined has implications for who or what is entitled to receive such payments, which has a significant impact on how the money is spent and how a community is able to undertake financial planning. Further definitional difficulties surround the very term, 'fracking', and Lampkin illustrates that what actually constitutes *fracking* and whether or not shale gas extraction operations that fall outside of specific legal boundaries still constitute fracking are important questions insofar as they may determine whether or not a community is entitled to receive associated financial payments in return for the right to use sub-surface resources. In many respects, then, Lampkin raises more questions than he answers. But in so doing, he lends support to his pleas for green criminologists to engage more thoroughly with the often-legal harms created by energy extraction processes.

Nicholas Kristof (2018: SR9), the Pulitzer-Prize-winning journalist and political commentator, asked recently, 'Does honoring animal rights come at the expense of human rights?' Kristof posed his question after considering studies (Herzog 2015; Kohn 2015; Levin et al. 2017) that seemed to suggest that news reports about non-human animal abuse often generate more empathy and expressions of outrage than those regarding violence directed toward humans. Kristof wondered whether we (humans) were 'betraying our own species when we write checks to help gorillas (or puppies or wild horses)' or whether it was 'wrongheaded to fight for elephants or rhinos'—as expressed by the two poems, 'The Wrinkled Rhinoceros' (2015) and 'The Rising Rhino' (2019), written four years apart by two different seven-year-old boys— 'while five million children still die each year before the age of 5' (Kristof 2018: SR9). Kristof determined that 'conserving rhinos or gorillas—or speaking up for tortured farm animals at home—is good for humans, too'—that '[a]t the broadest level, it's a mistake to pit sympathy for animals against sympathy for humans. Compassion for other species can also nurture compassion for fellow humans. Empathy isn't a zero-sum game'. Kristof (2018: SR9) concluded his article by stating:

> one of the most important resources some poor countries have is wildlife. Northern white rhinos are on the verge of extinction because of poaching to feed Chinese demand for rhino horn, with the last male in the world dying recently in Kenya.

This is a reference to the death of 'Sudan', who passed away on 19 March 2018 at the Ol Pejeta Conservancy (Dixon 2018; see also Nuwer 2018). 'When the animals are gone', Kristof (2018: SR9) ended, 'economic prospects for humans diminish as well'.

While Kristof's conclusion was that we, as humans, do not—or *should* not—possess a finite reserve of compassion and empathy, he seemed to suggest that we can care for both animals and humans because concern for the former *leads to* consideration and kindness for the latter. Under this formulation, then, compassion for animals is a stop on the path to empathy for humans, not an end or state of being into and of itself.

Part V, 'Relationships in green criminology: Humans and non-human species', probes and ponders the kind of questions raised by Kristof, providing a small representation of some of the green criminological issues arising from human abuse and mistreatment of animals, including interspecies sexual contact and animal sexual assault; the traffic and trade of animals, children and women; and the illegal trade in endangered species of wild fauna and the range and scope of (militarised) responses thereto. In Chapter 28, 'A violent interspecies relationship: Case of animal sexual assault', Jennifer Maher and Harriet Pierpoint submit that animal abuse creates challenges for traditional criminology once we move beyond the typical anthropocentric focus on animal abuse as, for example, a predictor of violent behaviour against humans. While the sexual assault of both humans and animals will usually be regarded as morally objectionable, Maher and Pierpoint assert that it is indefensible that criminologists have almost completely abandoned the study of animal victims. They ask: if it is not the duty of criminologists to expose the harm with a view to prompting change, then who? Maher and Pierpoint attempt to assume this responsibility by giving equal consideration to the interests of all sentient beings, that is, by highlighting animals as victims of sexual assault and by describing the impact of the multifarious harms they experience.

Maher and Pierpoint provide legal and philosophical reasons for taking animal sexual assault (ASA) seriously (considering both welfarist and rights-based approaches to animal abuse), and they document the nature and prevalence of the physical and psychological harm caused by ASA to animals. While they note that humans also suffer harm when ASA occurs, thereby providing an additional rationale for devoting increased attention to ASA, their larger point is that, regardless of the links to human suffering, ASA is an important area of inquiry because of the physical and psychological harms caused to *animals*. Following Beirne (2002), Maher and Pierpoint contend that human–animal sex is wrong and worthy of our concern for the same reasons as inter-human sexual assault—because it involves coercion, because consent cannot be given, and because it violates the rights of another.

Maher and Pierpoint's conclusion—that inequality, injustice and power are concerns central to ASA, just as they are to many, if not most, environmental harms—is illustrated further in Chapter 29, 'The victimisation of women, children and nonhuman species through trafficking and trade: crimes understood through an ecofeminist perspective', by Ragnhild Sollund. In this chapter, Sollund considers how women, children, non-human animals and nature more generally, are the victims of patriarchal actions, ideology and philosophy. After some prefatory comments about human–animal relationships, Sollund sketches out how international conventions seek to prevent trafficking and trade in human and animal bodies. As Sollund explains, a major difference between the goal of the conventions and protocols pertaining to human trafficking and those relating to animal trafficking and wildlife trade is that the former—the UN Palermo Protocol (a voluntary supplement to the United Nations Convention against Transnational Organized Crime) and the Council of Europe Convention —seek a *total ban* on the trafficking and trade in human victims, while the latter—the Bern Convention on the Conservation of European Wildlife and Natural Habitats 1979 and the Convention on International Trade in Endangered Species of Wild Fauna and Flora (or CITES)—seek only to *control* the trafficking and trade of animals, thereby preserving such activities and practices until the covered species have reached a critical state, at which time greater protections come into play.

Drawing on ecofeminist theory (e.g., Birkeland 1993; Collard and Contrucci 1989; Donovan 1993, 1996; Gaard 1993; Gruen 1993; Kheel 1996; Vance 1993), Sollund analyses why women, children and animals are regarded as commodities or exploitable resources, rather than perceived and treated as beings with rights to freedom and lives without physical and psychical abuse. In so doing, she contemplates why humans may benefit from legal instruments prohibiting them from trade and trafficking, while the instruments aiming to protect animals may have less power and efficacy.

Daan van Uhm continues this Handbook's consideration of the role of power in the worldwide wildlife trade in Chapter 30, 'Wildlife trafficking and criminogenic Asymmetries in a globalised world'. According to Passas (1999), criminal activities occur when 'criminogenic asymmetries'—structural disjunctions, inequalities and matches in the spheres of culture, economy, law and politics—are present; borrowing from Passas (1999), van Uhm puts forth that criminogenic asymmetries in the realms of ecology, economy, law, politics and power have created conditions ripe for global defaunation and enabled large flows of the illegal wildlife trade to flourish. To demonstrate how such criminogenic asymmetries contribute in complex ways to the absence of controls and provide opportunities for illegal wildlife trafficking, van Uhm offers three case studies: the illegal trade of rhino horn and tiger bone for use in Traditional Chinese Medicine (TCM); the smuggling of Barbary macaques, found in the Atlas Mountains of Algeria and Morocco, for sale as pets in Europe; and the poaching of sturgeon to satisfy the demand for caviar. The three case studies illustrate that in the context of global anomie and criminogenic asymmetries, structural discrepancies between the source and destination countries provide opportunities for crimes against nature—where legal and illegal entrepreneurs from countries of the Global North exploit poverty and inequality to entice people to participate in criminal activities, from poor farmers in Southeast Asia who hunt opportunistically endangered species for TCM to Berber communities in Morocco, who poach monkeys for the pet industry, to poor fishermen in Dagestan who catch sturgeon for caviar.

Whereas van Uhm reveals how the geopolitical and socioeconomic background of three biodiverse regions provides fertile breeding grounds for criminal networks driven by criminogenic asymmetries—and how, despite the differences between the three geographies of his case studies, the destruction of nature has, essentially, become a feature of an increasingly globalised world—Siv Rebekka Runhovde in Chapter 31, 'Myths of causality, control and coherence in the "war on wildlife crime"', considers the security implications of poaching and trafficking, and the ways in which the response from controlling authorities has become increasingly militarised. 'War' is now a common model and metaphor for approaches to biodiversity conservation across Africa, Runhovde explains, and this development is comparable to the 'wars' on crime, drugs and terrorism—as discussed by Ayres in Chapter 13—where use of strong language regarding criminals and zero tolerance is common and employed to promote and justify harsh repressive measures. Runhovde explores such questions as whether the current conceptualisations of wildlife crime reflect the situation at ground level, what the influence of a 'war' discourse has on the practices of law enforcement officers, whether the process of securitisation is driving the generation of effective responses, what the influence of securitisation has been on judicial processes, and whether suspected poachers and traffickers are treated fairly, in accordance with legal procedures and with respect to human rights. To answer these questions—and to provide insights into the wildlife crime/security nexus more generally—Runhovde draws on her previous research (see Runhovde 2017) in which she observed a disconnect between the authoritarian approach associated with the 'war on wildlife crime' and the everyday enforcement problems highlighted by officers in the East African state of Uganda.

Runhovde begins with an overview of the threats that wildlife face, noting that while the destruction of natural habitats by humans is the main cause of biodiversity loss, others include the introduction of alien invasive species, climate change, intensive agriculture, ozone depletion and pollution, as well as poaching and illegal trade. With this backdrop, Runhovde turns to the assumptions, metaphors, narratives and terms used to describe wildlife crime, describing how, in general, the 'war' metaphor represents a dramatic way to draw attention to a perceived serious threat and the response deemed necessary for tackling it. In the context of wildlife crime, however, Runhovde points out that the 'war on wildlife crime' discourse has material consequences insofar as the assimilation of biodiversity conservation into wider sets of policy debates and initiatives linked to global security has led to an emphasis on militarised responses and to increased possibilities for authoritarian control in enforcement. Runhovde thus argues that militarisation strategies in response to wildlife crime are unlikely to resolve the principal challenges at the ground level, where the need for basic equipment and conventional capacity building appears most critical. Indeed, while many forms of illegal wildlife trade are transnational, Runhovde notes that law enforcement officers experience and respond to it primarily as a local phenomenon. And with the majority of wildlife crime offenders in Uganda being opportunistic and poorly equipped locals, already under threat of arrest and sanctioning (Tumusiime et al. 2011), militarisation strategies are unlikely to deter these hunters and do little to provide alternative means of survival.

For Runhovde, the capacity of the 'war' metaphor to further blur the line between warfare and security, on one side, and criminality and crime control, on the other, is problematic given the different notions of risks and objectives between these types of activity. As her chapter suggests, the war metaphor may distort more than it illuminates and Runhovde reminds us that the distortion occurs, in part, because when discussing social policies and practices in the language of war, we tend to forget the moral conditions for resorting to and waging war. In sum, Runhovde warns, how we address wildlife crime has consequences for how we seek to deal with it: our interpretation of what is transpiring and our actions in response are structured by language, and eventually the line is crossed from metaphorical war to actual war. An inflated rhetoric of warfare that depersonalises poachers and traffickers as enemies, Runhovde concludes, should be used with caution because it serves to construct an image of wildlife crime that is misleading, that oversimplifies the challenges, and that fails to encourage responses that are effective in the long term.

David N. Pellow's Chapter 32, 'Environmental justice, animal rights and total liberation: From conflict and distance to points of common focus', the last chapter in Part V 'Relationships in green criminology: Humans and non-human species', further illustrates some of the challenges we face in addressing harm to animals. Here, however, the focus is not on the implications and consequences of war as metaphor in public policy or the effect of militarisation strategies in response to wildlife crime, but on the obstacles of conjoining social movements. As Pellow explains, the environmental justice (EJ) and animal rights (AR) movements would, at first glance, seem to be entirely distinct and unrelated social causes, whose struggles and goals reflect different ecophilosophies. Pellow considers the bases for divergences and conflicting visions across the environmental justice and animal rights movements before exploring how 'total liberation' (TL)—liberation from all forms of inequality—could represent a point of convergence and a place of possible collaboration between the two movements. While innovative and optimistic, Pellow is pragmatic and recognises the social differences between the EJ movement (traditionally composed of poor or working-class communities of colour) and the AR movement (frequently comprised of white middle-class men). Nevertheless, Pellow asserts that and demonstrates how social difference can become a resource, rather than a liability, for activists seeking to create alliances across these movements. At the end of the day, although members of the EJ and AR movements may hold different attitudes, beliefs and goals with respect to human–animal species relationships, both movements—and, indeed, all the chapters in this part—reflect a concern for the role played by power differentials, including class, gender and race-based inequalities, in the social construction of environment, nature, environmental crimes and harms, and environmental regulation and laws (or the dearth thereof).

As Pellow makes clear in his chapter, the EJ movement is comprised largely of people from communities of colour, Indigenous communities, and working class communities who are focussed on combating environmental racism and injustice. The term, 'environmental racism', as Angus Nurse explicates in Chapter 33, 'Environmental justice and the rights of

Indigenous peoples'—the first chapter in Part VI, 'Relationships in green criminology: Environment and culture'—covers various activities but has been defined as

> racial discrimination in environmental policy making, the enforcement of regulations and laws, the deliberate targeting of communities of color for toxic waste facilities, the official sanctioning of the life-threatening presence of poisons and pollutants in our communities, and the history of excluding people of color from leadership of the ecology movements.
>
> *(Mohai et al. 2009: 406–407 (footnote omitted))*

Environmental racism, Nurse continues, exists when governments and corporations pursue policies that disproportionately impact marginalised groups and minorities, including Indigenous peoples, or engage in racial discrimination in environmental decisions or policy implementation (Bullard 2007; Bullard et al. 2008; Park 1998; Schlosberg 2007).

Nurse's goal in Chapter 33 is to consider how Indigenous people often suffer disproportionately from the negative impacts of environmentally harmful activities but may also have their traditional rights upheld through exemptions in law—a situation whereby Indigenous people may be marginalised with respect of access to (some) natural resources (e.g., clean air, clean water), but, due to their ethnic and cultural status, may be able to continue with some activities that might otherwise be prohibited under environmental and wildlife legislation. In particular, Nurse contemplates examples of culturally endorsed animal harm, such as the whaling practices of ethnic minorities and Indigenous peoples, that would otherwise be unlawful under contemporary environmental protection legislation. This entails a consideration of the extent to which contemporary perspectives on environmental and ecological justice can apply where environmental protection policies may be in conflict with the rights of Indigenous peoples. Nurse discusses existing perspectives on Indigenous rights and how these align—or not—with contemporary ecological (and species) justice discourse. In doing so, Nurse highlights the cultural importance of certain natural resource exploitation practices in relation to specific ethnic or cultural identities such that, for example, animal killing activities continue despite legislative or political efforts to eliminate them. Drawing on some of his previous work (e.g., Nurse 2013)—and with a nod to van Uhm's earlier chapter—Nurse illuminates how animal harm is socially constructed to have different meanings according to the society in which it occurs and thus the same act (for example, the killing of a whale) may have multiple meanings: illegal wildlife crime in the view of animal activists and legislators or legitimate cultural practice in the eyes of the Indigenous person committing the act. Nurse's purpose is not to develop a cookie-cutter approach to future issues or tensions of this nature, but to shed light on how Indigenous people's historical environmental rights have been criminalised or become subject to challenge by contemporary environmental justice perspectives.

Environmental justice scholars often emphasise how toxic factories and pollution and waste sites disparately affect communities of colour—and Nurse is no different in this respect. But what Nurse's chapter adds is a reminder that environmental injustice and racism entails *both* disproportionate exposure to environmental 'bads' or 'harms' and the denial of access to environmental 'goods' (e.g., natural resources)—and, in his example of the Makah Indian Tribe of the Pacific Northwest of the United States, the opportunity to hunt grey whales in furtherance of their customs and traditions (but prohibited under domestic and international law). Thus, Nurse's chapter serves to illustrate a complexity—indeed, an apparent paradox—that seems to exist whereby Indigenous people are marginalised with respect to access to natural resources, but, due to their ethnic and cultural status, may be able to continue with some activities that might otherwise be prohibited under environmental and wildlife legislation.

The clash between Euro-centred Western values and Indigenous or Native American values is explored further in Chapter 34, 'Green crime on the reservation: A spatio-temporal analysis of U.S. Native American reservations 2011–2015', by Tameka Samuels-Jones, Ryan Thomson and Johanna Espin. As Samuels-Jones and her co-authors explain, non-Indian landowners have different priorities than tribes regarding the use and management of natural resources. Thus, an examination of environmentally harmful activities on reservations usually reveals the location of capitalist systems of production on or close to reservations or, in other cases, when state actors effectively designate reservations as 'sacrifice zones' in the name of national interests.

In their chapter, then, Samuels-Jones, Thomson and Espin explore this unequal relationship between Western societies and Indigenous peoples, which has resulted in a higher occurrence of environmental or 'green' crimes on tribal lands. More specifically, they offer an analysis of environmentally criminal behaviour on and around Native American reservations in the United States using geospatial cluster analysis to examine prolonged case studies that instantiate and highlight the relevance of the historical processes and lasting effects of hazardous exposures. (For the spatial distribution and occurrence of green crimes in or close to reservations they rely on data from the EPA's Enforcement and Compliance History Online (ECHO) database (https://echo.epa.gov).) Samuels-Jones and her co-authors also consider key court rulings and environmental laws to illustrate characteristics of the legal-procedural framework that continue to enable colonial power relations throughout the United States that facilitate unequal toxin exposure. Their findings are then used to advance a critique of policies that have enabled the expansion of environmental crimes in and around reservations, providing evidence that much of the green crime on Native American lands may be traced to corporate and military activity (Smith et al. 2014).

All in all, Samuels-Jones, Thomson and Espin's chapter offers an exploration of the uneven spatial distribution and lasting temporal effects of environmental injustices affecting the environmental and community health of a wide variety of Native American tribes. Using geospatial analysis and case study analysis, they discuss both the statistically significant concentrations of green crime on reservations and offer an overview of the historical and political factors guiding these green criminal trends. The examination of environmental harm from this perspective highlights the ways in which colonisation and capitalism have contributed to the flourishing of environmental crimes on reservations. While the three authors' spatial analysis captures evidence of widespread harm, we must emphasise that there are equally devastating cultural and traditional impacts which do not meet the legal definition of crime but also require further investigation and study—and thus this is one of the reasons why we have placed their chapter, along with Nurse's, in Part VI, 'Relationships in green criminology: Environment and culture'. Indeed, whereas Western capitalists view the accumulation of material wealth as an indicator of success, Indigenous peoples/Native Americans view the preservation of the environment as paramount to their cultural and spiritual survival.

Because it is clear that political and economic forces, not tribes, determine the value of natural resources, Samuels-Jones and her co-authors argue, an explanation for environmental crimes occurring on reservations must include a historical and multifaceted analysis of laws and regulations, cultural norms, social values and economic and environmental practices. In a similar vein, Lieselot Bisschop, Staci Strobl and Julie Viollaz, in Chapter 35, 'The disappearing land: Coastal land loss and environmental crime', claim that in order to understand fully who is harmed by environmental plundering, as well as who benefits from such activities, the economic, political and social context needs be taken into account. Drawing on their case study of the Isle de Jean Charles (a small island located in Terrebonne Parish in the Louisiana bayou in the southeastern part of the United States)—in particular, interviews with key stakeholders regarding their perceptions of ecological harm, who is responsible for the harm (if anyone), and what are potential solutions—Bisschop and her co-authors demonstrate that coastal land loss is an environmental crime both in terms of its causes and consequences. (About 1.5 million people in Louisiana live in an area that is at risk of coastal land loss and sea level rise, the authors note, and about 40 per cent of the at-risk inhabitants are members of, or descendants from, minority groups.) Bisschop, Strobl and Viollaz then connect their findings to two other locations that face this fate with disturbingly similar causal dynamics: the Wadden Sea (the Netherlands) and the Sundarbans Delta (India and Bangladesh). Although the causes that Bisschop and her co-authors discuss in the context of Louisiana are legal activities (such as canal digging for oil exploration and river manipulation to serve industrial development), the authors note that these activities reflect the capacity of states and corporations to use their power to perpetuate significant social harms. From a state-corporate crime perspective, then, Bisschop and her co-authors maintain that such harms at the hand of elite actors should be considered crimes and they put forth that regional-level corporate behaviours have likely contributed more to coastal land loss problems than the often-cited sea-level rise due to global climate change (though this too is a contributing factor).

What makes Bisschop, Strobl and Viollaz's chapter particularly relevant to Part VI's examination of the impact of environmental crimes and harms on culture is that for a long time, residents of Isle de Jean Charles engaged in subsistence fishing, farming and trapping. There was enough land to grow vegetables and raise livestock, and crawfish, oysters, and shrimp were plentiful to catch and eat. Today, those livelihoods are disappearing: whereas the island once measured about 160 square kilometres in 1950, it is now barely 1.2 square kilometres. The harm to the community, though, extends beyond just the threats to residents' livelihoods that Bisschop and her co-authors describe. It has affected the sense of community, as well as the culture of the island. For instance, floods have damaged old cemeteries, destroying Native American tribes' cultural heritage. Many inhabitants are members of the Biloxi-Chitimacha-Choctaw and Houma Native American tribes and the land loss endangers their spiritual relationship with their land and resources. For them, the issue of land loss is entangled with issues of sovereignty, human rights and inequality. This leaves Bisschop, Strobl and Viollaz to lament that those responsible for a region's plans for coastal restoration often seem to forget about the cultural impacts of land loss, especially for the poorest in that region. Indeed, when decision-makers base their determinations primarily on economic cost-benefit analyses that provide for technical restoration efforts—or when ecological issues are approached solely as engineering or scientific problems to be solved—socio-cultural impacts on communities are ignored.

Bisschop and her co-authors' chapter is significant for extending our understanding of environmental (in)justice and environmental racism—and the ways in which the economic benefits of exploiting the Earth for profit have costs that are disproportionately paid by the poor. Their chapter is also vital for illuminating how, in the overarching category of 'Relationships in green criminology: Environment and culture', culture can be both a *driver* of environmental harm (discussed further by Nurse (above) in his chapter, and Ferrell (below) in his chapter) and a *tragedy* or *victim* of environmental harm (discussed further by

Samuels-Jones and her co-authors, and by Brisman, South and Walters in their observation of how rising global temperatures and the concomitant loss of biodiversity results in 'cultural extinction').

Two additional points that emerge from Bisschop, Strobl and Viollaz's comparative examination of coastal land loss in Louisiana, the Netherlands, and India and Bangladesh—an under-researched topic of study in green criminology—bear mention. First, while the specific reasons for coastal land loss may vary from community to community—or from country to country—*some* combination of natural processes and human activities is always at work. This means that while the extent of coastal land loss is generally not disputed—coastal land loss denial is far less pervasive than, say, climate change denial (see Kramer and Bradshaw, this volume, Chapter 9) and thus is much less of an 'invisible crime' (Davies et al. 2014)—identifying the main cause of coastal land loss remains contentious, and anthropogenic causes (sea level rise and the subsiding of land) tend to be downplayed.

Second, for Bisschop, Strobl and Viollaz, what is striking in the case of Isle de Jean Charles is the lack of a formal legal framework for responding to coastal land loss. This, the authors maintain, has had discursive consequences for how stakeholders imagine the problem, its causes and its solutions. Quite often, climate change is erroneously named as the main culprit for Isle de Jean Charles coastal land loss, probably due to the presence of the climate change problem in popular media and political discourse: it is an easy culprit, they note. Indeed, climate change has had a greater effect in the Sundarbans Delta than Isle de Jean Charles, Bisschop and her co-authors emphasise, but even there it remains a lesser force when compared with river manipulation by the state (the Farakka Barrage). Bisschop, Strobl and Viollaz thus underscore the importance of attending to the social construction of environmental crimes and harms—an area of particular interest for *green cultural criminology* (Brisman et al., 2014) and the topic of Chapter 36.

In Chapter 36, 'Toward a green cultural criminology of the south', Avi Brisman and Nigel South remind readers how green cultural criminology—a cross-fertilisation of green criminology and cultural criminology—has attempted to: (1) examine the way(s) in which environmental crimes, harms and disasters are constructed and represented by the news media and in popular cultural forms; (2) highlight and analyse patterns of consumption, constructed consumerism, commodification of nature, and related market processes; and (3) explore the contestation of space, transgression and resistance, in order to understand the ways in which environmental harms are opposed in/on the streets and in day-to-day living. Reflecting criminology more generally (see Brisman, South and Walters, this volume, Chapter 10; Goyes, this volume, Chapter 12), green cultural criminology has developed with somewhat of an urban and northern bias, Brisman and South admit. While some efforts have been undertaken to address the former—such as Brisman, McClanahan and South's article, 'Toward a Green-Cultural Criminology of "the Rural"' (2014)—Brisman and South take the opportunity in this chapter to tackle green cultural criminology's northern bias. The authors weave together green, cultural and southern criminologies through the exposition of several key issues, including 'the south' as a context in which exploitative global forces may exercise power (e.g., biodiversity loss due to patterns and practices of resource extraction; the theft of nature and the pollution of land, water and air from agribusiness and the food/profit chain). Focussing on the first of the three areas of green cultural criminological interest—the construction of environmental crimes, harms and disasters in popular cultural forms—Brisman and South contemplate examples of Latin-American cultural narratives of human–environment relationships (from the nineteenth century (e.g., Sarmiento 1845) to twentieth- and twenty-first-century presentations of tales old and new (such as *The Magic Bean Tree: A Legend from Argentina* (Van Laan 1998) and *The Future According to Luz*, a two-book graphic novel series by the Chilean-born Claudia Dávila (2011, 2012)). Brisman and South conclude by identifying several examples of possible directions in which the intersection of green, cultural and southern criminologies might proceed, including studies of energy integration and diversification in Latin America and critical interpretations of media and popular narrative depictions of environmental issues within the Global South. But they stop short of offering an agenda, blueprint or guide, emphasising that a genuinely *Southern* criminology cannot be prescribed from the North.

Part VI, 'Relationships in green criminology: Environment and culture', continues with Chapter 37, 'Consumed by the crisis: Green criminology and cultural criminology' by Jeff Ferrell —a chapter consonant with the theoretically integrative efforts of Agnew (Chapter 2), Burton and colleagues (Chapter 3), Lynch and colleagues (Chapter 4), and Natali and McClanahan (Chapter 5), among others. Ferrell begins by noting how green criminology and cultural criminology both push against the conventional boundaries of criminology, and so tend to upset the definitional and epistemic order of the discipline. Both green criminology and cultural criminology, Ferrell continues, are open to exploring a range of social harms and social consequences, whether these harms are defined as criminal, currently left outside the orbit of law and criminality, or even, themselves, propagated by the criminalisation process. At their best, Ferrell asserts, both green criminology and cultural criminology link their overt substantive concern—environmental harm in the case of green criminology, meaning and representation in the case of cultural criminology—with broader issues of power and inequality. And both attempt to situate their subject matter historically—in terms of its long-range development and its current residency within the crisis of late modernity and late capitalism.

Drawing on Brisman and South (2013, 2014), Ferrell demonstrates the potential for a convergence of green criminology and cultural criminology through a consideration of consumer culture as ecological harm. Like the authors in Part IV, who analyse corporate pollution and the pervasive corporate violation of environmental and health regulations, and who connect particular corporate practices and their representations (profit-taking, privatisation, unregulated manufacturing processes) to the particular environmental harms that are their consequences, Ferrell seeks to locate cases of environmental destruction within the exploitative dynamics of contemporary economic arrangements. Ferrell argues that as a result of these processes, late capitalism promotes both consumption and a pervasive *culture of consumption*—an increasingly globalised consumerist way of life defined by advertised meaning, constructed need, cycled fashion, and conspicuously acquired status. This late capitalist consumer culture—this culture of consumption—not only serves to mask the environmental abuses (and labour abuses) that underpin the manufacture of its products (corporate pollution and degradation of natural resources are made all but invisible to privileged consumers), but produces 'waste as pervasive as it is predictable'. As Ferrell reveals, the endless advertised construction of new needs and insatiable insecurities not only promotes the (over)consumption of natural resources to generate whatever products are currently being marketed as their solution, but the discarding of products accumulated by the consumer once those products come to be reconstructed as inadequate in the next round of marketing.

The dynamics, features and processes of everyday ecological resistance and everyday criminalisation serve as a second point of a convergence of green criminology and cultural criminology. Here, Ferrell draws on more than a decade of ongoing research into, and participation with, the various contemporary subcultures of trash picking, urban scrounging and dumpster diving. While his focus is on the United States, he notes that the globalisation of capitalism and the ongoing ecological and financial crises that have accompanied it have helped spur worldwide subcultures of scrounging and trash picking. Such trash pickers and activists, Ferrell contends, can be understood as participants in an eclectic, wide-ranging global phenomenon that intertwines alternative economic arrangements, environmental activism and desperate day-to-day survival. But despite their environmentally benevolent activities (see Brisman 2010)—or perhaps because such informal waste scrounging threatens to expose the very logic of consumer capitalism and its concomitant environmental harm—those participating in informal recycling and environmental reclamation frequently find their activities criminalised.

Cultural criminology's examination of popular culture constructions (especially mass media constructions) of crime and crime control, and its investigation of how the dynamics of media and popular culture, the lives and activities of criminals and their subcultures, and the operations of social control and criminal justice converge in everyday life serve as a lodestar for a healthy number and range of scholarly articles, books and chapters in edited volumes—as well as inspiration for a growing number of green criminologists. But it is cultural criminology's concern with the impact and meaning of consumer culture—for our purposes, the role of consumer culture in and on ecological harm—that leads us to Chapter 38. Thus, Part VI's theoretically innovative ways of exploring cultural dimensions to the means in which environmental harm is contested, depicted, represented, resisted and understood ends with Kelly Johnson, Tanya Wyatt, Sarah Coulthard and Cassandra O'Neill's chapter, 'Littering in the northeast of England: A sign of social disorganisation?'

Littering and fly-tipping appear to be getting worse in the United Kingdom (Reality Check team 2018; see generally Bodkin 2018; Thompson et al. 2019), perhaps reflective of larger global issues with respect to garbage or rubbish (see generally Gutierrez 2019). As Johnson and her co-authors describe, not only does the presence and accumulation of litter in public spaces have a negative social effect on the environment and reduce the aesthetic appeal of such places, but it also has devastating impacts on local ecosystems, contributes to environmental disasters such as flooding, and creates health risks and extra expense for tax payers.

Recognising that criminology has had little to say about littering—Nic Groombridge's (2013) chapter in the first edition of this Handbook being a notable exception—Johnson, Wyatt, Coulthard and O'Neill report on a study they conducted at four different sites in the northeast of England in the summer of 2016 to explore the nexus of personal wellbeing linked to the environment and to anti-social behaviour. In particular, Johnson and her colleagues sought to answer: (1) What is the nature and extent of litter at four observation sites (e.g., lone or group littering)? (2) What are the demographics of litterers (e.g., gender, estimated age)? and (3) Does sense of ownership of space (e.g., resident or visitor) affect whether a person litters? The authors begin by distinguishing 'fly-tipping' and 'littering', and then turn to a consideration of evolving perspectives on fly-tipping and littering, as well as legislative efforts to address these phenomena. From here, Johnson and her co-authors present their research questions and methodology, followed by their findings and analysis of their data in relationship to social disorganisation theory. While Johnson, Wyatt, Coulthard and O'Neill demonstrate how the act of littering has evolved throughout history from a consequence of consumerism and mobility to a global environmental concern—and make clear that the lack of attachment to place(s) may be contributing to the noticeable litter problem in the northeast of England and elsewhere—their work implies that additional criminological study of littering (including both an investigation of the role that a lack of effective informal and formal social control plays in littering and the impact of beautifying small swathes of the landscape through the 'ordinary act' of picking up trash or not littering in the first place) could make a contribution to improvement of human health and the vitality of the environment. As such, their chapter offers a somewhat more sanguine outlook on the potential of green criminological research to effect positive change—and thus is a fitting end to the substantive chapters in this second edition.

The chapters in the Handbook in no way represent the full range of environmental crimes, harms, risks and threats in the world. Nor does the Handbook include all of those researchers and scholars writing about environmental crimes and harms from a criminological perspective. Indeed, an entire third volume could be composed of scholars whom we would have liked to have included in the Handbook but whose other obligations prevented them from doing so. Nonetheless, the Handbook is 'international' in its discussion of the multiple origins of some problems and the multiple locations where other problems are experienced and felt, and the Handbook is 'international' in the ways in which geography plays a role in the values, perspectives and consciousness of the individual contributors to the volume, not to mention the individual, corporate and governmental contributors to—and victims of—environmental problems. What follows, then, is a representative, rather than exhaustive, Handbook—one that will hopefully inspire research and the study of new topics in new ways. At the same time, we hope that the Handbook will spur necessary action so as to render some environmental problems to historical fact, while bearing in mind the maxim of Michael Brune (2019: 6), Executive Director of the Sierra Club, that 'environmental victories are never final'—that 'the next pipeline proposal or oil-drilling permit is always around the corner [...]'.

Notes

1 See, e.g., Leiserowitz (2004), Lowe et al. (2006), and Reusswig and Leiserowitz (2005) for analyses of the impact of *The Day After Tomorrow* on moviegoers' perceptions of climate change risk.

2 Humans are animals and share many of the same characteristics with animals that are not human, such as the capacity to feel pain and suffering (see Sollund 2017). As such, some find it problematic to refer to all animals other than humans as 'animals'—grouping millions of species together—while excluding human animals from this category. Accordingly, some contend that a different term should be employed, such as 'nonhuman animals' (or 'non-human animals'). This term, however, is not without its own difficulties because it simply reproduces the very duality that those employing it wish to overcome and because it defines animals other than human animals through a negation—somewhat akin to calling a female human a 'non-man', rather than a 'woman' (see Beirne 2009). 'Animals other than human animals' (or 'AOTAs') has also been suggested (see, e.g., Beirne 2007), but it also privileges the *Homo sapiens* species and suffers from obscurity, thereby running the risk of confusing readers. Beirne's (2007: 18) 'practice is to juxtapose "humans" with "nonhuman animals" and then, at a suitably proximate point, to attach "(hereinafter, 'animals')" after the term "nonhuman animals"'. Following Beirne—and for lack of a good alternative (while still recognising its limitations)—we employ the term 'animals' in our authored chapters when speaking of animals that are not human animals. Other authors have been granted the freedom to choose different terminology and to comment on their choice (or not) as they see fit.

3 The loss of biodiversity extends beyond plants; according to the United Nations' Food and Agriculture Organization, 'a traditional breed of livestock dies out every week' (D'Auria 2019: 25).

4 Criminology has often referred to both 'environmental crime', in the singular, and 'environmental crimes', in the plural, with little consideration of the difference. Recently, however, Levi (2017: 4) has suggested that 'environmental crimes' is preferable—'the plural here being deliberate to avoid artificial homogenisation and confusion from ambiguity'. While one of the very purposes of this Handbook is to demonstrate the heterogeneity of crimes and harms in and to the environment, we

adopt Levi's pluralisation suggestion in order to emphasise quantity. We stop short, however, of imposing such a decision on the contributors to this volume.

5 More recently, Wu (2019: 17, 19), in a brilliant critique of academic computer science, laments that as an undergraduate and a master's student, 'our job was to solve whatever problems we were given, not to question what problems we should be solving in the first place'.

6 According to Schoenfeld (2018: 3), the incarceration rate in the United States grew from approximately 161 per 100,000 in 1972 to 760 per 100,000 in 2008 at the height of imprisonment—figures that amount to 1 in 100 adults and well over 2,000,000 people confined in a jail or prison in the United States. Racial minorities are overrepresented significantly in America's prisons, and in the early 1990s, at the height of the 'War on Drugs' in the United States, 60 per cent of the prison population was African American (Schoenfeld 2018: 18).

7 The 'fluid' used in fracking is 'a mixture of water (98–99.5 per cent) and a proprietary cocktail of organic and inorganic additives including sand and fluids (0.5–2.0 per cent): acids to improve gas flow, biocides to prevent clogging, corrosion and scale inhibitors to prevent leaks, gels or gums to add viscosity, and friction reducers to maintain pressure from surface pumps to the furthest reaches of the wells' (Michaels and Simon 2013: 12 (footnote omitted)). As Michaels and Simon (2013: 12) point out, 'the specific composition of fluids is unknown, however, because the gas drilling industry has guarded the composition of fracking fluids'. Some claim that the mysterious fluid includes toxic chemicals, resulting in adverse health effects for people living in close proximity to drilling sites (Davis and Fisk 2017; Michaels and Simon 2013).

References

Anderson, R. 2015. 'Greenwashing Washington state's prison system in a river of sewage,' *Prison Legal News*, 26(8) [August]: 1, 3–11.

Beirne, P. 2002. 'On the sexual assault of animals: A sociological view,' in A. Creager and W. Jordan (eds.) *The Animal/Human Boundary: Historical Perspectives*, pp. 193–227. Rochester, NY: University of Rochester Press.

Beirne, P. 2007. 'Animal rights, animal abuse and green criminology,' in P. Beirne and N. South (eds.) *Issues in Green Criminology: Confronting Harms against Environments, Humanity and other Animals*, pp. 55–83. Cullompton, Devon, UK: Willan.

Beirne, P. 2009. *Confronting Animal Abuse: Law, Criminology, and Human-Animal Relationships*. Lanham, MD: Rowman & Littlefield.

Berg, J. and Shearing, C. 2018. 'Governing-through-Harm and public goods policing,' *The Annals of the American Academy of Political and Social Science*, 679(September): 72–85.

Birkeland, J. 1993. 'Ecofeminism: Linking theory and practice,' in G. Gaard (ed.) *Ecofeminism: Women, Animals, Nature*, pp. 13–60. Philadelphia, PA: Temple University Press.

Bisschop, L. 2012. 'Is it all going to waste? Illegal transports of e-waste in a European trade hub,' *Crime, Law and Social Change*, 58(3): 221–249.

Bisschop, L. 2013. 'Go with the e-waste flows. The governance reality of illegal transports of e-waste in a European trade hub,' in P. van Duyne, J. Harvey, G. Antonopoulos, K. von Lampe, A. Maljević and J. Spencer (eds.) *Human Dimensions in Organised Crime, Money Laundering and Corruption*, pp. 393–424. Nijmegen: Wolf Legal Publishers.

Bisschop, L. 2015. *Governance of the Illegal Trade in E-Waste and Tropical Timber. Case Studies on Transnational Environmental Crime*. Surrey, UK: Ashgate.

Bisschop, L. and Huisman, W. 2018. 'Waste crime from three criminological perspectives. Implications for crime control and harm prevention,' in T. Spapens, R. White, D. Uhm and W. Huisman (eds.) *Green Crimes and Dirty Money*, pp. 148–176. Abingdon, Oxon, UK: Routledge.

Bodansky, D., Brunnee, J. and Hey, E. (eds.) 2007. *The Oxford Handbook of International Environmental Law*. Oxford: Oxford University Press.

Bodkin, H. 2018. Fly-tipping and Speeding: Rural communities living in fear as confidence in police drops. *The Telegraph*. July 23. Available at: www.telegraph.co.uk/news/2018/07/22/fly-tipping-speeding-rural-communities-living-fear-confidence/.

Brisman, A. 2010. 'The indiscriminate criminalisation of environmentally beneficial activities,' in R. White (ed.) *Global Environmental Harm: Criminological Perspectives*, pp. 161–192. Cullompton, Devon, UK: Willan.

Brisman, A., McClanahan, B. and South, N. 2014. 'Toward a green-cultural criminology of "the rural",' *Critical Criminology: An International Journal*, 22(4): 479–494.

Brisman, A., McClanahan, B., South, N. and Walters, R. 2018. *Water, Crime and Security in the Twenty-First Century: Too Dirty, Too Little, Too Much*. London: Palgrave Macmillan.

Brisman, A. and South, N. 2013. 'A green-cultural criminology: An exploratory outline,' *Crime Media Culture*, 9(2): 115–135.

Brisman, A. and South, N. 2014. *Green Cultural Criminology: Constructions of Environmental Harm, Consumerism, and Resistance to Ecocide*. Abingdon, Oxon, UK: Routledge.

Brune, M. 2019. 'One planet, one vote,' *Sierra Magazine*, 104(2) [March/April]: 6.

Bullard, R. D. 2007. Wasted people: Environmental racism: A 20-year Saga. *Black Agenda Report* (April 4, 2007). Available at: www.blackagendareport.com/content/wasted-people-environmental-racism-20-year-saga.

Bullard, R. D., Mohai, P., Saha, R. and Wright, B. 2008. 'Toxic wastes and race at twenty: Why race still matters after all of these years,' *Lewis & Clark Environmental Law Journal*, 38(2): 371–411.

Collard, A. and Contrucci, J. 1989. *Rape of the Wild: Man's Violence against Animals and the Earth*. Bloomington and Indianapolis, IN: Indiana University Press.

D'Auria, P. 2019. 'Saving seeds,' *Oberlin Alumni Magazine*, 114(1) [Spring]: 22–27.

Davies, P., Francis, P. and Wyatt, T. (eds.) 2014. *Invisible Crimes and Social Harms*. Basingstoke, Hampshire, UK: Palgrave Macmillan.

Dávila, C. 2011. *Luz Sees the Light*. Toronto: Kids Can Press.

Dávila, C. 2012. *Luz Makes a Splash*. Toronto: Kids Can Press.

Davis, C. and Fisk, J. M. 2017. 'Mitigating risks from frackingrelated earthquakes: Assessing state regulatory decisions,' *Society & Natural Resources*, 30(8): 1009–1025. DOI: 10.1080/08941920.2016.1273415.

del Olmo, R. 1993. 'The geopolitics of narcotrafficking in Latin America,' *Social Justice*, 20(3/4): 1–23.

del Olmo, R. 1998. 'The ecological impact of illicit drug cultivation and crop eradication programs in Latin America,' *Theoretical Criminology*, 2(2): 269–278.

Dixon, R. 2018. The last male Northern White Rhino has died, spelling probable extinction for the species. *Los Angeles Times*. March 20. Available at: www.latimes.com/world/la-fg-kenya-white-rhino-20180320-story.html.

Donovan, J. 1993. 'Animal rights and feminist theory,' in G. Gaard (ed.) *Ecofeminism: Women, Animals, Nature*, pp. 167–195. Philadelphia, PA: Temple University Press.

Donovan, J. 1996. 'Attention to suffering: Sympathy as a basis for the ethical treatment of animals,' in J. Donovan and C. J. Adams (eds.) *Beyond Animal Rights: A Feminist Caring Ethic for the Treatment of Animals*, pp. 147–170. New York: Continuum.

Dunne, T. 2009. 'How do we secure the environment: Review of 'security and environmental change' by S. Dalby, Polity, 2009,' *Times Higher Education*, October 8: 46.

Egan, T. 2019. Until we get real action on climate, try some fake meat. *The New York Times*. 22 June: A22. Published online as 'Fake Meat Will Save Us' on June 21, 2019, at www.nytimes.com/2019/06/21/opinion/fake-meat-climate-change.html.

Gaard, G. 1993. 'Living interconnections with animals and nature,' in G. Gaard (ed.) *Ecofeminism: Women, Animals, Nature*, pp. 1–13. Philadelphia, PA: Temple University Press.

Gregory, R. and W. Trousdale. 2009. 'Compensating aboriginal cultural losses: An alternative approach to assessing environmental damages,' *Journal of Environmental Management*, 90(8): 2469–2479.

Griffin, P. 2017. *The Carbon Majors Database: CDP Carbon Majors Report 2017*. CDP. Available at: https://b8f65cb373b1b7b15feb-c70d8ead6ced550b4d987d7c03fcdd1d.ssl.cf3.rackcdn.com/cms/reports/documents/000/002/327/original/Carbon-Majors-Report-2017.pdf.

Groombridge, N. 2013. 'Matter all over the place: Litter, criminology and criminal justice,' in N. South and A. Brisman (eds.) *The Routledge International Handbook of Green Criminology*, pp. 394–408. Abingdon, Oxon, UK: Routledge.

Gross, D. 2010. 'Fracking, oil sands, and deep-water drilling'. *Slate*. June 6. Available at: https://slate.com/business/2010/06/the-dangerous-new-era-of-extreme-energy.html.

Gruen, L. 1993. 'Dismantling oppression: An analysis of the connection between women and animals,' in G. Gaard (ed.) *Ecofeminism: Women, Animals, Nature*, pp. 60–91. Philadelphia, PA: Temple University Press.

Gutierrez, J. 2019. 'Trash collection day,' *The New York Times*. May 24: A4.

Herzog, H. 2015. Why people care more about pets than other humans. *Wired*. April 15. Available at: www.wired.com/2015/04/people-care-pets-humans/.

Jarrell, M. L. 2013. 'Book review: Nigel South and Avi Brisman (eds), Routledge international handbook of green criminology,' *Theoretical Criminology*, 17(4): 585–588. DOI: 10.1177/1362480613506638.

Jewkes, Y. and Moran, D. 2015. 'The paradox of the "green" prison: Sustaining the environment or sustaining the penal complex,' *Theoretical Criminology*, 19(4): 451–469.

Kheel, M. 1996. 'The liberation of nature. A circular affair,' in J. Donovan and C. J. Adams (eds.) *Beyond Animal Rights: A Feminist Caring Ethic for the Treatment of Animals*, pp. 17–34. New York: Continuum.

Klare, M. 2010. The relentless pursuit of extreme energy: A new oil rush endangers the Gulf of Mexico and the planet. *The Huffington Post*. May 19. Available at: www.huffpost.com/entry/the-relentless-pursuit-of_b_581921?guccounter=1. Updated December 6, 2017.

Kohn, S. 2015. Americans care more about cecil the lion (and dogs, too) than Syrian refugees. *Quartz*. November 20. Available at: https://qz.com/555858/americans-care-more-about-cecil-the-lion-than-syrian-refugees/.

Kristof, N. 2018. 'Choosing animals over people'. *The New York Times*. April 8: SR9. Published online as 'Choosing Animals Over People?' on April 7, 2018, at www.nytimes.com/2018/04/07/opinion/sunday/wildlife-central-african-republic.html.

Leiserowitz, A. A. 2004. 'Before and after the day after tomorrow: A U.S. study of climate change risk perception,' *Environment*, 46(9): 24–37.

Levi, M. 2017. 'Emerged from the American shadows? Reflections on the growth of criminology in the UK,' *Criminology in Europe: Newsletter of the European Society of Criminology*, 16(2): 4–8. Available at: https://escnewsletter.org/newsletter/2017-2/emerged-american-shadows-reflections-growth-criminology-uk AND https://escnewsletter.org/sites/escnewsletter.org/files/newsletter/2017/esc_newsletter_2017_2_online_final.pdf.

Levin, J., Arluke, A. and Irvine, L. 2017. 'Are people more disturbed by dog or human suffering?' *Society & Animals*, 25(1): 1–16. DOI: 10.1163/15685306-12341440.

Lowe, T., Brown, K., Dessai, S., de França Doria, M., Haynes, K. and Vincent, K. 2006. 'Does tomorrow ever come? Disaster narrative and public perceptions of climate change,' *Public Understanding of Science*, 15(4): 435–457.

Lynch, M. J., and Stretesky, P. B. 2010. 'Global warming, global crime: a green criminological perspective,' in R. White (ed.) *Global Environmental Harm: Criminological Perspectives*, pp. 62–84. Cullompton, Devon, UK: Willan.

Lynch, M. J., Long, M. A., Barrett, K. L. and Stretesky, P. B. 2013. 'Is it a crime to produce ecological disorganization? Why green criminology and political economy matter in the analysis of global ecological harms,' *The British Journal of Criminology*, 55(6): 997–1016.

Michaels, R. A. and Simon, R. W. 2013. 'Fracking in New York: Weighing risks and benefits. Albany, New York state bar association,' *NYSBA Municipal Lawyer*, 23(3) [Fall]: 12–16.

Mohai, P., Pellow, D. and Roberts, J. T. 2009. 'Environmental justice,' *Annual Review of Environment and Resources*, 34(1): 405–430.

Moreto, W. D. (ed.) 2018. *Wildlife Crime: From Theory to Practice*. Philadelphia, PA: Temple University Press.

Nurse, A. 2013. *Animal Harm: Perspectives on Why People Harm and Kill Animals*. Surrey, UK: Ashgate.

Nuwer, R. 2018. A subspecies of Rhino has lots its last male. *The New York Times*. March 21: A8. Published online as 'Sudan, the Last Male Northern White Rhino, Dies in Kenya' on March 20, 2018, at www.nytimes.com/2018/03/20/science/rhino-sudan-extinct.html.

Nuwer, R. 2019. 'What the world knows,' *Sierra Magazine*, 104(2) [March/April]: 32–39. Available at: https://digital.sierramagazine.org/publication/?i=568875&article_id=3309413&view=articleBrowser&ver=html5#{%22issue_id%22:568875,%22view%22:%22articleBrowser%22,%22article_id%22:%223309413%22}.

Park, R. S. 1998. 'An examination of international environmental racism through the lens of transboundary movement of hazardous wastes,' *Indiana Journal of Global Legal Studies*, 5(2): 659–709.

Passas, N. 1999. Globalization, criminogenic asymmetries and economic crime,' *European Journal of Law Reform*, 1(4): 399–424.

Paulson, N. 2018. 'An emergent "blue criminology"? Review of a new critical criminology book on water,' *Critical Criminology: An International Journal*. Online First October 12, 2018. DOI: 10.1007/s10612-018-9410-2.

Plumer, B. 2017. To slow deforestation, study offers an easy fix. *The New York Times*. July 21: A9. Published online as 'A Cheap Fix for Climate Change? Pay People Not to Chop Down Trees' on July 20, 2017, at www.nytimes.com/2017/07/20/climate/a-cheap-fix-for-climate-change-pay-people-not-to-chop-down-trees-uganda.html.

Plumer, B. 2019. Wildlife facing extinction risk all over globe. *The New York Times*. May 7: A1. Published online as 'Humans Are Speeding Extinction and Altering the Natural World at an 'Unprecedented' Pace', on May 6, 2019, at www.nytimes.com/2019/05/06/climate/biodiversity-extinction-united-nations.html?module=inline.

Rauber, P. 2019. 'The cost of doing business,' *Sierra Magazine*, 104(3) [May/June]: 18–19.

Reality Check team. 2018. 'Fly-tipping: Is it getting worse?' *BBC News*. January 15. Available at: www.bbc.com/news/uk–42689357.

Renkl, M. 2019. 'Surviving despair in the great extinction.' *The New York Times*. May 13. Available at: www.nytimes.com/2019/05/13/opinion/united-nations-extinction.html?action=click&module=Opinion&pgtype=Homepage.

Reusswig, F. and Leiserowitz, A. A. 2005. 'The international impact of the day after tomorrow (Commentary),' *Environment*, 47(3): 41–43.

Romero, S. 2011a. 'Brazil's long shadow vexes some neighbors.' *The New York Times*. November 5: A1, A8.

Romero, S. 2011b. 'Brazilian officials warn chevron over offshore spill.' *The New York Times*. November 19: A8.

Romero, S. 2012. 'World briefing: The Americas: Brazil: President vetoes major parts of bill to open up forests'. *The New York Times*. 26 May: A6.

Runhovde, S. R. 2017. 'Comparing discourse to officer perceptions: The problems of war and militarization in wildlife crime enforcement,' *Critical Criminology: An International Journal*, 25(2): 275–291. DOI: 10.1007/s10612-017-9360-0.

Sarmiento, D. F. 2003 [1845]. *Facundo: Civilization and Barbarism*, trans. Kathleen Ross Berkeley, CA: University of California Press.

Schept, J. and Mazurek, J.E. 2017. 'Layers of violence: Coal mining, convict leasing, and carceral tourism in central appalachia,' in J. Z. Wilson, S. Hodgkinson, J. Piché and K. Walby (eds.) *The Palgrave Handbook of Prison Tourism*, pp. 171–190. London: Palgrave Macmillan.

Schlosberg, D. 2007. *Defining Environmental Justice: Theories, Movements, and Nature*. New York: Oxford University Press.

Schoenfeld, H. 2018. *Building the Prison State: Race & the Politics of Mass Incarceration*. Chicago, IL: University of Chicago Press.

Schön, D. A. 1993. 'Generative metaphor: A perspective on problem-setting in social policy,' in A. Ortony (ed.) *Metaphor and Thought*, 2nd ed., pp. 137–163. New York: Cambridge University Press.

Short, D. 2016. *Redefining Genocide: Settler Colonialism, Social Death and Ecocide*. London: Zed Books.

Short, D., Elliot, J., Norder, K., Lloyd-Davies, E. and Morley, J. 2015. 'Extreme energy, "fracking" and human rights: A new field for human rights impact assessments?' *The International Journal of Human Rights*, 19(6): 697–736. DOI: 10.1080/13642987.2015.1019219.

Smith, C. L., Hooks, G. and Lengefeld, M. 2014. 'The war on drugs in Colombia: The environment, the treadmill of destruction and risk-transfer militarism,' *Journal of World-Systems Research*, 20(2): 182–203.

Sollund, R. 2017. 'The use and abuse of animals in wildlife trafficking in Colombia: Practices and injustice,' in D. R. Goyes, H. Mol, A. Brisman and N. South (eds.) *Environmental Crime in Latin America: The Theft of Nature and the Poisoning of the Land*, pp. 215–243. London: Palgrave Macmillan.

South, N. 2015. 'Anticipating the anthropocene and greening criminology,' *Criminology & Criminal Justice*, 15(3): 270–276.

Stretesky, P. B., Long, M. A. and Lynch, M. J. 2013. *The Treadmill of Crime: Political Economy and Green Criminology*. Abingdon, Oxon, UK: Routledge.

Stubbs, J. 2008. 'Critical criminological resarch,' in T. Anthony and C. Cunneen (eds.) *The Critical Criminology Companion*, pp. 6–17. Annandale, NSW: Hawkins Press.

Tarr, D. and Us-Sabah, N. 2019. 'The end of the line,' *Commune*, 2 (Spring): 79–91.

Thompson, B., Tseloni, A., Hunter, J., Tilley, N. and Tiwari, P. 2019. Street drinking, fly-tipping and nuisance neighbours: Who experiences anti-social behaviour? *The Conversation*. May 2. Available at: https://theconversation.com/street-drinking-fly-tipping-and-nuisance-neighbours-who-experiences-anti-social-behaviour–116316.

Tullis, P. 2019. 'How the Sapphire trade is driving lemurs toward extinction.' *National Geographic*. March 6. Available at: www.nationalgeographic.com/animals/2019/03/sapphire-mining-fuels-lemur-deaths-in-madagascar/.

Tumusiime, D. M., Vedeld, P. and Gombya-Ssembajjwe, W. 2011. 'Breaking the law? Illegal livelihoods from a protected area in Uganda,' *Forest Policy and Economics*, 13: 273–283.

United Nations Environment Programme (UNEP). 2006. *A High-Level Meeting on Compliance with and Enforcement of MEAs* [online], Available at: http://new.unep.org/Documents.Multilingual/Default.asp?DocumentID=466&ArticleID=5113&1=en.

Van Herk, W. 2016. *Is One Man's Trash Another Man's Treasure? On Social Constructions of Electronic Waste*. Utrecht: Utrecht University.

Van Laan, N. 1998. *The Magic Bean Tree: A Legend from Argentina*. Beatriz Vidal, illus. Boston, MA: Houghton Mifflin Company.

Vance, L. 1993. 'Ecofeminism and the politics of reality,' in G. Gaard (ed.) *Ecofeminism: Women, Animals, Nature*, pp. 118–145. Philadephia, PA: Temple University Press.

Wagner, G. 2011. 'Going green but getting nowhere.' *The New York Times*. September 8: A29.

Walters, R. 2007. 'Crime, regulation and radioactive waste in the United Kingdom,' in P. Beirne and N. South (eds.) *Issues in Green Criminology: Confronting Harms Against Environments, Humanity and Other Animals*, pp. 186–205. Cullompton, Devon, UK: Willan.

Walters, R. 2010. 'Eco crime,' in J. Muncie, D. Talbot and R. Walters (eds.) *Crime: Local and Global*, pp. 171–208. Collumpton, Devon, UK, Milton Keyes, UK: Willan/The Open University..

Weis, V. V. 2019. 'Por una criminología crítica verde del sur. Un análisis sobre selectividad penal, pueblos indígenas y daños ambientales en Argentina. [For a southern green critical criminology. An analysis on criminal selectivity, indigenous peoples and environmental damage in Argentina],' *Revista Crítica Penal y Poder*, 16 (Marzo): 53–74. Available at: http://revistes.ub.edu/index.php/CriticaPenalPoder/article/view/28573/29166.

White, R. 2010. 'Globalisation and environmental harm,' in R. White (ed.) *Global Environmental Harm: Criminological Perspectives*, pp. 3–19. Cullompton, Devon, UK: Willan.

White, R. 2018. *Climate Change Criminology*. Bristol: Bristol University Press.

Wu, J. 2019. 'Optimize what?' *Commune*, 2(Spring): 16–22.

Yee, A. 2019. 'Green tech takes hold in Africa, but its waste is a problem,' *The New York Times*. May 13: B3. Published online as 'Electronic Marvels Turn Into Dangerous Trash in East Africa' on May 12, 2019, at www.nytimes.com/2019/05/12/climate/electronic-marvels-turn-into-dangerous-trash-in-east-africa.html.

Part I

History, theory and methods

1

The growth of a field

A short history of a 'green' criminology

Avi Brisman and Nigel South

Our planet and its ecosystems face threats of increasing scale and complexity, mostly resulting from human activity. Yet, a stubborn commitment to 'business as usual' and growth economics—combined with either denial of anthropogenic emissions and pollutants, faith in Gaia's cornucopia, or an uncritical belief in our ability to save ourselves from the consequences of our actions—suggest that any responses may be a case of 'too little, too late'. As Pretty (2011: 50) submits, even when we do 'acknowledge … that it is indeed humans who have caused climate change, biodiversity extinction, pollution and cultural loss', we also maintain that 'we can invent ourselves out of any problem'.

It is now clear that criminology has much to contribute to debates about these threats and harms. As green criminology has developed, it has addressed epistemological, methodological, political and theoretical questions, and established a strong base and growing body of work. Among the challenges along the way has been the difficulty of moving beyond traditional criminological conceptions and definitions of 'crime'. This has been a vital step (although not one confined to green criminology) because definitions of 'crime' and 'offending' are often created or shaped by the powerful members of socio-economic elites, whose organisations and systems of production and reproduction initiate many, if not most, environmental harms. It is also they, like other powerful offenders, who will seek to reject definitions of 'crime' and 'offending' that might be applied to them and who will pass on the costs of avoiding environmental regulations, including safety standards for products and workers, to others who must bear the consequences. To that end, such firms and organisations invest enormous resources in efforts to persuade politicians and courts that the imposition of legislation and regulation clearly marking limits to environmental harm would be damaging to their profitable economic development, and therefore detrimental to the economic situation and stability of all (Ruggiero and South 2010: 246). All the while, multinational corporations and other corporate-state entities work to construct and reconstruct the public and social meaning of 'green' (see, e.g., Beder 1997; Benton 2007; Brisman 2009; Lynch and Stretesky 2003).

To review, beginning in the 1960s, some work in criminology and in sociological studies of deviance and power began to make significant contributions to critical thinking about environmental harm (Goyes and South 2017; and see various papers reprinted in South and Beirne 2006; White 2009). Only since the 1990s, however, has that momentum and wider interest gathered behind the efforts of criminologists to examine regulation, public policy and the diminution of legal protections, as well as issues of social responsibility and citizen empowerment regarding the preservation of the environment (Beirne et al. 2018; Beirne and South 2007; Lynch 1990; South and Beirne 1998). This work has developed into a new, identifiable green field within criminology that has promised—and continues to offer—enormous scope and potential. For example, South (1998: 226) has argued that

> [g]reen issues open up a wide range of possibilities for interdisciplinary work, both within the social sciences and with disciplines in the natural sciences, offering the potential for collaboration between criminologists and economists, geographers, biologists, health specialists, philosophers, human rights workers, lawyers and others.

Methodologically and theoretically, as White (1998: 214) suggests, the 'investigation of environmental harm requires analysis which is wide-ranging and multi-disciplinary, and which is sensitive to the inter-connectedness of social and ecological phenomena'. Essentially, if criminology is a 'rendezvous discipline' (Hayward and Young 2007) or 'rendezvous subject' (Downes 1988; see also Garland and Sparks 2000: 193, 202; South 2007: 231, 2010: 228), then this characterisation has become particularly appropriate as a description of criminology's engagement with environmental issues.

Introducing green criminology: terms and typologies

As alluded to above, green criminology has emerged as a fertile area of study bringing together a wide range of research interests and theoretical orientations (see, e.g., Beirne and South 2007; Brisman 2014b; Sollund 2008; South 2014; White 2010a). It has not been and is not intended to be a unitary enterprise. Diversity is one of its great strengths and it is most helpfully seen as a capacious and evolving *perspective* (see, e.g., South 1998: 212–213; see also White 2008: 14)—a loose framework or set of intellectual, empirical and political orientations toward problems (crimes, harms and offences related to the environment, different species and the planet). Importantly, it is also an 'open' perspective and framework, arising from within the tradition(s) of critical criminology; at the same time, it actively seeks inter- and multi-disciplinary engagement. It is both a network of interested individuals and a forum for sharing and debating ideas. Green criminology is thus *invitational*, to borrow from cultural criminology's self-description (Ferrell, Hayward and Young 2008).

Green criminology remains fluid and full of potential to link with other (both established and growing) areas within criminology (e.g., Agnew 2012; this volume, Chapter 2; Altopiedi 2019; Brisman 2014b, 2017a, 2018; Ferrell, this volume, Chapter 37). It also seeks to forge connections across the humanities, social sciences and natural sciences (e.g., Brisman 2011; Lynch and Stretesky 2011, 2014: 29–49). The 'naming' of the field has occasionally attracted debate and alternatives include 'environmental criminology', which White (2008) has argued could be reclaimed from what is more properly considered 'place-based criminology', to cover the study of environmental harms and threats, environmental legislation and related research activity. This usage is an obvious reflection of the way that the word 'environment' is frequently employed in everyday discussion and contemporary media but suffers the drawback of being too easily confused with its longer established usage in criminology to describe relationships between the incidence of crime and the spatial features of the built and urban environment.[1] Without expressly abandoning this endeavour, White (2010b: 6) has also offered the term 'eco-global criminology' to

> refer to a criminological approach that is informed by ecological considerations and by a critical analysis that is worldwide in its scale and perspective … one that expresses a concern that there be an inclusive definition of harm, and … a multidisciplinary approach … to the study of environmental harm.

In a related vein, Walters (2010a: 180) has suggested that the term 'eco-crime' is helpful and capable of 'encapsulat[ing] existing legal definitions of environmental crime, as well as sociological analyses of those environmental harms not necessarily specified by law'. Other formulations include 'conservation criminology' (Gibbs et al. 2010; Herbig and Joubert 2006). It seems, however, that criminologists most frequently employ the term 'green criminology' to describe the study of ecological, environmental or green crime or harm, and related matters of speciesism and of environmental (in)justice. Even so, as Goyes and South (2017: 178) argue, while the term and concept are very useful, their true value lies in drawing attention to concerns about the health and future of our environments and planet.[2]

Putting aside various names and nuances, all these terms represent similar frameworks and share a common interest in the bio-physical and socio-economic consequences of different sources of threat and damage to the environment, whether biodiversity loss, climate change, pollution or resource degradation. Whatever the descriptor—and ignoring questions of aetiology and different levels of individual, micro and macro analysis (which we touch on later in this chapter)—there is agreement on the need for research and debate on matters such as: pollution and its causes, consequences and control; corporate criminality and its impact on the environment; health and safety in the workplace where breaches have environmentally damaging consequences; involvement of organised crime and official corruption in the illegal disposal of toxic waste; the impact and legacy of law enforcement and military operations on landscapes, water supply, air quality and living organisms populating these areas—human, animal and plant; and the potential and scope of criminal law to prevent environmental despoliation and punish perpetrators of harm.

It is important to recognise that the way we identify and organize clusters of issues and problems can influence research agendas, policy priorities and methodologies (White 2010c: 415; see also Heckenberg and White, this volume, Chapter 6), and some simple but useful typologies can assist us in thinking about how to present the research directions and challenges relevant to green criminology (Lynch et al. 2017: 8–12). One typology derives from a distinction between 'primary' and 'secondary' green crimes (Carrabine et al. 2004) and has been developed further by Potter (2014). This is a straightforward but suggestive way of differentiating clusters of harms and crimes by classifying some as resulting directly from the destruction and degradation of the Earth's resources, and others as those crimes or harms that are symbiotic with or dependent upon such destruction and efforts made to regulate or prevent it.

Purely as an illustrative exercise, we can identify four 'primary' green crimes in which the environment and species other than humans are damaged, degraded or harmed by human actions—all of which, to add a positive note, have become the subject of some national and international legislative efforts to protect and intervene in recent years:

1. Crimes of air pollution	2. Crimes of deforestation
3. Crimes against animals	4. Crimes of water pollution

'Secondary' or 'symbiotic' green harms and crimes can arise from the exploitation of conditions that follow environmental damage or crisis (e.g., illegal markets for food, medicine, water) and/or from the violation of rules that attempt to regulate environmental harm and to respond to disaster. These can include numerous major and minor practices whereby states violate their own regulations (either by commission or omission) and, in so doing, contribute to environmental harms. Potter (2014: 11) takes this approach to a 'tertiary' level to add discussion of 'green crimes' that may be defined as those 'committed by environmental victims or as a result of environmental victimization … [e.g.] committed as a deliberate or direct response to environmental harm … [or] exacerbated by the experience of environmental victimisation', which might include: (1) crimes committed by those forced to migrate in response to environmental harms (e.g., Brisman 2019; Brisman, South and Walters 2018, this volume, Chapter 10; Hall and Farrall 2013); (2) increasing crime rates as environmental harm and changing environments (including access to natural resources) impact social and economic conditions that relate to crime (e.g. Agnew 2012); and (3) crimes relating to exposure to environmental pollutants, such as lead or other heavy metals, which can have behavioural effects (e.g., aggression, learning difficulties) that some criminological theories posit as causes of crime (see, e.g., Lynch and Stretesky 2014: 103–21; Muller, Sampson and Winter 2018; Sampson and Winter 2018).[3]

A different threefold typology is offered by White (2008: 98–99) in which 'brown' issues are defined in terms of urban life and pollution—air pollution, disposal of toxic/hazardous waste, oil spills, pesticides, pollution of beaches and water catchments, stormwater pollution; 'green' issues refer to conservation matters and 'wilderness' areas (e.g., acid rain, biodiversity loss, habitat destruction, invasive species introduced via human transport, logging practices, ozone depletion, toxic algae and water pollution); and 'white' issues include the impact of new technologies and various laboratory practices (e.g., animal testing and experimentation; cloning of human tissue; environmentally related communicable diseases; food irradiation; genetically modified organisms; in-vitro processes; and pathological indoor environments).

Rather than promote a particular categorisation or typology, we instead rehearse the substantive topics and themes addressed by the breadth of scholarship in green criminology, including harms to the environment, to humans and to animals. The following section considers theoretical developments and frameworks in green criminology. We end with some observations about future work.

Theoretical developments and frameworks of analysis

Conceivable theoretical positions concerned with environmental crimes and harms may draw upon existing traditions and developments within criminology, including feminism, Marxism and post-modernism, among many others (South 1998: 212). The idea of an approach unified simply as a 'perspective' affords flexibility. While as an entire discipline, academic criminology may be 'fragmented' (DeKeseredy 2010: 57), green criminology is decidedly not so: it combines investigation of both that which may be proscribed and that which may not be. While there is rarely 'any type of integration or accommodation between establishment and anti-establishment criminologies' (Barak 2003: 219)—or attempts to create such bridges—green criminology can accommodate both (see Brisman (2014b) for a discussion). It spans the micro to the macro—from work on individual-level environmental crimes to business/corporate violations to state transgressions—and includes research conducted from both mainstream and critical theoretical perspectives, as well as arising from interdisciplinary efforts (see, e.g., Brisman and South 2018b; Gibbs et al. 2010).

A number of criminologists have adopted a *legal-procedural approach* to their research on environmental issues, focussing on violations of existing environmental law (including civil and regulatory violations) designed to protect the health, safety and vitality of humans, animals, natural resources and ecosystems, while others pursue a *socio-legal approach*, contemplating environmental harms that may not be statutorily proscribed (for a discussion and examples of these approaches see, e.g., Brisman 2008; Burns, Lynch and Stretesky 2008; Halsey and White 1998; Walters 2007, 2010a; White 2008). Some scholars use different terminologies to describe these two approaches, but the conceptual divisions are effectively the same. For example, Lynch and Stretesky (2003) outline a 'corporate perspective' (akin to the legal-procedural approach) and an 'environmental justice perspective' (similar to the socio-legal approach) with the corporate perspective involving a recognition of the influence of corporate power structures on the creation or delineation of those unauthorised acts or omissions that violate the law, and which are therefore subject to criminal prosecution and sanctions. This 'corporate perspective' rests upon 'a very precise, exact and limiting definition of what can be considered a "crime"' while, by contrast, the 'environmental justice perspective' contemplates and includes acts or omissions that may not constitute a violation of an existing form of law but which result in, or have the potential to result in, harms to environments, to humans and to animals (Lynch and Stretesky 2003: 229, 227).

White (2010c: 411) notes that the 'spectrum of ideas and activities associated with green criminology' can encompass a variety of analytical frameworks:

> Some of these pertain to eco-philosophy, that is, to ways in which the relationship between humans and nature can be conceptualised. Academic work in this area might include consideration of gendered views of the natural and social worlds (Lane 1998; Plumwood 2005), exploration of anthropocentric, biocentric and ecocentric perspectives (Halsey and White 1998), through to postmodern versions of a constitutive green criminology (Halsey 2004). Less abstractly, however, most environmental criminology can be distinguished on the basis of who precisely it is that is being victimised.

The latter mission for a green criminology—to investigate and to advocate in cases of environmental victimisation and injustice (Hall 2013; Hall and Farrall 2013; Jarrell and Ozymy 2012, this volume, Chapter 8; Sollund this volume, Chapter 29; South 2010; Stephens 1996; Williams 1996)—places the idea of ecological and speciesist inequalities at 'the top of the environmental agenda' (White 2010c: 412). This is now articulated quite well in relation to environmental racism and to the 'toxic inequalities' and 'toxic struggles' of poor communities of colour (e.g., Bullard 1990, 1993; Hofrichter 1993; Muller, Sampson and Winter 2018; Sampson and Winter 2016, 2018; Winter and Sampson 2017), with respect to colonial exploitation in the developing worlds (e.g., Brisman and South 2016; Crook, Short and South 2018; Goyes 2016; Williamson 2003), and on behalf of those species who inhabit the planet with us but who have no voice (e.g., Beirne 1994, 1997, 1999, 2007, 2009, 2011; Benton 1998; Sollund 2008, 2011, 2012b, 2013, 2015a, 2015b, 2016, 2017a, 2017b; Wyatt 2009, 2011, 2013, 2014, 2016).

Given the connections and comparisons that can be made between male violence against nature and against women (e.g., Epstein 1993; Merchant 1980, 1996; Pellow, this volume, Chapter 32; Wachholz 2007), however, and the role that women have played in resistance and advocacy concerning the environment and intergenerational justice (Lane 1998), it is surprising that feminist criminology and related disciplinary areas have not played a more powerful role in the development of green criminology—though the works of Gaarder (2011, 2013), Maguire (2019), Sollund (2012a, 2012c, this volume Chapter 29), and Wonders and Danner (2015) all make serious and significant contributions to filling this gap.

The multifarious interdependencies among nature, humans and the other species inhabiting a shared planet, on the one hand, mean that we should consider all present and future harms when we damage any part of these complex systems. On the other hand, this is not to say that all parts can live together harmoniously. Inevitably, in current evolutionary and global arrangements, humanity exerts exploitative pressures on the planet and seeks, albeit so far in tentative ways, to take such misuse of power into space (littering it with space junk as we go). Rights discourses can clash in many areas (see, e.g., Beirne 2007; Brisman 2014a; South and Brisman 2013; Squires 2017) and this is likely to be highlighted further in the future as the pressures of demand are felt upon the availability of potable water, fertile land and clean air (Brisman et al. 2018a; Brisman, South and Walters, this volume, Chapter 10; Walters 2010b, 2013). Moral philosophy and ethics may have much to offer this area of criminology, especially as humanity faces the reality of and considers its role in driving so many species to extinction or the brink thereof (see, e.g., Brisman and South 2018a, 2018b, 2019).

Directions for future research

Green criminology needs to continue its efforts to forge connections that will take forward theory, policy and practice, developing the perspective both within criminology as well as across other disciplines. More importantly, a future programme of research is necessary, based on the fundamental and hugely significant challenges now posed with regard to the sustainability of societies, species and the planet. Such research will require commitment, imagination and creativity, including innovation in methodological approaches in order to synthesise existing and create new knowledge (see, e.g., Brisman and South 2017d; Sollund and Brisman 2017).

The open character of green criminology and the sweep of its research horizon—from the local to the global—mean it is easy to see how exciting new research directions and connections arise. For example, work on the role of media in presenting, reporting and imagining environmental harms and crimes has become an important area and, linked to studies of the cultural sphere, has given rise to a 'green cultural criminology' (see, e.g., Brisman 2014b, 2015, 2017a, 2017b, 2018, 2019; Brisman and South 2012, 2013, 2014, 2015, 2017a, 2017b, 2018a, this volume; Brisman, McClanahan and South 2014; Mazurek 2017; McClanahan 2014; Ningard 2018; Redmon 2018; Schally 2014, 2018). The sensory experience and interpreted aesthetics of environments and their features are being discussed in terms of the visual (Brisman 2017b, 2018; Carrabine 2018) and the sonic (Garcia-Ruiz and South 2018), and the 'sensory' more generally (McClanahan and South 2020). At the macro/global level, green criminology has always recognised global inequalities, the north-south divide and the weight of exploitation bearing down on Indigenous and colonised peoples, non-human species and resource-rich territories (whether above or below the sea). In so doing—and, we would note, rather recently—it has connected fruitfully and powerfully to the important new area of southern criminology and investigated the environmental contexts of migration, injustice against Indigenous peoples and forms of resistance (Carrington, Hogg and Sozzo 2016; Carrington et al. 2018; Crook, Short and South 2018; Goyes et al. 2017; Hogg,

Scott and Sozzo 2017). Concurrently and increasingly, attempts are being made to communicate across language barriers (e.g., Brisman and South 2012, 2017c; Mol et al. 2017; Natali 2015; South, Brisman and McClanahan 2018)—a welcome development, as well as a necessary one, given the transboundary nature of environmental problems and the need for collaborative, cross-boundary solutions.

Conclusion

Green crimes and harms are a part of everyday life and death on planet Earth, but that does not mean they should be accepted or are acceptable. As described in the Introduction, many of the chapters in this second edition of the *Routledge International Handbook of Green Criminology* urge that politics, policy and practice must engage with these issues and challenges as a matter of urgency. While Sampson and Winter (2018: 295) have recently suggested that '[t]he field of criminology would ... benefit by expanding its traditional focus on criminal justice institutions to include a more direct engagement with environmental policy' (citation omitted), green criminology has, in fact, been doing as much over the last three decades. Indeed, green criminology is taking a leading role in this regard and the contributors to this volume are among those at the forefront of this movement.

Notes

1 It bears mention that in the fifth edition of the *Oxford Handbook of Criminology*, the chapter on this area of criminology was titled 'Developing socio-spatial criminology' with one reason for this name change, the author explained, being that the use of 'environmental crime' as a description could generate confusion 'because it is sometimes used to refer to the important emerging field of "green" criminology' (Bottoms 2012: 451).

2 For accounts of the history and content of green criminology, as well as 'criminology's several environmentalisms', see Beirne (2009: 19 n.13) and the compilation of essays in South and Beirne (2006) that reflect the breadth of contributions that have built a green criminology.

3 Indeed, with respect to this last point—the relationship of crime(s) to environmental pollutants—Sampson and Winter (2018: 295) have recently argued:

> Criminological policy normally looks to actions governed by the *criminal justice system*, such as by the police or courts. But lead exposure is rightly categorized as an *environmental hazard*, and its distribution throughout the population is determined by business decisions (e.g., where to locate an industrial plant or whether to comply with local regulations) and myriad government policies and actions, such as federal policies set by the [U.S. Environmental Protection Agency], proper maintenance of the water supply by local municipalities, the remediation of contaminated soil, and the enforcement of restrictions on lead paint in rental units (Markowitz and Rosner 2013; Muller, Sampson and Winter 2018). Although these are 'non-crime' policies, they are potentially relevant to reducing crime. To paraphrase Reyes (2007), we suggest that *environmental policy is sound criminological policy as well* [emphases added].

To this, we might make the additional proposition that good *criminological policy* can be *sound environmental policy* (see, e.g., Mazurek et al., this volume, Chapter 14).

References

Agnew, R. 2012. 'Dire forecast: A theoretical model of the impact of climate change on crime,' *Theoretical Criminology*, 16(1): 21–42.

Altopiedi, R. 2019. 'Environmental crimes: Controversies and perspectives,' in T. Hall and V. Scalia (eds.) *A Research Agenda for Global Crime*, pp. 78–90. Cheltenham, UK: Edward Elgar.

Barak, G. 2003. 'Revisionist history, visionary criminology, and needs-based justice,' *Contemporary Justice Review*, 6(3): 217–225.

Beder, S. 1997. *Global Spin: The Corporate Assault on Environmentalism*. Melbourne: Scribe Publications.

Beirne, P. 1994. 'The use and abuse of animals in criminology: A brief history and current review,' *Crime and Social Justice*, 22(1): 5–31.

Beirne, P. 1997. 'Rethinking bestiality: Towards a concept of interspecies sexual assault,' *Theoretical Criminology*, 1(3): 317–340.

Beirne, P. 1999. 'For a nonspeciesist criminology: Animal abuse as an object of study,' *Criminology*, 37(1): 117–147.

Beirne, P. 2007. 'Animal rights, animal abuse and green criminology,' in P. Beirne and N. South (eds.) *Issues in Green Criminology: Confronting Harms Against Environments, Humanity and Other Animals*, pp. 55–83. Cullompton, Devon, UK: Willan..

Beirne, P. 2009. *Confronting Animal Abuse: Law, Criminology, and Human-Animal Relationships*. Lanham, MD: Rowman & Littlefield.

Beirne, P. 2011. 'On the facticity of animal trials in early modern Britain; or, the curious prosecution of farmer Carter's dog for murder,' *Crime, Law and Social Change*, 55(5): 359–374.

Beirne, P., Brisman, A., Sollund, R. and South, N. 2018. 'Editors' Introduction to the Special Issue: "For a Green Criminology"—20 Years and Onwards,' *Theoretical Criminology*, 22(3): 295–297.

Beirne, P. and South, N. (eds.). 2007. *Issues in Green Criminology: Confronting Harms Against Environments, Humanity and Other Animals*. Cullompton, Devon, UK: Willan.

Benton, T. 1998. 'Rights and justice on a shared planet: More rights or new relations?' *Theoretical Criminology*, 2(2): 149–175.

Benton, T. 2007. 'Ecology, community and justice: The meaning of green,' in P. Beirne and N. South (eds.) *Issues in Green Criminology: Confronting Harms against Environments, Humanity and Other Animals*, pp. 32–54. Cullompton, UK: Willan.

Bottoms, A. 2012. 'Developing socio-spatial criminology,' in M. Maguire, R. Morgan and R. Reiner (eds.) *The Oxford Handbook of Criminology*, pp. 450–489. Oxford: Oxford University Press.

Brisman, A. 2008. 'Crime-environment relationships and environmental justice,' *Seattle Journal for Social Justice*, 6(2): 727–817.

Brisman, A. 2009. 'It takes green to be green: Environmental elitism, "ritual displays," and conspicuous non-consumption,' *North Dakota Law Review*, 85(2): 329–370.

Brisman, A. 2011. '"GreenHarms" as art crime, art criticism as environmental dissent,' *Journal of Contemporary Criminal Justice*, 27(4): 465–499.

Brisman, A. 2014a. 'Environmental and human rights,' in G. Bruinsma and D. Weisburd (eds.) *Encyclopedia of Criminology and Criminal Justice*, Vol. 3, pp. 1344–1353. New York: Springer Verlag.

Brisman, A. 2014b. 'Of theory and meaning in green criminology,' *International Journal for Crime, Justice and Social Democracy*, 3(2): 22–35.

Brisman, A. 2015. 'Environment and conflict: A typology of representations,' in A. Brisman, N. South and R. White (eds.) *Environmental Crime and Social Conflict: Contemporary and Emerging Issues*, pp. 285–311. Surrey, UK: Ashgate.

Brisman, A. 2017a. 'On narrative and green cultural criminology,' *International Journal for Crime Justice and Social Democracy*, 6(2): 64–77.

Brisman, A. 2017b. 'Representations of environmental crime and harm: A green-cultural criminological perspective on *human-altered landscapes*,' in M. Brown and E. Carrabine (eds.) *Routledge International Handbook of Visual Criminology*, pp. 523–539. London and New York: Routledge.

Brisman, A. 2018. 'Representing the "invisible crime" of climate change in an age of post-truth,' *Theoretical Criminology*, 22(3): 468–491.

Brisman, A. 2019. 'The fable of *The Three Little Pigs*, climate change and green cultural criminology,' *International Journal for Crime, Justice and Social Democracy*, 8(1): 46–69. DOI: 10.5204/ijcjsd.v8i1.470.

Brisman, A. and South, N. 2012. 'Proposing a green-cultural criminology: A new perspective for 21st century criminology,' in G. Meško, A. Sotlar and K. Eman (eds.) *Ecological Crime and Environmental Protection—Multidisciplinary Perspectives*, pp. 17–35. Llubljana, Slovenia: Faculty of Criminal Justice, University of Maribor (Published as: Brisman, A. and South, N. 2012. 'Predlog ekološko-kulturne kriminologije: nov pogled za kriminologijo 21. Stoletja,'in G. Meško, A. Sotlar and K. Eman (uredniki). *Ekološka kriminaliteta in varovanje okolja – multidisciplinarne perspektive*, pp. 17–35. Ljubljana: Fakuleta za varnostne vede, Univerza v Mariboru).

Brisman, A. and South, N. 2013. 'A green-cultural criminology: An exploratory outline,' *Crime Media Culture*, 9(2): 115–135.

Brisman, A. and South, N. 2014. *Green Cultural Criminology: Constructions of Environmental Harm, Consumerism, and Resistance to Ecocide*. London: Routledge.

Brisman, A. and South, N. 2015. '"Life stage dissolution", infantilization and anti-social consumption: Implications for de-responsibilization, denial and environmental harm,' *Young – Nordic Journal of Youth Research*, 23(3): 209–221.

Brisman, A. and South, N. 2016. 'Water, inequalities and injustice: Social divisions, racism and colonialism – past and present,' in G. Meško and B. Lobnikar (eds.) *Criminal Justice Systems in Central and Eastern Europe – Safety, Security and Social Control in Local Communities*, pp. 359–366. Ljubljana: University of Maribor.

Brisman, A. and South, N. 2017a. 'Consumer technologies, crime and environmental implications,' in M. R. McGuire and T. J. Holt (eds.) *The Routledge Handbook of Technology, Crime and Justice*, pp. 310–324. London: Routledge.

Brisman, A. and South, N. 2017b. 'Criminología verde cultural,' in H. Mol, D. R. Goyes, N. South and A. Brisman (eds.) *Introducción a la criminología verde: Conceptos para nuevos horizontes y diálogos socioambientales* [*Introduction to Green Criminology: Concepts for New Horizons and Socio-Environmental Dialogues*], pp. 97–127. Bogotá, Colombia: Editorial Temis SA and Universidad Antonio Nariño, Fondo Editorial.

Brisman, A. and South, N. 2017c. 绿色犯罪学的起源、发展和研究方向 (Lǜsè fànzuì xué de qǐyuán, fāzhǎn hé yánjiū fāngxiàng ['Green criminology: Origins, directions of development and topics of study']), 河南警察学院学报 (Hénán jǐngchá xuéyuàn xuébào [*Journal of Henan Police College*]), 26(4): 89–98. Translated by: 徐永胜(译) (Xúyǒngshèng (yì) [Xu Yongsheng]).

Brisman, A. and South, N. 2017d. 'Methodological approaches and ethical challenges in green criminology,' in M. Cowburn, L. Gelsthorpe and A. Wahidin (eds.) *Research Ethics in Criminology: Dilemmas, Issues and Solutions*, pp. 166–182. London: Routledge.

Brisman, A. and South, N. 2018a. 'Green cultural criminology,' in W. DeKeseredy and M. Dragiewicz (eds.) *Routledge Handbook of Critical Criminology 2nd Edition*, pp. 132–142. Abingdon, Oxon, UK: Routledge.

Brisman, A. and South, N. 2018b. 'Perspectives on wildlife crime: The convergence of "green" and "conservation" criminologies,' in W. D. Moreto (ed.) *Wildlife Crime: From Theory to Practice*, pp. 17–37. Philadelphia, PA: Temple University Press.

Brisman, A. and South, N. 2019. 'A criminology of extinction: Biodiversity, extreme consumption and the vanity of species resurrection,' *European Journal of Criminology*. DOI: 10.1177/1477370819828307.

Brisman, A., McClanahan, B. and South, N. 2014. 'Toward a green-cultural criminology of "the rural",' *Critical Criminology: An International Journal*, 22(4): 479–494.

Brisman, A., McClanahan, B., South, N. and Walters, R. 2018. *Water, Crime and Security in the Twenty-First Century: Too Dirty, Too Little, Too Much*. London: Palgrave Macmillan.

Brisman, A., South, N. and Walters, R. 2018. 'Southernizing green criminology: Human dislocation, environmental injustice and climate apartheid,' *Justice, Power and Resistance*, 2(1): 1–21.

Bullard, R. 1990. *Dumping on Dixie: Race, Class, and Environmental Quality*. Boulder, CO: Westview.

Bullard, R. (ed.). 1993. *Confronting Environmental Racism: Voices from the Grassroots*. Boston, MA: South End Press.

Burns, R. G., Lynch, M. J. and Stretesky, P. 2008. *Environmental Law, Crime, and Justice*. New York: LFB.

Carrabine, E. 2018. 'Geographies of landscape: Representation, power and meaning,' *Theoretical Criminology*, 22(3): 445–467.

Carrabine, E., Iganski, P., Lee, M., Plummer, K. and South, N. 2004. *Criminology: A Sociological Introduction*. London and New York: Routledge.

Carrington, K., Hogg, R. and Sozzo, M. 2016. 'Southern Criminology,' *The British Journal of Criminology*, 56(1): 1–20.

Carrington, K., Hogg, R., Scott, J. and Sozzo, M. (eds.). 2018. *The Palgrave Handbook of Criminology and the Global South*. Cham, Switzerland: Palgrave Macmillan and Springer Nature.

Crook, M., Short, D. and South, N. 2018. 'Ecocide, genocide, capitalism and colonialism: Consequences for indigenous peoples and glocal ecosystems,' *Theoretical Criminology*, 22(3): 298–317.

DeKeseredy, W. 2010. *Contemporary Critical Criminology*. London and New York: Routledge.

Downes, D. (1988). 'The sociology of crime and social control in Britain, 1960–87,' *The British Journal of Criminology*, 28(2): 175–187.

Epstein, B. 1993. 'Ecofeminism and grass-roots environmentalism in the United States,' in R. Hofrichter (ed.) *Toxic Struggles: The Theory and Practice of Environmental Justice*, pp. 144–152. Philadelphia, PA: New Society Publishers.

Farrall, S., French, D. and Ahmed, T. (eds.). 2012. *Climate Change: Legal and Criminological Implications*. Oxford: Hart.

Ferrell, J., Hayward, K. and Young, J. 2008. *Cultural Criminology: An Invitation*. London: Sage.

Fussey, P. and South, N. 2012. 'Heading toward a new criminogenic climate: Climate change, political economy and environmental security,' in R. White (ed.) *Climate Change, Crime and Criminology*, pp. 27–40. New York: Springer Verlag.

Gaarder, E. 2011. *Women and the Animal Rights Movement*. Piscataway, NJ: Rutgers University Press.

Gaarder, E. 2013. 'Evading responsibility for green harm: State-corporate exploitation of race, class, and gender inquality,' in N. South and A. Brisman (eds.) *Routledge International Handbook of Green Criminology*, pp. 272–281. Abingdon, Oxon, UK: Routledge.

García Ruiz, A. and South, N. 2018. 'Surrounded by sound: Noise, rights and environments,' *Crime Media Culture*, 15(1): 125–141.

Garland, D. and Sparks, R. (2000). 'Criminology, social theory and the challenge of our times,' *The British Journal of Criminology*, 40(2):189–204.

Gibbs, C., Gore, M. L., McCarrell, E. F. and Rivers, L. III. 2010. 'Introducing conservation criminology: Towards interdisciplinary scholarship on environmental crimes and risk,' *The British Journal of Criminology*, 50(1): 124–144.

Goyes, D. R. 2016. 'Green activist criminology and the epistemologies of the South,' *Critical Criminology: An International Journal*, 24(4): 503–518.

Goyes, D. R., Mol, H., Brisman, A. and South, N. (eds.). 2017. *Environmental Crime in Latin America: The Theft of Nature and the Poisoning of the Land*. London: Palgrave Macmillan.

Goyes, D. R. and South, N. (2017) 'Green criminology before "Green Criminology": Amnesia and absences,' *Critical Criminology: An International Journal*, 25(2): 165–181.

Hall, M. 2013. *Victims of Environmental Harm: Rights, Recognition and Redress under National and International Law*. London and New York: Routledge.

Hall, M. and Farrall, S. 2013. 'The criminogenic consequences of climate change: Blurring the boundaries between offenders and victims,' in N. South and A. Brisman (eds.) *Routledge International Handbook of Green Criminology*, pp. 120–133. Abingdon, Oxon, UK: Routledge.

Hallsworth, S. 2011. 'Then they came for the dogs!' *Crime, Law and Social Change*, 55(5): 391–403.

Halsey, M. 2004. 'Against "green" criminology,' *The British Journal of Criminology*, 44(6): 833–853.

Halsey, M. and White, R. 1998. 'Crime, ecophilosophy and environmental harm,' *Theoretical Criminology*, 2(3): 345–371.

Hayward, K. J. and Young, J. (2007). 'Cultural criminology,' in M. Maguire, R. Morgan and R. Reiner (eds.). *The Oxford Handbook of Criminology*, 4th ed., pp. 102–21. Oxford: Oxford University Press.

Herbig F. J. W. and Joubert, S. J. (2006) 'Criminological semantics: Conservation criminology: Vision or vagary?' *Acta Criminologica*, 19(3): 88–103.

Hofrichter, R. (ed.). 1993. *Toxic Struggles: The Theory and Practice of Environmental Justice*. Philadelphia, PA: New Society Press.

Hogg, R., Scott, J. and Sozzo, M. 2017. 'Special edition: Southern criminology – guest editors' introduction,' *International Journal for Crime, Justice and Social Democracy*, 6(1): 1–7.

Jarrell, M. L. and Ozymy, J. 2012. 'Real crime, real victims: Environmental crime victims and the Crime Victims' Rights Act (CVRA), '*Crime, Law and Social Change*, 58(4): 373–389.

Lane, P. 1998. 'Ecofeminism meets criminology,' *Theoretical Criminology*, 2(2): 235–248.

Lynch, M. 1990. 'The greening of criminology: A perspective on the 1990s,' *The Critical Criminologist*, 2 (3–4): 11–12.

Lynch, M. and Stretesky, P. B. 2011. 'Similarities between green criminology and green science: Toward a typology of green criminology,' *International Journal of Comparative and Applied Criminal Justice*, 35(4): 293–306.

Lynch, M. J. and Stretesky, P. B. 2003. 'The meaning of green: Contrasting criminological perspectives,' *Theoretical Criminology*, 7(2): 217–238.

Lynch, M. J. and Stretesky, P. B. 2014. *Exploring Green Criminology: Toward a Green Criminological Revolution*. Abingdon, Oxon, UK: Routledge.

Lynch, M. J., Long, M. A., Stretesky, P. B and Barrett, K. L. 2017. *Green Criminology: Crime, Justice and the Environment*. Oakland, CA: University of California Press.

Maguire, R. 2019. 'Gender, climate change and the United Nations framework convention on climate change,' in S. H. Rimmer and K. Ogg (eds.) *Research Handbook on Feminist Engagement with International Law*, pp. 63–80. Cheltenham: Edward Elgar.

Markowitz, G. and Rosner,D. 2013. *Lead Wars: The Politics of Science and the Fate of America's Children*. Berkeley, CA: University of California Press.

Mazurek, J. 2017. 'Nemo's plight: Aquariums and animal abuse,' in J. Maher, P. Beirneand H. Peirpoint (eds.) *The Palgrave International Handbook of Animal Abuse Studies*, pp. 313–336. Basingstoke, Hampshire, UK: Palgrave Macmillan.

McClanahan, B. 2014. 'Green and grey: Water justice, criminalization, and resistance,' *Critical Criminology: An International Journal*, 22(4): 403–418.

McClanahan, B. and South, N. 2020. '"All knowledge begins with the senses": Toward a sensory criminology,' *The British Journal of Criminology* 60(1): 3–23. DOI: 10.1093/bjc/azz052.

McClanahan, B., Brisman, A. and South, N. 2017. 'Green criminology, culture, and the media,' in M. Brown and E. Carbine (eds.) *The Oxford Encyclopedia of Crime, Media, and Popular Culture*. Oxford: Oxford University Press.

Merchant, C. 1980. *The Death of Nature: Women, Ecology and the Scientific Revolution*. New York: Harper Collins.

Merchant, C. 1996. *Earthcare: Women and the Environment*. New York: Routledge.

Mol, H., Goyes, D. R., South, N. and Brisman, A. (eds.). 2017. *Introducción a la criminología verde. Conceptos para nuevos horizontes y diálogos socioambientales* [*Introduction to Green Criminology: Concepts for New Horizons and Socio-Environmental Dialogues*]. Bogotá, Colombia: Editorial Temis S.A. and Universidad Antonio Nariño, Fondo Editorial.

Muller, C., Sampson, R. J. and Winter, A. S. 2018. 'Environmental inequality: The social causes and consequences of lead exposure,' *Annual Review of Sociology*, 44: 263–282.

Natali, L. 2015. *Green Criminology: Prospettive emergentui sui crimini ambientali*. Torino: G. Giappichelli Editore.

Ningard, H. B. 2018. 'Attorney stories of environmental crime: Harms, agents, and ideal cases,' Ph.D. Dissertation, Department of Sociology, University of Tennessee, Knoxville, TN, USA (defended August 1, 2018).

Pellow, D. and Brulle, R. 2005. 'Power, justice, and the environment: Toward critical environmental justice studies,' in D. Pellow and R. Brulle (eds.) *Power, Justice and the Environment: A Critical Appraisal of the Environmental Justice Movement*. Boston: The MIT Press.

Plumwood, V. 2005. 'Gender, eco-feminism and the environment,' in R. White (ed.) *Controversies in Environmental Sociology*. Melbourne: Cambridge University Press.

Potter, G. (2014), 'The criminogenic effects of environmental harm: Bringing a "green" perspective to mainstream criminology,' in T. Spapens, R. White and M. Kluin (eds.). *Environmental Crime and Its Victims: Perspectives within Green Criminology*. Surrey, UK: Ashgate.

Pretty, J. 2011. 'Review of *Indra's Net and the Midas Touch: Living Sustainably in a Connected World* by L. P. Thiele, 2011,' *Times Higher Education*, October 27, 2011, pp. 50–51.

Redmon, D. 2018. 'Video methods, green cultural criminology, and the anthropocene: SANCTUARY as a case study,' *Deviant Behavior*, 39(4): 495–511.

Reyes, J. W. 2007. 'Environmental policy as social policy? The impact of childhood lead exposure on crime,' *The B.E. Journal of Economic Analysis & Policy*, 7(1): 1–41. https://doi.org/10.2202/1935-1682.1796.

Ruggiero, V. and South, N. 2010. 'Critical criminology and crimes against the environment,' *Critical Criminology: An International Journal*, 18(4): 245–250.

Sampson, R. J. and Winter, A. S. 2016. 'The racial ecology of lead poisoning: Toxic inequality in Chicago neighborhoods, 1995–2013,' *Du Bois Review: Social Science Research on Race*, 13(2): 261–283.

Sampson, R. J. and Winter, A. S. 2018. 'Poisoned development: Assessing childhood lead exposure as a cause of crime in a birth cohort followed through adolescence,' *Criminology*, 56(2): 269–301.

Schally, J. 2018. *Legitimizing Corporate Harm: The Discourse of Contemporary Agribusiness*. London: Palgrave Macmillan.

Schally, J. L. 2014. 'Agent of harm and good corporate citizen? The case of Tyson Foods,' PhD Dissertation, Department of Sociology, University of Tennessee, Knoxville, TN, USA (defended July 15, 2014).

Sollund, R. 2008. 'Causes for speciesism: Distance, difference and denial,' in R. Sollund (ed.) *Global Harms*, pp. 109–129. New York: Nova Science Publishers.

Sollund, R. 2011. 'Expressions of speciesism: The effects of keeping companion animals on animal abuse, animal trafficking and species decline,' *Crime, Law and Social Change*, 55(5): 437–451.
Sollund, R. 2012a. 'The essence of food and gender and the embodiment of migration,' in R. Sollund (ed.) *Transnational Migration, Gender and Rights*, pp. 77–98. Bingley, UK: Emerald Group Publishing Limited.
Sollund, R. 2012b. 'Speciesism as doxic practice versus valuing difference and plurality,' in R. Ellfesen, R. Sollund and G. Larsen (eds.) *Eco-global Crimes: Contemporary Problems and Future Challenges*, pp. 91–113. Surrey, UK: Ashgate.
Sollund, R.A. (ed.) 2012c. Transnational Migration, Gender, and Rights. Bingley, UK: Emerald Group Publishing Inc.
Sollund, R. 2013. 'Animal trafficking and trade: Abuse and species injustice,' in R. Walters, D. Westerhuis and T. Wyatt (eds.) *Emerging Issues in Green Criminology: Exploring* Power, *Justice and Harm*, pp. 72–92. Basingstoke, Hampshire, UK: Palgrave Macmillan.
Sollund, R. 2015a. 'The illegal wildlife trade from a Norwegian outlook: Tendencies in practices and law enforcement,' in R. Sollund (ed.) *Green Harms and Crimes: Critical Criminology in a Changing World*, pp.147–169. Basingstoke, Hamphsire, UK: Palgrave Macmillan.
Sollund, R. 2015b. 'With or without a license to kill: Human-predator conflicts and theriocide in Norway,' in A. Brisman, N. South and R. White (eds.) *Environmental Crime and Social Conflict: Contemporary and Emerging Issues*, pp. 95–124. Surrey, UK: Ashgate.
Sollund, R. 2016. 'The animal other: Legal and illegal theriocide,' in M. Hall, T. Wyatt, N. South, A. Nurse, G. Potter and J. Maher (eds.) *Greening Criminology in the 21st Century: Contemporary Debates and Future Directions in the Study of Environmental Harm*, pp. 79–99. Abingdon, Oxon, UK:: Routledge.
Sollund, R. 2017a. 'Legal and illegal theriocide of trafficked animals,' in P. Beirne, J. Maher and H. Pierspoint (eds.) *International Handbook on Animal Abuse Studies*, pp. 453–474. London: Palgrave MacMillan.
Sollund, R. 2017b. 'The use and abuse of animals in wildlife trafficking in Colombia: Practices, and injustice,' in D. R. Goyes, H. Mol, A. Brisman and N. South (eds.) *Environmental Crime in Latin America: The Theft of Nature and the Poisoning of the Land*, pp. 215–244. London: Palgrave Macmillan.
South, N. 1998. 'A green field for criminology?: A proposal for a perspective,' *Theoretical Criminology*, 2 (2): 211–234.
South, N. 2010. 'The ecocidal tendencies of late modernity: Transnational crime, social exclusion, victims and rights,' in R. White (ed.) *Global Environmental Harm: Criminological Perspectives*, pp. 228–247. Cullompton, Devon, UK: Willan.
South, N. 2014. 'Green criminology: Reflections, connections, horizons,' *International Journal for Crime, Justice and Social Democracy*, 3(2): 6–21.
South, N. (2007). 'The "corporate colonization of nature": Bio-prospecting, bio-piracy and the development of green criminology,' in P. Beirne and N. South (eds.). *Issues in Green Criminology: Confronting Harms against Environments, Humanity and Other Animals*, pp. 230–47. Cullompton, Devon, UK: Willan.
South, N. and Beirne, P. 1998. 'Editors' introduction,' *Theoretical Criminology*, 2(2): 147–148.
South, N. and Beirne, P. 2006. 'Introduction: Approaching green criminology,' in N. South and P. Beirne (eds.) *Green Criminology*, pp. xiii–xxvii. Surrey, UK: Ashgate.
South, N. and Brisman, A. 2013. 'Critical green criminology, environmental rights and crimes of exploitation,' in S. Winlow and R. Atkinson (eds.) *New Directions in Crime and Deviance*, pp. 99–110. London: Routledge.
South, N., Brisman, A. and McClanahan, B. 2018. 'Crimini e danni ambientali. La green criminology e la Earth jurisprudence,' ['Environmental crimes and harms: Green criminology and Earth jurisprudence,'] in C. Rinaldi and P. Saitta (eds.) *Criminologie Critiche Contemporanee*, pp. 105–131. Milano: Giuffrè Francis LefebvreS.p.A.
Squires, P. 2017. 'Hunting and shooting: The ambiguities of "country sports",' in J. Maher, H. Pierpoint and P. Beirne (eds.) *The Palgrave International Handbook of Animal Abuse Studies*, pp. 289–311. London: Palgrave Macmillan.
Stephens, S. 1996. 'Reflections on environmental justice: Children as victims and actors,' *Social Justice*, 23 (4): 62–86.
Wachholz, S. 2007. '"At risk": Climate change and its bearing on women's vulnerability to male violence,' in P. Beirne and N. South (eds.) *Issues in Green Criminology: Confronting Harms against Environments, Humanity and Other Animals*, pp. 161–185. Cullompton, Devon, UK: Willan.

Walters, R. 2007. 'Crime, regulation and radioactive waste in the United Kingdom,' in P. Beirne and N South (eds.) *Issues in Green Criminology*, pp. 186–205. Cullompton, Devon, UK: Willan.
Walters, R. 2010a. 'Eco crime,' in J. Muncie, D. Talbot and R. Walters, (eds.) *Crime: Local and Global*, pp. 171–208. Collumpton, Devon, UK: Willan, and Milton Keyes, UK: The Open University.
Walters, R. 2010b. 'Toxic atmospheres air pollution, trade and the politics of regulation,' *Critical Criminology: An International Journal*, 18(4): 307–323.
Walters, R. 2013. 'Air crimes and atmospheric justice,' in N. South and A. Brisman (eds.) *Routledge International Handbook of Green Criminology*, pp. 134–149. Abingdon, Oxon, UK: Routledge.
Walters, R. 2014. 'Organised crime and the environment,' in G. Bruinsma and D. Weisburd (eds.) *Encyclopaedia of Criminology and Criminal Justice*. New York: Springer Verlag.
White, R. 1998. 'Environmental criminology and Sydney Water,' *Current Issue Criminal Justice*, 10(2): 214–219.
White, R. 2008. *Crimes Against Nature: Environmental Criminology and Ecological Justice*. Cullompton, Devon, UK: Willan.
White, R. (ed.). 2009. *Environmental Crime: A Reader*. Cullompton, Devon, UK: Willan.
White, R. (ed.). 2010a. *Global Environmental Harm: Criminological perspectives*. Cullompton, Devon, UK: Willan.
White, R. 2010b. 'Globalisation and environmental harm,' in R. White (ed.) *Global Environmental Harm: Criminological Perspectives*, pp. 3–19. Cullompton, Devon, UK: Willan.
White, R. 2010c. 'A green criminology perspective,' in E. McLaughlin and T. Newburn (eds.) *The Sage Handbook of Criminological Theory*, pp. 410–426. London: Sage.
Williams, C. (1996), 'An environmental victimology,' *Social Justice* 23(4): 16–40.
Williamson, N. 2003. 'Illegal logging and frontier conservation,' in J. Spradley and D. W. McCurdy (eds.) *Conformity and Conflict: Readings in Cultural Anthropology* 11/e, pp. 191–200. Boston, MA: Allyn and Bacon.
Winter, A. S. and Sampson, R. J. 2017. 'From lead exposure in early childhood to adolescent health: A Chicago birth cohort,' *American Journal of Public Health*, 107(9) [September]: 1496–1501.
Wonders, N. A. and Danner, M. J. E. 2015. 'Gendering climate change: A feminist criminological perspective,' *Critical Criminology: An International Journal*, 23(4): 401–416.
Wyatt, T. 2009. 'Exploring the organisation in Russia Far East's illegal wildlife trade: Two case studies of the illegal fur and illegal falcon trades,' *Global Crime*, 10(1 & 2): 144–154.
Wyatt, T. 2011. 'Illegal raptor trade in the Russian Federation,' *Contemporary Justice Review*, 14(2): 103–123.
Wyatt, T. 2013. *Illegal Wildlife Trade: A Deconstruction of the Crime, the Offenders and the Victims*. London: Palgrave Macmillan.
Wyatt, T. 2014. 'Non human animal abuse and wildlife trade: Harms in the fur and falcon trades,' *Society and Animals*, 22(2): 194–210.
Wyatt, T. 2016. 'A comparative analysis of wildlife trafficking in Australia, New Zealand and the United Kingdom,' *Journal of Trafficking, Organised Crime and Security*, 2(1): 62–81.

2

The ordinary acts that contribute to ecocide

A criminological analysis

Robert Agnew

Mainstream criminologists focus on the explanation of 'street crimes', such as assault, robbery and larceny. But as green and other criminologists point out, there are a range of additional behaviours that also cause much harm, often far more serious than that caused by street crimes (e.g., Beirne and South 2007; Gibbs et al. 2010). This chapter focusses on the explanation of one such set of behaviours, the ordinary acts that contribute to ecocide—or the contamination and destruction of the natural environment in ways that reduce its ability to support life (South 2009). These ordinary acts have several characteristics: they are performed widely and regularly by individuals as part of their routine activities; they are generally viewed as acceptable, even desirable; and, collectively, they have a substantial impact on environmental problems.

Many specific acts meet these requirements; the most notable include living in a large suburban home, heated and cooled to comfortable levels; using a gasoline-powered automobile for most transportation; frequently purchasing consumer products; and regularly consuming meat. These activities are hereafter referred to as 'ordinary harms' for short. They contribute to ecocide by increasing air, water and soil pollution; destroying natural habitats and animal life; depleting natural resources; and helping to cause climate change (Worldwatch Institute 2010).

To illustrate, the livestock production that supports meat consumption is a major source of deforestation, water pollution and climate change—accounting for 14.5 per cent of greenhouse gas emissions (Gerber et al. 2013). The United States (US) leads the world in the commission of ordinary harms. For example, US residents comprise only 5 per cent of the world's population but account for 32 per cent of all global expenditures on consumption. If everyone lived at the same level as US citizens, the world could sustain only 1.4 billon people (the current population is 7.7 billon). For that reason, much of the discussion below focusses on the US, although the points made are generally applicable to all societies having market economies and a sizeable economic surplus.

Ordinary harms have not only been neglected by mainstream criminologists, but by many green criminologists as well—who more often focus on the environmental harms committed by states, corporations and organised criminal groups (for a discussion, see Brisman and South, this volume, Chapter 1). The focus on these latter harms is readily understandable given the tremendous damage they cause (e.g., White 2012). But ordinary harms also cause great damage. Furthermore, a full understanding of environmental harm requires that we consider both the actions of individuals and larger groups, for they are symbiotically related. Ordinary harms committed by individuals provide much incentive for those state and corporate behaviours that contribute to ecocide, such as deforestation and the generation of electricity in coal-powered plants. At the same time, states and corporations encourage and facilitate the commission of ordinary harms. I regularly refer to the ways in which this occurs in the discussion below. My focus, however, is on the more immediate factors that lead individuals to engage in ordinary harms (e.g., live in large homes, drive to work, consume meat).

In particular, I explain ordinary harms in terms of those individual-level theories that dominate criminology, including strain, social control, self-control, social learning/rational choice, biosocial and opportunity theories. One might question whether these theories can explain acts such as driving an automobile and consuming meat. Despite the harm they cause, such acts are instances of *conformity*, rather than *crime*. Therefore, it might seem doubtful as to whether they can be explained by the factors used to explain street crimes, such as strain, low social control and association with criminals. And, indeed, most efforts to explain ordinary harms have been carried out by researchers studying the causes of consumerism and environmentally responsible behaviour (the converse of ordinary harms), with these researchers drawing on theories designed to explain behaviour in general rather than criminal behaviour (e.g., Dietz et al. 2007; Iwata 2004; Kurz 2002; Larson 2010; Michaelis 2007; Patchen 2010; Smart 2010; Stearns 2001; Takacs-Santa 2007; Worldwatch Institute 2010). Nevertheless, I argue that the leading crime theories can help explain these ordinary harms, although they sometimes have to be applied in creative ways to do so. Where possible, I support my arguments with research from the environmental and consumerism literatures, although I argue that the crime theories have new insights to offer. Each of the major crime theories is discussed in turn below.

Strain theory

Strain theory states that individuals are pressured into engaging in crime by the strains they experience (Agnew 2006). Strains refer to events and conditions disliked by individuals, and they involve the inability to achieve one's goals (e.g., monetary success, high status), the loss or threatened loss of positively valued stimuli (e.g., financial loss, death of family members) and the presentation or threatened presentation of negatively valued stimuli (e.g., verbal and physical abuse). These strains lead to negative emotions, such as anger, frustration and envy. These emotions, in turn, create pressure for corrective action: individuals feel bad and want to do something about it. Crime is one possible response; crime may be used to reduce or escape from strain (e.g., theft to obtain money), to seek revenge against the source of strain or related targets (e.g., assaulting abusive peers) or to alleviate negative emotions (e.g., illicit drug use).

But can strain theory explain ordinary harms? On the face of it, it would seem that individuals do *not* have to be pressured into engaging in such harms; they are widely practiced, satisfy a range of needs and desires, are viewed as acceptable or desirable, and carry little risk of sanction. But with some modification, strain theory can shed much light on such harms. Although such harms are legal, they are nevertheless a method of coping with certain strains—including both experienced and anticipated strains. Furthermore, such harms are also a function of strains that are *not* experienced or at least not perceived.

Strains that increase the likelihood of ordinary harms

Relative deprivation

Individuals experiencing relative deprivation believe that they are materially deprived relative to those in their reference group. They experience emotions such as frustration and envy as a result. Relative deprivation is especially common in countries such as the United States, where success is defined in material terms, people are regularly exposed to more privileged others, and they are encouraged to compare themselves to these others (Messner and Rosenfeld 2007; Passas 1997). As such, both the poor *and* the wealthy may feel relatively deprived. The major way to cope with this feeling is through heightened levels of consumption, including consumption financed through borrowing and, occasionally, crime. This argument, it should be noted, does not predict a strong *cross-sectional* association between relative deprivation and ordinary harms. Those who score highest on ordinary harms (e.g., live in the largest houses, own the most automobiles) may have reduced their sense of relative deprivation. A longitudinal study, however, should find that relatively deprived individuals, at one point in time, are more likely than comparable individuals to engage in most ordinary harms at a later point in time.

Status frustration

Those experiencing status frustration believe that they lack sufficient respect and admiration from others, particularly those in their reference group (Cohen 1955). Status frustration is closely related to relative deprivation, given that material objects commonly function as status symbols in countries such as the US (Messner and Rosenfeld 2007; Smart 2010; Stearns 2001). Consequently, individuals experiencing status frustration often cope through excessive consumption. And research does suggest that individuals frequently use consumption—including the purchase of fashionable clothes, luxury cars and large homes—as a way to mask low status and/or to claim high status (e.g., Anderson 1999; Deutsch and Theodorou 2010; Dittmar 2005).

Accomplishing gender

Closely related to the desire for status is the desire to fulfill appropriate gender expectations—that is, to successfully 'accomplish masculinity or femininity' (Messerschmidt 1993). Consumption also plays an important role here. A critical part of being a 'man' in many societies is being a successful 'provider', which involves supplying one's family with a nice home, automobile and a range of possessions. And a critical part of being a woman in many societies is maintaining an attractive appearance, which involves the consumption of fashionable clothes, cosmetics and jewellery. Also, the consumption of meat, particularly red meat, is often linked to masculinity (Allen et al. 2000). A study by Deutsch and Theodorou (2010) provides some support for these arguments. When poor boys in the US were asked what they wanted in life, they often replied a nice house and car. Poor girls, on the other hand, more often replied that they wanted to go shopping and buy clothes.

Material deprivation

As numerous commentators have noted, businesses in market-oriented economies try to create a strong desire or 'need' for consumer products in order to fuel spending (e.g., Smart 2010; Stearns 2001; Worldwatch Institute 2010). Accordingly, individuals in such societies come to view products, such as air conditioning, dishwashers and cell phones, as 'essential' or as 'necessities'. So while these products may be desired to reduce feelings of relative deprivation, enhance status and/or accomplish gender, individuals also develop an independent need for them. This argument reflects the fact that individuals consume not only for display, but also for comfort. And this argument may be especially relevant to products that function as *primary* reinforcers, such as air conditioners and automobiles, and to individuals who have a genuine need for these products (e.g., those without access to public transportation). Consequently, individuals without these products feel a strong sense of material deprivation, and they typically cope by trying to obtain the products. (Note: the motives of display and comfort often overlap, but sometimes diverge—as when the desire for display leads to the consumption of uncomfortable products, such as high-heeled shoes.)

The threatened and actual loss of valued possessions/lifestyles

Once individuals are committing ordinary harms, an additional set of strains may become operative. In the first case, the strain involves the *anticipated* loss of valued possessions and lifestyles. In particular, individuals may *not* be high in relative deprivation, status frustration, gender-related strain or material deprivation. But they may experience great strain if they anticipate that their possessions and lifestyle are threatened. This perceived threat may stem from a variety of sources, including economic problems and government regulations designed to foster more environmentally responsible behaviour. As a consequence of this threat, individuals may do all that they can to protect their possessions and lifestyle. In the second case, the strain involves the *actual* loss of valued possessions and/or unwanted changes in their lifestyle (e.g., driving less, turning down the heat). This type of strain is especially likely to generate strong negative emotions because individuals have become accustomed to the products and lifestyles that they have lost. These individuals may cope by trying to replace their lost possessions and lifestyles, as well as taking actions to prevent further loss.

Consumption as a coping mechanism for other strains

The strains listed above are reduced by ordinary harms. For example, relative deprivation, status frustration and material deprivation are reduced by living in a large house and driving a luxury car. Certain other strains, however, may prompt individuals to engage in excessive consumption, even though these are strains that are *not* reduced by this consumption. In particular, individuals may purchase a range of products and services in order to *alleviate the negative emotions* associated with a wide range of strains (as opposed to reducing the strains themselves). That is, consumption may play a role similar to drug use. This idea is reflected in popular views such as the notion of 'retail therapy'. It finds support in the research on 'compulsive buying', which is often undertaken to alleviate the negative emotions associated with a range of problems or strains (Dittmar 2005; Ertelt et al. 2011). And this idea is a central theme in the research on consumerism, which finds that consumerism developed partly to compensate for problems such as the drudgery of industrial and clerical work (e.g., Smart 2010; Stearns 2001). It should be noted, however, that consumption does not necessarily result in the long-term alleviation of negative emotions. In fact, data suggest that increases in income (and energy consumption) are associated only with increases in psychological well-being up to a point; well-being no longer increases once individuals reach a certain minimal level of financial security (Csikszentmihalyi 2000; Michaelis 2007; Smart 2010; Worldwatch Institute 2010). Consumption appears to bring a *brief* increase in well-being, however. And the larger culture promotes the idea that consumption leads to happiness (Dittmar 2005).

Strains that are not experienced, are not perceived or are discounted

Finally, individuals may commit ordinary harms partly because they do not face immediate environmental threats; they are unaware of or discount the environmental threats they do face, perhaps because such threats are in the future; and they are unconcerned about the threats faced by others (e.g., Brody et al. 2008). It should be noted that environmental problems are now viewed as a serious threat by many in the US, with 55 per cent of the respondents in a 2017 survey stating that reducing such problems should be a 'top domestic priority' (Pew Research Center for the People & the Press 2017). But, at the same time, environmental problems ranked eleventh on the list of top priorities, with climate change ranked eighteenth. The environmental psychology and sociology literatures have examined many of the factors that influence the level of environmental strain, including factors such as media coverage and traits such as a short time horizon and self-interest (see the discussion of beliefs below, as well as the excellent overview by Takacs-Santa 2007). Those low in environmental strain should be more likely to engage in ordinary harms because these harms are less likely to be seen as problematic. Conversely, those high in environmental strain should be more likely to engage in environmentally responsible behaviours, such as recycling and using public transportation. Research provides some support for this argument, with environmentally responsible behaviour being more common among those high in environmental strain and the negative emotions prompted by such strain, such as anger, fear and sadness (e.g., Dietz et al. 2007; Patchen 2010; Takacs-Santa 2007). Environmental strain, however, is more likely to motivate environmentally responsible behaviour among those who care about the environment (Tribbia 2007; cf. Brisman 2009a, 2009b).

Factors conditioning the reaction to the above strains

Strain theory states that there are several ways to cope with strains, with certain factors increasing the likelihood of criminal coping (Agnew 2006). People are more likely to cope with the above strains by engaging in ordinary harms when:

- They have the resources and opportunity to engage in such harms, with financial resources being especially important for the more costly ordinary harms (e.g., buying a large house and car). Ordinary harms are also more likely when people *lack* the resources and opportunity to engage in alternative behaviours, particularly environmentally responsible behaviours (e.g., they are physically unable to walk long distances or public transit is not available in their community (see Tribbia 2007)). Most people in the US possess the resources and opportunity to engage in a range of ordinary harms, especially less costlier harms, while it is often more difficult to engage in many environmentally responsible behaviours (see Brisman 2009a, 2009b).
- The risk of sanction for engaging in ordinary harms is low, which is generally the case in the US given the conformist nature of such harms. Ordinary harms are also more likely when there is a significant risk of sanction for engaging in environmentally responsible behaviours, which is sometimes the case (see below).
- The disposition for engaging in ordinary harms is strong, while that for engaging in environmentally responsible behaviours is low. The disposition for ordinary harms is generally strong in the US. As described below, most people possess traits, beliefs and identities conducive to the harms (e.g., self-interest, materialism), are regularly exposed to others who model the harms, and are reinforced for engaging in the harms.

In sum, strain theory suggests that engaging in ordinary harms is a popular and at least temporarily effective coping strategy for a range of pressing strains. These strains are especially common in market-oriented societies with a large economic surplus that is broadly distributed, that define success largely in terms of material achievements and that encourage individuals to compare themselves with more privileged others. The US, as suggested, is an exemplar of such societies. While these ideas are compatible with the literatures on consumerism and environmentally responsible behaviour, strain theory provides a more complete description of the forces that pressure individuals into engaging in ordinary harms and the factors that influence the choice of ordinary harms as a coping strategy.

Social control theory

Social control theory focusses on the controls that prevent crime. According to control theory, crime requires no special explanation; it is often the easiest way to satisfy our needs and desires. What requires explanation is *conformity*. And we follow customs and norms, rules and regulations, because of the controls or restraints to which we are subject (Agnew and Brezina 2015). These controls include direct control or the fear of sanction. Direct control is high to the extent that others set clear rules that forbid crime, monitor behaviour and consistently sanction rule violations in a meaningful manner. The controls also include stake in conformity, which refers to those things that might be jeopardised by crime. Stake in conformity is high to the extent that individuals have close ties to conventional others, good reputations, a large investment in their education, well-paid jobs that they value and high expectations for the future. And controls include beliefs that condemn crime. When these social controls are present, crime should be low and conformity high. Ordinary harms involve conformist behaviour and so should be the result of high control.

Direct control

Ordinary harms, like other conformist behaviour, are generally *not* sanctioned. That is, one is not sanctioned for acts such as living in a large home, regularly driving long distances and consuming meat. (Certain jurisdictions and individuals, however, are beginning to sanction excessive instances of some ordinary harms, such as excessive water use (see Brisman et al. 2018; Funk and Kennedy 2016.) The fact that ordinary harms are not sanctioned helps explain their popularity. But unlike certain other conformist behaviour, *the failure* to commit ordinary harms is usually *not* subject to state sanction. For example, while the failure of children to attend school and of adults to care for their children is subject to state sanction, the failure to live in a large home or drive a luxury car is not. There are several reasons for this, perhaps the most notable being the fact that ordinary harms are frequently quite pleasurable—satisfying a range of needs and desires (see above). As such, their performance is less dependent on the threat of formal sanction—unlike the sometimes burdensome activities of attending school and raising children. Ordinary harms generally represent the positive side of conformity and, as histories of consumerism note, were emphasised in part to compensate for the negative side of conformity, particularly work in manufacturing jobs (e.g., Stearns 2001).

At the same time, the failure to engage in certain ordinary harms is subject to *informal* sanction. For example, those who wear out-of-date clothes or follow vegetarian diets are sometimes seen as deviant and subject to rebuke, ridicule and the loss of status. To illustrate this, certain vegetarians report that they encounter significant hostility from family members, especially male family members (Merriman 2010). Those who do not engage in ordinary harms may be seen as deviant and therefore deserving of sanction; they are atypical and their failure to partake of the benefits of conformity is difficult to understand, especially given that many of these benefits are viewed as necessities (e.g., air conditioning, meat). Also, those who fail to engage in ordinary harms may be seen as challenging the values and behaviours of those who do, again prompting sanction.

Stake in conformity

Individuals also engage in ordinary harms because the failure to do so might jeopardise their stake in conformity. For example, the failure to wear fashionable clothes, live in a large house and drive a 'nice' automobile may threaten their reputation. The failure to provide family members with a nice house and a range of possessions may jeopardise ties to them (see Deutsch and Theodorou 2010). In fact, advertisers regularly promote the idea that providing others with valued objects is how one expresses affection for them. And, as noted above, an essential part of the adult male role is providing family members with a range of objects; those who fail to do so are seen as bad husbands and fathers. Furthermore, ordinary harms directly benefit individuals (e.g., the comfort of air conditioning, the convenience of an automobile). As such, engaging in ordinary harms creates its own stake in conformity, providing individuals with possessions and a lifestyle that they are reluctant to relinquish.

Beliefs

Finally, individuals engage in ordinary harms because they hold beliefs that define them as acceptable or desirable. The nature of these beliefs is described in detail under social learning theory, but a core part of such beliefs is captured in the notion of 'materialism'. Individuals in the United States and many other developed countries are taught that it is desirable to accumulate material objects and lead the type of life made possible by such objects. Doing so is considered to be the major route to happiness, a mark of one's success and a means for self-expression and the realisation of one's potential (Messner and Rosenfeld 2007; Stearns 2001). Furthermore, engaging in such harms is said to provide some social benefit; most notably, such harms help provide employment, maintain a strong economy and support the free enterprise system. Such harms are seldom defined as harmful or undesirable, although this is *starting* to change with respect to some of the more extreme ordinary harms, such as driving certain 'gas guzzling' vehicles (see, e.g., Brisman 2004, 2007b, 2009b).

These ideas regarding social control have not been fully tested. In particular, researchers have not systematically examined the extent to which *not* engaging in particular ordinary harms is subject to direct control by various agents and jeopardises the different stakes in conformity. Researchers, however, have devoted much attention to the relationship between beliefs and engaging in environmentally responsible behaviours (see below). So once again, criminological theory can help guide the research on ordinary harms.

Self-control (and environmental control)

Those low in self-control have difficulty exercising self-restraint when tempted to engage in crime. Several traits contribute to this lack of restraint, including the tendency to act without thinking about the consequences of one's behaviour, a focus on the immediate rather than the delayed satisfaction of one's desires, a short time horizon, an attraction to risky activities, little concern for the rights and feelings of others, little motivation and perseverance, and irritability (Gottfredson and Hirschi 1990). Because ordinary harms are conformist rather than criminal in nature, we might expect that they are the result of high rather than low self-control. And having a moderately high level of self-control does facilitate the commission of the more costly ordinary harms—such as buying a large home and luxury car. Engaging in these harms generally presupposes that individuals have a good job, which requires some self-control. So in order to reap the rewards of conformity, individuals must have sufficient self-control to devote some effort to the work of conformity.

But to complicate matters somewhat, the traits comprising *low* self-control likely increase the *appeal* of ordinary harms. Ordinary harms result in the immediate satisfaction of one's needs and desires. Furthermore, the damage resulting from such harms is delayed and diffuse, affecting others as much as, if not more than, oneself. As such, ordinary harms may be more attractive to those who possess traits such as a desire for immediate gratification, a short time horizon, a tendency to act without thinking, and little concern for others. Reflecting this fact, those high-rate offenders who are low in self-control are usually quick to spend *all* of their money on consumer products, such as clothing and automobiles (e.g., Wright and Decker 1997). So those low in self-control have the will, but often not the way, to engage in ordinary harms. Those high in self-control have both the will, albeit to a more limited degree, and the way to engage in ordinary harms.

The will to engage in ordinary harms, however, might be better measured if the dimensions of self-control are considered in a more nuanced manner. In particular, we should examine whether individuals consider the *environmental* consequences of their behaviour; whether they are sensitive to the rights of people throughout the world, as well as those of non-human animals and the natural environment more generally; and whether their time horizon extends to future generations. Individuals with these traits might be said to be high in 'environmental control'—that is, they are able to restrain themselves from engaging in environmentally harmful behaviours when tempted. So while we would expect more costlier ordinary harms to be somewhat more common among those high in self-control, as traditionally defined, we would expect these harms to be lower among those high in environmental control. Research provides some support for this argument. For example, those with a long time horizon and a concern for the natural environment are more likely to engage in environmentally responsible behaviours (e.g., Dietz et al. 2007; Patchen 2010; Tribbia 2007).

Social learning/rational choice theory

Social learning theory states that individuals learn to engage in crime from others (Agnew and Brezina 2015; Akers 1998). These others are frequently members of criminal groups, such as gangs, but they also include parents, neighbours and the mass media (Brisman 2007a). Individuals learn to engage in crime in three ways: they are differentially reinforced for crime; they are exposed to criminal models, particularly admired others who experience reinforcement for their crime; and they are taught beliefs that approve of, justify or excuse crime in certain conditions. Rational choice theory is similar to social learning theory insofar as it suggests that people give some consideration to the costs and benefits of various actions, engaging in crime when they believe that its benefits exceed its costs (Akers 1990; Cornish and Clarke 1986). Social learning and rational choice theories were developed to explain all forms of behaviour, both conformist and criminal, and so can readily explain conformist acts such as ordinary harms.

The differential reinforcement (benefits and costs) of ordinary harms

Individuals engage in ordinary harms partly because of their many benefits. As noted above, ordinary harms often result in increased physical comfort and convenience, enhanced mental well-being (at least temporarily), status and social approval, including affection from others. The harms do have certain costs, including financial costs and environmental damage. But the environmental costs are frequently hidden, delayed and/or imposed on others; as such, they are heavily discounted (Kurz 2002). At the same time, engaging in environmentally responsible behaviour often results in high costs and delayed benefits. Installing solar panels, for example, involves a large upfront cost, one that is not repaid for many years (see Brisman 2009b). Forgoing one's car and walking imposes immediate physical costs and time delays; the health benefits only come later. And, as noted above, individuals who engage in environmentally responsible behaviours are sometimes subject to informal sanction. Research in environmental psychology provides some support for these arguments, suggesting that the decision to engage in environmentally responsible behaviours is influenced by a consideration of financial, physical and social costs and benefits (e.g., how much physical effort is required, do close others approve of the behaviour) (e.g., Dietz et al. 2007; Gockeritz et al. 2010; Kurz 2002; Tribbia 2007).

It is important to note that the extent to which ordinary harms and environmentally responsible behaviours are differentially reinforced varies across groups and over time (e.g., Michaelis 2007). In particular, groups differ in their evaluation of and reaction to ordinary harms and environmentally responsible behaviours. There has been some research in this area, focussing on national and sociodemographic groups. The results are somewhat mixed, although much data suggest that females are more approving of and likely to engage in environmentally responsible behaviours (e.g., Dietz et al. 2007; Dunlap and York 2008; Franzen and Meyer 2010; Gossard and York 2003; Kalof et al. 1999). The mixed results regarding other variables may partly stem from the fact that these variables have countervailing effects on the factors listed above. For example, those in the higher socioeconomic classes experience less material deprivation (decreasing their motivation for engaging in ordinary harms), but they also experience fewer environmental threats (increasing their motivation for ordinary harms) (see Dunlap and York 2008). But for most people in the United States, it still appears to be the case that the net benefits of ordinary harms exceed those of the environmentally responsible behaviours that might replace them (cf. Brisman 2009b).

Modelling

Individuals also engage in ordinary harms because they are regularly modelled by others, including admired others, who are reinforced for engaging in the harms. The media, in particular, regularly depicts fictional and non-fictional others who engage in ordinary harms and reap a range of benefits from doing so—particularly social approval and status. Much data suggest that exposure to such models increases the likelihood of imitative behaviour (Akers 1998). And research in environmental psychology and sociology indicates that views about whether others engage in environmentally responsible behaviour have a large impact on whether individuals engage in such behaviour themselves (see, e.g., Gockeritz et al. 2010; Patchen 2010; see also Brisman 2009b).

Attitudes favourable to ordinary harms

Finally, individuals learn attitudes favourable to ordinary harms, with such attitudes being taught by family members, friends, community members, politicians, religious figures, the media and others. The research in environmental psychology and sociology devotes much attention to the nature of these attitudes and their impact on behaviour, particularly environmentally responsible behaviour (e.g., Dietz et al. 2007; Gockeritz et al. 2010; Kaiser et al. 1999; Kurz 2002; Larson 2010; Patchen 2010; Schultz et al. 2005; Takacs-Santa 2007). Attitudes favourable to environmentally responsible behaviour have several components, including beliefs (e.g., the belief that driving less will reduce climate change), affect (e.g., the feeling that driving less is desirable) and behavioural intentions (e.g., the intention to drive less). Attitudes often have a strong effect on environmentally responsible behaviour, particularly when the attitudes and behaviour are measured at the same level of specificity (e.g., the belief that recycling is beneficial and actual recycling behaviour). Attitudes, however, have a stronger effect on behaviour when individuals believe that others perform and approve of the behaviour in question, the perceived cost of the behaviour is low, and individuals have the ability to perform the behaviour. Drawing on this research, I list *certain* of the attitudes that should increase ordinary harms below.

Ordinary harms cause little harm and much good

Ordinary harms should be more likely when individuals believe that they cause little or no harm (see Dietz et al. 2007; Frantz and Mayer 2009; Kurz 2002; Takacs-Santa 2007). This belief is common for several reasons. The damage caused when an individual engages in an ordinary harm is typically indirect, delayed, diffuse and trivial. Related to this, the damage is often hidden, particularly in developed countries, where consumption is removed from production (e.g., individuals who consume meat never see animals being slaughtered (see Smart 2010)) and from the problem of disposal of accumulated waste and unwanted consumables. Also, the leading figures of an individual's community engage regularly in such harms, making it difficult for many to believe that these 'harms' cause damage (i.e., 'good' people do not commit 'bad' acts). Furthermore, most individuals have a large investment—cultural, financial, psychological, religious and social—in the ordinary harms they commit. As such, they are motivated to ignore or discount information about the damage caused by such harms (Frantz and Mayer 2009). While the media sometimes report on the damage caused by ordinary harms, media coverage is uneven and an attempt is often made to provide 'balanced coverage', such that the views of those who deny harm are covered (McCright 2007; McCright and Dunlap 2000). Related to this, there is a well-funded and organised movement designed to deny and raise doubts about the seriousness of climate change and other environmental problems (Brisman 2012; Dietz et al. 2007; McCright and Dunlap 2000; Schwartz 2017; Takacs-Santa 2007; Wyatt and Brisman 2017). Ordinary harms should also be more likely when people believe that engaging in them has benefits of both a personal and social nature. As suggested above, this belief is also common, in part because it is promoted by corporations and states. For example, many believe that the consumption of animal products has health benefits and that the purchase of consumer products has economic benefits.

Ordinary harms are justifiable or excusable

Some individuals may believe that the costs of ordinary harms outweigh the benefits, but nevertheless justify or excuse their engagement in such harms. They may claim that they perform such harms out of necessity or under duress (e.g., public transit is unavailable, they are unable to live without air conditioning). And they may claim that there is little they can do as individuals to make a difference, perhaps noting that they are just one of millions engaging in these behaviours, that others engage in far worse behaviours, and that they are powerless to effect meaningful change (Frantz and Mayer 2009; Iwata 2004; Patchen 2010).

Environmentally responsible behaviours are ineffective or undesirable

Some believe that environmentally responsible behaviours are ineffective or undesirable. For example, behaviours such as recycling, using public transport and following a vegetarian diet may be viewed as having little impact on the environment; costlier in terms of money, time and/or effort; a threat to physical and mental well-being; a danger to the economy; and incompatible with cherished values (Dietz et al. 2007; Frantz and Mayer 2009; Iwata 2004; Kalof et al. 1999; McCright and Dunlap 2000).

General attitudes conducive to ordinary harms

Finally, certain more general attitudes contribute to ordinary harms (e.g., Dietz et al. 2007; Dittmar 2005; Ertelt et al. 2011; Franzen and Meyer 2010; Iwata 2004; Kaiser et al. 1999; Kalof et al. 1999; Larson 2010; McCright and Dunlap 2000; Patchen 2010; Schultz et al. 2005; Smart 2010; Takacs-Santa 2007; Tribbia 2007; Worldwatch Institute 2010). These include materialism or the view that the acquisition of material goods is a central life goal; a high value on economic growth, individual freedom, laissez-faire government and free enterprise; and the belief that the natural environment is to be exploited for one's benefit, as opposed to managed for all people or valued in and of itself.

Biosocial theories

The environmental literature often suggests that individuals engage in ordinary harms because they are self-interested and have a short time horizon (see Agnew 2012). As such, they are attracted to the immediate gratifications that result from ordinary harms and have little concern for their long-term consequences. It is further said that this self-interest and short time horizon emerged out of the evolutionary process, with these traits having some adaptive value as our ancestors struggled to cope with a host of immediate threats. Biosocial theories are attracting increased attention in criminology and can shed additional light on the role that biological factors play in promoting ordinary harms.

Biosocial theories state that certain individual traits conducive to crime have *some* genetic basis and are influenced by 'biological harms', such as serious head injury and drug use during pregnancy (Beaver et al. 2015; DeLisi and Vaughn 2015). These traits include self-interest, impulsivity, insensitivity to others/low empathy, sensation seeking and poor problem-solving skills. Individuals with such traits should be more attracted to ordinary harms, care less about the negative consequences of such harms and be less able and willing to seek alternatives to ordinary harms. As such, it can be argued that individual differences in the tendency to engage in ordinary harms are in part biologically based. These traits, however, are also influenced by environmental factors. Among other things, individuals are more likely to possess and display such traits when they are experiencing strains or stressors, are competing with others and are interacting with those they view as outgroup members. Such conditions promote self-interest and reduce concern for others (Agnew 2014). Unfortunately, environmental problems such as climate change may contribute to such conditions and thereby foster such traits (Agnew 2012).

The opportunity to commit ordinary harms

The above theories focus on those factors that dispose individuals to engage in ordinary harms. But individuals cannot engage in ordinary harms unless they have the opportunity to do so. Certain societies provide far more opportunity than others (e.g., Smart, 2010; Stearns 2001; Worldwatch Institute 2010). Most notably, ordinary harms are much easier to commit in market societies with a large economic surplus and an ideology comparable to that of the 'American Dream' (Messner and Rosenfeld 2007). Products in such societies are usually abundant, due to extensive trade and technological/organisational developments that permit their mass manufacture at low unit cost. These products are marketed aggressively to broad segments of the population, since manufacturers must sell what they produce. And cultural values strongly encourage their consumption. Within such societies, wealthy individuals are better able than poor individuals to engage in ordinary harms, particularly harms that are more costly (cf. Brisman 2009a, 2009b). Reflecting this fact, the wealthy are more likely to engage in many of the ordinary harms listed above, even though some research suggests that they have more concern for the environment (Harlan et al. 2009).

Furthermore, societies not only make it possible to engage in ordinary harms, but they often make it difficult not to do so. In particular, they may limit the choices available to individuals, with ordinary harms often the only viable option. For example, the layout of cities, lack of public transportation and absence of bicycle lanes mean that many individuals have little choice but to drive to work (see Kurz 2002; Patchen 2010; Rudel 2009). Related to this, certain environmentally responsible behaviours (e.g., hybrid cars, solar power) are expensive, effectively putting them out of reach of many consumers (see, e.g., Brisman 2009b).

Conclusion

The leading crime theories have much to say about why individuals engage in ordinary harms that contribute to ecocide, even though these harms represent conformist behaviour. Ordinary harms are a mechanism for coping with a range of strains and associated negative emotions. They are also a function of strains that are *not* experienced (i.e., environmental strains). The harms increase one's stake in conformity, since they provide a range of possessions and a lifestyle that most are reluctant to relinquish. *Not* engaging in ordinary harms, by contrast, may subject one to informal sanction, jeopardise one's stake in conformity and challenge one's beliefs. The harms are attractive to those low in self-control, particularly 'environmental control', although harms that are more costly are facilitated by high self-control. Individuals learn to engage in the harms. They are reinforced for the harms by others, frequently with social approval and status; the harms are intrinsically reinforcing; they are regularly modelled by admired others; and individuals learn a host of attitudes that approve of, justify and excuse these harms. The individual traits fostering such harms have some biological basis, although are also fostered by social conditions. Finally, individuals in many societies are given ample opportunity to engage in the harms; in fact, they frequently have little choice but to do so. Taken together, the crime theories point to multiple reasons why ordinary harms are so common (and environmentally responsible behaviours are uncommon).

The application of the leading crime theories to ordinary harms is important for several reasons. As noted above, these theories more fully describe certain of the factors that contribute to ordinary harms, building on the work on consumerism and environmental psychology and sociology. As next steps, researchers should test these ideas and, drawing on the results and the related research in other areas, attempt to develop an integrated theory of ordinary harms. It should be kept in mind that the specific variables in such a theory may differ somewhat depending on the ordinary harm that is being explained. For example, efforts to explain meat consumption will assign a central role to beliefs regarding animals, while efforts to explain automobile use will assign a central role to the availability of alternative forms of transportation.

The application of the leading crime theories also demonstrates that these theories can explain a broader range of behaviours than the street crimes to which they are commonly applied. The theories, however, sometimes have to be applied in creative ways to do so (e.g., the examination of strains *not* experienced and the focus on 'environmental control'). Also, the harms are the result of *high* rather than low social and self-control, as well as social learning that occurs through the *dominant* culture rather than through deviant subcultures. This, of course, reflects the conformist nature of the harms. Hopefully, this application will stimulate others to draw on the mainstream theories when explaining harmful acts that are not legally defined as crimes. Efforts to explain environmental harm now draw most heavily on critical theories, with such harms being explained in terms of the desire of powerful groups—particularly states and corporations—to advance their interests.

Finally, the focus on explaining why *individuals* routinely harm the environment supplements the work in green criminology, which focusses on the harmful acts committed by states, corporations and organised criminal groups. This latter focus is important but, as suggested above, individuals are also deeply implicated in environmental harm. One might argue that the harmful behaviour of individuals is a function of larger social forces, particularly the efforts of societies and corporations to encourage consumption with little concern for the environmental consequences. There is much truth to this, as noted above. And future work should build on this chapter by describing more fully the ways in which the larger cultural, economic, political and social environment promotes ordinary harms (see Dunlap and York 2008; Franzen and Meyer 2010 for an overview of certain work in this area). But at the same time, it is important to recognise that most individuals have become enthusiastic practitioners of ordinary harms. In addition, the harms they commit provide a market for much of the harmful behaviour committed by states and corporations. Furthermore, the commitment of individuals to these harms often makes them quite resistant to change, including change that will limit the ability of states and corporations to promote these harms (see Brisman and South 2014).

This is not to blame individuals for the harms they commit. As described above, a multitude of factors lead them to engage in these harms, with most individuals unaware of the harm they are causing. But it is to argue that any effort to understand the causes of environmental harm must consider both individuals as well as larger groups. The same is true of efforts to address environmental harm. This includes efforts to change state and corporate behaviour; if such efforts are to be successful, they require knowledge of the myriad ways in which states and corporations impact individuals. And this includes efforts that are directed at individuals. Changing individual behaviour will require changes in the culture, social structure and infrastructure of societies. The above discussions points to the types of changes that are necessary. For example, any successful change will require such things as the reduction in the status attached to ordinary harms, redefinition of gender roles in ways that place less emphasis on consumption, increased costs of engaging in ordinary harms, undermining the specific beliefs that foster the harms, and making alternatives to ordinary harms more available and less costly. These are of course major undertakings, but not impossible. Witness, for example, the dramatic reduction in cigarette smoking, stimulated in part by undermining the status of smoking, challenging the beliefs that foster smoking and increasing the costs of smoking (U.S. Department of Health and Human Services 2000). And just as crime theories can shed light on the causes of ordinary harms, the crime control research can shed light on ways to reduce such harms—a topic for subsequent research and scholarship.

References

Agnew, R. 2006. *Pressured into Crime*. New York: Oxford University Press.

Agnew, R. 2012. 'It's the end of the world as we know it: The advance of climate change from a criminological perspective,' in R. White (ed.) *Climate Change from a Criminological Perspective*, pp. 13–26. New York: Springer.

Agnew, R. 2014. 'Social concern and crime: Moving beyond the assumption of simple self-interest,' *Criminology*, 52(1): 1–32.

Agnew, R. and Brezina, T. 2015. *Juvenile Delinquency: Causes and Control*. New York: Oxford.

Akers, R. L. 1990. 'Rational choice, deterrence, and social learning theory in criminology: The path not taken,' *Journal of Criminal Law and Criminology*, 81(3): 653–676.

Akers, R. L. 1998. *Social Learning and Social Structure: A General Theory of Crime and Deviance*. Boston, MA: Northeastern University Press.

Allen, M. W., Wilson, M., Ng, S. H. and Dunne, M. 2000. 'Values and beliefs of vegetarians and omnivores,' *The Journal of Social Psychology*, 140(4): 405–422.

Anderson, E. 1999. *Code of the Street: Decency, Violence, and the Moral Life of the Inner City*. New York: W. W. Norton.

Beaver, K. M., Barnes, J. C. and Boutwell, B. B. (eds.). 2015. *The Nurture Versus Biosocial Debate in Criminology*. Los Angeles, CA: Sage.

Beirne, P. and South, N. (eds.). 2007. *Issues in Green Criminology: Confronting Harms Against Environments, Humanity and Other Animals*. Cullompton, Devon, UK: Willan.

Brisman, A. 2004. 'Double whammy: Collateral consequences of conviction and imprisonment for sustainable communities and the environment,' *William & Mary Environmental Law & Policy Review*, 28(2): 423–475.

Brisman, A. 2007a. 'Learning from "virtual" others: Fence plowers, methamphetamine cooks, and sex offenders on the internet,' Paper presented at 2007 American Society of Criminology Annual Meeting, Atlanta, GA. (November 16).

Brisman, A. 2007b. 'Toward a more elaborate typology of environmental values: Liberalizing criminal disenfranchisement laws and policies,' *New England Journal on Criminal & Civil Confinement*, 33(2): 283–457.

Brisman, A. 2009a. 'Food justice as crime prevention,' *Journal of Food Law & Policy*, 5(1): 1–44.

Brisman, A. 2009b. 'It takes green to be green: Environmental elitism, "Ritual Displays," and conspicuous non-consumption,' *North Dakota Law Review*, 85(2): 329–370.

Brisman, A. 2012. 'The cultural silence of climate change contrarianism,' in R. White, (ed.) *Climate Change from a Criminological Perspective*, pp.41–70. New York: Springer.

Brisman, A. and South, N. 2014. *Green Cultural Criminology: Constructions of Environmental Harm, Consumerism, and Resistance to Ecocide*. London and New York: Routledge.

Brisman, A., McClanahan, B., South, N. and Walters, R. 2018. *Water, Crime and Security in the Twenty-First Century: Too Dirty, Too Little, Too Much*. London: Palgrave Macmillan.

Brody, S. D., Zahran, S., Vedlitz, A. and Grover, H. 2008. 'Examining the relationship between physical vulnerability and public perceptions of global climate change in the United States,' *Environment and Behavior*, 40(1): 72–95.

Cohen, A. K. 1955. *Delinquent Boys: The Culture of the Gang*. New York: Free Press.

Cornish, D. B. and Clarke, R. V. 1986. *The Reasoning Criminal*. New York: Springer-Verlag.

Csikszentmihalyi, M. 2000. 'The costs and benefits of consuming,' *Journal of Consumer Research*, 27(2): 267–272.

DeLisi, M. and Vaughn, M. G. (eds.) 2015. *The Routledge Handbook of Biosocial Criminology*. London: Routledge.

Deutsch, N. L. and Theodorou, E. 2010. 'Aspiring, consuming, becoming: Identity in a culture of consumption,' *Youth & Society*, 42(2): 229–254.

Dietz, T., Dan, A. and Shwom, R. 2007. 'Support for climate change policy: Social psychological and social structural influences,' *Rural Sociology*, 72(2): 185–214.

Dittmar, H. 2005. 'A new look at "compulsive buying": Self-discrepancies and materialistic values as predictors of compulsive buying tendency,' *Journal of Social and Clinical Psychology*, 24(6): 832–859.

Dunlap, R. E. and York, R. 2008. 'The globalization of environmental concern and the limits of the postmaterialist values explanation,' *Sociological Quarterly*, 49(3): 529–563.

Ertelt, T. W., Marino, J. and Müller, A. 2011. 'Etiology of compulsive buying,' in A. Müller and J. E. Mitchell (eds.) *Compulsive Buying: Clinical Foundations and Treatment*, pp.19–26. New York: Routledge.

Frantz, C. M. and Mayer, F. S. 2009. 'The emergency of climate change: Why are we failing to take action?' *Analyses of Social Issues and Public Policy*, 9(1): 205–222.

Franzen, A. and Meyer, R. 2010. 'Environmental attitudes in cross-national perspective: A multilevel analysis of the ISSP 1993 and 2000,' *European Sociological Review*, 26(2): 219–234.

Funk, C. and Kennedy, B. 2016. 'Everyday environmentalism,' *Pew Research Center*. Available at: www.pewinternet.org/2016/10/04/everyday-environmentalism/.

Gerber, P. J., Steinfeld, H., Henderson, B., Mottet, A., Opio, C., Dijkman, J., Falcucci, A. and Tempio, G. 2013. *Tackling Climate Change through Livestock – A Global Assessment of Emissions and Mitigation Opportunities*. Rome: Food and Agriculture Organization of the United Nations (FAO). Available at: www.fao.org/3/a-i3437e.pdf.

Gibbs, C., Gore, M. L., McGarrell, E. F. and Rivers, L. III. 2010. 'Introducing conservation criminology,' *The British Journal of Criminology*, 50(1): 124–144.

Gockeritz, S. P., Schultz, W., Rendon, T., Cialdini, R. B., Goldstein, N. J. and Griskevicius, V. 2010. 'Descriptive normative beliefs and conservation behavior: The moderating roles of personal involvement and injunctive normative beliefs,' *European Journal of Social Psychology*, 40(3): 514–523.

Gossard, M. H. and York, R. 2003. 'Social structural influences on meat consumption,' *Human Ecology Review*, 10(1): 1–9. Available at: www.humanecologyreview.org/pastissues/her101/101gossardyork.pdf.

Gottfredson, M. R. and Hirschi, T. 1990. *A General Theory of Crime*. Stanford, CA: Stanford University Press.

Harlan, S. L., Yabiku, S. T., Larsen, L. and Brazel, A. J. 2009. 'Household water consumption in an arid city: Affluence, affordance, and attitudes,' *Society and Natural Resources*, 22(8): 691–709.

Iwata, O. 2004. 'Some psychological correlates of environmentally responsible behavior,' *Social Behavior and Personality*, 32(8): 703–714.

Kaiser, F. G., Wölfing, S. and Fuhrer, U. 1999. 'Environmental attitude and ecological behaviour,' *Journal of Environmental Psychology*, 19(1): 1–19.

Kalof, L., Dietz, T., Stern, P. C. and Guagnano, A. 1999. 'Social psychological and structural influences on vegetarian beliefs,' *Rural Sociology*, 64(3): 500–511.

Kurz, T. 2002. 'The psychology of environmentally sustainable behavior: Fitting together pieces of the puzzle,' *Analyses of Social Issues and Public Policy*, 2(1): 257–278.

Larson, K. L. 2010. 'An integrated theoretical approach to understanding the sociocultural basis of multidimensional environmental attitudes,' *Society and Natural Resources*, 23(9): 898–907.

McCright, A. M. 2007. 'Dealing with climate change contrarians,' in S. C. Moser and L. Dilling (eds.) *Creating a Climate for Change*, pp. 200–212. Cambridge: Cambridge University Press.

McCright, A. M. and Dunlap, R. E. 2000. 'Challenging global warming as a social problem: An analysis of the conservative movement's counter-claims,' *Social Problems*, 47(4): 499–522.

Merriman, B. 2010. 'Gender differences in family and peer reaction to the adoption of a vegetarian diet,' *Feminism & Psychology*, 20(3): 420–427.

Messerschmidt, J. W. 1993. *Masculinities and Crime*. Lanham, MD: Rowman and Littlefield.

Messner, S. F. and Rosenfeld, R. 2007. *Crime and the American Dream*. Belmont, CA: Wadsworth.

Michaelis, L. 2007. 'Consumption behavior and narratives about the good life,' in S. Moser and L. Dilling (eds.) *Creating a Climate for Change*, pp. 251–265. Cambridge: Cambridge University Press.

Passas, N. 1997. 'Anomie, reference groups, and relative deprivation,' in N. Passas and R. Agnew (eds.) *The Future of Anomie Theory*, pp. 62–94. Boston, MA: Northeastern University Press.

Patchen, M. 2010. 'What shapes public reaction to climate change? Overview of research and policy implications,' *Analyses of Social Issues and Public Policy*, 10(1): 47–68.

Pew Research Center. 2017. 'After Seismic Political Shift, Modest Changes in Public's Policy Agenda,' January 27. Available at: www.people-press.org/2017/01/24/after-seismic-political-shift-modest-changes-in-publics-policy-agenda/.

Rudel, T. K. 2009. 'How do people transform landscapes? A sociological perspective on surburban sprawl and tropical deforestation,' *American Journal of Sociology*, 115(1): 129–154.

Schultz, P. W., Gouveia, V. V., Cameron, L. D., Tankha, G., Schmuck, P. and Marek, F. 2005. 'Values and their relationship to environmental concern and conservation behavior,' *Journal of Cross-Cultural Psychology*, 36(4): 457–475.

Schwartz, J. 2017. 'Exxon misled the public on the risks of climate change, a study says,' *The New York Times*. August 24: B7. Published online as 'Exxon Misled the Public on Climate Change, Study Says,' on August 23, 2017, at www.nytimes.com/2017/08/23/climate/exxon-global-warming-science-study.html?_r=0.

Smart, B. 2010. *Consumer Society: Critical Issues and Environmental Consequences*. London and Thousand Oaks, CA: Sage.

South, N. 2009. 'Ecocide, conflict and climate change: Challenges for criminology and the research agenda in the 21st century,' in K. Kangaspunta and I. H. Marshall (eds.) *Eco-Crime and Justice: Essays on Environmental Crime*, pp. 37–53. Turin, Italy: UNICRI.

Stearns, P. N. 2001. *Consumerism in World History: The Global Transformation of Desire*. New York and Abingdon, Oxon, UK: Routledge.

Takacs-Santa, A. 2007. 'Barriers to environmental concern,' *Human Ecology Review*, 14(1): 26–38.

Tribbia, J. 2007. 'Stuck in the slow lane of behavior change? A not-so-superhuman perspective on getting out of our cars,' in S. C. Moser and L. Dilling (eds.) *Creating a Climate for Change*, pp. 237–250. Cambridge: Cambridge University Press.

U.S. Department of Health and Human Services. 2000. 'Reducing tobacco use: A report of the surgeon general.' Atlanta, GA: U.S. Department of Health and Human Services, Centers for Disease Control and Prevention, National Center for Chronic Disease Prevention and Health Promotion, Office on Smoking and Health. Available at: www.cdc.gov/tobacco/data_statistics/sgr/2000/complete_report/pdfs/fullreport.pdf.

White, R. (ed.) 2012. *Climate Change from a Criminological Perspective*. New York: Springer.

Worldwatch Institute. 2010. *State of the World 2010: Transforming Cultures: From Consumerism to Sustainability*. New York: W.W. Norton.

Wright, R. T. and Decker, S. H. 1997. *Armed Robbers in Action: Stickups and Street Culture*. Boston, MA: Northeastern University Press.

Wyatt, T. and Brisman, A. 2017. 'The role of denial in the "theft of nature": A comparison of biopiracy and climate change,' *Critical Criminology: An International Journal*, 25(3): 325–341 DOI: 10.1007/s10612-016-9344-5. FirstOnline: September 14 2016. Available at: http://link.springer.com/article/10.1007/s10612-016-9344-5.

3

Wildlife crime

A situational crime prevention perspective

Christina Burton, Devin Cowan and William Moreto

Introduction

The study of wildlife crime from an environmental criminology and crime science perspective has generated a considerable literature in recent years (Moreto and Pires 2018). For instance, scholars have examined the utility of theft concepts, which have proven to be useful in addressing wildlife crimes, such as parrot poaching (Pires and Clarke 2012) and illegal fishing (Petrossian and Clarke 2014). Others have assessed the spatiotemporal characteristics of poaching (Moreto and Lemieux 2015b) and wildlife markets (Kurland and Pires 2017). This growing body of work has even led to the development of a conceptual framework (e.g., the CAPTURED framework, which refers to whether a wildlife product is concealable, available, processable, transferrable, useable, removable, enjoyable and desirable), in which the desirable properties of wildlife products (e.g., rhino horn) are acknowledged in determining the actors, settings and logistics required for wildlife trafficking. For example, the role of a smuggler will vary and will be influenced by whether the product being transported is alive, dead or simply part of a whole (see Moreto and Lemieux 2015a). Such research has tended to focus on the proximal and situational characteristics of wildlife crime, complementing the macro-level assessments found within green criminological perspectives. Moreover, these studies have focused largely on activities that violate the law as opposed to activities that are legal, yet potentially harmful to wildlife populations (see White 2013).

The potential application of situational crime prevention (SCP) measures to prevent and reduce wildlife crime has led researchers and scholars to argue that such strategies can provide an alternative to—or, at least, can accompany—traditional approaches, which often rely primarily on law enforcement. Prior discussions, however, have tended to assess the utility of SCP with little discussion of the potential role and value of incorporating green criminological perspectives. In this chapter, we provide an overview of the literature, highlighting the potential role that SCP has in reducing and preventing wildlife crime. We then discuss how green criminology and SCP can be used in tandem to develop contextually appropriate strategies. We begin by defining and discussing wildlife crime.

Wildlife crime

Wildlife crime has occurred for centuries and is largely influenced by its socio-political and cultural context (Hopkins 1985). Recently, the International Consortium on Combating Wildlife Crime (ICCWC) defined 'wildlife crime' as 'acts committed contrary to national laws and regulations to protect natural resources and to administer their management and use' (ICCWC 2017). While wildlife crime can manifest in various ways, the illegal taking of fauna and flora, often referred to as 'poaching' (see Moreto and Lemieux 2015b), on its own or as a precursor to wildlife trafficking (Wyatt 2013), is often at the forefront of public debate and outcry. As such, we focus our attention on these two forms of wildlife crime in this chapter.

Wildlife crime is driven by a number of different factors, including subsistence (Moreto and Lemieux 2015a, 2015b), political economy (Gibson 1999), rebellion (Muth and Bowe 1997), cultural and traditional practices (Wyatt 2013), and human–wildlife conflict (Treves and Karanth 2003). Supply and demand markets have also been acknowledged as having a considerable influence on the domestic and international trade of 'wildlife products'.[1] While the aforementioned factors may play a role for particular wildlife crimes in specific settings, one component that is present for all types of wildlife crime is criminal opportunity (Moreto and Pires 2018). In other words, regardless of the distal or immediate factors that may motivate offenders, no crime can occur without the presence of crime opportunities. Recognising that crime opportunity is a viable driver of wildlife crime is therefore central in the understanding and development of crime-, setting- and product-specific prevention measures (Moreto and Pires 2018).

Situational Crime Prevention (SCP)

Situational crime prevention was created as a response to traditional crime prevention measures that stem primarily from a social perspective (Clarke 1980). Whereas traditional crime prevention measures would seek to address underlying problems, such as unemployment and disorderly communities, SCP, on the other hand, targets situational characteristics of the immediate environment in an effort to reduce the potential for criminal opportunities (Clarke 1980, 1983). The theoretical framework for SCP draws from four criminological perspectives (Cornish and Clarke 2003): routine activities (Cohen and Felson 1979), rational choice (Cornish and Clarke 1986), crime pattern theory (Brantingham and Brantingham 1993) and situational precipitators (Wortley 1997).

Briefly, the *routine activity perspective* proposes that, for a criminal event to occur, there must be the convergence, in time and space, of a motivated offender, a suitable target and a lack of capable guardianship (Cohen and Felson 1979). The *rational choice perspective* states that individuals decide to commit crime through a 'bounded' form of rational choice (Cornish and Clarke 1986). In other words, offenders have an imperfect calculus and are limited in their ability to assess fully the costs and benefits of the crime beyond the immediate circumstances. *Crime pattern theory* is a combination of the two previously mentioned perspectives (Brantingham and Brantingham 1993). This theory puts forth that individuals are interacting constantly with the environment, and that they occupy a series of infinite feedback loops where the individual and environment both adapt to the presence of the other (Brantingham and Brantingham 1993). Within these interactions, an individual forms an 'awareness space'—or the cognitive understanding of geographic locations based either on our own experiences or through information exchanges with others—in which a familiarity with the environment is created (Brantingham and Brantingham 1993). These interactions and the awareness space form an individual's crime template (Brantingham and Brantingham 1993). The crime template can be best thought of as a mental checklist that must be satisfied in order for the individual to seize a criminal opportunity (Andresen 2014). Finally, the concept of *situational precipitators* refers to how a situation can cause, or precipitate, certain behaviour. Wortley identifies four precipitators: prompts, pressures, permissibility and provocations (Andresen 2014). As the name implies, a 'prompt' would be a situational cue that induces an individual to commit a criminal act. Likewise, a situational cue that compels an individual to commit a criminal act is a 'pressure'. 'Permissibility' refers to a situational cue that permits an individual to commit a certain act, and a 'provocation' would be a situational cue that elicits an emotional response from an individual (Andresen 2014). This theoretical background provides specific crime prevention implications: increase the effort and risk, reduce the rewards and provocations and remove excuses for committing a criminal act (Cornish and Clarke 2003).

All crimes have unique characteristics. As such, SCP promotes the idea of crime specificity (Clarke 1983). This means that when attempting to apply SCP to a crime problem, one must be cognizant of the variation and differences in the characteristics and properties of seemingly similar crimes. The reason for this is that SCP calls for varying prevention efforts depending on the type of crime. For example, the crime prevention implications for residential burglary will be different than those for commercial burglary. Simply targeting burglary, in general, will not be sufficient when the crime problem is exclusive to residential areas.

SCP has been applied and evaluated within a variety of locations and for many crime types, including crime involving medicinal and illicit marijuana production (Clare et al. 2017), crime in nightclubs (Cozens and Grieve 2014), crime in fast food and convenience stores (Exum et al. 2010) and crime in criminal organisations (Gilmour 2016; von Lampe 2011; Weenink 2012). In large part, however, SCP has been applied mostly within a traditional urban setting. For example, Clare and colleagues examined whether current licensing practices in Surrey, British Columbia, Canada, adequately ensured that legal marijuana productions operated pursuant to regulations (Clare et al. 2017). From this evaluation, they found that current licensing practices did not adequately keep licensed growing operations within the code (Clare et al. 2017). The proposed SCP implications of these findings included increasing the risk of detection for individuals who are not operating up to code and removing any possible excuses for not following the law (Clare et al. 2017). Cozens and Grieve (2014) examined the situational characteristics of nightclub entrances that influence criminal activity within the nightclub itself. In this observational study, the authors questioned whether nightclub security had, in fact, taken situational crime prevention measures to an extreme. Specifically, this 'overfortressification' of nightclubs was theorised to have the potential to increase the stress of those experiencing these prevention measures (Cozens and Grieve 2014). Accordingly, the authors submitted that there must be a balance when controlling the various precipitators of criminal activity (Cozens and Grieve 2014). Finally, Exum and colleagues (2010) compared the SCP measures implemented by both fast food and convenience stores to identify whether there were commonalities between the two for preventing commercial robberies. Overall, they found that the operating procedures, environmental design and target hardening procedures varied between the two types of establishments. These results point to the efficacy of applying SCP by not only crime type but also by location (Exum et al. 2010).

In terms of the application to *organised crime*, SCP has been utilised to prevent financial crimes (Gilmour 2016; von Lampe 2011), as well as terrorism (Weenink 2012). Gilmour (2016) describes the money laundering process and proposes that efforts that are focused at the beginning stages of this process are more likely to prevent these activities from occurring.

Specifically, one must increase the effort and risk necessary to launder capital successfully (Gilmour 2016). In a critique and subsequent application of SCP to terrorism, Weenink (2012) asserts that SCP simply does not address terrorism sufficiently, primarily due to a narrow organisational task scope. Past applications of SCP to terrorism, Weenink (2012) argues, have largely been reactionary, and they have ignored the investigative nature of counter-terrorism. As a solution to this issue, Weenink (2012) proposes that SCP measures for terrorism take a more proactive focus in attempting to intervene as early as possible, such as when individuals are still in the preparatory stages of offending.

SCP has been criticised for suggesting unattractive crime prevention initiatives, such as installing barbed wire fences and padlocks, and the hiring of private security (Clarke 1980). In addition, due to the assumption that all individuals have the propensity to offend given the opportunity, SCP has been criticised for its pessimistic view of human behaviour (Clarke 1980). In addition to these common criticisms of SCP, Clarke (2009) also describes seven common concerns about and misconceptions regarding SCP: (1) SCP is simplistic and atheoretical; (2) it displaces crime and makes it worse; (3) it does not address the root causes of crime; (4) it is too conservative; (5) it promotes an exclusionary society; (6) it promotes the idea of 'Big Brother'; and (7) it blames the victim. To address a few of these misconceptions, SCP, as discussed above, is based on three criminological perspectives; therefore, it is hardly atheoretical (Clarke 2009). While SCP may not address root causes of crime, such as psychological or social influences of behaviour, it does provide society with visible reductions in criminal activity (Clarke 2009). Finally, SCP actually *empowers* crime victims by providing them with the knowledge of how to reduce criminal opportunity and the tangible means of doing so (Clarke 2009).

Utilising SCP to prevent wildlife crime: a review of the literature

Despite differences in terminology, conservationists' and criminal justice researchers' responses to the prevention of poaching share similarities. Most research on the nexus of SCP and wildlife crime has focused on the theoretical concepts of 'hot products' of specific animals (either as parts or the entire animal), such as in the illegal parrot trade (Pires 2015; Pires and Clarke 2012) or of wildlife in general (Petrossian et al. 2016; Pires and Moreto 2011). Other research has attempted to determine 'hot routes' and spatiotemporal characteristics of poaching (Kurland et al. 2017). Nevertheless, SCP offers an opportunity to use this prior research to prevent opportunities of wildlife crime. While this chapter will highlight only some of the different approaches to SCP with the current literature, Table 3.1 lists each of the 25 SCP techniques with applications to wildlife crime.

SCP offers a chance to incorporate *local* strategies to prevent poaching and the illegal wildlife trade, rather than relying on international- or national-level policies and regulations. Even then, reliance on national-level legislation to prevent wildlife crime leads to concerns regarding implementation in specific countries, as well as depending on those countries to manage their protected areas with their already strained resources (Broussard 2017). These international policies also fail to consider that most illegal trade operates through *internal* markets rather than across countries (see, e.g., Pires 2015; Runhovde 2017), misattributing the problem of wildlife crime to consisting mostly of international markets. In the context of wildlife crime SCP focuses on the prevention of poaching individual species (altering motivations), and one of the most significant approaches that has been utilised to reduce poaching through a SCP framework has been the creation and maintenance of protected areas. Theoretically, the use of protected areas is intended to increase the effort to obtain specific flora

Table 3.1 Applying situational crime prevention to reduce wildlife crime

Increase the effort	*Increase the risk*	*Reduce the rewards*	*Reduce provocations*	*Remove excuses*
Target harden	***Extend guardianship***	***Conceal targets***	***Reduce frustration and stress***	***Set rules***
Increasing law enforcement activities and presence around highly coveted targets (i.e., personal ranger guards for a wild rhino).	Utilise camera traps within protected areas to increase the monitoring of wildlife, as well as to provide an opportunity to record suspects.	Conduct 'early burnings' away from local communities.	Implementing a compensation scheme program to reduce frustration over problem species.	Educating locals on conservation objectives, informing citizens of laws and regulations and implementing awareness campaigns can aid compliance.
Control access to facilities	***Assist natural surveillance***	***Remove targets***	***Avoid disputes***	***Post instructions***
Protected areas can increase the effort of committing wildlife crime by creating boundaries, such as different types of fencing, to limit the ease of entry and exit from a protected area by potential offenders.	Provide anonymous reporting via email or phone.	Removing readily available and valuable wildlife products (i.e., dehorning rhinos at public zoos).	Create physical barriers (i.e., digging trenches to reduce elephant–people conflict) between wildlife and adjacent communities.	Protected areas post instructions to alert locals and outsiders that species within such areas are protected and cannot be hunted.
Screen exits	***Reduce anonymity***	***Identify property***	***Reduce emotional arousal***	***Alert conscience***
X-ray fluorescence scanners to assess legality of elephant ivory.	Publicise those who have been prosecuted for wildlife crimes.	CITES documents for legally traded wildlife.	Develop and participate in community conservation programs to address concerns raised by community members.	Provide information at groceries, markets, restaurants and stores about legal and illegal wildlife products.
Deflect offenders	***Utilise place managers***	***Disrupt markets***	***Neutralise peer pressure***	***Assist compliance***
Road blockades can be used to perform random car searches on highways or roadways that are identified as wildlife trafficking routes.	Encourage safari companies to report suspicious activity.	Close down local markets that sell illegally caught bushmeat.	Utilise local leaders as a means to spread the value of conservation initiatives and reduce peer pressure.	Community-based conservation programs can increase compliance of wildlife rules by incentivising locals to abide by the rules via direct or indirect benefits.

(*Continued*)

Table 3.1 (Cont.)

Increase the effort	*Increase the risk*	*Reduce the rewards*	*Reduce provocations*	*Remove excuses*
Control tools/ weapons Limit the sale of tools known to be used for animal trapping (e.g., metal traps).	***Strengthen formal surveillance*** Using science and technology, including SMART and DNA forensics, to increase law enforcement capabilities.	***Deny benefits*** Fining farmers if they are caught killing such predators and removing any compensation-based schemes.	***Discourage imitation*** Awareness campaigns by celebrities and other known individuals to reduce demand for illegal wildlife.	***Control drugs and alcohol*** During community conservation meetings, provide information and support for alcohol and substance abuse.

and fauna, while fencing provides its own set of SCP techniques. These areas require boundaries distinguishing the general environment from a conservation area that receives legal and law enforcement attention when compared with those areas beyond the borders.

Typically, conservation has focused on the use of protected areas to address poaching, namely as a location for law enforcement to patrol and safeguard against specific threats. Though regarded as vital to conservation efforts, few studies have determined their effectiveness in reducing poaching. Theoretically, placing barriers around these monitored areas (such as fencing) increases the effort required to access specific flora and fauna. Such barriers can be subdivided into or categorised as 'live fences' (use of animals or plants for a boundary), 'physical fences' and 'metaphysical fences' (Kurland et al. 2017). Live fences have been shown to be useful in preventing certain herbivores from attacking local crops (Hayward and Kerley 2009). Regarding physical fencing, there are several different types, including wire and electrified fencing, with research suggesting the latter as particularly useful in preventing wildlife from crossing into farms (O'Connell-Rodwell et al. 2000). Metaphysical fences include sound and chemical repellant to discourage animals and humans from crossing the barriers, and some studies have suggested they can be quite useful for preventing damage to farms (Kurland et al. 2017). One of those studies includes research on the use of non-traditional methods of fencing to prevent elephants from damaging crops in northeast India, such as chili fencing, noise and spotlights (Davies et al. 2011). That study found that both chili and electric fencing were the strategies most likely to have a lower probability of crop damage, followed by the use of fire and spotlights (Davies et al. 2011); such alternative methods of fencing can also provide viable ways to restrict access of animals to certain areas.

These physical (and sometimes metaphorical) barriers attempt to restrict access to specific hot targets (protected animals) while also reducing the likelihood of human–animal interactions. The key to their effectiveness, however, relies on limiting the damage they can cause to the ecological frameworks in which these animals reside. Furthermore, some physical barriers (such as metal wire fences) could counteract the intended side effects by providing a source of metal for the creation of snare traps (Lindsey et al. 2011). In addition, fencing could restrict animal migration to important resources like food and water, unintentionally reducing animal populations despite initial intentions of reducing animal–human interactions (Hayward and Kerley 2009).

Another SCP technique used in addressing wildlife crime is to reduce provocations and retaliatory killings that sometimes result from human–animal interactions and events. For instance, if a particular animal damages an individual's farm, that individual may seek revenge and target the animal to be killed. Knowledge of strategies that help reduce such provocations is limited however (beyond using different fencing and, as will be discussed shortly, incentive programs), suggesting a gap in the present literature (Kurland et al. 2017). An examination of human–felid (wild cat) conflicts by Inskip and Zimmerman (2009) suggests that research on those incidents requires more standardisation of measurements and that solutions to handling provocations need to focus on the unique situation rather than universal approaches.

Other ways of attempting to prevent illegal killing of animals include the use of community conservation programs to encourage other sources of income besides poaching. This strategy tries to reduce the impetus to pursue poaching as an income-generator while also changing the perception of animals from a single-source product to consistent income provider. One such program can be seen in Payments for Ecosystems Services—a program that focuses on giving money to local individuals who engage in conservation practices (Kurland et al. 2017). A study by Mishra and colleagues examined the impacts of an incentive program on retaliatory killings of snow leopards in India (Mishra et al. 2003); they found that the incentive program improved local support of conservation goals. Not only are individuals obtaining financial resources (reducing the benefits for poaching), but they are also involved personally in defending those protected areas (increased guardianship) and are less likely to poach (more likely to be compliant).

Legislation offers other methods for tackling wildlife crime. For example, legal sanctions can serve to remove excuses for engaging in wildlife crime, though actual enforcement of laws varies. Some jurisdictions have used fines as a sanction to reduce the rewards for poaching or illegal wildlife trade, however the effectiveness of these sanctions in deterring individuals has yet to be determined. (Some studies do attempt to explore the legal components of legislation and their impacts on wildlife crime prevention or deterrence (see, e.g., Broussard 2017).) Requiring compliance with wildlife regulations is another technique utilised in conservation efforts, and it attempts to remove excuses through known rules, as well as possibly increasing the risk for poachers through known sanctions. Part of achieving this compliance stems from interacting with the surrounding communities, increasing their awareness of laws and educating them about the purpose of conservation (Kahler and Gore 2012). Disrupting markets to reduce the rewards associated with wildlife crime and limiting access to specific areas via blockades constitute other techniques designed to increase the effort necessary for wildlife crime (Kurland et al. 2017).

While the use of sanctions to punish wildlife crime is important, so too is the incorporation of law enforcement for strengthening formal surveillance, which increases the risk of committing wildlife crime. Though literature on patrolling is beyond the scope of this chapter, it is necessary to state that increased patrolling in protected areas aids the prevention of wildlife crime by increasing the risk of capture. More patrolling from agencies has also been shown to be important for reducing poaching (Hilborn et al. 2006; Jachmann and Billiouw 1997), suggesting the importance of a law enforcement presence for formal surveillance.

Despite the above discussion on types of SCP applications to wildlife crime, there is still the possibility of displacement given these approaches. In other words, would-be poachers may select different targets if their initial efforts have been thwarted, or they may employ alternative methods of taking and killing wildlife after exposure to an intervention. As with most research on poaching and wildlife crime, the extent of the possibility of displacement is unclear due to a gap in the literature, though a meta-analysis of SCP interventions by Guerette and Bowers (2009) describes how most SCP interventions do not lead to displacement. In a case study observing the Wildlife Crimes Unit in North Sulawesi, Indonesia, researchers found that focusing on protected species through searches of vehicles at specific road blockades led to a decrease in the loss of protected species with an increase in unprotected species (Lee et al. 2005). While this does suggest displacement in the types of targeted species is possible, it does not mean that the net displacement of species exists after SCP interventions. In other words, a shift towards a different species in one location does not mean that all populations of that species in an entire country (or even region) are, collectively, targeted.

Integrating green criminological perspectives for SCP

Wildlife crime is a complex, 'wicked problem' (see Rittel and Webber 1973) that warrants a multi-faceted approach. The majority of discussions regarding SCP within the wildlife crime literature has tended to operate within the scope of crime science or conservation criminology. But the explicit integration of green criminological perspectives—particularly those sensitive to local cultures and viewpoints such as green cultural criminology (Brisman and South 2013, 2014)—can have a considerable and important place in guiding SCP measures (Moreto and Pires 2018). In other words, while SCP approaches are inherently crime-specific and require an in-depth assessment of the immediate setting, such approaches should be informed by the surrounding context. Indeed, long-term SCP strategies may require a better understanding of the overarching cultural, political and social factors influencing a problem and the place it occurs in order to be effective (Clarke 2004)—and ethical (Von Hirsch, Garland and Wakefield 2000). Furthermore, better contextualising crime prevention efforts may also help facilitate participatory involvement of vested local stakeholders, while also minimising unintended or harmful outcomes (Grabosky 1996). This may be especially vital for 'soft' strategies found within SCP, raising consciousness, assisting with compliance, and reducing frustration and stress (Moreto and Pires 2018; Pires and Moreto 2011). As such, scholars and policymakers who are interested in engaging in such applied research are recommended to put in the necessary time and effort to first appreciate and understand the context—cultural, ecological, political or otherwise—prior to the development of prevention strategies.

Integrating green criminology and SCP, as well as crime science and environmental criminology, should be viewed as a welcomed development. These perspectives—and the scholars who adhere to and promote such approaches—have tended to work in theoretical silos (Moreto 2018). Collaboration, however, has considerable benefits. In particular, the strengths of each approach can be heightened, while their respective limitations can be reduced (Brisman and South 2018; Brisman and South 2015; White 2018). In essence, far more can be gained in identifying areas for partnership as opposed to remaining in isolation (Moreto 2018). To encourage such collaboration, we argue that emphasis should be placed on the topic of interest as opposed to philosophical or theoretical orientation. Indeed, recent collaborations between environmental criminologists and green criminologists have demonstrated the products that can arise from such efforts (i.e., van Uhm and Moreto's (2018) recent study on the illegal wildlife trade and corruption is one example).

Summary

This chapter has described the potential role of SCP in preventing wildlife crime and has offered a guide for how to better situate SCP techniques within the broader and immediate context. Several key points have been presented. First, evidence suggests that SCP offers a viable strategy in the fight against wildlife crime. Because the SCP approach is inherently crime- and context-specific, these techniques provide local communities with the ability to address poaching within their area in a manner tailored specifically to the problem. In addition, and as described earlier in the chapter, the variety of approaches, from chemical repellants (Davies et al. 2011) on fencing to income-generating community programs (Kurland et al. 2017), allow for different solutions for different communities for a similar problem.

Second, proper implementation of SCP techniques requires the input from multiple stakeholders (Kurland et al. 2017), including the community, wildlife law enforcement and conservation biologists. Cooperation with community members and wildlife law enforcement is necessary not only for compliance with the former, but also for information gathering from informants about likely poachers. Conservation biologists are also vital for wildlife crime prevention because they are able to determine the overall health of an ecosystem and provide information on population numbers within those ecosystems.

Third, there are still plenty of gaps within the literature that should be explored to provide a more comprehensive understanding of the issue of wildlife crime and the outcomes that come from SCP approaches. While some of the techniques have been given extensive coverage, it is unclear which techniques yield greater reductions in wildlife crime than others in specific contexts or if there are certain effects that require multiple interventions at the same time. Furthermore, evaluations of interventions need to be conducted because it is important to ensure the program is producing the desired outcomes (Kurland et al. 2017; Moreto and Pires 2018). Programs that require or otherwise impose a significant cost to the surrounding communities could affect not only the implementation of the intervention or prevention technique, but also create undesirable effects associated with the intervention (such as creating wire snares from wire fencing). These deficits in research should, however, be seen as opportunities for future collaborations between practitioners and academics to create innovative and effective strategies for preventing, and ultimately reducing, wildlife crime.

Finally, SCP techniques will benefit from a better understanding of broader factors. Such knowledge will not necessarily be geared towards attempting to solve problems that extend beyond the capabilities of SCP (e.g., poverty), but could nevertheless provide valuable information that helps to contextualise and inform interventions and strategies. Recognising that SCP techniques require local input that sheds light on unique political, social and cultural circumstances may prove beneficial in avoiding ineffective, counterproductive or harmful results for both the targeted wildlife and surrounding communities.

Note

1 For the purposes of this chapter—and following Moreto and Lemieux (2015a)—we use the term "wildlife products" to refer to products made from wildlife for the purpose of clothing, food, medicine, etc.

References

Andresen, M. A. 2014. *Environmental Criminology: Evolution, Theory, and Practice.* Abingdon, Oxon, UK: Routledge.

Brantingham, P. L. and Brantingham, P. J. 1993. 'Environment, routine, and situation: Toward a pattern theory of crime,' in R. V. Clarke and M. Felson (eds.) *From Routine Activity and Rational Choice, Advances in Criminological Theory*, Vol. 5, pp. 1–14. Piscataway, NJ: Transaction Publishers.

Brisman, A. and South, N. 2013. 'A green-cultural criminology: An exploratory outline,' *Crime Media Culture: An International Journal*, 9(2): 115–135.

Brisman, A. and South, N. 2014. *Green Cultural Criminology: Constructions of Environmental Harm, Consumerism, and Resistance to Ecocide.* London and New York: Routledge.

Brisman, A and South, N. 2015. 'An assessment of Tonry and Farrington's four major crime prevention strategies as applied to environmental crime and harm,' *Journal of Criminal Justice and Security (Varstvoslovje)*, 17: 127–151.

Brisman, A. and South, N. 2018. 'Perspectives on wildlife crime: The convergence of "green" and "conservation" criminologies,' in W. D. Moreto (ed.) *Wildlife Crime: From Theory to Practice*, pp. 17–37. Philadelphia, PA: Temple University Press.

Broussard, G. 2017. 'Building an effective criminal justice response to wildlife trafficking: Experiences from the ASEAN region,' *Review of European Community & International Environmental Law*, 26(2): 118–127.

Clare, J., Garis, L. and Maxim, P. 2017. 'Medicinal marijuana production creates problem residential properties: A routine activity theory explanation and a situational crime-prevention solution,' *Canadian Journal of Criminology and Criminal Justice*, 59(2): 143–167.

Clarke, R.V.G. 1980. '"Situational" crime prevention: Theory and practice,' *The British Journal of Criminology*, 20(2): 136–147.

Clarke, R.V.G. 1983 'Situational crime prevention: Its theoretical basis and practical scope,' *Crime and Justice*, 4: 225–256.

Clarke, R. V. 2004. 'Technology, criminology and crime science,' *European Journal on Criminal Policy and Research*, 10(1): 55–63.

Clarke, R. V. 2009. 'Seven misconceptions of situational crime prevention,' in N. Tilley (ed.) *Handbook of Crime Prevention Community Safety*, pp. 39–70. Cullompton, Devon, UK: Willan.

Cohen, L. E. and Felson, M. 1979. 'Social change and crime rate trends: A routine activity approach,' *American Sociological Review*, 44(4): 588–608.

Cornish, D. B. and Clarke, R. V. 1986. *The Reasoning Criminal: Rational Choice Approaches on Offending*. New York: Springer-Verlag.

Cornish, D. B. and Clarke, R. V. 2003. 'Opportunities, precipitators and criminal decisions: A reply to Wortley's critique of situational crime prevention,' in M. Smith and D. B. Cornish (eds.) *Crime Prevention Studies: Theory for Practice in Situational Crime Prevention*, Vol. 16., pp. 41–96. Monsey, NY: Criminal Justice Press.

Cozens, P. and Grieve, S. 2014. 'Situational crime prevention at nightclub entrances in Perth, Western Australia: Exploring micro-level crime precipitators,' *Crime Prevention and Community Safety*, 16(1): 54–70.

Davies, T. E., Wilson, S., Hazarika, N., Chakrabarty, J., Das, D., Hodgson, D. J. and Zimmerman, A. 2011 'Effectiveness of intervention methods against crop-raiding elephants,' *Conservation Letters*, 4: 346–354.

Exum, M. L., Kuhns, J. B., Koch, B. and Johnson, C. 2010. 'An examination of situational crime prevention strategies across convenience stores and fast-food restaurants,' *Criminal Justice Policy Review*, 21(3): 269–295.

Gibson, C. C. 1999. *Politicians and Poachers: The Political Economy of Wildlife Policy in Africa*. Cambridge: Cambridge University Press.

Gilmour, N. 2016. 'Preventing money laundering: A test of situational crime prevention,' *Journal of Money Laundering Control*, 19(4): 376–396.

Grabosky, P. N. 1996. 'Unintended consequences of crime prevention,' in R. Homel and R. V. Clarke (eds.) *Crime Prevention Studies*, Vol. 5, pp. 25–56. Monsey, NY: Criminal Justice Press.

Guerette, R. T. and Bowers, K. J. 2009. 'Assessing the extent of crime displacement and diffusion of benefits: A review of situational crime prevention evaluations,' *Criminology*, 47(4): 1331–1368.

Hayward, M. W. and Kerley, G. I. H. 2009. 'Fencing for conservation: Restriction of evolutionary potential or a riposte to threatening processes?' *Biological Conservation*, 142(1): 1–13.

Hilborn, R., Arcese, P., Borner, M., Hando, J., Hopcraft, G., Loibooki, M., Mduma, S. and Sinclair, A. R. E. 2006. 'Effective enforcement in a conservation area,' *Science*, 314(5803) [24 November]: 1266.

Hopkins, H. 1985. *The Long Affray: The Poaching Wars in Britain*. London: Papermac.

ICCWC/CITES 2017. 'Wildlife crime,' Available at: https://www.cites.org/eng/prog/iccwc.php/Wild life-Crime.

Inskip, C. and Zimmerman, A. 2009. 'Human-felid conflict: A review of patterns and priorities worldwide,' *Oryx*, 43(1): 18–34.

Jachmann, H. and Billiouw, M. 1997. 'Elephant poaching and law enforcement in the Central Luangwa Valley, Zambia,' *Journal of Applied Ecology*, 34(1): 233–244.

Kahler, J. S. and Gore, M. L. 2012. 'Beyond the cooking pot and pocket book: Factors influencing noncompliance with wildlife poaching rules,' *International Journal of Comparative and Applied Criminal Justice*, 36(2): 103–120.

Kurland, J. and Pires, S. F. 2017. 'Assessing U.S. wildlife trafficking patterns: How criminology and conservation science can guide strategies to reduce the illegal wildlife trade,' *Deviant Behavior*, 38(4): 375–391.

Kurland, J., Pires, S. F., McFann, S. C. and Moreto, W. D. 2017. 'Wildlife crime: A conceptual integration, literature review, and methodological critique,' *Crime Science*, 6(4): 1–15.

Lee, R. J., Gorog, A. J., Dwiyahreni, A., Siwu, S., Riley, J., Alexander, H., Paoli, G. D. and Ramono, W. 2005. 'Wildlife trade and implications for law enforcement in Indonesia: A case study from North Sulawesi,' *Biological Conservation*, 123(4): 477–488.

Lindsey, P. A., Romanach, S. S., Tambling, C. J., Chartier, K. and Groom, R. 2011. 'Ecological and financial impacts of illegal bushmeat trade in Zimbabwe,' *Oryx*, 45(1): 96–111.

Mishra, C., Allen, P., McCarthy, T., Madhusudan, M. D., Bayarjargal, A. and Prins, H. H. T. 2003. 'The role of incentive programs in conserving the snow leopard,' *Conservation Biology*, 17(6): 1512–1520.

Moreto, W. D. (ed.). 2018. *Wildlife Crime: From Theory to Practice*. Philadelphia, PA: Temple University Press.

Moreto, W. D. and Lemieux, A. M. 2015a. 'From CRAVED to CAPTURED: Introducing a product-based framework to examine illegal wildlife markets,' *European Journal on Criminal Policy and Research*, 21(3): 303–320.

Moreto, W. D., and Lemieux, A. M. 2015b 'Poaching in Uganda: Perspectives from law enforcement rangers,' *Deviant Behavior*, 36(11): 853–873.

Moreto, W. and Pires, S. F. 2018. *Wildlife Crime: An Environmental Criminology and Crime Science Perspective*. Durham, NC: Carolina Academic Press.

Muth, R. M. and Bowe, J. F., Jr. 1997. 'Illegal harvest of renewable natural resources in North America: A typology of motivations for poaching,' *Society & Natural Resources*, 11(1): 9–24.

O'Connell-Rodwell, C. E., Rodwell, T., Rice, M. and Hart, L. A. 2000. 'Living with the modern conservation paradigm: Can agricultural communities co-exist with elephants? A five-year case study in East Caprivi, Namibia,' *Biological Conservation*, 93(3): 381–391.

Petrossian, G. A. and Clarke, R. V. 2014. 'Explaining and controlling illegal commercial fishing: An application of the CRAVED theft model,' *The British Journal of Criminology*, 54(1): 73–90.

Petrossian, G. A., Pires, S. F. and van Uhm, D. P. 2016. 'An overview of seized illegal wildlife entering the United States,' *Global Crime*, 17(2): 181–201.

Pires, S. and Clarke, R. 2012. 'Are parrots CRAVED? An analysis of parrot poaching in Mexico,' *Journal of Research in Crime and Delinquency*, 49(1): 122–146.

Pires, S. F. 2015. 'A CRAVED analysis of multiple illicit parrot markets in Peru and Bolivia,' *European Journal on Criminal Policy and Research*, 21(3): 321–336.

Pires, S. F. and Moreto, W. D. 2011. 'Preventing wildlife crimes: Solutions that can overcome the "tragedy of the commons",' *European Journal on Criminal Policy and Research*, 17(2): 101–123.

Rittel, H. W. J. and Webber, M. M. 1973. 'Dilemmas in a general theory of planning,' *Policy Sciences*, 4 (2): 155–169.

Runhovde, S. R. 2017. 'Merely a transit country? Examining the role of Uganda in the transnational illegal ivory trade,' *Trends in Organized Crime*, *21*(3): 215–234. DOI: 10.1007/s12117-016-9299-7.

Treves, A. and Karanth, K. U. 2003. 'Human-carnivore conflict and perspectives on carnivore management worldwide,' *Conservation Biology*, 17(6): 1491–1499.

von Lampe, K. 2011. 'The application of the framework of situational crime prevention to "organized crime",' *Criminology and Criminal Justice*, 11(2): 145–163.

Von Hirsch, A., Garland, D. and Wakefield, A. (eds.) 2000. *Ethical and Social Perspectives on Situational Crime Prevention*. Oxford: Hart Publishing.

Weenink, A. W. 2012. 'Situational prevention of terrorism. Remarks from the field of counterterrorism in the Netherlands on Newman and Clarke's *Policing Terrorism*,' *Trends in Organized Crime*, 15(2-3): 164–179.

White, R. 2013. *Environmental Harm: An Eco-Justice Perspective*. Bristol, UK: Policy Press.

White, R. 2018. 'Paradoxes of prevention: Situational, contextual, and political economy responses to wildlife crime,' in W. D. Moreto (ed.) *Wildlife Crime: From Theory to Practice*, pp. 62–80. Philadelphia, PA: Temple University Press.

Wortley, R. 1997. 'Reconsidering the role of opportunity in situational crime prevention,' in G. Newman, R. V. Clarke and G. Shohan (eds.) *Rational Choice and Situational Crime Prevention*, pp. 65–81. Aldershot: Ashgate Publishing.

Wyatt, T. 2013. *Wildlife Trafficking: A Deconstruction of the Crime, the Victims, and the Offenders*. London: Palgrave.

4

Expanding treadmill of production analysis within green criminology by integrating metabolic rift and ecological unequal exchange theories

Michael J. Lynch, Paul B. Stretesky, Michael A. Long and Kimberly L. Barrett

Introduction

Green criminology emerged as an extension of radical criminology and political economic analysis (Lynch 1990). Over time, some green criminologists have extended that original focus by drawing upon the treadmill of production (ToP) theoretical framework to better demonstrate how capitalism produces green crime at both the local and global level (e.g., Lynch et al. 2013; Stretesky, Long and Lynch 2013a). Specifically, such work has noted that green crimes are wide-ranging and include effects on humans and nonhuman animals (Lynch, Long and Stretesky 2015), as well as ecosystems (Long, Stretesky and Lynch 2014). These theoretical arguments are supported by empirical studies (e.g. Long et al. 2012; Lynch and Barrett 2015; Stretesky, Long and Lynch 2013b; Stretesky and Lynch 2009, 2011; Stretesky et al. 2017).

The present chapter extends the analysis of green crime by focusing on what we believe are important mechanisms for connecting ToP analysis to other political economic arguments in environmental sociology and ecological Marxism. We begin by reviewing the core components of the ToP framework. Next, we examine important political economic theories in ecological Marxism and environmental sociology that have not been widely addressed in the criminological literature, focusing attention on metabolic rift theory (MRT) and ecological unequal exchange theory (EUE). We present a brief illustration of how these frameworks and theories complement one another in a political economic explanation of green crimes involving the exploitation of nature using illegal wildlife trafficking as an example. Specifically, we propose that illegal markets are just as likely as legal markets to follow patterns within a global capitalist system of trade.

Treadmill of production and background assumptions

Treadmill of production arguments can be traced to the work of Schnaiberg (1980) and rest on both explicit and implicit Marxist and non-Marxist political economic assumptions

(Buttel 2004; Foster 2005; Gould, Pellow and Schnaiberg 2008, 2004). Schnaiberg makes little direct reference to Marx, but, as Foster (2005) notes, Schnaiberg's theoretical perspective has clear political economic commitments expressed in his use of Baran and Sweezy's (1966) and James O'Connor's (1973) Marxian analyses of monopoly capitalism. Extending the political economic dimension of Schnaiberg's approach, Foster (2005: 9) states that Marx himself used the example of a more literal treadmill of production 'as a relation of work and exploitation' in describing the process of capitalist production. Thus, to begin to understand ToP requires explaining its connection to capitalism and the Marxian view of capitalism.

As a system of production, capitalism promotes the unbridled pursuit of profit and the unequal ownership of the means of production, and in doing so generates an inequitable distribution of income and wealth. These economic relations of ownership, production and economic distribution give rise to a capitalist class structure based in inequality, which also translates into other forms of political and social inequality, favoring the owners of the means of production and further reinforcing class divisions. In Marx's (1976[1867]) view, the unequal distribution of economic power and the concentration of capital in the hands of the bourgeoisie translated into unequal access to social and political power, and promoted related forms of class conflict and inequality, as well as the objective existence and manifestations of class conflict over ownership and resource allocation.

The two main classes under capitalism—the owners and workers—have a 'natural' opposition in this system, as the interests of each class are strongly influenced by their structural relationship to ownership of the means of production. Ownership of the means of production, along with enhanced access to political power, facilitates exploitation of the laboring class (the proletariat). Under capitalism, the working class, lacking ownership of the means of production, must exchange their labor for wages that are then used to purchase a variety of basic necessities required for survival. According to Marx's (1976[1867]) labor theory of value, it is this unequal exchange that establishes conditions for the exploitation of the labor of the working class to generate surplus value and profits.

Enter the treadmill of production

With this background, we can now begin to connect capitalism and the ToP. Simply put, the ToP is a political economic system characterised by continuous increase in production, development and consumption (Gould, Schnaiberg and Weinberg 1996: 5), and, as Foster (2005) argues, accumulation. Schnaiberg argued that the structure of capitalism changed following World War II. Those changes were largely characterised by expanding ecological disorganisation (i.e., a condition that exists when ecosystems cannot reproduce and regenerate) and include an increased reliance on fossil fuel and chemical energy. This increased investment in ToP chemical technology and resource extraction expanded production and altered what Marxists call the 'organic composition of capital'—the ratio of capital investment in production (e.g., investment in machinery and technology) to the quantity of capital used to purchase labor. These changes in the production process expanded the exploitation of labor and increased the extraction of surplus value and profit (Gould, Pellow and Schnaiberg 2008; Marx 1976[1867], Ch. 25).

Speeding up the treadmill through increased fossil fuel consumption and machine labor reduces the relative volume of human labor used in production and laborers are 'cast off the treadmill' (see Gould, Pellow and Schnaiberg 2008). These additional non-human energy inputs (i.e., fossil fuel) also harm the environment. For example, Schnaiberg notes that when production expands, it not only releases harmful chemicals into the environment ('ecological additions'), but also demands that more raw materials are extracted for production, increasing the harmful effect of production by accelerating ecological withdrawals of raw materials. Together these withdrawals and additions are the cause of extensive ecological damage and ecological disorganisation. And, when production expands, as it must under capitalism, the level of ecological disorganisation also increases as the search for fossil fuels and raw materials becomes more and more destructive. For example, consider the extensive ecological impacts of contemporary methods of expanding extraction, such as hydraulic fracturing, mountaintop removal mining and sand tar development (see Heydon, this volume, Chapter 18; Lampkin, this volume, Chapter 27; Alexander, Shelley and Opsal, this volume, Chapter 19; Short, this volume, Chapter 26). Below we describe how these treadmill processes relate to theories of metabolic rift and ecological unequal exchange.

Taken together, this increase in the scope and speed of the ToP—and the acceleration of ecological withdrawals and ecological additions—are now creating a condition where ecosystems cannot reproduce and regenerate. In other words, when combined under ToP conditions, these processes (ecological withdrawals and additions) generate ecological disorganisation or an increased pace of ecological destruction that transforms (disorganises) the nature of the world around us.

Beyond the treadmill

With this overview, we can now turn to the relationship between capitalism and nature offered by Foster. Building on the 'two contradictions of capitalism' argument (O'Connor 1988, 1989, 1991), Foster (1992: 78, 78–79) posits the existence of an 'absolute general law of environmental degradation under capitalism', or the

> tendency toward ... amassing ... wealth at one pole and the accumulation of conditions of resource depletion, pollution, species and habitat destruction, urban congestion, overpopulation and a deteriorating sociological life-environment (in short, degraded 'conditions of production') at the other.

This second contradiction essentially means that nature and capitalism are in 'conflict' with one another, as the conditions which promote the healthy expansion of capitalism also produce ecological instability and the disorganisation of nature (Foster 2000).

Following Foster, and applying this observation to the ToP, we can suggest that the expansionary tendencies of the capitalist ToP are tied to its ability to exploit nature and to increase the pace of nature's exploitation over time, which is—at least in part—accomplished through technological advances in the portion of the treadmill designed to enable withdrawal of ecological resources. In addition, expanding the ToP requires increasingly using nature as a sink for pollution from production.

Building on Marx, Foster (2000, 2012) argues that the working class and nature are joined together by their exploitation under capitalism. Foster (1999, 2000, 2005) adds that neither labor nor nature can be exploited by capitalism without exploiting both simultaneously: in order to exploit labor, capitalism must exploit nature to provide the raw materials for production, while nature cannot be exploited without labor. Furthermore, under capitalism this dual exploitation of nature–labor is facilitated by unequal ownership of the means of production, the reorganisation of work in ways that intensify labor to make it more productive and through unequal class-based access to raw materials—a process supported by state regulations and mechanisms that protect these unequal access privileges (on the history of this argument see Marx 1842).

The general process described above is not only apparent within nations or in relation to any specific national application of capitalism, but also in the historical development of capitalism as a world system of production (Wallerstein 2011), or as part of a global or world capitalist ToP (Jorgenson and Burns 2007a; Kick and McKinney 2014). At the global level, the capitalist ToP possesses the ability to take advantage of differentials in the distribution of labor, wages and raw materials across nations, connecting these markets in a global class system of nations controlled by core (or developed) nations for their own advantage. In this way, the internationalisation of the world system of capitalist production improves the opportunity for profit-making by those who already own the means of production.

This international capitalist ToP allows owners of production in core nations to exploit the natural resources and raw materials of less developed nations, particularly those at the bottom of the class scale—the nations that are referred to as being in the peripheral, or as the least, lesser developed or 'underdeveloped' nations (see Deb, this volume, Chapter 20). Through this global system of ecological exploitation, ecosystems in peripheral nations are destroyed by ecological withdrawals for the production of commodities largely consumed in core nations. As a result, the consumption footprint of core nations rises, while the bio-capacity in peripheral nations declines to supply raw materials for commodity production. Understanding the complex and more complete picture of this process, as we explain below, also requires considering arguments from both metabolic rift and ecological unequal exchange theories.

In the ToP view, new, more efficient and more destructive methods of resource withdrawal are constantly being developed, allowing expanded ecosystem consumption and destruction to facilitate production and economic growth. This process has especially deleterious impacts on less developed nations. Between 2000 and 2005, for example, an average of more than 3.2 million hectares (7.9 million acres) of rainforest disappeared annually in Brazil under increased pressure from the global ToP, which also exemplifies both unequal ecological exchange and metabolic rift (see Boekhout van Solinge, this volume, Chapter 15). But ecological withdrawals account for only part of the ecological destruction caused by the ToP. The treadmill also increases the volume of ecological *additions* or the quantity of pollution added to the environment in less developed nations (Jorgenson 2003, 2006). Jorgenson (2006), for example, found that less developed nations with high levels of exports to developing nations experienced more significant deforestation (see also, Jorgenson 2008). Similar problems are seen with air and water pollution in less developed nations (Jorgenson 2007; see also Brisman, South and Walters, this volume, Chapter 10). Air pollution has become a significant global concern in many nations, particularly in Latin America where the Clean Air Institute reports that among 16 major Latin American cities examined, more than 100 million people are exposed to air pollution levels that exceed World Health Organization standards (www.cleanairinstitute.org/calidaddelaireamericalatina/index.php?id_sitio=1&p_idioma=ING&idp=60). (For a real-time example of global air pollution with readings from air monitoring stations around the world see: waqi.info; for ecological footprints of nations see Global Footprint Network, http://data.footprintnetwork.org, and studies by Jorgenson 2015a, 2015b, 2012, 2003.)

Below, we expand upon these observations, referring to metabolic rift and ecological unequal exchange and the ways in which these theoretical perspectives expand and supplement ToP analysis of ecological destruction and disorganisation. As we attempt to demonstrate, each view contributes important ideas useful for ToP analysis.

Metabolic rift

While Foster (1999) argues that the concept of metabolic rift originates in the work of Marx, this downplays the importance of Foster's elaboration of this concept. Here, we rely heavily on Foster's (1999) assessment of how Marx addressed metabolic rift, referring to this argument as *metabolic rift theory* (MRT).

In general terms, MRT posits that there is a divide between society (humans) and nature, and in the Foster/Marx version that schism is accelerated by capitalism. While important, this definition does not define or otherwise describe the features of metabolic rift. Specifically, but in a rather shorthand way, we can say that metabolic rift is the exploitation of the land or earth, and, in particular, the exploitation of nature or what Foster (1999: 379) refers to as the 'robbery' of metabolic materials from nature to benefit humans. In essence, this is similar to the ToP concept of ecological withdrawals but concentrates more specifically on the extraction of raw materials with energy components—raw materials that possess energy or can transfer energy through their use, or incorporate energy as a result of the way those raw materials are produced or 'manufactured' by nature through nature's production process. Foster argues that Marx's discussion of agricultural production is central to understanding the concept of metabolic rift. Here, Marx's point was that to produce food, metabolic materials must be absorbed from the land. Thus, food production required transferring metabolic materials that nature has produced to food production, exploiting nature for its metabolic materials, particularly in the context of expansion of the working class. With respect to the early stages of capitalist development, intensive or large-scale agricultural production of food was needed to feed and keep the working class alive, which began to strip the land of its productive ability, so, as Marx noted, 'exhausting the soil'.

In addition, MRT describes how capitalism undermines ecological organisation—creates ecological disorganisation—impairing the ability of the ecosystem to reproduce itself by removing metabolic material from nature. Moreover, given other aspects of the organisation of capitalism, this also leads to a transfer of metabolic materials from rural to urban areas, and from under-developed to developed nations through the process of ecological withdrawal. In other words, capitalist production unequally redistributes metabolic materials. This long-term process has occurred throughout the history of capitalism and its expansion into a global world system, beginning with what world system theorists call the 'long fifteenth century' (which began in the latter 1400s).

Capitalism must face this contradiction between capitalism and nature—that is, its exploitation of natural metabolic matter—because the limits of and the exhaustion of locally available natural resources (metabolic materials) eventually impede the ability of capitalism to expand. For example, early in the history of European capitalism, raw material resources near large urban centers of production began to be quickly eroded by the expansion of capitalism and its consumption of nature. As a result, to continue the expansion of capitalism, it was necessary for European nations to seek new, un-developed lands for ecological exploitation and as sources for metabolic materials, stimulating the search for those lands and the capture and settlement of un-developed lands in North, South and Central America (see Goyes et al. 2017).

Another method that capitalism employed to solve this capitalism–nature metabolic rift contradiction was through technological innovations. This led, as Foster (1999) notes, to the development of agricultural sciences—an issue Marx addressed through his research on soil science by nineteenth-century chemist Justus von Liebig, to develop an argument about capitalism, its requirement to exploit nature and the expansion of ecological destruction and a metabolic rift between man and nature. Important to this issue in relation to agricultural productivity was the need to understand the chemical composition of soil, and how plants absorbed metabolic/nutritional matter from soil. This new 'science of the soil' led to an understanding of how mass agricultural production and continuous use of a land site for agricultural purposes stripped the land of its metabolic materials, and made the land less agriculturally productive. Soil science also provided the basic information needed to learn how to supplement soil productivity.

An early response (prior to the nineteenth century) to this metabolic crisis of capitalism (i.e., the problem of soil fertility) was to employ natural fertilisers to supplement soil. This meant locating sources for natural fertilisers, and led to their discovery in colonies, and subsequently their transportation to colonising nations to supplement agricultural production to feed populations in those colonising nations (Clark and Foster 2009). Easily accessible natural fertilisers found in colonies were soon exhausted, and techniques of production that generated fertilisers through manufacturing processes—or inorganic fertilisers—were created to address soil fertility issues (Clark and Foster 2009), which then gave rise to the creation of a fertiliser industry in the mid-1800s (see also, Foster, Clark and York 2011).

Capitalism's creation of the fertiliser industry is one response to the contradictions of metabolic rift and the problem of feeding a growing working class (Foster 1999). This solution, however, contains its own set of contradictions and, as Marx noted, 'exhausted the soil' and eroded the productive ability of the land. That is, the expanding fertiliser industry and the mass application of fertilisers to farm lands (and later pesticides) produces unintended ecologically destructive consequences, such as extensive ecosystem pollution and run-off (Clark and Foster 2009; Foster 1999). These MRT observations concerning ecological disorganisation associated with the production and application of fertilisers are supported by numerous scientific studies: on the general negative effects of fertilisers on ecosystem health (Pimentel 2005); the negative effects of fertilisers on waterways (Ding et al. 2010; see also Brisman 2002), aquatic ecosystems (Camargo and Alonso 2006) and waterway species (Mercer, Mercer and Sayok 2013), including marine ecosystems (Clausen and Clark 2005); on the climate change effects of overuse and over-production of nitrogen fertilisers (Clark and Foster 2009); and on the generation of persistent organic pollutants from the production of fertilisers (Manz et al. 2001). Studies also connect this process to unequal nitrogen deposits globally (Fields 2004) and the nitrogen cascade effect (Galloway et al. 2003, 2008; Gruber and Galloway 2008); in addition, studies have noted the adverse effects of the production and application of fertilisers on plant species diversity (Bobbink et al. 2010); the tendency toward encroaching on global planetary boundaries (Rockstrom et al. 2009); the deleterious effect of excessive nitrogen on amphibians (Rouse, Bishop and Struger 1999); and negative human health impacts in the form of respiratory and cardiac diseases, and various cancers (Townsend et al. 2003).

MRT also applies to issues of energy withdrawals and use. Increasing production requires energy, and that energy has largely come from ecologically destructive fossil fuels. Using that kind of energy creates two kinds of energy waste streams that result from burning fossil fuels: chemical pollution waste streams and heat waste streams. Both waste streams contribute to ecological disorganisation through ecological withdrawals and additions (Masnadi and Brandt 2017).

This latter dimension of metabolic rift also has important implications with respect to the properties of physics (Foster, Clark and York 2011). As noted above, the more energy capitalism extracts from nature, the less energy is available for future work; moreover, the more energy capitalism extracts from nature, the more stored energy is turned into heat energy, resulting in the production of entropy. This alters the balance of energy in the world.

Technically, entropy is a form of disorder in physics and is an irreversible process. Thus, as capitalism expands and accelerates its use of energy, it increasingly disorganises nature by transforming potential energy into heat energy in ways that cannot be reversed, potentially contributing to problems such as climate change (Dyke and Kleidon 2010).

Metabolic rift and the treadmill of production

Metabolic rift theory and treadmill of production arguments are complimentary approaches. Integrating ideas from these views enhances our understanding of how the political economic organisation of capitalism generates ecological destruction/disorganisation. Integrating also allows discussions of the ways in which the ToP accelerates and extends metabolic rift. Both MRT and ToP describe how capitalism disorganises nature through ecological withdrawals. Schnaiberg discussed the importance of entropy to ecological disorganisation in early formulations of the ToP approach; less attention, however, is paid to entropy in later ToP work. MRT has returned focus to the importance of the relationship between entropy and environmental degradation. MRT also highlights the second contradiction of capitalism ('the absolute general law of environmental degradation under capitalism'), an argument overlooked by Schnaiberg—perhaps because he conceptualised ToP several years before discussions of the second contradiction of capitalism. Both approaches describe how technological change and innovation designed to expand worker productivity and profit-making accelerates ecological disorganisation. Compared with the ToP approach, current versions of MRT draw more heavily on scientific theories and evidence to explain the deleterious outcomes associated with expanded capitalist production, and better facilitate integrating political economic analysis of environmental problems with the findings of scientific literature. Perhaps the largest difference between these views is how they frame class conflict and analysis in relation to environmental problems. MRT provides a much more orthodox Marxian argument related to class conflict than is found in the ToP approach, which rarely makes reference to Marx.

Despite some technical-theoretical differences, there is little reason for green criminology to prefer one of these views over the other. We suggest it seems appropriate to draw insights from both views for the political economic analysis of environmental issues within green criminology, although in certain cases, one approach might be preferable. The choice between the two can also be influenced by the extent to which one wishes to remain more committed to a traditional/orthodox Marxian approach, in which case MRT should be the starting point for analysis.

Ecological unequal exchange

In recent decades, researchers in various fields (e.g., sociology, economics) concerned with what Foster and Holleman (2014) identified as explaining 'ecological imperialism'—or the asymmetrical exploitation and flow of ecological resources across nations in a capitalist world economy (Clark and Foster 2009)—have suggested the use of *ecological* unequal exchange theory (EUE). The EUE approach is an extension of *economic* unequal exchange theory, reviewed briefly below, which leans heavily on Foster and Holleman's (2014) discussion.

The earliest theory of unequal economic exchange can be traced to classical economist David Ricardo in the early nineteenth century. Ricardo's goal was to explain how a nation gains an advantage over another nation through unequal economic exchanges when the exchange involves unequal quantities of labor contained in the commodities being exchanged.

The nation that receives more labor in this unequal exchange nets an economic advantage with respect to profit-making ability (Foster and Holleman 2014).

As Foster and Holleman note, Marx added to these observations by applying his labor theory of value to explain this outcome. In the context of international trade, more developed nations take advantage of lower costs of production and reproduction in less developed nations and particularly the differential in the exploitation of labor between countries (which is greater in less developed nations) by importing products from less developed nations and selling them at increased market prices consistent with the costs of production in more developed nations. In more technical Marxian terms (see Foster and Holleman 2014: 203–204), we can state that unequal exchanges between nations are based on different compositions of the 'organic composition of capital' between nations. The organic composition of capital is a ratio of what Marx called *constant capital* (in money terms, the capital investment in physical production, such as costs of raw materials, rent, machinery) to variable capital (in monetary terms, the cost of labor)—and is used by Marx to describe a set of empirical conditions of capitalism, which have rarely been discussed or applied empirically in the criminological literature (cf. Lynch 1988, 2010; Lynch, Groves and Lizotte 1994).

Among Marxists, interest in unequal economic exchange expanded in the early 1970s. Competing explanations were offered by dependency and underdevelopment theorists (Amin 1976; Emmanuel 1972; Frank 1967), in Wallerstein's world systems theory (Hornborg 1998), and in relation to Baran and Sweezy's (1966) theory of monopoly capitalism (Foster and Holleman 2014: 203–205), and here we cannot describe these differences.

Marx had begun to explore the idea of ecological unequal exchange in relation to the problem of metabolic rift based upon his political economic reinterpretation of soil science research in the mid-1800s. For Marx, this involved a dual problem of unequal exchanges related to labor values and those related to the unequal exchange of metabolic materials or natural resources and energy (Burkett and Foster 2006). His approach connects unequal economic exchange, metabolic rift and ecological unequal exchange, in which unequal metabolic (material) exchange always accompanies an economic exchange (Foster and Holleman 2014: 206). This, as Foster and Holleman note, led Marx to conceptualise an unequal world economic order, with some nations (later described as 'dependent,' 'under-developed' or 'peripheral') being the source of materials for developed capitalist nations, with the nature of that system being determined by the accumulation process in developed nations. This interpretation explains the kind of expanding ecological disorganisation in less developed nations as being driven by accumulation processes (Long, Stretesky and Lynch 2017) and the direction of capitalist development in a handful of more developed nations.

More extensive development of the EUE idea did not emerge until the 1980s with Bunker's (1985) analysis of underdevelopment, which explained this process in the Amazon. Bunker's approach was then coupled with the emergence of ecological footprint analysis introduced in the early 1990s, which led to increased interest in developing EUE and to applying this approach empirically (Foster and Holleman 2014: 209).

In our view, the most important empirical EUE studies have been produced by Andrew K. Jorgenson (2006) and various colleagues. Jorgenson introduced a measure of weighted export flows across nations which empirically assesses the relative weight of exports a nation trades to more developed nations as a measure of EUE. For each nation, this procedure produces a complex set of measures of trade relations with other nations.

Jorgenson also modified the theoretical basis of prior EUE models. As he argued, dependency theories suggest that nations with high trade dependency on foreign nations are 'more vulnerable' to conditions in the world market, and, in such situations, trade dependency allows developed nations to create favorable trade relationships, which disadvantages less developed nations in trade partnerships. Based on his prior research, Jorgenson (2003, 2004, 2005) notes that developed nations, which have high ecological footprints, consume more natural resources than other nations. He then connects this observation to the ToP framework, noting that the ToP's expansionary economic tendencies expanded profit making and consumption in developed nations (2006: 688–690). Through this process, developed nations receive increasing quantities of consumable raw materials from less developed nations, which also allows developed nations to externalise pollution, environmental degradation and disorganisation onto developing/less developed/underdeveloped nations.

In this argument, the externalisation of pollution and ecological destruction/disorganisation that occurs through this global capitalist trade system can *make it appear* that an increasing proportion of the share of global ecological disorganisation (ecological withdrawals and additions) are being driven by economic development in less developed/developing nations as their economies expand. That appearance, Jorgenson noted, is misleading. Why? Because increased production in lesser developed nations is not driven by developing nations' internal consumption (i.e., an increase in the domestic ecological footprint), but rather is due to an increase in exports which support high levels of consumption (i.e., high ecological footprints) in developed nations through imports (for an empirical application of this argument by green criminologists, see Stretesky and Lynch 2009). In this way, EUE allows developed nations to not only externalise ecological disorganisation onto less developed nations, but to increase domestic ecological protection and reduce domestic ecological disorganisation evident, for example, in lower levels of pollution over time in developed nations.

In terms of the global capitalist ToP, the effect of unequal economic and ecological unequal exchange appears within the economic structure of less developed nations. For less developed nations, this translates into production for export, raw material/mining/timber extraction and agricultural and livestock production (Bunker 1985). Based on summaries of prior research, Jorgenson also notes the system of EUE has a long history connected to colonial exploitation (though that system and the relationships within that system have changed historically, and, as we suggest, also connects to points raised in MRT, see above). Moreover, given the nature of economic and ecological exploitation in the modern capitalist world system, semi-peripheral nations are also engaged in the exploitation of peripheral nations' ecological resources as part of the EUE supply cycle through intermediary manufacturing processes.

There is substantial and widespread support for EUE explanations. As examples, studies find a significant relationship between EUE and nations' ecological footprints (Jorgenson 2005, 2009a; Jorgenson, Austin and Dick 2009; Jorgenson and Burns 2007a, 2007b; Jorgenson and Clark 2011; Kick and McKinney 2014); cross-national carbon dioxide emissions (Jorgenson 2007, 2009b, 2012; Jorgenson and Clark 2010); levels of water pollution (Jorgenson 2007; Shandra, Shor and London 2009c); effects on footprints and carbon through a nation's level of militarisation (Jorgenson and Clark 2009); pesticide and fertiliser use (Jorgenson and Kuykendall 2008); deforestation rates (Jorgenson 2008; Jorgenson and Burns 2007b; Shandra, Shor and London 2009c); and biodiversity loss (Shandra et al. 2009a). As a result, it is important to consider how EUE theory can be employed to explain issues of concern to green criminologists.

ToP, MRT, EUE and green criminology

Of importance in the above is not simply the development of ToP, MRT and EUE theories, but the empirical literature these theories have generated. Those empirical studies document how EUE generates adverse ecological impacts related to ecological withdrawals, ecological additions, ecological footprints and ecological disorganisation across nations in the global capitalist ToP. Green criminologists should, we suggest, make reference to these empirical studies as support for the various arguments they make related to political economic explanations of green crime, as this research (as well as the theories described above) have far-reaching implications for green criminology.

We suggest that the focus of each theoretical perspective on the organisation of the world capitalist ToP can be clearly linked to explanations of green crimes, such as pollution, ecological resource withdrawal and ecological destruction and ecological disorganisation within and across nations. Accordingly, the expansionary and profit-oriented tendencies of capitalism described by Marx have now come to play out across nations in the global capitalist ToP, unevenly distributing ecological resource acquisition and ecological disorganisation, benefitting developed or core capitalist nations at the expense of lesser developed nations' ecosystems and peoples. Globally, these outcomes are seen in: extensive ecological destruction in lesser developed compared with core/capitalist nations; the export of raw materials from lesser developed to core nations; and excessive ecological consumption in developed nations compared with lesser developed nations. It is also possible that these processes can be seen within nations (i.e., across geographic units such as states), though to our knowledge, such models have yet to be tested empirically.

Related to these outcomes is the process of metabolic rift, which transfers natural ecological wealth—the resources that are and can only be produced by nature—from lesser to more developed nations as part of a series of related processes including those Marx and Foster describe as capitalism's robbery of nature (the idea that capitalism essentially steals or robs resources from nature without attending to the need to replace those resources to restore ecological balance and nature's reproductive capacities). In EUE and MRT terms, this constant transfer and harvesting of naturally occurring material resources from less to more developed nations creates inequalities in the transfer of wealth and in consumption (and patterns of excessive consumption) as peoples in developed nations exploit ecosystems in lesser developed nations. This not only results in high levels of ecological withdrawals and additions in lesser developed nations, but can lead to extreme cases of resource depletion (depletion hotspots) or pollution (pollution hotspots) from resource extraction and manufacturing. Future studies in green criminology could take up investigation of these issues, producing evidence of the connection between pollution and resource depletion and pollution hotspots as examples of green crimes that occur in the global capitalist ToP.

Less clear, perhaps, is how the explanations above apply to the study of green harms affecting wildlife. Below, we illustrate how EUE, MRT and ToP theories can be applied to understanding the global wildlife marketplace. Globally, there is extensive evidence of biodiversity loss across nations (Steffen et al. 2015; see also Brisman and South 2019). Research also indicates that patterns of biodiversity loss are not evenly distributed across the globe. These patterns have been modelled empirically (Hoffmann 2004; Naidoo and Adamowicz 2001) and further illustrate that there is what we call an 'anthropogenic species decline affect.' A similar argument (Ceballos et al. 2015) linking human development to species decline and biodiversity loss has been described in the green criminological literature (see, e.g., Lynch, Long and Stretesky 2015).

Shandra and colleagues argue that human activity has increased the threat to the viability of animal species due 'to agriculture, logging, pesticide use, pollution and population growth' in less developed nations (2009b: 286). They employ EUE theory to argue that current economic flows, especially those related to natural resource extraction and export, along with the expansion of agricultural production and urbanisation in lesser developed nations, accelerating deforestation and forest fragmentation, and the increased use of pesticides, have extreme deleterious impacts for wildlife species leading to species loss. Using data on export flows to represent EUE theory for a sample of 74 less developed nations and data on threatened mammal species from the International Union for the Conservation of Nature (the Red List), they find empirical evidence that a nation's export flow is positively related to species loss. In green criminological terms, this study illustrates how the current political economic structure of the global capitalist ToP linked to EUE affects green harms against animal species and causes increasing biodiversity loss in mammals.

We suggest that a similar argument can be applied to conceptualising the global wildlife trade within the complex political economic structure of the global ToP and EUE. This is an interesting approach because it moves beyond one of the limitations of current green criminological studies of wildlife trafficking, which tend to employ case study methods (e.g., related to generalisation of results). To be sure, case studies of wildlife trade are important, but have limitations. One of those limitations is the failure to produce generalizable data capable of generating broader theoretical models that link threats to wildlife to broader theories capable of explaining the commonalities among those case studies (see Lynch et al. 2017). We know, for example, from numerous green criminological and biological studies of wildlife trade that there is a widespread global animal trafficking problem (see, e.g., Burton et al., this volume, Chapter 3; Runhovde, this volume, Chapter 31; Sollund, this volume, Chapter 29), and likely that there are global wildlife trafficking networks. Green criminologists have attempted to make sense of this wildlife trafficking case study information by connecting the network of animal trafficking and the illegal drug trade networks (South and Wyatt 2011). The idea behind that approach is that perhaps these different types of illegal trade networks share some identifiable empirical similarities (South and Wyatt 2011), and that this may point toward identifying similar factors that structure both kinds of illegal trade markets. The similarity between these markets in a global capitalist economy is easy to identify—money-making. And groups that traffic drugs may overlap with or traffic animals for the sake of profit.

Here, our focus is on ecological disorganisation and its political economic origins, as well as on ecological resource flows. These flows of 'eco-commodities' (including wildlife species and other goods and resources), we suggest, involves both the legal and illegal transfer of metabolic material exchanges and unequal ecological exchanges. We are not the first to suggest that metabolic rift includes wildlife issues, and Clausen and Clark (2005) have empirically examined metabolic rift's connection to marine species depletion.

We suggest that illegal ecological material exchange networks associated with wildlife trafficking appear to *replicate* the characteristics of free-market capitalism—and perhaps ironically in the truest free-market sense because these illegal transactions occur in a marketplace free from internal constraints or rules that limit exchanges (though they are officially identified or labelled as illegal transactions externally). Illegal wildlife trade in the capitalist black market economy contains political economic influences. Following the theories described above, these influences include efforts to exploit labor and nature, and, in both cases, often relate to exploitation of labor and nature in less developed nations to source illegally traded wildlife. These transactions also involve the exploitation of marginalised labor in developed nations as part of these illegal exchanges. Just as in the 'legitimate' capitalist system of exchange, in the wildlife black market there is an attempt to increase profit-making through expanding production, which in the case of the illegal (and legal) wildlife market (and possibly, in some cases, in the 'pet' industry) includes escalating animal poaching (see generally Sollund 2017). While space precludes an extended analysis here, those interested in applying green criminological concepts to wildlife crimes like trafficking and poaching should consider the connection between the exploitation of labor and nature and profit making, and how metabolic 'exchanges' (i.e., in the form of animals or other illegally traded eco-commodities produced by nature) promote ecological unequal exchange and damages to ecosystems, biocapacity and biodiversity, especially in lesser developed nations. Such studies will help connect green criminology to the rich theoretical and empirical literature already developed in other disciplines.

Conclusion

Green criminology and its efforts to understand green crime and injustice was initially proposed as an extension of radical criminology and criminological applications of political economic analysis. In recent years, these ideas have been extended through the use of the ToP framework. The original application of ToP by Schnaiberg was not a true political economic theory derived only from Marx's political economic analysis of capitalism. Through various developments, the ToP framework has become more radicalised and has been introduced into the green criminological literature as a theoretical approach consistent with the radical political economic origins of green criminology.

The present chapter has extended the political economic orientation of ToP by connecting that approach to two other radical political economic theories designed to make the linkage between capitalism and ecological destruction more visible: metabolic rift theory and ecological unequal exchange theory. We have argued that these views help round out the ToP approach, and can be applied to understand any number of green crimes and green injustices associated with ecological disorganisation (though, in the interests of space, we limited our examples here). This approach awaits to be applied further by green criminologists. Doing so can help establish connections to the ecological Marxist and environmental sociology literatures, as well as to the growing number of empirical studies in those fields that support these approaches.

References

Amin, S. 1976. *Unequal Development.* New York: Monthly Review Press.

Baran, P. A. and Sweezy, P. M. 1966. *Monopoly Capital.* New York: New York University Press.

Bobbink, R., Hicks, K., Galloway, J., Spranger, T., Alkemade, R., Ashmore, M., da Cunha Bustamante, M. M., Cinderby, S., Davidson, E. A., Dentener, F., Emmett, B., Erisman, J. W., Fenn, M., Gillman, Frank S., Nordin, A., Pardo, L. and de Vries, W. 2010. 'Global assessment of nitrogen deposition effects on terrestrial plant diversity: A synthesis,' *Ecological Applications*, 20(1): 30–59.

Brisman, A. 2002. 'Considerations in establishing a stormwater utility,' *Southern Illinois University Law Journal*, 26(3): 505–528.

Brisman, A. and South, N. 2019. A criminology of extinction: Biodiversity, extreme consumption and the vanity of species resurrection. *European Journal of Criminology*. First published 28 February 2019. https://doi.org/10.1177/1477370819828307.

Bunker, S. J. 1985. *Underdeveloping the Amazon.* Chicago, IL: University of Chicago Press.

Burkett, P. and Foster, J. B. 2006. Metabolism, energy, and entropy in Marx's critique of political economy. *Theory and Society*, 35(1): 109–156.

Buttel, F. H. 2004. 'The treadmill of production: An appreciation, assessment, and agenda for research,' *Organization & Environment*, 17(3): 323–336.

Camargo, J. A. and Alonso, A. 2006. 'Ecological and toxicological effects of inorganic nitrogen pollution in aquatic ecosystems: A global assessment,' *Environment International*, 32(6): 831–849.

Ceballos, G., Ehrlich, P. R., Barnosky, A. D., García, A., Pringle, R. M. and Palmer, T. M. 2015. 'Accelerated modern human-induced species losses: Entering the sixth mass extinction,' *Science Advances*, 1(5): e1400253.

Clark, B. and Foster, J. B. 2009. 'Ecological imperialism and the global metabolic rift, unequal exchange and the guano/nitrates trade,' *International Journal of Comparative Sociology*, 50(3–4): 311–334.

Clausen, R. and Clark, B. 2005. 'The metabolic rift and marine ecology: An analysis of the ocean crisis within capitalist production,' *Organization & Environment*, 18(4): 422–444.

Ding, Y., Harwood, A. D., Foslund, H. M. and Lydy, M. J. 2010. 'Distribution and toxicity of sediment-associated pesticides in urban and agricultural waterways from Illinois, USA,' *Environmental Toxicology and Chemistry*, 29(1): 149–157.

Dyke, J. and Kleidon, A. 2010. 'The maximum entropy production principle: Its theoretical foundations and applications to the earth system,' *Entropy*, 12(3): 613–630.

Emmanuel, A. 1972. *Unequal Exchange*. New York: Monthly Review Press.

Fields, S. 2004. 'Global nitrogen: Cycling out of control,' *Environmental Health Perspectives*, 112(10): A556–A563.

Foster, J. B. 1992. 'The absolute general law of environmental degradation under capitalism,' *Capitalism Nature Socialism*, 3(3): 77–81.

Foster, J. B. 1999. 'Marx's theory of metabolic rift: Classical foundations for environmental sociology,' *American Journal of Sociology*, 105(2): 366–405.

Foster, J. B. 2000. *Marx's Ecology: Materialism and Nature*. New York: New York University Press.

Foster, J. B. 2005. 'The treadmill of accumulation: Schnaiberg's environment and Marxian political economy,' *Organization & Environment*, 18(1): 7–18.

Foster, J. B. 2012. 'The Planetary rift and the new human exemptionalism: A political-economic critique of ecological modernization theory,' *Organization & Environment*, 25(3): 211–237.

Foster, J. B. and Holleman, H. 2014. 'The theory of unequal ecological exchange: A Marx-Odum dialectic,' *The Journal of Peasant Studies*, 41(2): 199–233.

Foster, J. B., Clark, B. and York, R. 2011. *The Ecological Rift: Capitalism's War on the Earth*. New York: New York University Press.

Frank, A. G. 1967. *Capitalism and Underdevelopment in Latin America*. New York: New York University Press.

Galloway, J. N. Townsend, A. R., Erisman, J. W, Bekunda, M., Cai, Z., Freney, J. R., Martinelli, L. A., Seitzinger, S. P. and Sutton, M. A. 2008. 'Transformation of the nitrogen cycle: Recent trends, questions, and potential solutions,' *Science*, 320(5878): 889–892.

Galloway, J. N., Aber, J. D., Erisman, J. W., Seitzinger, S. P., Howarth, R. W., Cowling, E. B. and Cosby, B. J. 2003. 'The nitrogen cascade,' *Bioscience*, 53(4): 341–356.

Gould, K. A., Pellow, D. N. and Schnaiberg, A. 2004. 'Interrogating the treadmill of production everything you wanted to know about the treadmill but were afraid to ask,' *Organization & Environment*, 17 (3): 296–316.

Gould, K. A., Pellow, D. N. and Schnaiberg, A. 2008. *The Treadmill of Production: Injustice and Unsustainability in the Global Economy*. St. Paul, MN: Paradigm Publishers.

Gould, K. A., Schnaiberg, A. and Weinberg, A. 1996. *Local Environmental Struggles: Citizen Activism in the Treadmill of Production*. Cambridge, UK: Cambridge University Press.

Goyes, D. R., Mol, H., Brisman, A. and South, N. (eds.). 2017. *Environmental Crime in Latin America: The Theft of Nature and the Poisoning of the Land*. London: Palgrave Macmillan.

Gruber, N. and Galloway, J. N. 2008. 'An earth-system perspective of the global nitrogen cycle,' *Nature*, 451(7176): 293–296.

Hoffmann, J. P. 2004. Social and environmental influences on endangered species: A cross-national study,' *Sociological Perspectives*, 47(1): 79–107.

Hornborg, A. 1998. 'Towards an ecological theory of unequal exchange: Articulating world system theory and ecological economics,' *Ecological Economics*, 25(1): 127–136.

Jorgenson, A. K. 2003. 'Consumption and environmental degradation: A cross- national analysis of the ecological footprint,' *Social Problems*, 50(3): 374–394.

Jorgenson, A. K. 2004. 'Uneven processes and environmental degradation in the world-economy,' *Human Ecology Review*, 11(2): 103–113.

Jorgenson, A.K. 2005. 'Unpacking international power and the ecological footprints of nations: Aquantitative cross-national study,' *Sociological Perspectives*, 48(3): 383–402.

Jorgenson, A. K. 2006. 'Unequal ecological exchange and environmental degradation: A theoretical proposition and cross-national study of deforestation, 1990–2000,' *Rural Sociology*, 71(4): 685–712.

Jorgenson, A. K. 2007. 'Does foreign investment harm the air we breathe and the water we drink? A cross-national study of carbon dioxide emissions and organic water pollution in less-developed countries, 1975 to 2000,' *Organization & Environment*, 20(2): 137–156.

Jorgenson, A. K. 2008. 'Structural integration and the trees: An analysis of deforestation in less-developed countries, 1990–2005,' *The Sociological Quarterly*, 49(3): 503–527.

Jorgenson, A. K. 2009a. 'The sociology of unequal exchange in ecological context: A panel study of lower-income countries, 1975–2001,' *Sociological Forum*, 24(1): 22–46.

Jorgenson, A. K. 2009b. 'The transnational organization of production, the scale of degradation, and ecoefficiency: A study of carbon dioxide emissions in less-developed countries,' *Human Ecology Review*, 16(1): 64–74.

Jorgenson, A. K. 2012. 'The sociology of ecologically unequal exchange and carbon dioxide emissions, 1960–2005,' *Social Science Research*, 41(2): 242–252.

Jorgenson, A. K. 2015a. 'Lateral pressure and deforestation: A review essay of environmental impacts of globalization and trade,' *Journal of World-Systems Research*, 9(2): 393–402.

Jorgenson, A. K. 2015b. 'Inequality and the carbon intensity of human well-being,' *Journal of Environmental Studies and Sciences*, 5(3): 277–282.

Jorgenson, A. K. and Burns, T. J. 2007a. 'The political-economic causes of change in the ecological footprints of nations, 1991–2001: A quantitative investigation,' *Social Science Research*, 36(2): 834–853.

Jorgenson, A. K. and Burns, T. J. 2007b. 'Effects of rural and urban population dynamics and national development on deforestation in less-developed countries, 1990–2000,' *Sociological Inquiry*, 77(3): 460–482.

Jorgenson, A. K. and Clark, B. 2009. 'The economy, military, and ecologically unequal exchange relationships in comparative perspective: A panel study of the ecological footprints of nations, 1975—2000,' *Social Problems*, 56(4): 621–646.

Jorgenson, A. K. and Clark, B. 2010. 'Assessing the temporal stability of the population/environment relationship in comparative perspective: A cross-national panel study of carbon dioxide emissions, 1960–2005,' *Population and Environment*, 32(1): 27–41.

Jorgenson, A. K. and Clark, B. 2011. 'Societies consuming nature: A panel study of the ecological footprints of nations, 1960–2003,' *Social Science Research*, 40(1): 226–244.

Jorgenson, A. K. and Kuykendall, K. A. 2008. 'Globalization, foreign investment dependence and agriculture production: Pesticide and fertilizer use in less-developed countries, 1990–2000,' *Social Forces*, 87 (1): 529–560.

Jorgenson, A. K., Austin, K. and Dick, C. 2009. 'Ecologically unequal exchange and the resource consumption/environmental degradation paradox: A panel study of less-developed countries, 1970–2000,' *International Journal of Comparative Sociology*, 50(3–4): 263–284.

Kick, E. L. and McKinney, L. A. 2014. 'Global context, national inter-dependencies, and the ecological footprint: A structural equation analysis,' *Sociological Perspectives*, 57(2): 256–279.

Long, M. A., Stretesky, P. B., Lynch, M. J. and Fenwick, E. 2012. 'Crime in the coal industry: Implications for green criminology and treadmill of production,' *Organization & Environment*, 25 (2): 328–346.

Long, M. A., Stretesky, P. B. and Lynch, M. J. 2014. 'The treadmill of production, planetary boundaries and green criminology,' in T. Sapiens, R. White and M. Kluin (eds.) *Environmental Crime and Its Victims: Perspectives within Green Criminology*, pp. 263–276. Surrey, UK: Ashgate.

Long, M. A., Stretesky, P. B. and Lynch, M. J. 2017. 'Foreign direct investment, ecological withdrawls and natural resource dependent economies,' *Society and Natural Resources* 30(10): 1261–1276.

Lynch, M. 1990. 'The greening of criminology: A perspective on the 1990s,' *The Critical Criminologist*, 2 (3): 1–4.

Lynch, M. J. 1988. 'The extraction of surplus value, crime and punishment: A preliminary empirical analysis for the U.S.,' *Contemporary Crises*, 12(4): 329–344.

Lynch, M. J. 2010. 'Radical explanations of penal trends: The rate of surplus value and the incarceration rate in the United States, 1977–2005,' *Journal of Crime and Justice*, 33(2): 63–94.

Lynch, M. J. and Barrett, K. L. 2015. 'Death matters: Victimization by particle matter from coal fired power plants in the US, a green criminological view,' *Critical Criminology: An International Journal* 23 (3): 219–234.

Lynch, M. J., Barrett, K. L., Stretesky, P.B. and Long, M. A. 2017. 'The neglect of quantitative research in green criminology and its consequences,' *Critical Criminology: An International Journal* 25(2): 183–198.

Lynch, M. J., Groves, W. B. and Lizotte, A. 1994. 'The rate of surplus value and crime: Theoretical and empirical examination of Marxian economic theory and criminology,' *Crime, Law and Social Change*, 21(1): 15–48.

Lynch, M. J., Long, M. A. and Stretesky, P. B. 2015. 'Anthropogenic development drives species to be endangered: Capitalism and the decline of species,' in R. A. Sollund (ed.) *Green Harms and Crimes: Critical Criminology in a Changing World*, pp. 117–146. New York: Palgrave-Macmillan.

Lynch, M. J., Long, M. A., Barrett, K. L. and Stretesky, P. B. 2013. 'Is it a crime to produce ecological disorganization? Why green criminology and political economy matter in the analysis of global ecological harms,' *The British Journal of Criminology*, 55(6): 997–1016.

Manz, M., Wenzel, K. D., Dietze, U. and Schüürmann, G. 2001. 'Persistent organic pollutants in agricultural soils of central Germany,' *Science of the Total Environment*, 277(1): 187–198.

Marx, K. 1842. 'Debates on the law on theft of wood,' *Rheinische Zeitung*, 298, 300, 303, 305 and 307. Available at: www.marxists.org/archive/marx/works/1842/10/25.htm.

Marx, K. 1976[1867]. *Capital, Volume I*. New York: International Publishers.

Masnadi, M. S. and Brandt, A. R. 2017. 'Climate impacts of oil extraction increase significantly with oilfield age,' *Nature, Climate Change*, 7: 551–556. https://doi.org/10.1038/nclimate3347.

Mercer, E. V., Mercer, T. G. and Sayok, A. K. 2013. 'Effects of forest conversions to oil palm plantations on freshwater macroinvertebrates: A case study from Sarawak, Malaysia,' *Journal of Land Use Science*, 8(4): 227–245.

Naidoo, R. and Adamowicz, W. L. 2001. 'Effects of economic prosperity on numbers of threatened species,' *Conservation Biology*, 15(4): 1021–1029.

O'Connor, J. 1973. *The Fiscal Crisis of the State*. New York: St Martin's Press.

O'Connor, J. 1988. 'Capitalism, nature, socialism: A theoretical introduction,' *Capitalism Nature Socialism*, 1(1): 11–38.

O'Connor, J. 1989. 'Political economy of ecology of socialism and capitalism,' *Capitalism Nature Socialism*, 1(3): 93–107.

O'Connor, J. 1991. 'On the two contradictions of capitalism,' *Capitalism Nature Socialism*, 8(2–3): 107–109.

O'Connor, J. R. 1998. *Natural Causes: Essays in Ecological Marxism*. New York: Guilford Press.

Pimentel, D. 2005. 'Environmental and economic costs of the application of pesticides primarily in the United States,' *Environment, Development and Sustainability*, 7(2): 229–252.

Rockstrom, J., Steffen, W., Noone, K., Perrson, F. A., Chapin, S., Lambin, E., Lenton, T. M., Scheffer, M., Folke, C., Schellnhuber, H. J., Nykvst, B., de Wit, C. A., Hughes, T., van der Leeuw, S., Rodhe, H., Sorlin, S., Snyder, P. K., Costanza, R., Svedin, U., Falekmark, M., Karlberg, L., Corell, R. W., Fabry, V. J., Hanson, J., Walker, B., Liverman, D., Richardson, K., Crutzen, P. and Foley, J. 2009. 'Planetary boundaries: Exploring the safe operating space for humanity,' *Ecology and Society*, 14 (2): 32–47.

Rouse, J. D., Bishop, C. A. and Struger, J. 1999. 'Nitrogen pollution: An assessment of its threat to amphibian survival,' *Environmental Health Perspectives*, 107(10): 799–803.

Schnaiberg, A. 1980. *The Environment: From Surplus to Scarcity*. New York: Oxford University Press.

Shandra, J. M., Leckband, C. and London, B. 2009a. 'Ecologically unequal exchange and deforestation: A cross-national analysis of forestry export flows,' *Organization & Environment*, 22(3): 293–310.

Shandra, J. M., Leckband, C., McKinney, L. A. and London, B. 2009b. 'Ecologically unequal exchange, world polity, and biodiversity loss a cross-national analysis of threatened mammals,' *International Journal of Comparative Sociology*, 50(3–4): 285–310.

Shandra, J. M., Shor, E. and London, B. 2009c. 'World polity, unequal ecological exchange, and organic water pollution: A cross-national analysis of developing nations,' *Human Ecology Review*, 16(1): 53–63.

Sollund, R. 2017. 'Doing green, critical criminology with an auto-ethnographic, feminist approach,' *Critical Criminology: An International Journal*, 25(2): 245–260.

South, N. and Wyatt, T. 2011. 'Comparing illicit trades in wildlife and drugs: An exploratory study,' *Deviant Behavior*, 32(6): 538–561.

Steffen, W., Broadgate, W., Deutsch, L., Gaffney, O. and Ludwig, C. 2015. 'The trajectory of the Anthropocene: The great acceleration,' *The Anthropocene Review*, 2(1): 81–98.

Stretesky, P. B., and Lynch, M. J. 2009. 'A cross-national study of the association between per capita carbon dioxide emissions and exports to the United States,' *Social Science Research*, 38: 239–250.

Stretesky, P. B., and Lynch, M. J. 2011. 'Coal strip mining, mountain top removal and the distribution of environmental violations across the United States, 2002–2008,' *Landscape Research*, 36(2): 209–230.

Stretesky, P. B., Long, M. A. and Lynch, M. J. 2013a. *The Treadmill of Crime: Political Economy and Green Criminology*. Abingdon, Oxon, UK: Routledge.

Stretesky, P. B., Long, M. A. and Lynch, M. J. 2013b. 'Does environmental enforcement slow the treadmill of production? The relationship between large monetary penalties, ecological disorganization and toxic releases within offending corporations,' *Journal of Crime and Justice*, 36(2): 235–249.

Stretesky, P. B., Lynch, M. J., Long, M. A. and Barrett, K. L. 2017. 'Does the modernization of environmental enforcement reduce toxic releases? An examination of self-policing, criminal prosecutions and toxic releases in the United States, 1988–2012,' *Sociological Spectrum*, 37(1): 48–62.

Townsend, A. R., Howarth, R. W., Bazzaz, F. A., Booth, M. S., Cleveland, C. C., Collinge, S. K., Dobson, A. P., Epstein, P. R., Holland, E. A., Keeney, D. R., Mallin, M. A., Rogers, C. A., Wayne, P. and Wolfe, A. H. 2003. 'Human health effects of a changing global nitrogen cycle,' *Frontiers in Ecology and the Environment*, 1(5): 240–246.

Wallerstein, I. 2011. *The Modern World-system I: Capitalist Agriculture and the Origins of the European World-economy in the Sixteenth Century*. Berkeley, CA: University of California Press.

5

The visual dimensions of green criminology

Lorenzo Natali and Bill McClanahan

Introduction

Over the last 25 years, 'green criminology' has become known on an international level as a multiple/manifold perspective oriented towards the opening of criminological paradigms to issues of environmental harms and crimes (see Brisman and South, Introduction and Chapter 1, this volume). While emerging within the framework of critical criminology, green criminology is marked by a constitutive openness that allows it to extend beyond the boundaries of a specific criminological tradition to become a theoretical laboratory for thinking about environmental issues in the richest and broadest meaning of the word (see, e.g., Brisman and South, Introduction and Chapter 1, this volume; Sollund 2012: 4). In this sense, green criminology seems—indeed, *seeks*—to promote new 'ways of looking' at the human–environment relationship—a particular 'green gaze' or 'perspective' that can expand the criminological understanding and imagination of environmental crimes and harms beyond existing criminological frames (South 1998; White 2003; see also Brisman 2015).

It is through this green-tinted 'lens' that our chapter seeks to share some reflections designed to catalyse new visual explorations of environmental crimes and harms. In particular, we offer some suggestions for ways in which environmental crime and harm might be further analysed and understood using already existent images or images produced by the researcher or the participant (see Ferrell and Van de Voorde 2010: 37–38; Natali 2016a; Van de Voorde 2012: 215).[1] This proposal does not seek to take a normative stand—'how it should be done'. It is, after all, a *proposal*, rather than a *prescription*, for an explorative and interpretative approach (see also Pauwels 2015: 73–74)—one that represents a theoretical starting point for those who intend to develop qualitative visual research in the field of green criminology.

This chapter begins with some general notes about the potential for a green criminology with and about images. We then offer a discussion and exploration of photo-elicitation methods—one technique for a green criminology *with* images. Following that, we turn our attention to possible techniques for a green criminology *about* images with a consideration of a green analytical, methodological and theoretical approach, before suggesting ways in which a green-visual criminology can contribute to the development of new forms of participatory research and praxis. Finally, we conclude with some thoughts on the broad potential and applicability of a green visual mode of analysis and research.

A visual green criminology *with* images and *about* images

What new horizons are made available for green criminologists by the development and application of visual methodologies? The social sciences have long disregarded the study of the 'visual' (for a discussion, see, e.g., Becker 1974; Carrabine 2012; Ferrell and Van de Voorde 2010), and it is only recently that interest in the visual dimensions of social reality and in the use of visual methods of research has grown as a means for investigating contemporary socio-cultural transformations (see also Mirzoeff 1999; Pauwels 2011; Rose 2012). Specifically, if criminology is the study of crime, visual criminology may be defined as 'the study of ways in which all things visual interact with crime and criminal justice, inventing and shaping one another' (Rafter 2014: 129; see also Brown and Carrabine 2017). Visual criminology's aim, then, is to develop its own theoretical and methodological approaches, suggesting new visual ways of exploring and analysing critically social and power relations, harm, suffering and justice in the criminological field (see, e.g., Brown 2014; Rose 2012; Schept 2014).

Visual research methods in criminology embrace both research *on* or *about* images—where the focus is on the visual dimensions of the social and cultural worlds of crime—and conducting research *with* images—where visual images are used as a heuristic tool in order to explore more thoroughly specific criminological contexts.[2] In this regard, some criminologists have attempted not just to devote their attention to preexisting visual representations of criminal phenomena (Beirne 2015; Ferrell, this volume, Chapter 37; Van de Voorde 2012), but to generate *their own* visual images of crime and crime control (see, e.g., Brown and Carrabine 2017; Ferrell, Hayward and Young 2015: 228–235; Greek 2009; Natali 2016a). Moreover, even though in the specific field of green criminology other scholars have contemplated visual representations of environmental harms (e.g., Brisman 2017, 2018; Brisman and South 2014; Carrabine 2018; Kohm and Greenhill 2013; South 2017), the use of visual mediums for gathering data on environmental harms, rather than just as a subject of analysis, remains mostly unexplored (cf. Natali 2016a). As we have suggested elsewhere (Natali and McClanahan 2017), these theoretical and methodological sensibilities may be profitably put into dialogue with what Brisman and South (2013), 2014, this volume, Chapter 36) conceptualise as a 'green cultural criminology'—a criminological perspective that tries to imagine new modes of critically analysing the intersection of culture, crime, justice and environment.

An example of visual green cultural criminology *with* images: photo-elicitation

In a green criminological approach *with* images, the images employed during the research process may be those produced and then selected by the researcher or by the participants in order to facilitate posing 'visual questions' to the interviewees—a technique known as 'photo-elicitation'. As visual sociologist Douglas Harper (2001: 16) explains, photo-elicitation is 'a process of organizing interviews around photographs' (see also Kong et al. 2014; Rose 2012: 304–317; Van de Voorde 2012: 206). The assumption is that the meaning of the image rests in the mind of the viewer (see also Becker 1974; Holm 2008: 328; Pauwels 2011: 12). As Pauwels (2017: 67) remarks:

> in fact many types of images can be used (still and moving, paintings or drawings, etc.) [...] "image elicitation" or "visual elicitation" would be a more appropriate term. The visual materials used as "stimuli" to obtain unique kinds of information from respondents and informants may include pre-existing "societal imagery" [...] as well as researcher or respondent-generated materials.

Pauwels suggests that visual images can be used to elicit and probe meaning—as a means for the interviewer to delve deeper into the participant's verbal and visual narratives. This technique generates a kind of visual *verstehen*, creating a deeper unity between the subjects interviewed and the researchers (Harper 1988)—one favouring the sharing and creation of multiple—even conflicting—versions of reality. Specifically, photo-elicitation interviews prove useful in enhancing the active role of social actors and in placing their perceptions in the context of the social and cultural worlds in which they are embedded, starting directly from the perspectives of those who live specific environmental experiences. As Parkin (2014: 16) explains, 'photo-elicitation may reduce the gulf that often exists between the "emic" (insider/member) world of the respondent and the "etic" (outsider/non-member) world of the academic researcher'.

The idea of using visual images in order to conduct interviews was proposed for the first time by John Collier (1967). The reasons for introducing this novel element into an interview are based on some considerations, summarised briefly below:

- Interaction and collaboration between interviewer and interviewee can be (or become) more fluid. On some level, the interviewee allows himself/herself to be questioned *by the images*, rather than by the *interviewer*. The interviewee feels less controlled by the interviewer than inspired by the images, and thus he/she says what he/she sees and feels about the images, enhancing an active and reflexive role during the interpretative process (Harper 1988).
- Because photographs can afford a more accurate documentation of objects, people, and physical and socio-environmental contexts than other visual media, the statements of the interviewees after having viewed the images may result in more detailed and complete accounts (see also Rose 2012: 307).
- The use of photographs generates unique data not obtainable through verbal questions. In fact, photographic images offer the observer the opportunity of speaking about them in more than one way—in both a rational/argumentative way and an emotional/evocative one.
- The use of photographs can catalyse a personal interpretative process—one that transcends what is visible to the researcher. In spite of their self-evidence—their 'proof' of reality—images can be interpreted in various ways and thus generate potentially conflicting meanings (Barthes 2000 [1980]). It is thanks to this polysemy of visual images that it is possible to investigate more deeply the perspective of the observing social actor—the interviewee (Harper 2012: 155–187).
- The use of photographic images during the interview helps to override the binary distinction between what is often perceived to be or otherwise considered 'natural' and that which is 'social' (see also Natali 2016a, 2016b).

In the green criminological context, the importance of visual images is that they can become a bridge not only between the subjects and the researchers, but among other social actors. More generally, because these worlds are 'sensitive' worlds, where conflicts are expressed and suffering felt, a qualitative method, working with both images *and* words, will have a decisive role in the process of approaching and empathising with the different visions of others (Figure 5.1).

Figure 5.1 One of the authors—Natali (2016a)—created this photographic collage of Huelva (Spain)—a town overwhelmed by industrial contamination—and showed it to several inhabitants of the place. This resulted in a number of different stories. In particular, the historical photograph (in the centre of the picture) allowed the narratives to develop around a 'now and then' with reference to the creeping environmental disaster (case 30: female, 49 years old), while the satellite photo (middle row, far-right image) led the participants to reflect on the extent of contamination from a different perspective (case 38: female, 42 years old)

Case 30 (female, 49 years old): 'It's something I'll never forget … when I was a kid, my mother used to take us to bathe there … we knew nothing about pollution back then … I'll never forget going there as a teenager in my first bikini … and when I came out of the water it was filthy … covered in oil from the factories … an absolute mess … this is the memory I have.'

Case 38 (female, 42 years old): 'We know what is happening but when faced with this situation we see ourselves as powerless … It's well known how dangerous phosphogypsum [visible in the satellite photo) is but … it's something we know is there, but it's as if we wanted to escape from it … It's as if a curtain could be pulled in front of it so as not to see what's happening.'

Essentially, with photo-elicitation, the photograph serves as a tool for investigating and understanding others' social reality—as a means for activating an interpretative process of the visual and symbolic content of the perceived reality of the researcher and the interviewees (Natali 2016a). It is here that the visual image deploys one of its most significant capabilities —inviting the participant and the researcher to encounter and interpret symbolically and emotionally visual representations of environmental crime and harm. Because the nature of photography 'entails an *objective representation* (a mechanical record of something factual) and a *subjective interpretation* (a representation of the paradigm in which it was constructed) with meanings ascribed to the image by the photographer and the viewer' (Van de Voorde 2012:

212, emphasis in original; see also Ferrell and Van de Voorde 2010: 41–42), a qualitative interview 'with' images can capture the paradox typical of environmental phenomena: they are *socially defined and described* but at the same time they are *real* (Brisman and South 2013; Natali 2013b). A visual approach within green criminology can contribute to this cultural and scientific undertaking in its own unique way.

In addition to these considerations, Harper (2012: 167) underscores a further dynamic, which holds relevance for visual research in green criminology: the ability of the photograph to document a bygone time. When one wants to investigate the social perception of environmental contamination and catastrophe, the use of photographs allows one to introduce into the conversation the historical dimension of the phenomenon and, with it, the collective memory of the inhabitants of the area in question, granting broader narrative potential about the various ways of feeling, living, remembering and seeing the industrial history of a particular place. From this perspective, the choice of a method—in this case, photo-elicitation—is linked directly to the idea of a criminological imagination (White 2003; see also Ferrell, Hayward and Young 2015)—one capable of connecting the individual biographies and the historical frame in which they are located—the micro- and the macro-narratives in which the social actors perceive the dramatic transformations that have affected the human–environment relationship in the course of time. This does not mean reducing one level to the other, but establishing links and resonances between different scales of 'ecological crisis' (see Latour et al., 2011; Natali 2013b).

During this process, it is necessary that the borders between the researcher and the participants in the research remain porous. Introducing a photograph into a conversation, then, can help to ease or even remove conflicting relationships within diverse visions of the world—to explore the tensions and the ambiguities of what is taken for granted and to show their transformative potential (Natali 2016a: 96). This is because meanings are often fluid and open to change (Blumer 1969). Through this path, it will be possible to highlight the profound relationships each of us holds with our ecological worlds by listening actively to the narrative and visual dimensions of the phenomenon explored—environmental crime and harm—from the perspectives of lay people, as well as those of experts (Natali 2015b). Learning to pay more attention to these multiple narratives—understanding how to cultivate a perspective of 'elasticity' suitable for a sensitivity towards environmental issues that are not always immediately visible—is a necessary step. More analytically, visual research in green criminology may help in probing the silent knowledge of social actors and in bridging cultural and natural worlds, thereby crossing the dichotomous divide between what is natural and what is social. To this end, it is crucial to develop not only flexible methods, but also supple conceptual tools—instruments sensitive enough to capture critically the vagueness and elusiveness of environmental issues without severely diminishing their multiple dimensions.

Furthermore, the use of visual dimensions makes it possible to place more value on the spatial dimension(s) of environmental crimes and harms. Reflecting upon our mode of perceiving the environment and its possible destruction implies, in fact, recognition of the *concrete space* of which we are part. Each social actor is also, or perhaps above all else, a 'spatial' actor—one who moves in a physical, not just symbolic, space.[3]

Finally, photo-elicitation has been expanded 'to develop a participatory action research (PAR) approach called photovoice,' which uses participants' photographs 'to facilitate participants' critical reflection through group discussions, and members of the public including policymakers are engaged through public forums to bring about actions or changes on issues captured in the photographs' (Kong et al. 2014: 14; see also Harper 2012: 188–206). With photovoice, a visual method of participatory action research conceived by Caroline Wang

(2006) in the 1990s, participants are asked to take photographs of themes relevant to their daily life, to reflect on their community's concerns, to expose social problems and to ignite social change. The goal is to make the voices of the participants in the research heard in the political sphere in order to orientate policy decisions and to improve practices. The hope is that collaborative and participatory visual research, such as this, will enhance social actors' reflexivity and awareness of environmental change and harm.

An analytical green (cultural) criminology *on* or *about* (already existing) images

If the approach offered above represents a green criminology conducted *with* images in that it urges and suggests a methodology that explores the interpretive processes of those who witness and experience environmental change and harm, we can now turn our attention to the potential of a green criminology *about* images. Put simply, a green criminology *about* images proposes that images themselves (e.g., visual archival materials, images from popular visual culture, images taken by satellite or aerial photography) offer rich insight into the various phenomena that green criminology—and, particularly, green cultural criminology—so often explores and describes. This approach, we argue, could lead to increased criminological insight into the visual dimensions of environmental *change* and *harm*, environmental *conflict* and *resistance* to environmental harm. Before proceeding with a description of such an approach, though, we find it necessary to offer some critical thoughts on the dominant ways, methods and modes in which the visual is employed in criminological research.

Within criminology in particular—although we also note that other fields of visual study have been similarly troubled and contested—there is sometimes a tendency to employ images in a way that does not offer sufficient consideration of the various and complex theoretical and political realities and dimensions of visuality (or offered by 'the visual'). All too often, then, images serve as little more than an interlude to the main act of the text. Does such use of images (e.g., a photograph of a prison cell inserted, with minimal analysis, within the margins of a qualitative study on incarceration) pay adequate theoretical attention to the image and its production? While the image itself, stripped of theoretical analysis, is certainly important in that it represents and communicates a moment in time and space, the methodological tendency at play in such clichéd use of the image fails to interrogate its synecdochal qualities or adopt the innovative and inventive tendencies of cultural criminology. In response, we suggest that it is necessary to develop an integrated framework that makes room for *theories* of the visual, rather than simply approaching the image as 'mere "data" to be gathered' (Zaitch and de Leeuw 2010). In order to focus adequate attention on the image, we can follow the lead of photographers and visual theorists, such as Sekula (1981) and Mirzoeff (2011), who offer a more rich and challenging perspective that requires devoting attention to the meaning of not only the image itself, but also the conditions and processes—cultural, legal, mechanical or philosophical—that underlie, facilitate and empower its production. While there is currently a tendency in some criminological work to engage with the visual as just another data point, excellent and compelling scholarship within visual criminology engages the visual in a more theoretically informed way. For example, Brown (2014), Carrabine (2011, 2012), Linnemann and Wall (2013), Wall and Linnemann (2014) and others have produced work that reflects serious attention to the production and dissemination of images. There is, however, a paucity of this sort of scholarship within green criminology—with, of course, some exceptions (Beirne 2014; McClanahan, Brisman and South 2017; Natali 2010, 2013a, 2016a; Natali and McClanahan 2017).

Across the sensory and affective ways in which humans apprehend material ecologies, the visual is, perhaps, most dominant. Leaving aside, for now, the valid criticisms of an 'ocularcentric' approach to considerations of ecological apprehension (see generally Kavanagh 2013)—concerns that are grounded in a cultural critique of the domination of western cosmologies and ways of being in nature (see Brisman and South, Chapter 33, this volume; Brisman, South and Walters, Chapter 10, this volume; see also Goyes 2016; Goyes and South 2016, 2017)—we note that, for the vast majority of humans, the ecological world is felt and known most immediately and intensely on and in the register of the visual; it is in seeing that most of us locate knowing (see generally Brisman 2014, 2018; Natali and McClanahan 2017). Following that assertion, we maintain that it is in *seeing* change that we know it has happened. As we have noted elsewhere, without knowing what *was* we cannot know what *is*. Similarly, without knowing or seeing the relationship between what was and what is—a relationship of change—we cannot meaningfully know the significance of ecological and environmental change and harm.

Among the many ways in which we can imagine 'the image' is as a tool that provides and urges *frames* of understanding. As Judith Butler (2009: 51) describes in her work on the American invasion of Iraq and the ways in which lives are understood as 'grievable' or 'ungrievable,' frames of knowing derived from images operate on an affective level, operationalising the differences and tensions between the 'sights we can see and those we cannot'. With respect to environmental degradation, images thereof function as frames for knowing change and harm, capable of revealing the temporalities of human interactions with broader nonhuman ecologies. We must, though, remain mindful of the power of frames and their ability to, as Erving Goffman (1974) described, condition our interpretation of an event or phenomenon. Framing, then, following Butler and Goffman, is an essential component of the cultural intake and interpretation of images, and this is no less the case when we consider images of environmental destruction than it is when we experience images of war or human suffering.

Cultural criminology has long been interested in analysing the ways that images frame crime and crime control, influencing how we interpret and understand these phenomena. Indeed, in the introduction to the edited collection *Framing Crime* (2010), Hayward argues that 'it is increasingly important that *all* criminologists are familiar with the various ways in which crime and 'the story of crime' is imaged, constructed and 'framed' within modern society' (2010: 9 (emphasis in original)). Drawing inspiration from Hayward, we contend that green criminologists, in particular, should attend to the power and significance of the image and the visual in considering the ways that environmental harm and change are constructed and communicated.

Framing—and the image as frame—take on particular significance for ecological thought —and thus, we would hope, for green criminology—in the work of ecotheorist Timothy Morton, who asserts that in the interplay and tensions between 'frame and content', the nonhuman ecological world 'becomes audible as an echo, as afterimage'. Here, we can locate an opportunity to consider, through a simplification of Morton's thesis (which is too sprawling to provide the attention it deserves in a short chapter such as ours), the ways that examining existing images offers the green cultural criminological project an opportunity to establish and call attention to the temporalities of harm that we often find are the subject of our inquiries. Environmental *harm* is almost always connected to or evidenced by environmental *change*: harm occurs when the forces of the human world—whether intentionally or unintentionally, whether through addition or subtraction—reconfigure ecological spaces to suit particular needs or fulfill particular desires. The photographic or moving image, then, has significant power, insofar as it has unique command over establishing specific temporalities of such change(s), thereby offering immersion and insight into bygone times and providing a glimpse into the shift between what was and what is (see also Natali 2016a; Natali and McClanahan 2017). In short, following Morton, images of ecological systems changed by interaction with humans and contemporary modes of human social relations are *afterimages*—echoes of what those spaces once were.

In examining and juxtaposing images and afterimages of ecological spaces, green cultural criminologists can not only begin the process of locating the meaning(s) of environmental change—an essential part of the enterprise, as described by Brisman and South's outline of and call for the approach—but can also establish the very presence of change and harm. In archival images, for example, there is wide opportunity to find the sort of easily apprehendable 'data' that establish change and, as is so often the case, harm. Here, we suggest that green cultural criminologists that are attuned to the visual cultural register employ the power of the image to 'prove' temporal changes and harms. An analysis of images side by side, for example, can demonstrate that some transformation has occurred—a starting point for exploring and establishing the various meanings and significance of those changes. We argue, then, that while it is necessary that a visual green cultural criminology always work towards a theoretically informed consideration of the image as a force that transcends the material dimensions of a simple photograph, the green cultural criminological enterprise can nevertheless employ the sort of 'image-as-data' approach favoured by more mainstream criminological and sociological research described at the outset of this section.

Among the many ways in which ecological environments are harmed and changed is from—or through—extractive and productive capitalism, where the visual markers of environmental contamination and destruction are pronounced. One of us (McClanahan 2017) conducted research in the coal-producing region of Appalachia in the eastern part of the United States, creating and consulting images to establish widespread selenium contamination of creeks, lakes and ponds by comparing images taken over time to note the dramatic change in the colour of water. Similarly, environmental justice activists and scholars have long used images in order to establish and communicate the types of ongoing environmental harms faced by residents and ecologies of the industrial and postindustrial spaces so often affected by the siting of harmful industry (see generally Houston 2013; Scott and Oelofse 2005). We suggest that green criminologists continue to locate in existing images the opportunities to establish, analyse and communicate harm to human and nonhuman environments, ecologies and ecosystems.

Having considered in this section the potential for a green criminology on or about images to strengthen and support criminological analysis of environmental change and contamination, we now turn our attention to the final components of the three core areas of visual interest mentioned at the start of the section: environmental conflict and resistance to environmental harm. Because visual criminology shares common ground with cultural criminology, and because cultural criminology has been attuned to cultural modes and politics of resistance, we find here a reaffirmation of the assertions central to proposals for a green cultural criminology—namely that a green cultural criminology follow cultural criminology in its essential analytical attention to various meanings and forms of resistance (see Brisman and South 2013, 2014; McClanahan 2014, 2017). Movements and moments of resistance to environmental harm often employ and engage with the cultural visual register in order to communicate a resistant spirit, and so we find that attention to such images of resistance make up an essential component of a visually attuned green criminology.

Indeed, resistance to environmental harm, change and contamination is a fundamentally cultural affair, and may employ the visual in a number of ways. From protest signs to films, the politics of resistance are made strikingly clear on the visual register. Green criminologists, then, can locate in those images the dimensions of human–environment interaction that seek to resist ecological harm. In such a criminological approach—an approach attuned to the power of images of environmental harm and images of resistance to those harms—we find robust opportunity to heed the suggestions of the emergent green cultural criminology. Here, then, we suggest a green cultural criminology that takes seriously the images generated in order to resist environmental harm, change and contamination or images produced to communicate environmental conflict (Figure 5.2a and b).

How, though, can green cultural criminologists work towards or within a green cultural criminology *on* or *about* images? As this chapter has suggested, there have been significant shifts towards the visual in green criminological research, and in each moment of such engagement we find methodological opportunity. A visual green cultural criminology on or about images might, for example, employ the sort of cultural analysis favoured by cultural criminology (see, for example, McClanahan, Brisman and South 2016, 2017), or the sort of secondary analysis of images-as-data described at the outset of this section. Aerial and satellite photography, archival images, stills from popular cinema, multi-media visual art and the

Figure 5.2a and b The above images show some dimensions of resistance to environmental harm and affective dimensions of environmental conflict expressed through visual culture. Both images were taken by Bill McClanahan in Eastern Kentucky in July 2015

visual metaphors employed in literature—all hold the potential to offer documentation and representation of environmental change, contamination and conflict. The 'how', then, is answered in existing methodological approaches to the analysis of images, texts and other cultural products. Film, for example, can be engaged with analytically through the rigorous theoretical examination of themes, images and meanings of resistance (see, for example, McClanahan, Brisman and South 2017). Photographic images of change can, in turn, be employed to enrich field-based research (see, e.g., the discussion of photo-elicitation above and in Natali 2010, 2016b). Archival images can be located and interrogated for evidence of harmful transformation (e.g., McClanahan 2017), and aerial and satellite photography can be employed to explore the various ways that harm is hidden or rendered invisible by way of being ecologically embedded in material landscapes (McClanahan 2017; McClanahan and Linnemann 2018).

Towards new *visualisations* of environmental crime and harm?

In order to investigate and narrate with images and words the possible environmental scenarios that may enter the green criminological arena, it will be useful to design and use visual devices of criminological research that favour the learning of modes of listening to and seeing the manifold experiences of environmental destruction. The visual device thus becomes a real symbolic force that promotes new visions of the world through new forms of perception. Here, the interplay between and interpretation of images and their corresponding afterimages offers a unique form and site of *narrative* (see Brisman 2016, 2019; Carrabine 2016).

The partnership between social research and visual methods is characterised by a long tradition that finds innovative developments in proposals from within visual anthropology (Pink 2001) and visual sociology (see Becker 1981; Harper 2012; see also Carrabine 2017). The insights of these fields, we contend, can be employed in the field of green criminology. Different visual techniques work both as methodological instruments of research (as in the case of photo elicitation interviews) and as vehicles for communicating the results of the research to the public (see also Banks 2001; Stanczak 2007). Concerning this latter dimension, the visual essay (Grady 1991; Pauwels 2012, 2017), for example, allows the results of sociological research to come together in a video format that can be utilised outside the academic environment (see also Hayward 2017; Redmon 2017).

As we have suggested, investigating environmental harm lends itself to the use of images (fixed or moving), which help to take into account the ambiguity and relational nature of the ecological processes in play. Visual methodologies in environmental research might also allow working *with* the subjects of the research on the complexity of environmental issues. As we discussed above regarding 'photovoice', the adoption of visual methodologies in order to generate participation in social interactions and to co-construct knowledge through the direct experience of the participants represents a necessary bridge between theory and practice, as shown by the various forms of PAR (Participatory Action Research) (McIntyre 2008: 20).[4] This praxis can also contribute to creating the conditions for a shift away from a rigid anthropocentrism (Natali 2013b; see also Cianchi 2015). In particular, participatory filmmaking could help people to become sensitive to a socio-environmental reality different from their own, and is a methodological strategy capable of placing the spectator within the social and cultural (practical) experience of the (human or nonhuman) participants (see Ruby 2000). From this perspective, observing socio-environmental processes will also mean encountering them in their complex intertwining, in their ineradicable opaqueness, ambivalence and richness. To obtain these results, though, it is vital to promote a 'visual scientific literacy' (Pauwels 2011: 14) which would have to include the skills necessary to interpret and produce images, but, above all, would allow the development of a visual thinking capable of permeating and animating the whole research process.

Conclusion

The aim of this chapter has been to suggest the salience of the visual dimensions of crime within green criminology. Devoting greater attention to the 'visual' will add fresh narratives, improving our understandings of conflicted—and conflicting—relationships with the environment. By becoming even more familiar with the 'culture of the image' and with its possible uses, criminology could also discover unknown ways of 'originating "new"—insightful, open, moving—descriptions of the world' (Robins 1996: 167). These theoretical and methodological sensitivities could improve our awareness of planetary degradation and destruction.

Many questions remain and provide wide and exciting fields for future visual research in green criminology: what role is played by the *indirect* imaginary, the one made up of the images provided by culture? What will be the capacity of the individual imagination in the so-called 'civilization of the image' (see also Brown 2017)? As Italo Calvino (1988: 91–92) writes:

> At one time the visual memory of an individual was limited to the heritage of his direct experiences and to a restricted repertory of images reflected in culture. The possibility of giving form to personal myths arose from the way in which the fragments of this memory came together in unexpected and evocative combinations. We are bombarded today by such a quantity of images that we can no longer distinguish direct experience from what we have seen for a few seconds on television. The memory is littered with bits and pieces of images, like a rubbish dump, and it is more and more unlikely that any one form among so many will succeed in standing out.

These aspects open the door to a new line of comparative methods. As Harper (2012: 107) explains, '[t]he mind-numbing number of images now available via free Web sources would make it possible to experiment with comparative analysis in a newly creative way. Photos have the disarming capacity to ask what sociological concepts look like in the concrete.' The mutual relations and points of methodological and theoretical overlap between green, cultural, narrative and visual criminology can help negotiate the challenges Harper describes and can represent the starting point for the promotion of new imaginative explorations of environmental crimes, harms and conflicts (see also Natali and Budó 2018). Moreover, we argue and hope that in a world of increasingly dramatic environmental change and harm, green criminology, in general, and green cultural criminology, in particular, will continue to grow and find salience, and that the visual (and an appreciation of the intense and spectacular power of the image) will continue to find a place in their research approaches and agendas.

Notes

1 As Van de Voorde (2012: 215) reminds us, "the use of visual ethnographic analysis is a novel approach in criminology whereby images, instead of being mere illustrations, actually engage readers/viewers in a genuine analytical investigation of the visual."

2 The distinction between sociology *with* images (that is, images generated by the researcher and/or by the subjects of the research in order to investigate certain social phenomena) and sociology *about/on*

images (those that circulate within the daily life of social actors) is now well established (Harper 1988: 55), and a number of scholars have highlighted the importance of promoting a deeper dialogue between visual methodologies and visual culture (see, e.g., Rose 2014).

3 Many techniques are already employed to take into account this dimension. These include the "diary-photo" (Letham 2004) or experiments with a higher level of creativity, such as the "visual tours" (Peyrefitte 2012) and "itinerant soliloquies" (Natali 2016b).

4 McIntyre (2008: XII) explains: "Participatory action research *does* provide opportunities for codeveloping processes *with* people rather than *for* people. Its emphasis on people's lived experiences, individual and social change, the co-construction of knowledge [...] has the potential to create public spaces where researchers and participants can reshape their understanding of how political, educational, social, economic, and familiar contexts mediate people's lives" (emphasis in original). In the context of PAR, McIntyre (2008) uses the technique of "photo-voice." To co-produce knowledge—through PAR and/or "photo-voice"—means not only recognising the active role of the participants in the process of research, but explaining in what measure, in what forms and in which phases the actors exist as real and proper "co-researchers" (Phillips et al. 2013).

References

Banks, M. 2001. *Visual Methods in Social Research.* London: Sage.

Barthes, R. 2000 [1980]. *Camera Lucida. Reflections on Photography.* London: Vintage.

Becker, H. 1974. 'Photography and sociology,' *Studies in the Anthropology of Visual Communication,* 1(1): 3–26.

Becker, H. 1981. *Exploring Society Photographically.* Chicago, IL: University of Chicago Press.

Beirne, P. 2014. *Hogarth's Art of Animal Cruelty: Satire, Suffering and Pictorial Propaganda.* London: Palgrave Macmillan.

Beirne, P. 2015. *Hogarth's Art of Animal Cruelty: Satire, Suffering and Pictorial Propaganda.* Basingstoke, Hampshire, UK: Palgrave Macmillan.

Blumer, H. 1969. *Symbolic Interactionism: Perspective and Method.* Englewood Cliffs, NJ: Prentice Hall.

Brisman, A. 2014. 'The visual acuity of climate change,' in P. Davies, P. Francis,. and T. Wyatt (eds.) *Invisible Crimes and Social Harms,* pp. 61–80. Basingstoke, Hampshire, UK: Palgrave Macmillan.

Brisman, A. 2015. '"Multicolored" green criminology and climate change's achromatopsia,' *Contemporary Justice Review,* 18(2): 178–196.

Brisman, A. 2016. 'On narrative and green cultural criminology,' *International Journal for Crime, Justice and Social Democracy,* 6(2): 64–77.

Brisman, A. 2017. 'Representations of environmental crime and harm: A green-cultural criminological perspective on *human-altered landscapes,*' in M. Brown and E. Carrabine (eds.) *Routledge International Handbook of Visual Criminology,* pp. 523–539. Abingdon, Oxon, UK: Routledge.

Brisman, A. 2018. 'Representing the "invisible crime" of climate change in an age of post-truth,' *Theoretical Criminology,* 22(3): 468–491.

Brisman, A. 2019. 'The fable of *The Three Little Pigs,* climate change and green cultural criminology,' *International Journal for Crime, Justice and Social Democracy,* 8(1): 46–69. DOI: 10.5204/ijcjsd.v8i1.470.

Brisman, A. and South, N. 2013. 'A green-cultural criminology: An exploratory outline,' *Crime Media Culture,* 9(2): 115–135.

Brisman, A. and South, N. 2014. *Green Cultural Criminology. Constructions of Environmental Harm, Consumerism and Resistance to Ecocide.* London: Routledge.

Brisman, A., McClanahan, B. and South, N. 2014. 'Toward a green-cultural criminology of "the rural",' *Critical Criminology: An International Journal,* 22(4): 479–494.

Brown, M. 2014. 'Visual criminology and carceral studies: Counter-images in the carceral age,' *Theoretical Criminology,* 18(2): 134–158.

Brown, M. 2017. 'The criminologist as a visual scholar in a global mediascape,' in M. Brown and E. Carrabine (eds.) *Routledge International Handbook of Visual Criminology,* pp. 486–495. Abingdon, Oxon, UK: Routledge.

Brown, M. and Carrabine, E. (eds.) 2017. *Routledge International Handbook of Visual Criminology.* Abingdon, Oxon, UK:Routledge.

Butler, J. 2009. *Frames of War: When Is Life Grievable.* London: Verso.

Calvino, I. 1988. *Six Memos for the Next Millennium.* Cambridge, MA: Harvard University Press.

Carrabine, E. 2012. 'Just images. Aesthetics, ethics and visual criminology,' *The British Journal of Criminology*, 52(3): 463–489.
Carrabine, E. 2016. 'Picture this: Criminology, image and narrative,' *Crime Media Culture*, 12(2): 253–270.
Carrabine, E. 2011. 'Images of torture: Culture, politics and power,' *Crime] Media Culture*, 7(1): 5–30.
Carrabine, E. 2017. 'Social science and visual culture,' in M. Brown and E. Carrabine (eds.) *Routledge International Handbook of Visual Criminology*, pp. 23–38. Abingdon, Oxon, UK: Routledge.
Carrabine, E. 2018. 'Geographies of landscape: Representation, power and meaning,' *Theoretical Criminology*, 22(3): 445–467.
Cianchi, J. 2015. *Radical Environmentalism. Nature, Identity and More-Than-Human Agency*. London: Palgrave Macmillan.
Collier, J. 1967. *Visual Anthropology: Photography as a Research Method*. New York: Holt Rinehart and Winston.
Ferrell, J. 2001. *Tearing Down the Streets: Adventures in Urban Anarchy*. Basingstoke, Hampshire, UK: Palgrave Macmillan.
Ferrell, J. and Van de Voorde, C. 2010. 'The decisive moment. Documentary photography and cultural criminology,' in K. Hayward and M. Presdee (eds.) *Framing Crime. Cultural Criminology and the Image*, pp. 36–52. Abingdon, Oxon, UK: Routledge.
Ferrell, J., Hayward, K. and Young, J. 2015. *Cultural Criminology: An Invitation*, 2nd edn. London: Sage.
Goffman, E. 1974.*Frame Analysis: An Essay on the Organization of Experience*. Cambridge, MA: Harvard University Press.
Goyes, D. R. 2016. 'Green activist criminology and the epistemologies of the South,' *Critical Criminology: An International Journal*, 26(4): 503–518.
Goyes, D. R. and South, N. 2016. 'Land grabs, bio-piracy and the inversion of justice in Colombia,' *The British Journal of Criminology*, 56(3): 558–577.
Goyes, D. R. and South, N. 2017. 'Green criminology before "Green Criminology": Amnesia and absences,' *Critical Criminology: An International Journal*, 25(2): 165–181.
Grady, J. 1991. 'The visual essay and sociology,' *Visual Sociology*, 6(2): 23–38.
Greek, C. 2009. 'Documenting and framing police public interaction with citizens: A study in visual criminology,' *Criminal Justice Matters*, 78(1): 18–20.
Harper, D. 1988. 'Visual sociology: Expanding sociological vision,' *The American Sociologist*, 19(1): 54–70.
Harper, D. 2001. *Changing Works: Visions of a Lost Agriculture*. Chicago, IL: University of Chicago Press.
Harper, D. 2012. *Visual Sociology*. Abingdon, Oxon, UK: Routledge.
Hayward, H. 2017. 'Documentary criminology. A cultural criminological introduction,' in M. Brown and E. Carrabine (eds.) *Routledge International Handbook of Visual Criminology*, pp. 135–150. Abingdon, Oxon, UK: Routledge.
Hayward, K. and Presdee, M. (ed.). 2010. *Framing Crime: Cultural Criminology and the Image*. Abingdon, Oxon, UK: Routledge.
Holm, G. 2008. 'Visual research methods. where are we and where are we going?' in S. Hesse-Biber and P. Leavy (eds.) *Handbook of Emergent Methods*, pp. 325–341. New York: Guilford Press.
Houston, D. 2013. 'Environmental justice storytelling: Angels and isotopes at Yucca Mountain, Nevada,' *Antipode*, 45(2): 417–435.
Kavanagh, D. 2013. 'The limits of visualisation: Occularcentrism and organization,' in E. Bell, S. Warren and J. E. Schroeder (eds.) *The Routledge Companion to Visual Organization*, pp. 66–78. London: Routledge.
Kohm, S. and Greenhill, P. 2013. '"This is the north, where we do what we want". Popular green criminology and 'little red riding hood' films,' in N. South and A. Brisman (eds.) *Routledge International Handbook of Green Criminology*, pp. 365–376. Abingdon, Oxon, UK: Routledge.
Kong, T., Kellner, K., Austin, D., Els, Y. and Orr, B. 2014. 'Enhancing participatory evaluation of land management through photo elicitation and photovoice,' *Society & Natural Resources: An International Journal*, 28(2): 212–229.
Latour, B., Harman, G., and Erdélyi, P. 2011. *The Prince and the Wolf*. Winchester, UK: Zero Books.
Letham, A. 2004. 'Researching and writing everyday accounts of the city: An introduction to the diary-photo diary-interview method,' in C. Knowles and P. Sweetman (eds.) *Picturing the Social Landscape: Visual Methods and the Sociological Imagination*, pp. 117–130. London: Routledge.
Linnemann, T. and Wall, T. 2013. '"This is your face on meth": The punitive spectacle of "white trash" in the rural war on drugs,' *Theoretical Criminology*, 17(3): 315–334.

McClanahan, B. 2014. 'Green and grey: Water justice, criminalization, and resistance,' *Critical Criminology: An International Journal*, 22(3): 403–418.

McClanahan, B. 2017. 'Capturing Appalachia: Visualizing coal, culture, and ecology,' Doctoral thesis, University of Essex Sloman Library, Colchester, UK.

McClanahan, B. and Linnemann, T. 2018. 'Darkness on the edge of town: Visual criminology and the "black sites" of the rural,' *Deviant Behavior*, 39(4): 512–524.

McClanahan, B., Brisman, A. and South, N. (2017). 'Green criminology, culture, and cinema,' *Oxford Research Encyclopedia of Criminology*. October 9. Available at: http://criminology.oxfordre.com/view/10.1093/acrefore/9780190264079.001.0001/acrefore-9780190264079-e-151.

McIntyre, A. 2008. *Participatory Action Research*. London: Sage Publications.

Mirzoeff, N. 1999. *An Introduction to Visual Culture*. London: Routledge.

Mirzoeff, N. 2011. *The Right to Look: A Counterhistory of Visuality*. Durham, NC: Duke University Press.

Morton, T. 2007. *Ecology without Nature: Rethinking Environmental Aesthetics*. Cambridge, MA: Harvard University Press.

Natali, L. 2010. 'The big grey elephants in the Backyard of Huelva,' in R. White (ed.) *Global Environmental Harm. Criminological Perspectives*, pp. 193–208. Cullompton, Devon, UK: Willan.

Natali, L. 2013a. 'Exploring environmental activism: A visual qualitative approach from an eco-global and green-cultural criminological perspective,' *CRIMSOC: The Journal of Social Criminology*, Special Issue: 'Green Criminology', Autumn 2013: 64–100.

Natali, L. 2013b. 'The contemporary horizon of green criminology,' in N. South and A. Brisman (eds.) *Routledge International Handbook of Green Criminology*, pp. 73–84. Abingdon, Oxon, UK: Routledge.

Natali, L. 2015b. 'A critical gaze on environmental victimization,' in R. Sollund (ed.) *Green Harms and Crimes: Critical Criminology in a Changing World*, pp. 63–78. Basingstoke, Hampshire, UK: Palgrave Macmillan.

Natali, L. 2016a. *A Visual Approach for Green Criminology: Exploring the Social Perception of Environmental Harm*. London: Palgrave Macmillan.

Natali, L. 2016b. 'Soliloqui itineranti e «green cultural criminology». Un approccio visuale e sensoriale alle esperienze di vittimizzazione ambientale,' *Studi Culturali*, December 3: 339–368.

Natali, L. and Budó, M. D. 2018. 'A sensory and visual approach for comprehending environmental victimization by asbestos industry in Casale Monferrato,' *European Journal of Criminology*, July 26. DOI: 10.1177/1477370818788012

Natali, L. and McClanahan, B. 2017. 'Perceiving and communicating environmental contamination and change: Towards a green cultural criminology with images,' *Critical Criminology: An International Journal*, 25(2): 199–214.

Parkin, S. 2014. *An Applied Visual Sociology: Picturing Harm Reduction*. Surrey, UK: Ashgate.

Pauwels, L. 2011. 'An integrated conceptual framework for visual social research,' in E. Margolis and L. Pauwels (eds.) *The SAGE Handbook of Visual Research Methods*, pp. 3–22. London: Sage.

Pauwels, L. 2012. 'Conceptualizing the "visual essay" as a way of generating and imparting sociological insight: Issues, formats and realisations,' *Sociological Research Online*, 17(1): 1–11.

Pauwels, L. 2015. *Reframing Visual Social Science. Towards a More Visual Sociology and Anthropology*. Cambridge: Cambridge University Press.

Pauwels, L. 2017. 'Key methods of visual criminology. An overview of different approches and their affordances,' in M. Brown and E. Carrabine (eds.) *Routledge International Handbook of Visual Criminology*, pp. 62–73. Abingdon, Oxon, UK: Routledge.

Peyrefitte, M. 2012. 'Ways of seeing, ways of being and ways of knowing in the inner-city: Exploring sense of place through visual tours,' *Sociological Research Online*, 17(4): 1–17.

Phillips, L., Kristiansen, M., Vehviläinen, M. and Gunnarsson, E. (eds.) 2013. *Knowledge and Power in Collaborative Research: A Reflexive Approach*. London: Routledge.

Pink, S. 2001. *Visual Ethnography: Images, Media and Representation in Research*. London: Sage.

Rafter, N. 2014. 'Introduction to special issue on visual culture and the iconography of crime and punishment,' *Theoretical Criminology*, 18(2): 127–133.

Redmon, D. 2017. 'Going feral. Kamp Katrina as a case study of documentary criminology,' in M. Brown and E. Carrabine (eds.) *Routledge International Handbook of Visual Criminology*, pp. 151–165. Abingdon, Oxon, UK: Routledge.

Robins, K. 1996. *Into the Image: Culture and Politics in the Field of Vision*. London: Routledge.

Rose, G. 2012. *Visual Methodologies. An Introduction to Researching with Visual Materials*. London: Sage.

Rose, G. 2014. 'On the relation between "visual research methods" and contemporary visual culture,' *The Sociological Review*, 62(I): 24–46.
Ruby, J. 2000. *Picturing Culture: Explorations of Film and Anthropology*. Chicago, IL: University of Chicago Press.
Schept, J. 2014. '(Un)seeing like a prison: Counter-visual ethnography of the carceral state,' *Theoretical Criminology*, 18(2): 198–223.
Scott, D. and Oelofse, C. 2005. 'Social and environmental justice in South African cities: Including 'invisible stakeholders' in environmental assessment procedures,' *Journal of Environmental Planning and Management*, 48(3): 445–467.
Sekula, A. 1981. 'The traffic in photographs,' *Art Journal*, 41(1): 15–25.
Sollund, R. 2012. 'Introduction,' in R. Ellefsen, R. Sollund and G. Larsen (eds.) *Eco-global Crimes: Contemporary Problems and Future Challenges*, pp. 1–3. Surrey, UK: Ashgate.
South, N. 1998. 'A green field for criminology? A proposal for a perspective,' *Theoretical Criminology*, 2 (2): 211–234.
South, N. 2017. 'Monstrous nature. A meeting of gothic, green and cultural criminologies,' in M. Brown and E. Carrabine (eds.) *Routledge International Handbook of Visual Criminology*, pp. 553–565. Abingdon, Oxon, UK: Routledge.
Stanczak, G. C. (ed.) 2007. *Visual Research Methods: Image, Society, and Representation*. London: Sage.
Van de Voorde, C. 2012. 'Ethnographic photography in criminological research,' in D. Gadd, S. Karstedt and M. Steven (eds.) *The Sage Handbook of Criminological Research Methods*, pp. 203–217. London: Sage.
Wall, T. and Linnemann, T. 2014. 'Staring down the state: Police power, visual economies, and the "war on cameras",' *Crime Media Culture*, 10(2): 133–149.
Wang, C. 2006. 'Youth participation in photovoice as a strategy for community change,' *Journal of Community Practice*, 14(1): 147–161.
White, R. 2003. 'Environmental issues and the criminological imagination,' *Theoretical Criminology*, 7(4): 483–506.
Zaitch, D. and de Leeuw, T. 2010. 'Fighting with images: The production and consumption of violence among online football supporters,' in *K.J. Hayward and M. Presdee (eds.) Framing Crime: Cultural Criminology and the Image*, pp. 184–200. Abingdon, Oxon, UK: Routledge-Cavendish.

6

Innovative approaches to researching environmental crime

Diane Heckenberg and Rob White

Introduction

This chapter considers the different ways in which green criminology has—or might be—conducted. It asks critical questions about current approaches, including when and where study should take place, how research might be undertaken, with whose participation and in whose interests? Answering such questions requires an examination of existing conceptual and theoretical approaches to the practice of green criminology, with a view to identifying the complexities of researching transnational environmental crimes and harms. By understanding the challenges of working in this area, we also hope to identify directions for future methodological development. The chapter is not meant to provide a comprehensive overview of research methodologies and methods as such (readers can refer to general social science texts for this purpose). Rather, our intention is to concentrate on several key areas that are particularly important for green criminologists to consider as they undertake research on environmentally related topics.

Methodology here refers to the overall approach to the research process, including the theoretical approach that influences the way the research is designed and conducted, and the lens through which the researcher views the social world. *Method* refers to the technique used to gather and analyse the research data (Walter 2006: 377). We argue that studying environmental crimes and harms demands new ways of looking at the world. It involves considering our location in the world, recognising competing interests from the local to the global, shaping new knowledge alongside others, acknowledging the problems of difference and culture, understanding the impact of colonialism, crossing disciplinary and conceptual borders, coping with the pace of change (particularly new technologies), mapping sites of harm and transference, and discovering lost voices, to name a few.

At a practical level, methodology involves a series of decisions about which research questions to ask, which theories to use, what information and data to gather, how to manage, analyse and synthesise those data, and what interpretation to give to such information in the final analysis. These decisions are complicated by overall shifts in the field as a whole. For instance, developments over the past 25 years have led to new interests, concepts and analytical techniques, as well as new ways of conceptualising crime and harm. In addition to this volume, there are now a number of handbooks and textbooks devoted specifically to green criminology (e.g., Hall 2015; Lynch, Long, Stretesky and Barrett 2017b; Nurse 2016; White and Heckenberg 2014), as well as edited collections and authored books that provide increasingly global coverage of environmental crimes (Beirne and South 2007; Moreto 2018), including Europe and Africa (Potter, Nurse and Hall 2016; Sollund, Stefes and Germani 2016), Scandinavia (Meško, Sotlar and Eman 2012), Central and South America (Arroyo-Quiroz and Wyatt 2018; Goyes, Mol, Brisman and South 2017; Mol 2017), and Asia (Cao 2017). Among the non-English language publications are books in Italian (Natali 2015), Slovenian (Meško, Sotlar and Eman 2012), Spanish (Mol, Goyes, South and Brisman 2017) and a special 'environmental criminality' issue of a journal published in French (Manirabona and Koutouki 2016). There has been considerable interest in such topics in China, Indonesia and Iran, and these countries, too, are producing local versions of green criminology texts, as well as contributing to world literature on environmental crime. Who does green criminology and where they do so shape what is deemed to be important to study and how it is studied.

The dimensions of environmental harm pose challenges for researchers insofar as different types of knowledge are required for dealing with specific kinds of environmental harm. Moreover, analysis needs to take into account considerable diversity in terms of:

- who the victim is (human or non-human)
- where the harm is manifest (from local to global)
- where the harm is most apparent (built or natural environment)
- when, or the time frame within which, the consequences of harm can be analysed (immediate, delayed, intergenerational).

Concepts that inform why we think it is important to conduct research in this area include the precautionary principle (forestalling future harms), questions of justice (issues of fairness and rights), intergenerational equity (the wellbeing of future generations), and compensation and rectification of harms (fixing the harm). We also want to get to the bottom of what happened, how it happened, why it happened and who knew about it and when.

While the complexities of green criminological research need to be acknowledged, they should not deter researchers from engaging in such study. The point of discussing methodology and method is to orient researchers to important substantive and ethical issues, in order to critique and improve what we do now and into the future. Critical reflection on the practice of green criminology is a natural part of building knowledge and technique as we grapple with the challenges of studying environmental harm.

When to conduct research

We live in a constantly changing global society and, consequently, the forms of environmental crime are changing too. As such, we need to engage with more advanced and more flexible methodological approaches to aid our understanding of environmental crime (see Eman, Mesko and Fields 2009: 574). One of the first questions to ask is: at what point do we engage in such research—before something happens, as an event evolves, or after the event? The 'when' (or timing) of research is important methodologically to the extent that where we focus our research gaze has implications in terms of the tools we will use to undertake that research. Consider, for example, the following observations:

- If we choose to analyse harm, risk or crime *before* it occurs (e.g., climate change and the potential for natural disasters), then a method such as 'horizon scanning' may be appropriate because it is based upon extrapolating from what is currently known to forecast future environmental harms and crimes.
- If we choose to study harms and crimes *as they are presently evolving* (e.g., oil rig explosions in ocean settings), then a case study approach that brings together descriptive information and contemporary facts and figures may be the best method.
- If we choose to study a harmful event *after the fact* (e.g., land pollution from mining operations), then analysis of documents and use of interviews may be appropriate to reconstruct the factors that combined to create the problem.
- If we choose to examine an event that is *a number of years in the past* (e.g., poisoning of waterways over many years), then the historical method can be utilised, drawing upon documents, maps and photographs, and site records that facilitate a retrospective analysis of the phenomenon in question.
- If we choose to re-examine significant events or trends (e.g., release of poisonous gases into the atmosphere due to factory explosion), we may find it useful to adopt a *cold case* type of approach, one that re-examines old evidence as well as utilises new types of evidence-gathering, such as environmental DNA techniques, and new sources of evidence, such as narratives of retired factory workers, to provide fresh insights into older cases, and narratives of surviving victims of toxic harm.

If human, biosphere and non-human interests are to be protected in the future, environmental crime prevention must be forward-looking. This means implementing interventions *now* to guarantee environmental wellbeing later (White 2008). It also means learning from the past in order to prevent harmful events from re-occurring. For example, a study of lobster poaching in Canada found a complex underground economy, with alliances between outlaw poachers, hotels, restaurants, community groups and private citizens. This occurred in a social environment in which the taking of lobster was seen as the natural right (and yearly ritual) of locals (McMullan and Perrier 2002). A futures orientation means grappling with such entrenched practices through innovative thinking at both a policy and grounded intervention level.

An innovative temporal analysis might

> spotlight and compare categories of environmental crime that are presently tightly regulated, yet predicted to experience a resurgence in commission (e.g., illegal waste disposal); continue to be problematic in enforcing (e.g., native vegetation clearance); or that have been the recent target of substantial publicity and strengthening of penalties (e.g., water theft).
>
> *(Bricknell 2010: 115)*

In other words, not only can we approach research itself from the point of view of 'before the fact' and 'after the fact', but we can analyse how various activities are socially defined and re-defined over time, and why.

One example of a forward-looking methodological approach to the study of environmental crimes and harms that lie over the horizon involves integrating the core concerns of eco-global criminology (a framework of analysis concerned with ecological, transnational and justice matters) with the futures orientation of horizon scanning (a systematic form of critical thinking about future risks, harms and precautions) (White 2011). As part of this approach, a conceptual framework has been developed as a tool for assessing and analysing environmental risks and harms. The three orientations in the framework—*substantive* (risk, harm and cause), *justice* (environmental, ecological and species) and *futures* (intergenerational equity, the precautionary principle and transference over time)—provide the conceptual building blocks for more detailed analysis of specific issues and trends. As a whole, these three orientations constitute the basis for the particular questions that are relevant to an environmental horizon scanning exercise informed by eco-global criminology (White and Heckenberg 2011: 89–90).

In terms of practical research considerations, the conceptual framework for environmental horizon scanning (see White 2011) translates into a stepped approach, as illustrated in Table 6.1. This table describes a research process that is more or less generic to any social research project. That is, the study of environmental harm—whether retrospective or prospective—demands a systematic approach to data collection and analysis. In addition to matters of timing, consideration of the spatial dimensions of research is also important. Delimiting green criminological research in terms of spatial dimensions may be informed by the geographical scale of the harm or crime itself or by a decision to deliberately focus the research at a specific geographical level (from local through to global).

At what geographical scale to conduct the research?

Sometimes it is useful to concentrate on local area matters and to undertake research that delves into the complicated dynamics of the relatively small scale, while bearing in mind that what occurs on a small scale can have global implications. For example, environmental harm is frequently associated with activities that occur in specific places that exhibit certain local cultural or historical traditions (e.g., cray potting, duck hunting, bird harvesting, four-wheel driving on beaches). In such situations, these activities may simply be considered 'folk crime' (i.e., everyone does it, we have always done it, everyone enjoys the benefits) and perceived as 'harmless fun' in the context of sporting and leisure pursuits.

Other forms of environmental harm are notable for their propensity to cross borders. This may involve all nation-states on the planet, as in the case of ozone depletion or global warming. Or, it may involve the international transference of toxic waste from developed countries of the North to less developed countries of the South (Heckenberg 2010). Air and water pollution crosses national borders and its effects extend beyond the local. Particular regions of the world are subject to certain types of crimes (e.g., killing of elephants in Africa for their tusks, deforestation in the Amazon) that are specific to those regions.

Consideration of scale and focus are implicit in the framing of research into environmental crime. With this in mind, there are at least three different ways in which transnational research can be approached (White 2009):

- *Global research*—examines transnational harms, such as climate change and radioactive fallout, and includes transference of harms worldwide into the open seas of our oceans as well as to nation-states everywhere.
- *Comparative research*—examines particular differences and commonalities between nation-states and specific regions of the world, identifying where the more worrisome environmental harms reside, whether related to pollution, biodiversity or other issues.
- *Historical research*—examines fundamental changes in the global systems of production and consumption over time, such as the shift from feudalism to mercantile capitalism to industrial capitalism, and the different environmental harms associated with these such as global warming (which amongst other factors is linked to carbon emissions stemming from the coal and oil and gas industries).

Table 6.1 Steps to doing environmental horizon scanning

Process		*Example 1*	*Example 2*
Step 1	Identify broad ecological issue	Land use	Climate change
Step 2	Ask what harm is related to this now and in the future?	Types of land use that threaten ecological wellbeing and social justice	Differential effects of climate change on specific population groups, particular ecosystems and particular species
Step 3	Draw upon a wide variety of sources (e.g., cross-cultural, cross-disciplinary, multi-jurisdictional) to investigate a broad ecological issue	Different types of land use, including, for example, replacement of forests by biofuel crops, use of subterranean spaces for radioactive waste	Conflict over resources, climate-induced migration, radical shifts in weather patterns
Step 4	Refine analysis by drilling down to a specific topic	Analysis of specific forms of land use, such as those that diminish biodiversity	Analysis of natural disasters associated with changing weather patterns
Step 5	Read widely on specific topic	Literature on genetically modified organisms (GMOs) and the role of transnational corporations, including, for example, United Nations reports on global biodiversity and literature on de-forestation	Disaster studies literature that links climate change to specific types of disaster (e.g., cyclones, floods) and that expounds issues surrounding cause and effect
Step 6	Collect information and data relevant to specific topic	Information about GMO crop substitution in countries such as Argentina, Brazil and Indonesia	Information about specific natural disasters, such as floods in Pakistan or Hurricane Katrina and associated storms in the United States
Step 7	Systematically investigate the phenomenon in question using the conceptual framework of environmental horizon scanning (e.g., substantive, justice and futures orientations)	Identify which species are threatened, the reasons why this is so and the key variables that together have generated the harm in question (e.g., global agriculture markets)	Identify which places and populations are most at risk, the reasons why this is the case, the key variables that together have generated the harm in question (e.g., lack of infrastructure)
Step 8	Analyse and interpret the information and data in light of eco-global criminological considerations (e.g., transgressions against humans, ecosystems and animals)	Displacement of endemic species from habitat (including humans) and replacement of multiple species (plant and animal) with monoculture	Analysis of environmental victimisation involving particularly vulnerable groups (e.g., women, children, poor, ethnic minorities) and effects of disasters on local ecosystems and species composition
Step 9	Extrapolate the key emerging patterns associated with the information and data on the particular topic	Forced removal of people from traditional lands, substitution of existing species with single species and further diminishment of biodiversity	Breakdown in law and order, prevalence of chaotic living conditions and massive changes to local ecosystems and species composition

(*Continued*)

Table 6.1 (Cont.)

Process		*Example 1*	*Example 2*
Step 10	Analyse the information in light of the varied discourses surrounding cause, harm and victimisation from the point of view of relationships of power	Examine statements by governments, corporations, communities, experts and others about land use issues	Examine statements by media outlets, governments, non-government organisations and global agencies about a particular disaster
Step 11	Theorise the findings in relation to anthropogenic causes (e.g., human responsibility for harm, specific perpetrators and degrees of culpability)	Transnational corporations and governments that privilege sectional interests over those of local communities and particular species	Government officials and local building contractors who have a duty of care vis-à-vis requisite construction standards and provision of adequate preventive measures
Step 12	Reflect on possible avenues for action or strategic intervention that will best forestall or mitigate the impact and consequences of the future trend (e.g., application of the precautionary principle)	Community engagement in local and regional planning processes, including environmental impact assessments, United Nations involvement in protecting traditional ownership and land uses	Regulation of building codes and instigation of community policing models based around local participation and neighbourhood security
Step 13	Communicate the findings, bearing in mind the varied audiences for the particular research topic	Local communities, local councils, regional governments	Planning and municipal decision-makers, construction companies, law enforcement officials, non-government aid organisations

White and Heckenberg (2011: 98–99), by permission of Springer.

Expanding the scope and vision of research to include worldwide institutions, social processes and conduits of power (including resistance) is essential to contemporary green criminology. The important thing is that research needs to take place at different levels of scale from the local to the global. The international nature of issues, trends, comparisons and networks is vital and ought to complement work conducted at local, country and regional levels.

Studying environmental crimes and harms in a global context is one of the greatest challenges we face. Some issues are of a planetary scale (e.g., climate change), others regional (e.g., oceans and fisheries), some are national in geographical location (e.g., droughts in Australia), while others are local (e.g., specific oil spills). Table 6.2 outlines the types of geographical scale important to the study of environmental harm.

When we talk about scale, it is not just geography that matters. The notion of scale also applies to the nature, size and social organisation of specific criminal activities. Illegal fishing, for example, may involve huge factory ships that operate on the high seas, and which process thousands of tons of fish at any one time. Alternatively, it may be organised around dozens of smaller vessels, each of which is contracted to provide a catch that ultimately brings reward to the originating contractor. In other words, illegal production can be organised according to economies of scale (e.g., factory ships) or economies of scope (e.g., small

Table 6.2 Geographical scale of environmental harm

Scale	*Example*
Local	Lobster poaching in Nova Scotia, Canada Abalone theft in Tasmania, Australia
National	Nitrate pollution related to pastoral industry in New Zealand Issues of drinking water in Israel, Jordan and Palestine
Regional	Logging in the forests of the Amazon Killing of elephants as part of the ivory trade in Africa
Global	Climate change and natural disasters Formation of huge plastic dumps in oceans
Transnational	Global trade in toxic waste Shifting of dirty industries to developing countries

Source: adapted from White 2011.

independent fishers). In each case, however, there has to be a link to legitimate markets (e.g., for abalone, for lobsters) for the value of the commodity to be realised in monetary terms. In addition, in each case, the damage is manifest in phenomena such as over-fishing and destruction of habitat that, in turn, affect subsequent market prices for the commodity in question. Scarcity is a major motivator for illegal as well as legal forays into particular kinds of harvesting and production activity (White 2008, 2009).

In practical terms, we suggest that the question concerning 'what level to study something' be informed by prior knowledge of scale, more generally. To study transnational environmental crimes and harms, therefore, requires knowledge of geography (where countries are) and an awareness of the way in which the world is divided up (ecologically, geopolitically), as well as the geographies of power inherent in these divisions. We suggest, quite literally, that researchers post a map of the world (Figure 6.1) on their walls to familiarise themselves with:

- continents (e.g., Africa, South America)
- countries (e.g., Argentina, Cambodia, United States)
- blocks (e.g., European Union, Latin America)
- regions (e.g., Amazon, South East Asia)
- countries with shared borders and waterways (transference of harm)
- global zones and spaces (e.g., Arctic, ocean gyres, outer space, subterranean)
- direction of ocean and air currents (transference of harm).

Examine the variety of maps that divide the world up in different ways:

- climate
- crime rates (top ten countries with highest reported crime rates)
- electricity consumption
- exports/imports
- food consumption
- geographically (lowlands, mountains, rivers)

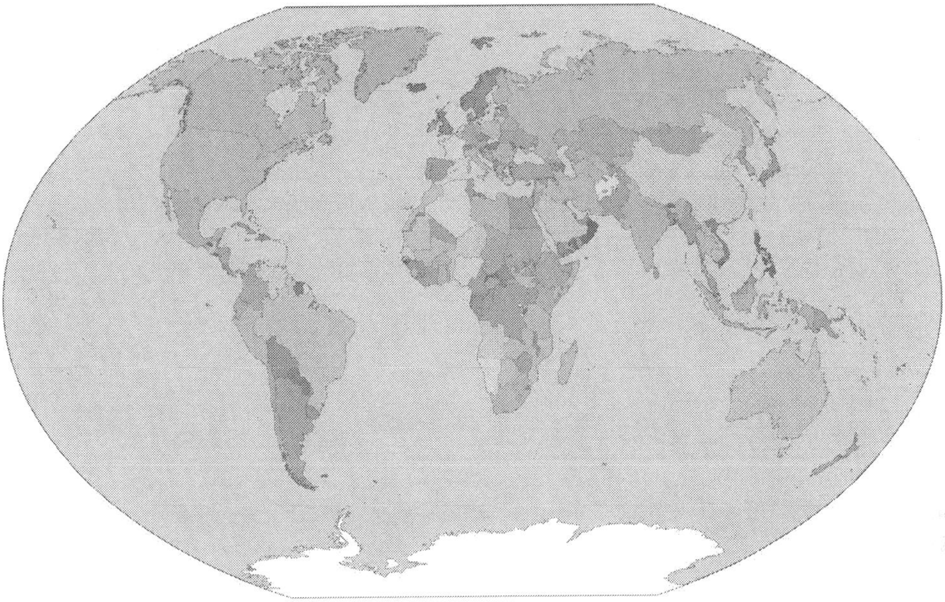

Figure 6.1 Map of the world

- gross domestic product
- language
- literacy
- militarily (top ten countries with armies)
- politically (nation-states)
- religion
- seaports
- vegetation
- wealth (richest/poorest countries)
- wind and pressure.

[See Mapsofworld.com, 2011 www.mapsofworld.com]

Part of this awareness involves locating ourselves as researchers in a global context, both geographically and in relation to the other features listed above. Studying environmental harms and crimes demands that we learn more about the world generally, how harm is circulated within this world, and where we fit into the overall global picture.

What data to collect and how

The study of transnational environmental harm requires appreciation of specific methodological and conceptual issues that impinge upon the data collection process. Some of these issues include the ethics and politics of 'outsiders' researching other people's cultures, patterns and practices, the differential availability and types of data in different jurisdictions, and the ways in which state denial and corporate resistance can impede the research process.

Technologies, such as satellites and DNA testing, are relevant to the discussion, as are considerations of the expertise provided by scientists, Indigenous peoples and local actors, such as fishers and farmers (White 2009).

A wide range of data sources can be drawn upon to substantiate claims about environmental crimes and harms and their causes. The principle of *triangulation* refers to the idea that any one data source should be cross-checked by drawing upon other sources so as to ensure accuracy, reliability and validity. Table 6.3 provides some examples of different types of data sources that can be useful for examining environmental crimes and harms.

There has been little sustained effort to bring together official and alternative sources of information, much less data between different government departments and criminal justice agencies (such as activist groups, animal welfare service providers, data collected by non-government

Table 6.3 Types of data sources

Data source	*Example*
Documents	Annual reports; correspondence such as emails, letters, memos; decision trees; flow charts; minutes of meetings; speeches; sustainability reports
Media reports	Articles; cartoons; letters to the editor; newspaper columns and editorials; opinion pieces; special documentaries
Official statistics	Bureau of Justice statistics, census, consumer product safety incident reports, crime commissions, occupational health and safety statistics
Court records	Briefs, opinions, sentencing reports
Official enquiries	Commissions, coronial inquests, panels, state inquiries
Web-based records	Blogs, corporate press releases, internet sites and home pages, video clips
Paper-based records	Diaries, journals, tracking records
Literature reviews	Community research, government reports and white papers, journal articles
Surveys	Questionnaires, telephone surveys, suggestion boxes
Group discussions	Invited respondents, public meetings, teleconferences
Focus groups	Specific sample groups, followed by briefing and de-briefing sessions
Life histories	Autobiographical narratives, storytelling
Field observations	Field research and visits, participant observation
Peer research	Friendship, family and kinship networks
Social media	Facebook, Instagram, Twitter
Maps	Geographical, networks, systems and flows, topographical
Victim statements	Victim impact statements, narratives of families and caregivers
Health information	Disease clusters, mortality statistics, toxicology reports
Self-reports	Emissions by industry to air, land and water
Images	Photographs of environmental disasters, images from closed-circuit cameras, videos
Cinema	Films about environmental issues (e.g., *The Day After Tomorrow*)
Documentaries	Films on topics such as climate change (e.g., *An Inconvenient Truth, Chasing Ice*) and fracking (e.g., *FrackNation, Gasland*)
Unobtrusive measures	Remote cameras, satellite pictures, tracking devices
Legislation and Enactment debates	Congressional and Parliamentary records (e.g., Hansard) to determine legislative intent
Television	Discovery Channel; National Geographic

organisations, journalist accounts, police files). Moreover, the quantity and quality of data collected is influenced by the capacity and resources available to agencies and/or countries for its collection, as well as by the political priority attached to the gathering and disseminating of such data (White 2009). The fact that specific data are generated in variable ways by a range of agencies inevitably means that wide disparities exist in the detail, geographic coverage, scale, scope and time frames of the data. This makes comparative studies difficult. Data collection therefore is always a social process in motion, a continuous 'work in progress'. At the heart of this process are a series of interrelated matters: namely, which questions and which information will provide the most meaningful data, from whom and what sources will it be collected, to whom will it be made available and for what purposes. 'Who' is collecting 'what', for 'whom' and 'why' are essential questions when it comes to data on environmental crimes and harms, and there are inevitably important ethical questions underpinning green criminological research (see Brisman and South 2017; White 2017).

The complexity of environmental issues demands responses that are multi-pronged, although this is easier said than done, especially if research has international dimensions. For instance, a number of issues and considerations must be taken into account in devising and implementing cross-national research projects. A brief summary of some of these is provided in Table 6.4. Several of the points raised in this table are worth considering in greater depth.

What we can learn from has to also include alternative sources which go well beyond conventional academic and 'official' bureaucratically provided material. This can include information from company records, the internet, media stories, medical information, non-government organisations and scientific studies of varying kinds, in addition to legends, myths, storytelling and traditions (see Table 6.3).

Table 6.4 Issues, limitations and constraints in data collection and analysis

Practical issues	• Language differences (and subtleties of culture)
	• Access to countries and regions
	• Expense of research
	• Expertise required for the research (e.g., 'local' or outsider)
Scientific limitations	• Availability and accessibility of data
	• Diverse definitions of crime and harm
	• Criteria used for comparisons
	• Technical equipment and expertise in data collection
	• Issues relating to the generalisation of findings
Political constraints	• Resistance to data collection
	• Denial of harm on the part of the powerful
	• State denial and corporate resistance to research process
	• Corruption of officials
	• Misinformation
Ethical issues	• Ethics and politics of 'outsiders' researching other people's territory
	• Issues of parochialism and paternalism
	• Whose knowledge is valued
	• Whose voices are heard

Source: drawing from White (2009).

Alternative sources of data, however, come in different forms and different guises, each with their own strengths and limitations. Three examples will illustrate this.

NGOs and data collection

Non-government organisations (NGOs) are often engaged in data collection based upon their own research and through devising innovative systems and methods of counting and recording environmental harms across national boundaries. Greenpeace, for example, has a physical presence in 40 countries, and the International Fund for Animal Welfare has staff in 15 countries and projects in more than 40 countries. NGOs such as these, in addition to well-known agencies such as Traffic and the Environmental Investigation Agency, provide extensive monitoring and data collection around issues (such as deforestation, illegal fishing, the illegal trade in natural resources and the illegal trade in wildlife) in specific regions as well as globally. Many transnational NGOs are in a prime position to provide cross-national insights into particular kinds of environmental crime and criminality. They also provide data on the interface between human rights and environmental protection, as illustrated, for example, by NGO-compiled reports on the murder of environmental defenders (see Global Witness 2018). Indeed, undertaking research in hostile social environments—such as non-democratic regimes and in relation to underground criminal networks—poses unique methodological challenges for green criminologists and environmental activists alike (Stefes and Theodoratos 2017; Wong, 2015).

Medical data to expose criminal harm

Lynch and Stretesky (2002) argue that: harm exists where evidence can be presented that the processes and products in question are reasonably expected to harm human health (e.g., medical data); toxic harms can be placed into context by comparing them with other harms that society considers serious (e.g., assault rifle homicide versus pesticide exposure deaths); and, criminal responsibility exists where there is evidence that corporations have had knowledge of the risks they create or are indifferent to those risks (e.g., silence or rejection of alternatives). Importantly, any claims along these lines are not reliant upon traditional criminological evidence (the usual crime data sets and criminal justice statistics) to be substantiated empirically. Medical records and epidemiological data can be drawn upon to establish the reality of the harm and to raise the possibility of criminal action against the perpetrators.

Photo elicitation

The use of visual methods (for example, the use and/or taking of photographs) in conducting green criminological research provides an innovative and thought-provoking method of investigation. The use of 'photo elicitation' involves research based on images generated by the researcher and/or by the subjects of the research in order to investigate social phenomena. In green criminology, for instance, this method has been used to investigate social perceptions of environmental contamination and thereby to better understand how people see, feel, react to and remember particular places (Natali 2010, 2016; Natali and McClanahan 2017, this volume, Chapter 5). By learning how to 'listen visually', green criminologists can gain rich insight into the varied dimensions of nature–human interaction. Importantly, this extends to historical relationships as well as the present; a picture is worth a thousand words, particularly when it evokes memory, emotion and sense of connection.

A robust methodology might include both quantitative and non-quantitative methods (Lynch et al., 2017a). Specific issues demand different approaches and the development of responses relevant to the nature of the problem, and there are bound to be complexities regardless of the approach taken. For example, qualitative criminological research, such as ethnographic study, demands that trust and rapport be formed with those with whom the researcher is engaged (Moreto 2017). A case study approach may be appropriate for some types of investigation; others will require statistical comparisons and analysis. A variety of research methods can and should be employed, especially for research that is interdisciplinary in nature.

The use of science and technology as part of researching environmental crimes and harms is crucial. This means that criminologists need to be aware of and work with a variety of sciences. Environmental forensics provides a case in point. Techniques relevant to green criminology include DNA testing of animals, fish, soils and timber in order to track their illegal movement; chemical fingerprinting in relation to oil spills; satellite surveillance and remote sensing in regards to land clearance and deforestation; site analysis and mapping in relation to air and water pollution; and toxicology and chemical analysis of contaminated landfill sites and factory outlets (see White and Heckenberg 2014). By drawing upon multiple scientific studies and knowledge production techniques, composite socio-ecological accounts of harm can be compiled.

Whatever methodology is selected, researchers need to be conscious of the diversity of social situations and situated knowledge—related to age, class, ethnicity, gender and race—that will have a bearing on their knowledge about the environment. A socially inclusive research programme is one that acknowledges this, as well as the intersections of age-based discrimination, class exploitation, colonial oppression, ethnic and racial injustice, and gender inequality with environmental degradation (White 2009: 245).

A typical case study (e.g., heavy metal pollution of soil in a mining town) involves interacting with key stakeholders (e.g., local doctors, local activists), being 'in the field' or conducting 'site' visits (e.g., to the town or affected community), 'participant observation' (observing first-hand in the research setting), conducting in-depth face-to-face interviews, and producing, sorting, transcribing and then analysing 'interview data'. A case study may also rely upon secondary data gained and distilled from the internet, including academic literature, company profiles on corporate websites, consumer and environmental activist voices, corporate press releases, media statements, statistics from wide-ranging sources, transcripts of government inquiries and video clips. One approach to the perennial issue of generalisation (i.e., how applicable is this one case to other instances of environmental harm?) is to consider the idea of 'naturalistic generalisation', which refers to context-specific knowledge gained by the *reader* of the case study. Melrose (2009) describes 'naturalistic generalisation' as the process by which the reader of the case study gains insight (or self-generated knowledge) by reflecting on the specifics of the case study and how the case resonates with his or her own experience. Thus, the reader reflects on how the details of a particular case study can be generalised to his or her own experience or research (Heckenberg 2011).

A specific case study, like the one suggested above for instance, may resonate with a reader examining a different form of harm, a different mode of transference or a different industry domain (e.g., with particular issues pertaining to power, evidence and control). Each case study undertaken may simultaneously add to an existing repository of similar stories and similar processes (e.g., thereby raising issues of time/space commonalities and differences). The findings from multi-disciplinary research can contribute to a 'research frontier' (Mjoset, 2009), in this case green criminology, while at the same time adding to a repository of work that examines specific environmental harms and crimes.

Which knowledge and whose voice?

All forms of knowledge are valuable. The key is to validate the various forms of knowledge in ways that are respectful to their contributors, and to integrate them into our work, while giving due acknowledgement to their strengths and limitations.

At the heart of investigations of transnational environmental harm is the question: whose knowledge of 'wrong' is right? In other words, whose voices are going to be heard and which kinds of evidence are to be given credibility? It is rare that scientific evidence is uncontested and proof of environmental harm is simply a matter of 'let the facts decide'. For example, what counts as 'science', what counts as 'evidence', who counts as being a 'scientific expert' and what counts as 'sensible' public policy are all influenced by factors such as economic situation, the scientific tradition within a particular national context, the scientific standards that are used in relation to specific issues and the style and mode of government (White 2008). There are several different types of knowledge including common sense, experiential, scientific and technical. There are many different sources of knowledge, in addition to scientific disciplines, including the knowledge of the layperson, the knowledge of workers, such as farmers, fishers and loggers, the knowledge of Indigenous peoples in diverse settings and the knowledge of technicians who use particular instruments to measure and appraise aspects of the world around them.

Knowledge is always tied to *someone* and *somewhere*. It is not socially neutral but reflects particular interests and relations of power. Accordingly, one task for green criminology is to identify the diverse and multiple discourses that collectively describe the world around us, in the context of particular environmental issues. These discourses are varied and many, and in many cases are in competition. Table 6.5 provides an outline of various types of discourse that we consider are useful to study in greater depth.

The issues associated with analysing the discourses and interests that underpin who is saying what (in this case, about environmental harms and crimes) are contained in the literature on discourse analysis. From a research perspective, we wish to highlight issues relating to the power relations that are pertinent to working with vulnerable population groups or groups outside the centres of world power.

Moving beyond one's own national borders to work with people in other locales and from other cultures is complicated by a range of factors. Gaining access to countries, regions and specific sites may be an issue, as is the expense associated with transnational study. University researchers may have to negotiate with relevant institutional review boards and human research ethics committees for permission to undertake research abroad. Language differences and the subtleties of culture may intrude into the research process by causing delays, leading to misunderstandings about substantive issues. The expertise required to undertake research is a perennial issue: outside 'experts' are the bane of many a developing country's existence insofar as local knowledge and capacity building is ignored in favour of relying on 'trained' personnel from the metropole (see Stanley 2008). On the other hand, the political realities within some nation-states suggest that it may be best that an 'outsider' carry out the research if issues of safety, security and independent knowledge production are at stake. Insider/outsider relationships are contingent, therefore, upon local resources, staff availability and political contexts, and thus require 'sensitivity to situation' on the part of 'outside' researchers (White 2009: 236).

Table 6.5 Discourses and language of environmental issues

Legal discourses
- How the law defines the issues (e.g., crime, culpability, liability, responsibility)
- Different legislation covering different aspects of the environment (e.g., health, environment, occupational health and safety, water)

Policing and regulatory discourses
- Including Environmental Protection Agencies (e.g., proof of wrongdoing)
- Assigning institutional responsibility for doing something
- Non-government organisations, watchdogs and advocates

Scientific discourses
- Including competing expertise (e.g., toxicology versus medical practitioners)
- In-house science and independent scientific review
- Industry experts and scientists

Community/lay discourses
- Competing claims regarding the 'best interests of the community'
- Including local 'experts' (e.g., general practitioners, Indigenous people, local residents)
- Social network sites and communication (e.g., Facebook, Instagram, Twitter, YouTube)

Tradition-based discourses
- Indigenous understandings of nature and social life
- Traditional ways of doing things and seeing things based upon longer-term settlement history
- Inter-generational acceptance of the way things are and ought to be

Occupation discourses
- Related to specific types of activities (e.g., farmers, fishers, loggers)
- Activities related to traditional and Indigenous living and subsistence practices

Litigation discourses
- Claims over damages from environmental victims (e.g., repairing the harm)
- Claims over damages to reputation and production by industry (e.g., Strategic Lawsuits Against Public Participation (SLAPP))

Media discourses
- Investigative journalism
- Current affairs shows and sensationalist accounts
- Internet sites, including blogs
- Live chat rooms associated with documentaries (e.g., *Sixty Minutes* in Australia and the United States)

Victim discourses
- Narratives of the victimised (men, women and children)
- Narratives of indirect victims (families, friends, overseas relatives)
- Human accounts on behalf of affected non-human animals

First responder discourses
- Narratives of rescuers (police, fire fighters, emergency services)
- International NGOs (Médicins Sans Frontières, Amnesty International)

Corporate discourses
- Annual reports and sustainability reports on websites
- Environmental and civic awards
- Media statements

International agency discourses
- Health and wellbeing (e.g., World Health Organisation)

(Continued)

Table 6.5 (Cont.)

- Economic issues and international development (e.g., International Monetary Fund, World Bank)
- Regulation, security and human rights (e.g., United Nations)

Activist discourses

- Environmental NGOs (e.g. Animal Liberation Front, Earth First!, Greenpeace, Sea Shepherd)
- Progressive radical movements (e.g. ecological, feminist, socialist)
- Reactionary social movements (e.g., neo-Nazi, religious fundamentalist)

Source: drawing from and adding to White and Heckenberg (2011: 96).

Such sensitivity, in turn, points to the importance of working alongside others and respecting their knowledge as guiding concepts in transnational research. How is it possible to be sensitive to situation and context if you are not actually talking and engaging with local people (including local intellectuals, broadly defined)? The notion of insider/outsider is a real and meaningful distinction that is forged in the crucible of local experiences, long-standing cultural traditions, relationship to imperial power and positioning in the wider global political economy. Bridging the gap requires dialogue (not monologue), listening (not lecturing) and give-and-take interchange (not just giving, or just taking) (White 2009: 236). Informed expertise is built upon processes that expand the horizons of knowledge and that, as part of this, incorporate the insights of people from many different backgrounds. This requires openness to the interplay between age, class, ethnicity, gender, race and other social variables in differentially positioning people (individually and collectively) in regards to social location and situated knowledge. It also demands adoption of multiple methods of study and a wide variety of ways in which to engage in dialogic social relationships (see, for example, Banerjee and Bell 2007).

There are ways to ensure that researchers are not simply 'taking'—that they are not exploiting the vulnerable and that they are not misleading in their representations of situated knowledge. For instance, Dodson and colleagues (2007) describe the dilemmas and opportunities associated with research about the lives and perspectives of marginalised people living in a variety of social settings. Interestingly, and usefully, they speak of a methodological practice called 'interpretive focus groups'. On the one hand, research is oriented toward involving a wide range of participants in the research practice (e.g., hearing the voices from below, including the voices of those groups which historically have been disregarded or excluded from such research conversations). On the other hand, people from the same localities and social backgrounds are asked to participate in panels to discuss and interpret the findings (e.g., assessing the meaning of what has been said in the first phase of the research). This acknowledges that marginalised populations will, on occasion, be silent or hide certain things due to fears or suspicions related to what might be revealed about themselves and their lives that could make them vulnerable in relation to authority figures and mainstream institutions. The experience and expertise of local residents helps us understand why and how respondents speak as they do, and is thus considered alongside that of the 'academic' per se. Without this interpretive lens, there may be misinterpretation of what people are actually saying. The process of utilising interpretive focus groups enables researchers to approach data analysis collaboratively, and thus to capture more accurately and ethically the 'truths' of those with whom they are interacting (White 2009: 237–238).

Ascertaining 'truth', however, works in more than one direction. It is not only 'hearing' what is really being said, but also involves interpreting and contextualising what is being conveyed. For example, specific groups who experience environmental problems may not always describe or see the issues in strictly environmental terms. This may be related to lack of awareness of the environmental harm, alternative explanations for the calamity (e.g., an act of God) and socio-economic pressures to 'accept' environmental risk in return for economic reward (see Julian 2004). Waldman (2007), for instance, describes a local community in South Africa that saw the contamination effects of asbestos as 'natural'. This was due to a combination of religious beliefs (that stressed a passive stance to the world around them) and the fact that often harms that are imperceptible to the senses only exist as a problem if they are constituted as such in public discourse (and, in particular, the public discourse of the village community). Otherwise, what is, simply is as it is. Something that is considered to be caused 'naturally' or created tends not to generate the same anger, angst and conflict as that which is perceived to be due to human error and/or conscious intervention. In these circumstances, appeal to scientific knowledge and a collaborative approach to making sense of what is happening is required. Otherwise, the 'common sense' knowledge belies the actual nature of the harm, and what is needed to address it. This is necessarily a highly political and sensitive process.

The imposition of outside frames of reference can also constitute a form of exploitation. This has both material and socio-cultural consequences, and can be seen, for example, in the acquisition of large areas of arable land in developing countries by foreign governments and private companies (Sutherland et al. 2009: 5). These land acquisitions are having major negative impacts on local people who are losing access and control over the resources on which they depend, and which are the rightful inheritance of future generations. Importantly, these problems are compounded in some cases by the ways in which 'conservation' is being foisted upon these same communities. As Duffy (2010: 11) points out:

> When wildlife reserves are established, local communities can suddenly find that their everyday subsistence activities have been outlawed and they have been redefined as criminals ... Some of the world's best-known pristine wilderness areas are, in fact, engineered environments. Creating a national park means drawing up new conservation rules which outlaw the everyday subsistence activities of local communities, such as hunting for food and collecting wood.

From an historical perspective, the imposition of colonial power was intrinsically a matter of resource colonisation—a phenomenon that affected many different Indigenous peoples in places such as Australasia, North America and South America, as well as the native inhabitants of Africa, Asia and beyond. In places such as Australia, Indigenous territories were considered frontier lands that were un-owned, under-utilised and therefore open to exploitation. The prior ownership rights, interests and knowledge of Indigenous inhabitants were treated as irrelevant by the European invaders. Environmental victimisation has been central to dispossession and maltreatment of Indigenous peoples over many continents and over a period of several centuries. Whose knowledge is privileged in interpreting 'the best interest' has been vital to dispossession and disregard in relation to Indigenous and traditional cultures.

Issues of understanding and exploitation must be kept in mind as green criminologists assert a more active role for themselves. Here the insights and approaches of 'southern criminology' are important. This refers to an approach to knowledge, knowledge production and knowledge consumption that emphasises the importance of dialogue between the (geographical and metaphorical) North and South (Carrington et al. 2019; Carrington, Hogg, Scott and Sozzo 2018; Carrington, Hogg and Sozzo 2016), the importance of listening to many voices, and of opening our minds to diverse ways of seeing, feeling and thinking. Inclusive research includes auto-ethnography (Sollund 2017). It also acknowledges forgotten or over-looked contributions from the South, and the longstanding connections between southern criminology and green criminology (Goyes and South 2017). It can involve calls for social action around ecological as well as human rights issues (Ruggiero and South 2010). How we do this depends upon various concrete factors, including who, precisely, is to be included in this advocacy work and how we approach it.

To talk about whose voices are heard means that we must also reflect critically on the dominant voices within our own field of green criminology itself. Key questions here include:

- Whose voices are heard?
- How and when are voices heard?
- Where are those voices located?
- What is the gender (or class, race, etc.) bias in those voices?
- Which topics are studied and which issues are given priority?
- What do we know about scholars in regions of the world other than our own?
- Do we silence dissenting voices by not quoting them?
- Do we discount certain voices because of a failure to grasp what it is they are saying?
- In what ways can we collaborate, in practice, with those living, working and researching elsewhere?
- What languages are not privileged in the global dialogue about environmental harm, and is universal translation possible?

Funding is one issue that can influence whose voice(s) are heard in the academic landscape. Larger universities in developed countries are more likely to attract substantial funding than smaller universities in the developed world, and some universities in the developing world may attract little or no funding at all. Innovative approaches to research might also consider more cost-effective ways of moving beyond the parochial. One way of accomplishing this is to engage in well-designed research projects and programmes of study. The best example of this that the authors are aware of is CoCoon.

CoCoon is an international knowledge, research and innovation programme on Conflict and Cooperation over Natural Resources in Developing Countries (see CoCoon at www.nwo.nl › content › wotro › CoCooN_programme_book_2015-pdf). The programme is jointly funded by the Directorate General of Development Cooperation (DGIS) of the Ministry of Foreign Affairs and the Netherlands Organisation for Scientific Research (NWO) and is part of the NWO's Conflict and Security theme. Projects funded by CoCoon are transdisciplinary and combine knowledge generation (through the sharing and the use of existing knowledge as well as research) and capacity development, with the ultimate goal of innovation in policy and practice for transforming conflicts over natural resources in developing countries. The CoCoon criteria for funding include:

- Coherence and synergy in project and process design
- Potential for capacity development
- Quality of knowledge generation and research and potential for innovation
- Relevance for development.

A project on land-use change in Columbia and Brazil provides an example of a CoCoon project's design (see Boekhout van Solinge and Zaitch 2010). Certain groups and local communities are suffering cultural, economic and social disadvantage, as well as environmental injustice, as a consequence of significant land-use changes linked to specific sectoral interests (such as mining and agricultural companies). As a result, there is a need to strengthen organisations and communities in the course of developing a rights-based approach to development. Accordingly, the project used many *different methods and approaches*—such as water testing and social mapping—in order to cover a number of *interrelated issues* relating to water and land use. It engaged a variety of *project participants* (North, South, activist, researcher), as well as *community-based stakeholders* (from the local areas within the identified regions). This kind of social action research provides an ideal model for what can be achieved when the parameters of that research are supported fully—and a requirement set by—the funding body.

The CoCoon project described here is also notable in that it involves both engagement with local communities as well as an element of 'studying up' (Connell 2007; Nader 1969), that is, focusing on the powerful as well as the less powerful in regards to regional issues. Extrapolating from this, we can make the argument that studying perpetrators is not only vital, but can be approached using a variety of techniques and methods, including:

- *Chronological analysis*—study of temporal developments, such as sequences of events, that can link the originator of the problem to the final criminal act (e.g., toxic dumping).
- *Company analysis*—study of specific company profiles in terms of history, activities and relationships to particular local communities (e.g., Trafigura, Monsanto).
- *Modus operandi analysis*—study of mode of operation of perpetrators and how this differs from the mode of operation of regulators (e.g., tends to be loose, transnational, motivated by singular purposes and involves networks on an ad hoc basis).
- *Stakeholder analysis*—study of particular industries and identification of who key suspects might be (e.g., financial backers of illegal logging, shipping companies).
- *Transaction analysis*—study of markets and understanding the social dynamics pertaining to the particular crime (e.g., illegal wildlife trade).

Resistance to data collection may accompany denial of harm on the part of the powerful (Brisman and South 2015a, 2015b; Kramer 2013; Wyatt and Brisman 2017). Research may also be seen as 'dangerous' to vested interests if corruption of officials is widespread. Research into environmental crimes and harms may well provoke negative reactions on the part of powerful interest groups. Many different strategies are used to silence critics, to dampen resistance and to minimise public outcry, including violation of human rights (Salama and White 2017; White 2011). This, too, is a challenge for those dedicated to doing green criminology research.

Conclusion

Green criminology is about studying the continuum of environmental transgressions from harmful to criminal and from local to global. To be truly global, we must not only foster the development of cross-disciplinary knowledge, but also capture the voices of criminologists from different parts of the world by considering their views and citing them in our research. Whether we work individually, in small groups or collectively, we are bound by the research endeavour itself and the ideals of social and environmental justice. Grounding research in the academic literature of different countries and cultures, incorporating the knowledge of diverse scholars, and engaging with the particular environmental crimes and harms that impact the lived realities of people in diverse places can bring a new energy and vitality to green criminological research. In other words, research on transnational environmental harm is carried out for a purpose—namely, to help address issues of pressing concern that are destroying environments, non-human species and human lives in the here and now, as well as those that threaten our planetary future.

We conclude this chapter by highlighting one other source of knowledge, information and data that we ignore at our peril. This is elder knowledge and expertise. It is from the older members of our community that we have so much to learn when it comes to environmental landscapes of the past and the beliefs, values and environmental histories and practices of former generations. One of our favourite elders is David Suzuki. In his book *Legacy* (Suzuki 2010: 61), he recounts the following anecdote:

> A documentary on fishing, *Empty Oceans, Empty Nets*, shown on PBS in 2002, featured an interview with a young skipper on a swordfish boat from Boston who stated that there are still plenty of swordfish. Based in Boston, she travels to Newfoundland, where she reported hearing that a 200-pound swordfish had been caught. 'There are still big ones', she said. The film then cut to an interview with a grizzled fisherman who must have been in his eighties. He recounted that he used to fish just 5 or 6 miles out of Boston and would throw back anything under 200 pounds! Two fishers with radically different baselines. To the young skipper, a trip all the way to Newfoundland was standard procedure, while a 200-pounder was a big fish. (In fact, the average size of swordfish before 1963 was 266 pounds; it had fallen to 133 pounds in 1973, and to 90 pounds in 1996).

The bottom line for research into environmental harms and crimes is that, ultimately, there is a need and an urgency to better identify, understand and deal with varying kinds of global harms. Building a better world for people, ecosystems, plants and non-human animals depends upon it. There is much to be done.

References

Arroyo-Quiroz, I. and Wyatt, T. (ed.). 2018. *Green Crime in Mexico: A Collection of Case Studies*. London: Palgrave Macmillan.

Banerjee, D. and Bell, M. 2007. 'Ecogender: Locating gender in environmental social science,' *Society and Natural Resources*, 20(1): 3–19.

Beirne, P. and N. South (eds.). 2007. *Issues in Green Criminology: Confronting Harms Against Environments, Humanity and Other Animals*. Cullompton, Devon, UK: Willan.

Boekhout van Solinge, T. B. and Zaitch, D. 2010. *Lands and Rights in Troubled Waters: Environmental* Harm *and* Conflict in the Tapajós (Brazil) and Cauca (Colombia) Basins. September 2011. Available at: http://landsandrights.blog.com/about/.

Bricknell, S. 2010. 'Environmental crime in Australia,' *AIC Reports: Research and Public Policy Series 109*. Available at: www.aic.gov.au/documents/2/1/1/%7B211B5EB9-E888-4D26-AED4-1D4E76646E4B%7Drpp109.pdf.

Brisman, A. and South, N. 2015a. '"Life stage dissolution", infantilization and anti-social consumption: Implications for de-responsibilization, denial and environmental harm,' *Young – Nordic Journal of Youth Research*, 23(3): 209–221.

Brisman, A. and South, N. 2015b. 'New "folk devils", denials and climate change: Applying the work of Stanley Cohen to green criminology and environmental harm,' *Critical Criminology: An International Journal*, 23(4): 449–460.

Brisman, A. and South, N. 2017. 'Methodological approaches and ethical challenges in green criminology,' in M. Cowburn, L. Gelsthorpe and A. Wahidin (eds.) *Research Ethics in Criminology: Dilemmas, issues and solutions*, pp. 166–182. London: Routledge.

Cao, N. 2017. *Timber Trafficking in Vietnam: Crime, Security and the Environment*. London: Palgrave Macmillan.

Carrington, K., R. Hogg, J. Scott and M. Sozzo (eds.). 2018. *The Palgrave Handbook of Criminology and the Global South*. London: Palgrave Macmillan.

Carrington, K., Dixon, B., Fonseca, D., Goyes, D. R., Liu, J. and Zysman, D. 2019. 'Criminologies of the global south: Critical reflections,' *Critical Criminology: An International Journal*, 27(1): 163–189. DOI: 10.1007/s10612-019-09450 -y.

Carrington, K., Hogg, R. and Sozzo, M. 2016. 'Southern criminology', *The British Journal of Criminology*, 56(1): 1–20.

Connell, R. 2007. *Southern Theory: The Global Dynamics of Knowledge in Social Science*. Sydney: Allen & Unwin.

Dodson, L., Piatelli, D. and Schmalzbauer, L. 2007. 'Researching inequality through interpretive collaborations: Shifting power and the unspoken contract', *Qualitative Inquiry*, 13(6): 821–843.

Duffy, R. 2010. *Nature Crime: How We're Getting Conservation Wrong*. New Haven, CT: Yale University Press.

Ellefsen, R., R. Sollund and G. Larsen (eds.). 2012. *Eco-global Crimes: Contemporary Problems and Future Challenges*. Surrey, UK: Ashgate.

Eman, K., Mesko, G. and Fields, G. B. 2009. 'Crimes against the environment: Green criminology and research challenges in Slovenia,' *Varstvoslovje - Journal of Criminal Justice and Security*, 11(4): 574–592.

Global Witness. 2018, July 24. 'At what cost? Irresponsible business and the murder of land and environmental defenders in 2017,' in *Global Witness*. London: Global Witness.

Goyes, D. and South, N. 2017. 'Green criminology before "green criminology": Amnesia and absences', *Critical Criminology: An International Journal* 25(2): 165–181.

Goyes, D., Mol, H., Brisman, A. and South, N. 2017. *Environmental Crime in Latin America: The Theft of Nature and the Poisoning of the Land*. London: Palgrave.

Hall, M. 2015. *Exploring Green Crime: Introducing the Legal, Social & Criminological Contexts of Environmental Harm*. London: Palgrave.

Heckenberg, D. 2010. 'The global transference of toxic harms,' in R. White (ed.) *Global Environmental Harm: Criminological Perspectives*, pp. 37–61. Cullompton, Devon, UK: Willan.

Heckenberg, D. 2011. 'What is a case study and what is it good for,' in L. Bartelsand K. Richards (eds.) *Qualitative Criminology: Stories from the Field*, pp. 190–202. Sydney: Hawkins Press.

Julian, R. 2004. 'Inequality, social differences and environmental resources,' in R. White (ed.) *Controversies in Environmental Sociology*, pp. 113–131. Melbourne: Cambridge University Press.

Kramer R. 2013. 'Public criminology and the responsibility to speak in the prophetic voice concerning global warming,' in E. Stanley and J. McCulloch (eds.) *State Crime and Resistance*, pp. 41–53. London: Routledge.

Lynch, M. J. and Stretesky, P. 2002. 'Toxic crimes: Examining corporate victimization of the general public,' *Critical Criminology: An International Journal*, 10(3): 153–172.

Lynch, M., Barrett, K., Stretesky, P. and Long, M. 2017a. 'The neglect of quantitative research in green criminology and its consequences,' *Critical Criminology: An International Journal*, 25(2): 183–198.

Lynch, M., Long, M., Stretesky, P. and Barrett, K. 2017b. *Green Criminology: Crime, Justice, and the Environment*. Oakland, CA: University of California Press.

Manirabona, A. and K. Koutouki (eds.). 2016. 'Criminalité environnementale,' *Criminologie*, 49(2): 5–347. Available at: www.erudit.org/fr/revues/crimino/2016-v49-n2-crimino02877/.

Mapsofworld.com. 2011. *World Maps in 800 Different Themes*. June 2011. Available at: www.mapsofworld.com/.

McMullan, J. and Perrier, D. 2002. 'Lobster poaching and the ironies of law enforcement,' *Law& Society Review*, 36(4): 679–720.

Melrose, S. 2009. 'Naturalistic generalization,' in A. J. Mills, G. Durepos and E. Wiebe (eds.) *Encyclopedia of Case Study Research*, pp. 599–601. Thousand Oaks, CA: Sage Publications.

Meško, G., A. Sotlar and K. Eman (eds.). 2012. *Ekološka kriminaliteta in varovanje okolja – multidisciplinarne perspective* [*Ecological Crime and Environmental Protection—Multidisciplinary Perspectives*]. Ljubljana: Fakuleta za varnostne vede, Univerza v Mariboru [Llubljana, Slovenia: Faculty of Criminal Justice, University of Maribor].

Mjoset, L. 2009. 'The contextualist approach to social science methodology,' in D. Byrne and C. Ragin (eds.) *The Sage Handbook of Case-Based Methods*, pp. 39–68. Thousand Oaks, CA: Sage.

Mol, H. 2017. *The Politics of Palm Oil Harm: A Green Criminological Perspective.* London: Palgrave Macmillan.

Mol H., D. R. Goyes, N. South and A. Brisman (eds.). 2017. *Introducción a la criminología verde. Conceptos para nuevos horizontes y diálogos socioambientales* [*Introduction to Green Criminology: Concepts for New Horizons and Socio-Environmental Dialogues*]. Bogotá and Colombia: Editorial Temis S. A. and Universidad Antonio Nariño, Fondo Editorial.

Moreto, W. (ed.). 2018. *Wildlife Crime: From Theory to Practice.* Philadelphia, PA: Temple University Press.

Moreto, W. 2017. 'Avoiding the tragedy of (un)common knowledge: Reflections on conducting qualitative criminological research in conservation science,' *Qualitative Research*, 17(4): 440–456.

Nader, L. 1969. 'Up the anthropologist—perspectives gained from studying up,' in D. Hymes (ed.) *Reinventing Anthropology*, pp. 284–311. New York: Random House.

Natali, L. 2010. 'The big grey elephants in the backyard of Huelva,' in R. White (ed.) *Global Environmental Harm: Criminological Perspectives*, pp. 193–209. Cullompton, Devon, UK: Willan.

Natali, L. 2015. *Green Criminology: Prospettive emergenti sui crimini ambientali.* Torino: G. Giappichelli Editore.

Natali, L. 2016. *A Visual Approach for Green Criminology: Exploring the Social Perception of Environmental Harm.* Basingstoke, Hampshire, UK: Palgrave Macmillan.

Natalia, L. and McClanahan, B. 2017. 'Perceiving and communicating environmental contamination and change: Towards a green cultural criminology with images,' *Critical Criminology: An International Journal*, 25(2): 199–214.

Nurse, A. 2016. *An Introduction to Green Criminology & Environmental Justice.* London: Sage.

Potter, G., A. Nurse and M. Hall (eds.). 2016. *The Geography of Environmental Crime: Conservation, Wildlife Crime and Environmental Activism.* London: Palgrave Macmillan.

Ruggiero, V. and South, N. 2010. 'Critical criminology and crimes against the environment,' *Critical Criminology: An International Journal*, 18(4): 245–250.

Salama, O. and White, R. 2017. 'Dissent, litigation, and investigation: Hitting the powerful where it hurts,' *Critical Criminology: An International Journal*, 25(4): 523–537.

Sollund, R. 2017. 'Doing green, critical criminology with an auto-ethnographic, feminist approach,' *Critical Criminology: An International Journal*, 25(2): 245–260.

Sollund, R., C. Stefes and A. Germani (eds.). 2016. *Fighting Environmental Crime in Europe and Beyond.* London: Palgrave Macmillan.

Stanley, E. 2008. *Torture, Truth and Justice: The Case of Timor-Leste.* London: Routledge.

Stefes, C. and Theodoratos, P. 2017 'Researching environmental crime in non-democratic regimes,' *Critical Criminology: An International Journal*, 25(2): 215–230.

Sutherland, W. J., Clout, M., Côté, I. M., Daszak, P., Depledge, M. H., Fellman, L., Fleishman, E., Garthwaite, R., Gibbons, D. W., De Lurio, J., Impey, A. J., Lickorish, F., Lindenmayer, D., Madgwick, J., Margerison, C., Maynard, T., Peck, L. S., Pretty, J., Prior, S., Redford, K. H., Scharlemann, J. P., Spalding, M. and Watkinson, A. R. 2009. 'A horizon scan of global conservation issues for 2010,' *Trends in Ecology and Evolution*, 25(1): 1–7.

Suzuki, D. 2010. *The Legacy: An Elder's Vision for our Sustainable Future.* Vancouver: Greystone Books, an Imprint of D and M Publishers.

Waldman, L. 2007. 'When social movements bypass the poor: Asbestos pollution, international litigation and griqua cultural identity,' *Journal of Southern African Studies*, 33(3): 577–600.

Walter, M. (ed.). 2006. *Social Research Methods: An Australian Perspective.* Melbourne: Oxford University Press.

White, R. 2008. *Crimes Against Nature: Environmental Criminology and Ecological Justice.* Cullompton, Devon, UK: Willan.

White, R. 2009. 'Researching transnational environmental harm: Ethical issues, technical problems & political dilemmas,' *International Journal of Comparative & Applied Criminal Justice*, 33(2): 229–248.

White, R. 2011. *Transnational Environmental Crime: Toward an Eco-Global Criminology*. London: Routledge.

White, R. 2017. 'Eco-Justice and the moral fissures of green criminology,' in J. Jacobs and J. Jackson (eds.) *The Routledge Handbook of Criminal Justice Ethics*, pp. 76–94. London: Routledge.

White, R. and Heckenberg, D. 2011, 'Environmental horizon scanning and criminological theory and practice,' *European Journal of Criminal Policy & Research*, 17(2): 87–100.

White, R. and Heckenberg, D. 2014. *Green Criminology: An Introduction to the Study of Environmental Harm*. London: Routledge.

Wong, R. 2015. 'A note on fieldwork in "dangerous" circumstances: Interviewing illegal tiger skin suppliers and traders in Lhasa,' *International Journal of Social Research Methodology*, 18(6): 695–702.

Wyatt, T. and Brisman, A. 2017. 'The role of denial in the "theft of nature": A comparison of biopiracy and climate change,' *Critical Criminology: An International Journal* 25(3): 325–341. DOI: 10.1007/s10612-016-9344-5. FirstOnline: September 14 2016. Available at: http://link.springer.com/article/10.1007/s10612-016-9344-5.

7

Environmental refugees as environmental victims

Matthew Hall

Introduction

This chapter sets out to marry two areas of discussion within the green criminological literature. The first is the development of a distinct current within that field which focuses attention specifically on the human and non-human victims of environmental harms—a so-called 'green victimology' (Hall 2013, 2017; Ozymy, Jarrell and Bradshaw, this volume, Chapter 8). The second is the ongoing debate and controversy around the issue of 'environmental refugees'. This second issue predates the development of green criminology as a distinct topic of academic inquiry but has nevertheless been widely commented on within that literature (Brisman 2019; Brisman, South and Walters 2018a, 2018b; Smith 2007; South 2010; White 2011), as well as outside of it (see, e.g., Westra 2009).

By discussing both issues concurrently, the chapter will seek to demonstrate: (1) how green victimology might assist with the incorporation of environmental refugees within green criminological discourse; and (2) how victimological insights might better aid us in understanding the plight of environmental refugees. This will be done with a view to improving how criminal justice and other agencies have tended to respond to such refugees, especially in so-called 'receiving countries'. More specifically, the argument will be made that conceiving of such persons as 'environmental victims' helps us move beyond formulistic debates around legal definitions of 'refugees' versus 'migrants' and focuses attention instead on the lived experience and the harms undergone by such people, along with the question of how national and international legal orders might address these. To this end, the chapter will draw on wider victimological insights to conceptualise environmental refugees and, most centrally, it will explore how the 1985 UN Declaration of Basic Principles of Justice for Victims of Crime and Abuse of Power (the '1985 UN Declaration') might apply in this area. Whilst this chapter will focus on the displacement of *human beings*, and is thus primarily anthropocentric in its orientation, this should not be taken to imply that this is an issue unconnected or easily discernible from disruptions to the wider ecosystem. Indeed, there is considerable evidence that the same environmental degrading activities and impacts which are compelling human populations to migrate are also having significant impacts on non-human animals, disrupting their migration and herding patterns (Avgar, Mosser, Brown and

Fryxell 2013). From an ecocentric perspective, therefore, there is no cogent reason to exclude such harms from the scope of 'environmental victimisation' save for the practical constraints of space within the present volume.

Green victimology and environmental victims

For many years victimology—the dedicated study of victims, victimisation and the impacts of crime (Hall 2013)—struggled to assert itself as a core component of wider criminological debate. Much of that debate was, of course, focused on *offenders* and the response of the criminal justice system to legally proscribed activities (Jones 2013). Arguably, it was not until the mid-1980s that dedicated investigations into the impact of crime on victims and their lack of a role in the criminal system process began to appear (see Shapland, Willmore and Duff 1985). Mirroring this trend, the advent of green criminology itself has arguably progressed for most of its history since the early 1990s (Lynch 1990) without dedicated consideration of victims, especially when one looks beyond the purely androcentric to consider non-human victims of environmental harm or indeed a true ecocentric approach whereby the environment itself may be classified as a victim (Williams 1996). The role or position of such 'environmental victims' in criminal justice and/or other regulatory processes has likewise rarely been the topic of academic debate until quite recently (Hall 2013).

In attempting to remedy this shortfall, a number of researchers and scholars, including myself, have advocated for the development of a distinct field of 'green victimology' (Flyn and Hall 2017; Hall 2013, 2017; Skinnider 2011; Sollund this volume, Chapter 29; Spencer and Fitzgerald 2013). In so doing, we have argued that the early[1] critical focus of green criminology on the *harms* caused by environmentally damaging activities—as opposed to considering only stringent legal classifications of such harm—makes a victimological focus sit well within this area given the very broad nature of the harms engendered by environmental degradation. Nevertheless, it remains clear that further development of victimological study within green criminology has been slow to progress, even as green criminology as a whole has gathered pace. Skinnider (2011: 26) emphasises the need for such specific research given the difficulties of applying broad-brush victim reforms to questions of environmental harm: 'The characteristic of the collective nature of this kind of victimization needs to be understood, particularly with its implications for victims to seek assistance, support and redress which have predominately developed for traditional crimes involving individual victims'.

In developing such debates, I have argued elsewhere that a key component of any 'green victimology' will necessitate a close interaction between victimologists and international legal scholars, including academics and practitioners (Hall 2013, 2017), because environmental pollution is so often constituting a cross-border issue (see, e.g., Passas 2005). This is one feature of green victimology that has important resonance with the issue of cross-border movements of peoples who are 'compelled' to move[2] by the impacts of climate change, environmental disasters or more gradual environmental degradations. A further key role for any green victimology, then, lies in unpicking the extent to which formal regulatory and justice mechanisms of the state appear incapable of responding adequately to cases of environmental victimisation (see Westra 2009).

Victimologists have long been concerned with the extent to which criminal justice practitioners—as a matter of occupational culture—construct ideas of their roles within the criminal justice system, and whether such roles include consideration for victims of crime (Hall 2010; Shapland et al. 1985). The ensuing discussion will in turn highlight how environmental refugees appear frequently to find themselves on the wrong side of the law and cut off from access to support and mechanisms of justice in both their 'home' jurisdiction for those internally displaced, and any 'receiving' jurisdictions for those compelled to cross borders. As such, it is argued that green criminologists need to focus greater attention on the plight of displaced human (and non-human) victims. Furthermore, this chapter will argue that the advent of green victimology, with its specific focus on causation and response to those harmed—as opposed to the prosecution or other censure of those responsible, or indeed those affected—represents a key opportunity for these issues to be incorporated fully within the green criminological lexicon and also become the focus of sustained policy attention across jurisdictions. Proceeding on this basis, the chapter will now turn attention to the complex and often controversial question of what is meant by 'environmental refugees'.

Deconstructing 'environmental refugees'

A collection of interrelated and sometimes overlapping terms has developed in recent decades attempting to describe and encompass in broad terms what Essam El-Hinnawi (1985: 5) labelled 'environmental refugees': 'people who have been forced to leave their traditional habitat, temporarily or permanently, because of a marked environmental disruption (natural and/or triggered by people) that jeopardizes their existence and/or seriously affects the quality of their life'.

What has followed is a protracted debate across a number of disciplines, including economics (Cameron and McConnaha 2006), international relations (Betts and Loescher 2011), law (McCue 1993) and sociology (Hunter 2005), as to the exact meaning of this and related terms, such as 'climate refugee' (Hartmann 2010), 'ecologically displaced person' (Boano, Zetter and Morris 2012) and 'environmental migrant' (Findlay 2011). In 2002, Myers 2002b: 609) wrote of environmental refugees that these are:

> people who can no longer gain a secure livelihood in their homelands because of drought, soil erosion, desertification, deforestation and other environmental problems, together with associated problems of population pressures and profound poverty. In their desperation, these people feel they have no alternative but to seek sanctuary elsewhere, however hazardous the attempt. Not all of them have fled their countries, many being internally displaced. But all have abandoned their homelands on a semi-permanent if not permanent basis, with little hope of a foreseeable return.

As a matter of international law, many legal experts have pointed out that 'refugees' are defined quite specifically in Article 1 of the 1951 United Nations Convention on Refugees and its 1967 Amendment as people with 'a well-founded fear of being persecuted for reasons of race, religion, nationality, membership of a particular social group or political opinion'.

For lawyers, then, the key difference is between 'refugees', who flee their homes by a compulsion *grounded in persecution*, and 'migrants' who, although often constrained, ostensibly leave by choice and not due to any particular persecution. Nevertheless, Bates (2002: 467) has pointed out the difficulties of distinguishing neatly between these two related ideas in the environmental context, arguing:

> Degrading environments affect human migration, but this may result from external compulsion or decisions made by migrants. The decision to relocate, usually made at the individual or household level, characterizes voluntary migration. Voluntary migrants have a variety of motives; the most common involves the desire for economic improvement. Other migrants

> are forced or compelled to relocate by external forces ... The distinction between voluntary migrants and refugees offers some theoretical power to differentiate between migrants. However, many important migratory flows are not easy to categorize as one or the other.

Others have tried to further deconstruct and categorise the degree of 'compulsion' involved in the 'decision' to migrate within various typologies. For example, the International Organisation for Migration (IOM) draws on an understanding presented by Hugo (1996: 107): 'Population mobility [in the context of environmental change] is probably best viewed as being arranged along a continuum ranging from totally voluntary migration [...] to totally forced migration'. The IOM also distinguishes between 'forced migration' and 'migrations influenced by environmental change', whereby 'environmental change can be identified as affecting the drivers of migration, and thus is a factor in the decision to migrate' (Foresight 2011: 34).

Koubi and colleagues (2016: 439) have offered a micro-level analysis of individual perceptions of different types of environmental events using Vietnamese survey data:

> Our empirical results ... show that individuals do not seem to migrate due to slow-onset environmental events, this type of events rather seem to decrease the likelihood of migration. In contrast, short-term events, such as floods or hurricanes, are associated with an increased likelihood of migration, although not in a statistically significant way. While non-migrants are slightly better in judging the actual extremeness of events such as floods and hurricanes, it is the migrants who are slightly better in judging the actual extremeness in the case of droughts.

Marshall (2016) discusses a continuum ranging from 'Imperative Environmental Migrants' (persons permanently and irrefutably displaced from their homes and/or livelihoods primarily as a result of environmental factors); 'Pressured Environmental Migrants' (peoples who are unable to continue effective lifestyles and are thus strongly pressured to migrate to more hospitable climates to sustain basic living requirements for food, water and shelter as a result of the slow-moving processes of climate change); 'Temporary Environmental Migrants' (migrants experiencing short-term forced migration resulting from a one-time severe environmental event); and finally 'Human Environmental Migrants' (residents displaced from their homes and/or livelihoods as a result of human conflict over environmental resources).

Further complexities derive from distinctions drawn between displacements precipitated by 'natural' events like earthquakes and hurricanes, and man-made natural disasters such as the pollution of the Ogoniland region in the Nigerian delta as a result of state-sanctioned oil excavation by Royal Dutch Shell (see Lindén and Pålsson 2013). Aside from the issue of what legal or social distinction (if any) is to be drawn between such groups, the very question of what is 'man-made' and what is 'natural' is often itself widely contested. For example, in the summer of 2017, many commentators attributed an apparently severe hurricane season and other extreme weather events around the globe (Stott 2016) to the impact of anthropogenic climate change (Greshko 2017). A related debate is also ongoing in the literature around the distinction between those who flee more 'creeping' environmental changes, such as the desertification of regions of central Africa, in contrast to more 'immediate' environmental disasters or polluting events. As noted by Bates (2002: 475): 'The most controversial type of environmental refugee flees gradual, anthropogenic degradation'.

For her part, Bates (2002) has attempted to classify different forms of what she calls 'human migrations caused by environmental change' into a designated scheme, allowing for comparisons based on the characteristics of the causes of the migration. For her, such migrations can be divided into the three 'top' categories of: (1) those caused by 'disasters' ('an unintended, catastrophic event'); (2) those caused by 'expropriations' (wilful destruction of the environment rendering it unfit for human habitation); and (3) those caused by 'deteriorations' (incremental deterioration of the environment as constraints to human survival increase). Bates then posits that such migrations may be further sub-divided by origin. Thus, 'disasters' can be either *natural* or *technological*. 'Expropriations' may constitute either *development* or *ecocide*. 'Deterioration' can also be traced back to either *pollution* or *depletion*.[3] Notably, all of Bates' 'origins' are anthropocentric, save for natural disasters, which she describes as 'unintentional and acute'. Here, she gives the example of the July 1995 eruption of the Soufrière Hills volcano on the Caribbean island of Montserrat, which led to the displacement of some 7,000 people.

In a similar vein, Mayer (2017: 37) has argued forcefully against the use of the term 'environmental refugees' on the basis that 'they are rarely forced and rarely international migrants, and are not distinct from other migrants'. Mayer's argument is rather that 'environmental migrants' must be seen as constituting part of a broader group of vulnerable peoples who are 'induced to move by a cluster of causes, who are generally not protected under international or national law' (2017: 45).

Legally, then, there is a degree of consensus that those fleeing the kinds of environmental impacts categorised by Marshall (2016) and Bates (2002) are not, as a matter of international law, 'refugees'. This is practically significant because people falling into this category do not automatically receive the same protections under international law nor, potentially at least, the attention of UN and nongovernmental organisations, including the Red Cross, dedicated to the 'refugee' cause.

In many ways, the debate around *migrants* who are 'compelled' but not 'forced' to move versus 'real' persecuted *refugees* is reminiscent of arguments around 'victim precipitation' which have been deconstructed in the victimological literature for many years. Thus, the earliest victimologists suggested that individuals could be prone to victimisation and even precipitated it through lifestyle choices (von Hentig 1948). Often labelled as 'victim blaming', such an approach continued to be a feature of early mainstream victimology until the late 1950s and early 1960s (see Fattah 1992). In the 1960s, these were overtaken by a so-called second wave of victimology driven by a host of 'strange bedfellows' concerned with different aspects of victimisation ranging from feminists and mental health practitioners to survivors of Nazi concentration camps (see Pointing and Maguire 1988; Young 1996).

In fact, the social and political conceptualisation of 'environmental migrants' as 'victims' has been discussed previously, although not from a victimological perspective per se. Here, Ransan-Cooper and colleagues (2015: 112) examine the 'social framing' of such individuals and groups as 'victims', 'security threats', 'adaptive agents' and 'optical subjects'—at different times in different jurisdictions—concluding that:

> Analysis of evolving framings of environmental migrants has revealed a high level of dynamism in the way the phenomenon has been constructed and understood. A framing analysis has also revealed that different frames have real implications for the scope and shape of policy options.

For these authors, framing environmental migrants as 'victims' is too simplistic given the complex social diminution of this form of harm:

> The victim framing as it has been construed is unlikely to promote a more nuanced understanding of the vulnerability of people experiencing climate extremes, nor will it necessarily be beneficial to the 'subjects' themselves. As we have discussed, the key problem is that the framing is rooted in notions of people (often racialised 'other') as passive and helpless in the face of changing environments. What might, perhaps, be worthwhile preserving from the victim frame is the element of compassion and care, which does not necessarily reproduce a binary saviour-victim relation, but instead, could inspire reflexivity on the inter-connected nature of vulnerabilities.
>
> *(Clark 2010, quoted in Ransan-Cooper et al. 2015: 106)*

Ransan-Cooper and colleagues' (2015) analysis demonstrates clearly that the manner in which societies and governments frame the issue of human displacement predicated by environmental change has a significant impact on how that society or government responds to the issue. As such, for the remainder of this chapter, I wish to defend the conceptualisation of such peoples as *victims*, arguing that critical and cultural strands of victimology have progressed to a point at which they are well capable of reflecting the more 'nuanced' understanding that Ransan-Cooper and colleagues (2015) rightly champion. Indeed, modern victimology fully acknowledges that the 'victim/offender' dichotomy is not a zero-sum relationship (Drake and Henley 2014). At the same time, retaining the label of 'victim' recognises that harm has been inflicted on such refugees even if they have made choices which ultimately put them in this position. For example, it is widely acknowledged that domestic violence victims frequently 'choose' to stay with their abusers for protracted periods. As a branch of social science rather than law, victimology also acknowledges that victimisation is often the product of many interrelated social and economic factors whilst, in the modern age, tending to steer away from notions of 'blaming'.

As already suggested, such a perspective would suggest that a social constructivist approach might be adopted by green criminologists and green victimologists—an approach which seems well suited to the exploration of the varying and complex precursors to environmental refugees discussed above. Indeed, it is for this reason that this chapter argues that conceptualising such people as environmental 'victims' might go some way to assisting their plight, especially if seen through the lens of 'abuse of power', as covered by the 1985 UN Declaration (discussed below). By seeing such people as victims, this chapter will also continue to refer to 'environmental refugees' despite the legalistic objections and the fact that I include within this discussion those people displace internally within regions in their own 'home' jurisdiction. This is not because, *from a legal perspective*, those objections are not well founded, but that, in line with Ransan-Cooper and colleagues' (2015) view concerning the practical significance of different modes of framing the issue, this language conveys more accurately the level of harm and direct or indirect compulsion inherent to such displacements as a form of environmental victimisation.

Examining environmental refugees as environmental victims

Most data sources and commentators agree that the scale of the problems relating to the displacement of people as a result of environmental degradation is escalating (Brzoska and Fröhlich 2016). With this realisation, there comes a need to rethink the approach taken to such individuals both domestically (in relation to the internally displaced) and transnationally (in the case of those displaced over national frontiers). Nevertheless—and as demonstrated above—the sheer diversity of opinion on how to properly conceptualise such groups makes definitive statistics difficult to collate. By 1989, the executive director of the United Nations

Environmental Programme (UNEP) estimated that 'as many as 50 million people could become environmental refugees' if the world did not act to support sustainable development (Tolba 1989: 25). Writing in 2002, Myers—himself one of the most widely-cited authors to focus on this area—argued that the most comprehensive assessment of the total number of 'environmental refugees' (his term) in 1995 had suggested a total of 'at least 25 million people, compared with 27 million traditional refugees (people fleeing political oppression, religious persecution and ethnic troubles)' (Myers 2002a: 1). In 2009, the Environmental Justice Foundation estimated that, by 2050, some 10 per cent of the world's population would be displaced, stating: 'Global warming will force up to 150 million "climate refugees" to move to other countries in the next 40 years' (Myers 2002a: 12).

In terms of internal, as opposed to cross-border displacement, in 2015 the International Displacement Monitoring Centre in Geneva estimated that an average of 22.5 million people had been displaced by climate- or weather-related events since 2008 (International Displacement Monitoring Centre 2015). More recently, Marshall (2016: 1) has noted:

> Some experts loosely estimate that there may be as many as 50 million Environmentally Displaced Persons (EDPs) today: a number which could grow to as high as 250 million by the end of this century, depending on how this group of migrants is defined and counted.

Other commentators have eschewed an approach to understanding the human displacement 'caused' by environmental degradation purely through an effort to arrive at global-level estimates of the numbers comprising these populations. For example, Black and colleagues (2013: 33) have tried to develop what they call an 'integrated assessment approach', which 'seeks instead to understand how and why existing flows from and to specific locations may change in the future, and provide a practical tool for climate adaptation planning'.

Whilst the true scale of the issue is therefore unknown, it is clear that the problem is persistent, ongoing and likely to escalate as we progress through the twenty-first century. Furthermore, from a (green) victimological perspective, the overriding evidence now points to endemic inequality in the distribution of environmental harms at local, national and global levels of the kind that may lead (and has led) to displacement (Dobson 1998). This inequality is in part geographically grounded. So, for example, the 1992 UN Framework Convention on Climate Change (UNFCCC) acknowledges the particular vulnerability of 'low-lying and other small island countries, countries with low-lying coastal, arid and semi-arid areas or areas liable to floods, drought and desertification, and developing countries with fragile mountainous ecosystems' in its preamble. This notwithstanding, a focus on the inequalities of environmental harm fostered by physical geography should not distract us from the more complex social, economic and cultural aspects of such victimisation. The unequal distribution of environmental degradation as a whole has been commented on by South (2010), who sees this as reflecting wider tendencies towards 'social exclusion' that have long been a topic of research and discussion in mainstream criminology (Byrne 1999). In relation to environmental victimisation, Lee (2009: 3–4) has summarised the situation in the following terms: 'Poor people are usually excluded from the environmental decision making process, and once a policy is made, they are usually powerless to change it'.

Thus, it is clear that many of the impacts of environmental degradation that seem to drive much of the displacement highlighted in earlier sections of this chapter tend to weigh most heavily on the poorest countries, as well as the poorest people within those countries. Mendelsohn and colleagues' (2006: 173) analysis of statistical data/prediction on climate change puts the matter succinctly: 'Overall, the poor [countries] will suffer the bulk of the damages from climate change, whereas the richest countries will likely benefit'.

One particular aspect of this that has been emphasised in a number of more anthropological studies is an inability for people living in such regions to continue practising traditional or culturally significant ways of life (Eller 2016). A key point for present purposes is that it is these traditional *cultures* which also provide these environmental victims with the *practical* necessities of living (e.g., food, income), as acknowledged by the 2012 Rio+20 UN Conference on Sustainable Development in its Outcome Document: 'many people, especially the poor, depend directly on ecosystems for their livelihoods, their economic, social and physical well-being, and their cultural heritage' (p. 30).

Mendelsohn and colleagues' (2006: 162) contention that rich countries may benefit from climate change is based on the observation that they are, for the most part, 'located in the mid to high latitudes and are currently cool' and thus warmer temperatures may actually be closer to optimum for crop production. Indeed, Deschênes and Greenstone (2007) suggest an increase in annual profits from agricultural land of $1.3 billion in the US as a direct result of climate change over the next decade. Such observations and estimations are, however, contestable, especially if one expands the scope of the discussion beyond crop production. For example, White (2011: 25) notes how 'countries of the West are now beginning to experience climate-related disasters'. Wachholz (2007), to offer another example, compiles evidence of an increase in violence following hurricanes, floods and droughts.

In a comprehensive review of knowledge gaps in this area, Brody and colleagues (2008: 3) conclude:

> There is also evidence that women and girls are more likely to become victims of domestic and sexual violence after a disaster, particularly when families have been displaced and are living in overcrowded emergency or transitional housing where they lack privacy. The increase in violence is often partly attributed to stress caused by men's loss of control in the period following a disaster, compounded by longer term unemployment or threatened livelihoods.

The mention here of family displacement links the question of the apparent inequality of impact on women to that of human trafficking, which will be discussed below. It is clear that the vast majority of these victims are indeed women and girls (Denton 2000). Jasparro and Taylor (2008) have commented specifically on the vulnerabilities of women in this regard as climate change and other environmental degradation expands. Indeed, to give one example, it has been reported that Masaai parents in the Mar region of Kenya, where climate change is already having noticeable effects on crops, are being forced to 'sell off' their young underage daughters to groups of human traffickers who are posing as foreign tourists (Women's News Network 2010).

Whilst the displacement of people due to environmental degradation can itself be considered directly harmful for the reasons given above, particular concerns have arisen in the victimological literature relating to the likelihood that displaced peoples will find themselves at risk of becoming the victims of human trafficking. The concern with trafficking in the context of the present discussion stems from the expected increase in displaced peoples and forced migrations, as well as a general increase in poverty in the parts of the world which are hardest hit by climate change (Mendelsohn, Dinar and Williams 2006). Indeed, the link between displaced peoples/forced migrations and human trafficking has been drawn by a number of researchers (see Lee 2007). The United Nations University's Institute for

Environment and Human Security (Warner, Afifi, Dun, Stal and Schmidl 2008) in particular has demonstrated specific connections between migrations *forced by environmental factors* and a susceptibility of these displaced individuals to human trafficking. Jasparro and Taylor (2008: 1) have also summarised the links between climate change, culture and the threat of human trafficking (as well as the trafficking in illicit drugs, wildlife and arms), arguing that:

> Southeast Asian livelihood and social systems will be pressured, while state and civil society capacity will be strained. This will intensify existing vulnerabilities to non-state security threats and raise the overall level of vulnerability and risk to both human and state security.

In Europe, too, the expectation of human trafficking has been of high concern for EU Member States for over a decade (Shelley 2007). It is submitted that the effects of climate change and other environmental degradation are likely to create a further pull in the direction of stringent collaborative action, with implications for the human rights of those trafficked, many of whom end up working in illegal and poorly regulated sectors of the economy.

The association between environmental refugees and trafficked individuals also has important implications for the way such people are viewed and treated within receiving countries. As is the case with many trafficked individuals, such victims will inevitably find themselves engaged in illegal activities (e.g., prostitution, selling drugs) in the 'receiving' country or region. To this end, Marmo and La Forgia (2008: 174) comment on how official and unofficial authorities in Australia have a tendency to characterise trafficked women as undesirables, regardless of the circumstances that left them in their present situation and regardless of whether such people are actively engaged in illegal activities:

> In Australia, trafficked women are portrayed and maintained as the 'other', as unbelonging matter of the moral and legal community. Trafficked women are dealt with as an external issue—to the point that their conditions and situation are unable to affect domestic policy objectives. Their status as irregular immigrants is used to re-establish a social and moral order, a social identity of the Australian system, which is disturbed by the unwanted presence of trafficked women.

It is worth noting that such an attitude is certainly against the spirit (and possibly the letter) of Article 25 of the 2005 UN Protocol to the United Nations Convention against Transnational Organized Crime of 2000, which obliges each State Party 'to take appropriate measures within its means to provide assistance and protection to victims of offences covered by this Convention in particular in cases of threat of retaliation or intimidation'. Yet, even non-trafficked refugees may be treated as criminal, both by the original population of a country or area and by the criminal justice system. Furthermore, it has been demonstrated by Sampson (2008) that the presence of minority groups in an area or country appears to increase the perception of crime and disorder amongst existing residents, even though crime itself shows little increase. In response, Smith (2007) has commented on how some countries have gone so far as to deploy their military forces in reaction to the flow of displaced human populations, perceiving them as a security threat.

In light of the above issues, Westra (2009) has written specifically on the lack of rights for those who are displaced by environmental catastrophes and changes and thus become what she calls 'environmental refugees' in other states. As noted already, such individuals and groups of individuals do not fall under the heading of 'refugees' under current international law. From a rights perspective, this lack of status can also be attributed to a broad consensus at present amongst international environmental lawyers that no definitive right to an unpolluted, green environment can yet be said to exist in international law (see Hall 2013). Rather, the most progressive developments concerning rights for environmental victims have, to date, come about in the European Court of Human Rights as a result of its interpreting existing, well-established, rights—such as the right to privacy and the right to a home life—to include environmental harms.[4] Moreover, in most cases, existing 'rights' for victims of crime have not been applied to victims of environmental harm given that the definition of 'victims' employed in most circumstances is often purposely narrow. Thus, such people are not, as a matter of legal theory, escaping 'abuses of their rights' in their own country or region.

Environmental refugees as victims of abuse of power?

In an attempt to reconcile some of the above complexities in both conceptualising and addressing the needs of 'environmental refugees', a possible way forward is to draw on the UN General Assembly's definition of 'victims of abuse of power' in the 1985 UN Declaration. Certainly the 1985 UN Declaration has been the most wide-ranging and influential document on the issue of victims' rights as a whole at the international level. It speaks of victims being afforded access to justice, fair treatment and of compassion and respect for their dignity. Whilst an essentially non-binding, soft-law instrument, the 1985 UN Declaration has, in turn, influenced most of the domestic provisions relating to the place of victims in criminal justice (which usually take the form of non-binding Codes of Practice) in the world today (Hall 2010). Nevertheless, in line with the general focus of the victim movement on human agency as opposed to legal structure, the 1985 UN Declaration is very much lacking in 'hard' mechanisms for the enforcement of the principles it champions (at the national and international levels), and is, in fact, a self-confessed aspirational document.

Williams (1996: 18) argued that the 1985 UN Declaration might serve as a useful starting point for ascribing recognition to environmental victims as a whole. A similar argument can be applied to the issue of environmental refugees more specifically. In defining 'victims', the 1985 UN Declaration reads that these are:

> [P]ersons who, individually or collectively, have suffered harm, including physical or mental injury, emotional suffering, economic loss or substantial impairment of their fundamental rights, through acts or omissions that do not yet constitute violations of national criminal laws but of internationally recognized norms relating to human rights.

The inclusion of victims of abuse of power within the instrument was intended to encompass victimisation by the state, thereby making this definition particularly relevant from the perspective of victims of environmental harms that are not yet recognised by national or international law as 'officially' criminal, as is the case with a great deal of the industrial activity fostering environmental degradation (Stretesky, Long and Lynch 2013). Indeed, Kauzlarich and colleagues (2001) have drawn on the 1985 UN Declaration to develop a framework 'victimology of the state', which includes 'International-International Governmental Crime', or crime which occurs outside a state's geographic jurisdiction against international law or human rights. Such an understanding would theoretically encompass victimisation not only by one's home state, but by other states as well. This would include environmentally destructive activities perpetuated by one state (or a group of states) against another. The reality of such a scenario is increasingly championed by commentators examining sea level rise and the 'sinking' of low-lying islands in Melanesia (Carteret Islands and Vanuatu), Micronesia

(Kiribati) and Polynesia (Tuvalu), as well as the Maldives; the argument is that rising sea levels (and the subsequent sinking of island nations) has come about as the result of human-induced climate change to which the affected populations have hardly contributed. The situation is already prompting the displacement of individuals and is widely predicted to be on the verge of creating large populations of not just metaphorically, but literally, stateless communities (see Doherty and Slezak 2017). Indeed, in the case of the Maldives, Kothari (2013: 132) points out that 'technocratic and de-politicised discourses of climate change have often been invoked to conceal underlying political agendas in which environmental concerns are drawn upon to justify unfavourable government policies of mobility and resettlement'. This is in the context of *government-driven* 'resettlement policies', 'where the [Maldivian] government is proposing the consolidation of a population dispersed over 200 islands onto 10–15 islands' (Kothari (2013: 138). Again, the examination of such official moves as potential abuses of power seems particularly apt.

Abuse of power is specifically conceived in the 1985 UN Declaration (p. 19) as actions and omissions that *do not* constitute crimes. As such, states are prompted in the document to:

> [P]eriodically review existing legislation and practices to ensure their responsiveness to changing circumstances, [and] should enact and enforce, if necessary, legislation proscribing acts that constitute serious abuses of political or economic power, as well as promoting policies and mechanisms for the prevention of such acts, and should develop and make readily available appropriate rights and remedies for victims of such acts.

On the face of it, 'abuses of political or economic power' has the potential to capture many of the state-sanctioned activities (conducted pursuant to neoliberal agendas) that green criminologists have argued lead to environmental harms (see Stretesky, Long and Lynch 2013). Importantly, the definition also employs the term 'harm' rather than 'injury', again giving it the breadth to encompass a wide range of environmental victimisations. As noted above, the activities leading to environmental harms and consequent displacements are often not illegal in nature. More significantly, however, one might consider this provision alongside the so-called 'no-harm' principle under customary international law, which essentially requires states to actively prevent causing environmental harm to other states. Thus, the case could be made that a state has abused its power by neglecting to fulfil its responsibilities under the 1985 UN Declaration to regulate activities (that is, failure to conduct 'due diligence' (see Barnidge 2006)) within its borders that lead to environmental victimisation and mass displacement of peoples across borders. In addition, Renaud and colleagues (2017) have argued that the *precautionary* principle of international law should apply as the basis for improving legislation concerning displaced persons in separate jurisdictions and ultimately these should be reflected in either a new convention or anchored in bilateral intergovernmental environmental treaties. For these authors, this approach is preferable to any attempt to amend the existing 1951 Convention to include such persons as a new category of refugee.

The above arguments notwithstanding, one barrier to the use of the 'abuse of power' definition for the purposes of recognising environmental refugees as environmental victims is its reliance on 'recognized norms relating to human rights' as a means of distinguishing abusive from non-abusive exercise of power. Although it is the topic of increasing debate, the difficulty in establishing the existence of any generally applicable human right to a clean environment recognised by the international legal order has already been noted. Furthermore, the 1985 UN Declaration's definition does little to address the political reality that, whatever understandings are employed by commentators, legal reform tends to be enacted for the benefit of 'ideal' and 'innocent' victims, as opposed to the many environmental refugees discussed above who may turn to, or find themselves forced into criminal activities. This is significant because, whilst more general evaluations of victim reform carried out by victimologists across jurisdictions suggest that understandings of victims based on 'harm suffered' rather than 'crime' are now widely circulated, in reality reform agendas across these same jurisdictions tend to emphasise certain kinds of victims (ideal, cooperative) and certain kinds of suffering.(Hall 2013). Indeed, although the 1985 UN Declaration has existed for over 30 years, only a very small percentage of reforms derived from it have related to victims of *abuse of power*, as opposed to victims of *crime* (see Rothe et al. 2009). In effect, therefore, the definitions of environmental victimhood in use in most jurisdictions are much narrower than they first appear (Hall 2013). It can be predicated that similar political pressures will certainly be in place as national and international legal systems are adapted to (ostensibly) cater for environmental refugees as victims of environmental harm, particularly given the recent proliferation of more nationalist sentiments across a number of jurisdictions. I will return to a dimension of this debate near the end of this chapter.

Whilst it may seem fanciful to read environmental victims, or environmental refugees, more specifically, into a document conceived long before either term was in popular use or the problem was widely accepted and understood, in domestic law, at least, there is precedent for such an adaptation in the form of the 2004 US Crime Victims' Rights Act (CVRA) (Ferguson 2011; Jarrell and Ozymy 2012; Ozymy et al., this volume, Chapter 8). Heralded as a major breakthrough by proponents of a more judiciable form of victims' rights (Doyle 2008), the CVRA introduced the concept of victims' rights into the US penal code for the first time. The Act contains provision for 'service rights' for victims (Ashworth 2000) including the provision of information to them by the justice system, protection and compensation, as well as a suite of procedural rights requiring that victims of crime 'be reasonably heard at any public proceeding in a district court involving release, plea, sentencing, or any parole proceeding'.[5]

The first application of the CVRA to victims of *environmental* crime followed an explosion of a BP Oil Refinery in Texas in 2005. In this case, the US Fifth Circuit court ruled that the government had violated victims' rights under the CVRA by failing to consult with those locals affected by the explosion (mostly in the form of personal injury and property damage) in the agreement of a plea bargain with BP (Starr, Flack and Foley 2008). This was despite the fact that the number of victims stretched into the hundreds and the CVRA neither includes nor, on the face of it, conceives harm caused by environmental damage. More recently, in the case of *In re Parker; U.S.* v *U.S. District Court and W.R. Grace & Co.*[6] the United States Court of Appeals for the Ninth Circuit ruled that potential victims of environmental harm are included within the ambit of rights provided under the CVRA. The case is interesting not only for the specific result, but as a demonstration of the breadth of the term 'victim' and for the weight given to the contention that it includes (or should include) environmental crimes even where there is no specific mention of this category of harms within the rights-enabling legal instrument.

This domestic application of (traditional) victims' rights to environmental harm is admittedly several steps away from the acceptance of individual victims of environmental harm or of environmental refugees into international law, but it does demonstrate how instruments usually presumed to extend only to victims of traditional domestic offences (and in this case, one based heavily on the 1985 UN Declaration) can be applied to environmental harm. The critique here is not that international law has considered and rejected this argument in relation to environmental refugees specifically, but that, through its championing of legal rules and process over substantive *outcome*, such arguments are rarely even considered. Whilst the 1985 UN Declaration remains non-binding, it can be argued that such principles espoused within it could form the basis of future international obligations relating to those affected by environmental harms conceived as victims of abuse of power. Although there is presently insufficient evidence to argue that this aspect of the 1985 UN Declaration has attained the status of customary international law, it is significant that the instrument has already prompted large amounts of reform and policy development at the national and international levels (Hall 2010).

Indeed, it should not be thought that the creation of *formally binding* principles of international law is a prerequisite to attaining justice or redress for environmental refugees framed as environmental victims. Some international lawyers have championed the concept of 'soft law' that has the capacity to form the material basis of customary law and can be converted into 'hard law' though its enshrinement in treaties. The concept of soft law is greatly contested in the relevant literature however (Boyle 2006). In practice, whether or not one chooses to call the 1985 UN Declaration soft law has little bearing on arguments concerning their potential either to become hard law or to constitute an important step in the process towards the establishment of internationally binding legal principles relating to environmental refugees. Indeed, d'Aspremont (2008: 1062) has reflected on the argument that, given the operation of policy networks, legally binding instruments are not always needed to achieve significant ends:

> Many recent developments, like networks among governmental officials or transnational law, have shown that non-legal instruments may prove more adapted to the speed and complexity of modern international relations and are more and more resorted to in practice. Non-legal instruments can be at least as integrative for a community as legal ones.

Given the generally non-binding nature of most national and international provisions and principles relating to *both* environmental harm *and* victims of crime as a whole, such insight is important for both fields of study. What victimology also contributes to these debates is a wealth of experience in dealing largely (indeed, almost totally) with such non-binding instruments in attempting to attribute rights or so-called 'legitimate expectations' (JUSTICE 1998) to environmental refugees. Such 'rights' are almost exclusively found in non-binding declarations and codes of practice issued by national governments and international organisations. The important observation is that such instruments have brought about significant changes in many jurisdictions concerning the place of victims in criminal justice, notwithstanding their non-binding or persuasive character (Groenhuijsen and Pemberton 2009; Hall 2010). This again implies that 'hard law' is not the only mechanism for enhancing the political and legal position of environmental refugees.

Moving beyond legal formalism: deterritorialisation and cultural integration of environmental refugees

Nicholson (2014: 157) has criticised existing literature on environmental refugees as being epistemologically vague and chaotic, drawing on such a wide range of understanding and approaches as to deplete it of scientific rigour:

> The effect of all this semantic fluidity is to render the field Teflon to critique: one can raise methodological, conceptual and even political objections to the use of a particular term by a particular actor in a particular context, but the moment the labels change, the criticism is neutralised and the process begins all over again.

In particular, Nicholson argues that most of the debates in this literature are predicated on underlying assumptions around climate, ethics and causation, which are socially and politically variable. Tellingly for the present discussion, Nicholson (2014: 155) also bemoans the fact that, for him, the dismissal of the term 'environmental refugee' by international lawyers has led only to the term being 'superseded by different terms, largely focusing on a process rather than a person'.

The core argument put forward in this chapter is that, in order to make progress towards the formation of workable protection mechanisms for environmental refugees, the debate on environmental refugees needs to be centred around such persons and that characterising these people as environmental victims (of abuse of power) can help states and the international community at large make this step. Importantly, this necessitates a departure from debates around both internal and cross-border displacement linked inextricably to concepts of statehood, recognising such groups as 'victims'. Such an approach has already found support in the literature, with Marshall (2016: 14) championing the need for:

> Pushing back on the traditional framing of migration around states, sovereignty, and their authority over citizenship and rights offers a viable pathway for the future of environmental migration rights. In the same way that environmental issues do not recognize the 'firmness' of state borders, so too must environmental migration rights recognize the arbitrariness of these human constructions.

For Marshall, the solution is the rollout in international law of 'universal migration rights' rather than more ecocentric rights per se. Blitz (2011), too, argues that the short-term solution to concerns around environmental migration lies in the uncoupling of the obligations placed on states for such individuals from their present 'national moorings', in light of the wider responsibilities of those states to respect the human rights (rather than environmental rights) of stateless people. A common understanding of such individuals as 'victims' (if not 'refugees') can only ease this transmission process.

In light of the notions of environmental victimisation discussed above, one cannot discuss the topic of displaced peoples in the contemporary context without reflecting on the political context in many jurisdictions, especially of the 'global North', which has been characterised by an apparent shift in support towards more nationalistic political ideals. This is evidenced by developments such as the population of the United Kingdom voting to leave the European Union in the referendum of June 2016 and the election of Donald J. Trump as President of the United States later that year, on the back of considerable anti-international rhetoric. Such developments have, in turn, cemented the impression already replete in the literature of a slowdown in the degree to which the world is becoming integrated, with some going so far as to predict the 'end of globalisation' and/or the end of 'internalisation' (see Rugman 2012). In particular, many countries have seen a strong backlash against 'migrants' of various descriptions. Politically, then, it seems we have moved into a period in which such displaced peoples are much more often 'framed' as security threats than victims (to use Ransan-Cooper and colleagues' (2015) language).

The above points notwithstanding, the contemporary political climate is also arguably characterised by what Hans Boutellier (2000) referred to as the 'victimalization of morality'. Boutellier observed that as the process of secularisation continues, shared standards of morality decline but common appreciation and sympathy for the impacts on those who have suffered harm remains and becomes the new benchmark on which we can judge a collective morality. In similar terms, recent years have seen the growth of a so-called 'cultural' trend in the victimological literature. At the forefront of this development, McGarry and Walklate (2015) characterise such 'cultural victimology' as broadly comprising of two key aspects: the wider sharing and reflection of individual and collective victimisation and the mapping of those experiences through the criminal justice process. Through both of these mechanisms, wider definitions of 'victimisation' become so culturally embedded that policy makers are prompted to respond with more targeted reform (Mythen and McGowan 2017). Space is lacking in the present chapter to delve into this development of cultural victimology in any depth but, for present purposes, its predicted acceptance by society of wider and fluid notions of victimhood, predicated on notions of harm and 'trauma' (Ellison and Munro 2016) rather than legalistic definitions, offers hope for the better understanding and acceptance of environmental refugees *as victims*. Indeed, from a political standpoint, educating the public and policy makers as to the strong 'victim' credentials of many environmental refugees may in such a cultural context be the most effective way of challenging and reversing the more nationalistic, anti-immigrant feelings discussed above.

Conclusions

Despite widespread debate and criticism of the exact nature and predicates of environmental displacement, most commentators are united in the belief that this will be a significant and escalating problem in the coming decades (cf. Brisman 2019). Indeed, for many of those already displaced, the crisis is a contemporary reality. This chapter has demonstrated that the people who are forced or compelled into this position often find themselves in what, at best, can be described as a legal limbo and, at worst, can constitute significant victimisation in the form of falling subject to human traffickers. Legal and conceptual compartmentalisations aside, it is clear that such people form a very vulnerable group in need of basic protections, which often seem to be lacking both in 'home' jurisdictions and when they cross borders. This chapter has advocated one solution—the reframing of such individuals as 'environmental victims' and, in so doing, drawing on the 1985 UN Declaration's definition of 'victims of abuse of power' as a means of recognising this group as victimised. The intention is not so much to use this approach as a means of establishing 'hard' legal regimes around such victims, but to reframe this debate around concepts of personal harm and the lived experience of being displaced. Whilst this is coming at a time when the contemporary political scene is often one of hostility to 'migrant groups', it has been argued in the last section that appealing to an equally tangible sense of shared understanding and empathy exposed by scholars of cultural victimology may well prompt governments into action to better protect these individuals. Although this is only a first step, such moves help direct debate towards more concrete recognition of environmental refugees *as* environmental victims, whether through the recognition of forms of environmental rights at the international level or else the development of more general rights and protections linked to migration.

Notes

1 Relative, that is, to 'mainstream victimology', where such a critical focus did not develop until well within the field's second century (see Hall 2010).
2 This chapter will return to the question of 'compulsion' below.
3 In the green criminological literature, Stretesky and colleagues (2013) have classified the former as 'ecological additions' and the latter as 'ecological subtractions'. See also Chapter 4 of this volume.
4 See *Baegen* v *Netherlands* Series A no 327-B (1995) 77; *Doorson* v *Netherlands* Reports of Judgments and Decisions 1996-II, [1996] 23 EHRR 330.
5 18 USC § 3771(a)(4).
6 Nos 09–70,529, 09–70,533 (9th Cir. 2009).

References

Ashworth, A. 2000. 'Victims' Rights, Defendants' Rights and Criminal Procedure,' in A. Crawford and J. Goodey (eds.) *Integrating a Victim Perspective Within Criminal Justice: International debates*, pp. 185–204. Aldershot, UK: Ashgate Dartmouth.

Avgar, T., Mosser, A., Brown, G. S. and Fryxell, J. M. 2013. 'Environmental and individual drivers of animal movement patterns across a wide geographical gradient,' *Journal of Animal Ecology*, 82(1): 96–106.

Barnidge, R. 2006. 'The due diligence principle under international law,' *International Community Law Review*, 8(1): 81–121.
Bates, D. 2002. 'Environmental refugees? Classifying human migrations caused by environmental change,' *Populatio and Environment*, 23(5): 465–477.
Black, R., Kniveton, D. and Schmidt-Verkerk, K. 2013. 'Migration and Climate Change: Toward an Integrated Assessment of Sensitivity,' in T. Faist and J. Schade (eds.) *Disentangling Migration and Climate Change*, pp. 29–53. London: Springer.
Betts, A. and Gil L. 2011. 'Refugees in international relations,' in A. Betts and G. Loescher (eds.) *Refugees in International Relations*, pp. 1–28. Oxford: Oxford University Press.
Blitz, N. 2011. 'Statelessness and environmental-induced displacement: Future scenarios of deterritorialisation, rescue and recovery examined,' *Mobilities*, 6(3): 433–450.
Boano, C., Zetter, R. and Morris, T. 2012. *Environmentally Displaced People: Understanding The Linkages Between Environmental Change, Livelihoods and Forced Migration*. Oxford: Refugees Studies Centre.
Boutellier, H. 2000. *Crime and Morality: The Significance of Criminal Justice in Post-Modern Culture*. AA Dordrecht: Kluwer.
Boyle, A. 2006. 'Soft Law in International Law-Making,' in M. Evans (ed.) *International Law*, 2nd Edition, pp. 141–158. Oxford: Oxford University Press.
Brisman, A. 2019. 'The fable of *The Three Little Pigs*, climate change and green cultural criminology,' *International Journal for Crime, Justice and Social Democracy*, 8(1): 46–69. DOI: 10.5204/ijcjsd.v8i1.470.
Brisman, A., South, N. and Walters, R. 2018a. 'Climate Apartheid and Environmental Refugees,' in K. Carrington, R. Hogg, J. Scott and M. Sozzo (eds.) *The Palgrave Handbook on Criminology and the Global South*, pp. 301–321. London: Palgrave Macmillan.
Brisman, A., South, N. and Walters, R. 2018b. 'Southernizing green criminology: Human dislocation, environmental injustice and climate apartheid,' *Justice, Power and Resistance*, 2(1): 1–21.
Brody, A., Demetriades, J. and Esplen, E. 2008. *Gender and Climate Change: Mapping the Linkages – A Scoping Study on Knowledge and Gaps*. Sussex: BRIDGE Institute of Development Studies.
Brzoska, M. and Fröhlich, C. 2016. 'Climate change, migration and violent conflict: Vulnerabilities, pathways and adaptation strategies,' *Migration and Development*, 5(2): 190–210.
Byrne, D. 1999. *Social Exclusion*. Buckingham: Open University Press.
Cameron, T. and McConnaha, I. 2006. 'Evidence of environmental migration: Housing values alone may not capture the full effects of local environmental disamenities,' *Land Economics*, 82(November): 273–290.
Clark, N. 2010. 'Acquiescence: Fluid realities and planned retreat,' *Reading Room: A Journal of Art and Culture*, 4: 42–59.
d'Aspremont, J. 2008. 'Softness in international law: A self-serving quest for new legal materials,' *The European Journal of International Law*, 19(5): 1057–1093.
Denton, R. 2000. '"Gendered impacts of climate change" – A human security dimension,' *Energia*, 3(3): 13–14.
Deschênes, O. and Greenstone, M. 2007. 'The economic impacts of climate change: Evidence from agricultural output and random fluctuations in weather,' *The American Economic Review*, 97(1): 354–385.
Dobson, A 1998. *Justice and the Environment: Conceptions of Environmental Sustainability and Dimensions of Social Justice*. Oxford: Oxford University Press.
Doherty, B. and Slezak, M. 2017. '"The island is being eaten": How climate change is threatening the Torres Strait,' *The Guardian* [online]. Available at: www.theguardian.com/environment/2017/jul/13/the-island-is-being-eaten-how-climate-change-is-threatening-the-torres-strait.
Doyle, C. 2008. *Crime Victims' Rights Act*. Hauppauge, NY: Novinka.
Drake, D. and Henley, A. 2014. '"Victims" versus "offenders" in british political discourse: The construction of a false dichotomy,' *The Howard Journal of Criminal Justice*, 53(2): 141–157.
El-Hinnawi, E. 1985. *Environmental Refugees*. New York: UNEP.
Eller, J. 2016. *Cultural Anthropology: Global Forces, Local Lives*. London: Routledge.
Ellison, L. and Munro, V. 2016. 'Taking trauma seriously: Critical reflections on the criminal justice process,' *International Journal of Evidence & Proof*. DOI: 10.1177/1365712716655168.
Fattah, E. 1992. 'Victims and victimology: The facts and the rhetoric,' in E. Fattah (ed.) *Towards a Critical Victimology*, pp. 29–56. New York: Palgrave Macmillan.
Ferguson, A. 2011. 'We're victims, too! The need for greater protection of environmental crime victims under the crime victims rights act,' *Pennsylvania State Environmental Law Review*, 19(2): 287–305.

Findlay, A. 2011. 'Migrant destinations in an era of environmental change,' *Global Environmental Change*, 21(1): 50–58.
Flyn, M. and Hall, M. 2017. 'The case for a victimology of nonhuman animal harms,' *Contemporary Justice Review*, 20(3): 299–318.
Foresight. 2011. *Migration and Global Environmental Change. Final Project Report*. London: Government Office for Science.
Greshko, M. 2017. 'Why this hurricane season has been so catastrophic,' *National Geographic* [online]. Available at: http://news.nationalgeographic.com/2017/09/hurricane-irma-harvey-season-climate-change-weather/ .
Groenhuijsen, M. and Pemberton, A. 2009. 'The EU framework decision for victims of crime: Does hard law make a difference?' *European Journal of Crime, Criminal Law and Criminal Justice*, 17(1): 43–59.
Hall, M. 2010. *Victims and Policy Making: A Comparative Perspective*. Cullompton, Devon, UK: Willan.
Hall, M. 2013. *Victims of Environmental Harm: Rights, Recognition and Redress under National and International Law*. Abingdon, Oxon, UK: Routledge.
Hall, M. 2017. *Victims of Crime: Constructions, Governance and Policy*. London: Palgrave Macmillan.
Hartmann, B. 2010. 'Rethinking climate refugees and climate conflict: Rhetoric, reality and the politics of policy discourse,' *Journal of International Development*, 22(2): 233–246.
Hugo, G. 1996. 'Environmental concerns and international migration,' *International Migration Review*, 30 (1): 105–131.
Hunter, L. 2005. 'Migration and environmental hazards,' *Population & Environment*, 26(4): 273–302.
Internal Displacement Monitoring Center. 2015. *Global Estimates 2015*. Geneva: Internal Displacement Monitoring Center.
Jarrell, Melissa .L. and Ozymy, Joshua. 2012. 'Real crime, real victims: Environmental crime victims and the Crime Victims' Rights Act (CVRA),' *Crime, Law, and Social Change*, 58(4): 373–389.
Jasparro, C. and Taylor, J. 2008. 'Climate change and regional vulnerability to transnational security threats in southeast asia,' *Geopolitics*, 13(2): 232–256.
Jones, S. 2013. *Criminology*. 5th Edition. Oxford: Oxford University Press.
JUSTICE Committee Victims in Criminal Justice. 1998. *Report of the JUSTICE Committee on the Role of Victims in Criminal Justice*. London: JUSTICE.
Kauzlarich, D., Matthews, R. and Miller, W. 2001. 'Toward a victimology of state crime,' *Critical Criminology: An International Journal*, 10(3): 173–194.
Kothari, U. 2013. 'Political discourses of climate change and migration: Resettlement policies in the Maldives,' *The Geographical Journal*, 180(2): 130–140.
Koubi, V., Stoll., S. and Spilker, G. 2016. 'Perceptions of environmental change and migration decisions,' *Climatic Change*, 138(3–4): 439–451.
Lee, M. 2007. *Human Trafficking*. Cullompton, Devon, UK: Willan.
Lee, T.-P.. 2009. 'A welfare approach to mitigating environmental justice,' in *Conference Proceedings of the Centre for International Policy Exchanges, Exploring Needs of Pollution Victims July 2009*, University of Maryland. Available at: http://www.welfareacademy.org/pubs/international/epckdi/2.pdf.
Lindén, O., and Pålsson, J. 2013. 'Oil contamination in ogoniland, niger delta,' *Ambio*, 42(6): 1–17.
Lynch, M. 1990. 'The greening of criminology,' *Critical Criminologist*, 2: 1–5.
Marmo, M. and La Forgia, R. 2008. 'Inclusive national governance and trafficked women in australia: Otherness and local demand,' *Asian Criminology*, 3(2): 173–191.
Marshall, N 2016. 'Forced environmental migration: Ethical considerations for emerging migration policy,' *Ethics, Policy and Environment*, 19(1): 1–18.
Mayer, B. 2017. 'Critical Perspective on The Identification of "Environmental Refugees" As A Category of Human Rights Concerns,' in D. Manou, A. Baldwin, D. Cubie, A. Mihr and T. Thorp (eds.) *Climate Change, Migration and Human Rights: Law and Policy Perspectives*, pp. 28–42. London: Routledge.
McCue, G. 1993. 'Environmental refugees: Applying international environmental law to involuntary migration,' *Georgetown International Environmental Law Review*, 6: 151–160.
McGarry, R. and Walklate, S. 2015. *Victims: Trauma, Testimony and Justice*. Abingdon, Oxon, UK: Routledge.
Mendelsohn, R., Dinar, A. and Williams, L. 2006. 'The distributional impact of climate change on rich and poor countries,' *Environment and Development Economics*, 11: 159–178.
Myers, N 2002a. 'Environmental refugees: A growing phenomenon of the 21st century,' *Philosophical Transactions of the Royal Society*, 357(1420): 609–613.

Myers, N. 2002b. 'Environmental refugees: An emergent security issue,' *Proceeds of the 13th Economic Forum*, Prague, May 23–27, 2005.

Mythen, G. and McGowan, W. 2017. 'Cultural Victimology Revisited Synergies of Risk, Fear and Resilience,' in S. Walklate (ed.) *Handbook of Victims and Victimology*, 2nd Edition, pp. 235–250. Abingdon, Oxon, UK: Routledge.

Nicholson, C. 2014. 'Climate change and the politics of causal reasoning: The case of climate change and migration,' *The Geographical Journal*, 180(2): 151–160.

Passas, N. 2005. 'Lawful but awful': Legal corporate crimes,' *Journal of Socio-Economics*, 24(6): 771–786.

Pointing, J. and Maguire, M. 1988. 'Introduction: The rediscovery of the crime victim,' in M. Maguire and J. Pointing (eds.) *Victims of Crime: A New Deal?*, pp. 1–13. Milton Keynes, UK: Open University Press.

Ransan-Coopera, H., Farbotkob, C., McNamara, K., Thornton, F. and Chevalier, E. 2015. 'Being(s) framed: The means and ends of framing environmental migrants,' *Global Environmental Change*, 35(1): 106–115.

Renaud, F., Bogardi, J., Dun, O. and Warner, K. 2017. *Environmental Degradation and Migration*. Berlin: Berlin Institut.

Rothe, D., Ross, J., Mullins, C., Friedrichs, D., Michalowski, R., Barak, G., Kauzlarich, D. and Kramer, R. 2009. 'That was then, This is now, What about tomorrow? Future directions in state crime studies,' *Critical Criminology: An International Journal*, 17(1): 3–13.

Rugman, A. 2012. *The End of Globalization*. London: Random House.

Sampson, R. 2008. 'Rethinking crime and immigration,' *Contexts*, 7(1): 28–33.

Shapland, J., Willmore, J. and Duff, P. 1985. *Victims and the Criminal Justice System*. Aldershot: Gower.

Shelley, L. 2007. Human Trafficking As a Form of Transnational Crime,' in M. Lee (ed.) *Human trafficking*, pp. 116–137. Cullompton, Devon, UK: Willan.

Skinnider, E. 2011. *Victims of Environmental Crime – Mapping the Issues*. Vancouver: The International Centre for Criminal Law Reform and Criminal Justice Policy.

Smith, P. 2007. 'Climate change, mass migration and the military response,' *Orbis*, 51(4): 617–633.

South, N. 2010. 'The Ecocidal Tendencies of Late Modernity: Polnational Crime, Social Exclusion, Victims and Rights,' in R. White (ed.) *Global Environmental Harm: Criminological Perspectives*, pp. 236–240. Cullompton, Devon, UK: Willan.

Spencer, D. and Fitzgerald, A. 2013. 'Three ecologies, transversality and victimization: The case of the British Petroleum oil spill,' *Crime, Law and Social Change*, 59(3): 209–223.

Starr, J., Flack, B. and Foley, A. 2008. 'New intersection: Environmental crimes and victims' rights,' *Natural Resources & Environment*, 24(1): 41–52.

Stott, P. 2016. 'How climate change affects extreme weather events,' *Science*, 352(6293): 1517–1518.

Stretesky, P., Long, M. and Lynch, M. 2013. *The Treadmill of Crime: Political Economy and Green Criminology*. Abingdon, Oxon, UK: Routledge.

Tolba, M. 1989. 'Our biological heritage under siege,' *Bioscience*, 39(1): 725–728.

von Hentig, H. 1948. *The Criminal and His Victim*. New Haven, CT: Yale University Press.

Wachholz, S. 2007. '"At risk": Climate change and its bearing on women's vulnerability to male violence,' in P. Beirne and N. South (eds.) *Issues in Green Criminology: Confronting Harms Against Environments, Humanity and Other Animals*, pp. 161–185. Cullompton, Devon, UK: Willan.

Warner, K., Afifi, T., Dun, O., Stal, M. and Schmidl, S. 2008. *Human Security, Climate Change and Environmentally Induced Migration*. Bonn: United Nations University – Institute for Environment and Human Security.

Westra, L. 2009. *Environmental Justice and the Rights of Ecological Refugees*. Abingdon, Oxon, UK: Routledge.

White, R. 2011. *Transnational Environmental Crime: Towards an Eco-Global Criminology*. Abingdon, Oxon, UK: Routledge.

Williams, C. 1996. 'An environmental victimology,' *Social Science*, 23(1): 16–40.

Women's News Network. 2010. '*Climate Change, Poverty and Tourists Put Maasai Daughters at Risk*'. womennewsnetwork.net [online]. Available at: http://womennewsnetwork.net/2010/04/16/kenya-climatechange-trafficking-892/.

Young, A. 1996. *Imagining Crime*. London: Sage.

8

How criminologists can help victims of green crimes through scholarship and activism

Joshua Ozymy, Melissa L. Jarrell and Elizabeth A. Bradshaw

Introduction

On December 2, 1984, a poisonous gas leak at the Union Carbide plant in Bhopal, India, killed over 4,000 people instantly, while more than 14,000 additional individuals died over the course of several years from the long-term effect of exposure to toxins (Pearce and Tombs 1998). On April 26, 1986, an explosion and fire at the Chernobyl Nuclear Power Plant, in the part of the Soviet Union that is now the sovereign nation of Ukraine, immediately killed 31 individuals and over 200 people died from radiation exposure within months of the disaster (Burns and Lynch 2004; Frank and Lynch 1992). Cancer deaths from the Chernobyl incident will likely exceed tens of thousands. On March 24, 1989, the Exxon Valdez oil tanker bound for Long Beach, California, ran aground on the Bligh Reef in Prince William Sound, Alaska, causing hundreds of thousands of barrels of crude oil to spill into the icy waters. The Exxon Valdez oil spill resulted in 11 million gallons of oil covering 1,300 miles of coastline and 11,000 square miles of ocean, killing millions of fish and wildlife in one of the world's most pristine natural environments (Jarrell 2007). On April 20, 2010, an explosion rocked the Deepwater Horizon drilling rig owned by British Petroleum plc (BP) in the Gulf of Mexico, causing a massive oil spill that affected millions of people along the U.S. Gulf Coast, and that resulted in 11 deaths and 17 direct injuries (Bradshaw 2014). Some five years prior, on March 23, 2005, an enormous explosion at the BP Texas City Refinery resulted in 15 deaths and 180 injuries (CSB 2008). Prior to all of these devastating events that resulted in numerous casualties to humans, nonhuman animals and the natural environment, BP had been fined repeatedly for environmental violations at many of its facilities.

The events described above are all examples of 'green crimes'—acts or omissions by a corporation that resulted in harms to the environment, including humans and nonhuman animals. The thrust of this chapter is to explore solutions to protect victims of green crime, both in the form of institutional remedies, as well as those stemming from citizen-based actions in civil society. In doing so, we hope to illustrate how green criminologists, through both scholarship and activism, can play a role in protecting and advocating for victims of green crimes, particularly state-corporate environmental crimes.

This chapter is divided into eight substantive sections. The first six sections are organised as follows: (1) Changing the frame (how to conceptualise green crimes as 'real crimes'); (2) Enforcing existing laws (problems with the current regulatory enforcement apparatus); (3) Better oversight (reducing victimisation through better environmental enforcement); (4) Legal recognition of victims (how to better protect victims under the law); (5) Removing victims from harmful environments (community buyouts and environmental justice); and (6) Non-human victims matter (the value of considering non-human animals as victims). From here, this chapter then devotes two sections to how criminologists can play a role in protecting and advocating for victims of green crimes: (7) Becoming involved through research (exploring avenues for new research) and (8) Becoming active (how we engaged in grassroots activism in our local community).

Changing the frame

State-corporate crimes include both illegal and legal (but socially injurious) actions that result from the policies and practices of one or more agencies of political governance in collaboration with one or more institutions of economic production and distribution (Michalowski and Kramer 2006: 20). The concept of *state-corporate crime* draws attention to the commission of organisational deviance through joint government and corporate endeavours; increasingly, it has been applied to describe and explain a range of environmental harms in the oil industry (Bradshaw 2014, 2015a, 2015b; Ruggiero and South 2013; Smandych and Kueneman 2010), as well as degradation of forests, land, soil and water—in addition to the loss of biodiversity—due to climate change (Brisman and South Introduction, this volume; Kramer 2013a, 2014; Kramer and Michalowski 2012; Lynch, Burns and Stretesky 2010).

Governments rarely if ever make moderate or major institutional changes without pressure from civil society. Before the state-corporate relationship can be disentangled to help victims in any meaningful way or to be overhauled structurally to stop the production of such harms in such vast quantities in the future, we first need to shift how we look at green crimes. In other words, if we want to draw significant attention to the plight of victims we have to change the way the public views victims.

Unfortunately, it is still the case that the general public is unaware of the presence of most green crimes unless there is widespread media attention and mass victimisation (Jarrell 2009). Most cases actually receive very little to no media attention (Jarrell 2007; see generally Krugman 2017). Green criminologists have brought conceptual weight to the idea that an act or omission that causes harm, even if not proscribed by law, should be treated as a serious criminal act (Frank and Lynch 1992; White 2008). We, as scholars, as well as all concerned citizens, need to view green crimes as serious crimes that have adverse impacts and produce victims. Indeed, we must continue to emphasise a social harms perspective to illustrate how victims can be produced through legal and illegal actions within a framework of state-corporate malfeasance. As Stretesky and Lynch (1999) note, the next logical step is to continue stressing the intentionality of these crimes. Oftentimes, the public perceives inaccurately green crimes as accidents or mere regulatory infractions, rather than as negligent, knowing or intentional behaviour (Ozymy and Jarrell 2016). In a regulatory framework, green crimes are often seen conveniently as chance mishaps under the law or companies are given variances or exceptions, for a variety of reasons, in order to excuse reckless behaviours that cause harm (Ozymy and Jarrell 2012). Not only is it important for the public to consider green crime victims as 'real' victims, but they must understand how and why these victims are produced and reproduced—because corporations often engage in patterns of criminal behaviour (Simon 2000) and, as such, their actions (and inactions) are allowed to persist as a matter of economic and political imperative (Stretesky, Long and Lynch 2014).

Enforcing existing laws

Fighting green crime is often left to a country's regulatory apparatus. Law enforcement agencies spend most of their time and funds on violent or property crime and are often poorly trained and equipped to combat environmental crimes. Governments often fail to fund and support adequately a sufficient regulatory and legal apparatus to properly protect victims of state-corporate environmental crime. A fairly robust solution for reducing victimisation through the current regulatory system in most countries is to simply support regulatory agencies in their efforts. Research has shown that regulatory agencies, such as the U.S. Environmental Protection Agency (EPA), often have a strong culture of environmental enforcement (Fiorino 2006; Mintz 1995, 2004, 2005) that can persist even under hostile political regimes. Yet these agencies, which are often underfunded to begin with, may experience additional budget cuts during administrations sympathetic to corporate interests (see Krugman 2017).

Corporations are often able to engage in patterned behaviours, where they victimise nearby communities, consumers, wildlife and the natural environment, and where fines for regulatory infractions are generally subsumed as the cost of conducting business. Given the costs of engaging in the criminal investigation and prosecution of large corporate offenders (Daley and Layton 2004), regulatory agencies submit to economic and political considerations—especially if the administration in power adopts a lenient approach to enforcement of pollution laws (see Lipton and Ivory 2017)—and generally resorts to administrative fines or negotiated settlements. These fines arguably have little deterrent effect on large corporations, who have the financial ability and incentive to challenge regulatory actions in court. As Ozymy and Jarrell (2016) have found, cases involving identifiable human victims often result in larger fines and penalties than those with non-human animal victims, whose suffering and loss of life have little impact on punishment. In most cases where regulators in the United States actually subsume the costs of taking environmental criminals to court (which is a small fraction of the overall cases that could be prosecuted criminally), the officers and managers of large corporations were rarely punished with incarceration.

If regulatory agencies had the resources and power to punish properly larger companies—as well as political pressure to do so—fewer of these state-corporate crimes would likely occur or at least there would be some realistic deterrent power to prevent them. While regulatory agencies can easily scare an *individual* who might have illegally disposed of asbestos with threats of prosecution, or intimidate a *small company* that was engaging in off-label use of restricted pesticides, the transaction costs of bringing criminal charges against corporate environmental criminals is simply too great for most agencies to bear. Unless regulators are sufficiently empowered to punish offenders—which would entail providing them with resources comparable to those given to the investigation and prosecution of street crimes—such regulators will remain weak and will find themselves limited to negotiating small fines with offenders, which will be unlikely to result in a change of behaviour.

Better oversight

Petroleum refineries provide an excellent example of how the regulatory system is often structurally unable to enforce environmental laws and protect victims. Refineries are vast complexes that heat crude petroleum at different temperatures to extract a range of byproducts that can be used for industrial, commercial and individual uses. By design, refineries release air and water emissions and produce toxic byproducts. Yet, in the United States, there is very little real-time monitoring of such facilities (Ozymy and Jarrell 2012). While companies often sink geo-probes into the ground to test for ground water contamination, pursuant to state and federal statutes, or regulators place air monitors outside of the facilities, regulators do not usually engage in real-time monitoring of these actual sensors, and many of the monitors, particularly air monitors, test only for certain emissions at particular locations. Regulators rarely make surprise visits to petroleum-refining complexes and they rarely situate regulators within the facilities. Because regulators are often not available in real-time, if a crime is committed the burden of reporting falls on employees, who may be more concerned for their future employment. Before better enforcement of environmental laws can occur, better oversight of industrial facilities and other corporate polluters is needed. In other words, before more stringent punishments for violations of environmental regulations and laws can be imposed, better *detection* of such violations needs to occur. To put this in perspective, consider that if a street crime occurs, such as an assault or robbery, either a witness or the victim can call 911 in the United States or an equivalent phone number in other countries. If a police officer has reasonable suspicion a street crime is occurring in plain sight, he or she can investigate and apprehend an individual. Ideally, the same would occur if a citizen sees a suspicious stack flare at a refinery. In reality, however, there are no such environmental police officers to patrol industrial facilities in any consistent way or to keep watch over known polluters.

To effectively shift the focus towards recognising environmental crimes as *real* crime, we must realise that employing a regulatory apparatus to police state-corporate environmental crime is conceptually and practically different than the manner in which the criminal justice system deals with street crime. Companies produce goods that benefit society, but they also produce negative externalities that occur unintentionally, intentionally, or negligently—and often with the state's knowledge and implicit consent. As a result, polluters are treated primarily as entities existing within a regulatory apparatus, rather than as offenders in a criminal justice framework. This structure is unlikely to change. Governments generally do not have the resources or impetus to treat industrial facilities like criminal enterprises. But they could —and *should*—work to provide clear guidelines to corporations and significant real-time monitoring for hazards. This approach recognises that regulators do not and will not play an equivalent law enforcement role or have such a relationship as police do to street criminals.

With a commitment to reducing victimisation and environmental harm, stricter real-time monitoring is relatively easy to achieve with existing technology. Such monitoring would also provide regulatory agencies with the evidence to prosecute offenders for environmental crimes. Without substantive evidence, criminal prosecutions must often rely, particularly in the United States, on charges related to the crime, such as conspiracy, false statements, etc. To facilitate transparency, this real-time monitoring should be made available to the public. This kind of action is not without precedent and is more feasible than changing the entrenched corporate-state alliance, noted above. The difficulty is getting the state to agree to substantive real-time monitoring, rather than limited symbolic monitoring. Quality monitoring not only aids environmental law enforcement, but it emphasises the responsibility of both the state and corporations for their activities (such as polluting) or their inactivity (such as failing to monitor or engaging in quality monitoring).

Legal recognition of victims

On the production end of the state-corporate environmental crime problem is the relationship between the state and corporations that allows victimisation to occur repeatedly over time. Changing how we think about crime from a broader social harm perspective helps us to understand that many acts considered regulatory violations are quite harmful and many times, if they are not intentional acts, they are acts of wilful negligence. Once we broaden our perspective, we can appreciate how better monitoring holds the state and corporations accountable for their actions and inactions that produce victims.

One significant hurdle towards reducing the number of victims of state-corporate environmental crime is that it is all too easy to pollute and injure human and non-human victims and very difficult to prove that the actions of a particular company *caused* a specific outcome. Currently, corporate entities generally face only marginal transaction costs after negotiating punishments with regulators. They rarely encounter serious regulatory or criminal penalties and seldom fear costly litigation by their victims in civil court. Corporate actors, such as those in the automobile, medical device and pharmaceutical industries, may factor liability costs into their decision-making, and at times this can result in significant civil damages, such as the case of the Ford Pinto's exploding gas tank in the 1970s or, more recently, with Toyota's $3.4 billion lawsuit over rusting truck and SUV frames (AP 2016). While corporate polluters can be sued (as, most famously, in the BP Deepwater Horizon disaster, noted at the outset), on a day-to-day basis the chance of a refinery or chemical plant being sued for injuring nearby fence-line communities for chronic exposure is very low because it is very hard to prove long-term emissions caused specific problems in a particular area or to a particular person(s).

The way forward is for courts to recognise environmental crime victims. In the United States, this has been a slow process. Until 2004, with the passage of the Crime Victims' Rights Act (CVRA), crime victims played (and still do to a large extent) only a minor and indirect role in court cases. The passage of the CVRA signalled that victims should have rights and a legal role within the court system (Cassell and Joffee 2011). While the intent of the CVRA was not to apply to victims of environmental crime (Jarrell and Ozymy 2012), efforts have been undertaken to expand its ambit, such as in *United States* v *BP Products* and *United States* v *W.R. Grace & Co.* In *United States* v *Citgo Petroleum Corporation*, the United States District Court for the Southern District of Texas recognised that residents of a nearby fence-line community were victims of Citgo's crimes. While the court did not award the plaintiffs any compensation, the court did acknowledge victims were created as the result of Citgo's crimes. *Citgo* is important for environmental crime victims because it sets a precedent in United States case law that residents of a fence-line community were victims and rendered such as a consequence of the corporation's criminal actions. Although courts in other jurisdictions in the United States are not bound by the decision in *Citgo*, the case does provide guidance for other prosecutors pursuing criminal cases against corporations in similar situations to consider whether there are victims in their cases and if they feel there is sufficient legal grounds for pushing to have them recognised under the CVRA in Clean Air Act (CAA) criminal prosecutions. Moving forward, court systems across the globe should work to recognise that state-corporate environmental crime victims do exist, that victims should have rights and that they should be awarded compensation for their injuries.

Removing victims from harmful environments

Living near polluting industries not only poses the risk of negative health impacts, but individuals and communities often find themselves trapped by their circumstances, unable to sell their homes and move to a different neighbourhood. The only option, then, is to rely on regulators to reduce the emissions coming into their neighbourhoods, which often proves unsuccessful for the reasons mentioned earlier in this chapter. While residents of such communities often find it difficult, if not impossible, to sell their homes without incurring financial loss, real estate can be bought and sold as part of settlement or through the power of eminent domain (which, in the United States, refers to the power of the federal or a state government to take private property for public use, while requiring the payment of 'just' compensation to the owner).

The difficulties inherent in such 'buyouts', for lack of a better term, fall along moral, economic, political and practical lines. From a moral perspective, the question is whether a person is responsible for where he/she lives. In many cases, residents may have lived in the area before industry or industrial expansion, older residents may have been zoned into the area through redlining, or low-income residents may simply have lacked other viable options when they moved to the area. None of these are intractable problems for removing people from harm.

Even if a community was to receive market value for its homes, there would be political and practical obstacles to doing so. Full-scale removal and relocation is rare in democratic societies with property rights, even under eminent domain. Many residents will not want to move, even if paid handsomely for their homes and even if their neighbours elect to depart. The authors' experiences with buyouts have shown that many residents understand the health risks of remaining in their homes, but love their community and do not wish to leave. This has been the case in Corpus Christi, where the second author helped to found the Environmental Justice Housing Fund (EJHF). This organisation helped to raise over $2 million dollars through regulatory permit battles to fund buyouts in areas near heavy industry. In this particular case, many residents, even when offered moving costs and buyouts well above market rate and pegged towards the cost of buying a similar home in a better area of the community or otherwise, were unwilling to move, wishing to remain in their community, despite the health risks. Others made unreasonable demands for compensation well above market value for a replacement home elsewhere in the city.

Governments have generally worried about setting a precedent for buying out communities in areas impacted negatively by pollution or other types of environmental degradation. Like most government action, buyouts often come as the result of economic imperative, where government needs the land, such as in the case of building a bridge, highway, or other infrastructure project. While such acquisitions are usually undertaken pursuant to the power of eminent domain, buyouts can also come as the result of lawsuits that force governments to acquire real property. All of these examples are not without precedent, however, as we will discuss later in the chapter. Moreover, there is a prevailing inclination in many industrialised democracies to ignore the problems of marginalised communities experiencing disproportionate environmental impacts and to simply 'wait it out' until the moral imperative to correct past wrongs dissipates as older residents die from natural causes and long-term chronic environmental crimes.

Non-human victims matter

Whether intentional or unintentional, when an industrial facility releases chemicals into a waterway and kills millions of aquatic species, it is often treated as a regulatory violation instead of a criminal act. Recent work by two of the authors of this chapter (Jarrell, Ozymy and Sandel 2017) found that in almost 1,000 environmental crime prosecutions in the United States, there were approximately 7 million deaths of non-human animals, but these individuals were not categorised as 'victims' by the government. In these cases, the presence of a non-human victim did not appear to have had any impact on punishment severity (Ozymy and Jarrell 2016). More research is needed, however, to gauge when and under what circumstances the presence of animal victims in environmental crime prosecutions might enhance penalties.

Generally speaking, environmental laws 'do not address the conditions or welfare of animals directly' (Frasch et al. 2011: 314; Moyle 2009; Nurse 2013; see also Sollund, this volume, Chapter 29). In the United States, killing protected animals is often prosecuted under major federal statutes, such as the Migratory Bird Act or Endangered Species Act. Such statutes, however, are considered 'wildlife law', rather than 'environmental law' (Jarrell, Ozymy and Sandel 2017). In some instances in the United States, animal deaths factor into certain federal prosecutions under major environmental statutes such as the Clean Water Act (CWA) or Clean Air Act, (CAA), but evidence suggests that this is somewhat rare (Jarrell and Ozymy 2014) and it is usually not the deaths, by themselves, that result in prosecution (Jarrell and Ozymy 2014). As Freyfogle and Goble (2009) note, U.S. law (state and federal) tends to protect animals as public assets, rather than for the sake of their inherent worth as autonomous beings. In fact, the death of an individual animal will not result in much interest from law enforcement officials. But when a large number of dead fish rise to the surface of a local water body or estuary, an investigation may lead to the discovery of illegal discharge of toxic chemicals from an industrial facility, reflecting U.S. environmental law's focus on human health, rather than non-human morbidity and mortality.

In such an example, the offender might be punished for exceeding the terms and limits of a permit, rather than harming animals. Without vocal human advocates, victimisation of animals and the natural environment generally goes unknown and unappreciated. Even then, there is the issue of standing: who will be able to not only speak for, but also be able to represent legally, non-human animals in court?

Lemieux and Clarke (2009) and Petrossian (2015) argue for the greater inclusion of animals under environmental law, and contend that corporations that destroy the natural environment and harm humans and animals should be punished appropriately. If we were to appreciate more fully harm to non-human animals and the environment, then we might recognise that a facility that routinely dumps toxic chemicals that poisons waterways and kills fish is also likely to harm humans and violate the law. By thinking about victimisation more systematically and more synergistically, we can create better policies and regulations.

The discussion above helps to ground our understanding of the processes that take place with environmental legislation and enforcement, and how those mechanisms protect (or fail to protect) victims. In the next section, we consider new directions in academic research that can help us to better understand victimisation conceptually and empirically. We then turn to a consideration of the steps one might take to apply this knowledge in one's own community to help those in need. Here, we explore possible avenues for research as well as discuss our own experiences over the last decade of becoming involved in activism to help victims in our local community. We hope this provides readers with some new insights and directions for policy-relevant research, as well as avenues they might explore to positively affect their own local geography.

Becoming involved through research

Since the emergence of 'green criminology' in the 1990s, scholars have sought to place it within the broader field of criminology in order to illuminate the causes and consequences of environmental crime in the world. Over the years, green criminologists have attempted to bring to the study of green crime the insights from the literatures on corporate crime and state-corporate crime (see Ruggiero, this volume, Chapter 23). Green criminology challenges the ways in which the capitalist economy produces environmental harm and the means by which the state plays a role in producing and reproducing victims of these harms. These include not only human victims, but harms against the environment and non-human animals (Beirne and South 2007: xiii; Brisman and South this volume, Part V). Understanding environmental victimisation from the capitalist economy means examining it through the lens of the state-corporate relationship. We seek to explore new directions for research on state-corporate environmental crime victimisation, as well as avenues for scholars to help victims. We begin with identifying gaps in the literature for future scholars to address.

The first area to address is the gap in our understanding of the scope of the problem: we need to conduct empirical studies of victimisation in order to quantify the extent of the harm that is occurring. There are no comprehensive databases on victims of environmental crime, which makes studying the results of prosecutions of state-corporate environmental crimes difficult. Studies, such as those conducted by two of us (Ozymy and Jarrell 2015), have examined environmental crime prosecutions as a mechanism to understand state-corporate environmental crime victimisation. More research along these lines is needed in order to provide estimates of victimisation across place and time. Other approaches may be to look at random cross-sectional studies on victimisation in order to understand the phenomena better within specific populations.

A second direction for future research is to expand the locus of inquiry to non-human victimisation. Studying how the state-corporate crime relationship impacts non-human victims is of critical importance. While research that involves case studies has moved in this direction, there is still much work that needs to be done to understand how and to what extent non-human animals and the environment are impacted by state-corporate interactions (Ozymy and Jarrell 2016; Petrossian 2015; Pires 2015; Runhovde this volume, Chapter 31; Sollund 2008, 2015, 2019, this volume, Chapter 29; van Uhm this volume, Chapter 30; Wyatt 2011).

A third possibility for future research in green criminology is for researchers to engage in comparative research to understand better how victims are treated differently by legal systems in different countries (Jarrell and Ozymy 2014). Such scholarship should attempt to differentiate what roles, if any, environmental crime victims are able to play in legal proceedings and what impact these roles have on punishment and deterrence.

Along the lines of the previous suggestion, a fourth avenue for scholars would be to try to assess empirically how non-human animals are treated within the existing environmental and wildlife regulatory frameworks in different countries. Such studies could look at which animals are protected under which regimes (and why), the nature and type of victimisation and the range of penalties for proscribed behaviour.

Getting active

Increasingly, criminologists have been challenged to advocate for legal and social justice (Belknap 2015; Goyes 2016). In addition to research, academics who care deeply about the plight of environmental crime victims may be able to engage in 'public criminology', working with victims, political actors, non-governmental organisations and the media as a means of resisting state-corporate environmental crimes (Kramer 2016, 2013b). To illustrate, we draw on our own experience here to illustrate how two of the authors were able to help victims of state-corporate environmental crimes.

Corpus Christi, Texas, is a coastal town of approximately 300,000 residents. It is home to the sixth largest port in the United States, and it is responsible primarily for the shipment of petroleum products. The shipping channel contains six petroleum refineries, operated by

Valero, Citgo Petroleum Corporation (Citgo, mentioned above) and Flint Hills Resources. In addition to the refineries, there are numerous associated industries, such as asphalt production, natural gas liquefaction and plastics manufacturing. There are three fence-line communities extremely close to these heavy industries, including Dona Park, Oak Park and the Hillcrest neighbourhoods.

About 12 years ago, one of the authors teamed up with Citizens for Environmental Justice (CFEJ), which was working on establishing the negative health effects caused by living near heavy industry. One of the first lessons learned when interacting with people in the community was that there had been a long history of environmental injustices in these communities. In the 1990s, local activists formed People Against Contaminated Environments (PACE). PACE worked with the League of United Latin American Citizens (LULAC), the Sierra Club and other groups to organise for political action. As the result of a civil rights lawsuit, part of the Oak Park Triangle area was bought out, which permitted some residents the option to relocate. CFEJ was formed later in 2000.

Citizens for Environmental Justice was able to pressure the state to examine birth defects in Corpus Christi relative to the rest of the state in the early 2000s; the study found elevated levels of birth defects in the babies born in Corpus Christi (Langlois 2006). CFEJ then worked with Denny Larson, the founder of Global Community Monitor (GCM), which helps grassroots organisations organise to monitor pollution in their own community. GCM also assists local organisations start 'Bucket Brigade' programs, which enable them to collect their own air samples using simple widely available materials. Later, in 2006, CFEJ worked with the Texas A&M University's School of Public Health to perform a bio-monitoring study for participant volunteers that lived in these communities. The study found extremely high levels of blood benzene in the participants (Donnelly 2008).

What united the work of local environmental justice activists was the need to find proof that a problem existed. We learned a few practical lessons here that are probably not reflected in most environmental science textbooks. First, we discovered that finding definitive scientific proof that a refinery is poisoning a nearby fence-line community—proof on which regulators, industry and the community can agree—is almost impossible. Regulators are conservative by design and elected officials in charge of regulatory agencies generally want them this way. In a decade of activism, we have yet to hear a regulator say, 'yes, we agree this is a serious problem and this corporation is responsible.' Second, we realised that industry will hire experts to cast doubt on *any* evidence produced by community activists, scholars and scientists. The result is an indefinite back and forth between the involved parties that leads to meetings, more meetings and generally not much else. Common sense or at least the most basic application of a precautionary principle would dictate that living across the street from a smelter is probably bad, but, strangely enough, trying to prove this to regulators to the extent that they will take any serious action is an uphill battle.

The third lesson we learned is that regulators are often unable to do much to help people in real-time. We found that air and water monitors are surprisingly misplaced in the landscape, that many times they test only for certain chemicals at certain times, that they can be difficult to locate after they have been placed, and that when one does locate them, it becomes obvious that nobody is actually reading them on a regular basis. Regulators are not law enforcement agents and so they provide very little real-time response when there is a crime occurring. By the time a refinery releases dangerous chemicals or poisons the groundwater, even if citizens are able to call a regulator immediately, it often matters very little. Around the refineries in Corpus Christi there are hundreds of geo-probes that catalogue groundwater contamination and air monitors that record harmful levels of emissions; rapid regulatory response remains lacking. Regulators might contact the responsible entity, talk to a representative and perhaps issue a fine, all the time knowing that if they were to pursue criminal prosecution, it could take years and millions of dollars, with the chance of success low.

Activists often engage in health-effects research and partner with sympathetic scientists, non-profit organisations, established environmental groups such as the Sierra Club and, if possible, partner with academics to obtain grant funding to conduct heath-effects studies in local communities. We found collaborating with all of these entities to be the only way to pool resources to draw attention to the relevant issues. Raising awareness is really all one can do, but it is an important first step. Still, activists, academics and other interested parties must be prepared to attend lots of public forums where nothing happens. In our experience, we felt that these forums, with all manner of federal, state and local agencies, served little more than providing community members with opportunities to vent frustrations; it seemed that satisfying public participation requirements of statutes was more important to some of the regulators than actually solving problems. In addition, we met many administrators whose job seemed to be to show up to different areas of the state during the week, suffer verbal abuse from local residents, nod their heads and ask innocuous questions over and over again.

Despite such challenges and frustrations, health-effects research can expose a problem, as well as help activists to join forces, pool resources and engage in collective political or legal action against the state or industry. For example, two of us (Ozymy and Jarrell) helped a coalition of groups to prevent the siting of the Las Brisas Energy Center (LBEC). In 2008, LBEC filed for an air permit to construct a 1,200-megawatt power plant fuelled by petroleum coke—a byproduct of the petroleum refining process (Jarrell, Ozymy and McGurrin 2012). Local politicians, such as the County Commissioner's Court, Port of Corpus Christi and Chamber of Commerce, supported the project, whose permit was initially approved by the state environmental regulator, the Texas Commission on Environmental Quality (TCEQ). Various national groups, such as the Sierra Club and Public Citizen, opposed the siting of the facility. From May 19, 2008, when the air permit was filed, to January 8, 2009, when it received preliminary approval from the TCEQ, and January 26, 2011 when it received final approval, proponents failed to consider the possible adverse impacts of building another industrial facility in an industrial port town. While the plant was originally scheduled for construction in 2009, using the legal system (procedural delays), regulatory system (exhausting all of the public input and comment sessions required by law) and political system (lobbying politicians to not support the project), opposition forces were able to delay the project to the point that the company abandoned it, unable to find investors and unwilling to keep fighting court battles with environmental groups (Doniger 2013).

What we learned from this experience is that local groups must organise with better-funded state and national environmental organisations. Regulators often side with industry, and local officials are swayed easily by arguments regarding economic development, particularly in less-affluent areas. We also learned that academics' social status can help with coordination and collaboration with other groups. Having a background in environmental science is not necessary to get involved. We found that, like any discipline, people often hide behind professional language and use it as a barrier to public participation. Science, however, never really solved the victims' problems because, ultimately, the issue at hand was political, not scientific. An academic's writing and speaking abilities, combined with doctoral credentials, automatically gives one some level of status in a community, particularly when low-income groups are socially marginalised by middle-class bureaucrats and private sector workers. Using one's academic status to gain access to different groups and employing one's research abilities to learn as much of the scientific language as one needs in order to prevent it from being a barrier to discussion are key; science itself is never enough anyway to win the debate.

Outside of working with CFEJ and collaborating with different environmental groups, we were involved in the *United States* v *Citgo* case, as discussed above. While this case received only marginal national attention, we hope that it will have an impact for victims of state-corporate environmental crime in the United States because it was the first federal court case to recognise victims of such crimes as crime victims under the CVRA. It is difficult standing in a neighbourhood like Hillcrest, watching refineries and chemical plants flaring next door, and realising that it is almost impossible to prove in court that these companies are victimising these communities; yet that is exactly what happens. *Citgo* is significant because it was the first case to confer procedural rights to victims in a criminal prosecution of a corporation for environmental crimes, even if it awarded them no compensation based on the strange logic above.

One of the authors attended the trial almost every day, talked with victims, the prosecution, and took copious field notes. The first two authors also watched as the prosecution gathered evidence, as people came and went over the years, such as prosecutors, plaintiff's lawyers, people active over the issue in the local community, and other environmental organisations outside the area, and as the decision was handed down. We helped to bring a well-known victim's rights lawyer together with other lawyers representing potential victims to file motions and support their legal defence to keep the victims' rights issue moving forward. The first two authors also collaborated and coordinated between the legal team and victims in the community. While Citgo was charged in May 2007, sentencing did not occur until 2014. Approximately 1,000 victims in the fence-line community petitioned the court to be recognised as victims under the CVRA. The authors observed and attended events where the prosecution gathered victim impact statements in the community and presented them to the court. The judge, in our view, acknowledged—albeit begrudgingly—that some of these individuals were victims as a result of the corporation's acts and omissions. While they did not receive direct restitution, this created an example for future communities in the United States—a strategy that they might employ in future legal actions—and one that we are happy to say we played a small part in helping to achieve.

We were also fortunate to play a part in one other groundbreaking effort to help victims in our community. More recently, local activists were involved in a permit challenge. In the United States, federal and state statutes generally require that any industrial facility that is seeking to expand or be constructed must apply for a series of environmental permits, such as air and water permits, depending on their operational scope. Challenging a permit is an effective way to prevent or stall the construction of new facilities that can harm the community, or to try to induce regulators to require industrial facilities that wish to expand to utilise better pollution controls. Thus, new or expanding industrial facilities in the United States often expect to have these permits challenged as a matter of form, as many large national environmental organisations, such as the Sierra Club or Public Citizen, frequently stay abreast of postings of permit applications. In our particular situation, local and state activists negotiated a halt to a permit challenge in exchange for an endowment to create a fund to buy out residents of the Dona Park neighbourhood.

Local activists, including one of the authors, and dedicated attorneys with environmental law backgrounds, formed the initial board of the Environmental Justice Housing Fund (EJHF). The primary and ongoing goal of EJHF has been to utilise its endowment to buy out individuals in the Dona Park community. After creating a board and obtaining insurance, the EJHF held a public meeting and started walking the neighbourhood block by block to speak to residents. It also began researching tax and title records and residential histories in the neighbourhood. We surveyed residents in order to learn how long they had lived in the area. The EJHF decided it could purchase roughly a handful of homes and decided to begin by buying out those residents that had owned their homes the longest and had the lengthiest consistent tenure in the community.

Many of the homes had unpermitted additions, were in poor physical condition, and all home values were depressed due to the proximity to industry. The EJHF settled on a price that was sufficient to allow them to purchase a home of a similar size in another area of town and that included moving costs. Offers were made to residents; some accepted, some declined and some wanted an unreasonable amount of money for their homes. The EJHF has already been able to purchase some homes, which means that some residents have been able to move; those homes and foundations have been demolished, and what remains are empty lots maintained by the fund. The EJHF hopes to continue to secure additional funds to purchase more properties with the goal of moving people away from harm and the longer-term goal of realising a buffer zone between the refineries.

EJHF has proved to be a rewarding experience, where a non-profit organisation has helped those residents who have lived near heavy industry the longest, and borne the greatest brunt of toxic exposures over the years, to leave. While it would be wonderful if the EJHF could assist additional individuals, what it has achieved has been important. The ongoing dilemma is what to do with the land. The goal is to keep industry from developing it or having other residents move back into the area. While a full-scale buyout is impractical for economic reasons and the fact that many residents would choose to stay anyway, these lots may be placed in a land trust and managed by the fund for the foreseeable future, sold to the city with restrictions, or other uses.

Conclusion

The most fruitful avenue to protect state-corporate environmental crime victims is to provide better funding for agencies and to improve the enforcement of existing laws. Laws without substantive enforcement are useless (Ozymy and Jarrell 2012). For the foreseeable future, environmental crime will be handled primarily under the regulatory system, rather than the criminal justice system. Green crimes will likely continue to be viewed by the mass public as *regulatory issues*, rather than *crimes* that are practically and conceptually similar to street crimes. Victims of green crime will be considered by many to be collateral damage from a necessary industrial and commercial process, rather than victims of patterned abuse allowed under the current accepted governmental practice. The way forward is to begin acknowledging them as true victims. This conceptual shift is well underway in the green criminological literature and is slowly gaining broader acceptance.

The state is often ill-equipped to help human and non-human victims of green crimes and it is all-too-frequently explicitly or implicitly culpable in creating such crimes or allowing them to occur through its own actions, inaction, or insufficient action on behalf of victims. Human victims must turn to a regulatory system to find protection and justice, and rarely do they encounter either in sufficient quantities. Non-human animals are often protected under wildlife law rather than environmental law, thereby limiting the options for protecting those that have been harmed or at risk.

While these barriers make the protection of victims of the state-corporate apparatus seem daunting, green criminologists still have a lot to offer. Through scholarship, they can continue to advance a broader conceptual and theoretical understanding of victimisation. Through empirical studies, they can bring attention to the plight of human and non-human animals. They can also become involved in their community in myriad ways to help assist state-corporate environmental crime victims. In a wonderful way, we can use our skills so that scholarship and activism can be united for the betterment of those that often suffer in silence.

References

Associated Press (AP). 2016. 'Toyota to pay up to $3.4 billion to settle a truck and SUV lawsuit,' *Los Angeles Times*, November 13. Available at: http://latimes.com/business/la-fi-toyota-rust-settlement-20161113-story.html.

Beirne, P. and South, N. (eds.) 2007. *Issues in Green Criminology: Confronting Harms against Environments, Humanity, and Other Animals*. Cullompton, Devon, UK: Willan.

Belknap, J. 2015. 'Activist criminology: Criminologists' responsibility to advocate for social and legal justice,' *Criminology*, 53(1): 1–22.

Bradshaw, E. 2014. 'State-corporate environmental cover-up: The response to the 2010 Gulf of Mexico oil spill,' *The State Crime Journal*, 3(2): 163–181.

Bradshaw, E. 2015a. '"Obviously, we're all oil": The criminogenic structure of the offshore oil industry,' *Theoretical Criminology*, 19(3): 376–395.

Bradshaw, E. 2015b. 'Blockadia rising: Rowdy greens, direct action and the Keystone XL pipeline,' *Critical Criminology: An International Journal*, 23(4) 433–448.

Burns, R. G. and Lynch, M. J. 2004. *The Sourcebook on Environmental Crime*. New York: LFB Publishers.

Cassell, P. G. and Joffee, S. 2011. 'The crime victims' expanding role in a system of public prosecution: A response to the critics of the crime victims' Rights Act," *Northwestern University Law Review Colloquy*, 105: 164–183. Available at: scholarlycommons.law.northwestern.edu/cgi/viewcontent.cgi?referer=www.northwesternlawreview.org/online/crime-victim%E2%80%99s-expanding-role-system-public-prosecution-response-critics-crime-victims%E2%80%99&httpsredir=1&article=1177&context=nulr_online.

Daley, D. M. and Layton, D. F. 2004. 'Policy implementation and the environmental protection agency: What factors influence remediation at superfund sites?' *Policy Studies Journal*, 32(3): 375–392.

Doniger, D. 2013. 'Las Brisas power plant is gone with the wind,' *Natural Resources Defense Council*, January 28. Available at: https://nrdc.org/experts/david-doniger/las-brisas-power-plant-gone-wind.

Donnelly, K. C. 2008. *Memo: Report on Results of Nueces County Family Health Study*. November.

Fiorino, D. J. 2006. *The New Environmental Regulation*. Cambridge, MA: MIT Press.

Frank, N. K. and . Lynch, M. J . 1992. *Corporate Crime, Corporate Violence: A Primer*. New York: Harrow and Heston.

Frasch, P. D., Hessler, K. M., Kutil, S. M. and Waismin, S. S. 2011. *Animal Law in a Nutshell*. St. Paul, MN: Thomson Reuters.

Freyfogle, E. T. and Goble, D. D. 2009. *Wildlife Law: A Primer*. Washington, D.C.: Island Press.

Goyes, D. R. 2016. 'Green activist criminology and the epistemologies of the South,' *Critical Criminology: An International Journal*, 26(4): 503–518.

Jarrell, M L., Ozymy, J. and Sandel, W. 2017. 'Where the wild things are: Animal victimization at the intersection of wildlife law and environmental law,' *Contemporary Justice Review*, 20(3): 319–335.

Jarrell, M. L. 2007. *Environmental Crime and the Media: News Coverage of Petroleum Refining Industry Violations*. New York: LFB Scholarly Publishing LLC.

Jarrell, M. L. 2009. 'Environmental crime and injustice: Media coverage of a landmark environmental crime case,' *Southwest Journal of Criminal Justice*, 6(1): 25–44.

Jarrell, M. L. and Ozymy, J. 2012. 'Real crime, real victims: Environmental crime victims and the Crime Victims' Rights Act (CVRA),' *Crime, Law, and Social Change*, 58(4): 373–389.

Jarrell, M. L. and Ozymy, J. 2014. 'Few and far between: Understanding the role of the victim in federal environmental crime cases,' *Crime, Law, and Social Change*, 61(5): 563–584.

Jarrell, M. L., Ozymy, J. and McGurrin, D. 2012. 'How to encourage conflict in the environmental decision-making process: Imparting lessons from civic environmentalism to local policymakers,' *Local Environment*, 18(2): 184–200.

Kramer, R. C. 2013a. 'Carbon in the atmosphere and power in America: Climate change as a state-corporate crime,' *Journal of Crime and Justice*, 36(2): 153–170.

Kramer, R. C. 2013b. 'Public criminology and the responsibility to speak in the prophetic voice concerning global warming,' in E. Stanley and J. McCulloch (eds.) *State Crime and Resistance*, pp. 41–53. New York: Routledge.

Kramer, R. C. 2014. 'Climate change: A state-corporate crime perspective,' in T. Spapens, R. White and M. Kluin (eds.) *Environmental Crime and its victims: Perspectives within green criminology*, pp. 22–39. Surrey, UK: Ashgate.

Kramer, R. C. 2016. 'State crime, the prohetic voice and public criminology activism,' *Critical Criminology: An International Journal*, 24(4): 519–532.

Kramer, R. C. and Michalowski, R. J. 2012. 'Is global warming a state-corporate crime?' in R. White (ed.) *Climate Change from a Criminological Perspective*, pp. 71–88. New York: Springer.

Krugman, P. 2017. 'Making America polluted again,' *The New York Times*, August 25: A27. Published online as 'Trump and Pruitt, Making America Polluted Again,' August 25, 2017. Available at: https://nytimes.com/2017/08/25/opinion/trump-pruitt-polluted-climate-.html.

Langlois, P. 2006. 'Birth defects elevated in zip codes of concern to citizens for environmental justice, 1996–2002,' *Texas Department of State Health Services Report*. July, 7.

Lemieux, A. M. and Clarke, R. V. 2009. 'The international ban on ivory sales and its effects on elephant poaching in Africa,' *The British Journal of Criminology*, 49(4): 451–471.

Lipton, E. and Ivory, D. 2017. 'Under Trump, E.P.A. has slowed actions against polluters, and put limits on enforcement officers,' *The New York Times*, December 10. Available at: www.nytimes.com/2017/12/10/us/politics/pollution-epa-regulations.html.

Lynch, M. J., Burns, R. G. and Stretesky, P. B. 2010. 'Global warming and state-corporate crime: The politicization of global warming under the Bush Administration,' *Crime, Law and Social Change*, 54(3-4): 213–239.

Michalowski, R. J. and Kramer, R. C. 2006. *State-Corporate Crime: Wrongdoing at the Intersection of Government and Business*. New Brunswick, NJ: Rutgers University Press.

Mintz, J. A. 1995. *Enforcement at the EPA: High Stakes and Hard Choices*. Austin, TX: University of Texas Press.

Mintz, J. A. 2004. 'Treading water: A preliminary assessment of EPA enforcement during the Bush II Administration,' *Environmental Law Reporter*, 34: 10912–10932.

Mintz, J. A. 2005. 'Neither the best of times nor the worst of times: EPA enforcement during the Clinton Administration,' *Environmental Law Reporter*, 35(1): 10390–10412.

Moyle, B. 2009. 'The black market in China for tiger products,' *Global Crime*, 10(1-2):124–143.

Nurse, A. 2013. *Animal Harm: Perspectives on why People Harm and Kill Animals*. Surrey, UK: Ashgate.

Ozymy, J. and Jarrell, M. L. 2012. 'Upset events, policy drift, and the regulation of air emissions at industrial facilities in the United States,' *Environmental Politics*, 21(3): 451–466.

Ozymy, J. and Jarrell, M. L. 2016. 'Why do regulatory agencies punish? the impact of political principals, agency culture, and transaction costs in predicting environmental criminal prosecution outcomes in the United States,' *Review of Policy Research*, 33(1): 71–89.

Ozymy, J. and Jarrell, Melissa L. 2015. 'Wielding the green stick: An examination of criminal enforcement at the EPA under the Bush and Obama Administrations,' *Environmental Politics*, 24(1): 38–56.

Pearce, F. and Tombs, S . 1998. *Toxic Capitalism: Corporate Crime and the Chemical Industry*. Surrey, UK: Ashgate.

Petrossian, G. A. 2015. 'Preventing illegal, unreported and unregulated (IUU) fishing: A situational approach,' *Biological Conservation*, 189(September): 39–48. DOI: 10.1016/j.biocon.2014.09.005.

Pires, S. F. 2015. 'A CRAVED analysis of multiple illicit parrot markets in Peru and Bolivia,' *European Journal on Criminal Policy and Research*, 21(3): 321–336.

Ruggiero, V. and South, N. 2013. 'Toxic state–corporate crimes, neo-liberalism and green criminology: The hazards and legacies of the oil, chemical and mineral industries,' *International Journal for Crime, Justice and Social Democracy*, 2(2): 12–26.

Simon, D. R. 2000. 'Corporate environmental crimes and social inequality: New directions for environmental justice research,' *American Behavioral Scientist*, 43(4): 633–645.

Smandych, R. and Kueneman, R. 2010. 'The Canadian-Alberta tar sands: A case study of state-corporate environmental crime,' in R. White (eds.) *Global environmental harm: Criminological perspectives*, pp. 87–109. Cullompton, Devon, UK: Willan.

Sollund, R. A. 2008. *Global Harms: Ecological Crime and Speciesism*. New York, NY: Nova Science Publishers, Inc.

Sollund, R. A. 2019. *The Crimes of Wildlife Trafficking: Issues of Justice, Legality and Morality*. Abingdon, Oxon, UK: Routledge.

Stretesky, P. B. and Lynch, M. J. 1999. 'Corporate environmental violence and racism,' *Crime, Law and Social Change*, 30(2): 163–184.

Stretesky, P. B., Long, M. A. and Lynch, M. J. 2014. *The Treadmill of Crime: Political Economy and Green Criminology*. London and New York: Routledge.

U.S. Chemical Safety Board (CSB). 2008. *Anatomy of a Disaster*, March 21. Available at: http://csb.gov/videos/anatomy-of-a-disaster/.

White, R. 2008. *Crimes Against Nature: Environmental Criminology and Ecological Justice*. Cullompton, Devon, UK: Willan.

Wyatt, T. 2011. 'The illegal trade in raptors in the Russian Federation,' *Contemporary Justice Review: Issues in Criminal, Social and Restorative Justice*, 14(2): 103–123.

Court cases:

UNITED STATES of America, Plaintiff vs. W.R. GRACE, Defendants. 445 F. Supp.2d 1122 (D. Mont. 2006).

UNITED STATES of America, Plaintiff vs. B.P. PRODUCTS, Defendants. S 4:07-CR-434 (S.D. Tex. 2009).

UNITED STATES of America, Plaintiff, v. CITGO PETROLEUM CORPORATION, Citgo Refining and Chemicals Company, L.P., Defendants. 893 F. Supp. 2d 841 (S.D. Tex. 2012).

Part II

International and transnational issues for a green criminology

9

Climate crimes

The case of ExxonMobil

Ronald C. Kramer and Elizabeth A. Bradshaw

While traditional criminologists have been slow to study the causes and consequences of anthropogenic climate change, green criminologists have led the way in mapping the intersection of crime, harm and climate change. As this volume demonstrates, green criminology encompasses the study of crime, harm, justice, law and victimisation as it relates to the degradation and destruction of the natural environment. Given that climate change may create new categories of offenders and victims—as well as new types of crime—it is only fitting that criminologists of different theoretical stripes consider current and future harms resulting from global warming and the causes, consequences and possible responses to climate change (e.g., Agnew 2012a; Kramer 2013b; White 2012).

This chapter will begin with an overview of the literature on green criminology and climate change. After defining the concept of *climate crimes*, the chapter will then develop a conceptual framework for understanding these types of crime by drawing on Agnew's notion of blameworthy harms. Next, four different types of climate crimes will then be identified: crimes of continuing extraction and emissions; crimes of denial; crimes of political omission; and crimes of unjust and militaristic adaptation. Finally, to demonstrate some of the theoretical and empirical questions of climate crimes, the chapter will conclude with a case study of the ExxonMobil Corporation's ('ExxonMobil') continuing extraction of fossil fuels and the greenhouse gas (GHG) emissions it produces particularly as it pertains to the process of hydraulic fracturing (or 'fracking').

Green criminology and climate change

Outlining some of the contours of green criminological research, Lynch and Stretesky (2010) direct our attention towards state crimes and global warming; global warming and criminal justice policy; the unequal distribution of global warming harms; and international laws, regulations and treaties related to climate change. Moreover, they argue that in the face of climate change, an increase in crime resulting from the hardships caused by global warming is likely to emerge geographically unevenly. Property crime or even violence might also result as social responses to climate change. The future of crime in the era of global warming therefore requires the development of policies and strategies that address the problem of climate change directly, rather than focusing on social control policies that fixate on potential crime-related outcomes (Lynch and Stretesky 2010).

Social conflict linked to climate change reflects broader patterns of social inequality, with the effects experienced differentially by the poor and vulnerable living in unstable states under poor governance. Climate change has been, is giving and will likely continue to give rise to a range of social conflicts: conflicts over environmental resources (e.g., water); conflicts linked to heatwaves and drought (e.g., climate-induced migration); conflicts over the differential exploitation of resources (e.g., biopiracy); and conflicts over the transference of harm (e.g., cross-border pollution) (see, e.g., Brisman, South and Walters 2018; Brisman, South and White 2015). These consequences will therefore have a significant impact on those with the fewest resources to cope with climate-related changes (White 2011: 39). As White (2011: 36) argues, '[i]n many ways, and from the vantage point of future generations, present action and lack of action around climate change will most likely constitute the gravest of transnational crimes … Failure to act, now, is criminal'.

Agnew (2012a) predicts that the changing climate will influence many types of crime at the individual, corporate and state levels, including acts of violence and theft, corporate environmental pollution and acts of state aggression. With higher temperatures, more frequent and extreme weather events, shortages of food and fresh water, increasing poverty and inequality, forced migration and exposure to armed conflict, climate change generates more stressors—or strains—that lead to crime as an attempt to escape from these strains, seek revenge or alleviate negative emotions. Given the possible breakdown of social order, Agnew (2012a) emphasises the urgent need to devote resources and action towards mitigating and adapting to climate change.

The edited book, *Climate Change from a Criminological Perspective*, by White (2012) is one of the first to deal explicitly and specifically with climate change from the perspective of criminology. Overall, climate change will increase both *crimes of the less powerful*, such as theft and violence in response to survival needs, as well as *crimes of the powerful*, for example, crimes related to profit motives (White 2012: 7). White (2012: 4–5) identifies three categories of offenses in relation to climate change. One category encompasses offenses that contribute to climate change, such as unlicensed pollution and destruction of habitat and forests. A second category of offenses includes those that arise from the consequences of climate change, such as environmental offenses (e.g., stealing water, overfishing), as well as associated offenses (e.g., civil unrest, criminal activities). The third set of offenses relates to regulation and law enforcement resulting from migration and adaptation strategies, including fraud in carbon trading, misreporting of carbon offsets and regulatory corruption. *Climate Change from a Criminological Perspective* also explores a number of other facets of climate change, such as charting a new general terrain for the study of climate change by criminology (Agnew 2012b; Brisman 2012; Fussey and South 2012); state involvement in climate change (Franz 2012; Kramer and Michalowski 2012; Pink and Lehane 2012; Sollund 2012); the relationship between climate change and various types of disasters (Heckenberg and Johnston 2012; Nobo and Pfeffer 2012; Takemura 2012); and the possibility of state action to reduce carbon emissions (Lynch and Stretesky 2012).

The special issue, 'Climate Change from a Criminological Perspective', in *Critical Criminology: An International Journal* (2015, Volume 23, Issue 4) delves further into the intersection of criminology and climate change by providing analyses of the problem and exploring possible solutions. In the lead article, White and Kramer (2015) highlight areas for concerted action by criminologists, both as activists and public criminologists. In the subsequent articles, Wonders and Danner (2015) examine how the gender inequalities associated with neoliberal capitalism help to produce global warming, gendered vulnerabilities and unequal effects (see also Wachholz 2007), while Bradshaw (2015) explores the direct action tactics used by environmental activists to oppose climate change and further oil infrastructure development through a case study of resistance to the Keystone XL pipeline. McClanahan and Brisman (2015) reject the discourse of a 'war on climate change' and instead propose a peacemaking approach that forges a 'peace treaty with the Earth' (see also McClanahan and Brisman 2013). Brisman and South (2015) extend the insights of Stan Cohen into green criminology by arguing that climate change deniers portray climate change as a moral issue and have turned climate scientists into 'folk devils'. Clements (2015) considers climate change from the prism of John Rawls' notion of justice and concludes that rich industrialised countries should take the lead in mitigation, adaptation and efforts to recover from the harms because they are disproportionately responsible for the causes of global warming. McKie, Stretesky and Long (2015) examine the ideology of the international voluntary carbon market and assess its effects on climate change and crime.

Within the first edition of the *Routledge International Handbook on Green Criminology*, two chapters considered climate change and its consequences. Halsey (2013) tests the applicability of conservation criminology by examining damage to carbon sinks and its associated implications for climate change. Hall and Farrall (2013) predict that as climate change becomes more apparent and as its effects become more pronounced, polluting activities will become more criminalised and new issues of environmental security, food security, insurance fraud and tax avoidance will emerge, which will generate new crimes, new criminals and new victims.

Beyond these key works, green criminologists have explored the issue of climate change through multiple perspectives and approaches. For example, Brisman (2012) analyses how the media perpetuates climate change contrarianism and assesses its implications for collective and individual responses. Relatedly, Wyatt and Brisman (2017) examine the role of denial in the theft of nature through a comparison of the manifestations of denial surrounding biopiracy and climate change. Considering climate change in ophthalmological terms, Brisman (2014) uses two types of visual impairments—*climate change micropsia* and *climate change myopia*—to explain why the effects of climate change are perceived to be smaller or farther off than they really are. In a similar way, Brisman (2015) argues that climate change is *achromatopsic*, or colour blind, in the sense that it affects everyone regardless of skin colour, even though its effects are experienced unequally.

Finally, the political and economic relationships contributing to climate change have been examined by green criminologists through the concept of state-corporate crime. Lynch and Stretesky (2010) analyse the politicisation of global warming during the George W. Bush presidential administration as a case study of state-corporate crime. Kramer and Michalowski (2012) make the case that global warming can be analysed as a form of state-corporate crime, particularly by denying that global warming is caused by humans, thwarting efforts to mitigate emissions, failing to consider policy options for ecologically just adaptations and adopting militaristic solutions in response to conflicts that arise. Similarly, Kramer (2013b) argues that the political failure of the U.S. government to mitigate GHG emissions, as well as the socially organised climate change denial, can be conceptualised as state-corporate crimes. In a subsequent piece, Kramer (2014) highlights the relationship between the fossil fuel industry and conservative think tanks that perpetuate climate denial narratives.

Climate crimes and blameworthy harms

The objective of this chapter is to extend the growing body of green criminological research through an examination of the concept of *climate crimes* and to present a brief case study of a particular form of climate crime. To offer a conceptual framework for understanding climate crimes, we draw on Agnew's (2011) integrated definition of crime and Michalowski and Kramer's (2006) concept of state-corporate crime, which focuses on the interactions between states and corporations that produce illegal or socially harmful acts. To illustrate some of the theoretical and empirical questions concerning climate crimes, we present a case study of certain actions of ExxonMobil related to the continuing extraction and marketing of fossil fuels and the resulting GHG emissions they produce.

Defining climate crimes

To classify behaviour that leads to global warming and climate change—or acts of omission related to the climate crisis as climate *crimes*—we need a broad and flexible definition that can incorporate many of the significant elements (various legal standards found in domestic law, international law, social injury and harm, human rights, social audience definitions) that have been part of the broader historical debate over the definition of 'crime' in criminology (Kramer 2013a). We use Agnew's 'integrated' definition of crime which combines norms of conduct, reactions of a social audience and legal enforcement actions. As Agnew (2011: 30) notes, while '[t]he integrated definition assigns a central place to violations of the criminal law and street crimes ... it also focuses on a range of harmful acts that are not legally defined as crimes, *including acts committed by states and corporations*' (emphasis added).

According to Agnew (2011: 37), the three general characteristics that should be used to classify behaviour as criminal are, 'the extent to which they are (a) blameworthy harms; (b) condemned by the public; and (c) sanctioned by the state.' A morally *blameworthy harm* is an act that threatens physical security (or is a failure to act to prevent harm when one has a moral or legal duty to intervene), is voluntary and intentional behaviour, and is unjustifiable and inexcusable. *Public condemnation* means that there is an emotional reaction to the blameworthy harm and a desire by citizens to sanction the act in some way. Finally, the notion of being *sanctioned by the state* means that some type of legal action, broadly defined, is undertaken in response to the harmful act. Thus, Agnew (2011: 38) argues that

> any behavior classified as a blameworthy harm, subject to at least modest condemnation by a significant portion of the public, or classified as a crime or 'crime-like' civil violation by the state, should be viewed as a proper part of the subject matter of criminology.

This integrated definition initially yields a list of what Agnew calls 'core crimes,' which are mostly traditional forms of street crime. Conventional criminologists generally confine themselves to the study of such behaviours. Of the several other forms of crime that Agnew discusses in relationship to the integrated definition of crime, the most important category in our view is 'unrecognized blameworthy harms'—a crucial distinction that allows him to incorporate much of the work of those who advocate for a broader social definition of crime. Unrecognised blameworthy harms are those harms that are not yet strongly condemned by the public at large and not sanctioned strongly by the state. Many climate crimes fit this description. According to Agnew (2011: 38), '[m]uch state and corporate harm falls into this category, since the power of state and corporate actors makes it easier for them to justify and excuse harm, hide harm, hide blameworthiness and prevent state sanction'. Incorporating these harms within the parameters of criminology is an important step towards Agnew's goal of expanding the core of the discipline. Because these harms are often 'unrecognized' by social audiences, bringing them within the boundaries of criminology requires that criminologists make an independent judgment that these behaviours are morally blameworthy harms.

Identifying climate crimes

Climate crimes are acts that are committed primarily by corporations in the fossil fuel industry, nation states operating within the international political community, military institutions, government agencies, conservative foundations and ideologically oriented think tanks. We identify four specific forms of state-corporate climate crime: (1) crimes of continuing extraction and emissions; (2) crimes of denial; (3) crimes of political omission; and (4) crimes of unjust and militaristic adaptation.

Crimes of continuing extraction and emissions

Crimes of continuing extraction and emissions are the blameworthy harms of extracting fossil fuels (such as oil, gas and coal)—*crimes of ecological withdrawal*—and the marketing and eventual burning of these fuels that then sends heat-trapping GHGs into the atmosphere—*crimes of ecological addition* (Stretesky, Long and Lynch 2014). Scientists have understood and have been warning that the emission of carbon dioxide (CO_2) into the air through the burning of fossil fuels causes global temperatures to rise since the mid-to-late nineteenth century (McKibben 2011). Both the science and the warnings grew stronger in the second half of the twentieth century. We now know, based on reports from *Inside Climate News* (Banerjee, Cushman, Hasemyer and Song 2015) and the *Los Angeles Times* (Jerving, Jennings, Hirsch and Rust 2015), that scientists working for corporations in the fossil fuel industry provided substantial documentation of the greenhouse effect and issued early warnings about the threat of global warming to society and the bottom line of the companies for which they worked. Despite the strong evidence that burning fossil fuels was causing the Earth to warm with potentially catastrophic environmental and social effects—and increasing demands from the climate justice movement to 'leave it in the ground'—the oil, gas and coal corporations continued to extract and burn these fuels, which caused global warming to continue unabated with increasingly dire consequences. The continued emission of GHGs, not only due to the actions of the fossil fuel industry but also those of the worst polluter on the planet, the U.S. military in its worldwide imperial operations (Brisman, South and White 2015; Klein 2014; Sanders 2009), is a blameworthy harm that can be considered as both a corporate and a state crime.

While the continued emission of GHGs that cause global warming and climate disruption is an important blameworthy harm, the consequences of the extraction of fossil fuels must also be considered. The extraction of fossil fuels has inflicted a staggering amount of ecological destruction and social harm since the beginning of the Industrial Revolution. These harms are also climate crimes. Furthermore, in recent decades, despite the growing evidence and concern about global warming and climate disruption, the fossil fuel industry has turned to even dirtier forms of energy and more extreme methods of extraction (Klare 2012). Offshore deep water drilling, mountain top removal to mine coal, the hydraulic fracturing of shale rock to release natural gas (fracking) (see Lampkin, this volume, Chapter 27) and the extraction of heavy bitumen oil from the Canadian tar sands (see Heydon, this volume, Chapter 18) all produce massive environmental harms, including the release of even more GHGs. Because these more extreme forms of extraction often require government cooperation and regulatory permits, these blameworthy ecological harms can also be analysed as state-corporate crimes (Bradshaw 2015; Smandych and Kueneman 2010).

Crimes of denial

As the evidence for human-caused global warming and associated climate disruption continued to mount, there emerged a socially organised ideological denial of climate science (Brisman 2012; Dunlap and McCright 2015; Hoffman 2015; Kramer 2013b)—what we call *crimes of denial.* Through a variety of deceptive tactics and narratives, this conservative political countermovement denied and has continued to deny that climate change is occurring at all, or, if it concedes that global warming is occurring, denies that it is caused by humans (see Brisman and South 2015; Wyatt and Brisman 2017). These efforts have been very effective in creating doubt and re-shaping public opinion concerning global warming (Brulle, Carmichael and Jenkins 2012). Even within public schools, the political fight over global warming has led several states to weaken or block teaching standards that included information surrounding climate science (Albeck-Ripka 2018). This highly organised disinformation campaign has been a key factor in the Republican Party's obstructionism on the issue in the U.S., successfully blocking actions that might mitigate GHG emissions. Climate change denial efforts are largely carried out by right wing think tanks, such as the Heartland Institute, which are funded by corporations in the fossil fuel industry, such as ExxonMobil and Koch Industries, and over 140 conservative foundations (Brulle 2013; Dunlap and McCright 2015). While climate change denial can be analysed at the *social psychological level* by examining ideological worldviews and cultural cognition (see South 2016), it is the *organised structural resistance* to climate science that has prevented strong political action to reduce emissions. This is also a blameworthy harm that can be identified as a climate crime.

Crimes of political omission

A crime of omission is a failure to act when one is legally or morally required to act to prevent harm (such as a parent failing to feed his/her minor child). The larger political failure to mitigate GHG emissions (which could have slowed global warming and limited climate disruptions) is a critical blameworthy harm that can also be classified as a climate crime. The failure to reduce carbon emissions has occurred both at the level of the individual nation state, as well as at the level of the international political community. The failure of the George W. Bush administration in the United States to do anything about climate change for eight years has been analysed as a state-corporate crime (Lynch, Burns and Stretesky 2010). Likewise, the failure of the international political community to negotiate an effective, binding treaty to reduce GHG emissions has been an ongoing climate crime (the Paris Agreement of 2015, however, is a step forward, even without the U.S.). While the climate change denial countermovement has played a huge role in aiding and abetting the climate crime of political omission (particularly in the U.S.), other structural or systemic factors must also be examined. One factor that deserves special attention is the creation and operation of free trade agreements (such as the North American Free Trade Agreement (NAFTA) or the Trans-Pacific Partnership (TPP))) within the global capitalist system that legally restrict states from acting to curb corporate carbon emissions and other ecological harms (Klein 2014).

Crimes of unjust and militaristic adaptation

Forms of unjust and militaristic adaptation to climate disruption can also be explored as a form of climate crime. As McKibben (2011) has pointed out, due to climatic changes that have occurred, we live on a planet today that is already significantly different from what it was at the end of World War II. Those who accept that climate change is already underway argue that it is imperative that we explore the least destructive ways to adapt to these changes while simultaneously seeking to mitigate the causes of global warming (Hertsgaard 2011).

Adaptation to climate disruption can take two major forms. One form is positive, progressive, cooperative and socially just, achieving what Tokar (2014) and others have called *climate justice*. The other is militarised and repressive, what Parenti (2011) calls the 'politics of the armed lifeboat.' We contend that the exclusion of the first type of adaptation to climate change from economic and political discourse, and the adoption of the second, are state-corporate crimes insofar as they will bring predictable and avoidable harm to large portions of the human population in order to benefit smaller segments in the richest and most powerful nations of the world.

While the failure to adopt socially just measures of adaptation is a crime of political omission, the state-corporate nexus is also guilty of the direct commission of a violent climate crime by 'responding to climate change by arming, excluding, forgetting, repressing, policing, and killing' (Parenti (2011: 11). As Parenti (2011: 7) notes, '[t]he current and impending dislocations of climate change intersect with the already-existing crises of poverty and violence'—crises that are the products of Cold War politics and neoliberal economic policies. In his view, this collision of global poverty and violence with climate change constitutes 'the catastrophic convergence'. States in the Global North are responding to this convergence primarily with militarism, violence and repression. We contend that a militarised response to climate conflicts is a form of state-corporate crime designed to benefit powerful economies and their governments at the expense of the rest of the world.

Who is responsible for greenhouse gas emissions?

There is consensus within the Intergovernmental Panel on Climate Change (IPCC) and the larger scientific community that the global warming that has occurred since the dawn of the industrial age is 'anthropogenic', that is, human-caused. It results from the extraction and burning of fossil fuels and the resulting emission of GHGs, not from natural planetary variations. Some notable Earth System scientists, such as Paul J. Crutzen (Nobel-Prize-winning chemist) and biologist Eugene F. Stoermer, have advanced the striking notion that we have left the Holocene, a period of relative climate stability which started about 11,700 years ago after the last ice age, and entered a new geological epoch in Earth's history—'the Anthropocene'—the epoch of humanity (see Brisman and South 2018). The Anthropocene is considered 'a new and dangerous stage in planetary evolution' (Angus 2016: 19). The concept suggests that humans are now a new geological force transforming the planet through their activities that put increasing pressure on the Earth System.

It should be noted that some scholars, such as Moore (2015) and Malm (2016), are critical of the Anthropocene concept on the grounds that the idea that all of humanity is to blame for global warming is, in the final analysis, an indefensible abstraction. If everyone is to blame, they argue, then no one is, and the broader structural and cultural forces and the specific classes, organisations and institutions that predominately drive climate disruption are shielded from view. Angus (2016: 227) has responded to these criticisms by pointing out the specific ways in which '[t]he scientists in the forefront of the Anthropocene project have repeatedly and explicitly rejected any 'all humans are to blame' narrative'. Angus (2016: 232) contends that the 'Anthropocene does not refer to all humans, but to an epoch of global change that would not have occurred in the absence of human activity'—human activity that involves 'the decisive issues of class and power.'

As sociologists Charles Perrow and Simone Pulver (2015: 61) point out: 'Through the direct emission of greenhouse gases (GHGs), or through the indirect encouragement of behaviors that result in GHG emissions, *organisations* are responsible for most of the world's carbon pollution' (emphasis added). A recent quantitative analysis by Richard Heede at the Climate Accountability Institute in Colorado and published in the journal *Climatic Change* helps to identify the specific organisations responsible for this form of climate crime. Heede (2014) documents that 63 per cent of cumulative global emissions of carbon dioxide and methane between 1751 and 2010 could be attributed to just 90 'carbon major' entities (organisations): 50 leading investor-owned, 31 state-owned and 9 nation-state producers of oil, natural gas, coal and cement. In a review of sociological research on major institutional sources of carbon emissions, Perrow and Pulver (2015) point to the disproportionate contributions of private sector, for-profit organisations (what they call 'market organizations') to environmental degradation, particularly carbon pollution. They note that coal accounts for 37 per cent of U.S. carbon dioxide emissions, while 44 per cent comes from the use of petroleum products. Both the coal and oil industries are dominated by large profitable corporations, such as the coal company Peabody Energy, and the Big Five independent oil companies: BP, Chevron, Conoco Phillips, ExxonMobil and Royal Dutch Shell.

As Heede's (2014) analysis shows, over half of the GHG emissions from these carbon-producing organisations have occurred since 1986, the year that Dr Hansen first testified before the U.S. Congress about the greenhouse effect and two years before his more famous Senate testimony brought the issue to greater public awareness. Moreover, a recent report from the Energy Information Administration (EIA) of the U.S. Department of Energy reveals that the extraction and consumption of oil, coal and natural gas continues to grow, fuelling even more GHG emissions (Klare 2016). According to the 2016 EIA report, *International Energy Outlook*, despite the fact that renewable forms of energy are expanding more quickly than expected, fossil fuels are still projected to control close to 80 per cent of the world energy market in 2040 and GHG emissions are expected to rise by an estimated 34 per cent between 2012 and 2040. As energy expert Michael Klare (2016: 3) points out:

> If such projections prove accurate, global temperatures will rise, possibly significantly above the 2 degree mark, with the destructive effects of climate change we are already witnessing today—the fires, heat waves, floods, droughts, storms, and sea level rise—only intensifying.

Slowing the transition to renewables and continuing with 'business as usual' means that these corporations and state agencies, despite their knowledge of the harmful effects, have made deliberate organisational decisions to continue to extract and burn fossil fuels with the result that GHG emissions continue to enter the atmosphere and heat the planet. It is important to reiterate that over half of all the GHG emissions produced by the carbon majors since the start of the industrial era have occurred within the last 30 years—'well past the date when governments and corporations became aware that rising greenhouse gas emissions from the burning of coal and oil were causing dangerous climate change' (Goldenberg 2013). These intentional actions fit the description of 'morally blameworthy harms' that can be called 'crimes'.

Extraction and emissions as blameworthy harms

The first and most central 'core characteristic' of crime in Agnew's (2011) integrated definition of crime—the definition that we are using to identify *climate crimes*—is that there must be a 'blameworthy harm'. While the other two core characteristics, 'public condemnation' and 'state sanction', are also important, the focus of this chapter is on blameworthy harm. Agnew states that blameworthiness involves both voluntary and intentional behaviour, broadly defined as purposeful, knowledgeable, reckless or negligent behaviour. Elaborating on the concept of blameworthiness, Agnew (2011: 25) explains:

> Criminologists draw heavily on the criminal law and legal theory in defining blameworthiness. Blameworthy harms have several key features, with these features reflected in a range of societies and in the international law. They are voluntary and intentional, ranging along a continuum from acts which are purposely committed to harm another, to those committed not to harm but with the knowledge that harm is a highly likely outcome, to those committed not to harm but with the knowledge that there is a risk of harm (reckless behavior), to those committed not to harm and without knowledge of the risk of harm—even though a 'reasonable person' should have been aware of the risk (negligent behavior).

Agnew adds that the harmful act must also be 'unjustified' and 'inexcusable' because most legal jurisdictions provide an array of justifications and excuses to criminal behaviour, such as duress, insanity, necessity and self-defence. In conclusion, Agnew (2011: 25) states that 'blameworthy harms are those for which individuals or groups bear some responsibility, are unjustified, and are inexcusable,' adding that 'researchers who employ these criteria for blameworthiness argue that many harmful acts which are *not* defined as crimes in the United States, *should* be defined as crimes' (emphasis in original).

The argument is that the organisational actions of extracting and marketing fossil fuels, which when burned release large amounts of carbon dioxide and other greenhouse gases into the atmosphere causing global warming and climate change, are voluntary and intentional actions, committed without justification or excuse, and thus should be defined as crimes. Although corporate executives in the fossil fuel corporations, and those in command in military institutions, did not purposely intend to harm others through their organisational decisions, they did have knowledge that ecological and social harm was a highly likely outcome of their actions, or had knowledge that there was a grave risk of harm in their decisions, or at the very least, as 'reasonable persons', should have been aware of the environmental risks their behaviour imposed. The capitalists who decided to utilise steam power during the early days of the Industrial Revolution in Britain did intend, as Malm (2016) documents, to advance their economic interests in the class struggle against the working class at that time. These men had no way of knowing that their fateful decision to shift from the flow (water and wind power) to the stock (fossil fuels) and create a fossil fuel economy would one day heat the planet and cause massive environmental harm, however. Their twentieth-century counterparts, especially the men and women who occupy the top positions within corporations in the fossil fuel industry, cannot claim ignorance. Since at least 1988, when the global warming issue became a major public and political issue (and as we will see, often much earlier), organisational decision-makers have had knowledge that ecological and social harm was a highly likely outcome of their actions. There is little doubt that the continuing extraction and marketing of fossil fuels and the subsequent emission of greenhouse gases after 1988 (and on into the future) are blameworthy harms of great magnitude and can be defined as climate crimes, even though public condemnation and legal sanctions have lagged behind. As Engelhardt (2014: 139) has argued concerning oil executives, '[t]heir prior knowledge of the damage they are doing is what should make this a *criminal activity*' (emphasis added).

The remainder of this chapter will describe some of the major voluntary and intentional organisational actions that have resulted in global warming and climate change ecocide. We present an empirical case study of the actions of ExxonMobil that have resulted in the crime of continued emissions of CO_2 into the atmosphere. Data will be presented, from numerous sources, concerning what ExxonMobil knew about global warming, when the company knew about it, and what ExxonMobil's executives did or did not do with this knowledge. Finally, ExxonMobil's involvement with extraction of natural gas through the fracking of shale rock will also be examined as a blameworthy harm that can be considered a climate crime.

What Exxon knew

ExxonMobil is the largest, most profitable and most powerful private corporation in the world. Pulitzer-Prize-winning journalist Steve Coll titled his penetrating examination of the mighty oil giant *Private Empire: ExxonMobil and American Power.* As Coll (2012) meticulously documents, this powerful 'private empire' sustains an extreme culture of resistance to government regulation that goes back to the early history of the company when it was split off from John D. Rockefeller's Standard Oil monopoly in 1911. First operating as Jersey Standard (Standard Oil of New Jersey), the company became Exxon in 1972, a new, unified brand name for all its former Enco, Esso and Humble outlets. In 1999, Exxon merged with another fossil fuel giant, Mobil (formerly known as Socony or Standard Oil of New York) to become today's ExxonMobil.

The story about what Exxon knew about the relationship between carbon dioxide and global warming and what it did and did not do with that important scientific information is well documented. Recently uncovered internal Exxon documents from the 1970s and 1980s demonstrate that the company's own researchers had confirmed the emerging consensus among outside scientists concerning the role that fossil fuels played in anthropogenic global warming and the threat of climate disruption. In response to this information, Exxon's Research and Engineering department launched an innovative ocean research program and began to develop computer models to predict global temperature increase. Based on this internal scientific information concerning global warming, Exxon also began to climate-proof its facilities and infrastructure, and plan for future oil exploration in the Arctic. At first, Exxon shared its scientific findings and participated in workshops and policy deliberations. But in the late 1980s, when global warming emerged as a major public policy issue, the company did an 'about face' and became a significant force in the global warming denial countermovement. Exxon played a central role in the larger effort to deny climate science and obstruct government policies to mitigate global warming. Exxon's extensive attempts to corrupt the debate on global warming through the funding of proxy groups that engage in denial and deception concerning climate science, corporate communications (advertorials) that misled the public, political lobbying activities that involved the dissemination of disinformation and campaign contributions to influence politicians has been well documented by environmental groups like Greenpeace (2011, 2013)), investigative journalists like Coll (2012), historians of science analysing ExxonMobil's climate change communications (Supran and Oreskes 2017), and sociologists studying the broader global warming denial countermovement (Brulle 2013; Farrell 2016; McCright and Dunlap 2000, 2003). These blameworthy organisational actions can be examined as climate crimes (Kramer 2013b). The focus in this chapter, however, is on the independent investigations that document the extensive scientific information that Exxon had in the 1970s and 1980s concerning the relationship between fossil fuels and global warming, and what the company did or did not do with this critical information. The internal company documents discovered in these investigations show that despite the knowledge that its current operations and future plans were jeopardising the planet, Exxon not only engaged in global warming denial and deception, but also continued to extract and market oil which ensured that carbon wastes would continue to pour into the atmosphere. Despite the fact that alternatives were available, Exxon continued with 'business as usual' that resulted in crimes of ecological withdrawal and ecological additions.

Evidence concerning these blameworthy harms has emerged from two separate and independent investigations. *Inside Climate News* (ICN), a Pulitzer-Prize-winning, non-profit, non-partisan news organisation dedicated to covering climate change, energy and the environment, conducted an eight-month investigation in to what Exxon knew about climate change science and what the corporation did with this knowledge. The investigation was based on interviews with former Exxon employees, scientists and federal officials, and hundreds of pages of internal Exxon documents, as well as documents from archives at the ExxonMobil Historical Collection at the University of Texas at Austin's Briscoe Center for American History, the Massachusetts Institute of Technology and the American Association for the Advancement of Science. This research resulted in the publication of nine articles on its website (http://insideclimatenews.org) in late 2015 that were then gathered together with additional materials and published as an e-book, *Exxon: The Road Not Taken* (Banerjee, Cushman, Hasemyer and Song 2015). In collaboration with *Inside Climate News*, a short PBS *Frontline* video was broadcast on this topic on September 16, 2015.

The *Los Angeles Times*, in collaboration with the Energy and Environmental Reporting Project at Columbia University's Graduate School of Journalism (CSJ), conducted a similar but independent investigation. The *Times*/CSJ investigation was based on: (1) documents housed in the Glenbow Museum in Calgary, Alberta, and at the ExxonMobil Historical Collection at the University of Texas at Austin's Briscoe Center for American History; (2) scientific journals; and (3) interviews with dozens of experts, including former Exxon employees. This investigation resulted in the publication of a series of articles in the *Los Angeles Times* (www.latimes.com) in late 2015 (October 9, October 23, December 31).

The *Inside Climate News* investigation revealed that top executives at Exxon were warned in no uncertain terms in the late 1970s that the burning of fossil fuels would heat the planet and cause climate disruptions that could eventually endanger humanity. In July of 1977, at a meeting in corporate headquarters, a senior company scientist named James F. Black delivered a sobering assessment to Exxon's Management Committee: '... there is general scientific agreement that the most likely manner in which mankind is influencing the global climate is through carbon dioxide release from the burning of fossil fuels' (Banerjee, Cushman, Song and Hasemyer, 2015: 1). A year later, Black, a top technical expert in Exxon's Research and Engineering division, delivered an updated version of his report to a broader audience of Exxon scientists and managers. According to Banerjee, Cushman, Song and Hasemyer (2015: 1), he warned that

> independent researchers estimated a doubling of the carbon dioxide concentration in the atmosphere would increase average global temperatures by 2 to 3 degrees Celsius (4 to 5 degrees Fahrenheit), and as much as 10 degrees Celsius (18 degrees Fahrenheit) at the poles. Rainfall might get heavier in some regions, and other places might turn to desert.

While Black noted some of the uncertainties about the details of global warming in the scientific literature, he nonetheless maintained, in the 1978 summary, that quick action was necessary: 'Present thinking holds that man has a time window of five to ten years before the need for hard decisions regarding changes in energy strategies might become critical' (Banerjee, Cushman, Song and Hasemyer 2015: 2).

Exxon responded quickly to Black's reports and other scientific information concerning the greenhouse effect by launching its own ambitious research program concerning the environmental impact of the release of CO_2 from fossil fuels. In 1979, the company outfitted its biggest supertanker, the *Esso Atlantic*, with custom-made instruments to measure concentrations of carbon dioxide in the air over the oceans and in the water. In 1980, Exxon funded elaborate computer models to investigate important questions about the climate's sensitivity to the buildup of CO_2 in the atmosphere. An official from the U.S. Energy Department lauded these corporate research contributions. Based on their interviews, Banerjee, Cushman, Song and Hasemyer (2015: 2) note that:

> Working with university scientists and the U.S. Department of Energy, Exxon strove to be on the cutting edge of inquiry into what was then called the greenhouse effect. Exxon's early determination to understand rising carbon dioxide levels grew out of a corporate culture of farsightedness, former employees said. They described a company that continuously examined risks to its bottom line, including environmental factors. In the 1970s, Exxon modeled its research division after Bell Labs, staffing it with highly accomplished scientists and engineers.

It seems clear that, at least at this time, some Exxon managers and scientists wanted to create a project of excellence concerning the greenhouse effect that could be 'aimed at benefitting mankind' (Banerjee, Cushman, Song and Hasemyer 2015a: 3).

One key result of this internal research program is that Exxon possessed clear and convincing information on the causes and effects of global warming in 1980 and knew of the public importance of that knowledge. A memo from that year laid out an ambitious public relations plan and indicated that Exxon wanted a seat at the policy-making table when this issue was to be addressed. The public relations plan aimed at 'achieving national recognition of our CO_2 Greenhouse research program'. The memo went on to state, with perhaps a bit of foreshadowing of a different approach in the future, that:

> It is significant to Exxon since future public decisions aimed at controlling the buildup of atmospheric CO_2 could impose limits on fossil fuel combustion. It is significant to all humanity since, although the CO_2 Greenhouse Effect is not today widely perceived as a threat, the popular media are giving increased attention to doom saying theories about dramatic climate changes and melting polar icecaps.
>
> *(Hasemyer and Cushman 2015: 3)*

The *Inside Climate News* investigation clearly shows that Exxon was very engaged in public policy deliberations about global warming in the early 1980s. One Exxon scientist, Henry Shaw, was invited by then-Colorado Democratic Senator Gary Hart to attend an October 1980 conference of the National Commission on Air Quality to discuss 'whether potential consequences of increased carbon dioxide levels warrant development of policies to mitigate adverse effects' (Hasemyer and Cushman 2015: 3). In the spring of 1981, Exxon's top climate researcher, Brian Flannery, attended a large gathering of well-known scientists at

Harper's Ferry, West Virginia, for a Department of Energy 'Workshop on First Detection of Carbon Dioxide Effects'. Flannery was one of only a few oil industry representatives invited to the workshop, where he sat on a panel with the soon-to-be famous climate scientist Dr. James Hansen from NASA (Hasemyer and Cushman 2015: 3). The workshop issued a declaration that indicated consensus among the scientists present that the build-up of CO_2 in the atmosphere was causing global warming and that this warming would bring about climate disruptions. Exxon's Flannery would also go on to co-author a 'highly technical 50-page chapter' to a U.S. Department of Energy report, projecting 'up to 6 degrees Celsius of warming by the end of the twenty-first century unless emissions of greenhouse gases were curtailed' (Hasemyer and Cushman 2015: 4).

The results of Exxon's extensive internal research program on carbon dioxide and climate change were organised and presented in a 1982 corporate primer prepared by the company's environmental affairs office and marked 'not to be distributed externally' (Banerjee, Cushman, Song and Hasemyer 2015: 4). The primer contained information that 'has been given wide circulation to Exxon management', and it concluded that despite many lingering unknowns, heading off global warming 'would require major reductions in fossil fuel combustion'. Unless those reductions were pursued, 'there are some potentially catastrophic events that must be considered', and the document noted, citing independent academic scientists, that 'once the effects are measurable, they might not be reversible' (Banerjee, Cushman, Song and Hasemyer 2015: 4). The primer and other documents uncovered by *Inside Climate News* made it very clear that by the early 1980s, before global warming became a major public issue, Exxon knew that the continued extraction and marketing of oil, business as usual, would result in dangerous environmental harms. Avoiding these harms would require reductions in fossil fuel combustion and the pursuit of alternative business paths for the company.

So, what did Exxon do with this knowledge? First and foremost, the company 'used its knowledge of climate change to plan its own future' (McKibben 2016: 2). As Columbia University's Energy & Environmental Reporting Project and the *Los Angeles Times* have documented, between 1986 and 1992, in the far northern regions of Canada's Arctic frontier, 'researchers and engineers at Exxon and Imperial Oil were quietly incorporating climate change projections into the company's planning and closely studying how to adapt the company's Arctic operations to a warming planet' (Jerving, Jennings, Hirsch and Rust 2015: 1). During these years, Ken Croasdale, a senior ice researcher for Exxon's Canadian subsidiary Imperial Oil, led a Calgary-based team of researchers and engineers on a project to, in his words, 'assess the impacts of potential global warming' on Exxon's Arctic oil operations (Jerving, Jennings, Hirsch and Rust 2015: 1). Croasdale, like many Exxon scientists at the time, was very much aware of the science linking the dangerous rise of greenhouse gases in the atmosphere to Exxon's primary product. In an interview, Croasdale acknowledged that '[t]he issue of CO_2 emissions was certainly well known at that time in the late 1980s'; to an audience of engineers at a conference in 1991, he stated that greenhouse gases are rising 'due to the burning of fossil fuels'. 'Nobody disputes this fact,' he went on to say, nor did anyone doubt that these levels would continue to rise in the future (Jerving, Jennings, Hirsch and Rust 2015: 3–4).

According to the *Los Angeles Times*/Columbia School of Journalism investigation, Croasdale's team eventually reported back that 'potential global warming can only help lower exploration and development costs'—good news for a company that had leased large tracts of the Arctic for oil exploration efforts that had turned out to be difficult and expensive due to the extreme conditions (Jerving, Jennings, Hirsch and Rust 2015: 1). A warming planet, with that warming being most pronounced at the polar regions, might make Arctic oil exploration and production easier and cheaper in the long run. While more drilling opportunities might result from global warming, internal research also suggested that a warmer and wetter Arctic with rising seas might pose risks to the industry's facilities and infrastructure. Thus, throughout the region, Exxon and other oil companies began 'raising the decks of offshore platforms, protecting pipelines from increasing coastal erosion, and designing helipads, pipelines and roads in a warmer and buckling Arctic' (Lieberman and Rust, 2015: 3). 'In other words', writes McKibben (2016: 3), 'the company started climate-proofing its facilities to head off a future its own scientists knew was inevitable'. So despite the company's knowledge that the burning of fossil fuels released greenhouse gases that result in dangerous climate change, and despite the clear recognition that to avoid climate disruptions, fossil fuel combustion must be reduced, Exxon planned to exploit the effects of global warming to drill for even more oil (and profit), all the while taking care to climate-proof its facilities. These efforts to continue to extract and market fossil fuels, with the full knowledge that this activity would cause more dangerous carbon emissions to be released, is a major climate crime. And it continues to this day. As Hertsgaard (2017: 3) declares: 'Knowing what we know in 2017'—and what Exxon already knew in the 1970s and 1980s—'expanding fossil-fuel production is like Big Tobacco continuing to addict people to its cancer sticks: technically legal but, in effect, premeditated murder.'

Exxon fracks the world

Exxon has engaged in further crimes of continuing extraction and emissions by expanding natural gas production through hydraulic fracturing in the U.S. and abroad. Hydraulic fracturing (or 'fracking') is a method of extracting oil and gas from shale formations found deep underground. Although the fracturing of shale formations dates back to the late 1940s, its more recent combination with horizontal drilling makes the process even more environmentally dangerous (see Lampkin, this volume, Chapter 27). The process of fracking involves injecting millions of gallons of water mixed with sand and hundreds of undisclosed chemicals into a well at high pressure, causing fractures in the shale whereby oil and gas is released. Fracking poses numerous environmental problems, such as ground water contamination, wastewater storage, seismic activity, air pollution and greenhouse gas emissions.

The U.S. has been in the midst of a fracking boom beginning in 2005. Over the past ten years, production of shale gas has increased to more than 40 per cent of national gas, as well as 14 per cent of fossil fuel energy in 2013 (Howarth 2015). Natural gas has been portrayed as a transitional or 'bridge fuel' that allows for continued dependence on fossil fuels, while reducing greenhouse gas emissions. Due to the methane emissions associated with flow back fluids and 'drill-out' (the stage in which plugs set during well drilling are removed to release gas for production) during well completion, the lifecycle GHG footprint of shale gas is significantly greater than that of oil or coal. Considering the fugitive methane emissions during well completion, routine venting and equipment leaks, and processing, transport, storage and distribution losses, Howarth and colleagues calculate that '… during the life cycle of an average shale-gas well, 3.6 to 7.9% of the total production of the well is emitted to the atmosphere as methane' (2011: 685). The authors conclude that '[t]he large GHG footprint of shale gas undercuts the logic of its use as a bridging fuel over coming decades, if the goal is to reduce global warming' (2011: 688).

Exxon's foray into hydraulic fracturing began in 2009 when it acquired XTO Energy, Inc. through a $41 billion all-stock takeover (O'Keefe 2012). Starting late in the game, then CEO Rex Tillerson (and current U.S. Secretary of State under President Donald J. Trump) opted to acquire a company with an established infrastructure in hydraulic fracturing rather than to start from scratch internally. This purchase netted Exxon eight million acres of holdings, roughly equivalent to the size of Massachusetts and Connecticut combined. In an era of globally declining oil and gas reserves, the primary driver for the deal was Exxon's ongoing challenge of having sufficient resources to replace annual production. Thanks to a 2009 weakening of the rules allowing unconventional oil and gas resources to meet more easily the requirements for proven reserves, Exxon could count XTO's extensive shale gas holdings as reserves (Hauter 2015: 191). In 2012, Exxon received about 50 per cent of its production from natural gas, as well as retaining 50 per cent of its reserves in natural gas (O'Keefe 2012). With the Exxon-XTO merger, all six of the world's largest publicly traded oil and gas companies became significantly invested in unconventional oil and gas (Schutt 2010). Globally, the U.S. became the largest producer of fracked gas, and Exxon became the largest producer of fracked gas in the U.S. and worldwide (Kusnetz 2011a).

Beyond the U.S., Exxon sought to pursue fracking in Germany, Hungary, Poland, Turkey and the Ukraine, but many of these ventures were met with resistance. In Germany, Exxon devoted enormous resources towards changing public opinion on fracking through propaganda campaigns that promoted the practice as environmentally friendly, safe and responsible. Moreover, the company sought to control community dialogue by presenting misleading information and limiting meaningful debate on the topic. Skeptical of Exxon's claims and concerned about access to fresh water, German activists and brewmasters alike united to oppose fracking and instead embrace more environmentally sustainable solutions. As Hauter 2015: 195) speculates,

> [t]he reason that Exxon has targeted Germany for fracking may in fact have little to do with future profits from gas and everything to do with co-opting—if not disrupting—the successful model of a major industrial nation shifting to a sustainable energy future.

Ultimately, Exxon's efforts were unsuccessful and Germany banned fracking nationwide in 2016.

Although the company acknowledges the environmental risks of fracking, they continue to defend the practice as a better alternative than other modes of energy production such as conventional oil and coal. Moreover, Exxon has also funded a series of deceptive advertisements seeking to assure people that shale gas extraction is much simpler and safer than it really is (Kusnetz 2011b). Despite these statements seeking to persuade the public to embrace fracking, in February 2012, Tillerson joined a lawsuit in opposition to the construction of a water tower in his home town of Bartonville, Texas, that would be used for fracking, arguing that the project would create 'a noise nuisance and traffic hazards' (Richter 2014). Apparently, although fracking is not acceptable in Tillerson's own backyard, the consequences of this environmentally harmful process are safe for everyone else.

Conclusion

Decades after internal documents showed that Exxon knew that its current operations were causing global warming, the company persisted in promoting climate change denial and continued on with 'business as usual'. The company went on to become significantly invested in hydraulic fracturing, a process which produces greater greenhouse gas emissions than conventional oil and gas drilling, further contributing to climate change. Paired with the company's early knowledge of the connection between fossil fuels, global warming and GHG emissions, these intentional, deliberate actions should and must be identified for what they are: climate crimes of continuing extraction and emissions.

As the literature within green criminology has shown, there are multiple avenues for criminologists to explore climate change. Given the dominance of climate change denial by powerful organisations and the general population, it is all the more important for green criminologists to not only produce academic research on the topic, but to more widely disseminate their findings to a broader public audience and to take action within the public arena. As Belknap (2015) asserts, criminologists have a responsibility to advocate for social and legal justice at the individual, organisational and/or policy levels. Activist criminology can involve countering the cultures of denial and normalisation that prevent action on climate change, contesting the global corporate capitalist system to achieve progressive policy reforms and structural changes in the global political economy and working towards the democratisation of the international political community by strengthening international legal institutions.

Identifying climate change as one of the most significant forms of state-corporate crimes faced today, Kramer (2012: 42) argues that 'criminologists can assist the effort to resist state-corporate crime by speaking in the prophetic voice to publicly identify, sociologically analyse and politically frame major forms of these crimes'. This 'public criminology' (Currie 2007; Kramer 2012, 2016; Kramer, Michalowski and Chambliss 2010; Loader and Sparks 2011) can take two forms, traditional or organic:

> Traditional public criminology attempts to initiate a conversation, instigate a debate, or provoke a critical questioning within or between publics through the publication of books and articles addressed to audiences outside the academy or opinion pieces in national or international newspapers (or other media forums) that identify and analyze state crimes or comment on important public issues related to such crimes. Organic public criminology, on the other hand, involves criminologists working directly with specific groups, organizations, social movements or state officials, engaging in a dialogue or a process of mutual education that may or may not lead to specific political actions or policies related to the prevention or control of state crime.
>
> *(Kramer 2016: 520–1)*

While continued research on green criminology and climate change has an important role to play in highlighting the problem, what is needed now more than ever is coordinated action by criminologists and citizens alike.

References

Agnew, R. 2011. *Toward a Unified Criminology: Integrating Assumptions About Crime, People, and Society*. New York: New York University Press.

Agnew, R. 2012a. 'Dire forecast: A theoretical model of the impact of climate change on crime,' *Theoretical Criminology*, 16(1): 21–42.

Agnew, R. 2012b. 'It's the end of the world as we know it: The advance of climate change from a criminological perspective,' in R. White (ed.) *Climate Change from a Criminological Perspective*, pp. 13–26. New York: Springer.

Albeck-Ripka, L. 2018. 'Idaho Stripped Climate Change From School Guidelines. Now, It's a Battle,' *The New York Times*, February 6. Available at: www.nytimes.com/2018/02/06/climate/idaho-schools-climate-change.html.

Angus, I. 2016. *Facing the Anthropocene: Fossil Capitalism and the Crisis of the Earth System*. New York: Monthly Review Press.

Banerjee, N., Cushman, J. H., Hasemyer, D. and Song, L. 2015. *Exxon: The Road Not Taken*. New York: Inside Climate News.
Belknap, J. 2015. 'Activist criminology: Criminologists' responsibility to advocate for social and legal justice,' *Criminology*, 53(1): 1–23.
Bradshaw, E. 2015. 'Blockadia rising: Rowdy greens, direct action and the keystone xl pipeline,' *Critical Criminology: An International Journal*, 23(4): 433–448.
Brisman, A. 2012. 'The cultural silence of climate change contrarianism,' in R. White (ed.) *Climate Change from a Criminological Perspective*, pp. 41–70. New York: Springer.
Brisman, A. 2014. 'The visual acuity of climate change,' in P. Davies, P. Francis and T. Wyatt (eds.) *Invisible Crimes and Social Harms*, pp. 61–80. Basingstoke, Hampshire, UK: Palgrave Macmillan.
Brisman, A. 2015. '"Multicolored" green criminology and climate change's achromatopsia,' *Contemporary Justice Review*, 18(2): 178–196.
Brisman, A. and South, N. 2015. 'New "folk devils", denials and climate change: Applying the work of Stanley Cohen to green criminology and environmental harm,' *Critical Criminology: An International Journal*, 23(4): 449–460.
Brisman, A. and South, N. 2018. 'Autosarcophagy in the Anthropocene and the obscenity of an epoch,' in C. Holley and C. Shearing (eds.) *Criminology and the Anthropocene*, pp. 25–49.. London and New York: Routledge.
Brisman, A., South, N. and Walters, R. 2018. 'Climate apartheid and environmental refugees,' in K. Carrington, R. Hogg, J. Scott and M. Sozzo (eds.) *The Palgrave Handbook on Criminology and the Global South*, pp. 301–321. London: Palgrave Macmillan.
Brisman, A., South, N. and White, R. (eds.). 2015. *Environmental Crime and Social Conflict: Contemporary and Emerging Issues*. Surrey, UK: Ashgate.
Brulle, R. J. 2013. 'Institutionalizing delay: Foundation funding and the creation of U.S. climate change counter-movement organizations,' *Climatic Change*, 122(4): 681–694.
Brulle, R. J., Carmichael, J. and Jenkins, J. C. 2012. 'Shifting public opinion on climate change: An empirical assessment of factors influencing concern over climate change in the U.S. 2002-2010,' *Climatic Change*, 114(2): 169–188.
Clements, P. 2015. 'Rawlsian ethics of climate change,' *Critical Criminology: An International Journal*, 23(4): 461–471.
Coll, S. 2012. *Private Empire: ExxonMobil and American Power*. New York: Penguin Books.
Currie, E. 2007. 'Against marginality: Arguments for a public criminology.' *Theoretical Criminology*, 11(2): 175–190.
Dunlap, R. and McCright, A. 2015. 'Challenging climate change: The denial countermovement,' in R. E. Dunlap, and R. J. Brulle (eds.) *Climate Change and Society: Sociological Perspectives*, pp. 300–332. New York: Oxford University Press.
Engelhardt, T. 2014. *Shadow Government: Surveillance, Secret Wars, and a Global Security State in a Single Superpower World*. Chicago, IL: Haymarket Books.
Farrell, J. 2016. 'Corporate funding and ideological polarization about climate change,' *Proceedings of the National Academy of Sciences*, 113: 92–97.
Franz, A. 2012. 'Climate change in the courts: A US and global perspective,' in R. White (ed.) *Climate Change from a Criminological Perspective*, pp. 89–108. New York: Springer.
Fussey, P. and South, N . 2012. 'Heading towards a new criminogenic climate: Climate change, political economy and environmental security,' in R. White (ed.) *Climate Change from a Criminological Perspective*, pp. 27–40. New York: Springer.
Greenpeace. 2011. *Who's Holding Us Back? How Carbon Intensive Industry is Preventing Effective Climate Legislation*. Amsterdam: Greenpeace International.
Greenpeace. 2013. *Dealing In Doubt: The Climate Denial Machine vs Climate Science*. Amsterdam: Greenpeace International.
Goldberg, S. 2013. 'Just 90 Companies Caused Two-thirds of Man-made Global Warming Emissions,' *The Guardian*. 20 November. Accessed at: https://www.theguardian.com/environment/2013/nov/20/90-companies-man-made-global-warming-emissions-climate-change.
Hasemyer, D. and Cushman, Jr., J. H. 2015. 'Exxon sowed doubt about climate science for decades by stressing uncertainty,' *Inside Climate News* [Online], October 22. Available at: https://insideclimatenews.org/news/22102015/Exxon-Sowed-Doubt-about-Climate-Science-for-Decades-by-Stressing-Uncertainty.

Hauter, W.. 2015. *Frackopoly: The Battle for the Future of Energy and the Environment*. New York: The New Press.

Heckenberg, D. and Johnston, I. 2012. 'Climate change, gender and natural disasters: Social differences and environment-related victimisation,' in R. White (ed.) *Climate Change from a Criminological Perspective*, pp. 149–172. New York: Springer.

Heede, R. 2014. 'Tracing anthropogenic carbon dioxide and methane emissions to fossil fuel and cement producers, 1854-2010,' *Climatic Change*, 122(1–2): 229–241.

Hertsgaard, M. 2011. *Hot: Living Through the Next Fifty Years on Earth*. Boston/New York: Houghton Mifflin Harcourt.

Hertsgaard, M. 2017. 'Climate denialism kills,' *The Nation*, 305(September 25/October 2): 3–4.

Hoffman, A. J. 2015. *How Culture Shapes The Climate Debate*. Stanford, CA: Stanford University Press.

Howarth, R. 2015. 'Methane emissions and climatic warming risk from hydraulic fracturing and shale gas development: Implications for policy,' *Energy and Emission Control Technologies*, 3: 45–54. Available at: www.eeb.cornell.edu/howarth/publications/f_EECT-61539-perspectives-on-air-emissions-of-methane-and-climatic-warmin_100815_27470.pdf.

Howarth, R., Santoro, R. and Ingraffea, A. 2011. 'Methane and the greenhouse-gas footprint of natural gas shale formations,' *Climatic Change*, 106(4): 679–690.

Jerving, S., Jennings, K., Hirsch, M. M. and Rust, S. 2015. 'What exxon knew about the Earth's melting arctic,' *Los Angeles Times* [Online], October 9. Available at: http://graphics.latimes.com/exxon-arctic/.

Klare, M. 2012. *The Race for What's Left: The Global Scramble for the World's Last Resources*. New York: Metropolitan Books.

Klare, M. 2016. 'Hooked! The unyielding grip of fossil fuels on global life,' *TomDispatch.Com* [online], July 14. Available at: www.tomdispatch.com/blog/176164.

Klein, N. 2014. *This Changes Everything: Capitalism vs. The Climate*. New York: Simon and Schuster.

Kramer, R. 2012. 'Public criminology and the responsibility to speak in the prophetic voice concerning global warming,' in E. Stanley and J. McCulloch (eds.) *State Crime and Resistance*, pp. 42–53. London: Routledge.

Kramer, R. 2014. 'Climate change: A state-corporate crime perspective,' in T. Spapnes, R. White and M. Kluin (eds.) *Environmental crime and its Victims: Perspectives within green criminology*, pp. 22–39. Abingdon, Oxon, UK: Routledge.

Kramer, R. 2016. 'State crime, the prophetic voice and public criminology activism,' *Critical Criminology: An International Journal*, 24(4): 519–532.

Kramer, R. and Michalowski, R. 2012. 'Is global warming a state-corporate crime?' in R. White (ed.) *Climate Change from a Criminological Perspective*, pp. 71–88. New York: Springer.

Kramer, R. C. 2013a. 'Expanding the core: Blameworthy harms, international law and state-corporate crimes,' *American Society of Criminology*: 2013 Annual Meeting Presidential Papers. Available at: www.asc41.com/Annual_Meeting/2013/Presidential%20Papers/ASC_2013_Presidential-Paper_Kramer,%20Ronald.pdf.

Kramer, R. C. 2013b. 'Carbon in the atmosphere and power in America: Climate change as state-corporate crime,' *Journal of Crime & Justice*, 36(2): 153–170.

Kramer, R., Michalowski, R. and Chambliss, W. 2010. 'Epilogue: Toward a public criminology of state crime,' in W. Chambliss, R. Michalowski and R. Kramer (eds.) *State Crime in the Global Age*, pp. 247–261. Cullompton, Devon, UK: Willan.

Kusnetz, N. 2011a. 'Who are America's top 10 gas drillers?' *ProPublica*, September 1. Available at: www.propublica.org/article/who-are-americas-top-10-gas-drillers.

Kusnetz, N. 2011b. 'Exxon Ad Makes Gas Drilling Seem Simpler-and Safer- Than It Really Is,' *ProPublica*, May 25. Available at: www.propublica.org/article/exxon-ad-makes-gas-drilling-seem-simpler-and-safer-than-it-really-is.

Lieberman, A. and Rust, S. 2015. 'Big oil braced for global warming while it fought regulations,' *Los Angeles Times* [online], December 31. Available at: http://graphics.latimes.com/oil-operations/.

Loader, I. and Sparks, R. 2011. *Public Criminology?* London: Routledge.

Lynch, M. J. and Stretesky, P. 2010. 'Global warming, global crime: A green criminological perspective,' in R. White (ed.) *Global Environmental Harm: Criminological Perspectives*, pp. 62–84. Cullompton, Devon, UK: Willan.

Lynch, M., Burns, R. and Stretesky, P. 2010. 'Global warming and state-corporate crime: The politicization of global warming under the Bush Administration,' *Crime, Law and Social Change*, 54(3–4): 213–239.

Lynch, M.J. and Stretesky, P. B. 2012. 'A proposal for a new vehicle-based carbon tax (V-CART): Vehicle-based global warming policy and green criminology,' in R. White (ed.) *Climate Change from a Criminological Perspective*, pp. 205–225. New York: Springer.

Malm, A. 2016. *Fossil Capital: The Rise of Steam Power and the Roots of Global Warming*. London: Verso.

McClanahan, B. and Brisman, A. 2013. 'A peace on climate change,' *The Critical Criminologist*, 22(1): 2–7.

McClanahan, B. and Brisman, A. 2015. 'Climate change and peacemaking criminology: Ecophilosophy, peace and security in the "war on climate change,"' *Critical Criminology: An International Journal*, 23(4): 417–431.

McCright, A. and Dunlap, R. 2000. 'Challenging global warming as a social problem: An analysis of the conservative movement's counter-claims,' *Social Problems*, 47(4): 499–522.

McCright, A. and Dunlap, R. 2003. 'Defeating Kyoto: The conservative movement's impact on U.S. climate change policy,' *Social Problems*, 50(3): 348–373.

McKibben, B. (ed.). 2011. *The Global Warming Reader: A Century of Writing About Climate Change*. New York: Penguin Books.

McKibben, B. 2016. 'Recalculating the climate math: The Numbers on global warming are even scarier than we thought,' *The New Republic* [online], September 22. Available from: http://newrepublic.com/article/136987/recalculating-climate-math.

McKie, R., Stretesky, P. and Long, M. 2015. 'Carbon crime in the voluntary market: An exploration of modernization themes among a sample of criminal and non-criminal organizations,' *Critical Criminology: An International Journal*, 23(4): 473–486.

Michalowski, R. and Kramer, R. C. 2006. *State-Corporate Crime: Wrongdoing at the Intersection of Business and Government*. New Brunswick, NJ: Rutgers University Press.

Moore, J. 2015. *Capitalism and the Web of Life: Ecology and the Accumulation of Capital*. London: Verso.

Nobo, C. and Pfeffer, R. 2012. 'Natural disasters and crime: Criminological lessons from Hurricane Katrina,' in R. White (ed.) *Climate Change from a Criminological Perspective*, pp. 173–184. New York: Springer.

O'Keefe, B. 2012. 'Exxon's big bet on shale,' *Fortune*, April 16. Available at: http://fortune.com/2012/04/16/exxons-big-bet-on-shale-gas/.

Parenti, C. 2011. *Tropic of Chaos: Climate Change and the New Geography of Violence*. New York: Nation Books.

Perrow, C. and Pulver, S. 2015. 'Organizations and markets,' in R. Dunlap and R. J. Brulle (eds.) *Climate Change and Society: Sociological Perspectives*, pp. 61–92. New York: Oxford University Press.

Pink, G. and Lehane, J. 2012. 'Environmental enforcement networks: Their role in climate change enforcement,' in R. White (ed.) *Climate Change from a Criminological Perspective*, pp. 109–134. New York: Springer.

Richter, M. 2014. 'Exxon Mobil CEO welcomes fracking, but not water tower in his backyard,' *Reuters*, February 26. Available at: www.reuters.com/article/us-usa-fracking-tillerson/exxon-mobil-ceo-welcomes-fracking-but-not-water-tower-in-his-backyard-idUSBREA1P24O20140226.

Sanders, B. 2009. *The Green Zone: The Environmental Costs of Militarism*. Oakland, CA: AK Press.

Schutt, B. 2010. 'Exxon Mobil-XTO Energy merger hearing centers on hydraulic fracturing,' *SNL Energy Daily Gas Report*, January 21.

Smandych, R. and Kueneman, R. 2010. 'The Canadian-Alberta tar sands: A case study of state-corporate environmental crime,' in R. White (ed.) *Global Environmental Harm: Criminological Perspectives*, pp. 87–109. Cullompton, Devon, UK: Willan.

Sollund, R. 2012. 'Oil production, climate change and species decline: The case of Norway,' in R. White (ed.) *Climate Change from a Criminological Perspective*. pp. 135–148. New York: Springer.

South, N. 2016. 'Free trade agreements, private courts and environmental exploitation: Disconnected policies, denials and moral disengagement,' *International Journal for Crime, Justice and Social Democracy*, 5 (4): 45–59.

Stretesky, P. B., Long, M. A. and Lynch, M. J. 2014. *The Treadmill of Crime: Political Economy and Green Criminology*. Abingdon, Oxon, UK: Routledge.

Supran, G. and Oreskes, N. 2017. 'Assessing ExxonMobil's climate change communications (1977–2014),' *Environmental Research Letters* [open access], 12(8) (August 23): 084019.

Takemura, N. 2012. 'Uncontrollable nuclear power accidents and fatal environmental harm: Why we have not been ready for the impacts of climate change,' in R. White (ed.) *Climate Change from a Criminological Perspective*, pp. 185–204. New York: Springer.

Tokar, B. 2014. *Toward Climate Justice: Perspectives on the Climate Crisis and Social Change*. Porsgrunn, Norway: New Compass Press.

Wachholz, S. 2007. '"At risk": Climate change and its bearing on women's vulnerability to male violence,' in P. Beirne and N. South (eds.) *Issues in Green Criminology: Confronting Harms Against Environments, Humanity and Other Animals*, pp. 161–185.Cullompton, Devon, UK: Willan.

White, R. (ed.). 2012. *Climate Change from a Criminological Perspective*. New York: Springer.

White, R. 2011. *Transnational Environmental Crime: Towards an Eco-Global Criminology*. Abington, Oxon, UK: Routledge.

White, R. and Kramer, R. 2015. 'Critical criminology and the struggle against climate ecocide,' *Critical Criminology: An International Journal*, 23(4): 383–399.

Wonders, N. and Danner, M. 2015. 'Gendering climate change: A feminist criminological perspective,' *Critical Criminology: An International Journal*, 23(4): 401–416.

Wyatt, T. and Brisman, A. 2017. 'The role of denial in the "theft of nature": A comparison of biopiracy and climate change,' *Critical Criminology: An International Journal*, 25(3): 325–341. DOI: 10.1007/s10612-016-9344-5 FirstOnline: September 14 2016. Available at: http://link.springer.com/article/10.1007/s10612-016-9344-5.

10

Global environmental divides and dislocations

Climate apartheid, atmospheric injustice and the blighting of the planet

Avi Brisman, Nigel South and Reece Walters

Introduction

The United Nations estimates that about 20 million people a year are displaced by 'natural disasters', global warming and climate change, with more than 85 per cent from poor and/or developing countries (UNHCR 2019; see also Brisman 2015; Guha-Sapir and Hoyois 2015).[1] Among the many consequences are new forms of social division, both within nations and across the globe, as the Global South suffers disproportionately from the effects of ecological crises that have been and continue to be caused largely by activities pursued in the interests of the Global North. This chapter examines some of the ways in which global warming and climate change may impact the (im)mobility of those who have contributed the *least* to anthropogenic climate change. In doing so, it engages with the related projects of southern criminology and green criminology, as they pertain to, *inter alia*, knowledge production and problems of bias, inequality and injustice. Because the causes and consequences of global warming and climate change are transboundary in nature, we assert that recognition of the shared concerns of southern criminology and green criminology could be helpful in responding to this complexity.

Before proceeding, we wish to be clear about the 'historic-futuristic' dimensions of this chapter. As Barnes and Dove note (2015: 8), 'environments have never been static and people have always not only affected their environments but also have been affected by them and have perceived, interpreted, and responded to these changes'—which we quote as a reminder that climate *change* is both old and new and that it is occurring in parallel (and sometimes, but not always, in causal relationships) with other factors contributing to the blighting of the planet. Warmer temperatures and drier landscapes lead to raging fires; rising sea-levels in some places and droughts in others, mean water availability can create disaster in various ways; polluted air and contaminated land lead to ill-health, disease and deaths. Signs of planetary stress, alongside decades-long economic policies and related practices of social exclusion, are all combining to create a world of environmental injustice and climate-related divisions and dislocations. Our starting point, however, is to note the significance of the overlapping interests of southern criminology and green criminology, both of which have been concerned with unequal distribution of harm and inequities of power.

Southern and green criminologies

Given that elsewhere in this volume (Chapter 12), Goyes outlines the relationship between, and shared projects of, southern criminology and green criminology (see also Brisman et al. 2018b), we consider each of these only briefly here. Carrington and colleagues (2016, 2018, 2019) argue that the development of criminology in the Global South has often occurred in a position subordinate to the metropolitan assumptions of a northern/western criminology. Importantly, they propose that a *southern* criminology does not seek to denounce, oppose or replace criminology as a field or subject, but to enable re-orientation and augmentation. An important part of this is the pursuit of a 'series of projects of retrieval' (Carrington et al. 2016: 3)—discovering, highlighting and recognising work that offers insight, theory and evidence that have been overlooked. For Carrington and colleagues (2018, 2019), it is important to recognise and harness the experiences and victimisations of peoples of the Global South and create knowledges that bridge the lived realities of ongoing and unheard suffering and exploitation with the disseminating and powerful voices of the Global North. This is not a project that seeks to supplant existing knowledges but to embellish and strengthen our understandings to identify, examine and reduce the overwhelming amount of crime, criminality and victimisation that occurs in the Global South (Carrington et al. 2016, 2018, 2019).

Within criminology, northern/western and metropolitan/urban dominance has also functioned as a means of exporting ideology, perpetuating the assumptions of colonialism and development-aid programmes that prescribed and imposed western ways in contexts of culture, knowledge and practice where this was unnecessary, inappropriate and often unwelcome (see Carrington et al. 2016, 2018, 2019; Hogg et al. 2017; Moosavi 2019; Walters 2003). For example, Bowling (2011: 362–63) points out that 'western' criminology can be 'criticized because its theoretical presumptions are often misleading when applied to other contexts, miss the point, or are unhelpful in other ways'. Cain (2000: 239–40) draws attention to two 'persistent problems' suffered by a sociology of crime: (1) a tendency to 'orientalism', in the sense outlined by Said (1978), of a discursive, romanticised, 'wayward and unknowing "other"' in need of guidance and instruction from the more advanced or sophisticated; and (2) the adoption of 'Occidentalism', the unreflective and insensitive assumption of 'sameness', leading to the imposition of theory, policy and practice from one (western/northern) context to everywhere else (see also Cohen 1982). As evidenced by this volume (see also Brisman 2014a; Brisman and South 2017a, 2017b), the significance of a *green* perspective for criminology (South 1998) has now been recognised widely in the criminological literature but, like southern criminology, it has grown out of recognition of bias and absence in the field (Goyes and South 2017). Although there had been various past studies exploring environmental damage, crime and victimisation,[2] the strength of engagement with green issues that was apparent in many other fields of study across the social and natural sciences and humanities was not being replicated in a criminology that, for a long time, remained very 'human and urban' centred (Lynch 1990; South 1998, 2014).[3] This has changed since the 1990s and there is now a substantial body of work in criminology on a wide range of ecological and environmental themes and topics (e.g., Beirne 2009; Beirne and South 2007; Brisman et al. 2015, 2018; Burns et al. 2008; Ellefsen et al. 2012; Goyes et al. 2017; Hall

2013, 2015; Hall et al. 2017; Lynch and Stretesky 2014; Mass et al. 2013; Mol et al. 2017; Nurse 2013, 2015; Sollund 2008, 2015, 2019; South and Brisman 2013; Spapens et al. 2018; Stretesky et al. 2014; Walters 2011; Walters et al. 2013; White 2008, 2009, 2010, 2011, 2013, 2018; White and Heckenberg 2014; Wyatt 2013).

Southern criminology and green criminology complement each other in various ways, not only in terms of their central concerns regarding that which has been overlooked (Brisman et al. 2018a), but also with respect to how their history is illuminated by the idea of reclamation—a 'project of retrieval', as noted above (see Carrington et al. 2016: 3; Goyes and South 2017; see also Brisman et al. 2018b). This is because, to some extent, both these 'new' criminologies are old: they are statements of the accumulation of thought and they necessarily draw upon earlier thinking that has questioned, resisted and called for re-balancing of knowledge-power and knowledge-claims. For example, there is a considerable amount of knowledge that could be regarded as a contribution to a 'green' perspective in criminology that has been either forgotten or overlooked, for reasons related to what Santos (2014) calls 'epistemological blindness' or due to language barriers and the dominance of English (for a discussion, see Carrington et al. 2019; Goyes 2016).

In an analysis that sets out the foundations and method for a southern criminology, Carrington and colleagues (2016: 15) have called for the acknowledgement of spatial particularities and for the democratisation of epistemologies 'by levelling the power imbalances that privilege knowledges produced in the metropolitan centres of the North'. As noted above, Goyes and South (2017) have undertaken a similar recovery endeavour regarding the history of 'green' thought in criminology and challenging the assumption that criminology has flourished only in Anglophone countries. In fact, while most of what is *acknowledged* as modern green criminology has been produced in English and in English-speaking countries, green criminological research has been conducted in a much wider range of countries. It is not merely incorrect but intellectually and politically impoverishing to accept a view or history of criminology that sees it as purely a product of the Anglophone north/west. Both southern and green criminologies call for a critical understanding of the past—of the impacts of global patterns of exploitation of knowledge and natural resources, and the legacies of colonialism—as a way of helping to understand the problems of the present and the unfolding future. Of course, this kind of critical approach is rejected and undermined by alternative discourses of denial. This is particularly so in the case of evidence regarding climate change.

Much has been written about climate change denial in green criminology (e.g., Brisman 2012; Brisman and South 2015; Kramer and Bradshaw this volume, Chapter 9; Wyatt and Brisman 2017) and in other fields (e.g., Weintrobe 2013). From a green southern criminological perspective, Walters (2018: 178) argues that,

> climate change denial is commercially and politically powerful. It is not a mere agenda that determines a willingness to see the planet spiral into imminent and impending peril; it is a politics of being that undermines the democratization of knowledge, the expression of free speech and the realization of inalienable rights.

Walters (2018) argues for the need to conceive of 'knowledge politics' as a key factor in determining the contours and outcomes of decisions and policies that both shape and influence the planetary futures of all species (see also South 2016). It is therefore necessary to discuss climate change and its impacts on global ecosystems.

Climate change, global dislocation, 'cultural extinction' and social exclusion

The impact of climate change on the future of our planet is a topic of daily scientific and political dialogue (Asadallahie and Ospina 2017). Amongst the emerging issues of global concern are issues of human dislocation and the rise of climate apartheid (Brisman et al. 2018). As Amster (2015: 159) remarks:

> Resource wars and patterns of economic colonization are often initiated by the nations of the Global North vis-à-vis those of the Global South, yielding a two-tiered world of privileged consumers at the top and vulnerable producers on the bottom. The false security created by such a system is reinforced by a mindset in which human cultures are seen as separate from nature, and where traditional societies that exist closer to nature are viewed (in Social Darwinist terms) as inferior to modern societies in their sociopolitical, economic, and moral development. These dichotomies (North/South, Nature/Culture, Traditional/Modern) are historically untenable, ecologically destructive and self-refuting even when taken at face value. … these dualisms … perpetuate an unsustainable world in which people are alienated from one another and are dislocated from the essential workings of the environment all at once.

We can see how this applies in the context of climate change. While the Earth's climate has cycled through many periods of warming and cooling over geologic time (Debinski and Cross 2009; Lee 2009), Orlove and colleagues (2015: 49) stress that the 'human influence on the climate is recent and of a planetary scale (Crutzen 2006; Latour 2004)'. The Fifth Assessment Report (AR5) of the Intergovernmental Panel on Climate Change (IPCC), finalised in 2014, describes unequivocal warming of the Earth's climate over the past 50 years—with further confidence since the Fourth Assessment Report (AR4), finalised in 2007, that the warming is the result of increases in anthropogenic greenhouse gas emissions. Indeed, the Earth reached its highest temperature on record in 2016, which exceeded the record established in 2015, which beat the one set in 2014 (Gillis 2017; see also Horton et al. 2017)[4]—leading Barron (2019) to remark that '[e]ach successive year incinerates the temperature figures of the previous one'. This milestone represents the first time in the modern era of global warming (which began around 1970, after a long stretch of relatively flat temperatures) that three records were established in three consecutive years (Gillis 2017). According to scientists from the National Aeronautics and Space Administration (NASA), the five warmest years in recorded history have been the last five and 18 of the 19 warmest years have occurred since 2001 (Schwartz and Popovich 2019; see generally Rauber 2019).

Rising global *average* temperatures (the magnitude of warming has varied across the Earth's surface) have resulted in greater variability with respect to precipitation trends: some regions of the world have experienced significant increases (high latitudes) and others significant decreases (subtropics) (see, e.g., Barnes 2015: 127, 129). In addition to changes in average temperatures and precipitation means, global warming has and will continue to lead to increased climate variability and heightened occurrences of climatic extremes, such as coastal erosion, severe droughts, floods, landslides and extreme heat events (see, e.g., Brisman 2012, 2013, 2014b, 2015). This intensity, frequency and duration of droughts, floods and heatwaves has—and will continue to have—a number of direct and indirect *geopolitical*, *cultural* and *criminological* effects. Taking these in turn, rising sea levels could wipe out entire atoll nations, such as Kiribati, the Maldives, the Marshall Islands and Tuvalu (Brisman 2013: 252 n. 32 and accompanying text;

Schultz 2017). As Maeed Mohamed Zahir, the director for Ecocare, an environmental organisation in Malé, the capital of the Maldives, cautions, 'If the Maldives don't exist, we're not losing just 400,000 people. We're losing a nationality, an identity, a cultural history, a language, a script. We're losing the beaches. We're losing the coconut palms. We're losing everything'. In response to rising sea levels, some nations have begun 'purchasing' land from other countries in order to resettle entire populations. This is occurring in relation to Kiribati, where 24 square km of land has been purchased from the Fijian Government to undertake entire wholesale population resettlement of Kiribati peoples. This process presents a host of legal and social dilemmas for the nation of Fiji, which itself already suffers from rising sea levels and the threat of population displacement (see Brisman et al. 2018).

Indeed the legal status in international law of those forced to flee their homelands due to climate change remains undetermined. The first case attempting to establish legal 'climate refugee' status under international refugee law was *Teitiota* v *Chief Executive, Ministry of Business, Innovation and Employment* (2015) the Supreme Court of New Zealand. The Supreme Court of New Zealand, which heard the case on appeal from the New Zealand Immigration Tribunal, accepted the evidence that 'life will no longer be sustainable on Tuvalu because of rising sea levels'; referring to the Convention Relating to the Status of Refugees (also known as the 1951 Refugee Convention), however, it ruled that 'there is no basis for finding that any harm they face as a result of the adverse impacts of climate change has any nexus whatsoever to any one of the five convention grounds' (2015: 107). In essence, the petitioner, a farmworker from Tuvalu, argued that he could not return to his homeland and work because his low-lying south-Pacific country was gradually sinking into the ocean. He asserted that because of circumstances outside of his control, notably climate change, he was no different from those fleeing war and persecution and, therefore, was a refugee—as defined by New Zealand's Immigration Act 2009 and the 1951 Refugee Convention. The Supreme Court of New Zealand rejected this argument and Teitota, who had lived with his family in New Zealand for nine years, was deported back to Tuvalu (McDonald 2015).

Despite this specific result, in 2018, in the aftermath of the case, New Zealand moved to create an 'experimental climate change visa' for Pacific nations' peoples displaced by rising sea levels (Cole 2018). Having signed the Global Compact for Safe, Orderly and Regular Migration—an inter-governmentally negotiated agreement prepared under the auspices of the United Nations—New Zealand continues to advocate on the international stage for the climate-displaced to be recognised under law as 'refugees', arguing that climate change 'is the root cause for forced and irreversible migrations' (New Zealand Minister for Climate Change, quoted in Anderson 2018).

In addition to forced migration, we are witnessing how rising global temperatures and the concomitant loss of biodiversity results in 'cultural extinction'—specifically, Indigenous groups' loss of arts, languages and traditions associated with various habitats and food practices, such as the way in which melting ice in and around the Inupiat Eskimo settlements of Kivalina and Shishmaref in Alaska have made it difficult, if not impossible, to hunt for seals—a mainstay of their traditional diet (Brisman 2013: 253 n. 33, 34 and accompanying text). We also note Westra's (2004: 309) point that 'harmful environmental actions committed in pursuit of free trade or progress are "attacks on the human person" that deprive civilians (notably the poor and marginalised) of the social, cultural and economic benefits of their environment' (quoted in Walters 2010: 181). Elsewhere, economic stress and crop failures could lead to increased competition for dwindling resources, such as food and water, sparking large-scale migrations and, in turn, escalating tensions, upheavals and violence (Brisman 2013: 254–256 and accompanying footnotes; see also; Zimmerer 2014: 267, 275, 276–277; cf. Barnes 2015:

10; Castles et al. 2014: 211, 212). Agnew (2012a, 2012b) is particularly helpful for understanding some of the criminogenic dimensions of global warming and climate-change-induced migration. As he describes,

> Drought will force farmers and herders off the land; sea-level rise will force coastal inhabitants to move; social conflict will force many to flee to safer areas … ; and extreme weather events and forest fires will destroy homes and livelihoods—again prompting migration … While a portion of this migration will cross borders, much of it will be internal. Many of the migrants will move to megacities in developing countries, which are often polluted, overcrowded, and lacking in basic infrastructure such as clean water and sewerage.
>
> *(2012a: 24 [internal citations omitted])*

If work and employment opportunities are limited and if resources are scarce in the receiving region, this could create strains for the migrants that could lead to criminal behaviour (e.g., theft, prostitution); at the same time, such migrants could also be susceptible to victimisation. Agnew is cautious, however, about assuming that migration will necessarily result in crime, either by or to the migrant population (see also Brisman 2019). Context is paramount and the likelihood of criminality is linked not only to the availability or absence of resources, but to pre-existing social divisions, the preparedness of the receiving area, and the degree of hostility to the migrants. The presence of such conditions exacerbates strains, Agnew predicts, thereby increasing the likelihood of illicit/illegal responses. Relatedly, Agnew (2012a: 29) points out that '[m]igration may … foster state crime and other harmful behaviours, such as closing borders to those desperate for basic necessities'. This, in turn, could create conditions ripe for human trafficking (see, e.g., White 2016) and widen circumstances of vulnerability and openness to victimisation. For example,

> the psycho-social impact of displacement and sense of 'loss' makes people vulnerable to exploitation—whether encouragement into crime, capture into human trafficking for sex and labour, or recruitment as disposable soldiers in wars that are often waged over the riches of the earth, in turn displacing more people.
>
> *(South 2012: 101)*

Efforts to smuggle people into nation-states with more/better resources could, in turn, lead to military assaults on migrant groups and, potentially, to genocide (Agnew 2012a; Crook et al. 2018; Zimmerer 2014).

It would be overly reductive, however, to assume that those who *leave* a given area would necessarily be the poorest. As Guy Jobbins, an expert on climate adaptation, resilient livelihoods, poverty reduction and natural resources management argues, 'It's always the poor who are hurt the most because they are less able to absorb the shocks and adapt because they have fewer assets' (quoted in Vidal 2011). While climate change may be hurting those who are most vulnerable (see Stewart and Garcia-Navarro 2019), this does not necessarily mean that such individuals have been or will be the first to leave when a hurricane or powerful storm or crippling heatwave strikes. As Dr Nicole Stephens (2018), a professor at the Kellogg School of Management at Northwestern University, points out with respect to hurricanes in the United States, we often

> presume everyone in harm's way has a clear ability to leave when, in reality, many lack reliable transportation or the money for gas and a hotel. Countless people don't have

> close friends or family to stay with outside the hurricane-threatened area, and others cannot take for granted having a job when they return in the days or weeks after the storm.

Thus, 'material reasons' and 'monetary constraints' may lead people *to stay* in their homes and face a dangerous storm involuntarily, rather than evacuate—rendering them the 'climate abandoned'. In other situations and locations, financial factors may force people *to leave* their families/friends/neighbours, home, livelihoods and land, making them 'climate refugees'.[5] Moreover, because 'people who migrate, whether by choice or not, still like to stick close to home, moving just far enough to get out of harm's way but often remaining within the same state or region' (Pierre-Louis 2019), some people may be 'climate refugees' multiple times over—needing to move again after their new home becomes threatened or living conditions become untenable. At the same time, those with financial resources may be able to enjoy a new type of separation from everyone else—the kind of 'gated leisure' or 'elite survivalism' promised to those on the privileged side of the climate apartheid divide (see generally Pierre-Louis 2019).[6] So, whilst the nations of the Global South experience disproportionate human dislocation (BBC 2019; Gross 2017), we are also witnessing the emergence of 'privatised green enclaves' created by the rich within those countries threatened by global warming and climate change (South 2019/20).

The 'Eko Atlantic' in Nigeria, for example, is a proposed vision for the future—an ultra-elite and privileged metropolis for the super-rich, protected by private security from the impoverished, who dwell beyond the guarded walls. This has been described by some as a signal of the new emerging 'climate apartheid'—in other words, 'a world in which the rich and powerful exploit the global ecological crisis to widen and entrench extreme inequalities and seal themselves off from its impacts' (Lukacs 2014; see also BBC 2019; Brisman et al. 2018). It is proposed that this project will involve a ten-square-kilometre, multi-billion USD development along the Lagos shoreline, funded by transnational corporations and banks that seek to establish a self-governing enclosed metropolis of unprecedented living splendour on land rescued from the threat of rising seas. Indeed, the project is premised on being a capitalist response to 'arresting the ocean's encroachment'. The developers describe the project as:

> an entire new coastal city being built on Victoria Island adjacent to Lagos, Nigeria, to solve the chronic shortage of real estate in the world's fastest-growing megacity. It is a focal point for investors capitalising on rich development growth based on massive demand—and a gateway to emerging markets of the continent.
>
> *(Eko Atlantic 2017)*

It is estimated that this mega 'ecofriendly' city, advertised as matching the magnificence of Paris' Champs-Elysees and New York's Fifth Avenue, will house 250,000 of Africa's wealthiest people in a location where two-thirds of the population live in poverty (Winsor 2015). Eko Atlantic was originally conceived in 2003 as a retaining wall to prevent shoreline erosion caused by climate change and rising seas. What was, therefore, designed to be an architectural feature to save coastal Nigeria *for everyone* has evolved into 'the African Dubai'—a walled sanctuary of grandeur where the country's richest 1 per cent have their futures secured, whilst the impoverished locals are evicted from their surrounding homes to make way for the world's most expensive development (Soles 2014). Those providing the financial backing for the development are banks, corporations and former political officers with dubious records of human rights abuse. As Lukacs (2014: 2) describes:

> Those behind the project—a pair of politically connected Lebanese brothers who run a financial empire called the Chagoury Group, and a slew of African and international banks—give a picture of who will be catered to. Gilbert Chagoury was a close advisor to the notorious Nigerian dictatorship of the mid 1990s, helping the ultra-corrupt general Sani Abacha as he looted billions from public coffers. Abacha killed hundreds of demonstrators and executed environmentalist Ken Saro-Wiwa who rose to fame protesting the despoiling of the country by Shell and other multinational oil corporations.

The Eko Atlantic is not a one-off. As Squire and colleagues (2018) observe, the construction of 'air domes' or 'climate shelters' are predicted to be an architectural and technological innovation response to problems of polluted air. These futuristic artificially constructed geospheres or 'dome cities' seek to create self-sustaining environments within large enclosed pressurised translucent synthetic bubbles. The concept was first devised in the 1990s but became popularised by the Beijing Yuedun Metaspace—an air purification system to combat dangerous air quality in rapidly industrialising Chinese cities (Ying 2014). At present, 'air domes' have been developed for indoor sports facilities and schools, yet large commercial manufacturers have more grandiose visions. Pacific Domes USA, for example, manages biosphere domes and argues that they are 'engineering marvels designed to maintain whole sustainable systems for the future of Biosphere living. Through Earth-based science, Biosphere Domes are forging a new era in sustainable living by integrating the innate Intelligence found in Nature's self-sustained ecosystems' (Pacific Domes 2017: 1). Yet, the ability to produce large-scale sustainable living within climate-controlled 'domes' remains unproven and untested. Our concern with seeking technological advances to resolve human-induced pollution is that, like the Eko Atlantic concept discussed above, 'air domes' will become the domain of the rich and powerful, to be built within confined enclaves of the wealthy. Frase (2019: 9) refers to these as the 'apocalyptic fantasies of the super rich', whom he describes as 'invest[ing] in various schemes to hide out from what they see as the looming collapse of civilization'. Whether it is the Eko Atlantic or 'air domes' or 'walled compounds' to protect the super-rich with 'killer drones, while the rest of us scramble for what is left of a ruined Earth', it is clear that a small segment of the population does not believe that 'we're all in this together and [share] an interest in protecting the Earth for all our sakes' (Frase 2019: 10)—because such futuristic visions of purified clean air within fabricated climate shelters, independent floating cities, and fortified compounds have not included the starving and impoverished in Africa, nor the people of the slums of India and South America.[7] Indeed, as Gasser (2016) decries,

> capitalism, by its very nature, is completely incompatible with a just and sustainable future. If capitalism has a 'solution' for the climate crisis, one can only imagine a dystopian world where elites survive in isolated islands of livability, protected from the masses of climate refugees on the outside.

'Climate reductionism' and the 'cascade' of ecological crises

Without diminishing the already-experienced and anticipated/expected impacts of climate change, some commentators (e.g., Barnes 2015; Barnes and Dove 2015) have cautioned that heightened political and scholarly attention to climate change runs the risk of ascribing *all* changes in environment and society to *climate*. As Hulme (2011: 247) argues,

> heightening anxieties about future anthropogenic climate change are fueling … 'climate reductionism,' a form of analysis and prediction in which climate is first extracted from

> the matrix of interdependencies that shape human life within the physical world. Once isolated, climate is then elevated to the role of dominant predictor variable.[8]

Thus Hulme acknowledges that some previous attempts to understand and theorise the relationship between climate and society have fallen prey to the fallacy of '"climate determinism", in which climate is elevated to become a—if not *the*—universal predictor (and cause) of individual physiology and psychology and of collective social organization and behavior'. The problem with 'climate reductionism' as 'a form of neo-environmental determinism', however, is that it is often accompanied by 'eschatological rhetoric … where human freedom and agency are extinguished by the iron grip of the forces of climate' (2011: 246, 265, 248). To be clear, Hulme does not suggest tacking in the opposite direction, which runs the risk of '"climate indeterminism", in which climate is relegated to a footnote in human affairs and stripped of any explanatory power' (2011: 246). But his point—and one that we find compelling—is that the future (whatever it may be) will not be determined 'by climate *alone*' (2011: 266; emphasis added). It becomes incumbent then on green criminologists to articulate a *balance* between identifying a 'cascade of events' (Debinski and Cross 2009: 560) that may occur due to/from/in conjunction with climate change, while at the same time situating climate change—and the repercussions thereof—'in the context of other processes that may actually have more immediate significance to people's lives, such as grinding poverty or the loss of arable land and biodiversity' (Barnes and Dove 2015: 10). In other words, some communities will be particularly vulnerable to the effects of climate change because of prior activities and impacts; elsewhere, climate change will generate new and unforeseen consequences. Climate change cannot, as Barnes and Dove (2015: 10) stress, for better or for worse (or for varying degrees of worse) 'be unraveled from the complex web of social and material relations that mediate people's interactions with their environments (Cassidy 2012)'.

Essentially, green criminologists must call attention to the environmental—and criminological—implications of climate change. But given that climate change may not be the central—or driving—factor in/for all present or future environmental issues, green criminologists must maintain the strong and broad research agenda that has developed the field so well to date. We attempt to illustrate how this might be done in the next section.

Atmospheric injustice and the health divide

The renowned sociologist Ulrich Beck once stated that 'smog is democratic' (Beck 1992)—arguing that air pollution knows no ethnic or social divides—that it respects no geopolitical boundaries—and that we are all potential victims from atmospheric harms and damage to the natural environment as we all depend on the air we breathe and the environment for food and water. Whilst this is true, we do not experience environmental victimisation equally. All too often, and as noted above, it is the poorer and the more powerless who will feel the most dramatic effects of environmental harm and its consequences (see, e.g., BBC 2019; Stewart and Garcia-Navarro 2019). In fact, this 'climate divide' (South 2012; White 2014; see also Brisman 2019; Brisman and South 2019; Fussey and South 2012) produces a local and global 'health divide', which connects to both environmental pollution and to the causes of global warming.

In recent years, air pollution has been referred to as an 'invisible killer' and 'an invisible health crisis' (Walters 2014). The devastating effects of toxic air are experienced at both a macro and micro level. For example, only 5 per cent of the world's population breathes clean air, with pollution from tailpipe emissions, coal-fired power plants and 'Big Ag' responsible for a purported one out of every nine deaths (Hahn 2019);[9] it is estimated that outdoor air pollution causes the annual premature death of more than two-and-a-half million people worldwide through respiratory infections, heart disease and lung cancer—all accelerated by, or the direct result of, poor air quality (Kinver 2013; cf. Hersher 2019).[10] Importantly, in terms of our earlier discussion, air pollution in the form of greenhouse gas emissions is a key contributor to global warming that threatens the very existence of low-lying Pacific nation states through unseasonal and unprecedented destructive climatic events. As a result, such emissions cause damage and death on a global scale. When environmental harm is considered within the context and concepts of damage, deprivation and dislocation that disrupt, devalue or extinguish the lives and habitats of human and non-human beings, then it can be conceived as both aggressive and violent. Here, we begin to see environmental harm not just as an injustice, but as a form of *violence*.[11]

The political theorist Steve Vanderheiden (2008) calls for 'atmospheric justice'—recognising that the vast majority of air pollution and greenhouse gas emissions are problems caused by fossil fuel combustion, deforestation and the industrial activities of the world's most economically wealthy and powerful nations—or, in the words of Tsoneva (2019), in her analysis of air pollution in Sofia, Bulgaria, '[p]ollution is a political question, which boils down to who pays the price for the consequences of economic development'. Such nations' 'growth economies', productivity and consumption continue to have devastating consequences for the world's lowest-emission-producing countries. To remedy this, Vanderheiden (2008) calls for internationally agreed air pollution targets, with a global oversight committee and with a system under which the largest polluters compensate low-emitting nations for the environmental and human impacts of the atmospheric injustices not of their creation. Vanderheiden's (2008) recommendations, while more than a decade old, remain salient. Although the 2015 Paris Agreement has set some pollution targets, we are far from an international regulatory regime that imposes penalties and seeks compensations.

Conclusion

In the future then, we must, on the one hand, anticipate *some degree* of inter- and intra-state dislocation as a result of climate change. Some who move will be forced to do so; others who move will be those with resources, leaving behind the 'climate abandoned'. At the same time—and in other places—climate-induced migration will simply be a matter of moving from one estate or gated community to another—an eco-enclave to protect the wealthy. In other words, those who do move may be the affluent, or the very poor, depending on specific circumstances. Moreover, climate-induced migration may or may not occur and may or may not be negative. As Castles and colleagues (2014: 213) remind us, 'people have always moved in search of better livelihoods, and this can bring benefits both for origin and destination areas'. This prompts a call for a more nuanced approach to the consequences of climate change. We need to illuminate the range of possibilities emerging from the impacts of global climate change, while, at the same time, remaining sensitive to the shades, uncertainties and vicissitudes of context.

Although the global market decline in the fossil fuel trade has witnessed an increase in renewables (cf. Barron 2019), it is expected that coal and oil will continue to play a significant role in international energy needs for the next three decades (International Energy Agency 2018). With international markets and existing regulatory and legal apparatus unable to secure the future from toxic atmospheres, many multinational corporations are turning to innovations in technology to provide clean air. In this respect, the 2015 Paris Agreement has been widely condemned by poorer nations for failing to secure funds to alleviate the consequences of climate change (drought, famine, rising sea levels and coastal erosion) caused by rich nations. Seen as favouring 'highly developed' industrialised and polluting nations of the Global North, the 2015 Paris Agreement has failed to provide legal mechanisms to hold polluting rich nations to account. 'Climate justice' is therefore compromised and significant instruments of international governance and strategy continue to serve the interests of dominant trading nations.

Locally, nationally, transnationally, we live in a world of feigned ignorance (McGoey 2012), simultaneously knowing that environmental and social problems are accumulating, yet denying the causes or urgency of response, and instead embracing the reassurance of populism and consumerism (see South 2016). Weintrobe (2013: 7), a psychoanalyst, refers to this as 'disavowal', a state in which we are aware of climate change and its effects, but find ways to remain undisturbed by the implications of it; we remain uninspired to effect any action. With 'business as usual', certain inequalities and vulnerabilities will become increasingly important as our environment degrades, pollution increases and climate change makes its impact felt. Now—and in the future—anthropogenic global warming and climate change—increasing air and ocean temperatures, altered precipitation and storm patterns, rising sea levels and growing desertification—will lead to an increase in global environmental divides and dislocations. In so doing, it will define not only *where* we are, but *who* we are.

Notes

1 Some scholars take pains to point out that it is unlikely that climate change *by itself* will cause massive migration. Castles and colleagues (2014: 211), for example, caution that 'climate-change induced migration should not be analysed in isolation from other forms of movement—especially economic migration and forced migration'. As such, it should come as little surprise that estimates for migration as a result of climate change vary widely: the International Organisation for Migration warned in 2014 that anywhere from *25 million* to *one billion* people could be displaced by 2050 due to climate change (BBC 2019).

2 See, e.g., articles reprinted in sections 2 and 3 of South and Beirne (2006) and in all three parts of White (2009).

3 This critique of 'absences' includes neglect of non-human animal life (see, e.g., Beirne 1995, 1997, 1999, 2009, 2014; Burton et al., this volume, Chapter 3; Maher and Pierpoint, this volume, Chapter 28; Nurse 2013; Pellow, this volume, Chapter 32; Runhovde, this volume, Chapter 31; Sollund 2011, 2012, 2013, 2015, 2017a, 2017b, 2019, this volume, Chapter 29; van Uhm, this volume, Chapter 30) and rural life (see, e.g., Brisman, McClanahan and South 2014, 2016; DeKeseredy 2013; DeKeseredy and Donnermeyer 2013; Donnermeyer 2012).

4 Note that global average temperatures in 2017 were 1.62 degrees Fahrenheit (0.90 degrees Celsius) warmer than the 1951 to 1980 mean—second only to global temperatures in 2016. Or, to put it another way, the Earth's global surface temperatures in 2017 ranked as the second warmest since 1880 (NASA 2018). The Earth's average surface temperature in 2018, in turn, was the fourth highest in nearly 140 years of record keeping (Schwartz and Popovich 2019). It is worth emphasising that not all areas of the Earth are warming at the same rate. According to the National Oceanic and Atmospheric Administration, the Arctic is warming approximately twice as fast as other parts of the world (Fountain and Popovich 2019).

5 Hulme (2011: 248) attributes the term 'climate refugees' to Norman Myers (1993), who estimated 150–250 million climate refugees by 2050. Hulme contends that this claim has translated into powerful rhetoric, whereby such refugees are predicted to 'threaten global, regional, and national security in a rerun of the Mongol invasions of Europe'.

6 Reporting on how some cities in the northern United States, such as Buffalo, New York, and Duluth, Minnesota, have begun marketing themselves as 'climate refuges' for 'climate migrants' eager to escape other parts of the United States (the sweltering South, the East with its floods and the West with its wildfires), Pierre-Louis (2019) observes that such approaches 'favor those who are financially able to move … select[ing] for the affluent'.

7 As Jenny Maher has pointed out (personal communication) the visual representations of such sites or communities emphasise flourishing flora but frequently seem to exclude images of fauna.

8 In a similar vein, Haruki Murakami, the Japanese writer, writes in his memoir,

> The weather's been strange in Japan this summer [2006]. The rainy season, which usually winds down in the beginning of July, continued until the end of the month [August]. It rained so much I got sick of it. There were torrential rains in parts of the country, and a lot of people died. They say it's all because of global warming. Maybe it is, and maybe it isn't. Some experts claim it is, some claim it isn't. There's some proof that it is, some that it isn't. But still people say that most of the problems the Earth is facing are, more or less, due to global warming. When sales of apparel go down, when tons of driftwood wash up on the shore, when there are floods and droughts, when consumer prices go up, most of the fault is ascribed to global warming. What the world needs is a villain that people can point at and say, 'It's all your fault!' [2008: 139].

9 In a perverse effort to capitalize on global air pollution—and in a seeming attempt to prey on people choking on pollution—a number of companies have emerged (e.g., Aethaer (www.aethaer.com), Breathe Swiss (www.breatheswiss.com), Pure Swiss Air (https://twitter.com/pureswissair?lang=en), Vitality Air (https://vitalityair.com/), Swiss Alpine Air (https://twitter.com/swissalpineair?lang=en), Swissbreeze (www.swissbreeze.com)) that now market expensive, high-end bottled fresh air to those who can afford it. For a discussion, see Moshakis (2018); Startupticker.ch (2017).

10 It bears mention that Kinver's (2013) figure 2.5+ million premature deaths per year may be a *conservative* number. Moshakis (2018), citing data from the World Health Organization (WHO), reports that air pollution costs 6.5 million premature deaths a year—or one in nine of the global total. (According to the WHO, in 2016 in China alone, more than one million people died from the effects of ambient air pollution (see Shea 2019).)

11 For a provocative argument that climate change is a form of terror, see Sutter (2015); see also Bastasch (2015).

References

Agnew, R. 2012a. 'Dire forecast: A theoretical model of the impact of climate change on crime,' *Theoretical Criminology*, 16(1): 21–42.

Agnew, R. 2012b. 'It's the end of the world as we know it: The advance of climate change from a criminological perspective,' in R. White (ed). *Climate Change from a Criminological Perspective*, pp. 13–25. London: Springer.

Amster, R. 2015. *Peace Ecology*. Boulder, CO and London: Paradigm Publishers.

Anderson, C. 2018. 'New zealand creating climate change refugees visas'. *The Guardian*. October 31, 2018. Available at: https://www.theguardian.com/world/2017/oct/31/new-zealand-considers-creating-climate-change-refugee-visas.

Asadallahie, A. and Ospina, A. V. 2017. *Facing the Climate Change Conundrum: A Pessimist's and Optimist's Perspective*. Geneva: International Institute for Sustainable Development. Available at: https://iisd.org/blog/facing-climate-change-conundrum-pessimist-s-and-optimist-s-perspective.

Barnes, J. and Dove. M. R. 2015. 'Introduction,' in Jessica Barnes and Michael R. Dove (eds). *Climate Cultures: Anthropological Perspectives on Climate Change*, pp. 1–21. New Haven, CT and London: Yale University Press.

Barnes, J. 2015. 'Scale and agency: Climate change and the future of egypt's water,' in J. Barnes, and M. R. Dove (eds). *Climate Cultures: Anthropological Perspectives on Climate Change*, pp. 127–145. New Haven, CT and London: Yale University Press.

Barron, J. 2019. 'How big business is hedging against the apocalypse,' *The New York Times Magazine*. April 11. Available at: https://nytimes.com/interactive/2019/04/11/magazine/climate-change-exxon-renewable-energy.html?action=click&module=Top%20Stories&pgtype=Homepage

Bastasch, M. 2015. 'CNN Op-Ed: Global warming is terrorism,' *Daily Caller*. December 1. Available at: https://dailycaller.com/2015/12/01/cnn-global-warming-is-terrorism/

Batasch, M. 2015. 'CNN Op-Ed: Global warming is terrorism'. *The Daily Caller*. December 1. Available at: https://dailycaller.com/2015/12/01/cnn-global-warming-is-terrorism/.

BBC. 2019. '"Climate apartheid" between rich and poor looms,' UN Expert Warns. *BBC News*. June 25. Available at: https://bbc.com/news/world-48755154.

Beck, U. 1992. *Risk Society*. London: Sage.

Beirne, P. 1995. 'The use and abuse of animals in criminology: A brief history and current review,' *Social Justice*, 22(1): 5–31.

Beirne, P. 1997. 'Rethinking bestiality: Towards a concept of interspecies sexual assault,' *Theoretical Criminology*, 1(3): 317–340.

Beirne, P. 1999. 'For a nonspeciesist criminology: Animal abuse as an object of study,' *Criminology*, 37(1): 117–147.

Beirne, P. 2009. *Confronting Animal Abuse: Law, Criminology, and Human-animal Relationships*. Lanham, MD: Rowman & Littlefield.

Beirne, P. 2014. 'Theriocide: Naming animal killing,' *International Journal For Crime, Justice And Social Democracy*, 3(2): 49–66.

Beirne, P. and South, N. (eds.). 2007. *Issues in Green Criminology: Confronting Harms against Environments, Humanity and Other Animals*. Cullompton, Devon, UK: Willan.

Bowling, B. 2011. 'Transnational criminology and the globalization of harm production,' in M. Bosworth and C. Hoyle (eds.) *What Is Criminology?*, pp. 361–379. Oxford: Oxford University Press.

Brisman, A. and South, N. 2015. 'New "folk devils", denials and climate change: Applying the work of stanley cohen to green criminology and environmental harm,' *Critical Criminology: An International Journal* 23(4): 449–460.

Brisman, A., and South, N. 2017a. 'Green criminology,' in A. Brisman, E. Carrabine, and N. South (eds.) *The Routledge Companion to Criminological Theory and Concepts*, pp. 297–300. London and New York: Routledge.

Brisman, A. and South, N. 2017b. 'Green criminology,' in A. Liebling, S. Maruna, and L. McAra (eds). *The Oxford Handbook of Criminology*, Sixth Edition, pp. 329–349. Oxford: Oxford University Press.

Brisman, A., and South, N. 2017c. 'Consumer technologies, crime and environmental implications,' in M. R. MaGuire and T. Holt (eds.) *The Routledge Handbook of Technology, Crime and Justice*, pp. 310–324. Abingdon, Oxon, UK: Routledge.

Brisman, A. and South, N. 2019. 'Green criminology and environmental crimes and harms,' *Sociology Compass*, 13(1): e12650. DOI: 10.1111/soc4.12650.

Brisman, A., South, N. and White, R. (eds.). 2015. *Environmental Crime and Social Conflict: Contemporary and Emerging Issues*. Surrey, UK: Ashgate.

Brisman, A., McClanahan, B., and South N. 2014. 'Toward a green-cultural criminology of "the rural," *Critical Criminology: An International Journal* 22(4): 479–494.

Brisman, A., McClanahan, B., and South, N. 2016. 'Fractured earth, forced labour: A green criminological analysis of rights and the exploitation of landscapes and workers in rural contexts,' in J. F. Donnermeyer (ed). *The International Handbook of Rural Criminology*, pp. 289–297. London and New York: Routledge.

Brisman, A., Goyes, D. R., Mol, H. and South, N. 2017. 'Introduction: The theft of nature and poisoning of the land in latin america,' in D. R. Goyes, H. Mol, A. Brisman, and N. South (eds). *Environmental Crime in Latin America: The Theft of Nature and the Poisoning of the Land*, pp. 1–9. London: Palgrave Macmillan.

Brisman, A., South, N, and Walters R. 2018a. 'Climate apartheid and environmental refugees,' in K. Carrington, R. Hogg, J. Scott, and M. Sozzo (eds.) *The Palgrave Handbook on Criminology and the Global South*, pp. 301–321. London: Palgrave Macmillan.

Brisman, A., South, N. and Walters, R. 2018b. 'Southernizing green criminology: Human dislocation, environmental injustice and climate apartheid,' *Justice, Power and Resistance*, 2(1): 1–21.

Brisman, A. 2012. 'The cultural silence of climate change contrarianism,' in R. White (ed.) *Climate Change from a Criminological Perspective*, pp. 41–70. New York: Springer.

Brisman, A. 2014a. 'Green criminology,' in Bruce A. Arrigo (ed.) *Encyclopedia of Criminal Justice Ethics*, Vol. 1, pp. 398–401. Thousand Oaks, CA: Sage.

Brisman, A. 2014b. 'The visual acuity of climate change,' in P. Davies, P. Francis, and T. Wyatt (eds.) *Invisible Crimes and Social Harms*, pp. 61–80. Basingstoke, Hampshire, UK: Palgrave Macmillan.

Brisman, A. 2015. '"Multicolored" green criminology and climate change's achromatopsia,' *Contemporary Justice Review*, 18(2): 178–196.

Brisman, A. 2019. The Fable of *The Three Little Pigs*, Climate Change and Green Cultural Criminology. *International Journal for Crime, Justice and Social Democracy* 8(1): 46–69. DOI: 10.5204/ijcjsd.v8i1.470.

Burns, R. G., Lynch, M. J. and Stretesky, P. 2008. *Environmental Law, Crime, and Justice*. New York: LFB.

Cain, M. 2000. 'Orientalism, Occidentalism and the sociology of crime,' *The British Journal of Criminology*, 40(2): 239–260.

Carrington, K., Dixon, B., Fonseca, D., Goyes, D. R, Liu, J. and Zysman, D. 2019. 'Criminologies of the global south: Critical reflections,' *Critical Criminology: An International Journal*, 27(1): 163–189. DOI: 10.1007/s10612-019-09450 -y.

Carrington, K., Hogg, R., and Sozzo, M. 2016. 'Southern Criminology,' *The British Journal of Criminology*, 56(1): 1–20.

K. Carrington, R. Hogg, J. Scott and M. Sozzo (eds.) 2018. *The Palgrave Handbook of Criminology and the Global South*. Cham, Switzerland: Palgrave Macmillan/Springer Nature.

Cassidy, R. 2012. 'Lives with others: Climate change and human-animal relations, *Annual Review of Anthropology*, 41: 21–36.

Castles, S., de Haas, H. and Miller, M. J. 2014. *The Age of Migration: International Population Movements in the Modern World*. 5/e. New York and London: The Guilford Press.

Cohen, S. 1982. 'Western crime control models in the third world,' in S. Spitzer and Rita J. Simon (eds). *Research in Law, Deviance and Social Control*, Vol. 4, pp. 85–199. Greenwich: JAI Press. reprinted in.

Cole, L. 2018. 'Climate change: A new refugee visa?' *Geographical*. Available at: http://geographical.co.uk/people/the-refugee-crisis/item/2539-changing-climate

Connell, R. 2007. *Southern Theory: The Global Dynamics of Knowledge in Social Science*. Sydney: Allen & Unwin.

Crook, M., Short, D. and N. South. 2018. 'Ecocide, genocide, capitalism and colonialism: Consequences for indigenous peoples and glocal ecosystems environments,' *Theoretical Criminology*, 22(3): 298–317.

Crutzen, P. J. 2006. 'The "Anthropocene",' in E. Ehlers and T. Krafft (eds.) *Earth System Science in the Anthropocene*, pp. 13–18. New York: Springer-Verlag.

de la Tierra, Albert and Henne, K. 2017. 'Southern theory,' in A. Brisman, E. Carrabine, and N. South (eds.) *The Routledge Companion to Criminological Theory and Concepts*, pp. 381–385. London and New York: Routledge.

Debinski, D. M. and Cross, M. S. 2009. 'Conservation and global climate change,' in S. A. Levin (ed.) *The Princeton Guide to Ecology*, pp. 557–565. Princeton, NJ and Oxford: Princeton University Press.

DeKeseredy, W. S. 2013. Pushing the envelope: The current states of North American critical criminology. Paper presented as part of the Presidential Panel: Key Perspectives in Critical Criminology at the Annual Meeting of the American Society of Criminology, Atlanta, GA (22 November).

DeKeseredy, W. S. and Donnermeyer, J. F. 2013. 'Thinking critically about rural crime: Toward the development of a new left realist perspective,' in S. Winlow and R. Atkinson, (eds.) *New Directions in Crime and Deviancy*, pp. 206–222. London and New York: Routledge.

Donnermeyer, J. 2012. 'Rural crime and critical criminology,' in W. S. DeKeseredy and M. Dragiewicz (eds.) *Routledge Handbook of Critical Criminology*, pp. 289–301. London and New York: Routledge.

Eko Atlantic. 2017. March 28 2017. Available at: http://ekoatlantic.com/about-us/.

Ellefsen, R., Sollund, R. and Larsen, G. (eds.). 2012. *Eco-global Crimes: Contemporary Problems and Future Challenges*. Surrey, UK: Ashgate.

Fountain, H. and Popovich, N. 2019. 'March temperatures in Alaska: 20 degrees hotter than usual,' *The New York Times*. April 9 Available at: https://nytimes.com/interactive/2019/04/09/climate/alaska-abnormally-hot-march.html?smid=nytcore-ios-share.

Fussey, P. and South, N. 2012. 'Heading toward a new criminogenic climate: Climate change, political economy and environmental security,' in White, R. (ed.). *Climate Change from a Criminological Perspective*, pp. 27–40. New York: Springer.

Gillis, J. 2017. For Third Year, the Earth in 2016 Set Heat Record. *The New York Times*. Jan. 19: A1. [Published online as 'Earth Sets a Temperature Record for the Third Straight Year,' January 18 2017 Available at: https://nytimes.com/2017/01/18/science/earth-highest-temperature-record.html.]

Goyes, D. R. 2016. 'Green activist criminology and the epistemologies of the south,' *Critical Criminology: An International Journal*, 26(4): 503–518.

Goyes, D. R. and South, N. 2017. 'Green criminology before "green criminology": Amnesia and absences,' *Critical Criminology: An International Journal*, 25(2): 165–181.

Gross, P. 2017. 'Refugee displacement at seven-decade high,' *Giz press*. June 25. Available at: http://gizpress.com/2017/06/25/united-nations-refugee-displacement-at-seven-decade-high.html.

Guha-Sapir, D. and Hoyois, P. 2015. *Estimating Populations Affected by Disasters' Review of Methodological Issues and Research Gaps*. Brussells: Centre for Research on the Epidemiology of Disasters. March 28

2017. Available at: https://sustainabledevelopment.un.org/content/documents/7774UN%20Note%20on%20affected%20-%20Final%20version.pdf.

Hahn, J. 2019. 'Airpocalypse now,' *Sierra Magazine*, 104(3)[May/June]: 9.

Hall, M., Maher, J., Nurse, A., Potter, G., South, N. and Wyatt, T. (eds.). 2017. *Greening Criminology in the 21st Century: Contemporary Debates and Future Directions in the Study of Environmental Harm*, pp. 219–232. Surrey, UK: Ashgate.

Hall, M. 2013. *Victims of Environmental Harm: Rights, Recognition and Redress under National and International Law*. London and New York: Routledge.

Hall, M. 2015. *Exploring Green Crime: Introducing the Legal, Social and Criminological Contexts of Environmental Harm*. London: Palgrave Macmillan.

Hersher, R. 2019. 'EPA science panel considering guidelines that upend basic air pollution science,' *National Public Radio (NPR): Morning Edition*. March 28. Available at: https://npr.org/2019/03/28/707166015/epa-science-panel-considering-guidelines-that-upend-basic-air-pollution-science and https://npr.org/templates/transcript/transcript.php?storyId=707166015.

Hogg R., Scott, J., and Sozzo, M. 2017. 'Special edition: Southern criminology guest editors' introduction,' *International Journal for Crime, Justice and Social Democracy*, 6(1): 1–7. Available at: https://crimejusticejournal.com/article/view/395/294.

Horton, R., Hayhoe, K., Kopp, R. and Doherty, S. 2017. 'The climate risks we face,' *The New York Times*. November 6 Available at: https://nytimes.com/2017/11/06/opinion/climate-report-global-warming.html?login=smartlock&auth=login-smartlock.

Hulme, M. 2011. 'Reducing the future to climate: A story of climate determinism and reductionism,' *Osiris*, 26(1) [Klima]: 245–266.

International Energy Agency. 2018. WEO Analysis: Asea Change in the Global Oil Trade. January 30 2019. Available at: https://iea.org/newsroom/news/2018/february/weo-analysis-a-sea-change-in-the-global-oil-trade.html.

Kinver, M. 2013. 'Air pollution kills millions each year, says study,'.BBC News Science and Environment. July 15 2013. Available at: http://bbc.co.uk/news/science-environment-23315781.

Latour, B. 2004. 'Why has critique run out of steam? From matters of fact to matters of concern,' *Critical Inquiry*, 30(2): 225–248.

Lee, J. R. 2009. *Climate Change and Armed Conflict: Hot and Cold Wars*. London and New York: Routledge.

Lukacs, M. 2014. 'New, privatized African City Heralds Climate Apartheid,' *The Guardian*. January 21. Available at: https://theguardian.com/environment/true-north/2014/jan/21/new-privatized-african-city-heralds-climate-apartheid.

Lynch, M. J. 1990. 'The greening of criminology: A perspective on the 1990s,' *Critical Criminologist*, 2(3–4): 11–12.

Lynch, M. J. and Stretesky, P. B. 2014. *Exploring Green Criminology: Toward a Green Criminological Revolution*. Surrey, UK: Ashgate.

Mass, A., Bodó, B., Burnley, C., Comardicea, I. and Roffey, R. (eds.). 2013. *Global Environmental Change: New Drivers for Resistance, Crime and Terrorism?* Baden-Baden, Germany: Nomos Verlagsgesellschaft.

McGoey, L. (2012) 'The logic of strategic ignorance,' *The British Journal of Sociology*. 63(3): 553–576.

Moosavi, L. 2019. 'Decolonising criminology: Syed Hussein Alatas on crimes of the powerful,' *Critical Criminology: An International Journal*, 27(2): 229–242.

Moshakis, A. 2018. 'Fresh air for sale,' *The Guardian*. January 21. Available at: https://theguardian.com/global/2018/jan/21/fresh-air-for-sale.

Murakami, H. 2008. *What I Talk About When I Talk About Running: A Memoir*. Philip Gabriel, trans. London: Vintage Books.

Myers, N. 1993. 'Environmental refugees in a globally warmed world,' *Bioscience*, 43: 752–761.

NASA. 2018. 'Long-term warming trend continued in 2017: NASA, NOAA,' *NASA: Global Climate Change: Vital Signs of the Planet*. January 18. Available at: https://climate.nasa.gov/news/2671/long-term-warming-trend-continued-in-2017-nasa-noaa/.

Nurse, A. 2013. *Animal Harm: Perspectives on Why People Harm and Kill Animals*. Surrey, UK: Ashgate.

Nurse, A. 2015. *Policing Wildlife: Perspectives on the Enforcement of Wildlife Legislation*. London: Palgrave Macmillan.

Orlove, B., Lazarus, H., Hovelsrud, G. K. and Giannini, A. 2015. 'How long-standing debates have shaped recent climate change discourses,' in J. Barnes and M. R. Dove (eds.) *Climate Cultures: Anthropological Perspectives on Climate Change*, pp. 48–81. New Haven, CT and London: Yale University Press.

Pacific Domes. 2017. 'Dome cities: A positive timeline for humanity future (Part 1)', February 1 2019. Available at: https://pacificdomes.com/dome-cities-a-positive-timeline-for-humanitys-future-part-1/.

Pierre-Louis, K. 2019. 'As the earth warms, duluth is looking pretty cool,'. *The New York Times*. Apr. 16: A11. Published online as '*Want to Escape Global Warming? These Cities Promise Cool Relief* April 15 2019. Available at https://nytimes.com/2019/04/15/climate/climate-migration-duluth.html?smid=nytcore-ios-share.

Rauber, P. 2019. 'Up to speed: Two months, one page,' *Sierra Magazine*, 104(2)[March/April 2019]: 20.

Said, E. 1978. *Orientalism*. New York: Pantheon Book.

Santos, de B. S. 2014. *Epistemologies of the South: Justice against Epistemicide*. Boulder, CO: Paradigm.

Schultz, K. 2017. As Tourists Flood the Maldives, So Does the Rising Sea. *The New York Times*. Mar. 31: A8.

Schwartz, J. and Popovich, N. 2019. 'It's Official: 2018 Was the Fourth-Warmest Year on Record,' *The New York Times*. February 6. Available at: https://nytimes.com/interactive/2019/02/06/climate/fourth-hottest-year.html.

Shea, R. H. 2019. 'Ma Jun,' *National Geographic*. June: 28. Available at: https://nationalgeographic.com/magazine/2019/06/ma-jun-fights-pollution-in-china/.

Soles, G. 2014. 'Walling in the one percent: Eko Atlantic,' *Urban Voices*. March 23 2017. Available at: www.urbanafrica.net/urban-voices/walling-one-percent-eko-atlantic/.

Sollund, R. 2011. 'Expressions of speciesism: The effects of keeping companion animals on animal abuse, animal trafficking and species decline,' *Crime, Law and Social Change*, 55(5): 437–451.

Sollund, R. 2013. 'The victimization of women, children and non-human species through trafficking and trade: Crimes understood through an ecofeminist perspective,' in N. South and A. Brisman (eds.) *Routledge International Handbook of Green Criminology*, pp. 317–330. London and New York: Routledge.

Sollund, R. A. 2015. 'The illegal wildlife trade from a Norwegian outlook: Tendencies in practice and law enforcement,' in R. A. Sollund (ed.) *Green Harms and Crimes: Critical Criminology in a Changing World*, pp. 147–169. Basingstoke, Hampshire, UK: Palgrave Macmillan.

Sollund, R. 2012. 'Speciesism as doxic practice versus valuing difference and plurality,' in R. Ellefsen, R. Sollund, G. Larsen (eds.) *Eco-global Crimes, Contemporary Problems and Future Challenges*, pp.91–113. Surrey, UK: Ashgate.

Sollund, R. 2017a. 'The animal other: Legal and illegal theriocide,' in M. Hall, J. Maher, A. Nurse, G. Potter, N. South and T. Wyatt (eds.) *Greening Criminology in the 21st Century: Contemporary Debates and Future Directions in the Study of Environmental Harm*, pp. 79–99. London: Routledge.

Sollund, R. 2017b. 'Doing green, critical criminology with an auto-ethnographic, feminist approach,' *Critical Criminology: An International Journal* 25(2): 245–260. DOI: 10.1007/s10612-017-9361-z.

Sollund, R. 2017c. 'The use and abuse of animals in wildlife trafficking in Colombia: Practices and injustice,' in D. R. Goyes, H. Mol, A. Brisman and N. South (eds.) *Environmental Crime in Latin America: The Theft of Nature and the Poisoning of the Land*, pp. 215–243. London: Palgrave Macmillan.

South, N. and Beirne, P. (eds.) 2006. *Green Criminology*. Dartmouth: Aldershot.

South, N. 1998. 'A green field for criminology? A proposal for a perspective,' *Theoretical Criminology*, 2 (2): 211–233.

South, N. 2007. 'The "corporate colonisation of nature": Bio-prospecting, bio-piracy and the development of green criminology,' in P. Beirne and N. South (eds.) *Issues in Green Criminology: Confronting Harms against Environments, Humanity and other Animals*, pp. 230–247. Cullompton, Devon, UK: Willan.

South, N. 2012. 'Climate change, environmental (in)security, conflict and crime,' in S. Farrall, T. Ahmed and D. French (eds.) *Criminological and Legal Consequences of Climate Change*, pp. 97–112. Oxford: Hart.

South, N. 2016. 'Free trade agreements, private courts and environmental exploitation: Disconnected policies, denials and moral disengagement,' *International Journal for Crime, Justice and Social Democracy*, 5 (4): 45–59.

South, N. 2014. 'Green criminology: Reflections, connections, horizons,' *International Journal for Crime, Justice and Social Democracy*, 3(2): 5–20. DOI: 10.5204/ijcjsd.v3i2.172. Available at: https://www.crimejusticejournal.com/article/view/722/476.

South, N. 2019. 'Arcologies, eco-shelters and environmental exemption: Constructing new divisions and inequalities in the anthropocene,' *International Journal for Crime, Justice and Social Democracy*. Published online on 17 September 2019, https://10.5204/ijcjsd.v9i2.1007.

Squire, R., Adey, P. and Jensen, R. B. 2018. Dome, Sweet Home: Climate Shelters, Past, Present and Future. *Nature*. Available at: www.nature.com/articles/d41586-018-07513-8. *doi:10.1038/d41586-018-07513-8.*

Stephens, N. 2018. Why Do People Stay When a Hurricane Comes? *The New York Times*. September 14. Available at: https://nytimes.com/2018/09/14/opinion/hurricane-maria-staying-home.html?rref=collection%2Fsectioncollection%2Fopinion&action=click&contentCollection=opinion&region=rank&module=package&version=highlights&contentPlacement=3&pgtype=sectionfront.

Stewart, I. and Garcia-Navarro, L. 2019. Florida, Doctors See Climate Change Hurting Their Most Vulnerable Patients. *National Public Radio (NPR)*. March 30. Available at: https://npr.org/2019/03/30/706941118/in-florida-doctors-see-climate-change-hurting-their-most-vulnerable-patients.

Stretesky, P., Long, M. A. and Lynch, M. J. 2014. *The Treadmill of Crime: Political Economy and Green Criminology*. London and New York: Routledge.

Sutter, J. D. 2015. Climate Change is a Form of Terror. *CNN*. November 29. Available at: https://cnn.com/2015/11/28/opinions/sutter-cop21-paris-preview-two-degrees/.

Tsoneva, J. 2019. 'Blackening our sky,' *Jacbobin*. March 17. Available at: https://jacobinmag.com/2019/03/bulgaria-pollution-environmental-hazard-real-estate.

UNHCR. 2019. 'Climate change and disasters,' January 29 2019. Available at. https://unhcr.org/climate-change-and-disasters.html.

Vanderheiden, S. 2008. *Atmospheric Justice. A Political Theory of Climate Change*. Oxford: OxfordUniversity Press.

Vidal, J. 2011. 'Drier, hotter: Can Egypt escape its climate future?,' *The Guardian*. November 18. Available at: https://theguardian.com/environment/blog/2011/nov/18/egypt-climate-change.

Walters, R. 2003. *Deviant Knowledge: Criminology, Politics and Policy*. Cullompton, Devon, UK: Willan.

Walters, R. (2010) 'Eco Crime,' in J. Muncie, D. Talbot and R. Walters (eds.) *Crime: Local and Global*, pp. 173–208. Cullompton, Devon, UK: Willan.

Walters, R. 2011. *Eco Crime and Genetically Modified Food*. Abingdon, Oxon, UK: Routledge.

Walters, R. 2014. 'Air pollution and invisible violence,' in P. Davies, P. Francis, and T. Wyatt (eds.) *Invisible Crimes and Social Harms*, pp. 203–222. London: Palgrave.

Walters, R. 2018. 'Climate change: 'Making ignorance great again,' in A. Barton and H. Davis (eds.) *Ignorance, Power and Harm. Agnotology and the Criminological Imagination*, pp. 163–189. London: Palgrave.

Walter, R., Westerhuis, S. and Wyatt, T. (eds.). 2013. Emerging Issues in Green Criminology: Exploring Power, Justice and Harm. Basingstoke, Hampshire, UK: Palgrave Macmillan.

Weintrobe, S. (ed.) 2013. *Engaging with Climate Change: Psychoanalytic and Interdisciplinary Perspectives*. Sussex: Routledge.

Westra, L. (2004) *Ecoviolence and the Law: Supranational Normative Foundations of Ecocrime*, Ardsley, NY: Transactional Publications.

White, R (ed.) 2009. *Environmental Crime: A Reader*. Cullompton, Devon, UK: Willan.

White, R. (ed.). 2010. *Global Environmental Harm: Criminological Perspectives*. Cullompton, UK: Willan.

White, R. 2008. *Crimes Against Nature: Environmental Criminology and Ecological Justice*. Cullompton, UK: Willan.

White, R. 2011. *Transnational Environmental Crime: Toward an Eco-global Criminology*. London and New York: Routledge.

White, R. 2013. *Environmental Harm: An eco-justice Perspective*. Bristol, UK: Policy Press.

White, R. 2014. 'Environmental insecurity and fortress mentality,' *International Affairs*, 90(4): 835–851.

White, R. 2016. 'Criminality and climate change,' *Nature Climate Change*, 6 [August]: 737–739. DOI: 10.1038/nclimate3052.

White, R. 2018. *Climate Change Criminology*. Bristol, UK: Bristol University Press.

White, R. and Heckenberg, D. 2014. *Green Criminology: An Introduction to the Study of Environmental Harm*. London and New York: Routledge.

Winsor, M. 2015. 'Nigeria's new city: EkoAtlantic construction in lagos fuels criticism and praise,' *IBTimes*. April 8 2017. Available at: http://ibtimes.com/nigerias-new-city-eko-atlantic-construction-lagos-fuels-criticism-praise-2048964.

Wyatt, T. 2013. *Wildlife Trafficking: A Deconstruction of the Crime, the Victims and the Offenders*. Basingstoke, Hampshire, UK: Palgrave Macmillan.

Wyatt, T. and Brisman, A. 2017. 'The role of denial in the "theft of nature": A comparison of biopiracy and climate change,' *Critical Criminology: An International Journal*, 25(3): 325–341. DOI: 10.1007/s10612-016-9344-5. FirstOnline: September 14 2016. Available at: http://link.springer.com/article/10.1007/s10612-016-9344-5.

Ying, L. 2014. 'Dome, sweet dome,' *Global Times*. January 25 2019. Available at: www.globaltimes.cn/content/848220.shtml.

Zimmerer, J. 2014. 'Climate change, environmental violence and genocide,' *The International Journal of Human Rights*, 18(3): 265–280.

Court Case

Teitiota v Chief Executive of the Ministry of Business, Innovation and Employment [2015] NZSC 107 (20 July 2015), www.courtsofnz.govt.nz/cases/ioane-teitiotoa-v-the-chief-executive-of-the-ministry-of-business-innovation-and-employment/at_download/fileDecision. The decision is also available through NZLII, *at* www.nzlii.org/nz/cases/NZSC/2015/107.html.

11

Food crime and green criminology

Wesley Tourangeau and Amy J. Fitzgerald

All across the world, food products are being altered, contaminated and mislabelled. Recent examples include the 2016 seizure of counterfeited foods by INTERPOL (one of the largest ever), which included olives painted with copper sulphate to enhance colouring and peanuts repackaged as pine nuts (INTERPOL, 2016); the 2017 Fipronil egg contamination case, where hundreds of thousands of eggs and egg-based products contaminated with a harmful insecticide were identified in 15 European Union (EU) countries, Switzerland and Hong Kong (Boffey and Connolly, 2017); and also in that same year, undeclared species, including horse, were found in Canadian sausage products (Naaum et al., 2018). Instances such as these, wherein certain regulations and laws are clearly violated, are easily grouped together as 'food crimes'—illegal actions (or inactions) that compromise food and/or drink products.

When exactly the term 'food crime' was first used is unclear. A key point at which it entered the green criminological lexicon, however, can be traced to Hazel Croall's (2007) chapter, 'Food crime', in Beirne and South's *Issues in Green Criminology: Confronting Harms Against Environments, Humanity and Other Animals*. Regardless of its actual birthdate, the topic of 'food crime' provides another point from which to observe the limitations and contradictions of the social and legal construction of 'crime'. It is also a site where the limitations of the construction of victims have become apparent; for instance, the victimisation of animals categorised as 'food animals' has generally been overlooked (Beirne, 2007; Fitzgerald and Tourangeau, 2018).

Examinations of harm vis-à-vis food can benefit from green criminology's critique of both speciesist conceptualisations of victimhood and narrow legalistic definitions of harm. Indeed, using a green criminological lens to examine food-related harms enables an exploration of instances wherein no laws are broken, but environmental, physical and social harms result nonetheless. The production of *foie gras*,[1] for example, is legal in many countries (e.g., Canada, France), even though it causes considerable harm and pain to the ducks and geese, who are confined and force-fed to produce this 'delicacy'. Moreover, green criminology has examined critically those actions that are criminalised, yet fail to pose any discernible danger or harm to persons, animals, or property (see Brisman, 2010), such as the case of a woman in Ontario, Canada, who was charged in 2015 with criminal mischief for giving water to pigs in a truck on their way to slaughter (Fitzgerald and Tourangeau, 2018). In short, green criminology can assist with challenging assumptions about what constitutes 'food crime' and who can be victimised by it.

In this chapter, we seek to highlight the ways in which green criminology can contribute to a more nuanced understanding of food crime and the harms it can entail. We begin with a survey of food crime typologies, focussing on two broad categories: (1) food crimes defined as such by legal standards; and (2) food crimes that represent violations of moral standards, but which may not be proscribed by law. Food adulteration, counterfeiting and poisoning fall into the first category; these comprise specific legal or regulatory infractions. The second category challenges the limits of legally defined food crimes and includes important systemic issues and individual actions that are harmful but not legally prohibited. We utilise recent cases from numerous national contexts to illustrate both the categorical distinctions and the applied real consequences of each. A brief case study of a recent update to Canada's 'livestock' transportation regulations is used to demonstrate the complexity and difficulty of defining what constitutes a 'food crime' (or any 'crime' for that matter) and the limitations of restricting the subject of 'food crime' (as well as green criminology and criminology more broadly) to legalistic definitions. The examination of changes to Canada's 'livestock' transportation regulations and the related consultative process helps to illuminate the sites where legal boundaries are drawn, as well as how these boundaries can be rather arbitrary and yet extremely impactful. This act of drawing boundaries is an inherently complex task involving the ethical and normative dimensions of law formation, in addition to the injection of public and private interests. This case study provides an examination of how these dimensions and interests are weighted in matters of animal welfare and economic profitability.

Food crimes by legal standards

We begin by examining a range of food crimes that are, in general, prohibited by law and subject to regulation and punishment. These crimes range from food adulteration to the mistreatment of 'livestock' animals. By way of organising the varying crimes that fit within this section, three categories of food crime victims are examined: (1) consumers; (2) food producers; and (3) animals and the environment.[2]

Crimes against food consumers

There is a range of food crimes that can potentially impact the health and safety of consumers—from intentional activities of food fraud and mislabelling to unintentional events, such as food contamination. Spink et al. (2015) and Spink and Moyer (2011) draw from criminological approaches, such as the 'crime triangle', to work through ways of categorising and conceptualising food crimes as types of public health risks based largely on intentionality and motivation. Briefly, *food fraud* refers to any intentional act of altering, mislabelling, misrepresenting, substituting, or tampering with any food product (e.g., raw material, ingredient, final product, food packaging) at any point in the farm-to-table supply chain for the purpose of financial gain (e.g., reducing its cost of production, increasing its apparent value). *Food defence* refers to the protection of food products from intentional adulteration or contamination for the purpose of causing harm (e.g., a resentful employee contaminating food to retaliate against his or her employer) (Spink and Moyer, 2011). The terms *food quality* and *food safety* are used in the context of unintentional food risks. Quality can be compromised by mishandling, such as the accidental bruising of fruit, and food safety compromises the welfare of consumers, such as in accidental *E. coli* contamination (Spink and Moyer, 2011). Food fraud is the primary focus of this section, as these acts are not only intentional but also pervasive and complex crimes.

In 2013, a scandal erupted in Ireland and the United Kingdom (UK) when the Food Safety Authority of Ireland (FSAI) announced that it had identified horse and pig DNA in beef products that it had tested (FSAI, 2013). The penalties that resulted included the jailing of two businessmen for conspiring to defraud customers (Rawlinson, 2017) and the fining of an abattoir manager for failing to abide by meat traceability regulations (BBC News, 2015). The discovery of horsemeat also helped prompt the UK government to commission an independent review 'into the integrity and assurance of food supply networks, and to make recommendations for how the systems used to deter, identify and prosecute food adulteration could be improved' (HM Government, 2014: 11). Referred to as the *Elliott Review*, this inquiry, led by Professor Chris Elliott, recommended providing government support for the creation of a new Food Crime Unit within the Food Standards Agency, 'which would become the lead agency for food crime' (HM Government, 2014: 64). The National Food Crime Unit was formally established at the end of 2014. The horsemeat scandal provides a valuable illustration of how food fraud is not only a matter of health and safety, but also involves social and dietary norms and impacts consumer trust and confidence. Instances of food fraud (as well as other food scares) have an important effect on the value consumers place on labelling and traceability and such standards are integral to the capacity consumers have to protect themselves (see Charlebois and Haratifar, 2015).

In addition to concerns over adulterated foods, consumers are also faced with deceptive marketing tactics designed to make food look more enticing. Croall (2007) explains that many descriptions used in food advertising are subject to regulation and breaches are common. For example, manufacturers may be breaking guidelines when using phrases like 'farmhouse', 'home-made' and 'traditional' if the production process does not reflect the presumed meaning of these terms (see Croall, 2007). Labelling issues also arise with regard to religious-based diets that require foods to be certified as halal or kosher, for example. Recently, the Canadian Food Inspection Agency (CFIA) filed criminal charges against a businessman who allegedly forged kosher certification documents for cheddar cheese sold to Jewish summer camps (Henry, 2017).

Crimes against food producers

From farms to slaughterhouses, producers of food are commonly entangled in circumstances of exploitation and harm. Brisman et al. (2016) point to the environmental and human rights consequences of forced labour, wherein rural workers are subjected to exploitive conditions that are deeply enmeshed in normalised, systemic aspects of the global industrial food system. Many of the harms endured by those who work in the food system are, in fact, legal (see Croall, 2007) and many of the risks they face are systemic. Seasonal migrant farmworkers, such as the Mexican population working in Leamington, Ontario, Canada, are at a high risk for work-related accidents and exposure to airborne dust, animal-borne diseases and toxic chemicals (Basok, 2002). While this type of labour may be legal, these are potential sites for criminal exploitation. For example, a recruiter in the Leamington area was found guilty of exploiting migrant workers by charging them illegal recruitment fees (Sacheli, 2017). Slaughterhouses, though obvious sites of animal violence and death, are also high-risk sites for workers. At least since Upton Sinclair's 1906 novel *The Jungle*, the general public has been warned of the significant negative conditions experienced in industrial slaughterhouses (see Nierenberg 2005). Current conditions in slaughterhouses across the globe are severely problematic, putting at risk workers' physical and mental well-being and also impacting the surrounding communities (Fitzgerald, 2010, 2015). Slaughterhouse employment levels in communities have even been linked to increased violent crimes (Fitzgerald, Kalof and Dietz, 2009).

Some of these more pervasive systemic issues straddle legal boundaries and, even where they are deemed illegal, enforcement is often woefully inadequate (Fitzgerald, 2015); when charges are brought, the associated penalties are often minimal in comparison with the profitability of the perpetrator. For example, in one case at a beef plant owned by JBS USA Holdings, Inc. ('JBS'), in Greeley, Colorado, United States (US), a slaughterhouse worker's death was linked to a missing machine guard and the fine for this violation of safety regulations worked out to be less than 40,000 dollars—a drop in the bucket for JBS, which is the world's largest meatpacker with multi-billion dollar net revenues (Runyon, 2016). The penalties are often also inadequate in relation to the scope of the infractions, which are often immense, particularly when the harms against animals and the environment are taken into consideration.

Crimes against animals and the environment

While a range of harms to animals and ecosystems occur throughout the food system, only particular actions are controlled through laws and regulations. In this section, two types of food crimes are discussed: (1) events of regulatory noncompliance within the food system that negatively impact animals and the environment; and (2) inhumane actions against animals designated as food that are prohibited by law.

The fishing industry provides a useful site for exploring issues of illegality and regulatory noncompliance. Effectively regulating this industry requires a complex and delicate weighing of interests, from fishers, processors and fishing communities, to environmentalists (see Brisman, 2003). There are several types of illegal fishing activities, including commercial fishers catching over their quota, recreational fishing without a license and the exploitation of endangered species (White, 2008). Overfishing can also be linked to organised crime where illegally caught 'black fish' are sold on the black market—illustrated in the recent Scottish 'Black-Fish-Scandal', which netted a criminal organisation £63 million from the illegal landing of undeclared fish (Smith, 2015). In the mid-1990s in South Africa, when the total allowable catch (TAC) for the abalone industry was being reduced in an effort to compensate for over-exploitation, both organised crime syndicates and recreational divers engaged in poaching (Hauck and Sweijd, 1999). The heightened controversy became known as the 'abalone war' due to violent police confrontations, gang activity and illegal trade (Hauck, 2009; Hauck and Sweijd, 1999). While the over-exploitation of abalone has an impact on the sustainability of these species and symbiotic species like sea urchins, the fact that reductions to the TAC have failed to prevent over-exploitation points to the complexity and limitations of legal mechanisms (see Hauck, 2009; Hauck and Sweijd, 1999). This problem is illustrative of White's (2008) reminder that harms transcend the legal–illegal divide—that harms can occur in spite of—and sometimes *because* of—the fact that they are not proscribed by law. The inability of certain laws and regulations to thwart or curb harm is also evident in the livestock industry.

Developed countries, such as Canada, the UK and the US, have a suite of laws and regulations that standardise and police the treatment of 'livestock'. These regulations can be breached through inhumane treatment and living conditions, inhumane transportation and inhumane slaughter. In 2014, Maple Leaf Farms was brought to court by the Canadian Food Inspection Agency after 2,000 chickens died during transportation due to exposure to cold winter conditions. Maple Leaf Farms received a fine of \$80,000 (CAD) for the inhumane transportation of chickens and were also required to invest $1 million (CAD) to make their transport trailers compliant with federal regulations (Perkel, 2014). In another case, Animals International, an Australian animal rights charity, revealed a range of abuses and illegal conditions in an investigation of animals exported from the EU. Undercover footage depicts sheep and cattle being beaten and prodded, held for days in overcrowded pens and slaughtered in abysmal facilities—evidence that demonstrates clear breaches of EU laws (Dale-Harris, 2017). While these two cases offer proof of the inhumane and illegal practices currently taking place throughout the global food system, there is debate over where the boundary lines should be drawn between inhumane and humane, illegal and legal and harmful and acceptable (see Fitzgerald and Tourangeau, 2018). Public contestation of this boundary was evident when, in 1995, thousands of UK residents gathered in a nine-month-long protest against the live export of animals, which some now refer to as the Battle of Brightlingsea (Leate, 2010). The legally permissible practice was derided as being offensive and immoral. The following section examines other activities that do not fit neatly into the categories of 'harmful', 'inhumane' and 'illegal' and instead challenge us to question their parameters, their points of overlap and the lacunae between them.

Food crimes by moral standards

This section unpacks the term 'food crime'—and by extension terms like 'environmental crime' (see Barclay and Bartel, 2015; Halsey, 2004)—continuing the dialogue advanced by previous food crime authors regarding the limitations of examining only those harms proscribed by law when examining the food system (see Cheng, 2012; Croall, 2007, 2013). In much the same way that the broader discipline of criminology has grappled with mapping its disciplinary boundaries (see Brisman and South, Introduction, this volume), green criminologists have struggled with the question of what the sub-field ought to cover. A *legalistic approach* would set the demarcating line at actions deemed unlawful by the state, thereby excluding all other concerns, and binding criminological investigations to the changing tides of law and politics. A *socio-legal* or *social harm approach*, however, would include harmful actions/inactions against/regarding the environment and non-human animals that are not (yet) legally prohibited. Arguably, these harms may be more detrimental than those proscribed by law (see White, 2008). Accordingly, many scholars in the field favour this more encompassing approach.

Challenges regarding terminology within green criminology, however, remain and have given rise to many questions. Should the term *environmental crime* be used, in spite of the embedded legalistic assumptions? Or should the terms *environmental crime* and *environmental harm* be used in conjunction to denote a more comprehensive approach to green criminological work? In our reading of the literature, employing these two options has been common practice. Is it possible, however, to reclaim the term *environmental crime* and untether it from its legalistic grounding? Or is there another, more encompassing term that could be used in place of *environmental crime* and *environmental harm*? These two possibilities warrant examination, as they are quite relevant in the context of describing the area that has come to be referred to as *food crime*. In grappling with these questions, we refer to Clifford and Edwards (1998), who, many years ago, introduced a term that has not really caught on in the literature: *offences against the environment*. The term is more capacious than *environmental crime* as it includes unintentional and non-criminal incidents, yet they do not elaborate upon its value and viability. We seek to do so briefly here.

Offence has several meanings that are quite complementary in this context. As a noun, it refers to: 'a breach of a law', 'a violation of what is judged to be right or natural' and 'the action of attacking someone or something' (*Oxford Reference Dictionary*). Applying it to describe legal and illegal harms against the environment might be particularly apt: the *word* 'offence' retains much of the critical and political force of using the term *environmental crime*, while also being inclusive, rather than excluding certain forms of harm based upon legal designations determined by the state. An action can be an *offence* without being *illegal*.

We think that this terminology might be extended to the field generally referred to as *food crime*. There are food-related harms that, although they do not violate laws or regulations, are nonetheless offences in the sense that they violate social norms and/or inflict harm. These *food offences* are the focus of this section and are broken down into the three victim groups described in the previous section: (1) consumers; (2) producers; and (3) animals and the environment. A case study is then provided to illustrate the value of using a green criminological lens to label and problematise food offences.[3]

The complexity of consumer choice

Food crimes prohibited by law may harm consumers (e.g., food poisoning from unsafe handling) or offend their beliefs (e.g., fraudulent kosher certifications), while other non-prohibited considerations, such as preferences related to diets and production processes, are left up to the market mechanism of consumer choice. For instance, the use of pesticides to grow food is generally not illegal, so consumers who wish to avoid such foods must rely on the organic food market to satisfy their buying preferences. Genetically modified (GM) foods are a key example of where consumer choice becomes part of a complex legal and moral debate. While the EU has passed laws requiring all GM products be labelled and traceable (Walters, 2007), countries such as Canada rely on voluntary labelling policies. Despite public opinion polls that suggest the majority of Canadians want GM foods labelled as such, the country's government continues to block bills for a mandatory labelling scheme (CBAN, 2017). According to the CFIA, mandatory labelling is reserved for health and safety concerns, whereas standards for voluntary labelling have been put in place to assist consumers with information not related to health and safety (CFIA, 2017). Issues such as this represent the complexity of consumer choice: contrary to the EU and several other countries, the laws in Canada appear biased against consumers hoping to avoid foods made from GM technologies. While withholding this information from consumers may not readily be labelled a *food crime*, it nonetheless could be labelled as a *food offence*, wherein the interests of private companies eclipse those of consumers. In addition to negatively impacting consumers, food offences can harm producers.

The plight of peasants as producers

It should first be stated that 'peasant' is not a pejorative term—at least not to organisations belonging to La Via Campesina (LVC) (Desmarais, 2008). LVC is an international grassroots movement that brings together 'millions of peasants, small and medium size farmers, landless people, rural women and youth, Indigenous people, migrants and agricultural workers from around the world' (La Via Campesina, n.d.). Among the various struggles of this movement are the global displacement and criminalisation of, and discrimination against, peasants (La Via Campesina, n.d.). According to Rosset (2013: 767),

> This criminalization of struggle and the repression, involving the police, the army and the private security of corporations, translates into assassinations, judicial persecution and a high level of impunity, because nothing is investigated nor are the responsible parties ever punished in spite of the evidence presented.

A key priority of LVC is the defence of *food sovereignty*, which (among other things) prioritises local food production and consumption, peoples' rights over food and agricultural systems, and small-scale production models that benefit local producers, communities and the surrounding environments (La Via Campesina, n.d.). *Food sovereignty* is deeply embedded in relations of power and control over the food system (Patel, 2009) and is a precondition for *food security* (La Via Campesina, 1996). This is an important distinction, as early definitions of food security avoided addressing the social control of the food system (Patel, 2009). As a corrective, Brisman and South (2017) explore the criminological aspects of defining food security, including its entanglement with state power, social control and the subordination of populations. It should come as little surprise, then, that LVC's pursuit of food sovereignty and security has been demonised in the media and their protests have been criminalised (Rosset, 2013).

Another important example of the domination and criminalisation of food producers is the biopiracy of genetic resources (see Goyes, this volume, Chapter 12). As Goyes and South (2015) explain, international agreements and treaties regarding trade and intellectual property have facilitated the corporate appropriation of the world's genetic resources. Biopiracy is the term used to describe the activities of companies that utilise patents (and other mechanisms) over seeds to effectively colonise nature (Walters, 2004). For instance, genetic materials have been taken from developing countries and commodified as intellectual property when altered, which gives corporations control over the replanting of protected seeds. Goyes and South (2015: 5) describe this as 'a dual injustice of theft and criminalization' and explain that such occurrences are legal processes based on policies that support the privatisation of traditional knowledge.

Walters (2004, 2007) has pointed to both the illegal activities within the GM food industry (e.g., illegal distribution and trade in GM food), as well as the legal but harmful political economy of GM food trade that promotes monopoly capitalism and the associated risks of GM foods that include superweeds and genetic pollution. Criminological inquiry into the GM food industry will benefit from the continued investigation of both the legal and illegal offences that produce harm and injustice. Continued investigations are also needed on the animal and environmental harms prevalent within the global food system.

Harm to animals and ecosystems

Food production, particularly at industrial scales, has severe negative consequences for animals and the environment. Much of this harm is legal, accepted and therefore difficult to examine from a traditional criminological standpoint. The killing of chickens for food, for instance, is not a *food crime*—although we suggest that it can be understood as a *food offence* that would benefit from criminological examination. In addition, non-human animals are generally not examined by criminology as *victim* groups, despite the extent to which human interests are intertwined with those of nonhuman animals (see Brisman and South, Introduction, this volume). Accordingly, Beirne (1999) and Cazaux (1999) have advocated for a non-speciesist criminology that would interrogate harms perpetrated against non-human species—harms that frequently intersect with human interests and well-being.

Industrial animal agriculture is responsible for a great deal of harm inflicted upon non-human animals and the environment. (It is also an area where the interests of green criminology and the study of food offences intersect in important ways.) CAFOs (Confined/Concentrated Animal Feeding Operations) are a primary method and location of production within industrial animal agriculture. They make possible the production of vast amounts of animals with minimal turn-over time (Weis, 2007). This type of production has given rise to many behavioural problems among animals (such as aggression and cannibalism) that have been addressed through further harmful practices, such as ear cropping, amputation of tails and horns and the searing of beaks (often without anaesthesia). Additional examples of suffering include confinement to cages, limited exposure to sunlight, over- and underfeeding, rapid growth that results in debilitating deformities and eventual slaughter (Fitzgerald, 2015; Lovell, 2016). CAFOs have had extraordinary impacts on the global environment, including deforestation for feed crops, water and energy use, greenhouse gas emissions and water supply contamination (Fitzgerald, 2015; 2019; Weis, 2013; see generally Brisman, South and Walters, this volume, Chapter 10).[4]

CAFOs and slaughterhouses have tended to be the focal points of the food and environmental offences created by industrial animal agriculture. There is another segment in the commodity chain that warrants examination, however. Livestock transportation links CAFOs with the slaughterhouses and animals often endure a great deal of harm at this juncture,[5] particularly in Canada. Although often lauded as a progressive country, Canada's laws dealing with animal abuse and welfare are some of the most antiquated. A brief case study of recent updates to the animal transport regulations in Canada illustrates the scope of food offences involved in this specific part of the commodity chain and the challenges inherent in mitigating them.

Attempts to ameliorate offensive food practices: The case of animal transport in Canada

In December 2016, the CFIA, which reports to the Minister of Health/Health Canada, released its proposed amendments to the *Health of Animals Regulations* governing the transport of animals (Government of Canada, 2016). The highlights of the proposed changes included tightening the language in the provisions (e.g., defining what compromised and unfit animals are) and reducing the amount of time that animals can be transported without rest and access to food and water. The proposed changes also meant that Canada's regulations would move closer to those in other developed countries, although they would remain well below the standards in the EU.

This public release of the proposed amendments began a public consultation period that ended February 15, 2017. Stakeholders and interested members of the public were invited to provide feedback. Consultations with industry stakeholders, however, had been transpiring for ten years prior. An Access to Information request (Access Request #A-2016-00190) was submitted by the Canadian Coalition for Farm Animals to obtain information regarding these consultations and the proposed regulatory changes. The resulting 312 pages of documents were shared with the authors. The documents provide details regarding the process of updating the regulations, which began in 2006[6] and included consultation with individual companies and industry groups, other governmental agencies and 'organizations with a balanced viewpoint on animal welfare'.

The documents consistently make reference to how outdated the current regulations are. A number of reasons are provided in the documents for why the transport regulations need to be updated, including advances in animal welfare science made since the regulations were implemented in the 1970s, increased concern among the public about animal welfare, regulatory changes in other jurisdictions and reducing food safety risks. Before delving into an examination of these reasons and what can be gleaned about the consultative process, however, it is worth noting another reason—mentioned only once in the documents—why these regulations required strengthening.

In one item of correspondence between the Agriculture and Agri-Food Minister's Office (hereafter referred to as the Ministry) and the CFIA,[7] it is clear that the government was aware that large numbers of animals were being killed and injured during transport and that improved regulations could mitigate this problem. In posing questions to the CFIA about the cost-benefit analysis of strengthening the regulations that they had undertaken, the Ministry made clear the connection between animal deaths and transport conditions, writing 'What is the economic loss associated with the 1.59 million animals that die every year from poor transport conditions? Would the producers would [sic] no longer be losing product and therefore, their investment, in raising those animals?' The CFIA responded in the affirmative and provided illustrative statistics from the year 2014:

> of the 19,298,055 hogs slaughtered there were 13,856 DOAs [Dead on Arrival] but an additional 6,986 animals condemned. Of those many have been linked directly or indirectly to transport stresses and would be decreased with the new requirements for fitness, training, handling, etc.

In another email, the Ministry asked what proportion of loads of spent hens (former commercial egg-laying chickens) exceeded the 4 per cent DOA threshold (a guideline for CFIA inspectors). The CFIA response was that in 2014, 64 out of 368 (17.4 per cent) inspected shipments had DOA proportions greater than 4 per cent; in addition, some were as high as 51.59 per cent. The number of animals dying needlessly without benefit (i.e., human consumption) is not technically a food crime and, instead, is an accepted cost of doing business. It is offensive, nonetheless, particularly given that many of these deaths could have been prevented through different transport practices.

It is unclear to what extent the public was aware of the scope of the problem, but it was apparent in the documents that the CFIA was concerned about the degree of public objection to these practices. The point made in the documents was that animal transport is unique in the animal food commodity chain in that it is relatively public (referred to as 'high visibility' in the documents) compared with other points in the process of turning animals into food. The CFIA also noted the growing ability of social media to mobilise the public on this issue: on one PowerPoint slide, under the heading 'Moving Forward', the CFIA states that 'Social media has increased the availability of information on animal transport incidents and the public is increasingly demanding improvements to the Transport Regulations'. In other words, pressure from the public on this issue had increased and was not expected to wane—something that was noted in a 2015 internal factsheet that appeared to have been created to brief the Deputy Minister prior to a Parliamentary Committee appearance:

> Public awareness and public opinion on the issue of animal welfare in general and humane transport in particular has increased dramatically … Humane transport is highly visible to the public. While other points in a food animal's life are relatively unknown to the public i.e. on farm and at slaughter; transport remains the one aspect that is accessible to the public … it is reasonable to accept [sic] that animal transport, which is considered to be one of the most stressful events in an animal's life, will continue to be

> a high priority issue for the public, and the CFIA will continue to be petitioned to amend the current outdated regulations.

The visibility of animal transport, both directly and mediated through social media, had clearly offended the senses of some members of the public, which had influenced the CFIA to act.

It was also evident in these documents that the CFIA was motivated to update the regulations in order to bring them closer in line with other jurisdictions. A great deal of attention was paid in the documents to comparing Canada's transport regulations with the standards of the World Organisation for Animal Health (OIE). The OIE does not provide specific standards for food, water and rest (FWR) times during transport; instead, it focusses on the outcomes for individual animals. In an email, the Ministry queried CFIA about whether the proposed changes were consistent with OIE standards. The CFIA wrote in response that

> As a member country of the OIE, Canada is expected to meet or exceed OIE Standards. The current animal transport regulations are outdated. The proposed regulations provide a balance between current science and industry practices, and better align with the standards of our international trading partners and the OIE.

In order to satisfy OIE standards, if an animal is observed to need FWR before the specified time limit has been reached, the animal(s) would need to be provided with FWR. The amendments to Canadian regulations arguably account for this with requirements for monitoring animals during confinement and transport. How this will be enforced is, however, less clear.

Tables were provided in the documents comparing the existing and proposed Canadian FWR intervals with those in other countries, such as the US and member countries of the EU (see Table 11.1 for a summary by species[8]). These tables make several details apparent. First, the existing FWR regulations in Canada lagged far behind those in other countries. Acknowledging this, the CFIA referred to how updating the regulations would result in an 'improved international reputation'. Second, the proposed FWR intervals and those ultimately settled on in 2019, which will go into effect in 2020 (Government of Canada, 2019), still put Canada well behind those in the EU, although more in line with the US. Third, the tables and accompanying text indicated that, originally, the CFIA proposed more stringent FWR intervals to the industry than those made available for public comment in 2016 (note the changes in Table 11.1).

The cattle industry's response in the documents to the revised FWR limits originally proposed can be summarised as follows: 'Industry had concerns with the need to unload twice during long-haul shipments which would be necessary with a 28 hour interval'. Part of the industry reaction to the proposed FWR times for horses was redacted and reads: '[redacted] asked for 24 hours or less and [redacted] asked for 36 hours'. The phrase 'No concerns expressed' is entered for broiler chickens, but the industry reaction for spent laying hens is redacted completely, although their reaction can be surmised from other documents, discussed below. The feedback on the proposed decreased FWR time for day-old chicks is summarised as follows: 'Industry did not support the reduced FWR time intervals because of nutrients provided by the yolk sac reserve which normally last up to 72 hours after hatching'. Finally, the documents reveal that 'Industry provided various responses opposed to a reduced interval' for pigs. Interestingly, the information in a column headed 'Information used to determine CFIA position' is redacted for all instances where the FWR intervals were increased beyond the original proposal, whereas a 'No changes needed' notation appears

Table 11.1 Original, proposed and approved Food, Water, Rest (FWR) intervals in Canada, the US and the EU

Species	*Canadian regulations at time of review (hours)*	*Original proposed changes (hours)*	*Proposed changes made public for comment in 2016 (hours)*	*Changes going into effect in 2020 (hours)*	*Current regulations in the US (hours)*	*Current regulations in the EU (hours)*
Cattle	52	28	36	36	28	8
Horses	36	24	28	28	28	8
Broiler chickens	36	24	24	24 for water, 28 for feed and rest	None	12
Spent hens	36	12	24	24 for water, 28 for feed and rest	None	12
Day-old chicks	72	24	72	72	None	12
Pigs	36	24	28	28	28	8

Note: in some instances, extensions of a few hours can be granted in the US by permission and times in the EU can be extended if the trucks are equipped to provide water, are insulated, are partitioned and have mechanical ventilation.

where industry did not voice concern about the proposed changes and modifications to the original proposals were therefore not made.

Elsewhere, the CFIA reports that it balanced 'scientific evidence, current industry practices and public concern' in determining the proposed FWR intervals. It is clear, however, that the feedback from industry to the original proposals resulted in significant concessions. That the CFIA was swayed by industry in the process was made clear in a statement contained in a PowerPoint presentation describing their consultations, wherein it is stated that 'Following industry comments during pre-consultation, the CFIA considered and addressed concerns for maximum intervals without FWR, wherever possible. Most industry stakeholders are now comfortable with the proposed FWR intervals'.

That most industry stakeholders were comfortable with the revised proposal is perhaps testament to how far the CFIA bent. In fact, it is estimated in the documents that the vast majority of animal transport had already met the 2016 proposed FWR times. As a result, the economic impacts of the proposed regulations on the industry were projected to be small, according to the CFIA. The conclusion of the economic analysis was that 'very few companies would be significantly impacted'. Perhaps this is why the CFIA obtained only a 7 per cent response rate to its survey measuring the economic impacts of the proposed changes distributed to 1,100 stakeholders in 2013–2014. Presumably, if industry stakeholders were threatened significantly by the proposed changes, they would have been more vocal. The CFIA was ultimately unable to decide whether the costs to business would be outweighed by the benefits of updating the regulations, because the benefits (which they cited as including improved animal welfare, reduced food safety risks and reduction in economic losses caused by current long transportation times—i.e., mitigating food offences)—were not easily quantified.

The point at which the welfare of animals without FWR begins to suffer *has* been quantified in research. An internal document, in which the CFIA responded to questions posed by the Ministry, contains a table summarising research findings outlining at what point various species of animals begin to show detrimental effects from not having FWR—all of which are well below the accepted FWR limits. According to its summary, studies indicate that horses show ill effects between 12 and 24 hours without FWR (the accepted FWR is 28 hours), cattle show ill effects between 24 and 29 hours (the accepted FWR is 36 hours), pigs demonstrate negative effects at 12 hours (the accepted FWR is 28 hours), broiler chickens exhibit problems at 12 hours and spent hens show negative signs at eight hours (the accepted limit for both is 24 hours for water and 28 hours for food and rest).

A statement made in an internal memo indicated that the FWR limits suggested by animal welfare science were surpassed in the revised proposal in the interests of industry:

> While a 12-hour maximum food and water deprivation time is supported by science, it is recognized that several factors occurring around transport may affect this requirement. Bearing this in mind, [redacted] the initial proposed maximum time of 12 hours has been significantly increased to 24 hours.

These numerical values indicate that they were referring to either spent laying hens or rabbits, however the context of this and similar references suggested that it was the chicken industry and/or specific poultry companies that were objecting.

Essentially, the documents provide evidence of a significant degree of consultation and negotiation with the stakeholders presumably concerned with spent laying hens. In order to defend the revised 24-hour FWR interval against further industry pressure, the CFIA cited animal welfare concerns and a potential risk to food safety caused by chickens deprived of food and water for long periods prior to slaughter. The CFIA's own review of expert literature concluded that 'Extending the length of feed withdrawal arbitrarily beyond the optimal 8–12 hours … *is not advisable*' (emphasis in original). Instead, the CFIA recommended slaughter occur between 8–12 and 20–24 hours after consumption of food, but did not mention if or how they would enforce this. The two time windows appear to be in response to food safety concerns: the gut becomes fragile and risks rupture after 12 hours without food, but once the gut becomes severely dehydrated the gut becomes resistant to rupture (presumed to be no less than 20 hours). Finally, if 8–12 hours really is the ideal in terms of food safety and animal welfare, it is unclear why the initial proposed FWR time for broiler chickens was set at 24 instead of the 12 hours proposed for spent hens, which would have made it consistent with regulations in the EU and CFIA's own research. Regardless, the finalised requirement to provide so-called broilers and spent laying hens with water at 24 hours and food and rest at 28 hours fall well outside of EU's regulations and what CFIA had deemed advisable based on their own review of the scientific literature.

To the CFIA's credit—at least, as of the end of 2016—the agency seemed to be standing its ground and remained unwilling to increase the FWR interval for chickens even further, as illustrated in correspondence between the Ministry and the CFIA. In this correspondence, the Ministry asked the CFIA a number of questions about the proposed regulations so that it might respond to industry concerns. For instance, the Ministry advised that the industry has accused the CFIA of writing the revised regulations for livestock instead of poultry (implying that the welfare needs of birds were different); the Ministry then inquired if this claim was valid. The CFIA responded rather forcefully:

> The regulations apply to all animals including birds. Bird suffering has not been found to impact them to a lesser degree than other species … Industry has suggested that compromised birds should be viewed differently from other species due to the numbers of

> animals involved. The challenges of handling large numbers of birds must not be prioritized over individual bird suffering. Poultry welfare research indicates that birds suffer transport stress in a manner similar to other species.

In an 'additional information' section to this response, the CFIA wrote: 'It is important to note that increasingly the animals referred to above (livestock and poultry) are recognised as being be [sic] sentient beings, and as such are capable of mental distress and physical suffering'. The CFIA then noted that exceptions had already been made for the poultry industry, such as making it permissible for them to have chickens squat during transport instead of requiring that they be able to stand in a natural position, in addition to increasing the proposed FWR to 24 from 12 hours for spent hens.

Furthermore, in an August 2016 email, the Ministry asked the CFIA if there is 'a middle ground' that can be found between them and the unnamed opposing stakeholder. The CFIA responded,

> The middle ground is the currently proposed 24 hours without feed, water, and rest. CFIA originally proposed 12 hours … this was based on research and the needs of [redacted]. CFIA is now proposing 24 hours as a result of industry concerns.

Nevertheless, one of the internal documents ended with a recommendation that 'senior management re-engage [redacted] to discuss potential mechanisms to comply with the feed and water deprivation times'. Another document made reference to the inability of the CFIA to secure consensus among stakeholders and stated that the agency was consequently 'continuing to work with the [redacted] with a view to securing industry support'. In the end, the CFIA bent even further past the 24 hour 'middle ground' and set the limit for food and rest at 28 hours.

Conclusion: Food offences and green criminology

Consumers as victims of illegal action tend to be the focus of traditional 'food crime' research. As demonstrated here, a green criminological lens encourages a more expansive view, revealing more of the systemic types of harms via food that occur today. First, the use of a social harm approach as advocated by many green criminologists can help to broaden the focus beyond the narrow confines of those activities deemed illegal by the state, making it possible to appreciate and better understand the continuum of food offences. Second, green criminology highlights the need to foreground power imbalances and extend the analysis beyond human actors, thus bringing to the fore food offences endured by producers, as well as animals and the environment.

Without the benefit of a green criminological lens, the case study of the on-going attempts to update the animal transport regulations in Canada undertaken herein would likely not be considered salient to the subject matter of food crimes, except perhaps in instances where the current regulations are being violated. Yet, our examination of the Canadian animal transport regulations demonstrates that the boundaries of what is legal and illegal are shaped not just by the state, but by industry stakeholders lobbying for their economic interests, as well as by public pressure and shifting social norms. In addition, the case study illustrates how the interests of humans and non-human animals intersect. This interest extends from the apparently growing public interest in animal welfare during transport and into food safety, as the analysis indicates that the proposed food, water and rest intervals for chickens in particular not only exceed what is recommended by animal welfare science but may also pose a risk to food safety. In highlighting the socially constructed nature of animal transport regulations, this chapter demonstrates the limitations of using legalistic definitions and designations in demarcating a criminological field of study and adds to ongoing efforts to develop new terminologies and understandings for offences against humans, animals and the environment. In short, 'food crimes' are but one point on the expansive continuum of food offences.

Notes

1 Foie gras is the liver of a duck or goose that has been fattened, often through methods of force-feeding. The harms caused by these production methods have led to its prohibition in several countries.
2 While we acknowledge that animals and the environment are different victim groups, because their victimisation frequently intersects, we have decided to group them together for the purposes of this chapter.
3 The authors recognise that the term 'food offences' appears in Croall (2001), where a legalistic definition is outlined to discuss offences such as fraud and marketing malpractice. The use of the term food offences in this chapter is distinct from Croall's application of the term, capturing a much broader definition of 'offence'.
4 Space constraints limit the degree to which these issues can be examined. See Fitzgerald (2015) for further details on the impacts of producing, processing and consuming animals as food; see Weis (2013) for an exploration of the global environmental impacts of industrial livestock production.
5 The environmental impacts of transportation of feed and animals within the industry are also significant, however, due to space constraints, we cannot address those here. Instead, interested readers should consult the *Livestock's Long Shadow* report prepared for the Food and Agriculture Organization of the United Nations by Steinfeld and colleagues (2006).
6 Based on the CFIA's own timeline of events contained in these documents, no new activities aimed at updating the regulations took place between 2007 and 2012. During this period, Bill C-468, a private member's bill that proposed shorter food, water and rest intervals for animals being transported, was tabled in the House of Commons. It did not become law.
7 In the released documents, in several instances reference is simply made to 'MinO'. Based on the context, we believe this refers to the Agriculture and Agri-Food Minister's Office.
8 This is not an exhaustive list of the species addressed in the regulations.

References

Barclay, E. and Bartel, R. 2015.'Defining environmental crime: The perspective of farmers,' *Journal of Rural Studies*, 39, June: 188–198.

Basok, T. 2002. *Tortillas and tomatoes: Transmigrant Mexican harvesters in Canada*. Vol. 37. Montreal, Quebec, and Kingston, Ontario: McGill-Queen's Press-MQUP.

BBC News. 2015. 'Horsemeat scandal: Slaughterhouse boss fined over records,' March 23. Available at: https://bbc.com/news/uk-england-leeds–32023036.

Beirne, P. 1999.'For a nonspeciesist criminology: Animal abuse as an object of study,' *Criminology*, 37(1): 117–148.

Beirne, P. 2007. 'Animal rights, animal abuse and green criminology,' in P. Beirne and N. South (eds) *Issues in green criminology: Confronting harms against environments, other animals and humanity*, pp. 55–83. Cullompton, Devon, UK: Willan.

Boffey, D. and Connolly, K. 2017. 'Egg contamination scandal widens as 15 EU states, Switzerland and Hong Kong affected,' *The Guardian*, August 11. Available at: https://theguardian.com/world/2017/aug/11/tainted-eggs-found-in-hong-kong-switzerland-and-15-eu-countries.

Brisman, A. 'A less tragic commons? Using harvester and processor quotas to address crab overfishing,' *Seattle University Law Review*, 26(4) (2003): 929–978.

Brisman, A. 2010. 'The indiscriminate criminalisation of environmentally beneficial activities,' in R. White (ed.) *Global Environmental Harm: Criminological Perspectives*, pp. 161–192. Cullompton, Devon, UK: Willan.

Brisman, A., McClanahan, B. and South, N. 2016. 'Fractured earth, forced labour: A green criminological analysis of rights and the exploitation of landscapes and workers in rural contexts,' in J. F.

Donnermeyer (ed.) *The International Handbook of Rural Criminology*, pp. 289–297. Abingdon, Oxon, UK: Routledge.

Brisman, A. and South, N. 2017. 'Food, crime, justice and security: (Food) security for whom?' in I. Werkheiser and Z. Piso (eds.) *Food Justice in US and Global Contexts: Bringing Theory and Practice Together*, pp. 185–200. New York: Springer.

Campesina, La Via n.d. 'The international peasant's voice'. Available at: https://viacampesina.org/en/international-peasants-voice/.

Campesina, La Via. 'Food Sovereignty: A Future without Hunger. The Right to Produce and Access to Land'. November 11–17, 1996 in Rome, Italy.

Canadian Food Inspection Agency (CFIA). 2017. 'Labelling of genetically engineered foods in Canada Factsheet,' *Government of Canada*. Available at: https://inspection.gc.ca/food/labelling/food-labelling-for-industry/method-of-production-claims/genetically-engineered-foods/eng/1333373177199/1333373638071.

Cazaux, G. 1999. 'Beauty and the beast: Animal abuse from a non-speciesist criminological perspective,' *Crime, Law and Social Change*, 31(2): 105–125.

CBAN – Canadian Biotechnology Action Network. 2017. 'Labelling'. Available at: https://cban.ca/gmos/issues/labeling/.

Charlebois, S. and Haratifar, S. 2015. 'The perceived value of dairy product traceability in modern society: An exploratory study,' *Journal of Dairy Science*, 98(5): 3514–3525.

Cheng, H. 2012. 'Cheap capitalism: A sociological study of food crime in China,' *The British Journal of Criminology*, 52(2): 254–273.

Clifford, M. and Edwards, T. 1998. 'Defining environmental crime,' in Mary Clifford (ed.) *Environmental Crime: Enforcement, Policy, and Social Responsibility*, pp. 5–30. Gaithersberg: Aspen Publishing.

Croall, H. *Understanding White Collar Crime*. Buckingham: Open University Press, 2001.

Croall, H. 'Food crime,' in P. Beirne and N. South (eds.) *Issues in Green Criminology: Confronting Harms against Environments, Humanity and Other Animals*, pp. 206–229. Cullompton, Devon, UK: Willan Publishing, 2007.

Croall, H. 'Food crime: A green criminology perspective,' in N. South and A. Brisman (eds.) *Routledge International Handbook of Green Criminology*, pp. 167–183. Abingdon, Oxon, UK: Routledge, 2013.

Dale-Harris, L. 'Revealed: Exported EU animals subject to abuse and illegal conditions,' *The Guardian*. March 1, 2017. Available at: https://theguardian.com/world/2017/mar/01/revealed-exported-eu-animals-subject-to-abuse-illegal-conditions.

Desmarais, A. A. 2008. 'The power of peasants: Reflections on the meanings of La Vía Campesina,' *Journal of Rural Studies*, 24(2): 138–149.

Fitzgerald, A. J. 2010. 'A social history of the slaughterhouse: From inception to contemporary implications,' *Human Ecology Review*, 17(1): 58–69.

Fitzgerald, A. J. *Animals as Food: (Re)connecting Production, Processing, Consumption and Impacts*. East Lansing, MI: Michigan State University Press, 2015.

Fitzgerald, A. J. *Animal Advocacy and Environmentalism Understanding and Bridging the Divide*. Cambridge: Polity Press, 2019.

Fitzgerald, A. J., Kalof, L. and Dietz, T. 2009. 'Slaughterhouses and increased crime rates: An empirical analysis of the spillover from "The Jungle" into the surrounding community,' *Organization & Environment*, 22(2): 158–184.

Fitzgerald, A. J. and Tourangeau, W. 2018. 'Crime versus harm in the transportation of animals: A closer look at Ontario's "pig trial"'. In R. Hinch and A. Gray (eds.), *A handbook of food crime: Immoral and illegal practices in the food industry and what to do about them*, pp. 213–228. Bristol, UK: Policy Press.

Food Safety Authority of Ireland (FSAI). 2013. 'FSAI survey finds horse DNA in some beef burger products,' *Press Releases*. Available at: https://fsai.ie/news_centre/press_releases/horseDNA15012013.html.

Government of Canada. 2016. 'Regulations amending the health of animals regulations,' *Canada Gazette*, 150(49) 3 December. Available at: https://gazette.gc.ca/rp-pr/p1/2016/2016-12-03/html/reg2-eng.php.

Government of Canada. 2019. 'Regulations Amending the Health of Animals Regulations: SOR/2019-38,' *Canada Gazette, Part II*, 153(4). Available at: http://www.gazette.gc.ca/rp-pr/p2/2019/2019-02-20/html/sor-dors38-eng.html

Goyes, David Rodríguez and South, N. 2015. 'Land-grabs, biopiracy and the inversion of justice in Colombia', *The British Journal of Criminology*, 56(3): 558–577.

Halsey, M. 2004.'Against "green" criminology', *The British Journal of Criminology*, 44(6): 833–853.
Hauck, M. 2009. 'Crime, environment and power: Revisiting the abalone fishery', *South African Journal of Criminal Justice*, 22(2): 229–245.
Hauck, M. and Sweijd, N. A. 1999. 'A case study of abalone poaching in South Africa and its impact on fisheries management,' *ICES Journal of Marine Science*, 56(6): 1024–1032.
Henry, M. 'Fake "kosher" cheese at kids' camps leads to criminal charges,' *The Toronto Star*. May 9, 2017. Available at: https://thestar.com/news/canada/2017/05/09/criminal-charges-laid-over-fake-kosher-cheese-at-kids-camps.html.
HM Government. 2014. 'Elliott review into the integrity and assurance of food supply networks – final report: A national food crime prevention framework'. Available at: https://gov.uk/government/publications/elliott-review-into-the-integrity-and-assurance-of-food-supply-networks-final-report.
INTERPOL. 2016. 'Largest-ever seizures of fake food and drink in INTERPOL-Europol operation,' *INTERPOL News and Media*. 20 March. Available at: https://interpol.int/News-and-media/News/2016/N2016-039.
Leate, F. 2010. '15 years on, how Battle of Brightlingsea tackled live export trade,' *Daily Gazette*. January 22. Available at: https://gazette-news.co.uk/news/4864136.15_years_on__how_Battle_of_Brightlingsea_tackled_live_export_trade/.
Lovell, J. S. 2016. 'Understanding farm animal abuse,' in J.F. Donnermeyer (ed.) *The Routledge International Handbook of Rural Criminology*, pp. 137–146. Abingdon, Oxon, UK: Routledge.
Naaum, A. M., Shehata, H. R., Chen, S.,Li, J.,Tabujara, N., Awmack, D., Lutze-Wallace, C. and Hanner, R. 2018. 'Complementary molecular methods detect undeclared species in sausage products at retail markets in Canada,' *Food Control*, 84 February: 339–344.
Nierenberg, D. and Mastny, L. 2005. *Happier meals: Rethinking the global meat industry*. Vol. 171. Washington, DC: Worldwatch Institute.
Patel, R. 2009. 'Food sovereignty,' *The Journal of Peasant Studies*, 36(3): 663–706.
Perkel, Colin. 2014. 'Maple Lodge to spend $1 million after chicken cruelty conviction'. *The Toronto Star*, 28 March. Available at: https://thestar.com/business/2014/03/28/maple_lodge_to_spend_1_million_after_chicken_cruelty_conviction.html.
Rawlinson, K. 2017. 'Two men jailed in UK for horsemeat conspiracy,' *The Guardian*, July 31 2017. Available at: https://theguardian.com/uk-news/2017/jul/31/two-men-jailed-in-uk-for-horsemeat-conspiracy.
Rosset, P. 2013. 'Re-thinking agrarian reform, land and territory in La Via Campesina', *Journal of Peasant Studies*, 40(4): 721–775.
Runyon, L. 2016. 'Fines for meat industry's safety problems are "embarrassingly low",' *NPR – All things considered*. August 10 2016. Available at: https://npr.org/sections/thesalt/2016/08/10/489468457/fines-for-meat-industrys-safety-problems-are-embarrassingly-low.
Sacheli, S. 2017. 'Thieving recruiter ordered to return illegal fees he charged migrant workers,' *The Windsor Star*. February 10 2017. Available at: http://windsorstar.com/news/local-news/thieving-recruiter-ordered-to-return-illegal-fees-he-charged-migrant-workers.
Smith, R. 2015. 'Documenting the UK 'Black Fish Scandal' as a case study of criminal entrepreneurship', *International Journal of Sociology and Social Policy*, 35(3/4): 199–221.
Spink, J. and Moyer, D. C. 2011. 'Defining the public health threat of food fraud', *Journal of Food Science*, 76(9): R157–R163.
Spink, J., Moyer, D. C., Park, H.,Wu, Y., Fersht, V., Shao, B.,Hong, M., Yeop Paek, S. and Edelev, D. 2015. 'Introducing food fraud including translation and interpretation to Russian, Korean, and Chinese language,' *Food Chemistry*, 189, December 15: 102–107.
Steinfeld, H., Gerber, P., Wassenaar, T., Castel, V., Rosales, M., and de Haan, C. 2006. *Livestock's long shadow: Environmental issues and options*. Rome, Italy: Food and Agriculture Organization of the United Nations.
Walters, R. 2004.'Criminology and genetically modified food,' *The British Journal of Criminology*, 44(2): 151–167.
Walters, R. 2007. 'Food crime, regulation and the biotech harvest', *European Journal of Criminology* 4(2): 217–235.
Weis, T. 2007. *The global food economy: The battle for the future of farming*. London: Zed Books, 2007.

Weis, T. 2013. *The ecological hoofprint: The global burden of industrial livestock*. London: Zed Books.
White, R. 2008. 'Environmental harm and crime prevention,' *Trends & Issues in Crime & Criminal Justice*, 360: 1–6.

Access to Information Request

Access Request #A-2016-00190. Access to Information Act request to the Canadian Food Inspection Agency.

12

Monopolising seeds, monopolising society

A guide to contemporary criminological research on biopiracy

David Rodríguez Goyes

Planting the seeds: the germination of an intellectual project

The place was chaotic. There were problems everywhere. A professor was being publicly accused of racism because he had been heard saying that the *afrodescendientes* were being self-discriminatory; indeed, the *afrodescendientes* did not want to discuss matters with the *campesinos* or the *indigenas*.[1] This altered the whole purpose of the event. The *campesinos* were concerned with the events happening outside the auditorium. The *indigenas* were worried about saying something that could contradict their group's position.

For two-and-a-half days in December 2012, the team of mediators, which included me, had been working hard. Our task was to listen and record the statements of more than a thousand Colombians, including Afro-descendants, peasants, Indigenous and *raizales*,[2] about the internal armed conflict that the country had endured for the last six decades. The mediators were expected to summarise those hearings, organise the discussion in categories, and, most challenging of all, prepare a final draft for the approval of these groups. Work was demanding, not just because of the large number of different Colombian ethnicities represented and thus a diversity of perspectives or because the rural communities present in the event had been silenced for many years and now felt they had much to say, but because it was the first step in a new effort to end the internal armed conflict that had claimed the lives of more than 220,000 Colombians.

Tempers were flaring in this first forum of the peace process negotiations between the *Fuerzas Armadas Revolucionarias de Colombia* (FARC-EP), the biggest guerrilla group in Colombia, and the government. Held in a central location in Colombia's capital city, Bogotá, this forum gathered representatives of the government, community leaders of all sectors of Colombian civil society, and mediators and professionals from the United Nations and the National University of Colombia. We (the mediators) were participating in order to identify what the Colombian civil society recognised as prerequisites for achieving a long-standing peace. The product of our labour would later be sent to La Havana, Cuba, where, based on that material, the guerrillas and the government would try to come to an understanding and agree to end the use of violence.

Work had been demanding and we were exhausted. Before the last session in which the final report would be read, we took a much-needed break. Seeking to find a moment of calm, I avoided the company of my colleagues and found a seat among community representatives. Indelible on my mind is the image of two *campesinas* talking at the table next to mine. 'This time they will feel it', said one of them. 'They will soon realise how important we are', replied the other. I did not know what they were talking about and had not the slightest idea of how their conversation would impact my professional life in the coming years.

It did not take me long, though, to find out what the women in the cafeteria were discussing. After the final report of the forum was read, the floor was opened to comments. Immediately a peasant raised his hand, took the microphone, and warned the auditorium: '*las semillas son patrimonio de los pueblos al servicio de la humanidad, si dejamos perder nuestras semillas, perdemos nuestra libertad, dignidad y autonomía alimentaria*' ('Seeds are peoples' heritage in the service of humanity. If we lose our seeds, we lose our freedom, our dignity and our food autonomy').

Seeds? Why did that *campesina* make reference to seeds in the middle of a peace process? It happened that at the same time as the peace process forum (December 2012), a huge peasant mobilisation was taking place in several Colombian regions. Roads were being blocked and confrontations between the police and peasants were taking place. It was the beginning of one of many *paros agrarios* (agricultural strikes) that were following the process of 'seed privatisation'. The *campesinos* alleged that seeds were becoming more and more expensive and were now controlled by a few multinational corporations, whereas in the past, the seeds were free and available for communal use. This phenomenon of seed monopolisation has been referred to as 'biopiracy' (e.g., Goyes and South 2019). The *campesinos* also maintained that because of continuously diminishing profits, they had to sell their lands and migrate to the city. Likewise, they mentioned that because they were now obliged to buy from corporations instead of exchanging seeds with other *campesinos*, the social fabric of their communities was in jeopardy.

In the back of my mind, a set of questions was starting to form. If the *campesinos*, along with the *indígenas*, the *afrodescendientes* and other ethnic groups who have been the most affected by war were asserting that seeds were connected with peace, should we not be paying attention to that? Furthermore, given that the peace process was supposed to address mass murders, the drug trade, illegal armed groups, state violence and so on—all of which were relevant for criminology—maybe *seeds* should be of interest to criminologists as well?

At the time when these questions were forming in my mind, I had been reading pivotal criminological books, such as *The New Criminology* (Taylor, Walton and Young 2007), *Critical Criminology and a Critique of Penal Law* (Baratta 2004) and *Control and Domination* (Pavarini 2008). Nowhere in those texts was any mention made that the natural environment was—or could be—of interest to criminologists. Therefore, why should I, being concerned with understanding topics of crime, deviance and social control, pay any attention to something as small as a seed?

Wandering in a library, I found that Indian activist Vandana Shiva (1997) had addressed 'seeds' almost two decades ago, where she denounced the privatisation of seeds and other natural products as unfair and harmful, claiming that it was more than merely a matter of privatisation; it was a case of plunder. Seeds and other natural products were being stolen by means of intellectual property rights regimes and with the support of Western science. Shiva referred to this situation as *biopiracy*—or the colonisation of life forms. In a detailed account, Shiva described the harmful consequences of biopiracy. Looking today at the notes I took when reading Shiva's book, I can see that they resemble a typology of harms. Even though none of my criminology professors in Colombia had ever mentioned the relevance of the natural environment for criminology, I was able to identify that critical criminologists I had met would be very interested in the fact that unjust behaviours related to seeds, like patenting them, were legal. I had also read Nils Christie's *Limits to Pain* (1984) and knew that he would be troubled knowing that this affected the social fabrics of communities.

Somehow the denunciation presented by the *campesinos* and Shiva's description of biopiracy matched what I then understood was of interest to critical criminology: to comprehend social events that harm life. My scepticism remained, however, and I was not able to convince myself that a simple seed could provide all the blood and violence that criminological subject matter seemed to require. What was so dramatic about the way seeds were being regulated? Was it drastic enough to count as criminology? That peasants risked their lives in demonstrations and used the limited time given to them during the peace process discussions to talk about seeds seemed to signal that the topic deserved at least further examination. At that point, I established a set of questions to help me evaluate the importance of the topic. First of all, were seeds indeed being privatised? If so, how was this affecting the quality of life of Colombia's population? Also, was the privatisation of seeds somehow connected to the deep and well-documented problems of mass forced displacement, extreme poverty and even the internal armed conflict? Finally, if all this was true, what, if anything, was being done to address these interrelated injustices?

Those were the questions that spurred the development of my study, which came to be called *Biopiracy from a Green Criminological Perspective*. Since the time of the peace process discussion, I have learned that the answer to those questions is much more complex than their formulation, but most importantly, I have come to understand that a seed is the origin of many things, including many topics that should be studied by criminologists. I addressed some of those questions in my research, but many require further research. Likewise, whereas criminology has recently contributed to a deeper understanding of biopiracy (Goyes and South 2016; South 2007; Wyatt 2015; Wyatt and Brisman 2017), biopiracy is like an iceberg whose depth and dimensions we are just beginning to discover. In this chapter, I present a broad overview of biopiracy, hoping to provide a guide, and to inspire new research.

Origins of the term 'biopiracy'

The term 'biopiracy' seems to have first been used in print by Pat Mooney in a relatively unknown article from 1993. With the term 'biopiracy', Mooney sought to make explicit an injustice and an inequality he alleged existed in cases in which big corporations earned massive revenues from marketing agricultural and pharmaceutical products derived from Indigenous knowledge and 'resources', while the 'source' communities lived in economic poverty, deprived of food and medicines. Mooney (1993: 5) used biopiracy as a synonym of 'klepto-monopoly', noting that both concepts reflect 'the drive to establish exclusive monopolies over life' (1993: 6). In the years since this initial foray, Mooney has expanded his ideas and published them more widely (e.g., Mooney 2000). This wider distribution has contributed to growing concerns over biopiracy, as well as continuing controversy regarding the term.

Scholars, activists and politicians have devoted increased attention to biopiracy since Mooney first published his article, and the controversy that it has generated has influenced the development and signing of international conventions, protocols and treaties. Indeed, within the last 25 years, allegations of biopiracy have increased in many arenas throughout the world (see, e.g., Kuruk 2015; Robinson 2010; Tobin 2014; Zedan 2005). Seeking to provide a comprehensive summary of the criminological significance of biopiracy, the remainder of this chapter is divided into three sections. The first section presents the discursive aspect of biopiracy, differentiating between 'biopiracy' and 'bioprospecting', identifying characteristics, elements and features of biopiracy, and delineating the harms produced by biopiracy. The second section distinguishes between 'actors' and the 'target market' or 'market destination' and the 'source material'. The third section presents some areas of biopiracy that remain under-researched and to which green criminologists might be able to contribute.

The discursive arena

Analytically, the biopiracy arena is composed of three levels: the discursive, the politico-legal and the practical (Goyes and South 2019). This chapter considers the first and third levels, which are interdependent, affecting each other and impacting each other. The discursive level takes into consideration discourses, narratives and stories.[3] At the discursive level, biopiracy has been conceptualised as a meta-narrative that counters the bioprospecting narrative (Svarstad 2002). This implies that the concepts of biopiracy and bioprospecting are linked discursively (Svarstad 2000, 2002; Svarstad and Dhillion 2000).[4] As such, it is necessary to start by providing a brief explanation of bioprospecting before exploring the biopiracy meta-narrative.

Bioprospecting

The causal driver for the appearance of the debates about biopiracy was the creation of the bioprospecting meta-narrative, with Eisner (1990) pioneering its construction (Takeshita 2001). This narrative depends on four main premises: (1) the existence of a biodiversity crisis that produces a mass extinction of species—a phenomenon that is portrayed as a problem of interest to all humanity; (2) the consequential disappearance of unique chemical compounds found in those species, which, it is argued, could be useful for the development of products for human benefit; (3) the assumption that 'poor' countries will stop destroying their natural environments if they develop economically (Takeshita 2001); and (4) the belief that humanity benefits from the use of intellectual property rights (IPRs) (Hayden 2007b). These premises have led to the conclusion that the best way to save threatened organisms and ecosystems is to treat them as property and to develop markets to commercialise the organisms (Kloppenburg 2000). Specifically, Eisner (1990) called on the scientific community to undertake a two-step chemical prospecting activity, where the first step was to assess the effects of a natural material of certain organisms, and the second was the purification of the chemical compound responsible for desired effects. The geographical target of these processes was so-called 'Third World' countries, identified as mass extinction sites, where screening laboratories should be established that would simultaneously help with conservation programmes (Eisner 1990). Since Eisner's proposal three decades ago, bioprospecting has come to be understood as the process by which corporations or researchers use biological resources for extracting, isolating and purifying marketable products, and in which traditional knowledges are sometimes tapped as a point of departure (Wynberg 2017).

Bioprospecting has been referred to as a win-win scenario insofar as it purports to benefit all parties involved (Svarstad 2002): local communities derive economic benefits from conserving their environments (Takeshita 2001), the environment is protected, and humankind, as a whole, profits from the new commodities produced. The bioprospecting narrative gains legitimacy by making reference to its contribution to conservation efforts (Hayden 2007a) and the direct improvements it brings for human health and wellbeing. In the process, capital allocates 'functions'—to local communities as 'guardians', to nature as a 'resource' and to knowledge as a 'thing' that can become 'private property' (Takeshita 2001). Simultaneously, science and biotechnology are portrayed as 'enhancers' of nature in the pharmaceutical and agricultural realms (Loots 2007), while part of the legitimacy-claim of the bioprospecting narrative is provided by the sustainable development discourse, which prescribes that nature—particularly threatened habitats—should be protected, managed and preserved for profit, as is done with other resources (Takeshita 2001).

Biopiracy

The biopiracy meta-narrative opposes the development of bioprospecting, as just described. Its construction relies heavily on criticisms of bioprospecting. 'Biopiracy' was a term coined as a counter-narrative to the accusations made by industries based in the Global North, who alleged that the Global South owed them millions of dollars for the theft of their pharmaceutical and agroindustry products (Shiva 1997). Proponents of the biopiracy narrative responded to these accusations of theft—or piracy—by saying that the corporations were the original pirates because they stole biological resources (Bender 2003). The narrative relied on the definition of piracy as morally ambiguous property seizure committed by organised groups (Dawdy and Bonni 2012).

The biopiracy counter-narrative begins by relating simplified versions of stories involving the use of natural resources by foreign corporations, highlighting the exploitation of traditional communities. It then denounces the harms brought about by these bioprospecting processes. The narrative concludes by offering an image of another world, as a proposal for the replacement of the sustainable development rationale.

Contributors to the biopiracy narrative use, as a starting point, a set of cases with which they seek to illustrate the harmful consequences of bioprospecting. These cases can be divided into three categories: (1) cases that denounce the patenting of a natural product whose use was already known by traditional communities, most often without prior consent or benefit-sharing agreements; (2) cases that condemn any kind of macro-projects in which corporations seek to identify natural active compounds with marketable potentiality; and (3) cases that decry the dependence produced by resource monopolisation.

The first category of cases is the most commonly used to provide support for the biopiracy narrative. In these cases, a single biological species is identified. Its use for/by traditional communities (often over the course of hundreds of years) is then explained. These cases usually end by denouncing the unfair actions through which a corporation has acquired a patent on a product derived from the species—most of the time without prior consent or benefit-sharing with the community that helped breed the species and knew about its uses. Some—but not all—of the cases included in this category result in a success story, where a traditional community defeats the biopirates by achieving revocation of the patent derived from a species. It can thus be said that proponents of the biopiracy narrative use this type of case broadly because it can be seen to exemplify a clear injustice and, at the same time, show the possibility of confronting biopiracy via litigation. The existence of success stories provides motivation to sustain the struggle. Table 12.1 offers a sample of the stories used to date in the biopiracy narrative.

The second category of cases consists of those involving agreements between institutions (e.g., a corporation, governmental agency, university) from the Global North and a biodiverse country of the Global South to prospect its natural resources. These cases often involve distribution agreements, which are criticised for their unequal terms and for a lack of participation by traditional communities in the decision-making processes. A representative case of this type is the Merck-INBio arrangement—a two-year agreement with a budget of

Table 12.1 Cases used to support the biopiracy narrative

Resource	*Traditional use*	*Injustice story*
Ayahuasca	Beverage used by Amazonian Indigenous communities for religious and healing purposes.	In 1986, the Loren Miller company received a US patent for what the company claimed was a variety of the *Banisteriopsis caapi* plant. In 1999, the patent was invalidated after the intervention of the NGO Center for International Environmental Law (Folkins 2003; Kuruk 2015) and as a result of widespread negative media exposure.
Epipedobates frog	Tricolour species found in Peru and Ecuador, whose secretion has an analgesic effect locally used as a painkiller.	Based on information received from local healers, John Daly, using a large number of frogs 'collected' without permission, isolated epibatidine. In 1998, Abbot Laboratories patented the active principle (Alter 2000; Lavín and Alarcón 2010/2011).
Quinoa	South American grain that contains a higher protein content than any other grain, as well as all vitamins, amino acids and minerals required in the human diet.	Scientists from the Colorado State University obtained a patent in 1994. In 1998, due to pressure from Andean farmers and various NGOs, the university dropped the patent (Sundaram 2005). It must be noted, nonetheless, that the grain is exported in such great quantities from the Andes that the peoples who depend on it no longer have access to it because it has become too expensive (Brisman, McClanahan and South 2014).
Solomon Islands' population cell lines	Samples obtained by the US National Health Institute.	The US Department of Commerce applied for a patent for these cell lines. This was allegedly done without prior consent. The application was withdrawn but the samples were not given back (Kariyawasam 2008).

US$1.135 million. In this agreement, INBio collected biological samples in Costa Rica and delivered them to Merck for their screening in drug development. Merck agreed to share benefits, including technical assistance, staff training and royalties from resulting commercial products. This agreement has been both celebrated and criticised in bioprospecting literature (Kim 2010): some highlighted the shared benefits of the 'technology transfer' from Merck-INBio to Costa Rica; others condemned the small share of profits given to Costa Rica in comparison with those received by Merck.

The third category of cases involves dynamics broader than the patenting of a single product or the establishment of a single research agreement. In these cases, corporations (frequently, Ciba, Dupont and Monsanto) have patented more than one product at a time (e.g., soybean or cotton in the case of Monsanto) and have used chemical products to grow their seeds (e.g., Monsanto's herbicide Roundup (Aoki 1998)). After securing the patents, such companies have sold the whole 'cropping package' to farmers, rendering the farmers in these traditional communities dependent on corporations for access to natural products. The spectrum of appropriation is evidently wider in these cases. For example, a wide range of laws and market dynamics have made Colombian farmers reliant on big corporations for access to seeds (Goyes and South 2016).

Most of the authors contributing to the construction of the biopiracy narrative rely on anecdotal evidence (Abramova and Greer 2013; Rabitz 2015), and there is a lack of comprehensive systematic assessment of the magnitude of the issue, both within certain countries and more globally (Soria-López and Fuentes-Páramo 2016). There are only a few examples of allegations of biopiracy based on large and systematic gathering of empirical information. One of them is the study developed by researchers from the Traditional Knowledge Digital Library, asserting that 4,000 patents or patent applications in the US Patent and Trademark Office database are based on the medical properties of plants already known in India, and that out of 762 medicinal plants on which there is a patent, 360 of them could be categorised as traditional (Sharma 2002).

Characteristics, elements and features of biopiracy

Because of the differences in the cases above, it is difficult to develop a single, satisfactory definition of 'biopiracy' (Kim 2010). Nevertheless, it is possible to identify three fundamental elements: (1) the material object of the controversy is always a biological or genetic resource; (2) the actors always entail representatives of the Western world[5] in opposition to representatives of traditional communities; and (3) biotechnology is always present, for example, when samples from species identified as valuable are taken to laboratories and transformed into commodities (Isaac and Kerr 2005). Moreover, I identify in the literature four different characteristics, features, or issues that commentators use to discern instances of biopiracy: appropriation; exploitation and injustice; origins of the actors and victims; and role of law.

1 **Appropriation**. Some commentators understand biopiracy as the direct or indirect appropriation or expropriation of biological and genetic resources and their associated traditional knowledge (e.g., Tobin 2014). Low-level appropriation can entail, for example, isolated cases of stealing seeds from a collection (Pierce 2008) or the illegitimate collection of germplasm for gene banks (Fowler, Smale and Gaji 2001). As the degree of appropriation increases, appropriation can lead to a monopoly (Kuruk 2015). When appropriation reaches such structural proportions, it is referred to as *biocolonialism* (Hawthorne 2007). In these situations, it is not the *means used* that is most important but the *consequence* of the act: the claiming of ownership of biological and genetic resources that previously had no specifically defined (or single) owner.
2 **Exploitation and injustice**. For many experts, exploitation and injustice are the defining features of biopiracy. Ultimately, these are perpetrated by a lack of fairness, such as the absence of informed consent and equity. Thus, biopiracy becomes the unauthorised, improper, or uncompensated exploitation or expropriation of traditional resources and knowledge for commercial or other gain (Folkins 2003; Wyatt 2015). Unfair practices entail, for example, disallowing communities that provided the resource or the

knowledge from enjoying the revenues or other benefits derived from the commercialisation of the product or inequitably distributing those benefits (Koopman 2005).

3 **Origins of the actors and victims**. Generally, the authors exploring instances of biopiracy allege that representatives of the Global North are usually those accessing the natural resources and accused of biopiracy. The 'victims', on the other hand, are most often traditional populations of the Global South, such as Indigenous peoples and peasants (Woods 2002). Thus, biopiracy becomes the plunder of natural resources and related knowledge from the Global South at the hands of powerful industrial Northern corporations and countries (Mgbeoji 2006). As such, biopiracy is closely related to struggles over sovereignty (Kloppenburg 2000; Rabitz 2015).
4 **Role of law**. Biopiracy can occur because of or in spite of the law. For example, biopiracy can be considered the use of biological resources in violation of laws or contractual obligations (Guiza and Bernal 2013). From this perspective, if the law is followed and equity ensured, biopiracy has not occurred. Rather, what has transpired is (or becomes) bioprospecting, which, for some, has positive connotations and outcomes. Biopiracy can also occur through the intellectual property system, such as when a corporation patents a natural product that had been developed previously by a rural community (Kelter 2014; Oyewunmi 2013). Here, the corporation 'abuses' the protection of intellectual property laws, benefiting from a natural product that used to belong to another group (Kelter 2014).

Harms produced by biopiracy (as identified in the biopiracy narrative)

The characteristics, elements and features of the biopiracy narrative outlined above can help identify whether biopiracy has occurred, how, and by whom/to whom. With this, we can consider more carefully the nature and types of harm that proponents of the biopiracy narrative allege have occurred. Table 12.2 delineates five different types of harm produced by biopiracy.

The distributive consequences of biopiracy

The monopolisation of a product implies that, first, local communities need to start paying fees for using a product that was previously theirs (Conforto 2004). Under such an arrangement, farmers are forced to buy raw materials, such as seeds, fertilisers and pesticides, from corporations in order to farm, rendering them dependent on these corporations for their livelihoods (Bender 2003). Second, such monopolisation impedes the community's ability to export and profit from a product that earlier was theirs to commercialise (Wyatt and Brisman 2017). Furthermore, it has been alleged that in some cases, the price of a product, i.e., a food source, like quinoa, increases so much that traditional communities can no longer afford access to the product that used to be an important part of their daily lives and that could be essential for their health (Brisman, McClanahan and South 2014). These effects result in a few big corporations controlling the market and production to the exclusion of communities (Aoki 1998). Because of their exclusion from the market, traditional communities become vulnerable to expulsion from their lands (Goyes and South 2016). This has important impacts on local communities and countries that rely heavily on agricultural production because when national producers are displaced from the market, the nation state itself no longer controls the production of its own food, rendering it dependent on international corporations to satisfy its needs (Lee 2006).

Table 12.2 Harms produced by biopiracy.

Type of harm	*Harmful effects*
Distributive	• Traditional communities are made dependent on corporations. • Traditional communities are excluded from the market. • Privatising natural products facilitates land grabs. • Loss of control over national production. • Lack of sharing of benefits by corporations with traditional communities.
Ecological	• Fewer incentives to preserve natural resources. • Loss of biodiversity caused by the implementation of a monoculture of species, in which some crops are favoured due to the profit they produce, while others are eliminated for being 'unproductive'. • Soil exhaustion. • Threat of biohazards derived from the large-scale modification of nature that aims to shape ecosystems in a way that increases the profit generated by privatised species.
Sociological	• De-ruralisation/urbanisation. • Social fabric of communities is damaged because of the replacement of horizontal trading dynamics by vertical supplier-consumer dynamics. • Alteration of communal memories, practices and traditions. • Social uprooting.
Symbolic	• Commodification of nature by promoting the ideology that ownership and profit are more important than satisfying social needs. • Implementation of a reductionist logic in which it is believed that the components of ecosystems can be isolated and controlled as independent entities, thus neglecting the interrelation and complexity of life. • Devaluation of the role of traditional communities in the contemporary world.
Epistemological	• Breach of a knowledge system. • Expansion of the gap between traditional knowledge and Western science.

The ecological consequences of biopiracy

When local communities stop benefiting from their natural surroundings, they have less incentive to preserve them (Wyatt and Brisman 2016). In addition, when farmers are dependent on corporations for their materials, like seeds and fertilisers, and the market dictates which crops the corporations should sell, the diversity of products planted is much smaller than when farmers were independent. This leads to a loss of biodiversity, rendering crops more vulnerable to pests (Zedan 2005). Moreover, with the repetitive planting of the same products, the soil is exhausted, affecting surrounding ecosystems (Conforto 2004).

The sociological consequences of biopiracy

Biopiracy has been seen as the cause of swift de-ruralisation, as fewer and fewer hands are needed to farm, thus changing the composition of societies (Highfield 2009). Biopiracy can also contribute to a breach of the social fabric of traditional communities in two ways: first, trading replaces bartering, so peasants and farmers must deal more with corporations than with one another (Shiva 1997); second, knowledge systems are disrupted and broken due to the imposition of new ways of producing and treating natural products, brought on by corporate interests (Ptqk 2013.) This affects community memory, altering deeply rooted traditions and practices, as well as shared awareness of the community's contribution to the preservation of biodiversity and the production of food and medicine (Aguila-Way 2014). These abrupt transformations in the lifestyles of traditional communities have meant communities have been forced to join commercial arrangements for which they were not prepared—namely, globalised market dynamics—resulting in a feeling of disempowerment (Sarma 1999) of the kind that Young referred to as 'vertigo' (2012) and which the communities themselves see as social uprooting.

The symbolic consequences of biopiracy

Biopiracy has been accused of reinforcing the ethically problematic commodification of nature in which 'life forms are treated as if they are mere machines' (Shiva 1997: 23). According to this harmful utilitarian logic, living organisms and their ecosystems are preserved for their economic utility, rather than for their own integrity and intrinsic value. Likewise, biopiracy depends on a reductionist logic based on the belief that the components of the universe can be isolated and rearranged in any way humans want in order to control nature. This conviction is seen as dangerous given that it ignores the complexity of life (Shiva 1997). Another symbolic consequence, which is connected to the epistemological ones presented next, is that biopiracy strengthens the belief that the intellectual contributions of corporate scientists are much more valuable than the contributions farmers can make in the areas of traditional breeding, conservation and domestication of species (Aguila-Way 2014).

The epistemological consequences of biopiracy

Due to the force and intervention of the market, knowledge systems within communities are disrupted and severed because knowledge becomes individualised rather than remaining communal (Takeshita 2001). Furthermore, the friction that exists between scientists and traditional communities because of biopiracy has been seen as the cause of communities' distrust of Western science, limiting the potential for collaboration and the exchange of information (Conforto 2004). Finally, when epistemological power is taken away from traditional communities, they become subject to the assignment of roles and functions with which they might not identify, for example, as 'stewards' or 'custodians' of the resources that science will later develop, thus depriving traditional communities of their right to self-determination (Takeshita 2001).

These five types of harms provide actors constructing the biopiracy narrative with a reason to mobilise for change. The struggle against biopiracy has been presented as an important cause in the protection of traditional communities that aims to return to them control over their traditional culture and natural resources, as well as to help prevent the further impoverishment of local communities (Folkins 2003). The struggle extends beyond mere opposition, however, and includes a set of narratives to be established as alternatives to the current dominant environmental institutions, organisations and practices (Kloppenburg 2000). As such, it produces a rationale that challenges the treatment of nature as merchandise, rejects the commodification of natural and intellectual resources, and demands the recognition of the value of Indigenous and peasant cultures.

Actors, markets and materials

In this section, I describe developments and events on the material level that have shaped the biopiracy-bioprospecting debate. In so doing, I distinguish between 'actors' and the 'target market' or 'market destination' and the 'source material'. Over the last few decades, the field of biotechnology has grown, with the coding and manipulating of genetic sequences of many living organisms. Such progress in biotechnology implies a shift of focus from 'species' and 'specimens' to the microphysical properties of biological materials and the genetic information contained by them—genetic *resources* (Rabitz 2015). The development of these techniques fits with the individualistic nature of intellectual property rights by allowing an individual actor to be identified as the innovator (Isaac and Kerr 2005). Concurrently, many governments around the world have restricted their budgets for public research—a gap that has been filled quickly by corporations who have taken the lead on research and innovation on genetic resources (Isaac and Kerr 2005). This has resulted in some significant ventures in the development of biotechnology in industrialised countries with the results being used by corporations in the agribusiness and pharmaceutical industries (Conforto 2004).

Actors

'Users' are those individuals and groups (corporations, governmental agencies, individual scientists, research centres) who access directly biological material. 'Suppliers' constitute the other main set of actors—mainly traditional communities in southern nations. This division is taken to a broader geopolitical level, such as that between 'user countries', like Germany or the United States, and 'supplier countries'. In general, the legal frameworks of supplier countries are often weak and unable to protect environmental resources and the needs of local inhabitants (Lee 2006). In addition to 'users' and 'suppliers', supranational organisations are also involved in the biopiracy debate. Organisations like the Food and Agriculture Organization of the United Nations, World Health Organization, the World Intellectual Property Organization and the World Trade Organization have been active in the debate and have facilitated users' interests. Self-identified representatives of the suppliers' interests are activists, advocacy groups and NGOs (Kloppenburg 2000). Universities in the Global South are another actor involved in these dynamics; they often play a pivotal role because a lack of government financial support may mean that they have to cooperate with corporations under unequal conditions (Lavín and Alarcón 2010/2011).

In studies about biopiracy, the focus often falls on supplier communities, which are often referred to as 'traditional communities'. The term 'traditional community' is a generic label that encompasses Indigenous communities, peasant communities and other rural groups (Soria-López and Fuentes-Páramo 2016). Traditional communities have developed 'traditional knowledge' (Finetti 2011) and, in particular, 'traditional ecological knowledges' (TEK) based on their close interaction with the environment (Clarke 2010). Traditional communities produce TEK for their survival; they rely on it for food and medicine production. Such communities view nature not as a commodity but as an essential element in life (Daya and Vink 2006: 2). From a TEK perspective, there is no concept of individual ownership of knowledge: no one can claim rights over it and individuals are not credited with the advancement of knowledge, as is often the case with Western knowledge[6] (Daya and Vink 2006). Nonetheless, traditional communities are not as cut off from the rest of the world as they once were; they are influenced by it and develop their activities in it (Oyewunmi 2013). This means that the borders between Western knowledge and TEK have become more porous. What is certain is that, at least in the South American context, there is a clear disparity in terms of economic and political capital when these communities confront wealthy corporations (Sundaram 2005). The vulnerability of these communities is more pronounced when one considers other problems they face, such as conflict, famine and land grabs (Folkins 2003).

Traditional communities and their knowledges are of importance to the biopiracy narrative because corporations take the knowledge developed by traditional communities and appropriate it, together with natural resources, while TEK is unfairly excluded from the protection granted by intellectual property systems (Koopman 2005). Allegedly, TEK is stolen by corporations that use it in screening processes to identify potential uses of genetic resources (Daya and Vink 2006), without recognising the importance of the communities that contributed to its creation—taking it as nobody's and yet everybody's knowledge (Isla 2007).

Target market and source material

Prospecting activities, whether referred to as bioprospecting or biopiracy, can be categorised either on the basis of the target market or product or on the basis of what basic resource is used in the process (see Table 12.3). Zelder (2005) proposes dividing between red bioprospecting (processes aimed to develop medical products), green bioprospecting (when the resource is used for the development of genetically modified herbicides and crops), and white bioprospecting (when the resource is used for the industrial development of chemical products and enzymes for a variety of industrial processes). Efferth and colleagues (2016) differentiate between ethnopharmacology used for the treatment of diseases and ailments; nutrition used for food; ethnobotany used for housing, cloth production and ritualistic uses; and phytochemistry, used to isolate chemical molecules as a subfield of botany. Other researchers focus on the raw material used in the process, where raw materials can be divided into: *human*; *plant*; *microorganisms*; and *animal resources* (Goyes et al. 2013). Still other researchers and commentators, without providing all-encompassing classifications, add cosmetic and personal-care-products markets to the list (see, e.g., Rabitz 2015). If we combine these classifications, we generate the following typology (as expressed in Table 12.3): green—or nutritional—bioprospecting seeks to improve productivity or increase the resistance of crop plants (Kuruk 2015); red bioprospecting—or ethnopharmocology—is directed towards the pharmaceutical market; white—or phytochemistry—is used as the base for several other processes, such as to complement scientific testing of drugs and food products, and to verify laboratory research results (Kuruk 2015); and pink—or cosmetic bioprospecting—is used to develop fashion products.

Contested dynamics and counter arguments

Bioprospecting and biopiracy are entangled in a contentious dynamic of meta-narrative versus counter-narrative. Some argue that the biopiracy narrative is not sustainable and that it produces more harm than good. For example, Chen (2006) asserts that the entire

Table 12.3 Bioprospecting by market destination and by source material

Green or nutrition bioprospecting	Red or ethnopharmacology bioprospecting
White or phytochemistry bioprospecting	Pink or cosmetic bioprospecting

biopiracy narrative is based on lies and is riddled with inconsistencies, so much so that it amounts to a 'rural legend'. Others, like Svarstad (2002), claim that there is lack of proof of the negative consequences for traditional communities resulting from the use of IPRs (particularly patents) over plants, and that accusations of biopiracy are moralising, rather than based on violations of law (Koopman 2005). This is complemented with more specific reactions against what the biopiracy narrative portrays as injustice. For example, Heald (2003) argued that the use of natural resources by corporations and the patenting of the derived products do not deprive local communities of access to raw products for traditional medicines and food.

Those who reject the label of 'biopiracy', like Nash (2001), also seek to attack the picture constructed by the biopiracy narrative, which relies on the portrayal of the Global South as rich in unique biodiversity. Nash has maintained that the Global South is not the only biodiverse region and that countries in the Global North have also contributed important resources for the development of drugs, such as taxanes and etoposide (a chemotherapy medication), which have had worldwide benefits (Nash 2001). This response has been interpreted as a form of literal denial (Cohen 2001), in which corporations do not admit that they have taken anything from the Global South (Wyatt and Brisman 2016) and, instead, insist that the Global South now contributes little in terms of raw materials to the Global North because gene banks are the contemporary centres of diversity and main suppliers of genetic resources (Fowler, Smale and Gaji 2001).

Nash, in his argument against the use of the label 'biopiracy', also points out that companies can buy synthetic chemicals ready for screening, which is much cheaper than developing a bioprospecting project (Nash 2001). Nash's reasoning, however, inverts the burden of debt—now industrialised countries are the ones giving living genetic resources for breeding (germplasm) to biodiverse countries—in a 4 to 1 ratio. Essentially, he seems to be maintaining that countries of the Global North are not plundering material from less-industrialised countries, and that if payments were required for access to germplasm, less-industrialised countries would stand to lose.

Wyatt and Brisman (2016), drawing on Cohen (2001), identify the use of interpretative denial in the efforts to debunk the accusations contained in the biopiracy narrative. Although they do not engage Nash directly, they explain that interpretative denial occurs when corporations and countries of the Global North assert that the contribution of traditional communities is too small in the development of products to be of any consequence. Within this 'modern bioprospecting paradigm' (Kim 2010), corporations and countries of the Global North rely less on traditional knowledge, regarding the genetic resource as the only source of knowledge, elicited by screening and sampling.

In addition to denying the evidence for/of 'biopiracy', critics of the biopiracy narrative also reiterate the benefits of bioprospecting, not least its productivity in providing medicines and food that benefit the entire world (Heald 2003). Critics of the biopiracy narrative, such as Verma (2002), have argued that application of the 'biopiracy' label has had negative consequences for science and for the populations of the Global South. In their view, rural communities' demand for payment for access to genetic resources has led to a decrease in genuine scientific collaboration (see, e.g., Verma 2002). They also describe the Indigenous communities as the losers in the biopiracy controversy because they seem to be silenced by action groups, whose participation can frustrate Indigenous groups' efforts to comment on the issue (e.g., Nash 2001). These Indigenous communities, it is alleged, lose revenues and other benefits that they would receive if they collaborated with industry (Sundaram 2005).

Conclusion: challenges for green criminology

As this chapter has attempted to reveal, the complexity of the biopiracy-bioprospecting dynamics—and the struggles between these two narratives—brings a set of challenges for criminological study. Some of the key tasks in the study of biopiracy to which criminology could contribute include: the development of systematic analyses of biopiracy (as opposed to anecdotal studies), where criminologists gather large amounts of empirical information on the issue. For instance, such systematic analyses could assess whether and the extent to which biopiracy-bioprospecting practices lead to situations of broad dependence on corporations. Criminologists could also help tease out how dynamics vary substantially depending on the raw material in question and its target market. In addition, criminologists could explore more broadly the harms alleged and denounced by the biopiracy narrative, thereby challenging the assertions that biopiracy is a misnomer and a myth.

On a more personal note, I have seen and documented the harms listed above and the ways in which they are, indeed, produced by biopiracy. I have observed and recorded how seeds are monopolised. I have borne witness to the ways in which the lifestyles of traditional communities have been destroyed by biopiracy. I have watched how traditional societies have been monopolised to serve the economic interests of corporations. Traditional communities are suffering the harms of biopiracy. I hope to inspire, with this chapter, new studies of biopiracy with the goal of finding new solutions.

Notes

1. *Afrodescendientes* (Afro-descendants), *campesinos* (peasants), *raizales* and *indígenas* (Indigenous peoples) are self-referential designations used to denote some of the Colombian ethnic affiliations.
2. *Raizales* are the community of Afro-descendants living on the islands of San Andrés, Providencia and Santa Catalina.
3. 'Discourses' are understood here as the broad frameworks that provide a set of assumptions and judgments to help us analyse the events of our daily lives and locate them in coherent accounts (Svarstad 2002). Discourses define allowed and forbidden modes of thinking, living and speaking (Takeshita 2001).
4. A third term that appears in this debate, and which is sometimes confused with bioprospecting, is that of 'biotrade' (see, e.g., Kelter 2014). Nonetheless, in contrast to the definitions provided here of 'bioprospecting' and 'biopiracy', 'biotrade' involves 'traditional' commodity trade in environmental resources (Wynberg 2017).
5. Curiously, actors from locations, such as China and Japan, have not been included in the biopiracy narrative in any of the existing roles.
6. This is not to say that each person in a traditional community possesses all (the) knowledge, but that the concept of one person owning an invention is generally not present in traditional communities.

References

Abramova, I., and A. Greer. 2013. 'Ethnochemistry and human rights,' *Chemistry & Biodiversity*, 10(9): 1724–1728.

Aguila-Way, T. 2014. 'The Zapatista "mother seeds in resistance" project', *Social Text*, 32(1): 67–92.

Alter, J. M. 2000. 'International biopiracy versus the value of local knowledge', *Capitalism Nature Socialism*, 11(2): 59–66.

Aoki, K. 1998. 'Neocolonialis, anticommons property, and biopiracy in the (not-so-brave) new world order of international intellectual property protection', *Indiana Journal of Global Legal Studies*, 6(1): 11–58.

Baratta, A. 192004. *Criminología crítica y crítica al derecho penal [Critical Criminology and a Critique to Penal Law]*. Translated by Álvaro Búnster. *Nueva Criminología y Derecho*. 1 edition. Buenos Aires: Siglo Veintiuno Editores. Original edition, 1982. Reprint, 1.

Bender, E. K. 2003. 'North and South: The WTO, trips, and the scourge of biopiracy', *Tulsa Journal of Comparative & International Law*, 11(1): 281–320.

Brisman, A., McClanahan, B. and South, N. 2014. 'Toward a green-cultural criminology of "the rural"', *Critical Criminology: An International Journal* 22(4): 479–494. DOI: 10.1007/s10612-014-9250-7.

Chen, J. 2006. 'There's no such thing as biopiracy ... and it's a good thing too', *McGeorge Law Review*, 37(1): 1–32.

Christie, N. 191984. *Los límites del dolor [Limits to Pain]*. Translated by Mariluz Caso. Buenos Aires: Fondo de Cultura Económica. Original edition, 1981.

Clarke, T. J. 2010. 'Finding a remedy and respect in equity: Traditional knowledge, inventorship, and perspective biosystems v. pharmacia biotech', *DePaul Journal of Art, Technology Intellectual Property Law*, 2(1): 131–184.

Cohen, S. 2001. *States of Denial: Knowing about Atrocities and Suffering*. Cambridge: Polity Press.

Conforto, D. 2004. 'Traditional and modern-day biopiracy: Redefining the biopiracy debate', *Environmental Law and Litigation*, 19(2): 357–396.

Dawdy, S. L., and Bonni, J. 2012. 'Towards a general theory of piracy', *Anthropological Quarterly*, 85(3): 673–699.

Daya, Y., and Vink, N. 2006. 'Protecting traditional ethno-botanical knowledge in South Africa through the Intellectual property regime', *Agrekon*, 45(3): 319–338.

Efferth, T., Mita Banerjee Paul, N. W.,Abdelfatah, S., Arend, J., Elhassan, G., Hamdoun, S., Hamm, R., Hong, C., Kadioglu, O., Naß, J., Ochwangi, D., Ooko, E., Ozenver, N., Saeed, Mohamed E.M., Schneider, M., Seo, Ean-Jeong, Wu, Ching-Fen, Yan, G., Zeino, M., Qiaoli Zhao Abu-Darwish, M. S., Andersch, K., Alexie, G., Bessarab, D., Bhakta-Guha, D., Bolzani, V., Else Dapat Donenko, F. V., Efferth, M., Greten, H. J., Leslie Gunatilaka Hussein, A. A., Karadeniz, A., Khalid, H. E., Kuete, V., Lee, Ik-Soo, Liu, L., Midiwo, J., Mora, R., Nakagawa, H., Ngassapa, O., Noysang, C., Omosa, L. K., Hwiemtun Roland, F., Shahat, A. A., Saab, A., Saeed, E. M., Shan, L., and Titinchi, S. J. J. 2016. 'Biopiracy of natural products and good bioprospecting practice', *Phytomedicine*, 23(2): 166–173. DOI: 10.1016/j.phymed.2015.12.006.

Eisner, T. 1990. 'Prospecting for nature's chemical riches', *Chemoecology*, 1(1): 38–40.

Finetti, C. 2011. 'Traditional knowledge and the patent system: Two worlds apart?' *World Patent Information*, 33(1): 58–66.

Folkins, P. E. 2003. 'Has the lab coat become the modern day eye patch—Thwarting biopiracy of indigenous resources by modifying international patenting systems', *Transnational Law & Contemporary Problems*, 13(1): 339–368.

Fowler, C., Smale, M., and Gaji, S. 2001. 'Unequal exchange? Recent transfers of agricultural resources and their implications for developing countries'. *Development Policy Review*, 19(2): 181–204.

Goyes, D. R., and South, N. 2016. 'Land-grabs, bio-piracy and the inversion of justice in Colombia', *The British Journal of Criminology*, 56(3): 558–577. DOI: 10.1093/bjc/azv082.

Goyes, D. R., and South, N. 2019. 'Biopiracy', in E. McLaughlin and J. Muncie (eds.) *The SAGE Dictionary of Criminology*, fourth edition, 36–38. Thousand Oaks, CA: Sage.

Goyes, D. R., Victoria Pérez-Martínez, L., Rodríguez-Figueredo, M. I., Romero-Torres, L. L., Beltrán Barrera, Y. J., and Melgarejo, L. M. 2013. 'Análisis comparativo de las experiencias internacionales en bioprospección con las determinantes CESA (científicas, económicas y socio-ambientales) en Colombia [Comparative analysis of the international experiences on bioprospecting with the CESA (scientific, economic and socio environmental) determinants in Colombia', in C. Toro Pérez and L. Marina Melgarejo (eds.) *Determinantes científicas, económicas y socio-ambientales de la bioprospección en Colombia*, pp. 235–303. Bogotá: Universidad Nacional de Colombia-Colciencias.

Guiza, L., and Bernal, D. 2013. 'Bioprospecting in Colombia', *Universitas Scientarum*, 18(2): 153–164.

Hawthorne, S. 2007. 'Land, bodies and knowledge: Biocolonialism of plants, indigenous peoples, women, and people with disabilities', *Signs: Journal of Women in Culture and Society*, 32(2): 314–323.

Hayden, C. 2007a. 'Kinship theory, property, and the politics of inclusion: From lesbian families to bioprospecting in a few short steps', *Signs: Journal of Women in Culture and Society*, 32(2): 337–345.

Hayden, C. 2007b. 'Taking as giving: Bioscience, exchange, and the politics of benefit sharing', *Social Studies of Science*, 37(5): 729–758. DOI: 10.1177/0306312706707801 2.

Heald, P. J. 2003. 'The rhetoric of biopiracy', *Cardozo Journal of International and Comparative Law*, 11(2): 519–546.

Highfield, J. 2009. 'Finding the voice of the peasant: Agriculture, neocolonialism and Mulk Raj Anand's Punjab Trilogy', *Journal on Interdisciplinary Studies in Humanities*, 1(2): 115–133.

Isaac, G. E., and Kerr, W. A. 2005. 'Bioprospecting or biopiracy? Intellectual property and traditional knowledge in biotechnology innovation', *The Journal of World Intellectual Property*, 7(1): 35–52.

Isla, A. 2007. 'An ecofeminist perspective on biopiracy in Latin America', *Signs: Journal of Women in Culture and Society*, 32(2): 1–10.

Kariyawasam, K. 2008. 'Protecting biodiversity, traditional knowledge and intellectual property in the Pacific: Issues and challenges', *Asia Pacific Law Review*, 16(1): 73–90.

Kelter, K. A. 2014. 'Pirate patents: Arguing for improved biopiracy prevention and protection of indigenous rights through a new legislative model', *Suffolk University Law Review*, 47(2): 373–396.

Kim, T. J. 2010. 'Expanding the arsenal against biopiracy: Application of the concession agreement framework to prevent misappropiation of biodiversity', *SMU Science and Technology Law Review*, 14(1): 69–126.

Kloppenburg, J. 2000. 'Biopiracy, witchery, and the fables of ecoliberalism', *Peace Review* 12(4): 509–516.

Koopman, J. 2005. 'Reconciliation of propietary interests in genetic and knowledge resources: Hurry cautiously!' *Ecological Economics*, 53(4): 523–541.

Kuruk, P. 2015. 'Regulating access to traditional knowledge and genetic resources: The disclosure requirement as a strategy to combat biopiracy', *San Diego International Law Journal*, 17(1): 1–74.

Lavín, R. R. A. 2010/2011. 'La biopiratería de los recursos de la medicina indígena tradicional en el Estado de Chiapas, México. El caso ICBG-Maya [Biopiracy of the resources of the traditional indigenous medicine in the State of Chiapas, Mexico. The ICBG-Maya case]', *Revista Pueblos y fronteras digital*, 6(10): 151–180.

Lee, M. I. G. 2006. '¿Al final, TLC con o sin biopiratería? [Finally, FTA with or without biopiracy?]', *Revista Opera*, 6(6): 189–218.

Loots, L. 2007. 'Women, food and biopolitics: Gender debates for southern Africa', *Agenda* 21(73): 79–91.

Mgbeoji, I. 2006. *Global Biopiracy: Patents, Plants, and Indigenous Knowledge*. Ithaca: Cornell University Press.

Mooney, P. 1993. 'Bio-pirates patent indigenous knowledge … and indigenous people too', *Echoes*, 4: 4–6.

Mooney, P. 2000. 'Why We Call it Biopiracy', in H. Svarstad and S. S. Dhillion (eds.) *Responding to Bioprospecting*, 37–44. Oslo: Spartacus Forlag.

Nash, Robert J. 2001. 'Who benefits from biopiracy?' *Phytochemistry*, 56(5): 403–405.

Oyewunmi, A. 2013. 'Sharpening the Legal Tools to Overcome Biopiracy in Africa through Pro-Development Implementation of Normative International Standards: Lessons from Brazil, South Africa and India', *African Journal of International and Comparative Law*, 21(3): 447–466.

Pavarini, M. 192008. *Control y dominación, teorías criminológicas burguesas y proyecto hegemónico [Control and Domination, Bourgeois Criminological Theories and Hegemonic Project]*. Translated by Ignacio Muñagorri. 9 edition, *Nueva criminología y derecho*. México D.F.: Siglo Veintiuno editores. Original edition, 1980.

Pierce, F. 2008. 'The great seed blitzkrieg', *Mew Scientist*, 197(2638): 38–41.

Ptqk, M. 2013. 'Biopatentes. El cercamiento de lo vivo', *Revista Teknokultura*, 10(1): 177–193.

Rabitz, F. 2015. 'Biopiracy after the Nagoya Protocol: Problem Structure, Regime Design and Implementation Challenges', *Brazilian Political Science Review*, 9(2): 30–53.

Robinson, D. F. 2010. *Confronting Biopiracy. Challenges, Cases and International Debates*. New York: Eathscan.

Sarma, L. 1999. 'Biopiracy: Twenieth Century Imperialism in the Form of International Agreements', *Temple International and Comparative Law Journal*, 13(1): 107–136.

Sharma, D. 2002. 'Digital Library on Indian Medicine Systems: Another Tool for Biopiracy', *Economic and Political Weekly*, 37(25): 2016–2017.

Shiva, V. 1997. *Biopiracy, the Plunder of Nature and Knowledge*. Boston: South End Press.

Soria-López, M., and Fuentes-Páramo, I. 2016. 'The identification of biopiracy in patents', *World Patent Information*, 47(C): 67–74.

South, N. 2007. 'The 'Corporate Colonisation of Nature': Bio-Prospecting, Bio-Piracy and the Development of Green Criminology', in P. Beirne and N. South (eds.) *Issues in Green Criminology: Confronting Harms against Environments, Humanity and other Animals*, pp. 230–247. Cullompton, Devon: UK: Willian.

Sundaram, S. 2005. 'Battling Bills, Beans & (and) Biopiracy', *Albany Law Journal of Science and Technology*, 15(2): 545–578.

Svarstad, H. 2000. 'Reciprocity, Biopiracy, Heroes, Villains and Victims', in H. Svarstad and S. S. Dhillion (eds.) *Responding to bioprospecting. From Biodiversity in the South to Medicines in the North*, pp. 19–35. Oslo: Spartacus Forlag.

Svarstad, H. 2002. 'Analysing Conservation-Development Discourses: The Story of a Biopiracy Narrative', *Forum for Development Studies*, 29(1): 63–92.

Svarstad, H., and S. S. Dhillion. 2000. 'Responding to Bioprospecting: Rejection or Regulation?' in H. Svarstad and S. S. Dhillion (eds.) *Responding to Bioprospecting. From Biodiversity in the South to Medicines in the North*, pp. 9–15. Oslo: Spartacus Forlag.

Takeshita, C. 2001. 'Bioprospecting and Its Discontents: Indigenous Resistances as Legitimate Politics', *Alternatives*, 26(3): 259–282.

Taylor, I., Walton, P., and Young, J. 2007. *La nueva criminología, Contribución a una teoría social de la conducta desviada [The neW Criminology: For a Social Theory of Deviance]*. Buenos Aires: Amorrotu editores.

Tobin, B. 2014. 'Biopiracy by law: European Union Draft Law Threatens Indigenous Peoples' Rights over their Traditional Knowledge and Genetic Resources', *European Intellectual Property Review*, 36(2): 124–136.

Verma, I. M. 2002. 'Biopiracy: Distrust Widens the Rich-Poor Divide', *Molecular Therapy*, 5(2): 95.

Woods, M. 2002. 'Food for Thought: The Biopiracy of Jasmine and Basmati Rice', *Albany Law Journal of Science and Technology*, 13(1): 123–144.

Wyatt, T. 2015. 'Invisible Pillaging: The Hidden Harm of Corporate Biopiracy', in P. Davies, P. Francis and T. Wyatt (eds.) *Invisible Crimes and Social Harms*, pp. 161–177. London: Palgrave.

Wyatt, T., and Brisman, A. 2017. 'The Role of Denial in the 'Theft of Nature': A Comparison of Biopiracy and Climate Change', *Critical Criminology: An International Journal* 25(3): 325–341. DOI: 10.1007/s10612-016-9344-5. FirstOnline: September 14 2016. Available at: http://link.springer.com/article/10.1007/s10612-016-9344-5.

Wynberg, R. 2017. 'Making sense of access and benefit sharing in the rooibos industry: Towards a holistic, just and sustainable framing', *South African Journal of Botany*, 110: 39–51. DOI: 10.1016/j.sajb.2016.09.015.

Young, J. 2012. *The Vertigo of Late Modernity*. London: Sage.

Zedan, H. 2005. 'Patents and Biopiracy: The Search for Appropriate Policy and Legal Responses', *The Brown Journal of World Affairs*, 12(1): 189–205.

Zelder, O. 2005. 'White biotechnology: Science, fiction and reality', *Journal of Biotechnology*, 118(1): 1.

13

The War on Drugs and its invisible collateral damage

Environmental harm and climate change

Tammy Ayres

Introduction

The harms arising from the War on Drugs are well documented, particularly in relation to violence and the emergence of organised crime (see Rolles et al., 2016). A largely overlooked area, however, is the environmental impact of drug prohibition generally, and the War on Drugs more specifically, which is causing ecological degradation and accelerating climate change (McSweeney, 2015a; TDP, 2015). Although the extent and nature of environmental damage arising from proscribing the manufacture and sale of illicit drugs is unknown and speculative, there is no denying that the illicit production and distribution of drugs[1] has a negative impact on the environment, which is exacerbated by global drug prohibitions and the failing War on Drugs —a war waged by developed Western countries against impoverished ethnic minorities and poor producer and transit countries. As an integral component of Western supply reduction initiatives—aimed at stopping drugs at the source, leading to a decrease in production, an increase in price and, eventually, reduced availability and use—developed nations have spent trillions of dollars[2] imposing their problems (and policies) on developing countries in Latin America and the Andean region, the Golden Triangle (Asia) and the Golden Crescent (Middle East), not always with the countries' consent, and sometimes in breach of international agreements and treaties (Del Olmo, 1998; McSweeney, 2015a). As McSweeney (2015b: 1) explains,

> Countries in the global South have been paying a huge ecological and human price for drug policies driven primarily by affluent nations of the global North. This disproportionate burden carried by poorer countries includes lost economic opportunities, pollution and health problems caused by defoliants, the enriching of militaries and elites, cities ravaged by violence—not to mention the steep environmental costs.

Drawing on green criminology, which encompasses 'those dimensions of damage, injustice and social harm often neglected by criminal law and by the criminal justice system' (Natali, 2010: 195, quoted in Brisman and South, 2013: 3), this chapter examines the 'ecological collateral damage' arising from the War on Drugs (Dávalos, Bejarano and Correa, 2009: 381). Although obtaining reliable data on the environmental impact of illicit drug production and its prevention across the globe is problematic, due to its clandestine nature and the fact that many of these harms are not systematically monitored (Buxton, 2006; Del Olmo, 1998), this chapter investigates the link between prohibition, forced eradication, deforestation and pollution on the environment and public health of Indigenous populations, which has largely been disavowed by national and international governments, despite causing untold harm and irreversible damage.

Global prohibition and the War on Drugs

It is acknowledged by many that global drug prohibition is more harmful than the drugs it purports to prohibit (e.g., MacCoun and Reuter, 2001; Rolles et al., 2016). The War on Drugs and its twin-track approach of attempting to reduce demand and cut off supply has accomplished neither over the last 50 years; its only noticeable effect is to cause harm on a global scale (e.g., corruption, environmental degradation, ill-health, political instability, violence) (see Rolles et al., 2016). While most of this harm has been attributed to organised crime, terrorists and guerrilla (rebel) insurgent groups (see generally Goyes, this volume, Chapter 12), nation-states and transnational corporations—operating under the imperative of capitalism—have largely been ignored, despite evidence suggesting that anti-drug policies sustain and prioritise the expansion of capitalism (Courtwright, 2001; Del Olmo, 1993; Meehan, 2011, 2015; Paley, 2014; Schneck, 2012).

Traditionally, in official (state) discourse, drugs have been associated with subverting and undermining the state and its dominant socio-political system, posing a threat that needs to be eradicated, despite evidence to the contrary; drug prohibition has always prioritised, or at least been tied to, the exigencies of capitalism and the interests of the state (Courtwright, 2001; Del Olmo, 1993; Paley, 2014; Schneck, 2012). Drugs (their use, prohibition and, increasingly, calls for decriminalisation and legalisation) are inextricably connected to the expansion of neoliberal capitalism and its ideology of deregulation, financialisation, economic instability, export-orientated industrialisation, free international trade agreements and the opening up of markets (see Del Olmo, 1993; Hall and Antonopoulos, 2016; Meehan, 2015; Paley, 2014). In fact, Paley (2014) argues that the War on Drugs offers a distraction from other more pressing issues, acting as 'a permanent shock' (see Klein, 2007), allowing controversial, often draconian and exploitative policies to be implemented (see also Chomsky, 1992)—a phenomenon she refers to as 'drug war capitalism'. These drug policies have transformed the political economy of countries, such as Colombia and Mexico, as well as those in the Caribbean and Africa. Indeed, Western countries implement coercive, self-interested strategies in the name of thwarting the drug trade and in the guise of foreign aid and investment—measures that are often accompanied by militarisation, which operates as a form of social control, and that are beneficial to the expansion of capitalism (see Paley, 2014). Thus, the carefully planned Western-backed initiatives are, in Paley's (2014: 16) words:

> a long-term fix to capitalism's woes, combining terror with policymaking in a seasoned neoliberal mix, cracking open social worlds and territories once unavailable to globalized capitalism … in this war, terror is used against the populations in cities and rural areas, and … parallel to this terror and resulting panic, policies that facilitate foreign direct investment and economic growth are implemented. This is drug war capitalism. Pillage, profit, and plunder have been mainstays of war since pre-colonial times, but there is little focus on the role of finance and economics in war.

Historically, capitalism and its exigencies underpinned the initial control and regulation of substances, some of which were lucrative global commodities (e.g., opium), with many corporations (e.g., the East India Trading Company) and states using the drug trade to create new markets and trade routes intended to generate revenue;[3] in contemporary society, nothing has really changed (see Meehan, 2011; Paley, 2014; Schneck, 2012). The complex processes surrounding the connection between corporations, insurgents, the legitimate and illegitimate economy, organised crime and the state have been and continue to be ignored by mainstream policy responses, alongside the systemic violence attributable to the political economy of neoliberal consumer capitalism and its state-backed anti-drug policies (Meehan, 2011; Žižek, 2008).

To illustrate, international drug control efforts implemented in the early 1900s were aimed at creating a global control system prioritising supply reduction via law enforcement and military intervention, which tended to serve the interests of those in power (Courtwright, 2001; Del Olmo, 1993; Paley, 2014). Widely used substances (such as cannabis, coca and opium) were deemed dangerous, their cultural and medicinal values dismissed, their cultivation and use became prohibited, and they were excluded from legal agriculture in a system that prioritised privileged substances (alcohol, sugar, tobacco) integral to the development of Western capitalism (Chomsky, 1992; Courtwright, 2001; Paley, 2014). Thus, prohibition, while premised officially on the harmfulness of the substances in question, was actually motivated by the desire for capital and power.[4]

Despite being predicated on protecting people from harm, the demarcation of legal and illegal substances and the prohibition of the latter is unscientific, creating what Julian Buchanan (2015: 63) has termed a 'global drug apartheid', which Taylor and colleagues (2016: 463) describe as 'a brutal system of inclusion and exclusion, rooted in the politics and culture of maintaining power and privilege'. Indeed, the global system of prohibition lacks an adequate evidence base and yet costs USD$100 billion a year to enforce (Rolles et al., 2016). Its ineffectiveness is well documented, however, while the evidence pertaining to its harmfulness is disavowed. The overall costs—or 'collateral damage', as it is referred to in the literature—have never been evaluated systematically, despite consistent contentions that drug prohibition causes more harm than the drugs[5] it purports to protect us from (Dávalos, Bejarano and Correa, 2009; Rolles et al., 2016). The United States (U.S.) and United Kingdom (U.K.) have poured trillions of dollars and pounds into tackling supply and funding eradication programmes aimed at stopping drugs at their source, yet little has changed (Buxton, 2006); in fact, the global drugs market is estimated to be worth between USD$426 and USD$652 billion a year (May, 2017)—and it continues to grow. According to the Global Commission on Drug Policy (GCDP 2012: 13),

> Overall drug supply (as evidenced by various indicators of increasing production, declining prices and increasing potency) has been largely unimpeded by the multibillion-dollar investments that have gone into trying to disrupt supply through costly policing, arrests and interdiction efforts.

In sum, the drug market is thriving and the production of drugs like cannabis, coca and opium have increased (UNODC, 2017a, 2017b, 2018a), despite the fact that international drug prohibition policies tend to be widely supported (both financially and politically). Thus, it is not just the drug *trade* that is profitable, but also the War on Drugs, which has been a source of profit for corporations, governments and states for many years (Meehan, 2011; Paley, 2014; Schneck, 2012). In other words, while the War on Drugs has done little, if anything, to curb the illegal drug trade, it has been a tremendous source of profit for state-corporate entities.

Global production of drugs: big business

Despite interdiction and eradication efforts, global evidence suggests drug markets are thriving and diversifying, with the illicit drug market estimated to be worth 1 per cent of the global GDP (May, 2017). In fact, despite the War on Drugs, drug trafficking and production have increased, with some drug markets expanding in recent years (UNODC, 2018a). Global opium production in 2017 increased by 37 per cent with most plant-based opium being produced in Afghanistan,[6] Burma (Myanmar) and Mexico, resulting in 10,500 tonnes—'the highest level since the United Nations Office on Drugs and Crime (UNODC) started estimating global opium production on an annual basis' (UNODC, 2018a: 12). This was attributed to a growth in the area under cultivation and an increase in opium yield per hectare (UNODC, 2016b, 2017d, 2018a, 2018b). This growth in global opium production was accompanied by a 30 per cent increase in cocaine production between 2013 and 2015—with production reaching its highest ever level in 2016 (UNODC, 2018a).

Cocaine is produced mostly in the three Andean countries of Bolivia, Colombia and Peru—with an estimated 1,410 tonnes produced in 2016 (UNODC, 2016b, 2017b, 2018a). Unlike coca and opium, which grow only in certain habitats, cannabis can be grown practically anywhere, which is reflected in its production diversity: it has been grown/produced in 135 countries—home to 92 per cent of the total global population (Dávalos and Bejarano, 2008; UNODC, 2017c). As such, estimating the global production of cannabis is challenging, with reports suggesting Morocco remains the main source of cannabis resin, followed by Afghanistan, while the cultivation of cannabis herb is more widespread (Afghanistan, Burma (Myanmar), Colombia, Ghana, India, Jamaica, Lebanon, Nepal, Nigeria, Paraguay). Even less is known about the production and supply of synthetic drugs, with data mostly coming from seizure statistics (UNODC, 2017a, 2017b). Although drug production and cultivation statistics are often 'guestimates' based on a range of indicators that are not always corroborative,[7] evidence suggests that the global production of cannabis is increasing. The increase in drug production is often used as justification for more punitive, militarised and draconian law-enforcement initiatives, aimed at prohibiting drug use (more widely) and eliminating their supply (more generally).

The War on Drugs has always prioritised supply reduction over demand reduction,[8] thus serving Western hegemonic interests and their foreign policy objectives. By refusing to acknowledge the logic of the market and the fact that Western demand drives supply, the West's concealed coercion disavows its role in the global drug trade: it fails to acknowledge that until demand is reduced in the West, any supply reduction initiatives implemented elsewhere are doomed to fail. Instead the West shifts the burden and financial cost of drug prohibition onto developing producer and transit nations,[9] which are affected adversely because these initiatives impact negatively on their communities, environment and political economy (Courtwright, 2001; Del Olmo, 1987; Mejía, 2016; Paley, 2014). By focussing on these developing nations, the War on Drugs adopts a 'them, not us' approach (Chomsky, 1992). Prohibition and the short-sighted supply reduction initiatives implemented to control drugs at their source not only exacerbate the harm arising from their production, particularly in relation to the environment, which is the focus of this chapter, but are also ineffective as they continually fail to stem the supply of drugs. Even where eradication efforts have been successful in reducing the cultivation of drugs as seen in Burma (Myanmar) and Colombia,[10] this is often short-lived and does not lead to an overall reduction in global production, as drug markets are merely displaced (McSweeney, 2015a; TDP 2015). For example, successful eradication in Colombia led to an increase in coca cultivation in Peru, while opium eradication in

Burma (Myanmar) led to an increase in the production of methamphetamine and precursor chemicals in the country (UNODC, 2009, 2017e) via a process known as the balloon effect.[11] Essentially, eradication and interdiction are ineffective while demand exists. Instead supply reduction initiatives merely displace production because drugs are lucrative commodities with a high-market value—one that generates huge profits alongside their prohibition.

Drugs and their prohibition are big business and make a lot of money for insurgent groups, private contractors, states and transnational corporations,[12] and disentangling the illicit trade in drugs from the legitimate economy has become increasingly problematic (Del Olmo, 1993; Hall and Antonopoulos, 2016; Meehan, 2015; Paley, 2014; Seelke, Wyler, Beittel and Sullivan, 2011). Opiates constitute 20–32 per cent of Afghanistan's total GDP and they exceed the value of licit exports; indeed, opiates are worth more than many countries' entire agricultural sector, meaning that these countries' legitimate economy relies on the drug trade[13] (Meehan, 2015; UNODC, 2018b). States—their agents and institutions—rely not only on the drug trade to generate revenue, but also use prohibition to advance their own self-interests, capitalising on the 'disaster-induced collective trauma' arising from the War on Drugs; whether that involves appropriating land and exploiting its natural resources or using state-backed interdiction initiatives to support their own legitimate economy,[14] drug prohibition is big business (Del Olmo, 1993; Meehan, 2011, 2015; Paley, 2014; Schneck, 2012). The cultivation of illicit drugs also provides an income for some of the poorest and most remote populations on the planet, who depend on the coca, poppy and/or cannabis plant for their livelihoods. In remote areas where legitimate economic opportunities are limited, drug crops provide a better standard of living than most other forms of work and offer a genuine economic survival strategy (Del Olmo, 1993; Kramer, Jensema, Jelsma and Blickman, 2014; Mansfield, 2002; Transform Drug Policy (TDP), 2015; UNODC, 2015, 2017d). Drugs, such as coca and opium, maintain a high market price; they have high market security 'with a guaranteed market outlet'; they can be used for credit or as a form of savings; they incur low start-up costs, and are easy to grow, sell and transport; they are a high-value crop that require less land than other crops; they provide a cash income; they are low maintenance; they can be harvested several times a year, making them a source of fast money over a short period of time, meaning that they are more competitive and less risky than other cash crops; and they provide high levels of employment, given that demand is wide and varied (Dávalos, Bejarano and Correa, 2009; Dávalos et al., 2011; Fjeldsa, Alvarez, Lazcano and Leon, 2005; Grisaffi and Ledebur, 2016; Mansfield, 2002). Because many drugs are still grown and used culturally for medical and/or spiritual purposes, drug eradication and interdiction efforts may undermine cultural traditions. Even where spiritual traditions do not involve drugs, drug eradication and interdiction efforts may destroy the livelihoods of some of the poorest and most marginalised people on the planet—people who are merely responding to their local economic and social forces, but who find themselves criminalised for growing traditional cultural plants, which is often their only source of income (Del Olmo, 1993; Kramer, Jensema, Jelsma and Blickman, 2014; UNODC, 2015, 2017d). As a result, the War on Drugs has become a 'War against certain People' or, as Paley (2014: 4) puts it, '*Guerra contra los pueblos*' (see also Buchanan and Young, 2000)—one which disproportionately affects poor ethnic minority migrant groups, developing countries and Indigenous populations, as people's livelihoods and habitats are destroyed systematically via Western-backed eradication and interdiction efforts.

Crop eradication: biological and chemical warfare against drugs

As mentioned above, crop eradication is an integral component of global drug prohibition and a key supply reduction initiative often backed by foreign aid. From the 'Helmand Food Zone Program' in Afghanistan[15] to 'Plan Colombia' in South America,[16] roughly 24 per cent of the U.S. State Department and U.S. Agency for International Development (USAID) counter-narcotics budget is spent on eradication (Beittel and Rosen, 2017). Eradication eliminates illicit drugs at their source, which is believed to be the most vulnerable point in the chain from grower to user. While there is some evidence to show that crop eradication reduces cultivation and the illicit drug trade,[17] eradication efforts (without addressing demand) can, as noted above, have the opposite effect, increasing production[18] and supply, while exacerbating levels of environmental harm and degradation.

Although crop eradication efforts have been undertaken in many producer countries (e.g., Afghanistan, Burma (Myanmar), Mexico), the most intensive eradication programmes have occurred in Colombia (via 'Plan Colombia'), where the total area sprayed increased from 870 hectares in 1986 to more than 130,000 hectares in 2005. When 'Plan Colombia' officially ended in 2015, giving way to 'Peace Columbia' (see note 16), it had succeeded in reducing coca cultivation by 18 per cent—from 110,000 hectares to 48,000 hectares—between 2000 and 2013 (Dávalos and Bejarano 2008; Mejía, 2016). This was not a sustained reduction, however (UNODC, 2018b). Despite mixed evidence pertaining to the efficacy of this approach, crops are destroyed either by the slash and burn technique or by biological or chemical spraying—all of which cause ecological harm.

Chemical spraying using a range of herbicides has been integral to many drug interdiction programmes (e.g., 'Plan Colombia', 'Helmand Food Zone Program', the 'Mérida Initiative', 'Operation Intercept'), where resources are often skewed in favour of law enforcement and prevention[19] despite their ineffectiveness (Buxton, 2006). A range of herbicides is used routinely to destroy cannabis, opium and coca plants, including *Paraquat* in Mexico and Colombia, *2,4-Dichlorophenoxyacetate* in Bolivia and Burma (Myanmar), *Tebuthiuron* (Spike) in Peru, and *Glyphosate* (Roundup) in Colombia, which was originally promoted as a safer alternative to many of the other herbicides (Buxton, 2006; Del Olmo, 1998; HRW 2010; Transform Drug Policy (TDP), 2015). All herbicides are harmful, however, having a detrimental impact on the environment as well as on human health, which is exacerbated by the process of delivery—aerial spraying.

Typically, herbicides are sprayed from low-flying aircraft so that larger areas of illicit cultivation can be destroyed, but also because illicit crops are grown in hard-to-reach, remote and often hidden locations, accessible only by air. Aerial spraying is supposed to occur at a height of ten metres in order to reduce the environmental impact. The planes, however, are often forced to fly higher than the recommended ten metres so as to avoid attacks from the ground by those wishing to protect the crops. Indeed, with bounties exceeding $200,000 to shoot spray planes and helicopters out of the sky, such aircraft must fly higher, resulting in inaccurate dispersal, which kills food crops, forests, rare plants and fauna (Jelsma, 2001; Seelke, Wyler, Beittel and Sullivan, 2011). The environmental impact of herbicides is also exacerbated by the use of concentrations that exceed the manufacturers' guidelines. For example, instead of the recommended 2.5 litres per hectare, dosages as high as 23.7 litres per hectare are sometimes used, while toxicity is enhanced by the inclusion of a surfactant, which enables the herbicide to penetrate further, making it more lethal to *all* plants, not just the targeted illicit crops (Buxton, 2006; Jelsma, 2001; Transform Drug Policy (TDP), 2015). Subsequently, chemical eradication has a detrimental impact on Indigenous populations, their health, and their food crops and livestock, as well as local ecologies and biodiversity (Buxton, 2006; Jelsma, 2001; Mejía, 2016; Sunshine Project, 2001).

Despite the issues associated with crop eradication via chemical spraying, there have also been efforts to use mycoherbicides, such as *Fusarium Oxysporum*, *Pleospora Papaveraceae/Crivellia Papaveracea* and *Dendryphion Penicillatum/Brachycladium Papaveris*, to control illicit opium crops. Supposedly, these mycoherbicides are environmentally safer than the human-made herbicide solutions because they occur naturally. They also proffer long-term solutions to eradication because mycoherbicides remain in the soil for many years, preventing the growth of any and all flora (Buxton, 2011; Jelsma, 2001). Their use is controversial, however, and has been criticised heavily (on both political and scientific grounds), inciting global objections for violating international laws and human rights, and for having an irreversible impact on the environment (e.g., soil sterility) (Buxton, 2006; Jelsma, 2001; Mansfield, 2011). Indeed, some mycoherbicides are toxic enough to be listed as biological weapons under the UN Convention on Biological and Toxic Weapons (Sunshine Project, 2001)—with some having been used in biological and chemical warfare (Spiers, 1989). Consequently, forced eradication has been described as a form of biological warfare, particularly because most of the producer regions where spraying takes place are also combat zones (Jelsma, 2001; Mansfield, 2011; Sunshine Project, 2001).

Because many countries, such as Colombia, have banned aerial spraying, manual eradication (and mechanical uprooting) is often utilised. This involves pulling the plant up by its roots and/or chopping the stalks of the plant before ploughing the field or setting it on fire (Gruenwald, 2015; Human Rights Watch (HRW), 2010). Manual eradication is also used to destroy crops grown in national parks, where other forms of eradication are prohibited (Seelke, Wyler, Beittel and Sullivan, 2011). Manual eradication is labour intensive, however, requiring between 3 and 20 workers per day per hectare, depending on the crop. In addition, it can be implemented only if it is possible to reach the cultivation site on foot. Manual extraction has also been associated with human rights abuses by the eradication teams (e.g., destruction of homes, plundering, sexual violence, torture), which is compounded by the impunity many of these government-backed teams enjoy (Human Rights Watch (HRW), 2010; Mansfield, 2011). Due to the potential revenue from drug sales, illicit drug crops are heavily protected (e.g., booby traps, landmines, tripwires), particularly in certain countries where paramilitary groups control their production. This has led to the deaths of numerous law enforcement officers and military personnel[20] (Eth, 2008; Mansfield, 2011; UNODC, 2018b). Differentiating paramilitary groups from the state and its actors, however, has become increasingly problematic, particularly because these groups are often paid by the state or offered 'impunity if their acts benefit the state, foreign policy and transnational capitalism' (Paley, 2014: 16).[21] Forced manual eradication also has harmful economic and social effects for the region and for local communities, where people are pushed into poverty and starvation; this, in turn, necessitates emergency aid or displaces Indigenous populations to areas where they can access emergency food aid (Gruenwald, 2015; Mansfield, 2011). Often the aid provided does not address the needs of the farmers or offer a suitable long-term alternative to growing illicit crops (Kramer, Jensema, Jelsma and Blickman, 2014).

In fact, many forms of crop eradication are counterproductive, ineffective and harmful. Aerial fumigation with herbicides or mycoherbicides has negative impacts on Indigenous communities and their health (mental, physical), their livestock (e.g., cattle lose their hair, chickens die), water supplies, the soil (e.g., long-term sterility) and legitimate crops;[22] indeed, aerial fumigation with herbicides or mycoherbicides has resulted in the destruction of food crops (e.g., banana, cocoa, papaya, yucca), which has led to food shortages (Buxton, 2006; Jelsma, 2001; Mejía, 2016; Sunshine Project, 2001; Transform Drug Policy (TDP), 2015). Although the exact impact on human health and risk to humans is contested and has been denied by those in power (see Human Rights Watch (HRW), 2010; Seelke, Wyler, Beittel and Sullivan, 2011), herbicides (and pesticides, discussed later) have been linked to birth defects, cancers, chromosomal aberrations, coughing, delayed development in children, diarrhoea, foetal death, eye infections, fertility issues, headaches, long-term illnesses, miscarriages and spontaneous abortions, respiratory issues, skin problems and vomiting (Buxton, 2006; Jelsma, 2001; Mejía, 2016; Sanborn et al., 2004).

Research has shown that *Nivalenol* causes leukaemia and vomiting, that *Fumonisin* B_1 is carcinogenic, and that *Deoxynivalenol* causes fever, diarrhoea, leukaemia and vomiting, while *Fusariotoxin* leads to toxicity and even death (human fusarium infection is emerging as a life-threatening illness with a high mortality rate ranging from 50–76 per cent), particularly among certain groups with low immunity and malnutrition, which is high among producer-country populations, particularly children (Buxton, 2006; Sunshine Project, 2001; Zain, 2015). Eradication with mycoherbicides also harms the environment and denigrates the entire ecosystem—its vegetation and fauna—leading to the extinction of rare and endangered species (Burns-Edel and Davis, 2016; Transform Drug Policy (TDP), 2015). With mycoherbicides, there are also issues relating to mutagenicity and propagation, which are impossible to predict or prevent. This means once mycoherbicides are introduced, they can move to other sites by human or other vectors, triggering negative and irreversible ecological impacts, destroying rare plants and Indigenous species, some of which might be related to the target plants and thus affecting the wildlife that relies on them (e.g., butterflies). Mycoherbicides also impact soil micro-organisms and non-human animals, producing dangerous toxins that might contaminate or kill food crops, thus presenting a risk to humans (Buxton, 2011; Jelsma, 2001; Sunshine Project, 2001; Transform Drug Policy (TDP), 2015). Effectively—and as noted elsewhere in this chapter—research has shown that eradication exacerbates poverty and negatively impacts education and health, contributing to higher infant mortality rates; it fuels corruption, violence and insecurity, increases support and recruitment for insurgent groups, and destroys the livelihoods of Indigenous communities, pushing them deeper into the rainforest and onto new land created by deforestation, while also intensifying their reliance on illicit crops, which is all some farmers can grow to make back the money lost via eradication (Jelsma, 2001; Mansfield, 2011; Rozo, 2014; UNODC, 2016b).[23]

Consequently, eradication is, by and large, costly, harmful and ineffective. Drug crops are replaced at much the same rate they are destroyed, while production is increased to compensate for the previous losses, suggesting that eradication may actually lead to an *increase* in cultivation (Higginson, Mazerolle and Thompson, 2013; Jelsma, 2001; Mansfield, 2011; Transform Drug Policy (TDP), 2015). Despite the harm caused by aerial fumigation, it is one of the most expensive but one of the least effective drug eradication strategies, having only a marginal impact that is unsustainable over time (Mejía, 2016).[24] The efficacy of aerial spraying is reduced further by the methods implemented by farmers to protect their crops—from spraying the leaves of plants (e.g., with molasses) to prevent herbicide from penetrating them—to manual defoliation and cutting the stem of a sprayed bush before the herbicide takes effect—to planting higher yielding varieties and using mixed planting (agroforestry) on smaller plots that are more likely to go unnoticed (Dávalos, Bejarano and Correa, 2009; Grisaffi and Ledebur, 2016; Mejía, 2016; Seelke, Wyler, Beittel and Sullivan, 2011). Even if spraying effectively destroys the coca harvest, the coca bush itself often survives and recovers in a few months, meaning farmers can produce a new harvest within 3–6 months (Diaz and Sanchez, 2004). Those processing the cocaine—the cocaine paste manufacturers (which consists of families, farmers, entire villages, civil society groups, traffickers and insurgents)—have also invented new ways of extracting more alkaloid from lower volumes of leaf to get round any shortages created by eradication (Dávalos, Bejarano and Correa, 2009; Grisaffi and Ledebur, 2016). Therefore, despite illegal experiments and secret trials with stronger, more harmful (banned) herbicides and controversial mycoherbicides (Buxton, 2006; Jelsma, 2001; Mansfield, 2011)—and despite increasing the intensity of spraying—eradication programmes have not proved more effective and have had a negative effect on the alternative crop substitution programmes implemented to help farmers to stop growing illicit drugs (Jelsma, 2001; McSweeney, 2015a).[25]

Crop substitution programmes are also problematic, ineffective and have undesirable effects (e.g., food shortages, humanitarian crises, internal displacement, land grabbing and land loss,[26] a reliance on food aid) (Kramer, Jensema, Jelsma and Blickman, 2014; UNODC, 2016a) that have increased, rather than reduced, the production of drugs. Most crop substitution programmes take place in remote villages, making access to markets difficult. The timing of such programmes may also be problematic because the eradication programmes sometimes occur before viable alternative livelihoods have been put in place. Crop substitution is also inadequate with some of the alternative cash crops, such as pineapple or rubber, not producing for the first few years. If these cash crops are also being grown elsewhere, then the emergence of new farmers/growers producing more of these crops will drive the market price down; this means that farmers, who lack the money and start-up capital, will have to wait for the harvest of a crop that is hard to sell and only produces one crop a year (as with pineapples)—unlike coca, which produces three crops a year (Bradley and Millington, 2008; Gautreau, 2012; Jelsma and Kramer, 2008). Unfortunately, legal crops do not pay as much as illicit drug crops, making the latter more financially rewarding and profitable than engaging in the formal economy—a fact compounded by the reality that the majority of illicit drug cultivation occurs in places where other forms of agriculture are economically or ecologically unviable (Alvarez 2001; Bradley and Millington, 2008; Buxton, 2006; Dávalos, Bejarano and Correa, 2009; Del Olmo, 1993; UNODC, 2015). One of the only viable alternatives to drug crops is cattle rearing, but this raises its own set of environmental issues, specifically deforestation and climate change due to methane production (Bradley and Millington, 2008; Dávalos, Bejarano and Correa, 2009; McSweeney, 2015a; Sesnie et al., 2017).

In sum, eradication as a supply reduction initiative is costly and ineffective. It does not reduce demand and it has little effect on reducing drug supply and availability in Western consumer markets (Mansfield, 2011; Seelke, Wyler, Beittel and Sullivan, 2011). Eradication also does not address the motivations underpinning the cultivation of illicit crops, which is largely due to necessity, poverty and a lack of legitimate viable alternatives (Buxton, 2006; Kramer, Jensema, Jelsma and Blickman, 2014). Instead, eradication targets the poorest farmers who cannot afford the bribes and protection, lack political support and are unable to provide for their families in any other way (UNODC, 2017f). Foreign debt incurred by developing countries has also been used to coerce them into implementing drug eradication initiatives supported by foreign aid that are not only harmful to the environment and Indigenous populations, but also counterproductive insofar as they lead to increased cultivation of illicit drug crops, often in the more remote and biologically diverse regions such as national parks and rainforests, as cultivation is displaced rather than eliminated (Blackwell, 2014; McSweeney, 2015a; Paley, 2014; Transform Drug Policy (TDP), 2015; UNODC, 2015). Often, illicit crop eradication pushes farmers deeper into the forest to avoid the eradication teams causing higher rates of deforestation and fragmentation (Alvarez 2001; Armenteras, Rodriguez and Retana, 2013; Bradley and Millington, 2008). Despite crop eradication impacting the environment and adjacent ecosystems, the effect pales in comparison with the removal of large areas of forest for cultivation.

Deforestation: a growers' paradise

Millions of hectares of forest, including some of the world's most precious and biologically diverse tropical rainforests, are destroyed to grow illicit crops (Armstead, 1992).[27] Deforestation can be a direct or indirect result of illicit drug cultivation. Cultivation has a *direct effect* when the forest is cleared to grow illicit crops (e.g., it is estimated that at least 60 per cent of illicit crops are grown on newly deforested land) or when tree and plant extracts, such as *sassafras* oil, are harvested and used directly to make drugs like ecstasy (Alvarez 2001; Kegö and Maïga, 2014; Kramer, Jensema, Jelsma and Blickman, 2014; Transform Drug Policy (TDP), 2015). Deforestation can also be *indirect* as a result of clearing for cattle pastures and housing, farm expansion, and other forms of development, such as access roads and landing strips for drug transportation (Dávalos et al., 2011; UNODC, 2006). Research has shown that deforestation rates 'increased as coca substitutes became dominant', demonstrating that crop substitution programmes result in larger areas of the forest being cleared compared with drug plantations (Bradley and Millington, 2008). Although illicit drug cultivation is not a significant determinant of deforestation rates, which is often attributable to other factors (e.g., legitimate agriculture, logging and timber extraction, mining (see Boekhout van Solinge, this volume, Chapter 15)), there is a definite link, with research showing that new coca cultivation is an indicator of new conurbations, where increasing populations have led to higher deforestation rates (Dávalos et al., 2011; Sesnie et al., 2017).

Although estimates of deforestation should be treated with caution, according to Alvarez (2001: 1087), 'abandoned fields, forest cleared for future illicit crops and/or subsistence crops, and airstrips amplify deforestation by a factor estimated at 2.5–3 times the area of the illicit crop alone'. Approximately 262,000 hectares are deforested in Colombia annually; illicit crops account for at least 50 per cent of all deforestation and 69–76 per cent of sub-Andean and Andean forests have lost their original cover, leading some to lament that the Andean region bears 'the brunt of drug war deforestation' (Alvarez, 2001; Transform Drug Policy (TDP), 2015; UNODC, 2006). Coca plantations have also accounted for 7 million hectares of deforestation in the Peruvian Amazon in the twentieth century, and between 2001 and 2013, over 290,000 hectares of forest were lost to cocaine production, while the expansion of coca in the Huallaga region of Peru has been responsible for nearly 1 million hectares of tropical forest being destroyed (Armstead, 1992; Burns-Edel and Davis, 2016). Although less is known about the Golden Triangle[28] or Golden Crescent[29] region—Asia's two principal areas of illicit opium production—the annual rate of deforestation along the Thai-Burma (Myanmar) border is approximately 130,000 hectares per year and deforestation rates in Thailand are estimated to be between 280,000 and 300,000 hectares per year (Buxton, 2006). In fact, Burma (Myanmar) has the third fastest deforestation rate in the world after Indonesia and Brazil (UNODC, 2017d).

It is not just the cultivation of illicit crops that leads to deforestation, however. Many illicit drug plots are abandoned every year due to eradication efforts because farmers are reluctant to implement land management techniques. Instead, they adopt more harmful farming practices (e.g., intensive farming, monocropping, pesticides, rodenticides, use of fertilisers alongside harmful weeding and harvesting practices) in order to maximise profit and thus the harvest, which threatens the long-term productivity of the soil (Armstead, 1992; Buxton, 2006; Dávalos et al. 2011; Mansfield, 2002; UNODC, 2006, 2017f).

Illicit drug crops can be a driver of forest fragmentation (small transient crop areas of 0.6 hectares)[30]—a phenomenon related to deforestation—which increases the number of forest edges, thus altering the sub-canopy humidity conditions, thereby threatening biodiversity and forest-dependent avian fauna (Alvarez 2001; Armenteras, Rodriguez and Retana, 2013). Although research shows deforestation and fragmentation results from cultivating illicit drug crops, crop eradication programmes and crop substitution programmes increase rates of deforestation and fragmentation exponentially because more land is required,[31] while also displacing farmers and pushing them into more remote areas, such as biosphere reserves, national parks, or deeper into the tropical rainforests (Armstead, 1992; Bradley and Millington, 2008; Dávalos et al., 2011; McSweeney, 2015a; Song, Huang, Saatchi, Hansen and Townshend, 2015; UNODC, 2016b).

The slash-and-burn method (clear-cutting) used to clear new plots of forest exacerbate the environmental harms further by increasing erosion and by releasing carbon dioxide into the atmosphere, which, globally, is one of the most significant sources of carbon emissions (Armenteras, Rodriguez and Retana, 2013; Burns-Edel and Davis, 2016; UNODC, 2015). In Jamaica, cannabis cultivation has permanently damaged some forest regions, exposing bare rock incapable of sustaining growth after the thin limestone soil has been washed away (Armstead, 1992). Clearing land this way leaves no vegetative material behind to enrich the soil, meaning that these areas are utilised only for a few years before the soil nutrient sources are depleted or intensive amounts of fertiliser are needed to sustain the crop—both of which are environmentally damaging (Armstead, 1992). In fact, deforestation is occurring on a global level at a rate of 0.6 per cent per year and is the second largest anthropogenic source of carbon dioxide in the atmosphere, with 13 million hectares of forest lost each year contributing to '20% of the annual greenhouse gas emissions' (Armenteras, Rodriguez and Retana, 2013; McSweeney, 2015a; Song, Huang, Saatchi, Hansen and Townshend, 2015). Not only does deforestation release large amounts of carbon as CO_2 directly into the atmosphere, but it also alters the terrestrial carbon cycle[32] because removing trees and vegetation decreases the amount of carbon uptake in the terrestrial biosphere and modifies the local ecosystem, causing ecological imbalances that have a negative impact on the environment. Thus, deforestation has environmental implications that include atmospheric issues (CO_2 emissions, drought, flooding and global warming); ecological imbalance; the extinction of plants and wildlife, particularly because much of the forest destroyed for illicit drugs is in biodiversity hotspots; hydrological concerns (loss of watershed, sedimentation and siltation of waterways and rivers leading to flooding and destruction of marine life); landslides; and soil erosion and leaching (Armstead, 1992; Burns-Edel and Davis, 2016; Buxton, 2006; Transform Drug Policy (TDP), 2015). Subsequently, deforestation has an effect 'beyond the ecosystem level', removing important carbon sinks and accelerating global climate change (Burns-Edel and Davis, 2016). The forests affected do not always recover and some plants and wildlife never return, meaning that some of the most important ecosystems and species-rich regions on Earth have already been destroyed[33] (Alvarez, 2001; Armstead, 1992; Burns-Edel and Davis, 2016; Buxton, 2006; Eth, 2008; Sesnie et al. 2017; UNODC, 2015).

Due to a dearth of data, judging the effects of drug prohibition on biodiversity is challenging (Fjeldsa, Alvarez, Lazcano and Leon, 2005). It is estimated, however, that 3,375 plant species are at risk due to deforestation, with 135 species of plants and animals lost daily (50,000 species a year); deforestation has also increased current extinction rates from 100 to 1,000 times that of natural rates (Ridgewell, 2017). In fact, 75 per cent of plant and animal species in Colombia are considered endangered and 15,000 medical plants are threatened, while water appropriation for drug crops and their subsequent pollution also impacts the animals and local ecosystem more generally (Ridgewell, 2017). Drug crops require lots of water, but because of their remote location water must be diverted from the rivers and waterways; this has led to reduced water flow and scarcity of water downstream, that has, in turn, had a detrimental impact on the environment and Indigenous people, and that continues to pose one of the greatest threats to aquatic biodiversity[34] (Bauer et al., 2015; Burns-Edel and Davis, 2016; Eth, 2008; UNODC, 2016b). Not only are wildlife threatened by the loss of habitat, but the growers and traffickers eat them to supplement their protein-deficient diet or sell them for profit, as many trade in multiple (illicit) commodities (e.g., gold, timber, wildlife) or use other commodities as a front for laundering drug money (Eth, 2008; Felbab-Brown, 2015; Fjeldsa, Alvarez, Lazcano and Leon, 2005; McSweeney, 2015a; Sesnie et al. 2017; South and Wyatt, 2011). In sum, deforestation exacerbates the environmental damage arising from drug production, contributing to pollution and adversely impacting biodiversity.

Drugs, pollution and the destruction of jungle labs

The illicit nature of drug cultivation and production, and the fact that many cultivators have been driven into increasingly remote and ungoverned areas due to eradication and interdiction efforts, means that a lot of the raw plant material is grown and processed in these biologically diverse ecosystems where there is no legal or safe mechanism for disposing of toxic chemical by-products generated during the cultivation and processing of drugs (Burns-Edel and Davis, 2016; Buxton, 2006). These chemicals are also discharged into the local ecosystems by local law enforcement officials, who are sent to dismantle and destroy these 'jungle drug labs' (McSweeney, 2015a). Referred to as 'toxification', which means 'the improper or illegal usage and disposal of fertilisers, pesticides, rodenticides, and chemical compounds employed during the production' of illicit drugs (Burns-Edel and Davis, 2016: 2), these chemicals have a significant impact on the environment and their local ecosystems, which has led to genetic mutation in animals and species decline (Burns-Edel and Davis, 2016; Dávalos and Bejarano, 2008).

As mentioned above, illicit crops are cultivated intensely, meaning that chemical fertiliser use exceeds normal levels so as to increase productivity, leaf size and potency,[35] and that herbicide, pesticide, plaguicide and rodenticide is applied liberally by farmers in order to recover the losses incurred from drug interdiction and eradication efforts (Jelsma, 2001). It is not just the chemicals used to increase crop yield that are leaked into these remote biodiversity hotspots, but also the precursor chemicals[36] used to transform and process the drugs (e.g., coca leaf to cocaine), including solvents (acetone, ethyl, kerosene, sulphuric ether and toluene), acids (hydrochloric, nitric, sulphuric), oxidisers (potassium permanganate) and bases (ammonia, calcium carbonate, sodium and potassium hydroxide and sodium), which also affect humans, resulting in the risk of fire and explosion, as well as numerous health complications, ranging from irritations (eye, nose, skin, throat) to liver and kidney impairments, bleeding and corrosion in the lungs (Buxton, 2006; Transform Drug Policy (TDP), 2015; UNODC, 2015, 2016b). Due to the remote locations of the drug operations, these chemicals, many of which are considered so toxic that they are controlled under federal laws (Eth, 2008), seep into surrounding soils, waterways and water tables, negatively impacting the local ecosystem's plants and wildlife, as well as the farmers and their livestock (Armstead, 1992). In fact, many waterways and tributaries are now devoid of plant and animal life (Armstead, 1992; Del Olmo, 1998; Eth, 2008; Transform Drug Policy (TDP), 2015), while over-fertilised vegetation exposes herbivores and scavengers that eat the infected carcasses to secondary poisoning (Burns-Edel and Davis, 2016; Thompson et al., 2014).

Often banned (harmful) anticoagulant rodenticides, alongside the chemicals used to process drugs, have been found in a number of species (e.g., badgers, bobcats, coyote, earthworms, fishers, mink, mountain lions, owls, raccoons, red-tailed hawks, snails, stoats), causing death to animals who ingest them via internal haemorrhaging and organ failure, as well as indirect mortality due to failure of thermoregulatory control, higher levels of infection, lowered immunological abilities, neurological disorders and mange, while also inhibiting their ability to recover from natural injuries and wounds (Burns-Edel and Davis, 2016; Thompson et al., 2014). The nitrogen and phosphorous residues from these chemicals also exacerbate soil sterility, making it difficult to grow other plants (Armstead, 1992), while their presence in rivers and waterways causes eutrophication.[37] Although more research is needed, the environmental effects of pollution from illicit crops and their economy are profound, and the ecological impact is exacerbated by drug prohibition and international eradication efforts—measures that drive farmers into more remote locations as they endeavour to hide their crops, earn a living and provide for their family (Grisaffi and Ledebur, 2016; Kramer, Jensema, Jelsma and Blickman, 2014; Mansfield, 2002; UNODC, 2015, 2017f).

Conclusion

As outlined in this chapter, drug prohibition causes environmental damage, such as biodiversity loss, climate change and pollution (air, soil, water). Much of this harm is disavowed and official discourse focusses on the harm caused by the drugs themselves and their link to organised crime, insurgency and violence, which is used to justify more draconian and harmful drug interdiction strategies. Thus, it seems that drug prohibition and the War on Drugs reflects not a concern about the human health consequences of illicit substances, but the prioritising of the exigencies of capitalism, including its territorial and social expansion, as well as improving the conditions for direct foreign investment and the free-market economy (Paley, 2014). Consequently, we must ask: is drug prohibition an eco-crime?

The policies implemented to reduce drug supply lack an empirical evidence base, which may explain their ineffectiveness. Instead, they are premised on unfounded assumptions about the behaviour of illicit crop farmers in the context of international markets and global capitalism. They ignore the market forces underpinning the drug trade and represent many of the contradictions inherent in consumer capitalism, as Western interests are prioritised and drug prohibition initiatives are implemented inconsistently. Although drugs are often seen as subverting states and the political economy, as this chapter has attempted to demonstrate, the opposite can occur. Drugs are desirable commodities with high global demand, low economic barriers to entry and a high exchange value, requiring few skills to produce and supply them. This means that their production is a market-driven process that provides huge revenues for both legitimate (corporations, governments, states) and illegitimate (insurgent groups and organised criminals) actors (Meehan, 2011). While there is demand for illicit drugs in consumer countries,[38] there will always be *someone* willing to grow drug crops to meet that demand and generate a profit—which is why drugs have been impossible to eradicate and why prohibition, by itself, does not work.[39]

Instead, we might observe the following:

1 Market forces are a major factor in the global drugs market (and its inherent fluctuations) and the intricacies of supply and demand, but global drug policies have ignored such forces, prioritising supply reduction.
2 The evidence base underpinning drug prohibition is missing.
3 Drug prohibition has always focussed on supply reduction initiatives, ignoring demand in Western countries, shifting the burden (financial and political) onto developing

producer and transit countries, as drugs have been seen historically as originating from a supposed 'external enemy' (Del Olmo, 1993).

4 Stemming supply from other countries has been prioritised, despite it being ineffectual, costly and harmful. Despite costing trillions of dollars, drug interdiction and eradication have had no noticeable impact on the availability of drugs or their price in Western consumer countries (Dávalos, Bejarano and Correa, 2009).

5 Global prohibition and its supply reduction initiatives have exacerbated the exact issues they have sought to address, with many drug prohibition policies contradicting other policies intended to protect the environment, human rights and warfare (McSweeney, 2015a; Transform Drug Policy (TDP), 2015). Drug eradication and interdiction actually increases drug production and exacerbates environmental harm by displacing crops to more remote and often biodiverse locations due to the balloon effect. It also increases the price, which incentivises an increase in production that feeds back into lower prices and an eventual return to market equilibrium similar to that which existed before interdiction, particularly because eradication does not always occur in the high-cultivating provinces (Kramer, Jensema, Jelsma and Blickman, 2014; Transform Drug Policy (TDP), 2015; UNODC, 2016a).

6 Many of the Western-backed initiatives actually exacerbate food insecurity and levels of poverty, while contributing to displacement, insurgency, landlessness, political instability and violence, as many peasant farmers have been forced off their land to make way for large-scale commercial farming, energy projects and the exploration and exploitation of natural resources, which largely benefit those in power (banks and local elites, governments and transnational corporations) (Grisaffi and Ledebur, 2016; Kramer, Jensema, Jelsma and Blickman, 2014; Paley, 2014)—something that is largely ignored in official policy and discourse.

Essentially, although forced or coerced eradication initiatives may reduce production, at least temporarily, they are unsustainable and increase levels of harm, including environmental harm, which is experienced mostly by producer and transit countries. This also explains why, in recent years, many producer and transit countries have been pushing back against prohibitionist drug policies as their own national security interests are ignored in favour of Western supply reduction, and as they bear the brunt of global drug prohibition and its subsequent harms. The environmental impact of drug prohibition is severe and has lasting consequences for biodiversity, climate change and global warming, ecosystems and human welfare—none of which are considered or accounted for in international drug policy. Instead, resources aimed at environmental protection are being reassigned to prioritise Western drug interdiction initiatives as stopping the supply of drugs to Western consumer societies takes priority despite causing harm in developing countries, in what has been described as a form of recolonisation (see Bowling, 2010).

The economic reforms concealed as foreign aid have been described as frontier capitalism as large swathes of these resource-rich countries are privatised, commercialised and opened to capitalist markets and international trade (see Meehan, 2015). Foreign aid and debt relief are used to justify the coercive implementation of more draconian prohibitionist anti-drug policies aimed at eradicating drugs at their source, while the systemic violence (e.g., environmental degradation, human rights abuses) arising from capitalism and its expanding markets is ignored (Žižek, 2008). Instead, capitalist development imposed by violence generates corruption, inequality and poverty, which fuels further violence, as developing producer and transit countries are assimilated into world markets. This assimilation has exacerbated local economic, political and social conditions (e.g., poverty, state building, spiralling food costs, liberalisation of imports that has ruined domestic production and led to a dependency on volatile international commodity markets), while prioritising Western hegemonic interests, all of which have contributed to more illicit drug production and supply in these countries.

As described throughout this chapter, drug prohibition, along with crop eradication, deforestation and the destruction of jungle labs, causes more environmental harm than the cultivation of illicit drugs. And as MacCoun and Reuter (2001: 62) remind us, a policy 'that causes more harm than it mitigates is difficult to justify'. Drug prohibition and policies and programmes aimed at supply (rather than demand) are contradictory, discriminatory, harmful and prioritise the expansion of capitalism and the interests of those in power. In fact, because of the War on Drugs' adverse impact on the environment (e.g., biodiversity loss, deforestation, pollution of air, soil and water), one could argue that it is an ecologically destructive intervention that amounts to state-induced ecocide—a prohibition scheme that causes untold harm and irreversible damage beyond the ecosystem level, disproportionately effecting developing (transit and producer) countries, many of which are located in the Global South.

Prohibition and the War on Drugs is big business, however, justified by the fallacies inherent in the reductionist discourse surrounding illicit drugs (production, use and supply), where profit generation seems to outweigh non-monetary priorities that are harmful and ignored. Indeed, drug policy and their prohibition focus on drugs as a scapegoat—a scourge on society that needs to be eradicated if things are ever to improve, thus keeping the ideological fantasy alive (Žižek, 2008). It is through these efforts to keep the ideological fantasy alive that we witness the widespread death of flora and fauna, environments and ecosystems, while the paradoxical nature of capitalism, its inherent inequalities and objective violence is disavowed.

Notes

1 This also applies to the licit cultivation and production of drugs by big pharmaceutical companies (see Arnold et al., 2013).
2 Over the last 40 years, the United States has spent more than $2.5 trillion on initiatives, both domestic and abroad, aimed at decreasing the international flow of illicit drugs to its shores (Blackwell, 2014).
3 According to Courtwright (2001: 4–5), 'by 1885 taxation on booze, tobacco, and tea made up half of the revenues of the British government'.
4 For example, the Single Convention on Narcotic Drugs of 1961 (the 'Convention') expresses 'concern [for] the health and welfare of mankind', and states that all parties have a 'duty to prevent and combat this evil', while referring to drugs as 'dangerous', their trade 'a danger of incalculable gravity'; the 'evil of drug addiction' and 'addiction to narcotic drugs', in the words of the Convention, 'constitutes a serious evil for the individual and is fraught with social and economic danger to mankind'. The Convention remains the foundation of contemporary drug policy and global drug prohibition today, despite its inherent fallacies and falsehoods (see Taylor, Buchanan and Ayres, 2016).
5 Some commentators have argued that prohibition creates and exacerbates crime (e.g., armed conflict, corruption, organized crime, terrorism, violence), discriminates against the poor and ethnic minority groups, undermines human rights (e.g., in draconian sentencing for violations), destabilizes producer countries, causes ecological harm, and overwhelms the criminal justice system and its agents, while wasting billions on ineffective law enforcement initiatives (see, e.g., Rolles et al., 2016).
6 Two-thirds of the estimated global area under illicit opium poppy cultivation in 2016 was in Afghanistan (UNODC, 2016a, UNODC, 2018b).
7 Often the statistics are biased and influenced by local governments; they may also be contradictory and disparate, varying as much as 100 per cent. In fact, 'the disparity in provincial statistics may be even higher and contradictory about trends over time. For example, U.S. government estimates of cultivation in the province of Kandahar in southern Afghanistan show a decline from 2008 to 2010

from around 22,100 ha to 14,500 ha while UNODC show an increase from 14,600 to 25,800 ha' (Mansfield, 2011: 4).

8 Although in 2017, for the first time ever, the United States proposed more funding for demand reduction than supply reduction due to the country's continued opioid crisis and exponential increase in drug-related deaths (Executive Office of the President, 2016).

9 According to Mejía (2016: 1), 'Colombia has paid a high price to fight the "war on drugs," with costs amounting to approximately 1.1 per cent of its GDP per year from 2000 to 2008', while it is estimated that drug policies cost countries between 0.7–1.7 per cent of their annual GDP, and most of these costs account for law enforcement (UNODC, 2016b).

10 In Burma (Myanmar), 3,533 hectares of opium poppy were eradicated in 2017 representing a decrease of 53 per cent compared with 2016 (UNODC, 2017e).

11 The balloon effect is when 'the production in one region is squeezed by law enforcement ... it expands in another region as drug producers mobilise to meet demand' (Transform Drug Policy (TDP), 2015: 2).

12 Examples include the company Monsanto, which produces the herbicide Roundup and which also produced Agent Orange during the Vietnam War, to banks, transnational oil and gas companies, not to mention the profits generated by the U.S. arms industry that supplies weapons to both legitimate (states and governments) and illegitimate (insurgents and organized criminals) parties (Paley, 2014; Schneck, 2012; Transform Drug Policy (TDP), 2015).

13 In 2009, cocaine profits constituted 4.1 per cent of Colombia's GDP. The drug industry in Mexico earns between USD$30–50 billion in profit annually, putting it second only to its oil industry (Schneck, 2012).

14 For example, in Burma (Myanmar), the state offered money-laundering services through its banks, which charged a 40 per cent (and later a 25 per cent) 'whitening tax' (Meehan, 2011), while 40 per cent of the USD$1.4 billion 'Mérida Initiative' (a security agreement between the U.S., Mexico and the countries of Central America to address drug trafficking and transnational organized crime) went to U.S. defence companies, such as Textron (Schneck, 2012). In fact, big banks profit across the globe from drug money and its resultant laundering: drug money 'essentially rescued banks during the market meltdown in 2008' (Paley, 2014: 107).

15 The 'Helmand Food Zone Program' was part of the Helmand Province counternarcotic strategy, which was funded by the United States Agency for International Development (USAID), the U. K. and Denmark at a cost of USDS$56 million from 2008 to 2012. It was comprised of three components aimed at creating poppy-free zones, and it introduced farmers to alternative livelihoods, providing fertilizer and better-quality wheat seeds, public information campaigns and increased crop eradication (see Greenfield et al., 2015).

16 'Plan Colombia', now called 'Peace Colombia': since the ceasefire with FARC-EP (Fuerzas Armadas Revolucionarias de Colombia—Ejército del Pueblo), this was a joint U.S.–Colombia anti-drug strategy aimed at reducing the production and trafficking of illicit drugs. It focussed mostly on cocaine with a goal of reducing coca cultivation by 50 per cent within a six-year period. It also attempted to tackle organized crime's involvement in drug production and trafficking in order to improve security and take back territory controlled by insurgent groups, such as FARC and Ejército de Liberación Nacional (ELN), because in the seven years prior to its implementation, coca cultivation had increased by over 300 per cent and opium production had increased by 75 per cent. Plan Colombia consisted of U.S. funding averaging USD$1.352 million a year; since 2000, the U.S. has provided over USD$46 billion to Plan Colombia in military and non-military assistance (Dávalos and Bejarano, 2008; Mejía, 2016).

17 Opium in Colombia declined by more than 90 per cent between 2000 and 2009, and coca bush cultivation in Colombia was 41 per cent lower in 2015 than at its peak in 2000 (Beittel and Rosen, 2017; Mejía, 2016; UNODC, 2017b).

18 In 2008, when Colombia reported an 18 per cent decrease in coca cultivation, Peru experienced an increase of 6 per cent and Bolivia an increase of 4.5 per cent (UNODC, 2009); meanwhile, eradication efforts in the Golden Triangle led to large increases in opium production in Afghanistan (see Blackwell, 2014).

19 Nearly 80 per cent of the financial backing for 'Plan Colombia' by the U.S. was for military assistance, which totalled USD$860.3 million, while USD$519.2 million was given to the police. Alternative development options (e.g., alternative livelihoods, crop substitution, initiatives that reduce poverty) totalled only

USD$68.5 million. The USD$300 million military assistance to Colombian armed forces made it the third largest recipient of U.S. defence aid after Egypt and Israel (Buxton, 2006).

20 According to Gruenwald (2015: 1), Colombia has lost 197 eradicators, '145 of which were members of the armed forces and 52 [civilian] eradicators, while in Afghanistan 6 people died, and 8 people were injured in 2017 during eradication campaigns (UNODC, 2018b). We have also had 687 injured with amputations that compromise their physical integrity'. In 2005, there were 29 fatalities in one day of eradication because fields are protected by both armed militia and landmines (Gruenwald, 2015; Mansfield, 2011).

21 Paramilitary groups may be involved in the drugs trade and/or may provide traffickers with protection. At the same time, however, they may also work for the state and its agents (such as politicians) or engage in joint operations with state military.

22 For example, in 2001 'more than 30,000 hectares of legal crops were destroyed within six weeks of aerial spraying' (Gautreau, 2012: 71).

23 In addition to destroying traditional livelihoods and exacerbating food insecurity, eradication has an adverse impact on health because many of the illicit drug crops targeted are used as a form of traditional medicine, as well as a source of food (e.g., roasted coca leaves) by Indigenous people and their livestock (Gautreau, 2012; Sunshine Project, 2001). It is worth adding that some officials also use the *threat* of eradication to extort money from farmers, who pay these officials not to destroy their illicit crops. This fuels corruption and state illegitimacy (Kramer, Jensema, Jelsma and Blickman, 2014).

24 For every kilogram of cocaine removed from the retail market, the cost is about USD$240,000; for every hectare sprayed, which costs USD$2,400, coca crops are reduced by 0.02–0.065 hectares, which means 'to eliminate just one hectare of coca … 32 hectares of coca need to be sprayed'. This, in turn, means it is only 4.2 per cent effective and costs more than the price of coca leaves from one hectare ($450) (Mejía, 2016: 9).

25 According to Jelsma (2001: 10) 'recent sprayings had affected no less than eleven alternative development projects … including Plante projects implemented with European development assistance, three UNDCP projects and one "manual eradication pact"'.

26 The opium substitution programmes run by China for Burma (Myanmar) and Laos have either benefitted Chinese business and local authorities, or pushed local farmers off their land, prioritizing larger Chinese agricultural companies (Kramer, Jensema, Jelsma and Blickman, 2014).

27 About 11 million hectares each year of tropical forest are cleared, which constitutes 1–2 per cent of the world's tropical forests—an area the size of the U.K., including Northern Ireland (Armstead, 1992).

28 The Golden Triangle refers to the area where the borders of Thailand, Laos and Burma (Myanmar) meet at the confluence of the Ruak River and Mekong River.

29 The Golden Crescent refers to the crossroads of central, south and western Asia—the mountainous region of Afghanistan, Iran and Pakistan.

30 Forest fragmentation is where small plots of land are cleared and farmed 'within the forests to create a patchwork landscape with considerable forest edge that is unfavourable to the survival of many species' (UNODC, 2006: 28).

31 For example, 14 hectares of palm would need to be cultivated to produce the same monetary value of palm hearts that could be obtained from one hectare of cocaine (Bradley and Millington, 2008).

32 The terrestrial carbon cycle is basically the exchange of carbon between the terrestrial biosphere, which is all organic matter including vegetation and soil, the majority of which is held in forests, and the atmosphere, and is the difference between carbon uptake by photosynthesis and its release by plant respiration, soil respiration and disturbance processes, such as deforestation and fire.

33 For example, of the 15–30 per cent of annual forest lost in Guatemala, Honduras and Nicaragua due to cocaine, 30–60 per cent of this loss occurred within nationally and internationally protected areas, such as biosphere reserves, national parks and world heritage sites (Sesnie et al., 2017).

34 In Afghanistan, the rich wetlands have disappeared, while the reduced water flow in other parts of the world has had lethal consequences for some forms of aquatic and amphibian life (e.g., coastal tailed frog, the southern torrent salamander) (Bauer et al., 2015; UNODC, 2016a).

35 Colombian coca growers use 95 million kg of fertilizers and 1.4 million kg of herbicides in their fields annually (Dávalos and Bejarano, 2008).

36 It is estimated that the runoff from prohibited drug-processing facilities in Colombia totals 20 million litres per year of acetone, ammonia, ethyl ether, hydrochloric acid and sulphuric acid,

while heroin and morphine production releases acetone, alcohol, ammonia, ammonium chloride, lime and tartaric acid (Armstead, 1992). It is also estimated that Colombia produces 8.7 million gallons a year and Peru produces 50,000m³ of kerosene and 2,000 tonnes of sulphuric acid, while 600 million litres of chemicals are used annually in cocaine production in South America and 2 metric tonnes of chemical waste is produced per every hectare of coca processed into cocaine (Armstead, 1992; Buxton, 2006).

37 Eutrophication is the excessive richness of minerals and nutrients in a body of water, most often due to runoff from land (e.g., nitrates and/or phosphates from fertilizers), causing dense growth of plant life and algae. When this plant life decomposes, it uses up the available oxygen in the water, causing the level of oxygen to fall to the point where the fish and other forms of aquatic life choke—a condition known as 'hypoxia' (Brisman, 2002: 514; see also Eth, 2008).

38 The demarcation between 'user' and 'producer' countries is becoming increasingly blurred due to an increase in drug use in both 'producer' and 'transit' countries.

39 If prohibition is to be maintained, instead of prioritizing supply reduction, supply and demand reduction initiatives need to be integrated (Kramer, Jensema, Jelsma and Blickman, 2014) and an evidence base used to inform both strands of drug policy.

References

Álvarez, M. D. 2001. 'Could peace be worse than war for Colombia's forests?' *The Environmentalist*, 21(4): 305–315.

Armenteras, D., Rodriguez, N. and Retana, J. 2013. 'Landscape dynamics in Northwestern Amazonia: An assessment of pastures, fire and illicit crops as drivers of tropical deforestation,' *PLoS One*, 8(1): 1–9.

Armstead, L. 1992. *Illicit Narcotics Cultivation and Processing: The Ignored Environmental Drama*. Vienna: UNODC.

Arnold, K. E., Boxall, A., Brown, A. R., Cuthbert, R. J., Gaw, S., Hutchinson, T. H., Jobling, S., Madden, J. C., Metcalfe, C. D., Naidoo, V., Shore, R. F., Smits, J. E., Taggart, M. A. and Thompson, H. M. 2013. 'Assessing the exposure risk and impacts of pharmaceuticals in the environment on individuals and ecosystems,' *Biology Letters*, 9(4): 1–4.

Bauer S., Olson J., Cockrill A., van Hattem M., Miller L., Tauzer M. and Lepping G. 2015. 'Impacts of surface water diversions for Marijuana cultivation on aquatic habitat in four Northwestern California watersheds,' *PLoS One*, 10(3): 1–25.

Beittel, J. S. and Rosen, L. W. 2017. *Colombia's Changing Approach to Drug Policy, CRS Report for Congress*. Washington: Congressional Research Service.

Blackwell, J. M. 2014. 'The costs and consequences of US drug prohibition for the peoples of developing nations,' *European Journal of Law Reform*, 16(1): 665–692.

Bowling, B. 2010. *Policing the Caribbean: Transnational Security Cooperation in Practice*. Oxford: OUP.

Bradley, A. V. and Millington, A. C. 2008. 'Coca and colonists: Quantifying and explaining forest clearance under coca and anti-narcotics policy regimes,' *Ecology and Society*, 13(1): 31–50.

Brisman, A. 2002. 'Considerations in establishing a stormwater utility,' *Southern Illinois University Law Journal*, 26(3): 505–528.

Brisman, A., and South, N. 2013. 'Introduction to the handbook: Horizons, issues and relationships in green criminology,' in N. South and A. Brisman (eds.), *Routledge International Handbook of Green Criminology*, pp. 1–23. Abingdon, Oxon, UK: Routledge.

Buchanan, J. 2015. 'Ending prohibition with a hangover,' *British Journal of Community Justice*, 13(1): 55–74.

Buchanan, J. and Young, L. 2000. 'The war on drugs - a war on drug users?' *Drugs: Education, Prevention and Policy*, 7(4): 409–422.

Burns-Edel, T. and Davis, U. C. 2016. 'Environmental Impacts of Illicit Drug Production,' *Global Societies Journal*, 4: 1–14.

Buxton J. 2011. *The Politics of Narcotic Drugs: A Survey*. London: Routledge.

Buxton, J. 2006. *The Political Economy of Narcotics*. Black Point, NS: Fernwood.

Chomsky, N. 1992. *Deterring Democracy*. London: Verso.

Courtwright, D. 2001. *Forces of Habit: Drugs and the Making of the Modern World*. Cambridge, MA: Harvard University Press.

Dávalos, L. M. and Bejarano, A. C. 2008. *Illegal Drugs versus Habitat in the Americas, State of the Wild 2008–2009*. Washington, DC: Island Press.

Dávalos, L. M., Bejarano, A. C. and Correa, H. L. 2009. 'Disabusing Cocaine: Pervasive myths and enduring realities of a globalised commodity,' *International Journal of Drug Policy*, 20(5): 381–386.

Dávalos, L. M., Bejarano, A. C., Hall, M. A., Correa, H. L., Corthals, A and Espejo, O. J. 2011. 'Forests and drugs: Coca-driven deforestation in tropical biodiversity hotspots,' *Environmental Science and Technology*, 45(5): 1219–1227.

Del Olmo, R. 1987. 'Aerobiology and the war on drugs: A transnational crime,' *Crime and Social Justice*, 30: 28–44.

Del Olmo, R. 1993. 'The geopolitics of narcotrafficking in Latin America,' *Social Justice*, 20(3/4): 1–23.

Del Olmo, R. 1998. 'The ecological impact of illicit drug cultivation and crop eradication programs in Latin America,' *Theoretical Criminology*, 2(2): 269–278.

Diaz, A. M. and Sanchez, F. 2004. *A Geography of Illicit Crops (coca leaf) and Armed Conflict in Colombia*. London: LSE.

Eth, W. 2008. 'Up in Smoke: Wholesale Marijuana Cultivation within the National Parks and Forests, and the Accompanying Extensive Environmental Damage,' *Penn State Environmental Law Review*, 16(2): 451–486.

Executive Office of the President. 2016. *National Drug Control Strategy: FY 2017 Budget Summary*. Washington, DC: Executive Office of the President.

Felbab-Brown, V. 2015. *Enabling War and Peace: Drugs, Logs, Gems and Wildlife in Thailand and Burma*. Washington, DC: Brookings.

Fjeldsa, J., Alvarez, M. D., Lazcano, J. M. and Leon, B. 2005. 'Illicit crops and armed conflict as constraints on biodiversity conservation in the andes region,' *Ambio*, 34(3): 205–211.

Gautreau, G. L. 2012. 'To rid the world of the drug scourge: A human security perspective on the war on drugs in Colombia and Mexico,' *Paterson Review of International Affairs*, 12: 61–83.

Global Commission on Drug Policy (GCDP). 2012. *The War on Drugs and HIV/AIDS*. Geneva: GCDP.

Greenfield, V. A., Crane, K., Bond, C. A., Chandler, N. M., Luoto, J. E. and Oliker, O. 2015. *Reducing the Cultivation of Opium Poppies in Southern Afghanistan*. Santa Monica: RAND.

Grisaffi, T. and Ledebur, K. 2016. 'Citizenship or repression? Coca, eradication and development in the andes,' *Stability: International Journal of Security and Development*, 5(1): 1–19.

Gruenwald, T. 2015. 'Nearly 200 have died in manual eradication of coca in Colombia,' *Colombia Reports*, May 27. Available at: https://colombiareports.com/nearly-200-have-died-in-manual-eradication-of-coca-in-colombia/.

Hall, A. and Antonopoulos, G. A. 2016. *Fake Meds Online: The Internet and the Transnational Market in Illicit Pharmaceuticals*. London: Palgrave Macmillan.

Higginson, A., Mazerolle, L. and Thompson, J. 2013. *The Effectiveness of Crop Targeting Interventions for Drug Control: A Systematic Review and Meta-Analysis*. Conference Paper presented at the International Society for the Study of Drug Policy (ISSDP). Colombia. Available at: https://espace.library.uq.edu.au/view/UQ:699214.

Human Rights Watch (HRW). 2010. *Human rights and drug policy: Crop eradication*. Available at: www2.ohchr.org/english/bodies/cescr/docs/ngos/IHRA_Colombia44.pdf.

Jelsma, M. 2001. *Vicious Circle: The Chemical and Biological war on Drugs*. Amsterdam: Transnational Institute.

Jelsma, M. and Kramer, T. 2008. *Withdrawal Symptoms, Changes in the Southeast Asian Drugs Market*. Amsterdam: Transnational Institute.

Kegö, W. and Maïga, A. 2014. Tallying the Hidden Environmental Costs of Drug Production. *The Institute for Security and Policy Development*, 149(March): 1–2.

Klein, N. 2007. *The Shock Doctrine*. London: Penguin Books.

Kramer, T., Jensema, E., Jelsma, M. and Blickman, T. 2014. *Bouncing Back: Relapse in the Golden Triangle*. Amsterdam: Transnational Institute.

MacCoun, R. J. and Reuter, P. 2001. *Drug War Heresies: Learning from Other Vices, Times, and Places*. Cambridge: Cambridge University Press.

Mansfield, D. 2002. *The Economic Superiority of Illicit Drug Production: Myth and Reality: Opium Poppy Cultivation in Afghanistan*. Paper prepared for the International Conference on Alternative Development in Drug Control and Cooperation, Feldafing, Germany. Available at: www.scottshelmandvalleyarchives.org/docs/nar-01-02.pdf.

Mansfield, D. 2011. *Assessing Supply-Side Policy and Practice: Eradication and Alternative Development*. Geneva: GCDP.

May, C. 2017. *Transnational Crime and the Developing World*. Washington: Global Financial Integrity.

McSweeney, K. 2015a. *The Impact of Drug Policy on the Environment*. New York: Open Society Foundations.

McSweeney, K. 2015b. 'The war on drugs is destroying the environment.' *US News*, December 9. Available at: www.usnews.com/opinion/articles/2015/12/09/global-drug-policy-is-destroying-the-environment.

Meehan, P. 2011. 'Drugs, insurgency and state-building in Burma: Why the drugs trade is central to Burma's changing political order,' *Journal of Southeast Asian Studies*, 42(3): 376–404.

Meehan, P. 2015. 'Drugs, local politics and the subversion of global counter-narcotics ideology in Burma's eastern borderlands, 1988-2012,' in O. Charnoz, V. D. Pedregal and A. L. Kolata (eds.), *Local Politics, Global Impacts: Steps to a Multi-Disciplinary Analysis of Scales*, pp. 79–103. London; Routledge.

Mejía, D. 2016. *Plan Colombia: An analysis of effectiveness and costs*. Available at: www.brookings.edu/wp-content/uploads/2016/07/Mejia-Colombia-final-2.pdf.

Natali, L. 2010. 'The big grey elephants in the backyard of Huelva, Spain,' in R. White (ed.), *Global Environmental Harm: Criminological Perspectives*, pp. 193–209. Cullompton, Devon, UK; Willan.

Paley, D. 2014. *Drug War Capitalism*. Edinburgh: AK Press.

Ridgewell, H. 2017. *Big Read: Loss of tropical forests threatens search for antibiotics*. Available at: www.wikitribune.com/story/2017/11/16/medicine/deforestation-risks-wiping-out-future-medical-cures/2779/.

Rolles, S., Murkin, G., Powell, M., Kushlik, D., Saunter, N. and Slater, J. 2016. *The Alternative World Drug Report*. 2nd editon. Bristol: TDPF.

Rozo, S. V. 2014. 'On the unintended consequences of anti-drug eradication programs in producing countries,' *California Centre for Population Research On-Line Working Paper Series*. Available at: www.appam.org/assets/1/7/On_the_Unintended_Effects_of_Spraying.pdf.

Sanborn, M., Cole, D., Kerr, K., Vakil, C., Sanin, L. H. and Bassil, K. 2004. *Pesticides Literature Review*. Ontario: OCFP.

Schneck, G. D. 2012. 'A war on civilians: Disaster capitalism and the drug war in Mexico.' *Seattle Journal for Social Justice*, 10(2): 927–979.

Seelke, C. R., Wyler, L. S., Beittel, J. S. and Sullivan, M. P. 2011. *Latin America and the Caribbean: Illicit Drug Trafficking and US Counterdrug Programs, CRS Report for Congress*. Washington, DC: Congressional Research Service.

Sesnie, S. E., Tellman, B., Wrathall, D., McSweeney, K., Nielson, E., Benessaiah, K., Wang, O. and Rey, L. 2017. 'A spatio-temporal analysis of forest loss related to cocaine trafficking in Central America,' *Environmental Research Letters*, 12(5): 1–19.

Song, X., Huang, C., Saatchi, S. S., Hansen, M. C. and Townshend, J. R. 2015. 'Annual carbon emissions from deforestation in the Amazon basin between 2000 and 2010,,' *PLOS One*, 10(5): 1–21.

South, N. and Wyatt, T. 2011. 'Comparing illicit trades in wildlife and drugs: An exploratory study,' *Deviant Behavior*, 32(1): 1–24.

Spiers, E. M. 1989. *Chemical Warfare*. London: Palgrave.

Sunshine Project. 2001. *Risks of Using Biological Agents in Drug Eradication*. Austin: Sunshine Project. Available at: www.mamacoca.org/docs_de_base/Fumigas/nr_04.pdf.

Taylor, S., Buchanan, J. and Ayres, T. C. 2016. 'Prohibition, privilege and the drug apartheid: The failure of drug policy reform to address the underlying fallacies of drug prohibition,' *Criminology and Criminal Justice*, 16(4): 452–469.

Thompson, C., Sweitzer, R., Gabriel, M., Purcell, K., Barrett, R. and Poppenga, R. 2014. 'Impacts of rodenticide and insecticide toxicants from marijuana cultivation sites on fisher survival rates in the Sierra National Forest, California,' *Conservation Letters*, 7(2): 91–102.

Transform Drug Policy (TDP). 2015. *Counting the Costs - The War on Drugs: Causing Deforestation and Pollution*. Bristol: TDP.

UNODC. 2006. *Andean Report – Part 2: Environmental Effects of Illicit Drug Cultivation and Processing*. Vienna: UNODC.

UNODC. 2009. *Columba Coca Cultivation Survey June 2009*. Vienna: UNODC.

UNODC. 2015. *Southeast Asia Opium Survey 2015*. Vienna: UNODC.

UNODC. 2016a. *Afghanistan Opium Survey 2016: Cultivation and Production*. Vienna: UNODC.

UNODC. 2016b. *World Drug Report, 2016*. Vienna: UNODC.

UNODC. 2017a. *World Drug Report: Executive Summary: Conclusions and Policy Implications*. Vienna: UNODC.

UNODC. 2017b. *Market Analysis of Plant-Based Drugs: Opiates, Cocaine, Cannabis*. Vienna: UNODC.

UNODC. 2017c. *Global Overview of Drug Demand and Supply*. Vienna: UNODC.

UNODC. 2017d. *Evidence for Enhancing Resilience to Opium Poppy Cultivation in Shan State, Myanmar*. Vienna: UNODC.
UNODC. 2017e. *Myanmar Opium Survey, 2017*. Vienna: UNODC.
UNODC. 2017f. *Sustainable Development in an Opium Production Environment: Afghanistan Opium Survey Report 2016*. Vienna: UNODC.
UNODC. 2018a. *Analysis of Drug Markets*. Vienna: UNODC.
UNODC. 2018b. *Afghanistan Opium Survey 2017: Cultivation and Production*. Vienna: UNODC.
Zain, M. E. 2015. Impact of mycotoxins on humans and animals. *Journal of Saudi Chemical Society*, 15(2): 129–144.
Žižek, S. 2008. *Violence*. London: Profile Books Ltd.

14

'Greening' injustice

Penal reform, carceral expansion and greenwashing

Jordan E. Mazurek, Justin Piché and Judah Schept[1]

Introduction

A central challenge faced by those who seek to abolish jails and prisons is the question of what role reform should play in such struggles. After all, while prison abolitionists fight for an end to incarceration, there are prisoners who are subject to its brutalities day in and day out. Confronted with the tension between reformist and revolutionary changes, abolitionists acknowledge the necessity of the former, while rejecting the idea that incarceration is necessary and inevitable. Guarding against 'reformist reforms' advanced by advocates of imprisonment that deepen and provide legitimacy to penal power, abolitionists pursue 'non-reformist reforms'—ones that aim to improve the material conditions of prisoners in the short term by eradicating repressive policies and practices, while challenging the need to incarcerate in the long term (Ben-Moshe 2013: 87; see also Gorz 1967).

Similar debates between advocates of reformist changes (e.g., Tomkins 2005) and those calling for revolutionary transformations (e.g., Pellow 2016, this volume, Chapter 32) are also on-going with respect to the sustainability and ecological health of local communities, nation states, and indeed the world in the context of neoliberal capitalism and its effects on climate change. While some propose measures to limit the damage of capitalist extraction and accumulation because they are ardent supporters of the existing order (e.g., Mol 2010), others advance proposals to reduce production and consumption as a means of saving the planet and lifeforms that occupy it (e.g., Brisman and South 2014). Here, again, debates about how to move forward are shaped by the ability of capitalism's supporters to entrench the status quo, thus limiting the choices for action to reforms that sustain a way of life that injures, maims and kills many to line the pockets of the few (see, for example, Bittle 2012).

In recent years, questions pertaining to ecological justice and 'criminal justice' have intersected, with some arms of carceral states integrating the language of sustainability and environmental responsibility into their policies and practices (Jewkes and Moran 2015; Lynch 2007; White and Graham 2015). For instance, in both Canada and the United States, there are often claims that new carceral spaces are being built using green construction materials and practices, along with infrastructure that will reduce energy consumption and waste, while improving the environment in which captives live and captors work (Piché, Kleuskens and Walby 2017).

As imprisonment remains a dominant social practice and political expression of neoliberal states, progressive reformers and abolitionists must ask themselves whether new 'green' jails and prisons contribute to the betterment of prisoners and the environment in which such facilities are located, or if such projects are instances of 'greenwashing' that co-opt discourses of ecological justice movements (Brisman and South 2014) as a means of caging more human beings, while normalising the idea that both carceral and neoliberal relations are necessary and can be made sustainable. Put differently, Graham and White (2015: 860) argue that the movement towards 'greening justice' holds considerable potential to contribute to veritable penal reform, whereby 'true sustainability hinges upon the impetus to decarcerate, diminish in size and de-commission, restricting the use of confinement as a genuine last resort'. They also warn, however, that there is potential that this could also result in 'justifying penal expansionism' (Graham and White 2015: 860).

In what follows, we take up the call issued by Jewkes and Moran (2015: 466) 'to address the paradox at the heart of the green prison ... that rather than challenging the hegemony of incarceration, advocates of green prisons are arguably perpetuating and legitimising the expanding penal estate'. We do so by exploring the emergence of 'green' jail and prison infrastructure projects in Canada and the United States. More specifically, we examine how claims concerning the sustainability of facility construction and operations have contributed to the establishment of new and bigger institutions designed to deprive people of their liberty. In addition, by examining the marketing materials of the agencies promoting green initiatives in 'criminal justice', we demonstrate that, at least in some cases, neither sustainability nor prison reform are primary or even normative goals. Rather, the 'green' components of these initiatives are driven by their ability to cut state or municipal costs. In so doing, we argue that—at least in the cases we have explored—future claims with respect to 'greening justice' should be met with great scepticism given their role in legitimating carceral expansion and emerging penal reforms that fail to challenge the persistence of human caging. Importantly, we explore an understudied dimension of the literature, engaging critically with the emergence of 'green imprisonment' by turning our attention to organisers that are taking the fight to those who seek to build new jails and prisons, in part through the campaigns that point to the social and ecological toxicity of such facilities. Before doing so, however, we begin the chapter with a review of some of the key claims found in the emerging literature on 'greening justice', which we subsequently challenge. Our ultimate point is rather simple: there is no greener approach to incarceration than not having jails and prisons in the first place.

'Greening justice', penal reform and carceral expansion: towards sustainable carceral states?

Our intervention in this chapter operates on multiple fronts. Our concern is with both the analytical and practical terrain of criminology's engagement with and co-production of 'greening justice'. Analytically, we question the conceptual implications of 'greening justice' and argue that scholars have to take seriously the possibility that in advocating for sustainable penal institutions and practices within them, they argue ultimately for the sustainability of carceral states. Even as some authors acknowledge explicitly this tendency for capital to infect and co-opt discourses of reform, those same authors nonetheless seem to embrace the 'green' prison agenda. For instance, Stohr and Wozniak (2014) present six benefits for prisons going 'green', including the claim that doing so can create jobs in the communities where jails and prisons are being retrofitted or newly constructed using environmentally sustainable designs and methods. Of course, to the extent that we have such institutions, it would be better for them to be built and run in ways that reduce their harm to both prisoners and surrounding communities, as well as the environment. Stohr and Wozniak, however, essentially make the case for a green jobs programme reliant on the development of new penal infrastructure, which at best sustains carceral states and at worst expands them.

Indeed, if one looks at what governments themselves are doing—producing, for example, reports like *The Greening of Corrections: Creating a Sustainable System* (Feldbaum et al. 2011)—we might pause to consider our adoption of the very logics of the system we wish to change radically. That report, commissioned by the National Institute of Corrections (NIC), describes in detail the current work and future prospects for prisons that would hold Leadership in Energy and Environmental Design (LEED) certifications, run on photovoltaic power installations, use grey water and rain catchments, along with other forms of sustainable waste and water management. Indeed, the NIC report offers the ambitious and perhaps visionary goal of achieving facilities with net zero impacts. It is worth noting that forcing carceral sites and other major consumers of energy and contributors to climate change to transition to sustainable methods is, on its face, worthwhile and even cuts against the grain of the more neoliberal approaches that moralise individual choice (Brisman 2013; Jensen 2009). In other words, to the extent that we have major institutions that contribute disproportionately to climate change, we should consider and prioritise methods to reduce their impact. Yet, it must be noted that the NIC report is committed to the *sustainability of the system itself*. Indeed, 'sustainable development' is the preferred reformist economic strategy of anthropocentric capitalism deriving from the United Nations' Brundtland Report (World Commission on Environment and Development 1987; see also Brisman 2011; Schept and Mazurek 2017: 178–179), where 'the aim … is to operate within the context of global capitalist markets, rather than to challenge the logic of these forms of production and consumption' (Halsey and White 1998: 351).

Looking more closely at current examples reveals the extent to which 'green justice' initiatives reinforce the carceral state—at times through expansion and at times through omission of any meaningful attempt at reform. For instance, in the Canadian context, the past decade has seen the construction of several new provincial-territorial jails and prisons (Piché, 2014), most of which were marketed as 'green' for (a) using recycled materials in construction; (b) employing cheaper or more efficient heating, water and electricity management systems; (c) providing captives and captors with greater access to natural light; (d) cutting vehicle emissions related to court appearances through video-streaming; (e) reducing waste through the introduction of recycling programmes within the facilities once operational; and/or (f) incorporating architectural and design principles that qualify for LEED certification upon opening (Piché, Kleuskens and Walby 2017: 41–43). As the table below indicates (Table 14.1), there was not one case where new penal infrastructure, including 'green' projects, were *smaller* than the facilities they replaced or were built as part of an effort to decrease overall capacity within the jurisdictions examined. These new carceral sites were also marketed as more secure, humane and rehabilitative sites of confinement (Piché, Kleuskens and Walby 2017), illustrating the degree to which progressive rhetoric is, on occasion, used to legitimate the deprivation of liberty (Schept 2015).

While the 'green' aspects of new carceral sites often occupy no more than a sentence in related marketing materials, Piché and colleagues (2017) have found that state authorities consider sustainability and purported environmental benefits to be integral to manufacturing consent for such projects in some instances. For instance, in preparation for the press release and announcement of the construction of the new Dalhousie Regional Correctional Centre, an e-mail exchange between New Brunswick Supply and Services (2009) officials titled 'Key messages–Dalhousie' included requests to 'bulk it up a bit by speaking to some of the environmentally-friendly features of the building' and to add 'a little extra info on the green elements of the building and we'll be good to go'. The following environmental benefits were cited:

Table 14.1 New provincial-territorial jails and prisons in Canada (2008 to 2017)[2]

Jurisdiction	*New facility and location*	*Total capacity*	*Net gain*	*Construction costs*
Nova Scotia	Northeast Nova Scotia Correctional Facility (Coalburn)	196 beds	+164 beds	$42.3 million
New Brunswick	Southeast Regional Correctional Centre (Shediac)	180 beds	+122 beds	$36 million
New Brunswick	Dalhousie Regional Correctional Centre (Dalhousie)	100 beds	+70 beds	$20 million
Quebec	Centre de détention de Sept-Îles (Sept-Îles)	71 beds	+28 beds	$90.9 million
Quebec	Centre de détention de Roberval (Roberval)	180 beds	+31 beds	$115 million
Quebec	Centre de détention d'Amos (Amos)	220 beds	+84 beds	$125.9 million
Quebec	Centre de détention de Sorel-Tracy (Sorel-Tracy)	380 beds	+149 beds	$267.1 million
Quebec	Centre de détention de Percé—retrofit and re-opening (Percé)	46 beds	+46 beds	$11.3 million
Ontario	Toronto South Detention Centre (Toronto)	1,650 beds	+1,100 beds	$1.1 billion
Ontario	New Elgin-Middlesex Intermittent Centre (London)	112 beds	+112 beds	$9.3 million
Ontario	South West Detention Centre (Windsor)	315 beds	+175 beds	$336 million
Manitoba	Women's Correctional Centre (Headingley)	100 beds	+45 beds	$60 million
Saskatchewan	New Regina Provincial Correctional Centre (Regina)	427 beds	+211 beds	$50.3 million
Alberta	New Edmonton Remand Centre (Edmonton)	1,944 beds	+1,218	$568.5 million
British Columbia	Okanagan Correctional Centre (Osoyoos First Nation)	792 beds	+792 beds	$200 million
British Columbia	Surrey Pretrial Services Centre (Surrey)	324 beds	+324 beds	$112.5 million
Nunavut	Rankin Inlet Healing Centre (Rankin Inlet)	46 beds	+46 beds	$20.4 million
Nunavut	Makigiarvik Correctional Centre for Women (Iqaluit)	8 beds	+8 beds	$2.9 million
Yukon	Whitehorse Correctional Centre (Whitehorse)	194 beds	+109 beds	$75 million

> The building will be designed to maximise energy efficiency and water use reduction.
> All building materials and products specified will contain no or low VOC's (volatile organic compounds).
> The project will strive to specify materials with recycled content and which are harvested and manufactured regionally (within 500 miles).
> A construction waste management plan and an erosion and sedimentation control plan will be put in place during all construction phases of the Project.
> And efforts will be made to minimized [sic] site disruption during construction.
> A recycling program will be put in place for when the facility is operational.
> Let me know if you need anything else or more explanation.

After refinement, New Brunswick Supply and Services/Public Safety (2009) included the following 'green' elements of the new Dalhousie Correctional Centre in their press release:

> As part of the Government of New Brunswick's Green Buildings Program, the correctional centre has been designed to achieve a silver rating under the principles of LEED (Leadership in Energy and Environmental Design), and will be registered with the Canada Green Buildings Council.
>
> The facility has been designed to maximize energy efficiency and minimize water use. It will be constructed with environmentally friendly building materials, and waste generated during the construction period will be strictly managed. A recycling program will also be put in place once the centre is operational.

As noted by Piché and colleagues (2017: 43), within hours of the 11 May 2009 announcement, the Government of New Brunswick received word that data suggested 'there is a potential wetland … on the back of the site … and visible evidence on aerial photography'. If the 'green' talking points were developed and communicated to the public before the full environmental assessment of the land slated for the facility was complete, what does that say about the potential perils of 'greening justice'?

There are also many carceral facilities around the United States that have, at least in name and in various ways, adopted a 'green' agenda. An article in *The New York Times* from 2009, perhaps presciently titled 'Greening the Prison Industrial Complex', notes that the Washington State Department of Corrections alone has 34 LEED-designed facilities. At that time, California had recently announced 'green' retrofitting projects at 16 different facilities (Schwartzapfel 2009). Private prisons seem to have joined the movement as well, with the GEO Group, Inc., the world's second largest private prison company, recently receiving funds through a public grant process to build a native landscape plan for water conservation at their facility in the Central Valley desert town of Adelanto, California. The project would seem to be a prime case of greenwashing, for as the Prison Ecology Project and Human Rights Defense Center have pointed out, the facility still draws 140,000 gallons of water every day for the 700 prisoners it houses (Prison Ecology Project 2015).

The Multnomah County Oregon Sustainable Jail Project (the 'Sustainable Jail Project'), based out of Portland, also boasts of $400,000 in cost savings through various green initiatives, including water re-use, composting, digitising the jail law library and repackaging cleaning supplies. The efforts for green re-design of the jail's system seem animated first and foremost by cost savings, rather than concerns about environmental sustainability and climate change—an example of the kind of 'greening justice' that White and Graham (2015) problematise. As the project boasts on its website, 'The Multnomah County Sustainable Jail Project really is the first of its kind, [an] innovative model for the rest of the nation around sustainable, cost-effective jail operations … The convenient truth is using resources wisely saves money' (Multnomah County Sherriff's Office 2012). These rather cosmetic changes to reduce costs reveal another telling absence: there is no mention on the website, nor in any other materials, about the potential cost savings and environmental benefits of downsizing the jail itself through policies of decarceration or diversion along the lines proposed by Knopp and colleagues (Knopp et al. 2005 [1976]).

Before moving on, it is important to point toward programmes that perhaps avoid some of the pitfalls we have thus far delineated. The Sustainable Jail Project in Oregon notes that it drew inspiration from the Washington-based Sustainability in Prisons Project (SPP), a partnership between Evergreen State College and the Washington Department of Corrections. The SPP is notably different and perhaps distinct. They partner with a variety of state 'correctional' agencies to provide substantial environmental education and training programmes to prisoners at a number of different prisons. Their educational and training agenda includes multiple different classes on gardening, bee-keeping, waste sorting and recycling and green building. In addition, they support and sometimes facilitate partnerships between individual prisons and the communities in which they reside through activities and programmes like growing food for local schools, composting and forestry. Importantly, the SPP (Sustainability in Prisons Project n.d.) also counts among its allies a number of organisations explicitly working on issues of racial, climate and economic justice (see also Stohr and Wozniak 2014). Yet, their work has been absorbed—that is 'picked up and implemented in a way which … fits into the prevailing structure without threatening it' (Mathiesen 1990: 39)—by the Multnomah County Oregon Sustainable Jail Project. The promotion of costs savings in 'corrections' associated with these ventures, rather than their environmental virtues in the first instance, should raise questions about what kind of sustainability is being promoted when 'green' confinement is invoked (see also Little 2015).

In another example, Schept (2015) found 'corrections' consultants were vague in their use of the word 'green' in their proposals for carceral expansion in a community that they read correctly as sympathetic to increasing confinement capacity if sustainable methods of design were followed (see also Lynch and Stretesky 2003). Schept (2015) notes that in this case, proponents imagined the expansion project—which bore the title of 'justice campus'—as embodying social and environmental justice because 'green' methods of design and therapeutic methods of incarceration were the two foundational discourses used to justify the project. This follows a particularly noxious form of greenwashing whereby advocates of imprisonment use the word 'green' without any explanation as to what they mean by the term, but nonetheless signal to much of the audience a commitment to sustainable design (Jewkes and Moran 2015: 4; Lynch and Stretesky 2003). In the context of penal growth justified through invocations of both green design and rehabilitation (also see Piché, Kleuskens and Walby 2017), the important observations by Jewkes and Moran (2015: 3) that 'the powerful construct the meaning of 'green', just as they define 'crime' and 'punishment'' ring true. Indeed, as Jewkes and Moran (2015: 454) argue regarding the 'greening' of prisons in the United Kingdom:

> Discourses of sustainability and green ideologies are embedded in the growth of the carceral estate and … environmental policies are enmeshed with broader goals of the criminal justice system within a political economic context that has vested interests in its continuation and expansion. Our conclusion is that the political and cultural hegemony of the green agenda is, perhaps counter-intuitively, serving to sustain both the prison system and the myriad private companies behind the consortia that tender for Design, Construct, Manage & Finance (DCMF) contracts, while espousing the value of sustaining the environment.

It is here, at the contradiction between well-intentioned efforts to address climate change and their effect at sustaining, or even growing, a system so violently threatening to the lives of so many, that we must take sides. Even as some scholars may see important opportunities for interventions in the form of 'green' design and meaningful environmental work opportunities for prisoners, we caution against embracing 'greening justice' as a kind of normative goal. Lynch's (2007: 213) call for 'small, localized, and environmentally friendly prisons' operated on sustainable energy sources and focussed on opportunities for growth and addressing needs is all well and good, provided there are far fewer of them, and that we are actually working towards eventually ending our reliance on incarceration. In other words, this model should be embraced if it contributes to decreasing our environmental footprint *primarily by* shrinking the carceral state out of existence.

Jewkes and Moran (2015: 453) have argued recently that '"sustainability" has already become deeply embedded in corporate discourse in response to standards, policies and mandates, and as a means to communicate specific messages about the purpose and functioning of the correctional complex'. As such, we contend that abolition remain a normative goal of our work, and argue for a vision of sustainability and green justice accountable to, and rooted in, redistributive, racial, gender and sexual justice. Indeed, we suggest that in the space opened up by a critique of the 'green justice' movement is the recognition of the importance of a vision and strategy that understands climate justice as foundational to abolition democracy (Davis and Mendieta 2005)—and abolition democracy as the goal toward which climate justice strives. Put another way, and recognising that the loss of the commons and the rise of the prison are historically intertwined, notions of transformative justice must include the repair of the commons, as well as the restoration of freedom to the prisoner. 'Since the commons and liberation are inseparable', Linebaugh (2014, 2) argues, 'the abolition of privatized, capitalist property and the abolition of prison must go together'.

Even as greenwashing justice may be a new development riding the wave of ecological justice activism and concern over climate change, there is a long history between imprisonment and environment. Of course, historians of convict leasing have pointed out the necessity of prisoner labour to the re-establishment of the southern economy and racial state, very much including agricultural labour. Indeed, as Oshinsky (1996, 137) reminds us, the first penitentiary in the south, Parchman Farm, 'looked like a typical Delta plantation, with cattle barns, vegetable gardens, mules dotting the landscape, and cotton rows stretching for miles'. In the north, scholars of the early juvenile justice system have found some of the earliest logic and discourse of the current 'greening justice' movement. In their histories of the juvenile justice system, they found that a common justification for imprisoning youth in rural communities was the inherent benefits that particular kinds of carceral institutions, such as cottages, would have in particular places—rural communities. As Platt (1969: 65) writes in *The Child Savers*, 'The aim of penal reformers was not merely to use the countryside for teaching agricultural skills. The confrontation between depraved delinquents and unspoiled nature was intended to have a spiritual and regenerative effect'.

In a context of penal intensification, some scholars of punishment have drawn from concepts often associated with environmental pollution to consider the broader work of prisons in managing relative surplus populations. Specifically, these scholars suggest the importance of the concept of 'social waste' or 'toxic waste' (e.g., Simon 1993, 2007; also see Bauman 2004) in work on incarceration. As Davis (2003: 16) has argued, 'the prison has become a black hole into which the detritus of contemporary capitalism is deposited'. In the next section, we note places where communities under the most acute threats from criminalisation and mass incarceration have made such links, forming important political coalitions with those experiencing the environmental threats of jail and prison placement.

Abolitionism, social and ecological justice: taking the fight to toxic jails and prisons

The fight against toxic prisons and jails is not new, with the first anti-prison environmental campaigns rising out of grassroots environmental justice (EJ) organisations. The momentum and important victories of recent years, spearheaded by members of the radical environmental movement, have derived direct inspiration from the political work occurring in California in the 1990s and early 2000s against the proposed Delano II state prison led by Madres del Este de Los Angeles (MELA) and Critical Resistance (Pellow 2016: 11–15). As documented by long-time environmental justice and anti-prison activists, Braz and Gilmore (2006), the work in the Central Valley—otherwise known as 'prison alley'—showcases the intimate links between threats traditionally understood as environmental—air pollution, toxic waste dumping, pesticide-riddled water tables—and those putatively non-environmental (i.e., prisons and police). In fact, Braz and Gilmore (2006) observed that among residents of the Central Valley, these threats are all understood as hazards from and to the local environment. As such, the work against pollution and pesticides can operate in coalition with the work against police and prisons to form an expansive movement against the broad dangers to the social ecology of communities.

Indeed, Braz and Gilmore (2006) describe the inspiring and at times painful work of building a coalition, and subsequently turning the coalition into a movement. The success of that movement in slowing prison construction significantly, along with forging a new common sense around the importance of allying environmental justice and anti-prison organising, hinged on recognising the prison's harms to all communities. The authors quoted scholar and activist Laura Pulido at the 'Joining Forces: Environmental Justice and the Fight Against Prison Expansion' conference organised by several groups, noting that 'we need to consider prisons as part of the landscape of everyday life, not something "out there" or removed. Even though they may be in rural communities, they involve all of us' (Braz and Gilmore 2006: 106). The authors argue that

> the Delano II campaign demonstrates that the use of a combined grassroots political and legal strategy, borrowing from and interweaving with the environmental justice movement, holds promise in moving a wide range of groups and individuals from education and awareness to involvement to mobilization against the many ill effects of imprisonment.
>
> *(Braz and Gilmore 2006: 106)*

But prisons, the broader carceral state and abolitionism have been largely underexplored in the EJ literature and movement to date. Perhaps this is a function of the EJ movement's historical focus on reformist reform tactics, 'look[ing] to the state and capital to accommodate demands via legislation, institutional reforms and other policy concessions' (Pellow 2016: 4). But, as Pellow (2016: 4) points out, 'such an approach leaves intact the very power structures that produced environmental injustice in the first place'. Indeed, green criminologists may draw inspiration and parallels from Pellow's (2016) anarchist-inspired challenge to EJ studies to 'push our analyses and actions beyond the human, the state, and capital via a broad anti-authoritarian perspective' (see also Pellow, this volume, Chapter 32).

It is from such anti-authoritarian and explicitly radical environmentalist roots that the largest current American-based effort to organise resistance around the intersections of incarceration and the environment has grown since 2015—the Campaign to Fight Toxic Prisons (FTP). As predicted by Braz and Gilmore (2006: 106) these intersections have proven fertile ground for cross-movement coalition building and grassroots campaign development. At the time of writing, FTP has blossomed into a national collective composed of radical environmentalists, environmental justice activists, academics, anarchists, communists, journalists and lawyers, along with former and current prisoners, and their loved ones. For the purpose of this chapter, we focus on the roots of FTP and its longest-running campaign against the construction of United States Penitentiary (USP) Letcher in Eastern Kentucky.

FTP traces its lineage directly from such de-centralised direct-action environmental groups as the Earth Liberation Front (ELF) and Earth First!, conceptualising its work as 'the radical environmental movement's contribution to prison abolition organizing' (Tsolkas 2016). It is telling that this contribution comes after a period of intense state-targeting of radical environmentalists. Capitalising on the United States post-11 September 2001 'War on Terror' rhetoric and its vastly expanded powers under the USA PATRIOT Act, the US Federal Bureau of Investigations (FBI) has justified both legal and illegal monitoring, infiltration, entrapment and incarceration of scores of radical environmentalists. This period, beginning with the 2002 Congressional hearings on 'The Threat of Eco-Terrorism' and continuing to the present day, marks the start of what environmentalists have deemed the FBI's 'Green Scare' initiative in which it employs the language of 'extremism' and 'terrorism' to redefine a broad range of environmental activist tactics, which federal judges can now apply as anti-terrorism sentence 'enhancements' to greatly increase the time the convicted spend behind bars (see Best and Nocella 2004; Laurendeau and Van Brunschot 2007; Tsolkas 2015).

Both imprisoned and non-incarcerated members of the radical environmental movement, who were engaged in eco-prisoner support during this period, facilitated by letters passing across prison walls, have turned their focus slowly towards the prison itself as a site of radical environmental struggle and critique. Through letters between former ELF prisoner Daniel McGowan during his time incarcerated in the Communications Management Unit at USP Marion and former *Earth First! Journal* editor Panagioti Tsolkas, the initial ideas that would turn into both the Human Rights Defense Center's (HRDC) Prison Ecology Project and FTP were planted (Panagioti Tsolkas, personal communication, 7 October 2015; McGowan 2016; Tsolkas 2015).

Honouring this legacy of inside-outside organising, FTP actively promotes 11 June as the International Day of Solidarity With Long-Term Anarchist Prisoners by organising its national gathering, the annual Fight Toxic Prisons Convergence, either on or during the weekends adjacent to 11 June to reinforce the J11 Organizing Collective's efforts. The 2016 Washington, DC, 2017 Denton, TX, and 2018 Pittsburgh, PA, national FTP Convergences each drew between 200–300 activists from a broad range of movement backgrounds, including animal liberation, environmental justice, prison abolition and radical environmentalism, as well as labour unions, political prisoner support committees and Black, Indigenous, Undocumented, Trans and Queer organisers (FTP 2017). In a commitment to advocating more confrontational forms of political engagement that are hallmarks of the radical environmental movement, each FTP Convergence has ended with a day of direct action and protest against either national or regional targets. The 2018 FTP Convergence, for example, culminated in an un-permitted but heavily policed march through the streets of Pittsburgh with demonstrations at the EQT Corporation, 'a major oil and gas company notorious for poisoning drinking water supplies across rural Appalachia', and the NRG Energy Center

> calling attention to the health and human rights atrocities occurring at SCI Fayette … built in 2003, directly on top of a toxic coal ash dump that has been in operation for

> decades, receiving millions of tons of waste from coal processing companies, including NRG.
>
> *(FTP 2018)*

FTP's national convergences have thus provided a radical hub at the intersections of prisons and the environment that resonates with a diverse range of movements.

FTP itself is becoming an increasingly hybrid collective. Half of FTP's advisory committee are current or former prisoners, including 'jail house environmentalist' Bryant Arroyo who organised prisoners at SCI Mahanoy and successfully stopped an $800 million coal plant (Pellow 2017: 15). Four advisory committee members—Daniel McGowan, Eric McDavid, Marius Mason and Jeremy Hammond—are current and former long-term anarchist prisoners, three of whom were incarcerated due to ELF-related charges. Finally, the advisory committee includes leading EJ scholar Dr David Pellow, a contributor to this volume, who founded the Prison Environmental Justice Project in 2015 at the University of California Santa Barbara in coordination with FTP and HRDC (Pellow 2017), and the widely recognised 'father of environmental justice', Dr Robert Bullard (Bullard 1983, 1990a, 1990b).

The momentum and capacity provided by this broad base of engagement has allowed FTP to pursue a number of different campaigns. Here, we focus on the largest and longest campaign in which the FTP has engaged against the only currently proposed Federal US prison—a 1,200-bed supermax slated to be built on top of a mountaintop removal site in Letcher County, KY, at a cost of $510 million. This site is within two kilometres downstream from a toxic coal slurry impoundment and active strip mine to the northeast; approximately two kilometres to the west is one of the last three old-growth forests in the state, the Lilley Cornett Woods (HRDC 2015b; Mazurek 2015; Schept 2017).

Nationally, despite reductions in the federal prison population, including a 14 per cent decrease since its peak in 2013, federal prisons continue to be built (Ghandnoosh 2017; United States Courts 2017). Central Appalachia, particularly in Eastern Kentucky, continues to be one of the fastest-growing prison construction sites in the country (Beale 1998; Schept 2014, 2017; Schept and Mazurek 2017). This is largely due to the confluence of a number of problems: the precipitous decline of coal jobs, largely due to mechanisation; the particular form mechanisation has taken, which creates flat land necessary for prisons to be imagined and built; and a well-crafted narrative that positions prisons as regional economic saviours. Of the 16 federal, state and private prisons in Central Appalachia, four of them are built on mountaintop removal sites, while others are built on old deep mining sites.[3] Nine of these prisons are located in the poorest 10 per cent of counties in the United States and two are located in counties among the poorest 10–25 per cent (Appalachian Regional Commission 2016).

Hal Rogers, the US Representative for Kentucky's 5th congressional district, has represented this region of Eastern Kentucky since 1981, and specifically, through his role as Chair of the House Appropriations Committee (2011–2017), helped to ensure the building of three federal prisons in his district; USP Letcher would be the fourth. Also worth noting is that coal contributions to his campaign (Arch Coal—$43,500 from 2004–2016) have remained lower than contributions from prison profiteers Corrections Corporation of America, now CoreCivic ($51,100 from 2002–2012), and the GEO Group, Inc. ($15,000 in 2006, 2012 and 2014) (see Center for Responsive Politics 2016). Meanwhile, studies indicate that this form of 'carceral Keynesianism' (Davis 1998: 416; see also Gilmore 1999, 2007)—or the building of prisons to stimulate rural economies—is a dubious strategy for economic development. Scholars examining national, state and Appalachian contexts have found significant evidence of net zero or net negative impacts on local economies (Hooks, Mosher,

Genter, Rotolo and Lobao 2010; King, Mauer and Huling 2003; Perdue and Sanchagrin 2016; Ryerson 2013).

FTP drew its tactical inspiration directly from MELA's fight against Delano II in that their primary strategy has been to delay the Federal Bureau of Prisons (BOP) Environmental Impact Statement (EIS) process required by federal law. This particular tactic is quite familiar to radical environmentalists and is referred to as 'paperwrenching', with a section of the *Earth First! Direct Action Manual* devoted to it (DAM Collective 2015: 283–289). Working directly with local organisers from the Letcher Governance Project, as well as lawyers from the Abolitionist Law Center and HRDC, FTP's paperwrenching strategy against the Letcher prison is not to engage with the processes of the state with the goal of reformist reform, but rather to engage with the state in such a way that slows down the overall construction process, thus allowing for more time to engage in oppositional and non-reformist grassroots and national organising.

With the goal of buying time, the tactic of paperwrenching has proven particularly effective. At the time that the Bureau of Prisons handed down its Record of Decision on 30 March 2018, which formally ended the EIS process and moved the project toward construction (US DOJ 2018), paperwrenching had succeeded in delaying the prison by 36 months since the first EIS challenge was submitted to the BOP on 30 March 2015 during the first EIS public comment period (HRDC 2015a). The BOP released the supposedly Final EIS in July 2015 (US DOJ 2015), followed by a Revised Final EIS in March 2016 (US DOJ 2016), a Draft Supplemental Revised Final EIS in May 2017 (US DOJ 2017a), and a Final Supplemental Revised Final EIS in November 2017 (US DOJ 2017b). At every stage of the EIS process where public comments were accepted, FTP and allied organisations submitted extensive critiques of the EIS under the heading of the HRDC (see Human Rights Defense Center 2015a, 2015b; Mazurek 2015), as well as organising 1,000 individual comments in opposition to the March 2016 EIS, and over 6,000 individual comments to the November 2017 EIS (see Posner 2017). Cardno, the company hired by the BOP to complete the EIS, engaged in a particular tactic worthy of note in regards to the individual opposition comments. That is, Cardno engaged in a 'dilution of dissent' in that they counted public comments in favour of the prison as individual comments for inclusion within the EIS (even comments with no signatures), while at the same time counting public comments critical of the prison as a single statement with multiple signatories.

An additional tactic was pursued in a meeting held with the United States Environmental Protection Agency (EPA) in Washington, DC, on 10 June 2016, focussing on the environmental justice implications of prisons. At the meeting, FTP and HRDC members argued that USP Letcher should not be allowed to be built because potential prisoners would be discriminated against unfairly in regards to federal EJ policy—specifically, Executive Order 12,898, which mandates that 'each Federal agency makes achieving environmental justice part of its mission by identifying and addressing, as appropriate, disproportionately high and adverse human health or environmental effects of its programmes, policies and activities on minority populations and low-income populations', as well as Title VI of the Civil Rights Act, which is meant to protect minority populations from discrimination. It was FTP and HRDC's argument that due to the federal criminal justice system being disproportionately Black, Latino and poor, and that USP Letcher would be located on top of a mountaintop removal site and less than two kilometres from an active strip mine and coal slurry impoundment, the prison would generate much higher risks of exposure to carcinogens and other environmental toxins, thus representing a clear violation of federal EJ and civil rights policy. EPA officials, however, claimed that because the prison was not yet built, it was therefore impossible to know if the risk to the population that would eventually reside in it would, indeed, be 'disproportionate' and therefore 'discriminatory' (Panagioti Tsolkas, personal communication, 10 June 2016)—an institutional technique of neutralisation reminiscent of classic 'denial of the victim' justifications (Cohen 2001; see also Kramer and Bradshaw, this volume, Chapter 9; Wyatt and Brisman 2017).

Three days after this EPA meeting, at the culmination of the first national FTP Convergence in Washington, DC, FTP members shut down the Federal BOP office in a protest against USP Letcher and the carceral state by blockading its main employee parking garage all morning. The demonstration then proceeded through the streets of the capital and ended with a blockade at the intersection in front of both the Department of Justice and FBI headquarters to further reinforce J11 solidarity. Chants included 'Burn prisons, not coal!' and 'Break the locks, no more cops!', while banners displayed 'Toxic Prisons = Death Sentence', 'Prison Abolition Now', and solidarity with numerous anarchist, Black liberation and Indigenous liberation political prisoners (Mazurek 2016).

It is through such demonstrations, convergences and campaigns that FTP actively rejects the neoliberal 'green' agenda pushing carceral expansion, as described by Jewkes and Moran (2015). This conflict reveals the prison itself, echoing Ferrell (2003: 79), as 'cultural space' subject to 'contested public meaning'. Of particular relevance here, then, is not only what green 'means' to established 'criminal justice' systems, but also the inverse: what does it mean to be 'green' when it comes to prisons? The anthropocentric approach outlined by Jewkes and Moran (2015) is complicit in the failings of 'sustainable development' (Halsey and White 1998; see also Schept and Mazurek 2017: 177–179 in relation to prisons), and stands in fundamental conflict with the biocentric radical abolitionist green agenda of the Earth First!—and ELF-derived networks working with FTP. Meanwhile, the EJ movement is arguably still developing a nascent ecocentric or potentially biocentric green agenda in regards to prisons (Pellow 2016, 2017, this volume, Chapter 32). In an instructive and inspiring development, a coalition of actors forced the BOP to withdraw the Record of Decision for USP Letcher, indefinitely postponing the prison. The collaboration between FTP, movement lawyers, incarcerated plaintiffs and organisers based in Letcher County suggests a bright future for work at the intersections of environmental justice, abolition and just economic transition. Brisman and South (2014: 90) would argue that the prison, then, is a prime site for green cultural criminology to explore, particularly in terms of "the various forms which resistance to this complex web of social control may take" (quoting Ferrell and Webster 1999: 12). Thus, the radical environmental prison abolition organising of FTP, which we have considered only briefly, serves as a key example of the 'widening horizons of resistance within late modernity' (Ferrell, Hayward and Young 2015: 60).

A polemical position against 'greening justice', coupled with an analytical position that considers incarceration and pollution together, can forge new spaces of politics. If we understand prisons in the Central Valley and Eastern Kentucky as providing what Gilmore (2007) calls 'a spatial fix' for the complex social problems of globalising racial capitalism—and not necessarily as institutions first and last about 'crime' and punishment—then potential pathways emerge to broaden the scope of actors involved in prison abolition struggles to include those leading struggles against the further destruction of our environment.

Conclusion

In contexts where an end to imprisonment seems a distant possibility, one may be inclined to hold on to the possibility that the stated shift towards 'greening' confinement may have some benefits. Perhaps new and 'greener' carceral spaces have 'the capacity to change the emotional geography' of imprisonment for both captives and captors alike (White and Graham 2015: 852), including offering basic improvements such as enhancing the mood within institutions via greater exposure to natural light (White and Graham 2015: 854). It is also possible that the new 'green' jails and prisons are incorporating opportunities for prisoners to access vocational training and post-prison job opportunities in the 'green' economy as is sometimes the case elsewhere, while sustainability—in environmental terms as opposed to carceral ones—is becoming a guiding principle of 'correctional' work (Graham and White 2015). These are all elements of new penal infrastructure development that merit further research.

Having said this, even if one found that the rhetoric matched the reality on the ground, a key question remains: if a new 'green' jail or prison is also bigger—that is, incarcerates more prisoners than the one it replaces—is such carceral expansion ever a step in the right direction? Is building facilities housing more human beings who feel better while confined and have access to 'green' job training, along with administrators and staff whose work is guided by a deep concern for the environment, anything more than an exercise in attenuating the depth of carceral violence experienced by individual prisoners as it extends its reach to more people, and, by connection, their families and communities?

One could look on the bright side and declare that '"good" things can indeed emerge from "bad" places and troubling histories' (Graham and White 2015: 859), but carceral expansion takes us *further* from reformist goals of penal moderation (Loader 2010), and certainly further from our abolitionist objective of realising communities and a world without cages for humans (Mazurek 2015; Piché, 2014; Schept 2015). If 'the most sustainable building is the one that is never built' (White and Graham 2015: 860; also see Jewkes and Moran 2015), then the shift towards 'greening' incarceration is unlikely to translate into its future demise, particularly when advocates of caging are successfully co-opting discourses of sustainability to advance 'penal expansionism', as Graham and White (2015: 860) fear. The cases we have discussed above from Canada and the United States should serve as a cautionary tale for advocates of 'greening justice', while also providing an impetus for more individuals to become involved in campaigns like FTP to resist, rather than sustain, carceral states and the injustices they perpetrate and perpetuate.

Notes

1 The authors contributed equally to this chapter.

2 The jurisdictions appear in order from east to west (Nova Scotia is farther east than New Brunswick, which is farther east than Quebec, and so on). The facilities in each jurisdiction are also listed from east to west. Thus, for example, the New Elgin-Middlesex Intermittent Centre (in London, Ontario) is farther east than the South West Detention Centre (Windsor, Ontario).

3 According to the Appalachian Regional Commission (ARC), Central Appalachia is one of the five sub-regions of Appalachia and consists of the entirety of eastern Kentucky plus southwestern Virginia, western West Virginia and northeastern Tennessee. Some scholars examining prison growth in the region have expanded the boundaries of Central Appalachia to include North Central and South Central, two other sub-regions identified by the ARC. This more capacious conception of 'Central Appalachia' brings the number of prisons in the region to 29.

References

Appalachian Regional Commission. 2016. *County Economic Status in Appalachia, Fiscal Year 2016*. Available at: https://arc.gov/assets/maps/related/County-Economic-Status_FY2016_Map.pdf.

Bauman, Z. 2004. *Wasted Lives: Modernity and Its Outcasts*. Cambridge: Polity Press.

Beale, Calvin L. 1998. 'Rural Prisons: An Update,' *Rural Development Perspectives*, 11(2): 25–27.

Ben-Moshe, L. 2013. 'The Tension between abolition and reform,' in Mecke Nagel and Anthony J. Nocella II (eds.) *The End of Prisons: Reflections from the Decarceration Movement*, pp. 83–92. Amsterdam and New York: Rodopi Press.

Best, S., and A. J. Nocella II (eds.) 2004. *Terrorists or Freedom Fighters? Reflections on the Liberation of Animals*. New York: Lantern Books.

Bittle, S. 2012. *Still Dying for a Living: Corporate Criminal Liability After the Westray Mine Disaster*. Vancouver: UBC Press.

Braz, R., and Gilmore, C. 2006. 'Joining forces: Prisons and environmental justice in recent california organizing,' *Radical History Review*, 86: 95–111.

Brisman, A., and South, N. 2014. *Green Cultural Criminology: Construction of Environmental Harm, Consumerism, and Resistance to Ecocide*. London: Routledge.

Brisman, A. 2011. 'Brundtland Commission,' in D. Chatterjee (ed.) *Encyclopedia of Global Justice*, Vol. 1, pp. 91–92. Heidelberg, Germany: Springer.

Brisman, A. 2013. 'Not a bedtime story: Climate Change, neoliberalism and the future of the arctic,' *Michigan State International Law Review*, 22(1): 241–289.

Bullard, Robert. 1983. 'Solid waste sites and the houston black community,' *Social Inquiry*, 53: 273–284.

Bullard, R. 1990a. *Dumping in Dixie: Race, Class, and Environmental Quality*. Boulder, CO: Westview Press.

Bullard, R. 1990b. 'Ecological inequities and the new south: Black communities under siege,' *Journal of Ethnic Studies*, 17(4): 101–115.

Center for Responsive Politics. 2016. *Rep. Hal Rogers- Kentucky District 05- Contributors*. Available at: https://opensecrets.org/members-of-congress/contributors?cid=N00003473&cycle=2018.

Cohen, S. 2001. *States of Denial: Knowing about Atrocities and Suffering*. New York: Polity Press.

DAM Collective. 2015. *Earth First! Direct Action Manual*, 3rd ed. Lake Worth, FL: Earth First! Journal.

Davis, A. Y. 2003. *Are Prisons Obsolete?* New York: Seven Stories Press.

Davis, A. Y., and Mendieta, E. 2005. *Abolition Democracy: Beyond Empire, Prisons, and Torture*. New York: Seven Stories Press.

Davis, M. 1998. *Ecology of Fear: Los Angeles and the Imagination of Disaster*. New York: Henry Holt.

Feldbaum, M., Greene, F., Kirschenbaum, S., Mukamal, D., Welsh, M., and Pinderhughes, R. 2011. *The Greening of Corrections: Creating a Sustainable System*. Washington, DC: National Institute of Corrections.

Ferrell, J. 2003. 'Cultural criminology,' in M. D. Schwartz and S. Hatty (eds) *Controversies in Critical Criminology*, pp. 71–84. Cincinnati: Anderson Publishing Company.

Ferrell, J., Hayward, K., and Young, J. 2015. *Cultural Criminology: An Invitation*. 2nd edition. London: Sage.

Ferrell, J. and Websdale, N. 1999. 'Materials for making trouble'. in J. Ferrell and N. Websdale, (eds.) *Making Trouble: Cultural Constructions of Crime, Deviance, and Control*, pp. 3–21. Hawthorne, NY: Aldine de Gruyter.

Fight Toxic Prisons. 2017. 'Following up on the FTP 2017 Convergence'. *The Campaign to Fight Toxic Prisons – June 29*. Available at: www.fighttoxicprisons.wordpress.com/2017/06/29/following-up-on-the-ftp-2017-convergence/.

Fight Toxic Prisons. 2018. 'Prison Abolitionists Rally for Human and Environmental Health at Pittsburgh Polluter's Offices'. *The Campaign to Fight Toxic Prisons* –June 11. Available at: www.fighttoxicprisons.wordpress.com/2018/06/11/prison-abolitionists-rally-for-human-and-environmental-health-at-pittsburgh-polluters-offices/.

Ghandnoosh, Nazgol. 2017. *Policy Brief: Federal Prisons at a Crossroads*. Washington, DC: The Sentencing Project.

Gilmore, R. W. 1999. 'Globalization and U.S. Prison Growth: From Military Keynesianism to Post-Keynesian Militarism,' *Race and Class*, 40(2–3): 171–188.

Gilmore, R. W. 2007. *Golden Gulag: Prisons, Surplus, Crisis, and Opposition in Globalizing California*. Berkeley, CA: University of California Press.

Gorz, André. 1967. *Strategy for Labor: A Radical Proposal*. Boston: Beacon Press.

Graham, H., and R. White. 2015. *Innovative Justice*. London: Routledge.

Halsey, M., and R. White. 1998. 'Crime, Ecophilosophy and Environmental Harm,' *Theoretical Criminology*, 2(3): 345–371.

Hooks, G., Clayton, M., Shaun, G., Thomas, R, and Linda, L. 2010. 'Revisiting the impact of prison building on job growth: Education, incarceration, and county-level employment, 1976–2004,' *Social Science Quarterly*, 91(1): 228–244.

Human Rights Defense Center. 2015a. 'Comment Bureau of Prisons Proposed USP/FPC Letcher County Draft Environmental Impact Statement,' Lake Worth (FL): HRDC Prison Ecology Project. Available at: https://prisonlegalnews.org/media/publications/Letcher%20Co%20KY%20HRDC%20comment%20on%20BOP%20Draft%20EIS%203-30-15.pdf.

Human Rights Defense Center. 2015b. 'Comment Bureau of Prisons Proposed USP/FPC Letcher County Final Environmental Impact Statement,' Lake Worth (FL): HRDC Prison Ecology Project. Available at: https://prisonlegalnews.org/media/publications/Final%20Letcher%20Co%20KY%20HRDC%20comment%20on%20BOP%20Final%20EIS%208-31-15.pdf.

Jensen, D. 2009. 'Forget shorter showers: Why personal change does not equal political change,' *Orion Magazine*. Available at: https://orionmagazine.org/article/forget-shorter-showers/.

Jewkes, Y., and Moran, D. 2015. 'The Paradox of the "Green" Prison: Sustaining the Environment or Sustaining the Penal Complex,' *Theoretical Criminology*, 19(4): 451–469.

King, R. S., Mauer, M., and Huling, T. 2003. *Big Prisons, Small Towns: Prison in Rural America*. Washington, DC: The Sentencing Project.

Knopp, F. H., Boward, B., Brach, M. J., Christianson, S., Largen, M. A., Lewin, J., Lugo, J., Morris, M., and Newton, W. 2005[1976]. *Instead of Prisons: A Handbook for Abolitionists*. Oakland, CA: Critical Resitance.

Laurendeau, J., and Van Brunschot, E. G. 2007. '"Home-grown Brand of Al Qaeda": Moral Panics and the Construction of "Eco-terrorism",' *International Journal of Crime, Criminal Justice and Law*, 2(1): 105–123.

Linebaugh, P. 2014. *Stop, Thief! The Commons, Enclosure and Resistance*. Oakland, CA: PM Press.

Little, P. 2015. 'Sustainability Science and Education in the Neoliberal Ecoprison,' *Environmental Education Research*, 21(3): 365–377.

Loader, I. 2010. 'For Penal Moderation,' *Theoretical Criminology*, 14(3): 349–367.

Lynch, M. and Stretesky, P. 2003. 'The Meaning of Green: Contrasting Criminological Perspectives,' *Theoretical Criminology*, 7(2): 217–238.

Lynch, M. 2007. *Big Prisons, Big Dreams: Crime and the Failure of America's Penal System*. New Brunswick, NJ: Rutgers University Press.

Mathiesen, T. 1990. *Prison on Trial*. London: Sage.

Mazurek, J. 2015. 'Between Sludge Pond and Old Growth: A Look at Glaring Oversights in the Proposal for New Federal Prison in Eastern Kentucky,' *Earth First! Journal*, 35(4): 19–21.

Mazurek, J. 2016. *Fight Toxic Prisons Convergence and Day of Action*. Photodocumentary. [Digital Images]. Washington, DC: The Campaign to Fight Toxic Prisons. Available at: https://fighttoxicprisons.wordpress.com/2016/06/28/june-13th-d-c-action-photos/.

McGowan, D. 2016. 'Defending the earth & abolishing prisons: Voices from the struggle,' in David A. Clarke School of Law June 11. *Fight Toxic Prisons Convergence*. Washington, DC: University of the District of Columbia.

Mol, A. P. J. 2010. 'Ecological Modernization as a Social Theory of Environmental Reform,' in M. R. Redclift and G. Woodgate (eds.) *The International Handbook of Environmental Sociology*. Second Edition, pp. 63–76. Cheltenham, UK: Edward Elgar Publishing.

Multnomah County Sherriff's Office. 2012. 'County jails go green, save money through new sustainable jail project,' Portland: Multnomah County April 20. Available at: https://multco.us/communications/news/county-jails-go-green-save-money-through-new-sustainable-jail-project.

New Brunswick Supply and Services. 2009. Obtained through provincial Right to Information request (no file number). Fredericton: Government of New Brunswick.

New Brunswick Supply and Services/Public Safety. 2009. 'Province unveils design plans for $16.3-million correctional centre in Dalhousie,' Fredericton: Government of New Brunswick May 11. Available at: http://gnb.ca/cnb/news/ss/2009e0659ss.htm.

Oshinsky, D. 1996. *Worse than Slavery: Parchman Farm and the Ordeal of Jim Crow Justice*. New York: Free Press.

Pellow, D. 2016. 'Toward a critical environmental justice studies: Black lives matter as an environmental justice challenge,' *Du Bois Review: Social Science Research on Race*, 13(2): 1–16.

Pellow, D. 2017. 'Some recent history on prison environmental justice struggles,' in D. Pellow (ed.) *Exposing Deliberate Indifference: The Struggle for Social and Environmental Justice in America's Prisons, Jails,*

Detention Centers, and Concentration Camps, pp. 11–15. University of California Santa Barbara: The Prison Environmental Justice Project.

Perdue, R. T. and Sanchagrin, K. 2016. 'Imprisoning appalachia: The socio-economic impacts of rural prison development,' *Journal of Appalachian Studies*, 22(2): 58–71.

Piché, J., Kleuskens, S. and Walby, K. 2017. 'The Front and Back Stages of Carceral Expansion Marketing in Canada,' *Contemporary Justice Review*, 20(1): 26–50.

Piché, J. 2014. 'A contradictory and finishing state: Explaining recent prison capacity expansion in canada's provinces and territories,' *Champ pénal/Penal Field*, Vol. XII, 26 pages.

Platt, T. 1969. *The Child Savers: The Invention of Delinquency*. Chicago, IL: University of Chicago Press.

Posner, E. H. 2017. 'Public comment: Final supplemental revised environment impact statement proposed united states penitentiary and federal prison camp,' New Orleans: Abolitionist Law Center. Available at: https://fighttoxicprisons.files.wordpress.com/2017/11/alc-comments-fseis-final.pdf.

Prison Ecology Project. 2015. 'GEO group's gulags grasping for green approval'. *Nation Inside*. Available at: https://nationinside.org/campaign/prison-ecology/posts/geo-groups-gulags-grasping-for-green-approval/.

Ryerson, S. 2013. 'Speak your piece: Prison progress?' *The Daily Yonder*. Available at: www.dailyyonder.com/speak-your-piece-prison-progress/2013/02/12/5651.

Schept, J. and Mazurek, J. 2017. 'Layers of industry, landscapes of violence: Coal seams, prison walls and craft bourbon,' in J. Z. Wilson, S. Hodgkinson, J. Piché and K. Walby (eds.), *The Palgrave Handbook of Prison Tourism*, pp. 171–190. London: Palgrave Macmillan.

Schept, J. 2014. '(Un)seeing like a Prison: Countervisual Ethnography of the Carceral State,' *Theoretical Criminology*, 18(2): 198–223.

Schept, J. 2015. *Progressive Punishment: Job Loss, Jail Growth, and the Neoliberal Logic of Carceral Expansion*. New York: New York University Press.

Schept, J. 2017. 'Sunk capital, sinking prisons, stinking landfills: Landscape, ideology and the carceral state in central appalachia,' in M. Brown and E. Carrabine (eds). *Routledge International Handbook of Visual Criminology*, pp. 497–513. New York: Routledge.

Schwartzapfel, B. 2009. 'Greening the prison industrial complex,' *The New York Times* March 3. Available at: green.blogs.nytimes.com/2009/03/03greening-the-prison-industrial-complex.

Simon, J. 1993. *Poor Discipline: Parole and Social Control of the Underclass, 1890-1990*. Chicago, IL: University of Chicago Press.

Simon, J. 2007. *Governing through Crime: How the War on Crime Transformed American Democracy and Created a Culture of Fear*. Oxford: Oxford University Press.

Stohr, M. K., and Wozniak, J. F. 2014. 'The green prison,' in F. T. Cullen, C. Lero Johnson and M. K. Stohr (eds.) *The American Prison: Imagining a Different Future*, pp. 193–212. Los Angeles, CA: Sage.

Sustainability in Prisons Project [SPP]. no date. 'We bring environmental education, science, & nature into prisons,' Olympia (WA). Available at: http://sustainabilityinprisons.org/contact-us/.

Tomkins, K. 2005. 'Police, Law Enforcement and the Environment,' *Current Issues in Criminal Justice*, 16 (3): 294–306.

Tsolkas, P. 2015. 'The Ecology of a Prison Nation,' *Earth First! Journal*, 35(2): 5–8.

Tsolkas, P. 2016. 'Incarceration, justice and the planet: How the fight against toxicprisons could shape the future of environmentalism,' *Earth First! Newswire*. Available at: http://earthfirstjournal.org/newswire/2015/07/25/prisons-ecology-and-the-birth-of-an-empire/

U.S. Courts. 2017. *Policy Shifts Reduce Federal Prison Population*. April 25th. Available at: http://uscourts.gov/news/2017/04/25/policy-shifts-reduce-federal-prison-population

U.S. Department of Justice, Federal Bureau of Prisons. 2015. *Final Environmental Impact Statement for Proposed United States Penitentiary and Federal Prison Camp Letcher County, Kentucky*. Washington, DC. Available at: https://prisonlegalnews.org/media/publications/FEIS_For_Proposed_US_Penitentiary_and_Federal_Prison_Camp_July_2015.pdf.

U.S. Department of Justice, Federal Bureau of Prisons. 2016. *Revised Final Environmental Impact Statement for Proposed United States Penitentiary and Federal Prison Camp Letcher County, Kentucky*. Washington, DC. Available at: http://fbopletchercountyeis.com/Resources/Documents/2016_Revised_Final_EIS/2016_Revised_Final_EIS_USP_and_FPC_Letcher_Co_KY.pdf.

U.S. Department of Justice, Federal Bureau of Prisons. 2017a. *Draft Supplemental Revised Final Environmental Impact Statement for Proposed United States Penitentiary and Federal Prison Camp Letcher County, Kentucky*. Washington, DC. Available at: http://fbopletchercountyeis.com/Resources/Documents/

March_2017_Draft_Supplemental_Revised_Final_EIS/2017_Draft_Supplemental_RFEIS_USP_and_FPC_Letcher_Co_KY.pdf.

U.S. Department of Justice, Federal Bureau of Prisons. 2017b. *Final Supplemental Revised Final Environmental Impact Statement for Proposed United States Penitentiary and Federal Prison Camp Letcher County, Kentucky*. Washington, DC. Available at: http://fbopletchercountyeis.com/Resources/Documents/September%202017%20Final%20Supplemental%20Revised%20Final%20EIS/2017_FinalSupplementalRFEIS_USPandFPCLetcherCoKY.pdf.

U.S. Department of Justice, Federal Bureau of Prisons. 2018. *Record of Decision: Proposed United States Penitentiary and Federal Prison Camp, Letcher County, Kentucky*. Washington, DC. Available at: www.federalregister.gov/documents/2018/04/12/2018-07311/record-of-decision-proposed-united-states-penitentiary-and-federal-prison-camp-letcher-county.

White, R. and Graham, H. 2015. 'Greening justice: Examining the interfaces of criminal, social and ecological justice,' *The British Journal of Criminology*, 55(5): 845–865.

World Commission on Environment and Development. 1987. *Our Common Future*. Oxford: Oxford University Press.

Wyatt, T. and Brisman, A. 2017. 'The role of denial in the "theft of nature": A comparison of biopiracy and climate change,' *Critical Criminology: An International Journal*, 25(3): 325–341. DOI: 10.1007/s10612-016-9344-5. FirstOnline: September 14 2016. Available at: http://link.springer.com/article/10.1007/s10612-016-9344-5.

Part III

Region-specific problems

Some case studies

15

The Amazon Rainforest

A green criminological perspective

Tim Boekhout van Solinge

Introduction: crime and violence on the frontier in the Brazilian Amazon

The Amazon Rainforest, by far the planet's largest tropical rainforest, stretches over nine countries in South America. Two-thirds of the Amazon Rainforest is located within the borders of Brazil. Since the 1960s, around 80 per cent of all Amazonian deforestation has occurred in Brazil (Malhi et al. 2008: 169). In the Brazil Amazon itself, some 20 per cent has been deforested since the late 1960s. While Brazilian policy makers often emphasise *the reduction* in annual forest loss in the Amazon in comparison with the 1980s, 1990s and early 2000s, Brazil still is, by far, the world's leading country in terms of total forest loss; in 2017, for example, worldwide forest loss occurred at the speed of 40 football pitches per minute and in Brazil alone, Amazonian rainforest disappeared with an average speed of more than one football pitch per minute (Seymour 2018; see also Boekhout van Solinge 2016: 374). A 2018 satellite data analysis by Global Forest Watch, an initiative of the non-profit organisation World Resources Institute, revealed that Brazil lost 4.5 million hectares of forest in 2017. This is three times more than the countries that ranked second and third in terms of forest loss: the Democratic Republic of Congo (1.4 million hectares) and Indonesia (1.3 million hectares), respectively.

Land conversion for creating cattle farms has been responsible for 70 per cent of deforestation in the Brazilian Amazon (Malhi et al. 2008: 169), and conversion for soy cultivation is a second and more recent cause of deforestation in the Brazilian Amazon. Both types of land conversion accompany timber extraction, and much of the logging, as well as much of the deforestation for agricultural land conversion, is illegal. Common estimates indicate that at least half, and probably 60–80 per cent of all logging and deforestation in the Brazilian Amazon is illegal (Boekhout van Solinge 2010b: 272; Lawson 2014: 24–36). Brazil's 2012 Forest Act, however, essentially legalised, via a retrospective amnesty, much of the illegal deforestation that took place prior to 2009, which makes it difficult to determine how much of the logging for timber and deforestation for agriculture can be considered illegal (Boekhout van Solinge 2015: 374).

Logging and land conversion often lead to disputes over land tenure, and frequently result in violent conflicts over land use. In Brazil's rural and forested areas, it is quite common for loggers and farmers to use gunmen, *pistoleiros*, to use or threaten to use violence against traditional communities when disagreements over land tenure occur. Other victims have included human rights and environmental activists, such as Chico Mendes in 1987, Sister Dorothy Mae Stang, S. N.D., in 2005, and João and Maria da Silva in 2011.[1] While these murders received much international attention, most of the violence that occurs in the Amazon in the context of deforestation and land conflicts happens almost unnoticed.

Since the late 1980s, more than 1,150 people have been killed in the Brazilian Amazon in disputes related to land conflicts. Only 100 cases have proceeded to court. While 80 hired gunmen have been convicted, only 15 people who ordered killings have faced charges (Brooks, 28 May 2011). In Brazil's Pará state alone, 772 human rights and forest activists were murdered between 1971 and 2004. Only three of their killers were brought to trial (Grandin 2010: 364). Hundreds have been living 'under the threat of murder because of their fight against a coalition of loggers, farmers and cattle ranchers' (Phillips 22 December 2008). *Deadly Environment*, a report by Global Witness (2014), reported that, globally, some 900 environmental protectors had been killed in the previous decade, and that about half of those murders (448) had occurred in Brazil. Two of Brazil's states stood out in the report as being particularly deadly: Pará and Mato Grosso. It is these two Brazilian states that have experienced the highest deforestation rates.[2] More recently, reports by Global Witness (2016, 2018) have confirmed that Brazil is, by far, the number one country in terms of murder of land and environmental defenders (57 murders in 2017); 80 per cent of these murders in Brazil have occurred in North Brazil, the Amazon Region (Global Witness 2018: 10).

Many of these murders occur over land conflicts, which take place on the encroaching frontier of economic—mostly agricultural—development and the creation of settlements, which slowly but consistently consume large portions of Amazon Rainforest. Brazilians from elsewhere move in and their land 'development' through deforestation leads to land conflicts with those who are already residing there. The frontier has moved from the southern Amazon, such as Brazil's Mato Grosso state, known for its large-scale deforestation for cattle and soy (noted above), into the northern Amazon, in particular to Pará state, which bears the distinction of being the state which, for years, has had the highest number of land conflicts (CPT 2009, 2011, 2018). It also has a notorious reputation for highly prevalent illegal logging, land grabbing, land conflicts, corruption, violence and lawlessness (Boekhout van Solinge 2014b; CPT 2018; Greenpeace International 2003).

While it seems easy to blame loggers and farmers for the illegal logging and violence on the Amazon frontier, one needs to ask: which actors, factors, or forces could be identified as contributing to or being responsible for the harms and crimes that are connected to deforestation in the Brazilian Amazon? This chapter focusses on the harms and crimes connected to deforestation in the Brazilian state of Pará—specifically, in the west of Pará, around the city of Santarém, at some 800 kilometres from the Amazon River's mouth, where conflicts have arisen over soy cultivation.

This chapter presents results from a project undertaken between 2010 and 2016, entitled 'Lands and Rights in Troubled Water' (or 'LAR'), funded by the Dutch NWO-WOTRO (Science for Global Development) Programme; the project focussed on understanding and mitigating conflicts over natural resources in Colombia and Brazil.[3] Under the umbrella of green criminology, different universities and NGOs, mainly from Brazil and Colombia, were involved in different activities in Colombia's Cauca valley and Brazil's Tapajós valley during this 2010 to 2016 period. This chapter discusses the situation in Brazil.

A number of different methods were employed to conduct the research described in this chapter. These included: (1) a review of the relevant literature in English and Portuguese from a variety of disciplines (e.g., archaeology, biology, criminology, history, sociology), as well as reports from public institutions, NGOs and press articles; and (2) qualitative methods, such as observations and interviews which were conducted during different research periods (of weeks and months) between 2011 and 2018—two years after the conclusion of the LAR project. Semi-structured interviews were also conducted in Santarém with representatives from NGOs, Indigenous communities and the (state and federal) prosecutor's office, in order to understand more about deforestation, soy cultivation and related crimes, such as conflict and human victimisation in the Santarém region. Overall, this chapter serves as an update to the chapter in the first edition of the *Routledge International Handbook of Green Criminology*, providing more recent information, based on annual (ethnographic) field visits and interviews between 2014 and 2018. For a discussion on this ethnographic research, see Boekhout van Solinge (2014b, 2016).

This chapter begins with a discussion of the scope and extent of deforestation worldwide before turning to an argument as to why tropical deforestation could and *should* be studied as a green criminological issue. Next, this chapter offers an historical overview of the Amazon's human population, demonstrating how Indigenous peoples, including 'uncontacted tribes', are disproportionally threatened and victimised by the deforestation frontier. It also shows, however, that Indigenous people are far from being the only human victims of deforestation. The Amazon's history of rainforest exploitations, migrations and economic development, means that the frontier of economic development is not new to the region. These earlier economic activities had a less dramatic environmental and social impact on the rainforest than more recent agricultural undertakings. This is illustrated in the case study on the recent soy frontier in Pará state. The final section discusses a criminological pilot or field experiment of GPS-supported community-based forest crime prevention. While forest-dependent Indigenous communities in the Brazilian Amazon are often victims of deforestation, as this chapter discusses, their presence in the forest also offers opportunities for better detection and prevention of illegal forest activities. This chapter concludes by trying to situate Brazil's deforestation for soy cultivation in the context of global consumer markets, thereby demonstrating that an ostensibly national or regional issue has international—indeed, worldwide—dimensions.

Deforestation as a (green) criminological theme

Logging and more generally deforestation are rarely regarded as criminological issues. Indeed, it is surprising how little criminological attention has been devoted to illegal logging, forest crime and deforestation given the extent to which it occurs across the globe. In 2009, an estimated 100 million cubic metres of illegal timber were being felled worldwide. If laid end-to-end, these illegal logs would circle the globe more than ten times (Lawson and MacFaul 2010: 102–103).

In 2012, a Rapid Response Assessment, published by UNEP and INTERPOL, on illegal logging, tax fraud and the 'laundering' of tropical rainforests, estimated the value of the annual worldwide illegal timber trade at USD $30–100 billion, representing between 10 and 30 per cent of global timber trade (Nellemann 2012). In a 2016 UNEP-INTERPOL report, the value of global forestry crimes, including corporate crimes and illegal logging, was estimated at USD $50–152 billion per year. These figures exceed those of the illegal wildlife trade, estimated at USD $7–23 billion per year, and illegal fishery, estimated at USD $11–24 billion. Forest crime is thus, according to UNEP and INTERPOL, the largest type of environmental crime (Nelleman et al. 2016). According to a report by INTERPOL (2016), illegal logging, facilitated by corruption, suppresses global timber prices by 7–16 per cent, and it costs the timber industry between USD $19–47 billion per year in lost company profits. INTERPOL (2016) estimates the annual global cost of corruption in the forestry sector to be in the order of USD $29 billion.

Although the world's largest forest, the taiga forest of Russian Siberia, suffers severely from illegal logging (Khatchadourian 2008), illegal logging is particularly prevalent in tropical regions. In many tropical countries with substantial areas of rainforests, a large part of all logging is illegal (Boekhout van Solinge 2008a, 2008b, 2014a; Lawson 2014). In some of these countries, illegal logging constitutes between 50 and 90 per cent of all logging operations (Oldfield 2005: 124; Goncalves, Panjer, Greenberg and Magrath 2012: 2). While timber extraction is a major driver of deforestation, in some places land conversion for agriculture is a more important cause of (illegal) deforestation. As mentioned earlier, in the Brazilian Amazon as a whole, between 60–80 per cent of all deforestation has been illegal (Lawson 2014: 24–36).

While deforestation in the Brazilian Amazon has decreased substantially over the last few years in comparison with previous decades (see, e.g., Boekhout van Solinge 2016), the official data from these last years still point at an area of around 5,000 km^2 that is deforested annually in the Brazilian part of the Amazon.[4] If one considers that much of the selective logging and some of the smaller-scale deforestation is not incorporated in these figures (see, e.g., Asner et al. 2005), the real figures and rates of deforestation may be substantially higher.

Areas or countries with very large tropical rainforests, such as the Earth's three largest tropical and equatorial rainforests—the Amazon (mainly Brazil), Central Africa (mainly the Democratic Republic of Congo) and South East Asia (mainly Indonesia)—are particularly vulnerable to illegal deforestation. Considering their sheer size, relatively low population densities and limited governmental presence (which is both a feature of their respective sizes and a result of weak governance), protecting these forests has proven challenging. The combination of low levels of law enforcement, high levels of corruption and an abundance of natural resources has further exacerbated the difficulties of protecting these forests and has made them even more susceptible to illegal extraction (Kolstad and Søreide 2009: 214).

Such limited risk is coupled with high reward. Indeed, the profits for illegal logging are significant. In a 2012 World Bank report, the illicit earnings of illegal logging were estimated at approximately USD$10–15 billion annually worldwide, with underpayment of royalties and taxes on legally sanctioned logging amounting to an additional US$5 billion (Goncalves, Panjer, Greenberg and Magrath 2012: 1).

A further reason for studying tropical deforestation from a criminological perspective is deforestation-related violence. As noted at the outset, the Brazilian Amazon has been the site of significant deforestation-related violence. Such violence is not peculiar to the Brazilian Amazon, however. The Peruvian Amazon has experienced outbreaks of state violence against Indians protesting against large-scale rainforest exploitation (Boekhout van Solinge 2010a: 20–26). In the other two largest tropical rainforests, the Congo basin and the Indonesian archipelago, a strong relationship between deforestation and violence also exists (Boekhout van Solinge 2014a, 2014b; French 2009; Tsing 2005; UNSC 2001).

The high levels of illegal logging, illicit earnings and violence associated with deforestation render it an appropriate subject of study from a conventional criminological perspective. It can, however, be studied even more fruitfully from a green criminological perspective, which frequently takes harm as a point of departure. The harmfulness of deforestation, especially in the tropics, can be established with ease, for humans and nonhumans, now and in the future.

Indeed, tropical rainforests are the most biodiverse ecosystems. Biologist Edward Wilson (2002: 59) calls them the headquarters of global diversity: 'Although they cover only about six per cent of the land surface, their terrestrial and aquatic habitats contain more than half of the known species and organisms'. Of the different tropical rainforests, Amazonia, as the region is also called, contains unparalleled biodiversity. It represents 40 per cent of the remaining tropical rainforest and contains the largest collection of plant and animal species on Earth. At least one in ten of every known plant and animal species is found there. On one hectare, 200 to 300 different types of tree species are commonly found—more than in Europe. Each tree hosts a unique variety of animals and insects, with some trees serving as home to 1,500 different types of insects (London and Kelly 2007: 24).

Moreover, many species of plants and animals are still unknown. Although scientists have studied Amazonia for centuries, our knowledge of species diversity and distribution in the Amazon is still in its infancy (Silva, Rylands and Da Fonesca 2005; Verweij, Schouten, Beukering, Triana, Leeuw and Hess 2009). What is known, however, is that biodiversity has geographical dimensions. Explorer and naturalist Alfred Russel Wallace studied monkey species in Amazonia and found that geographical barriers, such as rivers, often separated the ranges of closely allied species (Wallace 1852). He raised the so-called 'river hypothesis' that these waterways have led, over time, to the creation of geographical differentiation between species. This implies that the deforestation of a certain (large) area will almost certainly result in the disappearance of certain (sub)species.

Today, the tropical rainforests are not only among the most species-rich areas in the world, but also 'the leading abattoirs of extinction, shattered into fragments that are then being severely adulterated or erased one by one' (Wilson 2002: 59). From an ecological perspective, tropical deforestation contributes heavily to the current extinction crisis and to a continued biodiversity decline, which ultimately may develop into a new mass extinction (Butchart et al. 2010).[5]

Deforestation also contributes to soil erosion. Amazonia is vulnerable to erosion because the fertile layer of humus is very thin. As such, tree roots are mostly scattered horizontally, generally not growing deeper than half a meter (De Mello and Marigo 2007: 157). In some parts, Amazonia's forest even grows on rock, with tree roots forming a tapestry of roots covering the rocks, holding together the constellation of high trees above—as is the case around the small town of Presidente Figueiredo, 100 kilometres north of Manaus.

In addition to the harm caused to individual species and to biodiversity and ecology, deforestation in tropical regions threatens human health. About a quarter of modern medicines originally come from tropical plants or, more commonly, have been synthesised in imitation of them. The scientific community still does not know about many tropical plants, and thus when plant species disappear, so, too, do potential medicines.[6]

A potential harm concerns the effects of (future) deforestation on regional and global climate. When larger rainforest areas disappear, they become drier. In the humid Amazon ecosystem, most of the rain that falls is recycled back into the atmosphere through evaporation. Less rainforests means there is less rain. Today, almost 20 per cent of Amazonia has been deforested. If 30 to 40 per cent of the forest cover of the Amazon were to be removed, scientists fear it would be pushed into a permanently drier climate. This critical level of forest loss is referred to as a 'tipping point', beyond which return is unlikely (Verweij et al. 2007: 32).

It is possible that Brazil is already experiencing some of the negative consequences of Amazon forest loss. In 2014 and 2015, serious water crises occurred in Southern Brazil as a result of unusual low rainfall. São Paulo, Brazil's economic centre and South America's largest city with a population of more than 20 million, was also affected. The droughts led to a scientific and public debate about the possible causes. One study, by Antonio Nobre (2014) of Brazil's Centre for Earth Systems Science, was often mentioned in Brazil's (social) media. Nobre claims that deforestation in the Amazon Rainforest is a major cause of the droughts. He bases his argument partly on the idea of a 'biotic pump', put forth by

Makarieva and Gorshkov (2007), according to which land with extended natural forests, which have high levels of evaporation, attracts much more moisture from the sea than land without these forests.

Clouds from the Atlantic Ocean, carried by eastern winds, bring rain to the Amazon. Of all the rain that falls in the Amazon region, only 41 per cent of it eventually makes it to the sea; 59 per cent of it is recycled back into the atmosphere through evapotranspiration (Goulding, Barthem and Ferreira 2003: 24). Makarieva and Gorshkov's (2007) 'biotic pump', mentioned in the previous paragraph, has been applied by Nobre (2014) to the Amazon Rainforest: clouds from the Atlantic Ocean bring rain to the eastern Amazon, and this water is consequently recycled back through evapotranspiration several times before reaching the western Amazon, and other parts of Brazil and the continent. In this sense, the eastern Amazon represents the first phase of a series of water cycles of the Amazonian water pump. As much deforestation over the last years has taken place on the eastern side of the Amazon, namely in the Brazilian states of Pará and Mato Grosso,[7] this land, with less forest than before, would thus contain less water and, according to the 'biotic pump' theory, evaporate less and consequently attract fewer rainclouds than before. Indeed, there are indications that the Amazon is drier than it used to be as a result of less rain (see Hilker et al. 2014).

The Amazon may not be the 'lungs of the Earth', as sometimes thought, but it plays a crucial role in regulating the general circulation of the atmosphere. It is responsible for 15 to 20 per cent of all of the planet's freshwater flowing into the ocean. This water discharge equals that of the Earth's next six largest rivers combined. Together with the even larger water quantity that is in or above the forest, the Amazonian ecosystem represents so much water that it plays a crucial role in regulating the general circulation of the atmosphere. Disturbance of the rainforests may therefore also have major implications for the global climate (Verweij et al. 2007: 15).

An indirect way in which deforestation of Amazonia affects climate is through the release of carbon. As the largest tropical rainforest, Amazonia's soil and plants (trees) represent an enormous storage of carbon (Verweij et al. 2009: 7). Deforestation is already estimated to represent 18 per cent of all greenhouse gas emissions (IPCC 2007; Tollefson 2007). Considering the long-term effect on climate change, future generations can also be considered as potential victims of large-scale tropical deforestation. The direct human victims, however, are the people living in or near the forest.

The Amazon region and its human population

Documentaries about the Amazon often portray pristine and impenetrable jungles and huge rivers, inhabited by often dangerous and otherwise mysterious animals. The Amazon's human habitation is generally not emphasised. This historical section shows that the Amazon region is, in fact, inhabited by millions of people. Indigenous populations are a minority today, but they are clearly overrepresented among the human victims of deforestation. Later waves of migration into the Amazon Region have made the human population much more numerous and diverse, and understanding this is essential in order to understand why, today, there are so many conflicts over deforestation between inhabitants and others, often outsiders, wishing to commercially exploit the Amazon's natural resources, including its land and water.

The first outsiders to come in contact with Amazon Indians were colonisers (conquistadors), gold prospectors and missionaries. Amazon Indians still encounter prospectors and missionaries, but more common today is contact with loggers, who will cut into the forest to harvest an expensive tree such as mahogany. Locally, this will be worth thousands of dollars or Euros but when turned into furniture in Europe or North America, the ultimate retail value of the tree could be USD $250,000 (London and Kelly 2007: 138). Once a trail exists, settlers move in, first small farmers, later large-scale farmers.

Contact between Amazon Indians and large-scale farmers, in particular, is often unfriendly, due to conflicting interests. In general, the Amazon Indians wish to keep the forest intact, whereas farmers want to convert it into agricultural land. Indians often contend it is their ancestral land, while farmers argue, sometimes with paperwork, that they are entitled to exploit the land. Although in some cases Amazon Indians have established or been granted the right to live on ancestral land, the agricultural lobby in Brazil is very strong and Indians' rights are often violated. In many cases, these conflicts over land lead to violence. While Amazon Indians are not the only victims of violence from farmers, loggers and miners, they are clearly overrepresented as victims, considering their low, relatively powerless social position in society, and the fact that they are more likely to live in forested areas than in other regions. CIMI, Brazil's Missionary Indigenous Council, publishes yearly reports about violence against Indigenous people, including minors, who are killed, wounded, threatened, or chased away by farmers, loggers, or miners (CIMI 2014).

The Amazon region is the world's main and almost last refuge of humanity's oldest form of human societies—tribal societies of hunter-gatherers (Boekhout van Solinge 2010b; Middleton 2007: 37).[8] Some of these tribes are referred to as 'uncontacted' insofar as they live without contact with the modern world. In the 1960s, the number of uncontacted tribes living in the Brazilian Amazon was estimated at 250 (London and Kelly 2007: 35). Today, their number is estimated at around 60.

The existence of these societies is sometimes doubted and denied, however. Alan García, former president of Peru (from 1985–1990 and from 2006–2011), wishing to exploit Peru's Amazon Rainforest, stated that 'isolated Indians were a creation in the imagination of environmentalists and anthropologists' (quoted in Beaumont 2008). In 2008, Brazil's Indian Affairs Agency, Fundação Nacional do Índio (FUNAI), reacted by releasing pictures of a small isolated tribe, taken from an aeroplane flying over the Brazilian Amazon near Peru. News media around the world prominently showed the pictures. This particular small tribe probably fled from Peru as a result of illegal logging activities (Boekhout van Solinge 2010a, 2010b).

Hunter-gatherers are the oldest form of human societies. Anthropology, history and sociology books make mention of them, usually suggesting they are something from the distant past. They still do exist, some of them as uncontacted tribes, but agricultural and industrial society have increasingly destroyed their environments. Whether some of humanity's oldest societies can continue to exist depends on whether the rainforest around them will be preserved or destroyed.

While it is often assumed that the Amazon is inhabited mainly by Indigenous peoples, most humans living there today are not Indigenous. Of the 25 to 30 million Brazilians who live in the Amazon region, fewer than half a million are Indigenous.[9] Since the arrival of the European *conquistadores*, many children have been born from European men and Indigenous women. During the centuries of slavery, Brazil was a more important destination of African slaves than the United States. Some slaves fled the plantations—mostly located in Brazil's northeast—and found refuge in the rainforests where they founded Maroon communities (Mann and Hecht 2012).

Today, a majority of the population in the Brazilian Amazon are so-called *caboclos*, literally meaning the copper-coloured. This term refers to the people in the Amazon region who are of mixed white and Indian or Indian and black ancestry. Between 1800 and 1900, the population in the Amazon increased tenfold (Grandin 2010: 31) as rebels and later migrant workers came to the Amazon.

In 1835, 13 years after Brazil's independence from Portugal, the Cabanagem Revolt, Brazil's bloodiest uprising, broke out in the Brazilian Amazon. The rebellion had a long-lasting effect, especially in the lower Amazon and in the Tapajós Valley near Santarém. Runaway slaves deserted plantations en masse and found refuge in the forest. Many other rebels, such as caboclos, came to this part of the Amazon region as well and stayed. The rebellion, which had weakened the power of the white Portuguese elite, allowed provincial merchants and traders to become the new regional elite, setting up trading posts, claiming large parcels of jungle and laying the foundation of the later rubber boom (Grandin 2010: 112).

In the second half of the nineteenth century, the Brazilian Amazon supplied almost all of the world's rubber. Rubber was essential for the production of gaskets for steam engines and was used for a growing variety of products in the industrial age. Amazonian latex made up 40 per cent of Brazil's exports (Grandin 2010: 26). The rubber boom led to another wave of human migration into the Amazon. It attracted poor migrants from Brazil, especially from the northeast, as well as traders and merchants from Brazil and elsewhere, such as the Middle East and North Africa. The rubber boom led to the growth of Manaus and Belém, the Amazon's two major cities. Belém, near the river mouth, became the main rubber export harbour. Fifteen-hundred kilometres upstream, in the heart of the rainforest at the point where two large rivers meet,[10] Manaus developed as the rubber capital.

The Brazilian rubber boom also led to one of the most well-known cases of biopiracy. In 1876, British explorer Henry Wickham smuggled 70,000 rubber seeds out of the Brazilian Amazon to the UK (Jackson 2008). Wickham was based in Santarém, from where he had collected the seeds, in particular in the nearby Tapajós valley. Secretly at night, he loaded the seeds onto a British ship just outside the harbour of Santarém. In Belém, Wickham and the British consul misled Brazilian customs by declaring that the load contained 'delicate botanical specimens specially designated for delivery to Her Majesty's own Royal Gardens of Kew' (Jackson 2008: 189). In this way, they made an appeal to the Brazilian customs regulation that 'products destined for Cabinets of Natural History … be dispatched without opening the volumes in which they are encased'.

The smuggled rubber seeds from the Brazilian Amazon would become the source of rubber plantations in South East Asia, first in the British colonies and later in Dutch and French colonies. In the Amazon, large-scale rubber plantations are not possible, due to poor soil, insects and fungus. In tropical Asia these disadvantages are absent, which created the perfect conditions for large rubber plantations. Early twentieth-century Asian rubber production grew rapidly and by 1913 it was cheaper, breaking the monopoly of the Amazon, which subsequently entered a serious economic decline. In Brazil, Henry Wickham was dubbed the 'executioner of Amazonas' and 'the prince of thieves'. In the UK, however, he became a hero and was knighted (Jackson 2008: 191).

In the 1920s, Henry Ford, then the world's richest man, bought a large piece of land in the Tapajós Valley just south of Santarém and called it Fordlandia. Ford was the main car manufacturer and rubber was the only part of his supply chain that he did not control. *The Washington Post* wrote that Ford would bring 'white man's magic to the jungle'. A Brazilian writer called him the 'Jesus Christ of industry', another a 'New World Moses'. Ford was viewed as a saviour for Brazil's long-moribund rubber economy (Grandin 2010: 5).

Ford invested tens of millions of dollars in his jungle project: large rubber plantations, two company towns, a railroad, American-style houses, hospitals, movie theatres, golf courses and a 150-foot-high water tower (Grandin 2010: 9). Ford's investments and the high expectations led to another wave of migration, not only from other parts of the Amazon, but also from further away.

The working ethos of Fordlandia, however, with its time clocks, precise schedules and alcohol prohibition, led to rebellion and the departure of workers. In addition, large-scale rubber production began to fail when workers on the rubber plantations began to suffer from malaria and yellow fever, while frontline cutters were victims of fatal viper bites (Grandin 2010: 10). Ford's plan to build a jungle city with a large plantation eventually failed and, in the history of industry, it became known as an unsuccessful industrial megaproject. In 1945, Ford left. Ford's industrial rubber frontier was never realised and the impact of this particular venture on the people and environment proved limited.

In the 1960s, the military-led Brazilian government began constructing several roads through the Amazon. These roads allowed the frontier to move northwards from Brazil's southern, central and northeastern regions to the low populated rainforest areas in the north. Roads brought loggers, small farmers and later large landowners. This agricultural development was combined with industrialisation and urbanisation, although millions of people continued living in small (subsistence) communities. The Amazon's economy developed strongly on the pillars of industry, mining and especially agriculture.

Brazil's Amazonas state would develop industrially, with Manaus as Brazil's second industrial pole after São Paulo. The population of Manaus, the former rubber capital, grew rapidly from 200,000 in the 1960s to over two million in 2018, becoming the largest city in northern Brazil—an urban and industrial enclave surrounded by rainforest. Concurrently, the basis of the economy of the state of Pará, with over two million inhabitants in the metropolitan area of the state capital Belém, would become agricultural development, logging and mining. While the adjacent Amazonas state remained mostly forested, substantial areas of Pará state have been deforested. The agricultural frontier strongly and violently entered the Pará state from the Mato Grosso state in the south (Loureiro 2001) and several land conflicts can be distinguished (Boekhout van Solinge, Sauer, Vélez-Torres and Berrocal Vargas-van Den Brink 2016a; Loureiro 2001; Sauer 2018).

Of the nine Brazilian states in the Amazon, Pará and its largest harbour cities, Belém and Santarém, export the most timber. Pará is also the Brazilian state that experiences, by far, the most deforestation. The large extent of deforestation in Pará, combined with scattered human habitation at many places in and around forest and water, explain why Pará is also known for its land conflicts, land grabbing and conflicts stemming from (illegal) deforestation (CPT—Comissão Pastoral da Terra 2009, 2010; Greenpeace International 2003, 2011).

Deforestation for cattle farms, often by large landowners, has resulted in conflict between farmers and forest inhabitants. Mining (for both bauxite and gold) is a third source of conflict. In the last decade, deforestation by U.S. aluminium company Alcoa, near Pará's town Jurutí, along the Amazon River, has led to protests from traditional communities (Boekhout van Solinge 2010b: 271). A fourth source of conflict in Pará is the construction of hydroelectric power plants, which requires the flooding of large areas of land. In Brazil, most energy is hydroelectric and new dams continue to be planned. The federal government approved the construction of the large Belo Monte dam in the Xingu River, the fourth tributary of the Amazon River, but its construction has led to several (legal) battles. Although it has received less publicity, the federal government's plans for a series of dams in the Tapajós River, currently the only remaining undammed large tributary of the Amazon River, has led to protests from communities, some of which do not 'exist' on the maps of the dam. Finally, in the west of Pará, around the city of Santarém, mentioned above, deforestation for soy cultivation has become the main source of land conflict. Almost 60 years after Ford left Fordlandia, along the Tapajós just south of Santarém, Cargill, another large US company, came to Santarém, now a city of 300,000 inhabitants.

The last frontier in the Amazon: soy from Santarém

The old city of Santarém in Pará stands at the point where the Tapajós River flows into the Amazon River, some 800 kilometres upstream from the Atlantic Ocean. Since the beginning of the twenty-first century, the municipality of Santarém, which consists of both an urban area and much larger forest and rural areas, has become a new flashpoint of deforestation-related conflicts. Indeed, since the start of the century, soy production has been the main cause of deforestation in the Santarém area. Whereas, before, deforestation was mainly occurring in the southern and western Amazon, a new deforestation frontier is now found in the heart of the Amazon, around and near the Amazon River and Tapajós River.

This soy frontier has led to environmental problems, such as pollution from heavy and increasing use of herbicides (Meyer and Cederberg 2010). Such pollution from herbicides, especially glyphosate, affects neighbouring farmlands, natural reserves, residential areas and water reservoirs. Agrochemicals also end up in rivers and pollute vast areas of the Amazon biome (Verweij et al. 2009: 42). After heavy rain in the Tapajós valley, agricultural fertilisers flow into the Tapajós River, which increases the growth of algae and turns the normally blue Tapajós green. In three small (Indigenous) communities near Santarém—Ipaupixuna, Açaizal and São Francisco da Cavada—people complain about the quality of the water in the streams that are their sources of drinking water.[11] They fear that, during the rainy season, pollution from the nearby soy fields will enter their streams. The death of a boy after a bath in the stream has only increased the suspicion about soy and agrochemicals. Because the water quality has become such a concern, biologists and toxicologists of the LAR consortium have examined it. The researchers have found glyphosate residue in the water streams, but this has been within Brazil's allowable limits of 500 mg/l (see Passos et al. 2016). The quantities found, however, would surpass the permissible quantity limits in the European Union (EU) (of less than 1 mg/l). This large difference in (health) norms between Brazilian and European citizens (500 mg per litre in Brazil versus less than 1 mg per litre in the EU) has created some doubt and mistrust among community members about the health norms to which they are exposed.

How did the area of Santarém come to be afflicted with deforestation for soy and how did soy come to the Santarém area? As noted above, the construction of a soy export harbour in Santarém by Cargill at the beginning of this century has attracted soy farmers from other states from Central and Southern Brazil. In the slipstream of Cargill's port, the soy frontier has reached Santarém and the Tapajós valley (see Sauer 2018). Santarém is appealing for the soy industry, as well as for the timber industry, because it can be reached by ships. Moreover, two mostly paved roads, the BR-163 and the PA-370, connect Santarém to a large Amazonian hinterland, where soy beans are grown.

A review of the history and development of the port is necessary to understand the emergence of the soy industry in Santarém and the related deforestation that the area has suffered. In 2003, over opposition from some residents of Santarém, Cargill, one of the world's largest traders in agricultural commodities, built a port to reduce transport costs and facilitate soy exports. Soy from Brazil's largest soy-producing state, Mato Grosso, along with soy from states like Rondonia, could now be transported via the rivers and roads to Cargill's harbour in Santarém, where it is loaded on large cargo ships and exported (Steward 2007: 112).

When the port was first proposed, it drew criticism on the grounds that it would destroy an archaeological site, as well as a popular city beach. In 1999, the federal prosecutor's office started an investigation concerning Cargill's permit because no Environmental Impact Assessment (EIA) had been conducted. In 2000, a federal judge ordered Cargill to conduct an EIA for its port facilities (Santana 2010: 85–87). In the same year, in another court case, also initiated by the federal prosecutor's office, the judge came to the same conclusion and suspended the licenses given by Pará's Secretary for Environment (Santana 2010: 89; Procuradoria do Estado do Pará 2007). Cargill contested this verdict and appealed to Brazil's second highest court (Greenpeace International 2006a: 37).

Despite these legal hurdles, the port was built and in the first three years after its construction, the area planted with soy in the region of Santarém grew from 350 ha in 2002 to 36,600 ha in 2005, giving it the highest soy production in Pará (IBGE 2011). The arrival of Cargill further served as an incentive to attract soy farmers to the region, which increased deforestation and led to new land conflicts. In 2007, four years after the port had opened, Brazil's second highest court confirmed that the EIA should have been conducted before the construction of the port (Santana 2010: 92; Procuradoria do Estado do Pará 2007). But by that time the port was already in operation. As the judge declared: 'Cargill flagrantly assaulted this Tribunal's authority—until today—not carrying out the Pre-Environmental Impact Assessment it was obliged to' (Santana 2010: 93).[12]

Later, in 2007, another judge ordered the closing down of the port. Cargill contested this order and, a few days later, closure was suspended (Santana 2010: 93–4). In 2008, Cargill announced that it had contracted the consultancy firm CPEA to conduct the EIA (Santana 2010: 94–5). The final version of this EIA was published in 2010, but, in 2011, the police and the prosecutor's office claimed that faults and omissions had been found in the EIA (Polícia Civil do Estado do Pará 2011, Ministerio Público do Estado do Pará 2011). In 2011, the prosecutor's office opened a case against CPEA, but, despite protests in 2012 from civil society organisations in Santarém, Cargill managed to avoid prosecution (interview with João Camerini, a lawyer from Terra de Direitos, a local human rights organisation, Santarém, 4 April 2012). Cargill thus managed to build the harbour without an EIA. As Brazilian lawyer Santana (2010: 95) laments, the judicial authorities decide one thing 'but in reality, the things happen in the opposite way'. Economic interests sometimes seem to be stronger than the proper functioning of the judicial system and the protection of the Amazon and the Brazilian people (Santana 2010: 95–6).

The way in which Cargill managed to avoid a pre-construction EIA not only violated Brazil's environmental regulations (Santana 2010: 92), but the company's own ethical principles. On 26 April 2012, a Cargill delegation from São Paulo came to the little town of Belterra just south of Santarém along the Tapajós for a public hearing about Cargill's port. The hearing was organised by the prosecutor's office in Belterra, where American-style houses from the Ford era remain. Today, there is much soy production in the area. At the hearing, Cargill's director of ports, Clythio van Buggenhout, explained Cargill's ethical principles: 1) Cargill will comply with all laws of all countries in which it operates; and 2) Cargill will not intentionally support any third party's efforts to violate any law in any country (Cargill Brasil 2012).

Cargill clearly violated its own first principle. Whether Cargill has respected its second principle is a more difficult question. Obviously, the company does not overtly endorse (illegal) deforestation and land conflicts, but there is no question that the company benefits from soy produced on land that was deforested illegally.

To explicate, Cargill's port attracted soy farmers from Mato Grosso and Rio Grande do Sul to explore the Santarém area for the expansion of soy. The land was cheap and available. As Gilson Rego of the Pastoral Land Commission (CPT) explains, many people in the Amazon do not possess official land titles (interview in Santarém, 18 April 2012). Therefore, soy farmers invading the area claimed that it was 'empty' and suitable for soy (Schlesinger and Noronha 2006: 33). But, as noted above, the Tapajós Valley is far from being void of human habitation and the soy farmers were not the only ones to claim that enough land existed for soy. In 1996, after conducting a study on the potential for commercial agriculture in Santarém and neighbouring municipalities, the Pará state government declared that a potential 6.2 million hectares was available for soy in the Santarém region. Together with Santarém businessmen, Pará state government officials travelled to Mato Grosso. Armed with the results of the study, they tried to convince soy producers to invest in the region (Steward 2007: 113).

Thus, soy farmers came and started buying some land from local farmers. João Raimundo, chairman of the farmers' organisation Ceft-Bam,[13] explained that local farmers who were offered money and subsequently sold their land had never seen such quantities of money until the soy farmers arrived (interview, 16 April 2012) The price of a hectare of land skyrocketed—from US$25 in 2000 to US$500 in 2008 (Grandin 2010: 367). With the arrival of soy farmers, the real estate prices in Santarém increased as well.

Representatives of civil society who were interviewed in Santarém claimed that much of the land for soy cultivation in the Santarém area was not actually bought, but *grabbed*. They argued that soy farmers around Santarém grabbed publicly owned land from those who did not want to leave. Schlesinger and Noronha (2006) have asserted that land grabbing related to soy expansion around Santarém is a violent process: houses are burnt, people are killed and whole communities disappear. In line with the 'lawless' reputation of Pará, most of this violence goes unpunished. As João Raimundo explains, people who wish to stay have been and are increasingly pressured by soy farmers to leave (interview João Raimundo, Santarém, 16 April 2012). In some instances, soy farmers have used false land documents to claim new areas (CPT 2010: 7).

According to a study conducted by Santarém's Rural Workers' Union, about 600 families in the municipality of Santarém had left their land by 2003 (interview with Manoel Edivaldo Santos Matos, Santarém, 18 April 2012). By the end of 2003, approximately 200 agro-industrial farms had been established in Santarém (Steward 2007: 112). Santarém and neighbouring Belterra are now Pará's two main soy-producing municipalities. From there, the soy frontier is moving to other municipalities.

Satellite images of the Santarém area show that deforestation has grown rapidly since 2000 and is still continuing (Coordenação-Geral de Observação da Terra 2012; Global Forest Watch[14]). Cohenca (2005) claims that soy production is the main cause. Steward (2007: 113) argues that the Brazilian Institute for Environment and Natural Resources (IBAMA) largely overlooks soy farmers who do not abide by the Brazilian Forest Code and deforest land illegally. A shared opinion among the individuals I interviewed is that soy farmers generally start buying agricultural land that is already deforested, but then soon clear vast areas of forest surrounding the agricultural land.

Cargill and other members of ABIOVE (Brazilian Association of Vegetable Oil Manufacturers) signed a two-year moratorium on the purchase of soybeans produced on rainforest lands deforested after 2006. The moratorium has been extended and Cargill claims that it has reduced deforestation drastically (Cargill 2010: 6–7; see also Cargill, n.d.). For example, Cargill states on its website that it had resulted in 'zero deforestation in the Santarém area since 2006' (Cargill 2014). Cargill also stated that, thanks to collaborations with The Nature Conservancy, significant improvements have been made.

> 'Santarém was able to stabilize deforestation in just six years, a feat some predicted would take a century to accomplish. What's more, in 2014, Brazil announced that deforestation in the Amazon had dropped by nearly 80 per cent, and in recent years Santarém has not reported any instances of deforestation'.
>
> *(Cargill, n.d.)*

The fact that Cargill makes the blatant assertion that soy production in the Santarém region is 'sustainable' (when rainforest is being destroyed, communities suffer and glyphosate is being sprayed on a large scale) is another indication of greenwashing practices by this company (see Cargill, n.d.).

Locally, many claim that deforestation around Santarém has continued despite the moratorium (see, e.g., Coordenação-Geral de Observação da Terra 2012). Edilberto Sena is a vociferous critic of the moratorium:

> 'In the Amazon you just cannot do a moratorium of two, three years. Why? You don't destroy forest and plant soy the first year after. You first have to work the ground, so in the first year you plant rice, then you let the plot rest for a year and only in the third year you start planting soy'.
>
> *(interview 12 April 2012)*

Rego adds that, at the moment, many areas have been occupied or grabbed and will be planted with soy in the future, when the world market prices rise (interview 18 April 2012). In recent years, satellite data are increasingly being used for forest monitoring. Satellite monitoring and analysis confirms what locals are saying, namely that deforestation for soy has not stopped (see, e.g., Asher 2019).

The soy frontier has brought new conflicts over land and water to the region, next to the longer-standing conflicts over illegal logging. Ivete Bastos dos Santos, former president of the Rural Workers' Union and governor of Santarém, describes the soy frontier as 'one of the largest conflicts in Santarém's history'. She explains that in Pará, soy farmers, collaborating with timber traders and ranchers, have the power to hire *pistoleiros* to impose their will (interview, 23 April 2012). Most of this violence goes unpunished. Rego refers to the soy frontier as 'the wild west' (interview Gilson Rego, Santarém, 18 April 2012).

According to the Ministry of Agricultural Development, of all deaths related to agricultural expansion, 37.5 per cent have occurred in northern Brazil. Of these killings, 67 per cent have taken place in Pará (Schlesinger and Noronha 2006: 78). In recent years, Pará always appears as one of the Brazilian states with most land conflicts and related murders (see CPT—Comissão Pastoral da Terra 2009, 2011, 2018: 108, 115). In the Santarém region, rural workers who challenge soy expansion receive death threats and their homes and goods are burned; many disappear (Schlesinger and Noronha 2006: 78; Fiocruz and FASE 2012).

Since 2006, Ivete Bastos Santos has lived under constant police protection after receiving several death threats. Bastos Santos can still tell her story, but other local leaders have died (CPT 2011; Fiocruz and FASE 2012). Another person from the Santarém region who has been living under police protection for several years is the Indigenous *cacique* (chief), Odair 'Dadá' Borari of Maró Indigenous Territory, who is known in the region as an active and outspoken opponent of illegal logging and deforestation. Prior to receiving police protection, he had been kidnapped and tortured by gunmen (Boekhout van Solinge 2018a).

In 2017, media articles appeared about a new planned infrastructure in the Lower Amazon, including a network of railroads for transporting soy from land-locked Central Brazil to North Brazil in the Amazon Region (Brandford and Torres 2017). In 2018, criminologist and investigative journalist Karlijn Kuijpers (2018a, 2018b)[15] revealed that Dutch engineering and transport companies had actually been developing the master plan of this railroad network, named the Northern Corridor. This so-called multi-modal transport system would consist of 1,000+ km of railroads, ports of transhipments (on tributaries of the

Amazon River) and various additional soy export harbours (along the Amazon River). While framed as 'sustainable' by the Brazilian and Dutch policy makers, there is little doubt that this infrastructural network of ports and railroads will lead to more deforestation and related conflicts with traditional communities (Kuijpers 2018a, 29 May).

In October 2018, a Brazilian federal judge blocked the concession procedure of the *Ferrogrão*, the first 1,100-km-long branch of the Northern Corridor railroad, because he considered the environmental impact assessment insufficient. For example, the assessment did not mention that traditional (Maroon) communities would be affected by the railroad. Almost a year earlier, federal prosecutors had recommended cancelling a series of the public hearings about the *Ferrogrão* that were organised by Brazil's National Agency for Terrestrial Transport (ANTT). These federal prosecutors from the states of Pará and Mato wrote that the public hearings would be illegal because almost 20 traditional communities had not been informed properly (based on the principle of Free Prior and Informed Consent), and thus the hearings would constitute a breach of ILO Convention 169.

GPS-supported community forest watch

The question of whether deforestation has continued in the Santarém region can be answered by analysing satellite data, such as from the website Global Forest Watch, which allows visitors to the site to see the rate of deforestation over the years.[16] Zooming in on the Santarém region, the satellite map shows that deforestation has actually continued after the soy moratorium, albeit on a smaller scale. Cargill's zero-deforestation statements about the Santarém region are thus not supported by satellite data.

Another way to know whether deforestation has, indeed, stopped is by inquiring with the local communities themselves. During the period of 2013–2017, I visited several (forest) communities that are located on the deforestation frontline in the Santarém region. Some (Indigenous) communities living on the plains just southeast of Santarém were visited several times, due to the travel time of only one hour's drive from Santarém (as compared with some other communities for which one has to travel hours or some days by boat). People from (forest) communities, such as Açaizal, Ipaupixuna and São Francisco da Cavada, are obviously aware of the land-use changes in or near their communities. They can explain in detail which piece of forest was deforested by which (soy) farmer. Community members state that soy farmers have started more subtle and 'smarter' ways of deforestation. For example, some soy farmers no longer deforest larger areas, but take away and burn smaller strips of forests, which is less obvious and visible (Boekhout van Solinge 2014b: 46).[17] In fact, anyone who visits the area on a regular basis can observe that soy is, by far, the main crop in the area, and that soy is still the crop that is driving land conversion in the Santarém region. Moreover, community members confirm what satellite data show: deforestation in the Santarém region has continued but that the scale of deforestation is smaller than before (the soy moratorium).

These local findings lead to a discrepancy with the international representations of the effects of the soy moratorium, which suggest that there is hardly any deforestation for soy anymore (Cargill 2014; Gibbs et al. 2015). What can explain this difference? Is it a question of scale only? It is possible that the Santarém area is an exceptional region where deforestation is continuing more than elsewhere. It is also possible that the deforestation for soy in the Santarém region is on such a small scale that it is negligible or hardly detectable on the aggregate level of deforestation in the Brazilian Amazon as a whole (which is the focus of the study by Gibbs and colleagues (Gibbs et al. 2015)). Another potentiality is that the smaller-scale deforestation of the last years (as shown by Global Forest Watch, and which I confirmed in my conversations with locals) is not being detected by Brazil's satellite systems that currently detect deforestation only in amounts that exceed 25 hectares.[18] This discrepancy between international findings and representations, on the one hand, and local findings and impressions, on the other hand, shows the need for more precise monitoring.

As mentioned throughout this chapter, traditional communities in the Amazon are often victims of deforestation, but their presence in rainforests also offers opportunities for forest crime prevention. Increased security can result in decreased opportunities for crime (Van Dijk, Tseloni and Farrell 2012)—and, as situational crime prevention proponents have argued, such 'security' can be provided by non-law-enforcement actors (see Burton et al., this volume, Chapter 3). Could a rainforest equivalent of neighbourhood watch be developed? Could local intelligence be used to detect and, especially, to prevent forest crime?

In 2014, a criminological pilot study of community-based forest crime prevention was initiated at several deforestation hotspots in the Brazilian Amazon (since 2017, these efforts have continued under the name 'Forest Forces'[19]). Several communities were provided with waterproof GPS-cameras and efforts were undertaken to ensure that camera use would not increase the insecurity of people participating in the project (Boekhout van Solinge 2018a, 2018b). Those communities without electricity and access to a mobile phone network were given power banks and portable solar chargers. No one was paid. The study was undertaken with the understanding that it would function well only if GPS-referenced pictures of forest crime activities could reach law enforcement agents.

To explain, Brazil employs a satellite- and GPS-oriented forest protection system. Brazil's sophisticated rapid-response satellite system can detect and locate automatically large-scale deforestation. Perpetrators have adapted, however, to the satellite enforcement system by shifting to smaller-scale deforestation, by conducting their illegal forest activities at night, and by concentrating deforestation during the rainy season, when clouds block the view of most of the satellites.

The criminological pilot endeavoured to test whether (remote) forest communities would take GPS-referenced pictures of illegal forest activities to law enforcement and justice actors (in a distant town). The four-year pilot showed positive results in some, but not all of the communities. Indeed, success seemed dependent on the level of community organisation and also the courage of leaders (Boekhout van Solinge 2018a). This is not surprising, however, considering the level of violence that forest defenders have experienced. Indeed, the presence of armed guards or hired *pistoleiros* (gunmen) by logging companies influences the extent to which communities are able and willing to collect GPS evidence.

The experiment was effective in the (only) Indigenous Territory of the pilot. This did not come as a surprise because Brazil's Indigenous Territories have (invisible) GPS borders and outsiders are not allowed to enter without permission so as to help protect the areas from loggers and prospectors seeking access to the areas' diamonds, gold, timber and other natural resources. In fact, success was more or less expected in Maró Indigenous Territory because this Indigenous forest-dependent community had already formed surveillance teams to protect its territory of 44,000 hectares. For many years, the community had serious problems with trespassing and illegal invasions of logging companies, as well as other companies (such as, in 2017, when representatives of the US aluminium company Alcoa attempted to enter to look for bauxite in the soil).

A GPS camera indeed allowed the Maró Indigenous Territory's surveillance team to collect GPS evidence of illegal activities in their territory. The so-called second (vice) chief Odair 'Dadá' Borari then presented pictures, with GPS coordinates, of piles of logs and buildings of timber companies in their territory to the office of the Environmental Inspection

Agency IBAMA in Santarém, Pará. These GPS coordinates were subsequently entered into IBAMA's satellite system, which zoomed in on the crime spot. A helicopter was sent the same day. Eight logging concessions were cancelled and several timber companies expelled from the Indigenous territory.

The pilot study demonstrates how local forest protection can be effective—and undertaken relatively cheaply. For success to occur, however, there must be some level of community organisation, as well as access to law enforcement agents and officials whom the community members trust. The model can be replicated in other areas, such as the Indigenous community of Açaizal near Santarém. This community has been surrounded almost entirely by soy fields and it could better substantiate its case about deforestation and the glyphosate spraying with up-to-date GPS data.

Discussion and conclusion

What is driving the crimes and harms related to deforestation in the Brazilian Amazon and which actors or factors could be held responsible? The area around Santarém is one example of how the agricultural frontier has moved into the heart of Brazilian Amazon, near the Amazon River.

Brazil is a rapidly growing economy with the export of agricultural products an important pillar of economic development, making up 28 per cent of total exports (Mueller 2004; Verweij et al. 2009: 36). A powerful agricultural lobby has helped bring about numerous policies to further stimulate agricultural expansion (Rodrigues Da Cunha Soares 2007; Schlesinger and Noronha 2006). The Terra Legal Programme was implemented in 2009 to formalise land titles in the Amazon (Brito and Barreto 2011). Many of my interviewees have claimed that this programme mainly facilitates agro-industry and offers ways to legalise illegally grabbed land (interview with Gilson Rego, Santarém, 18 April 2012). All interviewees have also stated that the functioning of Brazil's judicial system facilitates the expansion of agro-industry. On the other hand, some recent actions by Brazil's federal prosecutor's office have had a positive impact for traditional communities. But governmental presence and law enforcement has been minimal in these large areas with relatively low population densities, further enabling illegal land grabs by force or threats thereof.

The planned paving of the rest of BR163 (noted above), a 1,500 km road from Mato Grosso, will reduce transportation costs of soy to the Santarém port. It will also open up ten million hectares of Amazon forest to exploitation. Eighty-five per cent of all deforestation in the Amazon occurs within a radius of 30 km from paved roads (Verweij et al. 2009: 29). The planned Brazilian–Dutch multi-modal transport systems of several railroads and (export) ports puts more pressure on the Amazonian ecosystem and its human and non-human inhabitants (Kuijpers 2018a). Davidson and colleagues (2012: 327) have argued that there is emerging evidence that Brazil not only faces a socio-economic transition, but an irreversible biophysical transformation of its rainforest system.

At the international level, Brazilian politicians and officials regularly express Brazil's commitment to fight and stop deforestation in the Amazon. The international objective is to cut deforestation in half by 2020 and to stop deforestation completely by 2030 (see, e.g., the New York Declaration of Forests).[20] Brazilian measures to stop deforestation are usually presented as relatively successful. Working on the deforestation frontline, however, one encounters a different reality. Cargill's illegally built harbour in Santarém acted as a catalyst for the deforestation for soy. In 2016, preparations began for more soy export ports in Santarém. The economic and political pressure to permit more deforestation in the region is strong.

Can Brazil's international promises to limit deforestation be fulfilled? How will Brazil deal with the tension between agricultural development and rainforest conservation? These questions raise a larger issue: to what extent are these entirely Brazilian issues? Land conversion for cattle and soy has been the main cause of Amazonian deforestation, often preceded by (illegal) logging. Where does all this meat and soy go? Most of Brazil's soy and an increasing percentage of its beef are exported abroad (Nepstad, Stickler and Almeida 2006: 1596–8). All soy from Santarém's port is exported abroad, mainly to China and Europe. Interviewees in Santarém, such as Ivete Bastos dos Santos, argue that consumers should become aware of where their food comes from and how it relates to deforestation.

Increasing meat consumption is driving Brazil's growing beef and soy exports. As mentioned before, the creation of cattle farms has been responsible for 70 per cent of deforestation in the Brazilian Amazon. Moreover, meat consumption elsewhere is also driving the demand for soy. Seventy to seventy-five per cent of all soy in the world is used as feed in the livestock industry—in particular feed for chickens, pigs, cows and farmed fish (Brack, Glover and Wellesley 2016: 24). Addressing deforestation in the Amazon therefore means confronting consumption patterns that involve so much meat (Pollan 2008). Many consumers do not know much about their food (see Tourangeau and Fitzgerald, this volume, Chapter 11) and do not associate deforestation and soy production with meat consumption. People know even less about agro-commodity chains. Many have never heard of Cargill, the world's largest trader in agricultural commodities. Brewster Kneen (2002) claims that it is a strategy chosen deliberately to remain invisible. Considering Cargill's dominance in the commodity chain (Kneen 2002; Schlesinger and Noronha 2006: 104–5), the company could improve its practices to become more in line with its stated ethical code and policy of corporate social responsibility. The fact that Cargill and four other giants in the agro-commodity market (ADM, Bunge, Glencore and Louise Dreyfus) have not wanted to engage in a dialogue with the UN Special Rapporteur on the Right to Food, as former Special Rapporteur De Schutter indicated in an interview, is not a sign of responsible conduct (Somers 2014).

International and national demand for cattle and livestock feed, in particular soy, are increasingly driving land-use change throughout the Amazon (Davidson et al. 2012: 323). The amount of soy that the Netherlands imports from Brazil is equivalent to roughly half the size of the country (Verweij et al. 2009). Governmental officials in Brazil often acknowledge the heavy toll that the agricultural industry is having on Amazon forests, but claim that, as an emerging global economic player, Brazil cannot compete with heavily subsidised agriculture in Europe and North America unless it exploits its available land, such as the Amazon Rainforest. The 2018 election of right-wing president Jair Messias Bolsonaro, who during the election campaigns vowed to give not one more centimetre of land to traditional communities, has only increased deforestation and land invasions of Indigenous land, as various Brazilian and international media report (such as in articles in the Brazilian daily newspaper *Folha de São Paulo*).

In the meantime, consumer markets are become more demanding about the origin of imported products that may contribute to tropical deforestation. The EU is increasingly insisting that commodity chains of products imported into the EU be *legal* (such as with timber in the years since the 2013 EU Timber Regulation). In 2015, during the Paris Climate Summit (where a specific Article 5 of the Paris Agreement[21] was being devoted to forests), a group of European countries signed the Amsterdam Declaration 'Towards Eliminating Deforestation from Agricultural Commodity Chains with European countries'.[22] In other words, European countries have begun demanding that products imported from the Amazon, like cattle, soy and timber, meet EU standards and therefore cannot be connected to activities that are illegal or detrimental to the biodiverse and carbon-rich tropical rainforest like the Amazon. It is one thing to *state* such a requirement and quite another to enforce it, however, and the extent to which implementation has occurred is subject to debate; this may be little more than greenwashing on the part of the EU.

Companies have become more aware of their responsibilities and have focussed increasingly on what they call sustainable or responsible production (see, e.g., Bleakley 2019; the so-called Round Tables on Sustainable Palm Oil and Responsible Soy).[23] Moreover, a growing number of companies is committing to so-called zero-deforestation commitments (ZDCs), such as the earlier mentioned soy moratorium and the New York Declaration on Forests. In an evaluation of corporate commitments to zero deforestation Jopke and Schoneveld (2018: vii) concluded that there still is

> significant room for further refining implementing mechanisms. Superficially it finds that weak commitment to full transparency, notably of disclosure of sourcing locations and suppliers, and to independent verification, undermine ZDCs transformative potential and ability to hold companies accountable for their failure to comply with their ZDCs.

With respect to Brazil, in particular, there is little doubt that the enforcement of forest and timber laws, and the monitoring of voluntary agreements and commitments, such as the soy moratorium, will be increasingly important. Better enforcement and monitoring are, indeed, necessary in order to prevent further illegal logging and deforestation. When it comes to effective monitoring, there remains the option of employing the people who live and are already present in and around the forest. One of the striking lessons that I have learned over the course of my research on deforestation in the Amazon, especially when I give presentations in Europe and the United States, but also in Rio de Janeiro, is that most people outside the Amazon have no idea that the Amazon is inhabited by so many people. Indeed, the belief that the Amazon is mostly inhospitable to humans persists (see also Boekhout van Solinge 2010b). At some (academic) conferences or seminars in the western world, where tropical forests are being discussed, the presence of humans in the discussed forests is never mentioned. If this observation is combined with the fact that nature documentaries about the Amazon usually show animals, and not (m)any humans, this picture of the Amazon will endure.

Involving communities in monitoring—communities that often have a direct interest in protecting the forest from which they obtain food and medicine—could help prevent deforestation from occurring. For example, in one Indigenous community that I visited, Maró, one of the hotspots of the deforestation near Santarém, illegal logging was accompanied by threats and violence from *pistoleiros*. In October 2014, three forest communities started patrolling their forest areas; no more incursions by loggers have been observed (personal communication by traditional leader Dadá, 21 February 2016).

To preserve Amazonia and its many inhabitants, humans and non-humans, and to prevent other harms related to deforestation now and in the future, not only are new land use practices and better enforcement and monitoring in Brazil needed, but also a new ethic (Singer 2002, 2004). As Wilson (2002: 149–50) observes,

> 'What humanity is inflicting upon itself and Earth is, to use a modern metaphor, the result of a mistake in capital investment. (…) Having appropriated the planet's natural resources, we choose to annuitize them with a short-term maturity reached by progressive increasing payouts. Why, our descendants will ask, by needlessly extinguishing the lives of other species, did we permanently impoverish our own?'

Notes

1 The murder of the husband-wife couple, João and Maria da Silva, prominent rainforest activists, occurred on the same day (24 May 2011) that the Brazilian House of Representatives voted overwhelmingly for the controversial 2012 Forest Act, which would allow farmers to deforest more of their land and give them a form of amnesty for much illegal deforestation that occurred prior to 2009.
2 The Brazilian government monitors deforestation in the Amazon by using satellites. While in itself this is a modern system, it currently detects only deforestation areas larger than 25 hectares (an area larger than 50 football fields). Smaller-scale deforestation and selective logging are therefore not captured by this system. Still, the official deforestation data give an indication of large-scale and longitudinal trends (see www.obt.inpe.br/prodes/index.php).
3 The 'Conflict and Cooperation over Natural resources in developing countries' Programme (known as the 'CoCooN programme') was part of the Dutch NWO-WOTRO Research for Global Development programme. See Bavink and colleagues (2014) for the conceptual approaches of the different CoCooN-consortia. See Boekhout van Solinge and colleagues (2016a) for research findings of the LAR project.
4 See www.obt.inpe.br/prodes/index.php.
5 Today's extinction crisis is sometimes called the 'sixth extinction' (Leakey and Lewin 1996). The current extinction rates are much higher than the fifth extinction of 65 million years ago, when many species of animals, such as the dinosaurs, became extinct. The causes of the current extinction are pollution, hunting/fishing, the introduction of species, fragmentation of landscapes, climate change and, primarily, habitat destruction (see, e.g., David Attenborough's documentary series, *The State of the Planet*; see also Brisman and South, Introduction, this volume; Brisman and South 2019).
6 Pharmaceutical companies are well aware of the potential profit of the species-rich tropical rainforests, which are for that reason a target for biopiracy—the appropriation, without payment, of Indigenous biological (often biomedical) knowledge and genes (see Goyes this volume, Chapter 12; South 2007; Wyatt and Brisman 2017). The profits for pharmaceutical companies, which patent (parts of) plants, can be worth millions and even billions of US dollars (London and Kelly 2007: 249). While the appropriation and patenting of tropical species is a relatively new phenomenon, biopiracy is, by no means, a recent occurrence. One of the earliest examples, discussed in greater detail below, involved the removal of rubber seeds from the Amazon—a British-government-backed endeavor to create more lucrative, large-scale rubber plantations in tropical portions of Asia.
7 Over the last five years, more than half of all deforestation in the Brazilian Amazon has occurred in two states. For example, in 2014, a total of 4,848 km^2 was deforested according to Brazilian statistics. Pará (1,829 km^2) and Mato Grosso (1,048 km^2) together accounted for 59 per cent of the total. Previous years show a similar image. Data on deforestation in each Brazilian state can be found at www.obt.inpe.br/prodes/index.php.
8 New Guinea is also home to isolated tribes (Middleton 2007). The country, however, is under 'attack' by loggers, who seek *intsia bijuga* (also known as merbau or ipil timber). EIA and Telapak (2004, 2005, 2006, 2010) have found that professional criminal networks are predominantly responsible for the large-scale, illegal merbau exploitation.
9 In the 2000 census, some 700,000 Brazilians classified themselves as Indigenous—0.4 per cent of the Brazilian population. A majority of them live in the Amazon (see IBGE, the Brazilian Institute of Geography and Statistics: www.ibge.gov.br).
10 At the Brazilian city of Manaus, the muddy, tan-colored, nutrient-rich waters of the Solimões River (the upper Amazon River) meet the black, nutrient-poor water of the Negro River.
11 Biologist Carlos Passos of the National University of Brasilia (UnB), a research partner to this LAR-project, has studied the water quality and the levels of (herbicide) in the streams near soy fields in the Santarém area.
12 Translation by the author. The statement by the judge (in Portuguese) is as follows: 'Cargill agrediu flagrantemente a autoridade deste Tribunal, descumprindo o acórdão que lhe impôs a realização de um Estudo Prévio de Impacto Ambiental, não realizado até hoje'.
13 Ceft-Bam stands for Centre for Study, Research and Education of Workers in Baixo Amazonas and is part of STTR Santarém, the Rural Workers' Union.
14 www.globalforestwatch.org.
15 Kuijpers was a co-author on the version of this chapter that appeared in the first edition of the *Routledge International Handbook of Green Criminology*.

16 See www.globalforestwatch.org.
17 One can draw a comparison to drug traffickers' adaptations to governmental crackdowns on international money transfers. When governments began requiring banks and other financial institutions to report the transfer of large amounts of money, drug traffickers—and others involved in illicit sales and markets—attempted to avoid detection by sending smaller amounts.
18 Brazil's most used satellite to detect deforestation is the DETER satellite, which automatically signals deforestation of areas larger than 25 hectares. The *Science* publication by Gibbs and colleagues (2015) on the effect of the soy moratorium on deforestation (or not) is also based on data from the DETER satellite and thus included deforestation over 25 hectares, and only of so-called primary forest, in the period 2007–2013. The background and methodological details of the study can be found at the website: www.sciencemag.org/content/suppl/2015/01/21/347.6220.377.DC1/aaa0181.Gibbs.SM.revision3.pdf.
19 www.forestforces.org.
20 https://nydfglobalplatform.org.
21 https://unfccc.int/process-and-meetings/the-paris-agreement/what-is-the-paris-agreement.
22 The signatory countries are Denmark, France, Germany, the Netherlands, Norway, the United Kingdom and, since 2017, Italy. See www.euandgvc.nl/documents/publications/2015/december/7/declarations.
23 See respectively https://rspo.org/ and www.responsiblesoy.org.

References

Asher, C. 2019. 'Brazil soy trade linked to widespread deforestation, carbon emissions', Mongabay 3 April 2019. Available at: https://news.mongabay.com/2019/04/brazil-soy-trade-linked-to-widespread-deforestation-carbon-emissions/ (Consulted5 April 2019).

Asner, G. P., Knap, D. E., Broadbent, E. N., Oliveira, P. J. C., Keller, M. and Silva, J. N. 2005. 'Selective Logging in the Brazilian Amazon', *Science*, 310: 480–482.

Bavinck, M., Pellegrini, L. and Mostert, E. 2014. *Conflicts over Natural Resources in the Global South. Conceptual Approaches*. London: Taylor & Francis.

Beaumont, P. 2008. 'Secret of the "lost" Tribe that Wasn't', *The Observer*, June 22, 2008.

Beirne, P. and N. South (eds.) 2007. *Issues in Green Criminology. Confronting Harms against Environments, Humanity and Other Animals*. Cullumpton, Devon, UK: Willan.

Bleakley, P. 2019. 'Big fish, small pond: NGO–corporate partnerships and corruption of the environmental certification process in tasmanian aquaculture', *Critical Criminology: An International Journal*, DOI: 10.1007/s10612-019-09454-8.

Boekhout van Solinge, T. 2008a. 'Eco-crime: The tropical timber trade', in D. Siegel and H. Nelen (eds) (2008) *Organized Crime. Culture, Markets and Policies*, pp. 97–112. New York: Springer.

Boekhout van Solinge, T. 2008b. 'Crime, conflicts and ecology in africa', in R. Sollund (ed.) (2008) *Global Harms. Ecological Crime and Speciesism*, pp. 13–34. New York: Nova Science.

Boekhout van Solinge, T. 2008c. 'The Land of the Orangutan and Bird of Paradise under Threat', in R. Sollund (ed.) (2008) *Global Harms. Ecological Crime and Speciesism*, pp. 51–70. New York: Nova Science.

Boekhout van Solinge, T. 2010a. 'Equatorial deforestation as a harmful practice and criminological issue', in R. White (ed.) (2010) *Global Environmental Harm. Criminological Perspectives*, pp. 20–36. Collumpton, Devon, UK: Willan.

Boekhout van Solinge, T. 2010b. 'Deforestation crimes and conflicts in the amazon', *Critical Criminology: An International Journal*, 18(4): 263–277.

Boekhout van Solinge, T. 2014a. 'Natural resources and organized crime', in L. Paoli (ed.) *Oxford Handbook of Organized Crime*, pp. 500–528. New York: Oxford University Press.

Boekhout van Solinge, T. 2014b. 'Researching illegal logging and deforestation', *International Journal for Crime, Justice and Social Democracy*, 3(2): 35–48.

Boekhout van Solinge, T. 2016. 'Deforestation in the brazilian amazon', in R. Sivanpillai (ed.) *Biological and Environmental Hazards, Risks, and Disasters*, pp. 373–395. Amsterdam/Oxford/Waltham: Elsevier.

Boekhout van Solinge, T., Sauer, S., Vélez-Torres, I. and Berrocal Vargas-van Den Brink, B. (eds.) 2016a. *Terra E Direitos En Áquas Turbulentas: Conflitos Socioambientais Em Brasil E Colombia*. Utrecht: Utrecht University/Lands and Rights in Troubled Waters [also in Spanish].

Boekhout van Solinge, T. 2018a. 'Georganiseerde Houtcriminaliteit in De Braziliaanse Amazone [organized Timber Crime in the Brazilian Amazon]', *Tijdschrift Voor Criminologie*, 2(60): 142–156. DOI: 10.5553/TvC/0165182X2018060002002. Available at: https://bjutijdschriften.nl/tijdschrift/tijdschriftcriminologie/2018/2/TvC_0165-182X_2018_060_002_002.

Boekhout van Solinge, T. 2018b. 'GPS-supported, Community-based Forest-crime Prevention in the Brazilian Amazon', *Trading Ideas* (newsletter), November 2018, Oxford Martin Programme on the Illegal Wildlife Trade, University of Oxford. Available at: http://illegalwildlifetrade.net/2018/11/22/gps-supported-community-based-forest-crime-prevention-in-the-brazilian-amazon/ (Consulted 22 November 2018).

Boekhout van Solinge, T., Zuidema, P., Vlam, M., Cerutti, P. O. and Emelin, V. 2016b. 'Organized Forest Crime. A Criminological Analysis with Suggestions from Timber Forensics', in D. Kleinschmit, S. Mansourian, C. Wildburger and A. Purret (eds.) *Illegal Logging and Related Timber Trade – Dimensions, Drivers, Impacts and Responses. A Global Scientific Rapid Response Assessment Report*. pp., 81–96. Wenen: IUFRO. Available at: https://iufro.org/science/gfep/illegal-timber-trade-rapid-response/report/

Brack, D., Glover, A. and Wellesley, L. 2016. *Agricultural Commodity Supply Chains. Trade, Consumption and Deforestation*. London: Chatham House. Available at: https://chathamhouse.org/sites/default/files/publications/research/2016-01-28-agricultural-commodities-brack-glover-wellesley.pdf.

Brandford, S., Torres, M. 2017. 'Getting there: The rush to turn the amazon into a soy transport corridor', *Mongabay*, February 15. Available at: https://news.mongabay.com/2017/02/getting-there-the-rush-to-turn-the-amazon-into-a-soy-transport-corridor/.

Brisman, A., and South, N. 2019. 'A criminology of extinction: Biodiversity, extreme consumption and the vanity of species resurrection', *European Journal of Criminology*. First published 28 February 2019. DOI: 10.1177/1477370819828307.

Brito, B, Barreto, P. 2011. *A Regularização Fundiária Avancou Na Amazônia? Os Dois Anos Do Programa Terra Legal*. Belém: Imazon.

Brooks, B. (28 May 2011) 'Like many before, amazon activists silenced by gun', *The Boston Globe*. Available at: http://articles.boston.com/2011-05-28/news/29601132_1_rain-forest-amazon-activists-amazon-state.

Butchart, S. H. M. et al. 2010. 'Global Diversity: Indicators of Recent Declines', *Science*, 328 (5982): 1164–1168.

Cargill Brasil. 2012. *Princípios Éticos*. Available at: http://cargill.com.br/pt/sobre-cargill-brasil/principios-eticos/index.jsp.

Cargill. 2010. *Growing Together. Cargill Corporate Sustainability Report 2010*. Minneapolis: Cargill.

Cargill. 2011. *Cargill completes acquisition of Provimi to create leading global animal nutrition business*. Available at: www.cargill.com/news/releases/2011/NA3052248.jsp.

Cargill. 2014. Statement *Responsible Soy Production: Respecting and Engaging with the Local Community in Santarém*. Available at: http://cargill.com/corporate-responsibility/pov/soy-production/local-community-santarem/index.jsp.

Cargill. n.d. 'Fighting deforestation & poverty witg sustainable soy', Available at: http://150.cargill.com/150/en/SUPPORTING-BRAZILIAN-FOREST.jsp.

CIMI—Conselho Indigenista Missionário. 2009. *Violene against Indigenous Peoples in Brazil*, Brasilia: CIMI (Indigenous Missionary Council). Available at: https://cimi.org.br/pub/relatorio/Report-Violence-against-the-Indigenous-Peoples-in-Brazil_2014-Cimi.pdf.

Cohenca, D. 2005. 'A Expansão Da Fronteira Agrícola E Seu Relação Com O Desmatamento Detectado Em Imagens Landsat TM E ETM+ Na Região Norte Da BR-163', *Pará entre os anos 1999 a 2004*. Available at: http://ibama.gov.br/flona_tapajos/download.php?id_download=136.

Coordenação-Geral de Observação da Terra. 2012. *DETER 01/2012- Resumo*. São José dos Campos: INPE.

CPEA—Consultoria Paulista de Estudos Ambientais. 2010. *Terminal Fluvial De Granéis Sólidos Da Cargill Agrícola S.A. RIMA. Relatório De Impacto Ambiental. Edição Revisada E Atualizada*, São Paulo: CPEA.

CPT—Comissão Pastoral da Terra. 2010. *Povos Da Floresta: Resistência Contra O Grande Capital No Baixo Amazonas*. Santarém: CPT Santarém.

CPT—Comissão Pastoral da Terra. 2011. *Conflitos No Campo Brasil 2010*. Goiânia: CPT.

CPT—Comissão Pastoral da Terra. 2018. *Conflitos No Campo Brasil 2017*. Goiânia: CPT. Online Available at: https://cptnacional.org.br/component/jdownloads/send/41-conflitos-no-campo-brasil-publicacao/14110-conflitos-no-campo-brasil-2017-web?Itemid=0 (Consulted 18 November 2018).
CPT—Comissão Pastoral da Terra. 2009. *Conflitos No Campo Brasil 2008*, Goiâna: CPT (Pastoral Land Commission).
Davidson, E. A., de Araújo, A. C., Artaxo, P., Balch, J. K., Brown, I. F., Bustamante, M. M. C., Coe, M. T., DeFries, R. S., Keller, M., Longo, M., Munger, J. W., Schroeder, W., Soares-Filho, B. S., Souza Jr, C. M., Wofsy, S. C. 2012. 'The Amazon Basin in Transition', *Nature*, 481: 321–328.
De Mello, T. and Marigo, T. L. 2007. *Amazonas. Patria Da Água – Amazonas Water Heartland*. São Paulo: Editora Boccota (publication in Portuguese and English).
EIA and Telapak. 2004. *Profiting from Plunder: How Malaysia Smuggles Endangered Wood*. London: EIA.
EIA and Telapak. 2005. *The Last Frontier. Illegal Logging in Papua and China's Massive Timber Theft*. London: EIA.
EIA and Telapak. 2006. *Behind the Veneer: How Indonesia's Last Rainforests are Being Felled for Flooring*. London: EIA.
EIA and Telapak. 2010. *Rogue Traders: The Murky Business of Merbau Timber Smuggling in Indonesia*. London: EIA.
Fiocruz and FASE. 2012. *Mapa da Justiça Ambiental e Justiça no Brasil*. Available at: http://conflitoambiental.icict.fiocruz.br/.
French, H. W. 2009. 'Kagame's Hidden War in the Congo', *The New York Review of Books*, September 24, 2009.
Gibbs, H. K., Rausch, L., Munger, J., Schelly, I., Morton, D. C., Noojipady, P., Soares-Filho, B., Barreto, P., Micol, L., Walker, N. F., 2015. 'Brazil's Soy Moratorium. Supply-chain Governance Is Needed to Avoid Deforestation', *Science*, 347(6220): 377, published January 23, 2015. Available at: http://sage.wisc.edu/pubs/articles/Gibbs/GibbsetalScience2015.pdf.
Global Witness. 2014. *Deadly Environment. The Dramatic Increase in Killings of Environmental and Land Defenders*. London: Global Witness.
Global Witness. 2016. *On Dangerous Ground*. London: Global Witness.
Global Witness. 2018. *At What Cost? Irresponsible Business and the Murder of Land Environmental Defenders in 2017*. London: Global Witness.
Goldsmith, P., Hirsch, R. 2006. 'The Brazilian Soybean Complex', *Choices*, 21(2): 97–103.
Goncalves, M. P., Panjer, M., Greenberg, T. S. and Magrath, W. B. 2012. *Justice for Forests. Improving Criminal Justice Efforts to Combat Illegal Logging*. Washington: The World Bank.
Goulding, M., Barthem, R. and Ferreira, E. 2003. *The Smithsonian Atlas of the Amazon*. Washington and London: Smithsonian.
Grandin, G. 2010. *Fordlandia. The Rise and Fall of Henry Ford's Forgotten Jungle City*, 2nd ed. London: Icon Books.
Greenpeace International. 2003. *State of Conflict. An Investigation into the Landgrabbers, Loggers and Lawless Frontiers in Pará State, Amazon*. Amsterdam: Greenpeace International.
Greenpeace International. 2006a. *Eating up the Amazon*. Amsterdam: Greenpeace International.
Greenpeace International. 2006b. *We're Trashing It. How McDonald's Is Eating up the Amazon*. Amsterdam: Greenpeace International.
Hilker, T., Lyapustin, A. I., Tucker, C. J., Hall, F. G., Myneni, R. B., Wang, Y., Bi, J., de Moura, Y. M., Sellers, P. J., 2014. 'Vegetation Dynamics and Rainfall Sensitivity of the Amazon', *Proceedings of the National Academy of Sciences of the United States of America*, 111(45): 16041e16046. DOI: 10.1073/pnas.1404870111.
IBGE—Brazilian Institute of Geography and Statistics. 2011. *Produção Agrícola Municipal 2010*, Rio de Janeiro: IBGE (Brazilian Institute for Geography and Statistics).
INTERPOL. 2016. *Uncovering the Risks of Corruption in the Forestry Sector*. Lyon: INTERPOL.
IPCC—Intergovernmental Panel on Climate Change. 2007. *Climate Change 2007. Summary for Policy Makers*. Geneva: IPCC.
Jackson, J. 2008. *The Thief at the End of the World: Rubber, Power, and the Seeds of Empire*. New York: Viking.
Jopke, P. and Schoneveld, G. C. 2018. *Corporate Commitments to Zero Deforestation*. Bogor, CIFOR.
Kaimowitz, D., Smith, J. 2001. 'Soybean technology and the loss of natural vegetation in brazil and bolivia', in A. Angelsen, D. Kaimowitz (eds.) *Agricultural Technologies and Tropical Deforestation*. Wallingford: CAB International.

Khatchadourian, R. 2008. 'The stolen forests. inside the covert war on illegal logging', *The New Yorker*, October 6, 2008.

Kishi, J. 20 April 2012. Exposição Apresenta Objetos Arqueológicos Tapajônicos, *Jornal De Santarém E Baixo Amazonas*, 5.

Kleinschmit, D., Mansourian, S., Wildburger, C. and A. Purret (eds.) 2016. *Illegal Logging and Related Timber Trade. Dimensions, Drivers, Impacts and Responses. A Global Scientific Rapid Response Assessment Report*. Vienna: International Union of Forest Research Organizations (IUFRO).

Kneen, B. 2002. Invisible giant: Cargill and its transnational strategies. London, UK: Pluto Press.

Kolstad, I. and Søreide, T. 2009. 'Corruption in natural resource management: Implications for policy makers', *Resources Policy*, 34: 214–226.

Kuijpers, K. 2018a, 25 April. 'Duurzaamheid Is Slecht Een Verhaaltje', *De Groene Amsterdammer*, Available at: https://groene.nl/artikel/duurzaamheid-is-slechts-een-verhaaltje.

Kuijpers, K. 2018b, 29 May. 'Dutch support soy mega-project, posing major risk to amazon, mongabay.' Available at: https://news.mongabay.com/2018/05/dutch-support-soy-transport-mega-project-posing-major-risk-to-amazon/.

Lawson, S. and MacFaul, L. 2010. *Illegal Logging and Related Trade. Indicators of the Global Response*. London: Chatham House.

Lawson, S., 2014. *Consumer Goods and Deforestation: An Analysis of the Extent and Nature of Illegality in Forest Conversion for Agriculture and Timber Plantations*. Washington: Forest Trends.

Leakey, R. E. and Lewin, R. 1996. *The Sixth Extinction. Patterns of Life and the Future of Humankind*. London: Weidenfeld and Nicolson.

London, M. and Kelly, B. 2007. *The Last Forest. The Amazon in the Age of Globalisation*. New York: Random House.

Loureiro, V. R. 2001. *Estado, Bandidos E Heróis. Utopia E Luta Na Amazônia*. Belém: Cejup.

Makarieva, A. M., Gorshkov, V. G., 2007. 'Biotic Pump of Atmospheric Moisture as Driver of the Hydrological Cycle on Land', *Hydrology and Earth System Sciences*, 11: 1013e1033.

Malhi, Y., Roberts, J. T., Betts, R. A., Killeen, T. J., Li, W. and Nobre, C. A. 2008. 'Climate Change, Deforestation, and the Fate of the Amazon', *Science*, 319(5860): 169–192.

Mann, C. C., Hecht, S. 2012. 'Where slaves ruled', *National Geographic*, April 2012. Available at: http://ngm.nationalgeographic.com/2012/04/maroon-people/mann-hecht-text.

Mendes, C. 1989. *Fight for the Forest. Chico Mendes in His Own Words*. London: Latin America Bureau.

Meyer, D. E., Cederberg, C. 2010. *Pesticide Use and Glyphosate-resistant Weeds. A Case Study of Brazilian Soybean Production*. Gothenburg: SIK (Swedish Institute for Food and Biotechnology).

Middleton, L. 2007. 'The last place on earth … to make contact with civilization', *New Scientist*, 194 (2608): 37.

Ministério Público do Estado do Pará. Procuradoria Geral de Justiça (29 July 2011) *MP denuncia empresa de consultoria por apresentar estudo ambiental enganoso*. Available at: http://mp.pa.gov.br/index.php?action=Menu.interna&id=320&class=N.

MPF—Ministério Público Fédéral (10 November 2017) MPF Recomenda Cancelamento De Audiências Públicas Sobre a Ferrogrão. Available at: http://mpf.mp.br/mt/sala-de-imprensa/noticias-mt/mpf-recomenda-cancelamento-de-audiencias-publicas-sobre-a-ferrograo (Consulted 10 November 2018).

MPF—Ministério Público Fédéral (31 October 2018) Justiça Paralisa Concessão Da Ferrogrão Por Insuficiência De Estudos Socioambientais. Available at: http://mpf.mp.br/pa/sala-de-imprensa/noticias-pa/justica-paralisa-concessao-da-ferrograo-por-insuficiencia-de-estudos-socioambientais (Consulted 10 November 2018).

Mueller, C. C. 2004. *Brazil: Agriculture and Agrarian Development and the Lula Government*, Paper for the 2004 Meeting of the Latin American Studies Association, 7-9 October 2004. Las Vegas, Nevada.

Nazareno, A. G. 2012. 'Call to veto brazil's forest-code revisions', *Nature*, 481: 29.

Nelleman, C., Henriksen, R., Kreilhuber, A., Stewart, D., Kotsovou, M., Raxter, P., Mrema, E., and Barrat, S., 2016. *The Rise of Environmental Crime. A Growing Threat to Natural Resources, Peace, Development and Security. A UNEP-INTERPOL Rapid Response Assessment*. United Nations Environment Programme and RHIPTO Rapid Response–Norwegian Centre for Global Analyses.

Nellemann, C. and Interpol. 2012. *Green Carbon, Black Trade. Illegal Logging, Tax Fraud and Laundering in the World's Tropical Forests*. Oslo: Norad.

Nepstad, D. C., Stickler, C. M., Almeida, O. T. 2006. 'Globalization of the amazon soy and beef industries: Opportunities for conservation', *Conservation Biology*, 20(6): 1595–1603.

Nobre, A. D. 2014. 'The Future Climate of Amazonia. Scientific Assessment Report', Articulación Regional Amazonica (ARA), São José dos Campos. Online at: http://ccst.inpe.br/wp-content/uploads/2014/11/The_Future_Climate_of_Amazonia_Report.pdf.

Oldfield, S. 2005. 'Regulation of the timber trade,' in S. Oldfield (ed.) *The Trade in Wildlife. Regulation for Conservation*. London: Earthscan, 121–131.

Ottaway, D., Stephens, J. (4 May 2003) 'Nonprofit Land Bank Amasses Billions', *Washington Post*, 4 May 2003. Available at: http://washingtonpost.com/wp-dyn/content/article/2007/06/26/AR2007062600803.html.

PAD (Processo de Articulação e Diálogo), MNDH (Movimento Nacional de Direitos Humanos). 2006. *A Criminalização Dos Movimentos Sociais No Brasil. Relatório De Casos Exemplares*. Brasília: MNDH (National Movements for Human Rights).

Passos, C. J. S., Infante Córdoba, C. M., Pires, N. L., Da Silva Caldas, B. M., Vélez-Torres, I., Barba Ho, L. E., Cruz Vélez, C. 2016. 'Residuos De Glifosato Y Ampa En Fuentes Naturales De Agua Y Límites Normativos Para Valorar La Contaminacion En Brasil Y Colombia,' in T. Boekhout van Solinge, S. Sauer, I. Vélez-Torres and B. Berrocal Vargas-van Den Brink (eds.) *Terra E Direitos En Áquas Turbulentas: Conflitos Socioambientais Em Brasil E Colombia*. Utrecht: Utrecht University/Lands and Rights in Troubled Waters [also in Spanish].

Phillips, T. (22 December 2008) 'Hundreds of brazil's eco-warriors at risk of assassination'. *The Guardian*. December 22, 2008. Available at: http://guardian.co.uk/world/2008/dec/22/brazil-activists-mendes.

Phillips, T. (24 May 2011) 'Amazon Rainforest Activist Shot Dead'. *The Guardian*. 24 May 2011. Available at: http://guardian.co.uk/world/2011/may/24/amazon-rainforest-activist-killed.

Polícia Civil do Estado do Pará. 2011. *Governo Do Estado Do Pará. Secretaría De Segurança Pública. Polícia Civil Do Estado Do Pará. Relatório. Inquérito Policial No. 273/2009.000082-4/DOA/DIOE*. Belém: Polícia Civil.

Pollan, M. 2008. *In Defence of Food. The Myth of Nutrition and the Pleasure of Eating*. London/New York: Penguin.

Procuradoria do Estado do Pará. 2007. Justiça Indefere Pedido De Censura Da Cargill. *Procuradoria do Estado do Pará, Ministério Público Federal*. Available at: http://prpa.mpf.gov.br/news/2007/noticias1/justica-indefere-pedido-de-censura-da-cargill.

Rangel, L. H. (ed.). 2014. *Violence against Indigenous Peoples in Brazil*. Brasilia: Conselho Indigenista Missionário – Cimi.

Red de Alta Dirección, The Nature Conservancy. 2005. *Amazonas. An Open Laboratory. Sustainability, Economy, Development, Social Justice. Exclusive CEO Expedition*. Santiago: Red de Alta Dirección.

Rodrigues Da Cunha Soares, M. 2007. *Lei Kandir: Breve Histórico*. Brasília: Consultoria Legislativa, Câmara dos Deputados.

Santana, R. R. 2010. *Justiça Ambiental Na Amazônia. Análise De Casos Emblemáticos*. Curitiba: Juruá Editora.

Sante Croix, de, S. (6 December 2011) IMF Praises Brazilian Economy on Visit. *Rio Times, 6 December 2011*. Available at: http://riotimesonline.com/brazil-news/rio-business/imf-praises-brazilian-economy-on-visit/#.

Sauer, S. 2018. 'Soy expansion into the agricultural frontiers of the brazilian amazon: The agribusiness economy and its social and environmental conflicts', *Land Use Policy*, 79: 326–338. DOI: 10.1016/j.landusepol.2018.08.030.

Schaan, D. P. 2012. *A Arqueologia Na Região De Santarém*. Universidade Federal do Pará (UFPA). Available at: http://marajoara.com/files/A_arqueologia_na_regi_o_de_Santar_m.pdf.

Schlesinger, S., Noronha, S. 2006. *O Brasil Está Nu! O Avanço Da Monocultura Da Soja, O Grão Que Cresceu Demais*. Rio de Janeiro: FASE.

SDDH (Sociedade Paraense de Defesa dos Direitos Humanos), MST (Movimento dos Trabalhadores/as Rurais sem Terra), CPT (Comissão Pastoral da Terra), MAB (Movimentos dos Atingidos/as por Barragens), Intersindical, Conlutas, CIMI (Conselho Indigenista Missionário). 2010. *Para Entender a Criminalização Dos Movimentos Sociais E Defensores De Direitos Humanos No Pará*. Belem: SDDH.

Seymour, F. 2018. 'Deforestation is accelerating, despite mounting efforts to protect tropical forests. what are we doing wrong?' Blog of Global Forest Watch, June 27, 2018. Available at: https://blog.globalforestwatch.org/data/deforestation-is-accelerating-despite-mounting-efforts-to-protect-tropical-forests-what-are-we-doing-wrong.

Silva, C., Rylands, A. B. and Da Fonesca, G. A. B. 2005. 'The fate of the amazonian areas of endemism', *Conservation Biology*, 19: 689–694.

Singer, P. 2002. 'Not for humans only. The place of nonhumans in environmental ethics' in A. Light, H. Rolston (eds.) *Environmental Ethics. An Anthology*, pp. 55–64. Oxford: Blackwell Publishing.

Singer, P. 2004. *One World. The Ethics of Globalization*. New Haven & London: Yale University Press.

Somers, M. 2014. 'Klem in the Voedselketen [translation: Stuck in the Food Chain], Interview with Olivier De Schutter, Special UN Envoy for the Right to Food, *NRC Handelsblad*, February 21, 2014.

SOS Florestas and WWF. 2012. *Código Florestal. Entenda O Que Está Em Jogo Com a Reforma Da Nossa Legislação Ambiental*. Rio de Janeiro: SOS Florestas.

South, N. 2007. 'The "corporate colonisation of nature": Bio-prospecting, bio-piracy and the development of green criminology', in P. Beirne and N. South (eds.) *Issues in Green* Criminology. *Confronting Harms against Environments, Humanity and Other Animals*, pp. 230–247. Cullompont, Devon, UK: Willan.

Steward, C. 2007. 'From colonization to "environmental soy": A case study of environmental and socio-economic valuation in the amazon soy frontier', *Agriculture and Human Values*, 24: 107–122.

The New York Times (14 June 2003). 'In Wake of Criticism, Nature Conservancy Changes Policies', *The New York Times*, 14 June 2003. Available at: https://www.nytimes.com/2003/06/14/national/in-wake-of-criticism-nature-conservancy-changes-policies.html.

Tollefson, J. 2007. 'Deforestation on the agenda at climate meeting?', *Nature*, 450(7170): 590–591.

Tsing, A. L. 2005. *Friction. An Ethnography of Global Connection*. Princeton: Princeton University Press.

UNEP—United Nation Environment Programme. 2006. *Brazil: Integrated Assessment and Planning in the Context of the Sustainable Amazon Plan: With Focus on the BR-163 Highway Area of Influence and the Soybean Sector*. UNEP. Available at: http://unep.ch/etb/areas/pdf/Brazil%20Report.pdf.

UNSC—United Nations Security Council. 2001. *Report by the Panel of Experts on the Illegal Exploitation of Natural Resources and Other Forms of Wealth of the Democratic Republic of Congo*. New York: United Nations Security Council (Report S/2001/357).

Van Dijk, J., Tseloni, A., and Farrell, G. 2012. *The International Crime Drop. New Directions in Research*. Basingstoke, Hampshire, UK: Palgrave Macmillan.

Verweij, P., Schouten, M., van Beukering, P., Triana, J., van der Leeuw, K. and Hess, S. 2009. *Keeping the Amazon Forests Standing: A Matter of Values*. Zeist: WWF Netherlands.

Wallace, A. R. 1852. 'On the monkeys of the amazon', *Proceedings of the Zoological Society of London*, 20: 107–110.

Wilson, E. O. 2002. *The Future of Life*. New York: Vintage.

Wyatt, T, and Brisman, A. 2017. 'The role of denial in the "theft of nature": A comparison of biopiracy and climate change', *Critical Criminology: An International Journal*, 25(3): 325–341. DOI: 10.1007/s10612-016-9344-5. FirstOnline: 14 September 2016. Available via Open Access at: http://link.springer.com/article/10.1007/s10612-016-9344-5.

16

Green issues in South-Eastern Europe

Katja Eman and Gorazd Meško

On 4 October 2010, the retaining wall of a caustic waste reservoir at the Ajka Timföldgyár Zrt alumina plant in Veszprém County in western Hungary collapsed, releasing more than one million cubic metres (38 million cubic feet) of highly alkaline red sludge (Taylor 2011; Williams 2014). The mud—a poisonous byproduct of aluminium extraction—rushed into the nearby villages of Kolontár, Devecser and Somlóvásárhely, claiming ten lives, flooding a 40 square km area and polluting the Danube River and its tributaries all the way to the Black Sea. This ecological disaster, which was caused by human negligence, reminded people in Hungary and neighbouring countries how fragile nature is and how easily human lives can be endangered. Unfortunately, it is just one of many examples of environmental crime and harm in South-Eastern Europe that has devastated and destroyed a wide range of ecosystems and life forms, with restoration taking decades, or even centuries.

While the Ajka accident received international attention (see, e.g., Bilefsky 2010a, 2010b; Rosenthal 2010a, 2010b), much environmental harm in South-Eastern Europe falls under the international radar, making an examination and analysis of the crimes, harm, risks and threats to the environment in South-Eastern Europe especially important. Although the number of studies on crime against the environment in the region is increasing gradually, more research is necessary. In this chapter, we provide an overview of environmental problems in the following countries: Albania, Bosnia and Herzegovina, Bulgaria, Croatia, Hungary, Kosovo, the Republic of North Macedonia, Romania, Serbia, Slovenia and the Ukraine. In so doing, we attempt to identify and draw upon green criminological work that has been conducted in these countries in the last two decades, in order to reveal some common and some specific characteristics of the environmental issues in South-Eastern Europe.

Green issues in specific countries of South-Eastern Europe

Before beginning our analysis of green issues in South-Eastern Europe, a word about terminology is in order. The area we refer to as 'South-Eastern Europe' is sometimes also referred to as the 'Balkans' or the 'Western-Balkans'.[1] Different definitions and descriptions of the geographical extent of the region exist, however. For example, Bufon (2006: 123) stresses that the area of South-Eastern Europe is not easily defined because there is no 'correct' geopolitical vision and that all terms are equally useful and used: South-Eastern Europe is 'basically a product of the definer's imagination, determined, not by its actual geographical position, but rather by its fluid geopolitical position among European regional powers'.

Approximately two decades ago, the term *South-Eastern Europe* was suggested to replace the negative connotations of the word *Balkans* for the region (for a discussion, see Lampe 2006). The Stability Pact for Southeastern Europe[2] and the Southeast Europe Transnational Co-Operation Programme[3] have influenced the 'form', growth and use of the term *South-Eastern Europe*. For the purposes of the present chapter, we employ the broadest form of the definition for the region of South-Eastern Europe to include the borders of the European Union and the 'Southeast Europe Transnational Co-Operation Programme' definition.[4] Therefore, our chapter provides a short analysis of the most important green issues and the role of green criminology (Clifford 1998; Eman, Meško and Fields 2009; Eman et al. 2013; Meško, Dimitrijević and Fields 2011b; South 1998; South, Eman and Meško 2014; White 2009) in Albania, Bosnia and Herzegovina, Bulgaria, Croatia, Hungary, Kosovo, the Republic of North Macedonia, Romania, Serbia, Slovenia and Ukraine.

Albania

In Albania, the protection of biodiversity (e.g., illegal poaching, illegal logging) and natural resources, as well as waste management, water management and energy resources, represent essential environmental issues (Todić 2011; Zenelaj and Elezi 2013). Since June 2014, Albania has been a candidate for entry into the European Union (EU) and, as such, has adopted the requirements of the specific EU directives on the protection of the environment through criminal law (Turkeshi 2015).

Albania is considered a country with lots of pollution, especially air pollution, where deterioration of air quality caused approximately 2,120 deaths in 2016 (European Environment Agency 2017). Waste management is another issue and hazardous waste (including radioactive and chemical materials), in particular, represents an enormous problem because there is a substantial illicit trans-national hazardous waste business involving a wide array of criminals, including private entities, corrupt public officials and organised crime groups. Furthermore, trafficking in animal and plant species (e.g., illegal logging) is also a very profitable business for organised crime groups (Liddick 2009; Zenelaj and Elezi 2013). In the last decade, the problems of illegal poaching and excessive deforestation have emerged as significant (Turkeshi 2015). These activities can have severely negative environmental and human health consequences, leading to forms of environmental victimisation and the death of innocent people. Albanian organised crime is globally known due to its power and 'business' operations, which extend beyond its borders across the Balkan Peninsula. Albanian organised crime families control all possible illegal activities, with logging, poaching, trafficking of animal and plant species and hazardous waste-trafficking being just some of the most profitable environmental crime activities in this part of South-Eastern Europe.

Bosnia and Herzegovina

The field of environmental protection and environmental harm has not been researched sufficiently in Bosnia and Herzegovina (Muratbegović and Guso 2011: 102), yet environmental harm in these regions has been acute in recent years. This has stemmed, in part, from the rapid development of technologies (Modly 1998) that use powerful new energy sources, as well as from the construction of new industrial plants in large urban areas that has also resulted in environmental harm (Muratbegović and Guso 2011; Petrović and Meško 2013).

The four key green issues in Bosnia and Herzegovina are as follows: 1) water pollution (specifically, household discharges and industrial wastewater (Eman 2016; Mujanović 2009); 2) air pollution (i.e., industrial plant emissions, along with increased amounts of ash and soot from thermal power plants (Balkan Insight 2015);[5] 3) de-forestation and illegal logging—both of which destroy natural habitats and contribute to poor air quality;[6] and 4) animal torture, poaching and trafficking (e.g., violent behaviour towards animals in the form of poaching and hunting endangered species for meat, trophies, or trafficking).

Finally, it is worth drawing attention to the continuing growth in industrial capacity as coal and natural mineral mines are opening, and construction of hydro-accumulations and travel communications is being undertaken. While there have been attempts to regulate these industries, new categories of crimes have emerged from the flouting of environmental laws (e.g., hazardous waste and the involvement of organised crime) (Golić 2005; Muratbegović and Guso 2011; Sućeska 2008; Variščić 2008).

Bulgaria

In Bulgaria, renewable and environmentally friendly energy resources are the most important environmental issues. Yarnal (1994) exposed the legacy of petrochemical complexes, coastal-zone hazards management and the Kozloduy nuclear facility as constituting Bulgaria's environmental threats. The energy sector is one of the main sources of pollution with its release of greenhouse gases from burning coal, gas and oil. Furthermore, nuclear power plants have produced, and continue to produce, nuclear waste, which presents disposal problems and which, as in other South-Eastern European countries, has provided opportunities for organised crime. Air quality improvement and the protection of forests, soils and water resources also represent key areas of concern (Gramatikov 2009). Bulgaria is one of the countries of the Danube-Carpathian region, where environmental crimes such as illegal fishing, illegal logging, poaching and a black market for caviar are putting 'high pressure' on ecosystems (European Commission 2019).

Croatia

With inefficient or non-existent waste management and waste disposal, people pollute the air, soil and water, and endanger animal and plant species. Such behaviour also presents a risk to human health. According to Kulišić (2011) and Levenat (1997), waste management and disposal is one of the most worrying environmental issues in Croatia, especially the manufacture and burning of hazardous waste in cement factories without sewage treatment. In many situations, water and soil remediation is impossible, leaving some areas virtually (and permanently) barren and uninhabitable. In addition to the issues regarding waste management and disposal, excessive hunting and over-fishing, along with poaching, animal torture (Bezuh et al. 2009), illegal logging and illegal excavation of minerals (Eman et al. 2013; Lonarčić-Horvat et al. 1998;) constitute the most prevalent environmental issues. Finally, the country has a long coastline and environmental threats, such as water runoff from urban areas and pollution in the course of oil transport, present risks to marine and coastal life (Morović 2008). An emerging issue—or series of issues—within the last decade is—or are—crime(s) against water (Moretti et al. 2017).

Hungary

As noted at the outset, an accident at the aluminium factory in Ajka on 4 October 2010 claimed ten deaths[7] and flooded a 40 square km area, polluting the Danube River and its tributaries all the way to the Black Sea.[8] The accident, which occurred as the result of the factory owner's negligence (i.e., insufficient repair and maintenance of parts) revealed the lack and inadequacy of environmental protection policies in the country.

Even before the October 2010 accident, waste management was an issue of concern in Hungary. Research conducted by Cserny, Utasi and Domokos (2009) reveals the problems of poorly maintained or located landfills causing soil and water pollution, and subsequently endangering animal and plant species in the Danube River basin. The same is happening with the world-famous Balaton Lake, where the human intervention (especially inadequate waste management (Dorn, Van Daele and Vander Beken 2007)) has caused irreparable environmental damage and devastation. Waste trafficking is an increasing problem, especially electronic and toxic waste (Kerezsi and Lévay 2008);[9] the same could be said for water crimes (Moretti et al. 2017).

Hungarian agriculture is very successful, but excessive use of (prohibited) fertilisers and pesticides has resulted in the acidification and salinisation of soil, soil erosion and water pollution. Finally, the so-called 'hunting tourism', while one of the most profitable sources of income for the Indigenous people, has endangered a number of wildlife species (e.g., brown hare, grey partridge, mountain goat, red, fallow and roe deer, and wild boar are endangered (Csányi 1997)). As with other countries in South-Eastern Europe, illegal logging is becoming an increasing problem.

Kosovo

Kosovo is one of the most impoverished and most polluted countries in the world. Environmental crime and harm in Kosovo are a consequence not only of the tragedy of war but also of endemic poverty and a weak state institutional system prone to corruption and organised crime (Fajardo del Castillo 2017). The environmental issues in Kosovo are numerous, most notably, air pollution, water pollution and soil contamination—all a result of poor infrastructure management and the lack of an environmental protection regime in the past (Hakaj, Balaj and Hoxha 2007). Air pollution, in the form of carbon dioxide, nitrogen oxide and dust from thermal power plants burning coal, is a particular problem. In addition, air quality is exacerbated by the transport sector, which possesses a large number of old vehicles that use low-grade fuel, and which employs trains running on diesel rather than electricity.

Due to the lack of regulation and infrastructure, power plants have been causing severe amounts of water pollution. Finally, coal exploration creates open mines of lignite, which are later filled with water. Due to their hazardous contents, almost no forms of life develop or survive in them. The coal that is extracted is usually transported in open wagons or truck-trailers, and is stored in containers or facilities where it is not prevented from spreading ash into the air, soil and water (Hakaj, Balaj and Hoxha 2007).

Finally, Fajardo del Castillo (2017: 161) has noted that Kosovo

> experiences serious problems of enforcement due to lack of human resources and expertise and weak governance as well as corruption and organized crime. These problems are at the root of illegal practices that are openly carried on in most of the territory of Kosovo: illegal logging, illegal hunting, illegal waste management, illegal building, destruction of cultural heritage of minorities, etc.

Republic of North Macedonia

In this successor state of the former Yugoslavia, almost all forms of environmental crime occur—from air, water and soil pollution, to illegal waste disposal and endangering animal and plant species. The most problematic forms of environmental crime, however, appear to be the devastation of forests due to illegal logging, as well as poaching and illegal fishing (Eman et al. 2013; Malis Sazdovska 2011). Illegal logging is one of the most productive organised crime activities in North Macedonia, where criminal groups protect their work with an impressive arsenal of weapons. Organised crime also thrives in North Macedonia as a result of bribery and corruption, undefined (or under-defined) criminal policies for environmental crimes, low penalties for those that do exist, lack of awareness on the part of the public, and, finally, organised crime's legal activities, which provide covers for their illicit endeavours. Malis Sazdovska (2009) has also indicated that eco-terrorism (i.e., terrorist acts targeting natural resources, such as soil and water, as well as food sources, with the purpose of harming people) is a security threat in this part of the Balkan Peninsula (Meško et al. 2011b).

Romania

In Romania, the situation is very similar to Hungary: both countries suffer from Danube River pollution and both are experiencing wildlife loss (e.g., brown bear, lynx, red and roe deer, wild boar, wolf) as a result of hunting by foreign tourists (Leslie et al. 1995). In particular, the ecosystems in the Danube River, in the Danube Delta and along the Romanian coast of the Black Sea, are under very strong European 'atrophic pressure'. Human activity in the upper Danube River system is causing pollution with inorganic constituents (e.g., nutrients, metals) and organic constituents (e.g., green waste, food waste, sewage), resulting in negative impacts on the lower Danube water system: high levels of nutrients in the Danube Delta contribute to excessive growth of some plants or species, dramatically affecting and damaging the ecosystems in the area (OCCRP 2017). In the last decade, Romania has had a huge problem with water resources and crimes against water (Eman and Humar 2017; Moretti et al. 2017).

Waste disposal is another issue for Romania. Besides domestic waste management, Romania, after joining the European Union, has experienced considerable increases in hazardous waste shipments from western European countries to the east by buses, trucks and vans that are not equipped properly or authorised to carry hazardous waste. Law enforcement personnel have found that, in many cases, shipments do not have the required documentation necessary for transporting hazardous substances. There is a very high possibility that this waste from France, Italy and Spain—which includes nuclear waste—is being dumped in the forested areas of Romania, as well as those in Hungary and Slovenia (Eman and Franca 2016; Eman et al. 2013).

Serbia

Legal protection of the environment in Serbia goes back to the middle of the nineteenth century and has evolved gradually to the present. That said, Serbia has, like other Balkan Peninsula countries, faced the challenges of governmental transition that, as a result, has affected the (criminal) legal provisions for environmental protection (Ljuština 2010).

In Serbia, the problem of excessive hunting and fishing without appropriate concern for habitat preservation or species restoration stands out the most. Poaching and illegal fishing are also problems. Serbia also suffers from hunting-tourism, which may involve agencies not only organising hunting expeditions for foreigners but also assisting in the smuggling of plant and animal species, such as deer, birds, turtles, falcons and even butterflies. Such activity can be facilitated by corruption at the highest level and can also be linked to corporate environmental crime (Jovašević 2011).

Corruption and incompetence have failed to prevent or respond adequately to illegal discharges of toxic factory effluent; air and water pollution has also been overlooked or otherwise ignored (Pešić 2011). Such corruption and incompetence, combined with the presence of organised crime, makes Serbia similar to its neighbours in the Balkan Peninsula (Eman et al. 2013; Meško et al. 2011a). Finally, the importation of dirty, obsolete technologies from the Western world and the theft of wood—both of which involve organised criminal groups—present additional environmental issues for Serbia.

Slovenia

For Slovenia, the most typical forms of environmental harm include air, water and soil pollution; illegal waste disposal; animal and plant species trafficking; animal torture and poaching (Meško et al. 2011a: 49–50). In last decade, illegal logging, (electronic) waste trafficking and water crimes have been detected (Barišić Jaman, Franca and Eman 2015; Eman and Franca 2016; Eman and Humar 2017; Eman, Kuhar and Meško 2016, 2017; Eman and Meško 2014).

Green criminology has been slow to develop in Slovenia. The only work from the end of the twentieth century in this field of expertise is that of Pečar (1981), who tried to warn about these new forms of criminality (see Eman, Meško and Fields (2009: 584) for a discussion of his attempt to define the terms environmental criminality and green criminology). Pečar offered an aetiology of the forms of environmental criminality found in Slovenia, defined the role of criminology and sciences related to it, and suggested the scope of duties for and tasks of governmental institutions. Despite his forecasts and prescriptions, there was little subsequent interest in green criminology (Eman 2011; South et al. 2013).

Recently, however, Slovenian scholars have begun to identify and analyse a number of different environmental crimes and harms (Eman 2008, 2011, 2012; Eman and Meško 2009, 2014; Eman, Meško and Fields 2009), including organised crime's involvement in environmental degradation (Dobovšek and Goršek 2007; Eman 2010; Klenovšek and Meško 2011; Meško & Eman 2012; Odar and Dobovšek 2011). Slovenian scholars have also entered into debates about (criminological) perspectives on the environmental threats to air, water and soil (Eman 2014; Eman et al. 2013; Meško, Eman and Sotlar 2012; Meško et al. 2011b), contemplated Slovenian environmental protection policies (Sotlar, Tičar and Tominc 2011), and considered situational crime prevention measures (Meško et al. 2011b).

A literature review also reveals that researchers in Slovenia have begun to explore: whether environmental crime represents a threat to security (Eman 2008; Eman, Meško and Fields 2013); how the media report environmental crime (Eman and Meško 2011a); the nature and extent of the psychological impacts of a polluted environment on humans (Areh and Umek 2011; Umek et al. 2011); types of justice protection for the environment (Eman and Meško 2011b, 2014; Rakar and Tičar 2011); and the ways in which Geographical Information Systems may be used to identify environmental crime hotspots (Eman, Meško and Ivančič 2011). With green criminology beginning to gain traction in Slovenia, a number of scholars have become attuned to the emergence of new forms of environmental crime, such as e-waste trafficking and water crimes (Eman and Franca 2016; Eman and Humar 2017; Eman, Kuhar and Meško 2016, 2017; Meško et al. 2017).

Ukraine

Green criminology is in its embryonic stages in the Ukraine. Nevertheless, Ukrainian scholars have begun to examine illegal waste disposal and environmental white-collar crime, in part as a result of the increase in environmental crime committed by corporations and factories that have identified legal loopholes. Furthermore, the movement of the metal industry from the West to South-Eastern Europe has posed problems in and for the Ukraine (Winkler and Zharykov 2011).

For the Ukraine, energy security has become a top priority because of the country's acute vulnerability. The Ukraine, like other South-Eastern European countries, lacks diversity of energy supplies. As a result, it is attempting to enhance energy security by building coal and nuclear energy power plants, despite the negative impact that these industries have on the environment. As noted above, coal mining results in water pollution (i.e., mine lakes full of wastewater affect animal and plant species; local rivers become polluted with mineral salt, metals and toxins)—one of a number of different crimes against water in the Ukraine (Moretti 2017). The subsequent burning of coal produces air pollution and contributes to global climate change.

Nuclear power has been a sensitive subject in the Ukraine since the Chernobyl disaster in 1986. With 13 operating nuclear power plants and more than 20 new ones planned for construction, nuclear waste management and disposal, in particular, represent growing environmental issues. The theft of radioactive material and its sale on the illegal market is also an emerging issue. In recent years, several criminals have been arrested in the Ukraine for attempting to sell stolen radioactive material (Milstein and Cherp 2009). Another growing issue is waste trafficking (Spapens n.d.).

Environmental criminological commonalities in the region of South-Eastern Europe

Environmental offenders have an incredible ability to change their *modus operandi* and to adapt to new socio-economic relations and legal changes governing the field of crimes against the environment. In addition, for countries in South-Eastern Europe, it is not atypical for perpetrators of environmental crime to take their activities to the limits of acceptable behaviour with only one goal—to make a profit (Eman et al. 2013). Using different loopholes in environmental protection legislation, as well as exploiting gaps in infrastructure and enforcement, criminals commit environmental offences without being detected, apprehended and punished. Convictions are rare (Eman and Meško 2014). Systematic prosecution of environmental crimes is necessary in order to ensure that much environmental damage is reduced or eliminated (Ljuština 2010). Making the risk of detection and the threat of severe punishment outweigh financial profit is integral to reducing organised crime's involvement in environmental crime (Dobovšek and Meško 2008; Eman et al. 2013; Ljuština 2010; Meško et al. 2011a).

As demonstrated throughout this chapter, while green criminology is still in its nascent stages in many countries in South-Eastern Europe, it is developing slowly (Eman et al. 2013; Eman and Meško 2014). As Muratbegović and Guso (2011: 101) explain, in these countries there are many legal and policy-related dimensions to environmental issues, but the criminal components are not considered important (enough) by the institutions of formal social control.

In the Republic of North Macedonia, Serbia and Slovenia, green criminology is a bit better established and has begun to be acknowledged as a significant area within criminology. In this process of development, academics, researchers and scholars in countries of South-Eastern Europe have relied on and built upon green criminological work that has emerged from Australia, the United Kingdom and the United States. Nevertheless, the particularities and specifics of their own environment means that green criminology in South-Eastern Europe will need to develop its unique flavour, as already evident from a number of past publications (Eman and Meško 2014; Eman et al. 2013; Meško et al. 2011b, 2013; Petrović and Meško 2013; South et al. 2014).

Despite differences between the countries of the South-Eastern European region, some common characteristics in the area can be identified: air, water and soil pollution caused by corporations and state-owned facilities are common forms of environmental damage. Coal dust and ash and thermal power-plant pollution of air and water are common in Albania, Bosnia and Herzegovina, Bulgaria, Kosovo, Moldova, Serbia and Ukraine, while the pollution of Lake Balaton is a problem in Hungary, and contamination of the Danube River has become increasingly troublesome in Hungary and Romania.

Waste trafficking and illegal waste disposal, white-collar environmental crime, animal and plant species trafficking and poaching and illegal fishing, are also pervasive in South-Eastern Europe. Unfortunately, our analysis shows the heavy influence of organised crime in the region (Eman et al. 2013a, 2013b; Meško et al. 2011a). In the last decade, water crimes as a 'new form' of environmental crime appeared in the region (Eman, 2016; Eman, Kuhar and Meško 2017; Meško, Migliorini, Segato, Kuhar and Eman 2017). Identifying environmental crime patterns in the region and then sharing these findings among other green criminology scholars in the region will hopefully help to enable cooperation between countries in order to protect and preserve the environment of the entire Balkans.

That said, the specific environmental and political nature of each country must not be ignored, and many issues (such as those pertaining to marine and coastal ecosystems pollution in Croatia, hunting tourism in Hungary and Serbia, nuclear and radioactive waste pollution in the Ukraine and illegal logging and waste trafficking in Albania, Bosnia and Herzegovina, Hungary and the Republic of North Macedonia) will have to be tackled by more focussed cooperation between and within countries, rather than as isolated initiatives.

Notes

1 *Balkan* is a historical and geographical term that describes South-Eastern Europe. The approximately 550,000 km^2 large area includes the entire landmass or parts of the following countries: Albania, Bosnia and Herzegovina, Bulgaria, Greece, Croatia, Macedonia, Serbia, Montenegro, Romania and the European part of Turkey (Bideleux and Jeffries 2007).

2 The Stability Pact for Southeastern Europe (the 'Pact') was an international coordinating body established to stabilise the region and to calm the crisis, war and conflicts of the past. The Pact, which included 11 countries (Albania, Bosnia and Herzegovina, Bulgaria, Canada, Croatia, Hungary, Japan, Romania, Russia, Slovenia and the United States) and 34 international institutions (e.g., EU, OECD, OSCE, UN), was in place from 1997 until 2008, when it was replaced by the Regional Cooperation Council (see EU, 2016: https://ec.europa.eu/neighbourhood-enlargement/policy/glossary/terms/stability-pact_en). The main goal of the Pact was the realisation of the vision of South-Eastern Europe (democracy, economic prosperity, peace and security), as well as integration policy and participatory policy approaches to overcome war and other barriers in the region. The basic task of the Pact was to stimulate the cooperation of South-Eastern European (SEE) countries and other states, and to promote and facilitate planned economic and other activities. The Pact was also established in order to provide all dimensions of European security (from economic and humanitarian to political and social) (Grizold, Vergles and Fišer 2000: 9–11).

3 A Southeast Europe Transnational Cooperation Programme (the 'Programme') was established and launched in March 2008 with the goal of developing a transnational partnership in order to improve the economic, social and territorial integration of the SEE region. The Programme involves 16 countries: eight EU member states (Austria, Bulgaria, Greece, Hungary, Italy, Slovakia, Slovenia and Romania) and eight non-EU member states (Albania, Bosnia and Herzegovina, Croatia, Republic of Macedonia, Serbia, Montenegro, Republic of Moldova and the Ukraine). The cohesion, cooperation and stability in the region were deemed to be of primary importance. Accessibility, environment, innovation, networking and sustainable development were placed at the top of the Programme agenda (South East Europe Transnational Cooperation Programme 2011).

4 The four possible 'conceptions', 'contours', 'definitions', or 'models' of *South-Eastern Europe* exist: 1) the old Balkan peninsula model (Mazower 2008); 2) the European territories of the former Ottoman Empire model, including the European Union-promoted initiative of this as a space with a northern delineation that respects actual borders (Bideleux and Jeffries 2007); 3) The 'Stability pact for South-eastern Europe' model (Stability Pact for Southeastern Europe 2011); and 4) the 'Southeast Europe trans-national co-operation programme' (South East Europe Transnational Cooperation Programme 2011).

5 Air quality has also been adversely affected by private furnaces, which are used for heating (e.g., by burning coal and wood) (Đongalić 2005). Research by Mujanović (2009) has also demonstrated that cars, especially those more than ten years old, are the third most significant air polluter in Sarajevo.

6 In Bosnia and Herzegovina, trees are often chopped down to provide wood for household stoves. The devastated land is subsequently used as a pasture for livestock and for plantations and settlements. Lack of reforestation results in landslides, which can further destroy ecosystems (Muratbegović and Guso 2011: 108; Đongalić 2005; Akers 2000.

7 Nine people drowned in the toxic red sludge and one person died later at a hospital as a result of the poisoning.

8 The Danube River flows through or acts as part of the borders of ten countries: Germany, Austria, Slovakia, Hungary, Croatia, Serbia, Bulgaria, Moldova, Ukraine and Romania. As a result, a great deal of industrial waste pollution occurs before it even reaches Hungary.

9 Fröhlich and colleagues (2003) analysed organised environmental crime in Hungary and neighbouring countries and identified the following illegal activities: 1) illegal pollution, dumping and storage of waste, including trans-frontier shipment of hazardous waste; 2) illegal commercial trade in ozone-depleting substances; and 3) illegal dumping and shipment of radioactive waste and potentially radioactive material.

References

Akers, L. R. 2000. *Criminological Theories: Introduction, Evaluation and Application*, 3rd ed. Los Angeles, CA: Roxbury Press.

Areh, I. and Umek, P. 2011. 'Psihološki Učinki Onesnaževanja Okolja,' *Varstvoslovje*, 13(1): 30–38.

Balkan Insighta. 2015. *Air Pollution is Choking Bosnia, Experts Warn*. Available at: https://balkaninsight.com/2015/12/01/air-pollution-reaching-alarming-levels-in-bosnia-experts-warn-11-30-2015/.

Bezuh, K., Domazetović, Z., Filipčić, H., Huiterna, A., Jakupić, I. and Javor, I. 2009. *Priručnik Prekogranični Promet I Trgovina Zaštićenim Vrstama I Cites Konvencija*. Zagreb: Ministarstvo kulture (Uprava za zaštitu prirode, Uprava za inspekcijske poslove zaštite prirode, Ministarsvo financija, Carinska uprava Republike Hrvatske, MUP RH, Ravnateljstvo policije).

Bideleux, R. and Jeffries, I. 2007. *A History of Eastern Europe*, 2nd ed. New York: Taylor & Francis.

Bilefsky, D. 2010a. 'Fears of more red sludge in Hungary, and more refugees,' *The New York Times*. 11 Oct.: A8.

Bilefsky, D. 2010b. 'Hungary arrests official, citing role in red sludge,' *The New York Times*. 12 Oct.: A6.

Bufon, M. 2006. 'South-Eastern Europe and bosnia and herzegovina between fragmentation and integration: A European challenge in the governance of convergence and divergence processes,' in M. Bufon, A. Grizold, S. Nurković and A. L. Sangurin (eds.) *The Western Balkans: A European Challenge: On the Decenial of the Dayton Peace Agreement = Zahodni Balkan: Evropski Izzivi: Ob Desetletnici Daytonskega Mirovnega Sporazuma*, pp. 123–144. Koper: Univerza na Primorskem, Znanstveno-raziskovalno središče.

Clifford, M. (ed.). 1998. *Environmental Crime: Enforcement, Policy, and Social Responsibility*, Gaithersburg, MD: Aspen Publisher.

Clifford, M. and Edwards, T. D. 1998. 'Defining "environmental crime",' in M. Clifford (ed.) *Environmental Crime: Enforcement, Policy, and Social Responsibility*, pp. 121–145. Gaithersburg MD: Aspen Publisher.

Cohen, M. A. 1998. 'Sentencing the environmental criminal,' in M. Clifford (ed.) *Environmental Crime: Enforcement, Policy, and Social Responsibility*, pp. 146–168. Gaithersburg, MD: Aspen Publisher.

Csányi, S. 1997. 'Challenges of wildlife management in a transforming society: Examples from hungary,' *Wildlife Society Bulletin*, 25(1): 33–37.

Cserny, A., Utasi, A. and Domokos, E. 2009. 'Using a decision support software in the course of the planning of a waste management system in hungary,' in L. I. Simenonov and M. A. Hassanien (eds.) *Exposure and Risk Assessment of Chemical Pollution – Contemporary Methodology*, pp. 473–486. Dordrecht: Springer.

Dobovšek, B. and Goršek, J. 2007. 'Ekološka Kriminaliteta – Ogrožanje Živalskih in Rastlinskih Vrst,' *Varstvoslovje*, 9(1/2): 47–57.

Dobovšek, B. and Meško, G. 2008. 'Informal networks in Slovenia: A blessing or a curse?,' *Problems of Post-Communism*, 52(2): 25–37.

Đongalić, M. 2005. *Energija I Okolina*. Tuzla: Printcom.

Eman, K. 2008. 'Uvod V Fenomenološko Analizo Ekološke Kriminalitete,' *Varstvoslovje*, 10(1): 220–239.

Eman, K. 2010. 'Organizirana Ekološka Kriminaliteta – Nekoč Teoretični Pojem, Danes Preteče Dejstvo,' *3. konferenca kazenskega prava in kriminologije 2010, Bled*, pp. 95–104.

Eman, K. 2011. 'Ekološka kriminaliteta v kriminologiji : razvoj nove veje kriminologije v Sloveniji,' *Revija za kriminalistiko in kriminologijo*, 62(4): 312–324.

Eman, K. 2012. 'Environmental crime trends in Slovenia in the past decade,' in G. Meško, A. Sotlar and B. Tominc (eds.) *Contemporary Criminal Justice Practice and Research: Conference Proceedings*, pp. 177–178. Ljubljana: Faculty of Criminal Justice and Security.

Eman, K. 2013a. 'Ekološka kriminaliteta v kriminologiji: razvoj nove veje kriminologije v Sloveniji,' *Revija za kriminalistiko in kriminologijo*, 62(4): 312–324.

Eman, K. 2013b. 'Environmental crime trends in Slovenia in the past decade,' *Varstvoslovje*, 15(2): 240–260.

Eman, K. 2014. 'Ekološka kriminaliteta kot priložnost za koruptivna ravnanja,' in Smolej, D. and Dobovšek, B. (eds.) *Korupcija kot pereča oblika okoljske problematike v Republiki Sloveniji*, pp. 37–55. Ljubljana: Ministrstvo za notranje zadeve, Policija, Uprava kriminalistične policije.

Eman, K. 2016. 'Water crimes – A contemporary (security) issue,' *Crimen*, 7(1): 44–57.

Eman, K. and Franca, B. 2016. 'Trgovanje z električno in elektronsko opremo – Problem moderne družbe,'*Revija za kriminalistiko in kriminologijo*, 67(3): 248–261.

Eman, K., Kuhar, S. and Meško, G. 2016. 'Providing water supply in local communities – Case study of Slovenia,' in G. Meško and B. Lobnikar (eds.) *Criminal Justice and Security in Central and Eastern Europe: Safety, Security, and Social Control in Local Communities: Conference Proceedings*, pp. 368–374. Ljubljana: Faculty of Criminal Justice and Security.

Eman, K., Kuhar, S. and Meško, G. 2017. 'Water crimes and policing,' *Varstvoslovje*, 19(2): 105–119. Available at: https://www.fvv.um.si/rV/arhiv/2017-2/01_Eman_Kuhar_Mesko_rV_2017-2.pdf.

Eman, K. and Meško, G. 2009. 'Ekološka Kriminologija – Poskus Opredelitve in Razprava,' *Varstvoslovje*, 11(3): 357–381.

Eman, K. and Meško, G. 2011a. 'Media reporting about environmental crime in the Republic of Slovenia,' in *Security in the post-conflict (western) Balkans, transition and challenges faced by the Republic of Macedonia. Book of abstracts: International scientific conference*. 27–28 May 2011, Ohrid, Ohrid: University "St. Kliment Ohridski" Skopje, Faculty of Security.

Eman, K. and Meško, G. 2011b. 'The issues of the protection of the environment through criminal law in the Republic of Slovenia,' in *The Issues of the Protection of the Environment Security in the Post-Conflict (Western) Balkans*, Transition *and Challenges Faced by the Republic of Macedonia. Book of Abstracts: International Scientific Conference*. 27–28 May 2011, Ohrid, Ohrid: University "St. Kliment Ohridski" Skopje, Faculty of Security.

Eman, K. and Meski, G. 2013. 'Green issues in South-Eastern Europe,' in N. South and A Brism (eds) *Routlede Hadnbook of Green Criminology etc.*

Eman, K. and Meško, G. 2014. *Environmental Crime and Criminology: Crime Phenomena and Development of a Green Criminology in Slovenia*. Saarbrücken: Scholar's Press.

Eman, K., Meško, G., Dobovšek, B. and Sotlar, A. 2013a. 'Environmental crime and green criminology in South Eastern Europe – Practice and research,' *Crime, Law and Social Change: An International Journal*, 59(3): 341–358. ISSN 0925–4994. DOI: 10.1007/s10611-013-9419-0.

Eman, K., Meško, G. and Fields, C. B. 2013b. 'Environmental crime: A new security challenge,' in A. Maas (ed.) *Global Environmental Change: New Drivers for Resistance, Crime and Terrorism?*, 1st ed., pp. 15–35. Baden-Baden: Nomos.

Eman, K., Meško, G. and Fields, C. B. 2009. 'Crimes against the environment: Green criminology and research challenges in Slovenia,' *Varstvoslovje*, 11(4): 574–592.

Eman, K., Meško, G. and Ivančič, D. 2011. 'Ekološka Kriminaliteta V Pomurju,' *12. slovenski dnevi varstvoslovja, 2.-3. junij 201, Moravske toplice*. Moravske toplice: Fakulteta za varnostne vede Univerze v Mariboru.

Eman, K., Meško, G., Dobovšek, B., & Sotlar, A. 2013. 'Environmental crime and green criminology in South Eastern Europe – Practice and research,' *Crime, Law and Social Change : An International Journal*, 59(3): 341–358. ISSN 0925–4994. DOI: 10.1007/s10611-013-9419-0.

European Comission. 2019. 'The environmental implementation review 2019: Country Report – Bulgaria,' Available at: https://ec.europa.eu/environment/eir/pdf/report_bg_en.pdf.

European Environment Agency (EEA). 2017. 'Albania,' Available at: https://www.eea.europa.eu/countries-and-regions/albania.

Fajardo del Castillo, T. 2017. *A Case Study on the EU's Promotion of Environmental Protection through Criminal Law in Kosovo*. EFFACE. Available at: https://www.ecologic.eu/sites/files/publication/2015/efface_a_case_study_on_the_eus_promotion_of_environmental_protection_through_criminal_law_in_kosovo.pdf.

Frohliche et al. 2003. *Organised Environmental Crime in the EU Member States*. European Commission. Available at: https://ec.europa.eu/environment/legal/crime/pdf/organised_member_states.pdf

Golić, B. 2005. *Ekologija I Ekološko Pravo*. Saravejo: Pravni fakultet.

Gramatikov, P. 2009. 'Bulgarian energetics management and environmental security,' in Stec, S. and Baraj, B. (eds.) *Energy and Environmental Challenges to Security*, pp. 211–224. Dordrecht: Springer.

Grizold, A., Vergles, E. and Fišer, Ž. 2000. 'Pakt Stabilnosti Za Jugovzhodno Evropo in Slovenija,' *Varstvoslovje*, 2(1): 9–16.

Hakaj, N., Balaj, N. and Hoxha, V. 2007. *Kosova-Energy and Environmental Challenges to Security*, [Online], Available: http://archive.rec.org/natoworkshop/draft_papers/hakaj_kosova.pdf [2 June 2011].

Jovašević, D. 2011. 'Environmental crime in the Republic of Serbia: Theory, practice and legislation,' *Law and Politics*, 9(2): 109–134.

Kerezsi, K. and Lévay, M. 2008. 'Criminology, crime and criminal justice in Hungary,' *European Journal of Criminology*, 5(2): 239–260.

Kirn, A. 1985. 'Ekološke Meje in Protislovja Družbenega Razvoja,' in A. Kirn (ed.) *Pasti Razvoja: Ekološke Študije*, pp. 9–66. Ljubljana: Komunist.

Klenovšek, A. and Meško, G. 2011. 'International waste trafficking: Preliminary explorations,' in G. Meško, D. Dimitrijević and C. B. Fields (eds.) *Understanding and Managing Threats to the Environment in South Eastern Europe*, pp. 79–99. Dordrecht: Springer.

Kulišić, D. 2011. 'The benefits from using professionally developed models of possible hazardous materials accident scenarios in crime scene investigations,' in G. Meško, D. Dimitrijević and C. B. Fields (eds.) *Understanding and Managing Threats to the Environment in South Eastern Europe*, pp. 9–32. Dordrecht: Springer.

Lampe, J. R. 2006. *Balkans into Southeastern Europe: A Century of War and Transition*. London: Palgrave Macmillan.

Leslie, D. M., Ionescu, O., Tissescu, A. and Nicolescu, N. V. 1995. 'Wildlife conservation and education in Romania,' *Wildlife Society Bulletin*, 23(1): 12–17.

Levenat, I. 1997. *Radioaktivni Otpad*. Zagreb: Agencija za poseban otpad.

Liddick, D. 2009. 'The traffic in garbage and hazardous wastes: An overview,' *Trends in Organized Crime*, 3(2–3): 134–146.

Ljuština, A. 2010. *Ekološki Delikti I Policija*. Beograd: Zadužbina Andrejević.

Lonarčić-Horvat, O., Cvitanovica, L., Glihe, I., Josipović, T., Medvedovica, D. and Omejec, J. in drugi. 1998. *Pravo Okoliša*. Zagreb: Ministarstvo zaštite okoliša i prostronog uređenja.

Lynch, M. L. and Stretesky, P. 2007. 'Green criminology in the United States,' in P. Beirne and N. South (eds.) *Issues in Green Criminology: Confronting Harms against Environments, Humanity and Other Animals*, pp. 671–708. Portland: Willan.

Malis Sazdovska, M. 2009. 'Elimination of ecological crimes as a part of organized crimes in the Republic of Macedonia,' *Review of International Affair*, 60(1135): 84–91.

Malis Sazdovska, M. 2011. 'Usage of special investigation measures in detecting environmental crime: International and Macedonian perspective,' in G. Meško, D. Dimitrijević and C. B. Fields (eds.) *Understanding and Managing Threats to the Environment in South Eastern Europe*, pp. 123–134. Dordrecht: Springer.

Mazower, M. 2008. *Balkan: Od Konca Bizanca Do Danes*. Ljubljana: Krtina.

Meško, G., Bančič, K., Eman, K. and Fields, C. B. 2011a. 'Situational crime-prevention measures to environmental threats,' in G. Meško, D. Dimitrijević and C. B. Fields (eds.) *Understanding and Managing Threats to the Environment in South Eastern Europe*, pp. 41–67. Dordrecht: Springer.

Meško, G., Dimitrijević, D. and Fields, C. B. (ed.). 2011b. *Understanding and Managing Threats to the Environment in South Eastern Europe*. Dordrecht: Springer.

Meško, G. and Eman, K. 2012. 'Organised crime involvement in waste trafficking – Case of the Republic of Slovenia,' *Kriminalističke teme: časopis za kriminalističku teoriju i praksu*, 12(5/6): 79–96.

Meško, G., Magliorini, M., Segato, L., Kuhar, S. and Eman, K. 2017. 'Kriminaliteta zoper vode in projekt Water crimes,' in L. Globevnik and A. Širca (eds.) *Zbornik*. Drugi slovenski kongres o vodah 2017, [19. in 20. april 2017, Podčetrtek], pp. 169–173. Ljubljana: SLOCOLD – Slovenski nacionalni komite za velike pregrade: DVS – Društvo vodarjev Slovenije.

Meško, G., Sotlar, A. and Eman, K. (Eds.) 2012. *Ekološka kriminaliteta in varovanje okolja – multidisciplinarne perspektive*. Ljubljana: Fakulteta za varnostne vede.

Michalowski, R. 1998. 'International environmental issues,' in M. Clifford (ed.) *Environmental Crime: Enforcement, Policy, and Social Responsibility*, pp. 315–340. Gaithersburg, MD: Aspen Publisher.

Milstein, D. and Cherp, A. 2009. 'Energy security and the environment in Eastern Europe: The case-study of Ukraine,' in S. Stec and B. Baraj (eds.) *Energy and Environmental Challenges to Security*. Dordrecht: Springer.

Modly, D. 1998. *Priručni Kriminalistički Leksikon*. Sarajevo: Fakultet kriminalističkih nauka.

Moretti, F., Segato, L., Capello, N., Mattioli, W., Monnier, C., Aleksic, D. et al. 2017. *European Report on Water Crimes*. Szentendre: The Regional Environmental Center for Central and Eastern Europe.

Morović, M. 2008. 'Natural and environmental risks in marine and coastal areas,' in H. G. Goskun, H. K. Cigizoglu and M. D. Maktav (eds.) *Integration of Information for Environmental Security*, pp. 291–300. Dordrecht: Springer.

Mujanović, A. 2009. *Kriminološki Aspekti Zaštite Životne Sredine U Bosni I Hercegovini*. Sarajevo: Fakultet kriminalističkih nauka.

Muratbegović, E. and Guso, H. 2011. 'Primary categories and symbiotic green crimes in Bosnia and Herzegovina,' in G. Meško, D. Dimitrijević and C. B. Fields (eds.) *Understanding and Managing Threats to the Environment in South Eastern Europe*, pp. 94–113. Dordrecht: Springer.

Muratbegović, E., Guso, H. 2011. 'Primary categories and symbiotic green crimes in Bosnia and Herzegovina,' in G. Meško, D. Dimitrijević and C. B. Fields (eds.) *Understanding and Managing Threats to the Environment in South Eastern Europe*, pp. 94–113. Dordrecht: Springer (Proceedings of the NATO Advanced Research Workshop on Managing Global Environmental Threats to Air, Water and Soil, Ljubljana, Slovenia, 28–30 June 2010).

Newburn, T. 2007. *Criminology*. Cullompton Cullompton, Devon, UK: Willan.

OCCRP. 2017. 'Annual report 2017,' Available at: https://www.occrp.org/documents/Annual-Report-2017.pdf.

Odar, V. and Dobovšek, B. 2011. 'Organizirana Ekološka Kriminaliteta,' *Varstvoslovje*, 13(1): 53–71.

Pečar, J. 1981. 'Ekološka Kriminaliteta in Kriminologija,' *Revija Za Kriminalistiko in Kriminologijo*, 34(1): 33–45.

Pešić, R. V. 2011. 'The role of economic instruments in eco-crime prevention,' in G. Meško, D. Dimitrijević and C. B. Fields (eds.) *Understanding and Managing Threats to the Environment in South Eastern Europe*, pp. 259–268. Dordrecht: Springer.

Petrović, B. and Meško, G. 2013. *Eko kriminal i eko kriminologija: osnovna razmatranja*. Sarajevo: Pravni fakultet.

Rakar, I. and Tičar, B. 2011. 'Nekatera Vprašanja Upravnopravnega Varstva Okolja V Republiki Sloveniji,' *Varstvoslovje*, 13(1): 5–19.

Rosenthal, E. 2010a. Hungarian Towns Begin Cleanup of Nightmarish Red Sludge. *The New York Times*. 7 Oct.:A6.

Rosenthal, E. 2010b. 'Hungarian waste pond was on list of risky sites,' *The New York Times*. 8 Oct.:A8.

Sotlar, A., Tičar, B. and Tominc, B. 2011. 'Slovenian environmental policy analysis: From institutional declarations to instrumental legal regulation,' in G. Meško, D. Dimitrijević and C. B. Fields (eds.)

Understanding and Managing Threats to the Environment in South Eastern Europe, pp. 11–39. Dordrecht: Springer.

South, N., Eman, K. and Meško, G. 2014. 'History of green criminology,' in G. Bruinsma and D. Weisburd (chief editors) *Encyclopaedia of Criminology and Criminal Justice*, pp. 2172–2181. New York: Springer Verlag.

South East Europe Transnational Cooperation Programme. 2011. [Online], Available: http://southeast-europe.net/hu/ [2 June 2011].

Spapens, A. C. M. 2011. 'Cross-border police cooperation in tackling environmental crime,' Available at: https://pure.uvt.nl/ws/portalfiles/portal/1347164/Spapens_Cross_Border_Police_Cooperation_110901_publishers_immediately.pdf

Stability Pact for Southeastern Europe 2011 [Online], Available: http://stabilitypact.org [2 June 2011].

Sućeska, M. 2008. *Metodika Otkrivanja Ekološkog Kriminaliteta*. Sarajevo: Fakultet kriminalističkih nauka.

Taylor, A. 2011. 'A flood of red sludge, one year later,' *The Atlantic*. [Online], Available: https://theatlantic.com/photo/2011/09/a-flood-of-red-sludge-one-year-later/100158/ [28 September 2011].

Todić, D. 2011. 'Social and environmental issues related to security in SEE countries,' in M. Montini and S. Bogdanović (eds.) *Environmental Security in South-Eastern Europe*, pp. 89–96. Dordrecht: Springer.

Turkeshi, E. 2015. *Crimes against Environment in Albania and the European Union's Approach to the Protection of Environment through Criminal Law*. Available at: http://dspace.epoka.edu.al/bitstream/handle/1/1329/Crimes%20against%20Environment%20in%20Albania%20and%20the%20European%20Union%27s%20Approach%20to%20the%20Protection%20of%20Environment%20through%20Criminal%20Law.pdf?sequence=1&isAllowed=y

Umek, P., Areh, I., Odar, V. and Šifrer, J. 2011. Psihološke Posledice Onesnaževanja Okolja. *12. Slovenski Dnevi Varstvoslovja, 2.-3. Junij 201, Moravske Toplice*. Ljubljana: Fakulteta za varnostne vede Univerze v Mariboru.

van Daele, S., Vander Beken, T. and Dorn, N. 2007. 'Waste management and crime: Regulatory, business, and product vulnerabilities,' *Environmental Policy and Law*, 37(1): 34–38.

Variščić, A. 2008. *Zaštita Prirode – Međunarodni Standardi I Stanje U Bosni I Hrecegovini*. Konjic: Neretva.

White, R. D. (ed.) 2009 *Environmental Crime: A Reader*. Cullompton, Devon, UK: Willan.

Williams, S. 2014. 'How the Hungarian town flooded by red toxic sludge went green,' *The Guardian* [Online]. Available: https://theguardian.com/environment/2014/jan/08/devecser-hungary-eco-town [8 January 2014].

Winkler, I. and Zharykov, G. 2011. 'Solid municipal wastes in Ukraine: A case study of environmental threats and management problems of the Chernivtsi Dump area,' in G. Meško, D. Dimitrijević and C. B. Fields (eds.) *Understanding and Managing Threats to the Environment in South Eastern Europe*, pp. 265–277. Dordrecht: Springer.

Yarnal, B. 1994. 'Socio-economic restructuring and vulnerability to environmental hazards in Bulgaria,' *Disasters*, 18(2): 95–106. DOI: 10.1111/j.1467-7717.1994.tb00291.x

Yarnal, B. (1994). 'Socio-economic restructuring and vulnerability to environmental hazards in Bulgaria,' *Disasters*, 18(2): 95–106. DOI: 10.1111/j.1467-7717.1994.tb00291.x

Zenelaj, E., Elezi, M. 2013. 'Geography of environmental crime in Albania-Demage, cutting and burned of forests,' *American Journal of Environmental Protection*. 1(4): 102–108.

17

The Flint water crisis

A case study of state-sponsored environmental (in)justice

Jacquelynn Doyon-Martin

Environmental justice has been a key concern of green criminologists since the outset (see, e.g., Brisman 2008; Ruggiero and South 2010; White 2009c). One of the more recent and visible cases is that of the water crisis in Flint, Michigan. Concerns regarding water safety began in 2014, when Flint, Michigan—a city comprised predominantly of minority and low-income residents—switched its water source from Lake Huron and the Detroit River to the Flint River. Officials failed to apply corrosion controls to the newly sourced water, leading to lead contamination and a public health state of emergency. An interesting dynamic present in Flint is the placement of Emergency Managers by the governor into positions of authority. This practice heightened already existing disparities in the lack of political capital among the residents of Flint—a dynamic that is frequently present in cases of environmental justice. Though the city has since returned to its original water source, this case of environmental (in)justice continues. The crisis has resulted in the erosion of public health, economic futures and public trust in government—and, thus, as this chapter will describe—the impact on Flint and its residents is far reaching and, for many, permanent.

Flint, Michigan

In order to better appreciate the length, scope and depth of the Flint water crisis, it is first necessary to consider Flint's geography and demography, as well as its recent history. The city of Flint, Michigan, is located roughly 60 miles north of Detroit and was once a booming automobile manufacturing hub for General Motors Company (GM). Deindustrialisation led to the closing of major GM factories in Flint, which decimated local job opportunities and, subsequently, the economy. A population exodus followed and the number of residents dropped from a peak of more than 200,000 in 1960 to fewer than 100,000 in 2014 (Flint Water Advisory Task Force 2016). In the most recently reported census data, the population of Flint was 97,386, 63 per cent of which were members of minority groups (over 56 per cent black) and approximately 27 per cent consisting of children under the age of 18 (U.S. Census Bureau 2017). In 2015, the average owner-occupied dwelling was valued at $32,600 and the median household income was $24,862—less than half the state average (which was $54,203 in 2015). Finally, 41.2 per cent of the population were living below the poverty line in 2015—nearly three times the national average (U.S. Census Bureau 2017).

The demographic makeup of Flint—primarily 'low-income and minority residents'—is particularly relevant here and in other instances of environmental (in)justice. In 1994, President Clinton issued Executive Order (EO) 12,898, 'Federal Actions to Address Environmental Justice in Minority Populations and Low-Income Populations', which was designed to 'focus federal attention on environmental and human health effects of federal actions' impacting these populations (U.S. EPA 2017a, n.p.; see Brisman 2002 for a discussion). EO 12,898 established an interagency working group consisting of 11 federal agencies, most notably the U.S. Environmental Protection Agency (EPA) and the Department of Health and Human Services (DHHS). This working group was designed to:

> provide guidance to Federal agencies on criteria for identifying disproportionately high and adverse human health or environmental effects on minority populations and low-income populations.
>
> *(Executive Order 12898 1994, 1)*

The EPA is the federal agency responsible for enforcing 'environmental justice', which it defines as the 'fair treatment and meaningful involvement of all people regardless of race, color, national origin, or income with respect to the development, implementation and enforcement of environmental laws, regulations and policies' (U.S. EPA 2017b, n.p.). The EPA highlights the importance of 'fair treatment and meaningful involvement' as populations impacted by environmental justice issues often suffer from a lack of social, economic and political capital. The EPA's definition is particularly ironic in the case of Flint because Michigan Governor Rick Snyder appointed a series of Emergency Managers in Flint between 2012 and 2015, thereby denying Flint residents the chance to have any 'meaningful involvement' in decisions pertaining to their drinking water.

Emergency management and environmental justice

State emergency management laws have existed across the United States for nearly a century and in Michigan in particular since 1988 (see Brisman, McClanahan, South and Walters 2018). While emergency management itself was not 'new' when implemented in Flint (in fact, it was the second time the city had been under emergency management), the increasing use of this disenfranchising management system itself played a major, if not the primary, role in the water crisis in Flint. Emergency management laws 'permit state officials, such as the governor, to appoint a receiver, state agency, or financial control board to oversee local (city) government' (Lee et al. 2016, 1). When this happens, decision-making authority usually granted to local, elected officials (such as mayors, school boards, or city councils) is transferred to appointed 'Emergency Managers' (EMs) (Lee et al. 2016). In principle, emergency management laws call for the scaling back of public expenses (most notably, services) in an effort to balance city budgets. In extreme circumstances, such as in the case of Detroit, Emergency Managers can even declare bankruptcy for a city (Michigan Legislature 2012; Michigan Radio 2011). In the State of Michigan, EMs have considerable control over city budgets and structural operations and can:

- change local budgets without local legislative approval;
- renegotiate, terminate, or modify labour contracts with state treasury approval;

- sell, lease, or privatise local assets with state treasury approval;
- revise contract obligations;
- hire/fire local government employees and support staff (Michigan Legislature 2012; Michigan Radio 2011).

In a democracy, there are natural concerns with a single appointed (rather than elected) official having control over a community, and the constitutionality of the EM law has been challenged repeatedly by citizens—both before, and as a result of, the Flint water crisis (Center for Constitutional Rights 2016; Lee et al. 2016; Michigan Radio 2015; Oosting 2016). Many argue that these laws disproportionately impact minorities and low-income citizens, and often negatively impact 'the wellbeing of children and families, particularly within economically distressed urban areas' (Lee et al. 2016, 1). Despite calls from concerned citizens to scale back or even eliminate the law, Michigan has implemented emergency management more than any other state (Lee et al. 2016).

The imposition of emergency management in Flint led to a series of what can be considered 'state crimes' against Flint residents at local, state and federal levels, and ultimately spawned an egregious case of environmental (in)justice. In general terms, 'state crimes' involve actions taken by the state against citizens (Green and Ward 2000; White 2009a). Green and Ward (2000) further refine this definition to focus more specifically on the combination of the violation of human rights and state organisational deviance. The marrying of these two aligns with both the federal definition of environmental justice outlined in EO 12,898, as well as conceptions of environmental justice found within green criminology (Schlosberg 2007; South and Brisman 2013; White 2008, 2009c) and elsewhere (e.g., Bullard 1990).

Almost 50 years ago, Schwendinger and Schwendinger (1970) outlined basic human rights, which they argued include the right to general well-being and, among other things, racial and economic equality. In a subsequent piece, they identified 'second generation' human rights, including entitlements to health, education and meaningful work opportunities. Inspired in part by the work of the Schwendingers, White (2008) identifies environmental rights as an extension of human or social rights, and acknowledges the pattern of victimisation perpetrated against vulnerable populations. Other scholars in this field have called for additional focus on issues of inequality, and more specifically, environmental injustice (see South 2010: 236–240; South and Brisman 2013 for further discussion and case studies), of which the Flint case is a fitting example.

In an attempt to rectify the budget crisis, the state violated basic human rights of the citizenry in Flint, disproportionately impacting an already marginalised population. While the appointing of Emergency Managers may have been well intentioned, it led to a pattern of decisions that were decidedly against the general well-being of Flint residents. Furthermore, given the legal action taken against EM laws in Michigan in the past, this government practice was already suffering from questions of legitimacy from citizens.

> In most contemporary states, the values on which the legitimacy of a state practice depends will include, *inter alia*, the state's real or nominal commitment to human rights. The conceptual link between legitimacy and human rights is regarded … as one that is valued for all times and cultures: only a legal order that upholds human rights can make a rationally justified claim to the voluntary obedience of its citizens.
>
> *(Green and Ward 2000, 109)*

In an effort to resist emergency management, and, later, to bring attention to the water quality issues in Flint, residents organised at the grassroots level, protesting and demonstrating against local and state governmental actions, and, in some cases, inactions. The failures of the state to respond to citizen concerns further degraded its legitimacy, weakening ties between the public and government in an already disenfranchised community.

Criminologists and green criminologists alike recognise both the impacts of state action (commission) and the failure to act (omission) as significant when considering harm (Huisman and van Erp 2013; Michalowski and Kramer 2006). Research has indicated that environmental crimes are generally crimes of *omission*, and, more specifically, the failure to perform a regulatory obligation (Huisman and van Erp 2013). Environmental regulation frequently imposes a duty on firms to take protective measures in their regular business processes. These measures involve extra time and money and therefore complicate routine services or processes, thus creating an incentive to avoid compliance. In other words, for the offender, it is easier and cheaper to offend than to comply (Huisman and van Erp 2013, 1184). In this way, environmental crimes are typically the result of a failure to follow guidelines or execute required actions. These omissions may be purposeful or the result of ignorance, and may be motivated by financial incentives or done with intent to expedite a desired action. Often, failure to ensure adherence to environmental regulations is the result of lax regulatory enforcement or oversight (Doyon 2014; Huisman and van Erp 2013): businesses and other corporate entities may see little benefit in investing time and money to comply with a regulation or rule when there is little chance of being investigated for a violation and little likelihood that a fine or penalty for non-compliance will exceed the cost of original adherence. A combination of these aforementioned omissions and motivations at local, state and federal levels led directly to the water crisis in Flint. The consequences of these actions and inactions, in tandem with the implementation of emergency management, resulted in the loss of confidence in government, economic hardships and grave impacts to human health. An abbreviated timeline of events is included below.

Timeline of emergency management and the water crisis in Flint[1]

- November 2011: Governor Rick Snyder appoints Michael Brown, the first of several EMs in Flint, to manage the financial problems facing the city. Discussions about possible cost-saving measures, including utilising an alternative water source, begin.
- January 2012: An initial study reveals that in order for Flint River water to be potable, anti-corrosion agents are needed.
- August 2012: Ed Kurtz (who had served previously as the EM of Flint from 2002–2004) replaces Michael Brown as EM. While in office, Kurtz and officials in the Michigan Department of Treasury discuss an alternative water source for Flint in an effort to save money. Initially, they consider the Flint River, but after reports regarding concerns over the quality of Flint River water and the need for anti-corrosive agents, it is decided that Flint will either switch to the planned Karegnondi Water Authority (KWA) or remain with Detroit Water and Sewage Department (DWSD) (Flint Water Advisory Task Force 2016).
- February 2013: While initial reports indicated that the KWA would present cost-savings for Flint, the Michigan Department of Treasury released a study providing detailed concerns about unexpected costs surrounding the changeover to KWA, which are about \$25.5 million more than originally assessed (Tucker, Young, Jackson, Tull, Inc. 2013). Furthermore, new offers from DWSD are about 20 per cent lower than anticipated KWA costs, suggesting remaining with the DWSD might be a more cost-effective strategy.

- April 2013: EM Kurtz decides to shift Flint from the DWSD to the KWA, citing unreliable rates from DWSD and a potential for significant cost saving for the city of Flint. At this time, the KWA pipeline is not yet under construction and estimates suggest it will not be able to supply Flint with water until 2016.
- April 2013: DWSD informs the City of Flint that because they have not signed another contract, their water service from DWSD will end in April of 2014, leaving Flint without a water source for over a year (Brush, Williams, Smith and Scullen 2015; Flint Water Advisory Task Force 2016).
- June 2013: After securing a contracting firm to prepare Flint to switch to the Flint River as their interim water source, Kurtz resigns as EM.
- July 2013: Michael Brown is once again appointed as the Flint EM, only to resign a second time three months later.
- October 2013: Darnell Earley (who had served as an EM for Flint in 2002) is appointed to replace Brown.
- April 2014: Flint officially switches to the Flint River as its interim water source. Less than a week after the switch, residents start complaining, reporting strange tastes, smells and a distinct colour to the water. Over the next couple of months they will report experiencing rashes, hair loss and mood swings.
- May 2014: Per policy, the first of two six-month monitoring cycles is put into place by the Michigan Department of Environmental Quality (MDEQ). These monitoring periods are required in order to be in compliance with the Lead Copper Rule (LCR)—a federal regulation issued by the EPA pursuant to the Safe Drinking Water Act (SDWA)—to determine whether corrosion controls are needed in order to ensure safe drinking water.[2]
- August 2014: Flint water tests positive for E. coli; residents are instructed to boil water prior to use periodically throughout August and September (Brush, Williams, Smith and Scullen 2015). Chlorine is added to the water to mitigate bacterial concerns.
- October 2014: The remaining GM plant in Flint switches its water source to Flint Township (which receives its water from Lake Huron), citing concerns about corrosion in its machines.
- October 2014: City and state officials continue to assure residents that the water is safe; meanwhile, preliminary testing finds lead levels in the water high enough to meet and exceed classification standards for 'hazardous waste' (Kennedy 2016); legionella cases begin to surface in the city (Flint Water Advisory Taskforce 2016; Michigan Radio 2015).
- January 2015: Governor Snyder appoints Jerry Ambrose as the new EM of Flint, even though the two have never met nor discussed (what has since become known as) the 'water crisis' (Committee on Oversight and Government Reform 2017; Fonger 2017).[3]
- January 2015: Despite increasing concerns surrounding lead contamination, EM Ambrose focusses primarily on budget issues and subsequently declines an offer from the DWSD to reconnect Flint (and waive the $4 million reconnection fee) to safe drinking water.
- January 2015: The second MDEQ six-month monitoring period for lead and copper in the water begins. Concurrently, email records indicate MDEQ staff discussions regarding the placement of water coolers in Flint state office buildings to provide potable drinking water for staff.
- January 2015: Flint Mayor Dayne Walling reassures residents the water is safe to drink; independent testing confirms extreme levels of lead contamination in Flint homes (Flint Water Advisory Task Force 2016; Michigan Radio 2015; Pieper, Tang and Edwards 2017).

- February 2015: Flint resident LeeAnne Walters makes local, state and then national headlines when it is revealed that her home and her children have tested positive for extreme levels of lead.[4]
- February 2015: The MDEQ continues to downgrade the severity of the issue in Flint, while the EPA begins collecting lead samples from LeeAnne Walters' home, and the Genesee County Health Department continues to investigate increased cases of legionella in the county, citing concerns that it is related to the water.
- April 2015: LeeAnne Walters' children test positive for lead poisoning (Brush, Williams, Smith and Scullen 2015).
- April 2015: Governor Snyder announces that the city of Flint is no longer under emergency management; control of the city shifts back to the Mayor and City Council.[5] Flint continues to receive its water from the Flint River, and residents and local media continue to express serious concerns over its quality and safety.
- August 2015: Results from the second six-month MDEQ lead and copper monitoring period are released, indicating the need for corrosion control in order for Flint to be compliant with the LCR. Under regulation, the city of Flint has six months from this time to fully implement corrosion controls, but is encouraged to begin 'as soon as possible' (Flint Water Advisory Task Force 2016, 98).
- September 2015: Dr Marc Edwards, Professor of Civil and Environmental Engineering, Virginia Polytechnic Institute and State University, who had been independently investigating and reporting on lead levels in Flint for months, publicly releases his findings and emails these results to Flint Mayor Dayne Walling.
- September 2015: Dr Mona Hanna-Attisha, Assistant Professor of Pediatrics, Michigan State University College of Human Medicine, and Director, Pediatric Residency Program, Hurley Children's Hospital, who had been independently monitoring blood lead levels (BLLs) in Flint children for over a year, continues contacting the Michigan Department of Health and Human Services (MDHHS) regarding her findings and urgent concerns. In addition, other local health officials express consternation over connections between Flint River water and Legionnaires' disease.
- October 2015: In spite of continued findings from the EPA and independent researchers over a myriad of health concerns, pleas from residents and the City Council to return to the DWSD, and increased coverage from local, state and national news media, Mayor Walling cites financial concerns as sufficient reason to avoid the switch back to DWSD water.
- October 2015: A 'State of Emergency' is declared in Flint, and filters and bottled water are distributed to residents (Pieper, Tang and Edwards 2017).
- October 16, 2015: Nearly 18 months after the switch and following months of consistent pressure from local, state and national parties, it is announced that Flint will shift back to the DWSD as its water source, a process that will cost $12 million and will take roughly three weeks to complete (Flint Water Advisory Task Force 2016).

  (The return to the DWSD does not solve the drinking water crisis in Flint. The corrosive water from the Flint River did irreversible damage; lead had begun leaching from service lines and pipes and faucets inside homes, and more and more lead continues to flow into Flint homes each time a faucet, shower, or washing machine is used. While filters offer some mitigation, a complete replacement of lead service water lines throughout the City of Flint is determined to be the only method for complete lead remediation.)
- November 2015: Flint residents file a class action lawsuit against the state of Michigan and city of Flint government employees, alleging personal injury, health problems and property damages (Brush, Williams, Smith and Scullen 2015).

Local, state and federal failures

A series of failures on local, state and federal levels began with the decision to use the Flint River and led directly to the Flint water crisis. Of primary note, four different Emergency Managers were appointed in Flint (with five different transitions), between November of 2011 and January of 2015, by the Office of the Governor. During this time, major decisions pertaining to Flint's water source were being considered and made, and information regarding the feasibility and safety of using the Flint River as an interim water source was being evaluated. The lack of stability in this office undoubtedly contributed to the overlooking or ignoring of critical information concerning financial and (more importantly) health risks associated with the Flint River. For example, findings were released which found that not only would the KWA pipeline take about two years to be functional, but the project would cost approximately $25 million *more* than originally reported by KWA (Tucker and Jackson 2013). Failure to recognise this may be attributable to the revolving door of Emergency Managers, or might suggest there were additional considerations (beyond cost saving for Flint) for the switch.[6] Furthermore, a series of studies, beginning in December of 2012 and continuing until the switch in 2014, raised concerns about the safety of using Flint River water (Flint Water Advisory Task Force 2016). Even MDEQ officials noted concerns in email exchanges regarding the decision: 'As you might guess we are in a situation with Emergency Financial Managers so it's entirely possible that they will be making decisions relative to cost' (Jim Sygo, MDEQ Chief Deputy Director, as quoted in Flint Water Advisory Task Force 2016, 88). What is interesting about the financial situation in Flint was that, while the KWA did seem to represent a cost-saving initially, the DWSD made multiple attempts to renegotiate with Flint presenting a final offer in April of 2013 that was 20 per cent less than the KWA proposal (Flint Water Advisory Task Force (2016). Nevertheless, analyses conducted by Flint EM Kurtz, the MDEQ and the Treasury's Office of Fiscal Responsibility independently concluded that the KWA was the cheaper option for the city of Flint (Flint Water Advisory Task Force 2016; Office of the Governor 2016).

Local failures: Flint Public Works and Flint Water Treatment Plant (FWTP)

At the local level, Flint Public Works employees and the Flint Water Treatment Plant (FWTP) were not prepared nor equipped to manage safe distribution of Flint River water, as the DWSD had previously been responsible for Safe Drinking Water Act (SDWA) compliance. In preparation for the switch, the old, outdated FWTP required upgrades in order to ensure proper functionality, and also needed to hire and train new staff in order to meet plant demands (Flint Water Advisory Task Force 2016). Employees at Flint Public Works failed to comply—and the MDEQ failed to ensure their compliance—with requirements of the Lead Copper Rule (LCR), which regulates the concentration of lead and copper in drinking water, as well as levels of pipe corrosion occurring because of the water itself (U.S. EPA 2017c). These omissions led directly to irreversible damage to the water system in Flint, and likely could have been prevented had a thorough review process been performed. An examination of Flint laboratory and water quality supervisor Michael Glasgow's e-mails to Adam Rosenthal, Stephen Busch and Michael Prysby of the MDEQ indicate the FWTP was rushed into operation during the switch to Flint River water. For example, on one occasion, Glasgow wrote:

> I am expecting changes to our Water Quality Monitoring parameters, and possibly our DBP on lead & copper monitoring plan … Any information would be appreciated, because it looks as if we will be starting the plant up tomorrow and are being pushed to

> start distributing water as soon as possible (Bridge Magazine 2016, n.p.; Flint Water Advisory Task Force 2016, 90) … If water is distributed from this plant in the next couple of weeks, it will be against my direction. I need time to adequately train additional staff and to update our monitoring plans before I will feel we are ready. I will reiterate this to management above me, but they seem to have their own agenda.[7]
>
> *(Flint Water Quality Supervisor Michael Glasgow, as quoted in Egan, Spangler and Shamus 2016, n.p.; Flint Water Advisory Task Force 2016, 90)*

Once water service began (followed, almost immediately, by complaints), Flint Public Works personnel failed to identify residences with lead service lines for testing, failed to secure an adequate number of tap water samples from high-risk homes, and failed to follow proper protocol for sampling practices (Flint Water Advisory Task Force 2016; Michigan Radio 2015). For instance, rather than taking samples immediately from the tap, FPW staff would 'flush' the lines first, significantly lowering lead levels in the sample. Meanwhile, advisory notices to residents to boil water before use for safety (issued by the city following the E. coli outbreak) may have helped to eliminate some bacteria in the water, but concurrently increased the concentration of lead,[8] making water use and consumption even more dangerous for residents (Centers for Disease Control and Prevention 2017; Smith 2016). In sum, the FWTP was simply not prepared to properly manage and treat Flint River water:

> Our interviews underscored several troubling aspects of the inexorable drive to leave the DWSD system and use the Flint River as an interim supply source for drinking water. Most obviously, the parties simply failed to adequately appreciate (or signal) the complexities involved in treating Flint River water, or the potential implications of water chemistry changes to the city's water distribution network. We note that Flint endured a series of water quality threats—from E coli contamination to high total trihalomethane (TTHM) levels—that could have been prevented. Increased lead exposure and increased incidences of Legionellosis likely are the most serious health consequences of a sustained period of water quality problems that clearly overwhelmed Flint staff.
>
> *(Flint Water Advisory Task Force 2016, 43)*

Aside from their own failures and omissions, Flint Public Works personnel acted (and over-relied) on improper guidance from the MDEQ, which the Flint Water Advisory Task Force, an independent review committee, subsequently found bears primary responsibility for the crisis.

State failures: the Michigan Department of Environmental Quality (MDEQ), the Michigan Department of Health and Human Services (MDHHS) and the Office of the Governor

At the state level, as early as January of 2013, MDEQ officials in the Office of Drinking Water and Municipal Assistance (ODWMA) raised concerns about utilising the Flint River as a water source (Bridge Magazine 2016; Flint Water Advisory Task Force 2016). Had proper protocol been followed, MDEQ could have greatly reduced if not entirely prevented the damage caused by the switch to the Flint River. The LCR outlines proper corrosion controls to be applied when treating water for public consumption. The MDEQ determined—incorrectly—that immediate corrosion controls were not necessary, and thus failed to meet regulatory statutes of the LCR. Rather than requiring corrosion control at the onset of the switch (despite the fact that the Flint Water had known corrosion issues), the MDEQ concluded that two six-month monitoring phases could be implemented instead to determine whether corrosion control would be necessary, and then Flint would have six additional months to implement these measures if needed (Flint Water Advisory Task Force 2016; Michigan Radio 2015; U.S. Environmental Protection Agency 2017c). This in itself seems illogical, as the Flint River was meant only as an interim water source, presumably for fewer than two years. At the conclusion of the first six-month monitoring period, MDEQ again failed to implement corrosion controls, even after results clearly demonstrated the need. Evidence suggests MDEQ officials used methods to reduce lead concentration in water samples, and intentionally excluded water samples that would exceed EPA action limits for lead (Flint Water Advisory Task Force 2016). These actions (and inactions) directly led to E. coli contamination and subsequently high levels of disinfection by-products (called 'total trihalomethanes'—or TTHMS—a result of over-chlorination), which then led to violations of the SDWA. Perhaps most significantly, the failure of MDEQ to implement corrosion controls allowed for the water itself to leach lead from pipes and plumbing fixtures, setting off a chain reaction that will impact the residents of the city of Flint for generations to come (Butler, Scammell and Benson 2016; Flint Water Advisory Task Force 2016; Shelson 2016).

The Michigan Department of Health and Human Services (MDHHS) also bears responsibility at the state level, failing to properly test and interpret data related to BLLs in Flint children. In addition, the MDHHS was often unwilling to share data with independent researchers seeking to determine the extent of lead contamination in Flint, which could have helped to bring attention earlier to the issue and may possibly have lessened exposure to lead, especially in children. The MDHHS failed to coordinate with the MDEQ to address concerns surrounding increased BLLs in Flint children, and the increase in cases of Legionnaires' disease in the county (Flint Water Advisory Task Force 2016; Hanna-Attisha 2017; Hanna-Attisha, LaChance, Sadler and Schnepp 2016; Salinsky 2016).

The Office of the Governor also bears some responsibility, as it was Governor Snyder who placed the city under Emergency Management, and who appointed multiple EMs (at least one of whom he had never met) to serve in place of locally elected officials. The Governor's office has also been accused of over-reliance on only a few staff members from the MDEQ and MDHHS for information regarding water concerns in Flint, and for failing to address concerns raised by its own executive staff. Following suggestions from the Governor's executive staff that Flint return to the DWSD as a water source in October of 2014, no review of the issue was considered 'because of cost considerations and repeated assurances [from MDEQ and MDHHS] that the water was safe' (Flint Water Advisory Task Force 2016, 11). Given that there was no meaningful public representation in Flint with the authority to act in the best interests of citizens, the Governor would have had the authority to effectively intervene on their behalf, had more attention been given to concerns regarding water quality.

Federal failures: the Environmental Protection Agency (EPA)

At the federal level, the EPA failed to act in its official capacity to oversee state adherence to environmental standards, namely the LCR and SDWA, citing ambiguity in federal law and a reluctance to overstep state regulatory rights. The Flint Water Advisory Task Force (2016) rejected this explanation for their omission:

> EPA's conduct casts doubt on its willingness to aggressively pursue enforcement (in the absence of widespread public outrage). EPA could have exercised its powers under Section 1414 and Section 1431 of the SDWA or under the LCR, 40 CFR 141.82(i).
>
> *(12–13)*

The EPA routinely deferred to the MDEQ, failing to require immediate corrosion control, prolonging the entire 'water crisis' (Flint Water Advisory Task Force 2016). Even though an EPA regulations manager raised concerns regarding lead contamination in June of 2015, the EPA did not officially intervene in lead sampling in Flint until January of 2016—nearly two years after Flint had switched water sources (Sanburn 2016a). Perhaps most importantly, the EPA failed to ensure that its state branch was upholding the protections offered by EO 12,898 providing for environmental justice:

> Environmental justice or injustice, therefore, is not about intent. Rather it is about process and results—fair treatment, equal protection, and meaningful participation in neutral forums that honor human dignity … The facts of the Flint Water Crisis lead us to the inescapable conclusion that this is a case of environmental injustice. Flint residents, who are majority Black or African American and among the most impoverished of any metropolitan area in the United States, did not enjoy the same degree of protection from environmental and health hazards as that provided to other communities. Moreover, by virtue of their being subject to emergency management, Flint residents were not provided equal access to, and meaningful involvement in, the government decision-making process.
>
> *(Flint Water Advisory Task Force 2016, 58)*

Lasting impacts of environmental (in)justice

Public health

The impact of the water crisis in Flint is far reaching and, for many, permanent. Lead is poisonous and can cause a myriad of health problems, including but not limited to issues with brain development, developmental delays and cognitive problems, behavioural issues, seizures, hearing impairments, anaemia and hypertension, kidney problems and complications/miscarriage during pregnancy. Furthermore, lead exposure is virtually untreatable (Zahran, McElmurry and Sadler 2017) and can lead to genetic mutations that can be passed down from generation to generation (Sen et al. 2015; Williams 2016). New research indicates that high blood lead levels can be carried through generations via epigenetic mutations. Dr Doug Ruden, one of the authors of a recent study on the topic (see Sen et al. 2015), spoke with Michigan Radio on implications this may have regarding victims in Flint.

> 'Mothers who are exposed to lead in the water, for instance, can not only affect their children's IQ but can also affect, potentially, the IQ of their grandchildren,' Ruden says. 'We know the DNA is affected, but we don't know right now … whether these changes in the DNA in the grandchildren can also affect their IQ'.
>
> *(Williams 2016, n.p.)*

It is widely recognised that the children of Flint will face physical and mental health challenges for decades to come (Campbell, Greenberg, Mankikar and Ross 2016; Cuthbertson, Newkirk, Ilardo, Loveridge and Skidmore 2016; Hanna-Attisha 2017; Hanna-Attisha, LaChance, Sadler and Schnepp 2016; Zahran, McElmurry and Sadler 2017), and that the policies and agencies designed to protect them bear responsibility.

> It has been said that pediatricians are the ultimate witnesses to failed policies. And as a pediatrician in Flint, I can attest to that. Our children were failed by every agency that was supposed to protect them.
>
> (*Testimony of Mona Hanna-Attisha, M.D., 114th Congress 2016*)

An estimated 8,000 children under the age of six suffered lead exposure in Flint and will likely need lifelong services as a result (114th Congress 2016). What is immeasurable is the loss of life directly related to the Flint water crisis. Studies are now beginning to link the lead contamination to increased infertility rates, miscarriages and foetal deaths. Grossman and David (2017, 32) estimate that 'between 198 and 276 more children would have been born had Flint not enacted the switch in water'. The authors also suggest that the change in water source caused a decline in the health of babies born in Flint during the water crisis (Grossman and David 2017), which can lead to future health complications and costs. In addition, over 80 illnesses and 12 deaths resulting from Legionnaires' disease are suspected to have been a direct result of contamination from the Flint River during this period (Flint Water Advisory Task Force 2016). To say this was a public health catastrophe would be an understatement.

Economic futures

The case in Flint centres on the intended cost-savings measures taken by the Emergency Managers. Financial decisions that would inevitably impact public health were made on multiple levels with the intent of saving the city of Flint money, not providing the safest water source. The irresponsible decision to not immediately implement anti-corrosives was exacerbated by the fact that it was economically driven. Estimates suggest it would have cost \$100–\$200/day to add this treatment, for a total of about \$75,000–\$150,000 during the roughly two-year time period that the Flint River was used. Failure to use corrosion control has now led to infrastructure replacement and health recovery costs estimated to be between \$80 and \$400 million (Salinsky 2016; Sanburn 2016b; Zahran, McElmurry and Sadler 2017). From a longitudinal perspective, the decline in births in Flint over the last few years will also impact school funding, as there will be a decline in student enrolment for a period of time. Given evidence which suggests foetal and birth health is directly related to long-term health, education and employment outcomes, there will also likely be extensive costs for additional health care (physical and mental) for the already disadvantaged residents of Flint. The economic impact of the Flint water crisis extends even to the housing and job markets, as new homebuyers and employers are now looking to invest elsewhere, and may continue to do so as long as social memory of the crisis remains (Wisely 2016). While the intentions motivating decisions made by Flint EMs may be understood in terms of fiscal responsibility, they have led unnecessarily to forced austerity measures on a population ill equipped to manage them.

Erosion of public trust in government

It is impossible to separate the water crisis in Flint from the failures on local, state and federal levels. The supplanting of local government with a series of Emergency Managers left Flint residents with little recourse when it came to voicing their concerns, and, ultimately, to seeking remedy. Their local elected officials were unable to intervene on their behalf; furthermore, when contacted, local, state and federal agencies—save for a few select individuals—not only did not intercede, but took steps to marginalise, or, in some instances, *conceal*, the severity of the situation (114th Congress 2016; Flint Water Advisory

Task Force 2016). Because of these actions, generations of Flint residents will rightfully lack faith in their public governments, as even children will grow up feeling a sense of betrayal, likely passing along these feelings to future generations (Brisman, McClanahan, South and Walters 2018). The removal of the system of 'checks and balances' via the Emergency Manager directive also eliminated public accountability for decision-making, as the EMs did not answer to and were not directly beholden to the citizens of Flint. In addition, decision-makers on all levels demonstrated reluctance to accept responsibility and continued to 'pass the buck' to the next agency (114th Congress 2016; Flint Water Advisory Task Force 2016). With an investigation into the actions of Governor Snyder and criminal charges pending against 15 defendants, the citizens of Flint are also paying (with their tax dollars) for the prosecution and legal representation of the very officials who failed them. Despite public outcry, legal assistance budgets of \$3.4m for the Governor and \$4.5m for MDEQ have been approved by the State Administrative Board (Fonger 2016). For a population that is already marginalised and lacking political and socioeconomic capital, a scenario such as this serves only to further distance citizens from their government. The erosion of public trust in elected officials (at all levels) undermines the entire system of democracy.

The future of Flint

The final finding of the independent Flint Water Advisory Task Force was that the water crisis has been 'a clear case of environmental injustice' (Flint Water Advisory Task Force 2016, 13) and has even been referred to by some as 'state sponsored child abuse' (Kristoff 2016, as quoted in Brisman, McClanahan, South and Walters 2018). Furthering the concept of basic human rights outlined by Schwendinger and Schwendinger (1970), White (2008) highlights the importance of 'intergenerational equity'—the idea that we have a responsibility and moral obligation to ensure environmental quality and sustainability for future generations (see also Brisman and South 2017). In Flint, it is clear that current and future generations now suffer the ramifications of decisions made by these state actors. In this instance, government has failed the people, and done so in a way that disproportionately impacted, and will continue to impact, minority and low-income populations in Flint, Michigan, for generations to come. Injured parties have filed over 16 lawsuits and class-action lawsuits against Flint EMs (Ed Kurtz, Darnell Earley and Gerald Ambrose), former mayor Dayne Walling, Governor Snyder, the State of Michigan, the MDEQ and the MDHHS, among others (Egan 2017; The Network for Public Health Law 2016), seeking financial recompense for their suffering. Citizens are also paying attention to pending criminal charges impacting 15 local- and state-level officials involved with the water crisis. While these cases cannot offer full reparation, they may help to offer some form of restitution to victims and hold accountable those who made the decisions regarding Flint water. Looking forward, it has been suggested that MDHHS should re-establish the Michigan Childhood Lead Poisoning Prevention and Control Commission to prevent future crises such as this, and establish a registry of children and adults who have been exposed to lead in Flint in order to track and treat them in the future (Campbell, Greenberg, Mankikar and Ross 2016; Flint Water Advisory Task Force 2016). Separately, funds are already being collected to provide treatment and care for victims of the Flint water crisis. The Foundation for Flint, a non-profit organisation, has raised and distributed funds to provide for the long-term health and development needs of Flint children, and has developed a separate fund dedicated specifically to cultivating future economic growth in the City of Flint (Community Foundation for Greater Flint 2017). While the case in Flint reflects and was compounded by many failures, it does reveal one 'success':

> The Flint water crisis [represents] something that did work: the critical role played by engaged Flint citizens, by individuals both inside and outside of government who had the expertise and willingness to question and challenge government leadership, and by members of a free press who used the tools that enable investigative journalism. Without their courage and persistence, this crisis likely never would have been brought to light and mitigation efforts never begun.
>
> *(Flint Water Advisory Task Force 2016, 5)*

Although the tragedy and scandal of Flint resulted from state action and subsequent inaction, Flint's path to recovery is instead the result of organisation within the community at the grassroots, which sends a strong statement about the state of the citizenry of Flint, Michigan.

Notes

1 This is a summary; for a more detailed timeline, see Flint Water Advisory Task Force (2016).
2 Given aforementioned knowledge of and concerns with the water quality of the Flint River, independent reviews of the situation have since indicated that had proper protocol been followed, corrosion controls would have been implemented immediately upon the switch to the Flint River, bypassing the monitoring cycles (Butler, Scammell and Benson 2016; Flint Water Advisory Task Force 2016; Michigan Radio 2015).
3 The Office of the Governor confirmed that the two had never spoken, and explained that '[e]mergency managers report to the Treasury Department' (Fonger 2017, n.p.).
4 Preliminary tests confirmed 104 parts per billion (ppb) of lead in her water, well above the EPA established 'safe' limit for drinking water (15 ppb) (Flint Water Advisory Task Force 2016; Michigan Radio 2015). It was later found that MDEQ conveniently, and without adequate investigation, excluded LeeAnne Walters' water quality test results for purposes of determining whether Flint sampling results exceeded EPA's action level (Flint Water Advisory Task Force 2016, 32).
5 In the list of accomplishments achieved by EMs between 2011 and 2015, there was no direct mention of the switch from DWSD to KWA as a cost-savings measure (Office of the Governor 2015).
6 Local news media have suggested the switch may have had more to do with an agreement between KWA, Mayor Dayne Walling and EM Kurtz. For example, Flint had agreed to purchase more water than necessary from the KWA, in order to ensure the company could justify a larger diameter pipeline, thus allowing it to distribute water to (and secure more profit from) other clients (Gross 2016; The Times Herald, USA Today 2016). In addition, Michigan legislators expressed concerns about justifications for the KWA project as well (Lynch and Ramirez 2017).
7 Further emails suggest Flint water quality supervisor Michael Glasgow was receiving pressure from local officials, EM Earley and Mayor Walling to begin water distribution (Egan, Spangler and Shamus 2016).
8 Water evaporates during the boiling process, leading to higher levels of lead concentration in the remaining water.

References

114th Congress. 2016. Flint Water Crisis: Impacts and Lessons Learned. House of Representatives Joint Hearing before the Subcommittee on Environment and the Economy and the Subcommittee on Health of the Committee on Energy and Commerce. 13 April 2016. Serial No. 114–131. Washington, DC: U.S. Government Publishing Office.

Bridge Magazine. 2016. 'Disaster day by day: A detailed flint crisis timeline,' *Bridge Magazine, The Center for Michigan*. 4 February 2016. Available at: https://bridgemi.com/truth-squad-companion/disaster-day-day-detailed-flint-crisis-timeline.

Brisman, A. 2002. 'EPA's disproportionate impact methodologies—RBA and COATCEM—and the draft recipient guidance and draft revised investigation guidance in light of *Alexander v. Sandoval,' Connecticut Law Review*, 34(3): 1065–1108.

Brisman, A. 2008. 'Crime-environment relationships and environmental justice,' *Seattle Journal for Social Justice*, 6(2): 727–817.

Brisman, A., McClanahan, B., South, N. and Walters, R. 2018. *Water, Crime and Security in the Twenty-First Century: Too Dirty, Too Little, Too Much*. London: Palgrave Macmillan.

Brisman, A. and South, N. 2017. 'Green cultural criminology, intergenerational (In)equity and "life stage dissolution",' in M. Hall, J. Maher, A. Nurse, G. Potter, N. South and T. Wyatt (eds.) *Greening Criminology in the 21st Century: Contemporary Debates and Future Directions in the Study of Environmental Harm*, pp. 219–232. Surrey, UK: Ashgate.

Brush, M., Williams, R., Smith, L. and Linsey S. 2015. 'Timeline: Here's How the Flint Water Crisis Unfolded,' *Michigan Radio*, 21 December 2015. Available at: http://michiganradio.org/post/timeline-heres-how-flint-water-crisis-unfolded.

Bullard, R. D. 1990. *Dumping in Dixie: Race, Class, and Environmental Quality*. Boulder, CO: Westview Press.

Butler, L. J., Scammell, M. K., and Benson, E. B. 2016. 'The flint, Michigan, water crisis: A case study in regulatory failure and environmental justice,' *Environmental Justice*, 9(4): 93–97.

Campbell, C., Greenberg, R., Mankikar, D. and Ronald, D. 2016. 'A case study of environmental justice: The failure in flint,' *International Journal of Environmental Research and Public Health*, *13*: 951–962.

Center for Constitutional Rights. 2016. 'Civil rights attorneys challenge michigan law that led to poisoning of flint water,' *Center for Constitutional Rights*. Available at: https://ccrjustice.org/home/press-center/press-releases/civil-rights-attorneys-challenge-michigan-law-led-poisoning-flint.

Centers for Disease Control and Prevention. 2017. 'Diseases and contaminants: Lead and drinking water from private wells,' (Available at: https://cdc.gov/healthywater/drinking/private/wells/disease/lead.html.

Committee on Oversight and Government Reform. 2017. 'Democrats call on oversight committee chairman to immediately re-open flint water investigation: Ranking members ask for vote on subpoena to michigan governor, refer emergency managers to DOJ for criminal prosecution,' Available at: https://democrats-oversight.house.gov/news/press-releases/democrats-call-on-oversight-committee-chairman-to-immediately-re-open-flint.

Community Foundation for Greater Flint. 2017. 'No title,' Available at: https://cfgf.org/cfgf/Home.

Cuthbertson, C. A., Newkirk, C., Ilardo, J., Loveridge, S. and Skidmore, M. 2016. 'Angry, scared, and unsure: Mental health consequences of contaminated water in flint, Michigan,' *Journal of Urban Health*, 93(6): 900–908.

Doyon, J. A. 2014. 'Corporate environmental crime in the electronic waste industry: The case of executive recycling, Inc,' in A. Nurse (ed.) *Internet Journal of Criminology*, pp. 68–89. 'Critical Perspectives on Green Criminology' Series.

Egan, P. 2017. 'Appeals court reverses federal judge; says Flint water lawsuits can proceed', *Detroit Free Press*. 28 July 2017. Available at: https://freep.com/story/news/local/michigan/flint-water-crisis/2017/07/28/flint-water-lawsuits-appeal/520206001/.

Egan, P., Spangler, T. and Shamus, K. J. 2016. E-mails: Flint Water Plant was Rushed Into Operation. *Detroit Free Press*. 12 February, 2016. Available at: https://freep.com/story/news/local/michigan/flint-water-crisis/2016/02/12/e-mails-flint-water-plant-rushed-into-operation/80300220/.

Executive Order 12898. 1994. 'Federal actions to address environmental justice in minority populations and low income populations,' 59 FR 7629; February 16, 1994. Available at: https://archives.gov/federal-register/executive-orders/1994.html#12898.

Flint Water Advisory Task Force. 2016. 'Flint water advisory task force final report, 2016,' Available at: https://michigan.gov/documents/snyder/FWATF_FINAL_REPORT_21March2016_517805_7.pdf.

Fonger, R. 2016. 'Budget for flint water crisis attorneys for Gov. Snyder, DEQ Rises to $7.9 million', MLive, 30 August 2016. Available at: https://mlive.com/news/index.ssf/2016/08/deq_gets_millions_more_for_leg.html.

Fonger, R. 2017. 'Flint emergency manager told congress he never met or talked to Gov. Snyder,' *MLive*, 23 January, 2017. Available at: https://mlive.com/news/flint/index.ssf/2017/01/flint_emergency_manager_told_c.html.

Green, P. J. and Ward, T. 2000. 'State crime, human rights, and the limits of criminology,' *Social Justice*, 27(1): 101–115.

Gross, A. 2016. 'New emails reveal the switch to the flint river was not about saving money,' *Detroit Metro Times*. Available at: https://metrotimes.com/news-hits/archives/2016/01/25/new-emails-reveal-the-switch-to-the-flint-river-was-not-about-saving-money.

Grossman, D. S. and Slusky, D. J. G. 2017. 'The effect of an increase in lead in the water system on fertility and birth outcomes: The case of flint, Michigan,' Working Paper. Available at: www2.ku.edu/~kuwpaper/2017Papers/201703.pdf.

Hanna-Attisha, M. 2017. 'Flint kids: Tragic, resilient, and exemplary,' *American Journal of Public Health*, 107(5): 651–652.

Hanna-Attisha, M., LaChance, J., Sadler, R. C. and Schnepp, A. Champney. 2016. 'Elevated lead levels in children associate with the flint drinking water crisis: A spatial analysis of risk and public health response,' *American Journal of Public Health*, 106(2): 283–290.

Huisman, W. and van Erp, J. 2013. 'Opportunities for environmental crime: A test of situational crime prevention theory,' *The British Journal of Criminology*, 53(6): 1178–1200.

Kennedy, M. 2016. 'Lead-laced water in flint: A step-by-step look at the makings of a crisis,' *NPR*. 20 April 2016. Available at: https://npr.org/sections/thetwo-way/2016/04/20/465545378/lead-laced-water-in-flint-a-step-by-step-look-at-the-makings-of-a-crisis.

Lee, S. J., Krings, A., Rose, S., Dover, K., Ayoub, J. and Salman, F. 2016. 'Racial inequality and the implementation of emergency management laws in economically distressed urban areas,' *Children and Youth Services Review*, 70: 1–7.

Michigan Legislature. 2012. 'MLC 141.1549: Local financial stability and choice act, state of Michigan,' Available at: https://legislature.mi.gov/(S(biagmjcdqhjwhtlkvcicg2wo))/mileg.aspx?page=getObject&objectName=mcl-141-1549.

Lynch, J. and Ramirez, C. E. 'Karegnondi water system rooted in frustration,' *The Detroit News*. Available at: https://detroitnews.com/story/news/michigan/flint-water-crisis/2016/03/24/kwa-pipeline-flint-water/82237222/.

Michalowski, R. J. and Kramer, R. C. 2006. *State-Corporate Crime: Wrongdoing at the Intersections of Business & Government*. New Brunswick, NJ: Rutgers University Press.

Michigan Radio. 2015. 'Can emergency managers be held accountable for their bad decisions?,' *Michigan Radio*. Availabe at: http://michiganradio.org/post/can-emergency-managers-be-held-accountable-their-bad-decisions.

Michigan Radio. 2011. '7 things to know about Michigan's emergency manager law,' *Michigan Radio*. Available at: http://michiganradio.org/post/7-things-know-about-michigans-emergency-manager-law.

The Network for Public Health Law. 2016. 'Flint water crisis – Summary of civil litigation,' The Network for Public Health Law. Available at: https://networkforphl.org/_asset/12x7ul/Flint-Litigation-Summary-Table.pdf.

Office of the Governor. 2015. 'Richard snyder, governor, press release: City of flint ready to move forward as financial emergency resolved,' *State of Michigan*. 29 April, 2015. Available at: https://michigan.gov/snyder/0,4668,7-277-57577_57657-353433–,00.html.

Office of the Governor. 2016. 'Richard snyder, governor, release of emails related to the flint water crisis 2014–2015,' *State of Michigan*. 20 January 2016. Available at: http://somcsprod2govm001.usgovcloudapp.net/files/snyder%20emails.pdf.

Oosting, J. 2016. 'Appeals court upholds michigan emergency manager law,' *The Detroit News*. Available at: https://detroitnews.com/story/news/local/michigan/2016/09/12/appeals-court-upholds-michigan-emergency-manager-law/90279788/.

Pieper, K. J., Tang, M. and Edwards, M. A. 2017. 'Flint water crisis caused by interrupted corrosion control: Investigating "ground zero" home,' *Environmental Science and Technology*, 51: 2007–2014.

Ruggiero, V. and South, N. 2010. 'Green criminology and dirty collar crime,' *Critical Criminology: An International Journal*, 18(4): 251–262.

Salinsky, J. I. 2016. 'Comparing the 2014–2016 flint water crisis to the 1993 Milwaukee *Cryptosporidium* outbreak,' *Environmental Justice*, 9(4): 128–199.

Sanburn, J. 2016a. 'Why the EPA is partly to blame for the flint water crisis,' *TIME*. 22 January, 2016. Available at: http://time.com/4190643/flint-water-crisis-susan-hedman-epa/.

Sanburn, J. 2016b. 'Flint water crisis may cost the city $400 million in long-term social costs,' *TIME*. 08 August, 2016. Available at: http://time.com/4441471/flint-water-lead-poisoning-costs/.

Schlosberg, D. 2007. *Defining Environmental Justice: Theories, Movements, and Nature*. New York: Oxford University Press.

Schwendinger, J. and Schwendinger, H. 1970. 'Defenders of order or guardians of human rights?' *Issues in Criminology*, 5(2): 123–157.

Sen, A., Heredia, N., Senut, M. C., Land, S., Hollocher, K. and Lu, Xiangyiet al. 2015. Multigenerational Epigenetic Inheritence in Humans: DNA Methylation Changes Associated with Material Exposure to Lead Can be Transmitted to the Grandchildren. Scientific Reports, 5: 1–10.

Shelson, J. 2016. 'Lead in the water—The flint water crisis,' *Defense Counsel Journal*, 83(4): 520–525.

Smith, L. 2016. 'Boil water advisory adds to confusion over how to make flint tap water safe to drink,' *Michigan Radio*. 11 February 2016. Available at: http://michiganradio.org/post/boil-water-advisory-adds-confusion-over-how-make-flint-tap-water-safe-drink.

South, N. 2010. 'The ecocidal tendencies of late modernity: Trans-National crime, social exclusion, victims and rights,' in R. White (ed.) *Global Environmental Harm: Criminological Perspectives*, pp. 228–247. Cullompton, Devon, UK: Willan.

South, N. and Brisman, A. (eds.). 2013. *Routledge International Handbook of Green Criminology*. New York: Routledge.

The Times Herald, USA Today. 2016. 'Flint crisis began with pipeline maneuvers,' *USA Today Network*. Available at: https://thetimesherald.com/story/opinion/editorials/2016/08/08/flint-crisis-began-pipeline-maneuvers/88413984/.

Tucker, Y., Jackson, Tull Inc. 2013. *City of Flint Water Supply Assessment, February 2013. For Submittal to: State of Michigan, Department of Treasury*. Detroit, MI: Tucker, Young, Jackson: Tull Inc. Consulting Engineers-Planners.

U.S. Census Bureau. 2017. 'U.S. census bureau quick facts: Flint City, Michigan,' Available at: https://census.gov/quickfacts/fact/table/flintcitymichigan/PST045216.

U.S. Environmental Protection Agency. 2017a. 'Summary of executive order 12898: Federal actions to address environmental justice in minority populations and low-income populations,' Available at: https://epa.gov/laws-regulations/summary-executive-order-12898-federal-actions-address-environmental-justice.

U.S. Environmental Protection Agency. 2017b. 'Environmental justice,' Available at: https://epa.gov/environmentaljustice/learn-about-environmental-justice.

U.S. Environmental Protection Agency. 2017c. 'Drinking water requirements for states and public water systems: Lead and copper rule,' Available at: https://epa.gov/dwreginfo/lead-and-copper-rule.

White, R. 2008. *Crimes Against Nature: Environmental Criminology and Ecological Justice*. Cullompton, Devon, UK: Willian.

White, R. 2009a. Environmental Victims and Resistance to State Crime Through Transnational Activism. *Social Justice*, 36(3): 46–60.

White, R. (ed.). 2009b. *Environmental Crime: A Reader*. Cullompton, Devon, UK: Willan.

Williams, R. 2016. 'Researchers investigating how lead exposure could affect DNA,' Michigan Radio. Available at: http://michiganradio.org/post/researchers-investigating-how-lead-exposure-could-affect-dna.

Wisely, J. 2016. 'Water woes could sink flint's property values even more,' *Detroit Free Press*. 7 February 2016. Available at: https://freep.com/story/news/local/michigan/flint-water-crisis/2016/02/07/flint-property-values/79823532/.

Zahran, S., McElmurry, S. P. and Sadler, R. C. 2017. 'Four phases of the flint water crisis: Evidence from blood lead levels in children,' *Environmental Research*, 157: 160–172.

18

Indigenous environmental victimisation in the Canadian oil sands

James Heydon

Introduction

Labelled the 'biggest environmental crime in history' (Milmo 2007), the extraction of bitumen from the oil sands of northern Alberta, Canada, has had a substantial impact on its surrounding environment. Situated under 54,000 square miles of boreal forest, the volume of proven reserves stands at 166 billion barrels—the third largest in the world after Venezuela and Saudi Arabia (Government of Alberta 2017). 'Oil sands' (also known as 'tar sands' or 'bituminous sands') are loose sands or partially consolidated sandstone that contain a mixture of clay, sand, water and bitumen—a semi-solid viscous form of petroleum. Extracting the bitumen from the ground requires strip-mining or 'in-situ' techniques, the latter of which involves injecting steam and solvents into the deposit to reduce its viscosity and allow it to be pumped to the surface. Because these extraction processes differ from 'conventional' well-drilling methods used for crude oil, oil sand reserves are considered an 'unconventional' oil source. The environmental costs of extraction are high, generating up to four times more carbon dioxide than conventional drilling techniques (National Aeronautics and Space Administration 2011), and producing waste-water ponds emitting levels of methane equivalent to half a million cattle per day (Timoney and Lee 2009: 66). As the reserves contain more than twice the total amount of oil burned in all of human history (Hansen 2012), continued expansion of these operations will guarantee the release of substantial quantities of emissions into the atmosphere for the foreseeable future. Indeed, extraction is due to accelerate from a rate of one million barrels per day in 2000 to five million per day by 2040 (National Energy Board 2016: 52), culminating in an expected 400 per cent increase in the production of a fossil fuel over a 40-year period.

The environmental impact of this extraction process has provoked widespread opposition from Indigenous peoples. In September 2016, over 50 U.S. Native American and Canadian First Nation leaders gathered in Musqueam Territory (Vancouver) and Mohawk Territory (Montreal), signing an agreement titled the Treaty Alliance against Tar Sands Expansion (Treaty Alliance 2016). This represented an unprecedented solidification of Indigenous opposition to expansive oil sands production across the breadth of Canada's landmass. While initially, and to some extent still, supportive of the industry as a means of channelling investment into their communities, First Nations in and around the deposit have since become vocal about its environmental consequences. Although opposition has differed in intensity both within and between communities, as attempts have been made to balance land preservation with the need for capital investment (see Taylor and Friedel 2010), when concerns have been expressed, as they have been for almost two decades now, they focus on the fact that contamination has reduced the quantity and quality of resources upon which traditional hunting, fishing and trapping practices depend.

Undermining the material activities underpinning their collective identities, this form of Indigenous environmental victimisation is encapsulated by the term 'cultural loss'. This refers to the 'adverse impacts on the range of traditional activities, emotional well-being or social relations engaged in by an individual and/or an Aboriginal community as a result of changes in the land' (Gregory and Trousdale 2009: 2470). As a form of harm, cultural loss fits uneasily into existing green criminological categorisations of environmental victimisation, which has been less attentive to the specific and interwoven relationship maintained by Indigenous peoples with the non-human environment.

This chapter begins by drawing out some of the conceptual contours of 'cultural loss', giving consideration to the 'land–culture' relationship maintained by Indigenous peoples more broadly, and the First Nations of Canada more specifically. Next, this chapter illuminates the more substantive aspects of the harm through an exploration of how contamination of the water, air and culturally significant species affects the traditional land-based practices of First Nations in and around the oil sands. The chapter concludes by calling for a green criminology more attentive to this relatively clandestine pattern of Indigenous environmental victimisation.

Indigenous environmental victimisation and 'cultural loss'

Emerging from the broad interpretation of what constitutes its basic subject matter, green criminology has made various efforts at categorising environmental 'crimes' or 'harms'. The diversity of these attempts ultimately stems from the fact that negative environmental impacts resulting from human activity 'are enormous in their range and variety' (South 2014: 9). Carrabine and colleagues (2014: 318) classify environmental 'crimes' and 'harms' as having 'primary' or 'secondary' forms, with the former referring to the more immediate consequences of ecological degradation and the latter those that follow, such as the creation of illegal markets for scarce basic commodities or the flouting of rules that seek to regulate environmental disasters. Building on this typology, Potter (2014: 11) develops the category of 'tertiary' green crimes, which he defines as those activities 'committed by environmental victims or as a result of environmental victimisation'. This has parity with Hall's (2013: 38) examination of '[v]ictims as offenders, offenders as victims', which focusses on those who commit criminal or harmful offences due to environmental pressures. Indeed, Hall (2013: 27–38) promulgates a four-pronged typology of specifically anthropocentric environmental victimisation: 'health impacts', 'economic impacts', 'social and cultural impacts' and 'security impacts'. White (2008: 98–99), in turn, adopts an alternative conception, opting to classify harms as 'brown' issues, which refer to pollution levels in urban locations, 'green' issues, which are harms associated with the biosphere, and 'white' issues, which involve the environmental impact of new technologies. Taken together, this body of literature provides a clear basis from which to describe a multitude of environmental harms and bring their study under the rubric of green criminology, or its fledgling counterpart, green victimology (see Hall 2014).

The environmental victimisation experienced by First Nations in the oil sands could be categorised using any one of these frameworks, as well as crossing many of the categories established within each. As described below, 'ecological disorganisation' resulting from oil sands expansion is reducing the quantity and quality of resources used by First Nations, the consumption of which has been associated with serious illnesses amongst their members (see Huseman and Short 2012), and has contributed to a decrease in traditional hunting, fishing and trapping activities. This varied impact would cross all of White's (2008) categories and at least three of Hall's (2013). It is also not difficult to see how the enclosure of land for oil sands projects may increase the likelihood of First Nation members being accused of trespass on newly designated private land, where hunting, fishing and trapping used to occur, thus raising the prospect of categorisation under Potter's (2014) 'tertiary' label. While these typologies provide a multifaceted basis from which to categorise specific forms of environmental harm, they tend to be broadly conceived, rendering them less sensitive to the specificities inherent to the Indigenous environmental victimisation under investigation here. As such, it is necessary to outline a more directly applicable thematic classification of 'cultural loss'.

According to the preamble of the United Nations Education Scientific and Cultural Organisation (UNESCO), 'culture' should be recognised as 'the set of distinctive spiritual, material, intellectual and emotional features of a society or a social group' and should encompass 'art and literature, lifestyles, ways of living together, value systems, traditions and beliefs' (UNESCO 2001: 1). The preamble notes that culture is 'at the heart of contemporary debates about identity … [and] social cohesion' (ibid), bringing the notion of collective identity pertaining to shared cultural characteristics to the fore. While each of the First Nation or Indigenous peoples are distinct, the legacy of colonialism in North America has generated a situation in which the myriad of cultural characteristics maintained by each is collapsed into an undifferentiated label, where the image of 'the Indian' operates as 'an entity that would stand for the whole' (King 2012: 83). Indeed, Brody (2001: 7) speaks of this caricature as at least partially resting on an imagined difference between highly mobile 'nomadic' hunters and 'settled' farmers who stay in one particular area. This, however, is actually an inversion of reality:

> the stereotype has it the wrong way round. It is agricultural societies that tend to be on the move; hunting peoples are far more firmly settled. This fact is evident when we look at these two ways of being in the world over a long time span—when we screen the movie of human history, as it were, rather than relying on a photograph.
>
> *(ibid)*

Such conceptual manipulation is related to settler attempts at constructing an identity around the fixity of territoriality—a process aimed at denying the authenticity of Indigenous claims to legitimate authority over land (see Veracini 2010). Yet, despite this, some cultural attributes are shared between these many, varied and specific cultures (see Berry 1999). One of the most significant is the 'deeply spiritual' relationship with the land maintained by Indigenous peoples globally (Anaya 2009: 69). As Cobo (1986/87: para 196), a previous UN Special Rapporteur for Indigenous Peoples, asserts, this is a relationship 'basic to their existence as such and to all their beliefs, customs, traditions and culture'.

The land–culture relationship also encompasses an ontological perception that views ecosystems as intrinsic to human life. Indigenous peoples' conceptions of nature and culture are 'braided' to one another, representing not simply a 'closeness' or reliance upon nature, but an 'embodied inscription', where land and wildlife form a central component to their collective

Indigenous identities (Woolford 2009: 91), meaning environmental destruction gradually erodes this relationship. Indeed, as the concept of identity 'usually implies a sense of attachment' (Berry 1999: 3), the cultural identity of a First Nation is derived not simply from recognition of others' membership of the collective, but simultaneous recognition of the attachment that collective maintains with the natural environment (ibid). By extension, this includes the myriad ways and means through which they engage with non-human nature. Put another way, material engagement with the landscape through hunting, fishing and trapping practices, for instance, underpins the more immaterial aspects of the collective cultural identities maintained by First Nations. In this sense, 'culture' should be conceived of as 'reflected and embedded in practices, the built and natural environment, and the relationships between people and their natural environment' (Gibson 2017: 8). It is for this reason that environmental degradation precipitated by expansionary extractive operations precedes cultural loss. It forcibly severs the connection Indigenous peoples maintain with non-human nature and is why, despite Indigenous people becoming increasingly involved in waged labour, throughout history 'the defining struggles of aboriginal peoples have been over land use' (Kulchyski 2013: 29).

This materiality also underpins the cultural identity of First Nations in and around the oil sands. Considering that 'different societies produce qualitatively different conceptions of space and time' (Harvey 1990: 418), Indigenous peoples maintain a relational concept of place (see Castree 2004) where spaces are not simply locations in and of themselves, but 'nodes in relational settings' (Aminy 2002: 391) or 'articulated moments in networks' (Massey 1994: 5). This emphasises connections between spaces rather than individual points, introducing the notion of 'topo-kinetic' knowledge as opposed to its 'topographical' counterpart. Indeed, for First Nations, travel through an environment is directly connected to the expression of oral traditions that encapsulate their cultural knowledge (McCormack 2012), where movement across the landscape has an iterative association with cognition, social relationships and interactions (see Turnbull 2007: 142–143). In noting that this relationship transcends the physical, being concurrently shaped by an understanding of the land as 'an autonomous living being' (Arnold 2001: 17, quoted in McCormack 2012: 115), McCormack (2012: 125) provides a detailed account of this spirituality for one First Nation in Northern Alberta, concluding that 'Chipewyan history, culture and religion are both encoded and demonstrated in the geography of their traditional territory'. It is for this reason that environmental degradation is so damaging to the land-based aspect of their collective identity. Impeding their ability to engage with traditional activities undermines the more immaterial aspects of culture with which they are entwined. This alienates First Nations from the land in the present, severs their ties with the past, and erodes culture over time by inhibiting its reproduction into the future. In this sense, cultural loss is an inherently intergenerational form of Indigenous environmental victimisation.

Several anthropological studies have described this specifically Indigenous form of victimisation as a type of 'loss' (see Berry 1999; Gregory and Trousdale 2009; Rose 1994). In examining the term, Kirsch (2001: 169) outlines two concepts to which such 'loss' may refer. The first of these denotes possession and the loss of 'objects or property for which one might claim rights or ownership' (ibid). As he is here discussing the loss felt by aboriginal peoples over land, and applying the concept of cultural property rights, this 'possession' is taken to include 'property, land and memory' (ibid). The second notion to which the term refers is that of 'kinship and belonging', which are together seen as a key feature of the social realm because of their productive possibilities. This productivity makes reference to 'the social relations organised through land, as well as the capacity for reproducing these relationships in place' (ibid). In deploying this conceptual foundation, Kirsch demonstrates that ecological destruction results in loss by destroying the former and disrupting the generative capacity of the latter. A similar concept is used by Turner and colleagues (2008) in relation to the environmental degradation experienced by Indigenous communities in western North America. They prefer to define this further as 'invisible loss' (ibid: 7), however, emphasising that the evidence of this impact goes unrecognised and unacknowledged by decision makers. It is in accordance with these positions that the term 'cultural loss' is deployed here.

Existing literature aimed at explaining the production of this harm in the oil sands, along with its less anthropocentric forms, can be found in a variety of fields. Using a socio-legal human rights perspective, Huseman and Short (2012) argue that ecological disorganisation breaches the historic hunting, fishing and trapping rights of First Nations, provide evidence of the adverse health effects of oil sands expansion, and use the notion of 'slow industrial genocide' to highlight the significance of cultural loss and draw out its relationship with the structural conditions of settler-colonial societies. Slowey and Stefanick (2015: 217) describe the 'dampening' of public and First Nation engagement in decisions pertaining to oil extraction over the last 50 years, explaining how the rise of neoliberalism has given priority to the 'indifferent, invisible hand of the market'. It is this, the authors contend, that has allowed industrial expansion to proceed uninhibited. From within green criminology, Lynch and colleagues (2016) consider ecological disorganisation in the oil sands as a consequence of the normative functioning of global capitalism, while Smandych and Kueneman (2010) use the state-corporate analytical model to position greenwashing, ineffective environmental monitoring and the constrictive influence of the North American Free Trade Agreement on federal government decision-making as implicative factors in the expansion of oil sands production.

Providing insightful contributions aimed at explaining the human and non-human consequences of oil sands extraction, this body of work tends to concentrate on nation-state or global actors and influences, or the abstract structures of capitalism and settler-colonialism. Positioning the analytical lens on these relatively macro-level influences highlights the importance of global processes of production and exchange in explaining ecological disorganisation, at the same time drawing attention to the absence or ineffectuality of mechanisms by which 'non-elite' populations can act to oppose or impede them. But as these approaches emphasise the forces perpetuating environmental harm, broadly conceived, they render existing explanations less attentive to the details of cultural loss as a specific form of victimisation. As such, they tend to collapse its different dimensions into a singular 'culture' without detailed consideration of its content, obscuring its specific facets and excluding more immediate considerations pertaining to each. In light of this, what follows here is an examination of the effects of low water levels, water contamination, air emissions and the degradation in quantity and quality of land and aquatic species, on the land-based practices of First Nations, with consideration also given to the some of the specific issues implicated in each.

Cultural loss in the Canadian oil sands

When examining the content of cultural loss, the political dimension of evidence needs to be accounted for as different claims to knowledge do not hold equal weight. As White (2008: 110) succinctly puts it, 'knowing' environmental harm is 'not just about gaining access to ... statistics'. Indeed, the traditional ecological knowledge of Indigenous peoples tends to be de-legitimated and given less credibility than 'scientific evidence', which is privileged for its apparent neutrality and objectivity (Sollund 2017; South 2007). As Mol (2013: 251) asserts:

> A propensity to render nonscientific, non-Western ways of thinking, seeing, and being invisible, or to case such systems of thought off as mere folklore or cosmovisions or belief systems of cultures, reduces these to objects of study, rather than being acknowledged as valid forms and producers of knowledge in their own right.

The credibility afforded to Western science is related to its 'northernness' (Connell 2006: 258; see also Goyes and South 2017) and associated claims to 'reason' (Tuhiwai Smith 2012), both of which produce questionable claims to universality as the theories developed in the metropole tend to be applied to the Global South (Aas 2012). Instead, it should be recognised that systems of traditional ecological knowledge may actually be *more holistic* than their Western counterparts, and better equipped to cope with the unpredictability of natural systems as this is considered intrinsic to ecological phenomena (Mazzocchi 2006). As such, there is a need to recognise what White (2008: 111) calls 'expertise from below', and use it alongside other forms of knowing to support the 'counter-hegemonic struggles against dominant socio-economic interests' (ibid: 112). After all, 'Western science and traditional knowledge constitute different paths to knowledge, but they are rooted in the same reality' (Mazzocchi 2006: 466). For this reason, evidence from both the natural sciences and Indigenous peoples are here used in conjunction with one another to demonstrate how changes to the land are generating cultural loss amongst the First Nations of Northern Alberta.

Water quantity and quality

Water has a central place in the ecosystem of northern Alberta and the lives of nearby First Nations. In explaining the importance of the Athabasca River to Indigenous existence, both the Mikisew Cree First Nation (MCFN) (MCFN 2016: 9) and Athabasca Chipewyan First Nation (ACFN) (ACFN 2016: 11) describe it as the 'transportation life blood ... providing access to Aboriginal territories for hunting, fishing and trapping, and other traditional-use activities'. Descriptions of the water as the 'life blood' of First Nation culture similarly reflect the fact that this river, along with Lake Athabasca, not only facilitates travel to hunting, fishing, trapping and ceremonial locations, but it also sustains each of the animal and plant species that are culturally significant to First Nations (Macdonald 2012). More specifically, concerns about water quantity centre on the amount of water drawn directly from the Athabasca River by the mining industry. In the oil sands, water is needed to separate the sand from the bitumen. While there is difficulty in determining 'acceptable' levels of water withdrawal due to natural fluctuations of the ecosystem in question, industrial extraction is contributing to low water levels across the delta system (Timoney 2013). Aside from the stress on the ecosystems, water withdrawal generates cultural loss for a number of reasons, not least because it renders areas upon which traditional practices depend inaccessible (ACFN 2016; MCFN 2016). As a previous Chief of the MCFN explains,

> When water levels are down, we can no longer access our Traditional Lands by boat, which limits our fishing, trapping and hunting. Our members have been stranded. We no longer drink the water. We see our rights along with our River deteriorating before us.
>
> *(Marcel, quoted in Parkland Institute 2010)*

Cumulative water withdrawal also generates a decrease in fish abundance and a restriction on harvesting activities (Ohlson et al. 2010: 98). As a recipient of 74.5 per cent of all surface water allocations in 2010 (Sauchyn et al. 2015: 12621), which equates to 13 times the provincial average (ibid), oil sands operators used 170 million litres of water in 2011 alone (Grant et al.

2013a: 26). Determined by the Phase 1 Water Management Framework in effect between 2007 and 2015, an evaluation of the framework concluded this to be 'inadequate to protect the Athabasca River system' (Schindler et al. 2007: 11). Phase 2 was never implemented as limits established under the Lower Athabasca Regional Plan were introduced in 2015. Considering that regulations governing water withdrawal have recently been deemed unfit for purpose due to a lack of evidential support (Sauchyn et al. 2015), however, and that freshwater use in mining operations is predicted to rise in accordance with industrial growth (Grant et al. 2013b: 3), the movement of First Nations away from the waterways upon which their cultural practices depend is likely to continue.

Water contamination is also an issue. As one member of the MCFN notes, 'you could drink water anywhere them days when I was younger, drinking off the river, and now you can't do that, you have to carry special water when you go anywhere' (Candler et al. 2010: 38). Following Timoney's (2007: 73) study of water and sediment quality in Fort Chipewyan, which concluded that the 'explosive growth' of northern Alberta's bitumen industry 'poses risks to environmental and public health that demand immediate attention independent of provincial and industrial oversight', several studies have reached similar conclusions. After observing elevated concentrations of contaminants upstream and downstream of the industry to be magnified two-fold in winter and twenty-fold in summer, Kelly and colleagues (2009: 4) likened the amount of bitumen deposited on the land, via air and waterways, to 'be equivalent to a major oil spill, repeated annually'. Following a conclusion made in its companion study, which stated that '[c]ontrary to claims made by industry and government in the popular press, the oil sands industry substantially increases loadings of toxic PPE (priority pollutant elements) to the AR (Athabasca River) and its tributaries via air and water pathways' (Kelly et al. 2010: 5), a report by the Royal Society of Canada on the environmental and health impacts of the oil sands criticised the research on the grounds of the sampling method used (Gosselin et al. 2010: 148). This criticism, however, was later rejected by the Water Monitoring Data Review Committee (Dillon et al. 2011: 11).

The licensed and unlicensed release of waste water into the Athabasca River is a particular concern when discussing water contamination. Although companies are prohibited from discharging untreated waste water, 'treated' waste water can be released according to provincial guidelines. Providing evidence of one of the flaws in water quality regulation, however, Timoney (2013: 411–413) highlights how the 11.9 billion litres of licenced waste water released into the river by Suncor in 2007 did not include the numerous unlicensed discharges from spills and leaks. Detailed research into the ecological and human health effects of these amounts has yet to be conducted. Indeed, tailings ponds, which hold the waste by-product from the oil sands extraction process, contribute heavily to this unlicensed pollution. Occupying an area of 25 square kilometres in 1998, the ponds are expected to fill an area of 250 square kilometres by 2020 (Simieritsch et al. 2009: 34). This is a particularly destructive pattern of development considering that latest estimates place unlicensed seepage from a single pond at 6.5 million litres per day (Frank et al. 2014). These figures gain prominence when considering that the content of tailings is acutely toxic to aquatic organisms and mammals (Gosselin et al. 2010), having implications for the hunting, fishing and trapping practices of First Nations.

Air quality

In addition to waste-water leaks and releases, another basis for Indigenous concerns about environmental contamination is air emissions. Although these have a less-direct influence on cultural loss, the environmental consequences of air emissions are experienced in other areas. This is because particles in air emissions accumulate on land and water through the process of wet and dry 'deposition'. This term refers to the means by which aerosol particles collect or deposit on solid surfaces via acidic rain, fog or snow, for the former, and acidic gases and particles for the latter (Hwang et al. 2008). Indeed, residents of the Indigenous town of Fort McKay have been complaining about air quality since the very inception of the industry in the 1960s (Boucher, quoted in CBC 2016a). As a local hunter and trapper explains, '[s]ometimes it smells like burnt plastic ... I won't go outside because you can feel it in your nostrils ... The only thing that worries me is how it affects my grandkids and the kids around here' (ibid). After receiving 165 complaints about odours from residents of the Indigenous town of Fort McKay, between 2010 and 2014, the Alberta Energy Regulator and Alberta Health (2016) conducted a study into the air quality at that location. Following an analysis of monitoring data, it found 19 thresholds for 'odour' to have been surpassed, along with 13 for 'odour and health' (ibid: 113–114). These include ozone and sulphur dioxide, toxins like hydrogen sulphide, and carcinogens like benzene. This echoes the findings of an earlier study into water quality, which found significant amounts of industrial particulates, including polycyclic aromatic hydrocarbons (PAHs) and heavy metals, such as mercury and arsenic, to be deposited on the landscape and waterways each year near Fort McKay (Kelly et al. 2010, 2009).

While the report from the energy regulator and Alberta Health states the need for a subsequent assessment of the health implications stemming from these threshold breaches, existing research does exist. Chronic exposure to particulates, such as PAHs and heavy metals, is related to increased risk of cardiovascular disease, respiratory symptoms and lung cancer (Rosenthal et al. 2008). Indeed, Canadian Natural Resources Limited (CNRL) was fined $500,000 for two large-scale releases of hydrogen sulphide gas, for failing to immediately report the incidents, and for providing misleading information to both the government and Fort McKay First Nation (CBC 2016b). Hydrogen sulphide, in particular, has, in various concentrations, been linked with asthma, cancer, pulmonary oedema, neurological difficulties, and a range of other health issues (Timoney 2013). An extensive array of scientific evidence exists warning that the impact of air contamination upon the health of flora and fauna should not be considered separate from its impact on the health of humans, especially if the human groups in question have a particularly close relationship with the natural environment (see Timoney 2007). This gains prominence when considering that heavy metals and PAHs have been found to 'bioaccumulate' within marsh and aquatic plants (Lafabrie et al. 2011; Meudec et al. 2006)—a process defined as the 'biological sequestering of a substance at a higher concentration than that at which it occurs in the surrounding environment' (United States Geological Survey 2007). As such, it is not only direct exposure to air and water pollution that poses a risk to human health, but also indirect exposure facilitated by subsistence based on wild food. The process of bioaccumulation presents a pathway by which these contaminants can enter the diets of various non-human animals and, in turn, the diets of humans, especially as the latter are at the very top of the food chain (National Aboriginal Health Organization 2008).

Species quantity and quality

Degradation of the aquatic ecosystem, through contamination and withdrawal, is causing First Nations to cease harvesting the culturally significant land and water-based species that rely upon its continued existence. Although ranking of certain species above others is antithetical to the holism of Indigenous worldviews, this section of the chapter will focus on 'cultural keystone' species. These can be defined as species that 'shape in a major way the cultural identity of a people, as reflected in the fundamental roles these species have in diet, materials, medicine, and/or spiritual practices' (Garibaldi and Turner 2004: 4). This is not to suggest that other species are insignificant, only that certain relationships vary in strength to others and, as such, so too do the effects that arise from their severance. For this reason, fish, caribou and moose will be focussed on as they are variously identified as species important to the First Nations.

Directly affected by the decline in water quality and quantity are fish—a 'subsistence mainstay' of some First Nations (McCormack 2012: 29). The reluctance to harvest fish in certain areas is linked to increasingly prevalent observations of fish deformities in the vicinity of Fort Chipewyan. Traditional users have identified 'lesions, internal and external tumors [sic], and deformed skulls, skeletons, and fins' (Timoney and Lee 2009: 77), with one elder describing deformed pickerel in Lake Athabasca as having '[p]ushed in faces, bulging eyes, humped back, crooked tails … never used to see that. Great big lumps on them … you poke that, it sprays water' (Ladouceur, quoted in Timoney 2007: 62). While fish abnormalities can result from natural causes, such as injury, disease, parasites, spawning, or poor nutrition, evidence links these defects with water quality in the region. Indeed, an increase in mortality rate, craniofacial irregularities, cardiac dysfunction and a reduction in size have all been observed in fish exposed to PAHs from the Athabasca River (Colavecchia et al. 2007), concentrations of which are now between 2.5 and 23 times greater than in 1960 as a direct result of oil sands developments (Kurek et al. 2012). Similarly, malformations and hatching alterations have been found to result from exposure to natural bitumen from the Athabasca River and waste water pond sediment, with haemorrhages, spinal malformations and oedemas, which is an excess of fluid beneath the skin, being observed in larvae (Colavecchia et al. 2006). These detrimental effects have been echoed by other studies (see Incardona et al. 2004; Parrott et al. 2004), supporting First Nation concerns surrounding the water contamination resulting from industrial operations.

Anxieties about the quality of land-based animal resources may also impact their pursuit by First Nation hunters. Species of particular concern are those of the muskrat, bison, migratory wildfowl, caribou and moose. Listed as some of the fundamental resources for the continuation of the MCFN's traditional knowledge (Centre for Indigenous Environmental Resources 2010), woodland caribou and wood bison have a central role in First Nation culture. As Chief Janvier of the Chipewyan Prairie Dene First Nation states:

> The extinction of caribou would mean the extinction of our people. The caribou is our sacred animal; it is a measure of our way of life. When the caribou are dying, the land is dying.
>
> *(quoted in Droitsch and Simieritsch 2010: 4)*

Similarly, Lameman of the Beaver Lake Cree First Nation notes that '[a]ll of the animals are starting to deplete … soon there will be nothing' (ibid: 7). While the ability to hunt woodland caribou has already been affected by lower water flows and declining populations (ACFN 2003), their need for 'large areas comprised of continuous tracts of undisturbed habitat rich in mature to old-growth coniferous forest, lichens, muskegs, peat lands, and upland or hilly areas' means that expansive oil sands developments compound the issue (Environment Canada 2012: vi). With the species already categorised as 'threatened' under both the Alberta Wildlife Act and the Federal Species at Risk Act (Athabasca Landscape Team 2009)—and Alberta's entire population of woodland caribou being classified as 'unlikely' or 'very unlikely' to be able to sustain itself without intervention (Hervieux et al. 2013: 872)—a report by the Athabasca Landscape Team (2009: i) emphasised that '[t]ough choices need to be made between the management imperative to recover boreal caribou and plans for ongoing bitumen development and industrial land-use'. Denhoff (2016) makes a similar point, noting that populations have been pushed close to extinction. McCormack (2012) builds on this, arguing that the majority of studies into the demise of the woodland caribou consider predators to be the problem without giving any consideration to habitat loss as a result of oil sands developments. Yet, the government's national species recovery strategy did recognise the importance of habitat, along with the need to reduce habitat disturbance, in its recommendation to maintain 'a perpetual state of a minimum of 65 per cent of the [national] area as undisturbed habitat' (Environment Canada 2012: vii). The issue with this, however, is that the policies intended to effect this change at the provincial level—the Alberta Woodland Caribou Recovery Plan (Alberta Woodland Caribou Recovery Team 2005) and the Woodland Caribou Policy for Alberta (Government of Alberta 2011)—have been criticised for failing to 'articulate clear and substantive steps towards reducing the amount of disturbed lands' and for focussing instead on mitigation efforts 'that appear unlikely to drastically reduce the disturbance footprint in Alberta's caribou ranges' (Unger 2012). In other words, the proposed solutions do not tackle the issue of industrial expansion, rendering them unlikely to result in the minimum standards needed to sustain caribou populations.

Similar in significance to caribou, moose is a 'highly desired and valued food by Athabasca Chipewyans for community dinners and feasts and other events that are culturally significant' (McCormack 2012: 31). They are also used to make moccasins, mitts and jackets, all of which are visible markers of First Nation identity (Centre for Indigenous Environmental Resources 2010). Human industrial activity on the landscape, however, and the associated habitat loss, has precipitated a reduction in the number of moose in the Alberta oil sands region (Wasser et al. 2011). In addition, low water levels are making it difficult to access the waterways needed to hunt the animals from boats and First Nations are expressing concerns about species contamination (McCormack 2012). These concerns are not unfounded. One Suncor study suggests consumption of arsenic-contaminated moose meat in the oil sands region risks an additional 453 cases of cancer per 100,000 people (The Ecumenical Council for Corporate Responsibility 2011: 7). This chemical element is linked to elevated risks of liver, lung, urinary tract and skin cancers; vascular diseases; and Type 2 diabetes (World Health Organization 2012). While the Suncor results have been disputed by Imperial Oil (CBC 2006)—and directly challenged by a subsequent government study which instead placed the cancer risk at 17–33 times the acceptable level (Alberta Health and Wellness 2007: iii)—the notable difference between results, coupled with a lack of rigorous peer-reviewed research, has done little to alleviate worries surrounding this traditional resource.

Conclusion

As this chapter has attempted to explain, expansion of the oil sands industry is having substantial multi-faceted effects on the traditional land-based practices of First Nations. With the withdrawal of waterways making it difficult to access hunting, fishing and trapping sites—and poor air and water quality acting to deter the harvesting and consumption of a wide range of culturally significant resources—it is clear that the First Nations are experiencing the very specific form of Indigenous environmental victimisation known as cultural loss. With more established conceptions of environmental victimisation being ill-equipped to represent accurately the specifically Indigenous form of harm under consideration here, the notion of cultural loss is of utility to a green criminology looking to the future—one more sensitive to Indigenous peoples, their rights and the specific forms of land-based victimisation experienced. As visible in the work of Goyes and colleagues (2017), Goyes and South (2015) and Mol (2013), the relationship between state-corporate power, Indigenous peoples and ecological disorganisation is likely to become more pronounced in the coming years. Indeed, this appears to be the case already, as communicated in the warning issued by the Chair of the UN Permanent Forum on Indigenous Issues:

> There are more and more arrests, killings and abuses [of Indigenous peoples]. This is happening in Russia, Canada, the Philippines, Cambodia, Mongolia, Nigeria, the Amazon, all over Latin America, Papua New Guinea and Africa. It is global. We are seeing a human rights emergency ... Much of the world's natural capital—oil, gas, timber, minerals—lies on or beneath lands occupied by Indigenous people.
>
> *(Tauli-Corpus, quoted in Mowforth 2014)*

In this context, green criminology can use the concept of cultural loss to examine Indigenous-specific forms of environmental victimisation outside the remit of criminal law. Having attracted scholarly attention, the analytical gaze can then shift from '*illuminating* and *describing* different types of harm' (Brisman 2014: 2, emphasis in original) to examining and exposing the structures, agents, policies and practices acting to produce and reproduce it. Considering that Indigenous peoples are frequently attempting to balance traditional land-based practices with the demands and conditions of late-modernity, however, such an agenda should also account for procedural rights and injustices. While this requires an attentiveness to the absence or efficacy of rights, and the availability or extent of the processes by which Indigenous peoples can meaningfully engage in environmental decision-making, it is only through such analyses that a nuanced explanation for the occurrence of Indigenous environmental victimisation can be reached.

References

Aas, F. 2012. '"The earth is one but the world is not": Criminological theory and its geopolitical divisions,' *Theoretical criminology*, 16(1): 5–20.

Alberta Energy Regulator and Alberta Health. 2016. *Recurrent Human Health Complaints Technical Information Synthesis: Fort McKay Area.* Calgary and Alberta: Alberta Energy Regulator.

Alberta Health and Wellness. 2007. 'Assessment of the potential lifetime cancer risks associated with exposure to inorganic arsenic among indigenous people living in the wood buffalo region of Alberta,' Available at: www.health.alberta.ca/documents/Wood-Buffalo-Arsenic-2007.pdf.

Alberta Woodland Caribou Recovery Team. 2005. 'Alberta woodland caribou recovery plan 2004/05 – 2013/14,' Available at: http://aep.alberta.ca/fish-wildlife/species-at-risk/species-at-risk-publications-web-resources/mammals/documents/SAR-WoodlandCaribouRecoveryPlan-Jul2005.pdf.

Aminy, A. 2002. 'Spatialities of globalisation,' *Environment and Planning*, 34(3): 385–399.

Anaya, J. 2009. *International Human Rights and Indigenous Peoples.* New York: Aspen Publishers.

Athabasca Chipewyan First Nation. 2003. *Footprints on the Land.* Calgary: Frabjous Books.

Athabasca Chipewyan First Nation. 2016. 'Written brief of the Athabasca Chipewyan first nation to the standing committee on transport, infrastructure and communities,' Available at: www.ourcommons.ca/Content/Committee/421/TRAN/Brief/BR8693005/br-external/AthabascaChipewyanFirstNation-e.pdf.

Athabasca Landscape Team. 2009. 'Athabasca Caribou Landscape Management Options Report,' Available at: www.albertacariboucommittee.ca/PDF/Athabasca-Caribou.pdf.

Berry, J. 1999. 'Aboriginal cultural identity,' *The Canadian Journal of Native Studies*, XIX(1): 1–36.

Brisman, A. 2014. 'Of theory and meaning in green criminology,' *International Journal for Crime, Justice and Social Democracy*, 3(2): 21–34.

Brody, H. 2001. *The Other Side of Eden: Hunter-Gatherers, Farmers, and the Shaping of the World*. London: Faber and Faber.

Candler, C., Olsen, R., DeRoy S. and the Firelight Research Co-Operative with the Athabasca Chipewyan First Nation. 2010. *As Long As the Rivers Flow: Athabasca River Knowledge, Use and Change*. Available at: http://s3-us-west-2.amazonaws.com/parkland-research-pdfs/aslongastheriversflow.pdf

Carrabine, E., Cox, P., Fussey, P., Hobbs, D., South, N., Thiel, D. and Thurton, J. 2014. *Criminology: A Sociological Introduction*, 3rd edition. London and New York: Routledge.

Castree, N. 2004. 'Differential geographies: Place, indigenous rights and "local" resources,' *Political Geography*, 23: 133–167.

CBC. 2006. 'Imperial, Gvm't say Arsenic Scare Unfounded,' *Canadian Broadcasting Corporation*. Available at: www.cbc.ca/news/canada/north/imperial-gov-t-say-arsenic-scare-unfounded-1.596524.

CBC. 2016a. 'Leaders vow to tackle Fort McKay air quality, odour complaints,' Available at: www.cbc.ca/news/canada/edmonton/leaders-vow-to-tackle-fort-mckay-air-quality-odour-complaints-1.3772373.

CBC. 2016b. 'Canadian natural resources fined $500,000 for hydrogen sulphide releases,' *Canadian Broadcasting Corporation*. Available at: www.cbc.ca/news/canada/edmonton/canadian-natural-resources-fined-500-000-for-hydrogen-sulphide-releases-1.3652379.

Centre for Indigenous Environmental Resources. 2010. *Sagow Pimachiwin: Plants and Animals Used by Mikisew Cree First Nation for Food, Medicine and Materials*. Manitoba: Centre for Indigenous Environmental Resources.

Cobo, M. 1986/87. *Study of the Problem of Discrimination against Indigenous Populations*. UN Doc E/CN .4/Sub.2/1986/7.

Colavecchia, M., Hodson, P. and Parrott, J. 2006. 'CYP1A induction and blue sac disease in early life stages of white suckers (*Catostomus Commersoni*) exposed to oil sands,' *Journal of Toxicology and Environmental Health Part A*, 69(10): 967–994.

Colavecchia, M., Hodson, P. and Parrot, J. 2007. 'The relationships among CYP1A induction, toxicity and eye pathology in early life stages of fish exposed to oil sands,' *Journal of Toxicology and Environmental Health Part A*, 70(18): 1542–1555.

Connell, R. 2006. 'Northern theory: The political geography of general social theory,' *Theory and Society*, 35(2): 237–264.

Denhoff, E. 2016. 'Setting Alberta on the path to caribou recovery,' Available at: http://aep.alberta.ca/fish-wildlife/wildlife-management/caribou-management/caribou-action-range-planning/documents/OnThePathtoCaribouRecovery-May-2016.pdf.

Dillon, P., Dixon, G., Driscoll, C., Giesy, J., Hurlbert, S. and Nriagu, J. 2011. 'Evaluation of four reports on contamination of the Athabasca river system by oil sands operations,' Available at: www.ceaa.gc.ca/050/documents/p59540/83233E.pdf.

Droitsch, D. and Simieritsch, T. 2010. *Canadian Aboriginal Concerns with Oil Sands: A Compilation of Key Issues, Resolutions and Legal Activities*. Calgary: Pembina Institute.

Environment Canada. 2012. *Recovery Strategy for the Woodland Caribou (Rangifer tarandus caribou), Boreal population*. Ottawa: Environment Canada.

The Ecumenical Council for Corporate Responsibility. 2011. *Oil Extraction – Risks to Health*. Surrey: ECCR.

Frank, R., Roy, J., Bickerton, G., Rowland, S., Headley, J., Scarlett, A., West, C., Peru, K., Parrott, J., Conly, M. and Hewitt, M. 2014. 'Profiling oil sands mixtures from industrial developments and natural groundwaters for source identification,' *Environmental Science and Technology*, 48(5): 2660–2670.

Garibaldi, A. and Turner, N. 2004. 'Cultural keystone species: Implications for ecological conservation and restoration,' *Ecology and Society*, 9(3): 1–18.

Gibson, G. 2017. 'Culture and rights impact assessment,' Available at: www.thefirelightgroup.com/thoushallnotpass/wp-content/uploads/2016/03/MCFN-303_MAPP-Report_Final.pdf.

Gosselin, P., Hrudey, S., Naeth, A., Plourde, A., Therrien, R., Van Der Kraak, G. and Xu, Z. 2010. *Environmental and Health Impacts of Canada's Oil Sands Industry*. A report by The Royal Society of Canada Expert Panel. Ottawa: The Royal Society of Canada.

Government of Alberta. 2011. 'A woodland caribou policy for Alberta,' Available at: http://esrd.alberta.ca/fish-wildlife/wildlife-management/caribou-management/documents/WoodlandCaribouPolicy-Alberta-Jun2011.pdf.

Government of Alberta. 2017. 'Facts and statistics,' Available at: www.energy.alberta.ca/OilSands/791.asp.

Goyes, D.R., Mol, H. Brisman, A. and South, N. (eds.). 2017. *Environmental Crime in Latin America: The Theft of Nature and the Poisoning of the Land*. Basingstoke, Hampshire, UK: Palgrave Macmillan.

Goyes, D.R. and South, N. 2015. 'Land-grabs, biopiracy and the inversion of justice in Colombia,' *The British Journal of Criminology*, 56(3): 558–577.

Goyes, D.R. and South, N. 2017. 'Green criminology before "green criminology": Amnesia and absences,' *Critical Criminology: An International Journal*, 25(2): 165–181.

Grant, J., Huot, M., Lemphers, N., Dyer, S. and Dow, M. 2013a. *Beneath the Surface: A Review of Key Facts in the Oilsands Debate*. Calgary: Pembina Institute.

Grant, J., Angen, E. and Dyer, S. 2013b. 'Forecasting the impacts of oil sands expansion,' Available at: www.pembina.org/reports/oilsands-metrics.pdf.

Gregory, R. and Trousdale, W. 2009. 'Compensating aboriginal cultural losses: An alternative approach to assessing environmental damages,' *Journal of Environmental Management*, 90: 2469–2479.

Hall, M. 2013. *Victims of Environmental Harm: Rights, Recognition and Redress under National and International Law*. Abingdon, Oxon, UK: Routledge.

Hall, M. 2014. 'Environmental harm and environmental victims: Scoping out a green victimology,' *International Review of Victimology*, 20(1): 129–143.

Hansen, J. 2012. 'Game over for the climate,' *The New York Times*. 10 May 2012.

Harvey, D. 1990. 'Between space and time: Reflections on the geographical imagination,' *Annals of the Association of American Geographers*, 80(3): 418–434.

Hervieux, D., Hebblewhite, M., DeCesare, N., Russell, M., Smith, K., Robertson, S. and Boutin, S. 2013. 'Widespread declines in woodland caribou (*Rangifer tarandus caribou*) continue in alberta,' *Canadian Journal of Zoology*, 91(12): 872–882.

Huseman, J. and Short, D. 2012. 'A slow industrial genocide: Tar sands and the indigenous peoples of Northern Alberta,' *International Journal of Human Rights*, 16(1): 216–237.

Hwang, W., Han, M., Jeong, H. and Kim, E. 2008. 'A predictive model for a radioactive contamination in an urban environment and its performance capability to the EMRAS project,' *Environmental Radiation Measures and Assessments*, 45(5): 594–597.

Incardona, J., Collier, T. and Scholz, N. 2004. 'Defects in cardiac function precede morphological abnormalities in fish embryos exposed to polycyclic aromatic hydrocarbons,' *Toxicology and Applied Pharmacology*, 196(2): 191–205.

Kelly, E., Schindler, D., Hodson, P., Short, J., Radmanovich, R. and Nielsen, C. 2010. 'Oil sands development contributes elements toxic at low concentrations to the athabasca river and its tributaries,' *Proceedings of the National Academy of Science of the United States of America*, 107(37): 16178–16183.

Kelly, E., Short, J., Schindler, D. H., Ma, P., Mingsheng, K. A. and Fortin, B. 2009. 'Oil sands development contributes polycyclic aromatic compounds to the athabasca river and its tributaries,' *Proceedings of the National Academy of Science of the United States of America*, 106(52): 22346–22351.

King, T. 2012. *The Inconvenient Indian*. Minneapolis: University of Minnesota Press.

Kirsch, S. 2001. 'Lost worlds: Environmental disaster, "culture loss", and the law,' *Current Anthropology*, 42(2): 167–198.

Kulchyski, P. 2013. *Aboriginal Rights Are Not Human Rights*. Manitoba: ARP Books.

Kurek, J., Kirk, J., Muir, D., Wang, X., Evans, M. and Smol, J. 2012. 'Legacy of a half century of Athabasca oil sands development recorded by lake ecosystems,' *Proceedings of the National Academy of Sciences of the United States of America*, 110(5): 1761–1766.

Lafabrie, C., Major, K., Major, C. S. and Cebrian, J. 2011. 'Arsenic and mercury bioaccumulation in the aquatic plant, vallisneria neotropicalis,' *Chemosphere*, 82(10): 1393–1400.

Lynch, M., Long, M. and Stretesky, P. 2016. 'A proposal for the political economy of green criminology: Capitalism and the case of the Alberta Tar Sands,' *Canadian Journal of Criminology and Criminal Justice*, 58(2): 1–24.

Macdonald, A. 2012. 'Supplemental social, economic and cultural effects submission for shell Canada's proposed Jackpine mine expansion,' Available at: www.ceaa.gc.ca/050/documents_staticpost/59540/82080/Appendix_D_-_Part_05.pdf.

Massey, D. 1994. *Space, Place and Gender*. Minneapolis: University of Minnesota Press.

Mazzocchi, F. 2006. 'Western science and traditional knowledge: Despite their variations, different forms of knowledge can learn from each other,' *European Molecular Biology Organisation Reports*, 7(5): 463–466.

McCormack, P. 2012. *An Ethnohistory of the Athabasca Chipewyan First Nation*. Edmonton: Alberta. Available at: www.ceaa-acee.gc.ca/050/documents_staticpost/59540/82080/Appendix_D_-_Part_03.pdf.

Meudec, A., Dussauze, J., Deslandes, E. and Poupart, N. 2006. 'Evidence for the bioaccumulation of PAH within internal shoot tissues by a halophytic plant artificially exposed to petroleum-polluted sediments,' *Chemosphere*, 65(3): 474–481.

Mikisew Cree First Nation. 2016. 'Written brief of the Mikisew Cree first nation to the standing committee on transport, infrastructure and communities,' Available at: www.ourcommons.ca/Content/Committee/421/TRAN/Brief/BR8708926/br-external/MikisewCreeFirstNation-e.pdf.

Milmo, C. 2007. The biggest environmental crime in history. *The Independent*. Monday 10 December 2007.

Mol, H. 2013. '"A gift from the tropics to the world": Power, harm and palm oil,' in D. Westerhuis, R. Walters and T. Wyatt (eds.) *Emerging Issues in Green Criminology*, pp. 242–260. Basingstoke, Hampshire, UK: Palgrave Macmillan.

Mowforth, M. 2014. 'Indigenous people and the crisis over land and resources,' *The Guardian*. 23 September 2014.

National Aboriginal Health Organization. 2008. *Resource Extraction and Aboriginal Communities in Northern Canada: Cultural Considerations*. Ontario: National Aboriginal Health Organization.

National Aeronautics and Space Administration. 2011. 'Athabasca oil sands,' Available at: http://earthobservatory.nasa.gov/Features/WorldOfChange/athabasca.php.

National Energy Board. 2016. 'Canada's energy future 2016: Energy supply and demand projections to 2040,' Available at: www.neb-one.gc.ca/nrg/ntgrtd/ftr/2016/2016nrgftr-eng.pdf.

Ohlson, D., Long, G. and Hatfield, T. 2010. 'Phase 2 framework committee report,' Available at: https://albertawilderness.ca/wordpress/wp-content/uploads/2015/12/20100131_rp_athabasca_p2fc.pdf .

Parkland Institute. 2010. 'Marcel. 2010. Treat rights impacted downstream of tar sands,' Available at: www.parklandinstitute.ca/media_treaty_rights_impacted_downstream_of_tar_sands.

Parrott, J., Sherry, J. and McMaster, M. 2004. 'Fish health effects from oil sands wastewater discharges and naturally-occurring oil sands compounds in the athabasca river system. Task 5 assessment of natural and anthropogenic impacts of oil sands contaminants within the Northern River Basins,' in F. M. Conly (ed.) *Compiler. Northern River Ecosystems Initiative: Collective Findings*, pp. 38–47. Saskatoon: Environment Canada.

Potter, G. 2014. 'The criminogenic effects of environmental harm: Bringing a "green" perspective to mainstream criminology,' in T. Spapens, R. White and K. Marieke (eds.) *Environmental Crime and Its Victims: Perspectives within Green Criminology*, pp. 7–22. Farnham: Ashgate.

Rose, C. 1994. *Property and Persuasion: Essays on the History, Theory and the Rhetoric of Ownership*. Boulder: Westview Press.

Rosenthal, F., Carney, J. and Olinger, M. 2008. 'Out of hospital cardiac arrest and airborne fine particulate matter: A case-crossover analysis of emergency medical services data in Indianapolis, Indiana,' *Environmental Health Perspectives*, 116(5): 631–636.

Sauchyn, D., St-Jacques, J. and Luckman, B. 2015. 'Long-term reliability of the athabasca river (Alberta, Canada) as the water source for oil sands mining,' *Proceedings for the National Academy of Sciences of the United States of America*, 112(41): 12621–12626.

Schindler, D., Donahue, W. and Thompson, J. 2007. 'Section 1: Future water flows and human withdrawals in the athabasca river,' in *Running out of Steam? Oil Sands Development and Water Use in the Athabasca River-Watershed: Science and Market based Solutions*, pp. 1–38. Edmonton: Environmental Research and Studies Centre, University of Alberta.

Simieritsch, T., Obad, J. and Dyer, S. 2009. 'Tailings plan review,' Available at: http://pubs.pembina.org/reports/tailings-plan-review-report.pdf.

Slowey, G. and Stefanick, L. 2015. 'Development at what cost? First nations, ecological integrity, and democracy,' in M. Shrivistava and L. Stefanick (eds.) *Alberta Oil and the Decline of Democracy in Alberta*, pp. 195–224. Edmonton: Athabasca University Press.

Smandych, R. and Kueneman, R. 2010. 'The Canadian-Alberta tar sands: A case study of state-corporate environmental crime,' in R. White (ed.) *Global Environmental Harm: Criminological* Perspectives, pp. 87–109. Devon: Willan Publishing.

Smith, L. T. 2012. *Decolonizing Methodologies*. London: Zed Books.

Sollund, R. 2017. 'Doing green, critical criminology with an auto-ethnographic, feminist approach,' *Critical Criminology: An International Journal*, 25(2): 245–260.

South, N. 2007. 'The "corporate colonisation of nature": Bio-prospecting, bio-piracy and the development of green criminology,' in P. Beirne and N. South (eds.) *Issues in Green Criminology*, pp. 230–247. Devon: Willan Publishing.

South, N. 2014. 'Green criminology: Reflections, connections, horizons,' *International Journal for Crime, Justice and Social Democracy*, 3(2): 5–20.

Taylor, A. and Friedel, T. 2010. 'Enduring neoliberalism in alberta's oil sands: The troubling effects of private-public partnerships for first nation and metis communities,' *Citizenship Studies*, 15(6–7): 815–835.

Timoney, K. 2007. *A Study of Water and Sediment Quality as Related to Public Health Issues, Fort Chipewyan, Alberta*. Alberta: Treeline Ecological Research.

Timoney, K. 2013. *The Peace-Athabasca Delta: Portrait of a Dynamic Ecosystem*. Alberta: University of Alberta Press.

Timoney, K. and Lee, P. 2009. 'Does the alberta tar sands industry pollute? The scientific evidence,' *The Open Conservation Biology Journal*, 3: 6–81.

Treaty A. 2016. 'First nation tribes sign new treaty joining forces to stop all tar sands pipelines,' Available at: www.treatyalliance.org/wp-content/uploads/2016/09/TAATSE-PR-Treaty-Signing-EN-FINAL.pdf.

Turnbull, D. 2007. 'Maps, narratives and trails: Performativity, hodology and distributed knowledges in complex and adaptive systems – an approach to emergent mapping,' *Geographical Research*, 45(2): 140–149.

Turner, N., Gregory, R., Brooks, C., Failing, L. and Satterfield, T. 2008. 'From invisibility to transparency: Identifying implications,' *Ecology and Society*, 13(2): 7–20.

Unger, J. 2012. 'Optimistic policy is not what woodland caribou need,' Available at: http://elc.ab.ca/optimistic-policy-is-not-what-woodland-caribou-need/.

United Nations Educational, Scientific and Cultural Organization. 2001. 'Universal declaration on cultural diversity,' Available at: http://portal.unesco.org/en/ev.php-URL_ID=13179&URL_DO=DO_TOPIC&URL_SECTION=201.html.

United States Geological Survey. 2007. 'Glossary,' Available at: http://water.usgs.gov/nawqa/glos.html.

Veracini, L. 2010. *Settler Colonialism: A Theoretical Overview*. Basingstoke, Hampshire, UK: Palgrave Macmillan.

Wasser, S., Keim, J., Taper, M. and Lele, S. 2011. 'The influences of wolf predation, habitat loss and human activity on caribou and moose in the alberta oil sands,' *Frontiers in Ecology and the Environment*, 9(10): 456–551.

White, R. 2008. *Crimes Against Nature*. Devon: Willan Publishing.

Woolford, A. 2009. 'Ontological destruction: Genocide and canadian aboriginal peoples,' *Genocide Studies and Prevention: An International Journal*, 4(1): 81–97.

World Health Organization. 2012. 'Arsenic,' Available at: www.who.int/mediacentre/factsheets/fs372/en/.

19

Fracking the Rockies

The production of harm

Kellie Alexander, Tara O'Connor Shelley and Tara Opsal

Introduction

Situated in the western portion of the United States (U.S.), Colorado is a geographically diverse state that is home to the Southern Rocky Mountain Range (i.e., the Rockies), the Great Plains and the Colorado Plateau (Huber 1993) (Figure 19.1). Indeed, Colorado is well known for its scenic beauty and varied landscape of forests, plains, rivers and canyons alongside 58 mountains exceeding 14,000 feet or 4,267 meters in elevation (Hamm 2017)—ranking it first in mean elevation (2,073 meters or 6,800 feet) among U.S. states (Colorado 2018). Approximately, 5.6 million people live in Colorado (U.S. Census Bureau 2019) with the majority residing in the region known by locals as the Front Range—a north to south urban corridor that includes Denver, the state's largest metropolitan city, and runs parallel to the eastern side of the southern Rocky Mountains (Cronin and Loevy 2017). Part of Colorado's unique charm is its diverse array of natural resources with over 24 million acres of forestland, 6,000 miles of streams, and more than 2,000 lakes and reservoirs, all of which are home to varied species of biota (Bank 2018).

Colorado also contains vast mineral reserves including uranium, coal, copper, gold, lead and silver, as well as natural gas and petroleum (Bank 2018; Colorado 2018). The oil and gas (O&G) industry in Colorado has expanded dramatically over the last decade after the discovery of two major resource reservoirs: the Piceance Basin on the western side of the Front Range and the Niobrara Shale area on the Denver-Julesburg Basin, located along the northeastern plains of the state (Opsal and Shelley 2014). These discoveries, coupled with developments in industry technologies, such as directional drilling (Yan, Ariaratnam, Dong and Zeng 2018), have allowed O&G companies to extract a greater amount of natural gas from existing reserves. These techniques facilitated much of the O&G drilling boom in Colorado between the early 2000s and the present day, spurring the expansion of large-scale industry development in the state. Since 2000, the amounts of natural gas produced in Colorado increased from 752,985 to 1,836,422 million cubic feet in 2018, a 144 per cent increase, while crude oil production increased 607 per cent from 2000–2017 (US EIA 2018; US EIA 2019). Currently, there are over 54,000 active drilling wells in the state, representing an increase of over 126 per cent in the last few years (COGCC 2016). The geographic spread of this development

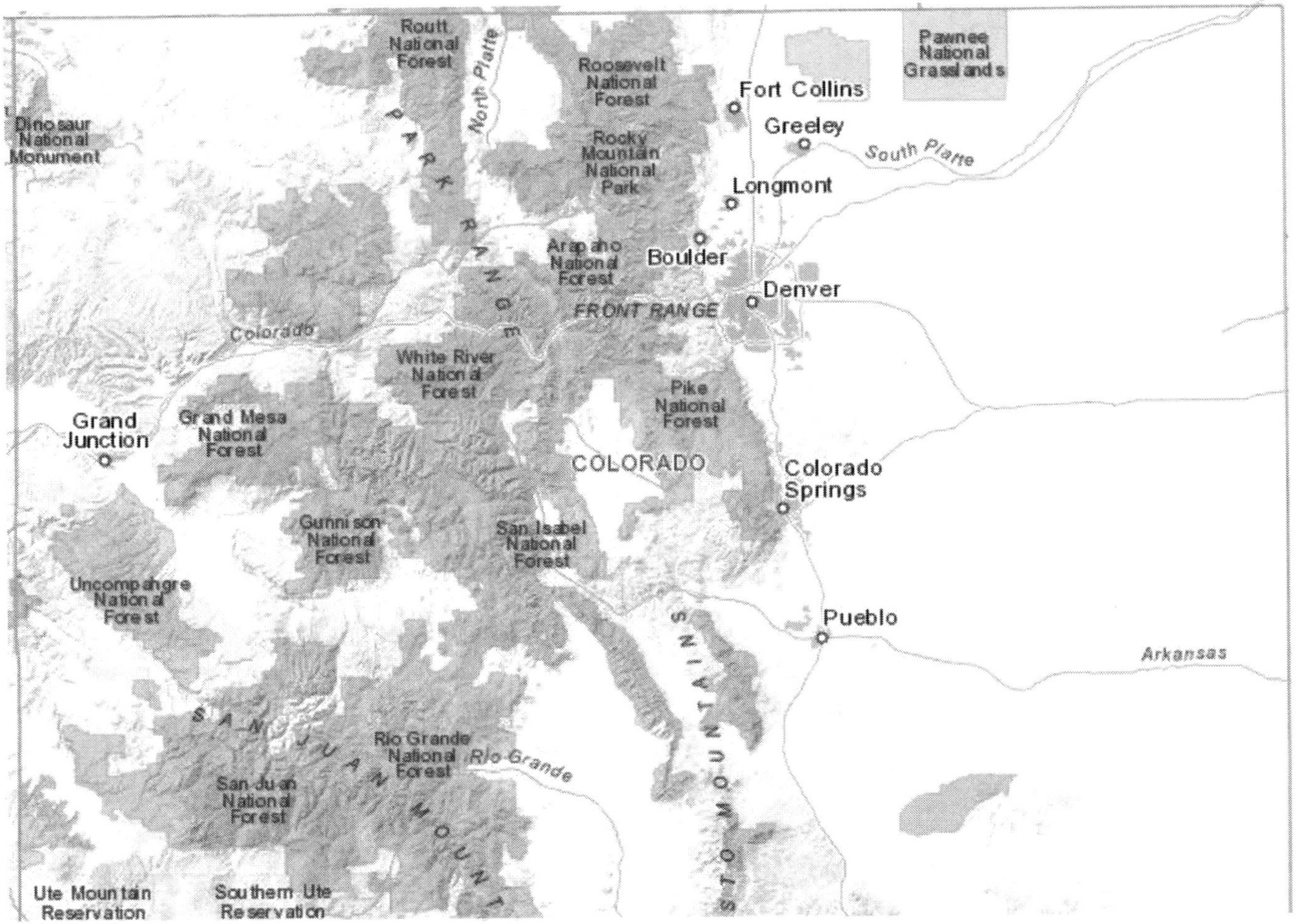

Figure 19.1 Map of Colorado

has been uneven; 87 per cent of active wells in the state of Colorado are in six counties, most of which are rural (COGCC 2016).

Not only has the expansion of O&G development led to the state granting more permits to O&G companies in Colorado, but it has also resulted in increased instances of spills on residents' property. For example, in 2000, there were 274 spills reported to the Colorado Oil and Gas Conservation Commission (COGCC)—the state's O&G permit-granting and regulatory enforcement agency—while in 2016, this figure increased to 524 representing a 91 per cent increase in spills from 2000–2016 (COGCC 2001; COGCC 2016). These spills, along with other accidents related to oil drilling and hydraulic fracturing (also known as 'fracking' or 'hydro-fracking'), have become points of concern, as well as contention, among Coloradans because they can create various harms. For instance, in March of 2013, workers removed over 1,500 cubic yards of petroleum-contaminated soil from the Western Slope of Colorado after a large spill leaked benzene and other contaminants into a major creek (Finley 2013a). Another spill occurred in Windsor, Colorado, in June of 2014 when a broken wellhead released at least 84,000 gallons of produced water over a 30-hour period (Finley 2013a). In addition to spills, a worker in Weld County died in May of 2017 after an oil tank battery exploded (Nicholson 2017). Despite these adverse events, the O&G industry has continued to grow; in 2016, the COGCC issued 2,565 new permits to corporations to drill and even established a fracking waste facility on the edge of the Colorado River, close to homes, a public water system, as well as a state wildlife area (Finley 2016).

Some Coloradans have taken notice of this O&G development and have responded with ballot initiatives[1] or proposed legislation at the local and state level calling for increasingly restrictive statewide and local regulations. For instance, in 2018, voters considered Proposition 112 that would have required new development to be set back at least 2,500 feet from occupied buildings rather than the current limit: 500 feet from homes and 1,000 feet from schools (Opsal and Malin 2018). Despite public concern, most of these ballot initiatives failed, including Proposition 112, as some Colorado residents support this form of energy development due to its potential economic benefits and perceive it as a path towards energy independence (Lee 2015; Munasib and Rickman 2015; Newell and Raimi 2015; Paredes, Timothy and Scott 2015; Weber 2014). Indeed, the political landscape in Colorado indicates that neither support nor opposition to hydraulic fracturing is universal (Kizewski 2015; Mayer 2016; Mayer 2018; Osher 2017).

Despite the contested nature of fracking in Colorado, as well as in the U.S. more broadly, there remains a paucity of research focussed on understanding individuals' direct experiences and perceptions of risk associated with fracking-related harm and externalities, particularly those associated with spills of fracking fluid and produced water. Rural and environmental sociologists have begun to examine citizen perceptions about the costs and benefits of hydraulic fracturing (Ladd 2013, 2018; Mayer 2016; Schafft, Borlu and Glenna 2013; Theodori 2013), as well as the social impacts of development on communities (e.g., Jacquet 2014; Malin, Opsal, Shelley and Hall 2018; Perry 2012). Criminologists have been slow to study these (and other) environmental harms, however. As noted in the first chapter of this volume, mainstream criminology emphasises legal definitions of offending and harm and focusses on the perpetration of and response to street crimes like murder, robbery and drug use (Burns and Lynch 2004; Hall 2014; Lynch, Long, Stretesky and Barrett 2017; White and Heckenberg 2014).

Green criminologists (as well as other critical criminologists) have demonstrated that this conception is limited given that societal constructions of crime link directly to economic, political and social power (e.g., Stretesky, Long and Lynch 2014). Indeed, green criminologists point out that externalities related to ecological harm can cause significantly more harm to people, animals, and the environment than these traditional forms of criminality (Burns and Lynch 2004; Lynch and Michalowski 2006). Thus, green criminology provides 'a space within criminology to examine the nexus between environmental problems, the definition of harms against nature as crimes', in addition to filling a need to 'reconsider the criminal justice practice and policy in relationship to the environmental harms they produce, the variety of victims environmental offenses create … and the effects of environmental toxins on ecological systems and species' health and behavior' (Stretesky and Lynch 2011: 210).

In furtherance of this goal, some green criminologists have turned their attention to resource extraction and its connection to social disorganisation (Lynch et al. this volume, Chapter 4; Stretesky, Long and Lynch 2014; White 2013), while others have examined the environmental harms resulting from resource extraction (Brisman, South and White 2015; Goyes, Mol, Brisman and South 2017; Jarell and Ozymy 2010; Shelley and Opsal 2017; Short, Elliot, Norder, Lloyd-Davies and Morley 2015; Van Gulijk 2014; see also Heydon, this volume, Chapter 18; Lampkin, this volume, Chapter 27). These issues are particularly magnified in the Global South (Gould, Pellow and Schnaiberg 2008; Goyes this volume, Chapter 12; Goyes, Mol, Brisman and South 2017). Less examined, especially in the context of O&G activity, is government regulation and response to environmental harms and degradation (but see Opsal and Shelley 2014; South 2015; Wyatt 2015). In this chapter, we extend this latter area of research and explore citizens' experiences with O&G activity, as well as regulatory responses after spills or leaks occur on or near their property.

Harms and hydraulic fracturing

Oil drilling and hydraulic fracturing are processes that both involve drilling and pumping of multiple liquids and chemicals into the ground to obtain the desired resource. Hydraulic fracking involves pumping a mixture of water, chemicals and sand or other fine-grained material at high pressure directly into the well through the horizontal well bore to release oil or gas resources that flow back to the wellhead.[2] The chemicals used in fracking fluid include friction reducers, anticorrosive agents and biocides, whereas the particulate matter works as proppants, which hold apart fractures within the rock. This helps increase porosity and facilitates the release of gas trapped within the shale (Gullion 2015; Yan, Ariaratnam, Dong and Zeng 2018).

Research has demonstrated that the chemicals used in hydraulic fracking are harmful to human health. A report by the United States House of Representatives Committee on Energy and Commerce Minority Staff (2011: 1) found that

> [b]etween 2005 and 2009, the O&G service companies used hydraulic fracturing products containing 29 chemicals that are (1) known or possible human carcinogens, (2) regulated under the Safe Drinking Water Act for their risks to human health, or (3) listed as hazardous air pollutants under the Clean Air Act.

Additional research has identified many of these chemicals as carcinogenic, linking them to a range of health problems, such as birth defects, respiratory ailments and endocrine dysfunction (Colborn, Kwiatkowski, Schultz and Bachran 2011; Davidson 2018; Hill 2014; Jemielita, Gerton, Neidell, Chillrud and Yan 2015; Kassotis, Tillitt, Lin, McElroy and Nagel 2016; McKenzie, Allshouse, Byers, Bedrick, Serdar and Adgate 2017; Rabinowitz, Slizovskiy, Lamers, Trufan and Holford 2015; Saunders, McCoy, Goldstein and Munroe 2018). Furthermore, living near O&G activity has been associated with mental health problems (Hirsch, Smalley, Selby-

Nelson, Hamel-Lambert, Rosmann, Barnes, Abrahamson, Meit, GreyWolf and Beckmann 2018; Short and Szolucha 2017).

In addition to other adverse effects of fracking on environmental quality (Ferrar, Michanowicz, Christen, Mulcahy, Malone and Sharma 2013; Grant, Weimer, Marks, Perow, Oster, Brubaker, Trexler, Solomon and Lamendella 2015; Holzman 2011; Meng 2017 Paulik, Donald, Smith, Tidwell, Hobbie, Kincl, Haynes and Anderson 2015; Rozell and Reaven 2012), social science illustrates how—as O&G development encroaches on neighbourhoods and businesses—residents of these communities report experiencing negative impacts on their quality of life, such as increased dust, light, noise and traffic, contributing to both congestion and road deterioration (Komarek 2014; Opsal and Shelley 2014; Theodori 2009). Many residents also experience and display concern about landscape despoliation, potential depreciation in property values of areas in proximity to well sites (Gibbons, Heblich and Timmins 2016), and increased use of large quantities of water in water-scarce areas (Cooley and Donnelly 2014).

Moreover, Perry's (2012) study of one rural community in Pennsylvania illuminates how these experiences—especially when felt persistently by residents—can result in collective trauma. Her research finds that the industrial development that is part of O&G activity deeply impacted residents' connection to their community alongside the community's local identity. In addition to broader impact to the community, Perry's research provides evidence that collective trauma can result in individual feelings of anger, depression and fear.

Community experiences with O&G activity are further complicated by Colorado's 'split estate' system, whereby residents may own the surface rights to their property but another person or entity may own the rights to develop the minerals below the surface (Ryder and Hall 2017). This system requires that surface owners provide mineral right owners necessary access to the resources that are beneath the surface, leaving landowners at a disadvantage compared with mineral rights owners and O&G companies, who have a vested interest in development due to potential economic benefit (Davis 2012). Research in Colorado indicates that the split estate system disempowers landowners and marginalises them from participating in decisions that affect their homes directly, leading to significant distress and frustration (Malin, Opsal, Shelley and Hall 2018).

In response to these issues, some communities along the Front Range[3] corridor north of Denver (see Figure 19.1 above) formed grassroots anti-fracking organisations in an effort to suspend or halt hydraulic fracking in their municipalities (Finley 2013b; Landman 2014; Quinn 2013). Indeed, five communities have passed moratoriums on fracking in the wake of expanded fracking (Kizewski 2015). In 2016, however, the Colorado State Supreme Court struck down two of the five community moratoriums, undermining efforts to ban fracking near communities in northern Colorado (Wines 2016). Since local attempts to restrict or ban fracking have been somewhat stymied, citizens must rely on the COGCC to resolve their problems.

Spill regulation

The COGCC is the primary regulatory agency responsible for overseeing O&G activity in the state of Colorado. This organisation has a dual mandate, meaning that while they serve to protect the public and environment, they must also promote O&G development in the state (Stokols 2013). Prior to the passage of the O&G Commission Reform Act in 2007, which necessitated an expansion and background diversification of its seven-member panel, the COGCC was comprised primarily of industry or industry-associated representatives. Shortly thereafter, the Colorado Habitat Stewardship Act of 2007, revised in 2016, mandated that the COGCC take part in conservation efforts. As a result, Colorado features some of the most stringent air emissions and water-testing regulations in the country; the effectiveness of these rules, however, is ultimately limited as the COGCC only has 31 inspectors to monitor and regulate 54,000 active wells around the state (COGCC 2018; Finley 2014; Maddaford 2013).

The ratio of inspectors to active wells in Colorado (i.e., one inspector per 1,741 wells) is cause for concern. While most accidents related to unconventional O&G development are due to human error, many accidents are caused by leaky wellheads, security equipment failure, blowouts and holding tank malfunctions (Howarth, Ingraffea and Engelder 2011; Sovacool 2014). Regarding leaks and spills—the focus of this chapter—the Center for Western Priorities, a Denver-based environmental group, found that, in 2015 alone, there were 615 oil and other chemical spills, and that 15 per cent of these spills contaminated groundwater. Companies most often spilled produced water, comprising 44 per cent of the total spills (Finley 2016).

Beyond occasional reports from local environmental groups and local newspapers, our knowledge about the nature and extent of leaks and spills in Colorado remains limited. Even more hidden from the public eye are accounts of citizen experiences with leaks and spills and the regulatory and/or industrial responses to these events. Thus, the goal of our chapter is to fill this research gap by addressing several research questions:

1 What is the nature and extent of leaks and spills in Colorado?
   a How often do they occur? What substances and chemicals are spilled and/or leaked?
2 Do citizens experience harms due to spills and/or leaks? If so, what types?
3 Are there conflicting narratives about harms (or the potential of harm) by stakeholders (e.g., industry, citizens and regulatory officials)?
4 Are leaks and spills resolved? If so, how? If not, do harms persist?

Methods

As noted by Hall (2014), there are a number of methodological challenges associated with collecting data from environmental victims. With this in mind, we employed a mixed methods approach that generated an array of data to answer our research questions, including: (1) a content analysis of the COGCC spill report database; (2) a survey of citizens (n=215) who had filed complaints with the COGCC regarding O&G activity; and (3) in-depth interviews with 65 environmental victims. In the next several sections, we discuss each of these sources of data in detail and then turn to findings organised by each source of data.

Content analysis of COGCC spill report database

The COGCC database is a state-run database containing information on complaints, spills and locational information on O&G wells (COGCC 2014). This database is available to the public and serves as a gateway for citizens to file complaints and to research well information. The database also includes official spill information reported by industry and regulatory officials. According to the COGCC, any observable release of exploration and production fluids or produced fluids spilled onsite is considered to be a 'spill', including materials such as oil, condensate, produced water, or diesel fuels used to power rig generators (COGCC 2019, Appendix I). Rule 906 of the COGCC establishes requirements for spills and releases in the State of Colorado. As of February 2014, Rule 906 asserts that an operator must report to the Director of the COGCC, verbally or in writing—and within 24 hours of discovery—a spill or release in which one barrel or more of waste or produced fluids is spilled or released outside berms or secondary containment, or any spill exceeding five barrels (COGCC 2019). Although spills under one barrel are not tracked by the state, we can assess them to some degree with our survey and interview data.

From 1 January 2016 through 31 December 2016, there were 524 official spill reports filed with the COGCC. The COGCC database, however, does not allow for the download of aggregate records (and supporting documents) and the state denied researcher requests for access to these data. Therefore, to conduct this research, we compiled data from all 524 official spill reports individually to create our own spill database derived from our content analysis of each spill report. Our content analysis consisted of analysing each individual spill report narrative and coding relevant information into a Microsoft Excel file. We completed this process in two stages. During the first stage, we coded for information, such as what material was spilled (e.g., drilling mud, oil, produced water) and the quantity of the material spilled. During the second stage of analysis, we narrowed our focus and examined spill narratives for mention of remediation plans, such as excavation of impacted soil.

We coded for as much detail as possible throughout the content analysis, however it is worth noting that 38 per cent (n=199) of all 2016 official spill reports were *brief* report narratives, meaning that the spill itself was summarised in just one or two sentences. Some 46 per cent (n=243) of all spill reports contained modest report narratives, usually involving two to four sentences to describe the spill. Finally, 16 per cent (n=82) of official spill reports included detailed spill narratives that were five or more detailed sentences to describe the spill incident.

Survey of environmental victims

In previous work, we engaged in a content analysis of 2,444 complaints filed with the COGCC from 2 November 2001–10 June 2013 (Opsal and Shelley 2014; Shelley and Opsal 2017). From these complaint data, we were able to identify 732 potential environmental victims with a working address. We surveyed these individuals in the summer and fall of 2014 regarding three central themes: (1) the harms these individuals experienced during the course of energy development often related to fracking; (2) their attitudes and satisfaction with state and industry response; and (3) their attitudes towards issues related to O&G activity and regulation.

Some 215 respondents completed and returned the survey—a 29 per cent response rate. The majority of the sample was white (87 per cent), male (57 per cent) and highly educated (at least 55 per cent had a college degree). Respondents were dispersed throughout the state and in ways that are consistent with O&G development insofar as 22 per cent of respondents were from Weld County—the most fracked county in the state. Our respondents ranged in age from 29–88 (mean 62) and the majority identified as politically conservative (44 per cent), while 24 per cent identified as liberal, and the remainder identifying as moderate (22 per cent). Some 50 per cent owned mineral rights, 38 per cent had signed a surface access agreement with industry to access their land, and 18 per cent did not identify experiencing a harm that would classify them as an environmental victim.

Next, we disaggregated this sample by those who had experienced a spill or leak on or near their land. Some 65 per cent (n=139) of our sample reported experiencing a spill or leak on or near their land and they are the focus of our analysis for this chapter.

Interviews with environmental victims

Individuals in the COGCC database who had complete mailing addresses (n=732) were invited to participate in face-to-face interviews during the summer and fall of 2013. Some 16 per cent or 120 individuals contacted us for an interview. Despite limited resources, we were able to complete interviews with 65 participants (32 male and 33 female) across 36 households or 54 per cent of those requesting an interview.[4] Our participants generally lived in rural areas and were, by our own estimates, most often members of the middle class, although some seemed far wealthier and others appeared to be living in poverty.[5] Twelve households (i.e., 33 per cent) in our interview sample experienced a spill or leak on or near their property, while one individual reported systematic dumping of O&G substances on his property over several years.

Before beginning each interview, we typically took a tour of the location where the incident occurred, and in order to document fully the extent of the problem we took photographs and detailed field notes.[6] In the interviews themselves, we relied upon an open-ended, semi-structured interview guide to review the events that led up to the complaints, the nature and extent of the complaints, and any harms experienced by the participant and/or non-human animals, and the extent of damage to the environment. These interviews were recorded, transcribed verbatim and uploaded into NVivo for subsequent coding and analysis. These results provide us with rich accounts of how citizens experience spills associated with O&G activity, while also providing thick narratives that contrast with the spill reports that are initiated by industry officials and collected by COGCC officials.

Findings

Findings from the COGCC spill report database

The content analysis of COGCC official spill reports revealed that, in 2016, a total of 524 spills were reported, most of which occurred in Weld County (N=251) and Las Animas County (N=53). The spills seemed to occur most often in December (n= 65) and least often in June (n =31) with a monthly mean of 43 spills. We speculate that spills may be more likely to occur in December due to increased instances of freezing temperatures that can cause cracks and leaks in holding tanks, or that can cause equipment to malfunction due to frozen lines, pipes, and pressure gauges. Of the total 524 official spill reports for 2016, 304 (58 per cent) listed the *quantity* of the substance spilled and 293 (56 per cent) indicated the *type* of the substance spilled, while 10 reports (2 per cent) included amount of spill but did not include information on the type of substance spilled (e.g., 10 bbls spilled, but no information about the substance of the 10 bbls). Only 222 (42 per cent) cases contained detailed information *about both categories*: volume and category of material.

Of the 304 complete reports that reported the *quantity* of the spill, the typical spill involved 51.9 barrels, while the median amount was 10 barrels and the mode was 5 barrels. The largest reported spill in the database from 2016 was 20,000 lbs of drilling mud, which was spilled from an overturned truck hauling the material away from the well site. We did not include this spill when calculating the average or typical spill size because it is a significant outlier. The following is an official narrative of this large spill obtained from the COGCC Spill Report Database in order to provide context and description of how these narratives read:

> On 26 April 2016 at approximately 1300 hours, a truck owned by Bar-S Services transporting water-based drill cuttings in a side-dump trailer from the Mutul 0780 4-7H

> well departed their facility in Walden, CO to deliver the cuttings to the Twin Emviro landfill in Milner, CO for disposal. While traveling southbound on CO Hwy 125 toward the intersection of CO Hwy 14, the truck driver applied his brakes to slow for the turn, resulting in approximately 10 tons of drill cuttings being discharged from the side dump trailer onto the ground. The resulting spill impacted approximately 300 linear feet of HWY 14 and the adjacent shoulder. Bar-S notified the CDOT, The Colorado Highway Petrol [sic] and SandRidge Energy of the incident, after which SandRidge dispatched its clean-up contractor to the spill site. The intersection was closed and traffic re-routed to allow contractor personnel safe access to the spill site. The spill was cleaned up and approved by CDOT. The road was open at 1940 hours.

This specific spill narrative, like several of the spill narratives, includes information such as the date, time and the location of the spill. Interestingly, there are several important aspects that are *omitted* including the broader consequences of the spill (for example, to what extent local vegetation or waterways were impacted) or *how* the state or industry remediated the spill. Further, the sterile language of the spill narrative reduces the significant magnitude of a spill that involved 10 tons of drill cuttings which is over nine thousand kilograms of impacted material. In addition, the description of *why* the spill occurred suggests that the brakes caused the spill ('The truck driver applied his brakes to slow for the turn'), rather than pointing to the speed at which the operator was driving, or proposing that the overfilling of the truck could have also contributed to the spill.

Finally, the Colorado Department of Transportation (CDOT) supervised the cleanup, rather than the COGCC. This means that the goal of clean-up for the CDOT, which was to re-allow traffic to pass through the roadway, did not correspond to the COGCC standards related to spill cleanup and remediation. Overall, this narrative (written by an industry official and submitted to the COGCC) is an example of how spills are documented, the types of information that are typically included and omitted, and the language that is often used—language that tends to sterilise the nature of spills.[7]

Of the spill reports that indicated the *type of substance* spilled (n=293), the most common types of substance spilled were: produced water (53 per cent), oil (20 per cent) and a mixture of oil and produced water (18 per cent). Produced water, which is drilling wastewater that contains contaminants such as grease, hydrocarbons, oil and production chemicals, is dangerous because these contaminants can pollute a landowner's water sources, endangering their livestock and harming their crops. Oil, which often leaks at production sites, is dangerous insofar as it has the potential to impact human health and well-being through pollution of water sources (particularly well-water in rural areas), harm domestic animals and livestock and cause damage to property or crops (D'Andrea and Reddy 2014).

Next, we examined how spills were reportedly resolved and found that in 44 per cent (n=233) of official spill reports, there was at least one mention of the initiation of remediation at the spill site while 21 per cent of official spill reports (n=107) included two or more mentions of remediation. The following narrative describes a typical remediation in spill reports:

> This spill occurred after a 3-inch injection line leaked, releasing 21 barrels of fracking injection fluid onto the well pad and surrounding area. In response, the COGCC disabled the injection line and used a vacuum truck to recover around 18 barrels of fluid, and used water to wash the affected area.

There was no mention of what happened to the three barrels of fluid that went unrecovered (run off, soil seepage, evaporation, etc.) Interestingly, some 35 per cent (n=184) of all spill reports *did not* discuss remediation in their spill summaries. The lack of information from 35 per cent of the spill reports could suggest that there was no need for remediation, that remediation occurred but was undocumented, or that simply *no* remediation occurred at all. Our data do not allow us to discern which explanation is most likely.

In sum, our analysis revealed an array of missing data and substantial inconsistencies in spill reports. Remarkably, some 42 per cent *did not* contain information about the volume of the spill, while 44 per cent of cases reported *no information* about the substance of the spill. The lack of reporting/missing data is particularly problematic given that Rule 906 *requires* the identification of spilled substances and their quantities.

Findings from the survey of environmental victims

As previously noted, some 65 per cent (n=139) of our survey sample reported experiencing a spill or leak on or near their land and they are the focus of this section. Interestingly, most of these respondents also reported a range of other problems related to O&G development (e.g., air pollution, damage to land and soil, illegal dumping, noise and light pollution, water pollution) that would qualify them in our view as 'extreme environmental victims';[8] in fact, the modal number of harms citizens reported experiencing was 21. Though we did not pose a structured closed-ended question about specific harms related to the spill or leak, we provided respondents with the opportunity to address this topic in an open-ended question. Many of them characterised the spill as causing harm: 'A pipeline leak ruined my domestic water well affecting my livestock' or 'our spring turned into a gray mud that stunk after a well went in across the road'. A small number of survey respondents regarded some spills as a routine and necessary part of development. For example, one respondent remarked, 'I'd rather deal with a few oil spills than have to deal with the Middle East'.

In addition to inquiring whether respondents experienced a leak or spill on or near their property, we asked respondents whether the spill *was reported to the COGCC*. We learned that while 65 per cent of respondents indicated that they had experienced a spill, only 14 per cent of them reported the problem to the COGCC, 5 per cent took the problem directly to industry and 12 per cent reported the issue to *both* the COGCC and industry (Figure 19.2).

For those survey respondents who reported a spill to the COGCC, we then asked if the spill was resolved to their satisfaction. The majority of respondents who reported a spill (55 per cent) expressed dissatisfaction with the response they received from the COGCC, while 45 per cent indicated some level of satisfaction (see Figure 19.3). It was common for survey respondents to write about the persistence of problems after reporting their spill to the COGCC. For example, one survey respondent explained:

> I have given COGCC coordinates, people have measured that gas that it expels as methane and it continue to deplete natural resources and contaminate our surface water which flows into the Colorado River. Nothing has been done to shut off this well and after being given the run around by this agency, you may be my last resort.

For those that reported a spill to industry, we also asked if they were satisfied with the industry response. As shown in Figure 19.3, some 63 per cent of survey respondents reported dissatisfaction with how industry addressed their concerns regarding or requests associated with the spill, whereas 37 per cent were satisfied or very satisfied with the response.

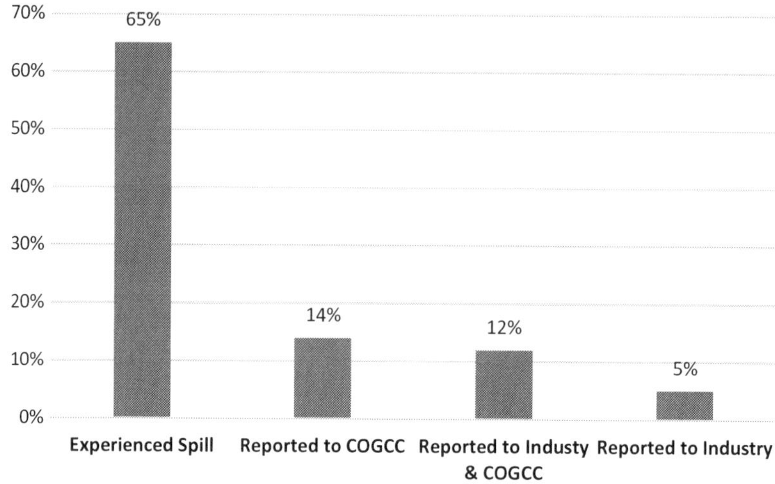

Figure 19.2 Frequency of spills and citizen reporting

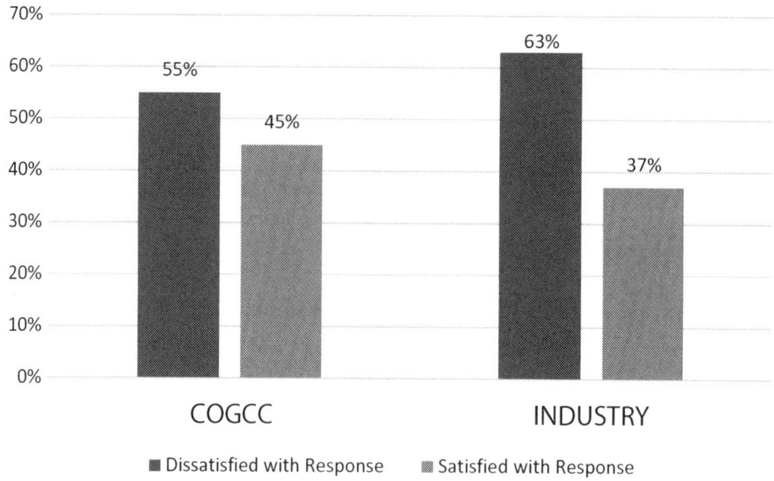

Figure 19.3 Citizen satisfaction with spill resolution

While the majority of COGCC spill reports indicate that remediation occurred (or was underway), citizens were less likely to report that the COGCC and/or industry resolved the spill to their satisfaction.

Findings from interviews with environmental victims

Similar to our survey results, interview participants reported experiencing a range of problems associated with O&G activity; indeed, nearly all reported being *repeat* victims. In comparison with our survey participants, however, a smaller proportion of our interview sample—33 per cent—experienced some kind of spill or leak. Most commonly, participants stated that broken or leaking gas or oil pipes were the cause of these problems. Phil, for example, explained that he knew that something was leaking from one of the two well pads on his property when he noticed a 'spot of oil on the ground, probably three feet in diameter' that plumed out significantly below the ground's surface.

Water pit breaks or overflows were the second most common way participants experienced a spill/leak. Carol and Roman, for example, described how a produced water pit up the canyon from their ranch broke and 'water ran down into the valley and washed down into the creek'; when this water flowed through their property, it displaced their horses because the creek was their central source of water.

Finally, a smaller number of participants reported spills associated with vehicles that were transporting produced water across their property. Paul, for example, described how his land was impacted by a spill when:

> A semi-truck transporting produced water, fracking fluids, drove off the road. There were no circumstances. It was dry. There was no weather, there were two witnesses. He drove right off the road and rolled a semi-truck over.

Paul explained that nauseating smells emanated from the fluids just spilled onto his land:

> You couldn't—one whiff of it and you were just like, 'Whoo!' … Actually I walked up underneath the truck and it was all runnin' down into the field, and I had, like, Sorrell's big winter rubber boots. It melted the glue in the boot.

Thus, participants experienced leaks and spills in two different ways: most commonly, the leak or spill occurred on their property; however, as illuminated by Carol and Roman's experience, a few participants experienced the 'after effects' of a spill that occurred off their property.

In contrast to the 14 per cent of our survey participants who indicated that they reported a leak or spill to only the COGCC, all of our interview participants—with the exception of one—proceeded directly to this state agency for assistance on this harm. The participant who did not report the leak on his property to the state did not actually report it to anybody because, as he/she explained,

> we were hesitant to make too big of a hubbub about it because they [the industry] help maintain roads on our ranch … We don't want to upset 'em. We like the fact that they come in and help us with the roads.

Participants who *did* report were more likely to report solely to the state if they thought the leak or spill was of a smaller quantity; however, for bigger leaks, participants contacted both the state and industry. One respondent also reported a large spill on his property to municipal officials (including the police) to no avail: 'there was no response by [the town of X], no public works responded, the town police officer did not respond because it was his day off'. Notably, though, as we have reported elsewhere (Opsal and Shelley 2014) and as illustrated next, citizens were overwhelmingly dissatisfied with these official responses.

Participants explained that when a spill occurred—especially one that they perceived to be of great magnitude—agents from the state and industry responded rapidly. For example, participants confirmed that state investigators often arrived onsite quickly, examined the problem, took samples of fluids and soils, and worked with industry representatives to determine the nature of the problem and the appropriate steps towards remediation. While the immediate response was quick, participants expressed their dissatisfaction with both the solutions that the state identified as appropriate and the long-term process associated with 'recovering' contaminated lands and waterways.

For example, in the case of the overturned semi-truck described earlier in this section, Paul described how, in the short-term, the state mandated regular soil testing of the impacted ground in order to ensure contamination levels were appropriately low before the corporation liable for the harm could cease remediation efforts. Paul, however, remained displeased with the long-term response because he believed the state was not holding the corporation responsible for ongoing needed remediation. As he explained:

> If you looked at the area today, you would see it's overgrown with weeds. The follow-up is not there. They come and spray for the weeds. Do they maintain that? Is this something they do on their own? No.

In addition, he believed the state should require the corporation to engage in longer-term testing of the groundwater to locate potential contamination, though he lamented that 'the state's not gonna mandate that [because of] politics'.

Similarly, Phil, who experienced a large leak on his property, illustrates these themes as well. He explained that immediately after reporting the incident, the state sent an 'environmental guy' to his farm and that the corporation who owned the well pad sent 'an attorney, a land man, an environmental guy, and whoever else they could find'. He explained that the remediation process involved excavating the contaminated soil, which extended six to eight feet below the surface, and filling sand back into the excavated area. While the O&G company was required to perform additional soil and groundwater tests (only in the direct spill area) and submit the results to the state, Phil decided to hire a private company to replicate and perform additional tests because:

> My honest opinion of the COGCC is, I think they're the fox in the henhouse. I think they're pro O&G. I don't think they're pro-surface owner. I don't think they're pro-environment. I think they just do the minimum to shut you up and really, as a land surface owner, you're almost powerless. That's how I felt. You have no power. 'Cause you're subservient. There's nothin' you can do except take it where the sun don't shine.

Thus, while many of the harms the participants experienced from leaks and spills were seemingly short-term—devaluation of their land, inability to use the land to grow crops, noxious smells and removal of livestock from contaminated areas—inadequate long-term response from state and industry exacerbated and extended harm and victimisation. Indeed, as Paul and Phil articulated clearly in these latter narratives, most participants expressed that, regardless of the harm corporations had caused to their health or land (including their livestock), the state failed in holding industry truly accountable because of the way their economic and political interests were bound together.

Discussion

Environmental victimisation is a growing area of interest among green criminologists (see, e.g., Hall 2014, this volume, Chapter 7; Ozymy et al. this volume, Chapter 8) but there is little research that explores citizen experiences with leaks and spills and the regulatory and/or industrial responses to these events. This chapter contributes to this research gap by drawing on multiple sources of data to elucidate the nature and extent of harm that corporations create as it relates to leaks and spills, as well as describing citizen perception of these harms and state and industry responses to spill incidents.

Our research sought to address several research questions regarding the nature and extent of leaks and spills as well as if, and how, citizens experience harms related to leaks and spills in Colorado. We also sought to learn if there were conflicting narratives about harms amongst stakeholders and if harms associated with leaks and spills were resolved in a satisfactory manner.

First, triangulating between multiple sources of data, we learned that leaks and spills occur frequently in Colorado. The COGCC reports that 524 spills occurred in 2016, our survey revealed that 65 per cent of respondents experienced a spill, and 33 per cent of our interview respondents reported a spill on or near their property. As demonstrated by our research, it is difficult to make firm conclusions about the nature of spills in Colorado due to substantial missing data regarding the quantity and the type of substance spilled in state records, even though Rule 906 requires this kind of information.

Second, this study sought to identify how Coloradoans experience harms related to leaks and spills. We learned that while 65 per cent of survey respondents reported experiencing a leak or spill on or near their property, only about one-third of those reported the leak or spill to state or industry officials, suggesting that the state (and possibly industry) accounts will underestimate significantly the nature and extent of spill incidents and their associated harms. In both the surveys and interviews, citizens provided detailed accounts regarding the harms they experienced, some of which produced trauma and feelings of loss. As one survey respondent put it, 'They have lost all sense of humanity and made this a Hunger Game … they have lost all sight of nature, their fellow human beings, food, water, air, soil, the insects, ancestry, past and future inheritance'.

We also compared narratives related to harms from industry and COGCC with those from our respondents. Broadly, the data presented in this chapter illuminate that citizens report experiencing a variety of harms because of leaks and spills and that there are serious gaps in the state's accounts of how citizens experience these harms. When we juxtapose citizens' general experiences with these harms and the state's documentation of these harms, we see clear evidence of both omission and dilution of the problem. Indeed, our interview accounts raise important questions about the extent to which justice is achieved, even when there is some attempt by the state or corporation to repair the harm associated with these leaks and spills. The lack of specific details about the remediation process after leaks and spills provided by the COGCC and the dissatisfaction with the COGCC that citizens report show a disparity between the stated goals of the COGCC and the reality of citizens' experiences after a leak or spill.

Finally, as with harms documented by the criminal justice system, our study reveals that the vast majority of harms citizens experience related to O&G spills are unaccounted for in official records. This finding was replicated in the comparisons made between our content analysis of the official COGCC records, survey data and qualitative interviews with citizens who filed those complaints. The gaps between what citizens are experiencing and what the official data represent functions to dilute the real and cumulative costs of energy development. Future research on long-term effects of short-term remediation efforts would be useful as our interview accounts suggest that there are continual and long-lasting environmental but also social-psychological impacts.

In particular, a deeper examination of the ways that extractive industries may produce long-term fractures in residents' understanding of and historical connection to their homes, land and communities would be useful. Given that research *does* provide evidence that extractive practices produce specific psychological consequences for individuals living amongst development, we wonder—as Kai Erikson saw in his observations of Buffalo Creek post-flood—if extractive industries carry away more than just minerals when they develop an area, including relationships, meaning and cultural practices (Erickson 1976).

Notes

1 In Colorado, citizens may initiate legislation through a constitutional amendment to the state constitution as part of a ballot initiative process. Ballot initiatives must receive a certain number of citizen signatures as part of the petitioning process for inclusion on the statewide ballot. After securing enough signatures, the proposed constitutional amendment then appears on the official state ballot in the next election, allowing residents to vote on the measure.
2 'Horizontal' is a bit misleading because, as Michaels and Simon (2013:12) point out, '[n]ew technologies now enable horizontal drilling in all radial directions, like spokes of a bicycle wheel, from the base of a vertical shaft, producing a shaped array of horizontal shafts miles beneath groundwater aquifers to deliver fracking fluids explosively'.
3 As described above, the Front Range is a north to south urban corridor that runs parallel to the eastern side of the Rocky Mountains (Cronin and Loevy 2017).
4 Those we could not reach for a face-to-face interview were later sent a survey to complete about their experiences.
5 We made these judgements based on our visits to participants' households, self-disclosure about their educational background, income and their discussion about other financial resources—especially as they related to being able to address the harm they experienced.
6 Although we would have liked to have included photographs with this chapter, because spills are high profile events—especially in small communities—we feared that including some visuals would run the risk of revealing the identity of our respondents.
7 See Opsal and Shelley (2014) for an analysis of landowners' reactions to these accounts.
8 We conceptualise 'extreme environmental victims' as those victims who experience repeat instances of victimisation or polyvictimisation. The harm experienced can come in the form of one-on-one harm and one-to-many harm (see Reiman 2008), as well as collective and secondary trauma.

References

Bank, E. 2018. 'Colorado natural resources,' *Sciencing*. Available at: https://sciencing.com/colorado-natural-resources-7056.html.

Brisman, A., South, N. and White, R. (eds.). 2015. *Environmental Crime and Social Conflict: Contemporary and Emerging Issues*. Surrey, UK: Ashgate.

Burns, R. and Lynch, M. 2004. *Environmental Crime: A Sourcebook*. New York: LFB Scholarly Publishing.

Colborn, T., Kwiatkowski, C., Schultz, K. and Bachran, M. 2011. 'Natural gas operations from a public health perspective,' *Human and Ecological Risk Assessment:An International Journal*, 17(5): 1039–1056. DOI: 10.1080/10807039.2011.605662.

Colorado (state). 'Funk & Wagnalls new world Encyclopedia,' January 1, 2018. Available at: https://zeus.tarleton.edu/login?url=https://search.ebscohost.com/login.aspx?direct=true&db=funk&AN=co178400&site=eds-live.

Colorado Oil and Gas Conservation Commission. 2001. '2000 annual report,' Available at: http://cogcc.state.co.us/documents/library/Technical/WQCC_WQCD%20Annual%20Reports/WQCC01RPT.pdf.

Colorado Oil and Gas Conservation Commission. 2014. 'Inspection/incident inquiry,' Available at: http://cogcc.state.co.us/cogis/.

Colorado Oil and Gas Conservation Commission. 2016. '2016 annual report,' Available at: http://cogcc.state.co.us/documents/library/Technical/WQCC_WQCD%20Annual%20Reports/2016%20ANNUAL%20REPORT%20WQCC_FINAL_12302016.pdf.

Colorado Oil and Gas Conservation Commission. 2018. 'GIS online map,' Available at: https://cogccmap.state.co.us/cogcc_gis_online/.

Colorado Oil and Gas Conservation Commission. 2019. 'Rules and regulations: Appendix I,' Available at: https://cogcc.state.co.us/documents/reg/Rules/LATEST/AppendixI.pdf.

Cooley, H. and Donnelly, K. 2014. 'Hydraulic fracturing and water resources: What do we know and need to know?' in P. Gleick (ed.) *The World's Water: The Biennial Report on Freshwater Resources*, pp. 63–81. Washington, DC: Island Press.

Cronin, T. and Loevy, R. 2017. 'The great majority of the state's voters reside in front range Colorado,' *The Gazette Telegraph*, 24 January 2017. Available at: https://gazette.com/news/the-great-majority-of-the-state-s-voters-reside-in/article_c36b0e27-5990-5187-b057-ede5e7aeb988.html.

D'Andrea, M. and Reddy, K. 2014. 'Crude oil spill exposure and human health risks,' *Journal of Occupational and Environmental Medicine*, 56(10): 1029–1041. DOI: 10.1097/JOM.0000000000000217.

Davidson, D. 2018. 'Evaluating the effects of living with contamination from the lens of trauma: A case study of fracking development in Alberta, Canada,' *Environmental Sociology*, 4(2): 196–209. DOI: 10.1080/23251042.2017.1349638.

Davis, C. 2012. 'The politics of "fracking": Regulating natural gas drilling practices in Colorado and Texas,' *Review of Policy Research*, 29(2): 177–191. DOI: 10.1111/j.1541-1338.2011.00547.x.

Erickson, K. T. 1976. *Everything in Its Path: Destruction of Community in the Buffalo Creek Flood*. New York: Simon & Schuster.

Ferrar, K., Michanowicz, D., Christen, C., Mulcahy, N., Malone, S. and Sharma, R. 2013. 'Assessment of effluent contaminants from three facilities discharging Marcellus Shale wastewater to surface waters in Pennsylvania', *Environmental Science & Technology*, 47(7): 3472–3481. DOI: 10.1021/es301411q.

Finley, B. 2013a. 'Colorado absorbs 179 oil and gas spills as parachute cleanup continues,' *The Denver Post*. Available at: www.denverpost.com/2013/06/22/colorado-absorbs-179-oil-and-gas-spills-as-parachute-cleanup-continues/.

Finley, B. 2013b. 'Colorado anti-fracking groups launches campaign for state ban,' *The Denver Post*. Available at: www.denverpost.com/environment/ci_27591553/colorado-anti-fracking-groups-launch-campaign-statewide-ban.

Finley, B. 2014. 'Colorado adopts tougher air rules for oil, gas industry,' *The Denver Post*. 23 February 2014. Available at: www.denverpost.com/environment/ci_25213661/colorado-adopts-tougher-air-rules-oil-gas-industry.

Finley, B. 2016. 'Oil and gas companies in Colorado reported 615 spills in 2015,' *The Denver Post*. 14 April 2016 Available at: www.denverpost.com/2016/03/17/oil-and-gas-companies-in-colorado-reported-615-spills-in-2015/.

Gibbons, S., Heblich, S. and Timmins, C. 2016. 'Fear of fracking: Earthquakes linked to shale gas exploration cause house prices to fall,' *Policy Bristol: Policy Briefing*, 16(22).

González Hernández, A. 2018. 'Shale gas extraction, energy reform, and environmental damage,' in I. Arroyo-Quiroz and T. Wyatt (eds.) *Green Crime in Mexico: A Collection of Case Studies*, pp. 39–48. Palgrave Studies in Green Criminology. Cham, Switzerland: Palgrave Macmillan. DOI: 10.1007/978-3-319-75286-0_1.

Gould, K., Pellow, D. and Schnaiberg, A. 2008. *The Treadmill of Production: Injustice and Unsustainability in the Global Economy*. Boulder, CO: Paradigm Publishers.

Goyes, D. R., Mol, H., Brisman, A. and South, N. (eds.). 2017. *Environmental Crime in Latin America: The Theft of Nature and the Poisoning of the Land*. London: Palgrave Macmillan.

Grant, C., Weimer, A., Marks, N., Perow, E., Oster, J., Brubaker, K., Trexler, R., Solomon, C. and Lamendella, R. 2015. 'Marcellus and mercury: Assessing potential impacts of unconventional natural gas extraction on aquatic ecosystems in Northwestern Pennsylvania,' *Journal of Environmental Science and Health, Part A*, 50(1): 482–500. DOI: 10.1080/10934529.2015.992670.

Gullion, J. 2015. *Fracking the Neighborhood: Reluctant Activists and Natural Gas Drilling*. Cambridge, MA: The MIT Press.

Hall, M. 2014. 'Environmental harm and environmental victims: Scoping out a "green victimology",' *International Review of Victimology*, 20(1): 129–143. DOI: 10.1177/0269758013508682.

Hamm, K. 2017. 'Map: Colorado Fourteeners,' *The Denver Post*. Available at: www.denverpost.com/2017/06/17/colorado-fourteeners-map-list/.

Hill, E. 2014. 'Three essays on the impacts of unconventional drilling on early life health,' Available at: www.ecommons.cornell.edu/handle/1813/38804.

Hirsch, J., Smalley, B., Selby-Nelson, E., Hamel-Lambert, J., Rosmann, M., Barnes, T., Abrahamson, D., Meit, S., GreyWolf, I. and Beckmann, S. 2018. 'Psychosocial impact of fracking: A review of the literature on the mental health consequences of hydraulic fracturing,' *International Journal of Mental Health and Addiction*, 16(1): 1–15. DOI: 10.1007/s11469-017-9792-5.

Holzman, D. 2011. 'Methane found in well water near fracking sites,' *Environmental Health Perspectives*, 119(7): a289. DOI: 10.1289/ehp.119-a289.

Howarth, R., Ingraffea, A. and Engelder, T. 2011. 'Natural gas: Should fracking stop?' *Nature*, 477(7364): 271–275. DOI: 10.1038/477271a.

Huber, T. 1993. *Colorado: The Place of Nature, the Nature of Place*. Niwot, CO: University Press of Colorado.

Jacquet, J. 2014. 'Review of risks to communities from shale energy development,' *Environmental Science and Technology*, 48(15): 8321–8333. DOI: 10.1021/es404647x.

Jarell, M. and Ozymy, J. 2010. 'Excessive air pollution and the oil industry: Fighting for our right to breathe clean air,' *Environmental Justice*, 3(1): 111–115. DOI: 10.1089/env.2009.0042.

Jemielita, T., Gerton, G., Neidell, M., Chillrud, S. and Yan, B. 2015. 'Unconventional gas and oil drilling is associated with increased hospital utilization rates,' *PLoS ONE*, 10(8): e0137371. DOI: 10.1371/journal.pone.0137371.

Kassotis, C., Tillitt, D., Lin, C.-H., McElroy, J. and Nagel, S. 2016. 'Endocrine-disrupting chemicals and oil and natural gas operations: Potential environmental contamination and recommendations to assess complex environmental mixtures,' *Environmental Health Perspectives*, 124(3): 256–264. DOI: 10.1289/ehp.1409535.

Kizewski, A. 2015. *'It's My Soul's Responsibility': Understanding Activist's Gendered Experiences in Anti-Fracking Grassroots Organizations in Northern Colorado*. Fort Collins, CO: M.A. Colorado State University.

Komarek, T. 2014. 'Crime and natural resource booms: Evidence from unconventional natural gas production,' *The Annals of Regional Science*, 1–25. Retrieved 28 March 2017. DOI: 10.1007/s00168-018-0861-x.

Ladd, A. E. 2013. 'Stakeholder perceptions of socio-environmental impacts from unconventional natural gas development and hydraulic fracturing in the Haynesville Shale,' *Journal of Rural Social Sciences*, 28 (2): 56–89. DOI: 10.1177/2329496514540132.

Ladd, A. E. 2018. *Fractured Communities: Risk, Impacts, and Protest against Hydraulic Fracking in US Shale Regions*. New Brunswick, NJ: Rutgers University Press.

Landman, A. 2014. 'Colorado citizen's launch class action lawsuit to protect Lafayette's fracking ban,' *Desmog*. Available at: www.desmogblog.com/2014/06/18/lafayette-citizens-launch-class-action-lawsuit-protect-community-s-fracking-ban.

Lee, J. 2015. 'The regional economic impact of oil and gas extraction in Texas,' *Energy Policy*, 87(1): 60–71. DOI: 10.1016/j.enpol.2015.08.032.

Lynch, M., Long, M., Stretesky, P. and Barrett, K. 2017. *Green Criminology: Crime, Justice, and the Environment*. Oakland, CA: University of California Press.

Lynch, M. and Michalowski, R. 2006. *A Primer in Radical Criminology*. New York: Criminal Justice Press.

Maddaford, B. 2013. 'Inspections of oil and gas development,' *Colorado Legislation Staff Council Issue Brief*, 13–09: 1–7. Available at: www.colorado.gov/cs/Satellite?blobcol=urldata&blobheader=application%2Fpdf&blobkey=id&blobtable=MungoBlobs&blobwhere=1251915389800&ssbinary=true.

Malin, S., Opsal, T., O'Connor Shelley, T. and Hall, P. 2018. 'The right to resist or a case of injustice? Meta-power in the oil and gas fields,' *Social Forces*, online first. DOI: 10.1093/sf/soy094.

Mayer, A. 2016. 'Risk and benefits in a fracking boom: Evidence from Colorado,' *The Extractive Industries and Society*, 3(1): 744–753. DOI: 10.1016/j.exis.2016.04.006.

Mayer, A. 2018. 'The fiscal impacts of energy: Perspectives from local governments in the Mountain West, USA,' *Energy Policy*, 122: 186–193. DOI: 10.1016/j.enpol.2018.07.043.

McKenzie, L., Allshouse, W., Byers, T., Bedrick, E., Serdar, B. and Adgate, J. 2017. 'Childhood hematologic cancer and residential proximity to oil and gas development,' *PLoS One*, 12(2): e0170423. DOI: 10.1371/journal.pone.0170423.

Meng, Q. 2017. 'The impacts of fracking on the environment: A total environmental study paradigm,' *Science of the Total Environment*, 580(15): 953–957. DOI: 10.1016/j.scitotenv.2016.12.045.

Michaels, R. A. and Simon, R. W. 2013. 'Fracking in New York: Weighing risks and benefits. Albany, New York State Bar Association,' *NYSBA Municipal Lawyer*, 23(3 [Fall]): 12–16.

Munasib, A. and Rickman, D. 2015. 'Regional economic impacts of the shale gas and tight oil boom: A synthetic control analysis,' *Regional Science and Urban Economics*, 50(C): 1–17. DOI: 10.1016/j.regsciurbeco.2014.10.006.

Newell, R. and Raimi, D. 2015. 'Oil and gas revenue allocation to local governments in eight states,' *National Bureau of Economic Research*. Available at: www.nber.org/papers/w21615.

Nicholson, K. 2017. 'One dead, three injured in Anadarko oil tank explosion in Weld County,' *The Denver Post*. 25 May 2017. Available at: www.denverpost.com/2017/05/25/anadarko-oil-tank-explosion-one-dead/.

Opsal, T. and Malin, S. 2018. 'Colorado voters will weigh in on drilling distances from homes and schools,' *The Conversation*. 29 September.

Opsal, T. and Shelley, T. O. 2014. 'Energy crime, harm, and problematic state response in Colorado: A case of the fox guarding the hen house?' Critical Criminology: An International Journal, 22(4): 561–577. DOI: 10.1007/s10612-014-9255-2.

Osher, C. 2017. 'What does $80 million buy oil and gas interests? Voter profiles, door knocking and influence at local and statewide levels,' *The Denver Post*. 16 July 2017. Available at: www.denverpost.com/2017/07/16/oil-gas-industry-public-influence-campaigns/.

Paredes, D., Timothy, K. and Scott, L. 2015. 'Income and employment effects of shale gas extraction windfalls: Evidence from the Marcellus region,' *Energy Economics*, 47(C): 112–120.

Paulik, B., Donald, C., Smith, B., Tidwell, L., Hobbie, K., Kincl, L., Haynes, E. and Anderson, K. 2015. 'Impact of natural gas extraction on PAH levels in ambient air,' *Environmental Science & Technology*, 49 (8): 5203–5210. DOI: 10.1021/es506095e.

Perry, S. 2012. 'Development, land use, and collective trauma: The Marcellus Shale gas boom in rural Pennsylvania. *Culture, Agriculture, Food and Environment*, 34(1): 81–92. DOI: 10.1111/j.2153-9561.2012.01066.x.

Quinn, M. 2013. 'New pro-fracking group forms in Broomfield,' *The Greeley Tribune*. Available at: www.greeleytribune.com/news/8388428-113/broomfield-fracking-group-ban.

Rabinowitz, P., Slizovskiy, I., Lamers, V., Trufan, S., Holford, T., Dziura, J., Peduzzi, P., Kane, M., Reif, J., Weiss, T. and Stowe, M. 2015. 'Proximity to natural gas wells and reported health status: Results of a household survey in Washington County, Pennsylvania,' *Environmental Health Perspectives*, 123(1): 1–21. DOI: 10.1289/ehp.1307732.

Reiman, J. 2008. *The Rich Get Richer and the Poor Get Prison: Ideology, Class and Criminal Justice*. Boston, MA: Allyn and Bacon.

Rozell, D. and Reaven, S. 2012. 'Water pollution risk associated with natural gas extraction from the Marcellus Shale,' *Society for Risk Analysis*, 32(8): 1382–1393. DOI: 10.1111/j.1539-6924.2011.01757.x.

Ryder, S. and Hall, P. 2017. 'This land is your land, maybe: A historical institutionalist analysis for contextualizing split estate conflicts in US Unconventional Oil and Gas Development,' *Land Use Policy*, 63(1): 149–159. DOI: 10.1016/j.landusepol.2017.01.006.

Saunders, P., McCoy, D., Goldstein, B. and Munroe, A. 2018. 'A review of the public health impacts of unconventional natural gas development,' *Environmental Geochemistry and Health* 40(1): 1–57. DOI: 10.1007/s10653-016-9898-x.

Schafft, K., Borlu, Y. and Glenna, L. 2013. 'The relationship between Marcellus Shale gas development in Pennsylvania and local perceptions of risk and opportunity,' *Rural Sociology*, 78(2): 143–166. DOI: 10.1111/ruso.12004.

Shelley, T. O. and Opsal, T. 2017. 'Environmental victimization: A case study of citizens' experiences with oil and gas development in Colorado, USA,' in M. Hall, J. Maher, A. Nurse, G. Potter, N. South and T. Wyatt (eds.) *Greening Criminology in the 21st Century: Contemporary Debates and Future Directions in the Study of Environmental Harm 2017*, pp. 100–119. New York: Routledge.

Short, D., Elliot, J., Norder, K., Lloyd-Davies, E. and Morley, J. 2015. 'Extreme energy, "fracking" and human rights: A new field for human rights impact assessments?' *The International Journal of Human Rights*, 19(6): 697–736. DOI: 10.1080/13642987.2015.1019219.

Short, D. and Szolucha, A. 2017. 'Fracking Lancashire: The planning process, social harm and collective trauma', *Geoforum*, 98(1): 264–276. DOI: 10.1016/j.geoforum.2017.03.001.

South, N. 2015. 'Environmental justice: The challenge posed by environmental crime for criminal justice,' *Scottish Justice Matters*, 3(1): 4–5. Available at: http://scottishjusticematters.com/wp-content/uploads/SJM_3_1_Mar2015_LoRes.pdf.

Sovacool, B. 2014. 'Cornucopia or curse? Reviewing the costs and benefits of shale gas hydraulic fracturing (fracking),' *Renewable and Sustainable Energy Reviews*, 37(1): 249–264. DOI: 10.1016/j.rser.2014.04.068.

Stokols, E. 2013. 'Strengthened bill to alter makeup, mission of Colo,' *Oil and Gas Commission Heads to Senate Floor*. 23 April 2013. Available at: http://kdvr.com/2013/04/29/strengthened-bill-to-alter-makeup-mission-of-colo-oil-and-gas-commission-heads-to-senate-floor/.

Stretesky, P., Long, M. and Lynch, M. 2014. *The Treadmill of Crime: Political Economy and Green Criminology*. Oxon, NY: Routledge.

Stretesky, P. and Lynch, M. 2011. 'Coal strip mining, mountaintop removal, and the distribution of environmental violations across the United States, 2002–2008,' *Landscape Research*, 36(2): 209–230. DOI: 10.1080/01426397.2010.547572.

Theodori, G. 2009. 'Paradoxical perceptions of problems associated with unconventional natural gas development,' *South Rural Sociology*, 24(3): 97–117.

Theodori, G. 2013. 'Perception of the natural gas industry and engagement in individual civic actions,' *Journal of Rural Social Sciences*, 28(2): 122–134.

U.S. Energy Information Administration. 2018. 'U.S. production of crude oil grew 5% in 2017, likely leading to record 2018 production,' Available at: www.eia.gov/todayinenergy/detail.php?id=35632.

U.S. Energy Information Administration. 2019. 'Natural gas gross withdrawals and production,' Available at: www.eia.gov/dnav/ng/NG_PROD_SUM_DC_SCO_MMCF_A.htm.

United States Census Bureau. 2019. 'QuickFacts Colorado,' Available at: www.census.gov/quickfacts/co.

United States House of Representatives Committee on Energy and Commerce Minority Staff. 2011. *Chemicals Used in Hydraulic Fracturing*. Washington, DC: US House of Representatives. Available at: http://ecolo.org/documents/documents_in_english/gas-_Hydraulic-Fract-chemicals-2011-report.pdf.

Van Gulijk, C. 2014. 'Oil spills: A persistent problem,' in T. Spapens, R. White and M. Kluin (eds.) *Environmental Crime and Its Victims: Perspectives within Green Criminology 2014*, pp. 133–148. Burlington, VT: Ashgate Publishing.

Weber, J. 2014. 'A decade of natural gas development: The makings of resource curse?' *Resource and Energy Economics*, 37(1): 168–183. DOI: 10.1016/j.reseneeco.2013.11.013.

White, R. 2013. 'Resource extraction leaves something behind: Environmental justice and mining,' *International Journal for Crime and Justice*, 2(1): 50–64. DOI: 10.5204/ijcjsd.v2i1.90.

White, R. and Heckenberg, D. 2014. *Green Criminology: An Introduction to the Study of Environmental Harm*. London and New York: Routledge.

Wines, M. 2016. 'Colorado court strikes down local bans on fracking,' *The New York Times*. 2 May. Available at: www.nytimes.com/2016/05/03/us/colorado-court-strikes-down-local-bans-on-fracking.html.

Wyatt, T. (ed.). 2015. *Hazardous Waste and Pollution: Detecting and Preventing Green Crimes*. London: Springer.

Yan, X., Ariaratnam, S., Dong, S. and Zeng, C. 2018. 'Horizontal directional drilling: State-of-the-art review of theory and applications,' *Tunnelling and Underground Space Technology* 72(1): 162–173. DOI: 10.1016/j.tust.2017.10.005.

20

Corporate capitalism, environmental damage and the rule of law

The Magurchara gas explosion in Bangladesh

Nikhil Deb

Introduction

In this chapter, I offer a political economic analysis of the Magurchara gas explosion in Moulvibazar, Bangladesh, where, on June 14, 1997, a shocking gas explosion took place during an exploration of a well at a site operated by Occidental Petroleum Corporation ('Occidental'), a multinational oil and gas exploration and production company. The gas in the Magurchara Gas Field continued to burn for 17 days, causing harm to the people living nearby, as well as infrastructure loss and grave environmental destruction, including damage to rainforests, farmlands and tea plantations (*BBC News*, February 16, 2005; Khan, Islam and Nasir 2014; Siddique 2016; *The Daily Star*, June 15, 2009). The consequences of the Magurchara gas explosion are continuing today and the demand for justice for socioecological damage remains largely obscured and unresolved.

The Magurchara gas explosion exemplifies the nature of capitalist resource exploitation, in which both national and global institutions contribute to disruptions in the socioecological system (Brisman 2014; Foster, Clark and York 2011; Gould, Pellow and Schnaiberg 2015). Despite the fact that the explosion occurred more than 20 years ago, it has received little media and academic attention on the national and international levels. Given that environmental organisations in Bangladesh were in a nascent stage at that time, the national response to the serious economic and environmental damage was muted. Importantly, the way the government of Bangladesh handled this socioecological tragedy has also contributed to an inattention to the Magurchara explosion. What factors prevented the Bangladeshi[1] government from acting in response to the explosion? The answer to this question cannot be found by focussing solely on the responsibility of the local Bangladeshi state. A political economic analysis integrating the role of the state, the corporation (Occidental) and law is required to (1) examine the causes of the gas tragedy; an d (2) analyse reasons for the tepid response undertaken afterward by the actors involved.

A plethora of research shows that the development of global capitalism is largely contingent upon its geographical expansion and the exploration and utilisation of natural resources (Bunker and Ciccantell 2005; Harvey 2003, 2006; Labban 2008; O'Connor 1998; Smith 1984). Although debate exists as to the nature of the underlying dynamic and material foundation of this continuous accumulation process, it is without dispute that the extraction of natural resources oftentimes causes enormous socioecological damage and disruption across the world (Foster, Clark and York 2011; Gellert 2010; Petras 2013; Watts 2001; White 2013). What is also evident in the research is that the people of poor countries suffer higher social and environmental risks than people living in developed countries (Beck 2016; Castleman 1983; Frey 2012, 2013). Accordingly, the implications surrounding social and environmental justice, following a disaster like the Magurchara explosion, appear to be different in poor countries compared with their rich counterparts. Not only were Occidental's acts of negligence evident in the Magurchara explosion, but, in the aftermath of the disaster, Occidental and other corporations' responses to calls for compensation for environmental damage demonstrate how law, as it pertains to environmental disasters, is not power-neutral: it favours systematically some groups at the expense of others (Walters 2010). Moreover, powerful economic actors, such as corporations, do not just shape environmental laws (Greife and Stretesky 2013); they can use law as a device to legitimise their works in poor countries, while at the same time remaining exempt from the rule of law.

Thus, this chapter examines the roles of three different yet inseparable actors—the state, the corporation (Occidental) and the law—in the Magurchara explosion, situating them in the specific political-economic context of Bangladesh. Modern states, as some scholars such as Foucault have argued, derive their power from the knowledge of their own constituent elements, including population and geography (see Lemke 2001; Scott 1998). For this reason, the state is capable of 'refashion[ing]' society and ecology by creating what Scott (1998) calls 'maps of legibility'. It is equally important to remember that the function of the local states in poor countries is complicated by their distinct economic and political contexts. For instance, democratic, economic and technological backwardness made the Bangladeshi government rely on foreign capital, which weakened its autonomy as a protector of its citizens, as well as in its negotiations with corporations, both before and after the disaster. Hence, it is hard to understand the role of the Bangladeshi state by using only a state-centric approach; both states and corporations are now what Barkan (2013) calls 'double bodies'—ontologically linked to establish each other's conditions of advancement by their joint efforts.

Questions concerning what role the rule of law played in and after the Magurchara explosion, why the legal process clouded the demands for and response to compensation, and why the Bangladeshi government was motivated to be lenient to Occidental remain difficult to investigate due to a lack of supporting evidence.[2] The legal conditions under which Occidental could conduct business in Bangladesh are still not completely known to the public. In this context, I argue that the law, as a mediating apparatus between the Bangladeshi state and involved corporations, has turned decisively into what Mattei and Nader (2008) call a 'product of the economy', in which the law has been used (1) as a rhetoric of democracy and development that enabled Occidental (and later other corporations) with the help of the Bangladeshi state, to extract natural resources from the Magurchara Gas Field (located inside a national reserve forest); and (2) as a legitimising force even in the wake of an explosion that resulted in enormous socioecological damage. It is well documented how corporate activities cause adverse socioecological consequences, as well as how the state is complicit with corporate interests. How the law is used as a mediating force between weak local states and powerful multinational corporations, however, remains largely under-emphasised in academic discourse.

This chapter proceeds as follows. First, to grasp the relationships between multinational energy corporations and the Bangladeshi state, I provide a brief history of exploration for and extraction of natural resources in Bangladesh, highlighting all major bidding rounds since the birth of Bangladesh in 1971. Next, I provide a short account of the Magurchara explosion with heightened attention to its socioecological consequences. Third, I offer a critical examination of corporate negligence in and after the disaster and why the Bangladeshi government is complicit with corporate interests. Fourth, I provide an analysis of why the negotiations over compensation fell through. This leads me to the final step—an analysis of what went wrong in the negotiations over compensation. I conclude this chapter with a discussion of implications for scholars studying the political economy of environmental harm.

Natural resources, Production Sharing Contracts (PSCs) and international oil companies (IOCs) in Bangladesh

Bangladesh (officially the People's Republic of Bangladesh) is a country in South Asia bordering India and Burma (Myanmar). The country is covered by the Ganges-Brahmaputra Delta (also known as the 'Bengal Delta')—the largest delta in the world. The total population of Bangladesh is roughly 156 million, living in its 56,000 square miles. Among countries having populations of more than 10 million in the world, Bangladesh is the most densely populated. Like other deltas in the world, Bangladesh has significant hydrocarbon (oil and gas) reserves, although significantly less than other major Southeast Asian countries, e.g., Brunei, Burma (Myanmar), Indonesia, Malaysia and Thailand (Iftekhar and Hoque 2005; Muhammad 2014a; Sovacool 2010). Natural gas and coal are two major mineral resources in Bangladesh (CPD Occasional Paper Series 2002; Rahman, Saha and Rahman 2010). Mineral resources are considered critical factors for the economic development of highly populated Bangladesh.

International oil companies have long been involved with the exploration and discovery of oil and gas in the territory known as Bangladesh today (Petrobangla 2015; CPD Occasional Paper Series 2002). After several major explosions, including the Magurchara gas disaster, the responsibilities and accountability of IOCs, national corporations and the Bangladeshi state have become highly questionable.

The history of oil and gas exploration in Bangladesh can be divided into three different periods: the British period (until 1947), the Pakistan period (1948–1971) and the Bangladesh period (1971–present). The search for natural resources in the territory of Bangladesh was first undertaken by the British in the middle of the eighteenth century, but was limited to geological mapping at that time. The first systematic attempt, however, was made in 1908 at the same place by the Indian Petroleum Prospecting Company. In British India, Assam (now a state in northeastern India) and what is now Bangladesh were well known for gas exploration efforts. In the 1920s, a leading, but now-defunct, Scottish oil corporation—the Burmah Oil Company (BOC)—conducted the first shallow drilling in Chittagong (Kazol 2016). This company explored at least five different sites in this region, however it abandoned its exploration because these sites were not beneficial in economic terms.

With the partition of India in 1947, which divided the country into Pakistan and India, exploration began in East Pakistan (now Bangladesh) with a renewed effort. The 1948 Petroleum Act generated larger interest in oil and gas exploration by foreign companies. A number of IOCs continued searching until the 1960s[3]—a significant decade for resource exploration primarily because the multinational oil and gas company, Shell, started working in the Bangladesh territory. Shell worked in at least ten sites located mostly in the eastern part of the country, one of which was next to Cox's Bazar, the world's longest sea beach.

Between 1960 and 1970, Shell explored five sites—Rashidpur, Kailastila, Titas, Habigonj and Bakhrabad—located in the Sylhet and Comilla districts.

After Bangladesh gained its independence from Pakistan in 1971, restructured national and international explorations for oil and gas in Bangladesh continued at a heightened pace and with a new set of agreements, as the previous discoveries had brought Bangladesh to the attention of IOCs. The Bangladesh Mineral, Oil and Gas Corporation (BMOGC) was established by the Bangladeshi president's order on March 26, 1972 to administer the exploration and development of natural resources in Bangladesh. Later, the BMOGC (nicknamed Petrobangla) was reconstituted under the Petroleum Act of 1974, to reinvigorate foreign companies' participation under Production Sharing Contracts (PSCs).[4] Under the Petroleum Act, the Bangladesh government owns all mineral resources and has the absolute right and authority to research, explore, develop, process and market mineral resources. In 1989, to further increase oil and gas exploration activities, the Bangladesh government terminated the Exploration Directorate of Petrobangla and created the Petroleum Exploration and Production Company Limited (BAPEX). In 2002, BAPEX became an exploration and production company that is now generating approximately 120 MMMcf gas daily from its six gas fields.

A series of historic events in the 1980s played a significant role in the future of the relationships between national and international oil companies. In 1986, the state corporation Petrobangla discovered its first oil site in Haripur, Sylhet. While various foreign companies had found other gas sites previously, this was the first discovery of an oil site by Bangladeshi geologists. The Haripur (Sylhet-7) was the first and only major oil-producing well of the country, and the people of Bangladesh saw this reserve as a source of national pride and a massive opportunity for the country's economic development. It became a big disappointment, however, when, in 1987, then-president Hussain Muhammad Ershad signed over control of the Haripur reserve to Scimitar Exploration Ltd ('Scimitar'). This act gave Scimitar the legal right to explore and extract oil from the 1,650 square-mile area, which erupted a widespread protest across the country. In the face of a nation-wide protest, Ershad stepped down in 1990. Scimitar left Bangladesh after the Ershad regime was ended.

The elected democratic regimes that began in 1991 after the resignation of Ershad did not fare any better than the former autocratic regime when it came to maximising the national interest. Because of a changed energy policy in 1996, coupled with a renewed PSC, Bangladesh was divided into 23 exploration blocks, which, according to a Petrobangla 2015 report, ushered in a new era of exploration of natural resources in the country. Since then, oil and gas exploration and discovery have undergone significant changes, and the government has awarded different blocks to a large influx of multinational oil corporations.

In 1997, both Cairn and Occidental managed to sign a gas purchase and sales agreement with Petrobangla to sell and deliver gas to the national gas distribution system. This development garnered the interest of both the Bangladeshi government and private corporations, resulting in renewed attention of multinational corporations in the energy sector of Bangladesh. In addition, although little exploration occurred for the next few years due to a maritime boundary dispute with Burma (Myanmar) and India, Bangladesh's maritime victory over these two neighbouring countries created the opportunity for more offshore drillings.

The involvement of IOCs for oil and gas exploration continues to grow in Bangladesh but is typified by questionable contracts that benefit multinational corporations. These contracts reduce the legal liability of the corporations in the case of explosions and diminish the host country's ability to fight for compensation. For instance, the latest deal with two Indian companies, ONGG Videsh Ltd and Oil India Ltd, would give Bangladesh a profit-sharing ratio of more than 50 per cent; according to this deal, however, Bangladesh cannot claim compensation if petroleum operation is suspended because of any disputes (*Dhaka Tribune*, February 18, 2016). This quagmire was evident in the events following the Magurchara gas explosion, which caused an enormous economic loss and serious socioecological damage. I turn my discussion to this specific, yet complex, set of events in the following sections.

The Magurchara gas explosion: socioecological consequences and forgotten stories

The gas explosion in the Magurchara Gas Field took place on June 14, 1997, during an exploration of a well operated by the Occidental Petroleum Corporation, a US-based international oil and gas exploration and production company. Although the Magurchara gas explosion was not the first gas field blowout accident in Bangladesh involving multinational corporations, it was the first to cause major socioecological devastation.[5] The explosion triggered a gas blowout (Figure 20.1) that continued for three weeks, and flames from the explosion reached 500 feet high (*Prothom Alo*, June 15, 2014). Not only did the explosion burn more than 250 billion cubic feet of gas, but the socioecological consequences of the Magurchara explosion, as experts argue, have been enormous and irreversible (Goswami 1997; Khan, Islam and Nasir 2014; Muhammad 2014b, 2014c).

The Magurchara Gas Field, located in the northeastern part of Bangladesh, is in the Upazila (sub-district) of Kamalgangj in the Moulvibazar district. This district is situated in the Surma River basin and is well-known for its hydrocarbon reserves. Importantly, and as

Figure 20.1 The flame from the explosion at the Magurchara gas field, which is located inside a national reserve forest, Lawachara Park.

noted above, the Magurchara Gas Field is situated inside an enormous, cherished national forest reserve area, known as the Lawachra National Park.[6] Biodiversity in this park consists of almost 500 species. The adjacent area to the Magurchara Gas Field is also famous for its tea plantations. In addition, there is a total of 18 villages nearby Lawachara, two of which lie within the park and are home to Indigenous people. Because of its critical socioecological location (Figure 20.2), the Magurchara gas explosion brought about serious damage to the local environment and caused massive biodiversity loss, leaving a legacy of human-induced environmental tragedy 'unprecedented' in Bangladesh.

According to an official report, and as noted above, the explosion burned approximately 250 billion cubic feet of gas causing irreparable environmental loss (*Prothom Alo* 2014; Siddiqui 2001; Siddique 2016). Several official and independent reports stated that the total monetary loss resulting from the Magurchara explosion has been approximately \$12 billion (*The Daily Star*, June 22, 2013). According to various reports published afterwards, about 120 acres of the forest reserve were destroyed by fire (Goswami 1997). A survey carried out by the Forest Department of Bangladesh shows the economic loss of forest resources alone was more than \$20 million (Goswami 1997). In addition, fire caused serious damage to adjacent parts of the reserve forest, affecting at least 30 tea plantations. It also impacted bamboo gardens, sugun gardens, jackfruit trees and the livelihoods of the people living on the Magurchara paan punji (betel leaf plantation). Several species of flora and fauna also suffered adverse consequences. Other damage to infrastructure included but was not limited to railway lines and electricity supply lines.

Figure 20.2 A green view of the Lawachara National Park. The explosion in the Magurchara gas field seriously damaged the socioecology of this forest and surrounding areas.

The cause of the gas explosion in the Magurchara Gas Field is still subject to debate. The reason provided by several investigators was that operators were expecting to drill almost 3,500 meters below the surface, but the well encountered a gas zone about 800 meters from the surface. When this occurred, the operator on duty started pulling out the drill and the gas flow became uncontrollable, leading to a fire. This technological failure, however, does not provide the full story of this disaster.

An official investigation carried out later found at least 15 acts of negligence by Occidental during the drilling process (*Prothom Alo*, June 14, 2014; *The Daily Star* 2013). After signing the contract with the Bangladeshi government, Occidental assigned Duetag, a German company, as sub-contractor to explore gas in the well at the Magurchara Gas Field. Duetag, however, lacked a sufficient number of experienced personnel. The poor quality of the technology used in drilling has been pointed out as a breach of the contract under which Occidental was supposed to be working (Rahman, Saha and Rahman 2010; *The Daily Star* 2013). In addition, the investigation report states that no drillers were present when the explosion took place, even though, as per contract, at least one driller was supposed to be on duty at all times.

What unfolded after the explosion of 1997 also deserves critical scrutiny. Despite the devastating accident in Magurchara, the Bangladesh government extended its contract with Occidental for two more years. Indeed, it was not until 1998, following a report of another gas emission at the Lakkatrua Gas Field, caused by Occidental's negligence, that Petrobangla, at the behest of the Energy and Mineral Resources Ministry of Bangladesh, decided not to renew the contract with Occidental.[7] Nevertheless, Occidental continued drilling at its own risk despite the Energy and Mineral Resources Ministry's order against the renewal of a further contract (*The Independent* 1998a). In 1999, two years after the Magurchara incident, Occidental left Bangladesh, selling its contract to Unocal, another U.S. corporation. In 2005, Unocal transferred its business to another U.S. energy giant, Chevron. Chevron began its operation at the Magurchara Gas Field in 2005 and started producing 62 million cubic feet of gas per day. In 2017, Chevron decided to sell its assets in Bangladesh to Himalaya Energy, a Chinese firm owned by the China ZhenHua Oil Ltd (*Reuters*, April 24, 2017). While the damaged well has been sealed, gas leakage was continuing in 2013 (*The Daily Star* 2013).

Even more than 19 years after the Magurchara explosion, the reserve forest and its nearby area have not recovered from their loss of biodiversity. To explore the issue of unresolved compensation, the following section sets up the political economic contexts of the Magurchara explosion.

The political economy of environmental harm: searching for a missing link

The argument that capitalism commodifies nature is nothing new. One of the major underpinnings of political economists is that capitalism expands by treating everything, including nature, as commodities, wreaking enormous damage to social life and to the environment (Brisman and South 2014; Castree 2008; Foster 2005; Gould, Pellow and Schnaiberg 2015; Moore 2015; Schnaiberg, Pellow and Weinberg 2002; Stretesky, Long and Lynch 2014; White 2013; White, Rudy and Gareau 2015). In capitalism's accumulation cycle, global hegemonic powers ensure and maximise their profits by trade and production (Arrighi 1994). This ever-expanding scale of economic production leads to the degradation of natural resources (Bunker and Ciccantell 2005) and an uneven development across geographical scales (Harvey 2007, 2006; Smith 1984). Questions about the roles of states and corporations and how law mediates between these two actors deserve critical attention in today's neoliberal, global economy. In this section, I argue that an analysis of how law is abused as a tool by corporations and states helps us grasp the underlying causes of environmental destruction, as well as helping us understand the ways in which compensation and remediation remain unresolved.

Pre-modern 'states' lacked a map to identify their borders and all of their constituents, whereas, in the modern state, socioecological aspects are 'refashioned by state maps of legibility' (Scott 1998: 3). Despite his critical purchase on the nature and purpose of the state, Scott's analysis does not help us to (1) analyse why states, particularly in poor countries, conduct their affairs in the way they do; and (2) understand the changing nature of the state's role in the specific context of neoliberal capitalism in poor countries. For instance, Marxist theories of the state differ in their explanations as to how and why states may collaborate with the interests of capitalists (Gold, Clarence and Wright 1975). The state may serve capitalism directly by performing two functions—accumulation and legitimation (O'Connor 1979)—or it may provide the structural mechanisms (Block 1987; Wallerstein 2004) that fulfill the capitalist ends, obviating the need for class consciousness by capitalists.

In addition, the role of the state in capitalism is not static; the changing nature of the state is evident throughout history. Specifically, capitalist states responded to the growing economic crises of the 1960s–1970s—when Keynesian economic policy, or what David Harvey calls 'embedded liberalism', appeared unviable—by inventing what is now known as 'neoliberalism'. Neoliberal actors use the state to control all domains of social life (Brown 2015; Johnson 2011; Swamy 2014). In addition, research also shows that the worldwide expansion of corporate capitalism has led to a transnational capitalist class (Robinson 2004; Toussaint and Millet 2010). Corporate power, therefore, can be viewed as a 'mode of political sovereignty' in which states and the corporations are conjoined as 'double bodies' and establish each other's conditions of advancement (Barkan 2013: 4).

How does this dynamic apply to the context of a poor, young country like Bangladesh? Poor countries cannot refuse to comply with the demands of corporations from developed countries because states in poor countries are (1) too weak to withstand the threats of retaliation from the hegemonic powers; and (2) too needy to refuse their offers of 'support'. Accordingly, state actors in poor countries—in some instances, despite their intentions otherwise—not only remain amenable to the corporate intervention, but also formulate laws favouring the interests of hegemonic powers.

Specifically, IOCs in poor countries work under legal contracts (PSCs), sometimes with the collaboration of national corporations (Goyes and South 2016) and sometimes on their own. Corporations use this legality under the PSCs to legitimise the work they are doing (Walters 2013, 2010), generating an opportunity to remain 'legally' exempted when their operations result in adverse social and environmental consequences. Highlighting this dark side of the law (Mattei and Nader 2008; Mignolo 2011), it can be argued that the corporations of powerful countries use law as a tool to (1) protect their 'extractive objectives' in poor counties; and (2) facilitate and legitimise the 'plunder' of poor countries.

Although the ways in which corporate activities cause adverse socioecological consequences are well documented, as are the ways in which the state is complicit with corporate interest, what remains largely ignored in academic discourse is how the law is used as a mediating force between weak local states and powerful multinational corporations. I use this missing link in the following discussion by shedding a critical light on the Magurchara explosion in Bangladesh.

Compensation negotiations after the Magurchara explosion: what went wrong?

In order to understand why the negotiations over compensation following the Magurchara explosion fell through, it is imperative to offer a brief, retrospective account of how much Occidental's negligence was responsible for the Magurchara explosion; how Occidental, and later other corporations, responded to the demand for compensation; and, importantly, how both these factors are intermeshed with the increased influence of neoliberalism, as well as with the distinct structures of Bangladesh's nascent democracy. As noted above, there have been four major exploration bidding rounds since 1971. One of the biggest was the 1993 bidding round that awarded Occidental three blocks for exploration. In a second round of bidding on January 11, 1995, Occidental signed a new PSC for gas exploration at the Magurchara Gas Field. On June 14, 1997, a massive explosion took place in this field, which left enormous socioecological damage in surrounding areas.

The blow-out in Magurchara was preventable because the geological information from the nearby gas wells, had Occidental considered it, should have been enough to extrapolate that their prediction about the safe depth of drilling at the Magurchara Gas Field was inaccurate (*Alexander's Gas and Oil Connections*, January 28, 1998). An investigation that was carried out after the Magurchara disaster by the Ministry of Mineral Resources Division found at least 15 instances of negligence in Occidental's operation at the Magurchara Gas Field. Due to this negligence, Occidental faced a scheduled termination of its contract in the year after the disaster.

Despite its negligence in the explosion, the Bangladesh government decided to extend the agreement with Occidental (*Chevron Press Release*, March 22, 1999), although the new agreement stipulated an additional 5 per cent share of gas for Petrobangla as a form of compensation for the loss of gas in the Magurchara explosion (*The Daily Star* 2013). In 1999, after another gas leak at a different site, Occidental sold its operation to Unocal, which, in turn, was acquired by Chevron, another U.S. multinational energy giant. Within two years of its operation at three different gas fields in Bangladesh, Chevron became the biggest investor in the energy sector of Bangladesh, doubling its gas production capacity (*Reuters*, August 2, 2007). The demand for compensation for both the economic and environmental losses amid all these dramatic events remains largely unresolved.

Occidental and later other corporations' refusal to pay the compensation led to protest in Bangladesh. In response, the Bangladeshi government vowed to take the issue of compensation to an international arbitration body in 2005 (BBC News 2005). The government never actually followed through with their promise, however, and they have yet to offer any explanations for this inaction. Why did the Bangladeshi government not fulfil its promise to take the issue of compensation to an international arbitration body? Why did the Bangladeshi government agree to Occidental's request for an extension of its contract in 1998 even after the devastating explosion caused by Occidental's substandard drilling and in the face of a nation-wide opposition and protest? To answer these questions, it may be helpful to consider the prevailing political-economic context of Bangladesh at the time—one consistent with the global neoliberal expansion of corporate capitalism.

According to the official estimate, 32 per cent of the population in Bangladesh now lives below the poverty line (Asian Development Bank 2016). The figure was even worse before 2000, at almost 50 per cent, with the gross national income (GNI) per capita approximately $400 (World Bank 2016).[8] Annual gross domestic product (GDP) growth, despite a recent trend upwards, is still much below the average of Southeast Asia. Arguably, an 'internal' democratic crisis has contributed to the political instability and economic impoverishment of the country. Major political parties in Bangladesh have played hardly any role to improve a democratic culture in Bangladesh (Khan, Aminul Islam and Imdadul Haque 2008);[9] rather, they have generated a culture of widespread corruption in Bangladesh.

In essence, Bangladesh really enjoyed only six years of democratic rule in the 26 years between achieving independence in 1971 and the Magurchara explosion in 1997. To explicate, Bangladesh suffered from 'internal colonialism' by its western counterpart Pakistan, until it liberated itself in 1971.[10] In its first two decades after independence, turbulent politics continued to be at the core of the problem in Bangladesh. The assassination of the architect of the nation, Sheikh Mujibur Rahman, who in 1974 initiated a one-party political system, aggravated the crisis. Bangladesh remained under several autocratic rulers until 1990, with the fall of the Ershad regime. Although a democratic regime finally took hold in 1991, socio-political stability has never really been the norm in Bangladesh. The corruption and non-accountability of the government is seemingly an indispensable feature of the nascent democracy of Bangladesh.

It was during this post-1971 time period that neoliberalism spread rapidly around the globe (Blyth 2008; Urry 2013, 2014). Neoliberalism links its economic logic with the advancement of human freedom and wellbeing, promoting an ideology of 'strong private property rights, free markets and free trades' (Harvey 2006), which has contributed to a democratic decline across the world (Brown 2015; Chomsky 1999; Crouch 2013). In the 1990s, this 'unchecked' western economic model contributed to deteriorating living conditions in Southeast Asia. More specifically, the onus of debt repayment crippled local economies, while pressures by international moneylenders increased. This pressure resulted in 'collusion between the ruling classes of North and South' (Toussaint and Millet 2010: 20–23), and the political elite of developing countries had few reservations about seeing their countries crushed by the burden of debt.[11] This explains why, on the one hand, an influx of foreign capital was increasing very rapidly in poor countries like Bangladesh, and, on the other, protecting the national interest and the environment was less of a concern for the government of poor countries.

The dynamic of neoliberal globalisation described above has coalesced with the political-economic context of Bangladesh. In 1997, when Occidental signed the contract with Petrobangla, the nascent democracy in Bangladesh was still very tenuous and was marred by widespread corruption. As a fragile country in the aftermath of its independence in 1971—one ruled by authoritative figures for two decades—it is no wonder that the people remained vulnerable to the rhetoric of democracy, economic development and the rule of law. This distinct situation, however, augurs well for foreign corporations in Bangladesh. In general, the invasion of foreign capital in local economies is often seen as a symbol of democratic and political stability, which is why Bangladesh experienced an influx of IOCs for natural resource exploration and discovery in the span of only one decade. In this process of market liberalisation, corporations used legal contracts (PSCs) as the means to earn profits in Bangladesh. In the case of the Magurchara explosion, these legal means helped corporations (Occidental, Unocal and now Chevron) evade their socioecological liabilities for the damage and disruptions left by Occidental's negligent activities, keeping the issue of who will pay for the damage unresolved. Moreover, this socioecological tragedy was viewed as little more than a mishap in a scheme designed to further advance corporations' interests.[12] Since the explosion little has changed, and conditions of vulnerability in Bangladesh have increased (Rahman 2009).

Conclusion

This chapter has attempted to demonstrate that in order to understand better the Magurchara gas explosion of 1997, one needs to consider various dynamics transpiring in Bangladesh and around the world at that time. First, the explosion took place when neoliberalism was accelerating globally, while poor countries, like Bangladesh, were struggling to find a viable way to ensure democracy and economic development. Second, although the environmental movement in the U.S. had made much progress by the 1990s, corporations still had a huge impact on people's environmental consciousness (Faber and O'Connor 1993; Lynch and Stretsky 2003), especially in the Global South. As a result of this corporate colonisation, the Bangladeshi state abdicated its responsibility to protect its environment, including the socioecology of its national rainforests, even in the wake of a devastating gas explosion caused by a corporation's negligence.

The distinct political-economic situation in Bangladesh and unencumbered corporate extraction of natural resources created conditions ripe for the Magurchara gas explosion. The undemocratic past of Bangladesh made the country vulnerable to the rhetoric of market democracy and to the influx of foreign capital, both of which promised to contribute to the economic advancement of Bangladesh. Given this context, Occidental—and later other corporations—took advantage of the weaknesses of the Bangladeshi state and managed to sign a legal contract favouring its interests over the socioecology of Bangladesh.

It is worth recalling two ways in which the rule of law became a mediating force between the weak Bangladeshi state and the powerful corporations. First, the rhetoric of economic development and law in the nascent democracy of Bangladesh set the stage for Occidental to exercise its dominance before and after the Magurchara explosion. Second, the PSC under which Occidental was permitted to explore and drill provided legitimate grounds for Occidental to leave Bangladesh without resolving the issue of compensation for environmental damage.

The Magurchara gas explosion demonstrates that an analysis of the combined role of weak states and powerful corporations is not enough; scholars must heed how law is used as a mediating tool between states and corporations to legitimate corporations' environmentally harmful activities across the world. Combining the role of the state, the corporation and the rule of law (or lack thereof) can shed light on the underlying causes of and responses to environmental harm, and the ways in which corporations can use law as a legitimising tool in their efforts to evade responsibilities in the wake of a deadly explosion.

Acknowledgement

I would like to express my gratitude to Dr Paul Gellert for his useful comments on earlier drafts of this chapter.

Notes

1 There is some confusion regarding the words 'Bangladeshi' and 'Bengali', which dates back to the colonial history of India. An in-depth explanation is outside the scope of this chapter, however 'Bengali' is a linguistic ethnic identity, and 'Bengali' people live both in India (Calcutta) and Bangladesh. The term 'Bangladeshi' is used as a state identity for the Bengali people in Bangladesh and, therefore, refers to a territorial identity, rather than the cultural identity, of the people living in Bangladesh.

2 The legal contracts under which Occidental was operating at the Magurchara gas field were never made public. Official investigation reports are also only partly known to the people of Bangladesh, which has made it difficult to offer a conclusive analysis of the causes and consequences of—and potential responses to—the Magurchara gas explosion. To corroborate my argument in this chapter, especially in relation to the legal contracts between the Bangladesh government and involved

corporations, I rely on the extensive use of (1) newspaper reports published nationally and internationally and experts' newspaper articles, in the period since the Magurchara explosion to December 22, 2016; (2) many relevant organizational documents such as from Petrobangla (www.petrobangla.org.bd/d), Banglapedia (http://en.banglapedia.org/index.php?title=Main_Page) and BAPEX (www.bapex.com.bd/); and (3) several writings by Anu Muhammad (including writings published in the Bengali language), the Member Secretary of the National Committee to Protect Oil, Gas, Mineral Resources, Power and Ports in Bangladesh. I used LexisNexis and Factiva, two online search tools, to access electronic journalistic documents.

3 In the middle of the 1960s, Pakistan Petroleum Limited started exploring in 12 sites in East Pakistan (what is now Bangladesh). During this course of exploration, a major historic site was found in Sylhet in 1955. The second one was found in Chattak, a sub-district in Sylhet. At that time, an American company, Stanback, started working at three different sites in the northwestern part of Bangladesh.

4 Petrobangla can enter into production-sharing contracts (known as PSCs) with IOCs. These PSCs are agreements between the Bangladeshi government and the IOCs, signed to enable the IOCs to explore and utilise mineral resources in Bangladesh.

5 Three major gas blowout incidents—the June 1997 Magurchara blowout, the January 2005 Tengratila blowout and the June 2005 Tengratila blowout—are considered major gas field disasters in Bangladesh. A second blowout in Tengratila took place on June 17, 2005, six months after the first explosion at the same site. The Tengratila gas field burned for a couple of months and forced the evacuation of at least 20,000 people. It caused enormous socioecological disruptions in local areas and the losses of natural resources worth billions of dollars. The demand for compensation for all these cases has been ignored (see Khan, Islam and Nasir 2014; Rahman, Saha and Rahman 2010).

6 Although the forest sector is not a large part of the national economy (1.9 per cent of GDP), forests play a very important role in the country's environment (especially with respect to biodiversity). Forest resources in Bangladesh are decreasing at a rate of 2.1 per cent. For unplanned neoliberal development activities that led to forest degradation and land grabbing in Bangladesh, see Adnan (2013) and Iftekhar and Hoque (2005).

7 The Energy and Mineral Resource Division of Bangladesh government reported that the Lakkatura gas emission could have been more dangerous than the Magurchara gas explosion. Occidental, however, placed the blame on Scimitar, which, as Occidental claimed, left the site without properly sealing the well in 1998 (see *The Independent* 1998b).

8 The GNI per capita is the value, in U.S. dollars, of a country's final income in a year, divided by its population. It thus reflects the average income of a country's citizens.

9 Khan et al. (2008) in *Political Culture, Political Parties, and the Democratic Transition in Bangladesh*, blame the nature of political parties for democratic failures in Bangladesh. The authors analyse how a culture of fragile party politics (fragmentation, merger and proliferation of political parties) resulted from the factional interest of certain leaders, failing to create a sustained democratic stability in Bangladesh.

10 During the 1971 Liberation War, the Pakistani Junta, with the assistance of the U.S. under the Nixon Administration, killed 3 million Bengali and raped 200,000 women. In addition, right before the humiliating defeat of the Pakistani Army, the Pakistani Junta killed many renowned Bengali intellectuals, who had participated in the war and supported Bengali freedom fighters. This war destroyed the infrastructure of Bangladesh. Although this genocide did not receive international attention, the Bengali people remember the unimaginable horror of this period in history (see Bass 2013; Blood 2002; Mamoon 2011).

11 Toussaint and Millet (2010), in *Debt, The IMF, and the World Bank*, offer a very revealing account of the consequences of debt practices in poor countries. They demonstrate how debt has become an instrument of domination and control because the policies of debt-receiving countries are very often decided by their creditors. Poor countries sometimes devote a third of their budget to debt repayment, which is often more than they spend on social sectors, including health and education. Poor countries' efforts to obtain foreign currencies result in increasing exploitation of resources. After a sudden rise of prices of basic food products, Bangladesh has become one of the poor countries that abandoned their food sovereignty due to the pressure from creditors such as the World Bank.

12 Hurricane Katrina revealed a similar trend in the U.S.: The disaster was used as a 'tipping point' to advance neoliberal goals. Several authors in *The Neoliberal Deluge*, edited by Cedric Johnson (2011), underpin how neoliberal policy choices before and after Hurricane Katrina are more at fault for the destruction and social misery experienced than were sheer forces of nature. See Swamy (2014) for how a discussion of the tsunami that hit the coastal town of Tharangampadi was used as an opportunity to further a neoliberal agenda.

References

Adnan, S. 2013. 'Land grabs and primitive accumulation in deltaic Bangladesh: Interactions between neoliberal globalization, state interventions, power relations and peasant resistance,' *The Journal of Peasant Studies*, 40(1): 87–128.

Alexander's Gas and Oil Connections. 1998. 'Occidental meets resistance in Bangladesh,' January 28, 1998. Available at: www.gasandoil.com/news/1998/03/cns81141.

Annual Report of Petrobangla. 2015. Kawran Bazar, Dhaka: Bangladesh. Available at: https://petrobangla.org.bd/?params=en/annualreport.

Arrighi, G. 1994. *The Long Twentieth Century: Money, Power, and the Origins of our Times*. New York: Verso.

Asain Development Bank. 2016. 'Poverty in Bangladesh,' Available at: www.adb.org/countries/bangladesh/poverty.

Barkan, J. 2013. *Corporate Sovereignty: Law and Government under Capitalism*. Minneapolis: University of Minnesota Press.

Bass, G. J. 2013. *The Blood Telegram: Nixon, Kissinger, and a Forgotton Genocide*. New York: Panguin Random House.

BBC News. 2005. 'Dhaka seeks $650m from gas losses,' February 16, 2005. Available at: http://news.bbc.co.uk/2/hi/south_asia/4271551.stm.

Beck, M. 2016. 'The risk implications of globalization: An exploratory analysis of 105 major industrial incidents (1971–2010),' *International Journal of Environmental Research and Public Health*, 13(3): 309.

Block, F. 1987. *Revisiting State Theory*. Philadelphia: Temple University Press.

Blood, A. K. 2002. *The Cruel Birth of Bangladesh*. Dhaka: University Press Ltd.

Blyth, M. 2007. 'One ring to bind them all: American power and neoliberal capitalism,' in S. Steinmo & J. Kopstein (eds.) *Growing Apart?: America and Europe in the 21st Century*, pp. 109–135. Cambridge: Cambridge University Press.

Brisman, A. 2014. 'Of theory and meaning in green criminology,' *International Journal for Crime, Justice and Social Democracy*, 3(2): 21–34.

Brisman, A. and South, N. 2014. *Green Cultural Criminology: Constructions of Environmental Harm, Consumerism, and Resistance to Ecocide*. London: Routledge.

Brisman, A., South, N. and Bernie, P. 2013. 'A guide to green criminology,' in edited by N. South and A. Brisman (eds.) *Routledge International Edition of Green Criminology*, pp. 27–42. London and New York: Routledge.

Brown, W. 2015. *Undoing the Demos: Neoliberalism's Stealth Revolution*. Cambridge, MA: MIT Press.

Bullard, R. D. 2005. 'Environmental injustice in the twenty-first century,' in R. D. Bullard (ed.) *The Quest for Environmental Justice*, pp. 19–42. San Francisco: Sierra Club.

Bunker, S. G. and Ciccantell, P. 2005. *Globalization and the Race for Resources*. Maryland: John Hopkins University Press.

Castleman, B. I. 1983. 'The double standard in industrial hazards,' *International Journal of Health Services*, 13(1): 5–14.

Castree, N. 2008. 'Neoliberalising nature: The logics of deregulation and reregulation,' *Environment and Planning A*, 40(1): 131–152.

Chevron Press Release. 1999. 'Occidental and unocal announce startup of Bangladesh gas project,' March 22, 1999. Available at: www.chevron.com/Stories/Occidental-and-Unocal-announce-startup-of-Bangladesh-gas-project.

Chomsky, N. 1999. *Profit over People: Neoliberalism and Global Order*. New York: Seven Stories Press.

CPD Occasional Paper Series. 2002. *An Exploratory Review of Bangladesh Gas Sector: Latest Evidence and Areas of Further Research*. Dhaka: Centre for Policy Dialogue.

Crouch, C. 2013. 'From markets versus states to corporations versus civil society?' in W. Streck and A. Schäfer (eds.) *Politics in the Age of Austerity*, pp. 219–238. London: Polity Press.

Dhaka Tribune. 2016. 'Govt. to allow gas export by IOCs.' October 2, 2016. Available at: www.dhakatribune.com/bangladesh/2016/10/02/govt-allow-gas-export-iocs/.

Faber, D. and O'Connor, J. 1993. 'Capitalism and the crisis of environmentalism,' in R. Hofrichter (ed.) *Toxic Struggles: The Theory and Practice of Environmental Justice*, pp. 12–24. Philadelphia: New Society Publisher.

Foster, J. B. 2005. 'The treadmill of accumulation schnaiberg's environment and marxian political economy,' *Organization & Environment*, 18(1): 7–18.

Foster, J. B., Clark, B. and York, R. 2011. *The Ecological Rift: Capitalism's War on the Earth*. New York: NYU Press.
Frey, S. R. 2012. 'The e-waste stream in the world-system,' *Journal of Globalization Studies*, 3: 79–94.
Frey, S. R. 2013. 'Breaking ships in the world-system: An analysis of two ship breaking capitals, Alang India and Chittagong, Bangladesh,' *Journal of World-Systems Research*, 21(1): 25–49.
Gellert, P. K. 2010. 'Extractive regimes: Toward a better understanding of indonesian development,' *Rural Sociology*, 75(1): 28–57.
Gold, D. A., Lo, C., and Wright, E. O. 1975. 'Recent developments in marxist theories of the capitalist state,' *Monthly Review*, 27(5): 29–43.
Goswami, R. K. 1997. 'Forest department likely to compensation from occidental co,' In *The Daily Star*, the issue of 31 July 2013.
Gould, K. A., Pellow, D. N. and Schnaiberg, A. 2015. *Treadmill of Production: Injusticeand Unsustainability in the Global Economy*. USA: Routledge.
Goyes, D. R., and South, N. 2016. 'Land-grabs, biopiracy and the inversion of justice in Colombia,' *The British Journal of Criminology*, 56(3): 558–577.
Greife, M. B. and Stretesky, P. B. 2013. 'Crude laws: Treadmill of production and state variations in civil and criminal liability for oil discharges in navigable waters,' in N. South and A. Brisman (eds.) *Routledge International Edition of Green Criminology*, pp.150–166. London and New York: Routledge.
Harvey, D. 2003. *The New Imperialism*. New York: Oxford University Press.
Harvey, D. 2006. *Spaces of Global Capitalism*. New York: Verso.
Harvey, D. 2007. *A Brief History of Neoliberalism*. New York: Oxford University Press.
Iftekhar, M. S. and Hoque, A. K. F. 2005. 'Causes of forest encroachment: An analysis of bangladesh,' *GeoJournal*, 62(1): 95–106.
Johnson, C. (ed.) 2011. *The Neoliberal Deluge: Hurricane Katrina Late Capitalism, and the Remaking of New Orleans*. Minneapollis: University of Minnesota Press.
Kazol, I. 2016. *Bangldesher Tel-Gas-Khonij Sompod: Bideshi Aggrassion (Oil, Gas, and Mineral Resouces in Bangladesh: Foreign Agression)*. Dhaka: Ittadi Publishing.
Khan, M. A. I. and Nasir, F. B. 2014. 'A review over major gas blowouts in Bangladesh, their effects and the measures to prevent them in future,' *International Journal of Scientific and Technology Research*, 3(9): 109–113.
Khan, S. I., Islam, S. A. and Haque, M. I. 2008. *Political Culture, Political Parties, and the Democratic Transition in Bangladesh*. Dhaka: The University Press Limited.
Labban, M. 2008. *Space, Oil and Capital*. London and New York: Routledge.
Lemke, T. 2001. 'The birth of bio-politics': Michel Foucault's lecture at the collège de France on neoliberal governmentality,' *Economy and Society*, 30(2): 190–207.
Lynch, M. J. and Stretsky, P. B. 2003. 'The meaning of green: Contrasting criminological perspectives,' *Theoretical Criminology*, 7(2): 217–238.
Mamoon, M. 2011. *1971 Chuknagar Genocide*. Dhaka: University Press Ltd.
Mattei, U. and Nader, L. 2008. *Plunder: When the Rule of Law is Illegal*. Hoboken, NJ: John Wiley & Sons.
Mignolo, W. 2011. *The Darker Side of Western Modernity: Global Futures, Decolonial Options*. Durham, NC: Duke University Press.
Moore, J. W. 2015. *Capitalism in the Web of Life: Ecology and the Accumulation of Capital*. New York: Verso Books.
Muhammad, A. 2014a. 'Natural resources and energy security,' *Economic & Political Weekly*, 49(4): 59.
Muhammad, A. 2014b. 'Bad deals makes Bangladesh vulnerable,' In *The Daily Star*, 22 May 2012.
Muhhamad, A. 2014c. 'Burden of development,' In *The Daily Star*, 27 February 2014.
O'Connor, J. 1979. *The Fiscal Crisis of the State*. New Brunswick, NJ: Transaction Publishers.
O'Connor, J. 1998. *Natural Causes: Essays in Ecological Marxism*. New York: Grossman.
Petras, J. 2013. 'Brazil: Extractive capitalism and the great leap backward,' *World Review of Political Economy*, 4(4): 469–483.
Prothom Alo. 2014. '19 Bochoreo Pawa Zayni Khotipuron (No compensation in 19 years),' In *Prothom Alo*, 14 June 2014.
Rahman, M. M., Saha, S. K. and Rahman, M. Z. 2010. 'Impact assessment of environmental consequences on a blowout at Chhatak -2 (Tengratila) gas field, Bangladesh,' in S. H. Rahman (ed.) *Bangladesh Journal of Environmental Research (Volume 8)*, pp. 15–22. Jahangirnagar University, Dhaka: Department of Environmental Sciences.

Rahman, S. 2009. 'Socio-economic vulnerability and neo-liberalism,' *South Asia Research*, 29(3): 235–254.
Reuters. 2007. 'Chevron doubles gas production capacity in Bangladesh,' August 2, 2007. Available at: www.reuters.com/article/bangladesh-chevron-gas-idUKDHA6146720070802.
Reuters. 2017. 'Chevron to sell Bangladesh gas fields to Chinese co,' April 24, 2017. Available at: www.reuters.com/article/china-bangladesh-chevron-idUSD8N16504W.
Robinson, W. I. 2004. *A Theory of Global Capitalism: Production, Class, and State in a Transnational World*. Maryland: John Hopkins University Press.
Schnaiberg, A., Pellow, D. N. and Weinberg, A. 2002. 'The treadmill of production and the environmental state,' *The Environmental State Under Pressure*, 10: 15–32.
Scott, J. C. 1998. *Seeing Like a State: How Certain Schemes to Improve the Human Condition Have Failed*. New Haven, CT: Yale University Press.
Siddique, S. 2016. 'Out of Tk 3,900 crore, only Tk 12 crore Realized,' October 27, 2016, *The Independent*. (www.theindependentbd.com/home/printnews/65704).
Siddiqui, J. 2001. 'Environmental non-accountability in Bangladesh? The striking case of the Magurchara gas field disaster,' *Social and Environmental Accountability Journal*, 21(2): 12–13.
Smith, N. 1984. *Uneven Development: Nature, Capital, and the Production of Space*. Athens,GA: University of Georgia Press.
Sovacool, B. K. 2010. 'The political economy of oil and gas in southeast asia: Heading towards the natural resource curse?' *The Pacific Review*, 23(2): 225–259.
Stretesky, P. B., Long, M. A. and Lynch, M. J. 2014. *The Treadmill of Crime: PoliticalEconomy and Green Criminology*. London: Routledge.
Swamy, R. 2014. 'Risk and opportunity in post-tsunami Tharangampadi,' in E. Fihl and Ā Irā Vē ka ācalapati (eds.) *Beyond Tranquebar: Grappling across Cultural Borders in South India*, pp. 148–177. New Delhi: Orient Blackswan.
The Daily Star. 2009.'Lawachara still bears the scars of magurchara blast,' June 15, 2009.
The Daily Star. 2013.'Damaged well sealed, but gas leakage continues,' June 22, 2013.
The Independent. 1998a. *Occidental Goes on with Drilling Despite Non-renewal of Contract*. May 9, 1998 issue of *The Independent*.
The Independent. 1998b. *Govt. Unhappy at Occidental Performance*. May 11, 1998 issue of *The Independent*.
Toussaint, E. and Millet, D. 2010. *Debt, the IMF, and the World Bank: Sixty Questions, Sixty Answers*. New York: Monthly Review Press.
Urry, J. 2013. *Societies beyond Oil: Oil Dregs and Social Futures*. London: Zed Books Ltd.
Urry, J. 2014. *Offshoring*. Hoboken, NJ: John Wiley & Sons.
Wallerstein, I. 2004. *World-systems Analysis: An Introduction*. Durham, NC: Duke University Press.
Walters, R. 2010. 'Toxic atmospheres air pollution, trade and the politics of regulation,' *Critical Criminology: An International Journal*, 18(4): 307–323.
Walters, R. 2013. 'Air crimes and atmospheric justice,' in N. South and A. Brisman (eds.) *Routledge International Edition of Green Criminology*, pp. 134–149. London and New York: Routledge.
Watts, M. 2001. 'Petro-violence: Community, extraction, and political ecology of a mythic commodity,' in N. L. Peluso and M. Watts (eds.) *Violent Environments*, pp. 189–212. New York: Cornell University Press.
White, D., Rudy, A. and Gareau, B. 2015. *Environments, Natures and Social Theory: Towardsa Critical Hybridity*. New York: Palgrave Macmillan.
White, R. 2013. 'Eco-global criminology and the political economy of environmental harm,' in N. South and A. Brisman (eds.) *Routledge International Edition of Green Criminology*, pp. 243–260. London and New York: Routledge.
World Bank. 2016. 'GNI per capita, Atlas Method (current US$),' Available at: https://data.worldbank.org/indicator/NY.GNP.PCAP.CD?locations=BD.

21

Authoritarian environmentalism and environmental regulation enforcement

A case study of medical waste crime in northwestern China

KuoRay Mao, Yiliang Zhu, Zhong Zhao and Yan Shan

Introduction

Medical waste[1] is a serious issue in many nations around the world, causing severe environmental and social harms. According to the World Health Organization (WHO) (2018), medical waste is waste generated by healthcare facilities, such as blood banks, community clinics, dental practices, hospitals and physicians' offices, as well as medical laboratories, research facilities and veterinary clinics; it includes chemicals, pharmaceuticals, sharp objects and a variety of wastes (e.g., cytotoxic, infectious, pathological and radioactive waste). Hazardous medical waste constitutes 15 per cent of the total amount of medical waste and its subsequent environmental harm and public health impacts have attracted increased attention worldwide. Untreated medical waste is connected to injuries from sharp objects and unintended exposure to biological, chemical and radioactive hazards for healthcare workers, patients and the public at large. The improper dumping and incineration of medical waste contaminates drinking water, surface water and groundwater and causes the emission of dioxins, furans and toxic metals in the environment (WHO 2018). Globally, there is a strong correlation between the formulation and implementation of medical waste regulations and the level of national economic development (Caniato, Tudor and Vaccari 2015). In developing nations, medical waste management systems are often constrained by deficient legislation and a lack of legal uniformity, which is connected directly to insufficient enforcement in classification, collection, storage, transportation and disposal practices (Ali, Wang, Chaudhry and Geng 2017; Yesilyurt, Nayır and Akbaba 2015). In addition, nations define and classify hazardous medical waste in different ways, which impedes law enforcement efforts in the regulation of domestic and international transference of risk and harm (Komilis 2016; Windfeld and Brooks 2015).

The transformation of China into the most prominent developing economy in the world has been accompanied by a rapid expansion in healthcare services. Between 2003 and 2012, the number of national healthcare facilities tripled from 305,000 to 961,830, leading to a rapid increase in medical waste and environmental harm in China (Nie, Qiao and Wu 2014). From 2010 to 2016, the generation of medical waste increased at an annual rate of 6.05 per cent, with an estimated 1.99 million tons of medical waste produced in 2017 alone (Liu 2018). From 2003 to 2016, the Chinese State Council, the Chinese Ministry of Health (MOH),[2] and the Chinese Ministry of Environmental Protection (MEP)[3] issued a series of regulations to govern the storage, transport, treatment and disposal of medical and hazardous wastes; non-compliance and violations have been widespread, however, especially in rural hinterland regions (Mao 2011; Zhang et al. 2013; Zhu 2017). Existing research has focussed primarily on the connection between deficient infrastructure investment, lack of proper training and the mismanagement of medical waste. In addition, such research has asserted that networks of illicit recyclers spanning multiple provinces in China have been the actors primarily responsible for the illicit trading of medical waste (Chai 2017; Ni 2017; Nie and Wu 2016; Wei 2016; Xin 2016). Few studies have examined critically the connection between deficiencies in China's regulatory apparatus and the criminality associated with illegal dumping and trading of medical waste. Accordingly, this chapter utilises a green criminological perspective to examine this key issue as it pertains to waste dumping in rural northwestern China. First, we offer a brief review of green criminology's approach to waste crime and summarise the literature on top-down environmental regulation enforcement in China. Next, we describe the development of the medical waste regulation framework and highlight the current obstacles to enforcement in China. The chapter then utilises a case study to illustrate how institutional incentives in the job performance evaluation system of bureaucrats shaped the under-enforcement of medical waste regulations at the 'grassroots' level of rural governance. Our chapter concludes with a discussion of how the study expands our understanding of waste crime and environmental regulation enforcement in an illiberal context.

Green criminology and waste crime

Green criminology has long examined the social and environmental harm caused by the generation, mismanagement, transport and disposal of waste (e.g., Bisschop 2012, 2016; Bisschop and Huisman 2018; Gibbs, McGarrell and Axelrod 2010; Groombridge 2013; Rothe 2010; Snider 2010; South 1998; Van Erp and Huisman 2010). Environmental issues related to waste might be considered as a form of 'brown crime', which refers to pollution caused by industrialisation and the expansion of global capitalism (South 2016; White 2008b). The social and environmental costs of waste are further exacerbated by the planned obsolescence of contemporary industrial economies (South and Brisman 2013), and the distribution of environmental and health risks associated with waste is structured not by the application of existing legal frameworks but by social inequality (Lynch, Stretesky and Long 2015; Mohai and Saha 2015). As such, waste management becomes 'a location problem for the state rather than a production problem for capital' (White 2008a: 116). To maintain the capitalist mode of production, nation-states choose to disguise the true cost of waste in production and focus only on a 'control instead of prevention' regulation approach, which results in an inverse incentive structure of waste treatment and subsequently the commodification of waste (Bisschop 2016; South 2016). The immense financial profits associated with the waste trade contribute to the emergence of 'dirty collar crime', in which corporations, state agents and illicit entrepreneurs involved with criminal organisations collude to form illegal or semi-legal waste disposal operations that perpetuate environmental harm (Ruggiero and South 2010, 2013). The externalisation of risk and environmental injustice caused by the global transference of harm are shaped directly by the pattern of stratification embedded within the global political economy, as less privileged populations suffer from asymmetrical information and regulation, in addition to gaps in domestic and international enforcement (Bisschop 2016; Gibbs, McGarrell and Axelrod 2010). The governance of waste disposal is thus a global issue because the interrelations between legal stakeholders and illicit enterprises in different social contexts directly affect the degree of regulation enforcement and compliance in different jurisdictions and at different administrative scales (Bisschop and Huisman 2018; White and Heckenberg 2014). Therefore, to understand properly the underlying causes of waste crime, green criminologists examine the cultural, economic, political and social contexts that have structured the environmental offenses related to the creation, treatment and disposal of waste (Bisschop 2012). Effective policy development requires criminological analysis to transcend the conventional state-corporate crime and organised crime approaches by examining the systematic causes that contribute to the complexity of regulation enforcement (Bisschop and Huisman 2018; Gibbs et al. 2011).

This chapter responds to the call for a more systematic analysis of waste crime by demonstrating how transformations in rural healthcare institutions and conflicts within the regulation enforcement apparatus contribute to an implementation gap in China's medical waste regulatory framework in rural areas. The study reveals how deficiencies related to the authoritarian model of environmental governance in China hinder the enforcement of environmental regulations at the grassroots level, and how, without institutionalised public oversight, the implementation of environmental regulations by the centralised regime will remain inefficient and unsatisfactory.

Environmental governance in China: an overview

Rapid economic development in China has generated severe environmental harm and ecological entropy. Correspondingly, the Chinese government has issued numerous environmental and resource protection laws, as well as hundreds of national environmental regulations and administrative orders, to address environmental pollution and natural resource depletion while maintaining rapid economic growth and promoting institutional reform (Kostka 2017; Qin and Zhang 2017).

It bears mention that the development of the Chinese environmental legal system has gone through four distinct phases. In 1979, China passed its first Environmental Protection Law (hereafter EPL), which established the Chinese central state as the sole legal authority responsible for formulating and enforcing environmental regulations pertaining to pollution prevention and natural resource conservation. The decentralisation of political decision-making and the depletion of central government budget finances, however, made the law largely symbolic and environmental regulations were seldom enforced in the early reform period. In 1989, China amended and enacted its second EPL, which created the legislative platform for continuous institutional innovation (Qin and Zhang 2017). The third phase was initiated by China's participation in the 1992 United Nations Conference on Environment and Development (UNCED), which promoted global sustainable development. From that point on, China gradually incorporated the principles of sustainable development into its environmental regulation regime. During its tenth Five-Year Plan (2001–2005), the Chinese central government proclaimed that the realisation of an 'ecological civilisation', which championed 'the harmonious relationship between citizens and nature', was central to the development of modern Chinese society (Zhang, Mol and Sonnenfeld 2007). The central government began to invest its fiscal resources in conservation programmes and impose more stringent nationwide environmental regulations. The central government's attempt suffered major setbacks, however, due to persistent implementation gaps in regulation enforcement.

According to some commentators, the implementation gap in China's environmental regulations can be attributed to China's fragmented authoritarian political system (Kostka and Mol 2013). The post-1978 economic liberalisation in China weakened the central government's control over budget and expenditure decisions, and contributed to the decentralisation of the authoritarian party-state (Lieberthal and Oksenberg 1988). Political authority became fragmented along the organisational interests of competing ministries at the national level, and the formulation of national policy goals was shaped by lengthy negotiations and bargaining between different administrative apparatus (Kostka 2017; Kostka and Mol 2013; Marks 2010). Moreover, policy implementation was frustrated by the complex fiscal transference system between the central and local governments. In the fragmented authoritarian political system, lower-level government agencies must follow orders from the local governments, which provide the operating budgets of the agencies' daily administration, in addition to the command of central and provincial government departments, which provide the funds for the implementation of special projects controlled by the central ministries. As such, local governments wield considerable influence over the implementation agencies, and the leaders of the local governments tend to prioritise the interests of economic and social stability over environmental policy goals imposed by the central state because of a reverse incentive structure that provides more concrete incentives for short-term economic gains than for long-term environmental protection (Eaton and Kostka 2014; Ran 2013). Subsequently, 'grassroots' state agents often interpret environmental regulations differently from the central government mandates and resist the enforcement of environmental regulations. Facing strong institutional inertia embedded within the authoritarian state, the central government must rely on short-term political campaigns to balance the competing interests in the fragmented bureaucracy. Consequently, support from central political leaders was crucial in shaping the design, implementation and enforcement of environmental regulations before 2014 (Mao and Zhang 2018).

To overcome the implementation gap in regulation enforcement, in recent years there has been a new trend of centralisation in China's environmental governance. The centralising trend can be perceived as a prominent example of what many observers refer to as 'authoritarian environmentalism', which is a non-participatory approach to policy formulation and implementation in environmental governance that combines the reduction of individual liberty and dominance with the administrative apparatus of a relatively autonomous central state (Beeson 2010; Eaton and Kostka 2014; Gilley 2012). In this model, the Chinese central state has leveraged its relatively autonomous position from corporate influence and public participation to formulate a series of environmental regulations based on deliberations among technocrats and relevant stakeholders within public institutions (Beeson 2010; Gilley 2012; Marks 2010). Essentially, the central government imposes a top-down implementation regime to ensure national policy goals can be fully enforced at the local level by setting binding environmental targets in the evaluation of state bureaucrats and by controlling its fiscal transfers to local governments (Kostka and Nahm 2017; Van Rooij et al. 2017). The binding targets are effective in imposing political control because they are crucial to personnel management decisions such as promotion and bonuses (Eaton and Kostka 2014). Moreover, the 'grassroots' governance of China has experienced a 'hollowing out of the state' as the 1994 tax reform has significantly reduced local tax revenue (Mao 2018; Smith 2010). Consequently, the operation of more than 51 per cent of environmental protection projects has relied on fiscal transfer funds from the central government (Van Rooij et al. 2017). Therefore, the success of binding targets is not only important to decisions for cadre promotion but also critical to maintaining revenue flow for local governments. Limited in funding, training and expertise, local governments are forced to impose political pressure to mobilise 'grassroots' state actors to focus on the meeting of binding environmental targets instead of the long-term sustainability of environmental projects (Mao and Zhang 2018).

In 2014, the People's Congress of China passed a thoroughly revised environmental protection law. This latest phase of environmental governance in China employs new policy instruments, such as environmental assessment, public hearings, information disclosure and adjudication, to reduce negative social and environmental harms. The formulation of the 2014 EPL went through three rounds of internal debates within the bureaucracy and incorporated multiple inputs from ministerial technocrats and university scholars (Zhang, He and Mol 2015). At the same time, the central government introduced stricter national environmental standards and elevated the status of binding environmental targets in the annual evaluation of bureaucrats and grassroots state agents. As a result, the enforcement of environmental regulations has gradually shifted from an administrative management-based approach to a system that relies on legal and economic instruments by mandating environmental assessment for new construction projects, as well as the sharing of environmental information by enterprises and public institutions. Polluters are also subject to daily fines, seizure and distrainment of property, restricted production and rectification (Qin and Zhang 2017). Institutional constraints and the varied contexts of development still present major obstacles in regulation enforcement at the local level (Van Rooij et al. 2017), however. The following section describes the development of medical waste regulations and the obstacles in the way of implementation of the regulatory framework.

Medical waste regulations in China

As noted in the previous section, based on the WHO's recommendation, the Chinese central government promulgated a series of laws and regulations to control pollution caused by solid and hazardous waste in the late 1990s. But there was no national regulatory framework regarding medical waste until the Severe Acute Respiratory Symptom (SARS) outbreak in 2003, which forced the State Council to issue the *Regulation on the Control of Medical Waste* (hereafter, the 'Regulation'). This significant legislation represented the first legal definition of 'medical waste' in China, provided clear guidelines for each stage of medical waste treatment, mandated centralised treatment by authorised entities, required waste generators to classify and manage medical wastes correctly, and mandated prefectural-level municipality that govern subordinate counties to complete the construction of medical waste treatment facilities by 2004 (Gai et al. 2009).[4] The Regulation defines the scope and content of medical wastes, designates the responsibilities of waste producers and relevant government agencies, and specifies technical requirements for appropriate management. For instance, Article 4 of the 2003 Regulation stipulates that county or higher level governments are responsible for establishing centralised infrastructure for medical waste treatment; Article 5 designates the local environmental protection bureaus (the 'EPBs') at the county or higher level to provide oversight over environmental pollution, and the local health and family planning committee (the 'HFPCs') to oversee disease prevention and intervention related to medical waste treatment. Furthermore, Article 11 requires healthcare providers and waste management entities to adhere to the Law of the People's Republic of China on the Prevention and Control of Environmental Pollution by Solid Waste and establish a tracking system for all medical waste generated. Article 12 specifies that the medical waste tracking system needs to monitor every step of the medical waste management process by recording the sources of waste generation, type and quantities produced, times of transference, means of storage and transportation and methods of final disposal. All records of the tracking system must be kept for at least three years and signed by the legal representatives of the healthcare and waste management facilities. Because of the lack of adequate infrastructure for medical waste treatment in the rural area, Article 21 explicitly allows rural healthcare providers to treat medical wastes locally but requires that single-use devices and sharps be sterilised and destroyed and that medical wastes should be incinerated in a timely fashion when feasible, or sterilised and buried in designated locations when incineration is not available. The Regulation also stipulates penalties for the violation of the national guidelines but leaves the financing of medical waste management unspecified. Instead, the Regulation states that healthcare providers must be responsible for the cost of waste treatment.

In 2003 and 2004, the MOH and the MEP issued *The National Guideline for Medical Waste Management in Healthcare Facilities, the Inventory of Medical Waste Classification* and *The National Hazardous Waste and Medical Treatment Facility Construction Plan*, which, collectively, set the technical standards for medical waste management procedures and infrastructure (Mao 2011). In 2013, the MEP implemented the *12th Five-Year Plan on Hazardous Waste Pollution Prevention*, which called for the promulgation of provincial-level regulations on medical waste and mandated the construction of medical waste treatment facilities at the county level (Sun et al. 2017). It was not until 2014, however, that the State Council issued an administrative order to officially criminalise violations of medical waste regulations in order to provide more incentive for enforcement. The order was further affirmed by China's Supreme People's Court and by the Supreme People's Procuratorate's decision concerning the applications of criminal laws to the violation of environmental regulations in China in 2016 (The Supreme People's Procuratorate of the People's Republic of China 2016).

Numerous case studies conducted in hospitals in China have found implementation gaps at every level of the medical waste regulatory system. In 2015, it was estimated that less than one-third of the 1.824 million tons of medical waste produced in China was treated properly and that more than 80 per cent of the counties in China do not have designated facilities to process medical waste (Zhu 2017). Research shows that there has been a severe discrepancy in waste treatment among different geographical regions and at different levels of hospitals and clinics. Healthcare facilities in coastal and urban areas have better access to comprehensive disposal treatment facilities, protective and transport equipment and budgetary support than healthcare facilities in the hinterland and rural regions (Li et al. 2013; Nie, Qiao and Wu 2014). In addition, the tracking system for transferring, storing and controlling medical waste was more likely to be enforced at provincial-level hospitals than the county- and lower-level facilities (Liu 2018; Nie and Wu 2016). Studies have also shown that, in China, medical professionals, waste management facilities and local governing authorities do not understand completely, or comprehensively adopt, national regulations and guidelines and that the general public's awareness of the hazardous nature of medical waste is low (Zhang et al. 2013; Zhang et al. 2009). Under the current system in China, the most common way to deal with medical waste is incineration, but this method has been impractical because most hospitals in hinterland regions find the costs prohibitive and their respective counties or municipalities lack centralised medical waste incineration centres (Zhang et al. 2009). In hospitals where incinerators are available, administrators often delegate waste disposal to general logistics departments or temporary workers instead of specialised personnel, resulting in the persistent misclassification and mixing of infectious waste with regular disposals (Zhang et al. 2013). Misclassification then causes serious secondary pollution as the incomplete combustion of polymer products generates carcinogenic dioxins in the exhaust, fumes and soot (Gai et al. 2009).

The lack of public awareness and the absence of an accurate tracking system for medical waste have created an extensive black market and the emergence of illicit medical waste recycling markets in China (Chai 2017). Medical waste enters the black market through two main channels: the reselling of used supplies and the illegal collection of medical waste to make recycled plastic granules, creating a dangerous source of infectious diseases. The lack of effective supervision, combined with asymmetric information between hospitals and patients, can lead to high-priced medical devices being re-utilised in major hospitals or repackaged as new supplies that are purchased by lower-level medical clinics through illegal channels. In addition, used catheters, syringes and transfusion bags are highly profitable in the illegal recycling market as the high-grade plastic content in medical supplies can be recycled as polypropylene and polyethylene granules and then used to manufacture consumer products (Xin 2016; Yang, Xia and Jia 2018). According to a recent report, police in the Hebei province discovered a criminal network consisting of 12 individuals who collected 140 tons of medical waste from five provinces at the price of 2,000 yuan per metric ton and then sold the processed polypropylene granules to buyers in Hebei at 5,000 yuan per ton (Shuai et al. 2017). In addition to the illegal recyclers, public hospitals in China play a major role in the domestic commodity chain of medical waste. For example, three suspects in Nanjing city paid 800 to 1,000 yuan per month to metro-area hospitals to collect their medical waste. From 2012 to 2016, the criminal network sold more than 3,000 tons of medical waste and earned more than 40 million yuan ($5.8 million). At the same time, it was estimated that hospitals producing 10 metric tons or more of medical waste a year could have saved more than 500,000 yuan annually in processing costs by using illegal disposable services instead of employing licensed companies. The proceeds from selling medical waste could have become informal compensation for workers in the general logistic departments of hospitals (Ni 2017; Wei 2016). Moreover, some licensed treatment companies also colluded with illegal recyclers and sold the medical waste they collected into the illicit market (Chai 2017).

All told, the commodity chain of waste in China is difficult to investigate because each criminal network may cover multiple provinces and regions where local governments protect revenue-generating hospitals and illicit recyclers, creating severe public health and environmental risks (Shuai et al. 2017). The literature and current reports indicate clearly that simply developing a legal framework and accelerating the construction of infrastructure have failed in regulation enforcement and comprehensive coverage of medical waste in China, especially in rural areas where most of healthcare activities occur in China. Unfortunately, the majority of research on medical waste in China focusses on cities, while published studies on the implementation of medical waste regulation in rural areas remain scarce and rely primarily on descriptive data gathered from quantitative surveys in specific locations.

Case study: the implementation of medical waste regulations in rural northwestern China

One major issue of medical waste management in China is the severe discrepancy of coverage in waste management between urban and rural areas and coastal and hinterland regions. Research has shown that, compared with urban areas, medical waste management in the countryside faces distinct challenges as rural healthcare facilities lack the professional knowledge, designated personnel and infrastructure support to implement regulation correctly (Mao 2011; Zhang et al. 2013; Zhang et al. 2009). Moreover, hinterland provinces have understaffed environmental protection and public health agencies that lack the administrative capacity to enforce medical waste regulations in rural regions, especially at the township and village-level

(Shuai et al. 2017; Yan 2015). The following case study contributes to the literature on the enforcement of medical waste regulations in rural China by providing a detailed qualitative analysis of how institutional incentives within the bureaucracy, coupled with the social dynamics of village and township communities, structure the implementation of medical waste regulations in rural northwestern China.

Data and methods

The data for this case study derive from a study of medical and hazardous waste management in two rural counties in northwestern China. Key research methods include in-depth interviews, focus groups and quantitative surveys from an ongoing 18-year (2013–2030) cohort study that explores how economic development and institutional transformation affect public health and environmental governance in hinterland China. The field sites are in the mountainous Loess Plateau region that faces significant water shortage and soil depletion (Figure 21.1).

A baseline survey using random cluster sampling was implemented in 2013 to understand the health conditions, environmental health behaviours and environmental awareness of 3,500 households in the field sites. During the survey, we built a network of volunteers consisting of village doctors and medical chiefs of township-level clinics. From 2015 to 2017, with support from health bureaus at the provincial and prefecture levels, we conducted 52 in-depth interviews with village doctors, township clinic medical chiefs and county health bureau officials to gather stakeholders' opinions about the implementation of medical waste management and disposal per the Regulations. The in-depth interviews were critical for identifying institutional constraints in several significant areas: *accountability* (of the environmental protection and public health agencies and waste generators); *attitudes and behaviours* (environmental awareness, perception of pollution and waste management practices); *economic impact* (cost, incentives and benefits to individual practitioners, clinics and local bureaucracy); *enforcement* (of existing laws and regulations); *legal authority* (accountability, jurisdictions and oversight); and *resources* (funding sources, technology, technical support and training for waste management). In addition, in 2015 and 2016, we conducted 31 interviews with village women and elders, who provided diverse perspectives on medical and hazardous waste management in the countryside.[5] The interviews were transcribed with the consent of the participants for later review and coding. In 2017, we conducted five separate focus groups consisting of village doctors and village officials, as well as interviews with three groups of women organised by our year-long intervention study to formulate an intervention programme capable of creating an incentive for community stakeholders to improve medical and hazardous waste management in the countryside.[6]

Illegal practices by village doctors and illicit entrepreneurs at the village level

The limited training village doctors receive has contributed directly to the under-enforcement of medical waste regulations in our field sites. Village doctors stated repeatedly in the interviews that the proper treatment of medical waste was extremely difficult to achieve because the training from township clinics failed to provide necessary legal knowledge and technical expertise to enable doctors to follow the requirements set by the Regulations. Though the village doctors had to attend annual workshops that stressed the importance of waste classification and the health and environmental hazards generated by the unregulated dumping of medical waste, there were no training opportunities that taught village doctors how to treat medical waste locally until our

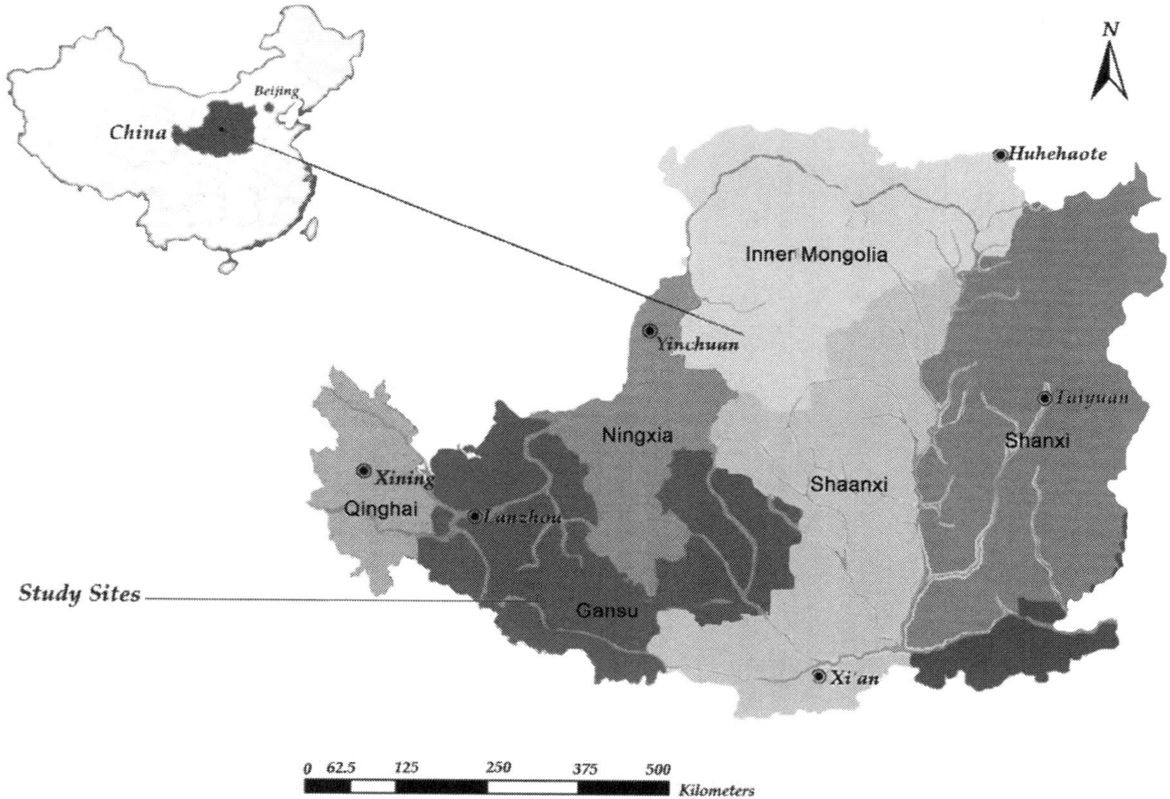

Figure 21.1 The Loess Plateau in China and the study sites

intervention study held three workshops in 2017. For example, 92 per cent of the village doctors we interviewed remarked that they did not have a useful disposal method for residues originating from the incomplete incineration of sharp objects and infectious wastes. Given the arid ecology of the region, many of the village doctors ended up dumping the half-incinerated residues on the usually dry riverbed and waited for the summer flash flood to wash the debris to downstream areas.[7] The patchy and conflicting regulatory guidelines also hindered the implementation of the Regulations, as one village doctor indicated:

> We are aware that intravenous glass bottles and the plastic infusion bags are legally considered to be recyclable unless the containers are contaminated with biochemical or pathological substances. But we do not have any guidelines to follow regarding the criteria of classification, storage, and disposal of these containers.

The lack of stable funding streams to treat medical waste was another major obstacle faced by village and township doctors, reflecting a fundamental transformation in the roles village and township clinics play in China's rural healthcare system. Before the 1980s, collective farming supported a commune-funded cooperative healthcare system where 'barefoot' doctors (villagers who received no formal education other than basic medical training in night schools) served as community health workers in villages. Economic reform during the 1980s, however, led to the collapse of the cooperative system, and by the 1990s, coverage of the community-based cooperative medical system was reduced to less than five per cent of the rural population (Ma, Lu and Quan 2008). The village and township clinics became profit-oriented because they had to generate their own operating costs. At the same time, village doctors became official state employees and had to complete training and licensing in provincial-level medical schools. The launch of the New Rural Cooperative Medical System (RCMS) in 2003 and the Basic Public Health Services (BPHS) in 2010 marked the next phase of rural healthcare in China. While the political will and financial investment of the Chinese government to improve rural healthcare has been laudable, many observers acknowledge difficulties translating policies into sustainable practices needed to further improve service delivery (China Joint Study Partnership 2016).

Specifically, RCMS and BPHS do not provide a clear funding stream and sufficient coverage for 'grassroots' medical care facilities. In the new system, village doctors' roles have been transformed from medical doctors to non-state-employed public health workers with most of their time devoted to the implementation of 14 national basic healthcare initiatives, including health records for villagers, maternity and newborn care, vaccination, senior care and chronic and mental illness monitoring. While the Chinese central government stated that village doctors would receive at least 40 per cent of the national public health expenditures, it did not provide thorough guidelines for regulating how the funding should be distributed at the county level. Subsequently, county HFPCs and township clinics began utilising various institutional loopholes to reduce the portion of public health funding transferred to village clinics, while simultaneously requiring village doctors to pay for supplementary services such as medical waste management and disposal (Xin and Liu 2018). In our field sites, village doctors' income consisted only of a stipend of 500 RMB[8] per month and an additional 1,000 RMB per month on average from the implementation of public health services, which had to be split in villages with more than one village doctor. The lack of funding caused village doctors to be unwilling and unable financially to treat medical waste out of pocket, as one doctor in a focus group meeting told us:

> It has become harder and harder to stay in this profession. We are no longer doctors recognized by the administrative apparatus, and we lost our status as state-employed workers (*bian zhi nei*). Why should we pay for something that ought to be included in the government's budget [the treatment of medical waste] while the county and townships found every excuse not to pay for our labor [public services].

In addition, county hospitals and township clinics encroached dramatically on the medical functions previous performed by village doctors. After the State Council promulgated the 2011 *National Guidelines of Strengthening the Profession of Village Doctors* ('National Guideline'), the village doctors were no longer allowed to provide intravenous medication or prescribe medication not included on the National Essential Medicine List, which contained only the most basic drugs available in the market. Studies have shown that after the implementation of the 2011 National Guidelines, 98.2 per cent of village doctors suffered reduced income with an average drop of 50.3 per cent, while more than 89.81 per cent of village doctors lost 20 per cent of their annual income. Worse, 72.5 per cent of the rural residents interviewed opted not to use village clinics for their healthcare needs because of the limited prescription drugs available there (PhiRDA 2012). In other words, under the new system, services provided by village clinics have no longer been able to fulfil the actual medical needs of the villagers, who often have limited resources to travel to county and township-level medical facilities for non-life-threatening illnesses (Yang 2012). To survive, some of the village doctors we interviewed admitted that they started to provide intravenous medication illicitly and prescription drugs outside of the government approved list. One village doctor admitted:

> We used to be the backbone of grassroots governance in our villages, and we were widely respected in the communities. After 2011, some villagers started to view us as swindlers who took advantage of them because we had to charge more for the off-list medications and injections than the fees publicized from RCMS that only covers drugs from the essential list. The economic reality forced me to break the law and prevented me from recording all the [medical] waste generated because we were not supposed to provide the services.

Worse still, the institutional constraints imposed on rural clinics created the space for the proliferation of 'black-market clinics'. According to our informants, black market clinics were often run by outsiders, who would visit remote villages periodically to provide intravenous treatment and prescription drugs at a low cost, before moving to neighbouring counties. Aside from concerns related to the quality of medical care and the sources of prescriptions, the illegal practices conducted by village doctors and black-market clinics created unregistered medical waste that caused profound environmental health threats in rural areas. As asserted by a township-level official:

> Since the unlawful practices of black clinics do not exist on paper, the syringes and transfusion bags they produce do not exist in our records. We are not responsible and are helpless to enforce relevant regulations in remote areas.

Fragmented enforcement and the collapse of rural environmental governance

There was limited supervision on how village doctors managed medical waste because there was little enforcement of the regulatory framework at the village level. The 2003 law and subsequent national guidelines delegated regulation enforcement to EPBs and

HFPCs at the prefectural and county levels. This created jurisdictional ambiguity that generated significant institutional barriers in regulation enforcement in the countryside. The EPBs cannot interfere with waste management within healthcare facilities, while the HFPCs lack the resources and expertise to investigate pollution caused by the haphazard dumping of hazardous waste. Medical waste from village clinics thus became unsupervised because the local EPBs had no authority over the daily operation of the clinics, and local HFPCs lack the governing capacity to prevent dumping in remote areas. Furthermore, though township clinics and county hospitals were now required by law to hire licensed contractors to transport medical waste to centralised waste treatment facilities in the prefectural city, according to the provincial law, prefecture EPBs were the only governing authority that could license private contractors and prefectural and county-level HFPCs were excluded from the evaluation of contractor qualifications. Because the county-level HFPCs could not serve as legal entities to sign contracts with private operators, they could not appropriate adequate budgets for medical waste treatment. Instead, township clinics had to sign individual agreements with private contractors without acknowledgment from the supervising administrative apparatus and, subsequently, township clinics had to produce their own funding to pay for the services. The institutional barriers created ample space for the falsification of management records at the village and township levels and limited stakeholder involvement in improving system-wide accountability. Our informants stated that, before 2016, the medical waste collected from the township clinics was frequently burned on the dry riverbed by the licensed contractors without any classification of the waste or proper treatment of the residues.

The county and township government's inability to enforce medical waste regulations to address illegal dumping reflects the dissolution of bottom-up oversight in environmental governance. According to a recent study covering five provinces in China, less than 30 per cent of the rural villages surveyed have collection services for general waste, while less than 10 per cent implement classification of hazardous or recycled waste (Wang et al. 2016). In the surveys and interviews we held in rural China, villagers reported that they routinely discarded dangerous agricultural waste and general waste into ravines and watersheds, even while acknowledging the environmental health threats that untreated waste creates in their drinking water. The village and township officials we interviewed implemented weak oversight of waste management because there were no binding targets related to environmental protection in their annual job performance evaluations. Consequently, the village and township officials had no incentive to organise bottom-up community action to promote the collection of hazardous waste or protect water sources. As described by one village secretary,

> The region is a nationally designated poverty area, and we [grassroots state agents] are already overburdened with various poverty alleviation and infrastructure building tasks. The best we can do about waste is to ask folks who are on public assistance to clean the major thoroughfare every month. We have no responsibility or resources to enforce the waste management laws at all.

The village officials we interviewed further stated that there was no point in implementing waste management regulations before the upper-level government invests in infrastructure and provides funding to promote classification and storage. In our field sites, the lack of environmental binding targets in the job performance review of village and township bureaucrats led to a lack of accountability in regulation enforcement on the ground. Grassroots state agents would rather devote their limited resources to projects that were designed to generate economic growth or promote social stability because of the pressure they receive from their supervisors. The villagers in our field sites were excluded from participating in grassroots environmental governance in a political system that provided little space for public deliberation policy implementation. Instead, the village and township officials we interviewed regarded the villagers as uneducated and stated repeatedly that bottom-up community actions to promote environmental protection were unfeasible because the villagers had no awareness of the environmental impacts of their acts and omissions. The enforcement of medical waste regulation in our field sites became ineffective and fragmented due to the lack of institutional incentives in the top-down administrative system and no public oversight over the pollution caused by medical and hazardous wastes.

Conclusion: green criminology and waste crimes in rural China

Our case study demonstrates the complex and interconnected components of a system that mismanages medical waste and that is failing to address associated environmental and social harms. Though China's Supreme People's Court criminalised waste dumping in 2016, the enforcement of medical waste laws has still relied on administrative penalties rather than criminal law. Consequently, the inaction of the prefecture and county EPBs and HFPCs constitutes a crime of omission that has caused the mismanagement of medical waste. The negligence of local state agents, the revenue concerns of village and township clinics, and the unlawful practices of licensed waste contractors and black-market clinic operators have all played a part in the perpetration of environmental offenses at the local level. Though we did not observe the transference and dumping of urban medical waste due to the field sites' remote locations, the inaction of the prefecture and county EPBs and HFPCs generated notable environmental health hazards in the underprivileged rural population, whose victimisation was further reinforced by the collapse of grassroots environmental governance in the local community. The waste crime in our case study does not fit entirely into the organised crime conceptualisation. Rather than the profit motives of 'an informal organisation of people working together with the sole purpose of committing crimes' (Bisschop and Huisman 2018), the criminality was structured by the interrelations of state agents, village doctors and illicit entrepreneurs operating at multiple levels of the unitary bureaucracy of the authoritarian state. As such, we need to examine critically the authoritarian environmental governance model, which shapes the cultural, economic and political contexts of the implementation gap in the enforcement of medical waste regulation in rural China.

The formulation and implementation of environmental policies in China are deeply affected by the unique dilemma faced by the authoritarian state. On the one hand, to maintain its legitimacy, the central government must provide swift policy responses to the rapid ecological deterioration caused by the expansion of global capitalism. On the other hand, China's geographical scale and its profound regional variations in climate, cultures, ecology and levels of economic development make environmental governance immensely complicated so that no one-size-fits-all approach exists. Policy formulation thus becomes a mostly non-participatory process, with decision-making authority concentrated on selected regulatory agencies in the central government, while implementation processes become highly dispersed and uneven. To bypass the time-consuming process of building consensus among various stakeholders located in different geographical regions, policymakers in the central government often create a degree of ambiguity in the legal language used in national regulations so that local governments can adapt enforcement to local conditions. As a result, environmental regulations often lack clear supplementary administrative instruments to standardise implementation procedures and supervision methods and therefore lack adequate measurement of intended outcomes (Ran 2017). In addition, the central government often splits enforcement between ministries and agencies that serve opposing functions to balance the interests of central ministries. This fragmented approach towards policy formulation and implementation may cause conflicting objectives for lower-level governments and generate institutional barriers during the implementation process.

The ambiguity embedded in China's top-down environmental governance model has contributed directly to two notable implementation gaps in rural medical waste regulation in China. First, though national-level regulations were promulgated in 2003 and 2004, it has taken over a decade for most provinces to develop the supplementary provincial regulations that establish the evaluation standards of policy outcomes. In our case study, the provincial government regulation has provided no clear funding streams for medical waste treatment because it has limited control over resource allocation of national-level RCMS and BPHS, which, in turn, has affected how the budgets for medical waste treatment were allocated at the county, township and village levels. Second, regulation enforcement has been divided between the domains of two regulatory agencies, and neither the local EPBs nor HFPCs have had the resources and expertise to cover the entire waste treatment and disposal process at the township level and below. Township and village officials have lacked the political clout to enforce compliance against township clinics because county-level HFPCs directly govern the clinics. These implementation gaps have eventually resulted in conflicts of interest among different regulatory parties in the bureaucracy and have caused grassroots state agents to view medical waste regulations as mostly unenforceable.

Moreover, because of the 1994 tax reform, rural governance in China's hinterland regions has had to deal with a significantly reduced tax base and revenues, resulting in limited state capacity to enforce environmental regulations (Mao 2018). As a result, county governments have become more and more dependent on fiscal transfer funds from the central government that is tied to binding targets in centrally controlled environmental projects (Van Rooij et al. 2017). Meeting these binding targets has become essential to the fiscal solvency of local governments, and, consequently, local governments have structured the criteria of state employee performance evaluation to prioritise the binding targets imposed by higher-level governments over the enforcement of the existing regulations that may generate long-term protection for the environment (Mao and Zhang 2018). The binding targets have created a crowding-out effect on state capacity in rural governance, and, in effect, have reinforced existing structural inequality in China, as poor counties have limited resources to complete basic governing functions that have not been listed as the binding targets in centralised programmes. The top-down policy implementation model of the fragmented bureaucracy, therefore, incentivises lower-level bureaucrats to identify with the political interests of their supervisors instead of serving the needs of their communities (Eaton and Kostka 2014). The medical waste and public health regulations failed to be implemented correctly in our field sites because adequate enforcement required the coordination of resources and personnel among multiple agencies across jurisdictions and administrative levels but would bring little job performance merits to the grassroots bureaucrats involved. From this perspective, the environmental victimisation experienced by the rural communities in our case study is no longer just the result of discrete episodes of environmental offenses conducted by networks of criminal actors; instead, the public health and environmental hazards of untreated hazardous medical waste are symptoms of a more systematic form of deviance embedded within the non-participatory policy formulation and the top-down implementation processes of authoritarian environmentalism. The crimes of omission by the 'grassroots' state bureaucrats, the falsification of waste disposal records by the village doctors and township clinic chiefs, the unlawful dumping of medical waste by the operators of black-market clinics and private waste contractors, and the utilisation of illicit healthcare services by the underserved rural community are intricately linked in the 'everyday acts of ecocide', and these social actors were all victimised by a policy context structured by the existing patterns of social stratification and the asymmetries in China's urban-rural divide (see Agnew this volume, Chapter 2; South 2014).

This chapter has provided a systematic analysis of the underlying causes of waste crime in an illiberal policy context. Our study has found that the changes in village and township healthcare institutions, the ambiguity in national environmental regulations, the confusion over jurisdictions within the regulatory apparatus, and the collapse of grassroots environmental governance have all contributed to the under-enforcement of medical waste regulations in rural northwestern China. The deficiencies in the top-down implementation process have exacerbated existing social inequality in resources and risk allocation, which has formed the political, social and economic background of environmental victimisation in rural China. From a green criminological perspective, the lack of bottom-up participation to ensure accountability in regulation enforcement and legitimacy in environmental governance will be the quintessential intergenerational challenge to authoritarian environmentalism. Accordingly, this chapter has expanded green criminology's approach to waste crimes by showing how the varied interests of a fragmented bureaucracy may become criminogenic as they generate institutional barriers to environmental regulation enforcement and create the structural conditions of environmental harm. The study thus builds on research by Bisschop (2012, 2016), Ruggiero and South (2010, 2013) and South (2016) and demonstrates how the authoritarian state's responses to the consequences of global toxic capitalism have shaped the interrelations of legal and illegal actors that have enabled the violations of medical waste regulations at the individual, organisational and institutional levels of analysis. This chapter, therefore, suggests that to study environmental offenses in China, green criminologists must examine how the institutional practices of the fragmented bureaucracy shape the political, social and economic contexts that have structured the complexity of environmental regulation enforcement in the illiberal society.

Notes

1 This chapter uses the term 'medical waste' instead of 'healthcare waste' because of the former term's prevalence in legal and academic publications in China.

2 In March 2018, the People's Congress changed the title of the 'Ministry of Health' to the 'National Health Commission'.

3 In March 2018, the People's Congress changed the title of the 'Ministry of Environmental Protection' to the 'Ministry of Ecology & Environment'.

4 The bureaucratic structure in China from top to bottom is as follows: national government—provincial governments—prefectural cities—counties—townships—administrative villages—natural villages.

5 The great majority of men under the age of 55 in our field villages were migrant workers who worked in coastal China or provincial capitals in northwestern China. The men would return to their villages only once per year during the Spring Festival, which prevented them from participating in our interviews and intervention programmes.

6 More specifically, we conducted participatory action research from May 2017 to June 2018 by organising groups of village women to undertake environmental assessment, promote environmental education and implement a bottom-up waste management programme.

7 The village clinics in our field sites were small operations and were usually run by one village doctor without support staff.

8 1 RMB roughly equals to $0.15 USD.

References

Ali, M., Wang, W., Chaudhry, N. and Geng, Y. 2017. 'Hospital waste management in developing countries: A mini review,' *Waste Management & Research*, 35(6): 581–592.

Beeson, M. 2010: 'The coming of environmental authoritarianism,' *Environmental Politics*, 19(2): 276–294.

Bisschop, L. 2012. 'Is it all going to waste? Illegal transports of e-waste in a European trade hub,' *Crime, Law and Social Change*, 58(3): 221–249.

Bisschop, L. 2016. 'How E-Waste challenges environmental governance,' in T. Wyatt (ed.) *Hazardous Waste and Pollution: Detecting and Preventing Green Crimes*, pp. 27–44. Switzerland: Springer.

Bisschop, L. and Huisman, W. 2018. 'Waste crime from three criminological perspectives. Implications for crime control and harm prevention,' in T. Spapens, R. White, D. Uhm and W. Huisman (eds.) *Green Crimes and Dirty Money*, pp. 148–176. London and New York: Routledge.

Caniato, M., Tudor, T. and Vaccari, M. 2015. 'International governance structures for health-care waste management: A systematic review of scientific literature,' *Journal of Environmental Management*, 153: 93–107.

Chai, H. 2017. 'Hu nan shou li fei fa chu zhi yi liao fei wu an bei hou: yi liao la ji chan ye lian [Behind the first case of illegal disposal of medical waste in Hunan: medical waste industry chain],' *Nan Fang Zhou Mo*. Available at www.infzm.com/content/127395 In Chinese.

China Joint Study Partnership. 2016. 'Deepening Health Reform in China: Building High-Quality and Value-Based Service Delivery.' Available at https://openknowledge.worldbank.org/bitstream/handle/10986/24720/HealthReformInChina.pdf?sequence=6.

Eaton, S., and Kostka, G. 2014. 'Authoritarian environmentalism undermined? Local leaders' time horizons and environmental policy implementation in China,' *The China Quarterly*, 218: 359–380.

Gai, R., Kuroiwa, C., Xu, L., Wang, X., Zhang, Y., Li, H., Zhou, C., He, J. and Tang, W. 2009. 'Hospital medical waste management in Shandong Province, China,' *Waste Management & Research*, 27(4): 336–342.

Gibbs, C., McGarrell, E. F. and Axelrod, M. 2010. 'Transnational white-collar crime and risk: Lessons from the global trade in electronic waste,' *Criminology & Public Policy*, 9(3): 543–560.

Gibbs, C., McGarrell, E. F., Axelrod, M., and Rivers III, L. 2011. 'Conservation criminology and the global trade in electronic waste: Applying a multi-disciplinary research framework,' *International Journal of Comparative and Applied Criminal Justice*, 35(4): 269–291.

Gilley, B. 2012. 'Authoritarian environmentalism and China's response to climate change,' *Environmental Politics*, 21(2): 287–307.

Groombridge, N. 2013. 'Matter all over the place: Litter, criminology and criminal justice,' in N. South and A. Brisman (eds.) *Routledge International Handbook of Green Criminology*, pp. 394–408. London: Routledge.

Komilis, D. P. 2016. 'Issues on medical waste management research,' *Waste Management*, 48: 1–2.

Kostka, G. 2017. 'China's local environmental politics,' in E. Sternfeld (ed.) *Routledge Handbook of Environmental Policy in China*, pp. 55–71. London and New York: Routledge.

Kostka, G., and Mol, A. P. J. 2013. 'Implementation and participation in China's local environmental politics: Challenges and innovations,' *Journal of Environmental Policy & Planning*, 15(1): 3–16.

Kostka, G., and Nahm, J. 2017. 'Central–local relations: Recentralization and environmental governance in china,' *The China Quarterly*, 231: 567–582.

Li, M., Qiu, M., Zhen, L., Zhong, F. and Wu, H. 2013. 'Xiao gan shi 40 suo yi yuan yi liao fei wu guan li xian Zhuang diao cha fen xi [Investigation and analysis of current situation of medical waste management in 40 hospitals in Xiaogan City],' *Hu Li Guan Li Za Zhi*, 7: 483–484. In Chinese.

Lieberthal, K., and Oksenberg, M. 1988. *Policy making in China: leaders, structures, and processes*, Princeton, NJ: Princeton University Press.

Liu, S. 2018. '2018 nian Zhong guo yi liao fei qi wu chu li hang ye xian Zhuang fen xi, hang ye wei lai fa zhan xu yao gui fan hua [Analysis of the current situation of China's medical waste treatment industry in 2018],' *Qian Zhan Yan Jiu Yuan*. Available at https://bg.qianzhan.com/report/detail/459/180129-ca8b0738.html. In Chinese.

Lynch, M. J., Stretesky, P. B. and Long, M. A. 2015. 'Environmental justice: A criminological perspective,' *Environmental Research Letters*, 10(8): 085008.

Ma, J., Lu, M. and Quan, H. 2008. 'From a national, centrally planned health system to a system based on the market: lessons from China,' *Health affairs*, 27(4): 937–948.

Mao, K. 2018. 'The treadmill of taxation: Desertification and organizational state deviance in Minqin Oasis, China,' *Critical Criminology: An International Journal*, 26(2): 271–288.

Mao, K., and Zhang, Q. 2018. 'Dilemmas of state-led environmental conservation in China: Environmental target enforcement and public participation in Minqin County,' *Society & Natural Resources*, 31 (5): 615–631.

Mao, Z. 2011. 'Waste Mismanagement: China's Struggle with Medical Trash,' *China Environment Forum*. July 11. Available at www.wilsoncenter.org/publication/waste-mismanagement-chinas-struggle-medical-trash.

Marks, D. 2010. 'China's climate change policy process: Improved but still weak and fragmented,' *Journal of Contemporary China*, 19(67): 971–986.

Mohai, P. and Saha, R. 2015. 'Which came first, people or pollution? Assessing the disparate siting and post-siting demographic change hypotheses of environmental injustice,' *Environmental Research Letters*, 10(11): 115008.

Ni, S. 2017. 'Shi ping: du jue yi liao la ji dao mai ying cong yi yuan zhuo shou [Commentary: Stopping medical waste reselling should start with the hospital],' *Sciencenet*. Available at http://news.sciencenet.cn/htmlnews/2017/6/379229.shtm. In Chinese.

Nie, L. and Wu, H. 2016. 'Investigation and analysis of rural medical waste management,' *Journal of Environmental Protection*, 7(1): 93–98.

Nie, L., Qiao, Z. and Wu, H. 2014. 'Medical waste management in China: A case study of Xinxiang,' *Journal of Environmental Protection*, 5(10): 803–810.

PhiRDA. 2012. 'Xin yi gai de yang guang he shi zhao dao xiang cun yi sheng shen shang [*The sun of the new medical reform will shine on the village doctor*].' Available at www.phirda.com/artilce_12516.html?cId=4. In Chinese.

Qin, T., and Zhang, M. 2017. 'Development of China's environmental legislation,' in E. Sternfeld (ed.) *Routledge Handbook of Environmental Policy in China*, pp. 17–30. London and New York: Routledge.

Ran, R. 2013. 'Perverse incentive structure and policy implementation gap in China's local environmental politics,' *Journal of Environmental Policy & Planning*, 15(1): 17–39.

Ran, R. 2017. 'Understanding blame politics in China's decentralized system of environmental governance: Actors, strategies and context,' *The China Quarterly*, 234: 634–661.

Rothe, D. L. 2010. 'Global E-waste trade: The need for formal regulation and accountability beyond the organization,' *Criminology and Public Policy*, 9(3): 561–567.

Ruggiero, V. and South, N. 2010. 'Green criminology and dirty collar crime,' *Critical Criminology: An International Journal*, 18(4): 251–262.

Ruggiero, V. and South, N. 2013. 'Green criminology and crimes of the economy: Theory, research and praxis,' *Critical Criminology: An International Journal*, 21(3): 359–373.

Shuai, C., Su, X., Shi, W. and Liu, L. 2017. '140 duo dun yi liao la ji liu ru shi chang [More than 140 tons of medical waste have entered the market],' *Outlook Weekly*, 24: June 11. In Chinese.

Smith, G. 2010. 'The hollow state: Rural governance in China,' *The China Quarterly*, 203: 601–618.

Snider, L. 2010. 'Framing E-Waste regulation: The obfuscating role of power,' *Criminology and Public Policy*, 9(3): 569–577.

South, N. 1998. 'A green field for criminology: A proposal for a perspective,' *Theoretical Criminology*, 2(2): 211–233.

South, N. 2014. 'Green criminology: Reflections, connections, horizons,' *International Journal for Crime, Justice and Social Democracy*, 3(2): 5–20.

South, N. 2016. 'Green criminology and brown crime: Despoliation, disposal and de-manufacturing in global resource industries,' in T. Wyatt (ed.) *Hazardous Waste and Pollution: Detecting and Preventing Green Crimes*, pp. 11–26. Switzerland: Springer.

South, N. and Brisman, A. 2013. 'The planned obsolescence of planet earth? How green criminology can help us learn from experience and contribute to our future,' in N. South and A. Brisman (eds.) *Routledge International Handbook of Green Criminology*, pp. 409–417. New York: Routledge.

Sun, N., Ren, Z., Sun, T., Zhu, W. and Si, S. 2017. 'Idea and countermeasures of comprehensive management on medical waste in the 13th five year period,' *Chinese Journal of Environmental Management*, 9(3): 78–82.

The Supreme People's Procuratorate of the People's Republic of China. 2016. 'Interpretation of Several Issues Concerning the Application of Law in Handling Criminal Cases of Environmental Pollution,' *Jiancha Daily*. Available at www.spp.gov.cn/zdgz/201612/t20161227_176817.shtml. In Chinese.

Van Erp, J. and Huisman, W. 2010. 'Smart regulation and enforcement of illegal disposal of electronic waste,' *Criminology & Public Policy*, 9(3): 579–590.

Van Rooij, B., Zhu, Q., Li, N., Wang, Q. and Zhang, X. 2017. 'Pollution law enforcement in China: Understanding national and regional variation,' in E. Sternfeld (ed.) *Routledge Handbook of Environmental Policy in China*, pp. 193–207. London and New York: Routledge.

Wang, A., Gao, Q., Shi, Y., Liu, C. and Zhang, L. 2016. 'Nong cun la ji guan li fu wu xian Zhuang ji ying xiang yin su yan jiu——ji yu 5 sheng 101 ge cun de shi zheng fen xi [The Situation of rural solid waste management and determination: Empirical analysis based on field surveys of 101 villages in 5 provinces],' *Issues in Agricultural Economy*, 4: 30-38+111. In Chinese.

Wei, C. 2016. 'Medical Waste Turned into Tableware, Toys,' *China Daily*, 21 December. Available at www.chinadaily.com.cn/china/2016-12/21/content_27728932.htm.

White, R. 2008a. 'Toxic cities: Globalizing the problem of waste,' *Social Justice*, 35(3): 107–119.

White, R. 2008b. *Crimes against Nature: Environmental Criminology and Ecological Justice*, London: Willan.

White, R. and Heckenberg, D. 2014. *Green Criminology: An Introduction to the Study of Environmental Harm*. Abingdon, Oxon, UK:: Routledge.

Windfeld, E. S. and Brooks, M. S. L. 2015. 'Medical waste management – A review,' *Journal of Environmental Management*, 163: 98–108.

World Health Organization. 2018. 'Health-care waste.' Available at www.who.int/news-room/fact-sheets/detail/health-care-waste.

Xin, L. 2016. 'Dai xue yi liao la ji zuo cheng can ju zai zhong guo da lu liu tong [Bloody medical waste made into tableware circulating in mainland China],' *Radio Free Asia*. Available at www.rfa.org/mandarin/yataibaodao/huanjing/xl2-04222016113355.html.

Xin, Y. and Liu, H. 2018. 'Cun yi liu he jie? Ji ceng gong wei bu zhu kan chang shi hu tu zhang, shou ru xia jiang cheng qun ti kun rao [How to solve the loss of village doctors? The grassroots public health subsidy and the income declines lead to a group trouble],' *Cai Jing*, March 25. Available at http://yuanchuang.caijing.com.cn/2018/0325/4424307.shtml. In Chinese.

Yan, F. 2015. 'Nong cun yi liao fei qi wu guan li gui fan [Rural medical waste management needs to be regulated],' *Zhong Guo Shen Ji Bao*, June 15, p. 6. In Chinese.

Yang, C., Xia, X. and Jia, X. 2018. 'People's Network unannounced visits to courier bags production: medical and chemical wastes as the source,' *Ren Min Wang*. Available at http://news.sina.com.cn/s/sd/2018-01-23/doc-ifyquixe6668352.shtml. In Chinese.

Yang, R. 2012. 'Cun yi liu shi diao cha: Yao pin ling cha jia shi hou shou ru rui jian [Village medical loss survey: income sharply declines after the implementation of zero price difference policy for medicine],' *Mei Jing Wang*. Available at www.nbd.com.cn/articles/2012-06-12/660144.html. In Chinese.

Yesilyurt, H., Nayır, T. and Akbaba, M. 2015. 'Medical waste management in Turkey and in the world,' *Turkish Journal of Occupational/Environmental Medicine and Safety*, 2(2): 22–34.

Zhang, H., Zhang, Y., Wang, Y., Yang, Y., Zhang, J., Wang, Y. and Wang, J. 2013. 'Investigation of medical waste management in gansu province, China,' *Waste Management & Research*, 31(6): 655–659.

Zhang, H., Zhang, Y., Wang, Y., Zhou, Y. and Zhang, J. 2009. 'Nong cun di qu yi liao fei qi wu chu li xian Zhuang de diao cha fen xi [Investigation and analysis on the status quo of medical waste treatment in rural areas],' *Chinese Journal of Nosocomiology*, 21: 2887–2888. In Chinese.

Zhang, L., He, G., and Mol, A. P. 2015. 'China's new environmental protection law: A game changer?,' *Environmental Development*, 13: 1–3.

Zhang, L., Mol, A. P. and Sonnenfeld, D. A. 2007. 'The interpretation of ecological modernization in China,' *Environmental Politics*, 16(4): 659–668.

Zhu, Q. 2017. 'The current situation of medical pollution is alarming'. *Qian Zhan Yan Jiu Yuan*. Available at www.qianzhan.com/analyst/detail/220/170310-cc8381ee.html. In Chinese.

Part IV

Relationships in green criminology

Environment and economy

22

E-waste in the twilight zone between crime and survival

Wim van Herk and Lieselot Bisschop

Introduction

The transport of discarded—non-functioning or outdated—laptops, refrigerators, televisions sets and other electronics—also known as 'e-waste'—from industrialised countries to developing countries has become common practice in the last decades (Baldé, Wang, Kuehr and Huisman 2015; Ferrell, this volume, Chapter 37). Discarded but reusable electronics are an important market share of the reusable electronics sold on the global second-hand market (Miller, Gregory, Duan, Kirchain and Linnel 2012). Many other discarded electronics are non-reusable, however; they never make it to the second-hand market and are disassembled immediately for recovery of their raw materials. The reusable share can be traded legally between OECD (Organization for Economic Cooperation and Development) and non-OECD countries, but the non-reusable share is traded illegally as 'second hand goods'. The dismantling of this trafficked e-waste happens in precarious circumstances, with toxins leaking into the air, soil and water, causing harm to the environment and human health (Bisschop 2014b; Brigden, Labunska, Santillo and Johnston 2008). Moreover, the dismantling is often performed by vulnerable groups (e.g., poor, minors, religious minorities), who are not provided with the proper means to protect themselves from the toxins that are released, such as when burning the plastic casings of devices to recover the valuable components (mainly precious metals) (Eidgenössische Materialprüfungs- und Forschungsanstalt (EMPA) 2009; Sepúlveda et al. 2010).

Several non-governmental organisations (NGOs) have targeted campaigns to producers, consumers and traders of (discarded) electronics to raise awareness about the social and environmental effects of trading and crudely dismantling these electronics (Brigden et al. 2008; Kuper and Hojsik 2008). E-waste has also been on the radar of policy makers, who consider it a 'hazardous waste' due to the fact that e-waste is a mixed waste that contains hazardous components, such as cooling gases, flame-retardants, lead and mercury. Accordingly, the e-waste trade is regulated strictly and is dealt with in increasingly punitive ways, although the actual implementation of e-waste trade legislation presents several challenges (Bisschop 2014a). Aside from the policy and NGO attention to the topic, e-waste dumping and trafficking has been a subject of study by green criminologists, as well as by criminologists interested in corporate crime, organised crime and regulation more generally (Brisman and South 2013b, 2018; Melvin and Mcgarrell 2009; van Erp and Huisman 2010).

This chapter builds on these earlier publications while also drawing from the findings of two empirical studies about e-waste. One of these studies focusses on illegal trade in e-waste between the port of Antwerp, Belgium and Accra, Ghana (Bisschop 2012, 2013; Bisschop 2015). A second study focusses on data from e-waste traders in Hong Kong (Van Herk 2016). This chapter includes quotes from respondents referred to by mentioning their function (trader, former trader, customs officer, director of waste facility, inhabitant) and a number. By comparing e-waste trafficking in these two different locations, we aim to illustrate, on the one hand, the importance of paying attention to locality when considering the global dimensions of the e-waste trade, and, on the other hand, to economic, political and socio-cultural factors that influence the definitional processes, social organisation and governance of e-waste. This chapter explores the wide range of characteristics of e-waste and its effects and uses, and contemplates the implications for control and prevention policy.

We begin this chapter by examining current international and European legislation for e-waste. This includes a discussion of the definitional challenges that are inherent to it. Next, we investigate the growing (informal) e-waste economy and illustrate the harm connected to the trafficking and informal recycling of e-waste. From here, we highlight the social organisation of the trafficking and informal recycling of e-waste by focussing on the roles played by formal as well as informal actors in the e-waste economy. This allows us to reflect, in the final section, about the complexities in implementing governance policy about e-waste and about the relevance of this topic for the field of green criminology.

Current legislation regarding the trade of e-waste

Many international governmental organisations, such as the Organization for Economic Cooperation and Development (OECD), the United Nations Environmental Programme (UNEP), the World Bank and the World Customs Organization (WCO), have developed policies pertaining to (hazardous) waste management. Waste management includes the trade in, treatment of, and disposal of discarded products originating from household or industrial processes. The most important piece of legislation on waste trade is the 1989 *Basel Convention on the Control of Transboundary Movements of Hazardous Wastes and Their Disposal* (the 'Basel Convention'). The Basel Convention intended to counter the increased international trade in (hazardous) waste, which started after the tightening of the waste treatment legislation in industrialised countries that led to skyrocketing prices for domestic treatment and disposal (Clapp 2001; Pellow 2007).

The Basel Convention was prescient insofar as it has since demonstrated its applicability to contemporary, as well as future, waste-related issues, such as the increased generation of electronic waste. The Basel Convention requires nations to ensure proper disposal of waste and to 'introduce appropriate national/domestic legislation to prevent and punish illegal traffic' (1989: 17). It defines 'illegal waste trade' as transboundary movements of waste, whereby the countries involved have not been notified or have not consented in writing—or have done so based on false information—or when the waste is deliberately disposed of 'in contravention of this Convention and of general principles of international law' (1989: 11–16). As is the case for all multilateral agreements, the Basel Convention requires implementation and operationalisation on regional and national levels. In this section, we focus on the definitional challenges that are inherent to the Basel Convention and the European Union's legislation on hazardous waste trade. The challenges that come with the actual implementation of waste trade policies will be discussed later in this chapter.

The Basel Convention leaves room for interpretation as to how nations should adhere to its requirements; section 4, General Obligations 7 (b), in particular, has been interpreted differently. Under this provision, each party shall:

> [r]equire that hazardous wastes and other wastes that are to be the subject of a transboundary movement be packaged, labelled, and transported in conformity with generally accepted and recognized international rules and standards in the field of packaging, labelling, and transport, and that due account is taken of relevant internationally recognized practices.
>
> *(1989: 11)*

In comparison, the European Union's *Directive on Waste Electrical and Electronic Equipment* (WEEE Directive) states explicitly that shipments of used EEE (second-hand electronic equipment) can actually contain or consist completely of e-waste. Consequently, the WEEE Directive applies 'minimum requirements' for shipments in order to 'avoid unwanted shipments of non-functional EEE to developing countries' (WEEE Directive, page 8, paragraph 15). These requirements reflect those found in the Basel Convention, but impose the additional requirement of demonstrating proof of testing of equipment (functionality) and ensuring correct packaging so as not to destroy the goods and thereby prevent them from becoming e-waste in transport. By being able to define shipments of EEE as possible e-waste, the WEEE Directive provides a better basis for crime control by its member states than the Basel Convention. The WEEE Directive leaves it to the member states, however, to develop specific regulations or guidelines as to what constitutes appropriate packaging, labelling and transportation. Should a washing machine be shrink- or bubble-wrapped or is it sturdy enough on its own? How high can a stack of computers be for it to pose a risk and be considered 'inadequately transported?' Should TVs have a cable attached to them or can those be cut? Technically, without a cable, the TVs are not functional, but shippers argue that cutting the cables facilitates transportation and is easily fixed at the destination to render it functional. Do we allow trucks or vans on roll-on/roll-off ships to be packed with used electronics or should those be shipped in containers? Loading trucks or vans with goods is prohibited in Rotterdam and (used to be) allowed in Antwerp—two ports a mere 100 kilometres removed from each other but located in different countries and jurisdictions. These are just some of the questions that arise when shipments of e-waste or second-hand electronics are inspected and that are not clearly answered by the legal guidelines. Because the law leaves room for interpretation, some member states implement stricter controls on e-waste trafficking, while others use more flexible operational procedures and strategies to monitor waste shipments. As a consequence of this divergence in interpretations, participants in the trade can effectively 'shop jurisdictions' and legally exploit these regulatory asymmetries (Passas 1999). Moreover, countries and ports sometimes see and experience a reputation for being more or less lenient as a competitive advantage (Eski 2011; Parola and Coppola 2011).

The Basel Convention aims to reduce the generation of hazardous waste, promotes environmentally sound waste management and restricts transboundary movements of hazardous waste unless it happens in line with principles of environmentally sound management (Basel Action Network (BAN) 2011 quoted in Pickren 2014). The Basel Convention devotes little attention to crime control and instead favours the regulation of legal types of waste trade. In an attempt to overcome some of the loopholes of the Basel Convention, the 1994 Basel Ban (also known as Decision III/1) was developed to amend the Basel Convention and impose a ban on the export of hazardous waste intended for disposal, recovery, or recycling from Annex VII countries (EU, OECD and Lichtenstein) to non-Annex VII countries. This amendment divided the world in two blocks: developed versus developing countries (Lepawsky 2015). Some countries wanted to keep trading in recyclables and in organic waste, whereas others wanted a total ban on all waste imports and exports. As a result, the 1994 Basel Ban has not been signed by enough countries for it to enter into force, which means we fall back on the requirements of the Basel Convention. This distinction between 'developing' and 'developed' countries is also rather problematic in the context of waste trade. Lepawsky (2015) even refers to the assumptions about origins and destinations of waste as specified in the 1994 Basel Ban as geographical imaginaries because it misconceptualises the transnational trade in (hazardous) waste as one primarily from the 'West to the rest'. Similar geographical imaginaries can be found in the EU's WEEE Directive because it groups countries as 'developed' or 'developing' without recognising the significant differences within those groups of countries and without recognition of the importance of regional trade in (hazardous) waste.

The distinction between the Global North and Global South, 'developed' and 'developing' countries, or 'West to the rest', also applies to a certain extent to academic research on hazardous waste trade. Although many accounts of hazardous waste trafficking and dumping are rightfully drawing attention to the injustices and the externalisation of harm by industrialised nations, the picture is more complex. It requires contextualisation of the scale of waste trade from OECD to non-OECD countries, as well as within regions of the world. It also requires investigation about what share of trafficked e-waste actually ends up dismantled in abysmal conditions or dumped in both OECD and non-OECD countries—an estimated 4 per cent of e-waste in developed countries is landfilled (Baldé, Forti, Gray, Kuehr and Stegmann 2017). It also relates to questions about who is involved in waste shipments and whether labelling the trade as 'environmental crime' is in the best interest of avoiding further harm to the environment. These and other questions are addressed in the following sections of this chapter based on case studies on the trade in and from Hong Kong and from Belgium to Ghana.

The legislation of e-waste trade has proven to be a complex and even controversial topic. The legal framework provides a basis but leaves room for interpretation. In other words, the criminalisation of e-waste trafficking is not clear-cut, similar to other types of (transnational) environmental crime (Halsey and White 1998).

The growing (informal) e-waste economy

This section discusses global estimates of illegal e-waste trade but also pays attention to the changes in consumption of electronics that influence the amount of discarded items. As for the geographical orientation, the focus is on the major regions and countries of origin, transit and destination. We consider both interregional (North–South) trafficking and the emerging intraregional trade among developing nations. Finally, a critical discussion on the difficulty of identifying waste streams and their volumes is provided.

In 2016, about 45 million metric tons of e-waste was generated globally (Baldé et al. 2017). The e-waste market is not only one of the fastest growing markets in scale but also in toxicity (CEC 2016; Pellow 2007). The growth rate for e-waste is between 3 and 5 per cent, which is up to three times that of other waste streams (Singh, Li and Zeng 2016). E-waste consists of both non-functional and unwanted 'old' electronic devices (Jaspers and Bisschop 2017) and has grown exponentially, keeping pace with the increased number of users of electronics and the internet globally and thus increased consumption, often of multiple devices (Brisman & South 2015). E-waste growth has also corresponded with the increasingly quick replacement cycles of computers, mobile phones and tablets driven by the marketing strategies of producers of electronics within the global free-market economy (Aladeojebi 2013). The sustainable use of resources in the development and production of new devices often takes a backseat when these would increase production costs (Singh et al. 2016).

Between 2010 and 2015, the volume of discarded electronics for (South) East Asia increased exponentially, driven by increased prosperity and totalling 18.2 metric tons in 2016 (Baldé et al. 2017; Khetriwal and Kuehr 2016). In comparison, Africa generated only 2.2 metric tons of e-waste but little is known about collection or trade. Studies show that, on a global scale, about 20 per cent of all e-waste is recycled and 74 per cent is unaccounted for, which means it was dumped, recycled, or traded in (or under) substandard circumstances (Baldé et al. 2017). It is important to emphasise that the above figures are estimates because most countries do not collect in any systematic fashion statistics on e-waste generation, recycling, or trade. In fact, e-waste has proven to be a problem that, both in scale and complexity, has outraced the policy attempts to contain it (Premalatha, Tabassum-Abbasi, Abbasi and Abbasi 2014, p. 1577).

As for our two research sites, Hong Kong and Accra, e-waste generation has both different and yet has strikingly similar dynamics. As a Special Administrative Region (SAR) of China, Hong Kong maintains separate administrative, judicial, and legal systems from the rest of the country, and has a more liberalised economy than that of the mainland (although this has been changing with China's economic reforms). Consumerism plays a major role in Hong Kong society, which means that goods may become 'waste' without becoming unusable. As a local citizen of Hong Kong remarked: 'People just want the newest gadgets. If you have iPhone 5 and someone at work shows up with the iPhone 6, you feel bad, you want to buy the new one too' (Inhabitant-1). Whereas Hong Kong is mostly an e-waste market with fairly new devices resulting from the formal electronics economy, Accra is mainly dealing with the largely informal consumption of imported and then refurbished equipment, which often has a very limited lifespan, as well as with the increased domestic consumption of new devices. As explained above, a portion of the imported electronics can be refurbished and reused, but many others are unsuitable for reuse and end up discarded (Prakash and Manhart 2010). Ghanaian importers have recognised the ease with which transhipments of e-waste, informal though not less organised than their formal counterparts, move between and through Africa's ports (Grant and Oteng-Ababio 2012). These developments have proven to be a significant challenge for effective governance of trading in e-waste.

Tracking the developments in the consumption of electronics, one finds not only large-scale consumption in the formal economy, but similar patterns of consumption among those participating in the informal economy or in the black market (Williams et al. 2013). In other words, consumerism takes place at all points on the economic spectrum, in which the buying and selling of discarded electronics not only feeds crude recycling operations, but also a growing market for second-hand goods in developing nations. This development is reflected in recent findings, which suggest that of those discarded goods arriving in West Africa or South East Asia, only a relatively small portion is actually destined for processing or recycling (between 9 per cent and 15 per cent) (Prakash and Manhart 2010; Schluep et al. 2011; Shinkuma and Huong 2009). The largest portion is destined for reuse or is refurbished for reuse. Some of those refurbished or reused products might work for only a few more months or years at best, which creates a recycling challenge.

With the demand for discarded objects in developing countries increasing, both for purposes of stripping for valuable components and for refurbishment, the number of ways in which waste is defined and valued by traders has also changed. Participants in the trade regularly redefine economic and practical value—and thereby the meaning of the objects they are trading—relative to the destination countries of their clients. Although the supply of e-waste originates from all regions of the world, demand is often more limited to specific countries. As one Hong Kong trader of Pakistani descent describes: 'Air conditioner, AC-compressor, refrigerator, these all go to UAE [United Arab Emirates]. Things like hospital beds, medical equipment, these things are wanted in Pakistan' (Trader-1). Interestingly, whereas legislative efforts on all levels use limited typologies to determine what constitutes 'waste' and what does not (e.g., devices with the wires cut off), traders conveniently employ significantly more diverse typologies, depending on their local supply and international customers. This fluidity allows for a diversity of explanations for calculating a certain value for an item, depending on the destination country's needs and wishes.

Whether a discarded hospital bed is waste or an object of value is contingent entirely on whether the Hong Kong trader to which the item becomes available is able to find a Pakistani buyer. Accordingly, the value one attaches to the hospital bed is dependent on the worth of the bed in Pakistan's market, rather than how the bed was regarded by the person or institution that initially discarded it. Similar examples were provided by a Nigerian man, who has experience in the e-waste trade, but who has since withdrawn from it: 'Ghanaians are very picky. In Ghana, the people keep track of what is the latest equipment and will select only the newest ones' (Former trader-1). This development opens up new possibilities for competition within the global informal market for discarded goods because differential demands give way to unconventional power struggles between developing countries.

Although it might seem as if legal definitions do not influence the social constructions of waste in the informal sector, several examples do exist where legal dynamics affect the route, cost and eventual risk of operations. One of these examples is provided by a Ghanaian trader from Hong Kong, who remembers an encounter that one of his clients had with a West-African customs agent.

> The agent, he wanted some money as well, you know. He wanted him to pay the money, so he would get his container into the country. But this man, he borrowed already all of the money for this transport. He could not pay for the bribe, you know? So this time, the officer took the container and sold the stuff himself! This happens, you know.
>
> *(Former trader-1)*

Accounts, such as the one above, make clear how important it is for green criminologists to pay attention to various dynamics of e-waste and to think beyond legal–illegal dichotomies or beyond the focus on harm to human health and the environment. Actions of traders are not informed solely by the formal context of e-waste—both legal and economic—but also by more informal conceptualisations that the traders themselves employ. The interconnectedness between informal and formal, between legal and illegal, is a tool that enables traders to connect, exchange and share beliefs, norms and values. It allows them (within their networks) to construct and uphold social boundaries that serve to legitimate their actions, where legalities remain locally bounded. Issues or questions of legality, which some participants in the e-waste trade ignore, are replaced by contextual legitimacy, empowering participants to design what can be seen as an alternative regime of truth, outside of a formal economy (Foucault 1980; Suchman 1995).

As suggested above, an important assessment to make is the interaction between intra-regional trafficking developments and other, mostly economic, developments in such regions. The consumption of electronic equipment in developing countries has increased significantly, with some scholars expecting the generation of obsolete computers in developing countries to soon exceed that of developed ones (Yu, Williams, Yu and Yang 2010).

E-waste generation correlates more strongly with a country's GDP than it does with the size of its population (Kumar, Holuszko and Espinosa 2017). Hong Kong and Singapore, for example, are regarded as non-OECD but enjoy significant economic development and, along with China, which is often viewed as a receiving rather than a source country, increasingly generate electronic waste due to increased consumption by their populations. India and China have similar populations but China's gross domestic product and purchasing power is higher, resulting in higher e-waste generation (Kumar et al. 2017). Such increases in domestic waste impact greatly on intra-regional trade because 'used-computer flows from Africa [e.g., South Africa, Nigeria, Tunisia] to Ghana skyrocketed in 2009, and traders expect this to continue' (Grant and Oteng-Ababio 2012: 9). Such flows, informal in nature and as novel as they are dynamic, are just some examples of waste streams not recognised in official trade data and not fitting within the Annex/non-Annex legal dichotomy. Currently, official trade data have not been able to account for manifests submitted incorrectly and illegal shipments (Lepawsky and McNabb 2010), revealing the need for empirical studies in providing estimates. Even though this might be culturally or politically difficult to undertake, it is necessary because the intricacy of this trade lies exactly in the legislative and cultural factors that are at play in each country.

Harm and livelihood

This section discusses the ecological and health damage that might occur in e-waste trafficking and substandard treatment and dismantling processes in destination countries. We also focus on economic and social harm that accompanies adverse environmental consequences. In so doing, however, we ask the question of whether e-waste might actually be an economically valuable opportunity for some informal workers, as a sole source of livelihood.

Gibbs and colleagues (2010) note that legally recycling a computer in the United States costs approximately $20. By selling that computer to an importer, however, the previous owner is able to *earn* $15 dollars. As discussed earlier, the proper recycling of e-waste is a costly process, so much so that it oftentimes costs more than it produces. So, why is the cost of recycling so low in undeveloped countries? The primary reason lies in less stringent or non-existent environmental and labour regulations in developing countries (Chi, Streicher-Porte, Wang and Reuter 2011; Oteng-Ababio 2012). Substandard recycling techniques allow for the extraction of precious metals: wires that contain copper are burned, while circuit boards are smelted in order to extract their gold. This highly toxic and hazardous labour is performed mostly by unskilled workers, who often have no knowledge of the dangers that their work entails (Oteng-Ababio 2012; Puckett and Smith 2002).

In the absence of well-equipped waste management systems, this imported and domestically generated e-waste harms the environment and the local population, but also affects the economy of the destination countries. Toxic substances remain in the environment for many years after they are absorbed in the air, water and soil, continuing to harm the ecosystem, animals and people living and working nearby (Eidgenössische Materialprüfungs- und Forschungsanstalt (EMPA) 2009; Premalatha et al. 2014). While one improperly discarded device may have minimal impact, the sheer quantity of waste makes the problem significant. Continued exposure to hazardous substances also plays a role. The inadequate health and safety measures in the dismantling and recycling of e-waste, often with no existing precautions or protection, impacts the health of workers (Puckett and Smith 2002; Puckett, Westervelt, Gutierrez and Takamiya 2005; Sepúlveda et al. 2010). In the Western African countries of Ghana, Ivory Coast, Nigeria and Togo, adults and children search barehanded through the heaps of dumped electronic and electrical equipment looking for valuable materials, and often dismantle them without protective equipment. These e-waste workers often do not know about the harms they face or, if they do, lack the ability to do anything about it (e.g., exert political pressure, obtain protective gear) (Hall 2013; Jarrell & Ozymy 2012).

People living near crude e-waste processing sites—using the water contaminated by burning or dumping, inhaling the toxic smoke of the burning e-waste and eating the crops grown on the toxic soil—feel the effects. The harm from e-waste also ties in to social and ecological inequalities. Several Ghanaian respondents explained that importers and sellers of second-hand goods constitute an important group of voters, causing reluctance among politicians to draft more stringent regulations (Bisschop 2012). Moreover, those most severely harmed by the burning and dumping—to be precise, those informal workers at the Agbogbloshie dump site in Accra—constitute a (religious) minority group who travelled from the north of Ghana to the capital in search of alternative sources of income which their region could no longer provide due to a loss of agricultural jobs (Bisschop and Vande Walle 2013; Konadu-Agyemang 2000).

These illegal transports of e-waste can also be harmful economically and politically. Cleaning up dumps is expensive and exacts a heavy toll on developing countries. Illegal transports also have economic advantages over legitimate transports due to lower processing costs, thereby adversely affecting trade and competition. Facilities that attempt to engage in environmentally friendly collecting and recycling practices experience these illegal transports as false competition.

Besides hazardous substances, electrical and electronic devices also contain valuable metals like copper, germanium, gold, indium, palladium and silver, which are inevitably lost if not recovered in an early stage of waste treatment. From a global perspective, the loss of scarce metals means intensified mining activities, which again lead to severe environmental impacts in mining areas worldwide. Moreover, the concentration of these metals in electronics is much higher than in the ores from mining, which implies that mining, smelting and refining e-waste results in fewer environmental impacts (Sthiannopkao and Wong 2013). The recovery of all types and quantities of metals is not possible, however, via crude processing. The informal 'recycling' sector has a lower recovery rate of (precious) metals, which means that more metals need to be extracted from the environment.

The picture, however, is more complex than the above description. Those who participate in the trade have very different conceptualisations of harm. A Nigerian client visiting Hong Kong to purchase equipment exhibits how the possible harms of improperly handling e-waste can be dismissed in the following interview excerpt:

I: Isn't it dangerous for workers to take apart the stuff that you send to these countries?
R: No, they have specialists for that, who know what they are doing.
I: But what about cancers, lead in the blood, or breathing problems?
R: Those people who have that, they were probably already sick.
(Client-1)

As simple and limited as the answer above might seem, preconceived notions of sickness and disease function as a form of denial and enable the trade to take place. For this trader, the e-waste that is sent to African countries is not what has caused the workers to experience lead poisoning and various forms of cancer. Several respondents mentioned that technicians, because of their expertise, are not harmed by the toxicity of electronic waste, nor do they expose others to it. This aligns with Oteng-Ababio's (2012: 13) findings about fieldwork in Ghana, in which he reports that individuals involved in scavenging valuable parts from discarded electronics did not fully recognise the causes of their sicknesses: 'Their perceived impact was restricted mainly to accident-related and other obvious effects (burns, cuts, etc.) that are in sharp contrast with those reported in other epidemiological studies'. During our own fieldwork in Ghana, a young e-waste scavenger mentioned that he could no longer run and play soccer, but he did not connect this to his 'job' of burning cables to get to the copper.

I: Do you think the average participant in this trade is aware of the consequences or cares about them?
R: They see no consequences. For them it's just about the money. They have no knowledge of the toxicity and pollution that they and their environment can be exposed to.
(Former trader-2)

A majority of respondents in the Hong Kong study (Van Herk 2016) indicated that, to them, harm to individual health is not necessarily connected to the trade and dismantling of e-waste. Instead, the traders seem to develop a 'spectrum of toxicity'. Some respondents seem to suggest that because dismantling and refurbishment was limited to specialist labourers (whom they often referred to as 'technicians'), the consequences of toxic substances were very limited. Although such a construction of hazardousness could be dismissed as a disregard for the problematic characteristics of discarded electronics—a form of denial or example of neutralisation—it shows how those actors outside of the formal economy uphold wholly different realities.

This alternative conception of harm is crucial to understanding the dynamics of the e-waste trade. Perhaps what is hampering policy and legislation to control this trade effectively is a limited understanding of the convictions and motivations for participating in the global informal network of e-waste trade. A comprehensive understanding of the e-waste trade requires acknowledgment of the possibilities and economic opportunities that this trade offers for participants with 'unconventional' livelihood strategies. In other words, in recognising the imminent harm caused by the e-waste trade, let us not dismiss participants' agency in utilising this trade as a vehicle to improve their economic mobility. 'If people notice that somebody is making money sending all of this scrap to Ghana, they think: "why not go there yourself, send the waste yourself and make more money?"' (Former trader-1). Based on his research among scavengers in Accra, Ghana, Oteng-Ababio (2012: 3) concludes that the current data deficiency on the topic of livelihood strategies in the e-waste trade 'tends to give justification for the occasional castigation of the practice by some media and environmental NGO's'. Therefore, any study of informal activity, including the trade in electronic discards, should take into account the concerns of those involved directly in the trade and how they conceptualise their participation and motivations for doing so.

In addition, in several locations, informal waste workers play a role in waste management (collection) that either supplements formal/official systems or exists in the absence of public waste collection or management (Coletto & Bisschop 2017; Davis, Akese, & Garb 2018). The informal waste workers' role in collecting waste and thus secondary raw materials is important in times of scarcity of natural resources. Moreover, informal e-waste workers in Ghana and other destination countries make up a considerable part of the population, which solely relies on these imports of e-waste for their livelihoods. Of course, recycling techniques could be improved and protective equipment worn and used. Actually, if a proper recycling infrastructure was to be developed, countries like Ghana might be able to avoid the environmental and human harm while, at the same time, benefiting from better materials recovery in times of resources scarcity (Amankwah-Amoah 2016). This would require sufficient influx of material to keep a processing facility operational and economical.

Essentially, a more nuanced study of e-waste trafficking requires the incorporation of the agency and experiences of participants in an analysis of causes, directions and developments concerning it. This warrants not only a more thorough exploration of the aforementioned factors, but indeed also exposes the fluidity of what actually constitutes waste, and how such definitions are constructed.

Social organisation

This section focusses on the social organisation of e-waste trafficking, paying attention to the different motivations of the participants in the trade. Given the complexity and global nature of transnational environmental crime, it is difficult to determine which actors are involved. In this regard, a local research setting, such as that of Ghana or Hong Kong, allows for an identification of the actors involved in these specific illegal trade flows and what their respective roles are or might be. Based on our research, as well as studies by others, we try to determine whether these actors and their roles can be considered legal or illegal (or perhaps both) and illustrate the legal–illegal interfaces in e-waste flows. This case study also analyses push and pull factors, considering what motivations and opportunities shape the flows of e-waste.

Various actors in different parts of the world play a role in the illegal transports of e-waste and their reasons to get involved are equally diverse. Earlier in this chapter we touched briefly on the role played by consumers and producers in generating increasingly larger quantities of e-waste. Consumers might discard e-waste in substandard ways due to a lack of awareness and due diligence or as a conscious choice for cheaper illegal disposal and for the externalisation of harm. The formal waste management sector also plays a role in e-waste trafficking. Corporations that treat e-waste legally and have environmentally sound management systems are few and their prices can be high. This makes it attractive to look for cheaper and less environmentally sound alternatives. This is the background against which potential interfaces between legal and illegal actors emerge. E-waste collection involves metal scrap dealers, urban recycling centres, refurbishers, official take-back systems, registered metal collectors (who pick up disposal skips from electronic hardware stores), and informal actors (e.g., waste tourists, charities). Many of these e-waste collectors and recyclers follow environmental and ethical standards, while others engage in direct or indirect export—often through brokers—to developing countries.

At the end of the e-waste flows—in countries of destination—legality, illegality and informality are inextricably connected. West African governments play a role in this when they allow substandard shipments to be imported, even levying import taxes on (used) electronics. Informal collectors and dismantlers are often the large majority of actors in the trade. E-waste is a massive industry, with recycling, second-hand EEE, parts, fixing and refurbishing; only a part of all discarded devices truly goes to waste. In this context, informality has actually become normalised and illegality might even be legitimised (Oteng-Ababio 2012; Suchman 1995). The informal trade in e-waste is, then, an economic strategy no different than formal entrepreneurship, moving beyond rationalisations of participation in illegal activity, towards explaining participation in activities to uphold livelihoods, whether legal or not. Arguably, participants find empowerment in their economic strategies in what is recognisable as an alternative regime of truth, outside of the formal economy (Foucault 1980).

> R: Ghana, this country is progressing. They don't even want the scraps, they have the new stuff now! And I think that's a good thing.
> I: If Ghana becomes more developed, doesn't that decrease your chances of finding business there?
> R: Yes! But if the country was doing well, I wouldn't have to do this!
> (Client-1)

Many of these informal actors, in turn, forge relationships with the legal recycling industry in supplying them with secondary raw materials. The extracted metals feed back into the production of electronics and other consumer products. Respondents in Ghana also referred to

Chinese organised crime groups buying copper for exorbitant prices. Similar findings were presented in a 2009 report on the linkages between organised crime and pollution crimes by Interpol (2009: 31), which stated that: 'the involvement of organised criminality in pollution crimes is more loosely structured'. It remains unclear, however, to what extent organised crime groups have been involved in e-waste trafficking.

In Hong Kong, the informal economy and its social impact are rather significant. Each and every person with both financial means and a strong network is able to participate. Although the smuggling of drugs, weapons and women is often attributed to one criminal organisation, the Chinese Triads, a custom officer explains why the e-waste business is egalitarian and small-scale rather than extortionate:

> Hong Kong is too small for criminal organizations to grow enough for them to become more powerful than others. There is simply so much competition on a small piece of land, that crime groups do not get to grow to a remarkable size.
>
> *(Customs officer-1)*

The absence of highly organised operations in Hong Kong can likely be explained by its size, contributing to a competitive market in which e-waste traders can be considered direct colleagues, working in the same conditions and depending on the same 'institutional boundaries' (Webb, Tihanyi, Ireland and Sirmon 2009). Furthermore, one may argue that such a competitive small-scale trade aids the perception of its legitimisation and normalisation. The relatively small size keeps the trade from being detected by formal control such as customs (which we will describe in the next section), while simultaneously reifying the importance of reliance on an informal economy. Such reliance presents itself in the form of interdependence and trust, as one Pakistani trader explains:

> From what I know, it's all legal, right? But that doesn't really matter, because what really matters is trust. Because if someone needs to be bribed, I need to know I can trust you. This is more important than whether something is legal or not.
>
> *(Trader-2)*

Although ethnic or other social ties play a role, repeat interaction and routinised market transactions are key in establishing trust (Van de Bunt, Siegel and Zaitch 2014). The social aspects of economic exchange seem most important to the social organisation of Hong Kong's e-waste trade. To illustrate how trust is utilised in the trade, consider the account of Popalzai (hereafter referred to as 'PZ'), a renowned trader in Hong Kong: 'You can always spot PZ's goods, because every piece has his initials written on them with a marker. Every television, AC, whatever, they all say 'PZ', 'PZ', 'PZ'' (Trader-1). As noted by one former trader, however: 'To a large extent, Pakistanis do most of the collecting and selling, whereas Nigerians do most of the exporting and, well, larger sales' (Former trader-3). Thus, social organisation seems to be characterised by *routine* as much as by social ties, with members of each respective ethnic group rarely venturing into those parts of the trade with which their group is not accustomed. One may argue that each group is able to count on the other, fortifying each other's trust.

Policy, governance and complexity

In this section, we shift our focus to the complexities inherent to the implementation of policy regarding e-waste and the difficulties that emerge in various interactions between governance actors in preventing harm and controlling crime related to e-waste. This section analyses which actors are involved in this legislative framework and provides insights into the facilitating and hindering factors for policy making throughout the e-waste flows. We devote attention to the importance and difficulty of involving local as well as international government actors, corporations and non-governmental organisations in addressing the e-waste issue. This also allows us to discuss how informal actors in countries of destination of trafficked e-waste might organise themselves and 'govern-from-below'. thereby contravening the stereotype of e-waste workers as victims of globalisation.

Enforcement targeted specifically at certain violations of law can have a twofold result in the informal economy (Webb et al. 2009). By focussing on a specific crime or misconduct, law enforcement warns the informal entrepreneur about the unlawfulness of his/her activities, yet in seeking to enforce the laws relevant to the trade of e-waste, the more visible and voluminous actors often offer enforcers a clear target, while the smaller shipments are not paid nearly as much attention. This minimises pressure on smaller actors, such as e-waste traders in Hong Kong, who seem to 'slip through the cracks' and remain relatively anonymous, as one trader explains:

> So when the client comes to Hong Kong, he goes to Sham Shui Po, you know, he buys some goods from a couple of businessmen there. Then he stores those goods, sometimes in my yard, sometimes he finds some other storage location, but eventually he will contact me. He will contact me and say that he wants this much stuff going to his country. I say 'okay', I call with the shipping company and I fill up the container, right? But that's it for me, after that, it is in the hands of the shipping company. I don't have anything to do with how the shipping company organizes the transport.
>
> *(Trader-3)*

This trader's comments are similar to those of other respondents in our Hong Kong research, who alluded to the important role of the shipping company. 'There is no need to lie, because this is all legal, so it is okay for us to put it like this (as is). The shipping company will take care of all of the paperwork' (Trader-1). In other words, traders rarely encounter repercussions from law enforcement entities. This is not to suggest that traders *never* encounter law enforcement officials, but that transnational legal loopholes offer a great advantage. This lack of legislative presence is not simply a misperception on the part of the traders because it can be argued that the various local, national and regional efforts that have been devised in and around Hong Kong are not in accordance with one another, thereby leaving regulatory gaps. As such, formal governance and its constructions of e-waste (and its shipments) are replaced by the experiences and social constructions of traders. This does not necessarily mean that participants in the informal e-waste trade are unaware of the legal boundaries of their trade. Actually, it is most likely the realisation that the boundaries are penetrable, if they are even met, that allowed these trades to autonomously develop an economic structure that reflects their interpretation of legitimacy.

> Actually, if you're talking about risk, it's the shipping companies that take the real risks, because if customs in another country captures the shipment, the shipping company's name is on the manifest, not mine. But they have to take those risks in order to keep getting enough clients.
>
> *(Trader-3)*

With risk within the trade of Hong Kong minimalised to shipping companies, one has to wonder to what degree formal stakeholders are effective, if at all. The problem seems to rest, in part, with the lack of congruence among different legislators. Compare, for example, the Food and Environmental Hygiene Department (FEHD) and the Customs Agency. A Hong Kong customs officer explains: 'Hong Kong's customs agency does not particularly focus on a single type of smuggled goods, in the sense that everything is monitored equally. No special attention is given to e-waste as such' (Customs officer-1). Similarly, one FEHD officer recognises how the rather partial enforcement of applicable laws contributes to a particularly opportunistic economic environment:

> If the EPD [Environmental Protection Department] wants to stop exports of dangerous waste, that is a very different area of law, that's not our job, to look at what people sell. We just make sure nobody is selling things in an illegal way.
>
> *(Customs officer-1)*

Any export of waste falls under the responsibility of Hong Kong's EPD, leaning on its Waste Disposal Ordinance (WDO), chapter 354 specifically, which states that:

> for the purpose of waste import and export control, any article or substance once given up by its original user is considered as waste under the WDO, irrespective whether it is still workable or can be sold for a value. As such, used electrical and electronic equipment having hazardous components or constituents (e.g. televisions, computer monitors and batteries) will likely be regarded as waste and fall within the said control unless they will be re-used for their originally intended purpose without repair.
>
> *(EPD 2012: 1)*

Non-governmental stakeholders seem to agree; a director of one large waste and recycling enterprise made this crucial observation:

> The economy is more important than the environment, essentially. That is why the Treasury Department can grant the rights to a piece of land to some company instead of a recycling facility. E-waste is essentially a problem of the Environmental Protection Agency (EPD), not Treasury.
>
> *(Director of waste facility-1)*

Without a combined effort by all agencies capable of intervening in the collecting, selling, or exporting processes, however, the probability of informal activity continuing is high. The importance of good relationships between enforcement agencies (e.g., networks) in order to be effective in tackling illegal trade is similar to what other studies about environmental enforcement agencies have found (e.g., Pink and Lehane 2012). Though not recognised by government agencies as such, the absence of effective cooperation can be viewed as a silent approval of the construction of alternative social realities, leaving their impacts on the global trade to be determined by others. As this director concludes accurately: 'Politicians worry about other stuff'.

The cooperation between enforcement agencies is equally important in countries of origin of hazardous waste flows. There, they are often faced with limited resources and rely on each other for expertise regarding topics on the outskirts of their responsibilities. Take the example of Belgium, which was the country of origin in our study of e-waste in Ghana. Customs, environmental inspectorates, maritime and environmental police and public prosecutors each play a key role in controlling for e-waste smuggling. Each of these government actors suffers from a lack of funding, with consequences for training, resources and the setting of enforcement and investigation priorities. Moreover, not all of these actors have the environment as their primary focus, which often hampers cooperation and information exchange between different agencies (Bisschop 2013). As a result, law enforcement is perceived as too slow to respond or imposes fines that are too low compared with the profits made with e-waste trafficking—a finding all too familiar in regulating the waste sector (Massari and Monzini 2004; Rucevska et al. 2015). Whereas coordination within countries can already be challenging, coordinated enforcement throughout the EU in view of implementing the EU's harmonised policy on waste and e-waste has proven to be even more daunting. It does not seem to result in harmonised implementation as of yet, which results in an unlevel playing field. Moreover, questions remain as to whether stopping all trafficked e-waste at the border of countries of origin is necessarily in the best interest of the environment when the legal shipments of second-hand electronics continue and have no way to be recycled properly once discarded. Moreover, stopping the inflow of e-waste to developing countries might make for an environmentally sound plan but does not necessarily guarantee a socially just outcome because it would take away the livelihood of already impoverished informal workers.

Private actors can also play a role in governing the e-waste flows. Corporations and non-governmental organisations are both involved in e-waste management today. First, producers can ensure that the recycling of e-waste is less harmful by phasing out hazardous components and can design their products in ways that facilitate fixing (Jaspers and Bisschop 2017). The engagement of producers and recyclers seems to depend on the potential benefits of being environmentally responsible—either in terms of shareholder profits or corporate image. The lack of raw materials (in the EU), for instance, serves as an incentive for European waste corporations to support policy that limits the exports of e-waste from the EU, but protecting the secondary raw materials and keeping those within Europe is increasingly accompanying the objective to avoid further environmental degradation in countries of destination of e-waste transports. Some companies have also started to invest in mining the e-waste that is generated in, for example, Western Africa, organising transports of motherboards or mobile phones to European smelters for the recovery for secondary raw materials.

Besides corporations, civil society representatives, such as NGOs, are crucial non-state actors; they already play a role in raising consumer awareness and in keeping both corporations and governments attentive. NGOs have also set up capacity-building projects to engage local actors, such as informal workers, in countries of destination. There are NGOs who have a system of renting out tools to dismantle electronics, which avoids burning to obtain the raw materials inside them. Capacity-building projects regarding sanitation in low-income countries have proven successful (van Welie and Romijn 2018), but evaluations of initiatives regarding e-waste are lacking. Increasingly, NGO initiatives recognise the agency of the individuals and groups in the informal e-waste sector. They stress the importance of not depriving 'vulnerable populations of a much-needed source of livelihood, while ignoring the underlying geo-political, historical and social determinants that fostered the emergence and growth of this [e-waste] industry in the first place' (Davis et al. 2018). There are initiatives that are looking to set up small-scale dismantling facilities in West Africa and then ship more difficult-to-recycle components to better-equipped countries (see above). It is important to keep in mind, of course, that this entails addressing the situation of informal recyclers rather than formalising their jobs and taking their sole source of livelihood away from them. Maybe by setting up monitored dismantling facilities and shipping more problematic components to Europe or other well-equipped processing sites, the work that is done in West Africa can be legitimised on a larger scale, thereby advancing social justice as well as avoiding environmental harm.

Conclusion

In this chapter, we have considered the problems accompanying legal definitions and policy-making regarding e-waste trafficking. We have demonstrated that these legal definitions are not necessarily a reflection of how participants and stakeholders involved in the e-waste business define boundaries or value e-waste—or waste, more broadly. Definitional processes of actors involved throughout the e-waste trade were demonstrated to be rather independent from 'official' definitions. A relative, culturally and socially sensitive definition is therefore instrumental to understanding the phenomenon of e-waste trafficking from a green criminological perspective.

We have tried to demonstrate that the governance of e-waste, both on a local and a global level, is inconsistent. Moreover, a large part of the situation regarding e-waste relates to the development of a parallel economy—an informal e-waste industry—in an attempt to fill the void left behind by an incongruent governance framework, influenced by a variety of geopolitical, historical and social factors. Developing stricter legislation and enforcement to counter the trade of e-waste from countries of origin to countries of destination—in other words a punitive approach—does not address the intraregional and domestic consumption and therefore ignores the environmental harms associated with it. Moreover, this does not address the issue of livelihood(s) and therefore risks strengthening the informality of working conditions and all social harms that might come with it. Therefore, efforts to address the e-waste challenge require an understanding of the economic, political and socio-cultural complexity of the e-waste issue in the twilight zone between legal and illegal, formal and informal.

Studying e-waste from a green criminological perspective entails more than the mere study of environmental crimes and harms. Making clear *which* environmental and social harms are associated with the practice of exporting e-waste to countries that lack processing facilities with the necessary environmental and health and safety safeguards in place is an important component of green criminological study (White 2011). A culturally sensitive approach towards the different meanings of waste, the different role played by actors in the formal and informal e-waste sector in different cultural, economic and social contexts, is essential to gain insights into the variety of catalysts of the (harmful) behaviour (Brisman and South 2013a).

Criminology has the benefit of being a discipline that brings different scientific perspectives such as geography, law and society, psychology, public administration and sociology together to understand crime and law enforcement. This is even more the case for green criminology because it draws on biology, chemistry, physics and toxicology, among other disciplines, to understand the complexity that lies at the basis of the environmental challenges that the world faces today. Based on our case studies of e-waste markets in two different locations, Hong Kong and Accra, we have aimed to illustrate the importance of considering locality when contemplating the global dimensions of the e-waste trade, as well as the economic, political and socio-cultural factors that influence the definitional processes, social organisation and governance of e-waste. Emancipating these 'polluters' might then go hand-in-hand with emancipating the study of crime to move beyond typologies and in order to embrace a broader approach. Such an approach will require green criminology to scrutinise not only actors and causes, but legislation all the same. It will ask us to incorporate meaning not only from the perspective of the researcher, but also from the vantage point of those actors who, on a day-to-day basis, experience what is being studied. Maybe in these particular locations, and on this particular topic, it would be worthwhile to explore possibilities of action research, engaging with (local) NGOs and stakeholders to determine what works in practice and what actually makes a difference in avoiding environmental and social harm. We leave that for another day.

References

Aladeojebi, T. 2013. 'Planned obsolescence,' *International Journal of Scientific & Engineering Research*, 4(6): 1504–1508.

Amankwah-Amoah, J. 2016. 'Global business and emerging economies: Towards a new perspective on the effects of e-waste,' *Technological Forecasting and Social Change*, 105: 20–26.

Baldé, C. P., Forti, V., Gray, V., Kuehr, R. and Stegmann, P. 2017. *The global e-waste monitor 2017*. Bonn, Geneva and Vienna: United Nations University (UNU), International Telecommunication Union (ITU) & International Solid Waste Association (ISWA). Available at: www.itu.int/en/ITU-D/Climate-Change/Documents/GEM%202017/Global-E-waste%20Monitor%202017%20.pdf.

Baldé, C. P., Wang, F., Kuehr, R. and Huisman, J. 2015. *The global e-waste monitor–2014*. Bonn, Germany: United Nations University, IAS–SCYCLE.

Basel Action Network (BAN). 2011. 'Annex VII expansion?—Say 'no' to attempts to undo the Basel Ban,' Available at: www.ban.org/wp-content/uploads/2011/10/BP3_Oct_2011_Final_A4.pdf.

Bisschop, L. 2012. 'Is it all going to waste? Illegal transports of e-waste in a European trade hub,' *Crime, Law and Social Change*, 58(3): 221–249.

Bisschop, L. 2013. 'Go with the e-waste flows. The governance reality of illegal transports of e-waste in a European trade hub,' in P. van Duyne, J. Harvey, G. Antonopoulos, K. von Lampe, A. Maljević and J. Spencer (eds.) *Human Dimensions in Organised Crime, Money Laundering and Corruption*, pp. 393–424. Nijmegen: Wolf Legal Publishers.

Bisschop, L. 2014a. 'How E-waste challenges environmental governance,' *International Journal for Crime, Justice and Social Democracy*, 3(2): 82–96. Available at: www.crimejusticejournal.com/index.

Bisschop, L. 2014b. 'Illegal e-waste transports: Exploring their harmfulness, scale, social organization and governance,' in R. White, T. Spapens and M. H. A. Kluin (eds.) *Environmental Crime and its Victims*, pp. 171–184. Surrey, UK: Ashgate.

Bisschop, L. 2015. *Governance of the Illegal Trade in E-waste and Tropical Timber. Case Studies on Transnational Environmental Crime*. Farnham and Burlington: Ashgate.

Bisschop, L. and Vande Walle, G. 2013. 'Environmental victimization and conflict resolution. A case study of e-waste,' in T. Wyatt, R. Walters and D. Westerhuis (eds.) *Debates in Green Criminology: Power, Justice and Environmental Harm*, pp. 34–54. Basingstoke, Hampshire, UK: Palgrave Macmillan.

Brigden, K., Labunska, I., Santillo, D. and Johnston, P. 2008. *Chemical Contamination at E-waste Recycling and Disposal Sites in Accra and Korforidua, Ghana*. Amsterdam: Greenpeace International.

Brisman, A. and South, N. 2013a. 'A green-cultural criminology: An exploratory outline,' *Crime Media Culture*, 9(2): 115–135. DOI: 10.1177/1741659012467026.

Brisman, A. and South, N. 2013b. 'Conclusion: The planned obsolescence of planet Earth? How green criminology can help us learn from experience and contribute to our future,' in N. South and A. Brisman (eds.) *Routledge Handbook of Green Criminology*, pp. 409–417. London and New York: Routledge.

Brisman, A. and South, N. 2015. 'Infantilization and anti-social consumption: Implications for de-responsibilization, denial and environmental harm,' *Young*, 23(3): 209–221. DOI: 10.1.1.831.1785&rep=rep1&type=pdf. Available at: http://citeseerx.ist.psu.edu/viewdoc/download?.

Brisman, A. and South, N. 2018. 'Green cultural criminology,' in W. S. DeKeseredy and M. Dragiewicz (eds.) *Routledge International Handbook of Critical Criminology*, 2nd ed., pp. 132–142. London and New York: Routledge.

Chi, X., Streicher-Porte, M., Wang, M. Y. L. and Reuter, M. A. 2011. 'Informal electronic waste recycling: A sector review with special focus on China,' *Waste Management*, 31(4): 731–742.

Clapp, J. 2001. *Toxic Exports: The Transfer of Hazardous Wastes from Rich to Poor Countries*. Ithaca: Cornell University Press.

Coletto, D. and Bisschop, L. 2017. 'Waste pickers in the informal economy of the global South: Included or excluded?,' *Journal of Sociology and Social Policy*, 37(5/6): 280–294. DOI: 10.1108/IJSSP-01-2016-0006.

Commission for Environmental Cooperation (CEC). 2016. *Quantitative Characterization of Domestic and Transboundary Flows of Used Electronic Products. Case Study: Used Computers and Monitors in North America*. Montreal, Canada: Commission for Environmental Cooperation. 126 pp. Available at: www3.cec.org/islandora/en/item/11673-quantitative-characterization-domestic-and-transboundary-flows-used-electronic-en.pdf.

Davis, J.-M., Akese, G. and Garb, Y. 2018. 'Beyond the pollution haven hypothesis: Where and why do e-waste hubs emerge and what does this mean for policies and interventions?,' *Geoforum*. DOI: 10.1016/j.geoforum.2018.09.020.

Eidgenössische Materialprüfungs- und Forschungsanstalt (EMPA). 2009. Ewasteguide.info: Hazardous substances in e-waste. Available at: http://ewasteguide.info/node/219.

EPD. 2012, October. Advice on import and export of used electrical and electronic equipment having hazardous components or constituents. Available at: http://www.epd.gov.hk/epd/sites/default/files/epd/english/environmentinhk/waste/guide_ref/ files/advice_on_e-waste.pdf.

Eski, Y. 2011. '"Port of call": Towards a criminology of port security,' *Criminology and Criminal Justice*, 11(5): 415–431. DOI: 10.1177/1748895811414593.

Foucault, M. 1980. *Power/Knowledge: Selected Interviews and Other Writings, 1972–1977*. Edited by C. Gordon. Translated by C. Gordon, L. Marshall, J. Mepham and K. Soper. New York: Pantheon.

Gibbs, C., McGarrell, E. F. and Axelrod, M. 2010. 'Transnational white-collar crime and risk. Lessons from the global trade in electronic waste,' *Criminology & Public Policy*, 9(3): 543–560.

Grant, R. and Oteng-Ababio, M. 2012. 'Mapping the invisible and real "African" economy: Urban e-waste circuitry,' *Urban Geography*, 33(1): 1–21.

Hall, M. 2013. *Victims of Environmental Harm: Rights, Recognition and Redress Under National and International Law. Frontiers of Criminal Justice*. London: Routledge.

Halsey, M. and White, R. 1998. 'Crime, ecophilosophy and environmental harm,' *Theoretical Criminology*, 2(3): 345–371.

Honda, S., Khetriwal, D. S. and Kuehr, R. 2016. *Regional E-waste monitor: East and South East Asia*. United Nations University & Japanese Ministry of the Environment. Available at: http://ewastemonitor.info/pdf/Regional-E-Waste-Monitor.pdf.

Interpol. 2009. *Electronic Waste and organized Crime. Assessing the Links. Phase II Report for the Interpol Pollution Crime Working Group* (pp. 49–49). Interpol.

Jarrell, M. and Ozymy, J. 2012. 'Real crime, real victims: Environmental crime victims and the Crime Victims' Rights Act (CVRA), '*Crime, Law and Social Change*, 1–17. DOI: 10.1007/s10611-012-9394-x.

Jaspers, J. and Bisschop, L. 2017. 'Planned obsolesence als organisatiecriminaliteit,' in R. Staring, R. Van Swaaningen, and K. Van Wingerde (eds), *Over de muren van stilzwijgen. Liber Amicorum Henk van de Bunt*, pp. 561–574. Den Haag: Boom Juridische Uitgevers.

Konadu-Agyemang, K. 2000. 'The best of times and the worst of times: Structural adjustment programs and uneven development in Africa: The case of Ghana,' *The Professional Geographer*, 52(3): 469–483.

Kumar, A., Holuszko, M. and Espinosa, D. C. R. 2017. 'E-waste: An overview on generation, collection, legislation and recycling practices,' *Resources, Conservation and Recycling*, 122: 32–42. DOI: 10.1016/j.resconrec.2017.01.018.

Kuper, J. and Hojsik, M. 2008. *Poisening The Poor. Electronic Waste in Ghana*. Amsterdam: Greenpeace International.

Lepawsky, J. 2015. 'The changing geography of global trade in electronic discards: Time to rethink the e-waste problem,' *The Geographical Journal*, 181(2): 147–159.

Lepawsky, J. and McNabb, C. 2010. 'Mapping international flows of electronic waste,' *The Canadian Geographer/Le Géographe Canadien*, 54(2): 177–195.

Massari, M. and Monzini, P. 2004. 'Dirty businesses in Italy: A case-study of illegal trafficking in hazardous waste,' *Global Crime*, 6(3–4):285–304. DOI: 10.1080/17440570500273416.

Melvin, J. and Mcgarrell, E. F. 2009. 'Electronic waste and organized crime-assessing the links,' *Trends in Organized Crime*, 12: 352–378. DOI: 10.1007/s12117-009-9076-y.

Oteng-Ababio, M. 2012. 'When necessity begets ingenuity: E-waste scavenging as a livelihood strategy in Accra, Ghana,' *African Studies Quarterly*, 13(1/2): 1.

Parola, F. and Coppola, G. D. 2011. 'Critical issues in managing port security across EU: Evidence from Italy,' *International Journal of Transport Economics*, 38(3): 311–335.

Passas, N. 1999. 'Globalization, criminogenic asymmetries and economic crime,' *European Journal of Law Reform*, 1(4): 399–423.

Pellow, D. 2007. *Resisting Global Toxics: Transnational Movements for Environmental Justice*. Cambridge, MA: MIT Press.

Pickren, G. 2014. 'Political ecologies of electronic waste: Uncertainty and legitimacy in the governance of e-waste geographies,' *Environment and Planning A 2014*, 46: 26–45. DOI: 10.1068/a45728.

Pink, G. and Lehane, J. 2012. 'Environmental enforcement networks: Their role in climate change enforcement,' in R. White (ed.) *Climate Change from a Criminological Perspective*, pp. 109–133. New York: Springer.

Prakash, S. and Manhart, A. 2010. *Socio-Economic Assessment and Feasibility Study on Sustainable E-waste Management in Ghana*. Freiburg: Öko-Instutut e.V.; Inspectorate of the Ministry of Housing, Spatial

Planning and the Environment of the Netherlands (VROM-Inspectorate) and the Dutch Association for the Disposal of Metal and Electrical Products (NVMP).

Premalatha, M., Tabassum-Abbasi, Abbasi, T. and Abbasi, S. A. 2014. 'The generation, impact, and management of e-waste: State of the art,' *Critical Reviews in Environmental* Science *and Technology*, 44(14): 1577–1678. DOI:10.1080/10643389.2013.782171.

Puckett, J. and Smith, T. 2002. *Exporting Harm: The High-tech Trashing of Asia.* Seattle and San Jose: The Basel Action Network (BAN) – Silicon Valley Toxics Coalition (SVTC).

Puckett, J., Westervelt, S., Gutierrez, R. and Takamiya, Y. 2005. *The Digital Dump. Exporting Re-use and Abuse to Africa.* Seattle: The Basel Action Network (BAN).

Reed Miller, T., Gregory, J., Duan, H., Kirchain, R. and Linnell, J. 2012. *Characterizing Transboundary Flows of Used Electronics: Summary Report.* Cambridge, MA: Material Systems Laboratory, Massachusetts Institute of Technology. Available at: http://contao.p153520.webspaceconfig.de/files/step/_bilder/Characterizing%20Transboundary%20Flows%20of%20Used%20Electronics%20Workshop%20Summary%20Report%201-2012.pdf.

Rucevska, I., Nelleman, C., Isarin, N., Yang, W., Liu, N., Yu, K., ... Nilsen, R. 2015. *Waste Crime: Low Risks – High Profits. Gaps in Meeting The Global Waste Challenge. A Rapid Reponse Assessment.* Nairobi and Arendal. Available at: www.grida.no/publications/default/6336.aspx.

Schluep, M., Manhart, A., Osibanjo, O., Rochat, D., Isarin, N. and Mueller, E. 2011. *Where are WEEE in Africa? Findings from the Basel Convention E-waste Africa Programme.* Berlin: Secretariat of the Basel Convention, UNEP, EU, EMPA, Öko-Institut, IMPEL.

Sepúlveda, A., Schluep, M., Renaud, F. G., Streicher, M., Kuehr, R., Hagelüken, C. and Gerecke, A. C. 2010. 'A review of the environmental fate and effects of hazardous substances released from electrical and electronic equipments during recycling: Examples from China and India,' *Environmental Impact Assessment Review*, 30(1): 28–41. DOI: 10.1016/j.eiar.2009.04.001.

Shinkuma, T. and Huong, N. T. M. 2009. 'The flow of E-waste material in the Asian region and a reconsideration of international trade policies on E-waste,' *Environmental Impact Assessment Review*, 29: 25–31.

Singh, N., Li, J. and Zeng, X. 2016. 'Global responses for recycling waste CRTs in e-waste,' *Waste Management*, 57: 187–197.

Sthiannopkao, S. and Wong, M. H. 2013. 'Handling e-waste in developed and developing countries: Initiatives, practices, and consequences,' *Science of the Total Environment*, 463–464: 1147–1153. DOI:10.1016/j.scitotenv.2012.06.088.

Suchman, M. C. 1995. 'Managing legitimacy: Strategic and institutional approaches,' *Academy of Management Review*, 20(3): 571–610.

Van de Bunt, H. G., Siegel, D. and Zaitch, D. 2014. 'The social embeddedness of organized crime,' in L. Paoli (ed.) *The Oxford Handbook of Organized Crime*, pp. 321–339. New York: Oxford University Press.

van Erp, J. and Huisman, W. 2010. 'Smart regulation and enforcement of illegal disposal of electronic waste,' *Criminology & Public Policy*, 9(3): 579–590.

Van Herk, W. 2016. *Is One Man's Trash another Man's Treasure? On Social Constructions of Electronic Waste.* Master's thesis. Utrecht: Utrecht University.

van Welie, M. J. and Romijn, H. A. 2018. 'NGOs fostering transitions towards sustainable urban sanitation in low-income countries: Insights from transition management and development studies,' *Environmental Science & Policy*, 84: 250–260. DOI: 10.1016/j.envsci.2017.08.011.

Webb, J., Tihanyi, L., Ireland, R. and Sirmon, D. 2009. 'You say illegal, I say legitimate: Entrepreneurship in the informal economy,' *Academy of Management Review*, 34(3): 492–510.

White, R. 2011. *Transnational Environmental Crime. Towards an Eco-global Criminology.* New York: Routledge.

Williams, E., Kahhat, R., Bengtsson, M., Hayashi, S., Hotta, Y. and Totoki, Y. 2013. 'Linking informal and formal electronics recycling via an interface organization,' *Challenges*, 4(2): 136–153. Available at: www.mdpi.com/2078-1547/4/2/136.

Yu, J. L., Williams, E., Yu, M. T. and Yang, Y. 2010. 'Forecasting global generation of obsolete personal computers,' *Environmental Science & Technology*, 44(9): 3232–3237. DOI: 10.1021/es903350q.

23

The environment and the crimes of the economy

Vincenzo Ruggiero

The notion that there is continuity between legality and illegality is crucial for an understanding of corporate, state, white-collar crime and crimes of the powerful in general. This notion of continuity is also apropos to the analysis of environmental harm because such harm may be produced by both criminal conduct and completely lawful initiatives. The study of environmental harm, in other words, presents the same theoretical predicament experienced by students of the crimes of the powerful and campaigners mobilising against them. As Sutherland (1949) realised, research on the crimes of the powerful is difficult without a willingness to expand one's sample well beyond the legal definitions of crime. Harm to the environment is caused by a series of interlaced conducts that are bad in themselves (*mala in se*) and conducts that are bad because they are prohibited by law (*mala prohibita*).

After some preliminary observations around the legal–illegal continuum, this chapter attempts to identify the novel traits of the crimes of the powerful which make the causes of environmental harm possible. It then examines how the very logic of economic development, supported by the 'science' of economics, may be, even if legitimate, equally or more harmful and destructive.

A schematic taxonomy

The environment has been among the theoretical and practical concerns of criminology for many years, but it could be argued that such concerns have long been only 'indirect' in nature. The real object of study, in past decades, was how organised and white-collar criminals operated in illicit businesses that had an environmental impact, for instance businesses relating to garbage disposal or the construction industry (Gruppo Abele 2005; Ruggiero 1996; Salzano 1994; Siegel et al. 2003). The former activity, as it was often found, was performed outside the statutory rules establishing the types of substances to be dumped and exactly where they were to be discarded. The latter, as investigators proved, led to illicit building on sites that are geologically hazardous and contrary to the guidelines regarding the precise materials to use and their proven safety. Not surprisingly, investigators and scholars focussing on these issues were experts in organised and white-collar crime, with the environment being a mere backdrop for law enforcement and academic analysis.

An understanding of how organised and white-collar delinquents jointly engage in environmental crime requires the appreciation, first, of a particular form of white-collar crime, and, second, a tentative classification of the ways in which these two different types of delinquents interact. To this effect, a preliminary delimitation of the analytical field is necessary, as individuals endowed with extremely varied degrees of power and reputation may be included under the rubric white-collar criminals. The delimitation proposed, therefore, confines the field of study to offences committed by actors such as states, corporations, financial institutions and other similarly powerful organisations and individuals. These offenders possess an exorbitant amount of material and symbolic resources when compared with those possessed by their victims. Theirs can be described as 'power crimes' that result from relatively larger opportunities offered to some social groups. Larger opportunities, in their turn, consist of wider choices among the potential actions to be carried out. The designation of 'power crimes' as crimes is controversial and highly problematic due to the higher capacity on the part of powerful actors to control the effects of their actions and to conceal (or negotiate) their criminal nature. The notion of 'power crime' is therefore used to refer to the acts and omissions of actors endowed with a wider range of behavioural choices and resources, a notion that echoes Sutherland's variables 'high status and respectability'. White-collar crime as 'power crime' is the type of delinquency we encounter when faced with environmental offences.

A different conceptualisation of power crime is found in criminological contributions from control balance theory. Tittle's theory (1995) takes as its organising theoretical variable the degree of control that actors exercise in relation to the amount of control they experience. According to his formulation, control surpluses (an excess of control exercised relative to control experienced) give rise to autonomous forms of deviance, namely deviance aimed at extending the existing control surplus. This includes offences which do not entail direct interaction with victims, ranging from acts of exploitation (e.g., corporate price-fixing, influence-peddling by political figures) to acts of plunder (e.g., pollution, destruction of forests and animals), and a variety of forms of indirect predation (Piquero and Piquero 2006). As Tittle (1995: 164) explains:

> An example of exploitative deviance [is] committed by corporate executives who authorize dumping of toxic waste into rivers after having carefully calculated that those who would be harmed most immediately—farmers and fishers along the river—will not be able to do much about it. Businesspeople do these things when they become aware that they, through the corporate vehicle, enjoy a surplus of control, which can be extended by any means.

As for a classification of how white-collar and organised criminals interact, it is necessary to try to isolate some of the distinct stages of the legal–illegal continuum, thus identifying a number of criminal conducts displaying their own specific characteristics. In the arena of environmental crime, for example, forms of 'gangster power crime' are encountered, namely behaviours of powerful actors committing conventional crime: for example, official actors directly violating environmental regulations. Environmental crime, on the other hand, may take the form of 'power crime by proxy', when criminality is 'contracted out' by legitimate powerful groups to criminal organisations: for example, official entrepreneurs paying organised crime for their illicit services that harm the environment. Finally, a 'criminal power partnership' may emerge when explicit consortia between the official overworld and the criminal underworld are established (Ruggiero 2007).

The categories mentioned above may be particularly suitable for the analysis of the illicit disposal of waste. In this respect, the notorious case of Naples has been well documented, with organised crime forging a partnership with industrialists and other official actors aimed at disposing illegally of both urban garbage and toxic waste (Ruggiero and South 2010). In this case, 'gangster power crime'—that is conventional crime committed by officials and enterprises, proved insufficient to complete the disposal operations. This presented an opportunity that favoured forms of 'crime by proxy' (with the dumping being contracted out to organised crime), and also 'criminal partnerships' (with officials, entrepreneurs and organised criminals involved on an equal footing in the operations).

In countries where conventional criminal groups are less able to access the official world, it is official actors themselves who provide the services needed. Research has shown that processing industrial and urban waste without a license and sidestepping environmental regulations is cheaper and faster than conventional and legal processes. In the Netherlands, for example, illegal enterprises may offer service packages which comprise false invoices, transport facilities, mendacious chemical reports as to the nature of the substances thrown away and the forged permits to dump. In most European countries, some legally registered companies also operate illegally, running their own in-house, parallel, illicit business. The choice between the two services is the result of how much the customer is prepared to pay. It is otiose, in this respect, to question whether customers are aware of the illegal nature of the cheaper option, as its very cheapness speaks for itself (Brants 1994; Moore 1994; van Duyne 1993). In the United States (U.S.), research has indicated that the involvement of organised crime reaches all aspects of the waste disposal business, from control over which companies are officially licensed to dispose of waste to the designation of which companies can earn contracts with public or private organisations. In such a context, organised crime members are in charge of paying bribes to dump site owners or, indeed, may be the proprietors of such sites themselves (Block and Scarpitti 1985; Salzano 1994; Szasz 1994).

Cases that have occurred in Germany demonstrate that even in countries where the legislation is progressive and clear, illegal disposal of waste is widespread. In one such instance, a mismatch was noted between the quantity of waste expected and that actually received by incinerators operating in the eastern regions of the country. The missing portion of waste was found to have been dumped in illegal disposal sites. Entrepreneurs utilising such dumps opted for the cheapest approach to waste management, thus circumventing the rules that impose a fee of approximately 200 euros per tonne of waste treated (Natale 2009). On other occasions, the composition of the waste treated was falsely certified, so that substances that should have been disposed of in special sites were instead dumped in inappropriate ones. It may be surprising that cases such as these occur in highly ecologically aware Germany. The paradox, however, is that the development of illegal dumping services runs parallel with the very increase in environmental awareness, the latter forcing governments to raise costs for industrial dumping, which indirectly encourages industrialists to opt for cheaper, if illicit, solutions.

Foundational crime

Along the legal–illegal continuum we find another category, which may help in the analysis of environmental crime and which I refer to as 'foundational power crime'. Crimes are 'foundational' when they occur in a grey area in which various conducts await the outcome of the criminalisation-decriminalisation conflict—in the sense that they may be subject to regulation or become accepted routine. Some acts or practices occur within vaguely regulated arenas and, while presenting themselves as legitimate conduct, are actually illegal but end up creating a precedent. Other criminal conduct implicitly invokes legal pragmatism, challenging legal reasoning and advocating departure from precedents (Waldron 2006). Crimes invoking legal pragmatism are foundational crimes insofar as the conduct is inspired by an 'experimental' logic and driven by a consequentialist philosophy. Powerful actors so driven adopt illicit practices with the awareness that they are indeed illicit but with an eye to the social and institutional reactions that might ensue. It is the intensity of such responses that will determine whether violations are to become part of a 'viable' routine or are to be carefully avoided. Some violations, in sum, possess a 'founding force', namely they are capable of transforming the previous jurisprudence and establishing new laws and new types of legitimacy (Derrida 1992). Foundational power crime restructures the legal and the political spheres while playing a legislative role.

A variety of foundational power crimes fall in the economic domain and pertain, specifically, to the environment, where enforcing the rules often results in new rules being devised, in a race which sees the law chasing the economy, rather than vice-versa. Let us consider some examples.

In Europe, carbon emissions are regulated by an emissions trading treaty whereby each country is expected to limit its production of carbon dioxide. Firms that overstep that limit are requested to buy the right to produce emissions from those who produce less. Purchases of such a right are supposedly discouraged by taxation but, in fact, are encouraged by the murky ways in which taxation is applied. Firms buying emissions credits have managed to avert taxes thanks to their negotiating strength relative to those selling them, leading to the charges being 'reversed', with the result that the most prosperous companies are also able to expand their emissions limit at will. An important precedent in corporate behaviour, this practice is rewriting the rules and 'founding' a new sense of legitimacy. The lack of control on emissions brokers, who act as intermediaries between firms, offers opportunities for adventurous and experimental initiatives, with improvised mediators, unqualified agencies and improbable in-betweens contributing to generalised violations. The emissions trading treaty, in brief, has failed to distinguish clearly between public and private interests: larger companies have been granted a chance to avoid investments aimed at reducing emissions and have been given the opportunity, instead, of enlarging their right to pollute. Fraudulent conduct has also emerged, with falsification of accounts and data relating to emissions trading and, finally, electronic theft of 'polluting' rights and credits (Giliberto 2011).

At the international level, cuts to carbon emissions by developed countries since 1999 have been cancelled out three times over by increases in imported goods from developing countries (Clark 2011). This is a way of 'outsourcing' emissions, so that the country producing the goods is made responsible for the emissions, while the country in which those goods are consumed can claim a reduction. Developed countries can claim to have reduced their collective emissions by almost 2 per cent between 1990 and 2008. But once the carbon cost of imports has been added to each country, the true change has been an *increase* of 7 per cent. The focus on territorial emissions in a subset of countries, in other words, is ineffective at reducing global emissions; without some mechanisms to monitor emissions from the production of imported goods, it encourages 'foundational' unorthodox conducts.

Toxic waste moves across increasingly porous borders, and this movement is determined by a set of business considerations (see van Herk and Bisschop, this volume, Chapter 22). Competing enterprises have to find cheap modalities for the disposal or concealment of their waste, which come in the form of purchasers situated in off-shore locations. Purchasers include communities whose priority is minimum income or survival rather than the environment. As a result, dangerous substances are relocated or transferred to developing and economically impaired regions. As Heckenberg (2010: 39) explains, '[e]conomic inequalities and social disparities create an uneven playing field, potentially conducive to opportunistic harms and crimes, particularly in political and commercial domains less open to regulatory and public scrutiny'. Transference of environmental harm may take place through the movement of substances or the relocation of specific segments of industrial activity that are proven to be highly hazardous. It may be accompanied by falsification or mislabelling of the substances being transferred, failure to analyse their nature and corruption of officials receiving them.

Ultimately, it makes perfect economic sense to transfer environmental harm to developing countries, where rates of ill health and loss of life are higher than in developed countries (see van Herk and Bisschop, this volume, Chapter 22). Migration of dirty industries and their hazardous waste to areas with low life expectancy, high morbidity and mortality implies a minimal economic cost (Morson and Schapiro 2017). But with this example, we have ventured into the realm of transnational crime, a specific form of power crime often associated with environmental harm. Let us discuss some of its traits.

Deregulation, mobility and invisibility

To what extent does transnationalism per se cause an increase in 'power crime'? This apparently new question, in fact, brings us back to similar, old concerns, for example: does corporate crime increase in periods of economic stagnation or in periods of economic growth? Are small firms operating in competitive markets more likely to commit crime than large companies enjoying a monopolistic condition? Students of corporate criminality have discussed these issues for decades, but the outcome of discussions has proven inconclusive. The reason, perhaps, lies in the extreme versatility of power crimes, which are capable of reproducing themselves within a wide range of diverse conditions.

There are three variables that provide the background to such versatility. The first falls in the normative domain, or, rather, it is associated with the lack of it. Transnational business benefits from what old colonialism has always enjoyed, namely the lack of clear, written rights protecting Indigenous populations. Just as colonialism built the Industrial Revolution on predation, new corporations and states build their profits on deregulation. Both, however, enjoy various degrees of complicity on the part of local elites who grant access to territories and peoples in exchange for status and private gains. In this respect, we seem to be faced with a new 'compradorial' class in developing countries that encourages or allows deregulation to develop. In brief, access to territories and peoples, in the present circumstances, does not translate into beneficial effects for developing countries (Kiely 2005). Far from reducing poverty, transnational economic activity generates criminal opportunities that lead to the type of conducts mentioned above. Paradoxically, when communities are inundated with dangerous substances in exchange for survival income, it is exactly their future survival that is undermined.

The second variable for the understanding of contemporary power crimes is mobility. This variable includes a notion of speed: financial and commercial conduits have to be identified quickly if quick profits are to be made. The task consists of reaching specifically suitable places, with fast, short-term operations, before their effects are perceived. Mobility is crucial for transference of environmental harm because the vagaries of the political climate in the receiving countries might bring change and therefore make regimes more unfavourable. New regulations may be devised and/or the international community may expose the damage produced, thus forcing dangerous activities to migrate elsewhere.

Invisibility is the third variable connoting transnationalism. Traditionally, invisibility is regarded as one of the characteristics of white-collar crime, and relates to the offender as well as the victim: in this respect, some power crimes appear to be offences without offenders. Victims may also be invisible, or they may even be unaware of being victimised (Davies et al. 2014). This is due to the fact that white-collar criminals often do not share the crime scene with their victim: the place in which the crime is committed and the place where its impact is experienced and suffered may not coincide. The same applies to time: the time when the crime is planned and the time when victimisation is experienced do not correspond. The Bhopal disaster is an example where the offence occurred at a certain point in time in one country and its effects were experienced at a different time in another.

Destroying through 'science'

At one extreme of the legal–illegal continuum, we find conduct that is detrimental to the environment but that enjoys the scientific sanction of economic thought. These are 'crimes of the economy' and deserve more attention than they are usually given by criminologists, some of whom still believe, by contrast, that economic development is in itself a key tool of crime *prevention*. Economists have often paid visits to the field of criminology, examining the rational logic of offending. It is time to return the visit in order to ascertain whether the traces of some familiar criminological concepts can be found there (Ruggiero 2009).

Green criminologists analysing global environmental harm straddle legal-procedural approaches, which define harm as the outcome of illegal practices, and ecological approaches, which contemplate environmental harm more broadly, 'by invoking notions of environmental morality, environmental ethics, and animal, ecological, or human rights' (Brisman 2010: 161). In doing so, they are faced with the dilemma known in ecological theory and practice as the distinction between 'shallow' and 'deep' ecologism. The former appears to believe that the technology which is destroying the environment may also rescue it: a managerial approach to environmental problems will be sufficient to solve problems, without fundamental changes in present values or patterns of production and consumption. Deep ecology, by contrast, embraces a holistic outlook, whereby humans are interconnected and are inextricably intertwined with everything around them: they are part of the flow of energy, the web of life. According to deep ecology, radical changes in production and consumption patterns, but also in the fundamental principles and values expressed by the undeservedly respected 'science' of economics, are necessary.

Is the environment a public good? 'Yes', if we, in abstract terms, equate it to other non-rival, non-excludable goods, in the sense that one person's enjoyment of the environment does not exclude its enjoyment by others, and in the sense that the environment is provided to one and all at the same time. The answer, however, is 'No' if we believe that goods and resources belong to those who turn them into wealth. Economic thought starts its 'scientific' arguments from the latter assumption, and in the texts of the founding fathers of economic liberalism, this assumption takes the form of rationalisation for the plunder and destruction of colonial regions. John Locke (1962), for example, laid the philosophical groundwork for human freedom in all its dimensions: free enterprise, free trade, free competition, and the freedom to invest. Freedom to destroy, in his thought, takes the form of exploitation of the Earth, which cannot be left undisturbed as an object of contemplation, but has to be turned into property as the result of improvement and work. By leaving fruits to rot and venison to putrefy, and, for that matter, by leaving the Earth untouched, we offend the common law of nature. Thrift, work and perseverance may replace inherited rights to property, but is there a limit in hoarding up more than one can make use of? By the same token, is there a limit beyond which the exploitation of the Earth constitutes a threat to the planet? Locke 1962 [1689]: 140) believed that the 'bounds of just property' have been removed with the invention of money—'some lasting thing that men might keep without spoiling'—which makes economic initiative boundless and infinite. Natural resources, in this view, must be turned into monetary value, because, if left idle, they will dissipate. Colonies were a substantial part of the natural resources to which this type of reasoning referred.

Today, the entire Earth can be likened to the resources of the old colonies, including slaves, all given to us not for the mere purpose of contemplation or for leading a good life, but with the implicit mandate to use and exploit them. The environment, therefore, is not a common good, but an arena where the capacity and ingenuity of humans is constantly tested, and such capacity and ingenuity appear to be the only limit to initiative and development. The ultimate resource, in brief, is the human mind, and throughout history, human genius always wins out against natural resource restraints.

Physiocrats, such as Quesnay (1972: 15), argued that

> the land employed in the cultivation of corn be brought together, as far as possible, into large farms worked by rich husbandmen; for in large agricultural enterprises there is less expenditure required for the upkeep and repair of buildings, and proportionally much less cost and much more net product than in small ones.

Small farms, instead, 'employ uselessly, and at the expense of the revenue of the land, a greater number of the families of farmers, the extent of whose activities and means hardly puts them in a position to carry on wealthy cultivation' (Quesnay 1972: 15). Wealthy cultivation, to be sure, consists of intensive and limitless exploitation of the soil, accompanied by enclosures and privatisation of the land, and the boundless use of resources. Growth is a permanent concern, as revenues cannot remain inert, 'to the detriment of the reproduction of the revenues and the well-being of the people' (Quesnay 1972: 5). Similarly, capital should not be taxed, otherwise growth is inhibited and development hampered.

Physiocracy contributed to the description of the material sphere of society, where wealth is created and consumed, as a living organism, with its own veins, arteries and blood circulation. Quesnay's economic tables offered an organic representation of economic life as an autonomous system, thus paving the way for the definitive divorce between economics and ethics. From then on, one sphere of human action increasingly distanced itself from other common values orienting social interaction: economics could no longer abide by the useless and damaging principles governing the socialisation of groups and individuals. Economics became a science. Adam Smith granted the final seal to this science, positing the existence of a universal, timeless individual engaged in the constant pursuit of material interests, thus turning the immorality of accumulation into an instinctive, biological necessity. According to Smith, infinite growth becomes a spontaneous mechanism involving productive agents who transform resources into commodities and wealth: such agents are the only representative of civility in that they provide the necessary livelihood for all. Adam Smith's glorification of producers goes hand in hand with ridiculing those whose activity does not yield quantifiable value or net profit, such as domestic servants, politicians, soldiers, judges, artists, teachers and clergy. Musicians, lawyers and other men of letters are equated with opera singers, opera dancers and buffoons (Smith 1976). Such unproductive individuals do not 'work' because they do not transform anything: their performance perishes as soon as it is delivered, leaving the surrounding environment unchanged. *Homo economicus* opposes sterility and is urged into developing innovative ideas leading to the relentless conquest and reshaping of the environment, in a process that coincides with innate desire and the search for human happiness. Access to the economy and its products links *homo economicus* with *homo laborans*, both chained to their own infinite material aspirations—the last human beings—the happy slaves 'replete with the goods that [they] produce and consume without any other ideal than ensuring [their] own comfort and tranquillity' (Hénaff 2010: 17).

With Adam Smith, necessity, not freedom, came to connote human history, as development was inscribed in the biological make up of humans. Whether such biological necessity generates waste and devastation did not concern the founding fathers of economics as a science because the spontaneous dynamic of growth was deemed capable of self-regulation. Human waste, in the form of labour cyclically expelled from the productive process, could sooner or later be absorbed into other, innovative, economic initiatives, while the harm caused to the environment would be mended by the very technology producing it (Ruggiero 2014). We have no alternative, Smith remarked, but to accept the distributional inequities and moral violence that accompany private property relations, as these are the only means for securing our survival.

Smith's argument, however, implies that selfishness should be the pivotal variable orienting our action, irrespective of how destructive this might be. Surely, there is a Christian-Hebraic stance in this suggestion, whereby a superior entity will arrange things so that every egoistic act will find its synthesis in a higher, inscrutable, harmony. This is a hubristic theory positing that we resemble the God who made us, and that we no longer need his judgement on our exploits. In sum, we are depicted as animals, full of instincts, innate desires and egoism, but, at the same time, as gods who turn their animal nature into universal harmony. This reveals a further contradiction: despite the adherence to the doctrine of laissez-faire in theory, Adam Smith maintains a strong interest in promoting policies that further accumulation and favour enterprise, whether both generate harm or not. Locke, Quesnay and Smith converge, then, in different fashions, into the practical philosophy that today we term neoliberalism.

It must be noted, however, that socialist theory is also, and equally, fascinated by development, growth and the economic sphere in a general sense. Saint-Simon and his followers focussed on technical advances and industrial production as necessities for the abolition of the last remainders of feudalism and its economic inefficiencies. Proudhon expressed his idea of freedom as cooperation between 'producing communities' (Honneth 2017), while Marx saw in the destruction of 'semi-barbaric and semi-civilised' economies the precondition of social revolution brought by the unstoppable development of the 'productive forces' (Ruggiero 2013: 33–36).

Axioms and risk

As an ideology, neoliberalism serves to legitimise economic conduct by conferring on it the character of inevitability—of a divine project aimed at the happiness of all. To hamper such a project is tantamount to sacrilege, and governments are still convinced that their role consists of civilising the economy and the human interactions this entails and that if they do not better adhere to the new ideology, they are doomed. The political sphere is required to forge its own philosophy through the concepts and axioms prompted by the economy, making society suitable to it, rather than the other way round. The marriage between economics and politics is so harmonious that representatives of the two realms swap functions and arenas, making them now perfectly interchangeable. Entrepreneurs become politicians while the latter, after their mandate expires, find comfortable positions within business boards of directors. Neoliberalist ideology posits that a 2–3 point growth per year is indispensable. Even for societies that have reached a satisfying degree of well-being, such growth is deemed necessary for the continued enjoyment of such well-being. A corresponding increase in consumption, inevitably, has to be stimulated. Whether permanent growth manifests dysfunctional aspects for humans and their environment should not concern us, because, so goes another axiom: (a) markets are perfectly able to self-regulate; (b) capital flows without hesitation where its utility is maximum; and (c) risks are always calculable (Gallino 2011). As for the enormous mismatch between technological and economic potentials and the actual life conditions of the population of the Earth, the 'trickle down' principle will soon display its healing capacity. Little attention is given to the growing signs that the use of natural resources implied by an economic model based on infinite development is unsustainable, and that the time left to change it is becoming dramatically brief. As Gallino (2011: 38–39) explains:

> The ecological footprint of the planet in 2008 was close to 1.3, namely the Earth was using all its own natural resources plus a third of those of another planet [...] If this tendency continues unaltered, the estimate is that in 2050 the Earth will need an entire second planet in order to satisfy its use of natural resources, including the capacity to absorb or recycle the waste thus produced [...] If developing countries came close to the levels of consumption of the EU, 2.1 planets would be necessary. If the entire world reached the levels of consumption of the US, the Earth would need the resources of four more planets.

Each society identifies a 'threshold of catastrophe' that derives from its perception of the utility brought by risky behaviour. Where this threshold is located is highly controversial. Societies and economies of subsistence, for example, may be highly opposed to risky decisions because they are constantly threatened by the loss of crops, the uncertainty of their productive system and ultimately by famine. Similarly, in monetary economies, entrepreneurs who hold limited finances may be deemed less prepared to run risks than their colleagues who own more funds.

On the other hand, one may suggest that lack and uncertainty may lead to riskier behaviour as a way of 'gambling' to achieve abundance and a secure future. In this sense, it is those endowed with fewer resources who might be prepared to run higher risks. In brief, the perception of risk and catastrophe is not only based on scientifically shared calculus, but is also heavily dependent on subjectivity.

In the seventeenth century, risk was associated with gambling, which entails simultaneous possibilities of loss and gains. Slowly, gains vanished from the equation, while the negative outcomes of gambling were linked to taboos and sins. The major moments of choice were signposted with danger. Later, the public politicised the subject, while scientists pretended to be neutral (Douglas 1992).

This politicisation of the subject matter occurs because society no longer runs risks in pursuit of what is necessary but of what is superfluous (Luhmann 1996). In this way, the identification of a threshold of catastrophe becomes increasingly dependent on who is likely to earn advantages from risky behaviour. Those who feel that risk or gambling will bring advantages to individuals other than themselves will move the threshold of catastrophe accordingly. In sum, the very perception of catastrophe and risk varies according to the position one occupies in 'gambling': some individuals may make decisions while others may just suffer the outcomes of those decisions (Ruggiero 2014).

'We spend money we don't have, on things we don't need, to make impressions that don't last, on people who don't care' (Kane 2011). Because we do not run risks in the pursuit of what is necessary, but of what is superfluous, neoliberalism needs to turn the superfluous into a natural product of human activity or even as an element of human organic reproduction. Hence the need of economics to imitate the natural sciences. Biologists, mathematicians, physicists and other scientists have been called upon to make economic theories more 'realistic and effective', namely to inject doses of dogma into them. As Gallino (2011: 94–95) has noted, the major opus of economics produced in the twentieth century, the *General Theory* of Keynes (1936), contained only three or four simple equations out of a total 400 pages—and those that did appear were mainly in the appendix. In 1950, only 2–3 per cent of the articles published by the influential *American Economic Review* contained mathematic formulas, which normally were not at all sophisticated. In 1980, the papers with mathematical calculations were 44 per cent and formulas had become much more complex. Currently, the percentage is close to 90 per cent. The only 'real' science within the human sciences, neoliberal economics dominates in university courses, in the specialist literature, and in most schools of management and business. It is the core religion of business administrators, large enterprises, financial institutions, ministries of the economy, central banks, international organisations, the World Bank, the International Monetary Fund and the European Commission. According to Gallino (2011: 92):

> The economy is seen as a physical system, implying flows of goods, information and energy, so that it might be useful to model the economy as a system, like physics does. However, while economic theory uses the concept of equilibrium, the same concept used by physics cannot be applied to the economy, because this is an open system and equilibrium refers to closed systems.

Neoliberalism does not observe and describe economic reality; it creates this reality. It also produces a new conceptualisation of risk—from risk as uncertainty for enterprise to risk as uncertainty for society at large. This shift contradicts one of the very axioms of free markets, namely that the full costs of a transaction must be borne by the involved parties. Many economic activities and transactions, however, exact a significant price on humans and ecosystems: the costs, which are borne by society but not the individual producers and consumers of the goods, are called externalities (Scorse 2010). Neoliberalism regards environmental harm as an externality.

Conclusion

In an autobiographical note, André Gorz (2010) recalls how the reading of a 1954 article in an American weekly contributed to his becoming an ecologist before the term even existed. The article explained that, if the U.S. was to make a return on investments, consumption would have to grow by at least 50 per cent in the following eight years, although people were quite incapable of identifying what that additional 50 per cent of consumption would consist of. 'It was up to the advertising and marketing experts to summon up new needs, desires and fantasies on the part of consumers, to deck out even the most trivial commodities with symbols that would increase the demand for them' (Gorz 2010: 6).

Sociologists and criminologists, including this author, have not shown similar precocious awareness, as the relatively recent development of green thought among them seems to confirm. The list of issues and conduct which, in the last decades, have compounded the dilemmas and expanded the arena of 'green criminology', includes climate change, deforestation, destruction of biodiversity, the disposal of toxic waste, illegal fishing, the illegal trade in reptile and endangered species and much more, as evidenced by the new chapters in the second edition of the volume in which this chapter appears. These acts and omissions reveal the complexity of the nexus environment–crime while displaying significantly original traits. First, it is their international, global, nature which is immediately manifest, thus leading us to equate them to forms of criminality with a transnational dimension. Second, they fall into the arena of conventional criminality, but also pertain to legitimate, wider, ecological notions of harm (White 2010).

This chapter has attempted to examine the traits of environmentally harmful conduct in two related dimensions, characterising them, namely, as forms of white collar and power crime, providing examples of how such conducts often result from partnerships between members of conventional criminal organisations and official actors operating in the economic and political spheres. After focussing on some variables which help us to understand the operations of transnational crime against the environment, the analysis has shifted onto the 'crimes of the economy', that is to say, the harm caused by economic initiative itself, aided by the philosophies underpinning and legitimising it. By locating environmental harm somewhere on the legal–illegal continuum, it has become clear that criminological analysis would be useless if confined to the examination of what is prohibited by law.

References

Block, A., and Scarpitti, F. R. 1985. *Poisoning for Profit: The Mafia and Toxic Waste in America.* New York: William Morrow.

Brants, C. 1994. 'The system's rigged—Or is it? The prosecution of white collar and corporate crime in the Netherlands,' *Crime, Law and Social Change*, 21(2): 103–125.

Brisman, A. 2010. 'The indiscriminate criminalisation of environmentally beneficial activities,' in R. White (ed.) *Global Environmental Harm: Criminological Perspectives*, pp. 161–192. Cullompton, Devon, UK: Willan.

Clark, D. 2011. 'Carbon cuts by developed countries cancelled out by imports,' *The Guardian*, 25 April. Available at: www.theguardian.com/environment/2011/apr/25/carbon-cuts-developed-countries-cancelled.

Davies, P., Francis, P. and Wyatt, T. (eds.) 2014. *Invisible Crimes and Social Harms.* Basingstoke, Hampshire, UK: Palgrave Macmillan.

Derrida, J. 1992. *Force De Loi Le Fondement Mystique De L'autorité.* Paris: Galilée.

Douglas, M. 1992. *Risk and Blame: Essays in Cultural Theory.* London: Routledge.

Gallino, L. 2011. *Finanzcapitalismo: La Civiltà Del Denaro in Crisi.* Turin: Einaudi.

Giliberto, J. 2011. 'Imprese in Allarme Sulla CO_2,' *Il Sole 24 Ore*, 23 January. Available at: www.ilsole24ore.com/art/economia/2011-01-23/imprese-allarme-081440_PRN.shtml.

Gorz, A. 2010. *Ecologica.* London: Seagull Books.

Gruppo Abele. 2005. *Dalla Mafia Allo Stato: I Pentiti: Analisi E Storie.* Turin: EGA-Edizioni Gruppo Abele.

Heckenberg, D. 2010. 'The global transference of toxic harms,' in R. White (ed.) *Global Environmental Harm: Criminological Perspectives*, pp. 37–61. Cullompton, Devon, UK: Willan.

Hénaff, M. 2010. *The Price of Truth: Gift, Money and Philosophy.* Stanford, CA: Stanford University Press.

Honneth, A. 2017. *The Idea of Socialism: Towards a Renewal.* Cambridge: Polity.

Kane, P. 2011. The '"I'm happy I'm green" consensus won't placate our lust for novelty,' *TheGuardian*, 26 April. Available at: www.theguardian.com/commentisfree/2011/apr/26/green-consensus-versus-consumerism.

Kiely, R. 2005. 'Globalization and poverty, and the poverty of globalization theory,' *Current Sociology*, 53 (6): 895–914.

Locke, J. 1962 [1689]. *Two Treatises on Civil Government.* London: J.M. Dent & Sons.

Luhmann, N. 1996. *Sociologia Del Rischio.* Milano: Bruno Mondadori.

Moore, R. H. 1994. 'The activities and personnel of twenty-first century organized crime,' *Criminal Organizations*, 9: 3–11.

Morson, G. S. and Schapiro, M. 2017. *Cents and Sensibility. What Economics can Learn from the Humanities.* Princeton, NJ: Princeton University Press.

Natale, S. 2009. 'Germania, Modello Napoli,' *Narco mafie*, 4[Aprile]: 20–23.
Piquero, N. L. and Piquero, A. R. 2006. 'Control balance and exploitative corporate crime,' *Criminology*, 44(2): 397–430.
Quesnay, F. 1972 [1758]. *Tableau Économique*. London: Macmillan.
Ruggiero, V. 1996. *Organised and Corporate Crime in Europe: Others that Can't Be Refused*. Aldershot: Dartmouth.
Ruggiero, V. 2007. 'It's the economy, stupid! Classifying power crime,' *International Journal of the Sociology of Law*, 35(4): 163–177.
Ruggiero, V. 2009. 'On liberty and crime: Adam Smith and John Stuart Mill,' *Crime, Law and Social Change*, 51(3–4): 435–450.
Ruggiero, V. 2013. *The Crimes of the Economy: A Criminological Analysis of Economic Thought*. London and New York: Routledge.
Ruggiero, V. 2014. *Movements in the City: Conflict in the European Metropolis*. London and New York: Routledge.
Ruggiero, V. and South, N. 2010. 'Green criminology and dirty collar crime,' *Critical Criminology: An International Journal*, 18(4): 251–262.
Salzano, J. 1994. 'It's dirty business: Organized crime in deep sludge,' *Criminal Organizations [International Association for the Study of Organized Crime]*, 8(3&4): 17–20.
Scorse, J. 2010. *What Environmentalists Need to Know about Economics*. New York: Palgrave Macmillan.
Siegel, D., van de Bunt, H. and Zaitch, D. (eds.) 2003. *Global Organized Crime: Trends and Developments*. Dordrecht: Kluwer.
Smith, A. 1976 [1776]. *An Inquiry into the Nature and Causes of the Wealth of Nations*, R. H. Campbell, A. S. Skinner, and W. B. Todd, eds. Oxford: Clarendon Press.
Sutherland, E. H. 1949. *White Collar Crime*. New York: The Dryden Press.
Szasz, A. 1994. *EcoPopulism: Toxic Waste and the Movement for Environmental Justice*. Minneapolis, MN: University of Minnesota Press.
Tittle, C. R. 1995. *Control Balance: Toward a General Theory of Deviance*. Boulder, CO: Westview.
van Duyne, P. C. 1993. 'Organised crime and business crime-enterprises in the Netherlands,' *Crime, Law and Social Change*, 19(2): 103–142.
Waldron, J. 2006. 'How judges should judge,' *The New York Review of Books*. August 10: 54–59.
White, R. (ed.) 2010. *Global Environmental Harm: Criminological Perspectives*. Cullompton, Devon, UK: Willan.

24

Green criminology and the working class

Political ecology and the expanded implications of political economic analysis in green criminology

Michael J. Lynch

Green criminology emerged as an extension of radical political economic analyses of crime and justice (Lynch 1990). That form of green criminology has expanded (e.g., Lynch, Long, Barrett and Stretesky 2013; Lynch, Long, Stretesky and Barrett 2017; Stretesky, Long and Lynch 2013a, 2013b) and now includes empirical studies of environmental injustice and the association between class, race and toxic exposure patterns (Lynch and Stretesky 2013; Lynch, Stretesky and Burns 2004a, 2004b; Stretesky and Lynch 2002, 1999). Despite its origins and those more recent contributions, a green criminological-political economic approach that addresses working class environmental concerns—or what is called 'political ecology' (Peet and Watts 2004)—remains underdeveloped. This chapter argues for expanding the political economic analysis of working class environmental issues within green criminology.

Political ecology draws attention to political expressions of ecological concerns, including the development of environmental social movements and race-based environmental justice movements (Stretesky, Shelia Huss, Lynch and Childs 2011; see also Ozymy et al., this volume, Chapter 8; Pellow, this volume, Chapter 32), many of which emerge in both urban and rural working class communities. Political ecology is important because through political expressions of environmental issues, the working class struggles with addressing how current political economic arrangements threaten their health and existence through various forms of ecological disorganisation. That struggle involves the working class's search for a solution to the deeply embedded structural constraints of capitalism that adversely impact the life-course and health of the working class. While the working class likely interprets these issues as *local* concerns, political economic analysis must connect these issues to the context of global capitalism. It must therefore also include analyses of environmental problems experienced by the working class (WC) and poor people in less-developed (LD) nations (WC-LD), and of how forms of capital penetration in the world economy keep the WC-LD dependent and unable to control the forms of ecological destruction capitalism brings.

For the working class, part of the issue involves (re)creating the means of production in ecologically sustainable ways while simultaneously maintaining sustainable employment—sufficient, well-paid, regular work conditions decoupled from variability in the cycles of capitalism. Both capitalism and ecological destruction have broad impacts on the world's working peoples, creating conditions in which traditional livelihoods are undermined and become hazardous, and in which adverse local environmental conditions (i.e., pollution and ecological destruction) impede the development of positive life conditions.

In developing this type of political ecology, attention must also be paid to the intersection of humans and nature under conditions of capitalism (O'Connor 1998). Capitalism exploits, as noted below, both workers and nature, which are joined together by capitalism as objects of exploitation.

Political economic analysis of ecological destruction and the working class should address limitations in traditional economic arguments about this relationship. In traditional economics, the poor/working classes are viewed as culprits behind ecological destruction (for a discussion see, e.g., Lynch, Stretesky and Long 2017). Especially vilified in this view are WC-LD peoples, who are depicted as producing forms of ecological destruction, and who then draw the attention of researchers and policy makers (see, Gray and Moseley 2005). Doing so detracts attention from the more significant ecologically destructive behaviours of the economically powerful. In reality, globally, there are many ecologically sustainable lifestyle options and philosophies detached from capitalism (Merchant 2005), and many ecologically active and conscious WC-LD peoples.

This chapter begins by connecting the exploitation of the working class and nature in political economic thought, and then describes working class responses to ecological destruction under capitalism. This is followed by a discussion of the linkages between workers and environmental movements from a political economic perspective, and then considers working class concerns with exposure to environmental toxins in workplaces and communities, and how these may develop into contested illness struggles. A brief discussion of the political economic analysis of environmental conflicts and struggles faced by the working class and poor in less-developed nations is also included.

Background part I: connecting Marxist political economy and the exploitation of workers and nature

Marx's political economy is a critique of capitalism that expresses concern for working class interests. Key to Marx's political economy is analysing exploitation of the working class under capitalism, which is organised around the exploitation of labour. For Marx, exploitation was not a subjective value judgement, but rather an empirical question. Marx (1974) measured working class exploitation using an empirical indicator—the rate of surplus value (the excess value produced by the labour of workers over and above the wages they are paid). The higher the rate of surplus value, the more exploited the working class (for a criminological example, see Lynch 1988).

In brief, working class exploitation (surplus value) tends to accelerate with the expansion of capitalism. For capitalists, the rate of profit (π) is limited or bounded by the rate of surplus value (the two measures share a common dimension mathematically) (Marx 1974). As a result, the maximum quantity *or mass of profit* (its aggregation) is limited by the *mass of surplus value*. Thus, if production and the mass of surplus value expand, the mass of profit also increases. Why does this matter? More production is better for the capitalist, but worse for the working class because it implies the expanded exploitation of labour (except in unusual short-term conditions).

Extending this argument, Foster (2000) argued that labour cannot be exploited unless nature is also exploited. This occurs because the process of industrial capitalist production requires raw material inputs, and those raw materials must first be extracted from nature using working class labour to initiate production. From this, it can be argued that the more nature is exploited for its resources, the more the working class will be exploited in the aggregate (Foster 2000). That is, the exploitation of nature allows the exploitation of the worker. As the exploitation of nature expands, the mass of surplus value also expands by increasing the mass of production. Consequently, the more nature is exploited for its resources, the more the working class can be exploited for its labour—through what can be described as a non-recursive relationship. This understanding is key to conceptualising the political economic analysis of the conjoined green victimisation of the working class and nature.

The exploitation of nature and the working class is also built around property relations that limit working class access to nature and natural resources, generating unequal class access to nature. As Marx (1842) argued in his essays on the theft of wood, restricting the access of the working class and the poor to nature causes those classes to be dependent on wage labour for survival because they are prevented from using natural resources that would allow people to survive outside of capitalist relations. In *Capital*, Marx referred to this as 'divorcing the producers from the means of production' (Marx 1974: 875). Removal of access rights is part of transforming the detached and independent person into a member of the working class, who must depend on engagement with capital relations of production for survival. This is a particularly important issue in the modern context of capitalism and the exploitation of natural resources in less-developed nations where limiting access to nature enhances the control of nature by capital and leads to conflicts with local peoples (Bryant 1992; Moore 1993; see also Goyes, this volume, Chapter 12; Goyes, Mol, Brisman and South 2017).

Background part II: ecological destruction and the working class

The previous part outlined the general connection between the exploitation of the working class and nature under capitalism to illustrate their joint exploitation. We now turn attention to the following question: how does the exploitation/destruction of nature create various adverse ecological consequences for the working class and affect working class responses to ecosystem *destruction*?

Under treadmill of production theory (ToP) (Schnaiberg 1980), two kinds of ecological destruction are important considerations: those associated with *ecological withdrawals* (natural resource extraction) and those involving *ecological additions* (pollution) (see Lynch et al., this volume, Chapter 4). As research indicates, both processes impact nature adversely and produce unequally distributed health effects that are more detrimental to the poor and working classes (see below). These conditions also generate working class environmental-social movements in response to detrimental environmental conditions (Barca 2012). A significant volume of research indicates that pollution and hazardous and toxic waste sites are unevenly distributed (Boyce, Klemer, Templet and Willis 1999; Daniels and Friedman 1999; Faber and Krieg 2002), and are located in closer proximity to communities of colour, the poor and the working class (Downey 2006; Downey and Hawkins 2008; Ozymy et al., this volume, Chapter 8; Pais, Crowder and Downey 2013; Young et al. 2012). Thus, production methods that exploit nature and return industrial waste to ecosystems are likely to generate detrimental environmental conditions for working class communities. The above is also likely true for ecological withdrawals. Due to the distribution of resources and social class, ecological withdrawal effects tend to be isolated geographically and have greater health impacts for the rural working class and the WC-LD. This occurs, as ecological Marxists argue, through the process of 'ecological unequal exchange' (Rice 2009, 2007) and 'metabolic rift' in the global capitalist world economy (Foster 1999) (for a discussion, see Lynch et al., this volume, Chapter 4).

The point: political economic analysis connects the exploitation of workers and nature. Workers and nature are joined as objects of capital's exploitation, while the exploitation of nature also creates adverse ecological conditions that are unequally distributed and have greater consequences for the working class. In this sense, two forms of ecological destruction—ecological withdrawals and additions—undermine the health of the working class. Capitalist production promotes both unhealthy ecosystem conditions and unhealthy conditions for the working class simultaneously through processes that link them together through exploitation. Because the working class and nature are joined together in these ways, working class responses to the adverse consequences of capitalism will necessarily also be responses to ecological destruction (O'Connor 1988).

Background part III: working class and environmental movement overlap

As noted above, the working class and nature are linked via forms of exploitation that characterise capitalism. As O'Connor (1988, 1998)) notes, working class responses to its exploitation can also be constituted as struggles against ecological destruction even when working class consciousness fails to perceive the connection between its own exploitation and nature's exploitation and degradation. Following Brisman and South (e.g., Brisman and South 2013, 2014), this type of analysis can be framed within the purview of green cultural criminology, focussing on how resistance to environmental harms emerge and are transformed and spread, but it has also been examined by green criminologists using social movements theory and empirical analyses (Stretesky, Huss and Lynch 2012; Stretesky, Huss, Lynch and Childs 2011).

At the conscious level, the working class perceives the exploitation of nature relative to its impacts on their health and general conditions of life. ToP theory recognises that this may occur in relation to the destruction of resources that provide working class jobs. But here, a contradiction may emerge when, for example, tree harvesting supplies jobs, while deforestation eliminates those jobs. Such struggles are often more visible for the rural working class and WC-LD, where they are confronted more directly by the contradiction between the destruction of nature through ecological withdrawals and their economic livelihoods—or how forms of ecological destruction that accompany ecological withdrawals create adverse ecological conditions that can impact public health. This situation (differential exposure of the working class to ecological destruction) may, as ToP theory suggests (Schnaiberg 1980), fragment working class responses to ecological destruction and even lead to a situation in which portions of the working class side with capital in ecological disputes to maintain conditions that provide employment despite the adverse ecological and health impacts created. In short, the working class is not always united in its responses to forms of ecological degradation caused by capitalism. In some cases, the working class cannot be united because much—if not all—of that class has limited alternatives or no option other than relying on the work capitalism provides, even if that work has adverse health consequences related to the destruction of nature (see, e.g., van Herk and Bisschop, this volume, Chapter 22). Thus, faced with the option of working and surviving in the present (short term) or promoting the long-term health of the community, some workers choose economic survival. Consequently, the working class is not likely to be single-minded when it comes to interpreting the effects of environmental policy or in responding to adverse ecological conditions through collective actions and social movements. Such tension is evident in battles over coal mining and especially mountaintop removal mining in rural America, where factions of the working class can be found on both sides of the issue (Bell and York 2010).

Political economic intersections: production, work and ecological struggles

Working class concerns with economic exploitation, and the effects of ecological disorganisation in the workplace and on working class communities sometimes connect to and affect working class responses toward ecologically destructive processes. O'Connor is among those who have addressed these issues, highlighting the idea that ecological Marxism 'unites the themes of culture and nature with the traditional Marxist category of labor or material production' (O'Connor 1998: 35). He points out the two-sided nature of this problem. On the one hand, there are 'technical relations' or 'productive force relations' that draw attention to the interaction of humans and nature through the technological means that humans use to withdraw and shape nature's raw materials into commodities. On the other hand, there are 'social relationships' of production issues that describe human production and the extraction and use of resources in a given mode of production (e.g., capitalism versus slavery). Cultural issues are subsumed here under social relations and are influenced strongly by the form of productive relations that dominate the productive system. While there is some variability in the specific appearance of productive relations across societies, and hence, in this view, some concept of 'cultural' variability (perhaps better addressed as 'political economic variability'), it must be recognised that all nations are currently part of the world capitalist system of production, and, therefore, one could argue that 'culture' has become a reflection of the composition of the productive structure of global capitalism (Robinson 2004: 30–33). In this sense, it is not so much *culture* as it is the *organisation of capitalism* that influences working class responses to the impacts of ecological destruction on their lives. The larger point, however, is to draw attention to how the political economic structure of capitalism shapes the ecological system and working class life opportunities, including exposure to environmental toxins.

Catton and Dunlap (1978) proposed understanding the sociological relevance of ecological forces as part of environmental sociology, arguing that environmental sociology should address how physical environments (i.e., natural ecology and ecosystems) affect human behaviour. This important statement laid the basis for distinguishing between environmental sociology and traditional sociological approaches. Drawing attention to the natural ecology–human behaviour interface, Dunlap and Catton (1979: 244) departed from the traditional sociological premise that social facts should be explained relative to other social facts, and stressed that the natural world influences the development and organisation of human societies (and, in so doing, they found common ground with economic and environmental anthropologists, although neither might admit as much). Expanding on this, Buttel (1978, 2003) drew political economic class analysis into environmental sociology, producing significant discussions of the relevance of environmental movements and the development of global anti-corporate movements (Buttel and Gould 2004) to illustrate social responses to deleterious ecological conditions generated by production. Importantly, both types of movements were influenced by working class participation.

These viewpoints reflect a political economic green perspective in which production and ecology intersect and influence each other. The context of that interaction involves recognition of working class exploitation as a codependent process attached to ecological exploitation, and the ways in which workers' and nature's exploitation are joined together by capitalism. In this sense, the political economy of production, work and environmental destruction also can be joined.

The workplace and beyond

Recognising that the working class and nature intersect in various ways creates the possibility of exploring a number of relevant issues from a radical-political economic approach to green criminology. From this perspective, the working class, nature, production and ecological issues appear in two primary forms that may elicit a working class response to ecological harms: as workplace concerns and as community concerns.

Toxins and the environmental workplace

Workers have long been concerned with the effects of exposure to toxins in the workplace (Robinson 1991). In the workplace, workers face the contradiction between employment and occupational safety. Numerous studies describe the forms of toxic exposure workers experience (see, e.g., Rosner and Markowitz 1987), and the struggles in which workers engage against toxic workplaces. These are not simply industrial struggles, but also extend to agricultural workers (Gordon 1999), and both kinds of workers' struggles against toxic workplaces can be examined in political economic terms (Elling 1989). A political economic approach to worker occupational exposure is an important aspect of investigating the intersection of workers and ecology under capitalism. This view has also been extended, in limited fashion, to environmental workplace issues affecting working women (e.g., Murphy 2000), including research on how women in developing nations struggle against toxic workplaces (Hippert 2002)—an issue largely ignored in green criminology (for a discussion, see Lynch 2017). Such analyses must also recognise that industry resists both workers' efforts to improve workplace environments and legislative efforts to limit toxic exposure in the workplace. In the United States (U.S.), for example, corporations have long campaigned to undo legislation protecting workers' health and safety (Szasz 1984).

The opposition of workers to toxic workplaces has been under-explored within green criminology (Shantz 2004). Workplaces are important environmental contexts for workers because they spend significant time there, and toxic workplaces can have serious detrimental consequences for worker health. The neglect of political economic approaches within green criminology may be one reason these struggles have been overlooked. Workplace environmental conditions, of course, are not limited to their direct impact on workers because toxic workplace conditions likely indicate the presence of toxic pollutants that spill over into working class communities.

A related problem is the definition of 'environment'. In general, green criminologists use the term 'environment' to mean the natural ecosystem or portions of the ecosystem. That definition excludes human-created environments, such as the workplace, which are important environmental locations related to toxic exposure (see Frank and Lynch 1992). Green criminologists can expand the concept of green crime substantially by addressing toxic exposure in the workplace in political economic terms—a point made by Brisman and South, in the first chapter of this volume, who note the need for research on 'health and safety in the workplace where breaches have environmentally damaging consequences'. Shantz (2004:

692) argues that an approach to environmental problems of/in workplaces can also produce analyses that recognise a 'dynamic understanding of people as workers and workers as activists'. Moreover, Shantz maintains that the literature on toxic workplaces has been rather insensitive to class analysis, even rejecting the class analysis of environmental social movements in workplaces (see also, Shantz and Adam 1999, and below). According to Shantz (2004: 696), '[p]erspectives that ignore or downplay political economy in favor of cultural issues or "postmodern values" and identities do a disservice by denying the ways in which the development of culture, values and identity are rooted in capitalist power relations'. Following Shantz's argument, concepts such as 'working class identity' have objective referents associated with the ways in which workers are attached to political economic relationships under capitalism. By recognising that connection, researchers call attention to the similarities in working class responses to toxic workplace environments, highlighting the effort of workers to respond to those negative conditions across time and place, and to the routine ways in which capital responds to or denies such efforts.

Toxins in the community

Shantz (2004: 698) also argues that 'if workers are to overcome their alienated class character ... they must ... confront the growing contradiction between their developing community consciousness and the material confinement and dehumanising experience on the job site', meaning they must interpret toxic exposure in the workplace and community as a consequence of the same structural conditions imposed by capitalism. This is an important point—one that recognises the intersection of working class community and workplace struggles against the ecologically destructive forces of capitalism.

Environmental social movement literature is divided with respect to the role of the working class in environmental movements. Schnaiberg (1980), for example, points out that workers occupy a contradictory place when it comes to ecological issues, sometimes supporting ecological legislation as *members of communities*, but often opposing them *as workers* because ecological legislation may restrict the expansion of production that has negative impacts on worker economic security within the confines of capitalism (see also Obach, 2004).

The social movement literature, however, indicates that workers' unions have played important roles in ecological movements, even in the founding of environmentalism in the U.S. (Dewey 1998). Organised worker movements have opposed: climate change (Fell 2014); deforestation (Bonanno and Blome 2001); the expansion of the treadmill of production (Obach 2004); surface mining (Montric 2000); numerous local environmental issues (e.g., Fine 2012); and those related to the globalisation of labour and capitalism (Fell 2014; Silverman 2006). To be sure, the relationship between workers/unions and environmentalism is complex (Kojola and Pellow 2018; Kojola, Xiao and McCright 2014), reaffirming the ToP argument that workers have interests on both sides of the environmental regulatory process. Fragmentation of working class responses to ecological issues does not mean, however, that political economic analysis has nothing useful to contribute to discussions of ecological worker movements within their communities, including fights against environmental injustice precipitated by production's adverse ecological consequences on working class communities and communities of colour. Indeed, these contradictory positions reflect the juxtaposition between the restrictions capitalism inscribes on the working class as a whole, and the desire of the working class to be freed from those restrictions in an effort to achieve what Marx described in his *Philosophical and*

Economic Manuscripts as a life consistent with the 'species being' of human. Worker struggles are not, in other words, always limited to issues that appear, at first glance, as struggles over the conditions of work, such as workplace exploitation or alienation. When workers confront environmental issues in their communities, it is easy to suppose that those are not work-related reactions against capitalism's deleterious conditions because they are located in the community rather than in the workplace. Correctly situating worker responses to environmental harms in their communities requires paying attention to the connection between the social and the economic. As a social force, the effects of capitalism are widespread—a point Marx made when he argued that social organisation reflects the characteristics of the means and mode of production. In his sense, workers who struggle against environmental problems in their communities are not engaged in cultural or identity conflicts, but in *economic* conflicts. In political economic terms, community-based working class struggles are activities that reflect the embeddedness of workers within the economic, political and social confines of capitalism, or in the forms of domination and control capitalism produces (Shantz 2004).

When analysing working class community ecological activism, researchers must be careful to separate those concerns from middle-class or liberal environmental reform efforts. Liberal environmental reform is more likely to focus attention on animal rights, taking animals as objects of study and policy in their own right (Loomis 2016; White 2008). Doing so tends to marginalise working class concerns with ecologically destructive behaviour in their communities, and sometimes academics suggest that research examining those issues harbours an anthropocentric bias. Importantly, as Adkin (1992) argues, working class environmental concerns have forced liberal environmental movements to recognise the role economic interests play in shaping ecological crises, and have altered responses to those crises. From a working class perspective, it is unfortunate that liberal reforms which target wildlife harms, for example, fail to develop a broader understanding of how ecological harms intersect under capitalism, and that the plight of wildlife species and humans are connected intimately to capitalism's growth imperative *and its disregard for the life of any species*. Consequently, green criminology must move beyond criticising research for its anthropogenic orientation, and instead recognise that political economic analysis, which recognises the joint exploitation of humans and nature by capitalism, is capable of addressing harms to humans, non-humans and ecosystems even if any particular application of that view is focussing attention on only one of these types of victims (cf. Sollund, this volume, Chapter 29). In short, all of these groups are united as *victims* by the expansion of capitalism. In relative terms, however, working class victims of capitalism's green crimes have received less attention than animals in the green criminological literature.

Drawing a wider circle: the political economy of contested illnesses

In exploring the uses of political economic theory and the subjects to which it applies, this part of the chapter directs attention to the literature on 'contested illnesses' as a process that occurs in working class communities. A 'contested illness' emerges when a claim that an ecological condition, such as pollution in a neighbourhood, is producing adverse health consequences for community members, *and* that claim is opposed by either or both the government and industry. The study of contested illnesses and the process involved in contested illnesses expanded significantly in 1999 with the formation of the Contested Illnesses Research Group at Brown University.

The contested illness literature draws attention to the dynamics process that occurs when a community—typically a working class community—asserts the existence of an ecological health hazard. Working class ecological struggles that involve contested illnesses are an example of working class responses to the detrimental ecological consequences of capitalist production.

Contested illness struggles often involve working class communities because it is these types of communities where industrial toxic waste is most likely to be located and to subsequently produce adverse health effects. In political economic terms, the importance of contested illnesses has to do with the ways in which responses to claims of adverse environmental health effects in working class communities are processed through the political system and how that process represents an important illustration of class conflict and the routine application of regulatory and legal powers capitalism generates.

The contested illnesses process begins when the environmental health claims of a community are lodged with some formal organisation charged with making regulatory decisions about the government's response to such claims, and whether such claims require further investigation to determine their veracity and the potential liability of corporate polluters who created the alleged circumstances. In this process, the government may request a response from industry to any government findings. Science plays a role at all levels of this process, as each actor recruits scientists or refers to scientific studies relevant to the matter. From a political economic perspective, it should be clear that class interest and access to assets and power play an important role in activating science. In comparison with corporations or industrial trade associations, working class communities have limited economic assets to wage such battles, and a community's economic assets limit its access to legal and scientific assistance (see, e.g., Brown, Morello-Frosch and Zavestoski 2011). On the political level, corporations and industries have much longer histories of association with regulatory agencies and individual regulators, who sometimes come from the regulated industries. In a political economic sense, the deck is stacked against working class communities, but this does not mean that the evidence is not sometimes so overwhelming that communities always lose these contests. While there is a significant literature on contested illnesses, this issue has barely penetrated the green criminological literature (for an exception, see South 2016). We suggest that greater attention to political economic theory within green criminology would help promote criminological study of contested illnesses and working class environmental concerns.

Drawing in the working class and poor in less developed (WC-LD) nations

Ecological harms come in a variety of forms and affect a variety of people. Perhaps most overlooked in green criminology are ecological harms affecting working class and poor peoples in less developed nations (WC-LD), as well as Indigenous/Native peoples (INP) (for exceptions, see, e.g., Goyes, this volume, Chapter 12; Goyes, Mol, Brisman and South 2017; Nurse, this volume, Chapter 33; Samuels-Jones, this volume, Chapter 34). Both groups have long resisted global capitalism's ecological destructive tendencies around the world. Some attention to this issue has been generated indirectly by studies of e-waste, which suggest that the international organisation of the e-waste trade has adverse effects on WC-LDs (see generally van Herk and Bisschop, this volume, Chapter 22). An extended analysis of the connection between political economy, e-waste and poverty, however, is absent from that literature. In addition, green criminology has hardly paid attention to ecological struggles in INP communities (Lynch and Stretesky 2012; Moloney and Chambliss 2014), an issue that requires more extensive green criminological analysis (for exceptions, see, e.g., Brisman, McClanahan, South and Walters 2018; Lynch, Stretesky and Long 2018).

Green criminologists are unlikely to object to the premise that e-waste deserves their attention. And in political economic terms, the production and distribution of e-waste reflects the structure of global capitalism and the division of nations on a development spectrum. Developed nations are centres of demand for electronic products. In developed nations, e-product turnover is rapid, and the production of e-waste from no-longer-desirable e-products is extensive. Many electronic products are produced in developing nations, while many of the raw materials needed for the production come from lesser-developed nations (Brisman and South 2017). Both the production of electronic products and the extraction of raw materials in developing regions are important sources of pollution in those areas—pollution that is unevenly disbursed and has greater impacts on the WC-LDs (Krishna and Kulshrestha 2008; see also South 2015).

In addition to the production/extraction concern above, the recycling of e-waste has important detrimental ecological and public health effects on WC-LDs. Those effects, widely reported in the media, impact WC-LD child-workers (Huo et al. 2007). Because political economic analysis situates the problem of e-waste within the context of global capitalism, it is important to explore the ways in which the global market place of capitalism and the penetration of capital into developing nations impacts ecological problems more generally (not just e-waste) in developing nations and creates adverse health problems for workers as part of the analysis of green crimes and injustice.

E-waste/e-product production is just one example of the forms of ecological harm that impact WC-LDs. As Foster (1993) suggests, orthodox economics justifies such harms, arguing that less-developed nations are 'under-polluted' relative to developed nations, and, moreover, that e-waste presents an 'opportunity' for economic growth in less-developed nations (Herat and Agamuthu 2012). Those types of morally questionable analyses overlook how the political economic process of uneven development produces the ecological crisis faced by WC-LDs (O'Connor 1989). There are many WC-LD issues green criminologists can address employing global political economic analysis, including: access to 'native' lands for subsistence (e.g., fishing, hunting); deforestation; mining; the production of pollution and exposure to pollution; and other traditional 'economic' relations; how regulatory and legal policies facilitate exclusion of the poor from environmental access; the transfer of traditional open access lands to corporate entities; the effects of the introduction of non-native agricultural species on WC-LDs; and the role the military sometimes plays in these arrangements. Additional studies can also address international working class environmental problems generated by the global treadmill of capitalism. There is, in other words, no shortage of opportunities to apply political economic analysis to green criminological problems.

Yet, green criminologists have paid minor attention to these concerns from a political economic perspective. As suggested above, green criminological discussions of WC-LD environmental issues have overlooked how those problems emerge in the context of uneven development and a highly stratified global division of labour that limits WC-LD responses to the deleterious ecological impacts of global capitalism (Adeola 2000; Smith 1994). Important to such discussion is the observation that global capitalism maintains WC-LDs in dependent economic conditions (Jorgenson 2009a; Jorgenson, Austin and Dick 2009; Rice 2007; Shandra, Shor and London 2009; Timmons and Parks 2009). Among many nations in that situation, average daily wages for the working poor are as little as $2/day (Santos-Paulino 2012) and, as a result, few economic resources exist to respond to ecological problems generated by capitalism. In taking this view, it is necessary that political economic analysis draws attention to the ways in which excessive consumption in developed nations generates environmental harm in underdeveloped and developing nations, and contributes to the green forms of victimisation experienced by WC-LDs.

While space precludes an extended discussion, relevant literature points to the need for further analysis of ecological destruction and INP responses to those circumstances. The research that has been undertaken has connected, for example, INP genocide to the history of ecological destructive tendencies of capitalism (Crook and Short 2014; Crook, Short and South 2018; Fenelon and Hall 2008; Fenelon and Murguía 2008; Hall and Fenelon 2015). With respect to the current subject, that approach situates INP within the context of global capitalism and as marginalised members of the working class.

Discussion and conclusion

This chapter has examined how the political economic analysis of green harms can be expanded to include more fully working class concerns and victimisation. The discussion has not covered all possibilities but has employed illustrative examples of potential research that green criminologists might explore. Questions related to the political economic distribution of and access to ecological assets are fruitful areas of investigation capable of expanding the scope of green criminology. Some of these potential ecological/environmental/social justice questions examine environmental degradation effects for the working class in less-developed/developing and developed nations, or in the context of world systems relationships. There is, I suggest, no shortage of issues to examine.

Such studies can, for example, draw attention to the political economy of the environment at the international level by focussing on international environmental and trade agreements and the processes governing environment–society intersections (Clapp and Helleiner 2012). Indeed, as Clapp and Helleiner (2012) point out, relevant work has provided important insights into how international environmental agreements are structured by global economic relationships, but they note that further studies are needed. As an example, China and India have emerged as important economic market actors with the capability of altering ecological trends either positively or negatively (see Mao et al., this volume, Chapter 21). These types of political economic analyses have long explored the global nature of these ecological crises and can be included within political economic green criminological research (Lynch 1990).

Of particular relevance to political economic green criminology is the literature produced by ecological Marxists. Here, the explanation of the human–nature intersection in relation to capitalism stands centre stage in the political economic framework of these explanations (e.g., Burkett 2008; Foster 1992, 1999, 2000; Foster, Brett and York 2010). Importantly, in addition to theoretical elaborations illustrating the importance of political economic analysis in relation to the intersection of capitalism and ecological destruction, this literature has produced numerous empirical analyses of that intersection (e.g., Jorgenson 2003, 2005, 2006a, 2006b, 2009a, 2009b). Many of those studies have particular relevance to developing discussions of ecological harm within the context of global capitalism. That literature and the issues of concern in those studies have received limited attention from green criminologists (Lynch, Long, Barrett and Stretesky 2013; Stretesky, Long and Lynch 2013a).

Despite three decades of development, green criminologists have barely scratched the surface of the variety of issues that they can explore. This point has been illustrated in this chapter by focussing on green political economic analysis of working class environmental issues. This connection to the working class is also important for establishing how green criminologists can contribute to efforts to organise the working class to resist ecological destruction.

The above arguments reinforce the theoretical origins of green criminology in political economic theory and analysis. Those roots provide an important theoretical foundation for green criminological analysis. As a theoretical approach, political economic analysis calls attention to class struggle and the economic origins of ecological disorganisation and destruction. Attending to those issues can strengthen the theoretical basis of green criminology and connect it to similar literatures in environmental sociology and ecological Marxism. Whether green criminologists heed this advice is another matter. But, whether they do or do not, environmental issues are connected inextricably to global and local political economic organisation. Unfortunately, ignoring that reality has meant overlooking how capitalism's ecological effects penetrate into the life of the working class and poor.

References

Adeola, F. O. 2000. 'Cross-National environmental injustice and human rights issues a review of evidence in the developing world,' *American Behavioral Scientist*, 43(4): 686–706.

Adkin, L. 1992. 'Counter hegemony and environmental politics in Canada,' in W. K. Carroll (ed.) *Organizing Dissent*, pp. 137–156. Toronto: Garamond.

Barca, S. 2012. 'On working-class environmentalism: A historical and transnational overview,' *Interface: A Journal for and about Social Movements*, 4(2): 61–80.

Bell, S. E. and York, R. 2010. 'Community economic identity: The coal industry and ideology construction in West Virginia,' *Rural Sociology*, 75(1): 111–143.

Bonanno, A. and Blome, B. 2001. 'The environmental movement and labor in global capitalism: Lessons from the case of the headwaters forest,' *Agriculture & Human Values*, 18(4): 365–381.

Boyce, J. K., Klemer, A. R., Templet, P. H. and Willis, C. E. 1999. 'Power distribution, the environment, and public health: A state-level analysis,' *Ecological Economics*, 29(1): 127–140.

Brisman, A., McClanahan, B., South, N. and Walters, R. 2018. *Water, Crime and Security in theTwenty-First Century: Too Dirty, Too Little, Too Much*. London: Palgrave Macmillan.

Brisman, A. and South, N. 2013. 'A green-cultural criminology: An exploratory outline,' *Crime Media Culture* 9(2): 115–135.

Brisman, A. and South, N. 2014. *Green Cultural Criminology: Constructions of Environmental Harm, Consumerism, and Resistance to Ecocide*. London and New York: Routledge.

Brisman, A. and South, N. 2017. 'Consumer technologies, crime and environmental implications,' in M. R. McGuire and T. J. Holt (eds.) *The Routledge Handbook of Technology, Crime and Justice*, pp. 310–324. London and New York: Routledge.

Brown, P., Morello-Frosch, R. and Zavestoski, S. (eds.) 2011. *Contested Illnesses: Citizens, Science, and Health Social Movements*. Oakland, CA: University of California Press.

Bryant, R. L. 1992. 'Political ecology: An emerging research agenda in third-world studies,' *Political Geography*, 11(1): 12–36.

Burkett, P. 2008. *Marxism and Ecological Economics: Toward a Red and Green Political Economy*. Chicago, IL: Haymarket Books.

Buttel, F. H. 1978. 'Environmental sociology, a new paradigm?,' *The American Sociologist*, 13(1): 252–256.

Buttel, F. H. 2003. 'Environmental sociology and the explanation of environmental reform,' *Organization & Environment*, 16(3): 306–344.

Buttel, F. H. and Gould, K. A. 2004. 'Global social movement(s) at the crossroads: Some observations on the trajectory of the anti-corporate globalization movement,' *Journal of World-Systems Research*, 10(1): 37–66.

Catton, W. R. and Dunlap, R. E. 1978. 'Environmental sociology: A new paradigm,' *The American Sociologist*, 13(1): 41–49.

Clapp, J. P. and Helleiner, E. 2012. 'International political economy and the environment: Back to the basics?' *International Affairs*, 88(3): 485–501.

Crook, M. and Short, D. 2014. 'Marx, Lemkin and the genocide–ecocide nexus,' *The International Journal of Human Rights*, 18(3): 298–319.

Crook, M., Short, D. and South, N. 2018. 'Ecocide, genocide, capitalism and colonialism: Consequences for indigenous peoples and glocal ecosystems environments,' *Theoretical Criminology*, 22(3): 298–317.

Daniels, G. and Friedman, S. 1999. 'Spatial inequality and the distribution of industrial toxic releases: Evidence from the 1990 TRI,' *Social Science Quarterly*, 80(2): 244–261.

Dewey, S. 1998. 'Working for the environment: Organized labor and the origins of environmentalism in the United States, 1948–1970,' *Environmental History*, 3(1): 45–63.

Downey, L. 2006. 'Environmental inequality in 14 major metropolitan areas in 2000,' *Sociological Spectrum*, 26(1): 21–41.

Downey, L. and Hawkins, B. 2008. 'Race, income, and environmental inequality in the United States,' *Sociological Perspectives*, 51(4): 759–781.

Dunlap, R. E. and Catton, W. R. 1979. 'Environmental sociology,' *Annual Review of Sociology*, 5: 243–247.

Elling, R. H. 1989. 'The political economy of workers' health and safety,' *Social Science & Medicine*, 28(11): 1171–1182.

Faber, D. R. and Krieg, E. J. 2002. 'Unequal exposure to ecological hazards: Environmental injustices in the Commonwealth of Massachusetts,' *Environmental Health Perspectives*, 110(S2): 277–288.

Fell, R. 2014. 'An alternative socio-ecological strategy? International trade unions' engagement with climate change,' *Review of International Political Economy*, 21(2): 372–398.

Fenelon, J. V. and Hall, T. D. 2008. 'Revitalization and indigenous resistance to globalization and neoliberalism,' *American Behavioral Scientist*, 51(12): 1867–1901.

Fenelon, J. V. and Murguía, S. J. 2008. 'Indigenous peoples globalization, resistance, and revitalization,' *American Behavioral Scientist*, 51(12): 1656–1671.

Fine, L. A. 2012. 'Workers and the land in US history: Pointe Mouillee and the downriver Detroit working class in the Twentieth century,' *Labor History*, 53(3): 409–434.

Foster, J. B. 1992. 'The absolute general law of environmental degradation under capitalism,' *Capitalism, Nature, Socialism*, 3(3): 77–82.

Foster, J. B. 1993. '"Let them eat pollution": Capitalism and the world environment,' *Monthly Review*, 44(8): 10–11.

Foster, J. B. 1999. 'Marx's theory of metabolic rift: Classical foundations for environmental sociology,' *American Journal of Sociology*, 105(2): 366–405.

Foster, J. B. 2000. *Marx's Ecology: Materialism and Nature*. New York: Monthly Review Press.

Foster, J. B., Clark, B. and York, R. 2010. *The Ecological Rift: Capitalism's War on the Earth*. New York: Monthly Review Press.

Frank, N. and Lynch, M. J. 1992. *Corporate Crime, Corporate Violence*. Albany, NY: Harrow & Heston.

Gordon, R. 1999. 'Poisons in the fields: The united farm workers, pesticides, and environmental politics,' *The Pacific Historical Review*, 68(1): 51–77.

Goyes, D. R., Mol, H., Brisman, A. and South, N. (eds.) 2017. *Environmental Crime in Latin America: The Theft of Nature and the Poisoning of the Land*. London: Palgrave Macmillan.

Gray, L. C. and Moseley, W. G. 2005. 'A geographical perspective on poverty–environment interactions,' *The Geographical Journal*, 171(1): 9–23.

Hall, T. D. and Fenelon, J. V. 2015. *Indigenous Peoples and Globalization: Resistance and Revitalization*. Abingdon, Oxon, UK: Routledge.

Herat, S. and Agamuthu, P. 2012. 'E-waste: A problem or an opportunity? Review of issues, challenges and solutions in Asian countries,' *Waste Management & Research*, 30(11): 1113–1129.

Hippert, C. 2002. 'Multinational corporations, the politics of the world economy, and their effects on women's health in the developing world: A review,' *Health Care for Women International*, 23(8): 861–869.

Huo, X., Lin, P., Xu, X., Zheng, L., Qiu, B., Qi, Z., Zhang, B., Dai H. and Piao, Z. 2007. 'Elevated blood lead levels of children in Guiyu, an electronic waste recycling town in China,' *Environmental Health Perspectives*, 115(7): 1113–1117.

Jorgenson, A. K. 2003. 'Consumption and environmental degradation: A cross-national analysis of the ecological footprint,' *Social Problems*, 50(3): 374–394.

Jorgenson, A. K. 2005. 'Unpacking international power and the ecological footprints of nations: A quantitative cross-national study,' *Sociological Perspectives*, 48(3): 383–402.

Jorgenson, A. K. 2006a. 'Unequal ecological exchange and environmental degradation: A theoretical proposition and cross-national study of deforestation, 1990–2000,' *Rural Sociology*, 71(4): 685–712.

Jorgenson, A. K. 2006b. 'The transnational organization of production and environmental degradation: A cross-national study of the effects of foreign capital penetration on water pollution intensity, 1980–1995,' *Social Science Quarterly*, 87(3): 711–730.

Jorgenson, A. K. 2009a. 'The sociology of unequal exchange in ecological context: A panel study of lower-income countries, 1975–2001,' *Sociological Forum*, 24(1): 22–46.

Jorgenson, A. K. 2009b. 'The transnational organization of production, the scale of degradation, and ecoefficiency: A study of carbon dioxide emissions in less-developed countries,' *Human Ecology Review*, 16(1): 64–74.

Jorgenson, A. K., Austin, K. and Dick, C. 2009. 'Ecologically unequal exchange and the resource consumption/environmental degradation paradox a panel study of less-developed countries, 1970–2000,' *International Journal of Comparative Sociology*, 50(3–4): 263–284.

Kojola, E. and Pellow, D. 2018. 'Empire of timber: Labor unions and the Pacific Northwest Forests, by Erik Loomis,' *Society and Natural Resources*, 31(3): 389–391.

Kojola, E., Xiao, C. and McCright, A. M. 2014. 'Environmental concern of labor union members in the United States,' *The Sociological Quarterly*, 55(1): 72–91.

Krishna, M. and Kulshrestha, P. 2008. 'The toxic belt: Perspectives on e-waste dumping in developing nations,' *International Law & Policy Journal*, 15: 71–92.

Loomis, E. 2016. 'Towards a working-class environmentalism,' *The New Republic*, 5 December. Available at: https://newrepublic.com/article/139132/towards-working-class-environmentalism.

Lynch, M. J. 1988. 'The extraction of surplus value, crime and punishment: A preliminary examination,' *Crime, Law and Social Change*, 12(4): 329–344.

Lynch, M. J. 1990. 'The greening of criminology: A perspective for the 1990s,' *The Critical Criminologist*, 2(3): 3–4, 11–12.

Lynch, M. J. 2017. 'Acknowledging the female victim of green crime: Environmental exposure of women to industrial pollutants,' *Feminist Criminology*. DOI: 10.1177/1557085116673172.

Lynch, M. J., Long, M. A., Barrett, K. L. and Stretesky, P. B. 2013. 'Is it a crime to produce ecological disorganization? Why green criminology and political economy matter in the analysis of global ecological harms,' *The British Journal of Criminology*, 55(3): 997–1016.

Lynch, M. J., Long, M. A., Stretesky, P. B. and Barrett, K. A. 2017. *Green Criminology: Crime Justice and the Environment*. Oakland, CA: University of California Press.

Lynch, M. J. and Stretesky, P. B. 2012. 'Native Americans and social and environmental justice: Implications for criminology,' *Social Justice*, 38(3): 104–124.

Lynch, M. J. and Stretesky, P. B. 2013. 'The distribution of water-monitoring organizations across states: Implications for community policing,' *Policing: An International Journal of Police Strategies and Management*, 36(1): 6–26.

Lynch, M. J., Stretesky, P. B. and Burns, R. G. 2004a. 'Determinants of environmental law violation fines against oil refineries: Race, ethnicity, income and aggregation effects,' *Society and Natural Resources*, 17(4): 333–347.

Lynch, M. J., Stretesky, P. B. and Burns, R. G. 2004b. 'Slippery business: Race, class and legal determinants of penalties against petroleum refineries,' *Journal of Black Studies*, 34(3): 421–440.

Lynch, M. J., Stretesky, P. B. and Long, M. A. 2017. 'Blaming the poor for biodiversity loss: A political economic critique of the study of poaching and wildlife trafficking,' *Journal of Poverty and Social Justice*. DOI: 10.1332/175982717X14877669275083.

Lynch, M. J., Stretesky, P. B. and Long, M. A. 2018. 'Green criminology and native peoples: The treadmill of production and the killing of indigenous environmental activists,' *Theoretical Criminology*, 22(3): 318–341.

Marx, K. 1842. 'Debates on the law on theft of wood,' *Rheinische Zeitung*. 298, 300, 303, 305 and 307. Available at: https://marxists.org/archive/marx/works/download/Marx_Rheinishe_Zeitung.pdf.

Marx, K. 1974. *Capital, Volume I*. New York: International Press.

Merchant, C. 2005. *Radical Ecology: The Search for a Livable World*. New York: Routledge.

Moloney, C. J. and Chambliss, W. J. 2014, September. 'Slaughtering the Bison, controlling native Americans: A state crime and green criminology synthesis,' *Critical Criminology: An International Journal*, 22(3): 319–338.

Montric, C. 2000. 'Expedient environmentalism: Opposition to coal surface mining in Appalachia and the United Mine Workers of America, 1945–1975,' *Environmental History*, 5(1): 75–98.

Moore, D. S. 1993. 'Contesting terrain in Zimbabwe's eastern highlands: Political ecology, ethnography, and peasant resource struggles,' *Economic Geography*, 69(4): 380–401.
Obach, B. K. 2004. 'New labor: Slowing the treadmill of production?,' *Organization & Environment*, 17 (3): 337–354. DOI: 10.1177/1086026604267939.
O'Connor, J. 1988. 'Capitalism, nature, socialism a theoretical introduction,' *Capitalism, Nature, Socialism*, 1(1): 11–38.
O'Connor, J. 1989. 'Uneven and combined development and ecological crisis: A theoretical introduction,' *Race & Class*, 30(3): 1–11.
O'Connor, J. 1998. *Natural Causes: Essays in Ecological Marxism*. New York: Guilford Press.
Pais, J., Crowder, K. and Downey, L. 2013. 'Unequal trajectories: Racial and class differences in residential exposure to industrial hazards,' *Social Forces*, 92(3): 1189–1215.
Peet, R. and Watts, M. 2004. *Liberation Ecologies*. Oxon, UK: Routledge.
Rice, J. 2007. 'Ecological unequal exchange: Consumption, equity, and unsustainable structural relationships within the global economy,' *International Journal of Comparative Sociology*, 48(1): 43–72.
Rice, J. 2009. 'The transnational organization of production and uneven environmental degradation and change in the world economy,' *International Journal of Comparative Sociology*, 50(3–4): 215–236.
Roberts, J. T. and Parks, B. C. 2009. 'Ecologically unequal exchange, ecological debt, and climate justice the history and implications of three related ideas for a new social movement,' *International Journal of Comparative Sociology*, 50(3–4): 385–409.
Robinson, J. C. 1991. *Toil andtToxics: Workplace Struggles and Political Strategies for Occupational Health*. Berkeley, CA: University of California Press.
Robinson, W. I. 2004. *A Theory of Global Capitalism: Production, Class, and State in a Transnational World*. Baltimore, MD: JHU Press.
Rosner, D. and Markowitz, G. E. (eds.) 1987. *Dying for Work: Worker Safety and Health in Twentieth century America*. Bloomington, IN: Indiana University Press.
Santos-Paulino, A. U. 2012. 'Trade, income distribution and poverty in developing countries: A survey,' Paper # 207. United Nations Conference on Trade and Development. Available at: http://ideas.repec.org/p/unc/dispap/207.html
Schnaiberg, A. 1980. *The Environment: From Surplus to Scarcity*. New York: Oxford University Press.
Shandra, J. M., Shor, E. and London, B. 2009. 'World polity, unequal ecological exchange, and organic water pollution: A cross-national analysis of developing nations,' *Human Ecology Review*, 16(1): 53–63.
Shantz, J. 2004. 'Radical ecology and class struggle,' *Critical Sociology*, 30(3): 691–710.
Shantz, J. and Adam, B. D. 1999. 'Ecology and class: The green syndicalism of IWW/Earth First! Local 1,' *International Journal of Sociology and Social Policy*, 19(7–8): 43–72.
Silverman, V. 2006. '"Green unionism in a grey world": Labor environmentalism and international institutions,' *Organization & Environment*, 19(2): 191–213.
Smith, D. A. 1994. 'Uneven development and the environment: Toward a world-system perspective,' *Humboldt Journal of Social Relations*, 20(1): 151–175.
South, N. 2015. 'Green criminology, brown crime and crime and problems of despoiling, disposal and de-manufacturing in global resource industries,' in T. Wyatt (ed.) *Hazardous Waste and Pollution: Detecting and Preventing Green Crimes*, pp. 11–25. London: Springer.
South, N. 2016. 'The contested planet: Global green criminology and environmental crime in transnational context,' in A. Spapens, W. Huisman and R. White (eds.) *Environmental Crime in Transnational Context: Global Issues in Green Enforcement and Criminology*, pp. 9–26. Farnham: Ashgate.
Stretesky, P. B., Huss, S. and Lynch, M. J. 2012. 'Density dependence and specialized environmental justice organizations, 1970–2008,' *The Social Science Journal*, 49(3): 343–351.
Stretesky, P. B., Huss, S., Lynch, M. J., Zahran, S. and Childs, B. 2011. 'The founding of environmental justice organizations across US counties during the 1990s and 2000s: Civil rights and environmental movement cross effects,' *Social Problems*, 58(3): 330–360.
Stretesky, P. B., Long, M. A. and Lynch, M. J. 2013a. *The Treadmill of Crime: Political Economy and Green Criminology*. Abingdon, Oxon, UK: Routledge.
Stretesky, P. B., Long, M. A. and Lynch, M. J. 2013b. 'Does environmental enforcement slow the treadmill of production? The relationship between large monetary penalties, ecological disorganization and toxic releases within offending corporations,' *Journal of Crime and Justice*, 36(2): 235–249.
Stretesky, P. B. and Lynch, M. J. 1999. 'Environmental justice and the prediction of distance to accidental chemical releases, Hillsborough County, Florida,' *Social Science Quarterly*, 80(4): 830–846.

Stretesky, P. B. and Lynch, M. J. 2002. 'Environmental hazards and school segregation in Hillsborough, 1987–1999,' *The Sociological Quarterly*, 43(4): 553–573.

Szasz, A. 1984. 'Industrial resistance to occupational safety and health legislation: 1971–1981,' *Social Problems*, 32(2): 103–116.

White, R. 2008. *Crimes against Nature: Environmental Criminology and Ecological Justice*. Cullompton, Devon, UK: Willan.

Young, G. S., Fox, M. A., Trush, M., Kanarek, N., Glass, T. A. and Curriero, F. C. 2012. 'Differential exposure to hazardous air pollution in the United States: A multilevel analysis of urbanization and neighborhood socioeconomic deprivation,' *International Journal of Environmental Research and Public Health*, 9(6): 2204–2225.

25

Insurance and climate change

Liam Phelan, Cameron Holley, Clifford Shearing and Louise du Toit

Insurers as shapers of climate risk

This chapter explores the role of the global insurance industry in creating, adapting to and mitigating climate risk. Since the early 1990s, insurance has been characterised repeatedly as the industry with the most to lose in a climate-changed world, and therefore the business sector most likely to take a lead in mitigation (Gelbspan 1998; Leggett 1993; Sachs et al. 1998). This characterisation of the industry as particularly vulnerable to climate change impacts has persisted (Pinkse and Kolk 2009: 93; Johannsdottir et al. 2014: 88). Yet, in the main, where insurers have responded to climate change, responses have emphasised adaptive and some weak, rather than strong, mitigative measures (Phelan et al. 2011b).

The insurance industry has been described as 'society's primary financial risk manager' (Hecht 2008: 1959). Given the magnitude of the risks that climate change (and many other environmental harms) present to human societies (Beck 1992), the ways insurers respond to climate change, including through shaping others' behaviour, are important. Insurers are significant regulators at both individual and institutional levels—something that the United Nations Environment Programme's (UNEP) Finance Initiative recognises (see, for example, UNEP-FI 2009; see also, UNEP-FI 2011).

Since 1988, 100 companies have been responsible for 71 per cent of global industrial greenhouse gas emissions (Griffin 2017: 8). In recognising the significance of insurance, this chapter is premised on a view that as well as creating harms, the private sector also has a role in addressing environmental harms and delivering public goods, like safety and environmental security (Harrington and Shearing 2017; Shearing 2015). This approach builds on a growing trend in criminology and policing scholarship to look beyond state visions of governance (Bayley and Shearing 2001) toward other providers of environmental security (Holley, Gunningham and Shearing 2012; Holley and Shearing 2016). This approach, however, has sometimes been at odds with green criminology's long history of critical narratives and resistance against corporate (and state) activities that harm humans and the environment (Walters 2010: 320).

It is within this broader debate that the insurance industry has become a growing site of interest for criminologists focussed on climate change harms and the many challenges posed by the age of the Anthropocene (Holley and Shearing 2017)—an age in which humans have been identified as 'geological agents' (Chakrabarty 2009). In today's risk society (Beck 1992), the insurance industry has been recognised as imposing new 'templates of control' on crime (Ericson and Carriere 1994) and, as O'Malley (2017) has argued, insurance was just as relevant to the nineteenth-century proposal by Jeremy Bentham to place a monetary value on harms and to focus 'criminal' justice on financial compensation. Others, such as Nel, Shearing and Reyers (2011), have also argued that insurance can positively shape societal behaviour, such as encouraging communities to actively manage and restore the ecological buffering capacity of landscapes, which can significantly reduce current and future risks associated with climate change (see also Herbstein et al. 2013).

Not everyone agrees that the regulatory power of the insurance industry will significantly reduce its clients' misbehaviour (South 2015: 273), however. For example, Hall and Farrall (2013: 126–127), in their chapter in the first edition of this volume, argue that climate risks will increase the likely costs of insurance coverage, and thus weaken trust in the insurance sector. This, it is argued, will lead customers to commit more economic crimes, such as over-claiming losses and fraud (Hall and Farrall 2013: 126–127). Furthermore, South (2015: 270) has cautioned that insurance can 'encourage "de-responsibilization" and hence risk-taking and anthropogenic damage to the environment'.

Examining these and other debates will require many more empirical studies to identify the conditions (e.g., the levels of awareness, motivations and pathways for institutional change (Holley and Lecavalier 2017; Petersen, Shearing and Nel 2015)) and consequences of insurance acting within broad networks of state and non-state nodes to address climate change (see, e.g., Honig et al. 2015; Shearing 2015). This chapter uses a desktop study to examine the insurance industry's potential as a 'fulcrum institution' (Shearing 2015) that can influence others to prevent and address environmental harms from climate change (Nel, Shearing and Reyers 2011). As this chapter will demonstrate, given insurance's central economic role, the relationship between insurers and climate change is complicated and conflicted (Herbstein 2015).

In the next section of this chapter, we explain how insurers are strongly implicated in creating climate change and attendant climate risk in the period since industrialisation through facilitating the accelerating fossil-fuel-based economic development and growth that causes climate change; this is the dominant dimension in insurers' relationship with climate change. Currently, and despite good and long-established understanding of climate change and associated risks (IPCC 2013; Wuebbles et al. 2017), insurers continue to facilitate increasing fossil-fuel-based economic growth and resultant greenhouse gas emissions that drive climate change.

In the third section of this chapter, we review insurers' responses over the past decade to increasing climate risk. Responses have been largely adaptive and aimed at increasing insurers' capacity to accommodate the climate risks faced by their policyholders. Some responses have been 'weakly mitigative', meaning that they provide for some mitigation, but on a very limited scale, and largely as side effects of initiatives unrelated to climate change (Phelan et al. 2011b). In marked contrast, a very limited number of recent 'divest and decline' actions by insurance industry actors can be described as 'strongly mitigative', noted in the fourth section. The fifth section concludes the chapter with some remarks on the prospects for further strong mitigation action from insurers on climate change and their role as governors of security beyond the state (Ericson and Carriere 1994).

Insurers' historical and continuing role in creating climate risks

Insurance has a long history (Trenerry 1926) of playing a central role in facilitating the conduct and expansion of trade and other economic activity: '[s]hips do not sail and capital is not deployed abroad without adequate insurance protection' (Pfeffer and Klock 1974: 272). Historians trace the beginnings of insurance's role in facilitating trade in monetary economies as far back as *c.*3000 BCE in China (Fink 2011), and insurance provisions in the Code of Hammurabi from 2250 BCE in Babylon (Pfeffer and Klock 1974: 27). The literature on historical aspects of insurance focusses on several key themes, primarily the functions of transferring risk (e.g., Clark 1999; Melone 1964; Pfeffer and Klock 1974) and pooling risk (e.g. Kulp and Hall 1968: 10).

Shifting focus forward to the Industrial Revolution and climate change's origin, insurance was already a long-established facilitator of economic activity and expansion. Supple (1984: 3) argues that insurance, understood as an economic and financial mechanism, is 'directly associated with ... modernisation of economic and social arrangements, and, therefore, with the growth of the British economy from the late eighteenth century'.

Shifting perspective forward again to the contemporary period, insurance is described 'as a business, a legal institution, a technique for averaging loss and an instrument of social planning, [with] many faces and forms, which continue to confound simple classificatory schemes' (Denenberg 1963: 323). Contemporary Western society is deeply dependent on insurance such that insurance is considered central to modern societies and economies. Lengwiler (2003) goes as far as to describe contemporary Western society as the 'insurance society', with the creation of welfare states (Harvey 2005) serving as the most comprehensive example of public policy reliance on insurance (Lengwiler 2003).

The dependence of fossil-fuel-based economic activity on insurance is evident in the sheer size of the insurance industry, the world's largest by revenue—larger than defence, electricity generation, oil, or pharmaceutical industries (Mills 2012). Revenue earned from premiums alone amounted to USD$4.7 trillion in 2016 (Swiss Re Institute 2017). In addition, insurance companies earn income from investments, which in 2009 was estimated at around USD$1 trillion (Mills 2009). In 2014, insurers held USD$29 trillion under management, including investments of third parties, which represent about one-third of global assets under management (Bosshard 2017: 8). Insurance provided through markets is complemented by social forms of insurance, including public expenditure in welfare states on health, unemployment benefits and age and disability pensions. In combination, commercial and social insurance provision has been estimated to be at least 15 per cent of the value of the global economy (Phelan et al. 2011b).

Climate change, as noted above and elsewhere (e.g., Kramer and Bradshaw, this volume, Chapter 9; Brisman, South and Walters, this volume, Chapter 10), is caused by fossil-fuel-dependent economic activity, and is not solely the responsibility of the insurance industry. Insurers have and continue to play a critical enabling role in the expansion of the fossil-fuel-based economic activity causing climate change and attendant climate risks (South 2015), however. As such, insurers—both historically and currently—are implicated strongly in the creation of climate change and climate risk.

Yet, as for all of humanity, the insurance industry is not immune to the impact of anthropogenic climate change. At present, insurers are able to manage financial risk in the global economy while the Earth system remains in a familiar, albeit precarious, state (Rockström et al. 2009). This is because familiar stable conditions and past experience provide a reasonable guide to the future, enabling insurers to calculate and price risks (Phelan et al. 2011a). A changing climate renders the Earth system unstable and characterised by unpredictable change (Schneider 2004).

On a timescale of interest to humans and our societies, the sum of climate-change-related feedbacks in the Earth system is positive, i.e., climate change leads to feedbacks that amplify rather than dampen changes in the climate (Allen and Frame 2007; Roe and Baker 2007; for a discussion of feedback in complex systems, see Meadows 1999). Net positive feedback leads to further increases in warming that push the Earth system further away from a familiar stable state to an alternate state which, whether stable or unstable, is unfamiliar. The non-linear quality of the change means the rate of the shift is increasing continually and, in practice, observed rates of climate change are repeatedly underestimated (Phelan, Henderson-Sellers and Taplin 2010). In addition, Earth systems thresholds result in rates of change that are uneven and unpredictable. Conventional predictive models and 'ever-finer scale risk assessments' thus have limited power in the context of non-linear change (UNEP-FI (UNEP Finance Initiative) 2011: 10). Over time, increasing unpredictability will tend to undermine the viability of the insurance industry (Phelan, Henderson-Sellers and Taplin 2010). The concept of 'the trillionth tonne' (see Allen et al. 2009) makes plain the importance of reducing quickly anthropogenic emissions, as does the defining of the Anthropocene and the challenges this poses for the future of environmental security (Shearing, Harrington and Holley forthcoming).

Insurers' adaptation to climate risk

In 1973, Munich Re, one of the world's largest reinsurers (key actors in the industry who assume some of the financial risk to which retail insurers are exposed), became the first in the industry to raise the possibility that climate change might present risks to insurers (Munich Re 1973). At the United Nations Conference on Environment and Development in June 1992, insurers were encouraged to support climate change mitigation efforts. For example, Greenpeace's Jeremy Leggett, with a background in the oil industry, presented the argument that climate change challenged insurers' capacity to manage risk (Paterson 1999), and that mitigation offered the only viable way for insurers to manage climate risk. Given that insurers maintain substantial financial investments to support their capacity to pay out claims as necessary, Leggett urged insurers to divest from fossil-fuel-intensive investments. Insurers, however, demurred.

Why insurers have not acted already—the views from international political economy and organisational studies

Paterson (1999, 2001) draws on international political economy (IPE) to explain why insurers did not respond favourably to Leggett and why they would in fact be unlikely to take strong action on climate change. Paterson (2001) argues that the industry has considered climate change a threat to itself that is manageable—in part because it considers itself as having at its disposal two apparent opportunities for limiting its own exposure to climate risk. The first strategy relates to system prediction and the potential for better prediction of extreme weather events over periods of 12–18 months, roughly congruent with standard reinsurance contract periods. This could allow reinsurers to increase premiums prospectively or limit exposures to large claims—by declining coverage in some years, for example. This approach is problematic, even where technically possible. First, market expectations limit insurers' capacity to move in and out of markets at will—doing so undermines insurers' reputations for dependable risk management. Second, regulatory frameworks are also constraining: transferring and pooling risk is a key function in modern economies, and commercial insurance markets are heavily regulated to ensure ongoing access to insurance.

The second strategy relates to insurers' capacity to carry climate-implicated risks. For example, catastrophe bonds and other insurance-linked securities are financial instruments that allow climate risk to be shifted outside the insurance system and onto capital markets (Cabral 1999; Guy Carpenter & Company LLC 2007; Tynes 2000). In the case of catastrophe bonds, a 'special purpose vehicle' (SPV) is created, which enters into a standard reinsurance contract with the insurer (or other risk carrier). Investors may then purchase bonds from the SPV, which invests the principal amount in low-risk money market instruments.

Investors then earn premiums and interest on the investment. If no catastrophe occurs, the principal amount is repaid to investors. If a catastrophe occurs before the bond matures (usually after three years), however, the principal amount is used to cover the costs of the insurer and payments to investors may be reduced or even terminated (Entropics Asset Management AB, n.d.; Tynes 2000). This strategy, in short, provides a way to spread financial risks that are traditionally managed within the industry to the substantially enlarged pool that capital markets provide.

Herbstein (2015) complements the IPE account of insurer inaction with a perspective that draws on organisational studies (e.g., March 1991). Herbstein (2015) argues, with reference to underwriting, that organisations can be expected to fully exploit strategies with which they are familiar before exploring alternative approaches. As an example, Herbstein (2015) identifies defensive underwriting, i.e., increasing premiums, tightening policy conditions and withdrawing cover, as a tried and tested approach that insurers will continue to employ prior to contemplating alternative approaches with which they have little or no prior experience (see also Herbstein et al. 2013). With reference to investment, Herbstein (2015) identifies a number of constraints on insurers' capacity and willingness to divest from fossil-fuel-intensive investments, as Leggett had proposed in 1992. Constraints centre on the obligation of commercial insurers to continually maximise returns to shareholders and the intricacy of insurers' relationships with businesses in the fossil fuel sector—as insurers, as investors and, in turn, as investees. As the size of the industry suggests, insurers have become located centrally and deeply in the fossil-fuel-dependent global economy, and have reaped financial reward accordingly.

What insurers have done

Where insurers have responded to climate change, responses have been largely adaptive and 'weakly mitigative', as opposed to 'strongly mitigative'. Through a global (but not comprehensive) review, Mills (2009a) identified 190 actors in the insurance industry taking 422 adaptation or weak mitigation actions—a figure that increased to 246 actors taking 643 actions in Mills' follow-up publication in 2009. Dlugolecki (2009: 17), however, describes this total as 'tiny' in the context of 'the tens of thousands of underwriting and intermediary firms in existence'. A more recent review identified 1,148 actions by 378 entities in 2012 (Mills 2012), but Dlugolecki's point is well made.

The adaptive responses, noted above, such as defensive underwriting and shifting financial risk onto capital markets, are made in the service of insurers' own capacity to adapt to climate change. Other responses are designed to support insurers' policyholders, who also seek to adapt to climate change. Some mitigate (i.e., reduce) losses, such as requiring more stringent building or land-use specifications. Others allow for some insureds' climate risks to be transferred, such as micro-insurance initiatives in low-income countries that allow small-scale farmers to mitigate catastrophic climate-implicated weather-related losses (see Phelan et al. 2011a for further detail).

A recent example of adaptive initiatives supported by insurers is the InsuResilience Global Partnership on Climate and Disaster Risk Finance and Insurance Solutions ('InsuResilience Global Partnership'), launched at the 23rd Conference of the Parties (COP) under the United Nations Framework Convention on Climate Change (UNFCCC) in November 2017. The InsuResilience Global Partnership is a project of the UN Environment's Principles for Sustainable Insurance Initiative, and it has the support of a number of states (e.g., Germany, Ethiopia, the United Kingdom), insurers (e.g., Allianz, Munich Re, Swiss Re), and large civil society, the United Nations, and other international organisations and institutions (e.g., the Nature Conservancy, UN Climate Resilience Initiative (A2R) and the World Bank).

The long-term viability of adaptation strategies is limited (Hallegatte 2009). Phelan and colleagues (2011b) note that adaptive responses are likely to be counter-productive in the medium and longer term. To the extent that adaptive strategies are effective in facilitating expanding fossil-fuel-based economic activity, these strategies serve to exacerbate the problem by accelerating climate change: what appears to be an adaptation may in fact prove to be a maladaptation (Barnett and O'Neill 2010) that ultimately increases vulnerability to climate risk for insurers, their policyholders and all of humanity.

'Weakly mitigative' responses can be organised into three broad groups: (1) insurance products that support limited reductions in policyholders' emissions or that support other emission-reduction initiatives; (2) public-policy-related research, lobbying and networking; and (3) support for corporate carbon disclosure initiatives. Activities in all three groups are described as weakly mitigative because they deliver incidental or otherwise minor climate benefits, rather than significant—i.e., deep and rapid—cuts in greenhouse gas emissions necessary to mitigate climate change seriously.

Products that support emission-reduction initiatives include those that align 'terms and conditions with risk-reducing behaviour' (Mills 2009b), such as retail insurers offering pay-as-you-drive insurance, which results in risk being priced more accurately and in reduced fuel consumption and emissions (Phelan et al. 2011b). Another example is insurers addressing climate change liability implications, such as the possibility of policy-holding directors and officers facing damages claims by shareholders for not having disclosed climate risks. Mills (2009b: 27) points to Swiss Re, which includes climate change risks 'amongst the many criteria ... used to evaluate its exposures under corporate [directors and officers] policies'. Mills (2009b: 27) goes on to note that 'to our knowledge, Swiss Re has yet to actually decline a policy or apply exclusions based on climate risks alone', and that in the absence of any teeth to this approach '[t]he potentially positive effect of this activity is to stimulate the policyholders to focus on their climate-related exposures'.

A number of insurers have also made significant investments in renewable energy projects (Herbstein 2015: 36; Mills 2009b: 44). For example, in 2009, Munich Re was involved in the founding of the ambitious Desertec Industrial Initiative (DII), which had the aim of developing a massive solar power park in the Sahara Desert to supply 15 per cent of Europe's electricity by 2050 (Seager 2009). For various reasons, however, this project has not progressed further (Stonington 2012).

Public policy initiatives have been pursued in national contexts (see Phelan et al. 2011b), as well as in international contexts, such as climate negotiations. One notable recent public policy and lobbying initiative in which some insurers have played a role is the consideration of insurance during the negotiations under the UNFCCC. Insurance received attention when the Alliance of Small Island States (AOSIS), during the International Negotiating Committee sessions preceding the formation of the UNFCCC, called for the introduction of an International Insurance Pool to provide compensation to small island states and low-lying countries for loss and damage due to rising sea levels (Vanuatu: Draft Annex 1991). While this proposal was not accepted, both the UNFCCC and Kyoto Protocol include references to insurance (UNFCCC 1992, art. 8; Kyoto Protocol 1998, art. 3(14)). The issue of insurance has received more attention in subsequent years due to the increased importance of adaptation (Wenta, McGee and Phelan 2016: 37–38).

In 2013, in Warsaw, the 19th COP under the UNFCCC established the Warsaw International Mechanism on Loss and Damage ('Warsaw International Mechanism'), which was subsequently included in the Paris Agreement (2015). The Paris Agreement calls on state parties to 'enhance understanding, action and support, including through the Warsaw International

Mechanism', and states that 'areas of cooperation and facilitation to enhance understanding, action and support may include … comprehensive risk assessment and management … [and] risk insurance facilities, climate risk pooling and other insurance solutions' (Paris Agreement 2015, art. 8(3)–(4)). There have been no concrete decisions on finance for this mechanism (Kreienkamp and Vanhala 2017: 9; Siddique and Darby 2017), however.

With regard to carbon disclosure initiatives, the most well-known voluntary initiative is the CDP (formerly known as the 'Carbon Disclosure Project'), which allows investors, companies and cities to disclose their greenhouse gas reduction actions, with the aim of improving awareness and management, culminating in 'leadership' (CDP 2017)—perhaps through reducing emissions. In 2017, 1,073 companies accounting for 12 per cent of global emissions disclosed data to the CDP. While a number of insurance companies participated in the CDP in 2017, including American International Group (AIG), Allianz, AXA, Munich Re and Swiss Re, only two (both Japanese) were included in the A-list, which includes those businesses 'leading on environmental performance'—assessed with reference to awareness, disclosure, management and leadership (CDP 2016: 56)—namely, MS&AD Insurance Group Holdings, Inc. and Sompo Holdings, Inc. (CDP 2017). One study showed that participants in the CDP experienced a number of benefits in addition to emission reductions, including increased transparency and efficiency and improved dialogue with stakeholders (Blanco, Caro and Corbett 2017). A further study found that carbon disclosure in the CDP was indicative of carbon performance and, thus, that CDP reports could be relied on by stakeholders to reflect practice accurately (Luo and Tang 2014).

Forty years later: the first examples of strong mitigation?

To be sure, insurers have a long history of engaging in mitigation of risks other than those related to climate change, such as conducting early materials safety research, establishing the first fire brigades and proposing and lobbying for the introduction of safety standards that apply across all facets of human endeavours (Herbstein 2015: 12; Mills 2009b: 67; O'Malley and Hutchinson 2007: 376–379). In the context of that history, and given the threat climate change presents, explanations for insurer inaction on climate change that date back almost 20 years (e.g., Paterson 1999, 2001) are sobering (South 2015) and remain compelling; and insurer behaviour in the period since then has remained largely unchanged. And yet, in very recent years, albeit 40 years after Munich Re first raised questions about the potential impact of climate change on insurers, several insurers have announced 'divest and decline' decisions that, in our view, constitute strong mitigation action.

Deciding to divest and decline coverage

In recent years, a number of insurers have announced their decisions to divest coal assets and decline coverage of coal infrastructure. In 2014, KLP, a Norwegian insurer and pension fund manager, became one of the first insurers to divest, announcing its decision to divest from 27 coal companies (defined as those companies deriving at least 50 per cent of their revenue from coal-based operations), and stating specifically that it 'decided to exclude coal companies from its investment portfolio because consumption of coal—at today's volumes—is not compatible with achievement of the two-degree target' (KLP 2014: 1–2). In 2015, KLP lowered the threshold to 30 per cent of revenue from coal-based operations (KLP 2015). In 2015, AXA also divested from coal, announcing at the Climate Finance Day (part of COP21 in Paris) that it would 'divest from companies most exposed to coal-related activities for the assets managed internally' (De Castries 2015). More specifically, AXA stated that investment in mining companies and electric utilities that generate more than 50 per cent of their revenue from coal production or the use of coal for their business 'should be avoided' (AXA Investment Managers 2017). Even more promising is that AXA has decided not to insure the companies in which it no longer invests. Two years later, in 2017, AXA announced that 'for reasons of consistency, the Group has also decided that the disengagement is applied to AXA's insurance operations', covering property and casualty insurance of the 'blacklisted companies' products, assets and liabilities' (AXA 2017).

In addition, just days before the UN climate change conference held in Paris in November 2015, Allianz announced its decision to divest 'equity stakes in coal-based business models by the end of March 2016' (Allianz 2015). 'Coal-based business models' were defined as mining companies earning at least 30 per cent of their revenues from coal mining or electric utilities generating at least 30 per cent of their electricity from coal (Allianz 2015).

While Munich Re has not made a public statement, it has reportedly decided to discontinue investing in companies earning at least 50 per cent of their revenue from coal or generating 50 per cent of their electricity from coal (Urgewald and Unfriend Coal 2017: 3–4). Another company, Swiss Re, also announced its decision to end investments in companies generating at least 30 per cent of their revenue from coal mining and generating at least 30 per cent of their power from coal (Swiss Re 2017: 27). In September 2017, yet another reinsurer, SCOR, declared that it would stop investing in coal companies earning 30 per cent of their revenue from coal. Significantly, SCOR also stated that it would 'not issue insurance or facultative reinsurance [the reinsurance of individual, specific risks] that would specifically encourage new greenfield thermal coal mines or stand-alone lignite mines or plants' (SCOR 2017).

In 2017, Zurich Insurance Group announced a 'divest and decline' decision, stating that it would divest from equity holdings in companies earning more than half of their revenue from thermal coal mining and utilities generating more than half of their energy from coal. In addition, it declared its intention to

> stop providing insurance or risk management services for new thermal coal mines or for potential new clients that derive more than half their revenue from mining thermal coal, and also for utility companies that generate more than half of their energy from coal.
>
> *(Kuchinski 2017)*

At the same time, Swiss Re and Lloyd's stated that they would prepare new policies on coal in the ensuing months (Harrell and Bosshard 2017: 3). Based on these more recent actions, the divestment movement appears to be gaining momentum 'and may be approaching a tipping point' (Harrell and Bosshard 2017: 3).

While such decisions have been welcomed (e.g., 350.org. 2015), they need to be considered closely. No divestment policies extend to funds managed on behalf of third parties. Furthermore, divestment from coal does not necessarily exclude divestment from other fossil fuels (Unfriend Coal 2017). Finally, Munich Re's policy disallows only investment in *bonds*, but still permits investment in *equities* (Urgewald and Urgewald and Unfriend Coal 2017: 3–4). This results in, amongst other things, the unsatisfactory situation where Munich Re holds bonds (but not equities) in Eskom (South Africa), which generates over 90 per cent of its electricity and earns more than 50 per cent of its revenue from coal (Urgewald and Urgewald and Unfriend Coal 2017: 4–5). Turning from divestment to declining coverage, the policies of Munich Re and Swiss Re still permit these insurers to insure coal companies. The announcement of SCOR has also been criticised as it stops short of denying insurance to all coal projects (Unfriend Coal 2017).

Decisions to divest and decline are a clear step beyond earlier but limited apparent interest in directors' climate liabilities. Though welcome, insurers' strong mitigation actions to date are extremely limited in number and are constrained in their scope. The insurance industry has certainly not led efforts to mitigate climate change and attendant risks, as it was encouraged to do 25 years ago. Indeed, in 2016, the top 15 European insurers held USD$130.74 billion in fossil fuel companies (Simons and de Wilde 2017: 11–12), while the top 40 US insurers held USD$459 billion in fossil fuel companies in 2014 (McHale and Spivey 2016: 24). It is reasonable to expect that these recent decisions to divest and decline coverage will be observed by others within and beyond the industry. The potential for these actions to inspire further actions remains to be seen. The possible exposure of insurers to climate change liability (Bank of England PRA 2015) and concern over the potential for stranded assets (Caldecott et al. 2017) may also now begin to motivate insurers to take further actions.

Conclusion: insurance in the Anthropocene

As Phelan and colleagues (2011b: 125) note,

> [t]he failure of the insurance system to respond appropriately to climate risk is consistent with broader societal inability to resolve the climate crisis. However, the insurance system's failure is notable to the extent that insurance is a primary risk governance instrument of industrialized economies and societies.

The loss of familiar Earth system stability does not necessarily mean the end of the insurance industry. Loss of familiar Earth system stability does, however, undermine the current linear basis for insurance, where history can be relied upon to serve as a guide to the future. A functioning insurance industry in a relatively unstable Earth system may or may not be recognisable in comparison with the insurance industry's current form, function and scale.

The divestment actions mentioned above are exceedingly limited in the context of a global industry comprising 'tens of thousands of underwriting and intermediary firms' (Dlugolecki 2009: 17), but noteworthy because of the otherwise total lack of strongly mitigative action from insurers, and especially so given the compelling explanations for insurer inaction first proposed almost 20 years ago. The fact of these new actions raises questions about what insurers might need in order to realise a stronger 'fulcrum' (Shearing 2015) role and influence others to take further stronger mitigative action. One possibility is that the broader divestment movement has provided an example which insurers may now be able to follow. The divestment movement has included participation from municipal governments, religious institutions, universities and other public institutions, together with banks and other financial bodies upon which divestment activists have focussed their attention (Ayling and Gunningham 2017; Healy and Barry 2017; Healy and Debski 2016; Neslen 2017; Richardson 2017). Insurers have demonstrated an inability to lead on divestment, but may be able to follow divestment leaders in the finance sectors. As they do so, they may, in turn, influence others. Looking ahead, as divestment is established more widely as an industry practice, it may be that insurers will increasingly be willing to decline cover for fossil-fuel-intensive projects, infrastructure and businesses, consistent with the first tentative steps, such as those noted above, that some insurers have taken to engage with their clients' evolving climate liabilities.

Climate change presents a societal challenge of unprecedented spatial and temporal magnitude. Moving—in an orderly manner—beyond several centuries of the accelerating fossil-fuel-based economic activity that causes climate change implies socio-economic challenges on an unprecedented scale and requires dramatic and rapid reductions in greenhouse emissions and protection of surviving carbon sinks such as forests. Insurers are not exclusively responsible for climate change, but neither is climate change a matter that can be resolved without effective participation of insurers, in the form of strongly mitigative action: we should expect nothing less from society's primary risk manager.

Insurers, of course, like all societal risk managers, operate within the context of nodal assemblages of other auspices and providers of security (Burris, Drahos and Shearing 2005). Criminology has traditionally concentrated its attention on responses to harm by professionals working within the criminal justice sub-assemblage (system). Within the context of the emerging 'harmscapes' that have begun to characterise the first quarter of the twenty-first century—harms that extend from climate change through to cyber-insecurities—it has become increasingly clear that criminology should extend its gaze beyond its established boundaries to include institutions outside of criminal justice (Shearing 2015).

In this chapter, we have contributed to this shift of criminological attention beyond these boundaries. We did so by picking up a theoretical thread identified by thinkers such as Ericson (see Ericson and Carriere 1994; Ericson, Doyle and Barry 2003), Ewald (1991), and O'Malley (2017), who have identified commercial insurance as a key node within nodal security assemblages and networks. In doing so, our hope is that others will also take up the long-standing invitation of criminologists, such as Ditton (1979) and Hillyard and colleagues (2004), to move beyond criminology's established edges.

References

350.org. 2015. 'World's largest insurance company allianz divests from coal,' 24 November. Available at: https://350.org/press-release/worlds-largest-insurance-company-allianz-divests-from-coal/.

Allen, M. R. and Frame, D. J. 2007. 'Call off the quest,' *Science*, 318(5850): 582–583.

Allen, M. R., Frame, D. J., Huntingford, C., Jones, C. D., Lowe, J. A., Meinshausen, M. and Meinshausen, N. 2009. 'Warming caused by cumulative carbon emissions towards the trillionth tonne,' *Nature*, 458: 1163–1166.

Allianz. 2015. 'Allianz statement on coal-based investments,' November. Available at: www.allianz.com/v_1448622620000/media/responsibility/Energy_Guideline_PublicVersion_final.pdf.

AXA. 2017. 'AXA group policy on coal mining and coal-based energy,' Available at: www-axa-com.cdn.axa-contento-118412.eu/www-axa-com%2F803065f4-200e-4d5f-ae5e-93a716b8e2d9_axa_coal_policy_201704.pdf.

AXA Investment Managers. 2017. 'Coal policy,' April. Available at: www.axa-im.com/documents/20195/607489/coal-policy-april-2017/545a5b09-8ce5-5467-de35-76cda8654728.

Ayling, J. and Gunningham, N. 2017. 'Non-state governance and climate policy: The fossil fuel divestment movement,' *Climate Policy*, 17(2): 131–149.

Bank of England PRA (Prudential Regulation Authority). 2015. 'The impact of climate change on the UK insurance sector,' Available at: www.bankofengland.co.uk/pra/Documents/supervision/activities/pradefra0915.pdf.

Barnett, J. and O'Neill, S. J. 2010. 'Maladaptation,' *Global Environmental Change*, 20(2): 211–213.

Bayley, D. and Shearing, C. 2001. *The New Structure of Policing: Description, Conceptualization, and Research Agenda*. Washington, DC: US Department of Justice.

Beck, U. 1992. *Risk Society: Towards a New Modernity*. Los Angeles, CA: SAGE.

Blanco, C., Caro, F. and Corbett, C. J. 2017. 'An inside perspective on carbon disclosure,' *Business Horizons*, 60(5): 635–646.

Bosshard, P. 2017. *Underwriting Climate Chaos: Insurance Companies, the Coal Industry and Climate Change*. Surry Hills, Australia: Friends of the Earth France, Greenpeace Switzerland, Market Forces, Re: Common, Sierra Club, The Sunrise Project and Urgewald.

Burris, S., Drahos, P. and Shearing, C. 2005. 'Nodal governance,' *Australian Journal of Legal Philosophy*, 30: 30–58.

Cabral, W. 1999. 'Securitisation out of the niche,' *Global Reinsurance*, 8(1). www.globalreinsurance.com.

Caldecott, B., Dericks, G., Pfeiffer, A. and Astudillo, P. 2017. 'Stranded assets: The transition to a low carbon economy – Overview for the insurance industry (Emerging risk report 2017: Innovation series: Society and security). Lloyd's,' Available at: www.lloyds.com/news-and-insight/risk-insight/library/society-and-security/stranded-assets.

CDP. 2016. 'Out of the starting blocks: Tracking progress on corporate climate action,' Available at: https://b8f65cb373b1b7b15feb-c70d8ead6ced550b4d987d7c03fcdd1d.ssl.cf3.rackcdn.com/cms/reports/documents/000/001/228/original/CDP_Climate_Change_Report_2016.pdf?1485276095.

CDP. 2017. 'CDP program scores,' Available at: www.cdp.net/en/scores-2017.

Chakrabarty, D. 2009. 'The climate of history: Four theses,' *Critical Inquiry*, 35(2): 197–222.

Clark, G. 1999. *Betting on Lives: The Culture of Life Insurance in England, 1695–1775*. Manchester: Manchester University Press.

De Castries, H. 2015. 'Climate change: It's no longer about whether, it's about when,' *AXA*, 22 May. Available at: www.axa.com/en/newsroom/news/about-whether-about-when.

Denenberg, H. S. 1963. 'The legal definition of insurance: Insurance principles in practice,' *The Journal of Insurance*, 30(3): 319–343.

Ditton, J. 1979. *Contrology: Beyond the New Criminology*. London: Palgrave Macmillan.

Dlugolecki, A. F. 2009. *Coping with Climate Change: Risks and Opportunities for Insurers*. London: Chartered Insurance Institute.

Ericson, R. and Carriere, K. 1994. 'The fragmentation of criminology,' in D. Nelken (ed.) *The Futures of Criminology*, pp. 89–109. London: SAGE.

Ericson, R., Doyle, A. and Barry, D. 2003. *Insurance as Governance*. Toronto, Buffalo and London: University of Toronto Press.

Ewald, F. 1991. 'Insurance and risk,' in G. Burchell, C. Gordon and P. Miller (eds.) *The Foucault Effect: Studies in Governmentality*, pp. 197–210. Chicago, IL: University of Chicago Press.

Fink, A. 2011. 'The origins of insurance,' Originally available at: http://insurancecoveragemonitor.com/cgl/the-origins-of-insurance/.

Gelbspan, R. 1998. *The Heat is on: The Climate Crisis, the Cover-up, the Prescription*. Reading, PA: Perseus Books.

Griffin, P. 2017. 'The carbon majors database: CDP carbon majors report 2017,' *CDP*. Available at: https://b8f65cb373b1b7b15feb-c70d8ead6ced550b4d987d7c03fcdd1d.ssl.cf3.rackcdn.com/cms/reports/documents/000/002/327/original/Carbon-Majors-Report-2017.pdf.

Guy Carpenter & Company LLC. 2007. *The Catastrophe Bond Market at Year-end 2006: Ripples into Waves*. New York: Guy Carpenter & Company LLC.

Hall, M. and Farrall, S. 2013. 'The criminogenic consequence of climate change: Blurring the boundaries between offenders and victims,' in N. South and A. Brisman (eds.) *Routledge International Handbook of Green Criminology*, pp. 120–133. Abingdon, Oxon, UK: Routledge.

Hallegatte, S. 2009. 'Strategies to adapt to an uncertain climate change,' *Global Environmental Change*, 19(2): 240–247.

Harrell, C. and Bosshard, P. 2017. 'Insuring coal no more: An insurance scorecard on coal and climate change.' *Unfriend Coal*. Available at: http://unfriendcoal.com/wp-content/uploads/2017/11/UnfriendCoal-Insurance-Scorecard.pdf.

Harrington, C. and Shearing, C. 2017. *Security in the Anthropocene: Reflections on Safety and Care*. London and Bielefeld: Transcript Press.

Harvey, D. 2005. *A Brief History of Neoliberalism*. Oxford: Oxford University Press.

Healy, N. and Debski, J. 2016. 'Fossil fuel divestment: Implications for the future of sustainability discourse and action within higher education,' *Local Environment*, 22(6): 699–724.

Healy, N. and Barry, J. 2017. 'Politicizing energy justice and energy system transitions: Fossil fuel divestment and a "just transition",' *Energy Policy*, 108: 451–459.

Hecht, S. B. 2008. 'Climate change and the transformation of risk: Insurance matters,' *UCLA Law Review*, 55(6): 1559–1620.

Herbstein, T. 2015. 'Insurance and the anthropocene: Like a frog in hot water,' PhD thesis, University of Cape Town.

Herbstein, T., Froestad, J., Nel, D. and Shearing, C. 2013. 'Insurance, climate-risk and the barriers to change,' in T. A. Börzel and R. Hamann (eds.) *Business and Climate Change Governance: South Africa in Comparative Perspective*, pp. 156–172. London: Palgrave Macmillan.

Hillyard, P., Pantazis, C., Tombs, S., Gordon, D. and Doring, D. 2004. *Beyond Criminology: Taking Harm Seriously*. London: Pluto Press.

Holley, C., Gunningham, N. and Shearing, C. 2012. *The New Environmental Governance*. Abingdon, Oxon, UK: Earthscan.

Holley, C. and Lecavalier, E. 2017. 'Energy governance, energy security and environmental sustainability: A case study from Hong Kong,' *Energy Policy*, 108: 379–389.

Holley, C. and Shearing, C. 2016. 'Policing and new environmental governance,' in B. Bradford, B. Jauregui, I. Loader and J. Steinberg (eds.) *SAGE Handbook of Global Policing*, pp. 552–572. London: SAGE.

Holley, C. and Shearing, C. 2017. 'Thriving on a pale blue dot: Criminology and the anthropocene,' in C. Holley and C. Shearing (eds.) *Criminology and the Anthropocene*, pp. 1–24. Abingdon, Oxon, UK: Routledge.

Honig, M., Petersen, S., Herbstein, T., Roux, S., Nel, D. and Shearing, C. 2015. 'A conceptual framework to enable the changes required for a one-planet future,' *Environmental Values*, 24(5): 663–688.

IPCC (Intergovernmental Panel on Climate Change). 2013. 'Summary for policymakers,' in T. F. Stocker, D. Qin, G.-K. Plattner, M. Tignor, S. K. Allen, J. Boschung, A. Nauels, Y. Xia, V. Bex and P. M. Midgley (eds.) *Climate Change 2013: The Physical Science Basis. Contribution of Working Group I to the Fifth Assessment Report of the Intergovernmental Panel on Climate Change*. Cambridge and New York: Cambridge University Press. Available at: www.ipcc.ch/site/assets/uploads/2018/02/WG1AR5_SPM_FINAL.pdf.

Johannsdottir, L., Davidsdottir, B., Goodsite, M. E., and Olafsson, S. 2014. 'What is the potential and demonstrated role for non-life insurers in fulfilling climate commitments? A case of nordic insurers,' *Environmental Science & Policy*, 38: 87–106.

KLP. 2014. 'Decision to exclude from investments,' 1 December. Available at: http://english.klp.no/polopoly_fs/1.29228.1417436452!/menu/standard/file/Beslutning_Kull_261114%20ENG.pdf.

KLP. 2015. '20 new companies excluded, 4 companies included,' Available at: http://english.klp.no/about-klp/press-room/20-new-companies-excluded-4-companies-included-1.32410.

Kreienkamp, J. and Vanhala, L. 2017. 'Climate change loss and damage,' *Global Governance Institute*. Available at: www.ucl.ac.uk/global-governance/downloads/policybriefs/policy-brief-loss-and-damage.

Kuchinski, R. 2017. 'Insurers can facilitate the transition to a low-carbon future,' *Zurich Insurance Group*. 13 November. Available at: www.zurich.com/en/knowledge/articles/2017/11/insurers-can-facilitate-the-transition-to-a-low-carbon-future.

Kulp, C. A. and Hall, J. W. 1968. *Casualty Insurance*. New York: The Ronald Press.

Kyoto Protocol (Kyoto Protocol to the United Nations Framework Convention on Climate Change). 1998. 37 *ILM* 22.

Leggett, J. 1993. *Climate Change and the Insurance Industry: Solidarity among the Risk Community?* Amsterdam: Greenpeace.

Lengwiler, M. 2003. 'Technologies of trust: Actuarial theory, insurance sciences, and the establishment of the welfare state in Germany and Switzerland around 1900,' *Information and Organization*, 13(2): 131–150.

Luo, L. and Tang, Q. 2014. 'Does voluntary carbon disclosure reflect underlying carbon performance?' *Journal of Contemporary Accounting & Economics*, 10(3): 191–205.

March, J. G. 1991. 'Exploration and exploitation in organizational learning,' *Organization Science*, 2(1): 71–87.

McHale, C. and Spivey, R. 2016. *Assets or Liabilities? Fossil Fuel Investments of Leading U.S. Insurers*. Boston, MA: Ceres.

Meadows, D. H. 1999. *Leverage Points: Places to Intervene in a System*. Hartland, VT: Chelsea Green Publishing.

Melone, J. J. 1964. 'Insurance: Transfer and pooling,' in H. S. Denenberg, R. G. Eilers, W. Hoffman, C. A. Kline, J. J. Melone and H. Wayne Snider (eds.) *Risk and Insurance*, pp. 141–151. Englewood Cliffs, NJ: Prentice-Hall.

Mills, E. 2009a. 'A global review of insurance industry responses to climate change,' *The Geneva Papers on Risk and Insurance: Issues and Practice*, 34(3): 323–359.

Mills, E. 2009b. *From Risk to Opportunity 2008: Insurer Responses to Climate Change*. Boston, MA: Ceres. Available at: https://pdfs.semanticscholar.org/4b64/527ad12e9cd5c57e290aa6f737e47152eb26.pdf.

Mills, E. 2012. 'The greening of insurance,' *Science*, 338(6113): 1424–1425.

Munich Re, M. 1973. *Flood Inundation*. Munich: Munich Re.

Nel, D. C., Shearing, C. and Reyers, B. 2011. 'Insurers could help address climate risks,' *Nature*, 476: 33.

Neslen, A. 2017. 'Catholic church to make record divestment from fossil fuels,' *The Guardian*, 3 October. Available at: www.theguardian.com/environment/2017/oct/03/catholic-church-to-make-record-divestment-from-fossil-fuels.

O'Malley, P. 2017. 'Bentham in the anthropocene: Imagining a sustainable criminal justice,' in C. Holley and C. Shearing (eds.) *Criminology and the Anthropocene*, pp. 109–132. Abingdon, Oxon, UK: Routledge.

O'Malley, P. and Hutchinson, S. 2007. 'Reinventing prevention: Why did "crime prevention" develop so late?' *The British Journal of Criminology*, 47(3): 376–379.

Paterson, M. 1999. 'Global finance and environmental politics: The insurance industry and climate change,' *IDS Bulletin*, 30(3): 25–30.

Paterson, M. 2001. 'Risky business: Insurance companies in global warming politics,' *Global Environmental Politics*, 1(4): 18–42.

Petersen, S., Shearing, C. and Nel, D. 2015. 'Sustainability transitions: An investigation of the conditions under which corporations are likely to reshape their practices to reverse environmental degradation,' *Environmental Management and Sustainable Development*, 4(1): 85–105.

Pfeffer, I. and Klock, D. R. 1974. *Perspectives on Insurance*. Englewood Cliffs, NJ: Prentice-Hall.

Phelan, L., Henderson-Sellers, A. and Taplin, R. 2010. 'Climate change, carbon prices and insurance systems,' *International Journal of Sustainable Development & World Ecology*, 17(2): 95–108.

Phelan, L., Henderson-Sellers, A. and Taplin, R. 2011a. 'Mitigation of the earth's economy: A viable strategy for insurance systems,' in W. Leal Filho (ed.) *The Economic, Social and Political Elements of Climate Change*, pp. 81–98. Berlin: Springer-Verlag.

Phelan, L., Taplin, R., Henderson-Sellers, A. and Albrecht, G. 2011b. 'Ecological viability or liability? Insurance system responses to climate risk,' *Environmental Policy and Governance*, 21(2): 112–130.

Pinkse, J. and Kolk, A. 2009. *International Business and Global Climate Change*. London and New York: Routledge.

Richardson, B. J. 2017. 'Divesting from climate change: The road to influence,' *Law and Policy*, 39(4): 325–348.

Rockström, J., Steffen, W., Noone, K., Persson, Å., Chapin III, F. S., Lambin, E. F., Lenton, T. M., Scheffer, M., Folke, C., Schellnhuber, H. J., Nykvist, B., de Wit, C. A., Hughes, T., van der Leeuw, S., Rodhe, H., Sörlin, S., Snyder, P. K., Costanza, R., Svedin, U., Falkenmark, M., Karlberg, L., Corell, R. W., Fabry, V. J., Hansen, J., Walker, B., Liverman, D., Richardson, K., Crutzen, P. and Foley, J. A. 2009. 'A safe operating space for humanity,' *Nature*, 461: 472–475.

Roe, G. R. and Baker, M. B. 2007. 'Why is climate sensitivity so unpredictable?' *Science*, 318(5850): 629–632.

Sachs, W., Linz, M., Loske, R. and Wuppertal Institute for Climate Environment and Energy. 1998. *Greening the North: A Post-Industrial Blueprint for Ecology and Equity*. London: Zed Books.

Schneider, S. H. 2004. 'Abrupt non-linear climate change, irreversibility and surprise,' *Global Environmental Change*, 14(3): 245–258.

SCOR. 2017. 'Press release No 23: SCOR announces further environmental sustainability initiatives,' 6 September. Available at: www.scor.com/sites/default/files/23_coal_disengagement_veng.pdf.

Seager, A. 2009. 'Solar power from sahara a step closer,' *The Guardian*, 1 November. Available at: www.theguardian.com/business/2009/nov/01/solar-power-sahara-europe-desertec.

Shearing, C. 2015. 'Criminology and the anthropocene,' *Criminology & Criminal Justice*, 15(3): 255–269.

Shearing, C., Harrington, C. and Holley, C. Forthcoming. 'Security and the anthropocene in law, international relations and criminology,' *Annual Review of Law and Social Science*.

Siddique, A. and Darby, M. 2017. 'Climate insurance website to be launched at Bonn talks,' *Climate Home News*, 10 November. Available at: www.climatechangenews.com/2017/11/10/climate-insurance-website-launched-bonn-talks/.

Simons, M. and de Wilde, J. 2017. *The Involvement of the European Insurance Groups in the Fossil Fuels Sector (A report for the Sunrise Project)*. Amsterdam: Profundo.

South, N. 2015. 'Anticipating the anthropocene and greening criminology,' *Criminology & Criminal Justice*, 15(3): 270–276.

Stonington, J. 2012. 'Desertec's promise of solar power for Europe fades,' *Spiegel Online*, 13 November. Available at: www.spiegel.de/international/europe/the-desertec-solar-energy-project-has-run-into-trouble-a-867077.html.

Supple, B. 1984. 'Insurance in British history,' in O. M. Westall (ed.) *The Historian and the Business of Insurance*, pp. 1–8. Manchester: Manchester University Press.

Swiss Re. 2017. 'Responsible investments: Shaping the future of investing,' Available at: http://media.swissre.com/documents/ZRH-17-11623-P1_Responsible%20Investments_WEB.PDF.

Swiss Re Institute. 2017. 'World insurance in 2016: The China growth engine steams ahead,' *Sigma*. No. 3/2017.

Trenerry, C. F. 1926. *Origin and Early History of Insurance*. London: P.S. King & Son.

Tynes, J. S. 2000. 'Catastrophe risk securitization,' *Journal of Insurance Regulation*, 19(1): 3–28.

UNEP-FI (UNEP Finance Initiative). 2009. *The Global State of Sustainable Insurance Understanding and Integrating Environmental, Social and Governance Factors in Insurance*. A report by the Insurance Working Group of the United Nations Environment Programme Finance Initiative Based on the IWG's pioneering 2009 global survey on ESG factors and insurance underwriting and product development. Geneva. Available at: www.unepfi.org/fileadmin/documents/global-state-of-sustainable-insurance_01.pdf.

UNEP-FI (UNEP Finance Initiative). 2011. *Insurance in a Changing Risk Landscape: Local Lessons from the Southern Cape of South Africa*. A report by the research partnership between the Santam Group, the WWF, the University of Cape Town and the Council for Scientific and Industrial Research in collaboration with the United Nations Environment Programme Finance Initiative, Geneva. Available at: www.unepfi.org/fileadmin/documents/insurance_changing_risk_landscape.pdf.

UNFCCC (United Nations Framework Convention on Climate Change). 1992. 31 *ILM* 849.

Unfriend Coal. 2017. 'Climate and coal policies of leading global insurers – Briefing papers,' 3 August. Available at: http://unfriendcoal.com/2017/08/03/climate-and-coal-policies-of-leading-global-insurers-briefing-papers/.

Urgewald and Unfriend Coal. 2017. 'Munich re needs to take bold action on climate change and coal,' 2 August. Available at: http://unfriendcoal.com/wp-content/uploads/2017/08/Briefing-paper-Munich-Re-0817-E.pdf.

Vanuatu: Draft Annex Relating to Article 23 (Insurance) for Inclusion in the Revised Single Text on Elements Relating to Mechanisms (A/ AC.237/WG.II/Misc.13) submitted by the Co-chairmen of Working Group II. 17 December 1991. UN Doc A/AC.237/WG.II/CRP.8.

Walters, R. 2010. 'Toxic atmospheres air pollution, trade and the politics of regulation,' *Critical Criminology: An International Journal*, 18(4): 307–323.

Wenta, J., McGee, J. and Phelan, L. 2016. 'Can a regional insurance mechanism enhance resilience to slow onset impacts of climate change?' *University of Tasmania Law Review*, 35(2): 23–57.

Wuebbles, D. J., Fahey, D. W., Hibbard, K. A., DeAngelo, B., Doherty, S., Hayhoe, K., Horton, R., Kossin, J. P., Taylor, P. C., Waple, A. M. and Weaver, C. P. 2017. 'Executive summary,' in J. W. Donald, D. W. Fahey, K. A. Hibbard, D. J. Dokken, B. C. Stewart and T. K. Maycock (eds.) *Climate Science Special Report: Fourth National Climate Assessment, Volume I*, pp. 12–34. Washington, DC: Global Change Research Program. Available at: https://science2017.globalchange.gov/downloads/CSSR2017_FullReport.pdf.

26

Energy harms

'Extreme energy', fracking and water

Damien Short

Introduction

This chapter discusses the social and environmental harms that are driven by humanity's reliance on fossil fuels. In particular, it examines the consequences of 'the process of extreme energy' (Short et al. 2015) and its use of one of the most precious resources, water. As Rob White noted in the first edition of the *Routledge International Handbook of Green Criminology*, environmental harm takes place within the overarching context of a distinct global political economy, but it is still rare to find a sustained political economy of environmental harm (White 2013: 243). This chapter makes a contribution to this perspective via a broad holistic inquiry that highlights the causal drivers and the environmental, political and social connections between the global capitalist economy, the limits to a growth economy, resource depletion, corporate 'externalities', political corruption, community collective trauma and the criminalisation of protest. It begins with a summary of the limits to growth, before turning to an explanation of the process of 'extreme energy' and the role of so-called 'unconventional energy' development, including its repercussions for societal use of key resources, such as water, which is vital for life as we know it.

The limits to growth

The Club of Rome is an organisation of notable business people, economists, high level civil servants and former heads of state and scientists 'who share a common concern for the future of humanity and strive to make a difference and promote understanding of the global challenges facing humanity and to propose solutions through scientific analysis, communication and advocacy' (Club of Rome, www.clubofrome.org). In 1972, it released a groundbreaking report entitled *The Limits to Growth* (hereafter *LtG*), which utilised a system dynamics computer model to simulate the interactions of population, food production, industrial production, pollution and consumption of non-renewable natural resources—five key global economic subsystems (Meadows et al. 1972). The results of the simulation raised very serious questions about long-term global sustainability. A scandalously under-publicised 2007 study sought to provide an update on where we are now in relation to the predictions of *LtG*, collating historical data for 1970–2000 (Turner 2007) and comparing the data with scenarios presented in *LtG*. The analysis showed that 30 years of historical data compare favourably with key features of the *LtG* 'standard run' scenario, which results in *collapse of the global system midway through the twenty-first century*. The key driver behind the *LtG* prediction—and arguably the one most poised to cause quickly global economic collapse—is the depletion of non-renewable energy sources, especially of oil and natural gas (Heinberg 2007). 'Too early' calls of 'peak oil and gas' proved incorrect due to the combined effects of extremely high oil prices, loose regulation and easy financing that would lead to increasing rates of extraction of *unconventional* and more marginal resources, like tar sands (see Heydon, this volume, Chapter 18) and tight oil, which began in earnest in 2011 (Heinberg 2007). Nevertheless, despite the best efforts of the fossil fuel industry to propagate a paradigm of energy abundance, especially in the United States (U.S.) (Heinberg 2014), global production of *conventional* oil has already peaked and—barring incredibly unlikely huge new discoveries of easily extracted oil—must soon decline as predicted in *LtG* (Murray and Hansen 2013: 245–252). Indeed, new discoveries of oil and natural gas liquids (Heinberg 2014: 25) have dropped dramatically since their peak in the 1960s, and the world now consumes four to five barrels of oil for every one discovered (Heinberg 2014: 25; Mobbs 2012). Even the largest Saudi oilfield has peaked and is fading much faster than predicted (Blas 2019). Because oil production from *conventional* fields drops globally by 5 per cent each year, it is thus assured that such fields will eventually 'run out' (Mobbs 2012). Accordingly, U.S. President Donald J. Trump issued an executive order to expand offshore oil and gas development, lifting the Obama-era ban on oil and gas drilling in the Arctic Ocean and parts of the North Atlantic coast, and relaxed the regulations for high-risk offshore drilling imposed after the devastating Deepwater Horizon oil disaster in 2010 (Rosane 2019).

This downward global trend in oil discovery and supply has not gone unnoticed by major international actors, namely nation-states and multi- and transnational corporations, who have taken various actions since the end of the Cold War to secure access to remaining conventional oil supplies. Conventional energy supplies have become so precious to many nation-states that 'energy security' (Barnett 2001) is now an overriding objective within which foreign and domestic policies situate the procurement of oil (and other energy sources) as a matter of national security (Wittenberg 2015; see also Amster 2015). Such a discourse often elevates concern for the global fossil fuel market over other considerations such as the environment and human rights.

This shift in rhetoric to enhance the perceived necessity of fossil fuels is furthered by the influence of major energy corporations upon state governments (Short et al. 2015). As numerous global corporations, such as ConocoPhillips and ExxonMobil, have developed economic revenues larger than the GDPs of many sizeable nation-states (Trivett 2011), their power has grown correspondingly. Because such companies' business models centre on fossil fuels, examples of corporate-state collaboration to further non-renewable energy use may be found in varying arenas. Examples include the more than 50 million U.S. dollars Koch Industries spent lobbying the U.S. government between 1998 and 2010 (Mayer 2010); the formation of the American Legislative Exchange Council (which brings private corporations together with elected U.S. state officials to draft new legislation) (Bedell 2014); and direct connections between advisors to the United Kingdom (U.K.) Cabinet Office and energy sector companies, such as Centrica and Riverstone (Mobbs 2013). Because of the overly close and arguably corrupt undemocratic relationships between politicians and corporate interests (Palast 2002), it could be argued that the following are—at the very least in part—results of the wishes of the energy sector: exclusion of 'the underground injection of natural gas for purposes of storage' and ' … of fluids or propping agents … pursuant to hydraulic fracturing ("fracking") operations related to oil, gas, or geothermal production activities' from the U.S. Safe Drinking Water Act (United States Congress 2019); the British government's determination to make unconventional energy extraction through hydraulic fracturing an 'urgent national priority' (BBC 2014); the failure of the European Union to create legally binding environmental legislation for hydraulic fracturing (Carrington 2014); and the Bush and Trump Administrations' policies of attempting to 'refute the science of global warming and install in its place economic and environmental policies that not only ignore but deny the views of the scientific community on climate change' (Lynch and Stretesky 2010; see also Kramer and Bradshaw, this volume, Chapter 9). Given that the 200 largest listed fossil fuel companies spent USD $674 billion on developing new energy reserves (five times as much as they spent returning money to shareholders) in 2012 (*The Economist* 2013), it becomes clear that the energy industry remains invested in pushing the 'limits' as far as they can go (Chomsky 2013).

Resource restraints and planetary boundaries are not the only significant, impending, ecological threats to humanity and ecosystems worldwide. Carbon dioxide atmospheric concentrations 'have increased by 40% since pre-industrial times'—with concentrations of carbon dioxide, methane and nitrous oxide at the highest in at least 800,000 years (IPCC 2013), and the rate of carbon dioxide release unprecedented, at least in the last 300 million years. The result of this level of pollution—tied inherently to an insistence on using and depleting non-renewable energy sources (Hönisch et al. 2012)—is the phenomenon of climate change, in this context represented by the anthropogenic increase in Earth's surface temperature (see Kramer and Bradshaw, this volume, Chapter 9). Since 1880, the average global temperature has increased by roughly 0.85 degrees Celsius, with most of the increase—0.72 degrees Celsius—occurring in the past 50 years (IPCC 2013). The effects of this global warming are diverse and range from shrinking glaciers and ice sheets to the highest rate of sea level rise in the past 2,000 years, as well as increasingly frequent extreme weather events—all of which clearly result from 'human influence on the climate system' (IPCC 2013).

Knowing that the effects of humanity's addiction to fossil fuels are imminently approaching (and, in some cases, have already arrived), it would seem obvious that the global use of coal, natural gas and oil should be curbed immediately. At present, however, fossil fuels still remain the world's main source of energy, accounting for around 87 per cent of global primary energy use, with the share of 'renewables' in meeting global energy demand expected to reach only 12.4 per cent in 2023 (International Energy Agency 2018). This is due, in no small measure, to the current, Western-propagated largely fossil-fuel-dependent neoliberal economic model, wherein corporations, being bound legally to pursue profit above all other considerations, continuously, and most often successfully, lobby for favourable legislation, deregulation and tax incentives. Bakan (2005), in the seminal text *The Corporation: The Pathological Pursuit of Profit and Power*, notes that under corporate law, the primary legal duty of the corporation is 'simply to make money for shareholders' and failing to pursue this end 'can leave directors and officers open to being sued' (Hinkley 2002). Thus, the multitude of multi-billion dollar companies that depend upon the continued global use of fossil fuels have not only a vested interest in advocating for further non-renewable energy extraction, but, in the current energy market, a legal duty to do so—and, at the very least, an *obligation* to continue pursuing coal, natural gas and oil extraction as long as it is profitable (and legal). And so, while the use of renewable energy sources is growing (U.S. Energy Information Administration 2019), such renewable energy sources are forced to compete with an established and highly subsidised (Bloomberg 2019) non-renewable market, rather than be allowed—or *encouraged*—to replace it (Carrington 2014; Grose 2013).

The process of 'extreme energy'

As conventional reserves are depleted and demand for energy rises, there is increasing pressure to exploit unconventional energy sources. Michael Klare (2011) has coined the term 'extreme energy' to describe a range of relatively new, higher-risk, non-renewable resource extraction processes that have become more attractive to the conventional energy industry as the more easily accessible supplies dwindle. Klare's notion of 'extreme energy' lacks 'explanatory or predictive power' (Short 2016), however, and leaves open the question of who decides which extractive techniques qualify. Elsewhere, colleagues and I (Short et al. 2015) have developed a different understanding of 'extreme energy'—one that acknowledges that extraction methods grow more intense (or 'extreme') over time, as resources that are easier to extract become depleted. The ontological foundation for this notion of 'extreme energy' can be found in both human and corporate logic, and in the empirical fact that those energy sources which require the least amount of effort to extract will be used first; only once those become more scarce will more effort be exerted to gain similar resources. Thus, the process of 'extreme energy', in this sense, is evident in the history of energy extraction itself—in the change from gathering 'sea coal' from British beaches and exploiting 'natural oil seeps' to opencast mining and deep-water oil drilling. Viewed in this light, the concept of 'extreme energy' becomes a lens through which current energy extraction efforts can be explained and the future of the energy industry predicted. Using this 'extreme energy' lens necessitates an understanding of 'the amount of energy which is needed to obtain energy', as in this process it is that value which is continually rising. This value may be calculated as either 'net energy' or 'energy return on investment (EROI)', whereby net energy is the available energy for use after subtracting the energy required for extraction, and EROI is the percentage of energy produced divided by the amount required for extraction. When charted together, the net energy available to society is seen to decrease along with EROI in a curved mathematical relationship, which forms the 'energy cliff'—the point at which EROI becomes increasingly low and net energy drops to zero (Short 2016).

In the extreme energy process, the economic system can be conceptualised as consisting of two distinct segments—the part which is extracting, refining and producing energy (the energy industry), and everything else, which just consumes energy. The energy industry is thus in the rare position where the commodity which it produces is also the main resource it consumes. Thus, as energy extraction becomes more extreme, the rest of the economy is squeezed by decreasing energy availability and rising prices. The energy industry's rising costs are then offset by the rising revenues it receives. The net result is a reallocation (through the market or otherwise) of resources from the rest of society to the energy industry in order to allow the energy industry to target ever-more-difficult-to-extract resources. Under the process of extreme energy, one of the most precious resources that is being reallocated away from society to industry is *water*, which we will examine later in this chapter.

As easier-to-extract resources are depleted, this process continues and data from recent extraction methods, such as hydraulic fracturing and tar sands extraction (see Alexander et al., this volume, Chapter 19; Heydon, this volume, Chapter 18; Lampkin, this volume, Chapter 27), show that industry is lurching towards the net energy cliff. Such action on the part of some of the largest and most commercially successful transnational corporations may be understood only as the logical result of the extreme energy process (Murphy 2010): in other words, there simply are not enough easier-to-extract resources available (Heinberg 2014).

Despite the obvious negative implications of these developments, the phenomenon shows no sign of stopping; it continues towards the precipice at an ever-increasing rate, fuelled by ever-increasing levels of energy consumption. Perpetuated by the global economic 'growth' fixation (Purdey 2010), increasing amounts of energy are consumed each year (IEA 2013), driving the process over the edge. Of course, industry is not willing to halt the process as intense demand further pushes up the price of energy,[1] allowing extraction to remain economical—provided that enough resource is extracted at each site and the price stays high. The result is that higher energy consumption leads to faster resource depletion, which in turn results in the acceleration of the extreme energy process. Within this neoliberal economic context of increasing demand and profit potential, the results of extreme extraction techniques (Heinberg 2014) and the consequences of continuing the process are easily trumped in the interest of short-term profiteering and 'energy security'. Indeed, as Malin (2014: 17–27) notes, neoliberal 'normalisation' of unconventional energy extraction emerges most saliently regarding environmental outcomes and economic development. Despite the prospective consequences of reaching our limits to growth, and with considerable evidence demonstrating a strong correlation between extraction effort and damage to both society and the environment, the extreme energy process continues to accelerate with potentially disastrous consequences (Short 2016).

For example, the tropics and subtropics have seen droughts increase in intensity and duration since the 1970s, and diseases such as malaria are affecting larger portions of the population (Patz et al. 2005). Two hundred thousand deaths in the U.S. each year result from air pollution, while a heatwave across Europe in 2003 (most likely resulting from global climate change) left roughly 30,000 people dead (Short et al. 2015). As predicted in the *LtG*, the effects of climate degradation will increase rapidly with temperature throughout the twenty-first century, resulting in large-scale deaths across Europe due to heat stroke (WHO 2009), worsening droughts across continents (IPCC 2014), further loss of food and water, and a potential, eventual, extinction-level event for humanity if global greenhouse gas emissions are not reduced in accordance with the latest climate science modelling. Such events, along with resulting unrest, wars and mass migrations (IPCC 2014), threaten people's rights to life and health worldwide.

As resources become more scarce, our scramble to use them grows, increasing the political prioritisation of fossil fuel extraction over ecosystems, human health and security; increasing demand also ensures that such resources will run out sooner, which in turn will result in further human rights violations as food, healthcare and other basic needs are no longer met, to say nothing of the abuses to human security which would also necessarily increase (Short 2016). These violations will most likely increase exponentially as resources are depleted—at least, that is, until the sharp population decline predicted in *The Limits to Growth* occurs.

Martin Crook and I (Crook and Short 2014) have shown how Karl Marx's classic critique of political economy, and his value analysis more specifically, helps explain the ecologically destructive forces unleashed by capitalist extractive industries. We argued that capitalism is geared structurally towards the social production of commodities in accordance with the imperatives of capital accumulation and exchange value and not in harmony with nature's laws of conservation, sustainability and natural metabolic cycles. The Athabasca 'tar sands' (Huseman and Short 2012; see also Heydon, this volume, Chapter 18) is an infamous example of the artificial division and fragmentation of the local ecosystem in an attempt to extract oil, with no regard for the anti-ecological effects this unnatural throughput and transfer of energy and materials has on the local environment and critically on downstream Indigenous peoples (Short 2016: 159; see also Heydon, this volume, Chapter 18).

One of the central ecological contradictions of capitalism is the exponential increase in the throughput of materials and energy required by the relentless need for 'growth' and the natural limits of production. Disequilibrium exists between capital's ferocious pace in the throughput of energy and materials, on the one hand, and nature's laws, temporal rhythms and metabolic cycles, on the other, which eventually provoke an inevitable shortage of materials and an accumulation crisis (Crook and Short 2014). The result is that the price of the relevant raw material will go up as the amount of socially necessary labour time objectified in each individual product or use value rises in relative terms. This process is exemplified by extreme energy as the supply of fossil fuels begins to encounter natural limits, thus raising the relative amount of objectified labour in a given quantity of fossil fuel, leading, in the medium to long-term, to a rise in the average price of fossil fuels. Indeed, within the process of extreme energy, where more complex and costly techniques are required for the extraction of ever-scarcer sources, the very same process unfolds. So extreme energy 'as a process' can be seen as both an expression of material shortages and a competitive market response in an attempt to correct the imbalance through the extraction of ever-more extreme substitutes. The net effect is to put further pressure on local ecosystems, as well as on the biosphere more generally (Crook and Short 2014).

Thus, capitalism sets in motion a rampant process of accumulation, which carves up nature and increases the material throughput of production to ever more ecologically unsustainable levels, disturbing the social metabolism of human civilisation and leading to a 'metabolic rift' of man from nature (Crook and Short 2014; see also Lynch, this volume, Chapter 24; Lynch et al., this volume, Chapter 4). The process of extreme energy, and the role of extractive industries within it, are manifestations of the anti-ecological imperatives of capital accumulation, and the drive towards 'unconventional' extraction techniques are a particularly virulent expression of the metabolic rift and the anti-ecological nature of the capitalist value–nature contradiction. The resort to more costly and more environmentally destructive forms of energy extraction within the 'extreme energy' process signifies a particular form of environmental crisis under capitalism caused by material shortages and the natural limits of production.

'Fracking' and green criminology

Opsal and O'Connor Shelley's (2014) article—one of the first green criminological studies of unconventional energy—investigated the social and ecological impacts of energy extractive practices on local communities through a study of thousands of official complaints. Additional green criminological examination of the harms of 'extreme energy' is urgently needed. We need to document not only illegal actions but also legal processes and outcomes that are harmful—or potentially so—to humans, animals and the environment. Of key relevance here is German sociologist Ulrich Beck's (1992) 'risk society' thesis (noted by Phelan et al., this volume, Chapter 25), whereby modern industrial societies create many new risks not found in nature but which are largely manufactured through new modern technologies that were unknown in earlier days. New technologies often generate new dangers to lives and to the planet itself. These dangers are anthropogenic in origin, can have massively unforeseen consequences, and may take many, many thousands of years to reverse. For Beck, these 'manufactured risks' are taking us to the edge of catastrophe, posing 'threats to all forms of life on this planet' and presenting us with an 'exponential growth of risks and the impossibility of escaping them' (Carrabine et al. 2008: 386). The emergence of 'green crimes and harms', such as those produced by extreme energy technologies, are part of these new risks, which bring new patterns of environmental harm and potential human rights abuses (Short 2016: 61).

According to de Rijke (2013b):

> the extraordinary expansion of the unconventional gas industry has … led to questions about social power and the rights of individuals and local communities, the role of multinational corporations in politics and rural service provision, as well as related questions regarding fundamental processes of democracy, capitalist economies and social justice, [while the] close relationship between governments and powerful multinational corporations brings to the fore questions about political influence and human rights.

Thus, to address these 'important conundrums', de Rijke has advocated further academic research into fracking from multiple perspectives, including social impact assessments.

Green criminology is well suited to respond to this call. In particular, we need more green criminological investigation into what could become the most widespread extreme energy technique—'fracking'. Indeed, in addition to the infamous 'tar sands' (Huseman and Short 2012) in Alberta, Canada (see Heydon, this volume, Chapter 18), the march towards the net energy cliff is arguably spearheaded in the West by 'fracking'—the most recently developed family of extreme energy extraction methods. 'Fracking' usually refers to the extraction of shale gas, coal-bed methane (CBM)—termed Coal Seam Gas (CSG) in Australia—and 'tight oil'. The term, however, has become somewhat loaded, such that it is necessary to outline the contrasting uses (Short et al. 2015). In public debates about 'fracking', different sides often talk past each other, due to very different understandings of what the issues are, and differing definitions of the term itself. These differences fall along a spectrum that can be understood in terms of the interests of the parties involved (Short 2016: 57).

Exploitation of unconventional oil and gas is a relatively new, more extreme form of fossil fuel extraction, targeting much less permeable rock formations than previous conventional oil and gas extraction. It is characterised by the drilling of dense patterns of, usually horizontal, wells (up to eight per square mile or more) in conjunction with other more intense processes, such as de-watering (a technique used to remove water from hydrocarbon streams). Different rock formations can be targeted, such as shale (shale gas and oil) and coal (coalbed methane (CBM)), but the negative impacts on the environment and society are very similar. For many people living where 'fracking' has taken place, 'fracking' has come to mean petroleum extraction companies overrunning their locality and coating the area in hundreds or thousands of well pads, compressor stations and pipelines, accompanied by large volumes of truck traffic—with some likening it to an 'invasion' and 'occupation' (Perry 2012: 81). The effect has been a large variety of negative consequences for them and their environment (see Alexander et al., this volume, Chapter 19).

The word 'fracking', however, is derived from 'fraccing'—industry slang for 'hydraulic fracturing' (noted earlier in this chapter and elsewhere in this volume), one particular stage of unconventional petroleum (oil or gas) extraction. A scaled-up form of hydraulic fracturing (high volume), involving injecting fluids under high pressure to crack the rock, is often used to release hydrocarbons during unconventional oil and gas extraction (Short 2016: 57). The communities living with the consequences of unconventional oil and gas extraction are concerned mainly with the impact it has on them and their environment. Unconventional oil and gas extraction is a complex process and, as mentioned in the previous paragraph, involving pad construction, the drilling of wells, casing, simulation (often including but not limited to hydraulic fracturing), extraction and transport, along with well plugging and abandonment (or failure to do so). All these stages have an adverse impact on their local environment and, due to the fact that fracking requires so many more wells covering much larger areas, these impacts exceed those of conventional extraction and production (Short 2016: 57).

In an era of peaked conventional supplies, extractive industries are concerned principally with finding new fossil fuels to extract in order to ensure continued profits, the cumulative impacts of which are likely to be seen as little more than simple 'externalities' for the companies involved. Focussed as they are on getting gas and oil out of the ground, regardless, the industry and its government supporters will utilise the technologies that can do just that. Moreover, the industry works on a drilling-site-by-drilling-site basis, thus the cumulative impact of the whole process across a country will be of little concern. It is also useful in their public relations to focus on micro details rather than the macro picture, and a narrow definition of 'fracking', as simply hydraulic fracturing, helps promote the impression that fracking is just conventional extraction plus hydraulic fracturing, rather than an entirely different process with very different impacts.

Quite possibly one of the reasons the term 'fracking' has become synonymous with unconventional oil and gas extraction more generally, lies in the choices made by the industry in its early promotional pitches to investors. Indeed, in the early part of the last decade, it seems that to raise funds for exploration, a simple technological explanation was preferred when pitching to non-experts. The industry chose to focus attention on hydraulic fracturing as the key ingredient out of a complex array of technological processes. It is not difficult to understand why the idea of a new, high-tech well completion method, 'massive slick-water hydraulic fracturing', which was going to single-handedly revolutionise the industry by allowing access to a wealth of previously untapped resources, was an attractive sales pitch to investors. In comparison, a more accurate view of unconventional oil and gas exploration—one requiring much more effort and drilling greater numbers of much more expensive wells in order to produce much less oil/gas—does not sound like such an attractive proposition. It is therefore unsurprising that the terminology used to describe the industry (and understanding of the issues involved) has become somewhat skewed by this initial spin.

For green criminology, with its focus on harms to people and the environment, the issues of interest go beyond those specific to the particular technologies the industry may or may not use, to the wider ones surrounding the overall effects of the entire more-intense extraction process. For this reason, it is far more appropriate to use this wider definition of 'fracking', rather than the more narrowly defined industry slang that has the effect of limiting discourse to just the narrow technical process of hydraulic fracturing itself, as if it could occur in an isolated vacuum without its necessary production infrastructure (Short 2016: 58). Even so, it should still be acknowledged that because there are often significant levels of confusion surrounding the use of the term, green criminologists should always make clear which definition they are adopting. In this chapter, then, I use 'fracking' in its wider sense to include all of the required industrial elements of hydraulic fracturing—from consumption of huge quantities of water to compressor stations to truck traffic to waste disposal.

In the countries where 'fracking' development has taken place, it has been controversial and divisive (see Alexander et al., this volume, Chapter 19). Supporters of unconventional gas development often claim that it reduces gas prices, creates employment opportunities and provides 'energy security', all the while producing lower carbon emissions than coal. Its detractors often contest all such claims, usually pointing to contrary data emerging from the US and Australia. Indeed, in numerous studies from both countries, local communities most affected by developments often cite considerable negative impacts on the environment and human health (see Brisman and South, this volume, Introduction), including air pollution, earthquakes, groundwater contamination (Fischetti 2013; Osborn et al. 2011), depletion of water sources

(Palmer, Short and Auch 2018), the industrialisation of rural landscapes (Anderson and Theodori 2009), methane migration (Howarth et al. 2014), negative economic impacts (Fleming and Measham 2014) and radioactive and toxic waste (Mobbs 2014c)—the cumulative effect of which has led to calls for the United Nations Human Rights Council (Environment and Human Rights Advisory 2011) to condemn fracking as a threat to basic human rights, particularly the rights to water and health. Indeed, fracking development is fast becoming a human rights issue (Short et al. 2015). The United Nations Environment Programme (UNEP 2012) has issued a 'Global Alert' on the issue of fracking development, warning of significant environmental risks to the air, soil and water (contamination and usage competition); ecosystem damage; habitat and biodiversity impacts; and fugitive gas emissions, which will endanger carbon reduction targets. In terms of public health, UNEP warned of risks of pipeline explosions, release of toxins into air, soil and water, and competition for land and water resources needed for food production; it also indicated that unconventional gas would likely be used 'in addition to coal rather than being a substitute' (Short et al. 2015) and would thus pose a threat to the development of sustainable economies.

Fracking harms

Most of the academic papers on the impacts of fracking have focussed on such issues as the macroeconomic benefits of a 'shale gas revolution', the 'green' credentials of shale gas (Howarth 2014; Howarth et al. 2011, 2012) and the levels of environmental impact and responsibility for it (Osborn et al. 2011). Over the last nine years or so, anthropologists and sociologists have started to document the social and political discourses of fracking, the surrounding social conflicts in discreet Australian communities (de Rijke 2013a, 2013b, 2013c) and perceptions of risk and opportunity in American communities (Anderson and Theodori 2009; Schafft et al. 2013, 2014), although such scholars have tended to engage in discourse and perception analysis rather than a harm or impact-based assessment. Malin's (2014) broader, more structurally aware approach, should be of more interest to green criminologists as it demonstrates that neoliberal logic has led stakeholders to self-regulate their behaviour in order to facilitate fracking, by seeing fracking's current role in rural industrialisation, alongside the potential negative economic, environmental and health outcomes, as part of a 'new normal'. The consequences of this normalisation of loss of agency raises fundamental questions about the ability of communities to resist extractive operations and make informed choices about the sources of their energy.

As an antidote to the dominance of perception studies within the social science of 'fracking', my colleagues and I have argued that there are at least ten areas of concern that would provide key 'indicator' data for harm-based approaches given their inherent connection with the fracking process and its social and political context: water, air, land, health, freedom of peaceful assembly, freedom of expression, liberty and security of the person, right to a fair trial, right to respect for the private and family life and anthropogenic climate change (Short et al. 2015). In the remainder of this chapter I will focus on perhaps the most contentious of these issues: water.

Water

The impact of unconventional energy extraction on water resources (e.g., contaminated water waste disposal, excessive water use, groundwater contamination) is highly contentious and widely publicised (Palmer, Short and Auch 2018). For example, unconventional gas production is a highly water-intensive process, with a typical single well requiring around

5–11 million gallons of water and an average well-pad cluster necessitating almost 60 million gallons (FracFocus 2012). The vast majority of this water is used during the fracturing process (although the exact amount depends on the particular basin and geological formation), with large volumes of water pumped into the well with 3,300–5,000 thousand tons of sand (i.e., proppant) and chemicals to facilitate the extraction of the gas; the remainder is used in the drilling stage, with water being the major component of the drilling fluids. Once that water is used by the industry, it is no longer a useful resource for society and must be disposed in Class II Salt Water or Brine Disposal wells (Palmer, Short and Auch 2018). This is a ubiquitous aspect of the process of extreme energy—the more energy and resource intensive an extraction technique, the less energy and resources there are for society to use.

While increasing quantities of water are being recycled and reused in the U.S., freshwater is still used in high quantities for the drilling operations as 'produced' (waste) water is more likely to damage the equipment and reduce the chance of a 'successful well'. The industry's requirements (Stark et al. 2012) for such quantities of freshwater is clearly a serious concern in water-scarce regions of the world and in places with high cumulative demand for water. The enormous amount of water used by the fracking industry is but one of many serious impacts. The contamination of groundwater sources (Fischetti 2013) from failure in the well casing over time (Ingraffea et al. 2014)—what industry refers to as 'zonal isolation' failure—is a very serious issue across regions that have experienced considerable fracking development to date, and has featured as a central propaganda battleground for industry and pro-fracking governments, who seek to downplay such failures (Short et al. 2015). Arguably, the most concerning issue with fracking's use of water is the issue of produced water disposal and waste water treatment, often referred to simply as 'waste water management'. And yet, the risks in this regard far outweigh the concerns of corporate risk minimisation.

The whole process of dealing with fracking's waste water is a highly risky business for local populations and the environment with considerable dangers of water or soil contamination from surface leaks and spills (Olmstead et al. 2013), but perhaps the most concerning issue with waste water is that it can contain significant amounts of radioactive material (Mobbs 2014c) due to the 'naturally occurring hypersaline brines associated with the formations targeted for natural gas production' (Warner et al. 2013)· For instance, radium has been found to be building up in rivers downstream of shale gas waste discharge points in Pennsylvania (Warner et al. 2013)·

Vengosh et al. (2014) have summarised the overall risks posed by fracking development:

- Contamination of shallow aquifers in areas adjacent to shale gas development through stray gas leaking from improperly constructed or failing gas wells.
- Contamination of water resources in areas of shale gas development and/or waste management by spills, leaks or disposal of hydraulic fracturing fluids and inadequately treated wastewaters.
- Accumulation of metals and radioactive elements on stream, river and lake sediments in wastewater disposal or spill sites, posing an additional long-term impact by slowly releasing toxic elements and radiation to the environment in the impacted areas. The water footprint through withdrawals of valuable fresh water from dry areas and overexploitation of limited or diminished water resources for shale gas development.

All these concerns have been exacerbated in the U.S. by the Energy Policy Act 2005 (infamously known as the 'Halliburton Loophole'), which, for example, exempts unconventional oil and gas production and delivery from the Safe Drinking Water Act (SDWA) (Vann et al.

2014). While the Halliburton Loophole exemplifies Vengosh and colleagues' concerns about water *quality*, there is a succinct link between water quality and quantity (Palmer, Short and Auch 2018; Brisman et al. 2018). If groundwater and shallow aquifers are contaminated by hydraulic fracturing and related oil and gas production activities—and are no longer viable as a freshwater resource—then water quantity is also diminished.

World Health Organization guidelines argue that states should ensure

> the safety of drinking water supplies through the elimination of, or reduction to a minimum concentration, of constituents of water that are known to be hazardous to health ... and water should also be of an acceptable colour, odour and taste for each personal or domestic use.
>
> *(Palmer, Short and Auch 2018)*

Given the incidents and complaints that have been reported to the Pennsylvania Department of Environmental Protection (DEP), it is clear that water quality is adversely impacted by 'fracking'. According to Inglis and Rumpler (2015):

> Drilling poses major risks for our water supplies, including potential underground leaks of toxic chemicals and contamination of groundwater. There are at least 243 documented cases of contaminated drinking water supplies across Pennsylvania between December 2007 and August 2014 due to fracking activities, according to the Pennsylvania Department of Environmental Protection (DEP).

In fact, it is commonplace for extraction companies to be required to bring in 'replacement water supplies for residents, construct new drinking water wells, or otherwise modify their existing water wells' in order to make water potable following 'fracking' operations. Some companies, however, have been 'cited' for neglecting to follow through on their promises. For instance, in November 2012, Carrizo (Marcellus) LLC was cited under state rules for failing to properly restore a contaminated drinking water supply following drilling operations in Forest Lake Township, Susquehanna County (Palmer, Short and Auch 2018). In cases like Forest Lake (and there are many), it is difficult to dispute that unconventional oil and gas affects both the quantity and quality of water resources.

Furthermore, worried citizens often see compelling scientific evidence introduced at planning hearings that suggests the risks are too high, only to then witness how those risks are ignored by decision-makers. This is accompanied by a regulatory framework that is not geared to respond to new science. It is clear that domestic laws are not prepared for either the new science that facilitates unconventional gas extraction or the scientific evidence that questions the safety and economic viability of unconventional resources. Arguably, existing regulation does not regulate such production adequately (for example, in most countries that require Environment Impact Assessments (EIAs), these EIAs do not have a category that covers fracking), and in some countries, such as the U.K., the regulations cover conventional extraction only; there is no fracking-specific regulation and the associated risks are quite simply not the same as conventional extraction. Existing regulations are often found wanting when it comes to mitigating harm, but many governments are promoting the technology aggressively.

At the outset of the 'Shale Revolution' in the U.S., there was considerable discussion about 'energy independence', jobs and tax revenue, and short shrift was paid to concerns about issues such as air quality, community cohesion, ecological effects and water quality and/or quantity (see Brisman and South, Introduction, this volume). In the five-to-fifteen years from the beginning of the unconventional resource revolution, however, we are seeing that the realised tax revenue is often an order-of-magnitude less than projections, job creation has been replaced by job *migration* from one shale play (area or site) to another shale play, and directional wells are proving short-lived (e.g., 85 per cent declines in productivity from year 1 to year 2) (Palmer, Short and Auch 2018). As a result, the unconventional resource industry has expanded into less productive plays, such as in Antrim County, Michigan, which has required more and more resources in the form of chemicals, sand (Carroll and Wethe 2016) and water to stimulate production in the name of shareholder return.

Furthermore, the exponential increase in water demand, as well as ever-longer lateral wells, has resulted in parallel rises in liquid and solid waste production. This waste increase has created tremendous stressors in states like Ohio and Oklahoma, where 'induced seismicity' or anthropogenic earthquake activity has increased from an average of 21 M3+ quakes between 1973 and 2008 to 659 of M3+ in 2014 alone, according to the United States Geological Survey (USGS). These seismic events are not limited to smaller events; magnitudes exceeding 5.8 have been witnessed in Pawnee and Cushing, Oklahoma. Incidentally Cushing happens to be the site of the U.S.'s largest strategic commercial crude oil storage terminal, prompting questions about whether the unconventional industry's excessive production of waste and demand for water may be compromising their own infrastructure and undercutting the notion that such resources will lead to 'energy independence'.

Examples of increasing resource demand include Chesapeake Energy's 'Propageddon' lateral in Louisiana, which required more than 25 tons of frac sand (5–6 times the average amount of sand needed in a typical fracked lateral) (Palmer, Short and Auch 2018). From a water demand perspective, names like 'Outlaw', 'Purple Hayes' and 'Walleye' have been given to so-called 'Super-Laterals' in Ohio and West Virginia, where they exceed 17–20,000 feet in length, or 2.3–2.6 times average lateral length in these two states. These lateral wells require more than 85 million gallons each, which translates into 4,470 gallons per lateral foot (GPLF). Assuming the average American uses 33,000 gallons of water per year, this is roughly equivalent to the annual water demand of 2,587 Americans (Palmer, Short and Auch 2018).

Traditionally, Appalachian West Virginia and Ohio laterals require 970–1,080 GPLF, with demand growing at a rate of 11–22 per cent per year. As an example of how much liquid—and potentially radioactive—waste is produced, it is estimated that 11–12 per cent of the freshwater used in the fracking process comes back to the surface as 'brine' and must be disposed of in Class II Salt Water Disposal Injection Wells (Palmer, Short and Auch 2018). An 85-million-gallon lateral well is likely to produce 9.8 million gallons of liquid waste, which is equivalent to the total amount of water in 15 Olympic-sized swimming pools.

These recent developments call into question our existing resource demand models, which estimate resource demand is increasing by 7–30 per cent per year, while oil and gas production is declining by 85 per cent per year per well. Yet, more importantly, these trends raise concerns about watershed ecological security and/or resilience, public water supply robustness and the increasing importance of the unconventional industry's water demand in predicting *any* given watershed's likely depletion in the face of less frequent and more intense precipitation events resulting from climate change.

Presently, the U.S. unconventional industry's water demand amounts to roughly 14 per cent of residential water demand but exceeds 65 per cent in counties as geographically disparate as Carroll County, Ohio, Richland County, Montana and Wetzel County, West Virginia. The most extreme example of how residential water demand is in conflict with unconventional oil and gas development's demand is in Doddridge County, West Virginia, where such unconventional oil and gas development demand is *nearly double* that of residential demand. These demands greatly exceed the 'precautionary principle setting 20%

of the natural runoff in a region as the upper limit of … consumptive use' by any one industry (Sposito 2013). The crux of the matter is that the industry is charged only $4.25–$6.25 per *thousand* gallons, which amounts to only 0.25–0.28 per cent of well-pad costs and is *less than half* of what *residential* users pay in the U.S. (Porter 2014). Furthermore, when the resulting liquid wastes are produced, the unconventional industry incurs charges of only $00.05–$00.20 per gallon disposed (e.g., 0.0044 per cent of well-pad costs) across the country's thousands of Class II Injection Wells (Palmer, Short and Auch 2018).

Data from Colorado on the pricing of water for the fracking industry is even more concerning. In a recent collaborative study, Palmer, Short and Auch (2018) found that the Windsor Town Council sold Great Western Oil & Gas (GWOG) up to 65 acre ft (1 acre foot of water = 325,851 gallons) per year for the next ten years. The Windsor Town Council reports that the cost that GWOG paid is $400/acre ft. That brings into the Town of Windsor a meagre $26,000 annually should the entire 65 acre ft be taken, and it seems likely that GWOG will use the water rather quickly, based on past consumption and the requirements of the industry (Palmer, Short and Auch 2018). Therefore, the cost per gallon for GWOG is $0.00122—or one tenth of one penny per gallon!

This is a considerable problem: there is no supply-side price signal demanding the unconventional industry reduce or stabilise its water demand per unit of energy produced. An additional issue concerns anecdotal evidence pointing towards the unconventional resource industry relying on highly fragile and ecologically critical 1st- and 2nd-order streams throughout Appalachia, when its demand cannot be met by documented water withdrawals agreements with conservancy districts (Palmer, Short and Auch 2018). Currently, research points to a 22–25 per cent gap in our understanding of where this industry's water demand is coming from, leaving frontline communities and policy makers in the dark regarding how this known 'unknown' environmental externality will manifest in the coming years and decades (Palmer, Short and Auch 2018).

Resource demand in the unconventional resource industry is related directly to the global price of oil and gas, with water demand increasing exponentially as the price of oil and gas declines. This forces the industry to rely on resources known to generate a disproportionate Return-On-Investment (ROI) relative to the price paid for the resources. As an example, the water demand increases in the Marcellus and Utica Plays of Southern Appalachia happened to coincide with a 50 per cent decline in the global price of Brent Crude and West Texas Intermediate Oil between Q1-2014 and the end of 2016. These significant problems over water can produce considerable localised harms, which can become national in scope when water is scarce in large regions, making the prioritisation of industry 'needs' over people a violation of the human right to water (Palmer, Short and Auch 2018).

There are correlative harms that flow from concerns over water. Local populations are increasingly aware of the dangers fracking can pose to local water supplies—from competition over the resource, to waste water spills and groundwater contamination. This knowledge can often lead to considerable local opposition, the like of which can be seen in the U.K., where fracking is still largely at the exploration stage. The epicentre of the fledgling industry is the county of Lancashire, which has seen overwhelming local opposition, including within the local government, but which is ignored by a central government seemingly intent on developing a fracking industry at all costs. Local opposition has been well organised and has sustained numerous challenges to the industry, involving successful opposition to the official planning process, unsuccessful judicial reviews of the central government decision to override local democracy and partially successful last-minute injunctions. The years of resistance have taken their toll on many concerned citizens, however. Indeed, it has caused a form of 'collective trauma' in the local community (Short and Szolucha 2019), which has unfortunately demonstrated that the industry can cause significant harm before it even enters full-scale production.

Another associated harm from fracking development that has attracted attention from criminologists is the criminalisation of peaceful protest (Jackson, Gilmore and Monk 2019). A groundbreaking report into the protests at the Barton Moss 'protection camp' (Gilmore, Jackson and Monk 2015; see also Jackson, Gilmore and Monk 2019) in the U.K. highlighted deeply worrying police behaviour. The study raised very serious questions about the proportionality of arrest patterns and bail conditions, as well as the dominant media and public portrayal of the protest and the protesters, including the role played by local police in influencing this depiction. The report documented protesters' experiences of police violence and harassment, including gendered violence experienced by women at the camp. In short, the report found that police behaviour had the effect of curtailing the right to protest, was violent, disproportionate to the size and peaceful nature of the protest, and carried out with impunity. More worrying is that preliminary research into the policing of protest nationally is finding this picture replicated across numerous protest sites across the country.

With the U.K. government committed to 'go all out for shale' (Short et al. 2015) and with the close relationship between the industry and the government (Mobbs 2013), it is likely that harms at the exploration and production stages will occur, resulting in many more protests in the years to come. What will be needed then is more critical and green criminological investigation into these energy harms.

Conclusion

This chapter discussed some of the social and environmental harms that are driven by humanity's reliance on fossil fuels, and, in particular, the consequences of unconventional energy extraction techniques, which devour precious resources such as water. From planetary boundaries and the limits to growth, to the process of extreme energy and its externalities, there is, unfortunately, much to engage the green criminologist. Indeed, there are currently, and will be, many considerable harms to be identified and analysed when it comes to the expansion of unconventional energy, as our more efficient resources dwindle and while governments seem incapable of extracting themselves from the influence of the extractive industries.

Note

1 Notwithstanding the current, inevitably temporary, geopolitically induced price reduction, prices will undoubtedly rise over time as supply declines (see Mobbs 2015a).

References

Amster, R. 2015. *Peace Ecology*. Boulder, CO and London: Paradigm Publishers.

Anderson, B. J. and Theodori, G. L. 2009. 'Local leaders' perceptions of energy development in the Barnett shale,' *Southern Rural Sociology*, 24(1): 113–129.

Barnett, J. 2001. 'Environmental security and U.S. foreign policy,' in P. G. Harris (ed.) *The Environment, International Relations, and U.S. Foreign Policy*, pp. 68–91. Washington, DC: Georgetown University Press.

Bakan, J. 2005. *The Corporation: The Pathological Pursuit of Profit and Power*. London: Constable and Robinson.

BBC. 2014. 'Lords: Fracking should be "urgent priority" for UK,' *BBC News: Business*, 8 May. Available at: www.bbc.co.uk/news/business-27312796.

Beck, U. 1992. *Risk Society: Towards a New Modernity*. Los Angeles, CA: SAGE.

Bedell, F. 2014. 'Economic injustice as an understanding of the existence of two Americas—Wealth and poverty,' *Open Journal of Political Science*, 4(3): 101–108. Available at: https://pdfs.semanticscholar.org/7e13/91ad73b7dd2d85d8ba236e00ab68165d2f93.pdf.

Blas, J. 2019. 'The biggest Saudi oil field is fading faster than anyone guessed,' *Financial Review*, 4 April. Available at: www.afr.com/news/world/middle-east/the-biggest-saudi-oil-field-is-fading-faster-than-anyone-guessed-20190404-p51alk.

Bloomberg: New Energy Finance. 2019. 'Subsidies for renewables, biofuels dwarfed by supports for fossil fuels,' *Bloomberg: New Energy Finance*. Available at: http://about.bnef.com/press-releases/subsidies-for-renewables-biofuels-dwarfed-by-supports-for-fossil-fuels/.

Brisman, A., McClanahan, B., South, N. and Walters, R. 2018. *Water, Crime and Security in the Twenty-First Century: Too Dirty, Too Little, Too Much*. London: Palgrave Macmillan.

Carrabine, E., Cox, P., Lee, M., Plummer, K. and South, N. 2008. *Criminology: A Sociological Introduction*, 2nd ed. Abingdon, Oxon, UK: Routledge.

Carrington, D. 2014. 'Fracking boom will not tackle global warming, analysis warns,' *The Guardian*, 15 October. Available at: www.theguardian.com/environment/2014/oct/15/gas-boom-from-unrestrained-fracking-linked-to-emissions-rise.

Carroll, J. and Wethe, D. 2016. 'Chesapeake energy declares 'propageddon' with record frack,' *Bloomberg Markets*, 20 October.

Chomsky, N. 2013. 'Can civilization survive capitalism?' *AlterNet*, 5 March. Available at: www.alternet.org/noam-chomsky-can-civilization-survive-capitalism.

Crook, M. and Short, D. 2014. 'Marx, "Lemkin and the Genocide Ecocide Nexus",' *The International Journal of Human Rights*, 18(3): 298–319.

Croteau, D. 2005. 'Which side are you on? The tension between movement scholarship and activism,' in D. Croteau, W. Hoynes and C. Ryan (eds.) *Rhyming Hope and History: Activists, Academics, and Social Movement Scholarship*, Vol. 24, pp. 20–40. Minneapolis, MN: University of Minnesota Press.

Croteau, D., Hoynes, W. and Ryan, C. 2005. 'Introduction: Integrating social movement theory and practice,' in D. Croteau, W. Hoynes and C. Ryan (eds.) *Rhyming Hope and History: Activists, Academics, and Social Movement Scholarship*, Vol. 24, pp. xi–xviii. Minneapolis, MN: University of Minnesota Press.

de Rijke, K. 2013a. 'Coal seam gas and social impact assessment: An anthropological contribution to current debates and practices,' *Journal of Economic and Social Policy*, 15(3): 3.

de Rijke, K. 2013b. 'Hydraulically fractured: Unconventional gas and anthropology,' *Anthropology Today*, 29(2): 13–17.

de Rijke, K. 2013c. 'The agri-gas fields of Australia: Black soil, food, and unconventional gas,' *Culture, Agriculture, Food and Environment*, 35(1): 41–53.

Environment and Human Rights Advisory. 2011. *A Human Rights Assessment of Hydraulic Fracturing for Natural Gas*. Oregon: EHRA. Available at: www.earthworksaction.org/files/publications/EHRA_Human-rights-fracking-FINAL.pdf.

Erikson, K. 1976. *Everything in Its Path: Destruction of Community in the Buffalo Creek Flood*. New York: Simon & Schuster, Inc.

Fischetti, M. 2013. 'Groundwater contamination may end the gas-fracking boom', *Scientific American*, 20 August. Available at: www.scientificamerican.com/article/groundwater-contamination-may-end-the-gas-fracking-boom/.

Fleming, D. A. and Measham, T. G. 2014. 'Local economic impacts of an unconventional energy boom: The coal seam gas industry in Australia,' *Australian Journal of Agricultural and Resource Economics*. DOI: 10.1111/1467-8489.12043.

FracFocus. 2012. 'FracFocus 2.0: Hundreds of companies. Thousands of Wells,' *FracFocus*. Available at: www.fracfocus.org.

Gilmore, J., Jackson, W. and Monk, H. 2015. 'Keep moving: Report of on the policing of the Barton Moss protection camp,' Available at: https://curbyork.files.wordpress.com/2016/02/bm_final_170216_email.pdf.

Gilmore, J., Jackson, W. and Monk, H. 2017. '"That is not facilitating peaceful protest. That is dismantling the protest": Anti-fracking protesters' experiences of dialogue policing and mass arrest,' *Policing and Society: An International Journal of Research and Policy*.

Grose, T. K. 2013. 'As U.S. cleans its energy mix, it ships coal problems abroad,' *National Geographic: News*, 15 March. Available at: http://news.nationalgeographic.com/news/energy/2013/03/130315-us-coal-exports/.

Heinberg, R. 2007. 'Peak coal: Sooner than you think,' *On Line Opinion*, 21 May. Available at: www.onlineopinion.com.au/view.asp?article=5869.

Heinberg, R. 2014. *Snake Oil: How Fracking's False Promises of Plenty Imperils Our Future*. West Sussex: Clairview Books.

Herman, E. S. and Chomsky, N. 1988. *Manufacturing Consent: The Political Economy of the Mass Media*. New York: Pantheon Books.

Hinkley, R. C. 2002. 'How corporate law inhibits social responsibility,' *Humanist*, 62(2): 26.

Howarth, R. 2014. 'A bridge to nowhere: Methane emissions and the greenhouse gas footprint of natural gas,' *Energy Science and Engineering*, 2(2): 47–60.

Howarth, R., Santoro, R. and Ingraffea, A. 2011. 'Methane and the greenhouse-gas footprint of natural gas from shale formations,' *Climatic Change*, 106(4): 679–690.

Howarth, R., Shindell, D., Santoro, R., Ingraffea, A., Phillips, N. and Townsend-Small, A. 2012. *Methane Emissions from Natural Gas Systems: Background Paper for the National Climate Assessment*. Available at: www.eeb.cornell.edu/howarth/publications/Howarth_et_al_2012_National_Climate_Assessment.pdf.

Hönisch, B. et al. 2012. 'The geological record of ocean acidification science,' *Science*, 335(6072): 1058–1063.

Huseman, J. and Short, D. 2012. '"A slow industrial genocide": Tar sands and the indigenous peoples of Northern Alberta,' *International Journal of Human Rights*, 16(1): 216–237.

IPCC. 2013. *Climate Change 2013: The Physical Science Basis. Contribution of Working Group I to the Fifth Assessment Report of the Intergovernmental Panel on Climate Change*. ed. T.F. Stocker et al. Cambridge: Cambridge University Press.

Inglis, J. and Rumpler, J. 2015. *Fracking Failures: Oil and Gas Industry Environmental Violations in Pennsylvania and What They Mean for the US*. Denver, CO: Environment America Research & Policy Center. Available at: https://environmentamerica.org/sites/environment/files/reports/EA_PA_fracking_scrn.pdf.

Ingraffea, A. et al. 2014. 'Assessment and risk analysis of casing and cement impairment in oil and gas wells in Pennsylvania, 2000–2012,' *Proceedings of the National Academy of the Sciences*, 111(30): 10955–10960.

International Energy Agency. 2013. *Key World Energy Statistics, 2013*. Available at: www.iea.org/publications/freepublications/publication/KeyWorld2013.pdf.

International Energy Agency. 2018. 'Renewables 2018: Market analysis and forecast from 2018 to 2023,' Available at: www.iea.org/renewables2018/

Jackson, W., Gilmore, J. and Monk, H. 2019. 'Policing unacceptable protest in England and wales: 'A case study of the policing of anti-fracking protests,' *Critical Social Policy*, 39(1): 23–43. DOI: 10.1177/0261018317753087.

Lynch, M.J., Burns, R.G. and Stretesky, P.B. 2010. 'Global warming and state-corporate crime: The politicization of global warming under the Bush administration,' *Crime, Law and Social Change*, 54(3/4): 213–239.

Malin, S. 2014. 'There's no real choice but to sign: Neoliberalization and normalization of hydraulic fracturing on Pennsylvania farmland,' *Journal of Environmental Studies and Sciences*, 4(1): 17–27. DOI: 10.1007/s13412-013-0115-2.

Marx, K. and Engels, F. 1967. *Capital*, vol. III. New York: International Publishers.

Mayer, J. 2010. 'Covert operations: The Billionaire brothers who are waging a war against Obama,' *The New Yorker*, 30 August. Available at: www.newyorker.com/magazine/2010/08/30/covert-operations.

McDermott-Levy, R., Kaktins, N. and Sattler, B. 2013. 'Fracking, the environment, and health: New energy practices may threaten public health,' *American Journal of Nursing*, 113(6): 45–51.

McKenzie, L. M., Guo, R., Witter, R. Z., Savitz, D. A., Newman, L. S. and Adgate, J. L. 2014. 'Birth outcomes and maternal residential proximity to natural gas development in rural Colorado,' *Environmental Health Perspectives*, 122(4): 412–417.

Meadows, D. H. et al. 1972. *The Limits to Growth: A Report for the Club of Rome's Project on the Predicament of Mankind*. New York: Universe Books.

Mobbs, P. 2012. '*Sheet E1*; Gaetano Maggio and Gaetano Cacciola, "when will oil, natural gas, and coal peak?"' *Fuel* 982012: 111–123. Available at: www.theecologist.org/News/news_analysis/2721027/frackingnbsppolicy_and_the_pollution_of_british_democracy.html.

Mobbs, P. 2013. 'Economically & politically fracked: 'Behind every picture lies a story' – Statistical reality versus PR-hype within the political project of unconventional gas in Britain,' *Extreme Energy Initiative*, Working Papers Series. Available at: http://extremeenergy.org/2013/07/25/economically-and-politic

ally-fracked-behind-every-picture-lies-a-story-statistical-reality-versus-pr-hype-within-the-political-project-of-unconventional-gas-in-britain/.
Mobbs, P. 2014a. 'Shale gas and public health – The whitewash exposed,' *The Ecologist*, 6 May. And for a detailed critique of Public Health England's methods and conclusions see Paul Mobbs 2014 'A critical review of Public Health England's report – "Review of the Potential Public Health Impacts of Exposures to Chemical and Radioactive Pollutants as a Result of Shale Gas Extraction – draft for comment"'. Available at: www.fraw.org.uk/mei/archive/phe_shale_gas_and_health_report-critical_analysis.pdf.
Mobbs, P. 2014b. 'With sub-$60 oil, fracking and tar sands losses threaten the whole financial system,' *The Ecologist*, 17 December. Available at: www.theecologist.org/News/news_analysis/2679765/with_sub60_oil_fracking_and_tar_sands_losses_threaten_the_whole_financial_system.html.
Mobbs, P. 2014c. 'An abuse of science – Concealing fracking's radioactive footprint,' *The Ecologist*, 8 July. Available at: www.theecologist.org/News/news_analysis/2469495/an_abuse_of_science_concealing_frackings_radioactive_footprint.html.
Mobbs, P. 2015a. 'Environmentalists' oil price panic reflects their own existential crisis,' *The Ecologist*, 8 January. Available at: www.theecologist.org/blogs_and_comments/commentators/2703420/environ mentalists_oil_price_panic_reflects_their_own_existential_crisis.html.
Mobbs, P. 2015b. 'Fracking policy and the pollution of British democracy,' *The Ecologist*, 20 January.
Murray, J. and Hansen, J. 2013. 'Peak oil and energy independence: Myths and reality,' *Eos*, 94(28): 245–252.
Olmstead, S. M. et al. 2013. 'Shale gas development impacts on surface water quality in Pennsylvania,' *Proceedings of the National Academy of the Sciences*, 110(13): 4962–4967.
Opsal, T. and O'Connor, S. T. 2014. 'Energy crime, harm, and problematic state response in Colorado: A case of the fox guarding the hen house?' *Critical Criminology: An International Journal*, 22(4): 561–577. DOI: 10.1007/s10612-014-9255-2.
Osborn, S., Vengosh, A., Warner, N. R. and Jackson, R. B. 2011. 'Methane contamination of drinking water accompanying gas-well drilling and hydraulic fracturing', *PNAS*, 108(20). Available at: www.pnas.org/cgi/doi/10.1073/pnas.1100682108.
Palast, G. 2002. *The Best Democracy Money Can Buy: An Investigative Reporter Exposes the Truth about Globalization, Corporate Cons and High Finance Fraudsters*. London: Pluto Press.
Patz, J. et al. 2005. 'Impact of regional climate change on human health,' *Nature*, 438: 310–317.
Palmer, R., Short, D. and Auch, W. T. 2018. 'The human right to water and unconventional energy,' *International Journal of Environmental Research and Public Health*, September, 15 (9): 1858.
Perry, S. 2012. 'Development, land use, and collective trauma: The marcellus shale gas boom in rural Pennsylvania,' *Culture, Agriculture, Food and Environment*, 34(1): 81–92, 81.
Peters, C. 2005. 'Knowing what's wrong is not enough: Creating strategy and vision,' in D. Croteau, W. Hoynes and C. Ryan (eds.) *Rhyming Hope and History: Activists, Academics, and Social Movement Scholarship*, Vol. 24, pp. 41–56. Minneapolis, MN: University of Minnesota Press.
Porter, E. 2014. 'The risks of cheap water,' *The New York Times*, 14 October.
Purdey, S. J. 2010. *Economic Growth, the Environment and International Relations: The Growth Paradigm*. Abingdon, Oxon, UK: Routledge.
Rosane, O. 2019. 'Trump weakens rules meant to prevent next deepwater horizon spill,' *EcoWatch*, 3 May. Available at: www.ecowatch.com/trump-offshore-driling-deepwater-horizon-2636183454.html.
Schafft, K., Borlu, Y. and Glenna, L. 2013. 'The relationship between Marcellus shale gas development in Pennsylvania and local perceptions of risk and opportunity,' *Rural Sociology*, 78(2): 143–166.
Schafft, K. A., Glenna, L. L., Green, B. and Borlu, Y. 2014. 'Local impacts of unconventional gas development within Pennsylvania's Marcellus shale region: Gauging boomtown development through the perspectives of educational administrators,' *Society & Natural Resources: An International Journal*, 27(4): 389–404.
Short, D. 2016. *Redefining Genocide: Settler Colonialism, Social Death and Ecocide*. London: Zed Books.
Short, D., Elliot, J., Norder, K., Lloyd-Davies, E. and Morley, J. 2015. 'Extreme energy, 'fracking' and human rights: A new field for human rights impact assessments?' *The International Journal of Human Rights*, 19(6): 697–736. DOI: 10.1080/13642987.2015.1019219.
Short, D. and Szolucha, A. 2019. 'Fracking Lancashire: The planning process, social harm and collective trauma,' *Geoforum*, 98(January): 264–276. DOI: 10.1016/j.geoforum.2017.03.001.

Sposito, G. 2013. 'Green water and global food security,' *Vadose Zone Journal*, 12(4). Available at: https://pubs.geoscienceworld.org/vzj/article-pdf/12/4/vzj2013.02.0041/2991488/vzj2013.02.0041.pdf.

Stark, M. et al. 2012. 'Water and shale gas development: Leveraging the US experience in new shale developments,' *Accenture*, December.

The Economist. 2013. 'Energy firms and climate change: Unburnable fuel,' 4 May. Available at: www.economist.com/news/business/21577097-either-governments-are-not-serious-about-climate-change-or-fossil-fuel-firms-are.

Trivett, T. 2011. '25 US mega corporations: Where they rank if they were countries,' *Business Insider*, 27 June. Available at: www.businessinsider.com/25-corporations-bigger-tan-countries-2011-6?op=1.

Turner, G. 2007. *A Comparison of the Limits to Growth with 30 Years of Reality*. Socio-Economics and the Environment in Discussion CSIRO Working Paper Series 2008–09.

United Nations Environment Programme. 2012. 'Gas fracking: Can we safely squeeze the rocks?' *United Nations Environment Programme*, Global Environment Alert Service.

United States Congress. 2019. *Energy Policy Act*, Pub.L. 109–58. U.S. Energy Information Administration, 'Renewable & Alternative Fuels', U.S. Energy Information Administration. Available at: www.eia.gov/renewable/.

Vann, A. et al. 2014. 'Hydraulic fracturing: Selected legal issues,' Congressional Research Service. Available at: https://fas.org/sgp/crs/misc/R43152.pdf.

Vengosh, A. Jackson, R. B. Warner, N. Darrah, T. H. and Kondash, A. 2014. 'A critical review of the risks to water resources from unconventional shale gas development and hydraulic fracturing in the United States,' *Environmental Science and Technology*. DOI: 10.1021/es405118y.

Warner, N. R., Christie, C. A., Jackson, R. B. and Vengosh, A. 2013. 'Impacts of shale gas wastewater disposal on water quality in western Pennsylvania,' *Environmental Science & Technology*, 47(20): 11849–11857. DOI: 10.1021/es402165b.

White, R. 2013. 'Eco-global criminology and the political economy of environmental harm,' in N. South and A. Brisman (eds.) *Routledge International Handbook of Green Criminology*, pp. 243–260. Abingdon, Oxon, UK: Routledge.

Wittenberg, A. 2015. 'Domestic oil, gas boom changes U.S. security posture—Experts,' *E&E News PM (E&E Publishing, Inc.)*, 26 June. Accessed at: www.eenews.net/eenewspm/2015/06/26/stories/1060020990.

World Health Organization (WHO). 2009. *Regional Office for Europe, Euroheat: Improving Public Health Responses to Extreme Weather Heat-Waves. Summary for Policymakers*. Copenhagen: World Health Organization.

27

The uncertainty of community financial incentives for 'fracking'

Pursuing ramifications for environmental justice

Jack Adam Lampkin

Introduction

The purpose of this chapter is twofold. First, while green criminology has gained recognition over the last 30 years, there has been insufficient research focussing specifically on *energy crime* (and energy harm), despite the fact that many energy extraction processes create environmental harm and ecological destruction. In order to contribute to green criminological literature on energy crime, this chapter explores the emergence of *unconventional hydraulic fracturing* (UHF) in the United Kingdom (U.K.) with a concurrent discussion of the global academic literature that has identified both social and environmental harm as a result of such technology overseas.[1] Second, this chapter offers an analysis of the *community financial incentives* (CFIs) that are provided to 'communities' in respect of the right to use underlying geology for the purposes of UHF and the subsequent ramifications that such payments may have for environmental justice in the communities that permit fracking to occur.

The chapter draws on empirical research (specifically, interviews) conducted with 20 key-informants. Key-informants are simply defined as *expert sources of information*—people who 'as a result of their personal skills, or position within a society, are able to provide more information and a deeper insight into what is going on around them' (Marshall 1996: 92). Participants consisted of: three academics; four consultants to the onshore oil and gas industry (geology and water); three regulators; two parish councillors; one journalist; five anti-fracking campaigners; one oil and gas professional; and one gas company director. I utilised three techniques to approach and arrange interviews with key-informants, all of which can be seen as forms of purposive sampling. These included utilising the social media professional networking site LinkedIn (30 per cent), non-LinkedIn public domain information (35 per cent) and face-to-face networking at conferences, debates and public meetings (35 per cent). This purposive sampling technique enabled me to approach prospective interviewees using the knowledge that I had gained through a comprehensive literature review undertaken prior to data collection.

Research rationale and methodology

This chapter draws upon interviews that I conducted between May 2016 and September 2017 as part of an empirical, qualitative, PhD project investigating the potential for environmental victimisation as a result of UHF processes in the UK. Prior to the commencement of interviews, I performed a literature review that identified seven central areas where environmental victimisation may occur, which included: chemical usage, greenhouse gas emissions, produced water, seismicity, water aquifers, water integrity and water resources. In addition, the literature review identified five further areas where the economic implications of UHF in the U.K. were uncertain. These included the potential economic impacts of UHF on community financial incentives, the economy, energy security, jobs and property values. As a result, the following research questions were formulated:

1 What are the most salient concerns regarding human victimisation in the U.K.?
2 What are the most salient concerns regarding environmental victimisation in the U.K.?
3 What are the economic implications of unconventional hydraulic fracturing in the U.K.?

This chapter begins with an explanation of the importance of green criminology as a discipline. Next, it considers the current lack of green criminological research into energy crime (and energy harm) despite the local and global impacts that energy production and consumption have on the environment and social and ecological justice. From here, the chapter examines the emergence of UHF in the U.K. and the social and environmental harms that have occurred on an international scale from UHF internationally. Finally, the chapter will draw upon empirical data to explain the implications that community financial incentives have on environmental justice in the U.K.

The importance of green criminological research into energy extraction processes

Environmental issues stayed mostly dormant within criminological discourse until Lynch's (1990) articulation of a *green criminology*. Consequently, since the late 1990s, the green criminological volcano has erupted to produce a body of research that encompasses a wide range of themes and topics that are encapsulated under the green criminological perspective. Despite the growth of green criminological research, as evidenced, in part, by the second edition of this volume, and despite a recognition that energy extraction processes often lead to environmental and social harm, there has been relatively little green criminological analysis of energy extraction methods (for exceptions, see, e.g., Alexander, O'Connor Shelly and Opsal, this volume, Chapter 19; Crook, Short and South 2018; Greife and Stretesky 2013; Lampkin 2016; Long et al. 2012; Ospal and O'Connor Shelly 2014; Ruggiero and South 2010a, 2010b; Short 2016, this volume, Chapter 26; Short and Szolucha 2019; Stretesky, Long and Lynch 2014; White 2013). Critically analysing energy extraction is exceedingly important in an era where many conventional fossil fuel resources have already been exploited, leaving corporations to search, identify and later exploit more unconventional (and essentially more difficult to extract) fossil fuel resources—all of which is fuelled by a global increasing demand for energy (Brisman 2013; Short, this volume, Chapter 26).

Energy is deemed by neoliberal society to be an indispensable and necessary component to modern civilisation. Energy creation not only satisfies the consumption lust of modern western culture (see Ferrell, this volume, Chapter 37), but is the fuel that drives the multiplicity of industries and corporations that keep the *treadmill of production* (ToP) running (see, e.g., Lynch this volume, Chapter 24; Lynch et al. this volume, Chapter 4). As Stretesky and colleagues (2014: 49–50) note, 'fossil fuels are important energy sources; when burned, they release large quantities of energy. Nevertheless, the withdrawal of fossil fuels causes significant ecological disorganization and ecological destruction'.

And the treadmill shows no signs of slowing down; indeed, it is running exponentially faster. The capitalist system requires more and more energy in order to satisfy continual—indeed, continuous—economic imperatives, such as larger shareholder dividends. Indeed, capitalism requires infinite resources and infinite economic growth in order to continue to be successful and to enjoy the same profiteering that has occurred post-World War II. Whilst the Earth is capable of supplying humans with seemingly infinite renewable energies (i.e., solar, water, wind), such usage is currently outweighed heavily by anthropocentric obsessions with non-renewable resources (i.e., coal, gas, oil). According to Jefferson (2015: 8), 'around 80% of the World's current energy supply comes from fossil fuels … coal accounts for about 29% of the total; oil for about 31%; and natural gas for about 21%'. The situation is exacerbated by the recent exponential increase in the global human population. In the past 50 years, the world population has doubled (to 7.5 billion), and world energy consumption has tripled (Global Energy Research Network Institute 2011: 32). Similarly, and looking ahead to the future, the global human population is set to rise to 9 billion by 2050 and to 12 billion by 2100 (Jefferson 2015: 7). Put simply, more energy will need to be supplied in order to provide enough energy to sustain everyone. If supply is unable to cater for such an increasing demand, the number of humans unable to access energy will increase (see generally Brisman 2015). Although a discussion of *access* to energy is not the goal of this chapter, it provides a necessary backdrop (not to mention an interesting and important avenue of research) for those green criminologists investigating energy crime or environmental justice issues.

An increasing energy demand for a growing global population raises pertinent practical and philosophical questions as to how humans can bridge the environment-energy nexus and perform an ecological balancing act. As of 2014, only 14.2 per cent of the global supply of energy was produced from renewable energy sources (O'Sullivan et al. 2017: 5). Although this is predicted to rise to 19.3 per cent by 2040 (O'Sullivan et al. 2017: 5), the rise in global human populations means energy demand will outweigh energy supply, particularly of (non-renewable) fossil fuel resources. One method for increasing the longevity of fossil fuel supply is to turn to more unconventional forms of fossil fuel energy extraction—a point made by Short in the previous chapter in this volume. Whilst unconventional methods may help extend the timeframe of human use of fossil fuels, such energy extraction methods are associated with higher levels of environmental and social harm than conventional energy extraction methodologies (see Carrara and Massetti 2014). Some authors are now referring to such unconventional energy extraction as processes of *extreme energy* (Crook, Short and South 2018; Gross 2010; Klare 2010/2017; Short 2016, this volume, Chapter 26; Short and Szolucha 2019)—the extensive environmental and social harms which can be seen to constitute a form of ecocide.

Despite this, several nations, including the U.K., are exploring unconventional energy generation options. The most recent of these options is the method of UHF, which is an engineering procedure that can be used to extract natural gas that exists in deep, impermeable shale reservoirs and combines conventional vertical drilling with unconventional horizontal drilling.

In order to conduct such drilling activities, fracking companies are required to make payments to communities in respect of such activities (Great Britain Infrastructure Act 2015). This chapter undertakes a critical analysis of such payments by analysing qualitative interview data from people who are involved with, or are knowledgeable about, fracking in the U.K. Before doing so, however, I offer an overview of the emergence of UHF in both a global and national sense followed by the extent to which fracking may produce both social and environmental harms.

The emergence of unconventional hydraulic fracturing in the U.K.

The U.K. has long relied on traditional fossil fuel energies, such as gas and oil, to provide U.K. consumers and industry with an expendable energy supply. In the post-World War II era, this supply has come from a mixture of North Sea gas and oil, conventional onshore gas and oil production, and the importation of gas and oil from various energy-abundant nations around the globe (either pipelined or in the form of Liquefied Natural Gas). With North Sea gas and oil exploration and production in steady decline (Mair et al. 2012: 18; Rogers 2013: 8), however, new ways of producing consistent, consumable energy are required in order to satisfy the current consumption demands of corporations and individuals in the U.K. (to avoid amplified reliance on fossil fuel from foreign countries).

Unconventional hydraulic fracturing is one technique, at least in the short term, that may help satisfy such an energy void, and the term 'unconventional' can, in this context, mean two entirely different things. First, unconventional can refer to the *type of resource* to which the method of UHF is being applied. Conventional gas and oil production targets permeable reservoirs (Speight 2013: 1)—locations where the hydrocarbons are the easiest to extract, such as in sandstone and limestone, which are relatively porous (Prud'homme 2014: 26). Unconventional gas and oil production, on the other hand, targets more impermeable formations (such as deep shale reservoirs). Because of the low permeability of shale (i.e., substances do not flow well), the rock needs to be stimulated in order to generate a flow, which leads to the second meaning of the term 'unconventional'. Here, 'unconventional' may refer to the specifically unconventional *technology* that is applied in the production of deep shale gas reservoirs. In conventional gas and oil production, wells are drilled only vertically and, consequently, access only a comparatively small pocket of hydrocarbon resource. In unconventional gas and oil production, the wells are drilled vertically (as with conventional drilling), but the drill-bit is gradually manoeuvred to a horizontal direction, which enables the well to continue to be drilled through the target (shale) formation (Speight 2013: 73).[2] This enables much more gas or oil to be extracted as more resource is exposed, enabling the formation to be hydraulically fractured multiple times (Stephenson 2015: 64). For the remainder of this chapter—and as mentioned in note 1—the term UHF, and 'fracking' more colloquially, will refer to a combination of both of these meanings.

It is important to note that UHF is not the only way of producing a consistent supply of consumable energy. Although there are some issues with storage capacity, renewable energy has the potential to provide the U.K. with a cleaner, greener energy supply from on-shore wind, off-shore wind, solar PV, tidal stream and wave technologies (Carbon Trust 2003). Conversely, there are also other less attractive technologies (in economic, environmental, moral and social terms), such as nuclear power, as well as increased reliance on traditional gas and oil resources from overseas. Despite these options, however, the U.K. government is attempting to implement a shale gas industry, where UHF is legally permitted, subject to a series of licenses, planning permissions and environmental and health and safety permits. Such implementation is continuing despite a lack of public acceptance of such technology (Department for Business, Energy & Industrial Strategy (DBEIS) 2017)[3] and the recognition that UHF can often create significant social and environmental harms (see, e.g., Jackson et al. 2014, 2013; Mooney 2011), which will now be analysed further.

Fracking—environmental and social harm

There is a growing body of evidence that suggests UHF has created multiple instances of both environmental and social harms in the areas where UHF has occurred (which largely includes Australia, Canada, Poland, South Africa, the U.K. and parts of the U.S. (see Alexander, O'Connor Shelley and Opsal, this volume, Chapter 19)). While this chapter concentrates on the economic implications of fracking in the U.K., it is important to recognise some of the research that identifies such environmental and social harm because this is especially significant in highlighting the purpose and importance of a green criminology. Although UHF creates environmental and social harm, traditional criminological approaches are not well-positioned to examine such harm because orthodox criminology is based on the premise that, if something is defined as legal, then no harm is taking place. As Stretesky and colleagues (2014: 3) note:

> there is a false assumption that if environmental damage is not defined as criminal, no serious harm is occurring. This idea is reinforced within criminology by the orthodox definition of crime as a violation of the criminal law, which excludes environmental crimes since these acts are often defined as violations of other, non-criminal forms of law.

So, what are the environmental and social harms that are associated with fracking? There are several official reports which address directly the potential impact of fracking on public health (see, e.g., Harrison, Parkinson and McFarlane 2014; McCoy and Saunders 2015; Public Health England 2014), as well as a body of organisational and academic research sharing similar concerns (see, e.g., Colborn et al. 2011; Down, Armes and Jackson 2013; McKenzie et al. 2012; Rabinowitz et al. 2015; Warhurst and Buck 2015; Reap 2015). The potential impacts on public health will depend on a variety of demographic, economic and geological factors and it is therefore not possible to say exactly what harms will occur prior to conducting UHF. Following the precautionary principle (and after learning from the harms that have already occurred as a result of UHF overseas), it is appropriate to consider what harms might transpire before such operations take place. Although public health impacts are manifold and complex, a common and, arguably the most obvious, impact comes in the form of air pollution. Srebotnjak (2014: 4–5), for example, cites a substantial body of research on air pollution involving diesel emissions from heavy trucks and machinery, toxic air pollutants originating 'from direct and fugitive emissions of hydrocarbons at the wells and from associated infrastructure' (Srebotnjak 2014: 4), and hazards from silica sand and ozone smog (Srebotnjak 2014: 4–5). In addition, there are other pollutions that are associated directly with the construction and development of a wellsite, such as 'traffic, dust, noise, odours, un-natural light and other nuisances' (McCoy and Saunders 2015: 16).

Alongside the detrimental impact of fracking on human health, another major social harm is evident in the concentrated truck traffic that is a necessary component to UHF. The very essence of unconventional hydraulic fracturing (using fluid to split open impermeable shale rock) requires a liquid (a mixture of water, sand and chemicals (see Brisman and South, this volume, Introduction)) to be brought to wellsites by trucks. Later, when some of this 'fracfluid' returns to the surface of the well as wastewater, more trucks are required to transport this fluid to the relevant storage unit or wastewater treatment facility. Trucks are also required in the construction and de-construction of wellsites themselves. As McCoy and Saunders (2015: 16) note:

> The amount of truck-heavy traffic required to build the wellpad and its surrounding infrastructure (e.g. offices, generators, compressors and tanks), drill the boreholes, and

> transport fluid, silica and various other materials is considerable. Estimates of the amount of traffic involved vary, with the critical factors being: the number of boreholes; whether water is piped or trucked in; and the volume of flowback needing to be transported away. The Institution of Civil Engineers estimated that a single well might require between 500 and 1,250 HGV lorry movements. The Royal Society for the Protection of Birds estimated a figure of between 4,300 and 6,600 truck trips per well pad. If a well pad were to generate as many as 40 boreholes, the number of truck movements could be of the order of 34,000 movements on and off a pad (over the typical two-year lifetime of a well, but with a concentrated period of about six months).

Such intense truck traffic has implications not only for human health due to air pollution from diesel fumes, which may affect local air quality, but on the enjoyment of one's property. When discussing air quality issues in relation to human rights, Short and colleagues (2015: 712) explain that 'when the rights to privacy, family, home and protection of property are read to include pollution ... it is apparent that the effects of fracking on the land are capable of legally violating human rights'.

Fracking also has the potential to contaminate groundwater and surface water. Accidental spillages may occur either onsite (during handling, mixing or wastewater treatment) or during fluid transportation (Warhurst and Buck 2015). Contamination may also occur from well-integrity failure, 'whereby some part of the well becomes damaged or degrades over time, opening up a potential contaminant pathway' (Harrison, Parkinson and McFarlane 2014: 5). These problems can lead to water contamination, which is well documented in the U.S. (see, e.g., Harrison, Parkinson and McFarlane 2014: 5; Jackson et al. 2013, 2014: 337–340; Osborn et al. 2011).

Fracking also increases seismicity (Jackson et al. 2014). While the U.K. is not prone to large earthquakes, fracking may produce micro-seismicity of the magnitude that causes damage to property (Short et al. 2015: 711). Although it is unlikely that seismicity will threaten human life in the U.K., the other explicit moral and philosophical concerns relating to fracking, such as air pollution, depletion of water reserves/sources, soil contamination and water contamination, are significant. Green criminology has exposed how legal acts may often create environmental harm or contribute to ecological destruction (see Ruggiero, this volume, Chapter 23), and fracking raises additional philosophical and jurisprudential issues regarding the relationship between the law, morality and environmental harm (particularly where energy creation is concerned). Drawing on 'Earth jurisprudence' (see, e.g., Burdon 2011) and ethics (see, e.g., Sagoff 2008; Weiss 1990) and applying such insights to fracking, green criminology could extend its analysis of the intersections of environmental harm and social injustice.

Corporate, governmental and gas and oil industry support and sponsorship for UHF technology is based on the philosophical premise that such development will be economically beneficial for the U.K. For example, several reports have alluded to the positive impact that shale gas production could have on energy security (Delebarre, Ares and Smith 2017; Tovey n.d.) and employment, especially considering job losses that are accruing from dwindling North Sea oil and gas production (Institute of Directors 2013; Mair et al. 2012: 18; Onshore Oil and Gas Industry 2014; Rogers 2013: 8), as well as local community benefits from community payments (Delebarre, Ares and Smith 2017). While it is not possible to discuss all of these, the remainder of the chapter will examine the final economic justification for fracking (the impact of community payments on local communities) and will address some of the environmental justice problems inherent with such a payment scheme.

Community financial incentives (CFIs): legal requirement, corporate good-will or financial bribery?

With respect to onshore energy generation, it is common for communities to receive financial payments in exchange for allowing access to their land for exploration and extraction. Such payments acknowledge that extraction may result in some short-term disturbance or longer-term visual blight. An illustration of this can be found in the onshore wind sector, where communities can receive financial investment in the form of community benefit funds (voluntary payments from the onshore wind developer), benefits in-kind (other one-off voluntary benefits, such as energy discount schemes), community investment or shared ownership (where the community has a financial stake in the scheme), socio-economic benefits (e.g., apprenticeships, jobs, skills training) and material benefits (steps taken to improve infrastructure, for example) (Department of Energy and Climate Change (DECC) 2014a: 8).

The production of sub-surface hydrocarbons onshore is no exception to such a situation. In February 2015, the U.K. government passed the Infrastructure Act 2015 (Great Britain Infrastructure Act 2015), which required 'relevant energy undertakings' (i.e., fracking 'companies' or fracking 'operators') to make payments to 'owners of relevant land' or 'interests in relevant land', 'for the benefit of areas in which relevant land is situated'. Essentially, this legislation created the requirement that operators must make payments to communities or individuals in exchange for the right to use their land to drill to access sub-surface hydrocarbons (subject to regulations by the Secretary of State):

> (1) The Secretary of State may, by regulations, require relevant energy undertakings to make payments in respect of the proposed exercise, or exercise, of the right of use.
> (2) The regulations may require payments to be made—
>
> (a) to owners of relevant land or interests in relevant land;
> (b) to other persons for the benefit of areas in which relevant land is situated.
>
> (3) The regulations may—
>
> (a) specify the amount or amounts of payments;
> (b) make provision for determining the amount or amounts of payments.
>
> (4) The regulations may require relevant energy undertakings to provide the Secretary of State, or any other specified person, with specified information about—
>
> (a) the proposed exercise, or exercise, of the right of use;
> (b) the making of payments in accordance with regulations under this section.
>
> (5) Before making any regulations under this section, the Secretary of State must consult such persons as the Secretary of State considers appropriate.
>
> *(Great Britain Infrastructure Act 2015)*

With regards to the regulations that concern the payment of such CFIs, the DECC (2014b) reported that:

In its Community Engagement Charter, the UKOOG committed to a community benefits package. The operator will:

- at exploration/testing stage, provide £100,000 in community benefits per well-site where fracturing takes place
- at production, pay 1 per cent of revenues to communities.[4]

According to one of my interviewees, an academic geologist, if UHF is to take place onshore in the U.K., 'it would seem very sensible to consider at least how a local community is impacted and whether there are financial aspects that can mitigate against any impact'.

There are, however, numerous concerns surrounding such CFIs, including the extent to which payments can be considered to represent corporate financial bribery, whether one-off grants actually distort community projects in the long term, problems with defining who and what constitutes the *community*, and the problematic relationship between CFIs and local economic loss. These issues will now be considered in turn, with further reference to my qualitative research.

During the course of my research, several interviewees expressed the view that CFIs represent corporate financial bribery. According to them, providing a monetary sum can be viewed as a financial exchange for the ability to conduct operations that result in environmental and social harm. Such payments are neither a 'win' for the environment, which may incur harm or contamination, nor a 'win' for people living within communities, who are subjected to disturbances in their community (e.g., dust, infrastructure damage, noise, traffic). The following interview excerpts represent such a view that CFIs represent a form of 'admission(s) of guilt', 'blood money' or 'bribe':

> I think it's very cynical, um, and it's also an admission of guilt really, an admission that fracking will have a very negative effect and so people need to be bribed. I don't actually think that that's working.
>
> *(anti-fracking campaigner)*

> And you know there are some quite interesting quotes in the papers that came immediately after the Third Energy application where there were people saying this is blood money you know we wouldn't accept it, er, we don't want it.
>
> *(journalist)*

> I think it needs to be made clear where it is going to go so that people know more about it and are more inclined to agree to it. Um, I know some people would see it as a bribe as well, because again, that's happened in North Yorkshire.
>
> *(consultant geologist)*

Although £100,000 may on first glance appear to be a large sum of money that may provide vital finances for local communities, such a one-off grant may actually distort the ability of local communities to provide essential goods and services in the long term. For instance, while £100,000 may help to build a community centre or provide an additional bus for a local bus service, many services (e.g., transport, youth services) require more long-term financial commitment in order to keep such services running. Such a situation can be seen in the following statement by an anti-fracking activist:

> if it's a one-off grant of £100,000, that is useless, local authorities run services and services require revenue costs. Ok you need new buses you need a bus replacement programme but

> you need the money to run the service, day in day out, year in year out, and a one-off grant just distorts that. £100,000 I think would buy you 1 and a half buses? Possibly? It's useless. Youth service the same. You can't just switch on a youth service for a year

Although there is a corresponding commitment of 1 per cent of revenues being provided to local communities, which may play a role in providing long-term solutions to communities to provide services, there is no indication as to exactly how much 1 per cent is in monetary terms. This 1 per cent depends entirely on the success of each particular site, which is unknown until shale gas is being produced. One per cent could turn out to be a significant amount of money, but could also turn out to be worthless if the wellsite turns out to be uneconomical:

> No way is it enough and neither is the fact that they will give 1 per cent of the revenue to the community. Um, because it is a carrot that they dangle but they can't define or quantify what that is. It could be a lot of money. It could be nothing at all. So, I always look at it as compensation.
>
> *(local parish councillor)*

In addition, significant problems arise from the failure of the U.K. government and industry to define what it means by *community* to which the CFIs are to be paid. Unlike official guidelines for onshore wind, which are extremely explicit with regards to what constitutes 'the community' and how 'the community is defined' (DECC 2014a),[5] both the UKOOG and U.K. government have failed to define what the term *community* means in relation to shale gas development.[6] This has implications for who or what is entitled to receive such payments, which has a significant impact on how the money is spent and how a community is able to undertake financial planning. This situation was brought up multiple times during data collection, as can be seen by the following two statements:

> So, you split that up and you might have £25,000 and suddenly it's not quite as much anymore. And, if you look at it, that's a one off payment of £100,000, it's not every year, that's just a one-off. It sounds like a lot but 25-grand doesn't really go very far at all. So, using that as a reason to say yeah, we think that's a good idea, and that your, you know, pay-off for that is you having to suffer the inconvenience and having a gas-field develop on your doorstep.
>
> *(local parish councillor)*

> There's the issue of how the money is used or distributed, who it goes to, because it is quite possible that you could be on a lorry route, um, to a fracking site, outside the Parish in which the site is based and you may not see any of that money. It may end up in a Parish which you don't belong to where you don't live, but actually the people that benefit from it haven't experienced the disturbance so I think there's a lot of very complicated issues, um, and questions that haven't been answered on this issue.
>
> *(journalist)*

A further definitional difficulty surrounds the term *fracking*—what actually constitutes *fracking* and whether or not shale gas extraction operations that fall outside of specific legal boundaries still constitute fracking. This is important insofar as it may determine whether or not a community is entitled to receive associated financial payments in return for the right to use sub-surface resources. For instance, the Infrastructure Act 2015 defines 'associated hydraulic fracturing' as hydraulic fracturing that takes place in shale that involves the injection of more than 1,000 cubic metres of fluid at each stage of hydraulic fracturing or more than 10,000 cubic metres of fluid in total (Great Britain Infrastructure Act 2015). Therefore, it is unclear, for example, whether operations that use less than 1,000 cubic metres of fluid per stage—or less than 10,000 cubic metres of fluid in total—will constitute associated hydraulic fracturing. This, in turn, will determine whether companies are legally obliged to provide CFIs in return for their activities.

In addition, there may be a troublesome relationship between CFIs and local economic losses that could reduce the local economic impact of such payments. Studies have found that UHF may decrease the property value of properties situated within communities where fracking occurs (Gibbons et al. 2016; Muehlenbachs, Spiller and Timmins 2015; Throupe, Simons and Mao 2013). This means that while a community, as a whole, may benefit from CFIs, these collective benefits could be undercut by individual losses in real property value, resulting in a community that is environmentally, financially and socially worse off than it was prior to the commencement of drilling operations. Short and Szolucha (2019; see also Short this volume, Chapter 26) have described such extensive and negative harms inflicted on a community subjected to UHF as a form of *collective trauma*. When discussing empirical research conducted with individuals from communities fighting fracking in Lancashire (with specific reference to the planning applications there), Short and Szolucha (2019: 269) describe participants as showing 'a sense of powerlessness and feelings of depression, a sense of loss, fear, betrayal, guilt, anger, and an emotional rollercoaster ride of highs and lows as the planning process ebbed and flowed through various stages and the appeal process'.

Finally, questions of environmental justice arise in determining who is liable for restoring the environment post-UHF, particularly if land has been contaminated and remedies prove expensive. Regulations are clear that mineral operators are responsible for the restoration and aftercare of sites, but in the event that a mineral operator is unable to pay, responsibility defaults to the landowner. This means that, should a situation occur where a fracking company is unable to pay restoration costs (for example, if a company is unable to produce shale gas in an economically successful manner), the landowner may face restoration costs. This can be seen in planning practice guidance provided by the Department for Communities and Local Government (DCLG) (2014): 'Responsibility for the restoration and aftercare of mineral sites, including financial responsibility, lies with the minerals operator and, in the case of default, with the landowner'. Such a situation would create a prime example of environmental injustice, whereby individuals, communities and the environment suffer at the expense of energy extraction industries, whose anthropocentric justification is to provide consumable energy and contribute to the national economy.

Conclusion

Energy extraction processes create a diverse range of harms from the environmental to the social. Green criminology has not sufficiently considered energy harms and energy crimes despite the obvious connections that exist between green criminological study and the often-legal harms created by energy extraction processes. ToP theory is one approach to understanding energy harms and provides a critical lens through which to analyse ecological withdrawals and ecological additions that lead to ecological disorganisation (see, e.g., Stretesky, Long and Lynch 2014: 13–16, 38–88). Such an approach, however, has been applied only rarely to UHF. The recent emergence of UHF in the U.K. presents a perfect opportunity for green criminologists to study both legal and illegal actions within fracking processes that lead to environmental and social harms. Similarly, UHF in the U.K. is also deserving of attention from treadmill theorists and traditional criminologists researching state-corporate crime.[7]

Through a combination of primary research and academic literature on UHF, this chapter has discussed the emergence of UHF in the U.K. and related environmental and social harms. In addition, this chapter has analysed CFIs and the subsequent ramifications that this may have for environmental justice in the communities where fracking occurs or might transpire. In order to do so, the chapter has considered the extent to which payments can be considered to represent corporate financial bribery, whether one-off grants actually distort community projects in the long-term, problems with defining who and what constitutes the *community*, and the problematic relationship between CFIs and local economic loss. Green criminologists should continue to probe these questions so that communities (however conceptualised or defined) understand how CFIs will affect them in the short and long term.

Notes

1 For the purposes of this chapter the terms 'fracking', 'hydraulic fracturing' and 'unconventional hydraulic fracturing' will be used interchangeably to describe the latter phrase 'unconventional hydraulic fracturing'. This terminology is explained in more detail in the section entitled 'The emergence of unconventional hydraulic fracturing in the UK'.

2 As Michaels and Simon (2013: 12) explain, '[n]ew technologies now enable horizontal drilling in all radial directions, like spokes of a bicycle wheel, from the base of a vertical shaft, producing a shaped array of horizontal shafts miles beneath groundwater aquifers to deliver fracking fluids explosively'.

3 DBEIS produces an *Energy and Climate Change Public Attitude Tracker* (established by the Department of Energy and Climate Change (DECC) in 2012). The 22nd edition of this tracker reported a continued decline for public support for fracking (at 16 per cent) with public opposition to fracking at 33 per cent (DBEIS 2017: 5).

4 UKOOG (United Kingdom Onshore Operators Group) is the representative body for the U.K. onshore oil and gas industry. For a critique of this payment scheme, see Cotton (2017).

5 For instance, the following quotation is taken from the DECC's best practice guidance for community benefits from onshore wind developments in England (DECC, 2014b: 22):

'identifying interested parties and defining the "community"—Engagement on community benefit schemes should reach at least the same geographical area as the consultation on the development itself. How the local community is then defined will be shaped by a number of factors, including physical and human geography and local culture, which plays a huge role in determining how a community defines itself. There are a number of different ways in which the community can be defined. Not all local residents will form a single community or group, for example, and there are also divergent forms of community belonging—communities of place and communities of interest (a shared outlook to faith, politics, social interaction, ethnicity or common interests)—both of which may be relevant in the context of community benefits around onshore wind energy projects'.

6 Some key texts that are accessible to the public that discuss directly CFIs' failure to actually address what is meant by a *community* include DECC (2014b); Delebarre, Ares and Smith (2017); UKOOG (2016).

7 An example would be the Secretary of State's decision to overturn Lancashire County Council's decision to not allow fracking in Lancashire in 2016 (DCLG 2016: 3) that, although technically legal, undercut the purpose of public consultation and community engagement.

References

Brisman, A. 2013. 'Not a bedtime story: Climate change, neoliberalism, and the future of the arctic,' *Michigan State International Law Review*, 22(1): 241–289.

Brisman, A. 2015. 'Environment and conflict: A typology of representations,' in A. Brisman, N. South and R. White (eds.), *Environmental Crime and Social Conflict: Contemporary and Emerging Issues*, pp. 285–311. Surrey, UK: Ashgate.

Burdon, P. (ed). 2011. *Exploring Wild Law: The Philosophy of Earth Jurisprudence*. South Australia: Wakefield Press.

Carbon Trust. 2003. *Building Options for UK Renewable Energy*. Available at: www.carbontrust.com/media/84916/ct-2003-08-building-options-for-uk-renewable-energy.pdf.

Carrara, S. and Massetti, E. 2014. *Should We Ban Unconventional Oil Extraction to Reduce Global Warming?* Fondazione Eni Enrico Mattei Research Paper Series No.105.2014. Available at: https://papers.ssrn.com/sol3/papers.cfm?abstract_id=2541691.

Colborn, T., Kwiatkowski, C., Schultz, K. and Bachran, M. 2011. 'Natural gas operations from a public health herspective,' *Human and Ecological Risk Assessment: An International Journal*, 17(5): 1039–1056.

Cotton, M. 2017. 'Fair fracking? Ethics and environmental justice in United Kingdom shale gas policy and planning,' *Local Environment*, 22(2): 185–202.

Crook, M., Short, D. and South, N. 2018. 'Ecocide, genocide, capitalism and colonialism: Consequences for Indigenous peoples and glocal ecosystems environments,' *Theoretical Criminology*, 22(3): 298–317.

Delebarre, J., Ares, E. and Smith, L. 2017. *Shale Gas and Fracking*. House of commons Briefing Paper: SN06073. Available at: http://researchbriefings.parliament.uk/ResearchBriefing/Summary/SN06073.

Department for Business, Energy & Industrial Strategy. 2017. *Energy and Climate Change Public Attitude Tracker: Wave 22*. Available at: www.gov.uk/government/uploads/system/uploads/attachment_data/file/634723/pat-wave-22-summary-report.pdf.

Department for Communities and Local Government. 2014. *Guidance: Minerals*. Available at: www.gov.uk/guidance/minerals#Restoration-and-aftercare-of-minerals.

Department for Communities and Local Government. 2016. *Recovered Appeals: Cuadrilla Bowland ltd and Cuadrilla Elswick Ltd (refs: 3134386, 3130923, 3134385 and 3130924-6 October 2016)*. Available at: https://assets.publishing.service.gov.uk/government/uploads/system/uploads/attachment_data/file/558278/16-10-06_DL_Cuadrilla.pdf.

Department of Energy and Climate Change. 2014a. *Community Benefits from Onshore Wind Developments: Best Practice Guidance for England*. Available at: www.gov.uk/government/uploads/system/uploads/attachment_data/file/363405/FINAL_Community_Benefits_Guidance.pdf.

Department of Energy and Climate Change. 2014b. *Fracking UK Shale: Planning Permission and Communities*. Available at: www.northyorks.gov.uk/sites/default/files/fileroot/About%20the%20council/Partnerships/Fracking_UK_shale_planning_permission_and_communities_%28Feb_2014%29.pdf.

Down, A., Armes, M. and Jackson, R. B. 2013. 'Shale gas extraction in North Carolina: Research recommendations and public health implications,' *Environmental Health Perspectives*, 121(10): 292–293.

Gibbons, S., Heblich, S., Lho, E. and Timmins, C. 2016. *Fear of Fracking? The Impact of the Shale Gas Exploration on House Prices in Britain*. Produced for: The National Bureau of Economic Research. Working Paper: No.22859. Available at: www.nber.org/papers/w22859.

Global Energy Research Network Institute. 2011. *The Population Picture: October 2011*. Available at: www.geni.org/globalenergy/research/population-picture/population-picture.pdf.

Great Britain. *Infrastructure Act 2015: Elizabeth II. Chapter 6 (2015)*. London: The Stationery Office. Available at: www.legislation.gov.uk/ukpga/2015/7/part/6/enacted.

Greife, M. B. and Stretesky, P. B. 2013. 'Crude laws: Treadmill of production and state variations in civil and criminal liability for oil discharges in navigable waters,' in N. South and A. Brisman (eds.) *Routledge International Handbook of Green Criminology*, pp. 150–166. Abingdon, Oxon, UK: Routledge.

Gross, D. 2010. *Fracking, Oil Sands, and Deep-Water Drilling*. Slate. June 6. Available at: https://slate.com/business/2010/06/the-dangerous-new-era-of-extreme-energy.html.

Harrison, G., Parkinson, S. and McFarlane, G. 2014. *Shale Gas and Fracking: Examining the Evidence*. Produced for: Scientists for Global Responsibility and the Chartered Institute for Environmental Health. Available at: www.sgr.org.uk/sites/sgr.org.uk/files/SGR-CIEH-Shale-gas-bfg.pdf.

Institute of Directors. 2013. *Infrastructure for Business: Getting Shale Gas Working*. Available at: www.igasplc.com/media/3067/iod-getting-shale-gas-working-main-report.pdf.

Jackson, R. B., Vengosh, A., Carey, W., Davies, R., Darrah, T., O'Sullivan, F. and Pétron, G. 2014. 'The environmental costs and benefits of fracking,' *Annual Review of Environment and Resources*, 39: 327–362.

Jackson, R. B., Vengosh, A., Darrah, T., Warner, N. R., Down, A., Poreda, R. J., Osborn, S. G., Zhao, K. and Karr, J. D. 2013. 'Increased stray gas abundance in a subset of drinking water wells near marcellus shale gas extraction,' *Proceedings of the National Academy of Sciences of the United States of America*, 110(28): 11250–11255.

Jefferson, M. 2015. 'A global energy assessment,' *Wiley Interdisciplinary Reviews: Energy and Environment*, 5(1): 7–15. Available at: http://onlinelibrary.wiley.com/doi/10.1002/wene.179/full.

Klare, M. 2010/2017. 'The relentless pursuit of extreme energy: A new oil rush endangers the Gulf of Mexico and the Planet,' *The Huffington Post*, May 19. Available at: www.huffpost.com/entry/the-relentless-pursuit-of_b_581921?guccounter=1 (Updated December 6, 2017).

Lampkin, J. 2016. 'Green criminology and fracking in the UK: An application of utilitarian ethics,' *Papers from the British Criminology Conference*, 16(2): 20–37. Available at: www.britsoccrim.org/wpcontent/uploads/2016/12/pbcc_2016_lampkin.pdf.

Long, M., Stretesky, P., Lynch, M. and Fenwick, E. 2012. 'Crime in the coal industry: Implications for green criminology and treadmill of production,' *Organization & Environment*, 25(3): 328–346.

Lynch, M. 1990. 'The greening of criminology: A perspective for the 1990s,' *The Critical Criminologist*, 2: 11–12.

Mair, R., Bickle, M., Goodman, D., Koppelman, B., Roberts, J., Selley, R., Shipton, Z., Thomas, H., Walker, A., Woods, E. and Younger, P. 2012. *Shale Gas Extraction in the UK: A Review of Hydraulic Fracturing*. Produced for: The Royal Society and The Royal Academy of Engineering. Available at: https://royalsociety.org/~/media/policy/projects/shale-gas-extraction/2012-06-28-shale-gas.pdf.

Marshall, M. 1996. 'The key informant technique,' *Family Practice*, 13(1): 92–97. Available at: http://fampra.oxfordjournals.org/content/13/1/92.short.

McCoy, D. and Saunders, P. 2015. 'Health and fracking. Produced for: Medact,' Available at: www.medact.org/wp-content/uploads/2015/04/medact_fracking-report_WEB4.pdf.

McKenzie, L. M., Witter, R. Z., Newman, L. S. and Adgate, J. L. 2012. 'Human health risk assessment of air emissions from development of unconventional natural gas resources,' *Science of the Total Environment*, 424: 79–87.

Michaels, R. A. and Simon, R. W. 2013. 'Fracking in New York: Weighing risks and benefits. Albany, New York state bar association,' *NYSBA Municipal Lawyer*, 23(3)[Fall]: 12–16.

Mooney, C. 2011. 'The truth about fracking,' *Scientific American*, 305(5): 80–85.

Muehlenbachs, L., Spiller, E. and Timmins, C. 2015. 'The housing market impacts of shale gas development,' *The American Economic Review*, 105(12): 3633–3659.

O'Sullivan, M., Overland, I., Sandalow, D., Begg, H., Behrens, A., Bhatiya, N., Clark, A., Cremer, T., Elkind, J., Fessler, M., Lemphers, N., Nakawa, M. S., Magdalena, S. C. and Vakulchuk, R. 2017. *Working Paper June 2017: The Geopolitics of Renewable Energy*. Published by: Center on Global Energy and The Geopolitics of Energy Project. Available at: http://energypolicy.columbia.edu/sites/default/files/energy/CGEPTheGeopoliticsOfRenewables.pdf.

Onshore Oil and Gas Industry. 2014. *Getting Ready for UK Shale Gas – Supply Chain and Skills Requirements and Opportunities: April 2014*. Available at: www.ey.com/Publication/vwLUAssets/Getting_ready_for_UK_shale_gas/$FILE/EY-Getting-ready-for-UK-shale-gas-April-2014.pdf.

Osborn, S. G., Vengosh, A., Warner, N. R. and Jackson, R. B. 2011. 'Methane contamination of drinking water accompanying gas-well drilling and hydraulic fracturing,' *Proceedings of the National Academy of Sciences of the United States of America*, 108(20): 8172–8176.

Ospal, T. and O'Connor, S. T. 2014. 'Energy crime, harm, and problematic state response in Colorado: A case of the fox guarding the hen house?,' *Critical Criminology: An International Journal*, 22(4): 561–577.

Prud'homme, A. 2014. *Hydrofracking: What Everyone Needs to Know*. New York: Oxford University Press.

Public Health England. 2014. *Public Health England's Draft Report on Shale Gas Extraction*. Available at: www.bmj.com/content/348/bmj.g2728.

Rabinowitz, P. M., Slizovskiy, I. B., Lamers, V., Trufan, S. J., Holford, T. R., Dziura, J. D., Peduzzi, P. N., Kane, M. J., Reif, J. S., Weiss, T. R. and Stowe, M. H. 2015. 'Proximity to natural gas wells and reported health status: Results of a household survey in Washington County, Pennsylvania,' *Environmental Health Perspectives*, 123(1): 21–26.

Reap, E. 2015. 'The risk of hydraulic fracturing on public health in the UK and the UK's fracking legislation,' *Environmental Sciences Europe*, 27(1): 1–7.

Rogers, H. 2013. *UK Shale Gas - Hype, Reality and Difficult Questions*. Oxford Energy Comment. Produced for: The Oxford Institute for Energy Studies. Available at: https://ora.ox.ac.uk/objects/uuid:cde70ad1-e701-4f32-b9a1-80cbb5182d01.

Ruggiero, V. and South, N. 2010a. 'Green criminology and dirty collar crime,' *Critical Criminology: An International Journal*, 18(4): 251–262.

Ruggiero, V. and South, N. 2010b. 'Critical criminology and crimes against the environment,' *Critical Criminology: An International Journal*, 18(4): 245–250.

Sagoff, M. 2008. *The Economy of the Earth: Philosophy, Law, and the Environment*. New York: Cambridge University Press.

Short, D. 2016. *Redefining Genocide: Settler Colonialism, Social Death and Ecocide*. London: Zed Books.

Short, D., Elliot, J., Norder, K., Lloyd-Davies, E. and Morley, J. 2015. 'Extreme energy, 'fracking' and human rights: A new field for human rights impact assessments?' *The International Journal of Human Rights*, 19(6): 697–736.

Short, D. and Szolucha, A. 2019. 'Fracking lancashire: The planning process, social harm and collective trauma,' *Geoforum*, 98(January): 264–276. DOI: 10.1016/j.geoforum.2017.03.001.

Speight, J. 2013. *Shale Gas Production Processes*. Oxford: Elsevier.

Srebotnjak, T. 2014. *Fracking Fumes: Air Pollution from Hydraulic Fracturing Threatens Public Health and Communities*. Produced for: US Natural Resources Defense Council. Available at: www.nrdc.org/sites/default/files/fracking-air-pollution-IB.pdf.

Stephenson, M. 2015. *Shale Gas and Fracking: The Science Behind the Controversy*. Oxford: Elsevier.

Stretesky, P., Long, M. and Lynch, M. 2014. *The Treadmill of Crime: Political Economy and Green Criminology*. Abingdon, Oxon, UK: Routledge.

Throupe, R., Simons, R. and Mao, X. 2013. 'A review of hydro "fracking" and its potential effects on real estate,' *Journal of Real Estate Literature*, 21(2): 205–232.

Tovey, K. n.d. *Fracking – A Solution to Solve Energy Security or an Unacceptable Step Too Far?* Available at: https://archive.uea.ac.uk/~e680/energy/ENV-2a84/Fracking_paper_for_Rotary.pdf.

United Kingdom Onshore Operators Group. 2016. *Community Engagement Charter: Oil and Gas from Unconventional Reservoirs*. [Online]. Available at: www.ukoog.org.uk/images/ukoog/pdfs/communi tyengagementcharterversion6.pdf.

Warhurst, M. and Buck, G. 2015. *Fracking Pollution: How Toxic Chemicals from Fracking Could Affect Wildlife and People in the UK and the EU*. Produced for: CHEM Trust. Available at: www.chemtrust.org.uk/wp-content/uploads/chemtrust-fracking-briefing-june2015.pdf.

Weiss, E. 1990. 'Our rights and obligations to future generations for the environment,' *American Journal of International Law*, 84(1): 198–207.

White, R. 2013. 'Resource extraction leaves something behind: Environmental justice and mining,' *International Journal for Crime, Justice and Social Democracy*, 2(1): 50–64.

Part V

Relationships in green criminology

Humans and non-human species

28

A violent interspecies relationship

The case of animal sexual assault

Jennifer Maher and Harriet Pierpoint

Introduction

Interspecies sexual contact has been and continues to be rare between 'animals'.[1] Historical accounts indicate, however, that animals have long been the focus of human sexual practices and that this has been a relatively common global phenomenon, evidenced by depictions in art, religious texts and self-reported prevalence studies in the mid-twentieth century. In fact, historians have traced the criminalisation of sexual acts by humans with animals back to the Code of Hammurabi in 1754 BCE (Miletski 2005). The offence of 'bestiality' (a penetrative sexual act between a human and an animal) was first prohibited by law in the United Kingdom (U.K.) by the Buggery Act of 1533. Although the few criminal justice statistics available across the developed world indicate little evidence that sexual assault on animals has been common practice, many countries have treated it as a serious offence carrying with it some of the most severe penalties and punishments (it would often command a death sentence pre-eighteenth century) or life sentence and penal servitude (in the eighteenth century) (Maher 2015). Furthermore, zoophilia—a paraphilia describing a human's preference for having a sexual relationship with an animal partner—has been common enough to be recognised in the psychiatric literature (DSM 4th ed. APA 2000). Official statistics do not reflect the social 'evidence' of human interest in sexual acts with animals, such as the prevalence of online animal pornography, the legal operation of animal brothels in Europe, and the presence of substantial political groups campaigning for the decriminalisation of interspecies sex (Maher 2015). Researchers have studied different types of 'animal sexual assault' (hereafter identified as 'ASA')[2] among the general public and specific populations, including self-identified 'zoophiles', prison inmates, college students and hospital patients. One such study found that 35 percent of adults reported that they had had sex with animals (Zequi et al. 2012).[3] Both sociological (Beirne 2009) and philosophical (Singer 2001) literature are in agreement that sexual abuse of animals is not uncommon, but their perspectives differ on how this impacts an animal and his or her right not to be used for human sexual gratification. According to Beirne (2009), legal definitions (and thereby statistical records) of bestiality fail to recognise the broad range of actions that constitute ASA and do not acknowledge that the victim simply cannot consent to *any* sexual acts. The complexity of this victimisation (discussed below) is one reason why it is impossible to provide an estimation of prevalence and impact of ASA on animals.

Although animal abuse studies were once of limited interest to the discipline of criminology, they have, particularly of late, attracted attention in mainstream journals and handbooks (Hall et al. 2016; Maher, Pierpoint and Piers 2017; Maher and Pierpoint 2012; Spapens, White and Marieke 2014). This growth may reflect the increasing number of regulations that place a range of constraints and obligations on the human–animal relationship, including the use of animals for human sexual gratification. Animal abuse, however, creates challenges for traditional criminology once we move beyond the typical anthropocentric focus on animal abuse as, for example, a predictor of violent behaviour against humans. Consequently, there are significant gaps in our understanding of animal abuse in general, and ASA in particular, with little data available on the types of offender, species of victim and kinds of abuse, the frequency of abuse and harm, the impact on the animal victims and human offenders, the motivation for abuse and successful treatments available. Indeed, ASA remains a poorly understood aspect of both the human–animal relationship and sexual assault research. While the sexual assault of both humans and animals will usually be regarded as morally objectionable, we argue that it is indefensible that criminologists have almost completely abandoned the study of animal victims. If it is not the duty of criminologists to expose the harm with a view to prompting change, then who?

In this chapter, we attempt to assume this responsibility by giving equal consideration to the interests of all sentient beings, that is, by highlighting animals as victims of sexual assault and by describing the impact of the multifarious harms they experience. We argue that ASA must be taken seriously for the following reasons:

- From a philosophical point of view, animals are sentient beings and should be recognised as victims accordingly. In recognising their victim status, we must consider the power-relations between humans and animals.
- From a legal and criminal justice system perspective, some acts of ASA are considered a crime and should be treated as such. More attention and resources are required to enable detection, enforcement, prosecution, sentencing and treatment. In addition, we must consider those sexual acts not (yet) criminalised and examine why they are not.
- From a research and academic perspective, ASA is worthy of consideration by critical criminologists interested in challenging discrimination, oppression and broader notions of harm.

Before making our case for the above, we will first consider the current philosophical and legal standing of animals.

Philosophical approaches and legal definitions

In line with Descartes' view of animals as *automata* (that is, as machines or controlled mechanisms), animals are generally recognised as commodities or objects in law (Regan 2004) and are, as a result, afforded little protection from harm. Other than a few domesticated animals, most animals receive little or no protection in law (see Francione 2008). Those animals that are more human-like are often valued more than those less like humans and, through regulation and mainstream social practices, are subsequently considered to be and treated as individuals who are 'subjects of life' (Regan 2004) and 'persons' (Francione 2008). Indeed, some animal species (such as primates and cetaceans) are being recognised increasingly in science and society as sentient beings with human-like cognitive and sophisticated mental capabilities (such as holding beliefs, having desires, possessing emotions), which makes them worthy of moral consideration, rights and, even, 'personhood'[4] (Nonhuman Rights Project 2018). Arguably, in countries where corporations are granted legal personhood, recognising personhood for some species should not be viewed as revolutionary. Whether society is prepared to embrace the full implications of this recognition is questionable, however. Nonetheless, as 'subjects of life', the suffering of certain animals is viewed as a crime by the laws of many countries. In the U.K., the Animal Welfare Act (AWA) 2006, for example, recognises that vertebrate animals under the care of humans may be victims of unnecessary harm. There is, however, a seemingly impenetrable 'glass ceiling' in the development of animal rights regarding an animal's ownership over its own body and life, which is central to the ASA argument. Specifically, if we can maim and kill animals for clothing, entertainment, food, or simply because we *can*, what is the basis for arguing they should be protected from gratifying human sexual desires? Protection and standards of care enshrined in law, according to Francione (2008: xiii), do not 'go beyond what is necessary to exploit the animals effectively'. By way of example, the bill to transfer the European Union (E.U.) protocol on animal sentience into U.K. law was defeated in the U.K. Commons by 313 votes to 295 on 15 November 2017. This defeat on whether animals are sentient[5] demonstrates that while we 'care' for animals, we also have a vested interest in denying their individuality and victim status. The long-standing debates on animals as victims of harm can be divided broadly into 'welfare' and 'rights' approaches, which are discussed below briefly with regards to ASA (for an extensive discussion, see Francione 2008; Regan 2004; Singer 1995). These two approaches are central to the human–animal relationship because they reveal the value that Western society places on animals and determine the protection received through legislation and practice.

Welfare approach

From a welfare perspective, animal abuse is defined as actions which cause *unnecessary suffering* to animals above and beyond the harm that accompanies their use (e.g., clothing, entertainment, food) or results in their destruction (e.g., due to their status as invasive species or pests) (see Maher, Pierpoint and Piers 2017). Under the U.K. AWA (2006), for example, which seeks to regulate the use of animals, it is an offence (§4.1) to cause 'unnecessary suffering' to an animal. The definition of 'unnecessary suffering' is open to interpretation and applies only to 'protected' vertebrate animals—'of a kind … commonly domesticated in the British Islands', 'under [human] control whether on a permanent or temporary basis', or 'not living in a wild state' (AWA 2006 §.2). This approach accepts harm to animals: they become victims if not treated 'humanely' in their lives and deaths, but only in specific contexts (Singer 1995). According to this approach, animals subject to sexual assault would be considered victims only if they belong to certain species and endure severe physical harm or are killed in the act. Many forms of penetration and sexual mutilation of animals are legitimated within this approach if, for example, performed for farming or scientific purposes (such as artificial insemination, induced ejaculation, or castration).

Rights approach

From a rights perspective, killing an animal for the benefit of humans is impermissible, unless doing so would relieve the animal of pain stemming from an untreatable illness or injury (akin to euthanasia). A rights perspective imposes a duty of protection on humans, which requires us to challenge the property status of animals and to recognise 'personhood' and an individual animal's *right* to life and to exist and reproduce naturally (Francione 2008; Regan 2004). Consequently, the rights approach seeks to abolish the use of animals by clarifying their role as victims if harmed for human gain. A few countries have enshrined human-like rights for animals in law: for example, the Spanish parliament has extended human rights to apes (Glendinning 2008), and the Law of Mother Earth (2010) in Bolivia affords nature equal rights to humans (Vidal 2010). Such rights are contentious for many reasons, such as the claim that animals lack human-like cognition and the moral accountability necessary to have or exercise rights. In fact, putting aside whether it is appropriate or not to compare performance of animals with humans on cognitive tasks, a body of evidence demonstrates that many groups of animals (e.g., Cetaceans, Corvidae, Hominidae, Octopoda and Psittaciformes) do possess human-like cognitive faculty (for example, Finn, Tregenza and Norman 2009). Moreover, a lack of or immature cognition does not afford humans fewer rights or protections. In fact, children, and some vulnerable adults, are sometimes not deemed 'responsible' for their actions and/or afforded strengthened rights or safeguards to reflect differential mental capacity. While these humans are not viewed as moral *agents*, they are moral *patients*: they deserve rights without needing to be accountable for their behaviour (Rowlands 2012). There is, therefore, a basis within some legal regimes for animals to be deemed moral patients with certain rights that moral agents must respect.

Under a rights approach, ASA could be treated as *interpersonal* sexual assault because any animal subject to sexual coercion would be considered a victim of harm. We see a semblance of this approach under the Swiss Constitution (1992), where the dignity of animals, including 'sexual integrity', is protected. While the spirit of the constitutional provision is appreciated, in practice, however, it becomes problematic because it would require an animal's consent. Moreover, the sexual manipulation of animals necessary for industrial farming would not be permissible.

Legal definitions

The positioning of animals in law gives rise to the ASA debate. The regulation of ASA exemplifies the paradoxes implicit in the human–animal relationship. We can, for example, torture, kill and consume animals legitimately and often penetrate their genitalia with force (e.g., using rape racks/stands), yet a human having sexual intercourse with an animal or even recording this behaviour is deemed to be criminal and evidence of a deviant mind. The fragile line that divides these behaviours in law is based on our perception of what is considered a *necessary* harm. In contrast to accepted practices, academic definitions recognise that direct vaginal or anal coitus with an animal, genital manipulation, masturbation, or synanthropic sexuality is ASA (Hvozdík et al. 2006). In the latter, the animal is 'groomed' or learns to tolerate the human sexual contact, without the application of force or additional physical maltreatment by the human. Animals may also be abused as part of a sexual fetish or sadism, whereby the killing of the animal is the sexual act, such as animals used in 'crush' or 'squish' videos (DeMello 2012). Also included in some definitions of ASA is the routine manipulation of sexual practices and organs in animal husbandry and research, as sexual assault (Adams 2010; Davis 2005). Still, of all the human–animal sexual behaviour across the world, intercourse is the act most commonly prohibited (Maher 2015).

In the U.K., the offence of 'intercourse with an animal' is defined under §69 of the Sexual Offences Act 2003 as 'intentionally penetrating a live animal's anus or vagina with the offender's penis or intentionally causing or allowing a person's anus or vagina to be penetrated by the penis of an animal'. This definition does not include oral sex, other non-penetrative or penetrative acts, or the killing or injuring of an animal for sexual gratification or other purpose. In addition, the possession of pornographic images of sexual conduct with animals is prohibited in the U.K. under §67 of the Criminal Justice and Immigration Act of 2008. Images are deemed obscene if it is both pornographic and extreme.[6] According to the 'Oliver scale', which is used to 'grade' pornographic images, animal pornography is placed in the most serious category (Sentencing Council 2014). The anthropocentric and speciesist nature of this legislation is evident when the definition and punishment of ASA is compared with the possession of materials depicting the act. While the Criminal Justice and Immigration Act of 2008 considers both penetrative and oral sexual acts on living or dead animals to be obscene, the Sexual Offences Act of 2003 recognises only penetrative sexual acts on living animals. Moreover, the act of possessing these materials carries with it a potential sentence that is more severe than for the actual perpetration of the act (imprisonment of two years and a fine compared with imprisonment of two years). The harm to the human viewer of sexual material is deemed more significant than the harm caused to the assaulted animal victim.

Internationally, there are many variations in the definition of ASA and countries differ as to which acts constitute ASA and which species of animals are covered. Some countries limit their definition to penetration (U.K.). Some include oral acts and masturbation (South Africa), whilst still others prohibit any sexual act with an animal (Sweden) (Maher 2015). Sentencing ranges from imprisonment of less than one year (U.S.) to up to five years (Australia, Kenya) to ten years (Canada) to life (Barbados) (see Maher 2015 for further analysis of global ASA regulations). Legal approaches to prohibiting sexual behaviour with an animal can be categorised in three ways: those countries that specifically prohibit a sexual act as part of their Animal Welfare legislation (Germany); those with general animal welfare legislation which *may* encompass sexual abuse (U.S.); those who include bestiality as part of their sexual offences legislation (U.K.); and those who do not recognise this behaviour as an offence (U.S.). Most countries do not specifically criminalise sexual acts with animals, although there is arguably some provision to respond to sexual conduct with animals if unnecessary suffering can be established. In the U.S., for example, there is no federal law against ASA, however 45 of the 50 states have some provision to respond to sexual offences. The limitations of responding to ASA through all-encompassing general welfare legislation is that there must be evidence of physical harm and, even then, welfare offences are typically punished less severely than sexual offences.

In sum, legal definitions of ASA are largely complex and deficient for the purpose of protecting animals from sexual abuse. Animals as the victims are rarely the focus, and this is evident in the type of legislation that covers ASA, the way in which this legislation is worded, and the penalties available. With general animal welfare legislation, for example, the inclusion of either an artfully or neglectfully chosen phrase can exclude entire species (such as wildlife) from legal protection and permit deviant acts (such as penetration with objects). Notably, all legislation excludes sexual acts required for commerce (artificial insemination in animal husbandry, forced masturbation); rather these behaviours are legally permissible, required and even state-funded. What separates these legal acts from illegal sexual acts is the intent of the person (suggesting commercial sexual exploitation is not perpetrated by deviant minds), rather than the impact on the animal involved. For those few animals conferred victim status, the need for physical evidence of *unnecessary* suffering reduces protection as their abuse must fit a very specific type of sexual abuse. Even where legislation extends the type of abuse, the protection granted remains questionable when those responsible for protecting the animal (such as 'owners' or 'government agencies') are also most likely to be the perpetrators of the abuse. Animals make ideal sexual assault victims as their survival relies upon those most able to abuse them and such abuse is very unlikely to come to the attention of an 'appropriate' guardian (see Cohen and Felson 1979). Current legislation does little to reduce the opportunities for these offences or the vulnerability of the victims. Indeed, neither the welfare approach nor the rights approach is realised or achieved through the minimal legislation protecting animals from ASA.

Making the case

What follows is our case for ASA to be taken seriously in green criminology by situating the argument that animals should be seen and treated as *victims* within a critically oriented green framework. To do so, we first establish the nature and prevalence of the physical and psychological harm caused by ASA to animals, before turning to a discussion of the impact of ASA on humans as victims and offenders.

Prevalence of ASA

It is difficult to ascertain the extent to which humans engage in ASA, the nature of the conduct and the number of animal victims. There are no victim surveys in this field: ASA is a crime in which the victim has no voice and, therefore, there is a significant 'dark figure'. It appears that the social taboo regarding the act(s) has contributed to lack of academic interest. The studies that do exist offer an incomplete picture on several levels. It is generally accepted that many of these studies must underestimate the extent to which ASA occurs. One reason is that few individuals will admit to socially unacceptable behaviour in self-report studies. Tallichet and colleagues (2005), for example, found that respondents who had sex with animals were more likely to conceal their cruelty toward animals by acting alone. Moreover, studies will often be interested only in certain types of ASA (for example, bestiality, sadistic acts or those involving domesticated animals), making comparisons between studies problematic. Other studies involve narrow sample sizes and focus on a particular type of offender—such as male prison inmates (Hensley, Tallichet and Dutkiewicz 2010; Miller and Knutson 1997), college students (Flynn 1999), institutionalised young offenders (Fleming, Jory and Burton 2002), young sex offenders (Gene G., Osborn and Twigg 1993), psychiatric patients (Alvarez and Freinhar 1991) or urology and oncology patients (Zequi et al. 2012)—limiting generalisability. It is, therefore, difficult to ascertain the number of animal victims, the number of incidences of victimisation, or range or seriousness of the harms suffered.

Research findings on ASA among specific populations vary greatly. In the most recent study, Zequi Sde and colleagues (2012), using a sample of 118 penile cancer patients and 374 controls (healthy men) recruited from 16 urology and oncology centres in Brazil, found that sex with animals had occurred among 35 percent (n = 171) of the participants. In terms of studies of the general population, Kinsey and colleagues (1948; Kinsey, Pomeroy, Martin and Gebhard 1953), who conducted a survey with 11,100 (5,300 male and 5,800 female) white adults in the mid-western United States (U.S.), reported that 8 percent of the male population and 3 percent of the female population had had sexual contact with an animal at least once in their lifetime. Hunt (1974) provides the only other study to report on the prevalence in the general population, wherein 5 percent of the men and 2 percent of the women in the study reported having engaged in bestiality (the term used in the study). If we take the conservative estimate (2 per cent) from these studies, we can infer that, based on the 2017 U.K. adult population (aged 20 and over), over a million people are engaging in some form of ASA in the U.K. alone. Studies focussing on the victims (through medical professionals or service providers) are rare because these practitioners are not required to report or record abuse (Pierpoint 2018). In 2011, a Danish Justice Ministry report surveying veterinarians found 17 percent suspected an animal they treated had been involved in intercourse with a human (BBC 2015), but such studies present only a fraction of the problem.

As previously suggested, official statistics—at least those few that exist—underestimate significantly the extent of ASA (Maher and Pierpoint 2012) as these offences are difficult to detect, are seldom enforced, and are unlikely to be reported. The results from freedom of information requests (MoJ 2015, 2018) reveal that the numbers of U.K. offenders cautioned and sentenced for the offence of sexual intercourse with an animal and the possession of animal pornography remain very small, particularly when compared with its incidence reported in academic studies. The data we received in response to our last Freedom of Information request showed that, in 2017, there were four offenders found guilty of the offence of intercourse with an animal under §69 of the Sexual Offences Act 2003, and 132 offenders found guilty of the possession of animal pornography under §63(7)(d) of the Criminal Justice and Immigration Act 2008 in England and Wales (MoJ 2018). Edwards (2019) recently studied bestiality-related arrests in the United States between 1975 and 2015. There were 456 arrests and, though the annual number of arrests was minimal between 1975 and 2001 (1–2 per year), this began rising sharply in 2004, peaking at 259 arrests during the period of 2011 to 2015. Of the 456 arrests, 133 resulted in bestiality convictions.

Impact of ASA on animal victims

There is insufficient information on the species of animals involved and the specific harms caused by ASA to animals. Even veterinary literature is lacking. Munro (2006: 195–196) questions why this is so:

> Is it that veterinarians have difficulty in facing up to the fact that an animal has been a victim of sexual abuse? Do they find it distasteful? Or is it that they regard the practice with amused, or bemused, tolerance, unthinking of the possibility of physical injuries?

Indeed, Munro and Thrusfield (2001) point out that sexual abuse is not included in the differential diagnosis of vaginal injuries in veterinary obstetrics/gynaecology textbooks. Data on the type of animal sexually assaulted suffer the same variability and from the same limitations as the findings on the prevalence of victimisation discussed above. Articles by veterinarians, Hvozdík and colleagues (2006), cite calves as victims of ASA, while Imbschweiler and colleagues (2009) point to sheep. Both the Humane Society of the United States (HSUS) (2011) and Beetz (2008) report that dogs and horses are the most commonly reported victims of ASA, but other animals are documented as victims in Beetz's review of literature, including domesticated animals (e.g., cats, rabbits), farm animals (e.g., cows, fowl, pigs, sheep) and wild animals (dolphins, large cats, wolves). In Edwards' (2019) study of bestiality-related arrests, dogs were the most frequent victims, followed by horses, farm animals (e.g., cattle, goats, chickens and pigs) and other species (e.g., reptiles, wildlife, cats and birds). The animal's age was reported in about half of all arrests (52.4 per cent) and, where known, they were most often under a year old.

The limited literature describing the impact on animal victims focusses mainly on physical injury and death. The injuries, according to Smith-Blackmore (quoted by DeGioia 2015) and Imbschweiler and colleagues (2009), include:

- loss of fur, abrasions or tears around the perineum, vaginal canal or rectum
- peritonitis (inflammation of the abdominal lining)
- injuries to the anus, nipples or genitalia
- recurrent vaginitis, proctitis or urinary infection.

Stern and Smith-Blackmore (2016) identify gross lesions in animal victims, including injuries to the anus, nipples, penis, rectum, scrotum and vagina; the presence of foreign bodies used in sexual contact; and abrasions and bruising indirectly related. Where animals do not resist (which may reduce evidence of sexual contact), they may be under the influence of sedatives or tranquilisers or have been stunned from blunt-force trauma. Bolliger and Goetschel (2008) explain that offenders can achieve submission by using physical force, such as with instruments that can result in major trauma or death. Animals can also contract human sexually transmitted diseases, bacterial or parasitic infections of the genital, intestinal or urinary tract, as well as cancer-causing viruses, such as human papillomaviruses (Smith-Blackmore quoted by DeGioia 2015). Such illnesses are often so severe that they lead to the animal's death in reported cases (Hvozdík et al. 2006; Imbschweiler, Kummerfeld, Gerhard and Pfeiffer 2009).

It is possible to sexually assault an animal without causing physical injury. Munro (2006) refers to the availability of information online on how to select and 'groom' animals to avoid physical harm. Hvozdík and colleagues (2006) refers to synanthropic sexuality. In this case, the animal learns to accept the human without the need for physical force, thereby decreasing the risk or incidence of physical injury, although general welfare can be impaired. Munro (2006) argues that evidence of psychological harm has not been investigated rigorously, therefore it would be wrong to assume that animal victims do not experience any psychological harm. Psychological impact may be exhibited through behavioural change, according to Smith-Blackmore (as quoted by DeGioia 2015), including unusual meekness in an animal. The similarity here to the injuries and impact on human victims of sexual assault is noticeable (Brayford, Cowe and Deering 2012), although we maintain that interpersonal sexual assault and ASA are not identical and thus require different levels of protection and consideration.

Impact of ASA on human victims and offenders

A human is typically viewed as a victim of ASA if he/she is: (1) a forced participant in sexual contact with an animal; (2) a forced or accidental viewer of ASA (e.g., of online animal pornography); or (3) a victim of a separate sexual, violent or other offence by a sexual abuser of animals. ASA may involve the offender coercing or forcing another person to participate in the act. Engaging in sex with an animal can cause injury to the humans (including physical injury and fatal diseases, such as echinococcosis and rabies). Thus, these individuals may endure both psychological and/or physical injuries—an issue also neglected in the literature.

It is this 'link' between animal abuse and interpersonal violence—the third category above—that makes up most research. The key messages from the literature are:

- There is some evidence that animal abuse at a young age appears to be predictive of later interpersonal violence (e.g., Henderson, Hensley and Tallichet 2011; Overton, Hensley and Tallichet 2012), although some (e.g., Beirne 2009) question this 'progression thesis'.
- In contrast to the progression thesis, there is strong evidence that individuals are often violent toward animals and people concurrently (e.g., Flynn 2012).
- There is some evidence of links between animal abuse and non-violent offending, such as drug sales, organised crime and street crime (Barnes, Boat, Harold and Mahlman 2006; Coonan 2006; Tapia 1971).
- Interpersonal violence found to be committed by ASA offenders includes child abuse, domestic violence, homicide, rape and robbery (Miller 2001).

Despite the focus on the association with animal abuse generally, the connection between ASA, as a specific type of animal abuse, and other offending has rarely been the subject of research and study. There are, however, a limited number of studies that consider this relationship. For example, Duffield and colleagues (1998 cited in Hensley, Tallichet and Dutkiewicz 2010), in their study of juvenile sexual offenders, found that those involved in bestiality (the term used in the study) may, in fact, be more at risk of sexually abusing humans in the future. In a study of a sample of 180 inmates at medium- and maximum-security prisons in the U.S., regression analyses revealed that the age at which offenders began committing animal cruelty and having sex with animals were predictive of adult interpersonal violence (Henderson, Hensley and Tallichet 2011). Fleming and colleagues' (2002) study supports the co-occurrence of animal and human sexual abuse. They found that 96 percent of those who reported ASA had also admitted to sexual offences against humans (at a rate in excess of that perpetrated by non-animal sex offenders). Moreover, in an analysis of the criminal histories of 150 adult males arrested for animal cruelty, neglect or sexual abuse in the U.S. between 2004 and 2009, a significant relationship was discovered between sexually abusing animals and sexual offending against humans (Levitt, Hoffer and Loper 2016). In Edwards' (2019) study nearly half (45.6 per cent) of all arrestees sexually exploited or offended against children and adults either in the current incident or as part of their criminal background.

The reason for summarising these studies' findings here is to provide evidence of the far-reaching harm of ASA and to establish it as a phenomenon worthy of study within green criminology, and beyond. While studies on its prevalence underestimate its extent, our understanding that ASA often occurs concurrently/sequentially with other crimes, coupled with our knowledge of the prevalence of those other crimes, lends weight to the argument that ASA is significant enough to merit further study. In addition, the fact that humans also suffer harm when ASA occurs provides an additional rationale for devoting increased attention to ASA. That said, regardless of the links to human suffering, ASA is an important area of inquiry because of the physical and psychological harms caused to *animals*. Following Beirne (2002), we contend that human–animal sex is wrong and worthy of our concern for the same reasons as inter-human sexual assault—because it involves coercion, because consent cannot be given, and because it violates the rights of another.

Situating ASA within green criminology

Having described the contours of the impact of ASA, we now turn to the question posed earlier—'If it is not the duty of criminologists to highlight this harm with a view to prompting change, then who?'—by examining how green criminology might undertake ASA studies and concerns. The critically oriented green criminological discourse challenges orthodox views of crime, inequality and notions of victimhood (Hall 2013, this volume; Hall and Farrall 2013; Jarrell and Ozymy 2012; Ozymy et al., this volume, Chapter 8; Sollund, this volume, Chapter 29), and resonates with Singer's (1995: xii) argument for animal rights:

> [a liberation movement demands] an expansion of our moral horizons. Practices that were previously regarded as natural and inevitable come to be seen as a result of an unjustifiable prejudice … If we wish to avoid being numbered among the oppressors, we must be prepared to rethink all our attitudes to other groups, including the most fundamental of them.

Both green criminologists and proponents of animal rights recognise that historical responses to non-traditional victims have been inadequate. Both also acknowledge the need to look beyond legalist definitions of crime, to issues of morals, rights, justice and victimisation. As such, our interest in and concern regarding ASA finds support in green criminology's and animal rights' discourses on inequality and victimhood.

Humans frequently exert control over animals' behaviour—and even their existence. This is possible through the 'othering' of animals, whereby animals are treated as separate and distinct from humans due to some biological or natural difference (such as the perception that animals lack human cognitive abilities). Similarities can be drawn between this 'othering' of animals and that of some human groups highlighted in imperialism, colonialism and postcolonialism (Sollund 2012). Othering is unmistakable in ASA responses, whereby our abhorrence is focussed on the *unnatural interspecies act*, rather than the *sexual exploitation and manipulation of vulnerable animals*. While bestiality (a penetrative sexual act by a human on an animal) has been criminalised across much of the world, it has seldom occurred in reaction to the impact on *the animals*. Rather, it has emerged as a moral or religious prohibition, overriding any concern or interest in protecting animals. For example, in England and Wales, bestiality was decriminalised in 1967 alongside homosexuality (i.e., sodomy). Animals, thereafter, were without legal protection from ASA until the Sexual Offences Act 2003.

ASA is a social taboo, treated differently from other sexual offences; indeed, it is often avoided or ignored. This response is characteristic of many green crimes, whereby green criminology places considerable emphasis on exposing, describing and explaining the nature of the harms and the related inequalities (Brisman and South, this volume, Chapter 1). The reaction to ASA and environmental crimes is awash with moral contradictions and cynicism. For example, as long as oppression facilitates the interests of the elite or capitalism, it is seldom defined as crime (and may, in some instances, be considered a *solution* to (a) crime—see Ayres, this volume, Chapter 13). In agriculture, animals are exploited systematically as objects of trade, and their sexual manipulation (used to maximise profit in industrial farming) is not a crime. Furthermore, it is easy to ignore the inequality implicit in ASA acts, whereby those in positions of power charged with the duty of protection are commonly the offenders. Nibert (2013) links the oppression of animals and people through the concept of 'domesecration', arguing that the domestication (and thereby exploitation) of animals is a precondition for the oppression of humans, particularly Indigenous people. He explains that the idyllic notion that domestication has promoted the betterment of all humans largely masks a history of violence and deprivation as:

> the exploitation of large groups of domesecrated animals throughout the centuries has resulted in deadly violence; displacement; enslavement or exploitation of the labor of the displaced; deaths from diseases brought on by domesecration, hunger, and malnutrition; impoverishment; marginalization; and, frequently, sexual exploitation.
>
> *(2013: 223)*

Nibert's (2013) suggestion that we examine indirect and unidentified victims and victimisation is consistent with a green criminological approach sensitive to a more capacious conception of 'victimhood' (see, e.g., Hall 2013, this volume, Chapter 7; Hall and Farrall 2013; Jarrell and Ozymy 2012; Ozymy et al. this volume, Chapter 8; Sollund, this volume, Chapter 29). Industrial animal farming, which cannot exist without institutionalised sexual practices (see Cudworth 2017), is a useful example. Artificial insemination is used in more than 90 percent of pigs and dairy cattle bred in the European Union and North America (Morrell 2011: 1). This constitutes a situation in which sexual manipulation of animals is commodified and the related hazardous by-products have a negative impact on humans[7] (Institute for Agriculture and Trade Policy and GRAIN 2018).

Although a more complete discussion of the institutionalised sexual manipulation of animals is not possible within the scope of this chapter, this does not mean that it should be viewed as a less problematic form of animal abuse or animal sexual assault. Rather, we intend this chapter to facilitate further exploration of ASA, including linking it to ongoing discussions on climate change, global warming, deforestation and pollution (Nurse 2016; Boekhout Von Solinge 2014; Wyatt 2014). By establishing ASA as a green concern, we challenge and expand traditional 'othering' and stereotypes central to the inequality implicit in environmental crimes.

As mentioned above, green criminology recognises the need to move beyond strict legalist definitions of crimes (Beirne and South 2007; Brisman and South, this volume, Chapter 1; Hall et al. 2016) to reveal inequalities and victims. One need not embrace a rights perspective to recognise that the legal responses to ASA and the protections these confer are inadequate in many ways. While it is not possible to measure or compare the severity of harm experienced by legally protected animal victims to those animal victims who do not enjoy the protection of the law, it is evident that current definitions err in denying victimhood to the majority of animals. Even those animals requiring a duty of care are denied victimhood as the welfare approach explicitly rejects the need for consent (e.g., we do not ask for cows' consent to be milked or killed for food; we do not require consent for sexual acts used in selective breeding). With human sexual assault, if one party lacks the capacity to communicate consent to the other, then there can be no consent/consent cannot occur (Adams 2010). Animals are incapable of clearly communicating 'yes' or 'no' to our sexual advances. Assuming they wished to, there is no agreement on how an animal would communicate consent, thereby precluding the possibility of consent. The absence of consent is central to the argument for recognising victimhood in ASA. Arguably, even if animals could communicate consent, this cannot be free from coercion. Because animals are so thoroughly dependent on us for their very survival, the validity of such consent and the appropriateness of acting on it must be challenged.

Discussion and conclusion

This chapter has argued that ASA is a substantial problem resulting in serious harms to sentient animal victims. To date, ASA has received negligible attention in criminology. It is likely, as Munro (2006) suggests above regarding veterinary inattention, that many find the subject 'distasteful' or perhaps 'they regard the practice with amused, or bemused, tolerance, unthinking of the possibility of physical injuries?' If so, it is a poor excuse for this dereliction of duty, not only because ASA is the cause of such pain and suffering, but also because it is a violation of a voiceless sentient being's basic rights. ASA is deserving of serious attention from criminologists and practitioners alike. There is much potential for further investigation of the nature and extent of abuse and abusers, offender motivations, the impacts upon the animal victims and offenders and successful responses and treatments, in addition to the wider-reaching impacts of institutionalised sexual manipulation of companion, farm and wild animals. This chapter is a call to green criminologists to undertake such studies: if not us, then who?

Emphasising the need to look at harmful behaviours that exist outside the traditional criminologists' gaze, green criminologists are increasingly positioning animals as victims of crime, harm and oppression (Beirne and South 2007; Ragnhild 2008; Ellefsen, Sollund and Larsen 2012; South and Beirne 2006; Walters, Westerhuis and Wyatt 2013; White 2013; Spapens, White and Marieke 2014). While providing a useful focal point for those interested in environmental harms and victimisation, green criminology has given rise to extraordinary and diverse areas of criminological research. It is this broad scope that makes green contributions both significant, insightful and a home for ASA scholars. While there remains debate over what should be defined as green crime (see, e.g., Brisman and South, this volume, Chapter 1; Nurse 2016), it is vital to focus on what unites the various branches. Sollund (2016: 3) argues that one of the underlying currents in green criminology is the 'insistent awareness of exploitative relationships and injustice'. Importantly, green criminology has called consistently for fundamental changes to how we conceive rights and wrongs; accordingly—and in order to 'avoid being numbered among the oppressors' (Singer 1995: xii)—our green colleagues should be prepared to rethink their attitudes to all other groups, including the most fundamental of them—our fellow animals. Inequality, injustice and power are, after all, concerns central to ASA, just as they are to many, if not most, environmental harms.

By naming the abuse as animal sexual assault, we aim to avoid dissecting and justifying animal abuse according to its impact on *people* (for example, human immorality and harm) and to move away from legal definitions that are too restrictive and too constraining of our ways of thinking about and responding to this harmful and far-reaching behaviour. By challenging accepted norms around the use of animals as objects of sexual gratification and gain, we strengthen the case made in other areas of interpersonal and institutional abuse (for example, racism, sexism, xenophobia). There is no need to prioritise human over animal or animal over human harms. Rather, by emphasising the interconnectedness of human, animal and ecological concerns, we challenge definitions of crime to ensure that all harms be treated as such. This call, for a greater focus on detection, enforcement, prosecution, sentencing and the treatment of offenders and victims of ASA, is in the interest of all.

Notes

1 A quick note is required here on the language used in this chapter. While there is widespread recognition that the terms commonly used in criminology when discussing animals are problematic and speciesist (e.g., pets, animal), we do not have the space here to engage in these discussions. For simplicity and clarity, we use some of this terminology—for example, non-human animal is shortened to animal—with the hope that future developments in animal abuse studies in criminology will facilitate a common use and understanding of better terminology.

2 Beirne proposes the term 'animal sexual assault' (Beirne 2009) in recognition of the similarities to human sexual assault. We adopt Beirne's term in recognition of animals as *victims* rather than *objects of abuse*.

3 These findings should be treated with caution given the methodological limitations of the research conducted and the significant difficulty involved in illuminating the dark figure surrounding this socially abhorrent and deviant behaviour.

4 Efforts have been undertaken in Bolivia (with respect to nature as a whole), India (with regards to cetaceans and elephants), Spain (apes) and the United States (U.S.) (chimpanzees and elephants) to define certain animals as persons, with human-like rights. See www.nonhumanrights.org/.

5 In 1997, the U.K., during their presidency of the E.U., submitted that E.U. law should recognise explicitly that animals are sentient beings. The resulting protocol (1999), was then incorporated into the Lisbon Treaty as Article 13 of Title II. Despite their support for animal welfare, the U.K. has no legal instrument other than Article 13 of the Lisbon Treaty to provide that animals are sentient beings. The Bill to transfer the E.U. protocol on animal sentience into U.K. law was brought to Parliament on 15 November 2017.

6 A pornographic image is defined as one 'of such a nature that it must reasonably be assumed to have been produced solely or principally for the purpose of sexual arousal' (§63.3). Extreme is defined as an image that portrays, in an explicit and realistic way, 'a person performing an act of intercourse or oral sex with an animal (whether dead or alive), and a reasonable person looking at the image would think that any such person or animal was real' (§63.7d).

7 According to the IATP and GRAIN (2018) report, meat and dairy companies are on track to be the world's biggest contributors to climate change outpacing even the fossil fuel industry.

References

Abel, G. G. Osborn, C. and Twigg, D. 1993. 'Sexual assault through the lifespan: Adult offenders with juvenile histories,' in H. Barbee, W. Marshall and S. Hudson (eds.) *The Juvenile Sex Offender*, pp. 104–117. New York: Guilford Press.

Adams, C. J. 2010. *The Sexual Politics of Meat: A Feminist-vegetarian Critical Theory*. 20th Anniversary Edition. New York: Continuum.

Alvarez, W. A. and Freinhar, J. 1991. 'A prevalence study of bestiality (zoophilia) in psychiatric patients, medical in-patients, and psychiatric staff,' *International Journal of Psychosomantics*, 38: 1–4.

American Psychiatric Association. 2000. *Diagnostic and Statistical Manual of Mental Disorders*. 4th ed. Washington, DC: American Psychiatric Association.

Barnes, J. E. Boat, B., Putnam, F., Dates, H. and Mahlman, A. 2006. 'Ownership of high-risk ('vicious') dogs as a marker for deviant behaviors – Implications for risk assessment,' *Journal of Interpersonal Violence*, 21(12): 1616–1634.

BBC. 2015. 'Denmark passes law to ban bestiality,' *BBC*. Available at: www.bbc.co.uk/newsbeat/article/32411241/denmark-passes-law-to-ban-bestiality.

Beetz, A. M. 2008. 'Bestiality and zoophilia: A discussion of sexual contact with animals,' in F. Ascione (ed.) *The International Handbook of Animal Abuse and Cruelty: Theory, Research, and Application*, pp. 201–220. West Lafayette, IN: Purdue University Press.

Beirne, P. 2002. 'On the sexual assault of animals: A sociological view,' in A. Creager and W. Jordan (eds.) *The Animal/Human Boundary: Historical Perspectives*, pp. 193–227. Rochester, NY: University of Rochester Press.

Beirne, P. 2009. *Confronting Animal Abuse: Law, Criminology and Human-Animal Relations*. Lanham, MD: Rowman & Littlefield.

Beirne, P., Maher, J. and Pierpoint, H.2017. 'Animal sexual assault,' in J. Maher, H. Pierpoint and P. Beirne (eds.) *Palgrave International Handbook of Animal Abuse Studies*, pp. 59–85. London: Palgrave Macmillan.

Beirne, P. and South, N. 2007. *Issues in Green Criminology: Confronting Harms against Environments, Humanity and Other Animals*. Collumpton, Devon: Willan.

Bolliger, G. and Goetschel, A. F. 2008. 'Sexual relations with animals (zoophilia): An unrecognized problem in animal welfare legislation,' in A. M. Beetz and A. L. Podberscek (eds.) *Bestiality and Zoophilia: Sexual Relations with Animals*, pp. 23–45. West Lafayette IN: Purdue University Press.

Brayford, J., Cowe, F. and Deering, J. (eds.) 2012. *Sex Offenders: Punish, Help, Change or Control? Theory, Policy and Practice Explored* (Routledge Frontiers of Criminal Justice series). Abingdon, Oxon, UK: Routledge.

Cohen, L. and Felson, M. 1979. 'Social change and crime rate trends: A routine activity approach,' *American Sociological Review*, 44(4): 588–608.

Coonan, C. 2006. 'Illegal wildlife trade is worth £6bn a year,' *Independent*. Available at: www.independent.co.uk/environment/illegal-wildlife-trade-is-worth-1636bn-a-year-5329949.html.

Cudworth, E. 2017. 'Breeding and rearing farmed animals,' in J. Maher, H. Pierpoint and P. Beirne (eds.) *Palgrave International Handbook of Animal Abuse Studies*, pp. 159–177. London: Palgrave Macmillan.

Davis, K. 2005. *The Holocaust and the Henmaid's Tale: A Case for Comparing Atrocities*. New York: Lantern Books.

DeGioia. 2015. 'Recognizing sexual abuse in animals,' Available at: www.vin.com/news/VINNews.aspx?articleId=35718.

DeMello, M. 2012. *Animals and Society: An Introduction to Human-Animal Studies*. New York: Columbia University Press.

Duffield, G., Hassiotis, A. and Vizard, E. 1998. 'Zoophilia in young sexual abusers,' *Journal of Forensic Psychiatry*, 9: 294–304.

Edwards, M. J. 2019. 'Arrest and prosecution of animal sex abuse (bestiality) offenders in the United States, 1975–2015,' *Journal of the American Academy of Psychiatry and the Law Online*, 47(3): 335–346.

Ellefsen, R., Sollund, R. and Larsen, G. (eds.) 2012. *Eco-global Crimes: Contemporary Problems and Future Challenges*. Surrey, UK : Ashgate.

Finn, J. K., Tregenza, T. and Norman, M. D. 2009. 'Defensive tool use in a coconut-carrying octopus,' *Current Biology*, 19(23): 1069–1070.

Fleming, W., Jory, B. and Burton, D. 2002. 'Characteristics of juvenile offenders admitting to sexual activity with nonhuman animals,' *Society and Animals*, 10(1): 31–45.
Flynn, C. 1999. 'Animal abuse in childhood and later support for interpersonal violence in families,' *Society and Animals*, 7(2): 161–172.
Flynn, C. 2012. *Understanding Animal Abuse. A Sociological Analysis*. New York: Lantern.
Francione, G. L. 2008. *Animals as Persons: Essays on the Abolition of Animal Exploitation*. New York: Columbia University Press.
Glendinning, L. 2008. 'Spanish parliament approves 'human rights' for apes,' *The Guardian*. Available at: www.theguardian.com/world/2008/jun/26/humanrights.animalwelfare.
Hall, M. 2013. *Victims of Environmental Harm: Rights, Recognition and Redress under National and International Law*. London and New York: Routledge.
Hall, M. and Farrall, S. 2013. 'The criminogenic consequences of climate change: Blurring the boundaries between offenders and victims,' in N. South and A. Brisman (eds.) *Routledge International Handbook of Green Criminology*, pp. 120–133. Abingdon, Oxon, UK: Routledge.
Hall, M., Maher, J., Nurse, A., Potter, G., South, N. and Wyatt, T. (eds.) 2016. *Greening Criminology in the 21st Century*. London: Ashgate.
Hensley, C., Tallichet, S. and Dutkiewicz, E. L. 2010. 'Childhood bestiality: A potential precursor to adult interpersonal violence,' *Journal of Interpersonal Violence*, 25(3): 557–567.
Henderson, B., Hensley, C. and Tallichet, S. 2011. 'Childhood animal cruelty methods and their link to adult interpersonal violence,' *Journal of Interpersonal Violence*, 26: 2211–2227.
Hvozdík, A., Bugarský, A., Kottferová, J., Vargová, M., Ondrašovičová, O., Ondrašovič, M. and Sasáková, N. 2006. 'Ethological, psychological and legal aspects of animal sexual abuse,' *The Veterinary Journal*, 172(2): 374–376.
Humane Society of the United States [HSUS]. 2011. 'Fact sheet,' Available at: www.humanesociety.org.
Hunt, M. 1974. *Sexual Behavior in the 1970s*. Chicago, IL: Playboy Press.
Imbschweiler, I., Kummerfeld, M., Gerhard, M. and Pfeiffer, I. 2009. 'Animal sexual abuse in a female sheep,' *The Veterinary Journal*, 182(3): 481–483.
Institute for Agriculture and Trade Policy and GRAIN. 2018. 'Emissions impossible,' Available at: www.iatp.org/emissions-impossible.
Jarrell, M. L. and Ozymy, J. 2012. 'Real crime, real victims: Environmental crime victims and the Crime Victims' Rights Act (CVRA),' *Crime, Law and Social Change*, 58(4): 373–389.
Maher, J., Pierpoint, H. and Beirne, P. (eds.) 2017. *Palgrave International Handbook of Animal Abuse Studies*. London: Palgrave Macmillan.
Miller, K. and Knutson, J. 1997. 'Reports of severe physical punishment and exposure to animal cruelty by inmates convicted of felonies and by university students,' *Child Abuse and Neglect*, 21(1): 59–82.
Overton, J., Hensley, C. and Tallichet, S. 2012. 'Examining the relationship between childhood animal cruelty motives and recurrent adult violent crimes toward humans,' *Journal of Interpersonal Violence*, 227: 899–915.
Kinsey, A. C., Pomeroy, W. and Martin, C. 1948. *Sexual Behavior in the Human Male*. Philadelphia, PA: W. B. Saunders & Co.
Kinsey, A. C., Pomeroy, W., Martin, C. and Gebhard, P. 1953. *Sexual Behavior in the Human Female*. Philadelphia, PA: W. B. Saunders & Co.
Levitt, L., Hoffer, T. and Loper, A. 2016. 'Criminal histories of a subsample of animal cruelty offenders,' *Aggression and Violent Behaviour*, 30: 48–58.
Maher, J. 2015. 'Animal sexual assault,' in A. Ackerman and R. Furman (eds.) *Sexual Crimes: Transnational Problems and Global Perspectives*, pp. 226–242. New York: Columbia University Press.
Maher, J. and Pierpoint, H. 2012. 'Animal abuse and sex offending,' in F. Cowe and J. Brayford (eds.) *Sex Offenders, Punish, Help, Change or Control? Theory, Policy and Practice Explored*, pp. 150–169. London: Routledge.
Miletski, H. 2005. 'A history of bestiality,' in A. M. Beetz and A. L. Podberscek (eds.) *Bestiality and Zoophilia: Sexual Relations with Animals*, pp. 1–22. West Lafayette, IN: Purdue University Press.
Miller, C. 2001. 'Childhood animal cruelty and interpersonal violence,' *Clinical Psychology Review*, 21: 735–749.
Ministry of Justice [MoJ]. 2015. *Replies to Freedom of Information Requests 18 August (FOI 98889, 16 June, 28 September (FOI 72179) and 6 Oct (FOI 72644)*. London: MoJ.
Ministry of Justice [MoJ]. 2018. *Replies to Freedom of Information Requests 13 April (FOI180319013) and 2 June (180514028)*. London: MoJ.

Morrell, J. M. 2011. 'Artificial insemination: Current and future trends,' in Dr M. Manafi (ed.) *Artificial Insemination in Farm Animals*, pp. 1–14. London: InTechOpen.
Munro, H. 2006. 'Animal sexual abuse: A veterinary taboo?' *The Veterinary Journal*, 172: 195–197.
Munro, H. and Thrusfield, M. 2001. 'Battered pets: Sexual abuse,' *Journal of Small Animal Practice*, 42: 333–337.
Nibert, D. 2013. *Animal Oppression and Human Violence: Domesecration, Capitalism and Global Conflict*. New York: Columbia University Press.
Nonhuman Rights Project. 2018. 'Litigation,' Available at: www.nonhumanrights.org/litigation/
Nurse, A. 2016. *An Introduction to Green Criminology and Environmental Justice*. London: Sage.
Pierpoint, H. 2018. 'Dog fighting: A role for veterinary professionals in tackling a harmful and illegal practice,' *Vet Record*, 183(18): 563–566.
Regan, T. 2004. *The Case for Animal Rights*. Los Angeles, CA: University of California Press.
Rowlands, M. 2012. *Can Animals be Moral*. Oxford: Oxford University Press.
Sentencing Council. 2014. 'Sexual offences definitive guideline,' Available at: www.sentencingcouncil.org.uk/wp-content/uploads/Final_Sexual_Offences_Definitive_Guideline_content_web1.pdf.
Singer, P. 1995. *Animal Liberation*. London: Pimlico.
Singer, P. 2001. 'Heavy petting,' *Prospect Magazine*. Available at: www.prospectmagazine.co.uk/magazine/heavypetting.
South, N. and Beirne, P. 2006. *Green Criminology. International Library of Criminology, Criminal Justice and Penology (Second Series)*. Sussex, UK: Ashgate.
Sollund, R. (ed.) 2008. *Global harms: Ecological Crime and Speciesism*. New York: Nova Science.
Sollund, R. 2012. 'Speciesism as doxic practice versus valuing difference and plurality,' in R. Ellefsen, R. Sollund and G. Larsen (eds.) *Eco-Global Crimes: Contemporary Problems and Future Challenges*, pp. 91–114. Surrey, UK: Ashgate.
Sollund, R. 2016. 'Introduction: Critical green criminology — An agenda for change,' in R. Sollund, (ed.). *Green Harms and Crime: Critical Criminology in a Changing World*, pp. 1–26. London: Palgrave Macmillan.
Spapens, T., White, R. and Kluin, M. (eds.) 2014. *Environmental Crime and Its Victims: Perspectives within Green Criminology*. Surrey, UK: Ashgate.
Stern, A. W. and Smith-Blackmore, M. 2016. 'Veterinary forensic pathology of animal sexual abuse,' *Veterinary Pathology*, 53(5): 1057–1066.
Tallichet, S., Hensley, C. and Singer, S. 2005. 'Unraveling the methods of childhood and adolescent cruelty to nonhuman animals,' *Society and Animals*, 13(2): 91–108.
Tapia, F. 1971. 'Children who are cruel to animals,' *Child Psychiatry and Human Development*, 2(2): 70–77.
Vidal, J. 2010. 'Bolivia enshrines natural world's rights with equal status for mother earth,' *The Guardian*. Available at: www.theguardian.com/environment/2011/apr/10/bolivia-enshrines-natural-worlds-rights.
Von Solinge, T. B. 2014. 'Researching illegal logging and deforestation,' *International Journal for Crime, Justice and Social Democracy*, 3(2): 36–49.
Walters, R., Westerhuis, D. and Wyatt, T. (eds.) 2013. *Emerging Issues in Green Criminology: Exploring Power, Justice and Harm*. Basingstoke, Hampshire, UK: Palgrave Macmillan.
White, R. 2013. *Crimes against Nature: Environmental Criminology and Ecological Justice*. London: Routledge.
Wyatt, T. 2014. 'The Russian far east's illegal timber trade: An organized crime?' *Crime, Law and Social Change*, 61(1): 15–35.
Zequi, S. de C., Guimarães, G. C., Da Fonseca, F. P., Ferreira, U., de Matheus, W. E., Reis, L. O., Aita, G. A., et al. 2012. 'Sex with animals (SWA): Behavioral characteristics and possible association with penile cancer. A multicenter study,' *Journal of Sex Medicine*, 9(7): 1860–1867.

29

The victimisation of women, children and non-human species through trafficking and trade

Crimes understood through an ecofeminist perspective

Ragnhild Sollund

Introduction

A number of feminist scholars claim that the exploitation of the Earth and non-human species is rooted in patriarchal power structures and androcentrism (the placement of male human beings or the masculine perspective at the centre of one's view of the world, its culture and history) (e.g., Adams 2003; Birkeland 1993; Collard and Contrucci 1989; Donovan 1996; Donovan and Adams 1996; Gaard 1993; Gålmark 2008; Kheel 1993, 1996; Merchant 1992, 1995a, 1995b; Noske 1989, 1997). This feminist interpretation of human nature critiques the assumed universality of the masculine model of 'Man' and its associated values. As a result of this dominance by males and emphasis on masculine interests, feminist scholars argue that 'the masculine' and 'the feminine' are archetyped and polarised: what are regarded as masculine values and traits are elevated, whereas women are associated with nature in an instrumentalist way: they (and their contributions to society) 'are valued only to the extent that they have value to Man' (Birkeland 1993: 24). To grossly simplify these perspectives and positions, animals, children, nature and women are the victims of patriarchal philosophy, ideology and actions.

While it has been demonstrated that women and children are the first to suffer from acid rain, chemical waste(s), radiation, toxic pesticides and other pollution—in part, because of their detrimental effects on women's reproductive systems (Collard and Contrucci 1989; Gaard 1993: 5)—in this chapter, I focus on what may be more direct examples of androcentric power structures: the trade and trafficking of animals, children and women. I explore whether an ecofeminist approach may shed light on these phenomena and the implicit abuse, exploitation and suffering. These acts cannot be disconnected from the exploitation of nature, ecofeminists argue, because all species of the Earth (human and non-human alike) are part of nature and should not be regarded as merely other forms of 'natural resources' (e.g., Collard and Contrucci 1989; Noske 1989, 1997). Similarly, predominantly poor women and children should not be regarded as commodities and sources of financial gain, regardless of their own needs and wishes. In ecofeminism, animals, children and women are considered to have a common cause (e.g., Adams 1993; Birkeland 1993; Collard and Contrucci 1989; Donovan 1996; Gaard 1993; Gruen 1993; Kheel 1996). As Walker states, 'The oppression that … people of color, and children face all over the world—is the same oppression animals endure every day to a greater degree' (in Adams 1994: 119).

After some prefatory comments about the human–non-human animal relationships,[1] I sketch out how international conventions seek to prevent trafficking and trade in human and animal bodies (which are used, in whole or in part, for food, fur, medicine and 'pets', as well as for experiments, entertainment—e.g., in circuses, in the sex industry). I then consider whether such trafficking and trade can be understood from the perspective of ecofeminism. Prior ecofeminist projects have endeavoured to document the poor quality of life for women, children, people in the Global South, as well as all animals and the environment more generally, and have demonstrated how classism, racism and sexism are mutually reinforcing systems of oppression (see, e.g., Gaard 1993). Drawing on the ecofeminist theory of Birkeland (1993), Collard and Contrucci (1989), Donovan (1993), 1996), Gaard (1993), Gruen (1993), Kheel (1993) and Vance (1993), among others, I contemplate both legal and illegal examples of exploitation, and reflect on why and how animals, women and children are objectified as commodities rather than perceived and treated as beings with rights to freedom and lives without physical and psychical abuse.

Human–animal relationships

Because there may exist similarities in the ways human victims are regarded by those who exploit them, and the far more dispersed victimhood of animals in relation to humans, my point of departure in this chapter is the human–animal relationship, as this may serve to accentuate forms of taken-for-granted exploitation. As the different forms of oppression may be mutually reinforcing, so, too, may the liberation of the oppressed. Indeed, it has been suggested that the liberation processes are interdependent (see, e.g., Birkeland 1993; Gaard 1993; see also Pellow this volume, Chapter 32), although the liberation processes for animals still seem far off and have lagged tremendously behind the development of rights for women and children.[2]

The human–animal relationship is commonly understood as one in which animals are regarded as property, thereby lacking individual rights (see, e.g., Beirne 1999; Brisman 2014; Ellefsen 2009; Francione 2005 [1996]; Regan 1983; Singer 2002; Sollund 2008a, 2012a). In human–animal relationships, animals are regarded as a means to an end, such as for clothing, food, medicine, research subjects and for use in or as part of sport activities (see generally Brisman 2019). Although animals appear to have protection in animal welfare legislation, at least in most states in the Western world, many claim that such legislation serves to legitimate animal abuse and exploitation (Beirne 1999; Francione 2005 [1996]; Maher and Pierpoint this volume, Chapter 28; Svärd 2008; Sollund 2008b, 2015a). What is commonly referred to as 'welfare' for animals in this kind of legislation,[3] would, if applied to humans living under the same conditions (e.g., in cages with extremely limited freedom of movement, lack of exposure to daylight, no contact with offspring), constitute a gross and obvious breach of most state law, as well as various international conventions adopted to safeguard human interests. The suffering of many animals under human control, such as foxes and minks used in fur farms in Norway, calves and pigs—so called 'production animals'—kept in crates for the meat industry in Denmark and the United States (U.S.), would not be acceptable for the animals we regard as important for human companionship (e.g., dogs). If animals in this category are subject to such treatment, it would, in most cases, be a breach of law (Beirne 1999, 2009; Sollund 2008a, 2012a). Indeed, the real meaning of the word 'welfare'—to 'fare well'—which should be central in animal 'welfare' legislation, seems not to apply to many animals used by humans because 'faring well' is incompatible with torture and death.

The 'Five Freedoms', which were developed in response to a 1965 report in the United Kingdom (U.K.) by the government on animal husbandry, and which have been adopted by professional groups (such as the American Society for the Prevention of Cruelty to Animals and the Royal Society for the Prevention of Cruelty to Animals), are: (1) freedom from hunger or thirst; (2) freedom from discomfort; (3) freedom from pain, injury, or disease; (4) freedom to express (most) normal behaviour; and (5) freedom from fear and distress (Nekaris et al. 2015; Engebretson 2006). These freedoms are often not enjoyed, as is the case of animals living in factory farms or in research laboratories, to say nothing of those animals who have been subject to trafficking. Thus, the concept 'animal welfare' serves to mitigate and mask the painful treatment administered to animals. Humans, on the other hand, are entitled to *rights*, such as those set forth in the Universal Declaration of Human Rights (discussed below). This demonstrates the extent to which humans hold different standards for acceptable treatment of other humans in comparison with animals.

There is also considerable difference between the ways in which the 'right' to welfare is ensured to different categories of animals, and how breaches of legal rights not to suffer from human-inflicted abuse are enforced: 'companion animals' have more rights in this regard than 'captive animals' used for various kinds of exploitation, or 'free-born animals', whose interests in welfare are seldom recognised and who, despite legislation stating all animals have intrinsic value (such as in Norwegian animal welfare legislation) are valued only insofar as their species is threatened with extinction (Goyes and Sollund 2016; Sollund 2013b, 2015b; 2017a, 2017b; Sollund 2017c, 2019). This also becomes clear when examining the international conventions prohibiting the trafficking in humans and animals, which I turn to next.

Trafficking and trade in animals and humans

Before I proceed to these conventions, and establish what the terms 'trafficking' and 'trade' refer to, I attempt to demonstrate, with an example, how different forms of oppression, such as sexism and speciesism, may interlink. In particular, the case that I discuss demonstrates the relatedness between the trafficking in women and children for sexual exploitation and the trafficking in non-human animals. The case also illustrates the objectification of the victims involved, and the role that human male and patriarchal ideology play in this objectification, thus revealing how instrumentalist perspectives lead to the oppression of non-human animals, children, nature and women (Birkeland 1993; Collard and Contrucci 1989; Donovan 1996; Gruen 1993; Noske 1989, 1997). The case involves the orangutan *Pony*, who, after abduction, was held captive in a village in Indonesia where she was kept in a brothel and sold to men for sex. Chained to a wall and kept on a mattress, she was trained to exhibit sexualised behaviour if men approached her. She was, after several attempts, saved by the Borneo Orangutan Survival Foundation—a difficult task given that the villagers who kept her captive were reluctant to relinquish their popular sex slave.[4] In sum, not only was *Pony* a victim of enslavement and sexual abuse, she was a victim of the so-called 'wildlife trade'.[5] As a closer parallel, until 2015, when Denmark criminalised bestiality in their legislation, the country was also known for attracting men who wanted to have sex with animals, allegedly kept in animal brothels.[6]

Before proceeding further, a note about terminology is in order. South and Wyatt (2011: 546) suggest the following definitions for the terms *trade, wildlife trafficking* and *illegal wildlife trade*:

> *Trade* encompasses collection, harvesting, possession, processing, acquiring or transporting of wildlife for the purpose of purchasing, importing, exporting, selling, bartering or exchanging (Burgener et al. 2001). *Wildlife trafficking* or the *illegal wildlife trade* is the specific name of the green crime that involves the illegal trade, smuggling, poaching, capture or collection of endangered species, protected wildlife (including animals or plants that are subject to harvest quotas and regulated by permits). [emphasis added]

I accept these understandings, although with some serious reservations. The terms 'harvesting' and 'poaching' are highly anthropocentric and should therefore be avoided because they imply and support (indirectly) the perspective that animals can be the property of humans—indistinguishable from crops, plants and natural resources. Accordingly, I suggest the term 'abduction', rather than 'harvesting' or 'poaching' (Sollund 2011); when animals are killed, I recommend that we follow Beirne (2007; 2009, 2014; see also Sollund 2015a) and employ the term 'theriocide'. Furthermore, in my view, all animals that are subject to abduction from their habitats, trafficking,[7] and trade are *victims*—independent of their species' status as threatened or endangered—because their suffering is the same, though often not lexically illegal (Sollund 2017b; Sollund 2017c). I nonetheless regard it as a *crime* (cf. Sollund 2008a, 2008b; White 2008: 36). Therefore, I do not distinguish between legal and illegal species abduction, although I recognise that the *crime* of abduction and trade of animals may be regarded as more severe when the animals are considered endangered species (Svärd 2008), or when the abduction and trade of a particular species results in the destruction of an entire ecosystem (Teclaff 1994)—what are often referred to as 'keystone' species (see, e.g., Paine 1995; Scott, Soulé and Doak 1993). Thus, I conceive of 'wildlife trade' as the abduction, acquisition, collection, destruction, possession, or transportation of animals (e.g., amphibians, birds, reptiles, mammals) for the purpose of barter, exchange, export, import, or purchase. I conceive of 'animal trafficking' as the legal and illegal abduction, capture, collection, smuggling, or transport of free born animals, whether or not 'domesticated'[8] (alive or dead) or parts thereof (i.e., derivatives or products made from their bodies).

With this terminological backdrop, but before turning to the conventions that protect animals and humans from trafficking, I wish to set forth my notion of 'human trafficking'. The United Nations Economic and Social Commission for Asia and the Pacific (ESCAP) defines *human trafficking* as:

> The recruitment, transportation, transfer, harbouring or receipt of persons, by means of the threat or use of force or other forms of coercion, of abduction, of fraud, of deception, of the abuse of power or of a position of vulnerability or of the giving or receiving of payments or benefits to achieve the consent of a person having control over another person, for the purpose of exploitation.[9]

'Trafficking' is linked to the *purpose of exploitation* (Skilbrei and Tveit 2008);[10] 'exploitation', in turn, may be for labour, for the sex industry, for marriage, in war (as soldiers or for demining/ mine clearance) (Tiefenbrun 2007). As is the case with animal trafficking, human trafficking is based on supply and demand. The demand-side comes from men (usually) who are willing to purchase women and children in a variety of ways: directly (in long- or short-term arrangements, such as prostitution) or indirectly through the use of pornography (Skilbrei and Tveit 2008; see also Adams 2003). The supply-side, whether of human or animal victims, comes from those willing to abduct, recruit, 'poach' and traffic, and includes all individuals involved in the various stages of these processes (e.g., the abductors, the middlemen, the pimps) (cf. Meredith in Warchol, Zupan and Clack 2003: 7; Sollund 2019; Maher and Sollund 2016; Wyatt 2013).

Conventions protecting animals and humans from trafficking

Just as animal welfare legislation provides animal consumers with a sense of legitimacy for their consumerism—as they are comfortingly misled into believing that animals under human custody enjoy protection (see, e.g., Beirne 1999; Svärd 2008)—international conventions aimed at securing basic human rights can serve to create a false image of the protection of humans, especially of women and children. I support this position through an examination below of some of the international conventions regarding 'wildlife' trafficking and human trafficking.

While many nation-states are governed by national (or federal) legislation, a discussion of which is outside the scope of this chapter, the most important international conventions pertaining to 'wildlife trafficking' are: (1) the Bern Convention on the Conservation of European Wildlife and Natural Habitats 1979[11] (the Bern Convention), signed not only by most European states, but also by a few African states; and (2) the Convention on International Trade in Endangered Species of Wild Fauna and Flora (CITES),[12] whose purpose is to regulate the trade in 'wildlife' and which has been signed by 183 member parties (states, including the European Union (E.U.) as one party).[13] Both conventions aim to monitor and protect endangered species, including flora and fauna, so that the international trade in 'specimens'[14] of wild animals and plants does not threaten the survival of the species as a whole. What determines whether a species can be traded legally is its degree of threat of extinction. Those listed in the three Appendices of CITES either should not be traded at all or the trade is controlled depending on the degree of threat; the Bern Convention places a special emphasis on migratory species.

The most important international conventions to prevent human trafficking, in turn, are: (1) the UN Palermo Protocol;[15] and (2) the Council of Europe Convention.[16] Both conventions aim to establish and safeguard the rights of trafficking victims (May-Len and Tveit 2008) by making states responsible for victims' rights, such as the right of return and access to legal, physical and psychological aid, as well as meeting their security needs (Skilbrei 2012). The purpose of the Palermo Protocol, which is a voluntary supplement to the United Nations Convention against Transnational Organized Crime, is twofold: a) to prosecute offenders; and b) protect victims (Skilbrei 2012). The purpose of the Council of Europe Convention is set forth in its explanatory introduction:

> Trafficking in human beings, with the entrapment of its victims, is the modern form of the old worldwide slave trade. It treats human beings as a commodity to be bought and sold, and to be put to forced labour, usually in the sex industry but also, for example, in the agricultural sector, declared or undeclared sweatshops, for a pittance or nothing at all.[17]

A major difference between the goal of the protocols and conventions relating to human trafficking and those relating to 'wildlife' trade and animal trafficking is that the former seek a total ban of the trafficking and trade in human victims, while the latter seek only to *control* the trafficking and trade of animals, thereby preserving such activities and practices until the covered species have reached a critical state, at which time greater protections come into play. Animals (and other species) thus enjoy only apparent protection under CITES and the Bern Convention; by *regulating*, rather than *proscribing*, trade and trafficking may be encouraged and may provide opportunities for illicit trade (see, e.g., Lemieux and Clarke 2009; Sollund 2019; South and Wyatt 2011; Warchol, Zupan and Clack 2003; Wyatt 2009: 145). Furthermore, by permitting trade and trafficking in animals, the conventions send a strong message that animals are not to be regarded as individuals, but as 'objects', 'natural resources', 'specimens' and 'values'.

Failure to enforce the provisions of the wildlife trafficking conventions is also a problem (Warchol, Zupan and Clack 2003; Zimmerman 2003). As such, it is worth considering whether more strict provisions will have the perverse effect of creating more expansive black markets—as has often been the case with drugs (see Ayres this volume, Chapter 13)—because the lucrative incentives for trafficking and trade may outweigh the risk of detection and prosecution. Already, we have witnessed how traders in animals pay attention to CITES listings, knowing that once a species is listed (or once it moves from one Appendix to another with greater protection), it is perceived as being (more) rare, thereby increasing the black market for the remaining members of the species (Hall, Milner-Gulland and Courchamp 2008; Warchol, Zupan and Clack 2003; Zimmerman 2003). Similarly, while no one would condone *regulating* human trafficking along the lines of wildlife trafficking, human trafficking remains a profitable industry despite its illegality.[18]

The contrast between animals as objects and humans as subjects is strengthened when examining state legislation and international conventions protecting humans in general, such as in the Universal Declaration of Human Rights[19] and the United Nations Convention of the Rights of the Child,[20] both of which are rights-based regimes. CITES and the Bern Convention are not rights-based; animals and other species are regarded as exploitable resources under CITES and the Bern Convention, and their sustainability and survival are deemed desirable only to the extent that they serve human interests (Sollund 2011; cf. Hutton and Dickson 2000).

The pain inflicted on humans and animals when they are abducted—and often drugged or gagged and concealed in boxes, suitcases, trucks, or whatever form of container is available for the purpose of transportation (see, e.g., Wyatt 2011: 114)—is comparable: both humans, including those who are smuggled 'voluntarily' (see Skilbrei and Tveit 2008), and animals are 'subjects of a life' (Regan 1983) and are equally able to experience dehydration, fear, pain, starvation and suffocation.

Animal and human trafficking: victims or exploitable resources?

As noted above, the human trafficking conventions seek to protect women and children from trafficking based on notions of individual and human rights, whereas the conventions governing non-human animals do not reflect notions of rights. For example, the fact that 75 per cent of parrots who are victims of abduction from their habitats die during transport seems to be of less importance to traffickers—whether in legal or illegal trade—and those condoning it, as long as the species as a whole survives (Sollund 2011). The Bern Convention states specifically that wild flora and fauna have intrinsic value, as well as aesthetic, cultural, economic, recreational and scientific value.[21] It is, however, a question as to how those values are balanced, and whether intrinsic value is or will be sacrificed for economic and scientific values. Because the gains of the trade are so enormous, even 90 per cent mortality rates do not deter animal traffickers (Sollund 2019; Wilson-Wilde 2010). As long as the animal trade prevails with the blessing of CITES, species' survival cannot be secured.

To further illustrate this point, in Mexico, fieldwork has led to the estimate that half of the parrot species is threatened (Weston and Memon 2009; see also Pires and Clark 2011, 2012). Another study has estimated that up to 25 per cent of the tropical rainforest 'wildlife' may become extinct by 2020. Despite the international conventions, as well as specific nation-state legislation, there is a thriving trade in threatened and endangered species. In fact, estimates regarding the economic value of the illegal trade range from 6 billion USD annually (Warchol, Zupan and Clack 2003; Zimmerman 2003) to 10–20 billion USD. Van Uhm (2016: 91) confirms that 'if there is an assumed legal wildlife trade of € 86 billion, the illegal wildlife trade would be roughly estimated at € 21.5 billion worldwide from which € 9.5 billion relates to the EU'. This makes it the second largest illegal trade in the world, following the drug trade, and more lucrative than the illegal arms trade (Zimmerman 2003). Yet, as South and Wyatt (2011: 540) explain: 'The financial capital assigned to the wildlife trade does not reflect the external costs of damage to the environment nor consider other value beyond or besides the instrumental worth to humans'. It is also worthwhile mentioning that the *legal* 'wildlife' trade includes more than 350 million animals and plants (Warchol, Zupan and Clack 2003: 3). Thus, both human trafficking and animal trafficking, whether legal or illegal, are contemplated in *economic* terms, rather than with respect to pain, suffering and death.

Although it is difficult to generate estimates due to the illegal and thus clandestine character of the trade, the abduction of animals and plants is on a par with deforestation as the largest threats to animal and plant species, resulting in the extinction of many (TRAFFIC 2008). To complicate matters further, the illegal trade and trafficking in animals varies broadly from the poor peasant abducting parrots from their nests (Goyes and Sollund 2016; Maher and Sollund 2016; Pires and Clark 2011; Sollund 2019) to organised criminal networks that take advantage of lax law enforcement, where the risk of detection is low and the penalties, if caught, are negligible (South and Wyatt 2011; van Uhm 2016; Warchol, Zupan and Clack 2003; Wilson-Wilde 2010; Wyatt 2009; Zimmerman 2003). As observed by Sollund (2019), South and Wyatt (2011), Warchol and colleagues (2003: 21) and Zimmerman (2003), animal trafficking may occur in tandem with drug trafficking, following the same transportation routes and reaching the same destinations (e.g., Europe and the U.S., where markets exist for cocaine and exotic pets). Such 'tandem trafficking' can make the detection and prosecution of either more difficult because it can create jurisdictional overlaps and gaps—a phenomenon somewhat akin to Buzbee's (2003) notion of a 'regulatory commons' problem. Wyatt (2011, 2013, 2015) has found that the illegal trade in raptors is used to fund terrorist operations in the Middle East and Central Asia.

As with animal trafficking, the trafficking of humans has been identified as one of the largest growing illegal markets, with estimates ranging from 5 to 9 billion USD annually.[22] A UN report addressing the issue of trafficking in women and children states that approximately 700,000 persons are trafficked across borders annually—numbers that do not include domestic trafficking.[23] As with the case of animal trafficking, the illegal nature of these activities renders any estimate particularly imprecise. Denisova (2004) ranks the trafficking in women and children for the sex industry as the third largest illegal trade behind the arms and drugs trades, thereby placing human trafficking on a par with animal trafficking.

Both the conventions regarding human trafficking and those concerning animal trafficking present challenges for law enforcement and prosecutors at the national level. For example, judges may have difficulty in delineating trafficking from procuring and pimping (Skilbrei 2010).[24] In the case of humans, *all* trafficking for exploitation is illegal, but prostitution is permitted in some states that are members of the human trafficking conventions. Some women—especially those who are poor—may be forced into prostitution if they cannot secure the funds and proper paperwork to enter countries legally. While conventions distinguish smuggling and human trafficking, distinguishing between the two can be difficult and '[i]t is necessary to discuss under what circumstances smuggling is exploitation because the consequences of this debt [incurred as "payment" for being transported across a border illegally] are grave as the women are prevented from leaving prostitution because of it' (Skilbrei and Tveit 2008: 25).

Women and children may be persuaded and lured into migration, and subsequently forced into prostitution, but animals will *always* be abducted and traded by use of physical force. In the case of animals, the *values* represented in CITES and the Bern Convention are likely to induce animal victimisation. In CITES, only passing concern is expressed for the well-being of the individual victims of the trade, and both conventions serve and seek to perpetuate trafficking and trade in animals through legitimating and controlling processes (Goyes and Sollund 2016; Maher and Sollund 2016; Sollund 2011, 2013). The human exploitation of animals and 'natural resources' are perceived as 'normal'—as accepted and expected—as a *right*—and the rationale behind this perspective is not questioned—a point to which I return. Although the conventions fail to recognise the inherent value of all beings, the strength of CITES may lie in its ability to impose restrictive sanctions on the trade of protected species by countries which are not complying with this convention (Birkeland 1993; Gruen 1993; Lemieux and Clarke 2009; Reeve 2002). These sanctions may hurt the ability of non-compliant countries to profit from the regulated market for so called 'wildlife'.

Legal versus illegal trade and trafficking in animal and human victims

As mentioned throughout this chapter, the animal conventions attempt to *control*, rather than *prohibit*, the trafficking and trade of non-human species. This facilitates various ways of making the trade *appear* legal (Sollund 2019; South and Wyatt 2011; Warchol, Zupan and Clack 2003; Wilson-Wilde 2010; Wyatt 2009; Zimmerman 2003). A number of techniques are applied to 'legalise' the illegal trafficking of various species, such as bribery; disguising birds' true colours using dyes; false import/export permits; fictitious breeding documents; forgery of and fraud in CITES permits; and mislabeled shipping invoices (Sollund 2019; Warchol, Zupan and Clack 2003: 21; Wilson-Wilde 2010). False certificates may be produced stating that the animal or bird in question belongs to another species, one that is not CITES listed, or one that is listed on a less restrictive CITEX Appendix.[25] Thus, bribery, corruption, forgery and fraud represent other ways of smuggling animals, in addition to the above-mentioned clandestine acts of hiding species in bottles and suitcases, or sewing them into waistcoats (see, e.g., Wyatt 2011). The legal trade of birds, for example, which is worth 2 million USD per month, is inextricably intertwined with the illegal trade of birds that are moved in planeloads from South Africa and Zambia to Europe and the U.S., and organised, among others, by Liberian criminal groups (Warchol, Zupan and Clack 2003: 21).

Like animals whose trafficking is facilitated with documents that falsely legalise their trafficking, humans need documents to legally cross borders between states. This has entailed a market in which middlemen procure forged documents for women who are trafficked—both in situations where the women are abducted by force and in situations where women are pushed into servitude by circumstances (e.g., poverty) (Skilbrei and Tveit 2008). For humans, the lack of access to legal documents to enter Europe or the U.S., for example, may endanger their safety and liberty precisely because they become dependent on persons who exploit their need for those documents (Sollund 2012b). Legal documents, such as a Shengen Visa (which facilitates cross-border travel between the 22 E.U. states and three non-E.U. members), can serve to protect migrants from exploitation as these may serve to legalise their stay and facilitate work in the formal sector; living as undocumented migrants makes them dependent on intermediary organisations and channels for migration and survival—so-called 'bastard institutions' (Engebretson 2006: 231; Mahler 1995). This also makes them easy victims for traffickers and pimps (see, e.g., Denisova 2004).

In the case of non-human animals, their 'travel documents' will in no way secure their survival or prevent them from suffering. In fact, the opposite appears to be true. For birds, for example, the difference between being a legal object for trade, or an illegal victim of trafficking, may be nil. An exploration of exports in CITES-listed 'wildlife' from the South American Amazon countries, Bolivia, Brazil, Colombia, Ecuador, Guyana, Peru, Suriname and Venezuela, showed, for example, that on average, 12,000 parrots were trafficked per year between 2005–2014, mainly to Mexico, Russia, Singapore and Thailand, which were the largest single importers, importing nearly half of live parrots (Sinovas, Price, King, Hinsley and Pavitt 2017). Without a doubt, being a victim of this kind of legal abduction and trafficking represents a breach of the Five Freedoms previously mentioned. Regardless of whether they are travelling legally or illegally, women, children and non-human species suffer from objectification when trafficked and traded. The 'paperwork' required may expose both humans and non-human species to dangerous confines and conditions if such paperwork is lacking, or such paperwork may only protect them superficially—essentially amounting to a form of state-sanctioned pain, suffering, torture and death.

With this backdrop, I turn to the perspectives of ecofeminism to analyse why women, children and animals are regarded as exploitable resources. In so doing, I contemplate why humans may benefit from legal instruments prohibiting them from trade and trafficking, while the instruments aiming to protect animals may have less power and efficacy.

Ecofeminist perspectives on humans and animals as 'resources'

Animals, women and children are systematically devalued as individuals through the objectification of their bodies. Animals are regarded as (being part of) nature and therefore something for the taking. Women—at least from an androcentric perspective—are also regarded *as* nature, and thus are seen as more legitimate victims of exploitation than men (see, e.g., Adams 1993; Birkeland 1993; Gaard 1993; Gruen 1993; Merchant 1992, 1995a, 1995b).[26]

Though women, like other animal mothers, usually and naturally take care of their offspring, this feminine role of caregiver is also one into which women have been forced culturally, which, in turn, has also frequently curtailed their education and careers outside of motherhood (see Vance 1993: 138; Wachholz 2007). Because caregiving is associated with the female for both human and non-human animals, women (and their wards—children) are held in contrast to men and perceived as 'other', thereby helping to legitimise their mistreatment and exploitation (see generally Lynch, Burns and Stretesky 2014: 67). As Gruen (1993: 61) explains, the categories 'women' and 'animals' serve the same symbolic function of being constructed as the dominated, submissive, 'other', thereby sustaining human (white) male dominance. Women, children and nature are typically positioned in contrast to men and masculinity, which creates the dualistic hierarchy so central to the organisation of patriarchal thought and culture (e.g. Adams 1993; Birkeland 1993: 37; Noske 1989, 1997). Once designated the role of 'caretaker' and 'nurturer', and once viewed as 'bearers of nature', it becomes all that much easier to justify and legitimise their exploitation.

To further establish the link between women and nature, and thus convey how men legitimise their exploitation, women are commonly referred to in 'animalistic' terms as bird, bitch, cow, fox, heifer, hen, shrew (see, e.g., Adams 2003; Cazaux 1998: 383). In addition, they are often 'sexualised' by being encouraged to wear fur or fur-like outfits (e.g., bunny ears, boas), which serve to emphasise the connection between women, nature and other animals. This not only denigrates women but also confirms their inferior status—one on a par with animals who are systematically denigrated due to doxic speciesism (Sollund 2012a). As Adams (1993: 204) explains, '[i]n the prevailing dualistic ontology, equation of any human group with other animals serves to facilitate the humans' exploitation'.

The 'sexualisation' of women frequently means that they are *only sexualised*—that other facets of their bodies, minds and souls are ignored—thereby making the idea of exploiting women much more palatable (and, in fact, defensible) to many men. Children, in turn, may have even more in common with nature as they are not fully grown, and are thus malleable—capable of being shaped to meet their exploiters' desires as (sexual) slaves or child soldiers (Tiefenbrun 2007). For example, until the 1950s, physicians in Norway regarded babies as not sufficiently sentient to recognise pain, and thus babies were operated upon without anesthesia just as, due to Cartesian ideals for vivisection, it was believed that animals did not experience pain (Sollund 2008a, 2008b).

Through this objectification of animals (and nature), women and children are regarded as property: 'the exploitation of nature is intimately linked … a parallel in men's thinking between their "right" to exploit nature on one hand, and the use they make of women on the other' (Salleh, quoted in Birkeland 1993: 18). The property status of women is also exemplified by their being treated as 'chattels to be bought' and sold in many countries, such as in India and Pakistan, where they are frequently victims of violence by their fathers, husbands and strangers (Birkeland 1993: 34).

The similar or comparable objectification of animals and women is further illustrated by the extensive use of animals in painful, deadly experiments (see, e.g., Collard and Contrucci 1989; Gruen 1993; Noske 1989, 1997; Regan 2004; Sollund 2008a, 2008b). During World War II under the androcentric Nazi regime, animals, women and other humans regarded as inferior (such as Gypsies, Jews and homosexuals) were classified as suitable research tools (Gruen 1993; Sollund 2008a, 2008b). Today, such experimentation is prohibited, but poor people—often women—frequently agree to participate in risky scientific studies and trials. These processes follow those already conducted on animals in laboratories, thereby doubling the objectification and victimisation of the living research tools.

Powerful male versus powerless nature, children and animals

Patriarchal cultures frequently elevate, glorify and otherwise reward violence (see, e.g., Brisman 2010/2011; Sollund 2017a, 2017c, 2017d, 2019). A man's ability to hunt, for example, may determine his status in his society (see, e.g., Collard and Contrucci 1989; Gruen 1993: 62; Noske 1989, 1997; Sollund 2017a, 2019). By rewarding violence, victims of this violence (whether in hunting or in war) are devalued, lose status and are turned into 'prey'. By making violence the domain of men and by linking power and status to successful displays of violence, patriarchal societies have created histories in which man is separate from and superior to animals, as well as separated from women, thereby facilitating male dominance and exploitation (Birkeland 1993; Collard and Contrucci 1989; Gruen 1993; Lynch, Burns and Stretesky 2014; Noske 1989, 1997; Sollund 2017a, 2017c, 2019).

While women, children and animals in varying degrees are deemed powerless in relation to men—a set of relationships that is then often written into law—nature is, at times, powerless to resist exploitation by humans who cause deforestation, species eradication and other forms of ecocide. One strategy to counteract male exploitation and abuse of power could be to detach oneself from nature—to 'play the game' of the patriarchal culture and those who adhere to it. This appears to be the strategy of many women who, rather than advocating for the value of 'feminine properties', such as altruism, care, communication, empathy and love, choose, instead, to adopt or otherwise subscribe to various 'patriarchal values' (see, e.g., Adams 1993; Birkeland 1993: 27; Kheel 1993, 1996; Sollund 2017a, 2017c). This can be seen, for example, with the increase in the number of female hunters in Norway,[27] where 6.3 per cent of those who paid fees for hunting licenses in the last hunting year were women, as well as in instances where women adopt or adapt to (rather than contest) masculine standards for leadership.

The detachment from 'feminist values and properties' is also obvious in the context of dietary practices, in which many women—and many feminists—eat meat (Adams 1994; Gålmark 2008), as well as in the context of wearing fur and using makeup that has been tested on animals (see, e.g., Collard and Contrucci 1989; Regan 2004; Singer 2002). In using fur and wearing makeup tested on animals, women indirectly accept the extensive pain experienced by these animals. In so doing, they not only contribute to the objectification of animals, but also to their own objectification: they respond to male standards of beauty and turn themselves into the sex symbols that males desire (Gruen 1993).

Towards a worldwide change in mentality?

Ecofeminists choose not to 'play the game', but employ an oppositional strategy. Recognising the disastrous consequences that patriarchy has had for our planet and its species, ecofeminists emphasise the connection between humans, animals and nature. Kheel (1993, 1996), for example, promotes a holistic world-view. She proclaims:

> As we disengage from patriarchal discourse, we begin to hear larger and fuller stories. Hearing these bigger stories means learning to listen to nature. The voice of women and the voice of nature have been muted under patriarchy, and others do not speak, objects do not feel, and objects have no needs. Objects exist only to serve the needs of others.
>
> *(Kheel 1993: 260)*

Kheel (1993, 1996) argues not only for the interdependence, but for the *quality* of the relation and interaction that should be in this interdependence. Empathy is essential (Donovan 1996; Donovan and Adams 1996; Kheel 1993, 1996; Sollund 2017d), and by emphasising that all humans (men, women and children) are part of nature, ecofeminists hope to achieve a better future.

More than 25 years have passed since the publication of *Ecofeminism, Women, Animals and Nature* (Gaard 1993), one of the books upon which I have relied heavily in this chapter. While in many instances, the plight of women and children has improved, we have also witnessed a growth in the trafficking of women and children. While better enforcement of existing conventions protecting women and children could result in a decrease in human trafficking, animal trafficking is likely to persist because there is little hope that the legal markets for animals (e.g., as clothing, food, 'pets', research tools) will be banned in the near future. Speciesism is part of doxa (Bourdieu 1995; Sollund 2012a) and consequently so is the (ab)use of non-human species.

The self-claimed rights of humans to exploit other species and nature has proved disastrous over the past decades with deforestation, global climate change and species extinction as evidence thereof. This is precisely why conventions and other legal instruments are necessary to protect all those who are regarded as commodities and resources—whether human or non-human—from exploitation. Legislation and treaties, however, will never be effective by themselves. What is required is a worldwide change in the relationship many men have to women, and humans in general have to nonhuman animal species and nature. This requires *banning*, rather than merely *regulating*, the trade in animals.

Notes

1 The term 'animal' can be criticised for implying that all animals other than humans are the same, while only humans are unique, and not to be regarded as animals. Authors arguing for non-speciesist language have solved this difficulty in different ways, for example by using the term 'non-human animal' and 'animals other than humans' (e.g., Beirne 1999: 118; Nibert 2002: 23). As observed by Beirne, both of these formulations still leave us with the problem of 'othering' non-human animals, categorising them all in one group without acknowledging the huge variation of animal species of which a 'human' is one. Except where it is necessary to draw a distinction, for stylistic reasons, however, I will use the term 'animal' when referring to animals other than humans, trusting that my readers will not assume that my word choice reflects a belief that species other than humans lack the capacity to think, enjoy pleasure and wish to avoid pain and deprivation (Regan 1983).

2 The Declaration of the Rights of the Child was adopted by the UN General Assembly in 1959 (see www.cirp.org/library/ethics/UN-declaration/). 'Childhood' is a modern construct and it was not until the previous century that children were given the predominant role they have in modern, western society (Christie 1982). In Norway, at least, children were supposed to work and otherwise keep quiet; women received the right to vote in 1913—one of the first countries in the world to extend this. By comparison, in Switzerland, women became enfranchised only in 1971; in Liechtenstein, the wait lasted until 1984.

3 www.regjeringen.no/en/doc/laws/Acts/animal-welfare-act.html?id=571188 (last visited 19 February 2016). The Norwegian animal welfare law was amended in 2009. Although section 3 states that animals are beings with intrinsic value, this does not prevent animals from being used as a means to an end. Human interest in using animals is given priority, and what is not *unnecessary* pain is determined by humans.

4 www.viceland.com/int/v14n10/htdocs/yo1.php?country=us .

5 To refer to animals that are not domesticated as 'wildlife' is anthropocentric in that this alienates them and treats them as 'other' or different from domesticated species and humans. The term 'wildlife' suggests that animals that are not under human control are somehow acting only according to their needs. Much 'wildlife' poses no threat to humans, but the term suggests that such animals may be dangerous or harmful to humans—a perspective that often leads humans to kill or mistreat such 'wildlife.'

6 www.aftenposten.no/verden/i/On25k/Nordmenn-drar-til-danske-dyrebordeller.

7 Carol Adams (1993: 197) uses the term 'trafficking' differently—to refer to buying and consuming animal parts.

8 With some reservations, I use this term to distinguish between animals that have not previously been subject to human control and dominion, and those who have, although I realise the anthropocentric connotation of the word 'undomesticated' (i.e., the word 'domestic' refers to the home, the household, household affairs, or the family (see http://dictionary.reference.com/browse/domestic)). Animals living in the forest logically also regard their habitat as a 'home' and their offspring as family. Although human-made concepts make no difference to animals, their experiences of what they refer to do.

9 www.unescap.org/esid/gad/issues/trafficking/index.asp.

10 Although outside the scope of this chapter, it is worth noting that the wording of various conventions has been criticised for grouping women with children, thus regarding women as being unable to protect themselves. As a consequence, women (and children) are turned into passive victims

lacking agency (Skilbrei and Tveit 2008: 14–15). Animals, of course, are frequently regarded as lacking agency and will, and are assumed to act 'on instinct' alone.

11 http://conventions.coe.int/treaty/en/treaties/html/104.htm (last visited 19 February 2016).
12 www.cites.org/eng/disc/what.shtml (last visited 19 February 2016).
13 For more details about how CITES works, see, e.g., Hutton and Dickson (2000); Wyatt (2011); Zimmerman (2003).
14 The term 'specimen' used in CITES, as well as in the Bern Convention, underscores how animals and other species are objectified, rather than treated as individuals.
15 www2.ohchr.org/english/law/protocoltraffic.htm.
16 http://conventions.coe.int/treaty/en/reports/html/197.htm (last visited 19 February 2016). Those readers wishing to explore other instruments relating to the trafficking of persons may wish to consult the following theme paper for the 2nd World Congress Against the Commercial Sexual Exploitation of Children, Yokohama, December 2001: https://childhub.org/en/system/tdf/library/attachments/aa_no_author_undated_t.pdf?file=1&type=node&id=16243 (last visited 26 October 2017).
17 http://conventions.coe.int/treaty/en/reports/html/197.htm (last visited 19 February 2016).
18 www.unece.org/press/pr2004/04gen_n03e.htm (last visited 19 February 2016).
19 www.un.org/en/universal-declaration-human-rights/index.html (last visited 26 October 2017).
20 The International Convention on the Rights of the Child was adopted by the UN General Assembly on 20 November 1989.
21 http://conventions.coe.int/Treaty/en/Treaties/Html/104.htm (last visited 19 February 2016).
22 www.unece.org/press/pr2004/04gen_n03e.htm (last visited 19 February 2016).
23 www.unfpa.org/sites/default/files/pub-pdf/Trafficking.pdf (last visited 19 February 2016).
24 For example, in Norway, it is possible to be convicted of procuring/pimping without ever having earned money or benefits from prostitution by another. In cases of exploitation, the trafficking section should apply (Skilbrei 2010: 47).
25 Species may also be listed on Appendix II because they resemble species listed in Appendix I, i.e., those in serious danger of extinction. Look-alikes are monitored to prevent trading of Appendix I-species disguised as non-regulated 'wildlife'. Species listed in Appendix III may not be threatened on a global scale but may be threatened in some specific states (Zimmerman 2003: 1663–1664).
26 This, of course, has long cultural and religious roots (see, e.g., Gålmark 2008; Kheel 1996; Noske 1997; Vance 1993).
27 www.ssb.no/english/subjects/10/04/10/jeja_en (last visited 19 February 2016).

References

Adams, C. J. 1993. 'The feminist traffic in animals,' in G. Gaard (ed.) *Ecofeminism. Women, Animals, Nature*, pp. 195–219. Philadelphia, PA: Temple University Press.

Adams, C. J. 1994. *Neither Man Nor Beast: Feminism and the Defense of Animals*. New York: Continuum.

Adams, C. J. 2003. *The Pornography of Meat*. New York and London: Continuum.

Nekaris, K. A. I., Musing, L., Vazquez, A. G. and Donati, G. 2015. 'Is tickling torture? Assessing welfare towards slow lorises' (Nycticebus spp.) within Web 2.0 videos,' *Folia Primatologica*, 86(6): 534–551.

Beirne, P. 1999. 'For a nonspeciesist criminology: Animal abuse as an object of study,' *Criminology*, 37(1): 117–147.

Beirne, P. 2007. 'Animal rights, animal abuse and green criminology,' in P. Beirne and N. South (eds.) *Issues in Green Criminology: Confronting Harms Agains Environments, Humanity and Other Animals*, pp. 55–87. Cullompton, Devon, UK: Willan.

Beirne, P. 2009. *Confronting Animal Abuse. Law, Criminology and Human-Animal Relationships*. Lanham, MD: Rowman & Littlefield Publishers.

Beirne, P. 2014. 'Theriocide: Naming animal killing,' *International Journal for Crime. Justice and Social Democracy*, 3(2): 49–66.

Birkeland, J. 1993. 'Ecofeminism: Linking theory and practice,' in G. Gaard (ed.) *Ecofeminism: Women, Animals, Nature*, pp. 13–60. Philadelphia, PA: Temple University Press.

Bourdieu, P. 1995. *Outline of a Theory of Practice*. Cambridge: Cambridge University Press.

Brisman, A. 2010/2011. 'Fictionalized criminal law and youth legal consciousness,' *New York Law School Law Review*, 55(4): 1039–1071.

Brisman, A. 2014. 'Environmental and human rights,' in G. Bruinsma and D. Weisburd (eds.) *Encyclopedia of Criminology and Criminal Justice*, Vol. 3, pp. 1344–1345. New York: Springer Verlag.
Brisman, A. 2019. 'Are you serious?' *Sports Criminology: A Critical Criminology of Sport and Games: A Review. Critical Criminology: An International Journal*, 27(2): 373–392.
Buzbee, W. W. 2003. 'Recognizing the regulatory commons: A theory of regulatory gaps,' *Iowa Law Review*, 89(1): 1–64.
Burgener, M., Snyman, N. and Hauck, M. 2001. 'Towards a sustainable wildlife trade: An analysis of nature conservation legislation in South Africa with particular reference to the Wildlife trade,' Available at: http://www.lib.uct.ac.za.criminology/sjrp.
Cazaux, G. 1998. 'Legitimating the entry of "the animals issue" into (critical) criminology,' *Humanity and Society*, 22(4): 365–385.
Christie, N. 1982. *Hvor tett et samfunn? [How densely knit a society?]*. Oslo: Universitetsforlaget.
Collard, A. and Joyce C. 1989. *Rape of the Wild: Man's Violence Against Animals and the Earth*. Bloomington and Indianapolis: Indiana University Press.
Denisova, T. A. 2004. 'Trafficking in women and children for purposes of sexual exploitation. [This report has not been published by the US Department of Justice. To provide better customer service, the National Criminal Justice Research Service NCJRS has made this document available electronically in addition to traditional paper copies] Document no. 204371,' Available at: www.ncjrs.gov/pdffiles1/pr/204371.pdf.
Donovan, J. 1993. 'Animal rights and feminist theory,' in G. Gaard (ed.) *Ecofeminism: Women, Animals, Nature*, pp. 167–195. Philadelphia, PA: Temple University Press.
Donovan, J. 1996. 'Attention to suffering: Sympathy as a basis for the ethical treatment of animals,' in J. Donovan and C. J. Adams (eds.) *Beyond Animal Rights: A Feminist Caring Ethic for the Treatment of Animals*, pp. 147–170. New York: Continuum.
Donovan, J. and Adams, C. J. (eds.) 1996. *Beyond Animal Rights: A Feminist Caring Ethic for the Treatment of Animals*. New York: Continuum.
Ellefsen, R. 2009. *Ny dyrevelferdslov: Beskyttes dyr eller næring? Interessekonflikt og motstridende syn på dyrs status i lovprosessen forut for dyrevelferdsloven*. MA thesis in Sociology of Law, University of Oslo, Dept of Criminology and Sociology of Law, Oslo, Norway.
Engebretson, M. 2006. 'The welfare and suitability of parrots as companion animals: A review,' *Animal Welfare*, 15(3): 263–276. Available at: http://citeseerx.ist.psu.edu/viewdoc/download?doi=10.1.1.522.1843&rep=rep1&type=pdf.
Francione, G. 2005 [1996]. *Rain without Thunder: The Ideology of the Animal Rights Movement*. Philadelphia, PA: Temple University Press.
Gaard, G. 1993. 'Living interconnections with animals and nature,' in G. Gaard (ed.) *Ecofeminism: Women, Animals, Nature*, pp. 1–13. Philadelphia, PA: Temple University Press.
Gålmark, L. 2008. 'Aritstotle revisited: Anthro- androcentrism and meat normativity,' in R. Sollund (ed.) *Global Harms: Ecological Crime and Speciesism*, pp. 87–109. New York: Nova Science Publishers, Inc.
Goyes, D. R. and Sollund, R. 2016. 'Contesting and contexualizing CITES. Wildlife trafficking in Colombia and Brazil,' *International Journal for Crime, Justice and Social Democracy*, 5(4): 87–102.
Gruen, L. 1993. 'Dismantling oppression: An analysis of the connection between women and animals,' in G. Gaard (ed.) *Ecofeminism: Women, Animals, Nature*, pp. 60–91. Philadelphia, PA: Temple University Press.
Hall, R. J., Milner-Gulland, E. J. and Franck C. 2008. 'Endangering the endangered: The effects of perceived rarity on species exploitation,' *Conservation Letters*, 1(2): 75–81.
Hutton, J. and Barnabas, D. (eds.) 2000. *Endangered Species, Threatened Convention: The Past, Present and Future of CITES*. London: Earthscan.
Kheel, M. 1993. 'The ecofeminist challenge,' in G. Gaard (ed.) *Ecofeminism. Women, Animals, Nature*, pp. 243–272. Philadelphia, PA: Temple University Press.
Kheel, M. 1996. 'The liberation of nature. A circular affair,' in J. Donovan and C. J. Adams (eds.) *Beyond Animal Rights: A Feminist Caring Ethic for the Treatment of Animals*, pp. 17–34. New York: Continuum.
Lemieux, A. M. and Clarke, R. V. 2009. 'The international ban on ivory sales and its effects on elephant poaching in Africa,' *The British Journal of Criminology*, 49(4): 451–501.
Lynch, M. J., Burns, R. G. and Stretesky, P. 2014. *Environmental Law, Crime, and Justice*, 2nd ed. El Paso, Texas: LFB Scholarly Publishing LLC.

Maher, J. and Sollund, R. 2016. 'Law enforcement of the wildlife trafficking: A comparative strengths, weaknesses and opportunities and threats analysis of the UK and Norway,' *Journal of Trafficking, Organized Crime and Security*, 2(1): 82–99.

Mahler, S. J. 1995. *American Dreaming: Immigrant Life on the Margins*. Princeton, NJ: Princeton University press.

Merchant, C. 1992. *Radical Ecology: The Search for a Livable World*. New York: Routledge.

Merchant, C. 1995a. *Earthcare: Women and the Environment*. Abingdon, Oxon, UK: Routledge.

Merchant, C. 1995b. 'Reinventing eden: Western culture as recovery narrative,' in W. Cronon (ed.) *Uncommon Ground: Toward Reinventing Nature*, pp. 132–159. New York and London: W.W. Norton & Company.

Nibert, D. 2002. *Animal Rights/Human Rights: Entanglements of Oppression and Liberation*. Lanham, MD: Rowman & Littlefield.

Noske, B. 1989. *Humans and other Animals: Beyond the Boundaries of Anthropology*. London: Pluto.

Noske, B. 1997. *Beyond Boundaries: Humans and Animals*. Montreal: Black Rose Books.

Paine, R. T. 1995. 'A conversation on refining the concept of keystone species,' *Conservation Biology*, 9(4): 962–964.

Pires, S. F. and Clark, R. V. 2011. 'Sequential foresting, itinerant fences and parrot poaching in Bolivia,' *The British Journal of Criminology*, 51(2): 314–335.

Pires, S. F. and Clarke, R. V. 2012. 'Are parrots CRAVED? An analysis of parrot poaching in Mexico,' *Journal of Research in Crime and Delinquency*, 49(1): 122–146.

Reeve, R. 2002. *Policing International Trade in Endangered Species*. The Royal Institute of International Affairs: Sustainable Development Program. London: Earthscan.

Regan, T. 1983. *The Case for Animal Rights*. Berkeley, CA: University of California Press.

Regan, T. 2004. *Empty Cages: Facing the Challenges of Animal Rights*. Lanham, MD: Rowman and Littlefield Publishers.

Scott, M. L., Soulé, M. E. and Doak, D. F. 1993. 'The keystone-species concept in ecology and conservation,' *BioScience*, 43(4): 219–224.

Singer, P. 2002. *Dyrenes Frigjøring [Animal Liberation]*. Oslo: Spartacus.

Sinovas, P., Becky, P., Emily, K., Amy, H. and Alyson, P. 2017. *Wildlife Trade in the Amazon Countries: An analysis of trade in CITES listed species*. Technical report prepared for the Amazon Regional Program (BMZ/DGIS/GIZ). UN Environment – World Conservation Monitoring Centre, Cambridge, UK. Available at: https://wcmc-my.sharepoint.com/personal/pablo_sinovas_unep-wcmc_org/Documents/Wildlife%20trade%20in%20Amazon%20countries.pdf?slrid=c7fc319e-80f5-4000-c87a-88e625e47e02.

Skilbrei, M–L and Marianne T. 2008. 'Defining trafficking through empirical work: Blurred boundaries and their consequences,' *Gender Technology and Development*, 12(1): 9–30.

Skilbrei, M. L. 2010. 'Taking trafficking to court,' *Women & Criminal Justice*, 20(1): 40–56.

Skilbrei, M. L. 2012. 'Moving beyond assumptions? The framing of anti-trafficking efforts in norway,' in R. Sollund (ed.) *Transnational Migration, Gender and Rights*, pp. 211–227. Bingley, UK: Emerald Group Publishing Limited.

Sollund, R. 2008a. 'Introduction,' in R. Sollund (ed.) *Global Harms: Ecological Crime and Speciesism*, pp. 1–12. New York: Nova Science Publishers, Inc.

Sollund, R. 2008b. 'Causes for speciesism: Difference, distance and denial,' in R. Sollund (ed.) *Global Harms: Ecological Crime and Speciesism*, pp. 109–131. New York: Nova Science Publishers, Inc.

Sollund, R. 2011. 'Expressions of speciesism: The practice of keeping companion animals in terms of animal abuse, trafficking and trade of animals and species decline,' *Crime, Law and Social Change*, 55(5): 437–451.

Sollund, R. 2012a. 'Speciesism as doxic practice or valuing difference and plurality,' in R. Ellfesen, R. Sollund and G. Larsen (eds.) *Eco Global Crimes: Contemporary Problems and Future Challenges*, pp. 91–113. Surrey, UK: Ashgate.

Sollund, R. 2012b. *Transnational Migration, Gender and Rights*. Bingley, UK: Emerald Group.

Sollund, R. 2013. 'Animal trafficking and trade: Abuse and species injustice,' in R. Walters, D. Westerhuis and T. Wyatt (eds.) *Emerging Issues in Green Criminology: Exploring Power, Justice and Harm*, pp. 72–92. Basingstoke,Hampshire, UK: Palgrave Macmillan.

Sollund, R. 2015a. 'With or without a licence to kill: Human-predator conflicts and theriocide in Norway,' in A. Brisman, N. South and R. White (eds.) *Environmental Crime and Social Conflict: Contemporary and Emerging Issues*, pp. 95–121. Surrey, UK: Ashgate.

Sollund, R. 2015b. 'The illegal wildlife trade from a Norwegian outlook: Tendencies in practices and law enforcement,' in R. Sollund (ed.) *Green Harms and Crimes: Critical Criminology in a Changing World*, pp. 147–170. London: Palgrave.

Sollund, R. 2017a. 'Perceptions and Law Enforcement of Illegal and Legal Wolf Killing in Norway: Organized Crime or Folk Crime?' *Palgrave Communications* 3 July. Available at: https://ssrn.com/abstract=2997457 or 10.1057/palcomms.2017.59.

Sollund, R. 2017b. 'Legal and illegal theriocide of trafficked animals,' in J. Maher and H. Pierpoint and P. Beirne (eds.) *The Palgrave International Handbook of Animal Abuse Studies*, pp. 453–474. London: Palgrave Macmillan.

Sollund, R. 2017c. 'The animal other. Legal and illegal theriocide in Norway,' in M. Hall, T. Wyatt, N. South, A. Nurse, G. Potter and J. Maher (eds.) *Greening Criminology in the 21st Century: Contemporary Debates and Future and Future Directions in the Study of Environmental Harm*, pp. 79–99. Abingdon, Oxon, UK: Routledge.

Sollund, R. 2017d. 'Doing green, critical criminology with an auto-ethnographic, feminist approach,' *Critical Criminology: An International Journal*, 25(2): 245–260.

Sollund, R. 2019. *The Crimes of Wildlife Trafficking: Issues of Justice, Legality and Morality*. Abingdon, Oxon, UK: Routledge.

South, N. and Wyatt, T. 2011. 'Comparing illicit trades in wildlife and drugs: An exploratory study,' *Deviant Behavior*, 32(6): 538–561.

Svärd, P. A. 2008. 'Protecting the animals? An abolitionist critique of animal welfarism and green ideology,' in R. Sollund (ed.) *Global Harms: Ecological Crime and Speciesism*, pp. 167–186. New York: Nova Science Publishers, Inc.

Teclaff, L. A. 1994. 'Beyond restoration – the case of ecocide,' *Natural Resources Journal*, 34(4): 942–956. Available at: http://digitalrepository.unm.edu/cgi/viewcontent.cgi?article=1847&context=nrj.

Tiefenbrun, S. 2007. 'Child soldiers, slavery and the trafficking of children,' *Fordham International Law Journal*, 31(2): 415–486. Available at: ir.lawnet.fordham.edu/cgi/viewcontent.cgi?article=2091&context=ilj and www.tjsl.edu/sites/default/files/susan_tiefenbrun_child_soldiers_slavery_and_human_trafficking_31_fordham_intl_l.j._415_2008.pdf.

TRAFFIC. 2008. 'What's Driving the Wildlife Trade? A Review of Expert Opinion on Economic and Social Drivers of the Wildlife Trade and Trade Control Efforts in Cambodia, Indonesia, Lao PDR and Vietnam. East Asia and Pacific Region. Sustainable Development Discussion Papers,' Washington, DC: East Asia and Pacific Region Sustainable Development Department, World Bank. Available at: www-wds.worldbank.org/external/default/WDSContentServer/WDSP/IB/2008/12/12/000333037_20081212005813/Rendered/PDF/467910WP0Box3310wildlife1fullreport.pdf.

Vance, L. 1993. 'Ecofeminism and the politics of reality,' in G. Gaard (ed.) *Ecofeminism: Women, Animals, Nature*, pp. 118–145. Philadephia, PA: Temple University Press.

Van Uhm, D. P. 2016a. *The Illegal Wildlife Trade: Inside the World of Poachers, Smugglers and Traders (Studies of Organized Crime)*. New York: Springer.

van Uhm, D. P. 2016a. *The Illegal Wildlife Trade: Inside the World of Poachers, Smugglers and Traders (Studies of Organized Crime)*. New York: Springer.

van Uhm, D. P. 2016b. 'Illegal trade in wildlife and harms to the world,' in A. C. M. Spapens, .R. White and W. Huisman (eds.) *Environmental Crime in Transnational Context*, pp. 43–65. Farnham: Ashgate Publishing, Ltd.

van Uhm, D. P. 2016c. 'Monkey business: The illegal trade in Barbary macaques,' *Journal of Trafficking, Organized Crime and Security*, 2(1): 36–49.

Wachholz, S. 2007. '"At risk": Climate change and its bearing on women's vulnerability to male violence,' in P. Beirne and N. South (eds.) *Issues in Green Criminology: Confronting Harms against Envirionments, Humanity and other Animals*, pp. 161–185. Cullompton, Devon, UK: Willan.

Warchol, G. L., Linda L. Z. and Clack, W. 2003. 'Transnational criminality: An analysis of the illegal wildlife market in Southern Africa,' *International Criminal Justice Review*, 13(1): 1–26.

Weston, M. K. and Memon, M. A. 2009. 'The illegal parrot trade in latin america and its consequences to parrot nutrition, health and conservation,' *Bird Populations*, 9: 76–83, Available at: www.birdpop.org/docs/journals/Volume-9/BPJ09-10_Weston_and_Memon.pdfandwww.birdpop.org/docs/journals/Volume-9/BPJ09-10_Weston_and_Memon.pdf.

White, R. 2008. *Crimes Against Nature: Environmental Criminology and Ecological Justice*. Collumpton, Devon, UK: Willan.

Wilson-Wilde, L. 2010. 'Wildlife crime: A global problem,' *Forensic Science, Medicine and Pathology*, 6(3): 221–222.

Wyatt, T. 2009. 'Exploring the organization of Russia Far East's Illegal wildlife trade: Two case studies of the illegal fur and illegal falcon trades,' *Global Crime*, 10(1–2): 144–154.

Wyatt, T. 2011. 'The illegal raptor trade in the Russian Federation,' *Contemporary Justice Review*, 14(2): 103–123.

Wyatt, T. 2013. 'Uncovering the significance of and motivation for wildlife trafficking,' in N. South and A. Brisman (eds.) *Routledge International Handbook of Green Criminology*, pp. 303–316. Abingdon, Oxon, UK: Routledge.

Wyatt, T. 2015. 'Mapping the links between conflict and illegal logging,' in A. Brisman, N. South and R. White (eds.) *Environmental Crime and Social Conflict: Contemporary and Emerging Issues*, pp. 41–56. Surrey, UK: Ashgate.

Zimmerman, M. E. 2003. 'The black market for wildlife: Combating transnational organized crime in the illegal wildlife trade,' *Vanderbilt Journal of Transnational Law*, 36(5): 1657–1689.

30

Wildlife trafficking and criminogenic asymmetries in a globalised world

Daan van Uhm

Introduction

In the twentieth century, with advancements in technology and transportation, wildlife trafficking developed into a professional global enterprise. Indeed, with technological innovation as a result of the Industrial Revolution, people succeeded in transporting large numbers of exotic animals from the Global South to the Global North from as far away as Antarctica, New Zealand and South Africa (Broad et al. 2003; Simons 2012). Strengthened colonial relationships and overall growth in post-WW II economies helped ensure expanding markets for wildlife and wildlife products (Collard 2013). Consequently, large flows of endangered species became important to the global economy and were traded as commodities for a wide range of purposes (e.g., for food; for use as/in medicines; as pets) (van Uhm 2018a). This was the beginning of the specialist animal trade, as we know it today in the twenty-first century, in which commercial and specialist traders foresaw the increasing demand for exotic species.

Gradually, the trade in exotic animals has evolved as a trend-sensitive market that responds to consumer demand (Kalof 2007; Ryhiner and Mannix 1958).[1] The transformation of the world order through globalisation—through the multiplication and intensification of linkages and interconnectedness—has not only facilitated the massive boom in the demand for exotic animals, but has also had a devastating effect on species' populations and ecosystems (Collard 2013). The international demand for ivory, for example, has led to the extinction of elephant populations in many parts of Africa (Blanc et al. 2003), while three out of the nine tiger species have disappeared in Asia due to human activities in the twentieth century (Abbott and van Kooten 2011). While the value of wildlife is socially constructed by scarcity and social meanings (van Uhm 2018a), the market dynamics for these products depend on global anomie and criminogenic asymmetries. According to Passas (1999), criminogenic asymmetries mean that structural discrepancies and inequalities in a globalised world provide new opportunities for crime. This chapter shows how *criminogenic asymmetries* in the realms of ecology, economy, law, politics and power have enabled large flows of the illegal wildlife trade to flourish.

Worldwide wildlife flows and crimes of the powerful

Traditionally, conditions such as poverty and unemployment appear to be important incentives for poaching in the source countries (Duffy 2010; Martin and Martin 2006; Nurse 2015; van Uhm 2016a). According to Mainka and Trivedi (2002), on a global basis, rural poverty and the exploitation of resources are often closely connected. Research conducted by wildlife experts, who have examined the economic and social driving forces of the trade in wildlife, have concluded that most poachers originate from the poorest one-third of all households. Middle- and upper-income groups are involved far less in the harvesting of wildlife (e.g. World Bank 2008). This section will reflect upon the illegal wildlife trade in the context of the dynamic of inequalities between the Global North and Global South, partly based on previous research on confiscations of illegal wildlife.

Willingness to engage in poaching often originates as a result of the impacts of economic inequalities and, subsequently, frustration and strain experienced by the affected communities. While local people are often involved in harvesting illegal wildlife, they usually work for 'outsiders' (e.g., Milliken and Shaw 2012; Nooren and Claridge 2001; Pantel and Chin 2009; Raymakers 2002). Such outsiders are able to capitalise on the poor socio-economic conditions in the source countries to recruit potential poachers to meet the demand from developed countries (e.g., Duffy 2010; Roe et al. 2002).

Several studies have identified relatively poor African and Asian countries as the main countries of origin for illegal wildlife (van Uhm et al. 2019; Lawson and Vines 2014; Rosen and Smith 2010; UNODC 2010; World Bank 2008). Data from more than 20,000 seizures (N = 22,204) in the European Union (E.U.) between 2001 and 2010 reveal a marked concentration of seizures of illegal wildlife emanating from African and Asian countries (van Uhm 2016b).[2] An exception is the illegal trade in reptile products from the United States (U.S.). North African countries seem to play an important role in the trade in live animals, such as reptiles and monkeys, to the E.U., partly because of geographical advantages: the Strait of Gibraltar, for example, offers the possibility of a quick border crossing. China, Thailand and Vietnam are major exporters of illegal (animal parts for) traditional Asian medicine and reptile products, while caviar is mostly smuggled from Russia to the E.U. (Figures 30.1 and 30.2).

Wildlife confiscations (N = 40,113) in the U.S. between 2003 and 2012 demonstrate the significant role of Southeast Asian countries.[3] Besides the neighbouring countries that play the most important role in the illegal wildlife trade heading to the U.S., more than 20 per cent of the seizures were from Southeast Asia. The data show that 52 per cent of the seizures were from six countries alone, which included the U.S.' neighbouring countries, Canada and Mexico and the Southeast Asian countries, China, Indonesia, Thailand and the Philippines (Petrossian et al. 2016). A disproportionate share of the U.S. reptile seizures, for example, were from the Asian countries of China, Indonesia and Thailand, while relatively high numbers of seizures of traditional Asian medicines made from parts of endangered mammals that took place in the U.S. were from China and Vietnam (Figure 30.2).

Whereas the data and figures noted in the previous paragraph reflect the role of African and Southeast Asian countries as sources, traditionally the demand market for the illegal trade has been in wealthy countries in the Global North (Sollund and Maher 2015; Wyatt 2013). Similar patterns of exploitative trade from the Global South to the Global North have been identified where powerful Northern countries overexploit poor Southern countries and profit from their resources (e.g., Bavinck et al. 2014; Passas and Goodwin 2005). These 'crimes of the powerful', which often encompass a combination of criminal, illegal, legal and unethical practices, are not always defined

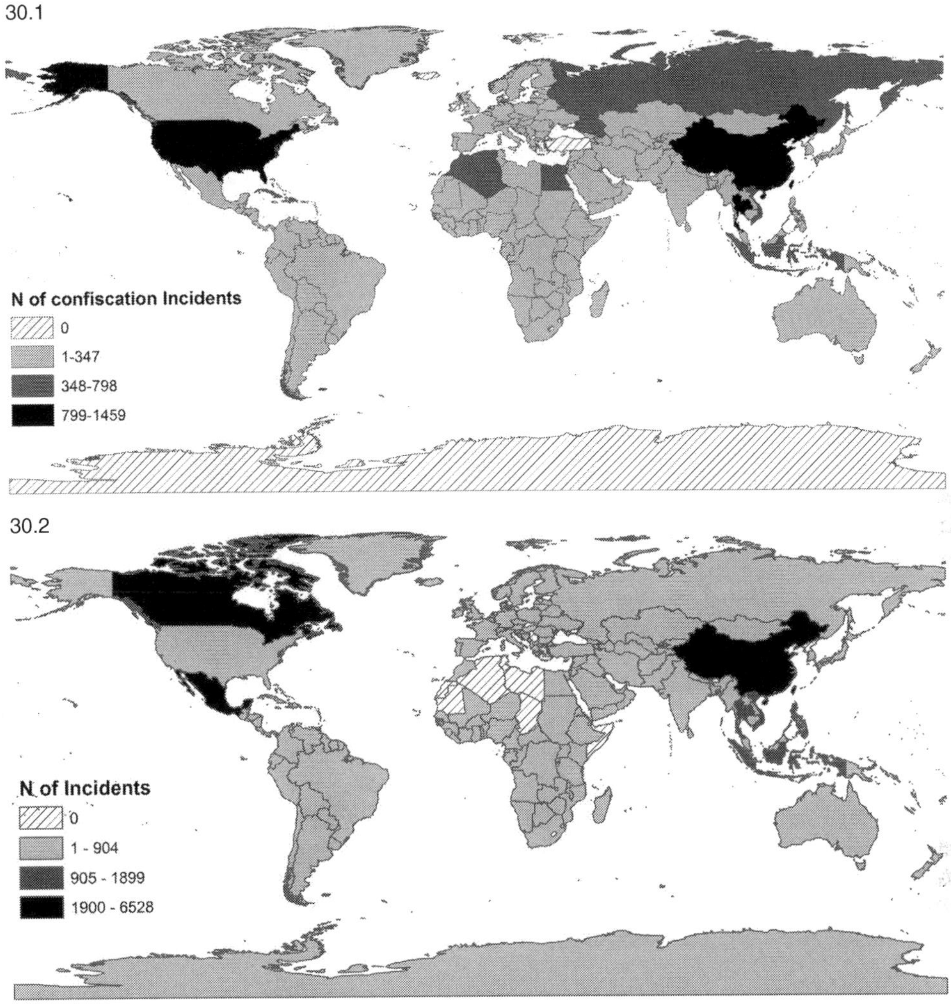

Figures 30.1 and 30.2 Source countries for illegal wildlife based on confiscations; EU confiscations between 2001–2010 (30.1), US confiscations between 2003–2012 (30.2).

Sources: van Uhm (2016b) (30.1); Petrossian et al. (2016) (30.2).

as criminal offences (e.g., Friedrichs 1996; Friedrichs and Rothe 2011). This allows processes of 'accumulation by dispossession' to perpetuate, whereby the Global South is stripped of its commons, while the Global North profits, illustrating the power dynamics and discrepancies in and of a globalised world (Harvey 2003). At the same time, international law enforcement endeavours focus primarily on the countries of origin, instead of the Northern countries—including Europe and the U.S.—which are the most important importing regions (e.g., Engler and Parry-Jones 2007). While each market is distinct, one can summarise the illegal trade of flora and fauna as follows: the illegal trade is driven by the demand from the rich North (Passas 2000), while the accusing finger points at the countries of origin (Boekhout van Solinge 2010).

Global anomie and misconduct

Global anomie has emerged as a result of growing inequalities between poor countries of the Global South and powerful industrialised countries of the Global North, creating a fertile breeding ground for crime (Friedrichs 1996; Passas 2000).[4] In the context of global communication and improved trade lines, entrepreneurs abuse economic and power inequalities in illegal ways; indeed, both organised crime syndicates and powerful corporations overexploit natural resources and leave the damage behind (Lynch and Stretesky 2014; Lynch and Stretsky 2003; Passas and Goodwin 2005). Contrary to growing conventional wisdom and efficient market ideologies that promise global economic growth, globalisation also contributes to dysnomie, misconduct and criminogenic asymmetries (Passas 1999). These criminogenic asymmetries—structural discrepancies, inequalities and mismatches within the realms of economy, law, politics and power that provide new opportunities for crimes—create conditions ripe for global defaunation.[5]

According to Passas (2000), criminogenic asymmetries can cause crime by fuelling the demand for illegal goods and services, generating incentives for people and organisations to engage in illegal practices, and reducing the ability of authorities to control crime. Passas (2000) refers to regulatory discrepancies, along with economic and political asymmetries, that have given rise to a variety of environmental crimes. For instance, developing nations frequently do not regulate environmental degradation or do so much less rigorously than industrial states, which provides opportunities for companies from rich countries to benefit in those areas where rules are lax or non-existent (Bisschop 2015; van Uhm 2016a).

Moreover, asymmetries are multiplied, intensified and their criminogenic potential is activated during globalisation. As Giddens (1991) explains, the process of 'disembedding' social relations enables people to leave their local contexts and reconstitute across space and time. Essentially, the world becomes smaller with technological advances and the dismantling of trade barriers, both of which facilitate the development of new criminal alliances (Aas 2007; Miklaucic and Brewer 2013). In this way, asymmetries contribute in complex ways to the absence of adequate controls and provide opportunities for crime. To understand the criminogenic asymmetries providing opportunities for illegal wildlife trafficking, three case studies will be discussed.

Case study 1 (traditional Chinese medicine): (a) crime to cure

The first case study involves the illegal trade in Traditional Chinese Medicine (TCM). TCM, which involves animal and plant products, has existed for thousands of years and is deeply rooted in Chinese society. In the context of globalisation, the trade in TCM has increased significantly—in particular in the second half of the twentieth century and the beginning of the twenty-first century—as China has slowly developed a more open market economy (Goodman 1998). The combination of decentralisation, privatisation and open borders has created new opportunities for both legal and illegal entrepreneurs. The recent plans to improve the Silk Road, the ancient trade route that ran between China and the West during the days of the Roman Empire, is believed to start a new era of globalisation by reopening channels between China and its neighbours in the West (van Uhm 2019).

Simultaneously, the increasing economic prosperity in China has allowed more people to afford traditional Chinese medicines made from endangered wildlife products (e.g., van Uhm and Wong 2019; Von Moltke and Spaninks 2000). Indeed, as a result of a sharp decrease in inflation between 1995 and 1999 in China, a rapidly expanding middle class emerged with the ability to purchase expensive TCM containing endangered species (Nooren and Claridge 2001: 41; Zhang et al. 2008). Besides the purported curing effects, medicine derived from endangered species also came to be seen as a cultural symbol of status and pride (Swan and Conrad 2014). The use of endangered species in TCM has, however, resulted in the criminalisation of possession and use of protected animal parts,[6] and, after more than 1,500 years, animal parts, such as rhino horn and tiger bone, have become prohibited from use in TCM (Mainka and Mills 1995; Martin and Martin 1982).

Unfortunately, the combination of scarcity and criminalisation forced prices on the black market to reach new heights; for example, the same quantity of rhino horn is nowadays valued at more than gold and cocaine (van Uhm 2012).[7] An international wildlife trafficking syndicate that hired Thai prostitutes from clubs in South Africa to pose as 'hunters' in sham rhino trophy hunts on their rhino farm illustrates how legitimate players have misused permits issued for hunting white rhinos (Rademeyer 2012).[8] Moreover, 'rhino wars' are now being waged with organised criminal groups using helicopters, night vision equipment, rifle silencers and tranquilisers to capture their prey, while, at the same time, members of such groups carry automatic weapons to threaten (and, if necessary, kill) park rangers in order to gain profits from those endangered species (van Uhm 2016a).

Case study 2 (pets): monkey business

The second case study concerns another driver of the wildlife trade: the social phenomenon of keeping animals as pets (Sollund 2019; van Uhm 2018a). Historically, the keeping of exotic pets has been associated with the upper-classes of society (Herzog 2014; Kisling 2001). Post-WW II economic growth in Europe, however, led to a high demand for exotic animals as pets (as a representation of status and prosperity) (Kalof 2007; van Uhm 2015). Indeed, the increased demand by the middle classes for exotic animals resulted in a lucrative global market for illegal endangered species. While in the past, famous examples in the illegal trade in wildlife included Great Apes (e.g., chimpanzees; orangutans), the most seized endangered mammal in Europe nowadays consists of a lesser-known monkey species—the Barbary macaque—found in the Atlas Mountains of Algeria and Morocco (van Uhm 2016c). This species is threatened, with an estimated remaining wild population of only several thousand individuals (Majolo et al. 2013).

The large-scale illegal trade began in the 1990s when Barbary macaques were obtained legitimately from the wild for biomedical research. Sometimes hunters misused the obligatory certificates to catch additional macaques for the retail trade: for example, ten monkeys might be captured when only one was needed for biomedical research, enabling the hunter to sell the remaining monkeys illegally (van Uhm 2016c). Currently, capturing Barbary macaques for biomedical research is no longer legal because the species is excluded from the list of biomedical research primate species (van Lavieren 2004), which reflects the controversies about using monkeys for biomedical research (see also Maldonado and Lafon 2017). Today's poachers usually consist of relatively poor local people from Berber villages in the Azrou area of Morocco; they target young monkeys because they become better accustomed to people than older ones and are easier to smuggle in suitcases or bags. In order to keep the macaque quiet and to decrease its stress levels, the monkeys are drugged with a sleeping aid for children. Hundreds of baby monkeys are estimated to be smuggled from Morocco each year to fuel the pet industry in the European Union (van Uhm 2016c).

The criminalisation of the trade in Barbary macaques has had a clear influence on the (criminal) organisation of the actors involved. Traditionally, the monkeys were sold openly at the *souks* (Moroccan informal markets); today, legitimate animal shops order the monkeys secretly on demand from Western entrepreneurial criminal groups. The deterrence of imprisonment has also ensured that the illegal activities have become more sophisticated in order to evade law enforcement. For instance, semi-structured networks transfer the wildlife through the Strait of Gibraltar with the assistance of corrupt officials, truck drivers and professional local smugglers to avoid being uncovered (van Uhm 2016c).

Case study 3 (food): black caviar

The last case study shows that wildlife is also traded as luxury food. The demand for caviar has a long and rich history, from the food of the poor to a delicacy for the Tsars and upper classes in Europe. Historically, the symbolic value of caviar—unfertilised sturgeon roe—has been determined in the context of changing environmental, political and social circumstances. With the dissolution of the Soviet Union in the 1990s, many individuals in the Republic of Dagestan, who were already poor, became unemployed and resorted to poaching (Birstein et al. 1997; Shadrina 2007). Sturgeon—one of the oldest families of fish—have now become the most endangered group of animals on the Red List of endangered species[9] (IUCN 2010; Musing et al. 2019).

The low standard of living conditions in poaching towns in Dagestan makes the business attractive not only for organised crime, but also for fishery inspectors, senior government officials and even law enforcement—they all have a stake in the business. Militias from the republic sometimes even protect the poachers during conflicts with the federal authorities, using 'security vessels' to escort the poachers and to distract the police (van Uhm and Siegel 2016). Every illegal boat trip supposedly costs around $800–1,500 USD in bribes to officials in Dagestan (Nellemann et al. 2014). The use of violence and counterstrategies is not uncommon in the caviar business, as is illustrated by numerous threats of violence and reports of gunfights between fishery inspectors, border guards and poachers (Knapp et al. 2006; Lagutov 2007; van Uhm and Siegel 2016).

Today, the 'caviar mafia', as it might be called, is also embedded in legal businesses, whereby the infrastructure of farms and legitimate companies are used to launder illegal caviar. In the post-Soviet period, several official directors of the current fish farms in Russia have been the alleged 'big fish' in the illegal trade in caviar (van Uhm and Siegel 2016). They have invested their illegally obtained money in real estate (Volkov 2002), such as sturgeon farms to produce caviar. Some of these companies still buy illegal caviar from poachers in remote villages near the Caspian Sea in order to sell it as being produced by captive-bred sturgeon. There are even examples where sturgeon are caught illegally under the pretence of scientific purposes, demonstrating the extremes to which some are willing to go to perpetuate their illegal activities (van Uhm and Siegel 2016).[10]

Criminogenic asymmetries and crimes against nature

The three case studies illustrate that in the context of global anomie and criminogenic asymmetries, structural discrepancies between the source and destination countries provide opportunities for crimes against nature. In this scenario, legal and illegal entrepreneurs from Northern countries exploit poverty and inequality to lure people into criminal activity, from poor farmers in Southeast Asia who hunt opportunistically for endangered species for TCM, to Berber communities in Morocco who poach monkeys for the pet industry, to poor fishermen in Dagestan who catch sturgeon for caviar. The poachers are supplied with loans, expensive equipment and weapons in order to conduct their activities for criminal organisations and corporations (van Uhm 2016a). Increased economic prosperity in the destination countries has also made it possible to afford growing numbers of luxury wildlife products (e.g., van Uhm 2016b; Von Moltke and Spaninks 2000). In other words, the economic asymmetries between relatively wealthy and relatively poor countries ensure a fertile breeding ground for criminal organisations to exploit both the natural resources and the local communities. The socio-economic discrepancy between such wealthy consumers and such poor poachers is perhaps best illustrated by the illegal trade in caviar. While poor fishermen poach sturgeon in the Caspian Sea and risk their lives to feed their families, upper-class society nevertheless consumes the illegally obtained black caviar without knowledge or consideration of the environmental and social impacts (van Uhm and Siegel 2016).

In addition, political changes, such as the dissolution of the Soviet Union, have provided new opportunities for crime (Passas 1999; Shelley 1995). In the early 1990s, the existing regulatory systems collapsed and informal criminal systems were developed to replace the formal state services in Russia (Dinerstein et al. 1994). According to Varese (1997: 580), the end of socialism resulted in a high amount of corruption and 'Mafia-style crime'. Illegal activities, such as the illegal drug and wildlife trades, emerged. Consequently, wildlife populations suffered overexploitation by those criminal networks. The emergence of organised crime, in combination with levels of corruption, caused a lucrative illegal trade in products, such as caviar and saiga antelope horns, to fuel the global demand markets (e.g., Birstein et al. 1997; Kühl et al. 2009; van Uhm 2016a).

Another example is the 'liberation' of the Chinese market that provided new opportunities for both legal and illegal entrepreneurs. The Chinese economy has transformed slowly into a more open market. With new middle 'capital-owning' classes in China enlarging the demand for all kinds of goods and services, there has been a growth in legal and illegal businesses (Goodman 1998). The illegal wildlife industry is no exception (Nooren and Claridge 2001; Zhang et al. 2008).

The implementation of laws and regulations also created criminal opportunities for all three case studies in the context of legal or 'law-related' asymmetries. Although the use of rhino horn and tiger bone in TCM has a long and widespread history, these products became prohibited under Chinese national law in 1993. In order to supply the demand for endangered species used in TCM, illegal businesses emerged. There are several examples in which 'traditional' criminal organisations diversified or transformed completely to direct their activities into the illegal trade in rhino horn (e.g., Christy 2014; Europol 2011; van Uhm 2016a). Criminalising the poaching of Barbary macaques with harsh custodial sentences has ensured another dynamic in which criminal groups have become more sophisticated in order to evade law enforcement (van Uhm 2016c).[11] After the political transformation of the Soviet Union, when the large-scale poaching of sturgeon without restriction became commonplace, the trade in caviar became restricted by the Convention on International Trade in Endangered Species of Wild Fauna and Flora (CITES)—the international treaty that regulates the trade in wild animal and plant species or products thereof through permits (see Sollund, this volume, Chapter 29).[12] Subsequently, all Caspian countries (the coastline of the Caspian Sea is shared by Azerbaijan, Iran, Kazakhstan, Russia and Turkmenistan) joined a ban on fishing sturgeon in the entire Caspian Sea (Nellemann et al. 2014; Raymakers 2006), while Russian criminal groups became increasingly involved in the context of these legal or 'law-related' asymmetries (van Uhm and Siegel 2016).

The historically dominant position of countries of the Global North with respect to wildlife conservation issues illustrates the influence of power asymmetries. Many regulations and the first game reserves were developed to protect Western interests and to introduce the moral values of Western elites. This resulted in disadvantages for the local people with regard to their access to and use of natural resources, as well as social differentiation with settler communities (Grove 1995; MacKenzie 1988). Several authors see this development as a continuation of the colonial 'white man's burden' approach[13] to conservation in a post-colonial world (e.g., Dickson 2003). Duffy (2010) clarifies that instead of centring on the creation and continuation of wildlife demand markets by the wealthy world, the focus has shifted to coercion and enforcement in the world's poorest communities. Conservation and enforcement efforts are embedded largely in identifying problems in the source countries and, consequently, this has produced exclusion, marginalisation and violence towards the local communities. Focussing on poaching in the local communities neglects the actual problem—the demand for wildlife (van Uhm 2016a). From this perspective, the traditional power asymmetries between wealthy powerful countries and relatively poor developing countries are still being used to distract attention from responsibility for the illegal *demand* for wildlife.

The processes of globalisation also intensify the intertwined relationship between the 'overworld' or 'upperworld' and 'underworld'. The economic, legal and political asymmetries between countries have given rise to illicit markets for the uncontrolled exploitation of natural resources by corporations (Brisman and South 2017; Passas 2000). Legitimate companies that exploit local people in their search for illegal wildlife illustrate the overlaps with economically and politically powerful actors involved in the plundering of natural resources (Carrabine et al. 2004; Lyons and Natusch 2011). Furthermore, powerful legal enterprises misuse structural weaknesses in existing regulations in source countries (see, e.g., Ruggiero and South 2010, 2013). This means that both antithetical relationships and symbiotic relationships between legal and illegal actors facilitate wildlife trafficking. For instance, competition between legal and illegal actors is present when legally registered wildlife companies offer illegal wildlife products for less money than their competitors. Symbiotic relationships occur when interests are shared and enhance mutual benefits between the 'underworld' and the 'overworld' or 'upperworld' (e.g., cooperation between police and caviar poachers) (van Uhm and Moreto 2018). Clearly, companies that are legally registered use their legal infrastructures to hide, launder, or trade in illegal wildlife (e.g., Knapp et al. 2006; Li et al. 2007; Nijman and Shepherd 2009; Lyons and Natusch 2011; Pantel and Chin 2009; van Uhm 2018b; Vinke and Vinke 2010).

Finally, the concept of *ecological asymmetries* may help our understanding of the way in which new opportunities for crimes emerge. Paradoxically, the presence of many natural resources appears to be detrimental to a country's development (Kolstad and Søreide 2009). Those countries that are rich in biodiversity often experience lower economic growth rates, lower levels of human development and more inequality and poverty—the so-called 'resource curse' (Kolstad and Søreide 2009: 214; Sachs and Warner 2001). The presence of abundant natural resources also seems to correlate with crime and violence (Boekhout van Solinge 2014: 501, this volume, Chapter 15). Brisman and South (2013: 57) show that 'the damaging and divisive exploitation of environmental wealth in forms such as illegal trades in diamonds, timber, and wildlife ...[has] ... generated funds that have supported and perpetuated internal conflicts, corruption, and the externalising of economic surplus'. Defaunation in the Anthropocene[14] may even lead to both ecological disorganisation and trophic cascades (Courchamp et al. 2006; Lynch and Stretesky 2014; Power 1990; Wilson 1993). Not only is defaunation harmful for ecosystems and their species, but it also ensures that the economic and social value of the land decreases. Almost 30 years ago, Beck (1992: 38) observed that '[p]roperty is being devalued, it is undergoing a creeping ecological expropriation'. This reflects the process of the accumulation of dispossession that has obvious repercussions for local people, ecosystems and their species (Harvey 2003; Hornborg 1998). Moreover, the ecological asymmetries where the destruction of nature leads to the increasing scarcity of endangered species (e.g., rhinoceros, sturgeon, tigers) have proved to create rising values on the black market that attract transnational criminal groups worldwide.

Conclusion

This chapter shows that the destruction of nature has become a feature of an increasingly globalised world. Structural discrepancies between wealthy consumer countries and relatively poor countries with rich biodiversity density activate several criminogenic asymmetries, resulting in the plundering of natural resources. Wildlife traffickers exploit poverty and inequality to entice people to poach in territories without government presence. In addition, they benefit from legal loopholes and political apathy to facilitate and professionalise their illegal wildlife trafficking. Crimes by powerful legal enterprises that misuse structural weaknesses in laws and regulations in the source regions illustrate the intensified symbiotic relationship between the underworld and the 'overworld' or 'upperworld' in times of globalisation. Furthermore, crime groups thrive particularly well in such socio-economically and politically weak regions with a high level of biodiversity where the government is unable to effectively apply the monopoly of violence. For instance—and as discussed above—the struggle for political and economic power in the Republic of Dagestan in the North Caucasus region of Russia has created a cover for the poaching of sturgeon, while Berber monkeys are smuggled through the Rif Mountains in northern Morocco, traditionally known as a 'smuggling paradise' due to political instability and poverty. All the while, endangered animals used in Chinese medicine are transported through the Golden Triangle in Southeast Asia—one of the most underdeveloped areas in the region. It comes as no surprise, then, that in such areas other forms of crime also occur.[15] Thus, the socio-economic and geopolitical backgrounds of these biodiverse regions clearly provide fertile breeding grounds for criminal networks driven by criminogenic asymmetries in a changing world.

Notes

1 In post-WW II Western countries, middle- and upper-class individuals and families began to keep and collect a wide range of exotic animals. Various department stores in Europe offered monkeys, lions and even elephants for sale, while luxury coats made from the skins from big cats or bears emerged as symbols of wealth and status (van Uhm 2018a).

2 To obtain an overview of the illegal trade to the E.U., data on confiscations in the E.U. were obtained from the European Union Trade in Wildlife Information eXchange database (EU-TWIX)—a database of information on wildlife seizures in the E.U. (van Uhm 2016b).

3 In the U.S., confiscated wildlife is recorded in the Law Enforcement Management Information System (LEMIS) database. The LEMIS dataset was obtained through the Freedom of Information Act (FOIA) request made on 23 September 2013 to the USFWS—LEMIS division (Petrossian et al. 2016).

4 As Passas (2000: 27) explains, in societies that do not encourage high social mobility, there are disjunctions between socially induced goals and the legal means of achieving them: 'In such societies, people may not feel that they are lacking anything, even when they are "objectively" deprived'; with globalization and neoliberalism, needs and normative models have become more 'harmonized' and 'people become conscious of economic and power asymmetries, and directly experience their impact'. Thus, processes of globalisation and neoliberalism (and global neoliberalism) have brought about 'relative deprivation as well as absolute immiseration of masses of people'. This has both generated new sources of criminogenesis and removed existing antidotes to it.

5 Defaunation is the equivalent of deforestation and the term is used to refer to the loss of species, populations and local declines in the abundance of individual wildlife (van Uhm 2017).
6 In China, the population of wild tigers decreased from 4,000 in 1949 to approximately 40–50 in 2012; meanwhile, the tigers in China's farms increased from roughly 8–13 in 1986 to 6,000 in 2010 (EIA 2013). In the 1980s, the Chinese government established tiger farms for the commercial supply of tiger bone for TCM (Nowell 2000). Since 1993, the sale has become officially banned by Article 22 of the Law of the People's Republic of China on the Protection of Wildlife. Dubious certificates are still provided by officials to sell tiger bone products through these farms, however (van Uhm 2019).
7 According to Traffic (2011), rhino poaching peaked after claims that rhino horn powder cures cancer.
8 In another instance of exploitation, the Polokwane (South Africa) game farmer Dawie Groenewald claimed to have kept rhinos for conservation purposes for years, when, in actuality, he engaged in an elaborate scheme of dehorning and killing of rhinos to make profits from the sale of their horns (Ayling 2013; Hübschle 2016). He was out on bail in the 'Groenewald case' when he was re-arrested after being caught in the illegal possession of 11 rhino horns.
9 The International Union for Conservation of Nature's Red List of Threatened Species is the world's most comprehensive inventory of the global conservation status of biological species.
10 Statistical data covering several years after the ban demonstrate that 600 t of caviar from sturgeon were fished out of the Caspian Sea for 'scientific purposes' (Zabyelina 2014).
11 In 2016, the commercial trade in Barbary macaques became prohibited completely by CITES.
12 Appendix I includes species threatened with extinction. Trade in Appendix I specimens is permitted only in exceptional circumstances. Appendix II includes species not necessarily threatened with extinction, but controlled in order to avoid utilization incompatible with their survival. Appendix III are protected in at least one country, which has asked other CITES parties for assistance in controlling the trade.
13 The 'white man's burden' approach refers to the supposed or presumed responsibility of white people to govern and impart their culture to non-white people, often advanced as a justification for European colonialism.
14 Anthropocene refers to a proposed new geological era characterized by the unprecedented impact of human activities on the Earth (see, for a discussion, Brisman and South 2018; Phelan et al. this volume, Chapter 25).
15 For example, the North Caucasus region is home to much trafficking of drugs, people and weapons (e.g., Arasli 2007); the Rif Mountains are known as a key area in Europe for the smuggling of hashish and immigrants (e.g., Lehtinen 2008; Soddu 2006); and the Golden Triangle is notorious for the booming opium and timber trade (e.g., Felbab-Brown 2011; Zhang and Chin 2011).

References

Aas, K. F. 2007. *Crime and Globalization*. London: Sage.

Abbott, B. and Van Kooten, G. C. 2011. 'Can domestication of wildlife lead to conservation? The economics of tiger farming in China,' *Ecological Economics*, 70(4): 721–728.

Arasli, J. 2007. 'The rising wind: Is the caucasus emerging as a hub for terrorism, smuggling, and trafficking?' *The Quarterly Journal*, 6(1): 5–26.

Ayling, J. 2013. 'What sustains wildlife crime? Rhino horn trading and the resilience of criminal networks,' *Journal of International Wildlife Law & Policy*, 16(1): 57–80.

Bavinck, M., Pellegrini, L. and Mostert, E. (eds.) 2014. *Conflicts over Natural Resources in the Global South*. London: CRS Press.

Beck, U. 1992. *Risk Society: Towards a New Modernity*. London: Sage.

Birstein, V. J., Bemis, W. E. and Waldman, J. R. 1997. 'The threatened status of acipenseriform species: A summary,' in V. J. Birstein, W. E. Bemis and J. R. Waldman (eds.) *Sturgeon Biodiversity and Conservation*, pp. 427–435. Dordrecht: Springer Netherlands.

Bisschop, L. 2015. *Governance of the Illegal Trade in E-waste and Tropical Timber: Case Studies on Transnational Environmental Crime*. Surrey, UK: Ashgate Publishing.

Blanc, J. J., Thouless, C. R., Hart, J. A., Dublin, H. T., Douglas-Hamilton, I., Craig, C. G. and Barnes, R. F. W. 2003. *African Elephant Status Report 2002: An Update from the African Elephant Database*. Gland: IUCN/SSC African Elephant Specialist Group.

Boekhout van Solinge, T. 2010. 'Deforestation crimes and conflicts in the Amazon,' *Critical Criminology: An International Journal*, 18(4): 263–277.

Boekhout van Solinge, T. 2014. 'The illegal exploitation of natural resources,' in L. Paoli (ed.) *The Oxford Handbook of Organized Crime*. Oxford: Oxford University Press.

Brisman, A. and South, N. 2013. 'Resource wealth, power, crime, and conflict,' in R. Walters, D. S. Westerhuis and T. Wyatt (eds.) *Emerging Issues in Green Criminology: Exploring Power, Justice and Harm*, pp. 57–71. Basingstoke, Hampshire, UK: Palgrave Macmillan.

Brisman, A. and South, N. 2018. 'Autosarcophagy in the anthropocene and the obscenity of an epoch,' in C. Holley and C. Shearing (eds.) *Criminology and the Anthropocene*, pp. 25–49. London and New York: Routledge.

Broad, S., Mulliken, T. and Roe, D. 2003. 'The nature and extent of legal and illegal trade in wildlife,' in S. Oldfield (ed.) *The Trade in Wildlife, Regulation for Conservation*, pp. 3–22. London: Earthscan.

Carrabine, E., Cox, P., Lee, M., South, N., Plummer, K. and Turton, J. 2004. *Criminology: A Sociological Introduction*. London: Routledge.

Christy, B. 2014. *Convicted Drug Dealer Indicted for Selling Rhino Horns. Undercover Investigation Nets Alleged Wildlife Trafficker with Ties to Former Medellín Drug Cartel*. Washington, DC: National Geographic. April 17, 2014.

Collard, R. C. M. S. 2013. *Animal Traffic: Making, Remaking and Unmaking Commodities in Global Live Wildlife Trade*. Vancouver: University of British Columbia.

Courchamp, F., Angulo, E., Rivalan, P., Hall, R. J., Signoret, L., Bull, L. and Meinard, Y. 2006. 'Rarity value and species extinction: The anthropogenic allee effect,' *PLoS biology*, 4(12): e415.

Dickson, B. 2003. 'What is the goal of regulating wildlife trade? Is regulation a good way to achieve this goal?' in S. Oldfiels (ed.) *The Trade in Wildlife. Regulation for Conservation*, pp. 23–32. London: Earthscan Publications.

Dinerstein, E., Krever, V., Olson, D. M. and Williams, L. 1994. 'An emergency strategy to rescue Russia's biological diversity,' *Conservation Biology*, 8(4): 934–939.

Duffy, R. 2010. *Nature Crime: How We're Getting Conservation Wrong*. New Haven, CT: Yale University Press.

EIA. 2013. *Hidden in Plain Sight: China's Clandestine Tiger Trade*. London: EIA.

Engler, M. and Parry-Jones, R. 2007. *Opportunity or Threat: The Role of the European Union in Global Wildlife Trade*. Brussels: Traffic Europe.

Europol. 2011. *Organised Crime Threat Assessment (OCTA)*. The Hague: Europol.

Felbab-Brown, V. 2011. *The Disappearing Act: The Illicit Trade in Wildlife in Asia*. Washington, DC: The Brookings Institution.

Friedrichs, D. 1996. *Trusted Criminals: White Collar Crime in Contemporary Society*. Belmont, CA: Wadsworth, Cengage Learning.

Friedrichs, D. O. and Rothe, D. L. 2011. *Crimes of the Powerful. Routledge Handbook of Critical Criminology*. London: Routledge.

Giddens, A. 1991. *Modernity and Self-Identity: Self and Society in the Late Modern Age*. Stanford: Stanford University Press.

Goodman, D. S. 1998. 'In search of China's new middle classes: The creation of wealth and diversity in Shanxi during the 1990s,' *Asian Studies Review*, 22(1): 39–62.

Grove, R. 1995. *Green Imperialism*. Cambridge: Cambridge University Press.

Harvey, D. 2003. *The New Imperialism*. Oxford: Oxford University Press.

Herzog, H. A. 2014. 'Biology, culture, and the origins of pet-keeping,' *Animal Behavior and Cognition*, 1(3): 296–308.

Hornborg, A. 1998. 'Towards an ecological theory of unequal exchange: Articulating world system theory and ecological economics,' *Ecological Economics*, 25(1): 127–136.

Hübschle, A. M. 2016. *A game of Horns: Transnational Flows of Rhino Horn*. Köln: Universität zu Köln.

IUCN. 2010. *Sturgeon More Critically Endangered than any Other Group of Species*. Gland: IUCN.

Kalof, L. 2007. *Looking at Animals in Human History*. London: Reaktion Books.

Kisling, V. N. 2001. *Zoo and Aquarium History: Ancient Animal Collections to Zoological Gardens*. Boca Raton, FL: CRC Press.

Knapp, A., Kitschke, C. and von Meibom, S. (eds.) 2006. *Proceedings of the International Sturgeon Enforcement Workshop to Combat Illegal Trade in Caviar. Prepared by TRAFFIC Europe for the European Commission*. Brussels: Traffic.

Kolstad, I. and Søreide, T. 2009. 'Corruption in natural resource management: Implications for policy makers,' *Resources Policy*, 34(4): 214–226.

Kühl, A., Balinova, N., Bykova, E., Arylov, Y. N., Esipov, A., Lushchekina, A. A. and Milner-Gulland, E. J. 2009. 'The role of Saiga poaching in rural communities: Linkages between attitudes, socio-economic circumstances and behavior,' *Biological Conservation*, 142(7): 1442–1449.

Lagutov, V. (ed.) 2007. *Rescue of Sturgeon Species in the Ural River Basin*. Dordrecht: Springer Science & Business Media.

Lawson, K. and Vines, A. 2014. *Global Impacts of the Illegal Wildlife Trade: The Costs of Crime, Insecurity and Institutional Erosion*. London: Chatham House.

Lehtinen, T. 2008. 'At the Gates of El Dorado,' in F. Söderbaum (ed.) *Afro-Regions: The Dynamics of Cross-Border Micro-Regionalism in Africa*, pp. 121–135. Villavägen: The Nordic Africa Institute.

Li, L., Zhao, Y. and Bennett, E. L. 2007. 'Report of a survey on Saiga horn in markets in China,' CoP14 Inf, 14.

Lynch, M. J. and Stretsky, P. B. 2003. 'The meaning of green: "Contrasting criminological perspectives",' *Theoretical Criminology*, 7(2): 217–238.

Lynch, M. J. and Stretesky, P. B. 2014. *Exploring Green Criminology: Toward a Green Criminological Revolution*. Surrey, UK: Ashgate Publishing.

Lyons, J. A. and Natusch, D. J. 2011. 'Wildlife laundering through breeding farms: Illegal harvest, population declines and a means of regulating the trade of green pythons (Morelia viridis) from Indonesia,' *Biological Conservation*, 144(12): 3073–3081.

MacKenzie, J. 1988. *The Empire of Nature*. Manchester: Manchester University Press.

Mainka, S. and Trivedi, M. 2002. *Links between Biodiversity Conservation, Livelihoods and Food Security: The Sustainable Use of Wild Species for Meat (No. 24)*. Gland: IUCN.

Mainka, S. A. and Mills, J. A. 1995. 'Wildlife and traditional Chinese medicine: Supply and demand for wildlife species,' *Journal of Zoo and Wildlife Medicine*, 26(2): 193–200.

Majolo, B., van Lavieren, E., Maréchal, L., MacLarnon, A., Marvin, G., Qarro, M. and Semple, S. 2013. 'Out of Asia: The singular case of the Barbary macaque,' in S. Radhakrishna, A. H. Michael and S. Anindya (eds.) *The Macaque Connection. Cooperation and conflict between Humans and Macaques*. New York: Springer.

Maldonado, Á. M. and Lafon, T. 2017. 'Biomedical research vs. biodiversity conservation in the Colombian-Peruvian Amazon: Searching for law enforcement where there is lack of accountability,' in D. R. Goyes, H. Mol, A. Brisman and N. South (eds.) *Environmental Crime in Latin America*, pp. 261–294. London: Palgrave Macmillan.

Martin, E. B. and Martin, C. 1982. *Run, Rhino, Run*. London: Hodder & Stoughton.

Martin, E. B. and Martin, C. 2006. 'Insurgency and poverty: Recipe for rhino poaching in Nepal,' *Pachyderm*, 41: 61–73.

Miklaucic, M. and Brewer, J. 2013. *Convergence: Illicit Networks and National Security in the Age of Globalization*. Washington, DC: Government Printing Office.

Milliken, T. and Shaw, J. 2012. *The South Africa-Viet Nam Rhino Horn Trade Nexus: A Deadly Combination of Institutional Lapses, Corrupt Wildlife Industry Professionals, and Asian Crime Syndicates*. Cambridge: Traffic.

Musing, L., Harris, L., Williams, A., Parry- Jones, R., van Uhm, D. and Wyatt, T. 2019. *Corruption and Wildlife Crime: A Focus on Caviar Trade*. A TRAFFIC, WWF, U4 ACRC. Oxford: Utrecht University and Northumbria University report.

Nellemann, C., Henriksen, R., Raxter, P., Ash, N. and Mrema, E. (eds.) 2014. *The Environmental Crime Crisis – Threats to Sustainable Development from Illegal Exploitation and Trade in Wildlife and Forest Resources*. A UNEP Rapid Response Assessment. Nairobi and Arendal: United Nations Environment Programme and GRIDArendal.

Nijman, V., Shepherd, C. R. and van Balen, S. 2009. 'Declaration of the Javan hawk eagle Spizaetus bartelsi as Indonesia's national rare animal impedes conservation of the species,' *Oryx*, 43(01): 122–128.

Nooren, H. and Claridge, G. 2001. *Wildlife Trade in Laos: The End of the Game*. Gland: IUCN-The World Conservation Union.

Nowell, K. 2000. *Far From a Cure: The Tiger Trade Revisited*. Cambridge, UK: Traffic International.

Nurse, A. 2015. *Policing Wildlife. Perspectives on the Enforcement of Wildlife Legislation*. Basingstoke, Hampshire, UK: Palgrave Macmillan.

Pantel, E. B. S. and Chin, S. 2009. *Proceedings of the Workshop on Trade and Conservation of Pangolins Native to South and Southeast Asia*. Singapore: Traffic.

Passas, N. 1999. 'Globalization, criminogenic asymmetries and economic crime,' *European Journal of Law Reform*, 1(4): 399–424.

Passas, N. 2000. 'Global anomie, dysnomie, and economic crime: Hidden consequences of neoliberalism and globalization in Russia and around the world,' *Social Justice*, 27(2): 16–44.

Passas, N. and Goodwin, N. 2005. *It's Legal But It Ain't Right: Harmful Social Consequence of Legal Industries*. Ann Arbor, MI: University of Michigan Press.

Petrossian, G. A., Pires, S. F. and Van Uhm, D. P. 2016. 'An overview of seized illegal wildlife entering the United States,' *Global Crime*, 17(2): 181–201.

Power, M. E. 1990. 'Effects of fish in river food webs,' *Science*, 250(4982): 811–814.

Rademeyer, J. 2012. *Killing for Profit: Exposing the Illegal Rhino Horn Trade*. Cape Town: Random House Struik.

Raymakers, C. 2002. *Study on the Social and Economic Aspects of Illegal Fishing in the Caspian Sea*. Brussels: Traffic Europe.

Raymakers, C. 2006. 'CITES, The convention on international trade in endangered species of wild fauna and flora: Its role in the conservation of acipenseriformes,' *Journal of Applied Ichthyology*, 22(s1): 53–65.

Roe, D., Mulliken, T., Milledge, S., Mremi, J., Mosha, S. and Grieg-Gran, M. 2002. *Making a Killing or Making a Living. Wildlife Trade, Trade Controls and Rural Livelihoods*. London: IIED and Cambridge: Traffic.

Rosen, G. E. and Smith, K. F. 2010. 'Summarizing the evidence on the international trade in illegal wildlife,' *EcoHealth*, 7(1): 24–32.

Ruggiero, V. and South, N. 2010. 'Green criminology and dirty collar crime,' *Critical Criminology: An International Journal*, 18(4): 251–262.

Ruggiero, V. and South, N. 2013. 'Green criminology and crimes of the economy: Theory, research and praxis,' *Critical Criminology: An International Journal*, 21(3): 359–373.

Ryhiner, P. and Mannix, D. P. 1958. *The Wildest Game*. New York: J.B. Lippincott Company.

Sachs, J. D. and Warner, A. M. 2001. 'The curse of natural resources,' *European Economic Review*, 45(4–6): 827–838.

Shadrina, E. 2007. 'The great Caspian caviar game,' *Security Index: A Russian Journal on International Security*, 13(1): 55–78.

Shelley, L. I. 1995. 'Post-soviet organized crime,' *European Journal on Criminal Policy and Research*, 3(4): 7–25.

Simons, J. 2012. *The Tiger that Swallowed the Boy: Exotic Animals in Victorian England*. Oxford: Libri Publishing.

Soddu, P. 2006. *Ceuta and Melilla: Security, Human Rights and Frontier Control*. Institut Europeu de la Mediterrània (eds.) Barcelona: IEMED Mediterranean Yearbook Med, pp. 212–214.

Sollund, R. 2011. 'Expressions of speciesism: The effects of keeping companion animals on animal abuse, animal trafficking and species decline,' *Crime, Law and Social Change*, 55(5): 437–451.

Sollund, R. A. 2019. *The Crimes of Wildlife Trafficking: Issues of Justice, Legality and Morality*. Abingdon, Oxon, UK: Routledge.

Sollund, R. and Maher, J. 2015. *The Illegal Wildlife Trade. A Case Study Report on the Illegal Wildlife Trade in the United Kingdom, Norway, Colombia and Brazil*. Oslo and Wales: University of Oslo and University of South Wales.

Swan, K. and Conrad, K. 2014. 'The conflict between Chinese cultural and environmental values in wildlife consumption,' in P. G. Harris and G. Lang (eds.) *Routledge Handbook of Environment and Society in Asia*, pp. 321–336. London: Routledge.

Traffic. 2011. *Creative Experts Meeting on Messaging to Reduce Consumer Demand for Tigers and Other Endangered Wildlife Species in Vietnam and China*. Hong Kong: Traffic.

UNODC. 2010. *The Globalization of Crime: A Transnational Organized Crime Threat Assessment*. Vienna: UNODC.

UNODC. 2016. 'World wildlife crime report: Trafficking in protected species,' Available at: www.unodc.org/documents/data-and-analysis/wildlife/World_Wildlife_Crime_Report_2016_final.pdf.

Van Lavieren, E. 2004. *The Illegal Trade in the Moroccan Barbary Macaque (Macaca sylvanus) and the Impact on the Wild Population (Master's thesis)*. Oxford: Oxford Brookes University.

Van Uhm, D. P. 2012. 'Organised crime in the wildlife trade,' *Centre for Information and Research on Organised Crime Newsletter*, 10(2): 2–4.

Van Uhm, D. P. 2015. 'Towards moral principles regarding non-human animals: A green criminological perspective,' in F. de Jong et al. (eds.) *Overarching Views of Crime and Deviancy. Rethinking the Legacy of the Utrecht School*, pp. 565–587. The Hague: Eleven International.

Van Uhm, D. P. 2016a. *The Illegal Wildlife Trade: Inside the World of Poachers, Smugglers and Traders (Studies of Organized Crime)*. New York: Springer.

Van Uhm, D. P. 2016b. 'Illegal trade in wildlife and harms to the world,' in A. C. M. Spapens, A. C. M. R. White and W. Huisman (eds.) *Environmental Crime in Transnational Context*, pp. 43–65. Surrey, UK: Ashgate Publishing, Ltd.

Van Uhm, D. P. 2016c. 'Monkey business: The illegal trade in Barbary macaques,' *Journal of Trafficking, Organized Crime and Security*, 2(1): 36–49.

Van Uhm, D. P. 2017. 'A green criminological perspective on environmental crime: The anthropocentric, ecocentric and biocentric impact of defaunation,' *Revue Internationale de Droit Pénal*, 87(1): 323–340.

Van Uhm, D. P. 2018a. 'The social construction of the value of wildlife: A green cultural criminological perspective,' *Theoretical Criminology*, 22(3): 384–401.

Van Uhm, D. P. 2018b. 'Wildlife and laundering: Interaction between the under and upper world,' in T. Spapens, R. White, D. P. Van Uhm and W. Huisman (eds.) *Green Crimes and Dirty Money*, pp. 197–214. London: Routledge.

Van Uhm, D. P. 2019. 'Chinese wildlife trafficking networks along the silk road,' in T. Wing Lo, D. Siegel and S. Kwok (eds.) *Organized Crime and Corruption Across Borders*, pp. 114–133. Abingdon, Oxon, UK: Routledge.

Van Uhm, D. P. and Moreto, W. D. 2018. 'Corruption within the illegal wildlife trade: A symbiotic and antithetical enterprise,' *The British Journal of Criminology*, 58(4): 864–885.

Van Uhm, D. P., Pires, S. F., Sosnowski, M. and Petrossian, G. A. 2019. 'A comparison of seizures of illegal wildlife between the US and the EU,' in M. J. Lynch and S. F. Pires (eds.) *Quantitative Studies in Green and Conservation Criminology*, pp. 127–145. Abingdon, Oxon, UK: Routledge.

Van Uhm, D. P. and Siegel, D. 2016. 'The illegal trade in black caviar,' *Trends in Organized Crime*, 19(1): 67–87.

Van Uhm, D. P. and Wong, R. W. Y. 2019. 'Establishing trust in the illegal wildlife trade in China,' *Asian Journal of Criminology*, 14(1): 23–40.

Varese, F. 1997. 'The transition to the market and corruption in post-socialist Russia,' *Political Studies*, 45(3): 579–596.

Vinke, T. and Vinke, S. 2010. 'Do breeding facilities for chelonians threaten their stability in the wild?' *Schildkröten im Fokus Online*, 1: 1–18.

Volkov, V. 2002. *Violent Entrepreneurs. The Use of Force in the Making of Russian Capitalism*. Ithaca and London: Cornell University Press.

Von Moltke, K. and Spaninks, F. 2000. *Traditional Chinese Medicine and Species Endangerment: An Economic Research Agenda*. London: International Institute for Environment and Development/Amsterdam: Institute for Environmental Studies.

Wilson, E. O. 1993. 'Biophilia and the conservation ethic,' in S. R. Kellert and E. O. Wilson (eds.) *The Biophilia Hypothesis*, pp. 31–41. Washington, DC: Island Press.

World Bank. 2008. *What's Driving the Wildlife Trade? A Review of Expert Opinion on Economic and Social Drivers of the Wildlife Trade and Trade Control Efforts in Cambodia, Indonesia, Lao PDR, and Vietnam*. Washington, DC: The World Bank.

Wyatt, T. 2013. *Wildlife Trafficking: A Deconstruction of the Crime, the Victims, and the Offenders*. Basingstoke, Hampshire, UK: Palgrave Macmillan.

Zabyelina, Y. G. 2014. 'The "fishy" business: A qualitative analysis of the illicit market in black caviar,' *Trends in Organized Crime*, 17(3): 181–198.

Zhang, L., Hua, N. and Sun, S. 2008. 'Wildlife trade, consumption and conservation awareness in Southwest China,' *Biodiversity and Conservation*, 17(6): 1493–1516.

Zhang, S. and Chin, K. 2011. 'Ants moving houses. Cross-border drug trafficking in the Golden Triangle,' in C. J. Smith, S. X. Zhang and R. Barberet (eds.) *Routledge Handbook of Criminology*, pp. 237–247. Abingdon, Oxon, UK: Routledge.

31

Myths of causality, control and coherence in the 'war on wildlife crime'

Siv Rebekka Runhovde

Throughout the last decade, the illegal trade in endangered species of wild fauna and flora has received increasing attention in both discursive and material terms. At international and national policy levels, within intergovernmental organisations (IGOs), non-governmental organisations (NGOs) and in the media, the urgency for action due to the level of corruption and violence associated with the trade and the involvement of organised crime networks and non-state armed groups is frequently highlighted. The United Nations Security Council has acknowledged the connection between transnational organised crime, wildlife trafficking and regional security, and has recognised poaching[1] as one of the factors fuelling crises in Central Africa (CITES 2015). As a result of the security implications of poaching and trafficking, the response from the controlling authorities is becoming increasingly militarised[2] (Duffy 2014, 2016a; Humphreys 2012; Lunstrum 2014; McClanahan and Wall 2016; Wall and McClanahan 2015). 'War' is now a common model and metaphor for approaches to biodiversity conservation across Africa (Neumann 2004). This development is comparable to the 'wars' on crime, drugs and terrorism (Runhovde 2017a; Ayres this volume, Chapter 13), where use of strong language regarding criminals and zero tolerance is common and employed to promote and justify harsh repressive measures (Delmas-Marty 2007).

Appropriate and timely questions to ask include: do the current conceptualisations of wildlife crime reflect the situation at ground level? What influence does the discourse have on the practices of law enforcement officers and is a process of securitisation driving the development of effective responses? From a rule of law perspective, what is the influence of securitisation on judicial processes? Are suspected poachers and traffickers treated fairly, in accordance with legal procedures, and with respect to human rights? In this chapter, I explore the wildlife crime/security nexus by drawing on perspectives within theories on discourse, discretion and deterrence. The discussion builds on previous observations of a disconnect between the authoritarian approach associated with the 'war on wildlife crime' and the everyday enforcement problems highlighted by officers in the East African state of Uganda (see Runhovde 2017a). The chapter focusses on some key issues in securitisation, seeking to discuss the appropriateness and implications of the combative rhetoric and the growing demand for repressive and militarised strategies in conservation policies. Taking inspiration from Childress' (2001) broader work on war as metaphor in public policy, this chapter asks: 'Does [the military metaphor] generate insights, or does it obscure what is going on, and what should be done' (Childress 2001: 195)?

The threats of wildlife crime

'Wildlife',[3] which this chapter defines as all forms of non-domesticated animals and plants living in the wild (Lemieux 2014), are facing many threats, most of which are attributable to human encroachment into habitats and human activity therein (Ceballos et al. 2015). While destruction of natural habitats is recognised as the greatest threat to wildlife, others include the introduction of alien invasive species, climate change, intensive agriculture, ozone depletion and pollution, as well as over-exploitation for economic gain, such as domestic and international trade (Ceballos et al. 2015; Reeve 2002). Thus, although poaching and illegal trade are not the main causes of biodiversity loss, the pressure from international consumer demand has an adverse impact on many wildlife species and on the welfare of individual animals, which, in turn, has had negative long-term effects on human social and ecological well-being (Schneider 2012). Due to the prospect of high profit margins, many assume that organised crime is involved in the trade (Pires et al. 2016). Often presented as a threat to national, regional and global security, as well as a mechanism for financing terrorism, wildlife crime is believed to contribute to political instability in many African and Asian countries (see, e.g., CITES 2015; Nellemann et al. 2016; Vira & Ewing 2014; UNODC 2016).

The development is therefore two-fold. A material increase in illegal sourcing and trade in wildlife contributes to species extinction and loss of biodiversity at an alarming and unparalleled rate. At the same time, the gravity of wildlife crime, the possible link to organised crime, and national security issues that the supposed link raises, all lead to increased attention at the international policy level and from the wider law enforcement community. The 'tipping point' for the extinction for many wildlife species is fast approaching (see, e.g., Brisman and South, Introduction, this volume; Rademeyer 2016; Sellar 2014). Combined with the limited human and logistical resources compromising law enforcement agencies in many countries (see, e.g., Nurse 2015; Wellsmith 2011), there is urgent need for tangible and efficient responses.

The discourse has material consequences

The discourse—the assumptions, metaphors, narratives and terms used to describe wildlife crime—signifies the importance and severity of the issue. Among available metaphors, the 'war' metaphor represents a dramatic way to draw attention to a perceived serious threat and the response deemed necessary for tackling it (see, e.g., Childress 2001; McClanahan & Brisman 2015). For instance, the former Director of the Kenya Wildlife Service, Richard Leakey (Leakey & Morell 2001), entitled his memoirs *Wildlife Wars*. The South African Environment Minister has often referred in press briefings to the 'war on rhino poaching' (Shaw and Rademeyer 2016), and news articles contain headlines such as 'The Wildlife War' (Smith 2015) and 'On the frontline of Africa's wildlife wars' (Vidal 2016). The term 'wildlife genocide' has been proposed as another way of raising the profile because equating wildlife crime with genocide and war crimes could lead to its classification as an international crime and eventually resolve existing jurisdictional conflicts (see Asian Development Bank 2014). Recently, 'traitor' was added to the list when Malaysia's Minister of Tourism, Culture and Environment referred to poachers as not merely misguided souls or criminals but as *traitors* 'doing a great disservice to their own state and country' (Clean Malaysia 2017). Finally, the 'poaching funds terrorism' narrative or trope, although controversial and disputed (Duffy et al. 2015; Maguire & Haenlein 2015), shapes policies and has material consequences on the ground by integrating conservation within a global security agenda (Duffy 2016b), meaning that the use of militaristic rhetoric in relation to wildlife crime and conservation is not limited to metaphor.

Within this context, *discourse theory* emerges as central to the securitisation debate. Discourse theory emphasises the intrinsic connection between linguistic and social processes, and its implications for the way we think and act (George 1994: 191; Milliken 1999). In their influential book on the role of metaphors in language, Lakoff and Johnson (1980) argue that metaphors, often subconsciously, shape how we think, what we experience and what we do. And, indeed, we should become conscious of them and can engage in a critical assessment of their appropriateness (Childress 2001). For example, one might seek to explain how a discourse articulated by authorities legitimises and produces certain policy practices (Milliken 1999: 236).

As indicated by Childress (2001) in the context of health care budgets, the military metaphor tends to assign priority to critical care over preventive and chronic care, to deadly diseases over disabling and crippling ones, and to technological interventions over less technical approaches. Hallsworth and Lea (2011) explain that in the context of security, criminal justice systems likewise tend to focus on short-term coercive solutions as opposed to long-term structural changes, such as investment in education and jobs. The 'war on wildlife crime' discourse and the assimilation of biodiversity conservation into wider sets of policy debates and initiatives linked to global security has led to an emphasis on militarised responses and to increased possibilities for authoritarian control in enforcement (Duffy 2016a, 2016b; Neumann 2004). The discourse, therefore, encourages direct (militarised) action. Similarly, while there is considerable debate regarding the meaning of 'organised crime' (see Ruggiero this volume, Chapter 23), in general, raising the spectre of organised crime's involvement has important practical implications as it may attract additional resources and allow for more intrusive and authoritarian methods and increased penalties (Abraham and van Schendel 2005; Larsson 2016). At the same time, however, suggesting the possibility of organised crime's involvement on an international level (Korsell 2013) runs the risk of making the challenge seem vague and undefeatable, deterring national law enforcement agencies from responding effectively at local levels (Runhovde 2017b). It may conjure up stereotypical images that make it hard to convince policy makers and law enforcement officers that locals, rather than large international crime rings, may in fact be responsible, and may prevent intimidated citizens from reporting crimes (Pires et al. 2016).

(Mis)understandings of local challenges

Research has rarely explored the impact of global forces on ordinary local policing (Bowling 2009: 156) and the question of what, if any, positive impact the heightened attention to wildlife crime has had on the daily work activities of law enforcement officers around the world remains largely unanswered. Policy decisions are made above the local level, and the connection between decisions at management levels and actual ground-level work activities is complex. Looking at transparency and accountability in professional organisations, Bromley and Powell (2012) consider the concept of 'decoupling'—commonly understood as a gap between policy and practice. Maintaining that the external environment creates myths of causality, control and coherence that structure organisations, Bromley and Powell (2012) argue that taken-for-granted assumptions encourage organisational behaviours that may be counterproductive. In turn, such assumptions may generate what is termed 'means-ends decoupling' by leading to implementation of practices with little or no relation to the intended outcome and overall goals of the organisation. The effects of militarisation strategies in response to wildlife crime, even if motivated by a desire to save species, have been widely disputed (Duffy 2014; Tumusiime et al. 2011; Wall and McClanahan 2015) and have been referred to as a 'counterproductive distraction' that serves to lessen support for conservation in local communities (Duffy 2016a). In Uganda (Runhovde 2017a) and Zimbabwe (Duffy 1999), such strategies are unlikely to resolve the principal challenges at ground level, where the need for basic equipment and conventional capacity building appears most critical. With the majority of wildlife crime offenders in Uganda being opportunistic and poorly equipped locals, already under threat of arrest and sanctioning (Tumusiime et al. 2011), militarisation strategies are unlikely to deter these hunters and do little to provide alternative means of survival. Militarisation thus represents a form of means-ends decoupling because the causal link between the methods employed and organisational effectiveness or intended outcomes is weak and undocumented.

While many forms of illegal wildlife trade are transnational, law enforcement officers experience and respond to it primarily as a local phenomenon. Official statements establishing that such crimes are international, organised and a threat to national or global security are of limited interest, relevance, or use if local law enforcement officers are not given the appropriate tools and tactics for dealing with the crimes (Runhovde 2017b). It may therefore be argued that, rather than stressing to local law enforcement officials the 'global' and 'transnational' side of the trade, improved understanding of the dynamics and importance of the trade might be achieved by studying it at the local level, where it 'manifests itself as a tangible process of activity' (Hobbs 1998: 408). Focussing on the particularities and implications of illegal wildlife trade on/at the local level might also foster interest in addressing the problem locally (Korsell 2013). People involved in wildlife crime may be individuals acting alone as the opportunity presents itself or they may be employees of a larger informal or formal criminal network (Wyatt 2013: 86). Such networks have been found to vary from opportunistic flexible trade networks to long-term highly organised criminal groups with considerable rationality and use of violence (van Uhm 2015). While there are indications that organised crime and rebel militias are reaping the rewards of the poaching, trafficking and selling of elephant ivory and rhinoceros horn from Africa to Asia (see, e.g., Rademeyer 2016; Wasser et al. 2015, 2008, 2007), the level of involvement by 'organised crime' may be overstated and based on largely anecdotal evidence (Warchol et al. 2003; Wyler and Sheikh 2008; Zimmerman 2003). This is important because differentiating between the various actors involved and the level of organisation has significant implications for what strategies will be most effective in reducing or disrupting illegal trade (Pires et al. 2016).

Undermining discretion and voluntary compliance

Importantly, the nature and extent of 'policing' as a process and 'the police' as an organisation varies between countries (Mawby 2008), and understanding contemporary policing in former colonies or protectorates should begin with recognising their history. For instance, while policing in England was developed in the direction of service-oriented functions and crime prevention, a different policing model was preferred for the control of subjugated populations in the British colonies. Characterised as defenders of the government rather than the people, the police were militaristic and authoritarian in their emphasis on law and order (Mawby 2008). This colonial-style paramilitary police force was inherited by independent Uganda and its legacy survives today, leaving contemporary policing a complex pattern of overlapping policing agencies, with the line between the conventional police, the military and other security agencies unclear (Kagari & Edroma 2006). The capacity of the 'war' metaphor to further blur the line between warfare and security on one side, and criminality and crime control on the other, is problematic given the different notions of risks and objectives between these types of activity (Delmas-Marty 2007; Hallsworth & Lea 2011; McCulloch & Wilson 2016; Zedner 2009). For example, Zedner (2010) warns that the security discourse may lead to the construction of suspects as *presumptive enemies* who can be punished in advance of wrongdoing because enemies by definition are guilty of hostile intentions.

Because decision-making at the individual level is often based on limited information and a biased set of possible solutions, a gap is created between policy and action (Bromley & Powell 2012). Hence, research on policing has afforded considerable attention to the concept of 'discretion', which broadly refers to the exercise of individual judgement in making a decision outside of the direct command of superiors (Lipsky 2010; Reiner 2010). The nature of the interactions that take place between law enforcement officers and wildlife offenders may be an important determinant for compliance in the future. Criminal justice policy is often premised on the idea that compliance is secured by the presence of formal policing and the threat of negative sanctions. Experts have argued convincingly that wildlife crime is treated too leniently in the criminal justice system and that current punishment levels are too weak to act as a deterrent (see, e.g., Nurse 2015; Wellsmith 2011; Wyatt 2013c). Personal commitment to law-abiding behaviour is just as important and when institutions obey the rule of law and act according to principles of prosecutorial fairness, citizens are more likely to follow the law (Jackson et al. 2012; Tyler 2006). For example, in his study of game wardens in the United States (U.S.), Filteau (2012) employed *deterrence theory* (Sherman 1993) to explain how traditional law enforcement undermined its primary goal of voluntary compliance by inciting defiance from poachers against wardens and creating incentives for future poaching. Filteau (2012) discovered that while the determination of unfair treatment encouraged defiance, would-be poachers were deterred from future or further poaching when they perceived their interactions with game wardens to be fair or procedurally just.

As such, establishing voluntary compliance through flexibility, trust and procedural justice may provide a more proactive way to combat wildlife crime, while unfair treatment or exceedingly strict punishment may inadvertently contribute to individuals' decisions to continue poaching, thereby escalating the problem further. In a policing model that is essentially authoritarian and militaristic, a process of securitisation may bring about or heighten tensions and influence negatively how law enforcement officers interact with suspected wildlife offenders, in turn instigating more anger and hostility, and leading to confrontations between officers and people in the communities. In many African countries, where rural communities have relied on forest resources for cash income or subsistence for generations, conservation policies are often viewed as illegitimate and oppressive and as a continuation of colonial practices (Duffy 2010; Siurua 2006). Illegal hunting could therefore be regarded as a form of resistance, and while such crimes may receive a degree of law enforcement accommodation (von Essen et al. 2014; White 2016), there is limited knowledge regarding how law enforcement officers in African countries are influenced by the perceived characteristic and motivation of wildlife offenders.[4] White (2016: 305) notes that when it comes to the poaching of elephants and rhinoceroses, little latitude is granted to offenders, despite the fact that commercially driven offenders are often poor rural individuals employed by larger traders (Harrison et al. 2015).

Subsistence-hunters *and* rangers risk becoming victims in a 'war on wildlife crime'

A homogenous categorisation of wildlife crime fails to recognise the complexity of motivations that are driving offenders (Nurse 2015: 110) and that subsistence-driven offenders cannot be pursued with the same strategies as those driven by large-scale profit-making (Duffy 1999; Harrison et al. 2015; Hill 2015). The complex relationship between poverty and wildlife crime requires the development of initiatives tailored for the specific context in which they are intended and that may benefit both wildlife *and* people. In Uganda, human rights concerns have been raised following the forceful evictions of local people from protected areas by the Uganda Wildlife Authority (UWA)[5] (UHRC 2015) and the implementation of 'shoot-to-kill' policies upon suspected hunters that target animals in these areas (Tetana 2014). Such orders have previously been given in the Central African Republic, Malawi, Tanzania and Zimbabwe (Neumann 2004), and security and military personnel play an increasingly central role in conservation and wildlife crime enforcement in Africa. Amongst the concerns raised by the ranger communities themselves in response to this development are a lack of coordination, lack of ecological sensitivity, limited knowledge of legal frameworks, as well as lack of proper vetting of such personnel (Duffy 2017).

From a moral and human rights perspective, it is highly problematic if law enforcement officers are not able to discriminate between 'legitimate' and 'illegitimate' targets (see Childress 2001), i.e., between those poachers involved in large-scale organised wildlife crime and those who are subsistence-driven (see Childress 2001). This requires, among other things, knowledge and understanding of the ecological and social environment in which one is operating. If officers fail to make this distinction, small-scale subsistence hunters risk becoming collateral damage in the 'war on wildlife crime', subjected to excessive punishment designed to deter organised criminals involved in lucrative large-scale poaching. Indeed, this happened in 2014, when an anti-poaching campaign in Tanzania resulted in serious violence towards people and the killing and maiming of livestock when armed security forces indiscriminately targeted the local population (Makoye 2014). The risk also extends to law enforcement rangers because 'shoot to kill' policies put rangers and anti-poaching units at greater risk of death than those operating in areas without such policies, especially in regions where the poaching is organised and well-armed (Messer 2000: 55). Poachers, rangers and associated military personnel are increasingly locked into the use of lethal force, making rangers participants in some of Africa's most complex regional conflicts (Duffy 2014)—roles outside the rangers' original job descriptions. Indeed, the rangers themselves may not support military strategies and tactics (Duffy 2017), and, as a result, conservation agencies risk losing valuable well-trained staff (Duffy 2016b). On the other hand, with a lack of other employment and economic opportunities, many rangers may not feel that they have the option to resign even if they want to and, as such, are forced to remain in a dangerous job, often without necessary equipment and for poor wages.

Discussing rhetoric as a driver of securitisation

Many of the concepts associated with transnational wildlife crime are inherently ambiguous and malleable, often lacking universal definitions. This ambiguity may advance the securitisation process. First, there is no commonly agreed upon definition of 'wildlife crime' (UNODC 2016) or of the broader term 'environmental crime' (Nellemann et al. 2016). Neither is there a consensus on a precise international definition of 'corruption' (Wyatt 2013: 52), 'organised crime' (Hagan 2006; von Lampe 2016), 'security' (Zedner 2009: 121), or 'terrorism' (Jackson 2011). Although specialists and non-specialists alike commonly employ the term 'transnational crime', it is not a legal concept but one that is employed to describe a social phenomenon (Felsen & Kalaitzidis 2005). The convenient lack of definitional clarity permits expansive interpretation of these concepts and support for measures and policies that would otherwise be hard to justify. The flexibility also has the ability to avoid substantive criticism of interventions

(Jackson 2013: 155). In fact, Hallsworth and Lea (2011) list *diffusion* as one of the processes in the 'drift' towards securitisation, having particular impact on the criminal justice system: 'Legislation targeting seemingly specific activities such as terrorism is couched in vague forms amenable to a widening use' (Hallsworth & Lea 2011: 152), and, as mentioned above, the line between security and crime control gradually becomes distorted (Delmas-Marty 2007; Hallsworth & Lea 2011; McCulloch & Wilson 2016; Zedner 2009).

The conceptual ambiguity may also provide an opportunity to accommodate a diversity of political and institutional interests (van Duyne 2004; von Lampe 2002) and may legitimise the development and continuation of organisations mandated to address related issues (see Hobbs and Dunnighan 1998; Sheptycki 2002). As stated by Bowling (2009: 151), while increasing global criminal activity leads to a growth in transnational policing, it is also evident that police and governments are actively *driving* the globalisation of policing. Emphasising and potentially exaggerating the prevalence of organised crime results in increases in the resources made available to state agencies, leading Korsell (2013: 161) to identify organised crime as the 'ideal enemy' of our time (Christie & Bruun 1985). In the context of wildlife crime, Duffy (2016b) maintains that the association between wildlife crime, terrorism and security has gained traction because it intersects with pre-existing concerns about global security and the expansion of terrorist networks.[6] Nation-states engage in militarisation in the name of conservation in order to ensure 'security', while making biodiversity conservation increasingly integrated with the U.S.-led War on Terror. In turn, the association allows states, conservation NGOs and private security organisations to tap in to the greater resources available for security and anti-terrorism initiatives from donors, governments and the private sector (Duffy 1999, 2016b). The academic community, by articulating and supporting such narratives, are also inadvertently contributing to advancing a global security agenda (see, e.g., Hutton et al. 2005; Neocleous 2008: 161; White & Heckenberg 2014: 115), signalling the range of participants that, directly and indirectly, are driving the process of securitisation.

Conclusion

As suggested throughout this chapter, the war metaphor may distort more than it illuminates. Childress (2001) claims that the distortion occurs in part because, when discussing social policies and practices in the language of war, we tend to forget the moral conditions for resorting to and waging war. These include the legitimate authority to undertake war, that it is a last resort or necessity (where all other alternatives have been exhausted), that there is a reasonable chance of success and that the probable long-term benefits outweigh the likely bad effects. As such, unlike crime, war is a highly rule-governed activity (Childress 2001).

The situation in many protected areas in Africa and Asia is acute and desperate, and poachers represent a real threat to both rangers and wildlife. The specific framing of the problem that dominates public debates—one that integrates security and biodiversity conservation—is unlikely to lead to relevant long-lasting solutions because it calls for displacing more conventional law enforcement strategies and community-oriented approaches. Resisting this march to militarisation is challenging, however, because to be opposed to security is almost unthinkable; anything in the name of security appears as an unquestionable good (Rigakos 2011: 144; Zedner 2009), and the more security fails, the more it succeeds, as security breaches are met with security enhancements (Linnemann 2013).

In sum, there is no simple solution to wildlife crime and Christie's (1971) statement that our role as criminologists is not primarily to be 'problem solvers' but 'problem raisers' is somewhat reassuring in this respect. Undoubtedly, the wildlife crime/security nexus calls for close attention from criminologists, as the development is likely to lead to new forms of criminalisation, victimisation and intervention. How we address wildlife crime has consequences for how we seek to deal with it. Our interpretation of what is transpiring and our actions in response are structured by language, and eventually the line is crossed from metaphorical war to actual war. An inflated rhetoric of warfare that depersonalises poachers and traffickers as enemies should be used with caution because it serves to construct an image of wildlife crime that is misleading, that oversimplifies the challenges, and that fails to encourage responses that are effective in the long term.

Notes

1 While the definition and use of the term 'poaching' is contested (see Sollund 2013, 2017), for the purposes of this chapter, 'poaching' is defined as the *illegal* taking of wildlife (Moreto & Lemieux 2015).
2 'Militarisation' is the extension of military approaches, equipment and techniques to wildlife protection, including the deployment of armed forces in conservation activity (Duffy 2016a).
3 According to Sollund (2015), the term 'wildlife' is problematic because it creates a gap between humans and non-humans, and implies that non-human animals are uncivilised and unpredictable in contrast to humans, who are therefore positioned above them. Sollund (2015) therefore offers the term 'freeborn animals' as an alternative. For the purposes of this chapter however, Lemieux's (2014) definition is adopted.
4 Both Eliason (2003) and Filteau (2012) have found that U.S. game wardens' discretion is influenced by factors such as the severity of the infraction, previous offence history, the demeanour and social class of the offender, the threat to health and safety and the detriments to the resource. According to Forsyth and colleagues (1998), U.S. game wardens' sympathy and level of tolerance decreases significantly when poachers target endangered species (Forsyth et al. 1998).
5 UWA is a semi-autonomous, paramilitary government agency responsible for conservation and management of wildlife and wildlife-protected areas in Uganda.
6 Other scholars have explored how crimes related to food and water increasingly are taking on new discursive and material roles and dynamics in global conflicts (see, Brisman et al. 2017, 2018).

References

Abraham, I. and van Schendel, W. 2005. 'Introduction: The making of illicitness,' in I. Abraham and W. van Schendel (eds.) *Illicit Flows and Criminal Things: States, Borders, and the Other Side of Globalization*, pp. 1–37. Bloomington: Indiana University Press.

Asian Development Bank. 2014. *Symposium on Combating Wildlife Crime: Securing Enforcement, Ensuring Justice, and Upholding the Rule of Law. The Proceedings*. The Philippines: Asian Development Bank.

Bowling, B. 2009. 'Transnational policing: The globalization thesis, a typology and a research agenda,' *Policing: A Journal of Policy and Practice*, 3(2): 149–160. DOI: 10.1093/police/pap001.

Brisman, A., McClanahan, B., South, N. and Walters, R. 2018. 'Too insecure: Water and security,' in A. Brisman, B. McClanahan, N. South and R. Walters (eds.) *Water, Crime and Security in the Twenty-First Century: Too Dirty, Too Little, Too Much*, pp. 149–182. London: Palgrave Macmillan.

Brisman, A. and South, N. 2017. 'Food, crime, justice and security: (Food) security for whom?' in I. Werkheiser and Z. Piso (eds.) *Food Justice in US and Global Contexts: Bringing Theory and Practice Together*, Vol. 24, pp. 185–200. New York: Springer.

Bromley, P. and Powell, W. W. 2012. 'From smoke and mirrors to walking the talk: Decoupling in the contemporary world,' *Academy of Management Annals*, 6(1): 483–530. DOI: 10.1080/19416520.2012.684462.

Ceballos, G., Ehrlich, P. R., Barnosky, A. D., García, A., Pringle, R. M. and Palmer, T. M. 2015. 'Accelerated modern human-induced species losses: Entering the sixth mass extinction,' *Science Advances*, 1(5). DOI: 10.1126/sciadv.1400253.

Childress, J. F. 2001. 'The war metaphor in public policy: Some moral reflections,' in J. Carl Ficarrotta (ed.) *The Leader's Imperative: Ethics, Integrity, and Responsibility*, pp. 181–197. West Lafayette, IN: Purdue University Press.

Christie, N. 1971. 'Scandinavian criminology facing the 1970s,' *Scandinavian Studies in Criminology*, 43: 121–149.

Christie, N. and Bruun, K. 1985. *Den gode fiende: narkotikapolitikk i Norden*. Oslo: Universitetsforlaget.
CITES. 2015. 'Increasing attention on illegal trade in wildlife – A visual summary of key events and measures since 2012'. Available at: https://cites.org/sites/default/files/eng/news/sundry/2015/IWT-events.pdf
Clean Malaysia. 2017. 'Poachers in Sabah are 'Traitors''. Available at: http://cleanmalaysia.com/2017/08/05/poachers-sabah-traitors/
Delmas-Marty, M. 2007. 'The paradigm of the war on crime. Legitimating inhuman treatment?' *Journal of international Criminal Justice*, 5(2007): 584–598.
Duffy, R. 1999. 'The role and limitations of state coercion: Anti-poaching policies in Zimbabwe,' *Journal of Contemporary African Studies*, 17(1): 97–121. DOI: 10.1080/02589009908729640.
Duffy, R. 2010. *Nature Crime: How We're Getting Conservation Wrong*, New Haven, CT and London: Yale University Press.
Duffy, R. 2014. 'Waging a war to save biodiversity: The rise of militarized conservation,' *International Affairs*, 90(4): 819–834. DOI: 10.1111/1468-2346.12142.
Duffy, R. 2016a. 'Militarising conservation: A triple 'fail' for security, people and wildlife'. Available at: https://sustainablesecurity.org/2016/06/23/militarising-conservation-a-triple-fail-for-security-people-and-wildlife/
Duffy, R. 2016b. 'War, by conservation,' *Geoforum*, 69: 238–248. DOI: 10.1016/j.geoforum.2015.09.014.
Duffy, R. 2017. 'We need to talk about the militarisation of conservation'. Available at: www.greeneuropeanjournal.eu/we-need-to-talk-about-militarisation-of-conservation/
Duffy, R., St John, F., Büscher, B. and Brockington, D. 2015. 'The militarization of anti-poaching: Undermining long term goals?' *Environmental Conservation*, 42: 345–348.
Eliason, S. L. 2003. 'Throwing the book versus cutting some slack: Factors influencing the use of discretion by game wardens in kentucky,' *Deviant Behavior*, 24(2): 129–152. DOI: 10.1080/01639620390117219.
Felsen, D. and Kalaitzidis, A. 2005. 'A historical overview of transnational crime,' in P. Reichel (ed.) *Handbook of Transnational Crime & Justice*, pp. 3–20. Thousand Oaks, CA: SAGE.
Filteau, M. R. 2012. 'Deterring defiance: "Don't give a poacher a reason to poach",' *International Journal of Rural Criminology*, 1(2): 236–255.
Forsyth, C. J., Gramling, R. and Wooddell, G. 1998. 'The game of poaching: Folk crimes in Southwest Louisiana,' *Society & Natural Resources*, 11(1): 25–38. DOI: 10.1080/08941929809381059.
George, J. 1994. *Discourses of Global Politics: A Critical (Re)introduction to International Relations*. Boulder, CO: Lynne Rienner Publishers.
Hagan, F. 2006. '"Organized crime" and "organized crime": Indeterminate problems of definition,' *Trends in Organized Crime*, 9(4): 127–137. DOI: 10.1007/s12117-006-1017-4.
Hallsworth, S. and Lea, J. 2011. 'Reconstructing Leviathan: Emerging contours of the security state,' *Theoretical Criminology*, 15(2): 141–157. DOI: 10.1177/1362480610383451.
Harrison, M., Roe, D., Baker, J., Mwedde, G., Travers, H., Plumptre, A., Rwetsiba, A. and Milner-Gulland, E. J. 2015. *Wildlife Crime: A Review of the Evidence on Drivers and Impacts in Uganda*. London: IIED Research Report.
Hill, J. F. 2015. 'A systems thinking perspective on motivations and mechanisms that drive wildlife poaching,' in R. A. Sollund (ed.) *Green Harms and Crimes. Critical Criminology in a Changing World*, pp. 189–219. Basingstoke, Hampshire, UK: Palgrave Macmillan..
Hobbs, D. 1998. 'Going down the glocal: The local context of organized crime,' *The Howard Journal*, 37 (4): 407–422.
Hobbs, D. and Dunnighan, C. 1998. 'Glocal organized crime: Context and pretext,' in V. Ruggiero, N. South and I. Taylor (eds.) *The New European Criminology: Crime and Social Order in Europe*. London: Routledge.
Humphreys, J. 2012. 'Resource wars: Searching for a new definition,' *International Affairs*, 88(5): 1065–1082. DOI: 10.1111/j.1468-2346.2012.01119.x.
Hutton, J., Adams, W. M. and Murombedzi, J. C. 2005. 'Back to the barriers? Changing narratives in biodiversity conservation,' *Forum for Development Studies*, 32: 341–370.
Jackson, R. 2011. 'In defence of "terrorism": Finding a way through a forest of misconceptions,' *Behavioral Sciences of Terrorism and Political Aggression*, 3(2): 116–130. DOI: 10.1080/19434472.2010.512148.
Jackson, W. 2013. 'Securitisation as depoliticisation: Depoliticisation as pacification,' *The Journal of the Society for Socialist Studies*, 9(2): 146–166.

Jackson, J., Bradford, B., Hough, M., Myhill, A., Quinton, P. and Tyler, T. R. 2012. 'Why do people comply with the law? Legitimacy and the influence of legal institutions.' *The British Journal of Criminology*, 52(6): 1051-1071.

Kagari, M. and Edroma, E. 2006. *The Police, The People, The Politics: Police Accountability in Uganda*. Nairobi: Commonwealth Human Rights Initiative (CHRI).

Korsell, L. 2013. 'Local organised crime,' in U. Töttel, G. Bulanova-Hristova and H. Büchler (eds.) *Research Conferences on Organised Crime at the Bundeskriminalamt in Germany (Vol. II) Organised Crime – Research and Practice in Western and Northern Europe 2011–2012*, pp. 161–173. Köln: Luchterhand Verlag.

Lakoff, G. and Johnson, M. 1980. *Metaphors We Live By*. Chicago: University of Chicago Press.

Larsson, P. 2016. 'The big scare: Bikers and the construction of organized crime in Norway,' in G. A. Antonopoulos (ed.), *Illegal Entrepreneurship, Organized Crime and Social Control: Essays in Honor of Professor Dick Hobbs*, Vol. 14, pp. 205–217. Switzerland: Springer.

Leakey, R. E. and Morell, V. 2001. *Wildlife Wars: My Fight to Save Africa's Natural Treasures*. New York: St Martin's Press.

Lemieux, A. 2014. *Situational Prevention of Poaching*. New York: Routledge.

Linnemann, T. 2013. 'Governing through meth: Local politics, drug control and the drift toward securitization,' *Crime Media Culture*, 9(1): 39–61. DOI: 10.1177/1741659012454125.

Lipsky, M. 2010. *Street-level Bureaucracy: Dilemmas of the Individual in Public Services (30th Anniversary Expanded ed.)*. New York: Russell Sage Foundation.

Lunstrum, E. 2014. 'Green militarization: Anti-poaching efforts and the spatial contours of Kruger National Park,' *Annals of the Association Of American Geographers*, 104(4): 816–832. DOI: 10.1080/00045608.2014.912545.

Maguire, T. and Haenlein, C. 2015. 'An illusion of complicity. Terrorism and the illegal ivory trade in East Africa [Online],' *Royal United Services Institute for Defence and Security Studies*. Available at: https://rusi.org/sites/default/files/201509_an_illusion_of_complicity_0.pdf.

Makoye, K. (2014). 'Anti-poaching operation spreads terror in Tanzania'. Available at: www.ipsnews.net/2014/01/anti-poaching-operation-spread-terror-tanzania/

Mawby, R. C. 2008. 'Models of policing,' in T. Newburn (ed.), *Handbook of Policing*, 2/e., pp. 17–46. New York: Willan Publishing.

McClanahan, B. and Brisman, A. 2015. 'Climate change and peacemaking criminology: Ecophilosophy, peace and security in the "war on climate change",' *Critical Criminology: An International Journal*, 23(4): 417–431. DOI: 10.1007/s10612-015-9291-6.

McClanahan, B. and Wall, T. 2016. '"Do some anti-poaching, kill some bad guys, and do some good": Manhunting, accumulation and pacification in African conservation,' in G. R. Potter, A. Nurse and M. Hall (eds.) *The Geography of Environmental Crime: Conservation, Wildlife Crime and Environmental Activism*, pp. 121–147. London: Palgrave Macmillan.

McCulloch, J. and Wilson, D. 2016. *Pre-Crime: Pre-Emption, Precaution and the Future*. Abingdon, Oxon, UK: Routledge.

Messer, K. 2000. 'The poacher's dilemma: The economics of poaching and enforcement,' *Endangered species update*, 17(3): 50–56.

Milliken, J. 1999. 'The study of discourse in international relations: A critique of research and methods,' *European journal of international relations*, 5(2): 225–254.

Moreto, W. D. and Lemieux, A. M. 2015. 'Poaching in Uganda: Perspectives of law enforcement rangers,' *Deviant Behavior*, 36(11): 853–873, DOI: 10.1080/01639625.2014.977184.

Nellemann, C., Henriksen, R., Kreilhuber, A., Stewart, D., Kotsovou, M., Raxter, P., Mrema, E. and Barrat, S. (eds.) 2016. *The Rise of Environmental Crime. A Growing Threat to Natural Resources, Peace, Development and Security*. Oslo, Paris and London: United Nations Environment Programme and RHIPTO Rapid Response - Norwegian Center for Global Analyses.

Neocleous, M. 2008. *Critique of Security*. Edinburgh: Edinburgh University Press.Neumann, R. P. 2004. 'Moral and discursive geographies in the war for biodiversity in Africa,' *Political Geography*, 23(7): 813–837. DOI: 10.1016/j.polgeo.2004.05.011.

Nurse, A. 2015. *Policing Wildlife: Perspectives on the Enforcement of Wildlife Legislation*. London: Palgrave Macmillan.

Pires, S., Schneider, J. and Herrera, M. 2016. 'Organized crime or crime that is organized? The parrot trade in the neotropics,' *Trends in Organized Crime*, 19(1): 4–20. DOI: 10.1007/s12117-015-9259-7.

Rademeyer, J. 2016. *Tipping point. Transnational Organised Crime and the 'War' on Poaching. Part 1 of a 2-Part Investigation into Rhino horn Trafficking in Southern Africa.* Geneva: The Global Initivative against Transnational Organized Crime.

Reeve, R. 2002. *Policing International Trade in Endangered Species. The CITES Treaty and Compliance.* London: Earthscan.

Reiner, R. 2010. *The Politics of the Police*, 4th ed. Oxford: Oxford University Press.

Rigakos, G. S. 2011. 'To extend the scope of productive labour: Pacification as a police project,' in M. Neocleous and G. S. Rigakos (eds.) *Anti-Security*, pp. 57–83. Ottawa: Red Quill Books.

Runhovde, S. R. 2017a. 'Comparing discourse to officer perceptions: The problems of war and militarization in wildlife crime enforcement,' *Critical Criminology: An International Journal*, 25(2): 275–291. DOI: 10.1007/s10612-017-9360-0.

Runhovde, S. R. 2017b. 'Merely a transit country? Examining the role of Uganda in the transnational illegal ivory trade,' *Trends in Organized Crime*, 21(3): 215–234. DOI: 10.1007/s12117-016-9299-7.

Schneider, J. L. 2012. *Sold into Extinction. The Global Trade in Endangered Species.* CA: Praeger.

Sellar, J. M. 2014. *Policing the Trafficking of Wildlife: Is There Anything to Learn from Law Enforcement Responses to Drug and Firearms Trafficking?* Geneva, The Global Initiative Against Transnational Organized Crime.

Shaw, M. and Rademeyer, J. 2016. 'A flawed war: Rethinking "green militarization" in the Kruger National Park,' *Politikon*, 43(2): 173–192. DOI: 10.1080/02589346.2016.1201379.

Sherman, L. W. 1993. 'Defiance, deterrence, and irrelevance: A theory of the criminal sanction,' *Journal of Research in Crime and Delinquency*, 30(4): 445–473. DOI: 10.1177/0022427893030004006.

Sheptycki, J. 2002. *In Search of Transnational Policing : Towards a Sociology of Global Policing*, Surrey, UK: Ashgate.

Siurua, H. 2006. 'Nature above people: Rolston and "fortress" conservation in the South,' *Ethics & the Environment*, 11(1): 71–96.

Smith, D. 2015. 'Africa is centre of a 'wildlife war' that the world is losing,' Available at: www.theguardian.com/environment/2015/mar/21/wildlife-war-lost-in-africa

Sollund, R. 2015. 'The illegal wildlife trade from a Norwegian outlook: Tendencies in practices and law enforcement,' in R. Sollund (ed.) *Green Harms and Crimes: Critical Criminology in a Changing World*, pp. 147–169. Basingstoke, Hampshire, UK: Palgrave Macmillan.

Sollund, R. 2017. 'The animal other: Legal and illegal theriocide,' in M. Hall, J. Maher, A. Nurse, G. R. Potter and T. Wyatt (eds.) *Greening Criminology in the 21st Century: Contemporary Debates and Future Directions in the Study of Environmental Harm*, pp. 79–100. Abingdon, Oxon, UK: Routledge

Sollund, R. A. 2013. 'Animal trafficking and trade: Abuse and species injustice,' in R. Walters, D. S. Westerhuis and T. Wyatt (eds.) *Emerging Issues in Green* Criminology. *Exploring Power, Justice and Harm. Critical Criminological Perspectives*, pp. 72–92. Basingstoke, Hampshire, UK: Palgrave Macmillan.

Tetana, P. 2014. 'Shoot poachers on sight – Museveni'. Available at: http://busiweek.com/index1.php?Ctp=2&pI=678&pLv=3&srI=

Tumusiime, D. M., Vedeld, P. and Gombya-Ssembajjwe, W. 2011. 'Breaking the law? Illegal livelihoods from a Protected Area in Uganda,' *Forest Policy and Economics*, 13: 273–283.

Tyler, T. R. 2006. *Why People Obey the Law.* Princeton, NJ: Princeton University Press.

UHRC. 2015. *The 17th Annual Report of the Uganda Human Rights Commission.* Kampala: Uganda Human Rights Commission.

UNODC. 2016. *World wildlife Crime Report. Trafficking in Protected Species.* New York: United Nations.

van Duyne, P. C. 2004. 'The creation of a threat image. Media, policy making and organized crime,' in P. C. van Duyne, M. Jager, K. von Lampe and J. L. Newell (eds.) *Threats and Phantoms of Organised Crime, Corruption and Terrorism. Critical European Perspectives*, 4th ed., pp. 21–50. Nijmegen: Wolf Legal Publishers.

van Uhm, D. 2015. 'Uncovering the Illegal Wildlife Trade,' Phd, Utrecht: Universiteit Utrecht.

Vidal, J. 2016. 'On the frontline of Africa's wildlife wars'. Available at: www.theguardian.com/environment/2016/may/07/africa-frontline-of-wildlife-wars

Vira, V. and Ewing, T. 2014. 'Ivory's curse: The militarization and professionalization of poaching in Africa [Online],' *Born Free USA and C4ADS.* April. Available at: http://7a1eb59c2270eb1d8b3d-a9354ca433cea7ae96304b2a57fdc8a0.r60.cf1.rackcdn.com/Ivorys-Curse-2014.pdf.

von Essen, E., Hansen, H. P., Kallstrom, H. N., Peterson, M. N. and Peterson, T. R. 2014. 'Deconstructing the poaching phenomenon: A review of typologies for understanding illegal hunting,' *The British Journal of Criminology*, 54(4): 632–651.

von Lampe, K. 2002. 'Afterword. Organized crime research in perspective,' in P. C. van Duyne, K. von Lampe and N. Passas (eds.) *Upperworld and Underworld in Cross-Border Crime*, pp. 189–197. Netherlands: Wolg Legal Publishers.

von Lampe, K. 2016. *Organized Crime: Analyzing Illegal Activities, Criminal Structures, and Extra-Legal Governance*. Los Angeles, CA: Sage.

Wall, T. and McClanahan, B. 2015. 'Weaponising conservation in the "heart of darkness": The war on poachers and the neoclassical hunt,' in A. Brisman, N. South and R. White (eds.) *Environmental Crime and Social Conflict: Contemporary and Emerging Issues*, pp. 221–240. Surrey, UK: Ashgate Publishing Ltd.

Warchol, G. L., Zupan, L. L. and Clack, W. 2003. 'Transnational criminality: An analysis of the illegal wildlife market in Southern Africa,' *International Criminal Justice Review*, 13(1): 1–26.

Wasser, S. K., Brown, L., Mailand, C., Mondol, S., Clark, W., Laurie, C. and Weir, B. S. 2015. 'Genetic assignement of large seizure of elephant ivory reveals Africa's major poaching hotspots,' *Science*, 349(6243): 84–87.

Wasser, S. K., Joseph Clark, W., Drori, O., Stephen Kisamo, E., Mailand, C., Mutayoba, B. and Stephens, M. 2008. 'Combating the illegal trade in African elephant ivory with DNA forensics,' *Conservation Biology*, 22(4): 1065–1071. DOI: 10.1111/j.1523-1739.2008.01012.x.

Wasser, S. K., Mailand, C., Booth, R., Mutayoba, B., Kisamo, E., Clark, B. and Stephens, M. 2007. 'Using DNA to track the origin of the largest ivory seizure since the 1989 trade ban,' *Proceedings of the National Academy of Sciences of the United States of America (PNAS)*, 104(10): 4228–4233.

Wellsmith, M. 2011. 'Wildlife crime: The problems of enforcement,' *European Journal on Criminal Policy and Research*, 17: 125–148.

White, R. 2016. 'Re-conceptualizing folk crime in rural contexts,' in J. F. Donnermeyer (ed.) *The Routledge International Handbook of Rural Criminology*, pp. 299–308. Abingdon, Oxon, UK: Routledge

White, R. and Heckenberg, D. 2014. *Green criminology: An introduction to the study of environmental harm*. Abingdon, Oxon, UK: Routledge.

Wyatt, T. 2013. *Wildlife Trafficking: A Deconstruction of the Crime, The Victims, and the Offenders*. Basingstoke, Hampshire, UK: Palgrave Macmillan.

Wyler, L. S. and Sheikh, P. A. 2008. *International Illegal Trade in Wildlife: Threats and US Policy*. [Online.] Washington, DC: Congressional Research Service, The Library of Congress. Available at: https://apps.dtic.mil/dtic/tr/fulltext/u2/a486486.pdf.

Zedner, L. 2009. *Security*. London: Routledge.

Zedner, L. 2010. 'Security, the state, and the citizen: The changing architecture of crime control,' *New Criminal Law Review: In International and Interdisciplinary Journal*, 13(2): 379–403. DOI: 10.1525/nclr.2010.13.2.379.

Zimmerman, M. E. 2003. 'The black market for wildlife,' *Combating Transnational Organized Crime in the Illegal Wildlife Trade Vanderbilt Journal of Transnational Law*, 36: 1657–1689.

32

Environmental justice, animal rights and total liberation

From conflict and distance to points of common focus

David N. Pellow

Introduction

At first glance, the environmental justice (EJ) and animal rights (AR) movements would seem to be entirely distinct and unrelated social causes. There are many reasons why observers might draw this conclusion. The EJ movement is comprised largely of people from communities of colour, Indigenous communities and working-class communities who are focussed on combating environmental racism and injustice—the disproportionate burden of environmental harm facing these populations. For the EJ movement, the battle for global sustainability cannot be won without addressing the ecological violence imposed on vulnerable human populations; thus, social justice (that is, justice for humans) is inseparable from environmental protection. The AR movement, on the other hand, is comprised largely of middle-class white activists whose primary goal is the protection and liberation of non-human animals. For AR activists, any struggle for global sustainability must prioritise the plight of non-human animals. In this chapter, I consider the basis for these divergences and conflicting visions across these movements, and also explore several points of convergence and possible collaboration between them. These possibilities emerge when one shifts the focus from animal rights (AR) to radical animal liberation (AL)—a movement that calls attention to the ways in which human beings are harmed by intra- and inter-species hierarchies, and that strives for 'total liberation' (TL)—liberation from all forms of inequality (e.g., ageism, disablism, heterosexism, patriarchy, racism). This chapter considers ways in which these differences might become an asset, rather than a liability, for activists seeking to create alliances across these movements. Moreover, I explore the ways in which these differences tend to mask considerable common ground between these movements. Using a variety of source materials, I argue that the AL and EJ movements could learn a great deal from each other and already share plenty of unrealised common ground. I conclude with implications these arguments raise for the field of green criminology.

Methods

I draw on three principal research methods. My primary method is semi-structured interviews, which I conducted with 100 activists across AR and AL movements between the winter of 2009 and summer of 2011. I also conducted fieldwork at activist gatherings, conferences, meetings and other related public events where AR and AL activists convened. Finally, I conducted content analyses of thousands of pages of newsletters, journals, websites and zines produced by activists. Overall, the three components—interviews, fieldwork and document analysis—offer an opportunity to triangulate sources of evidence to provide a more complete consideration of the data (Denzin 2009; Lofland et al. 2005). In this chapter, I make use of a small sample of these sources. I also draw on experiences and insights I have gained over the years as an animal rights activist, environmental justice activist and person of colour.

Two movements

The EJ movement gained visibility and strength in the United States (U.S.) beginning in the late 1970s and early 1980s, as activists and movement networks confronted a range of toxic locally unwanted land uses (LULUs) that were disproportionately located in communities of colour and working-class neighbourhoods. This movement fused discourses of anti-racism, civil and human rights, ecological sustainability, public health and social justice, with tactics like civil disobedience, legal action and public protest to prevent the construction or expansion of undesirable and controversial facilities and developments, such as chemical plants, incinerators, landfills and mines. Activists also demanded that owners of existing facilities shut them down or improve their operational safety, reduce pollution levels and provide economic benefits to local residents. This movement sought to openly integrate campaigns for justice on behalf of vulnerable human beings with the goal of ecological sustainability (see, e.g., Brisman 2007, 2008; Bullard 1990; Bullard 1994; Gottlieb 1993; Shabecoff 1993).

Various forms of animal welfare and AR movements have been in existence in the U.S. since the early nineteenth century. The animal welfare component of the AR movement is the most dominant and is led by groups like the American Society for the Prevention of Cruelty to Animals (ASPCA) and the Humane Society of the United States (HSUS). So-called 'welfarists' generally accept most of the exploitative uses of non-human animals, but they seek to minimise their pain and suffering (see Maher and Pierpoint, this volume, Chapter 28). Their primary approach to achieving these goals is through public education and lobbying elected officials for protective legislation (Jasper and Nelkin 1992). Beginning in the late 1970s, in the U.S., groups with a more radical approach emerged to redefine animal welfare concerns as a struggle for animal *rights* and animal *liberation*. Instead of accepting most practices of animal exploitation, these new groups called for the immediate cessation of animal oppression in all forms. While welfarist groups are the most politically influential, the radical groups have left an indelible and significant mark on the broader environmental movement's terrain and on the public discourse about human–non-human animal relations. Because the radical movement was disillusioned with limited reformist approaches associated with lobbying and animal welfare politics, many of these activists engaged in direct action to liberate non-human animals from fur farms, research laboratories and other facilities, often destroying property and scientific data, dealing major financial blows to industries practicing animal exploitation (see, e.g., Brisman 2008, in press). This movement continued to grow in visibility and impact in the 1990s, as the Animal Liberation Front (ALF), People for the Ethical Treatment of Animals (PETA) and other groups launched animal rescue operations and produced videos of numerous actions for media release and public education (see, e.g., Best and Nocella 2004; Brisman, in press; Rosebraugh 2004). Perhaps even more critical than the considerable property damage and losses they caused was the message they promoted that speciesism (in this case, the view that non-human species exist to serve the needs of humans) was not only unethical, but a threat to public and global environmental health. The federal government soon responded by launching numerous investigations and jailing many activists (see, e.g., Pellow 2010, 2014; Scarce 1990).

Sources of difference, points of contention

While it is true that the EJ movement's lack of focus on AR issues makes it difficult to find common ground between these movements, I place the majority of the burden on the AR movement because many AR activists have, for years, engaged directly and publicly in activities that have offended EJ and social justice advocates. In this part, I examine a few examples.

Single-issue politics and culturally offensive practices

Many elements within the AR movement have long adopted a single-issue orientation. Within this framework, the movement's goal is to save non-human animals from abuse, exploitation and/or extinction—a goal that supersedes all others. For these activists, it makes strategic sense to focus only on these issues without linking them to other social causes because humans are perceived to have a voice to advocate for themselves, while non-human animals generally do not (Jasper and Nelkin 1992). In many cases, within this narrative, concerns for justice for humans are an impediment to the goal of protection for non-human animals, particularly because the poor and people of colour are viewed as implicitly part of the problem due to the fact that such a small percentage of those populations are vegan and even fewer are supporters of AR movements. Paul Watson, founder of the Sea Shepherd Conservation Society (SSCS) and star of the hit television show *Whale Wars*, once declared when asked why he opposed immigration to the U.S.: 'I'm not here to represent people, people are well represented … I don't allow any human politics to influence my decisions … I'm here to represent non-human species and ecosystems'. This statement emerged in the context of the Sierra Club's contentious debate on whether Latin American immigration and population growth damage U.S. ecosystems and wildlife habitat (see, e.g., Brisman 2007: 292; Gottlieb 1993). That debate—which occurred in the late 1990s and the mid-2000s—was costly for the organisation (which remains the largest environmental group in the U.S.) and led many leaders of the EJ movement to denounce the Sierra Club as nativist and racist (Park and Pellow 2011).

The single-issue approach to AR politics has often alienated potential supporters when AR activists have collaborated with individuals and groups involved in behaviours that are an affront to the non-AR community. Consider the fact that a number of AR activists and groups worked with the notorious nativist Joe Arpaio, who served as Sheriff of Maricopa County from 1993–2016, to support a campaign to ban veal crates in the state of Arizona. Arpaio remains an internationally recognised figure within the immigration control movement for supporting the most stringent U.S.–Mexico border control policies, and, while in office, he publicly paraded detained undocumented immigrants in shackles, and enthusiastically embraced racial profiling of Latinos in Arizona (Gaffey 2017). An AR activist explained this problem at a recent Animal Rights Conference:

> I think we're a movement that sometimes falls short in our understanding of where people of communities of colour are coming from and what they are dealing with. I think that—to

> me … this was [highlighted] when the Proposition was worked on in Arizona to ban the veal crate and the gestation crate. And one of the main spokespeople for this campaign was Sheriff Joe Arpaio. And if you don't know who Sheriff Joe Arpaio is, just google "Sheriff Joe" and "racist," and lots of articles will come up. They used him as a spokesperson for this campaign, which alienated many people of colour in Arizona. I talked to the leaders of the campaign in Arizona who led the effort. They understood my concerns, and I understood that they felt, you know, as is understandable, animal rights groups have a *single purpose*. They have a single mission, and I understand that, and I think they need to stick to their mission. I just would like a lot of these organizations to be more understanding of not alienating other people.

Many elitist, patriarchal, racist and homophobic elements are quite strong in AR movements (Kim 2015). Specifically, in actions, speeches and writings, numerous activists reproduce these inequalities and social hierarchies, whether consciously or otherwise. For example, many activists informed me that a small number of high profile men in the AR movement are infamous for their sexism and/or sexual harassment of women. These are sources of internal embarrassment, but other leaders in the movement have quietly taken the position that to confront these men would compromise the 'more important' goals of the cause. This, of course, is an old story that we have seen in prior social movements throughout much of history (Oropeza 2005), but it is disappointing for many activists that this movement—which some view as the 'final frontier' of all social movements—still reflects this traditional problem (Best and Nocella 2004: 11).

Much of the racism in the AR movement is unconscious and unintentional, but no less harmful than blatant racism. At a recent national animal rights conference, on a panel titled 'Engaging Ethnic Minorities', a panelist boldly told the audience the following regarding his approach to cross-cultural cooperation: 'And you also get drunk with them … Latin people love to dance. They love to party. Go dance and party with them. Get to know each other on a basic, basic level. I mean, it's really silly to say, but no, it's really true'.

I believe the above activist genuinely wants to work toward animal rights, but offers a longstanding racist approach to working with people of colour populations to achieve that end. The stereotype of Latinos dancing and drinking heavily is offensive and would likely be met with revulsion if this target population knew this was a viewpoint held by any participants in this movement.

The Faroe Islands case

The 1988 film *Black Harvest* tells the story of the controversial annual pilot whale slaughter in the Faroe Islands (near Denmark), and of the local people who seek to preserve this centuries-old tradition. The film also features the stories of wildlife activists and conservationists who are members of the SSCS, who work to save the pilot whales (also known as 'Common Calderon') from extinction. Apparently, the annual slaughter or 'harvest' is a tradition that dates from several centuries ago, when the Faroe Islanders first sought out an abundant protein source as a staple of their diet. Every year, young men from the island wade into the shallow waters of the bay and kill hundreds of whales, haul them to shore, butcher them and distribute the flesh to the community for consumption. For years, AR activists and conservationists have tried to put an end to this practice on the grounds that it is cruel and unnecessary (because the Islanders have multiple sources of protein in the contemporary era).

In the spring of 2009, a colleague sent me an email that had been circulating among activists in the AR and environmentalist communities for a number of years. The message she forwarded to me read:

> The Red Sea in Denmark: APPALLING, SHOCKING and UNBELIEVABLE!!! Why is the European Union so quiet about this? Where is Greenpeace, who make so much noise in other countries … This happens only in uncivilized Denmark.
>
> DENMARK: WHAT A SHAME, A SAD SCENE. THIS MAIL HAS TO BE CIRCULATED. THERE IS NO WORSE BEAST THAN MAN!!!!
>
> While it may seem incredible, even today this custom continues … in the Faroe Islands, (Denmark). A country supposedly 'civilised' and an EU country at that. For many people this attack to life is unknown—a custom to 'show' entering adulthood. It is absolutely atrocious. No one does anything to prevent this barbarism being committed against the Calderon, an intelligent dolphin that is placid and approaches humans out of friendliness. Make this atrocity known and hopefully stopped.

As an AR activist and vegetarian myself, I must admit that the photos accompanying this message were deeply disturbing. The images were of pilot whales being slaughtered by the dozens and the surrounding seawater turning bright red with blood, while those villagers not killing the whales looked on, apparently awaiting their share of the meat. But as I separated the images from the message, I became troubled by its content as well, particularly for those of us who seek to build the movements for AL and EJ. Indeed, the message from AR activists about the whale slaughter was problematic in three ways: (1) it insulted the people of the Faroe Islands by assuming they were simply a cruel and vile group, referring to them as an uncivilised culture, and not asking them directly why they carry out this slaughter in the first place (thus avoiding questions of sustenance and historical practices); (2) it offended the rest of the world with its racist implications—suggesting that Europeans must be civilised, while other regions of the globe presumably are not; and (3) ironically, it also offended non-humans by implying that these particular whales should be spared because they are allegedly more intelligent than other species. The depths of insensitivity, racism and even speciesism in this message are astounding and present little hope for building common cause with environmental and social justice movements.

The list of such examples is endless, and includes a notorious PETA action outside the Westminster Kennel Club convention that involved AR activists wearing Ku Klux Klan robes, handing out flyers protesting against what they described as the dog breeders' efforts to create a 'master race' of purebred canines. PETA also produced an infamous exhibit that drew parallels between human slavery and the lynching of African Americans and the treatment and exploitation of non-humans, which was at least as controversial as PETA's 'Holocaust on a Plate' campaign that drew parallels between the Nazi Holocaust and the human consumption of non-humans (Patterson 2002). Each of these actions was meant to connect speciesism and non-human exploitation to more familiar examples of human exploitation, but largely failed to build alliances with people of colour and exploited human populations for a number of reasons.

First, in a speciesist world, any suggestion that human exploitation of non-human animals bears a resemblance to human exploitation of other humans requires a great deal of work, and sloganeering and flyers are likely to be entirely inadequate. So, if AR activists wish to make these connections clear to other people, they must be prepared to delve into history, philosophy and the politics of trans- and intra-species hierarchies.

Second, the problem with comparing people of colour's exploitation to the suffering of non-human animals is that people of colour have struggled for centuries to resist such violent practices directed at them *and continue to do so*. As an AR activist and person of colour, I find this to be one of the most challenging points of engagement. When many people of colour are asked whether we support the notion that humans and non-human animals should be treated the same—that is, afforded rights—we might justifiably reply that people of colour have historically been (mis)treated like non-human animals anyway, so this is nothing new and has been a part of a violent past and present circumstances. Many AR activists see no problem here because they generally view the notion that humans are animals as a universal truth that applies to all of humankind. But if we actually examine the histories of different human populations, we find that certain people have long experienced an involuntary flattening of hierarchies between humans and non-humans through violently imposed systems of racism, chattel slavery and mass incarceration (see generally Brisman and South, this volume, Introduction; Mazurek et al., this volume, Chapter 14). In other words, a fundamental problem here is that some AR activists attempt to build support for their cause by appearing to challenge white supremacy, while unwittingly embracing one of its fundamental tenets—that there should be no hierarchy between people of colour and non-humans (because, after all, we are all animals). People of colour have, ironically, been struggling to maintain the boundaries between humans and non-humans because our dignity and survival have depended on it (despite the inherent speciesism of that stance), while privileged and largely unaware AR activists wish to dismantle these borders without careful attention to the historical and contemporary contexts in which they have evolved.

Finally, many leaders and activists in communities of colour view these actions by AR activists as disingenuous and problematic because they seem to appropriate (some people have used the term 'pimp') social justice movements for the cause of animal rights without respecting or working in solidarity with those movements. Specifically, for AR activists to make the claim that animal exploitation has strong parallels with chattel slavery, they must do so with the understanding that people of colour often view such statements as arrogant declarations that white AR activists know our history better than we do, and that they are using it for their own ends, rather than in a genuine effort to build and support racial justice movements. That is, drawing parallels between human slavery and non-human slavery might appear to link speciesism and white supremacy, but many people of colour tend to view this effort as concerned only with dismantling speciesism, largely because the implicit message is that the worst manifestations of racism are in the past.

The single-issue 'Animals First' orientation that characterises much of the discourse and action within the AR movement reflects a serious absence of attention to social and environmental justice concerns, and is a primary reason for the need for a transformative movement that more forcefully sees and challenges the entangled oppressions of humans, non-humans and ecosystems (Nibert 2002). As indicated above, the AR movement often perpetuates social injustices in numerous ways—namely, by reinforcing white privilege and ignoring class, gender, national and racial inequalities. Fortunately, many criticisms of the 'Animals First' narrative have, in part, given rise to what some activists have recently termed the 'total liberation' perspective (Best 2010, 2011).

While TL activists are certainly not immune to racism and unacknowledged privilege (because they remain largely white and primarily focussed on non-humans), they tend to have a much more informed approach to multi-issue politics, making them more probable and capable of being allies of EJ and social justice movements than animal welfarists and other AR groups. This is where the possibility of hope rests because the TL frame is productive for imagining the possibilities of creating common ground with EJ politics.

Sources of unrealised common ground and potential collaboration

Revolutionary environmentalism and total liberation

In their anthology *Igniting a Revolution*, Best and Nocella (2006: 23) embrace what they call 'revolutionary environmentalism', which they describe as 'a class, race, gender, and culture war that aims to abolish every system of domination, including that of human beings over nature'. The editors explain: 'revolutionary environmentalism is not a single group, but rather a collective movement rooted in specific tactics and goals … and organized as multi-issue, multiracial alliances that can mount effective opposition to capitalism and other modes of domination' (2006: 22). While this framework is still wedded to the language of environmentalism, it is refreshing in its anti-capitalist, anti-racist and feminist intersections. In fact, it embraces a politics set against all forms of domination, something that neither the AR nor the EJ movement has pursued.

Four years after *Igniting a Revolution* was published, Steven Best (2010) gave a presentation at the International Meeting for Environmental Ethics, in which he employed the term 'total liberation' to describe the concept embodied in his earlier use of the term revolutionary environmentalism:

> it is imperative that we no longer speak of human liberation, animal liberation, or Earth liberation as if they were independent struggles; rather, we need to speak of total liberation. By 'total liberation' … I refer to the theoretical process of holistically understanding movements in relation to one another, to capitalism, and to other modes of oppression, and to the political process of synthetically forming alliances against common oppressors, across class, racial, gender, and national boundaries, as we link democracy to ecology and social justice to animal rights. A truly revolutionary social theory and movement will not just emancipate members of one species, but rather all species and the Earth itself. It will merge animal, Earth, and human liberation in a total liberation struggle against global capitalism and domination of all kinds. It must dismantle all asymmetrical power relations and structures of hierarchy, including that of humans over animals and the Earth. It must eliminate every vicious form of prejudice and discrimination—not only racism, sexism, homophobia, and ablism, but also the scientifically false and morally repugnant lies of speciesism and humanism.

Best's words partially echo the well-established concept of 'intersectionality' (see Henne and Troshynski 2017, 2019). Critical legal theorist Kimberlé Crenshaw's work on intersectionality reminds us that various forms of inequality—such as classism, heteropatriarchy and racism—interrelate and work together to produce advantages and disadvantages for people. Class, gender, race and sexuality are also what feminist theorist Anne McClintock (1995) calls 'articulated categories'—that is, we define each of these categories through others. While scholars have done an admirable job of pursuing this line of theorising among and across the above categories, Best's work suggests that there remain many ways in which we might expand this concept.

For example, the 2011 Eastern Sociological Society conference theme was 'Intersectionality and Complex Inequalities'. The call for papers (CFP) read:

> The concept of intersectionality … has enriched and transformed academic research across many disciplines. Its application allows scholars to explore the simultaneous and

> multiplicative interaction of class, race, ethnicity, gender, age, religion, sexuality, disability, citizenship and other axes of inequality in people's lives as mutually constructing systems of power.

From a TL perspective, categories like non-human animal, land and nature are virtually absent from this CFP and related literatures, and including such categories might be useful for deepening our analysis of intersectionality. That is, what happens when we incorporate non-human categories in this framework, particularly when we think about them as 'articulated categories'? For example, if we define class, gender, race and sexuality through each other, do we not also define these categories by drawing on images and popular understandings of land, nature and non-human animals? Decades of research on class, gender, race and sexuality reveal that we tend to naturalise and reify those categories and the social difference associated with them by implicitly or explicitly linking them to biological and non-human processes and actors (see Collins 2008; Santa Anna 2002). Furthermore, ecofeminist theory and environmental justice studies have argued that the exploitation of land and non-human animals is inseparable from the exploitation of women, people of colour and Indigenous persons (Gaard 1997, 2017; Smith 2005; see also Lynch, this volume, Chapter 24; Nurse, this volume, Chapter 33; Sollund, this volume, Chapter 29).

This widening of intersectionality's scope is evident in the work of many ecofeminists and activists calling for TL (e.g., Gaard 1993; Merchant 1980; Warren and Cheney 1991). More recently, ecofeminists have challenged the nature/culture dualism that serves to oppress both women and non-human nature, and they extend this analysis to understand how women's oppression intersects with other oppressions, such as classism, colonialism, heterosexism, patriarchy and racism (Mack-Canty 2003; Regan 2006; see also Gaard 1997; Lahar 1991; Sollund, this volume, Chapter 29). Thus, drawing on ecology as a model for human behaviour, ecofeminism offers a politics that recognises our interdependency with all other beings. Ecofeminism, however, may be limited in that its analysis is rooted largely in a theory of gender power, while other scholars have argued that there are numerous other driving forces behind the problem of unsustainability that extend beyond patriarchy and androcentrism (see generally Runhovde, this volume, Chapter 31).

Building on ecofeminism and other radical intellectual and political traditions, the TL perspective argues that the domination of non-human nature is necessarily linked to the domination of human beings, and that there can be no liberation of one without the other. This narrative seeks to counter the 'Animals First' narrative tradition of AR movements that has been critiqued as nativist, patriarchal and racist. The TL narrative draws explicitly and implicitly from biocentrism/deep ecology, ecofeminism, environmental justice studies and intersectionality and TL activists articulate a theory of intersectionality that expands the traditional concept to include non-human ecosystems, land, species and trees.

In the course of my research, I interviewed many activists who have adopted and promote the TL perspective. One activist told me her story of teaching a class at a major U.S. university that reflects her support of TL:

> I started teaching a multi-disciplinary course on the theory and practice of social change … And I taught that course from the perspective of the intersection of the oppressions, weaving race, class, sex all the way through. But the point was that I was finding, consistent with this whole intersection of the oppressions thing, you know, I couldn't explain whiteness without sexism. I could not explain racism without

> patriarchy. I simply could not. It turned out I couldn't explain patriarchy without explaining pastoralism. [So] … speciesism is part of the matrix.

Building on the analysis above, another activist stated, 'It's a matter of understanding the commonalities of oppression—how different systems of power overlap. You can't fight sexism or racism without fighting speciesism and contrariwise. So total liberation tries to unite these standpoints'.

Another activist linked these forms of oppression to institutional forces in our society:

> our government, our country was founded upon exploitation. And so the capitalist system … treats not only workers, but the environment and animals as, essentially, commodities to be exploited—our entire culture is based on exploitation of human and non-human animals.

While activists offered this TL narrative of an expanded view of intersectionality, there was also a strategic choice driving their thinking. As one activist told me:

> Why we need to do it is, first of all, for all of the problems that we have to work on, and none of us have enough people. None of us have enough people; none of us have enough resources. So we kind of need the mutual support.

The 'Animals First' and TL narratives exist in deep tension with one another and represent an internal struggle within the various AR/AL movements over whether they will remain elitist, exclusive and incapable of engaging issues of social difference and justice, or whether they will confront these questions and attempt to build alliances with other movements. While not without its own shortcomings, the TL perspective seeks to unpack and challenge the myriad forms of power that gain strength and legitimacy from hierarchies within and across species, offering perhaps one of the most comprehensive theories of power of any existing social movement. For that reason, I believe there are significant points of overlap and possibilities for building common ground with EJ movements.

In the next section, I consider some of the broad contours of EJ movements to explore the possibilities of affinities, connections and collaboration with AR and TL movements and activists.

Environmental justice movements

In this section, I demonstrate that many ideas at the root of EJ movements are consonant with TL. In fact, the ideas that radical AL activists express in their public and internal movement conversations are almost entirely reflective of concepts contained at the heart of the Principles of Environmental Justice—a sort of founding document of the U.S. EJ movement (www.ejnet.org/ej/principles.html). As I have shown above, while many AR activists frequently reproduce social hierarchies, a growing number—although certainly not all—of radical AL movement activists seek to challenge all forms of inequality and domination through the lens of TL. This philosophical and political orientation offers hope for building conversations and alliances with EJ movements. Contrary to the dominant approach within AR movements, I make this argument not just based on the enlightened efforts of this largely socially privileged cause, but also on the basis of the work that EJ activists themselves have undertaken for decades.

Let us consider the Principles of Environmental Justice, adopted by activist delegates to the First National People of Color Environmental Leadership Summit in 1991. The Preamble to the Principles reads in part:

> WE, THE PEOPLE OF COLOR, gathered together at this multinational People of Color Environmental Leadership Summit, to begin to build a national and international movement of all peoples of color to fight the destruction and taking of our lands and communities, do hereby re-establish our spiritual interdependence to the sacredness of our Mother Earth.

Principle #1 affirms 'the interdependence of all species', while Principle #5 supports 'the fundamental right to political, economic, cultural and environmental self-determination of all peoples'. The delegates to that meeting—commonly referred to as the first Environmental Justice Summit—set forth in these three statements their opposition to racism and ecological destruction and recognised the inherent and cultural worth of non-human nature.

Principle #2 reads: 'Environmental Justice demands that public policy be based on mutual respect and justice for all peoples, free from any form of discrimination or bias'. Principle #3 states that 'Environmental Justice mandates the right to ethical, balanced and responsible uses of land and renewable resources in the interest of a sustainable planet *for humans and other living things*'. Principle #15 'opposes military occupation, repression and exploitation of lands, peoples and cultures, *and other life forms*'. These principles embrace the idea of ethical relations between and among all beings, both human and non-human—a cornerstone of AL.

Principle #17 speaks to key AL issues focussed on making changes in lifestyles in order to reduce harmful impacts on ecosystems and non-humans:

> Environmental Justice requires that we, as individuals, make personal and consumer choices to consume as little of Mother Earth's resources and to produce as little waste as possible; and make the conscious decision to challenge and reprioritize our lifestyles to ensure the health of the natural world for present and future generations.

While this principle might indeed reflect anthropocentric or speciesist tendencies, its intention is to underscore the interdependence and linked fates of all living beings. I therefore contend that many of the Principles of Environmental Justice are largely consistent with the politics of radical AL movements, despite the fact that there has been little effort to build a space for conversation or collaboration.

The EJ movement in the U.S. does have significant limitations, however, that make it challenging to imagine bridge-building with AL and TL activists. While EJ activists have demonstrated repeatedly a willingness to challenge state and corporate policy making through various tactics and strategies, the EJ movement is ultimately rooted in a reformist model of social change. That is, activists generally seek to push the state and corporations to embrace some degree of EJ practices, while accepting the fundamental legitimacy and existence of those institutions, including the legal system (Benford 2005). If, as philosopher David Theo Goldberg (2002) argues, states are inherently racist and exclusionary social forces, then anti-racist social movements should not expect such institutions to be capable of securing a world in which racial justice prevails. Yet, this is exactly the view that EJ movements implicitly support as they work to introduce (or undo) legislation, state and corporate policies and pursue claims through the courts. In this regard, the EJ movement's strategic orientation mirrors more closely the animal welfarist approach. The radical AL and TL movements generally adopt an anarchist and anti-capitalist perspective that rejects states and capitalism as inherently authoritarian and violent systems of appropriation, governance and control. In this respect, the EJ movement has a long way to go.

Total liberation and environmental justice

EJ and TL movements *do* have a good deal in common, however, which might escape the casual observer or narrowly focussed activist. For example, both movements challenge and oppose myriad forms of domination, hierarchy and inequality, which can include classism, colonialism, heterosexism, nativism, naturism/dominionism, patriarchy, racism and speciesism. Not only do these movements reject certain forms of hierarchy, they also challenge the violence those hierarchies embody and authorise. The list is long and includes war, the slaughter and consumption of non-human animals and the appropriation and/or destruction of forests, rivers and threats to air and water quality. These movements may oppose such violence for different reasons and with different emphases, but their focus on these practices suggests possibilities for cross-movement conversation, analysis and collaborative action.

Both movements also oppose the violence associated with states and dominant economic systems like capitalism and socialism. As I noted earlier, the EJ movement tends to take a reformist approach to these social institutions, but it nevertheless refuses to stand for their excessive abuses of vulnerable human populations and their associated ecosystem bases. The EJ movement's support of civil rights, human rights and the sacredness of non-human nature reflects these values.

Both movements also view human society as the source or point of origin for the harm visited upon vulnerable bodies, whether they are human or non-human. In that sense, both movements adopt a biocentric and/or posthumanist orientation to varying degrees. While the TL movement pursues a thoroughly posthumanist worldview, the EJ movement is perhaps best described as a hybrid of humanism and posthumanism.

Broadly, both movements view threats to ecological sustainability as harmful to all life forms. While much of the AR movement has been rightly criticised for its general lack of attention to ecosystem defence, the TL movement makes clear connections among risks to ecosystems, humans and non-human animals. As one activist told me, 'I'm an animal liberation activist, but that means I must also be in favor of forest protection and preservation because that's home for countless animals'. As for the EJ movement, the first of 17 Principles of Environmental Justice affirms 'the interdependence of all species', underscoring that movement's commitment to protecting the future of all life forms.

Both the EJ and total liberation movements practice what scholars have called 'dissident citizenship', because they 'publicly challenge prevailing structures of power … [through] extra-institutional, oppositional tactics … [and adopt views] that are not consistently entering the dominant political discourse' (Boykoff 2007: 20; see also Maira 2009). Boykoff (2007: 20) views dissident citizenship as a key force that 'challenges privilege … and seek[s] out forms of authority and domination … vigorously questioning their legitimacy'. The state often responds by ignoring, appeasing, or co-opting such dissident groups, or it can choose to suppress them directly. Piven and Cloward (1971) argue that the state suppresses dissent not only to protect its political and social interests, but also to preserve capitalism itself, so that dissident groups that adopt an anti-capitalist orientation are likely to be on the receiving end of both state and corporate repression (see also Brisman 2012). As a result, many TL and AL activists have been imprisoned while many EJ activists are placed under surveillance and frequently co-opted.

Finally, both the TL and EJ movements are important actors in broader efforts to attribute accountability and responsibility for harms visited upon ecosystems, non-human animals and marginalised people—all of which are key concerns of the field of green criminology (Beirne and South 2007; Brisman and South 2017a, 2017b; Brisman and South, this volume, Chapter 1; White 2008, 2010). The EJ movement tends to focus its attention on the problems associated with the negative externalities of production and consumption by states, corporations and privileged human communities because these institutions and groups routinely make decisions that cause considerable harm to other people and their environments. And those decisions are often well within the bounds of existing law—a reminder that the definition of 'crime' is a social construction and rarely if ever universally accepted (see, e.g., Brisman 2011, 2016). For TL activists, virtually any form of hierarchy—whether among humans or between humans, non-humans and ecosystems—authorises an enormous range of violent and routine practices.

We must note that what TL activists might define as 'criminal' would be viewed as legal, normal and morally appropriate by most human denizens of almost any given nation. Thus 'crime'—green or otherwise—is not a given and must be understood as socially constructed and often deeply contested. Any effort by scholars or movement activists to define certain routine institutional and widespread social practices as 'criminal' will require a great deal of energy. Not surprisingly, it has been much easier for states, corporations and media organisations to label the actions of activists challenging threats to vulnerable human populations, non-human animals and ecosystems as 'criminal' and even 'terrorist', and the 'green scare' offers ample evidence to that effect. The 'green scare' is the term AR and radical environmental activists have given to the recent increase in state repression directed at these movements. These measures generally include surveillance, infiltration, intimidation and imprisonment. A major part of this effort has also included state and federal legislation that increases penalties for animal rights and radical environmental activism, often by labelling such activities as 'terrorist' (Pellow 2014; see generally Brisman, in press). Counter efforts by activists to label states and corporations as 'the real eco-terrorists' have enjoyed limited success.

Discussion and conclusion

The goal of this chapter has been to explore points of tension and possibilities for building common ground between AR and EJ movements. What I have found in my research and in interactions among these movements over the decades is that, while there are barriers to initiating conversations and collaboration on both sides, they exist largely within the AR movement. That movement tends to adhere to a single-issue emphasis to the neglect of other critical issues, while the EJ movement is necessarily a multi-issue effort that integrates ecological sustainability with civil rights, human rights, women's rights, Indigenous peoples' rights and public health. While it is certainly the case that the EJ movement has not embraced an AR perspective, EJ activists have long supported the protection and preservation of non-human species. This, however, has been on the grounds that these species are often integral to the ecosystems that people depend upon for food and other resources. That is indeed a divide that is unlikely to be bridged because Indigenous communities and other vulnerable peoples tend to rely on a multiplicity of food sources (see generally Nurse, this volume, Chapter 33).

More problematic, however, is that many elitist, homophobic, patriarchal and racist elements are quite evident in AR movements. As indicated earlier in this chapter, numerous parts of the AR movement perpetuate social injustices in various ways by reinforcing white privilege and paying little attention to class, ethnic, gender and racial inequalities. These tendencies produce barriers to even considering a conversation—let alone *collaboration*—between AR and EJ movements because the foundation of EJ politics is a commitment to social justice for vulnerable human communities, while the core of the AR movement is what I have called the 'Animals First' narrative. Fortunately, many criticisms of the latter perspective have, in part, given rise to what some activists have called the TL perspective.

Total Liberation is a framework that a growing number of animal (and Earth) liberation activists promote—one that challenges all forms of domination and hierarchy, within and across species. This perspective offers a real sign of hope and possibility for linking some of the key concepts from both the AR and EJ movements and pushing them forward intellectually and politically.

Like the AL movement, however, the TL movement is burdened by the following dilemma with regard to building alliances with people of colour: in their efforts to confront the socially constructed hierarchies and divisions between human and non-humans, they run up against the historically entrenched and presently taboo subject of the association of non-Europeans with a 'state of nature', as highlighted in the writings of philosophers like Hobbes, Locke, Pufendorf and Rousseau (see Goldberg 2002). That is, every step toward fighting speciesism and anthropocentrism is also a step that comes dangerously close to what David Theo Goldberg calls 'naturalism'—those theories of humanity that place non-Europeans in an inherent state of inferiority because of their supposed subhuman (read 'animal' or 'natural') qualities. I view this as a formidable, if not intractable, challenge for the foreseeable future. Most TL activists are white and seek to work as allies with vulnerable human populations, but many do not seem to acknowledge this issue. Instead, they appear to circumvent it by emphasising that the association with non-human nature must be applied to *all* humans as one of many interdependent species. This is a universalist approach to politics that ignores or glosses over the deeply entrenched histories of differentiation and oppression *within* the human community.

Another way of putting this is that TL activists are attempting to challenge the socially constructed hierarchies between humans and non-human animals (and non-human nature, more generally) with the goal of liberating all sides. The problem is that some of these barriers were actually already flattened and broken down via centuries of European and Euro-American racism that placed people of colour on a level with non-human animals and in a state of nature—precisely as part of a unified project of dominating both. This, in fact, is the root of the problem of environmental racism: people of colour are generally associated with non-human nature—with impure and socially contaminated spaces—so ecological violations against these people and their environments are deemed normal and appropriate. The dilemma, then, is that TL activists are trying to confront those divides for all of humanity in a way that might ignore the long-standing legacies of earlier efforts to do so (albeit for different reasons), which was central to the rise of European modernity. These groups then run the risk of re-introducing or reproducing the foundational problems of racism and anthropocentricism that gave rise to the present-day socio-ecological crises.

This dilemma may be irresolvable, but it is one that we must be aware of in our intellectual and political engagements within and across these intellectual fields and movements. Following White (2003, 2013) and Brisman (2008), perhaps any conversation between EJ movements and TL activists might begin with the goal of connecting *environmental* justice (the intersection of social inequality and environmental harm) with *ecological* justice (the relationship of human beings to the broader non-human world). These two concepts are infinitely productive for each other.

While the EJ movement has challenged racism and the symptoms of capitalism, it is not clear that the movement in the U.S. has linked the two in a way that seeks to confront them head on. In other words, like the civil rights movement, the EJ movement tends to place a primary emphasis on challenging institutional racism (within environmental policy making) through the legal system and political system (i.e., legislation). As a small number of scholars have argued (Benford 2005; Cole and Foster 2001), working within an inherently racist and anti-ecological capitalist-state system is likely to yield limited results and might possibly prove counterproductive. This is where I think the most useful links among the EJ, AL and TL movements may exist—at the intersection of anarchist, anti-capitalist and anti-racist politics. The EJ movement has a great deal to teach the AL and TL movements about race and the history of how communities of colour have been violated by states and corporations, while the AL and TL movements have embraced thoroughly an anarchist and anti-capitalist orientation that is missing in the EJ movement. The EJ and AL/TL movements are not just focussed on the goals of liberating certain populations from oppression; they are also implicitly focussed on challenging dominant *property* relations, which necessarily suggests a critique of the state and capitalist systems, albeit with important variations across these movements.

In closing, I would like to return to the question of green criminology and make a few observations. In my view, perhaps the greatest promise of green criminology is that it draws inspiration from the admirable work of critical criminologists and applies those insights to the myriad interfaces between human and non-human bodies and ecosystems. Critical criminologists have historically questioned dominant definitions, labels, explanations and theories of crime, consistently exploring not only the causes and consequences of crime, but asking how criminalisation itself serves particular interests and works against others (Gilmore 2007; Rodriguez 2006). The way in which 'crime' becomes a terrain of power tells a far more interesting story than do the actions in question.

For the EJ, AL and TL movements, green criminology offers a discourse and theory that pulls back the veil of dominant concepts of crime to expose a world in which hierarchy and power play a determining role in defining crime, criminals, justice, punishment and remedies. The hope is that a critical approach to crime will contribute to building a world in which power imbalances are challenged at every juncture and scale. This is a formidable task because these movements are under fire from many quarters. The EJ movement is threatened by the erosion of civil rights laws, the gutting of the U.S. Environmental Protection Agency (see, e.g., Whitman 2017) and policies that routinely pit economic growth against ecological sustainability and human rights. The AL and TL movements are threatened by direct state repression from the Federal Bureau of Investigation (via the 'green scare', mentioned above), the criminalisation of above-ground activism and the public labelling of activism as 'terrorism'. As much as the actions of these movements matter considerably, it will surely be the ideas and discourse around what actually constitutes crime and justice in relation to protecting humans, non-humans and ecosystems that will matter a great deal more.

References

Beirne, P. and South, N. (eds.) 2007. *Issues in Green Criminology: Confronting Harms Against Environments, Humanity and Other Animals*. Cullompton, Devon, UK: Willan.

Benford, R. 2005. 'The half-life of the environmental justice frame: Innovation, diffusion, and stagnation,' In D. N. Pellow and R. J. Brulle (eds.) *Power, Justice, and the Environment: A Critical Appraisal of the Environmental Justice Movement*, pp. 37–53. Cambridge, MA and London, UK: MIT Press.

Best, S. 2010. Total liberation: Revolution for the 21st century. Proceedings of the 2nd International Meeting for Environmental Ethics in Athens, Greece. Retrieved from http://drstevebest.wordpress.com/2010/12/31/total-liberation-revolution-for-the-21st-century-4/.

Best, S. 2011. Our Task. Posted on the North American Animal Liberation Front Press Office website. August 4.

Best, S. and A. J. Nocella, II (eds.) 2004. *Terrorists or Freedom Fighters? Reflections on the Liberation of Animals*. New York: Lantern Books.

Best, S. and A. J. Nocella, II (eds.) 2006. *Igniting a Revolution: Voices in Defense of the Earth*. Oakland, CA: AK Press.
Boykoff, J. 2007. *Beyond Bullets: The Suppression of Dissent in the United States*. Oakland, CA: AK Press.
Brisman, A. 2007. 'Toward a more elaborate typology of environmental values: Liberalizing criminal disenfranchisement laws and policies,' *New England Journal on Criminal & Civil Confinement*, 33(2): 283–457.
Brisman, A. 2008. 'Crime-environment relationships and environmental justice,' *Seattle Journal for Social Justice*, 6(2): 727–817.
Brisman, A. 2011. 'Advancing critical criminology through anthropology,' *Western Criminology Review*, 12 (2): 55–77.
Brisman, A. 2012. 'Ritualized degradation in the twenty-first century: A revisitation of Piven and Cloward's *Regulating the Poor*,' *Seattle Journal for Social Justice*, 10(2): 793–814.
Brisman, A. 2016. *Geometries of Crime: How Young People Perceive Crime and Justice*. London: Palgrave Macmillan.
Brisman, A. in press. 'Direct action as conceptual art: An examination of the role of the Communiqué for eco-defense,' *Radical Criminology*.
Brisman, A. and South, N. 2017a. 'Green criminology,' In Sixth Edition A. Liebling, S. Maruna and L. McAra (eds.) *The Oxford Handbook of Criminology*, pp. 329–349. Oxford: Oxford University Press.
Brisman, A. and South, N. 2017b. 'Green criminology,' In A. Brisman, E. Carrabine and N. South (eds.) *The Routledge Companion to Criminological Theory and Concepts*, pp. 297–300. London and New York: Routledge.
Bullard, R. D. 1994. *People of Color Environmental Groups*. Flint, MI: Charles Steward Mott Foundation.
Bullard, R. D. 1990. *Dumping in Dixie: Race, Class and Environmental Quality*, Third Edition. Boulder, CO: Westview Press.
Cole, L. and S. Foster. 2001. *From the Ground Up: Environmental Racism and the Rise of the Environmental Justice Movement*. New York: New York University Press.
Collins, P. H. 2008. *Black Feminist Thought: Knowledge, Consciousness, and the Politics of Empowerment*. Abingdon, Oxon, UK: Routledge.
Denzin, N. 2009. *The Research Act: A Theoretical Introduction to Sociological Methods*. Chicago: Aldine Transaction.
Gaard, G. 1993. *Ecofeminism* (Ethics in Action). Philadelphia, PA: Temple University Press.
Gaard, G. 1997. 'Toward a Queer Ecofeminism,' *Hypatia*, 12(1): 114–137.
Gaard, G. 2017. *Critical Ecofeminism*. Lanham, MD: Lexington Books.
Gaffey, C. 2017. 'Who Is Joe Arpaio, 'America's Toughest Sheriff' and the Man President Trump Wants to Pardon?' *Newsweek*. August 15.
Gilmore, R. W. 2007. *Golden Gulag: Prisons, Surplus, Crisis, and Opposition in Globalizing California*. Berkeley and Los Angeles: University of California Press.
Goldberg, D. T. 2002. *The Racial State*. Malden, MA: Blackwell Publishers.
Gottlieb, R. 1993. *Forcing the Spring: The Transformation of the American Environmental Movement*. Washington, DC: Island Press.
Henne, K. and Troshynski, E. I. 2017. 'Intersectionality,' In A. Brisman, E. Carrabine and N. South (eds.) *The Routledge Companion to Criminological Theory and Concepts*, pp. 316–320. London and New York: Routledge.
Henne, K. and E. I. Troshynski. 2019. 'Intersectional criminologies for the contemporary moment: Crucial questions of power, praxis and technologies of control,' *Critical Criminology: An International Journal*, 27(1): 55–71.
Jasper, J. M. and Nelkin, D. 1992. *The Animal Rights Crusade: The Growth of a Moral Protest*. New York: The Free Press.
Kim, C. J. 2015. *Dangerous Crossings: Race, Species, and Nature in a Multicultural Age*. New York: Cambridge University Press.
Lahar, S. 1991. 'Ecofeminist theory and grassroots politics,' *Hypatia*, 6(1): 28–45.
Lofland, J., D. Snow, L. Anderson and L. H. Lofland. 2005. *Analyzing Social Settings: A Guide to Qualitative Observation and Analysis*, Fourth Edition. Belmont, CA: Wadsworth.
Mack-Canty, C. 2003. Third-wave feminism and the need to reweave the nature/culture duality. *NWSA Journal*, 16(3): 154–179.
Maira, S. M. 2009. *Missing: Youth, Citizenship, and Empire after 9/11*. Durham, NC: Duke University Press.
McClintock, A. 1995. *Imperial Leather: Race, Gender, and Sexuality in the Colonial Contest*. New York and London: Routledge.

Merchant, C. 1980. *The Death of Nature: Women, Ecology and the Scientific Revolution*. New York: HarperCollins.

Nibert, D. 2002. *Animal Rights/Human Rights: Entanglements of Oppression and Liberation*. Lanham, MD: Rowman and Littlefield.

Oropeza, L. 2005. *Raza Si! Guerra No! Chicano Protest and Patriotism During the Viet Nam War Era*. Berkeley and Los Angeles: University of California Press.

Park, L. S. and Pellow, D. N. 2011. *The Slums of Aspen: Immigrants vs. the Environment in America's Eden*. New York: New York University Press.

Patterson, C. 2002. *Eternal Treblinka: Our Treatment of Animals and the Holocaust*. New York: Lantern Books.

Pellow, D. N. 2010. The Animal Enterprise Terrorism Act and the Assault on Academic Freedom. *Earth First! The Radical Environmental Journal*. 30th Anniversary Special Edition, Volume 1. November/December, pp. 30–31.

Pellow, D. N. 2014. *Total Liberation: The Power and Promise and Animal Rights and the Radical Earth Movement*. Minneapolis, MN: University of Minnesota Press.

Piven, F. F. and Cloward, R. A. 1971. *Regulating the Poor: The Functions of Public Welfare*. New York and Toronto: Vintage Books.

Regan, T. 2006. *Defending Animal Rights*. Champaign, IL: University of Illinois Press.

Rodriguez, D. 2006. *Forced Passages: Imprisoned Radical Intellectuals and the US. Prison Regime*. Minneapolis, MN: University of Minnesota Press.

Rosebraugh, C. 2004. *Burning Rage of a Dying Planet: Speaking for the Earth Liberation Front*. New York: Lantern.

Santa Anna, O. 2002. *Brown Tide Rising. Metaphors of Latinos in Contemporary American Public Discourse*. Austin, TX: University of Texas Press.

Scarce, R. 1990. *Eco-Warriors: Understanding the Radical Environmental Movement*. Chicago: The Noble Press, Inc.

Shabecoff, P. 1993. *A Fierce Green Fire: The American Environmental Movement*. Washington, DC: Island Press.

Smith, Andrea. 2005. *Conquest: Sexual violence and American Indian genocide*. Cambridge, MA: South End Press.

Warren, K. and Jim, C. 1991. 'Ecological feminism and ecosystem ecology,' *Hypatia* 6(1): 179–197.

White, R. 2003. 'Environmental issues and the criminological imagination,' *Theoretical Criminology*, 7(4): 483–506.

White, R. 2008. *Crimes Against Nature: Environmental Criminology and Ecological Justice*. Cullompton, Devon, UK: Willan.

White, R., ed. 2010. *Global Environmental Harm: Criminological Perspectives*. Cullompton, Devon, UK: Willan.

White, R. 2013. *Environmental Harm: An Eco-justice Perspective*. Bristol, UK: Policy Press.

Whitman, C. T. 2017. 'How Not To Run The E.P.A.,' *The New York Times*. Sept. 8: A27. Retrieved from www.nytimes.com/2017/09/08/opinion/how-not-to-run-the-epa.html?action=click&pgtype=Homepage&clickSource=story-heading&module=opinion-c-col-left-region&region=opinion-c-col-left-region&WT.nav=opinion-c-col-left-region&_r=0.

Part VI

Relationships in green criminology

Environment and culture

33

Environmental justice and the rights of Indigenous peoples

Angus Nurse

This chapter examines potentially contrasting perspectives on environmental justice, considering how Indigenous people often suffer disproportionately from the negative impacts of environmentally harmful activities but may also have their traditional rights upheld through exemptions in law. As a result, a complexity (and apparent paradox) exists where Indigenous people are marginalised with respect of access to natural resources, but, due to their ethnic and cultural status, may be able to continue with some activities that might otherwise be prohibited under environmental and wildlife legislation.

The term 'environmental racism' covers various activities but has been defined as

> racial discrimination in environmental policy making, the enforcement of regulations and laws, the deliberate targeting of communities of color for toxic waste facilities, the official sanctioning of the life-threatening presence of poisons and pollutants in our communities, and the history of excluding people of color from leadership of the ecology movements.
>
> *(Mohai et al. 2009: 406–7 (footnoted omitted))*

Environmental racism exists when governments and corporations pursue policies that disproportionately impact marginalised groups and minorities, including Indigenous peoples, or engage in racial discrimination in environmental decisions or policy implementation (Bullard 2007; Bullard et al. 2008; Park 1998; Schlosberg 2007). Activists and scholars argue that toxic factories and pollution and waste sites affect communities of colour more than Caucasians (Cutter 1995; Ozymy et al. this volume, Chapter 8; Schlosberg 2007), and their short-term goals are to achieve race-linked theory and action, which means considering positive racially oriented action to combat discrimination.

This chapter examines the social construction of environmental justice for Indigenous peoples through a green criminological lens. It considers examples of culturally endorsed animal harm, such as the whaling practices of ethnic minorities and Indigenous peoples, that would otherwise be unlawful under contemporary environmental protection legislation. Thus, the chapter contemplates the extent to which contemporary perspectives on environmental and ecological justice can apply where environmental protection policy might be in conflict with the rights of Indigenous peoples.[1] The chapter discusses existing perspectives on Indigenous rights and how these align—or not—with contemporary ecological (and species) justice discourse. In doing so, the chapter also highlights the cultural importance of certain natural resource exploitation practices in relation to specific ethnic or cultural identities such that, for example, animal killing activities continue despite legislative or political efforts to eliminate them. Animal harm, socially constructed to have different meanings according to the society in which it occurs (Nurse 2013), can allow the same act (for example, the killing of a whale) to have multiple meanings: illegal wildlife crime in the view of animal activists and legislators, or legitimate cultural practice in the eyes of the Indigenous person committing the act (Nurse 2013; Schaffner 2011). The chapter thus examines inequality by exploring various conceptions of how Indigenous people's historical environmental rights have been criminalised or become subject to challenge by contemporary environmental justice perspectives.

Environmental justice and environmental racism

Low-income and minority communities are often discriminated against in respect of access to environmental justice (Cutter 1995; Ozymy et al. this volume, Chapter 8; Pellow this volume, Chapter 32; Pullido 2010; see also Brisman 2013). Delegates to the First National People of Color Environmental Leadership Summit held on October 24–27, 1991, in Washington DC, drafted and adopted 17 Principles of Environmental Justice which sought:

> to ensure environmental justice; to promote economic alternatives which would contribute to the development of environmentally safe livelihoods; and, to secure our political, economic and cultural liberation that has been denied for over 500 years of colonization and oppression, resulting in the poisoning of our communities and land and the genocide of our peoples.
>
> *(Network 2018)*

The Principles of Environmental Justice identify the significance of the problems faced by people of colour due to alleged institutional and cultural racism, which results in discrimination in access to goods, opportunities, resources and services. Research shows consistently how people of colour are marginalised with respect to access to environmental resources and in the context of the siting of environmentally harmful operations within their communities (Pellow this volume, Chapter 32; Schlosberg 2007; Scott 2014). As noted above, institutional racism may be a factor, and various policies, practices and procedures adopted by a range of institutions have had a disproportionately negative effect on racial minorities' access to and quality of goods, services and opportunities (Brisman 2013). Accordingly, when considering environmental racism as a bar to environmental justice, there is a need to consider the extent to which individual and institutional racism are part of systemic societal systems that support and allow discrimination, whether consciously or unconsciously. Arguably, intent is irrelevant; the result of the behaviour, policies and practices and their impact on members of minority groups and on the group as a whole are the core concerns of environmental racism. Thus, racial discrimination can occur even where an institution, such as a state environmental agency, has no intention of race-based discrimination, but the effect of its policies and practices results in a racially disproportionate impact. Blanton (2011) notes, for example, how racist municipal practices caused pollution and deterioration of the areas in which the black community in Oklahoma resided, thereby marking those spaces as 'black' and arguably in receipt of differential treatment. In the context of racism, power is a necessary precondition for discrimination. Racism depends on the ability to give or withhold social benefits, facilities, opportunities and services from someone who is entitled to them, and is denied on the basis of race, colour or national origin. The source of power can be formal or informal, legal or illegal, and is not limited to traditional concepts of power.

While the disproportionate impact of toxic factories, pollution and waste sites borne by communities of colour constitutes one form of environmental injustice and racism (Kay and Katz 2012; Scott 2014), environmental racism can also occur in situations where a dominant group in society imposes its will on Indigenous groups in a manner that threatens their cultural survival or requires them to conform to societal norms that they may not share. This is especially the case when considering the conflict between Western or colonial governments and the Indigenous groups they have supplanted (see, e.g., Goyes this volume, Chapter 12; Brisman and South this volume, Chapter 36). Dhillon and Young (2010), for example, highlight how the deliberate siting of hazardous waste sites, incinerators, landfills, and polluting industries in communities inhabited by First Nations communities (in Canada) represents a social justice issue of considerable magnitude. Similarly, because natural resources and the environment are often considered to belong to no one (Weston and Bollier 2013), they can effectively be seized by governments and exploited against the wishes of Indigenous people who have traditionally lived off the land and who have considerable investment in natural resources.[2] Human rights norms can potentially come into play, however, given that there are international human rights instruments that also protect the environmental rights of Indigenous peoples.

Legal protection for Indigenous peoples

Different cultures possess different attitudes, beliefs, customs, laws and practices regarding animal killing (see, e.g., Nurse 2013; Preece 1999; van Uhm this volume, Chapter 30), although there is no unitary term for the killing of animals. Criminologists have proposed the term 'theriocide' to refer to diverse human actions that result in animal death (see, e.g., Berine 2014; Sollund 2017). Indigenous peoples may, therefore, have developed cultural practices arguably at odds with contemporary environmental protection legislation (discussed later in this chapter). Thus, legislation pertaining to the protection of the environment, which can include non-human animals, risks threatening the cultural expression and identity of Indigenous peoples where their traditional practices might be criminalised under such environmental and wildlife protection laws. Many Western countries, for example, generally prohibit unsustainable use of animals and unnecessary suffering caused to animals in food production. Killing of animals for food is also tightly controlled (Croall 2007, 2013; Tourangeau and Fitzgerald this volume, Chapter 11) such that much killing of animals outside of the regulated activity of animal processing operations risks giving rise to legal problems in the taking and use of animals.

Human rights law, however, explicitly recognises the 'difference' of Indigenous practices via its incorporation and classification of the rights of Indigenous peoples into a framework of exemptions from certain legislative provisions. Human rights generally attach to *individuals* and frequently concern the relationship between the individual and the state or state institutions. The recent recognition of human rights attaching to groups, however, is consistent with other human rights considerations on the right to self-determination and to preserving traditional cultures and cultural activity (Nurse 2017). Specifically, human rights law provides land rights and rights of cultural preservation that sometimes recognise that Indigenous peoples should be exempt from the confines of national environmental or animal law where this is considered necessary in order to give effect to cultural self-preservation and expression.

Indigenous peoples are broadly recognised as distinct ethnic groups by international and regional regulatory bodies. They are given a legal status in international law that acknowledges both historic and present threats and the assimilation and alienation of their traditional way of life. The International Labour Organisation's (ILO) 1953 guidelines (still in force today) describe Indigenous peoples as:

> descendants of the original aboriginal population living in a given country at the time of settlement or conquest (or successive waves of conquest) by some of the ancestors of the non-Indigenous groups in whose hand political and economic power at present lies. In general these descendants tend to live more in conformity with the social, economic and cultural institutions which existed before colonisation or conquest … than with the culture of the nation to which they belong; they do not fully share in the national economy and culture owing to barriers of language, customs, creed, prejudice, and often out-of-date and unjust systems of worker-employer relationship and other social and political factors.
>
> *(ILO 1953: paras 25–26)*

The International Covenant on Civil and Political Rights (ICCPR) of 1966 also states that:

> In those States in which ethnic, religious or linguistic minorities exist, persons belonging to such minorities shall not be denied the right, in community with the other members of their group, to enjoy their own culture, to protect and practice their own religion or to use their own language.
>
> *(Article 27)*

Further protection for Indigenous peoples and clarification of their rights has been provided by the United Nations Declaration on Indigenous Peoples (UNDRIP), which was adopted by the UN General Assembly on 13 September 2007, by a majority of 144 states in favour, 4 votes against (Australia, Canada, New Zealand and the United States (U.S.)) and 11 abstentions (Azerbaijan, Bangladesh, Bhutan, Burundi, Colombia, Georgia, Kenya, Nigeria, Russian Federation, Samoa and Ukraine). The four countries originally voting against UNDRIP subsequently reversed their position and by 2017 were all in support of the declaration.

Arguably, the UNDRIP is the most comprehensive contemporary international instrument pertaining to the rights of Indigenous peoples. The United Nations (2018) maintains that

> it establishes a universal framework of minimum standards for the survival, dignity and well-being of the Indigenous peoples of the world and it elaborates on existing human rights standards and fundamental freedoms as they apply to the specific situation of Indigenous peoples.

The basis of the UNDRIP is to affirm that Indigenous peoples are equal to all other peoples, while recognising 'the urgent need to respect and promote the inherent rights of Indigenous peoples which derive from their political, economic and social structures and from their cultures, spiritual traditions, histories and philosophies, especially their rights to their lands, territories and resources' (Annex to the Declaration, United Nations 2018). Accordingly, Article 5 of the UNDRIP states that 'Indigenous peoples have the right to maintain and strengthen their distinct political, legal, economic, social and cultural institutions, while retaining their right to participate fully, if they so choose, in the political, economic, social and cultural life of the State'. Article 8 provides that states shall provide for effective mechanisms for prevention and redress for (among other things):

> (a) Any action which has the aim or effect of depriving [Indigenous peoples] of their integrity as distinct peoples, or of their cultural values or ethnic identities;
> (b) Any action which has the aim or effect of dispossessing [Indigenous peoples] of their lands, territories or resources.

Several articles of UNDRIP also set out the framework for forms of access to environmental justice, including Articles 24, 25 and 26, which arguably protect the right of Indigenous peoples to exploit natural resources (including wildlife) located within their community and to have their Indigenous knowledge recognised and protected:

> Article 24—Indigenous peoples have the right to their traditional medicines and health practices, including the right to the protection of vital medicinal plants, animals and minerals.
>
> Article 25—Indigenous peoples have the right to maintain and strengthen their distinctive spiritual and material relationship with the lands, territories, waters and coastal seas and other resources which they have traditionally owned or otherwise occupied or used, and to uphold their responsibilities to future generations in this regard.
>
> Article 26—Indigenous peoples have the right to own, develop, control and use the lands and territories, including the total environment of the lands, air, waters, coastal seas, sea-ice, flora and fauna and other resources which they have traditionally owned or otherwise occupied or used. This includes the right to the full recognition of their laws, traditions and customs, land-tenure systems and institutions for the development and management of resources, and the right to effective measures by States to prevent any interference with, alienation of or encroachment upon these rights.
>
> *(United Nations 2018)*

Accordingly, the UNDRIP provides a framework for a form of environmental justice for Indigenous peoples and indicates to states the importance of protecting their rights.

In addition to the general provisions in international law, such as the ICCPR and the UNDRIP, which put states under an obligation to protect minority rights, specific provisions exist in national laws to provide aboriginal subsistence rights. Such rights are the main route through which aboriginal people may achieve food security, and thus the animal killing, which takes place in exercising those rights, constitutes legal activity that would otherwise be unlawful. Such activity, however, is usually subject to strict controls, mainly through the use of quotas that determine the number of animals that can be killed and permits which specify who is authorised to carry out this form of animal harm. Where either quotas are exceeded or animal hunting, trapping, or killing is carried out in contravention of the regulations, unlawful animal harm occurs. Such ostensibly unlawful animal harm, however, may still be argued to be a form of cultural self-expression, raising questions about both the mechanisms through which cultural identity is controlled and regulated, as well as the cultural necessity of such animal harm. In common with other forms of legitimised animal harm (such as the trade in wildlife), legal animal harm may exist alongside illegal animal harm in subsistence and 'cultural' killing. Where animal killing has importance as cultural self-expression, it may stand in conflict with conservation and animal protection priorities and give rise to animal crime (Nurse 2013).

As a result of the considerations afforded under human rights legislation, 'whale hunting, reindeer husbandry and a variety of other usufructory rights' can be granted to Indigenous peoples to the exclusion of others (Smith 2010: 583). These rights allow Indigenous peoples to kill, hunt and harvest otherwise protected animals where doing so is considered necessary to their cultural expression and to preserve a specific way of life that is otherwise under threat (Nurse 2013). In theory, at least, affording rights to Indigenous peoples in this way distinguishes culturally based forms of animal harm carried out by Indigenous peoples from sport and trophy hunting carried out as a leisure pursuit or the commercial killing and trade in wildlife conducted mostly for profit (see Runhovde this volume, Chapter 31; Sollund this volume, Chapter 29; van Uhm this volume, Chapter 30) in that it represents an integral part of a particular 'ethnic' lifestyle. In practice, however, despite its acceptance by courts in numerous countries, there are questions over the extent to which animal harm of this type remains a cultural necessity that should be allowed to continue. Under Article 27 of the ICCPR, minority cultural rights can be secured only by persons belonging to the specified minority group; the right of self-determination provided under Article 1 of the ICCPR is a *group* right, rather than an *individual* right, however. As a result, Indigenous people wishing to carry out animal husbandry activities may need to demonstrate compliance with certain criteria determining their participation in the cultural life of a defined ethnic minority, rather than claiming an individual right to be exempt from national laws that prohibit animal killing. This raises the question of how to determine which animal killing is (legally) acceptable as part of the expression of Indigenous cultural identity and which animal killing may be undertaken by individuals under the cloak of self-expression. As with other forms of animal harm discussed in previous research (e.g., Nurse 2013; Sollund 2017), illegal animal harm exists alongside or under the guise of legal animal use activities. The examples of fishing, whaling (discussed later) and reindeer herding by Indigenous peoples help to clarify the social construction of this form of animal harm.

Animal killing, environmental justice and Indigenous peoples

The U.S. Environmental Protection Agency (EPA) provides the following overview of the conflict between contemporary lifestyles, which exploit the environment, and the more 'natural' environmentally conscious lifestyles of Indigenous people:

> Advanced knowledge, innovation, technology and wealth have accelerated the insatiable need to feed, finance and advance growth and development, consuming natural resources at a rate that exceeds Mother Earth's ability to restore. At the same time, Indigenous peoples whose communities and nations pre-date the settler-state have maintained their unique relationships with the land, rivers, seas and sky. But in the 500 years since western contact, Indigenous peoples have experienced dispossession and disenfranchisement, rendering them one of the most vulnerable subgroups on standard measures for quality of life and sustainability such as: poor health, obesity, unemployment, teen pregnancies, high school drop-out rates, drug abuse, incarceration, etc.
>
> *(EPA 2013: 8–9)*

Firestone and colleagues (2005: 222) suggest that when one culture is heavily outnumbered, marginalised, or subjugated by another (as often happens with Indigenous cultures located within a dominant non-Indigenous population), problems can arise even when the non-dominant culture exists within a democratic state. Accordingly, states have begun to introduce laws that protect Indigenous people, even going so far as to allow the harvesting of protected animals that would otherwise be unlawful. As noted above, animal harm, socially constructed to have different meanings according to the society in which it occurs, can allow the same act (for example, the killing of a whale) to have multiple meanings: illegal wildlife crime in the view of animal activists and legislators, legitimate cultural practice in the eyes of the Indigenous person committing the act (Nurse 2013). Fisher (2008: 17) claims that Indigenous people comprise around 4 per cent of the world's population and that pockets of Indigenous peoples still carry out 'sacred ways handed down from their remote ancestors and adapted to contemporary circumstances'. As a result, forms of animal killing, such as fishing, reindeer herding, whaling and even big game hunting, have cultural significance to Indigenous peoples and are integral to their ethnic identity, persisting even where such practices might otherwise be considered unlawful.

While many legal systems prohibit animal killing (except with respect to so-called 'invasive' or 'pest' species and certain species, classified as legitimate field sports quarry, killed within the scope of regulated hunting activity), exceptions are sometimes made for Indigenous peoples to engage in animal killing practices recognised as culturally significant. Some animal killing is also socially justified when individuals either do not recognise the legitimacy of the law or consider its restrictions to be unnecessarily harsh (von Essen and Allen 2017a). Robinson and Redford (1985) point out that the goals of animal conservation and those of Indigenous peoples wishing to hunt are not always compatible. They suggest that animal harm seen as integral to cultural identity often trumps legislation prohibiting animal harm from taking place where the legislation is perceived as lacking cultural legitimacy. This perspective is later echoed by White's (2008) view that human interests become privileged in determining the relationship between nature and society. While legislation may in some respects preserve species justice as a conservation priority, cultural expression rights may dictate that animal harm should continue (Nurse 2013; von Essen and Allen 2017b).

Recognising that government decisions do not always take into account the needs of Indigenous people (particularly Native Americans), a report issued by the EPA recommended the following:

> The EPA should better incorporate the wishes of state-recognized tribes and other Indigenous people in its decision-making processes through consultation and meaningful engagement/involvement in policies;
> EPA should work effectively with tribal governments regarding on-reservation environmental justice issues;
> EPA should continue to recognise and support tribal authority to set environmental standards, make environmental policy decisions and to manage environmental programs; and
> EPA should create a standing Indigenous Peoples Environmental Justice Committee to help advise EPA to address Environmental Justice concerns.

The EPA's recommendation reflects the fact that federal governments and Indigenous peoples' interests are often in conflict. Firestone et al. (2005: 220) suggest, however, that

> a fundamental change is occurring in the way Indigenous peoples' rights, aspirations and knowledge influence international environmental law. Whereas historically, international environmental law was state-centred and did not concern the rights and the role of Indigenous communities regarding environmental issues, recently a number of debates have emerged touching on issues central to Indigenous peoples.

The debates referred to by Firestone et al. (2005) include questioning: whether Indigenous people should be encouraged or forced to change their customs so that they align with broader society's mores and laws; how best to define an Indigenous practice; how to distinguish between culturally essential and merely desirable or 'cosmetic' traditional practices; and to what extent should the law permit practices to continue that perhaps should have been discontinued many years ago? The following discussion and the case study explored later in this chapter illustrate some of the complexity inherent in these questions.

Perspectives on environmental and animal harm and Indigenous peoples

As mentioned above, some forms of animal harm are an integral part of cultural and ethnic identity. While contrary to Western notions of animal welfare and animal protectionism, some cultures embrace animal harm as integral to their cultural identity, adopting attitudes towards animals that incorporate different perspectives on animal use. Practices ranging from subsistence fishing to full-scale harvesting of wild animals and their derivatives (internal organs, skin, tusks) are deeply ingrained in some cultures and can have significant religious and social significance for Indigenous people. Animal use or exploitation, including killing, when carried out in accordance with the law, may be recognised as a fundamental human right of Indigenous peoples and ethnic minorities. Activities that are claimed as distinct characteristics of ethnic identity can come into conflict with the animal protectionism of contemporary legislation, which would define some of those cultural practices as unlawful animal harm.

In some cultures, animal harm through the hunting, trapping and killing of animals was historically a necessity for subsistence: people hunted, fished and harvested animals as a means of survival (Schmidt 1998). Particularly in remote areas of the world, where the availability of other food sources was limited even as society began to develop the means of mass production and distribution of food, animals remained critical to the subsistence needs of native peoples. In addition, animals sometimes carried spiritual significance for Indigenous peoples, whose philosophy was one of living in harmony with the land, such that animals were considered almost to be kin (McLuhan 1971)—part of an extended family (Matthews 2013)—or thought to possess a spiritual power or consciousness equal or even superior to that of humans (Gill 1983; Harrod 1987). As a result, the killing of animals for sustenance was of cultural and spiritual significance to Indigenous people, such that, for many Indigenous peoples, fishing, hunting and the killing of wildlife achieved special significance as part of rituals and as a sacred responsibility entrusted only to particular members of a tribe.

Arguably, the necessity of subsistence hunting by Indigenous peoples has been altered as a result of globalisation processes and attempts to integrate (or assimilate) Indigenous peoples into a state's mainstream society (see generally Goyes this volume, Chapter 12). There still exist, however, Indigenous cultures where subsistence hunting remains a necessity (Fisher 2008: 17). Hunting and animal killing practices also hold cultural importance to some groups even where subsistence hunting is not a necessity. In a contemporary environment where environmental justice is denied to some groups and the need to assert cultural identity takes on added importance, conflict between contemporary environmentalism and Indigenous rights is perhaps inevitable. The following case study illustrates this.

Case study: the Makah whale hunt

Despite the general ban on whaling introduced in 1986 under the International Convention for the Regulation of Whaling (ICRW), aboriginal groups are allowed to harvest otherwise protected species by way of fishing and hunting whales in order to meet 'cultural and subsistence' needs—an exception that recognises centuries-long traditions of killing whales by Indigenous (native) peoples. Indigenous whale-hunting traditions are recognised by the International Whaling Commission (IWC) as being distinct from commercial whaling. The IWC regulations thus permit aboriginal subsistence whaling and the IWC sets limits for aboriginal subsistence hunts that cover a five-year period and are reviewed on this basis. Under ICRW and IWC regulations, aboriginal subsistence whaling is permitted for Inuit and Bequian people (International Whaling Commission (IWC) 2011), allowing hunting of whales within the territorial waters of Denmark (Greenland: fin and minke whales), the Russian Federation (Siberia: grey and bowhead whales), St. Vincent and the Grenadines (Bequia: humpback whales) and the U.S. (Alaska: bowhead and grey whales). Whaling carried out in accordance with IWC regulations and subject to IWC monitoring is therefore considered lawful, although strict adherence to regulations is required and a number of examples exist where Indigenous people have harmed animals in violation of the exceptions to ICRW.

The IWC recognises that whaling may be important for cultural reasons and thus permits certain Indigenous groups to engage in it provided the whaling is carried out humanely. The Makah Indian Tribe (the 'Makah') of North America contend that whaling is central to their culture and social organisation, and that 'the conduct of a whale hunt requires rituals and ceremonies which are deeply spiritual' (Makah Tribal Council and Makah Whaling Commission 2005: 5). Whaling, which has been conducted by the tribe for over 1,500 years, is a right guaranteed to them under U.S. law, specifically the Makah Treaty of Neah Bay 1855 (the 'Treaty'), signed between four Makah villages and the Governor of Washington. In essence, the Treaty established the Makah reservation, while ceding lands to the United States, providing some monetary recompense for the ceded land (Article 5 of the Treaty specifies a sum of 30,000 dollars), while also providing education and health care for the Makah. Crucially, while the Treaty required the Makah to adhere to various standards of behaviour (Article 9 specifies a dependence on the U.S. government, while Article 10 contains a prohibition on liquor on the reservation), the Treaty secures the right for the Makah to continue fishing, sealing and whaling according to their customs (Governor's Office of Indian Affairs 2018). Article 4 of the Treaty provides the rights of taking fish, whaling and sealing 'at usual and accustomed grounds'. While the Marine Mammal Protection Act of 1972 (MMPA) (16 U.S.C. 1361–1407, P.L. 92–522, 21 October 1972, 86 Stat. 1027) established a moratorium on the taking and importation of marine mammals as well as products derived from them, amendments to the MMPA in 1994 expressly preserved aboriginal fishing and whaling rights. Section 14 of the MMPA states that 'nothing in this Act including any amendments to the Marine Mammal Protection Act of 1972 made by this Act alters or is intended to alter any treaty between the United States and one or more Indian Tribes'. Thus, provisions exist in U.S. law (and which are replicated in the laws of certain other jurisdictions) that acknowledge, specifically, the cultural difference between the taking of wildlife by Indigenous people and that of (commercial) mainstream society.

According to the IWC, the Makah people's whale hunt 'invokes ancient rituals and ceremonies that are deeply spiritual to the tribe' (International Whaling Commission (IWC) 2006: 1). In the 1920s, the tribe had suspended the exercise of their whaling rights enshrined in the 1855 Treaty of Neah Bay, due to a decline in grey whale stocks, but reasserted these rights in 1999 when grey whale stocks had recovered sufficiently for whale hunting to be considered sustainable. Thus, in 1999, the Makah, with the permission of the IWC and the US government, harvested a grey whale. Following litigation concerning the new conservation status of grey whales, which had become protected under the U.S. Endangered Species Act in 1994, hunts were again temporarily suspended. Following the decision in *Anderson* v *Evans*, 371 F.3d 475 (9th Cir. 2004), however, the Makah were allowed to once again engage in whaling, subject to regulations that required the tribe to either make an application or obtain an exemption under the MMPA before they could hunt grey whales.

The nature of the animal harm involved in Makah hunts was assessed by the IWC in 2006. The IWC considered the Makah's hunting techniques, which now involved 'substituting the traditional killing lance for a large calibre rifle both to eliminate a prolonged pursuit and because the use of the killing lance would be considered inhumane by modern standards' (International Whaling Commission (IWC) 2006: 2). Gosho (1999, cited in Makah Tribe 2007) noted that the whale that had been harvested in 1999 had expired eight minutes after being harpooned and that the IWC concluded on the basis of its evidence that the .50BMG or .577 calibre firearms proposed to be used in the grey whale hunt would be 'more than adequate to humanely dispatch' grey whales during the Makah hunt (International Whaling Commission (IWC) 2006).

The question of whether the revised hunt constituted traditional subsistence hunting or commercial hunting was also considered by the IWC, which concluded that:

> The Tribe's current harvest methods retain all of the ceremonial aspects of the spiritual, physical, and mental preparations required for a traditional Makah whale hunt. The substitution of a high caliber rifle over the traditional killing lance is necessary to ensure a safe and humane harvest and eliminates a prolonged pursuit. The Tribe's harvest techniques are more than sufficient to quickly and humanely dispatch gray whales.
>
> *(International Whaling Commission (IWC) 2006: 3)*

On 8 September 2007, however, five members of the Makah tribe conducted a hunt and killed a grey whale in the Strait of Juan de Fuca in the Pacific Northwest. The hunt had been authorised by neither the tribe nor the National Marine Fisheries Services (NMFS), a division of the National Oceanic and Atmospheric Administration (NOAA), a U.S. federal agency. While there was scope for whales to be hunted lawfully in accordance with the regulations, the unauthorised hunt failed to comply with various elements of the tribe's application and the restrictions on hunting and killing grey whales contained within legislation and environmental protection policy; it thus constituted unlawful animal harm (Nurse 2013). The permit issued to the tribe restricted hunting of whales to specific areas of Makah territory on the north Olympic Peninsula at Neah Bay, and prohibited the taking of whales within the Strait of Juan de Fuca (the international boundary between Canada and the U.S. that runs through the strait). Permit restrictions 'also required the whale to be secured with a harpoon from a traditional canoe before being dispatched with shots from a high-powered rifle' (Mapes and Ervin 2007).

On 5 October 2007, the five tribal members involved in the unlawful killing of the grey whale were indicted in federal court on charges of unauthorised whaling, unauthorised taking of a marine mammal and conspiracy to engage in unlawful whaling. Civil penalties under the MMPA consisted of a $20,000 fine, with the options for criminal prosecution and seizure of vessels and equipment used in the illegal act. On 16 November 2007, the five members of the tribe were also charged in tribal court for violating the tribe's grey whale management plan, violating state and federal laws and reckless endangerment.

In March of 2008, three out of five of the tribal members involved in the illegal whaling entered guilty pleas to unlawful taking of a marine mammal in violation of the MMPA. Two members declined to make guilty pleas, however, arguing that they had not committed any crime. Despite contravening the regulatory requirements of the MMPA, the two remaining members declined to accept a plea deal that would have resulted in a probation sentence rather than a jail term on the grounds that, from their point of view, they had not done anything wrong. Clarridge (2008) reported in *The Seattle Times* that the two tribesmen believed they should be allowed to carry out their traditional hunting activities without U.S. governmental oversight of any sort. Both were convicted on federal misdemeanour charges.

In 2015, NOAA published the *Draft Environmental Impact Statement (DEIS) on the Makah Tribe Request to Hunt Gray Whales* following the Makah's proposal to resume treaty-based hunting of eastern North Pacific grey whales (*Eschrichtius robustus*) for ceremonial and subsistence purposes (National Marine Fisheries Service, West Coast Region, National Oceanic and Atmospheric Administration, U.S. Department of Commerce [NOAA] 2015).[3] The Makah proposed harvesting up to 24 whales over a six-year period, with no more than five grey whales harvested in any single year. In order to develop a full range of action alternatives, NOAA (National Marine Fisheries Service, West Coast Region, National Oceanic and Atmospheric Administration, U.S. Department of Commerce [NOAA] 2015: ES-1)

> considered the principal components associated with a hunt, including: the time when whale hunting would occur; the area where whale hunting would occur; the annual and six-year limits on the number of whales harvested, struck, and struck and lost; cessation of whale hunting if a predetermined number of Pacific Coast Feeding Group (PCFG) whales were harvested; and the method of hunting.

Drawing on pages ES-1 to ES-3 of the Executive Summary of the 1,230-page DEIS, I summarise the resultant alternatives below:

Alternative 1: the 'No-Action Alternative'. Makah grey whale hunt not authorised.

Alternative 2: the 'Tribe's Proposed Action Alternative'. This would allow harvest of four grey whales per year on average (with a maximum of five in any one year) and up to 24 whales in any six-year period. This alternative specified some exclusions on where and when hunting would be allowed to take place (the hunting season would be 1 December to 31 May) and limited the number of whales that could be taken.

Alternative 3: this alternative would have the same conditions as Alternative 2 regarding numbers of whales taken (struck), struck and lost, and harvested; seasonal restrictions; and regulatory conditions and would have the same hunt area as Alternative 2, but it would prohibit Makah hunters from making an initial strike on a grey whale within 5 miles (8 km) of shore, and assumes an all-motorised hunt with no use of a canoe. Alternative 3 also differs from Alternative 2 in its approach to managing impacts to the whale population known as the Pacific Coast Feeding Group (PCFG).

Alternative 4: this alternative would have the same conditions as Alternative 2 except the hunting season would be from 1 June through 30 November, to avoid killing a Western North Pacific (WNP) whale (because such whales would be feeding in the WNP at this time). Alternative 4 would also include restrictions specifically intended to manage impacts to the PCFG. Key restrictions include avoiding female whales, setting an annual total mortality limit using the potential biological removal approach (PBR[4]) described for Alternative 3 (but using a lower recovery factor and accounting for other sources of human-caused mortality), and the presumption that all whales struck but not landed are PCFG whales.

Alternative 5: this alternative would have the same conditions as Alternative 2, except there would be two hunting seasons of three weeks each: one from 1 December through 21 December and one from 10 May through 31 May. This split-season approach is intended to avoid killing a WNP whale and to minimise the chance of killing a PCFG whale. Alternative 5 would also differ from Alternative 2 by setting an annual PCFG mortality limit at 10 per cent of PBR.

Alternative 6: this alternative would have the same conditions as Alternative 2, except that strikes would be limited to seven over two years and an annual PCFG mortality limit would be set. Under Alternative 6 the waiver of the MMPA take moratorium would expire ten years after adoption, and regulations governing the hunt would limit the term of any hunt permit to not more than three years.

At the time of writing this chapter, the situation appears to be at an impasse. Legally, the Makah need to wait for the approval or rejection of the DEIS before their proposal is resolved and a decision is made as to whether they can resume whaling (and if so, under what conditions).

Conclusions on environmental justice and the rights of Indigenous peoples

Brisman (2014: 1353) explains that 'environmental degradation and environmental protection are intertwined with both human rights and environmental rights'—a contention that becomes more pronounced when considering the environmental rights and access to environmental justice concerns of Indigenous peoples. The Makah case (and, indeed, Canadian seal culling studies and other incidences of 'illegal' subsistence hunting) highlights the conflicting interests of ecological and species protection with the rights of Indigenous peoples. Environmental activists might argue that the actions of the Makah not only should be but actually *are* 'illegal' under international law (see, for example, Johnson 2015). Brisman (2014: 1352) notes that 'the Makah Nation is not an international legal entity separate from the United States', which means that 'as a matter of international law, the Treaty of Neah Bay is simply a domestic legal matter to be worked out between the US government and the Makah Tribe'. Arguably, this creates a situation where the Makah's domestic legal arrangement could be challenged as being contrary to international law.

The hunting, such as that carried out by the Makah, also raises issues of environmental justice. As described at the outset, Indigenous peoples are often denied access to justice in a general sense similar to that of other marginalised groups (Schlosberg 2007). Killing of animals by Indigenous people is inextricably linked to their cultural identities such that legislative efforts by governments and international regulatory bodies might be resisted as a way of asserting cultural identity and environmental rights. Environmental regulation might be seen by activists within the Indigenous community as a further attempt to impose a Westernised view of animals and animal exploitation on Indigenous peoples that is inconsistent with their beliefs about animals and animal killing. In extreme cases, one can view the imposition of Western laws prohibiting the killing of animals as a continuation of colonial attempts to 'civilise' lesser-developed societies (Bolt 1971; Winthrop 1968). Thus, regulatory control of

Indigenous hunting practices could be seen as a form of racism practiced by predominantly Anglo-American and Anglo-Saxon governments towards ethnic minority groups—a form of subjugation that requires submitting of permit applications, making traditional practices subject to monitoring, control and modernisation, and also making the people subject to the jurisdiction of federal rather than tribal courts.[5] Brisman (2014) notes that under the IWC, an Aboriginal Subsistence Whaling (ASW) quota could be granted, but the strict criteria that (would) accompany it conflict with the Makah's whaling practices, leaving them vulnerable to the consideration of national policies administered by bodies like the NOAA.

Of course, resistance to regulation is not just a response by Indigenous cultures; it also occurs in contemporary societies, where international legislative or political acts are viewed as unwanted foreign interference. Where cultural acceptance of animal harm is strong—and legal and regulatory regimes are weak or implemented poorly—animal harm will continue as a means of resistance and as a way of reasserting cultural identity (von Essen and Allen 2017a, 2017b). In this respect, contemporary environmental protection risks denying Indigenous societies their historical rights, whilst, at the same time, human rights legislation attempts to uphold their rights of self-determination and cultural expression. Accordingly, a contested and complex notion of environmental justice continues to exist for Indigenous communities.

Notes

1 A similar discussion of competing visions in relation to Arctic land and sea mammals is found in Brisman et al. (2015: 8–10) as part of a proposal for a 'criminology of environment-conflict relationships'.

2 It bears mention that the notion of *terra nullius*, translated as 'nobody's land', is applicable in international law to describe land that nobody owns and so the first nation to discover it can claim ownership. Weston and Bollier discuss 'oceans, outer space, biodiversity and the Internet as resources that belong to no one, or [exist] as *res nullius*, therefore justifying unchecked private exploitation in the Lockean tradition, while simultaneously calling such resources "global commons" that belong to everyone, or are *res communes*' (Weston and Bollier 2013: 129).

3 NOAA had issued a previous draft EIS in May 2008 and requested public comment. Despite ending the public comment period in August 2008, NOAA announced in May 2012 that it would be terminating the 2008 EIS and would begin a process to develop a new draft EIS which was subsequently published three years later in 2015.

4 'PBR' stands for 'potential biological removal' level and can be defined (broadly) as the maximum number of animals, not including natural mortalities, that may be removed from a marine mammal stock, which not allowing that marine mammal stock to maintain or reach its optimum sustainable population level (Amanda et al. 2018: 298).

5 Although in the Makah case, it should be noted that, initially, the Makah tribal court determined that the federal court should hear the case when there were difficulties in empanelling a tribal jury; ultimately, the tribe upheld the decision in *Anderson* v *Evans*, noted above (Brand 2009; Mapes 2008).

References

Bradford, A. L., Baird, R. W., Mahaffy, S. D., Gorgone, A. M., McSweeney, D. J., Cullins, T., Webster, D. L., Zerbini, A. N. 2018. 'Abundance estimates for management of endangered false killer whales in the main Hawaiian Islands,' *Endangered Species Research*, 36: 297–313. DOI: 10.3354/esr00903.

Berine, P. 2014. 'Theriocide: Naming animal killing,' *International Journal for Crime, Justice and Social Democracy*, 3(2): 49–66.

Blanton, R. 2011. 'Chronotopic landscapes of environmental racism,' *Anthrosource*, 21(1): E76–E93. DOI: 10.1111/j.1548-1395.2011.01098.x.

Bolt, C. 1971. *Victorian Attitudes to Race*. London: Routledge and Kegan Paul.

Brand, E. 2009. 'The struggle to exercise a treaty right: An analysis of the Makah Tribe's path to whale,' *Environs Environmental Law and Policy Journal*, 32(2): 287–319.

Brisman, A. 2013. 'The violence of silence: Some reflections on access to information, public participation in decision-making, and access to justice in matters concerning the environment,' *Crime, Law and Social Change*, 59(3): 291–303.

Brisman, A. 2014. 'Environmental and human rights,' in G. Bruinsma and D. Weisburd (eds.) *Encyclopedia of Criminology and Criminal Justice*, Vol. 3, pp. 1344–1353. New York: Springer Science+Business Media. DOI: 10.1007/978-1-4614-5690-2.

Brisman, A., South, N. and White, R. 2015. 'Toward a criminology of environment-conflict relationships,' in A. Brisman, N. South and R. White (eds.) *Environmental Crime and Social Conflict*, pp. 1–38. Surrey, UK: Ashgate.

Bullard, R. D. 2007. 'Wasted people: Environmental racism: A 20-year saga,' *Black Agenda Report*, [April 4, 2007]. Available at: https://blackagendareport.com/content/wasted-people-environmental-racism-20-year-saga.

Bullard, R. D., Mohai, P., Saha, R. and Wright, B. 2008. 'Toxic wastes and race at twenty: Why race still matters after all of these years,' *Lewis & Clark Environmental Law Journal*, 38(2): 371–411.

Clarridge, C. 2008. '3 Makah whale hunters plead guilty,' *The Seattle Times*, 27 March. Available at: https://seattletimes.com/seattle-news/3-makah-whale-hunters-plead-guilty/.

Croall, H. 2007. 'Food crime,' in P. Beirne and N. South (eds.) *Issues in Green Criminology: Confronting Harms Against* Environments, *Humanity and Other Animals*, pp. 206–229. Cullompton, Devon, UK: Willan.

Croall, H. 2013. 'Food crime: A green criminological perspective,' in N. South and A. Brisman (eds.) *Routledge International Handbook of Green Criminology*, pp.167–183. Abingdon, Oxon, UK: Routledge.

Cutter, S. 1995. 'Race, class and environmental justice,' *Progress in Human Geography*, 19(1): 111–122.

Dhillon, C. and Young, M. 2010. 'Environmental racism and first nations: A call for socially just public policy development,' *Canadian Journal of Humanities and Social Sciences*, 1(1): 23–37.

Energy Justice Network. 2018. 'Environmental justice/environmental racism.' Available at: https://ejnet.org/ej/.

Firestone, J., Lily, J. and Torres de Noronha, I. 2005. 'Cultural diversity, human rights, and the emergence of indigenous peoples in international and comparative environmental law,' *American University International Law Review*, 20(5): 219–292.

Fisher, M. P. 2008. *Living Religions: A Brief Introduction*. Englewood Cliffs, NJ: Prentice-Hall.

Gill, S. D. 1983. *Native American Traditions: Sources and Interpretations*. Belmont, CA: Wadsworth.

Governor's Office of Indian Affairs. 2018. 'Treaty of Neah Bay, 1855.' Available at: https://goia.wa.gov/tribal-government/treaty-neah-bay-1855.

Harrod, H. L. 1987. *Renewing the World: Plains Indian Religion and Morality*. Tucson, AZ: Univeristy of Arizona Press.

International Whaling Commission (IWC). 2006. *A Review on the Technique Employed by the Makah Tribe to Harvest Gray Whales*. Cambridge: IWC.

International Whaling Commission (IWC). 2011. *Report of the International Whaling Commission*. Cambridge: IWC.

Johnson, L. 2015. 'Makah tribe grey whale hunt question reopened by NOAA report,' CBC News. Available at: https://cbc.ca/news/canada/british-columbia/makah-tribe-grey-whale-hunt-question-reopened-by-noaa-report-1.2987811.

Kay, J. and Katz, C. 2012. 'Pollution, poverty and people of color: Living with industry,' *Scientific American*. Available at: https://scientificamerican.com/article/pollution-poverty-people-color-living-industry/.

Makah Tribal Council and Makah Whaling Commission. 2005. *The Makah Indian Tribe and Whaling*. Neah Bay and Washington, DC: Makah Tribal Council.

Makah Tribe. 2007. *Report on concerns raised at September 11, 2007 meeting on unauthorized whale hunt*, Neah Bay and Washington, DC: Makah Tribal Council. Available at: https://turtleisland.org/resources/makah07.pdf.

Mapes, L. 2008. 'Tribal Judge rejects Whalers plea deal,' *The Seattle Times*. Available at: https://seattletimes.com/seattle-news/tribal-judge-rejects-whalers-plea-deal/.

Mapes, L. V. and Ervin, K. 2007. 'Gray whale shot, killed in Rogue tribal hunt,' *The Seattle Times*, 9 September. Accesssed at: www.seattletimes.com/seattle-news/gray-whale-shot-killed-in-rogue-tribal-hunt.

Matthews, W. 2013. *World Religions*, 7th ed. Belmont, CA: Wadsworth.

McLuhan, T. C. 1971. *Touch The Earth*. New York: Promontory.

Mohai, P., Pellow D. and Timmons Roberts, J. 2009. 'Environmental justice,' *Annual Review of Environment and Resources*, 34(1): 405–430.

National Marine Fisheries Service, West Coast Region, National Oceanic and Atmospheric Administration, U.S. Department of Commerce [NOAA]. 2015. *Draft Environmental Impact Statement on the Makah Tribe Request to Hunt Gray Whales*. Seattle, WA: NOAA. Available at: https://westcoast.fisheries.noaa.gov/publications/protected_species/marine_mammals/etaceans/gray_whales/makah_deis_feb_2015.pdf.

Nurse, A. 2013. *Animal Harm: Perspectives on Why People Harm and Kill Animals*. Surrey, UK: Ashgate.

Nurse, A. 2017. 'Criminalising the right to hunt: European law perspectives on anti-hunting legislation,' *Crime, Law and Social Change*, 67(4): 383–399. DOI: 10.1007/s10611-016-9669-8.

Park, R. S. 1998. 'An examination of international environmental racism through the lens of transboundary movement of hazardous wastes,' *Indiana Journal of Global Legal Studies*, 5(2): 659–709.

Preece, R. 1999. *Animals and Nature: Culture Myths, Cultural Realities*. Vancouver: University of British Columbia.

Pullido, L. 2010. 'Rethinking environmental racism: White privilege and urban development in Southern California,' *Annals of the Association of American Geographers*, 90(1): 12–40. DOI: 10.1111/0004-5608.00182.

Robinson, J. G. and Redford, K. 1985. 'Hunting by indigenous peoples and conservation of game species,' *Parks and People*, 9(1). Available at: https://culturalsurvival.org/ourpublications/csq/article/hunting-by-Indigenous-peoples-and-conservation-game-species.

Schaffner, J. 2011. *An Introduction to Animals and the Law*. Basingstoke, Hampshire, UK: Palgrave Macmillan.

Schlosberg, D. 2007. *Defining Environmental Justice: Theories, Movements, and Nature*. New York: Oxford University Press.

Schmidt, R. 1998. *Exploring religion*. Belmont, CA: Wadsworth.

Scott, D. N. 2014. 'Environmental justice?,' in D. Coghlan and M. Brydon-Miller (eds.) *The Sage Encyclopedia of Action Research*, pp. 299–302. London: SAGE Publications Ltd.

Smith, R. K. 2010. *Texts and Materials on International Human Rights*. Abingdon, Oxon, UK: Routledge.

Sollund, R. 2017. 'Legal and illegal theriocide of trafficked animals,' in J. Maher, H. Pierpoint and P. Beirne (eds.) *The Palgrave International Handbook of Animal Abuse Studies*, pp. 453–474. London: Palgrave Macmillan.

United Nations. 2018 'United nations declaration on the rights of indigenous peoples.' Available at: https://un.org/development/desa/indigenouspeoples/declaration-on-the-rights-of-indigenous-peoples.html.

von Essen, E. and Allen, M. 2017a. 'A reluctant right-wing social movement: On the 'good sense' of Swedish hunters,' *Journal of Rural Studies*, 50(February): 139–147.

von Essen, E. and Allen, M. 2017b. 'Interspecies violence and crimes of dissent: Communication ethics and legitimacy in message crimes involving wildlife,' *Critical Criminology: An International Journal*, 25 (2): 261–274.

Weston, B. and Bollier, D. 2013. *Green Governance: Escological Survival, Human Rights, and the Law of the Commons*. Cambridge: Cambridge University Press.

White, R. 2008. *Crimes Against Nature: Environmental Criminology and Ecological Justice*, Cullompton, Devon, UK: Willan.

Winthrop, J. 1968. *White Over Black: American Attitudes toward the Negro*, pp. 1550–1812. Baltimore, MD: Penguin.

34

Green crime on the reservation

A spatio-temporal analysis of U.S. Native American reservations 2011–2015

Tameka Samuels-Jones, Ryan Thomson and Johanna Espin

Introduction

The 2016 grassroots movement initiated by the Standing Rock Sioux against Energy Transfer Partners and the Army Corps of Engineers' construction of the Dakota Access Pipeline (#NoDAPL) ignited a larger discussion surrounding issues of colonialism, environmental harm, natural resources and power. A year later, the protests had been repressed violently, the pipeline had been constructed through numerous sacred sites, and it had sprung leaks at least five times in 2017 alone. This case represents one of thousands of green crimes and injustices that have occurred in or around Native American reservations. In this chapter, we employ an environmental justice perspective to explore the unequal relationship between Western societies and Indigenous peoples, which have resulted in a higher occurrence of environmental or 'green' crimes on tribal lands. The acts and omissions recognised by law as crimes ('environmental crimes' or 'green crimes') and broader instances of environmental harm discussed in this study speak to the numerous limitations of the legal-procedural approach (see Brisman and South, this volume, Chapter 1) and continued need for an explicit environmental justice perspective, which stands for equal protection from environmental health hazards and participatory decision-making in environmental governance (Brisman 2008, 2013, 2014; Schlosberg 2007). The use and integration of insights from this approach can undoubtedly further the development of Indigenous studies within green criminology.

More specifically, this chapter offers an analysis of green criminal behaviour on and around Native American reservations using geospatial cluster analysis to examine prolonged case studies that instantiate and highlight the relevance of the historical processes and lasting effects of hazardous exposures. Key court rulings and environmental laws are also used to illustrate characteristics of the legal-procedural framework that continues to enable colonial power relations throughout the United States (U.S.) that facilitate unequal toxin exposure. Findings are then used to advance a critique of several policies which have enabled the expansion of environmental crimes in and around reservations.

Sacrifice zones and the treadmill of crime

The historically dependent relationships created by colonialism have resulted in the distribution of environmental burdens in such a way that environmental injustice appears systemic. We characterise these asymmetrical relations and corresponding injustices surrounding Native American reservations as 'sacrifice zones' (also commonly referred to as 'national sacrifice areas' or 'national sacrifice zones'). As a term, 'sacrifice zones' is used to describe the toxic hotspots or corridors where industrial burdens are concentrated geographically (Lerner 2012). The term emerged among scholars and engineers in the 1970s as a way to describe the long-term temporal effects of strip-mining coal (Atwood 1975; National Research Council 1974). These zones are most commonly found in low-income and minority communities because hazardous industries follow the path of least resistance with regards to social pressures and environmental law. The socio-environmental problems and injustices generated in these zones (areas and people sacrificed to toxins and then neglected) are viewed as an acceptable price of industrial development (Collin and Collin 2005).

While the literature on sacrifice zones has offered rich analytical depictions of the processes and experiences associated with concentrated toxin exposure, we introduce a new way of approaching this concept. We advance theorisation on the treadmill of production (ToP) hypothesis regarding political-economic factors associated with expanding production and profits to the detriment of the environment and human health (Lynch et al. this volume, Chapter 4; Stretesky, Long and Lynch 2013) as a way of enriching the concept of sacrifice zones. Based on the extent of green crimes on reservations, our geospatial analysis reflects that the emergent patterns are in keeping with the treadmill of production's notions of environmental inequality. Further, the case studies in this chapter provide evidence that much of the green crime on Native American lands may be traced to corporate and military activity (Hooks and Smith 2004). The long-term environmental harm that often results from continued capitalist and military practices on reservations have been referred to as Native American contributions to the collective good (Hooks and Smith 2004). These unwilling contributions—these 'sacrifices' of environmental health—are required to support the adverse environmental impacts of the treadmill's steady production of capital goods and military arms testing.

Native American reservations in the United States

From an environmental justice perspective, Bullard and his colleagues (2007) describe Native American reservations as the 'new dumping grounds' for toxic waste disposal. This body of work, which proposed a broader understanding of justice (Schlosberg 2007), builds directly on the first generation of environmental justice research examining toxin exposure among minority communities (Bullard 1990; United Church of Christ 1987; U.S. Government Accounting Office 1983). According to Bullard and colleagues (2007), Native Americans are 1.8 times more likely to reside near commercial toxic waste facilities as a result of continued marginalisation by state and corporate actors. This hazard exposure has been linked with a variety of different health issues, such as cancer, chronic lower respiratory diseases and kidney disease. Superfund sites, the most serious of federally recognised contamination threats to public health, pose the greatest risk to Native American communities (Anderton 1997). Gowda and Easterling (2000) found a significant link between reservations and nuclear waste disposal. Orr and colleagues (2002) discovered that Native Americans throughout California experienced disproportionately high birth defects as the result of their immediate proximity to hazardous waste sites. Oil and lead dust pollution waste was also found to pose a greater concern to Native Americans than any other group (Malcoe, Lynch, Kegler and Skaggs 2002).

Native American reservations are geo-political constructs resulting from centuries of colonial reorganisation. Although most tribes maintain their own governing bodies, they are still subordinate to federal and state laws (Berger 2017; Nurse this volume, Chapter 33). Therefore, while reservations have a separate legal framework, they operate within and under the purview of the U.S. court system (Pevar 2012). Thus, these quasi-autonomous spaces are still subjected to U.S. law and influenced heavily by a wide variety of external interests. These tribal groups are even classified by the federal government along different administrative, geographic and legal lines. For instance, the U.S. Census Bureau uses the categories of American Indian, Alaska Native and Native Hawaiian areas (AIANNHAs), and differentiates between tribal subdivisions that can constitute American Indian reservations, state-recognised American Indian reservations, Alaska Native regional corporations (ANRCs) and Hawaiian home lands (HHLs). While many of these areas are commonly referred to as 'reservations', half of California's tribes call them 'Rancherías', many tribes throughout New Mexico refer to them as 'Pueblos', and around greater Nevada they are 'Indian Colonies', which retains terminology introduced by the Indian Reorganization Act of 1934.

It is also important to note the difference between a 'reservation' and a 'trust territory'. A 'reservation' is a legal designation for an area of land managed by a Native American tribe that is federally recognised under the U.S. Bureau of Indian Affairs (BIA). A 'reservation', then, tends to be directly associated with a nation. This differs from off-reservation 'trust territories', which are lands owned and protected by the U.S. government for the benefit of a tribe (tribal trust land) or an individual Native American (individual trust land). Most reservations are surrounded entirely by non-tribal lands, although some reservations such as the Hopi Reservation are tribal enclaves contained within a larger tribal territory (the Navajo Nation Reservation).

Currently, there are 573 tribes legally recognised by the BIA at the federal level, and an additional 62 recognised only at the state level (Hilleary 2018; Library of Congress 2016). The 14 states that have granted recognition to tribes are concentrated in the east of the Mississippi River, where the largest tribe is the Lumbee Tribe of North Carolina, followed by the United Houma Nation of Louisiana (Department of the Interior 2015; Library of Congress 2015). The size of these reservations is smaller compared with their federally recognised counterparts as a result of the 1830 Indian Removal Act, which forced many tribes in this area to undertake a series of death marches heading west while rounding up any remaining Native Americans into camps (Pevar 2012).

The size of reservations ranges substantially from the Pit River Tribe's cemetery in California (1.32 acres) to the 16-million-acre (27,413 square miles) Navajo Nation Reservation, which is comparable in size with the state of West Virginia. Currently, there are still over 500 additional landless tribes who are petitioning for recognition and land rights.

In addition to tribes' rights to land and self-determination, the clash between Euro-centred Western values and Native American values has also impacted the ways in which tribes interact with the environment. Non-Indian landowners have different priorities than tribes regarding the use and management of natural resources. Thus, examinations of environmentally harmful activities on reservations usually stem from the process of locating capitalist systems of production on or close to reservations or, in other cases, when state actors effectively designate them as 'sacrifice zones' in the name of national interests. These types of sacrifice zones have been used primarily for military testing and the storage of toxic wastes and have contributed to the pollution of both air and water in such territories (Hooks and Smith 2004). Native American lands have been popular choices for sacrifice zones as illustrated by the fact that 75 per cent of the U.S. national uranium reserve is under the control of major oil companies located on Native American lands (Moore-Nall 2015). The Four Corners area of the Navajo nation (Southwest Colorado, Northwestern New Mexico, Northeastern Arizona and Southeastern Utah) has also been designated as a national sacrifice area. Mining activities in that region from the 1940s to 1960s resulted in extensive mine waste, which is believed to have contributed to cases of lung cancer among Navajo uranium miners (Lynch and Stretesky 2011). The irony is that Native Americans have not been the primary recipients of the profits from these economic activities nor has the 'sacrifice' of their sacred lands been consensual.

The misappropriation of tribal lands has also paved the way for environmental regulatory gaps. A tribe's environmental management is hindered by disparities in jurisdiction with non-Indian facilities. This disparity exists despite the treaties between the federal government and Native American tribes, which grant tribes a special legal status that authorises them to set environmental standards that could be more stringent than state and federal standards (Grijalva 2008). The jurisdiction of non-Indian lands in close proximity to reservations remains contentious for a number of reasons. Most important is that the capacity to enforce tribal regulations is hampered by a history of colonialism and federal neglect that has reduced the tribes' financial resources for implementing their own environmental regulatory programmes. In the absence of their own regulatory mechanism, reliance is placed on the U.S. Environmental Protection Agency (E.P.A.) for environmental protection. With approximately 850 facilities to monitor on tribal lands, however, the E.P.A.'s intervention and support has failed to account for much of the environmental and cultural harms produced.

Because it is clear that political and economic forces, not tribes, determine the value of natural resources (as raw materials or commodities), an explanation for environmental crimes occurring on reservations must include a historical and multifaceted analysis of laws and regulations, cultural norms, social values and economic and environmental practices.

Data and methods

Despite the serious consequences for communities that experience prolonged toxic exposure, the geographic distribution of criminal activity with respect to the environment remains understudied. In fact, green criminology has relied primarily on descriptive case studies, while underutilising quantitative methods traditionally associated with orthodox criminology (Lynch, Barrett, Stretesky and Long 2017). Our methodological approach couples these case studies with a quantitative geospatial account to address the need for more quantitative analysis assessing different hypotheses from a green criminology perspective (Lynch and Stretesky 2011).

Applying spatial methods to analyse the unequal distribution of environmental crimes on or close to Native American reservations can help shed light on the existing relationships between green crime, land use and boundaries of tribal lands. Such quantitative visual tools also facilitate the examination of notions of capitalism, colonialism, justice and territoriality, which are connected to the exploitation of natural resources in such areas. Geospatial analysis thus draws green criminologists' attention to areas with the greatest vulnerabilities, such as tribal lands. Furthermore, mapping green crime on reservations provides a significant opportunity to include a contextually sensitive understanding of green crime as a socio-spatial process.

For examining the spatial distribution and occurrence of green crimes in or close to reservations, we rely on data from the E.P.A.'s Enforcement and Compliance History Online (ECHO) database (echo.epa.gov). This dataset compiles violations in all 50 states, including those on and around Native American reservations and territories. We identified spatial clusters and concentrations of cases across three different types of violations: air, water and solid waste pollution. These types of legal violations are not only common but also relatively reliable in terms of reporting. We then coupled the case numbers within the data with the E.P.A.'s 'Criminal Case' summary of prosecutions for additional descriptive details. The data provide information on the perpetrator, such as their address, case number, statute violation, resolution outcome—whether formal (in court settlements) or informal (settled out of court), present E.P. A. violation status (high/low exposure threat), type and amount of hazard, number of inspections, number of repeated offenses, latitude and longitude coordinates, last inspection date and description of the violation.

Because we rely on data from the E.P.A.'s ECHO database, the definition of environmental or green crime is limited and refers only to acts proscribed by law, which excludes numerous forms of environmental harms. Hence, by using the E.P.A.'s definition, an environmental harm that is not designated, reported and registered as an environmental crime, cannot be mapped. The lack of registration and regulation of such environmentally harmful but legal incidents represents a blind spot in environmental protection. This means that while it can be used to measure the occurrence of green crimes, the data do not provide evidence of the real impacts of such acts, for instance the number of people affected or the ecological harms generated. Therefore, we complement the ECHO data with an analysis of specific case studies that illustrate the historical processes that have led to and maintained an unequal distribution of green crimes.

Findings

Toxic colonialism: national summary of violations on reservations

Of approximately 3.75 million industrial facilities reported within the ECHO database, 19,564 are located on a reservation, while 21,160 additional industrial facilities are located within one mile of a reservation. These figures mean that no more than 0.5 per cent of the total facilities in the U.S are located in Native American reservations. Of the total number of facilities with formal enforcement actions in the last five years, however, 1.5 per cent are located in Native American reservations. Likewise, 1.5 per cent (612 cases) of the total of significant environmental violations committed nationwide in 2017 were located on Native American reservations (see Table 34.1). Most of the violations against environmental regulations are perpetrated by private companies, followed by state actors and, in some cases, by tribes themselves.

Transitory dumping (such as pushing barrels of hazardous waste from the back of a truck or draining coal ash into a river) is also a prevalent strategy among polluters, especially along remote stretches of highways. It represents a desperate attempt to externalise the costs of hazardous disposal while concealing the identity of its perpetrator. This evokes the kind of environmental harm that began the initial environmental justice movement of Warren County, North Carolina, where Ward's Transformer Co. dumped thousands of gallons of toxic waste alongside Route 401.

Case studies of green crimes on Native American reservations

Because green crimes can be related to natural resource extraction, industrial expansion of urban areas, fragmentation of reservation lands or dumping, we chose six case studies with unique features that illustrate clearly these environmentally harmful practices. The cases of Oklahoma, the Navajo and Hopi reservations and North Dakota are illustrative of green crimes caused by natural resource extraction, while the cases of Puget Sound in Washington and greater Oklahoma illustrate the negative environmental impacts of industrial expansion of urban areas. The case of Enterprise Product Operating LLC within the cracks of the

Table 34.1 2017 statistical summary of ECHO violations in and around Native American reservations

	On a reservation	*On or 1 mile from a reservation*	*On or 5 miles from a reservation*	*United States*
Number of permitted facilities	19,564	40,724	137,153	3,754,492
Current violations	612	1,079	2,500	67,285
Current significant violations	118	198	375	7,983
Facilities with violations (3 years)	1,290	2,179	5,283	147,260
Facilities with formal enforcement actions (5 years)	634	853	1,649	42,154
Facilities with informal enforcement actions (5 years)	626	1,215	3,282	131,207

Navajo trust offers a sound illustration of how the fragmentation of reservation lands enables a decrease of environmental regulations. The lasting effects of nuclear waste and modern mining practices throughout Alaska emphasise the long-term effects of common legal and harmful behaviours. Finally, two atypical cases in the eastern part of the U.S. illustrate how waste infrastructure frequently exposes tribal communities in North Carolina and Louisiana.

Oklahoma: a long history of environmental harm

Historically, many major conflicts between Native Americans and the oil industry have occurred in Oklahoma. Several tribes (Cherokee, Chickasaw, Choctaw, Creek and Seminole) were removed from eastern parts of the U.S. where European colonisers settled and they were forced to relocate to what was to become Oklahoma. At the time, the Europeans did not realise that there were valuable oil reserves on the lands to which they were rehoming the Native American tribes. Once the oil reserves were discovered, the tribes attempted to maintain their autonomy by organising an Indian state, Sequoyah. This effort was rejected by the federal government, which had its own interest in oil extraction. Eventually, the tribes were forced to give up their lands under the Dawes Act and to accept individual property allotments (Grijalva 2008).

Environmental injustice entails both the denial of access to environmental 'goods' (e.g., natural resources) and disproportionate exposure to environmental 'bads' or 'harms'. The previous paragraph represents an example of the former and we describe here an example of the latter. One of the most polluted Superfund sites named by the E.P.A. is located in Tar Creek, Oklahoma, where extensive lead mining occurred in order to supply the armament and ammunition industry in both world wars. Seven tribes (including the Cherokee, Ottawa and Quapaw) and three states (Kansas and Missouri, in addition to Oklahoma) have been impacted significantly by toxic contamination from lead and zinc mines at Tar Creek. In terms of cultural harm, the impacts have been devastating as acid mine drainage has poisoned many of the sacred sites belonging to these tribes. Any claim for the protection of sacred sites, however, presents complications because many tribes cannot disclose the exact location of their sacred sites to non-tribal members and therefore the entire area in which these sites are located must be protected (Gould and Ross 2006). Naturally, Native Americans' demand for protection of their sacred land conflicts with more Eurocentric perspectives that consider that land should be used in accordance with its economic value (Gould and Ross 2006).

Hence, in many cases (see, for example, *Sequoyah* v *TVA*, 620 F.2d 1159 (6th Cir. 1980)), the U.S. government has denied Native Americans religious protection for sacred sites located on lands that are deemed to be economically viable. Any further attempt by Native Americans to continue to use the sacred sites has been seen as illegal, but the destruction of these sites for income generation is not (Gould and Ross 2006).

Oklahoma represents one of the densest pockets of green criminal activity occurring on the reservations across a combination of Apache, Blackfeet, Cherokee, Chickasaw and Seminole tribal lands (see Figure 34.1). This area also includes Arapaho and Cheyenne tribes (sharing reservations), Caddo Nation, Ponca Tribe (and their affiliates with the Kaw Nation), Muscogee (of the Creek) nation, the Absentee-Shawnee Tribe and Otoe-Missouria tribe. In total, Oklahoma reports 49 violations of the Clean Air Act (CAA), 57 violations of the Clean Water Act (CWA) and seven violations of the Resource Conservation and Recovery Act (RCRA). Some of the facilities that violate environmental regulations are strategically located within a few hundred feet of a reservation.

Green crimes and environmental harms in Puget Sound

In many cases, tribal communities have been prevented from accessing traditional hunting and sacred grounds, which is not considered to be a green 'crime' by any strict legal definition. For Native Americans in the Pacific Northwest however, salmon and other foods that are gathered and hunted represent an important part of their deep-rooted relationship with nature. Cantzler and Huynh (2016) analysed the case of tribal families in the Puget Sound area, which

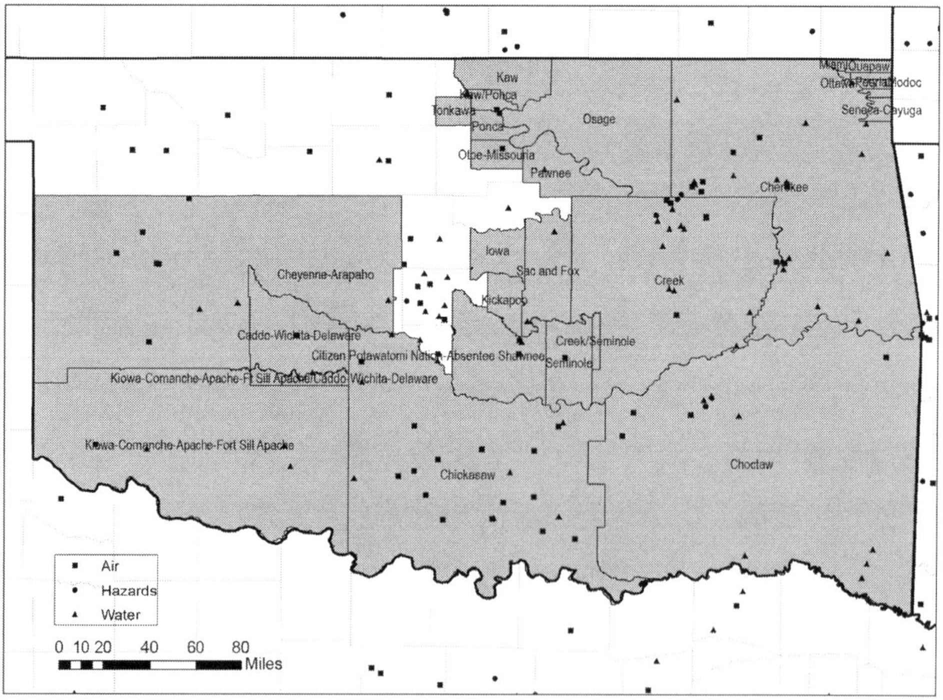

Figure 34.1 Green crime on and around Oklahoma Native American reservations.

at the time of the European colonisation consumed about 500 pounds of salmon per year. More than just a food source, Native Americans in this region view salmon as central to their cultural identity. In the mid-1800s, when the presence of colonial settlers began to increase in the region, Native Americans were pressured to relinquish their land because it had become valuable real estate. Twenty-five tribes sold almost 64 million acres of land but with the explicit provision that they would still be permitted to fish for salmon. By the end of the century, non-Indian fish traps placed strategically above tribal fishing sites resulted in the rapid decline in the availability of fish for Native Americans. Nevertheless, this situation set the stage for a landmark decision regarding environmental justice for tribal peoples because the tribes, with the assistance of the federal government, sued the state of Washington for recognition of the tribes' fishing rights. In *United States* v *Washington*, 384 F. Sup. 312 (W.D. Wash. 1974), *aff'd*, 520 F.2d 676 (9th Cir. 1975) (known as the 'Boldt Decision' after George Hugo Boldt, the trial judge), the court ruled in favour of the tribes. Despite this victory for Native Americans, the resolution of new and ongoing fish wars between corporate entities and Native Americans, such as the proposed Pebble Mine in Bristol Bay in Alaska, are often subject to the E.P.A.'s determination. The concentration of green crime violations along the Puget Sound are primarily towards the south emanating to the north into the Whidbey Basin and west along the South Basin (see Figure 34.2). Furthermore, such rights for Native Americans are often dismissed based on arguments disputing the basis on which tribes should be viewed as a sovereign government with separate hunting rights (Berger 2011).

More recent environmental violations throughout the Puget Sound area are characterised by an outward spread of industrial projects from Everett, Olympia, Seattle and Tacoma toward

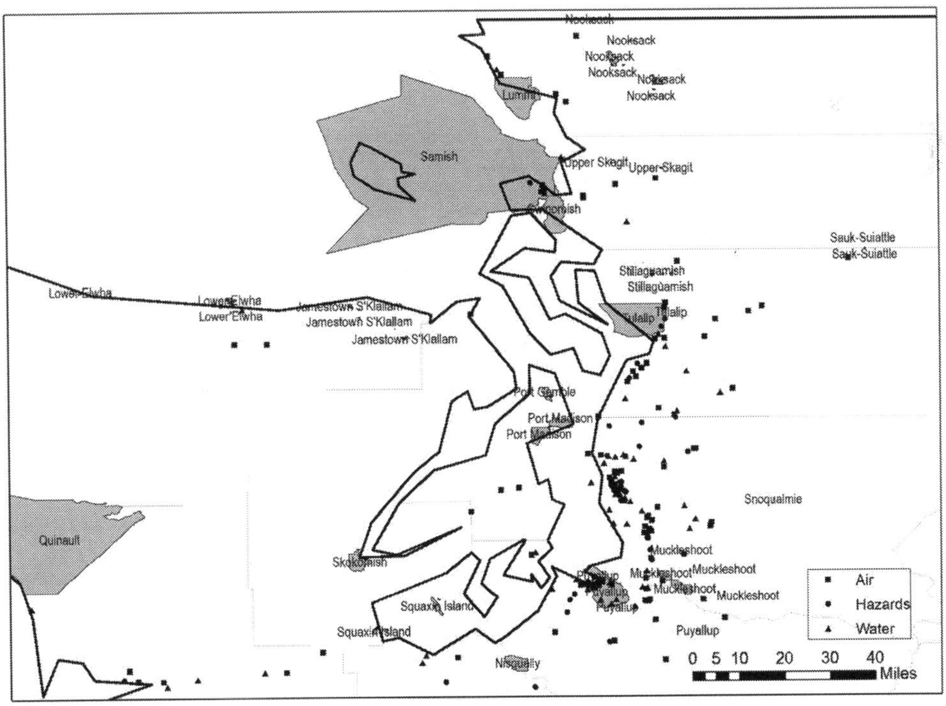

Figure 34.2 Green crime on and around Puget Sound Native American reservations.

a series of different smaller reservations. Starting from the northern part of the Sound, the Samish and Lummi reservations and the island located to the west of Bellingham, Washington, are bordered by a variety of different industrial facilities, including chemical companies, oil refineries, paper companies and timber processing plants. The nearby Tulalip Reservation is also subject to violations by two surrounding sewage treatment plants and granite extraction companies. The Musckelshoot and Puyallup reservations (and nearby trust lands) have been adversely impacted by 21 water, 13 hazard and 32 air violations. The larger industrial park lists a wide variety of private actors, including Boeing, a dozen waste management (e.g., Murrey's Disposal Co.) and seafood packaging companies (e.g., Supervalue Distribution), as well as U.S. Oil and Phillips 66.

Beyond anthropocentric frameworks, the ongoing struggle of the Tulalip and Suquamish Tribes has grown into a legal challenge to the U.S. Coast Guard's management of Washington State's inland waters. As tanker traffic has spiked in the area, the tribes are seeking to challenge the agency's shipping traffic regulations as a potential violation of the Endangered Species Act because of the immediate threats they pose to orcas for oil spills throughout the Salish Sea (Earthjustice 2018a).

Coal mining on the Navajo nation's lands

The Navajo and Hopi tribes have been similarly impacted by mining on their reservations. The Navajo and Hopi reservations are located in the Black Mesa area of northeastern Arizona, where Peabody Energy, the largest private-sector coal company in the world, operates the Kayenta and Black Mesa mines (see Figure 34.3). These mines supply coal to the Mohave Generating Station in

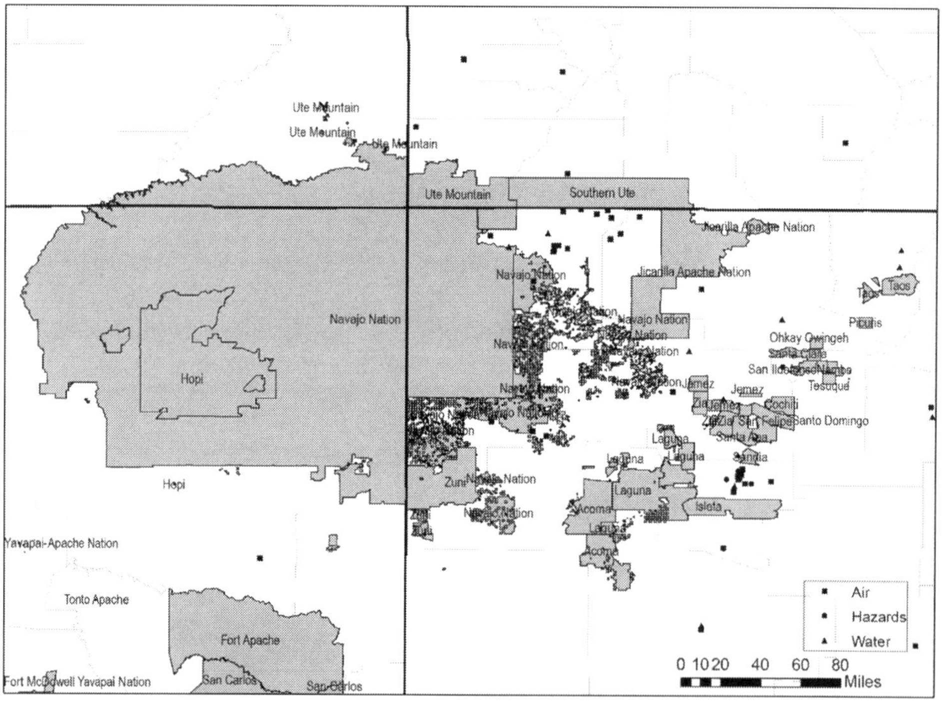

Figure 34.3 Green crime on and around Navajo Native American reservations.

Nevada, which is burned in power plants in Southern California, Las Vegas and Central Arizona. Yet ironically, the Navajo and Hopi tribes that live on Black Mesa do not have electricity or running water.

Navajo and Hopi families have been routinely relocated to the reservations' borders to facilitate the extraction of 7.8 million tons of coal per year through strip mining. The coal mine has been described as the dirtiest in the western United States, emitting up to 40,000 tons of sulphur dioxide per year (www.sourcewatch.org/index.php?title=SourceWatch). The main evidence of such contamination is the black lung diagnosis that commonly afflicts Native Americans on those reservations. It has been estimated that between 500 and 600 Native American uranium miners from the Navajo tribe alone have died of lung cancer between 1950 and 1990 (Brugge and Goble 2002). The Black Mesa plant was shut down after the Hopi and Navajo tribes passed resolutions to end Peabody Energy's use of the Navajo Aquifer. The company, however, is able to reopen and recommence business activity at any time because their permit allows them to take both coal and water from the reservation indefinitely.

In the U.S., drinking water is typically derived from either the Earth's surface (lakes, rivers) or from underground aquifers. On Native American reservations, almost 90 per cent of drinking water comes from aquifers, which makes contamination of this water source particularly detrimental to those living on the reservation. Hence, the temporary protection of the underground water supply is a victory for the Hopi and Navajo tribes, but there is still a constant threat to the tribal communities' water supply based on the possible reopening of the mine. The lack of autonomy of these tribes to prevent a threat to their depleted water supply illustrates that dominant legal and political institutions often reinforce environmental racism (Bullard 1993).

In addition, the eastern border of the Navajo Nation's off-reservation trust lands has been fragmented by piecemeal sales. Enterprise Products Operating LLC owns a small parcel of land within the Navajo trust, which operates Chaco Gas plants. Its two processing units have repeatedly violated the Clean Air Act by discharging volatile organic compounds comprised of lead, ozone, particulate matter and sulphur dioxide. The fragmentation of the Navajo trust territories in many ways constitutes a legal loophole because it has enabled industries to situate themselves within the cracks of these boundaries while circumventing the trust's regulatory protections. The toxic emissions inevitably spill into the surrounding territories because the facility is surrounded by Navajo land. This case, comparable with cases affecting the Kalaeloa in Hawaii, the Crow in Montana and the Mississippi Choctaw, demonstrates how territorial fragmentation enables industrial facilities to penetrate tribal lands and produce serious environmental harms.

Water toxicity in North Dakota

In 1943, Colonel Lewis Andrew Pick and William Sloan of the Bureau of Land Management developed the 'Pick-Sloan Project' to construct four dams—Big Bend, Fort Randall, Garrison and Oahe—on Native American soil in North Dakota. The reservoirs destroyed approximately 550 square miles of tribal land which resulted in the dislocation of almost 1,000 tribal families. Under the 'Pick-Sloan Project', the reservations located on the Upper Missouri Basins were treated as national sacrifice areas. Of course, tribal members were never consulted regarding their water rights, the environmental sacrifices to be made or the impact that building these dams would have on their way of life. The large dams built under this project utilised over 356,000 acres of the Standing Rock Reservation and, when the dams on the Missouri River flooded, they destroyed 203,457 acres of Sioux land, which resulted in the loss of pastures, sacred grounds, timber and wildlife.

Armed with this historical insight, the opposition of the Sioux tribe in 2017 to the Dallas-based Energy Transfer Partners' (now officially Energy Transfer Operating L.P.) Dakota Access Pipeline was clearly not without precedent. Extensive media coverage of the Standing Rock Sioux tribe's protest against the construction of the Dakota Access Pipeline, noted earlier in this chapter, heightened awareness of the risks of environmentally harmful practices on tribal lands, but the construction of the pipeline continued. This area already has a few pockets of industrial factories with a handful of noteworthy environmental regulations (see Figure 34.4).

The pipeline was projected to facilitate the transportation of 470 thousand barrels of crude oil per day between Bakken, North Dakota and Patoka, Illinois. The Sioux argued, however, that the construction of this project would destroy burial and prayer sites and, in the event of a breach, would undoubtedly contaminate the water supply on which the tribe relies. In response to the Standing Rock Sioux tribe's peaceful protest, tensions rose and on September 3, 2017, law enforcement officials pepper-sprayed and released dogs that attacked the protesters, including women and young children. Despite the tribe's opposition, Energy Transfer Partners received approval to proceed with the construction of the pipeline, which became operational in June 2017. This case demonstrates how power, particularly capitalist power in alliance with the state, continues to create environmental policies that have the potential to cause significant environmental harm on tribal lands. This environmental harm as promoted by large corporations and protested by Native Americans is symbolic of broader notions of wealth among the two groups. Whereas capitalists view the accumulation of

Figure 34.4 Green crime on and around North Dakota Native American reservations.

material wealth as an indicator of success, Native Americans largely view the preservation of the environment as paramount to their cultural and spiritual survival (Means 1999).

Oil extraction, military exercise and climate change in Alaska

Point Hope, a city in North Slope Borough in Alaska, more accurately known as Tikigaq, is the oldest continuously occupied human settlement in North America, going back at least 1,500 years. Tikigaq was a landmark to the first Americans and is also the site of one of the first most obvious cases of environmental injustice. At this site, Edward Teller of the U.S. Atomic Energy Commission (AEC) decided that the agency would use nuclear explosions to create a new harbour in Northwestern Alaska. The project, named the Plowshare Program, took place approximately 30 miles away from the Inupiat Eskimo village of Point Hope. Shortly after this project, the AEC developed new plans to add an experimental harbour excavation called Project Chariot. As these plans were drafted and executed, the Native Americans who resided in these lands were never consulted; rather, they were only informed that they had to relocate.

Misinformation was common in this case. The tribal people of Point Hope were told that the fish in the Pacific Proving Grounds, where the AEC tested nuclear explosions, were not affected by the radiation of nuclear weapons tests and were thus safe for consumption. In addition, they were misinformed that the nuclear weapons tests would not generate any side effects or seismic shocks. With the assistance of researchers from the University of Alaska, the Native Americans presented scientific data to support their claims and, using their own Indigenous knowledge, explained the impacts of the nuclear testing in 1961. The tribe thus successfully appealed to President Kennedy to end any further nuclear testing on this reservation (Kirsch 2005).

This case is important for two reasons. First, tribal people are not passive 'victims' that have acted as bystanders in relation to the occurrence of green crimes on their reservations. Second, the role of researchers in academia extends beyond reporting the results of empirical work (see Ozymy et al. this volume, Chapter 8). Research from a green criminology perspective represents an opportunity to take proactive measures to prevent crime through activism, collaborate with affected groups to disseminate information to the public, and increase awareness of environmental issues (see Ozymy et al. this volume, Chapter 8).

Currently, it is also gaining more relevance to apply a green criminology perspective to the analysis of increasing environmental threats generated by potential impacts of climate change, as in the case of the Inupiat village of Shishmaref located in the Srichef Island, five miles off the coast of the Seward Peninsula in Alaska. Beginning in the 1990s, ice in this area started to form later in the fall and dissolve sooner in the spring. The impact of this temperature change on the Inupiat tribe has been significant. Tribal members used to be able to travel up to 20 miles onto the snow in search of the bearded seal, which comprises the majority of their diet; now, they are limited to fishing and hunting within only a few miles of the shore (Kolbert 2015), thereby demonstrating how the impacts of environmental harms produced by climate change affect vulnerable tribal communities even when environmentally harmful practices are not taking place on their land.

Other recent violations across Alaska are related to activities associated with fishing, metal mines, military bases and oil extraction. In the case of fishing, the most common violations are perpetrated by private seafood companies (Salamatof Seafoods Inc., Silver Bay Seafoods LLC, Trident Seafoods) dumping 'seafood waste' along the southern coasts in highly significant violations of their National Pollutant Discharge Elimination System (NPDES) permits. Trident Seafoods based out of Seattle, for example, received two sizeable fines, the first for USD$2.5 million for numerous CWA violations and a second recently resolved violation for

$300,000. The latter ruling requires the company to remove over three acres of fish waste from the sea floor and placed discharge limits on another (U.S. Department of Justice 2011).

In the case of oil extraction, several oil drilling and refinery companies, some of which operate as far north as the Arctic Circle, have received fines for violations of various federal statutes. Notable RCRA perpetrators include: CVEA's Glennallen Diesel Plant, the Valdez Marine Terminal and BP's North Slope exploration. ConocoPhillips, which operates the Kuparuk River Unit (North America's second largest oil field) received a fine of USD-$312,000 in 2012 for a pair of oil spills resulting from corroded pipelines. The first spill released roughly 500 gallons of crude oil, while the second released 1,386 gallons and 2,870 gallons of contaminated water in sub-zero temperatures (Anchorage Daily News 2012). A number of gold and copper mining operations have also been caught violating their NPDES permits for discharges into Alaskan rivers, such as the Sumitomo Corporation's Pogo Mine, Coeur Mining's Kensington gold mine and Mystery Creek Resource, Inc.'s Nixon Fork Mine. Finally, CAA violations include the University of Alaska Fairbanks power plant, Nome Joint Utility System's Snake River power plant, Flint Hills Resources' North Pole Refinery, Eielson AFB and Clear Air Force Station. ConocoPhillips and BP's North Slope locations were also among the most serious (and steeply fined) air violations reported.

Contaminated waters in North Carolina and Louisiana

Green crimes on large reservations in the western U.S. can differ significantly from those in the eastern part of the country. The Lumbee of the Carolinas (recognised in 1957) and the United Houma Nation (recognised in 1972) in southern Louisiana present a unique situation because both are recognised at their respective state levels but lack federal recognition. Although both states constitute green crime havens (concentrated areas of green crime), these reservations are subject to an even more disproportionate frequency of water-related offenses resulting from poor infrastructure activity (Thomson, Espin and Samuels-Jones in press). These historic tribal lands have been devalued as the result of state water policies and industrial development patterns. Water Treatment Plants (WTP) and Waste Water Treatment Plants (WWTP) violations occur throughout the U.S. but take place even more frequently in Louisiana and Central Carolina. The most common water-related offence tends to be total suspended solids (TSS) and fecal waste with a high pH balance.

In Louisiana, Total Environmental Solutions, Inc. (TESI), which owns and operates individual sewage treatment plants, was cited for five notable environmental crimes in and around Houma land. In addition to those violations (which occurred between 2011 and 2015), nine other water violations related to municipal entities were also reported. A total of 31 CWA violations, coupled with 11 CAA violations, has turned the once rich Atchafalaya, Terreboon and Barataria Rivers into a relatively uninhabitable environment for nearby Houma communities (see Figure 34.5).

The Lumbee, as well as nearby Coharie, Pee Dee and Waccamaw Siouan reservations, all of which are in the Carolinas, have been exposed to a similar dense concentration of chemicals found in local rivers. There are 29 WWTP located in this area and a variety of industrial actors emit high levels of ammonia, chlorine, chloroform, mercury and zinc into the Cape Fear, Lumber and Pee Dee River basins (see Figure 34.6).

Limitations

The E.P.A.'s database presents several weaknesses in terms of broken URLs, inaccuracies, lags, omissions in certain regions and validity (Golden 2012). We find that the quality of the

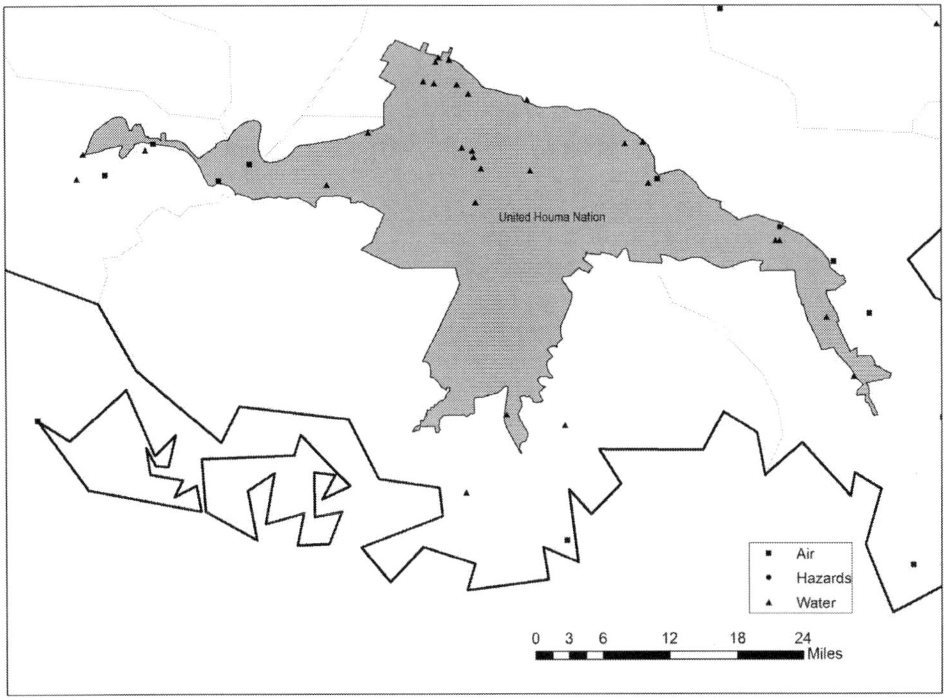

Figure 34.5 Green crime on and around Southern Louisiana Native American reservation.

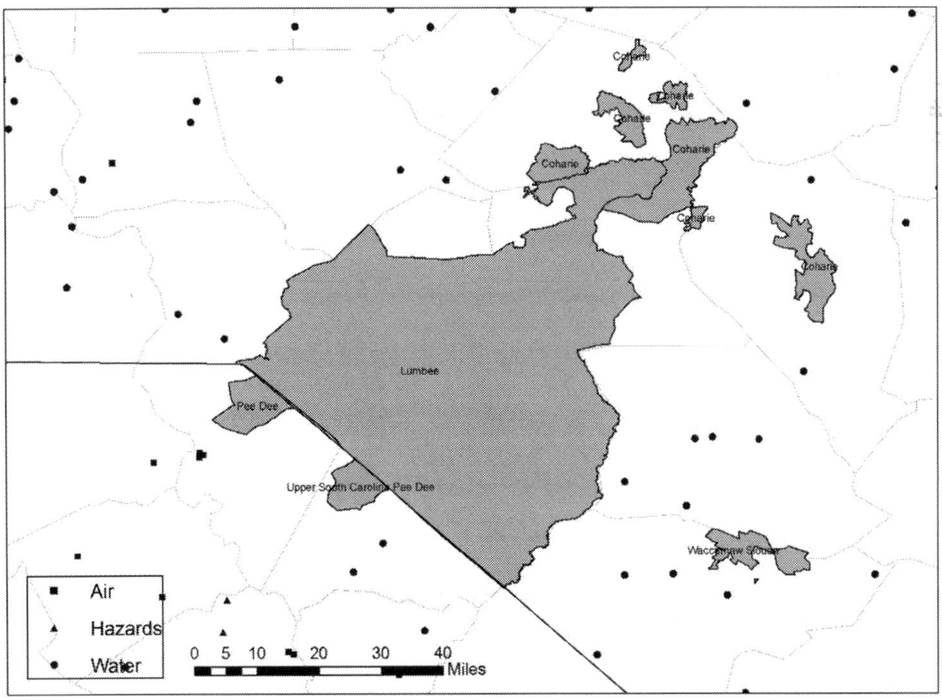

Figure 34.6 Green crime on and around Carolina Native American reservations.

reporting has improved within recent years but, during the completion of this analysis, administrative changes at the E.P.A. resulted in challenges that impacted data collection. We faced a number of difficulties finding details for informal enforcement actions which tend to be limited or entirely absent from E.P.A. legal reports.

Nevertheless, despite its current statistical deficiencies, some progress must also be acknowledged. The E.P.A. has made notable efforts to accommodate tribal perspectives in environmental discussions. The most significant is the Environmental Justice for Tribes and Indigenous People's programme. While this programme seeks to incorporate the perspectives of Native Americans on how their practices and concerns may be incorporated into federal regulatory policy, this is insufficient. These discussions must materialise into meaningful change through adequate and consistent enforcement. Furthermore, the restructuring of the E.P.A., specifically the merging of the Office of Environmental Justice and Office of Federal Activities into the Office of Policy, has been reflected in the approval of numerous federal large-scale development permits. The green light for corporate extractivist projects, such as the Atlantic Coast Pipeline or the Keystone XL oil pipeline, can be expected to exacerbate problems in the daily lives of Native Americans.

Discussion and conclusions

This chapter has explored the uneven spatial distribution and lasting temporal effects of environmental injustices affecting the environmental and community health of a wide variety of Native American tribes. Using geospatial analysis and case study analysis, we discussed both the statistically significant concentrations of green crime on reservations and offered an overview of the historical and political factors guiding these green criminal trends. The examination of environmental harm from this perspective highlighted the ways in which colonisation and capitalism have contributed to the flourishing of environmental crimes on reservations. While our spatial analysis captures evidence of widespread harm, it must be noted that there are equally devastating cultural and traditional impacts which do not meet the legal definition of crime but also require further review and exploration. Despite this blind spot, it is not unusual that a hierarchy of economics and politics over environmental concerns exists across spatial scales for environmental justice (Simmons 2004). In many respects, Native American lands experience many of the environmental injustices suffered by other marginalised communities. Arguably, these crimes impact Native Americans more because Native Americans enjoy less financial, legislative and political power than other minority groups (Newton 1984). In addition, their rural location on expansive lands make them primary targets for environmental exploitation.

Through boundary creation, colonialism has created a series of different geographic patterns which, alongside a capitalist system of production, have resulted in an uneven accumulation of green criminal behaviours (and corresponding exposure) on and around Native American reservations. While the uneven geopolitical patterns and corresponding unequal exposure and green criminal behaviours surrounding Native American reservations differ substantially, our findings suggest that the treadmill of crime depends significantly on political-economic factors. In particular, resource extraction occurring in the western U.S. and throughout Alaska differs from the many infrastructural shortcomings observed in the eastern part of the U.S. These geographic differences emerge from the federal relocation of tribes to the west relative to the more recent land-use decisions made at the state level.

Policy recommendation

From an environmental justice approach, we examined the high occurrence of environmental or 'green' crimes in tribal lands as a result of an existing unequal relationship between Western societies and Indigenous peoples. Our findings lead us to conclude that environmental regulation of tribal lands would benefit more from a non-legalistic approach to crime. It means not only the creation of regulations that incorporate the definition of harm, but also regulations that include the normative values of those impacted by such regulations. This proposal would require that policymakers adopt an environmental justice framework to best address the environmental risks and harms that marginalised groups, such as Native Americans, experience. At present, a regulatory perspective based solely on the environmental measurements required by law fails to provide equal protection by not accounting for cultural and traditional Indigenous values. An inclusive approach may mitigate the inequality between tribal people on their lands and capitalists who transform these lands into sacrifice zones justified through political-economic expansion (Schnaiberg, Pellow and Weinberg 2002; see also Heydon this volume, Chapter 18; Lampkin this volume, Chapter 27).

The example of Menominee hardwood forests in Wisconsin presents one illustrative case for moving forward (Earthjustice 2018b). When the federal government terminated Menominee reservation status in 1920, they forced the tribe to sell off parts of their ancestral lands to developers. The disastrous experiment ended decades later with the Menominee Restoration Act of 1973. The Menominee reservation, like so many others, was carved up selectively—in a manner that attracted capitalist exploitation along the borders of areas protected previously by tribal conservation efforts. The Menominee Restoration Act of 1973 reunited these fractured lands resulting in tribal sovereignty and better environmental stewardship. Similar reparative policies could offer comparable benefits to the fragmented reservations and trust territories previously mentioned. Other successful actions realised within the courts include the Havasupai Tribe's recent victory having the 20-year ban on new uranium mining bordering Grand Canyon National Park (Earthjustice 2018b).

In addition, the current regulatory gap that exists between protected state lands and reservations should be addressed through local–state collaborations that incorporate cultural and legal autonomy. Healthy legally pluralist societies are characterised by a delicate balance of sovereignty and accountability. Our findings show, however, that historically, Native Americans lack sovereignty while the E.P.A. lacks mechanisms of accountability. The E.P.A. and BIA might consider increasing the enforcement measures around marginalised communities (whether communities of colour, low income communities, reservations, or trust territories). These varied and heightened sanctions would reflect the increased normative value of the land to these groups. This recommendation speaks to the roots of environmental justice efforts by emphasising a community defense framework aimed at deterring environmentally harmful activity on their lands. Notably, hundreds of tribes are still petitioning for state and federal level status, which will grant them the legal autonomy to implement tribal regulation and enforcement. Even when the status of these tribes is recognised, however, they will then be subject to the deference to Congressional authority that federally recognised tribes face in environmental cases. Therefore, environmental law, whether at the state or federal level, constitutes a sort of shifting sands for Native Americans. A radical approach could be to recognise tribal autonomy and grant the governing bodies of a reservation the option to revoke the permits bordering on or near their communities. Another indirect route could be simply increasing tribal participation in the juries of green crime cases.

Research recommendations

Criminology has largely ignored Native American issues, thereby suggesting that Native American issues are not important. As such, we argue for research from a green criminology perspective, that considers the particularities of Indigenous issues within the larger process of environmental inequality formation (Crook, Short and South 2018; Lynch, Stretesky and Long 2018; Nurse this volume, Chapter 33; Pellow 2000, this volume, Chapter 32). Due to the complex, dynamic and historical processes related to the disproportionate environmental burdens faced by marginalised Native American people, future analysis of green crimes should examine multiple forms of social inequalities shaping exposure to green crimes, as well as regulatory decision-making and enforcement procedures that may reinforce power dynamics and reproduce environmental injustices.

Scholars should prioritise the analysis of uneven stakeholder relationships to obtain a deeper understanding of unequal exposure to different types of hazards. There are also a variety of research areas that could be explored, such as redefining the acceptable types and volume limits of toxins permitted within existing legislation or prioritising tribal voices. The prioritisation of Indigenous voices would undoubtedly aid in grounding green criminological understandings within the complex mechanisms and first-hand effects being experienced by tribal communities.

References

Anchorage Daily News. 2012. 'ConocoPhillips will pay Alaska $312,000 after North Slope Oil Spills,' Available at: www.adn.com/alaska-news/article/conocophillips-will-pay-alaska-312000-after-north-slope-oil-spills/2012/12/18/.

Anderton, D. 1997. 'Environmental equity in superfund: Demographics of the discovery and prioritization of abandoned toxic sites,' *Evaluation Review*, 21: 3–26.

Atwood, G. 1975. 'The strip-mining of Western coal,' *Scientific American*, 233(6): 23–29.

Berger, B. R. 2011. '"Williams v. Lee" and the debate over indian equality,' *Michigan Law Review*, 8: 1463.

Berger, B. R. 2017. 'Hope for Indian tribes in the U.S. Supreme Court?: Menominee, Nebraska v. Parker, Bryant, Dollar General ... and Beyond,' *University of Illinois Law Review*, 5: 1901.

Brisman, A. 2008. 'Crime-environment relationships and environmental justice,' *Seattle Journal for Social Justice*, 6(2): 727–817.

Brisman, A. 2013. 'The violence of silence: Some reflections on access to information, public participation in decision-making, and access to justice in matters concerning the environment,' *Crime, Law and Social Change*, 59(3): 291–303.

Brisman, A. 2014. 'Environmental and human rights,' In G. Bruinsma and D. Weisburd (eds.) *Encyclopedia of Criminology and Criminal Justice*, Vol. 3, pp. 1344–1353. New York: Springer Verlag.

Brugge, D. and Goble, R. 2002. 'The history of uranium mining and the Navajo People,' *American Journal of Public Health*, 92(9): 1410–1419.

Bullard, R., Mohai, P., Saha, R. and Wright, B. 2007. 'Toxic wastes and race at twenty 1987–2007: Grassroots struggles to dismantle environmental racism in the United States. United Church of Christ Justice and Witness Ministries,' Available at: www.nrdc.org/sites/default/files/toxic-wastes-and-race-at-twenty-1987-2007.pdf.

Bullard, R. D. 1990. *Dumping in Dixie*. Boulder, CO: Westview Press.

Bullard, R. D. 1993. *Confronting Environmental Racism: Voices from the Grassroots*, 1st ed. Boston, MA: South End Press.

Cantzler, J. M. and Huynh, M. 2016. 'Native American environmental justice as decolonization,' *American Behavioral Scientist*, 60(2): 203–223.

Collin, R. and Collin, R. 2005. 'Environmental reparations,' In R. D. Bullard (ed.) *The Quest for Environmental Justice: Human Rights and the Politics of Pollution*, pp. 209–221. San Francisco, CA: Sierra Club Books.

Crook, M., Short, D. and South, N. 2018. 'Ecocide, genocide, capitalism and colonialism: Consequences for indigenous peoples and glocal ecosystems environments,' *Theoretical Criminology*, 22(3), 298–317.

Dunn, J. P. 1909. *True Indian Stories*. St. Cloud, MN: Sentinel Printing Company.

Earthjustice. 2018a. 'Saving orcas from oil tankers,' *Earthjustice* Summer, 2018: 9.

Earthjustice. 2018b. 'Court nixes new uranium mines near Grand Canyon,' *Earthjustice*, Spring 2018: 8–9.

Golden, K. 2012. 'EPA's ECHO database: Your two-faced best friend,' *Society of Environmental Journalist*. Available at: www.sej.org/publications/sejournal-su-fall12/epas-echo-database-your-two-faced-best-friend.

Gould, L. A. and Ross, J. I. 2006. *Native Americans and the Criminal Justice System*, n.p. Boulder, CO: Paradigm Publishers.

Gowda, M. V. and Easterling, D. 2000. 'Voluntary siting and equity: The MRS facility experience in native America,' *Risk Analysis*, 20(6): 917–930.

Grijalva, J. M. 2008. *Closing the Circle: Environmental Justice in Indian Country*. Durham, NC: Carolina Academic Press.

Hilleary, C. 2018. 'US Recognizes 6 Virginia Native American Tribes,' *VOA News*, January 31. Available at: www.voanews.com/a/us-recognizes-six-virginia-native-american-tribes/4232989.html.

Hooks, G. and Smith, C. L. 2004. 'The treadmill of destruction: National sacrifice areas and native Americans,' *American Sociological Review*, 69(4): 558–575.

Jacoby, K. 2014. *Crimes against Nature: Squatters, Poachers, Thieves, and the Hidden History of American Conservation*. Berkeley, CA: University of California Press.

Kirsch, S. 2005. *Proving Grounds: Project Plowshare and the Unrealized Dream of Nuclear Earthmoving*. New Brunswick, NJ: Rutgers University Press.

Kojola, E. 2019. 'Indigeneity, gender and class in decision-making about risks from resource extraction,' *Environmental Sociology*, 5(2): 130–148.

Kolbert, E. 2015. *Field Notes from a Catastrophe: Man, Nature, and Climate Change*. New York, NY: Bloomsbury Publishing USA.

Lawson, M. L. 1994. *Dammed Indians: The Pick-Sloan Plan and the Missouri River Sioux, 1944–1980*. Norman, OK: University of Oklahoma Press.

Lerner, S. 2012. *Sacrifice Zones: The Front Lines of Toxic Chemical Exposure in the United States*. Cambridge, MA: MIT Press.

Library of Congress. 2015. 'Federal register notices,' 80(9). Available at: www.loc.gov/catdir/cpso/biaind.pdf.

Library of Congress. 2016. 'Federal register notices,' 81 (19). Available at: www.gpo.gov/fdsys/pkg/FR-2016-01-29/pdf/2016-01769.pdf.

Lynch, M., Barrett, K., Stretesky, P. and Long, M. 2017. 'The neglect of empirical research in green criminology and its consequences,' *Critical Criminology: An International Journal*, 25(2): 183–198.

Lynch, M. and Stretesky, P. and Long, M. 2018. 'Green criminology and native peoples: The treadmill of production and the killing of indigenous environmental activists,' *Theoretical Criminology*, 22(3): 318–341.

Lynch, M. J., and Stretesky, P. 2011. 'Native Americans and social and environmental justice: Implications for criminology,' *Social Justice*, 38(3): 104–124.

Malcoe, L. H., Lynch, R. A., Kegler, M. C. and Skaggs, V. J. 2002. 'Lead sources, behaviors, and socioeconomic factors in relation to blood lead of native American and White Children: A community-based assessment of a former mining area,' *Environmental Health Perspectives*, Supp 2: 221.

Means, R. 1999. 'For America to Live, Europe Must Die,' *American Journey Online: The Native American Experience U.S. History in Context*. Available at: https://theanarchistlibrary.org/library/russell-means-for-america-to-live-europe-must-die.

Moore-Nall, A. 2015. 'The legacy of uranium development on or near Indian reservations and health implications rekindling public awareness,' *Geosciences*, 5(1): 15–29.

National Research Council. 1974. 'Study Committee on the potential for rehabilitating lands surface mind for coal in the Western United States,' In *Rehabilitation Potential of Western Coal Lands*. Cambridge, MA: Ford Foundation Energy Policy Project.

Newton, N. J. 1984. 'Federal power over Indians: Its sources, scope, and limitations,' *University of Pennsylvania Law Review*, 2: 195.

Orr, M., Bove, F., Kaye, W. and Stone, M. 2002. 'Elevated birth defects in racial or ethnic minority children of women living near hazardous waste sites,' *International Journal of Hygiene and Environmental Health*, 205: 19–27.

Pellow, D. 2000. 'Environmental inequality formation: Toward a theory of environmental injustice,' *American Behavioral Scientist*, 43(4): 581–601.

Pevar, S. L. 2012. *The Rights of Indians and Tribes*. Oxford: Oxford University Press.

Robyn, L. and Alcoze T. in J. I. Ross and Gould, L. 2015. *Native Americans and the Criminal Justice System: Theoretical and Policy Directions*. Abingdon, Oxon, UK: Routledge.

Schlosberg, D. 2007. *Defining Environmental Justice: Theories, Movements, and Nature*. Oxford: Oxford University Press.

Schnaiberg, A., Pellow, D. and Weinberg, A. 2002. *The Treadmill of Production and the Environmental State: The Environmental State under Pressure*. Bingley, UK Emerald Group Publishing Limited.

Sikor, T. and Lund, C. (eds.) 2010. *The Politics of Possession: Property, Authority, and Access to Natural Resources*. Hoboken, NJ: John Wiley & Sons.

Simmons, C. S. 2004. 'The political economy of land conflict in the Eastern Brazilian Amazon', *Annals of The Association of American Geographers*, 94(1): 183–206.

Smith, C. L., Hooks, G. and Lengefeld, M. 2014. The war on drugs in Colombia: The environment, the treadmill of destruction and risk-transfer militarism. *Journal of World-Systems Research*, 20(2): 185–206.

Stretesky, P., Long, M. and Lynch, M. 2013. *The Treadmill of Crime: Political Economy and Green Criminology*. Abingdon, Oxon, UK: Routledge.

Thomson, R., Espin, J., Samuels-Jones, T. in press. Green crime havens: A spatial cluster analysis of environmental crime. *Social Science Quarterly*.

U.S. Department of Justice. 2011. 'Trident Seafoods Corp. to Pay $2.5 Million to Resolve Clean Water Act Violations and Spend More Than $30 Million to Upgrade Processing Plants,' Available at: www.justice.gov/opa/pr/trident-seafoods-corp-pay-25-million-resolve-clean-water-act-violations-and-spend-more-30.

U.S. Department of the Interior. 2015. 'DOI News Release December 10, 2015,' Available at: www.indianaffairs.gov/sites/bia.gov/files/assets/public/press_release/pdf/idc1-032765.pdf.

U.S. General Accounting Office. 1983. 'Siting of hazardous waste landfills and their correlation with racial and economic status of surrounding communities'.

United Church of Christ. 1987. *Toxic Waste and Race in the United States: A National Report on the Racial and Socioeconomic Characteristics of Communities with Hazardous Waste Sites*. New York: Commission for Racial Justice. United Church of Christ.

35

The disappearing land

Coastal land loss and environmental crime

Lieselot Bisschop, Staci Strobl and Julie Viollaz

Introduction

Coastal land loss brings to mind images of beaches giving way to the sea, but its consequences extend far beyond this. Bays, estuaries, freshwater marshes and wetlands can also be lost to the sea, which harms coastal regions' fauna and flora and also has impacts on its communities and their economies. Although coastal land loss has been a chronic issue for several regions worldwide, it has become acute in the last few years. The Mississippi Delta region of the United States (U.S.) has lost an average of 55 square kilometres of land per year in the last 80 years (Day et al. 2007), while the Huang He Delta (China) lost 67 square kilometres of coastal wetland on average per year between 1989 and 2000 (Coleman, Huh and Braud 2008). Many citizens have moved from these regions because they no longer see a future for themselves or their families (Gramling and Hagelman 2005; Syvitski et al. 2009). While coastal megacities receive the most attention, many smaller communities are also at risk.

A green perspective has made criminology more sensitive to the harm that results from criminal activities but, more importantly, to the fact that similar harms might result from lawful activities (Brisman and South, this volume, Introduction; Ruggiero 2013; South 1998). These harms from lawful activities, often associated with the relentless pursuit of economic growth, are considered neither accidental, unintentional, or external to the society that experiences them, nor fair (Ruggiero and South 2013). Green criminology often focusses squarely on how—and the extent to which—these harms are accepted and normalised (Bernat and Whyte 2016). In order to understand fully who is harmed by environmental plundering, as well as who benefits from this, the economic, political and social context needs be taken into account (McDowell 2013), which requires a proactive and prospective approach to longer-term potential harm (Potter 2012).

In this chapter, drawing on our case study[1] of the Isle de Jean Charles in Louisiana (in the southeastern part of the U.S.) (Bisschop, Strobl and Viollaz 2018) among other research noted here, we argue that coastal land loss is an environmental crime both in terms of its causes and consequences. We then connect our findings to other places in the world that face this fate with disturbingly similar causal dynamics: the Wadden Sea (the Netherlands) and the Sundarbans Delta (India and Bangladesh). Although the causes we discuss for Louisiana, such as canal digging for oil exploration and river manipulation to serve industrial development, are legal activities, they also reflect the capacity of states and corporations to use their power to perpetuate significant social harms. From a state-corporate crime perspective, such harms at the hand of elite actors should be considered crimes (Barak 2015). We also put forth that regional-level corporate behaviours have likely contributed more to coastal land loss problems than the often-cited sea-level rise due to global climate change (though this too is a contributing factor). While researching the Isle de Jean Charles in 2016, we performed semi-structured interviews with key stakeholders, including members of the affected communities, civil servants, climate scientists, levee engineers, politicians and representatives of oil companies.[2] We asked about perceptions of ecological harm, who is responsible for the harm (if anyone), and what are potential solutions. Our exploration of the other two places (the Wadden Sea and the Sundarbans Delta) is based on document analysis.

The Isle de Jean Charles

Southern Louisiana, home of the Mississippi Delta, loses approximately a football field of land per day to the adjacent Gulf of Mexico, and the same amount per hour in hurricane season (June to October). The fate of the people living on Isle de Jean Charles, a small island located in Terrebonne Parish in the Louisiana bayou, is especially dire. Whereas the island once measured about 160 square kilometres in 1950, it is now barely 1.2 square kilometres. This island and the broader Barataria-Terrebonne Estuary now face regular storms and flooding on top of seasonal hurricanes. The levee system and floodgates are not sufficient to save the Isle. The 'Morganza to the Gulf Hurricane Protection Project'—a system of levees and floodgates that is intended to protect the Gulf region from hurricanes and floods—does not protect the island; it remains outside the system. In 2016, the U.S. Department of Housing and Development (HUD) granted 50 million USD to relocate the whole community—bringing together the 24 remaining families with an additional 48 families that had already moved since 2002.

For Louisiana's coastal land loss, the harms appear to be known and recognised widely (Hester, Spalding and Franze 2005; Laska, Wooddell, Hagelman, Gramling and Teets Farris 2005; O'Connell, Franze, Spalding and Poirrier 2005). There is much disagreement, however, about their causes and about whether particular communities, corporations, governments, or people should be held responsible. None of the human behaviour associated with land loss has been adjudicated as criminal because most of these activities, from oil extraction to insufficient levee protection, are legal.

Harm to ecology

Land loss impacts different aspects of the ecology of the region. The coastal environment is a complex interplay of habitats. For instance, barrier islands are crucial for the ecology of the bays and wetlands that they protect (Penland, Williams, Davis, Sallenger and Groat 1992), creating a complex ecosystem of dunes and marshes with unique biodiversity (Hester, Spalding and Franze 2005). Vegetation provides habitats for animals while also improving island stability. Many animals, including keystone species (e.g., American oyster, Rangia clam), endangered or threatened species (e.g., brown pelican) and other estuary organisms in the food web, rely on this complex habitat to thrive. Today, however, many nutrients are disappearing and plants are dying (Science respondent 1). About 350 species of waterfowl and migratory, sea-, song- and shorebirds live, breed, rest, or winter in coastal Louisiana and 22 amphibian, 48 mammalian and 51 reptilian species live there year-round (Lindstedt 2005)—all threatened by shoreline changes (O'Connell, Franze, Spalding and Poirrier 2005).

The harm to ecology in Southern Louisiana is inextricably connected to damage caused by oil and gas infrastructure. Many of today's pipelines are either crossing wetlands or open water but their construction is not always appropriate for these conditions. Given continued land loss and erosion, the pipelines run the risk of being damaged and becoming the source of spills that would be disastrous for the local ecology (Cruciotti and Matthews 2006; Gavenus, Tobin-Gurley and Peek 2013; Spencer and Fitzgerald 2013). For Isle de Jean Charles, the loss of land has homogenised the aquatic habitat that surrounds the island and has decreased the biodiversity of both plants and animals (Figure 35.1).

Harm to humans

For a long time, residents of Isle de Jean Charles engaged in subsistence fishing, farming and trapping. There was enough land to grow vegetables and raise livestock, and crawfish, oysters, and shrimp were plentiful to catch and eat. Today, those livelihoods are disappearing.

> There is an ongoing attempt to hold on to culture but it is not exactly the same because you now need to actively go out for it (fishing, trailing) whereas it used to be at our doorstep. It does not happen as a main source of livelihood anymore.
>
> *(Citizen respondent 2)*

Figure 35.1 Ghost trees near Isle de Jean Charles—June 2016—Lieselot Bisschop.

The harm to the community, though, extends beyond just threats to residents' livelihoods. It has affected the sense of community, as well as the culture of the island.

> Our community was once one of several hundred people, it was thriving, and people took pride in their home and their boats, invested in sustainable living and grew their own vegetables. There was also a real sense of community.
>
> *(Citizen respondent 1)*

For instance, floods have damaged old cemeteries, destroying Native American tribes' cultural heritage. Many inhabitants are members of non-federally-recognised Biloxi-Chitimacha-Choctaw and Houma Native American tribes that are, however, both recognised by the state of Louisiana. The land loss endangers their spiritual relationship with their land and resources (Maldonado, Shearer, Bronen, Peterson and Lazrus 2013; Rivard 2015). This community has faced systematic impoverishment and injustice, economic oppression and political disempowerment (Maldonado, Shearer, Bronen, Peterson and Lazrus 2013). For them, the issue of land loss is therefore inherently entangled with issues of sovereignty, human rights and inequality (Rivard 2015).

Isle de Jean Charles is not alone in this regard as other coastal communities in Louisiana are experiencing similar losses and facing comparable uncertain futures. About 1.5 million people in Louisiana live in an area that is at risk of coastal land loss and sea level rise. About 40 per cent of the at-risk inhabitants are members of, or descendants from, minority groups. All told, the residents of coastal Louisiana reflect a diverse ancestry, including Acadian,[3] African, early Anglo-American settlers, French, German, Spanish and original Native Americans, as well as later-arriving immigrants from China, Croatia, Haiti, Ireland, Vietnam and the former Yugoslavia (Gramling and Hagelman 2005). Native American presence dates back 10,000 years, although the tribal make-up of the region has changed dynamically over these centuries due to war and migration. Historically, these communities have depended on the coastal environment for their livelihood and the region has experienced the development of a deeply rooted, diverse and distinctive culture (Laska, Wooddell, Hagelman, Gramling and Teets Farris 2005). Given the damage to the physical environment, this unique culture is at risk as well.

> [My dad] is 81 years old and has seen the coast change to open water, with the biggest changes in the last few years. He used to trawl the bayou and knows every part by heart [...] Many people used to raise cattle and horses but that is no longer possible with the rising water. The view from the back porch is very different.
>
> *(Citizen respondent 1)*

Those responsible for the region's plans for coastal restoration seem to forget about the cultural impacts of land loss, especially for the poorest in the region. Such decision-makers base their determinations primarily on economic cost-benefit analyses that provide for technical restoration efforts, but pay limited attention to social or cultural dynamics. Approaching ecological issues purely as science or engineering problems means that the socio-cultural impact on communities is ignored (Colten 2015; see also Samuels-Jones et al., this volume, Chapter 34). While the communities whose land is disappearing are obviously affected, those communities receiving the influx of residents from other parishes moving in to avoid the rising waters are also impacted. In other words, both coastal communities and 'receiving' communities experience change and loss, albeit somewhat differently (Brisman 2018). A citizen at the State of the Coast conference, held in June of 2016 in New Orleans, summarised this concern: 'How can we avoid Southern Louisiana from becoming a land with great levees but no people, no culture?'

Coastal communities also face the consequences of changing lifestyles. The change from subsistence fishing and farming to buying food and a more sedentary lifestyle, together with the pollution of the coast and the poisoning of seafood by oil spills, has negatively impacted their health.

> Every household has some form of cancer but there are also many non-life-threatening illnesses such as diabetes or sinus infections. There are now many treatment centers across the Bayou to address this but there is no addressing of the causes.
>
> *(Science respondent 3)*

Although we have argued that economic loss should not be the sole or primary concern, coastal communities throughout Southern Louisiana have experienced the economic consequences of land loss. For years, many people relied on crabbing, fishing and shrimping for their livelihoods. Indeed, since the 1800s, fishing has been a core component of Louisiana's culture and economy. Louisiana supplies one fifth of the seafood consumed by humans in the U.S., including blue crab, crawfish, oysters and shrimp, as well as wild and farmed alligators (O'Connell, Franze, Spalding and Poirrier 2005). The state also supplies one third of the fish (menhaden) for poultry and livestock feed for the lower 48 states. Louisiana's seafood industry has an economic impact of 2.4 billion USD annually, and accounts for about one in every 70 jobs. Crabbing, fishing and shrimping are full-time occupations for many residents, but they are also important activities during time off from other vocations (e.g., from offshore oil work). The sustainability of these renewable resources has diminished due to coastal land loss. Changes in salinity levels, for instance, have impacted crab, oyster and shrimp populations, as have decades of minor and major oil spills. Generally, though, the economic interests of fishing communities seem to have taken a backseat in coastal restoration projects (Colten 2015), which could prove disastrous for these communities because 'the way of life in south Louisiana is inseparable from the ecosystem' (Gramling and Hagelman 2005: 131).

Previous studies have shown that the exploitation of natural resources and the exploitation of minorities often go hand in hand (Goyes, Mol, Brisman and South 2017; Mohai and Saha 2007; Nurse, this volume, Chapter 33; Park and Pellow 2004; Pellow, this volume, Chapter 32; Samuels-Jones et al., this volume, Chapter 34). Those most likely to be harmed by environmental crime are communities of low socio-economic status or racial minorities (McDowell 2013; Stretesky and Lynch 1998). This also rings true for Isle de Jean Charles. Due to coastal land loss, this minority community risks losing access to food, livelihood and shelter, as well as education and cultural life. In other words, coastal land loss impinges on their human rights.

Causes of coastal land loss in Louisiana

While the specific reasons for coastal land loss may vary from community to community, some combination of natural processes and human activities is always at work. At the same time, while the extent of coastal land loss is generally not disputed, identifying its main cause remains contentious (Jones et al. 2016). Anthropogenic causes especially tend to be downplayed (Turner 2014). In this part of the chapter, we discuss the two primary natural causes of coastal land loss: sea level rise and subsiding land. These are two distinct, yet interconnected, natural processes (Anderson, Wallace, Simms, Rodriguez and Milliken 2014) that we will show are exacerbated by human interventions. We then discuss the purely human-made cause: the effect of the withdrawal of minerals, particularly oil and gas extraction.

Sea level rise

Sea level rise refers to higher sea levels due to global climate change and the melting of the polar icecaps as the planet warms. The global average sea level rise is currently at 2 to 3 millimetres per year, but recent modelling has shown a potential acceleration to 2–3 *centimetres* per year (resulting in a sea level rise of 3 meters in the next 100 years). Conservative modelling for Louisiana predicts a sea level rise of 0.65 of a meter by 2062, doubling the land loss of the past 80 years (CPRA 2012; Olea and Coleman 2013).

Journalistic accounts and popular media reports frequently point to climate change as the reason for Isle de Jean Charles' land loss (Hasemyer 2016; Van Houten 2016; Zanolli 2016). Famously, the film *Beasts of the Southern Wild* (Zeitlin 2012), based on Isle de Jean Charles and nearby Pointe-aux-Chênes, interprets storm-related social dislocations through a depiction of a young girl's graphic ruminations on glaciers melting and dislocated mega-fauna roaming the Earth.

Indeed, tying coastal land loss to climate change likely facilitated the Isle de Jean Charles community's successful application for a HUD grant to relocate. This narrative also tied the fate of Isle de Jean Charles and Southern Louisiana to that of other low-lying places in the world, giving their narrative more traction in the media and garnering more support worldwide (Farbotko and Lazrus 2012; Maldonado, Shearer, Bronen, Peterson and Lazrus 2013; Sarwar and Woodroffe 2013). Many of our respondents, however, expressed the belief that climate change was a secondary cause that only exacerbated the effects of other causes.

Subsidence

'Subsidence' refers to the sinking of the ground, which, under natural conditions, is offset by sediment coming from upstream locations along the rivers or brought in with the tides from other coastal areas. Subsidence is accelerated when material is removed from underground, such as when oil or gas is extracted. For Southern Louisiana, both a lack of sediment and the removal of underground material has contributed to coastal subsidence. Neither of these contributing factors are purely natural causes in Louisiana, however. Humans are responsible for the removal of underground material as discussed below.

The lack of sediment results from the re-routing of the Mississippi's waters since the early twentieth century. The US Army Corps of Engineers ('Army Corps') constructed river levees and other flood-control mechanisms in response to the Great Mississippi Flood of 1927—the most destructive river flood in U.S. history (Coleman, Roberts and Stone 1998). They were meant to provide flood-control, to ensure a stable river course and to facilitate economic opportunities in transportation and oil and gas (Bisschop, Strobl and Viollaz 2018). The Mississippi River (and its many smaller tributaries) drains rainwater and other runoff from approximately 45 per cent of the landmass in the continental U.S., bringing along an abundance of sediment and nutrients (Olea and Coleman 2013). Before the Army Corps' activities, approximately 100 meters of coastal sediment built up for every 1,000–2,000-year cycle (Day et al. 2007). Now, however, sediment is not widely dispersed by the river water, so most parts of the coastline are receding rather than rebuilding themselves (Blum and Roberts 2012). Although the region has always faced natural subsidence from storm activity, the sediment deposits previously offset this.

Since the patterns of river manipulation in the early twentieth century, much of the sediment travels to the end of the Mississippi River and ends up deep in the Gulf of Mexico. Instead of depositing at the mouth of the river, the sediment falls off the underwater plateau and becomes submerged in deep waters, thereby not contributing to the formation of coastal land (Olea and Coleman 2013). The limited amount of sediment that does reach the wetlands today is washed away by increasingly fierce storms and snowmelt runoff. This sediment loss, in turn, contributes to additional environmental problems, such as the loss of freshwater that acts to stabilise levels of salinity, and the loss of nutrients that maintain coastal biodiversity (Olea and Coleman 2013)—all of which impact coastal Louisiana's ecosystem. In particular, the Isle de Jean Charles is cut off completely from any sediment delivered through river flows and receives only minimal sediment through storm activity. The Isle is thus especially vulnerable to land subsidence.

When major construction began on the levees of the Mississippi River in the 1920s, the trade-offs were possibly not fully understood, though some scientists and local governments had previously predicted both immediate and long-term consequences for river flow and the bayou communities (Corthell 1897). The interests of cities, industry and transportation, though, were favoured over those of rural communities (Colten 2015). Adding insult to injury, limited investment in maintaining the levee infrastructure over the long-term left rural communities vulnerable to severe storm damage, as was the case with hurricane Katrina. One government respondent (number 9) indicated that the damage to New Orleans and points 60 miles inland by Hurricane Katrina was pronounced precisely because public money was slated to fix levees only when failure occurred rather than investing in maintaining structural integrity. He added that 'Louisiana's levees and dykes infrastructure is designed for storms that occur once every 100 years because designing for storms that occur once every 1000 years, as in the Netherlands, is too expensive'.

Canal building

Throughout the twentieth century, private enterprises dug 16,000 kilometres of canals in Southern Louisiana in pursuit of oil and gas to extract. The dredging of these canals also meant the creation of spoil banks (banks of excavated refuse or so-called 'waste earth') next to canals. Although initially 8 to 10 meters wide, many canals are now 100 meters wide as the water eroded the spoil banks and open water encroached. Together, these canals and spoil banks are responsible for 12 to 16 per cent of subsidence and wetland losses (Turner 2014). The canals and banks change water flow, cause erosion, increase salinity and kill nutrients, thereby harming freshwater ecosystems up to 2 kilometres away from the canal (Day et al. 2007). For 30 years, state officials ignored these harmful consequences of canals and spoil banks. In 1982, as a result of new federal laws enacted to protect America's wetlands, the Louisiana government was compelled to track the canal dredging and require permits for new canal creation. In theory, explorers were required to backfill canals once they become inactive for oil exploration or extraction, allowing the wetlands to recover. A legal loophole in effect to the present day, however, allows companies to avoid backfilling as long as these canals could be reactivated. By referring to technological innovations in oil and gas drilling—and thus potential re-exploitation in the future—companies have avoided having to backfill canals or restore wetlands,

> Part of the problem is that the tax structure is very generous for industry but there are less and less positives and they are recalcitrant to fix what they broke. For instance they do not backfill the canals despite this being a requirement. The state is friendly to oil and gas and is also designed this way. If they had to transition there would be billions of stranded assets.
>
> *(NGO respondent 3)*

Currently, oil and gas corporations own about 90 per cent of the land in Terrebonne Parish, where many of these canals are located. At the start of oil exploration in Louisiana in the 1930s, these lands were the domain of Native Americans and other residents, many of whom were not consulted before drilling happened or were tricked out of their land ownership. Bayou resident respondents in our prior study (Bisschop, Strobl and Viollaz 2018) talked about how their ancestors and relatives were presented with papers to sign by representatives of oil and gas companies. In some cases they could not read or did not fully understand what they were signing. One respondent said:

> I call [this corporate behaviour] an environmental crime because they took advantage of isolated people who were desperate for work; it was a depressed area with merely subsistence living and they illegally and knowingly took land for oil and mineral purposes.
>
> *(Citizen respondent 3)*

Oil and gas extraction

Oil and gas extraction contributes to coastal land loss because it changes land's underground pressure, resulting in subsidence (Day et al. 2007). Several studies have shown that coastal land loss is doubled or tripled in certain areas during active oil and gas production (Olea and Coleman 2013). In fact, the effects of petroleum extraction can accelerate subsidence for several decades (Mead et al. 2016):

> The oil and gas exploration and exploitation causes the damage to spread exponentially like a disease. There are natural causes, which together with the extracting of oil created funnels as wide as anything. Many aspects are not rocket science, just gravity.
>
> *(Public participant comment, State of the Coast conference, New Orleans, Louisiana, June 3, 2016)*

> Oil and gas hastened the process [of subsidence] and caused the symptoms to be seen quicker.
>
> *(Government respondent 5)*

Some argue that the economic interests of the oil and gas industry hinder discussions about whether oil and gas is causing subsidence. Coastal Louisiana has approximately 50,000 oil and gas wells, which produce about one third of U.S. crude oil and one fifth of its natural gas, a major source of revenue for the state (Laska, Wooddell, Hagelman, Gramling and Teets Farris 2005; Scott and Richardson 2015). Oil and gas is also an important employer, although several respondents referred to these jobs as a 'deal with the devil' insofar as they allow them to provide for their families now that sustenance fishing and farming are no longer viable given pollution levels and land loss from oil and gas extraction.

> Oil and gas is the only game in town so of course they will work for it, but they have to watch out with blaming because it is often the only source of livelihood remaining.
>
> *(Science respondent 3)*

Ever since the 1940s, government regulation of the oil and gas industry has failed to keep pace with industrial growth (Houck 2015). Prior to the Clean Water Act of 1973, Louisiana did not require permits for oil and gas exploration or extraction on privately owned land. Since 1973, permits are required and only granted when industry promises to undertake mitigation, but there is limited monitoring of actual mitigation. This lax regulation and monitoring is consistent with a history of corruption, anaemic transparency laws, industry-friendly tax regimes and an institutional culture of complacency when it comes to environmental regulations.

> Generally in the process we are helpful and cooperative with industry. If all impacts will be mitigated then the permits are usually granted.
>
> *(Government respondent 8)*

Local governments (such as those in Cameron, Jefferson, Plaquemines, St. Bernard and Vermilion Parishes) have filed lawsuits recently against oil and gas companies for ignoring the wetland mitigation requirements spelled out in permits or for working without permits (Mufson 2013). Whereas previous state governments (i.e., those under Republican Governor Bobby Jindal) discouraged parishes from suing, the current government (that of Democratic Governor John Bel Edwards) has changed course, and has even foreshadowed that the state might also sue industry actors. Accountability efforts remain difficult, however, as local governments and affected citizens are rarely successful against corporations in the courtroom (e.g., *Barasich* v *Columbia Gulf Transmission Co.* [E.D. La., 2006]; Houck 2015), with the exception of some restitution money from the British Petroleum (BP) Oil Spill of 2010. The pro-industry political climate is clear given that the state tax incentives continue to heartily encourage development of the oil and gas industry on coastal land (Bisschop, Strobl and Viollaz 2018; Bradshaw 2015), while the federal government does not directly regulate this development (it only directly regulates off-shore oil drilling).

Other examples of coastal land loss

Isle de Jean Charles may be the poster child of coastal land loss, but other communities throughout the world face similar challenges. In the following sections, we describe two additional examples, the Wadden Sea in the Netherlands and the Sundarbans in India and Bangladesh, to further demonstrate the relevance of coastal land loss as a research topic for green criminology.

Wadden Sea

In the north of the Netherlands and Germany and to the west of Denmark lies the Wadden Sea, a UNESCO world heritage site that translates to the 'mud flats sea' (Figure 35.2). This combination of dunes, mussel beds, saltwater marshes and sandy low-lying islands of high ecological value constitutes the world's biggest tidal coast. The area is crucial for migratory birds and seals. During the twentieth century, the Wadden Sea ecosystem suffered significant damage from pollution and overexploitation, but efforts to save the area demonstrated that changes can be reversed with sufficient habitat restoration and species diversification (Lotze et al. 2005). Yet, it is currently facing an environmental change of a different magnitude: it risks disappearing by 2100 due to coastal land loss (Neslen 2017).

The Wadden Sea area is a largely closed system with only a limited influx of sediment, but one that can offset a sea level rise of 15 centimetres per century. In view of protecting the other low-lying areas of the Netherlands, a world-renowned system of levees and dykes—the *Delta Works*—was constructed along the coast. Construction started after the major floods of 1953 and finished in 2010.

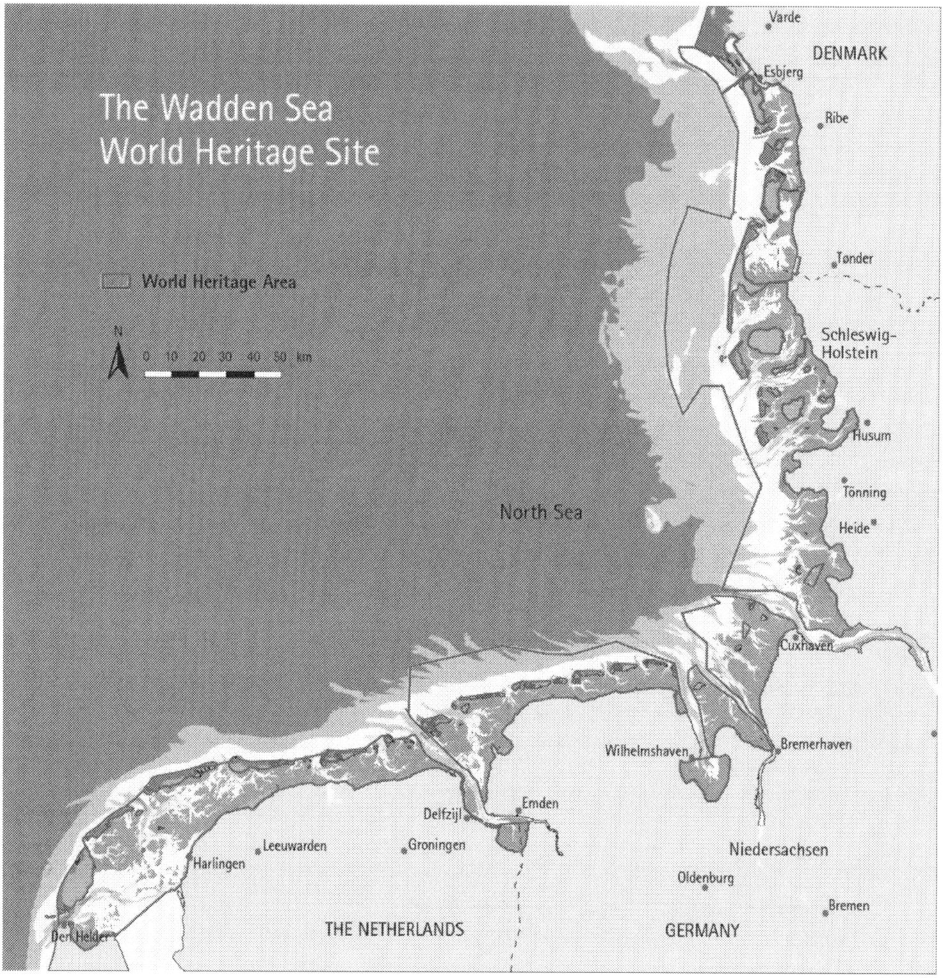

Figure 35.2 Wadden Sea World Heritage Site, map source: UNESCO.

Withdrawal of minerals (gas) and of salt in the region has increased land subsidence from a couple of centimetres naturally to several decimetres in specific locations, with effects extending far out into the delta. The ongoing drilling for gas in the Groningse and Frisian fields (since 1959) and offshore near Ameland (since 1986) has already impacted the sediment loss buffer of the Wadden Sea. Permits for these activities are often granted based on outdated sea level rise scenarios and fail to take into account the longer-term effects of mineral withdrawal. A recent study by Schuttenhelm (2017) now calls into question these scenarios, replacing them with more realistic data, which found that the benefits of allowing gas drilling are not worth the risk of using up the limited sediment buffer remaining.

While obtaining a drilling permit requires a check of the subsidence level at the extraction location, those measurements are conducted by the extraction industry. This is especially troubling, given that Schuttenhelm's research suggests the extraction industry and the permit system suffer from 'insight inertia'; they ignore updated predictions of sea level rise or land loss from independent scientists. The industry also uses five-year predictions that focus on the short-term benefits of gas drilling instead of looking at the potential long-term harm.

This lack of industry oversight is reminiscent of the situation of Isle de Jean Charles. Fishermen from coastal communities near Friesland describe similar concerns and feelings of distrust as Isle de Jean Charles residents. They worry about the effects of drilling on fish habitats and on dykes that protect their communities, and believe that industry growth is being prioritised over their welfare:

> It's all about the money. We had one talk with [*Dutch oil and gas company*] and they constantly repeated that they would help us make the clean energy transition. But it's crap. We don't buy it. They only want to invest in it when they are drilling. They hold on to their old ways and destroy everything for the sake of money.
>
> *(Willem Schoorstra, citizen/novelist (cited in: Neslen 2017: 2))*

Extraction companies have implied that they will shut down operations as soon as geological monitoring demonstrates that land is subsiding faster because of their drilling (NAM 2018). The Dutch government and involved municipalities, though, got increasingly worried that these measures were insufficient given that it may take years to understand the full effect of drilling on land subsidence. By that point, the damage would likely already be significant and irreversible. The supervisory board of mining activities asked the oil and gas companies for realistic subsidence predictions with adequate methodologies. In case they do not comply, drilling permits will not be granted.

The oil and gas industry argues that drilling is necessary for a safe, secure and affordable energy supply. Meanwhile, the Dutch government believes that gas is essential to transition to a low-carbon society. Citizens, though, have been increasingly worried that financial gain, rather than a cautious scientific study of harms, drives the decision to issue drilling permits, especially because the negative effects of drilling are felt mostly far away from the epicentre of decision-making in The Hague. Nevertheless, some government and industry actors are taking a stand with citizens. The Governor of Friesland has joined several protests after earthquakes increased in the Groningen region due to gas drilling. Some financers of gas-drilling projects have also joined with the citizens, deciding to no longer finance gas-drilling activities under the Wadden Sea. Moreover, new housing developments in the Netherlands will no longer have a gas connection for heating and cooking but will instead connect to the district heating networks, which uses surplus heat from industrial activities, or will use electric heating and cooking. This fits the plans of becoming a climate neutral society by 2050. These initiatives are promising, but the Dutch government must overhaul industry regulations significantly to ensure the survival of the Wadden Sea and its communities.

In March 2018, the Dutch Minister of Economic Affairs and Climate, Eric Wiebes, decided that natural gas extraction from the Groningen field will be significantly reduced by 2022 and terminated by 2030 (www.government.nl/latest/news/2018/03/29/dutch-cabinet-termination-of-natural-gas-extraction-in-groningen). In July 2018, the Dutch Parliament approved an amendment, led by political representatives of the Wadden Sea communities, to stop granting permits for drilling there. A similar proposal submitted to Parliament in 2017 failed but, since then, public awareness and outrage about the gas drilling and its consequences have increased. Drilling in the Wadden Sea is no longer allowed, but drilling for gas from shore is still possible if the subsidence by gas extraction can be compensated for by the sand and silt brought in with the natural tide, so-called 'extraction with the hand on the tap' (Waddenvereniging 2018). Moreover, a permit process was recently started for one field in the Wadden Sea (Ternaard), which had been inactive for years because of cost inefficiency. As a result, drilling will likely still take place for decades in this field and many others. This reopening of old oil and gas fields is similar to the situation of Isle de Jean Charles.

> It is astonishing that activities which cause subsidence are still allowed in the Wadden Sea, an area so vulnerable to accelerated sea level rise due to climate change. The technique of supplementing with extra sand is used to mitigate the effects of these activities, but this is ecologically harmful and the long term effects and sustainability are unclear. The advice of the Delta Commission to stop all activities that cause subsidence in lower lying areas seems like the logical next step to protect the Netherlands' only natural World Heritage site.
>
> *(NGO respondent quote)*

Sundarbans

In India and Bangladesh, the Sundarbans contains the world's largest contiguous mangrove forest and is another UNESCO World Heritage Site due to its exceptional biodiversity. It is also the only home of the Royal Bengal Tiger, a threatened species (Aziz and Paul 2015; Dasgupta, Soghan and Wheeler 2016; Ghosh 2015). The region is approximately 10,000 square kilometres and consists of flat forestland with ground elevation of 0.9 to 2.11 meters above sea level. Three rivers spill into the delta—the Bahmaputra, Ganges and Surma-Kushiara—plus their tributaries, which bring water and sediment from the Himalayan mountain range. During the last 100 years, the Sundarbans ecosystem has suffered significant damage from pollution and the shipping industry—both associated with the region's relatively dense population of approximately 5 million people. By 2050, coastal land loss could lead to a complete disappearance of the entire region if trends cannot be reversed (Aziz and Paul 2015).

The Sundarbans region, like the Mississippi Delta, was formed over several thousand years by the gradual layering of sediment from upriver onto the coastal shelf at the mouths of the delta's three rivers. More recently, human manipulation of the three-river system, in particular the effects of the Farakka Barrage, a diversion dam built in 1975 on the Ganges in West Bengal designed to prevent sediment accumulating in Kolkata Harbour, has obstructed the natural sedimentary build-up within the delta. Currently, the sediment volume is diminished and falls off the coastal shelf into deep waters instead of forming coastal layers. Among many other contributors to land loss, the loss of sediment is among the major causes of the overall problem (Aziz and Paul 2015). Tidal patterns during the dry season (December to May) create almost no sedimentary build-up during that part of the year. Between 1986 and 2007, the Sundarbans' coastlines lost an average of 0.2 and 1.7 kilometres, with the worst loss occurring in the southern part of the delta. On the other hand, new islands have been forming at the mouth of the Beshawar River, though they are not enough to offset the region's overall losses. Withdrawal of groundwater to support the population has contributed to land subsidence, exacerbated by sea level rise associated with global climate change. In addition, patterns of erosion have made the Sundarbans more susceptible to climate-change-related coastal land loss than most other regions on Earth (Shearman, Bryan and Walsh 2013).

The lack of freshwater available to the Sundarbans is the second major driver of land loss in the region (Aziz and Paul 2015). With land loss comes the destruction of mangrove forests, which are also suffering from increased salinity due to the encroachment of the Bay of Bengal further inland. Of the Ganges' tributary, the Gorai is a major source of freshwater in the region because of the Farakka Barrage and other human manipulations of the system's rivers.

The increased salinity from the lack of freshwater negatively affects most species of mangrove, which require influxes of both freshwater and seawater. In addition, freshwater and sedimentary decreases have led to reduced forest canopy (Giri, Pengra, Zhu, Singh and Tieszen 2007) as has over-exploitation of forests for timber (Dasgupta, Soghan and Wheeler 2016).

Local people's livelihoods are connected to the forest and to the water. This is particularly true for the millions of poor inhabitants of the region who live adjacent to the Sundarban Biosphere Reserve (SBR)—an area protected from human activity for conservation purposes in West Benghal, India—as well as the larger subsistence communities in Bangladesh (Dasgupta, Soghan and Wheeler 2016; Ghosh 2015). These communities rely on crabs, fish, honey, shrimp, timber and wax for their livelihoods. Migrations of whole communities are expected to become more frequent as people relocate to places where subsistence opportunities are greater (Dasgupta, Soghan and Wheeler 2016). Meanwhile, illegal fishing and trapping in conservation zones is on the rise and human–tiger conflicts have also increased as competition for resources intensifies and tigers pass through or move into areas of high human density (Ghosh 2015). Both of these issues further damage the ecosystem, precipitating the need for these community migrations.

Ironically, those most directly affected by the disappearing Sundarbans have seen little if no economic benefit from global, industrial development. The same socioeconomic global order that promotes resource exploitation and over-consumption among the privileged, at the same time creates conditions of environment degradation that compound the economic struggles of the poor—a macro-level concern of the environmental justice perspective within green criminology (Ozymy et al. this volume, Chapter 8; Nurse this volume, Chapter 33; Pellow this volume, Chapter 32; Samuels-Jones this volume, Chapter 34; White 2013). Furthermore, as relatively poor countries with relatively high populations, the governments of India and Bangladesh appear ill-equipped to offer major solutions to offset harms or reverse the environmental damage other than to wait for the upheaval of mass internal migration and the collapse of subsistence livelihoods.

While, in the Wadden Sea and Southern Louisiana, direct corporate responsibility for environmentally unfriendly oil and gas industries, coupled with insufficient governmental oversight, provides a potentially blameworthy target for the criminalisation of coastal land loss, such blameworthiness appears less straightforward in the case of the Sundarbans (although the oil and gas industry might be responsible for the 2014 oil spill in a protected mangrove estuary) (Alexander 2014). Nevertheless, green criminology's focus on the harms, and their human footprint in a general sense, suggests that coastal land loss, in all three of these cases, can be labelled a 'crime of the powerful'. The land loss can be linked to the business-friendly institutional arrangements that favour industrial and investor interests over those of local communities. According to the state-corporate crime perspective, the state does not merely *legitimise*, but also *cooperates* with industries in creating territories and jurisdictions oriented toward resource extraction and profit (Bernat and Whyte 2016; Tombs 2012). Under this notion of state-facilitated crime, governmental regulatory agencies fail to restrain businesses, which cause substantial injury to the well-being of people (Kramer, Michalowski and Kauzlarich 2002) and their environment (Simon 1999, 2009).

Conclusion: coastal land loss as environmental crime

To better understand the underlying dynamics of coastal land loss, theories focussing on crimes of the powerful are most useful. As the cases above have illustrated, a complex interplay of economic, political and social dynamics between government and corporate actors has contributed to coastal land loss. Notions of state-corporate crime apply well to the cases of the Isle de Jean Charles and the Wadden Sea, even though the acts and omissions of responsible parties are not always labelled as criminal (Kramer, Michalowski and Kauzlarich 2002; Tombs 2012). In all three cases presented here, environmental harms and crimes are committed—or at least facilitated—by state and/or corporate actors, even if they are seldom held accountable for them (Bradshaw 2015). Meanwhile, the degradation of the Sundarbans Delta speaks to global inequality where the economic benefits of exploiting the Earth for profit have costs that are disproportionately paid by the poor—a more abstract and far-reaching crime of the powerful, and one of concern to those activists, researchers and scholars (green criminologists or otherwise) interested in exposing and ameliorating environmental injustices.

What is striking in the Isle de Jean Charles case, in particular, however, is that the lack of a formal legal framework for responding to coastal land loss has had discursive consequences for how stakeholders imagine the problem, its causes and its solutions. Quite often, climate change is erroneously named as the main culprit for Isle de Jean Charles coastal land loss, probably due to the presence of the climate change problem in popular media and political discourse (i.e., it is an easy culprit) (see generally Brisman, South and Walters this volume, Chapter 10). Indeed, climate change has had a greater effect in the Sundarbans Delta (Shearman, Bryan and Walsh 2013), but even there it remains a lesser force when compared with river manipulation by the state (the Farakka Barrage). Our prior case study found that citing climate change as the cause seemingly blames the entire industrialised world for the problem, while at the same time ensuring that no one in particular is held responsible (Bisschop, Strobl and Viollaz 2018). This dynamic is why a green cultural criminological focus on the social construction of environmental harm and environmental crime is vital to coming up with workable responses to and/or accountability mechanisms for these harms and crimes (Brisman and South 2013, 2014, this volume, Chapter 1).

Narratives describing Isle de Jean Charles' land loss influence stakeholders' perceptions. Though most agree on the extent of harm, very few frame the problem as state-corporate crime (Bisschop, Strobl and Viollaz 2018). Both what is reported and what is not reported affects responses to the regional environmental problem (Brisman 2010). The Isle de Jean Charles community is really only an indirect victim of climate change. They are more likely the direct victims of capitalism, engineering, industrialism and other man-made interventions perpetuated in a particularly problematic way in the region. Understanding this complex interplay of who is harmed, how and by whom would not have been possible without examining the economic, political and social context of Isle de Jean Charles (Brisman and South 2015; Stretesky, Long and Lynch 2013). Only once this interplay is clear, can policy makers and governments produce solutions that hold those responsible accountable.

Notes

1 Research was funded by a Postdoctoral Fellowship grant by the Research Foundation Flanders (Belgium) to Lieselot Bisschop and a grant from the Liberal Arts and Education Dean's Fund at the University of Wisconsin-Platteville (United States) to Staci Strobl.

2 Quotations from these respondents are used throughout this chapter and referred to as 'citizen respondent', 'government respondent', 'NGO respondent' and 'science respondent', followed by a number. We refer to a more general category because reference to specific government agencies or towns would compromise the confidentiality we guaranteed our respondents (see also Bisschop, Strobl and Viollaz 2018).

3 'Acadians' are descendants of Indigenous peoples of Acadia in the northeastern region of North America.

References

Alexander, C. 2014. 'After oil spill in Bangladesh's unique mangrove forest, fears about rare animals,' *National Geographic*. Available at: http://news.nationalgeographic.com/news/2014/12/141216-sundarbans-oil-spill-bangladesh-tigers-dolphins-conservation.

Allison, M. A., Yuill, B., Törnqvist, T., Dixon, T., Erkens, G., Stuurman, R., ... Teatini, P. 2016. 'Global risks and research priorities for coastal subsidence,' *EOS*, 97. DOI: 10.1029/2016EO055013

Anderson, J., Wallace, D., Simms, A., Rodriguez, A. and Milliken, K. 2014. 'Variable response of coastal environments of the Northwestern Gulf of Mexico to sea level rise and climate change: Implications for future change,' *Marine Geology*, 352(June): 348–366.

Aziz, A. and Paul, A. R. 2015. Bangladesh Sundarbans: Present status of the environment and biota. *Diversity*. DOI: 10.3390/d7030242

Barak, G. 2015. *The Routledge International Handbook of the Crimes of the Powerful*. Abingdon, Oxon, UK: Routledge.

Bernat, I. and Whyte, D. 2016. State-corporate crime and the process of capital accumulation: Mapping a global regime of permission from Galicia to Morecambe Bay. *Critical Criminology: An International Journal*, 25(1): 71–86. DOI: 10.1007/s10612-016-9340-9

Bisschop, L. C. J., Strobl, S. and Viollaz, J. S. 2018. Getting into deep water: Coastal land loss and state-corporate crime in the Louisiana Bayou. *The British Journal of Criminology*, 58(4): 886-905 DOI: 10.1093/bjc/azx057

Blum, M. D. and Roberts, H. H. 2012. 'The Mississippi Delta Region: Past, present, and future,' *Annual Review of Earth and Planetary Sciences*. DOI: 10.1146/annurev-earth-042711-105248

Bradshaw, E. A. 2015. '"Obviously, we're all oil industry": The criminogenic structure of the offshore oil industry,' *Theoretical Criminology*, 19(3): 376–395.

Brisman, A. 2010. 'The indiscriminate criminalisation of environmentally beneficial activities,' in R. White (ed.) *Global Environmental Harm: Criminological Perspectives*, pp. 161–192. Collumpton, Devon, UK: Willan.

Brisman, A. 2018. The fable of *The Three Little Pigs*, climate change and green cultural criminology. *International Journal for Crime, Justice and Social Democracy*, 8(1): 46–69. DOI: 10.5204/ijcjsd.v8i1.470.

Brisman, A. and South, N. 2013. A green-cultural criminology: An exploratory outline. *Crime Media Culture*, 9(2): 115–135. DOI: 10.1177/1741659012467026

Brisman, A. and South, N. 2015. 'State-corporate environmental harms and paradoxical interventions: Thoughts in honour of Stanley Cohen,' in R. Sollund (ed.) *Green Harms and Crimes*, pp. 27–42. Basingstoke, Hampshire, UK: Palgrave Macmillan.

Coleman, J., Huh, O. K. and Braud, D. 2008. Wetland loss in world deltas. *Journal of Coastal Research*. DOI: 10.2112/05-0607.1

Coleman, J., Roberts, H. and Stone, G. 1998. 'Mississippi river delta: An overview,' *Journal of Coastal Research*, 14(3): 698–716.

Colten, C. E. 2015. 'The place for humans in Louisiana coastal restoration,' *Labor & Engenho*, 9(4): 6–18.

Corthell, E. 1897. 'The Mississippi river delta,' *National Geographic*, VIII(12): 351–354.

CPRA. 2012. *Louisiana's Comprehensive Master Plan for a Sustainable Coast*. Baton Rouge, LA: Coastal Protection and Restoration Authority of Louisiana. Available at: http://coastal.la.gov/a-common-vision/2012-coastal-master-plan/

Cruciotti, T. and Matthews, R. A. 2006. 'The Exxon Valdez oil spill,' in R. Michalowski and R. Kramer (eds.) *State-Corporate Crime: Wrongdoing at the Intersection of Business & Government*, pp. 149–171. New Brunswick, NJ: Rutgers University Press.

Dasgupta, S., Soghan, D. and Wheeler, D. 2016. 'Impact on Climate Change and Aquatic Salinization on Mangrove Species and Poor Communities in the Bangladesh Sundarbans,' Available at: https://openknowledge.worldbank.org/handle/10986/24653.

Day, J. W., Boesch, D. F., Clairain, E. J., Kemp, G. P., Laska, S. B., Mitsch, W. J., ... Whigham, D. F. (2007). Restoration of the Mississippi delta: Lessons from Hurricanes Katrina and Rita. *Science*, 315 (5819): 1679 LP–1684. Available at: http://science.sciencemag.org/content/315/5819/1679.abstract

Farbotko, C. and Lazrus, H. 2012. 'The first climate refugees? Contesting global narratives of climate change in Tuvalu,' *Global Environmental Change*, 22(2): 382–390.

Gavenus, K. A., Tobin-Gurley, J. and Peek, L. 2013. 'Children of the spills-phase II: The Gulf coast and the BP/deepwater horizon oil spill,' *Children Youth and Environments*, 23(1): 167–179.

Ghosh, P. 2015. 'Conservation and conflicts in the Sundarban Biosphere Reserve, India,' *Geographical Review*. DOI: 10.1111/j.1931-0846.2015.12101.x

Giri, C., Pengra, B., Zhu, Z., Singh, A. and Tieszen, L. L. 2007. 'Monitoring mangrove forest dynamics of the Sundarbans in Bangladesh and India using multi-temporal satellite data from 1973 to 2000,' *Estuarine, Coastal and Shelf Science*. DOI: 10.1016/j.ecss.2006.12.019

Goyes, D., Mol, H., Brisman, A. and South, N. 2017. *Environmental Crime in Latin America: The Theft of Nature and the Poisoning of the Land*. London: Palgrave/Macmillan.

Gramling, R. and Hagelman, R. 2005. 'A working coast: People in the Louisiana wetlands,' *Journal of Coastal Research*, 44(Spring): 112–133.

Hasemyer, D. 2016. 'Native American tribe gets federal funds to flee rising seas,' *Inside Climate News*, 28 (2): 185–455. Available at: https://insideclimatenews.org/news/15032016/native-americans-federal-funds-isle-de-jean-charles-relocation-climate-change-sea-level-rise

Hester, M., Spalding, E. and Franze, C. 2005. 'Biological resources of the Louisiana Coast: Part 1: An overview of coastal plant communities of the Louisiana Gulf shoreline,' *Journal of Coastal Research*, 44 (Spring): 134–145.

Houck, O. A. 2015. 'The reckoning: Oil and gas development in the Louisiana coastal zone,' *Tulane Environmental Law Journal*, 28: 185–455.

Jones, C. E., An, K., Blom, R. G., Kent, J. D., Ivins, E. R. and Bekaert, D. 2016. 'Anthropogenic and geologic influences on subsidence in the vicinity of New Orleans, Louisiana,' *Journal of Geophysical Research: Solid Earth*, 121(5): 3867–3887. DOI: 10.1002/2015JB012636

Kramer, R., Michalowski, R. and Kauzlarich, D. 2002. 'The origins and development of the concept and theory of state-corporate crime,' *Crime and Delinquency*, 48(2): 263–282.

Laska, S., Wooddell, G., Hagelman, R., Gramling, R. and Teets Farris, M. (2005). At risk: The human, community and infrastructure resources of coastal Louisiana. *Journal of Coastal Research*, 44(Spring):90–111.

Lindstedt, D. 2005. 'Renewable resources at stake: Barataria-Terrebonne estuarine system in southeast Louisiana,' *Journal of Coastal Research*, 44(spring): 162–175.

Lotze, H. K., Reise, K., Worm, B., van Beusekom, J., Busch, M., Ehlers, A., ... Jensen, C. (2005). Human transformations of the Wadden Sea ecosystem through time: A synthesis. *Helgoland Marine Research*, 59(1): 84.

Maldonado, J. K., Shearer, C., Bronen, R., Peterson, K. and Lazrus, H. 2013. 'The impact of climate change on tribal communities in the US: Displacement, relocation, and human rights. *Climatic Change*, 120(3): 601–614.

McDowell, M. G. 2013. 'Becoming a waste land where nothing can survive': Resisting state-corporate environmental crime in a "forgotten" place,' *Contemporary Justice Review*, 16(4): 394–411. DOI: 10.1080/10282580.2013.857094

Mohai, P. and Saha, R. 2007. 'Racial inequalities in the distribution of hazardous waste: A national-level assessment,' *Social Problems*, 54: 343–370.

Mufson, S. 2013, July 24. 'Louisiana flood-control agency sues oil and gas firms, seeking wetland restoration,' *Washington Post*. Available at: www.washingtonpost.com/business/economy/la-flood-control-authority-to-sue-major-oil-gas-companies-seeking-wetland-restoration/2013/07/24/6e4cf5ae-f459-11e2-aa2e-4088616498b4_story.html?utm_term=.b174daa9e2ba.

NAM. 2018. 'Onze historie,' Available at: www.nam.nl/over-ons/onze-historie.html%0A.

Neslen, A. 2017, June 16. 'Gas grab and global warming could wipe out Wadden Sea heritage site,' *The Guardian*. Available at: www.theguardian.com/environment/2017/jun/1.

O'Connell, M., Franze, C., Spalding, E. and Poirrier, M. 2005. 'Biological resources of the Louisiana coast: Part 2: Coastal animals and habitat associations,' *Journal of Coastal Research*, 44(spring): 146–161.

Olea, R. A. and Coleman, J. L. 2013. 'A synoptic examination of causes of land loss in Southern Louisiana as related to the exploitation of subsurface geologic resources,' *Journal of Coastal Research*, 30(5): 1025–1044. DOI: 10.2112/JCOASTRES-D-13-00046.1

Park, L. S.-H. and Pellow, D. N. 2004. 'Racial formation, environmental racism, and the emergence of Silicon Valley,' *Ethnicities*, 4(3): 403–424.

Penland, S., Williams, S. J., Davis, D. W., Sallenger, A. H., Jr. and Groat, C. G. 1992. 'Barrier island erosion and wetland loss in Louisiana,' in S. J. Williams, S. Penland and A. H. Sallenger, Jr. (eds.) *Louisiana barrier island erosion study-atlas of barrier shoreline changes in Louisiana from 1853 to 1989, U.S. Geological Survey Miscellaneous Investigations Series I-2150-A*, pp. 2–7. Denver, CO: U.S. Geological Survey.

Potter, G. 2012. 'Pushing the boundaries of (a) green criminology: Environmental harm as a cause of crime,' Available at: http://greencriminology.org/2012/11/the-green-criminology-monthly-3-november-2012/.

Rivard, C. 2015. 'Archival recognition: The Pointe-au-Chien's and Isle de Jean Charles Band of the Biloxi-Chitmacha Confederation of Muskogees' fight for federal recognition,' *Settler Colonial Studies*, 5(2): 117–127.

Ruggiero, V. 2013. 'The environment and the crimes of the economy,' in A. Brisman and N. South (eds.) *Routledge International Handbook of Green Criminology*, pp. 261–271. Abingdon, Oxon, UK: Routledge.

Ruggiero, V. and South, N. 2013. 'Toxic state–corporate crimes, neo-liberalism and green criminology: The hazards and legacies of the oil, chemical and mineral industries,' *International Journal for Crime, Justice and Social Democracy*, 2(2): 12–26.

Sarwar, M. G. M. and Woodroffe, C. D. 2013. Rates of shoreline change along the coast of Bangladesh. *Journal of Coastal Conservation*, 17(3): 515–526.

Schuttenhelm, R. (2017). *De toekomst van de Waddenzee. Een stijgende zeespiegel over een dalende bodem. Wetenschappelijke inzichten over zeespiegelstijging, sedimentatie en bodemdaling - en een concreet verdrinkingsrisico binnen de 21ste eeuw.* Harlingen, Netherlands: de Waddenvereniging.

Scott, L. C. and Richardson, J. A. 2015. *The Louisiana Economic Outlook: 2016 and 2017.* Baton Rouge, LA: Division of Economic Development, E. J. Ourso College of Business, Louisiana State University. Available at: www.oneacadiana.org/sites/default/files/2018-09/LEO_2019-20.pdf.

Shearman, P., Bryan, J. and Walsh, J. P. 2013. 'Trends in deltaic change over three decades in the Asia-Pacific Region,' *Journal of Coastal Research.* DOI: 10.2112/JCOASTRES-D-12-00120.1

Simon, D. 1999. *Elite Deviance*, 6th ed. Needham, MA: Allyn & Bacon.

Simon, D. 2009. 'Corporate environmental crimes and social inequality: New directions for environmental justice research,' in R. White (ed.) *Environmental Crime*, pp. 103–115. Portland, OR: Willan.

South, N. 1998. 'A green field for criminology: A proposal for a perspective,' *Theoretical Criminology*, 2(2): 211–233. DOI: 10.1177/1362480698002002004

Spencer, D. C. and Fitzgerald, A. 2013. 'Three ecologies, transversality and victimization: The case of the British Petroleum oil spill,' *Crime, Law and Social Change*, 59(2): 209–223.

Stretesky, P., Long, M. and Lynch, M. 2013. *The Treadmill of Crime: Political Economy and Green Criminology.* London and New York: Routledge.

Stretesky, P. and Lynch, M. 1998. 'Corporate environmental violence and racism,' *Crime, Law and Social Change*, 30(2): 163–184. DOI: 10.1023/a:1008393401769

Syvitski, J. P. M., Kettner, A. J., Overeem, I., Hutton, E. W. H., Hannon, M. T., Brakenridge, G. R., … Nicholls, R. J. 2009. 'Sinking deltas due to human activities,' *Nature Geoscience*, 2(10): 681–686.

Tombs, S. 2012. 'State-corporate symbiosis in the production of crime and harm,' *State Crime Journal*, 1 (2): 170–195.

Van Houten, C. 2016, May. 'The first official climate change refugees in the U.S. race against time,' *National Geographic.* Available at: http://news.nationalgeographic.com/2016/05/160525-isle-de-jean-charles-louisiana-sinking-climate-change-refugees/.

Waddenvereniging. 2018. De strijd tegen gaswinning. Available at: https://waddenvereniging.nl/ons werk/gaswinning.

White, R. 2013. *Environmental Harm: An Eco-Justice Perspective.* Bristol, UK: Policy Press.

Zanolli, L. 2016, March 15. 'Louisiana's vanishing island: The climate "refugees" resettling for $52m,' *The Guardian.* Available at: www.theguardian.com/environment/2016/mar/15/louisiana-isle-de-jean-charles-island-sea-level-resettlement.

Zeitlin, B. 2012. *Beasts of the Southern Wild.* USA: Fox Searchlight.

36

Toward a green cultural criminology of the South

Avi Brisman and Nigel South

Introduction

Humanity has an ambivalent relationship with other species, 'nature' and the shared environment (Benton 1998; see also Maher and Pierpoint, this volume, Chapter 28; Pellow, this volume, Chapter 32; Runhovde, this volume, Chapter 31; Sollund, this volume, Chapter 29; van Uhm, this volume, Chapter 30). As demonstrated by other chapters in this second edition of the *Routledge International Handbook of Green Criminology* and elsewhere (e.g., Brisman and South 2019; Lynch, Long, Stretesky and Barrett 2017; Lynch and Stretesky 2014; White and Heckenberg 2014), a 'green perspective' in criminology has encouraged exploration of various aspects of this relationship. The idea of a 'perspective' was a recognition of the absence of an obvious or dominant theory underpinning the criminological study of environmental crimes and harms, and, concomitantly, that a number of 'diverse theoretical positions' might be relevant, drawing, for example, 'upon existing traditions and developments within criminology, including Marxism, feminism, anthropology, functionalism, or post-modernism, among, no doubt, many others' (South 1998: 212). Since then, green criminology has borrowed and taken inspiration from—and sought integration with—elements of gothic, narrative and visual/sensory criminologies (e.g., Brisman 2017a, 2017b, 2018, 2019a, 2019b; Carrabine 2018; García Ruiz and South 2018; McClanahan and South 2020; Natali and McClanahan, this volume, Chapter 5; South 2017)—and, as we discuss in the next section, cultural criminology.

On reflection, however, these theoretical developments have been and continue to be statements arising from research traditions rooted in the Global North. As Goyes and South (2017: 172) have observed,

> green criminology has—like most of the field of criminology—tended to reflect a very "western" character and set of concerns, and has largely communicated these in English. Yet, it is obvious that other "green" research literatures in other languages must exist and be highly relevant. The problem perhaps has been that in the absence of translations, the western English-language literature does not "see" or "hear"; but in addition, there is a failure of intellectual curiosity and willingness to search and learn from "elsewhere".

This requires, not just in green criminology, but across criminology more generally, some remembering, renewing and re-visioning of criminological theory—a project that has been stimulated in recent years by the emergence and elaboration of a 'Southern criminology' (Carrington, Hogg and Sozzo 2016; Carrington, Hogg, Scott and Sozzo 2018; Carrington et al. 2019).

Green criminology has always taken an approach that emphasises the links between the local and the global—how, for example, forms of local and international environmental victimisation are connected; how wildlife, timber and waste are trafficked through transnational commodity chains; and how air and water pollution cross borders and circle the planet. Indeed, green criminology has appreciated 'the South' as a context in which exploitative global forces may exercise power, causing biodiversity loss due to patterns and practices of resource extraction (Boekhout van Solinge this volume, Chapter 15; Brisman, South and Walters, this volume, Chapter 10); and where the theft of nature and the pollution of air, land and water follow from ever more intensive agribusiness and the food/profit chain (Goyes this volume, Chapter 12; Goyes, Mol, Brisman and South 2017). It has therefore been very receptive to the arguments of a Southern criminology.

In this chapter, we recognise the complementarity of green and Southern criminologies (e.g., Brisman, South and Walters 2018a, 2018b, 2019, this volume, Chapter 10; White 2018) and follow through the implication that there is much work to be undertaken in order to develop green criminology further and in new directions. This chapter takes an existing direction in green criminology—green cultural criminology—and makes tentative and modest suggestions about how this theoretical framework can be enriched by engaging with examples of literary cultural productions of various kinds from Latin America. The chapter is structured as follows. After a brief overview of the projects of green cultural criminology and Southern criminology, we turn to a discussion of power, violence and suppression (including conquest and colonialism) in the tropes of nature in Latin American literature. Here, we consider literature 'of' and 'about' 'nature' in Latin America—specifically, eco-critical scholarship on both fiction and non-fiction—although we note that the two domains often blur in this kind of imagining, reporting and writing. This discussion leads us to contemplate examples of Latin American cultural narratives of human–environment relationships from the nineteenth century, as well as twentieth- and twenty-first-century presentations of tales old and new. We conclude by identifying several examples of possible directions in which the intersection of green cultural criminology and Southern criminology might proceed. We stop short of offering an agenda, blueprint, or guide, stressing that a genuinely *Southern* criminology cannot be prescribed from the Global North/West.

A green cultural criminology and a Southern criminology

A green cultural criminology provides a lens through which to view representations of nature, paying attention to the 'mediated and political dynamics surrounding the presentation of various environmental phenomena' (Brisman and South 2014: 6). Importantly, our cultural, literary and visual worlds are saturated with 'images' of nature and the natural, both positively and negatively presented—as sources of life and sustenance but also of danger and fear (see generally Brisman and Rau 2009). This is a common feature of most, if not all, cultures, but may be presented in different ways to different degrees. The development of Southern Theory (Connell 2007, 2014; Connell, Collyer, Maia and Morrell 2017) and of a Southern criminology (Carrington, Hogg and Sozzo 2016; Carrington, Hogg, Scott and Sozzo 2018; Carrington et al. 2019) emphasises the need for sensitivity to such differences. Within criminology, Northern/Western and metropolitan/urban dominance has functioned as a means of exporting ideologies and perpetuating colonialist assumptions—imposing

Northern/Western ways of doing things in contexts of culture, knowledge and practice where this was inapplicable, inappropriate, unnecessary and often unwelcome.

A *Southern* criminology does not seek to offer a form of denunciation or opposition regarding 'traditional' criminology, but to enable re-orientation and augmentation (Carrington, Hogg and Sozzo 2016; Carrington, Hogg, Scott and Sozzo 2018; Carrington et al. 2019). While green criminology has roots in critical criminology (e.g., Lynch 1990), it has developed healthy relationships with a range of criminological orientations (e.g., Agnew, this volume, Chapter 2; Burton et al., this volume, Chapter 3; Natali and McClanahan, this volume, Chapter 5). As such, Southern criminology and green criminology complement each other in various ways and our intention here is to admit and address northern bias in thinking about a 'green cultural criminology'—and thus, if 'green cultural criminology' is a 'perspective within a perspective' (Brisman 2018: 469), then our goal here might be considered a 'perspective within a perspective within a perspective'. To emphasise the 'cultural' here, we aim, in particular, to make inter-disciplinary links. This is important in helping us to acknowledge the Eurocentric imposition and importation of 'understandings' of 'nature' and 'culture' within nations-states of the Global South. One starting point for this project is to explore cultural narratives of human–environment relationships in the Latin American context.[1]

Power, violence and suppression in the tropes of nature in Latin American literature

We begin by considering literature 'of' and 'about' 'nature' in Latin America, principally eco-critical scholarship on both fiction and non-fiction, although the two domains often blur in this kind of imagining, reporting and writing. This is necessarily a short exercise in signalling thoughts and directions, but it should become apparent that there is much in the literary academic review of historical and creative accounts of borders and place, boundaries and space, memory and folklore, language and geography and so on, that should be immensely stimulating for a future green cultural criminological project engaging with the countries and continent of Latin America as representative of the Global South.

As Gudynas (2010: 269) remarks,

> In the first stages of European conquest and colonisation, according to available information, the dominant conception of the environment [in literature] was as a "savage" space. The prevalent testimonies are about uncontrollable nature imposing itself over human beings, who would then suffer the rhythms of rains and droughts, of soil fertility, of water availability, or plagues affecting crops. The spaces left to colonise were savage spaces, potentially dangerous due to the wild beasts and diseases that could be present.[2]

So, as Boling (2006: 245) writes: 'As part of the colonizing process, the Spaniards conceived the New World as "the passive *object* of transplantation and grafting" (O'Gorman [1961]: 142)' and

> [t]he literature of discovery and conquest reiterate[d] the motif of a utopian land of plenty *in which natural phenomena, including the Indigenous populations, were to be named and catalogued.* Nature as abundance is transformed into resource; discovery gives way to conquest.
>
> *(our emphasis).*

Conquest and colonialism

With Boling's perspective in mind, we must, then, see conquest and colonialism as far more complex than simply the imposition of economic, military, or religious rule. Conquest and colonialism granted 'rights' not only of ownership but also of 'conceptualisation' and 'interpretation'—or 'ways of seeing' and 'ways of not seeing'. The resulting epistemological distortions and injustices have been elaborated by de Sousa Santos (2014) and drawn upon by Goyes and South (2017: 168) in the following way: '"representation", much like the drawing of a map', often involves

> selecting a limited amount of phenomena to include in the depictions of reality we make, and consequently disregarding a vast amount of other phenomena ... In order to represent something, its origins and traits need to be identified first. How we detect and recognize these will determine what we see and what we do not ... we sift reality through theories and methods and what appears at the end is what we "see" ... this process ... means that we are "blind" to everything that has not made it through the "sifting" process and is therefore absent from our knowledge. Spotting the phenomena to which we have been blind can open the doors to new knowledge acquisition.

The ways in which the 'natural world' were conceived, received and understood were influenced by a meeting of *external politics* and new *interiors*—new landscapes, peoples, species and the interior lives of 'different' imaginations based on different stories and legends. 'In the founding literature of the Americas', explains Boling (2006: 246),

> the expansionism of discovery and conquest and subsequently of nation building foregrounds the image of *borders*, and this *delimitation and reconceptualization of nature* creates various conflicts and oppositions that come to characterize the state and the political, economic, and social concept of that state.
>
> *(our emphasis).*

The border between 'civilization' and 'barbarism'—a 'northern' border imported and imposed—is a familiar point of recognition in post-colonial studies and in the sociologies and criminologies of divisions and divides, cores and peripheries. But it is also important to recall how such 'borders' were extended into the categorising, phenotyping and differentiating of 'nature' and 'peoples'. To illustrate, in the famous non-fiction (yet partly fictionalised) work '*Facundo*', subtitled 'Civilization and Barbarism', written in 1845 by Domingo Faustino Sarmiento (writer, journalis and 7th President of Argentina), themes of *culture, development, modernisation* and *power* are central. They are, in large part, so central because European 'ideas' or 'knowledge' are elevated here above local and Indigenous nature, practice and understandings. Sarmiento, Boling (2006: 247) contends, was '[s]trongly influenced by *positivistic and deterministic perspectives*, convinced that the milieu determines the character of those that inhabit it' (our emphasis)—so 'the natural world (along with its original inhabitants)' is distrusted because it is a source of subversion of 'the goals of enlightenment and modernization'. This narrative of determination or discrimination between sources of 'danger' (nature and indigeneity) and 'purity' (European religion and enlightenment) (see Douglas 1966), is also noted by Stepan (2001) in her book, *Picturing Tropical Nature*, which, as Carey (2009: 231) observes, shows how

> nineteenth-century natural history influenced European views of tropical nature and societies. Scientists often portrayed tropical flora and fauna as enlarged, exotic, prehistoric, and unconquered. They depicted local people as racially distinct and degraded, as backward and incapable of taming their natural environments, as emasculated men and exploitable female specimens, and as mixed race (particularly "dangerous" with the rise of eugenics).

According to Boling (2006: 247), in nineteenth-century Argentina, the dominant proposition, as promoted by Sarmiento and like-minded leaders, was that 'In order … to ensure mankind's dominance … over nature and the land, the pampas are to be incorporated as a resource into the national project by their modification and use, and the original inhabitants are to be eradicated'. This was, as Boling (2006: 248) maintains, a 'symbolic, political conceptualization' that differentiated between populations in ways that were very much based on notions of the kind of nature with which they were associated. Hence, as Boling (2006: 248) continues, people

> of Northern European descent were to be transplanted to the wilds of Argentina and the figurative "weeds" of Indigenous origin were to be eradicated. This binary opposition of civilization (represented by the city based on European models and by specific populations or races) and barbarism (… the natural world and … those elements—including the Indigenous … associated in the Europeanized Argentine's mind with the natural world) dominates much of the discourse of 19th- and 20th-century narratives.

This narrative is powerful and, as Baumann (1989) shows, is the basis of thinking that justifies genocide—and, by extension, ecocide (see Crook, Short and South 2018). Baumann (1989: 92) analyses how modern European culture viewed itself as a 'garden culture', defining itself in terms of 'perfect' arrangements for human conditions: '[It] constructs its own identity out of distrust of nature. In fact it defines itself and nature, through its … longing for a better and necessarily artificial, order'.

Boling (2006: 248) suggests that in South America, 'The modernization project requires the domination of man over nature, and nature—no longer a Paradise but rather the image of fallen man—is associated with evil, with primitivism, and constitutes an obstacle to progress'. It is no surprise, then, that the 'fallen' and the sources of corruption of what is 'civilized' appear in Latin American versions of European monsters, albeit sometimes appropriated as critique. There are further directions here that a green cultural criminology could explore, perhaps, again, making connections with a gothic criminology and psychoanalytic explorations of hauntings (Frosh 2013). We offer an initial foray in the next section.

Nature, hauntings and the gothic in Latin American literature

Ghosts, monsters and the undead appear in Latin American gothic film, literature and media in various guises and with various purposes (Casanova-Vizcaíno and Ordiz 2017), but prominent among these are roles as representatives of fantasy, legends and nightmares that aim to fascinate and repel. Indeed, they are products of anxieties—of attempts to impose control over uncontrollable forces (death, human resistance, nature)—but they may also often represent political critique. In this literature, these stories involve 'the gothic'—ghosts and magical realism—which may all give voices to the silenced and can provide critique of past and present (Armitt 2014). There is the basis here for further criminological connections, to new writings on ghost criminology and hauntology (e.g., Ferrell 2018; Fiddler 2007; Fiddler, Kindynis and Linnemann 2020; Linnemann 2015) and to Picart and Greek's pioneering outline of a gothic criminology, where they have suggested we can conceive of this as a concern with 'The ongoing fascination with evil, as simultaneously repellent and irresistibly attractive' (2007: 11; South 2017).

There are many other directions and connections to pursue once we start to see how a green cultural criminology of the South can learn to explore art, film, literature and other media that intertwine 'nature', the spiritual and portrayals of human endeavour and human folly. We should remember that, as Stepan (2001: 15) puts it, 'nature is always culture before it is nature' insofar as 'nature is not just "natural" but is created *as* natural by human desires and intentions' (our emphasis). For a green cultural criminology, making connections with what might be the concerns of a Southern cultural criminology opens up a new methodology and body of data and knowledge with which to engage. It will be very fruitful to link this to the field of 'eco-criticism' and its connections to, and interest in, environmental injustice (see, e.g., Buell et al. 2011; Hsu 2011). As Buell and colleagues argue (2011: 418):

> By themselves, creative depictions of environmental harm are unlikely to free societies from lifestyles that depend on radically transforming ecosystems. But reflecting on works of imagination may prompt intensified concern about the consequences of such choices and possible alternatives to them.

This can be accomplished in many forms of storytelling. By way of illustration, we offer two examples in the next section.

The Magic Bean Tree *and* The Future According to Luz *series*

In *The Magic Bean Tree: A Legend from Argentina*, Nancy Van Laan retells the story of how, in the middle of the wide Argentine pampas (a vast grassland/lowland in South America that stretches from the Atlantic coast to the Andes Mountains), there once grew a magic tree. Above this tree slept the Great Bird of the Underworld—a bird so evil, it could stop the rain from falling by hiding the skies, stars and heavens behind its wings. And not far from this tree, there lived a brave Quechuan boy named Topec, who one day set out to save his village and all the creatures from dying of thirst.

In the story, geared towards children 4–8 years of age, Topec asks a once-deep river whether it has seen rain. The river responds that it has not and that it will soon dry up and die. Topec promises to find rain and 'bring it back', but the river admonishes him: 'Hide from the sun, little one. Curl up like the armadillo. Cover your head like the rhea, or you will die, too!' Topec, however, ignores the river's cautionary advice and continues on until he comes to the Carob Tree, who tells him of the Great Bird of the Underworld. That night, Topec leads his people to the tree, where they attempt to scare off the Great Bird of the Underworld by 'beat[ing] their drums, bang[ing] on sticks, rattl[ing] rattles, and rais[ing] their voices, shrieking, screaming, filling the air with such noise that the Earth shook'. By themselves, the people cannot affect the bird, but '[t]hen, from all over the pampas animals c[o]me running, leaping, hopping, jumping, adding their voices to those of the people. SNORT HISS! YAP YEOW!' Frightened by the sound of so many voices, the bird flies away. With the bird gone, the people pray for rain, which comes, filling the rivers and turning the brown grass green. As a sign of gratitude to Topec for his bravery, the Carob Tree shakes its branches, covering the ground with golden-red beans: 'From the beans came fodder to feed the llamas. From the beans came flour to make porridge and cake. And from the seeds of the beans grew many more carob trees ...'.

At the most basic level, this Argentine legend conveys the importance of rain to the people of the Argentine pampas and helps explain why Argentineans believe that good luck can be found in the shade of a carob tree. But the story also raises a number of important questions, such as: to whom—or to what—do we attribute loss of environmental resources—that which we need from the Earth in order to survive? What is the role of the individual in addressing environmental problems, such as lack of sufficient, clean water? What is the role of the group or collective?

Although the legend conveys the importance of courage and faith—both of which are important (albeit insufficient, by themselves, as we point out in the Conclusion to this volume) —the legend also makes three additional points with wide applicability. First, the legend suggests that in times of scarcity, there is a tendency to focus on self-preservation. Topec's people urge him not to seek rain because he 'might crumble like the plants' or 'turn into dust like the earth'. And the river, as noted above, advises Topec to focus on his own survival. Only by eschewing such warnings does Topec learn why there is no rain and what he must do.

Second, Topec enlists the help of his people—the very people who initially discouraged Topec from making the effort to find (the) rain. The people, by themselves, cannot solve the situation; they need the help of all the animals from the pampas. While this is not to suggest that we need to recruit non-human nature in our efforts to address environmental problems (many of which stem from human activity), the joint effort serves as a reminder that we are not the only species that relies on the Earth to support life—a point that is underscored by the way in which the beans are used not just for human consumption, but to feed the llamas.

Third, the last sentence of Van Laan's version reminds readers that 'it takes a carob tree a long time to grow'. This can be interpreted as a recognition that while nature is resilient and does (often) recuperate, it takes time (and patience) and that misuse of its resources may mean that recovery does not happen during human lifetimes. The image that accompanies the last page—of a small child planting a carob tree—can thus be seen as a suggestion to take steps *now* for the benefit of future generations—that efforts to conserve and preserve, mitigate and replenish, may well have more pronounced impacts on those who come after us.

The messages of conservation and eco-activism are presented considerably differently in *The Future According to Luz*—a two-book, young adult (geared to children 8–12 years of age) graphic novel series by Chilean-borne Claudia Dávila. *Luz Sees the Light* (2011), the first of the two books, begins with a blackout and soaring gas prices. Twelve-year-old Luz (whose name means 'light' in Spanish) is hardly electrified by the prospects of having to *walk* to the mall, rather than drive. And she is more than a little unnerved when the rising cost of gas impacts the price of imported groceries, forcing her mother to buy local dairy and produce. (She balks at the thought of eating lettuce, tomatoes and zucchini from nearby farms instead of 'Chocky cookies' from China.) Rather than get frustrated with Luz's sense of entitlement, Luz's mother explains why they will have to change the way they shop:

> Oil is running out and getting very expensive, so now it costs more to import goods than it used to. If we keep relying on imports, eventually we won't be able to afford the things we need. So we should buy from local farms and businesses and produce our own stuff. Plus, if farms and factories were closer to our stores, they'd use less gas to deliver their goods. So things would become more affordable. The same should be true in other countries. And they could actually eat what they grow instead of selling it all to us!
>
> *(2011: 34)*

Luz seems to understand and interjects: 'And less transportation means less pollution, too, right?' (2011: 34).

Or so it would seem. It takes a blackout at the mall—right as Luz discovers that the sneakers she has wanted so desperately have nearly doubled in price due to import costs—as well as the realization that her downstairs neighbours, the DeSouzas, 'grow food and make everything they need themselves, so they don't need to buy as much from stores' (2011: 51), for Luz to realise the need for change.

Luz decides to be more 'self-sufficient', like the DeSouzas, and attempts to solicit help from her friends and other members of the community to transform an abandoned city lot into a garden where she and her neighbours can grow their own fruits and vegetables. At first, Luz encounters little support for her project: her friends (Anika and Robert) think she is crazy, her community is dismissive and she struggles trying to remove some of the larger items that have been discarded on the lot. Gradually, however, Luz's friends join her cause, as do other members of her community, who help remove refuse and rubbish, lay down grass, plant trees, turn old tyres into planter boxes and build a concert area and a playground.

'This place was a path of concrete with no sign of life', Luz (2011: 84) explains at the opening of 'Friendship Park', 'right where our neighborhood could have a place for people to hang out and play ...'.

'... And look at birds and flowers instead of traffic and ads for things we don't need!' Anika continues.

Later, Luz says to Anika: 'this park is proof that we're not alone, and we can all work together and help each other to learn stuff and grow stuff and make stuff and build stuff ... So that in the end, whatever happens, we can rely on ourselves for the things we really need! No more imports or giant malls!' (2011: 85).

The book concludes with a bonus chapter or short vignette in which 'Gord', a doomsdayer member of the community who warns of future blackouts early on in the book and who stockpiles canned foods, teaches Luz how to make compost for the food garden. Luz learns which items can go in the compost and how to aerate the pile to make new soil, reminding her that '[i]n nature there's no such thing as waste' (2011: 96).

While *Luz Sees the Light* is compelling because Luz is appealing—a fearless, fiery, intelligent, resourceful and spunky heroine—the book is persuasive because it operates on a number of different levels. First, more than one environmental problem is presented—or, to put it another way—multiple dimensions of a particular environmental issue—in this case, fossil-fuel dependency—are unpacked. The blackouts are caused by high demand for electricity; at the same time, mounting gas prices impact everything from the cost of food (a need) and sneakers (a want) to transportation decisions. As a result, young adult/preteen readers come to understand the interconnectedness of environmental issues in ways that some other books intended for this age readership do not.[3]

Second, while the plot in *Luz Sees the Light* builds towards the communal effort to transform the rundown city lot, over the course of the book we encounter other efforts to affect positive environmental change. At one juncture, after Luz's mother refuses to drive her to the mall, Luz uses public transportation and admits to Anika, 'Man, why didn't I think of taking the bus on the way to the mall?'—to which Anika replies, 'Ha-ha! Yeah, good thing they run even during blackouts' (2011: 43). Later, Gord explains to Luz and Robert that he has been 'biking instead of driving because gas is a problem and biking is free ... ' (2011: 48)—a statement that foreshadows Gord's successful attempt to gain city approval for 'Car-Free Sundays' (2011: 79). In other words, not only are the efforts to steer a community/neighbourhood/society towards (self-)sustainability not undertaken solely by one individual—as is often the case in *The Magic Bean Tree* and other literature for children and young adults—

but the changes that transpire occur *throughout* the book. This feature helps to illuminate eco-consciousness and environmentally beneficial behaviour as habitual, on-going, quotidian, rather than epiphanous.

Third, Luz tries to change the world—or, at least, change her locality—by soliciting the help of her neighbours to create a more sustainable community. What is important here is not just that she has to overcome resistance from her friends and neighbours—a point alluded to above—but that the book describes her very willingness to marshal public support. All too often, stories of environmental harm suggest that the solutions must be—or are—individualistic. Dávila's approach here reflects the Quechua peoples' of the Andes notion of *sumak kawsay* or *buen vivir* (in Spanish), which loosely translates as 'good living' or 'well living', although, as Gudynas (mentioned above) points out, such translations veer too close to Western ideas of 'wellbeing' or 'welfare' and these, he claims, 'are not equivalents at all. With buen vivir, the subject of wellbeing is not [about the] individual, but the individual in the social context of their community and in a unique environmental situation' (quoted in Balch 2013). As Balch (2013), citing Gudynas, explains, 'harmony' is a defining characteristic of *buen vivir*[4]—'harmony between human beings, and also between human beings and nature'. 'A related theme', Balch (2013) continues,

> is a sense of the collective. Capitalism is a great promoter of individual rights: the right to own, to sell, to keep, to have. But this alternative paradigm from South America subjugates the rights of the individual to those of peoples, communities and nature.

This is a theme that runs through *Luz Sees the Light*—not just at the end, when the community comes together to create 'Friendship Park', but during the blackouts earlier in the book. Indeed, Dávila seems to invoke ideas that humans are stewards, rather than owners of the Earth and its resources, as well as notions of 'collaborative consumption' (see Bristow 2011)—without ever using the terms *sumak kawsay* or *buen vivir*.

Luz Makes a Splash (2012), the second book in *The Future According to Luz*, follows a similar pattern, only here the environmental problem is water scarcity, stemming not only from 'the hottest summer on record' and a 'record-breaking drought' (2012: 4) in 'Petroville', but from a multinational corporation's acquisition of a local water source to make its soda. Friendship Park is suffering, as is 'Spring Pond'—'the watering hole just outside of town' (2012: 12). Luz is already more environmentally conscious and aware than in *Luz Sees the Light* (as evidenced, for example, by the fact that Luz, Anika and Robert take public transportation to the pond). Other differences include the identification of a corporate actor responsible for environmental degradation ('Top Cola') and a multi-pronged solution that involves, *inter alia*, engagement with the political process: at one juncture, Luz's mother states, 'I'm going to call city council and our local Sierra Club. If what you say is true, we're going to boycott Top Cola!' (2012: 21), and later she explains to Luz that '[w]e need to campaign against them [Top Cola] draining the groundwater and wrecking Spring Pond' (2012: 35), while Anika's father declares, '[w]e're also starting an online petition. We want to get this from every angle!'

As in *Luz Sees the Light* (2011), *Luz Makes a Splash* (2012) offers readers an explanation of how an ecological process interacts with socio-political dynamics. As Mr DeSouza explains to Luz,

> In nature, there is always water deep underground. Rivers and streams trickle into the soil along with rainwater. It spreads all over, and plants can drink it up through their roots to keep healthy and growing. So plants get watered by rain above, as well as from

> below! But in the city, there's very little groundwater—instead, we have basements and subways and sewers. When it rains, water can't land on the soil because buildings and roads cover the ground! Rain is lost into sewer pipes.
>
> *(2012: 42)*

Mr DeSouza's description of the relationship of groundwater and rainwater eventually leads Luz and her neighbours to set up rain barrels, as well as hoses and a bathtub 'mini-marsh' to filter greywater from local businesses for gardens. And in the bonus chapter at the end, Gord teaches Luz about xeriscaping and creating a 'water-wise' lawn.

One could argue that *Luz Makes a Splash* (2012) is a slightly less convincing book than *Luz Sees the Light* (2011) on the grounds that the company, Top Cola, responds to public pressure. As Anika proclaims at the end: 'See this? "Top Cola has announced its Spring Pond Initiative. The company will slow production to help replenish groundwater levels ... It will also restore the pond habitat near its production plant by reintroducing flora and fauna"' (2012: 83). Gudynas reminds us, however, that, in the context of corporate social responsibility, 'CSR ... is a good strategy for improving the brand of a company, but that it doesn't have much impact on the social performance of the sector' (quoted in Balch 2013). Corporations, Gudynas continues, 'aren't made to be responsible ... They are made to generate profits' (quoted in Balch 2013). Admittedly, then, Top Cola's response renders the book a little less believable, but it is important to remember that *Luz Makes a Splash* is geared towards young adult readers and that there may be some benefit to leaving open for them the *possibility* that corporations can change.

While *Luz Makes a Splash* may seem a bit shallow with respect to its depiction of corporate responsibility (i.e., it is to its shareholders, not the environment), the book deserves praise for connecting the problems Luz and her community face to others in different locations. When Luz reports to her mother and grandmother (abuela) that Spring Pond has dried up because Top Cola has used the pond's spring to make soft drinks, her grandmother replies, 'This happened in our homeland. A mining company bought land and pumped water out of the ground. Many people suffered without clean water' (2012: 20). Later, Anika's father recounts a similar experience: 'This is outrageous! A giant textiles company did that in my homeland, too. Not only did our town end up with no water, the company pumped out polluted waste, too!' (2012: 28). These shared experiences lead Anika's father and Luz's mother to locate examples of other communities that have filed complaints against Top Cola and to 'look for other cases of water rights abuses around the world' (2012: 34).

Herein, then, lies one of the strengths of *Luz Makes a Splash* and of the series—*The Future According to Luz*—more generally. Not only do the books describe how environmental problems are often interrelated and multifactorial—and thus require multidimensional responses and solutions—but they accentuate that the issues are not peculiar to one place. From a narrative perspective, this allows readers to identify more closely with Luz. From a green cultural criminological perspective, this allows us to underscore the spatial and geographic aspects, components and commonalities of environmental crimes, harms and hazards. When green cultural criminology opens itself up to examples of cultural narratives of human–environment relationships from the Global South, this allows it to develop not only a deeper and more elaborate understanding of the construction of environmental crimes, harms and disasters in popular cultural forms, but an opportunity to learn about new problems, draw connections to similar concerns and gain exposure to new paradigms for responses.

Conclusion: possible future directions for a green cultural criminology of the South

In this chapter, we have attempted to explore examples of literary cultural productions of various kinds from Latin America and to illustrate the richness of their internal messages as well as the inter-disciplinary and inter-cultural connections they can suggest for a green cultural criminology. Looking ahead, a few possible directions in which the intersection of green, cultural and Southern criminologies might proceed, include: (1) critical interpretations of media and popular narrative depictions of environmental issues within the Global South—along the lines suggested here with respect to *The Magic Bean Tree: A Legend from Argentina* and *The Future According to Luz*; (2) instances and examples of protest against environmental degradation in the Global South, and critical analysis thereof to identify its peculiar dynamics and salient features; and (3) studies of energy integration and diversification in Latin America and the implications for (patterns of) consumption, constructed consumerism, commodification of nature and related market processes. We are reluctant, however, to offer too much in the way of an agenda or blueprint or guide because—and as we hope we have suggested in this chapter—a genuinely *Southern* criminology cannot be prescribed from the Global North, and neither should an authentically green cultural criminology of the South.

Notes

1 We wish to emphasize that we pursue this project as learners not experts. We are not specialists in Latin American literature or the environmental or cultural characteristics of the continent, although elsewhere we have been fortunate to work with scholars who are better qualified (see Goyes, Mol, Brisman and South 2017; McClanahan, Parra and Brisman 2019; Mol, Goyes, South and Brisman 2017). We wish to extend our thanks for assistance, encouragement and suggestions to various colleagues and friends, none of whom can be held responsible for any of our misreading and misunderstanding. We are, however, particularly grateful to David Rodríguez Goyes for his advice. The chapter was presented as a paper entitled *Toward a Green Cultural Criminology of the 'South'* at two panels convened by Maximo Sozzo in 2018: at the 18th Annual Conference of the European Society of Criminology, Sarajevo, Bosnia and Herzegovina (30 August 2018), and 'Delito, Derecho y Justicia Penal en el Sur Global' [Crime, Law and Justice in the Global South], Workshop Internacional [Southern Criminology Workshop], Co-Hosted by Universidad Nacional del Litoral, Facultad de Ciencias, Júridicas y Socciales [Faculty of Social and Juridical Sciences, National University of Litoral] and the Faculty of Law, Queensland University of Technology, Santa Fe, Argentina (7 November 2018). We thank audience members for their comments, insights, and suggestions.

2 This is a translation from the Spanish by David Rodríguez Goyes and we are grateful to him for drawing our attention to the work of Gudynas. The original text is:

> En las primeras etapas de la conquista y colonización europea, según la información disponible, parece haber predominado una concepción del entorno como espacios «salvajes». Prevalecen testimonios sobre una Naturaleza que era incontrolable y se imponía sobre los seres humanos, quienes debían sufrir los ritmos de lluvias y sequías, la fertilidad del suelo, la disponibilidad de agua o las plagas de los cultivos. Los espacios sin colonizar eran, a su vez, sitios salvajes, potencialmente peligrosos por las fieras y enfermedades que pudieran cobijar.

3 Many of the books and stories—which we have written about elsewhere—seem geared solely towards Western audiences; they tend to reflect environmental problems peculiar to or of primary relevance to the West, treating them as discrete issues with singular causes and just one solution (see, e.g., Brisman 2013, 2019b; Brisman and South 2015, 2017).

4 See also www.pachamama.org/sumak-kawsay.

References

Armitt, L. 2014. 'The gothic and magical realism,' in Jerrold E. H. (ed.) *The Cambridge companion to the modern gothic. Cambridge Companions to Literature*, pp. 224–239. Cambridge, UK: Cambridge University Press.

Balch, O. 2013. 'Buen vivir: the social philosophy inspiring movements in South America,' *The Guardian*, 4 February. Available at: www.theguardian.com/sustainable-business/blog/buen-vivir-philosophy-south-america-eduardo-gudynas.

Baumann, Z. 1989. *Modernity and the Holocaust.* Ithaca, NY: Cornell University Press.

Benton, Ted. 1998. 'Rights and justice on a shared planet: More rights or new relations,' *Theoretical Criminology*, 2(2): 149–175.

Boling, B. 2006. 'The trope of nature in Latin American Literature: Some examples,' *Studies in 20th & 21st Century Literature*, 30(2): 245–262. DOI: 10.4148/2334-4415.1632. Available at: https://newprairiepress.org/cgi/viewcontent.cgi?article=1632&context=sttcl.

Brisman, A. 2013. 'Not a bedtime story: Climate change, neoliberalism, and the future of the arctic,' *Michigan State International Law Review*, 22(1): 241–289.

Brisman, A. 2017a. 'On narrative and green cultural criminology,' *International Journal for Crime, Justice and Social Democracy*, 6(2): 64–77.

Brisman, A. 2017b. 'Representations of environmental crime and harm: A green-cultural criminological perspective on *human-altered landscapes*,' in M. Brown and E. Carrabine (eds.) *Routledge International Handbook of Visual Criminology*, pp.523–39. London and New York: Routledge.

Brisman, A. 2018. 'Representing the "Invisible crime" of climate change in an age of post-truth,' *Theoretical Criminology*, 22(3): 468–491.

Brisman, A. 2019a. 'The fable of *the three little pigs*, climate change and green cultural criminology,' *International Journal for Crime, Justice and Social Democracy*, 8(1): 46–69. DOI: 10.5204/ijcjsd.v8i1.470.

Brisman, A. 2019b. 'Stories of environmental crime, harm and protection: Narrative criminology and green cultural criminology,' in J. Fleetwood, L. Presser, S. Sandberg and T. Ugelvik, (eds.) *The Emerald Handbook of Research in Narrative Criminology*, pp.153–72. Bingley, UK: Emerald Group Publishing Limited.

Brisman, A. and Rau, A. 2009. 'From fear of crime to fear of nature: The problem with permitting loaded, concealed firearms in national parks,' *Golden Gate University Environmental Law Journal*, 2(2): 255–272.

Brisman, A. and South, N. 2014. *Green Cultural Criminology: Constructions of Environmental Harm, Consumerism, and Resistance to Ecocide.* Abingdon, Oxon, UK: Routledge.

Brisman, A. and South, N. 2015. '"Life stage dissolution", infantilization and anti-social consumption: Implications for de-responsibilization, denial and environmental harm,' *Young– Nordic Journal of Youth Research*, 23(3): 209–221.

Brisman, A. and South, N. 2017. 'Green cultural criminology, intergenerational (In)equity and "Life Stage Dissolution",' in M. Hall, J. Maher, A. Nurse, G. Potter, N. South and T. Wyatt (eds.) *Greening Criminology in the 21st Century: Contemporary Debates and Future Directions in the Study of Environmental Harm*, pp. 219–32. Abingdon, Oxon, UK: Routledge.

Brisman, A. and South, N. 2019. 'Green criminology and environmental crimes and harms,' *Sociology Compass*, 13(1): e12650. DOI: 10.1111/soc4.12650.

Brisman, A., South, N. and Walters, R. 2018a. 'Southernizing green criminology: Human dislocation, environmental injustice and climate apartheid,' *Justice, Power and Resistance*, 2(1): 1–21.

Brisman, A., South, N. and Walters, R. 2018b. 'Climate apartheid and environmental refugees,' in K. Carrington, R. Hogg, J. Scott and M. Sozzo (eds.) *The Palgrave Handbook on Criminology and the Global South*, pp. 301–21. London: Palgrave Macmillan.

Bristow, R. 2011. 'Collaborative consumption – Rachel Botsman live Q&A,' *The Guardian*, June 10. Available at: www.theguardian.com/sustainable-business/online-q-a-rachel-botsman-collaborative-consumption.

Buell, L. Heise, U. K. and Thornber, K. 2011. 'Literature and environment', *Annual Review of Environment and Resources*, 36: 417–40.

Carey, M. 2009. 'Latin American environmental history: Current trends, interdisciplinary insights, and future directions,' *Environmental History*, 14(2): 221–252.

Carrabine, E. 2018. 'Geographies of landscape: Representation, power and meaning,' *Theoretical Criminology*, 22(3): 445–467. DOI: 10.1177/1362480618787172.

Carrington, K., Dixon, B., Fonseca, D., Goyes, D. R., Liu, J. and Zysman, D. 2019. 'Criminologies of the global south: Critical reflections,' *Critical Criminology: An International Journal*, 27(1): 163–189. DOI: 10.1007/s10612-019-09450-y

Carrington, K., R. Hogg, J. Scott and M. Sozzo (eds.) 2018. *The Palgrave Handbook of Criminology and the Global South*. Switzerland: Palgrave Macmillan/Springer Nature.

Carrington, K., Hogg, R. and M. Sozzo. 2016. 'Southern criminology,' *The British Journal of Criminology*, 56(1): 1–20.

Casanova-Vizcaíno, S. and I. Ordiz (eds.) 2017. *Latin American Gothic in Literature and Culture*. Abingdon, Oxon, UK: Routledge.

Connell, R. 2007. *Southern Theory: The Global Dynamics of Knowledge in Social Science*. Sydney: Allen and Unwin.

Connell, R. 2014. 'Rethinking gender from the South,' *Feminist Studies*, 40(3): 518–539. DOI: 10.15767/feministst udies.40.3.518

Connell, R., Collyer, F., Maia, J. and Morrell, R. 2017. 'Toward a global sociology of knowledge: Post-colonial realities and intellectual practices,' *International Sociology*, 32(1): 21–37. DOI: 10.1177/0268580916676913

Crook, M., Short, D. and South, N. 2018. 'Ecocide, genocide, capitalism and colonialism: consequences for indigenous peoples and glocal ecosystems,' *Theoretical Criminology*, 22(3): 298–317.

Dávila, C. 2011. *Luz Sees the Light*. Toronto: Kids Can Press.

Dávila, C. 2012. *Luz Makes a Splash*. Toronto: Kids Can Press.

De Sousa Santos, Bd S. 2014. *Epistemologies of the South: Justice against Epistemicide*. Boulder, CO: Paradigm Publishers.

Douglas, M. 1966. *Purity and Danger: An Analysis of the Concepts of Pollution and Taboo*. London: Routledge and Kegan Paul.

Ferrell, J. 2018. *Drift: Illicit Motion and Uncertain Knowledge*. Berkeley, CA: University of California Press.

Fiddler, M. 2007. 'Projecting the prison: The depiction of the uncanny in. *The Shawshank Redemption*,' *Crime Media Culture*, 2(2): 192–208.

Fiddler, M., Kindynis, T. and Linnemann, T. 2020. *Ghost Criminology*. New York: New York University Press.

Frosh, S. 2013. *Hauntings: Psychoanalysis and Ghostly Transmissions*. London: Palgrave.

García Ruiz, A. and South, N. 2018. 'Surrounded by sound: Noise, rights and environments,' *Crime Media Culture*, 15(1): 125–141.

Goyes, D. R., Mol, H., Brisman, A. and South, N. (eds.) 2017. *Environmental Crime in Latin America: The Theft of Nature and the Poisoning of the Land*. London:Palgrave Macmillan.

Goyes, D. R. and South, N. 2017. 'Green criminology before 'Green Criminology': Amnesia and absences', *Critical Criminology: An International Journal*, 25(2): 165–181.

Gudynas, E. 2010. 'Imágenes, ideas y conceptos sobre la naturaleza en América Latina,' in L. Montenegro (ed.) *Cultura y Naturaleza*, pp. 267–292, Bogotá: Jardín Botánico J.C. Mutis.

Hsu, H. 2011. 'Fatal contiguities: Metonymy and environmental justice', *New Literary History*, 42(1): Winter, pp. 147–168.

Linnemann, T. 2015. 'Capote's ghosts: Violence, media and the spectre of suspicion,' *The British Journal of Criminology*, 55(3): 514–533.

Lynch, M. J. 1990. 'The greening of criminology: A perspective on the 1990s, @ *Critical Criminologist*, 2(3): 1–4; 11–12.

Lynch, M. J., Long, M. A., Stretesky, P. B. and Barrett, K. L. 2017. *Green Criminology: Crime Justiceand the Environment*. Oakland, CA: University of California Press.

Lynch, M. J. and Stretesky, P. B. 2014. *Exploring Green Criminology: Toward a Green Criminological Revolution*. Surrey, UK: Ashgate.

McClanahan, B., Parra, T. S. and Brisman, A. 2019. 'Conflicto ambiente y transición. Colombia, ecología y turismo después de la desmovilización,' *Revista Crítica Penal y Poder*, 16(Marzo): 99–120.

McClanahan, B. and South, N. 2020. '"All knowledge begins with the senses": Toward a sensory criminology,' *The British Journal of Criminology*, 60(1): 3–23. DOI: 10.1093/bjc/azz052.

Mol, H., Goyes, D. R., South, N., Brisman, A. (eds.) 2017. *Introducción a la criminología verde. Conceptos para nuevos horizontes y diálogos socioambientales* [*Introduction to Green Criminology: Concepts for New Horizons and Socio-Environmental Dialogues*].Bogotá, Colombia: Editorial Temis S.A. and Universidad Antonio Nariño, Fondo Editorial.

O'Gorman, E. 1961. *The invention of America, an inquiry into the Historical nature of the New World and the Meaning of its History*. Bloomington, IN: Indiana University Press.

Picart, C. J. and Greek, C. E. (eds.) 2007. *Monsters In and Among Us: Toward a Gothic Criminology*. Madison, NJ: Fairleigh Dickinson University Press.

Sarmiento, D. F. 2003. *Facundo: Civilization and Barbarism*. trans. Kathleen Ross. Berkeley, CA: University of California Press (published 1845), ISBN 0-520-23980-6 The first complete English translation.

South, N. 1998. 'A green field for criminology? A proposal for a perspective', *Theoretical Criminology*, 2(2): 211–33.

South, N. 2017. 'Monstrous nature: A meeting of gothic, green and cultural criminologies,' in M. Brown and E. Carrabine (eds.) *Routledge International Handbook of Visual Criminology*, pp. 553–66. Abingdon, Oxon, UK: Routledge.

Stepan, N. L. 2001. *Picturing Tropical Nature*. Ithaca, NY: Cornell.

Van Laan, N. 1998. *The Magic Bean Tree: A Legend from Argentina*. Beatriz Vidal, IL and Boston, MA: Houghton Mifflin Company.

White, R. 2018. 'The global context of transnational environmental crime in Asia,' in K. Carrington, R. Hogg, J. Scott and M. Sozzo (eds.) *The Palgrave Handbook on Criminology and the Global South*, pp. 281–300. London: Palgrave Macmillan.

White, R. and Heckenberg, D. 2014. *Green Criminology: An Introduction to the Study of Environmental Harm*. London and New York: Routledge.

37

Consumed by the crisis

Green criminology and cultural criminology

Jeff Ferrell

Over the past couple of decades, two new types of criminological analysis have developed: green criminology and cultural criminology. Both remain emergent perspectives—still in the process of sharpening their theoretical and substantive focus—though in the case of cultural criminology, at least, this inchoate state is itself valued for its anarchic and inclusionary dynamics, for keeping cultural criminology 'a loose federation of outlaw intellectual critiques' (Ferrell 2007: 99). Even in these emergent stages, though, particular orientations can be identified—proclivities that create fertile ground for the intertwining of green criminology and cultural criminology. By the nature of their subject matter, both green criminology and cultural criminology push against the conventional boundaries of criminology, and so tend to upset the definitional and epistemic order of the discipline. Likewise, both are open to exploring a range of social harms and social consequences, whether these harms are defined conventionally as 'criminal', currently left outside the orbit of law and criminality, or even, themselves, propagated by the criminalisation process. At their best, both link their overt substantive concern—environmental harm in the case of green criminology, issues of meaning and representation in the case of cultural criminology—with broader questions of power and inequality. Certainly, both attempt to situate their subject matter historically, in terms of its long-range development and its current residency within the crisis of late modernity and late capitalism.

This potential for a convergence of green criminology and cultural criminology has already been anticipated by green criminologists, as in South's (1998: 226) invocation of a green cultural politics, Brisman's (2010) work on the criminalisation of pro-environmental activities and activism and White's (2002) linking of environmental harm to the political economy of capitalist consumption. More recently, Brisman and South (2013b, 2014) have outlined explicitly the contours of this convergence in the form of a 'green cultural criminology', as per the title of their 2013 article, their 2014 book and other works (e.g., Brisman 2017a, 2017b, 2019; Brisman and South, 2017b, 2017c, 2018, this volume, Chapter 34). In their book, Brisman and South (2014: 6) argue that a fully-developed green criminology must account not only for environmental harm as such, but for 'the mediated and political dynamics surrounding the presentation of various environmental phenomena ... the commodification and marketing of nature and the construction of the insatiable consumption that underpins this; and examples of resistance to environmental harm'. Incorporating these themes into green criminology, they argue, both sharpens its critical lens and, at the same time, begins to develop a distinctive green cultural criminology.

As these themes suggest, cultural criminology can be defined by its attunement to the interplay of crime, crime control and cultural dynamics. In particular, cultural criminology attempts to theorise the ongoing intersections of crime, crime control, media, popular culture and subcultures in everyday life. In this context, cultural criminology argues that both crime and crime control operate as cultural processes, and increasingly so—processes whose consequences emerge from contested symbolism and collective interpretation. An analysis of 'crime' or 'criminal justice', then, also necessitates an examination of mediated anti-crime campaigns, alternative forms of justice or resistance circulating within subcultures and social movements, public displays of law and policing and the cultural conventions of everyday life. Of particular importance for the convergence of cultural criminology and green criminology is cultural criminology's exploration of seemingly 'objective' or 'taken-for-granted' phenomena—public concerns over crime, the amount of damage committed or done by one sort of crime or another, the characteristics of 'criminals' or 'nature' or 'society'—as contested cultural and political constructions. Rejecting the allegedly 'objective' reality of law and crime, cultural criminologists investigate the ways in which political institutions constitute acts as legal or illegal; the ways in which media institutions portray (or ignore) particular acts so as to spawn varying perceptions of them; and the ways in which law enforcement agencies negotiate social situations so as to shape dynamics of arrest, conviction, criminal identity and incarceration. From this view, cultural dynamics construct the reality of crime, crafting its meaning and consequences and charging crime and crime control with the energy of power, conflict and resistance.

Cultural criminology, in this way, casts a distinctly critical eye toward official explanations of crime and crime control and toward popularly accepted narratives regarding crime and criminals. Cultural criminologists also question academic and governmental accounts that reduce experiences of criminality and criminal victimisation to statistical summaries. Such accounts, they argue, rest on a series of questionable epistemic and methodological assumptions, and in any case, miss the meaning and emotion, the mix of pleasure, pain and outrage that animates crime and crime control. In all of this, cultural criminology, like green criminology, seeks to attune criminology to the particular structures, processes and problems of the late modern/late capitalist world (Ferrell, Hayward and Young 2015; see also Ferrell 2018). As White (2002) argues, for example, the global reach of contemporary consumerism necessitates not only a broad analysis of 'culture and crime', but a focussed examination of consumer culture as a locus of criminality and social harm. Similarly, Brisman's (2010) work suggests that the global degradation of work and the dislocation of global populations, coupled with the emergence of a punitive neoliberal state, point to the necessity of exploring new forms of late modern political activism, as well as new forms of punishment and political repression. Of equal significance for cultural criminologists is the incursion of multiple media forms into everyday life: indeed, the contemporary saturation of everyday life by advertising images, media technology and manufactured political discourse means that any useful criminology must account for an ongoing process in which criminal events, their mediated images and public perceptions of crime spiral around and amplify one another. If 'real' is taken to mean *real effects* and *real consequences*, then the cultural construction of crime and crime control is now as real as crime and policing itself—to the extent that the two remain distinguishable at all (Ferrell 1999; Ferrell, Hayward and Young 2015; Ferrell and Sanders 1995).

Across this range of concerns, cultural criminology can be seen to share with green criminology a deeper agenda as well: the revitalisation of the criminological imagination. Following from C. Wright Mills' (1959) classic conceptualisation of the sociological imagination, the late cultural criminologist Jock Young (2011: 2, 5) called for the return of 'the criminological imagination', noting that 'for Mills, the key nature of the sociological imagination was to situate human biography in history and in social structure', and arguing that, 'in a late modern world of heightened insecurities and competing fundamentalisms, the necessity for a sociological imagination becomes that much greater' if we are to link 'personal troubles in various parts of the world with collective issues across the globe, to make the personal political'. Likewise, green criminologist Rob White (2003: 483–484), writing on 'environmental issues and the criminological imagination', has noted that green criminology

> demands more than simply talking about the environment in general and what needs to be done to protect or preserve it: instead, it requires an appreciation of how harm is socially and historically constructed [and] understanding and interpreting the structure of a globalized world; the direction(s) in which this world is heading; and how diverse groups' experiences are shaped by wider social, political and economic processes.

For both cultural and green criminologists, then, the criminological imagination means not only situating the personal in the social and the historical, and the local in the global, but also engaging in an imaginative reconsideration of criminology's contemporary subject matter and modes of analysis. With each new historical period—with each shift in the social composition of everyday life and the cultural construction of crime—the criminological imagination must itself be re-imagined if criminologists are to regain the 'capacity for astonishment' (Mills 1959: 8; see also Wender 2004). As emergent perspectives, both green criminology and cultural criminology seem well-positioned to assist in reviving this criminological imagination; together, they can perhaps collaborate in restoring the criminological capacity for astonishment, analysis and critique.

Consumer culture as ecological harm

Green criminologies of capitalism and its complicity in environmental harm have followed a number of analytic paths, each critically important in locating cases of environmental destruction within the exploitative dynamics of contemporary economic arrangements. Some research, for example, addresses corporate pollution stemming from pervasive violation of health and environmental regulations (for example, Shuqin 2010). Other research explores the increasing commodification of nature—from farm animals to genetically modified seed stock—and the concomitant privatisation of essential natural resources like water (for example, Brisman et al. 2018; McClanahan, Brisman and South 2015; South 2007; Walters 2011; White 2002, 2003). Still other research attempts to expose the dynamics of corporate 'greenwashing' campaigns, whereby dangerous corporate practices are recast as environmentally beneficial or genuinely pro-environmental activism is co-opted in the service of corporate profit and legitimation (see Bleakley 2019). In each of these arenas, green criminology's task is to connect particular corporate practices and their representations—profit-taking, privatisation, unregulated manufacturing—to the particular environmental harms that are their consequence.

While these are indisputably essential areas for green criminological inquiry, a cultural criminological perspective perhaps contributes a different frame for approaching them. This analytic framework begins with the understanding that contemporary capitalism—globalised 'late capitalism'—operates as an essentially cultural enterprise, one 'whose economic and political viability, and its crimes and transgressions, rest precisely on its cultural accomplishments' (Ferrell 2007: 92–93; see also Ferrell, Hayward and Young 2015). This later form of capitalism manufactures physical products less than it manufactures and markets the *meanings* of these products and the images of their appropriate use; in this way, the advertising industry operates not as an adjunct to capitalist dynamics but as capitalism's essential motor force. Moreover, advertising itself is designed not to address existing needs but to create new ones, which are then to be filled, allegedly, by the advertised product. This ongoing creation of meaning, need, anxiety and status insecurity produces a predictable consumer insatiability, and with it elastic markets to be expanded with each new advertising campaign. Widening markets further still is the planned obsolescence of contemporary consumer goods—obsolescence that is accomplished not only by building in technical limitations, but by creating ever more rapid cycles of fashion trends and product 'improvements', such that yesterday's purchase is certain to be out of style or out of date come tomorrow (Brisman and South 2013a, 2017a). Vance Packard (1960: 71) memorably referred to this cultural process as 'planned obsolescence of desirability'—the ability 'to wear the product out in the owner's mind'. Within this late capitalist universe, a phenomenon that Thorstein Veblen (1953 [1899]: 61, 64, 70) first identified amidst an emerging 'leisure class' a century ago now comes to pervade everyday life: consumption as status acquisition. Here, consumption takes on a 'ceremonial character'—becoming 'honorific'—more a matter of displaying and confirming one's status than of addressing an innate need for, say, shelter or warmth. With this 'conspicuous consumption', as Veblen called it, consumer items come to be purchased and displayed for the status that they carry and communicate—and so, once this status evaporates, so does their social and cultural worth.

As a result of these processes, late capitalism promotes both consumption and, more to the point, a pervasive *culture of consumption*—an increasingly globalised consumerist way of life defined by advertised meaning, constructed need, cycled fashion and conspicuously acquired status. This consumer culture can be investigated usefully for the social and cultural harms it produces—the syndromes of personal and bodily insecurity, the ontological vacancy and the financial indebtedness it spawns, for example, or the interplay of crime and consumption that comes to pervade urban life (Hayward 2004). But it can also be investigated for its environmental harms in two primary dimensions.

First, as a carefully orchestrated constellation of meanings and perceptions, this late capitalist consumer culture serves to mask the environmental abuses (and labour injustices) that underpin the manufacture of its products. With the globalised divorcing of production from consumption—and the wall of corporate advertising that is erected between the two—widespread corporate pollution and degradation of natural resources are made all but invisible to privileged consumers (see generally Davies, Francis and Wyatt 2014). Inside the swirl of first-world status associated with Nikes or iPhones or DeBeers diamonds, the conditions of their third-world production are rendered all but unimaginable (see Redmon 2005). In this sense, consumer culture itself operates as an ongoing, everyday machinery of corporate greenwashing. On occasion, focussed corporate greenwashing campaigns may be needed to finesse particular environmental abuses that come to light. But, in general, the pervasiveness of corporate advertising and the consumer culture it engenders is such that no such campaigns are necessary. In this kind of cultural climate, the greenwash is ongoing; ecological harm remains, in Jenkins' (1999) terms, 'unconstructed'. Every advertisement hides its own ecological crisis—and taken collectively, the ongoing saturation of everyday life by corporate advertising ensures that, for consumers, the environmental harms endemic to consumer products exist as vague abstractions, if they exist in the minds of consumers at all.

A second environmental harm is the consumer waste that this system produces—waste as pervasive as it is predictable. The endless, advertised construction of new needs and insatiable insecurities not only promotes the (over)consumption of whatever products are being marketed presently as their resolution, it also ensures the widespread discarding of products already accumulated by the consumer once the next round of advertising reconstructs these existing products as inadequate. Each new iPhone, then, is accompanied by the discarding of the old. The planned obsolescence built into poorly made goods and promoted by carefully engineered fashion cycles likewise spawns a throwaway culture of ongoing dissatisfaction and disposal. The microwave oven imported from China might be repaired, but where, and by whom and likely at a cost greater than that of a newly imported one; the tear in last year's Italian dress pants might be sewn, but why bother, when the pants are already out of style anyway? And if, as Veblen suggested, an item is purchased in the first place primarily for the status it confers—for the sheen of its newness and the cultural desirability of its design—then the exhaustion of the item's status leaves it culturally worthless, and so disposable, no matter its remaining physical utility. Indeed, Veblen (1953 [1899]: 71, 77) contended that waste is inherent in the process of conspicuous consumption; the 'element of waste', the 'waste of goods', he argued, is the key to 'demonstrating the possession of wealth' to others:

> Throughout the entire evolution of conspicuous expenditure, whether of goods or of services or human life, runs the obvious implication that in order to effectually mend the consumer's good fame it must be an expenditure of superfluities. In order to be reputable, it must be wasteful. No merit would accrue from the consumption of the bare necessities of life, except by comparison with the abjectly poor who fall short even of the subsistence minimum; and no standard of expenditure could result from such a comparison, except the most prosaic and unattractive level of decency.

Waste is the heart of consumer culture, and triply so: conspicuous consumption builds from the wasteful over-exploitation of natural resources, promotes the wasteful over-consumption of manufactured items beyond basic human need, and then spawns the widespread disposal of these items, sooner than later, as social waste (see Varul 2006; White 2002). The designer coat, bought not for its warmth but for its fashionable status, will not be kept for its warmth, either; it will be wasted once its value as a status symbol wears thin.

Here, the sociological and criminological imagination offers insights into otherwise inexplicable individual behaviours—and into the deep roots of consumerism's ecological crisis. The consumer's willingness to purchase a product with origins in human and environmental destruction—and thus the readiness to partake in that destruction by way of the product—may well reflect the sort of mindset that emerges amidst the shallow, self-centred satisfactions of consumer culture. But it also reflects the power of that culture—and the advertising that animates it—to mask successfully such destruction behind ideologies of status, style and convenience. Likewise, the consumer's decision to then dispose of that product wastefully and unnecessarily—with no regard to its remaining utility for the consumer or others in need—may well reflect the hurried, insatiable and status-driven nature of consumerist identity. But this decision also echoes and exists within the larger patterns of waste and disregard that are hardwired into an individualistic, consumerist society. No matter how calloused the consumer, the ecological crisis of late capitalism does not begin with the consumer's poor choices; it begins amidst a globalised system of production and distribution, and inside the cultural dynamics and consumerist ideologies that structure these choices and the system itself.

The material consequences of this system are mountainous. Across the globe, in developed and developing societies, the removal and disposal of waste present intractable problems and result in engorged landfills, sprawling illegal dump sites and the pervasive pollution of land and water (see generally van Herk and Bisschop, this volume, Chapter 22). The problems of consumer waste reinforce and redouble other social problems as well, producing particularly virulent forms of environmental racism and ecological injustice—ranging from the disproportionate disposal of consumer waste in impoverished pockets of American cities to the illegal transport of northern Italian waste to southern Italy (see, e.g., Pellow 2004; Ruggiero 2010, 2013). These patterns cut across global capitalism as well, as with the shipping of electronic consumer waste from Europe and the United States (U.S.) to China and West Africa, there to be 'reclaimed' through open-air burning and other environmentally destructive practices, and the illegal shipping of discarded automotive batteries from the U.S. to Mexico, where the poorly regulated extraction of lead from them exposes both workers and residents to soaring levels of toxicity (Rosenthal 2011; South 2010; Takemura 2010; see also Bisschop 2012, 2013, 2014, 2015a, 2015b; Coletto and Bisschop 2017; van Herk and Bisschop, this volume, Chapter 22).

The particular content of the trash that accumulates within consumerist economies, that fills these sprawling landfills and spreads out across global dumpsites, confirms the profligate wastefulness of contemporary consumerism. Within consumer culture, 'trash' is conventionally associated with filth, decay and dysfunction—in no small part because such association serves, once again, to push the consumer back towards consuming the new and the immediately marketable (Strasser 1999). But as my ongoing research has shown, a large proportion of everyday consumer waste is neither decayed nor dysfunctional. Instead, it is made up of commodity packaging, like-new clothing, functional appliances—and many purchased items that retain their wrappers, having never been worn nor used (Ferrell 2006). Over the course of several decades of daily trash picking and trash sorting—decades dedicated to an ongoing archaeology of consumer waste—I have consistently found that 'waste' is defined less by its physical deterioration than by its cultural obsolescence.

In formulating his theory of conspicuous consumption among the leisure class, Veblen (1953 [1899]): anticipated—in a sense, predicted—what would become this particular form of wastefulness within a larger late capitalist consumer economy. In his analysis of clothing and fashion, for example, he argued that

> No one finds difficulty in assenting to the commonplace that the greater part of the expenditure incurred by all classes for apparel is incurred for the sake of a respectable appearance rather than for the protection of the person … And the commercial value of the goods used for clothing in any modern community is made up to a much larger extent of the fashionableness, the reputability of the goods than of the mechanical service which they render in clothing the person of the wearer … That the alleged beauty, or 'loveliness', of the styles in vogue at any given time is transient and spurious only is attested by the fact that none of the many shifting fashions will bear the test of time.
>
> *(1953 [1899]: 119, 125)*

Failing to bear the test of time and their fashionableness made obsolete by the next cycle of marketing and consumption, wearable clothes accumulate in trash bins and curbside trash piles. Not surprisingly, given that women remain the primary target of the fashion industry, women's clothes in particular are discarded; in fact, they constitute the single most common type of discarded consumer goods that I have collected and documented over the past decades. Again, these and other trashed clothes are often found with their price tags still attached; never worn, purchased perhaps as part of an 'impulse buy', whose impulsivity was in reality an orchestrated consequence of consumer culture—their fashionableness worn out over time even if their stitching has not. In this sense, the 'ecocidal tendencies' (South 2010: 228) of the fashion industry are not confined to wildlife trafficking and the fur and leather trades (see van Uhm, this volume, Chapter 30); instead, such tendencies are put into play with every change in the height of hem lines or the width of lapels. And when clothes discarded due to outdated hemlines or lapels do not end up in the landfill, they are often shipped to Africa for resale, where they, in turn, overwhelm local garment-making economies (de Freytas-Tamura 2017).

Similarly, Brisman (2010), Brisman and colleagues (2018), Croall (2007), Goyes (this volume, Chapter 12), McClanahan and colleagues (2015), South (2007), Tourangeau and Fitzgerald (this volume, Chapter 11), White (2002, 2003) and other green criminologists have highlighted the pervasive corporate privatisation and commodification of water, as well as animals, plants, seeds and the food that comes from them. As they have shown, such privatisation and commodification spawn social harms ranging from systemic animal abuse at factory farms to food adulteration, deprivation of essential human resources and the destruction of local knowledge and local economic sustainability (Goyes and South 2016). This commodification has consequences for waste as well, and for its content. The commodity chains through which global capitalism manufactures and moves these products mean that they arrive at their destinations not in their 'natural' state, but encased in cardboard, bubble wrap and plastic—all to be discarded upon arrival. Water as a bottled commodity embodies, among a host of other social harms, a wasted bottle (Brisman et al. 2018; Brisman and South 2013b, 2014). A sandwich as corporate product—enclosed in its cardboard and plastic shell, lined up alongside a hundred others at an airport food shop or motorway convenience store—differs from a homemade sandwich not only in flavour and freshness, but in the amount of attendant packaging waste. And commodified food itself is also more likely to be wasted: manufactured and shipped in large quantities, bought in mass by retailers, it is disposed of en masse as a result of expiration dates or overstocking—a fact to which most any trash picker can attest. To the many 'food crimes' that Croall (2007, 2013; Tourangeau and Fitzgerald, this volume, Chapter 11) documents can be added another: the foundational crime of food commodification itself, and with it the inevitable waste of food and packaging alike.

As a whole, the consumer culture of late capitalism produces any number of social harms—inequality, insatiability, insecurity—but certainly central among them is a 'constant and escalating pressure on the world's nonrenewable resources', and with this, 'a huge waste of existing human and natural resources and potentials' (White 2002: 88). This advertising-driven culture of consumption serves both to mask initial environmental harms of extraction, exploitation and commodity production, and to ensure the subsequent and ongoing environmental harms of waste and misuse. Significantly, the pervasively wasteful logic of this system is such that it is more than capable of engulfing alleged 'alternatives'—even green alternatives—that do not confront it directly. Green shopping is, after all, still *shopping*, and even within a 'greener' system of consumption, green products must still be marketed, packaged, sold and sold again (Brisman 2009). And as regards this commodifying tendency, perhaps one item is the most revealing—an item that my research has turned up time and again, regularly thrown away in trash bins and trash piles: the stylishly reusable shopping bag. As these widely discarded reusable bags suggest, the 'greening' of consumer culture would seem a self-defeating project—a small green life preserver tossed into a torrent of advertising, planned obsolescence and waste. Instead, for green criminologists and cultural criminologists alike, subcultures and social movements that confront consumer culture directly and radically—and that promote fundamental ecological alternatives to it—can be explored productively, and with them, emergent issues of crime, policing and social control.

Everyday ecological resistance and everyday criminalisation

As already noted, Brisman and South's (2014: 6) elaboration of a 'green cultural criminology' calls for green criminology to engage with the mediated dynamics, marketing and cultures of commodification; each of these thematic interactions draws on a cultural criminology that focusses on media and meaning. But green criminologists draw from cultural criminology another theme as well: 'resistance to environmental harm'. Highlighting meaning, symbolism and interpretation, cultural criminology undertakes to resurrect the notion of resistance in criminology and related disciplines (Ferrell 1996, 2001, 2007, 2018). Exploring the top-down politics of crime and criminalisation, cultural criminologists attune their analysis to the ways in which criminal or criminalised actions can, at times, constitute resistance to law and power. Notably, cultural criminologists decline to measure such resistance against some stern template of political purity; instead, they look for resistance as it blossoms, often imperfectly, amidst the shared situations of crime and crime control in everyday life.

As a cultural criminologist, my decades of investigating consumer waste, for example, have not been undertaken in isolation; they have been part of my ongoing research into, and participation with, the various contemporary subcultures of trash picking, urban scrounging and reclamation, and, as it is called in the U.S., 'dumpster diving'. Such trash picking is pervasive in the U.S., and the title of my book on the subject, *Empire of Scrounge* (Ferrell 2006), was meant to reflect the widespread and varied nature of this subterranean world. The homeless scrounge trash piles and trash containers for discarded backpacks, clothing, food and shoes; many of them also search for aluminium cans to be sold for small amounts of cash at urban recycling centres (Botha 2004; Pritchett 2009). Train-hopping gutter punks dumpster dive—'run trash cans', as they call it—in search of the clothes, food and supplies they need for survival on the rails. Others, impoverished but not homeless, drive old pickup trucks or ride rebuilt bicycles around urban and rural areas, searching for brass, copper and other metals that can be extracted from discarded appliances and machinery, and sold for a bit of cash. Among the working poor, parents mine trash piles and trash containers as repositories of building materials for home repair or school clothes for their children. Freegans and like-minded young punks gather, cook and eat discarded food in an attempt to withdraw from the harms of consumer capitalism—to 'act as a living challenge to waste and over-consumption' (http://freegan.info/what-is-a-freegan/freegan-philosophy/). The group Food Not Bombs likewise mixes social movement activism with on-the-street action, gleaning discarded food so as to cook and serve vegetarian meals to the homeless across the U.S. and beyond (Butler and McHenry 2000; Clark 2004).

These subcultures and social movements are hardly confined to the U.S. In fact, with the globalisation of capitalism and the ongoing financial and ecological crises that have accompanied it, subcultures of scrounging and trash picking are flourishing worldwide. As already noted, electronic waste and other consumer trash from Europe and the U.S. are shipped regularly to Asia and Africa, where communities of scavengers engage in the dangerous work of reclaiming metals and other materials. In India's major cities, a complex 'urban informal economy' revolves around the scavenging and recycling of scrap materials ranging from Pepsi cups to jerrycans (Gill 2010). In Buenos Aires, Argentina, the economic crisis of the past two decades has spawned tens of thousands of *cartoneros*; making at best a meagre living from salvaging cardboard and other waste materials, they have nonetheless formed cooperatives and schools, and staged Somos Todos Cartoneros festivals (Ferrell 2006: 15, 170). Trash pickers from a Paraguayan slum have built complex musical instruments from everyday landfill garbage, and have built an orchestra as well: the Recycled Orchestra of Cateura (Allgood and Townsley 2015). For many years, Jardim Gramacho—located outside Rio de Janeiro, Brazil, and one of the world's largest and busiest landfills—hosted a community of *catadores*—trash pickers who first squatted the landfill during the economic crisis of the 1970s and 1980s and later organised for improved labour and health conditions (Walker, Jardim and Harley 2010). Notably, the sheer volume of the trash itself eventually overwhelmed their subsistence as trash pickers; with liquid waste from the towering landfill leaking into the nearby bay, authorities closed Jardim Gramacho in 2012.

Trash pickers and activists, then, can be understood as participants in an eclectic, wide-ranging global phenomenon that intertwines alternative economic arrangements, environmental activism and resistance and desperate day-to-day survival. From Argentina, Brazil and Mexico to China, Malaysia and Vietnam, they constitute a vast informal army of everyday environmentalists, unsalaried and uninsured, working the trash heaps of consumer capitalism, salvaging countless tonnes from urban landfills, feeding the hungry and clothing the homeless, inventing imaginative forms of community and, in the process, producing for local governments significant savings in trash disposal and social service costs.

And for all this, they are rewarded, increasingly, with criminalisation. Across the U.S., cities now ban public trash picking, outlaw the off-premises possession of the shopping carts utilised by homeless scroungers, aggressively enforce ordinances banning accumulations of scrap materials, meticulously regulate the materials that scrap yards can accept, require special identity cards for those selling to the yards, threaten to seize vehicles utilised in illegal scrounging and deploy police 'scavenger patrols' to search for recalcitrant trash pickers (Ferrell 2006: 178–183, 2011; see also Brisman 2010: 171). For Food Not Bombs' efforts to feed scrounged food to the homeless, city and police officials require that Food Not Bombs obtain permits and then deny their requests for those permits, arrest Food Not Bombs servers en masse, seize Food Not Bombs food supplies and complain that, if not stopped, Food Not Bombs will continue with the 'visible, blatant, and untimely distribution of food'. As a result, the group disseminates, along with Tofu Dill Dip and Potato-Pea Curry recipes to serve a hundred people, guidelines on what to do 'if the police start taking your food' (Butler and McHenry 2000: 93–103, 110, 114).

City and police officials justify such actions on grounds ranging from identity theft and metal poaching to public health and public safety. As Brisman (2010) argues in his analysis of 'the indiscriminate criminalization of environmentally beneficial activities', though, and as I have shown in a series of case studies (Ferrell 2001, 2006, 2018), this pervasive criminalisation is, in fact, founded in contemporary political economy. Brisman (2010: 172–173) notes, for example, that municipalities often earn income from city-run recycling programmes and garner additional income from fines levied against those who scrounge or recycle outside the framework of such programmes. In these cases, illicit scavenging is perceived as threatening not only the rationalised governmental control of city life but city budgets as well. Moreover, everyday informal trash scrounging and do-it-yourself recycling and reuse, along with the intentional consumerist interventions staged by freegans and groups like Food Not Bombs, threaten the larger dynamics of consumer capitalism. Physically, such activities may well salvage tons of waste from engorged landfills. From the view of corporations and their political allies, however, they also deflect potential consumers, allowing them to acquire food and materials without the cost, and corporate profit, of purchase. (This view underlies the intentional fouling of discarded retail items, with shoes and clothes often cut or torn by retail outlets prior to disposal, and food adulterated with bleach or other pollutants.) Culturally, the viability of informal waste scrounging threatens to expose the very logic of consumer capitalism itself, revealing that yesterday's items may, in fact, function as well as tomorrow's, and awakening consumers to the notion that their trash may be made up not of the deteriorated but of the needlessly discarded (Ferrell 2006).

A distinct contemporary constellation of cultural, economic and urban politics also drives the criminalisation of informal waste reclamation. With the withering of urban industrial production in American and European cities, and the exportation of production to developing countries, these cities rely increasingly on service economies organised around consumption, entertainment and tourism. Researchers like Markusen and Schrock (2009: 345, 353) promote this sort of 'consumption-driven urban development', arguing that 'superior local consumption-based offerings help to attract skilled workers, managers, entrepreneurs, and retirees', and emphasising that 'economists and geographers have recently stressed the significance of lifestyle preferences of skilled workers as an important determinant of economic development'. More critically, radical geographers, such as David Harvey (2008: 31), conclude that 'quality of urban life has become a commodity, as has the city itself, in a world where consumerism, tourism, [and] cultural and knowledge-based industries have become major aspects of the urban political economy'. To protect this 'quality of life' image and its privatised urban 'consumption spaces' (Zukin 1997, 2010) from those who might trespass on their intended meanings, the policing of urban life has, in turn, come to focus as much on perception as on populations. In the midst of an urban revitalisation campaign, for example, an economic official in the U.S. contends that panhandling is a problem precisely because 'it's part of an image issue for the city' (Ferrell 2001: 45); an American legal scholar agrees, arguing that 'the most serious of the attendant problems of homelessness is its devastating effect on a city's image' (in Mitchell 2003: 201). As Aspden (2008: 13) concludes in regard to the transformation of a British industrial city into a 'corporate city of conspicuous consumption': 'There seems to be no place in the new Leeds for those who disturb the rhythms of the consumer-oriented society'.

Within this contemporary cultural economy of the city, there is indeed 'no place' for peripatetic dumpster divers, for freegans picking food from trash piles, for Food Not Bombs activists gathering homeless folks in city parks for salvaged meals; such groups must be excluded by law from the spaces of 'consumption-driven urban development' so that they will not befoul the appeal of such spaces to the desired sorts of consumers. Noting a new city ordinance banning dumpster diving and other street activities, the *Houston Chronicle* (Turner 2002) explained that 'the redevelopment of downtown as a retail, entertainment, and residential centre has nurtured an urban spirit less hospitable to the poorest of the poor'. Likewise, in decades as a daily trash picker, I have documented a direct correlation between the aggressiveness of police and private security responses to my presence and the degree to which an area is under consumption-oriented redevelopment—to the point that, in one of my city's newly developed retail zones, I am now on a police list of 'known troublemakers'. This criminalisation of informal recycling and reclamation is further reinforced by contemporary models of risk-based urban policing—models that emphasise a rationalised, actuarial web of crime prevention through systematic surveillance, information collection and pre-emptive intervention. By this logic, the unregulated and the unpredictable invite criminality and the breakdown of crime control. Likewise, for conservative criminologists like Wilson and Kelling (1982), homeless trash pickers or panhandlers are, in fact, defined only as signs of social disorder—as metaphorical 'broken windows'—to be policed aggressively, lest they dispirit citizens and invite violent criminality.[1] In this way, consumerist urban economies and the risk-based policing that protects them combine to make outlaws of those who would engage day-to-day with the very waste that such economies spawn (Ferrell 2018). The ecological harms of consumer culture double down, ensuring that its waste must not benefit even those willing to wade through it.

The efforts of everyday waste scroungers and street-level environmentalists to glean sustenance for themselves and others, and the legal and political campaigns to criminalise and contain these practices, suggest further intersections of cultural and green criminologies. The first builds from cultural criminology's revitalisation of the labelling theory tradition in sociological criminology, and with it the notion that power is often exercised through the imposition of meaning. Cultural criminologists argue that an analysis of this labelling process—the process of assigning meaning and enforcing identity around issues of crime and justice—is more important than ever in a contemporary world shaped by mediated images and high-profile 'wars' on crime (Ferrell 1999; Ferrell, Hayward and Young 2015; Ferrell and Sanders 1995; see generally Ayres, this volume, Chapter 13; Brisman and South, this volume, Introduction; Runhovde, this volume, Chapter 31). From this view, contemporary economies of conspicuous consumption and 'consumption-driven urban development' sell meaning—that is, they sell the lifestyles and status cycles by which such goods are defined, and the consumerist experiences of urban 'authenticity' (Zukin 2010) and 'quality of life' through which goods are acquired. Maintaining these profitable meanings, though, requires a parallel process of meaning construction—one focussed on justifiably policing those who would intrude. As a result, law enforcement and political authorities label homeless trash pickers, freegans and Food Not Bombs activists as 'criminals' and, through a process of 'cultural criminalisation' (Ferrell 1999), advertise them as outcasts who would paw through filth, thieve away consumer identities and proffer unhealthy food. During a legal campaign against Food Not Bombs, the mayor of Orlando, Florida, takes this labelling a step further still; for him, Food Not Bombs activists constitute 'food terrorists' (Donohoe 2011). In the contemporary political economy, then, the longstanding historical ambiguity of the scrounger identity is resolved in the direction of a particular label: criminal (Ferrell 2006; Strasser 1999). This sort of analysis of labelling—of meanings imposed or ignored—would, likewise, seem applicable to corporate greenwashing campaigns, state and corporate recalcitrance in defining ecological harms and similar core concerns of green criminology. Certainly, the everyday phenomenon of trash scrounging and its criminalisation can be understood in this light.

A careful examination of contemporary trash picking and the cultures that surround it reveals another aspect of labelling as well. Like their global counterparts, who have created cooperatives and staged trash-picking festivals, many trash scroungers in Europe, the U.S. and elsewhere aim not only to pick valuables from consumer waste, but to reverse the very dynamics by which trash and trash pickers are defined. In this sense, they engage in ecological resistance—resistance defined not simply as disobeying the rules, but resistance undertaken so as to turn the logic of the dominant system back on itself. At a basic level, this involves utilising the essence of consumer capitalism—the proliferation of consumer goods and their inevitable waste—as a foundation for creating alternative communities, alternative economic arrangements and alternative forms of survival. As the Industrial Workers of the World (1973 [1908]) famously put it, this is a matter of 'forming the structure of the new society within the shell of the old'. Yet, this reversal operates at the level of labelling as well—that is, at the level of meaning and perception. Freegans, as already noted, attempt to survive on scrounged food, and so to 'act as a living challenge to waste and over-consumption'. Food Not Bombs groups certainly undertake the practical work of feeding the hungry from discarded food, but they do so as part of a 'decentralized, non-hierarchical movement' designed to publically 'create new alternatives and life-affirming structures from the ground up' (Butler and McHenry 2000: xii, 72). In this sense, both groups reverse conventional notions of soiled food waste by 'cleansing' discarded food of its exploitative origins and resurrecting it as a force for social change (Clark 2004). Likewise, as part of my own ongoing trash scrounging, I collect and donate scrounged goods to charities, but I also quite intentionally work with various media to craft a disconcerting portrait of a 'Dumpster diving professor' dedicated to confronting consumer waste. While trash picking across America, the anonymous anarcho-punk author of the book *Evasion* (2003: 74) began to question

> who the barbarians were, the contemptible. Those operating the machine, enslaving the people, and bleeding the Earth dry. Producing things only to throw them away, digging a hole only to fill it up again. Or those who saw the absurdity of it all, and chose to humbly wait in the shadows of that machine and pick up the crumbs.

The larger world of informal waste scrounging serves to raise that question as well, and so to resist consumer capitalism and its machineries of meaning. After all, if consumer capitalism operates as a cultural enterprise—as a manufacturer of perceptions and identities, with its ecological crimes hidden behind walls of advertising—then it must be confronted on those terms, too.

This discussion of a 'decentralised, non-hierarchical' Food Not Bombs movement—this invocation of the old Industrial Workers of the World and the new anarchist punks—suggests yet another potential intersection of cultural and green criminologies. White (2003, 2008, 2009–2010) and other green criminologists have offered productive examinations of legal and regulatory responses to environmental harm, transnational organisation and resistance around environmental issues, state repression of environmental protest and other aspects of green activism. Decentralised, anarchic, do-it-yourself movements that emphasise fluid forms of everyday activism can be more difficult to account for, but as groups like the freegans and Food Not Bombs demonstrate—and as cultural criminologists have documented in related contexts (Ferrell 1996, 2001, 2018)—they embody a powerful contemporary model for environmental activism. Building from anarchist traditions of 'direct action' and 'the propaganda of the deed', they mix practical, on-the-ground activism with the notion that such activism can itself embody and demonstrate the viability of alternative arrangements (Botha 2004: 78–102). In this sense, such groups are less interested in protesting for environmental justice or lobbying for environmental regulation than they are in confronting environmental harms directly; they are determined to enact alternative, environmentally just relationships within the spaces of daily life (Hayward 2012). Freegans, Food Not Bombs activists and urban 'guerrilla gardeners' share this orientation; so do groups like Critical Mass and Reclaim the Streets, with their 'disorganised' direct actions against automotive harms to the environment, their innovative forms of playful cultural resistance and redefinition, their disavowal of political and legal authority and their commitment to 'live the way we wish it could be' through 'assertive desertion' (in Ferrell 2001: 114; see Brisman and South 2013b, 2014, 2017b; Carlsson 2002; Carlsson and Manning 2010). Given that Occupy Wall Street and the larger, subsequent Occupy movement have drawn on this anarchic direct action orientation as well (Naegler 2016), it would seem a propitious time for green criminology to investigate, perhaps even affiliate with, such groups, and so to fulfil the promise of 'a green perspective [as] particularly sensitive to cultural politics and the emergence of new social movements concerned with lifestyle, identity and visionary protest' (South 1998: 226).

Coda: lost ecologies large and small

Consumer culture and its wasteful consequences are among the defining dynamics of late capitalism, and for this reason, a primary node of confluence between cultural and green criminologies. Yet, this focus by no means exhausts the possibilities of interweaving cultural criminology's attention to meaning, symbolism and power with green criminology's critical environmental analysis. Other important areas of research, some of them already being explored within cultural criminology and elsewhere, would include the sort of reverse green-washing by which alleged environmental harm is invoked in the criminalisation of graffiti, drug use and other subcultural practices (for example, Ferrell 1996); the contested cultural and legal politics of water and waterfront spatial environments (Kane 2009, 2012); and the ecological consequences of changing rural cultures and economies (Brisman, McClanahan and South 2014; Mazurek et al., this volume, Chapter 14; Tunnell 2011). Beyond this, the overblown fear of crime that is manufactured by media and political institutions would itself seem an ecological issue, promoting as it does the 'safety' of the automobile in preference to the perceived vulnerability of walking or bicycling, along with the hyper-consumption of personal and home safety devices (Brisman 2004; Lauer 2005). The aesthetics of manicured lawns and corporate landscaping would seem an appropriate focus for a criminology of ecological commodification. Likewise, the prim aesthetics of middle class professionalism would seem to mitigate against bicycle riding, guerrilla gardening, trash digging and other everyday ecological practices, and so might be investigated as a 'personal' style with serious ecological implications.

The cultural construction of meat, with its seared-in masculinity and conspicuous culinary consumption, certainly intertwines with the vast ecological harms of factory farm meat production (see generally Sollund, this volume, Chapter 29). If meat is murder, then these factory farms constitute mass murder on an unimaginable scale—unimaginable, in large part, because their brutal, ecocidal practices are hidden behind a daily onslaught of fast food advertising and protected from exposure by 'ag gag' laws and the labelling of animal rights activists as terrorists (see Tourangeau and Fitzgerald, this volume, Chapter 11). Most certainly, as groups like Critical Mass and Reclaim the Streets emphasise, confronting the culture of the automobile—the constellation of meanings promulgated by automobile manufacturers, advertisers, city planners and associated culture industries—is essential to understanding the automobile as ongoing environmental disaster. Within this culture, neighbours' front gardens, and indeed whole neighbourhoods, seem inevitably to give way to pavement; Middle-Eastern oil wars and their ecological consequences seem somehow disconnected from the drive to work; the indebtedness and conspicuous consumption of automotive ownership seems only necessary and normal; and most miraculously, the everyday automotive carnage of dead drivers, dead bicycle messengers, dead pedestrians, dead dogs and squirrels and dead urban and rural ecologies seems somehow to disappear behind myths of 'safe driving' and ecologically friendly automobiles (see, for example, Bohm et al. 2006; Burns, Ferrell and Orrick 2005; Carlsson 2002; Ferrell 2001, 2003; Fincham 2006; Furness 2010; Lutz and Lutz Fernandez 2010; Muzzatti 2010).

These issues, and countless others, coalesce into a series of lost ecologies large and small. Ruined rural landscapes, fake plastic trees and gas-powered leaf blowers, middle-class lawns made a deeper shade of green by overdoses of water and fertiliser, sedentary children driven to and from schools three blocks away, professors and other professionals fearful of sweat or rain or dirt, diners digging into double-meat fast food hamburgers, swatches of land cut off from public use by motorway onramps, multiplying 'ghost bike' memorials to bicyclists mowed down by speeding autos—all intertwine the cultural and the environmental, and all confirm ecological possibilities lost to us, isolated from us, misplaced from our lives. In all of these, we can also see yet another potential cultural criminological contribution to green criminology: the cultural criminological focus on everyday life and on developing a criminology of the everyday that discovers the momentous in the momentary (Ferrell 2007; Ferrell, Hayward and Young 2015; Presdee 2000, 2004). We can, after all, visit vast electronics dumps in China to study consumer culture's environmental consequences—but we can also look into our own dustbins. We can, and should, document the ongoing ecological criminality of the global auto industry, but we can also kneel before a single roadside shrine that commemorates a loved one lost to automotive violence (Ferrell 2003). We can, and should, develop a wide-ranging green criminology of animal abuse, but along the way, we can also take note of the shoes we wear, the food we eat and the pets we pick for companionship (Beirne 2007; Sollund 2017, this volume, Chapter 29; van Uhm, this volume, Chapter 30). We can, and should, confront the toxic interplay of contemporary imprisonment and environmental destruction (Brisman 2004, 2007; Mazurek et al., this volume, Chapter 14), but we can also find this interplay dispersed throughout the situations of everyday life (Story 2016). In these small moments, we discover again Mills' (1959: 7) sociological imagination—the 'capacity to shift from one perspective to another', to discover 'the minute points of the intersections of biography and history within society'—and sow the sociological seeds of intertwined cultural and green criminologies.

In that light, this chapter ends not with words but with images. Cultural criminology has long emphasised the power and importance of the visual, not only as an essential criminological subject matter in an increasingly mediated world, but as a mode of criminological documentation and analysis (Hayward and Presdee 2010; Redmon 2005; Sabin and Redmond 2009); now, a fully realised visual criminology has taken shape (Brown and Carrabine 2017; see also Natali and McClanahan, this volume, Chapter 5). This sort of cultural and visual criminology seems particularly appropriate for capturing small moments of environmental harm, little lost ecologies of everyday life (see Brisman 2017b; Carrabine 2018; Natali and McClanahan, this volume, Chapter 5)—lost ecologies like that of a small stream a few miles west of my home in Texas. Over the centuries, this stream cut a channel through the open prairie, finding the limestone bedrock a few feet down. Now this little stream has been enveloped by economic development and by consumer culture, in particular. A concrete viaduct today constitutes its headwaters; from there, it flows down a concrete culvert in the middle of a roadway and then into and around a series of Texas-size shopping centres. Upon arrival at the last of these shopping centres, it is made to disappear beneath a vast parking lot, and by the time it reappears a thousand yards later the stream has not simply been affected by consumer culture. It has been lost to it, and has become it.

Figure 37.1 Untitled photograph by the author

Figure 37.2 Untitled photograph by the author

Figure 37.3 Untitled photograph by the author

Note

1 Jorgensen (2011: 2) notes that,

> In an effort to make the Summer Olympic Games greener, Chinese authorities moved more than one hundred thousand of Beijing's garbage pickers out of town. China does not have any formal beverage container recycling system. Instead, garbage pickers have collected bottles and cans—along with other waste—from the street to sell them to recycling stations. While these workers contribute to one of the most effective recycling economies in the world, they did not fit into Beijing's campaign to present a modern, sanitised city to the world during the Olympics. Nor do they fit Western conceptions of greenness and recycling. The hordes of Western Olympic visitors in Beijing preferred both their trash and their recycling systems to be invisible—out of sight, out of mind.

References

Allgood, B. and Townsley, G. (dirs.). 2015. *Landfill Harmonic (documentary film)*. Paraguay: Hidden Village Films.

Anonymous. 2003. *Evasion*. Atlanta, GA: CrimethInc.

Aspden, K. 2008. *The Hounding of David Oluwale*. London: Vintage.

Beirne, P. 2007. 'Animal rights, animal abuse, and green criminology,' in P. Beirne and N. South (eds.) *Issues in Green Criminology: Confronting Harms against Environments, Humanity and Other Animals*, pp. 55–83, Cullompton, Devon, UK: Willan.

Bisschop, L. 2012. 'Is it all going to waste? Illegal transports of E-waste in a European trade hub,' *Crime, Law & Social Change*, 58(3): 221–249.

Bisschop, L. 2013. 'Go with the E-waste flows. The governance reality of illegal transports of E-waste in a European trade hub,' In P. van Duyne, J. Harvey, G. Antonopoulos, K. von Lampe, A. Maljevic and J. Spencer (eds.) *Human Dimensions in Organised Crime, Money Laundering and Corruption*, pp. 393–424, Nijmegen: Wolf Legal Publishers.

Bisschop, L. 2014. 'Illegal E-waste transports: Exploring their harmfulness, scale, social organization and governance,' in A. Spapens, W. Huisman and M. Kluin (eds.) *Environmental Crime and its Victims: Perspectives within Green Criminoloy*, pp. 171–184, Surrey, UK: Ashgate.

Bisschop, L. 2015a. *Governance of the Illegal Trade in E-Waste and Tropical Timber: Case Studies on Transnational Environmental Crime*. London: Routledge.

Bisschop, L. 2015b. 'How E-waste challenges environmental governance,' in T. Wyatt (ed.) *Hazardous Waste and Pollution: Detecting and Preventing Green Crimes*, pp. 27–44, London: Springer.

Bleakley, P. 2019. 'Big fish, small pond: NGO–corporate partnerships and corruption of the environmental certification process in Tasmanian aquaculture,' *Critical Criminology: An International Journal*. doi: 10.1007/s10612-019-09454-8. First Online: 20 June 2019.

Bohm, S., Jones, C., Land, C. and Paterson, M. (eds.) 2006. *Against Automobility*. Malden, MA: Blackwell.

Botha, T. (ed.) 2004. *Mongo: Adventures in Trash*. New York: Bloomsbury.

Brisman, A. 2004. 'Double whammy: Collateral consequences of conviction and imprisonment for sustainable communities and the environment,' *William & Mary Environmental Law & Policy Review*, 28(2): 423–475.

Brisman, A. 2007. 'Toward a more elaborate typology of environmental values: Liberalizing criminal disenfranchisement laws and policies,' *New England Journal on Criminal & Civil Confinement*, 33(2): 283–457.

Brisman, A. 2009. 'It takes green to be green: Environmental elitism, "Ritual displays," and conspicuous non-consumption.' *North Dakota Law Review*, 85(2): 329–370.

Brisman, A. 2010. 'The indiscriminate criminalisation of environmentally beneficial activities,' in R. White (ed.) *Global Environmental Harm: Criminological Perspectives*, pp. 161–192, Cullompton, Devon, UK: Willan.

Brisman, A. 2017a. 'On narrative and green cultural criminology,' *International Journal for Crime, Justice and Social Democracy*, 6(2): 64–77.

Brisman, A. 2017b. 'Representations of environmental crime and harm: A green-cultural criminological perspective on human-altered landscapes,' in M. Brown and E. Carrabine (eds.) *Routledge International Handbook of Visual Criminology*, pp. 523–539, London and New York: Routledge.

Brisman, A. 2019. 'The fable of *the three little pigs*, climate change and green cultural criminology,' *International Journal for Crime, Justice and Social Democracy*, 8(1): 46–69. doi:10.5204/ijcjsd.v8i1.470.

Brisman, A. and South, N. 2013a. 'Conclusion: The planned obsolescence of planet earth? How green criminology can help us learn from experience and contribute to our future,' in N. South and A. Brisman (eds.) *Routledge International Handbook of Green Criminology*, pp. 409–417, London and New York: Routledge.

Brisman, A. and South, N. 2013b. 'A green-cultural criminology: An exploratory outline,' *Crime Media Culture*, 9(2): 115–135.

Brisman, A. and South, N. 2014. *Green Cultural Criminology: Constructions of Environmental Harm, Consumerism, and Resistance to Ecocide*. London and New York: Routledge.

Brisman, A. and South, N. 2017a. 'Consumer technologies, crime and environmental implications,' in M. R. McGuire and T. J. Holt (eds.) *The Routledge Handbook of Technology, Crime and Justice*, pp. 310–324, London and New York: Routledge.

Brisman, A. and South, N. 2017b. 'Criminología verde cultural,' in H. Mol, D. R. Goyes, N. South and A. Brisman (eds.) *Introducción a la criminología verde. Conceptos para nuevos horizontes y diálogos socioambientales* [*Introduction to Green Criminology: Concepts for New Horizons and Socio-Environmental Dialogues*], pp. 97–127. Bogotá, Colombia: Editorial Temis S.A. and Universidad Antonio Nariño, Fondo Editorial.

Brisman, A. and N. South. 2017c. 'Green cultural criminology, intergenerational (In)equity and "Life stage dissolution",' in M. Hall, J. Maher, A. Nurse, G. Potter, N. South and T. Wyatt (eds.) *Greening Criminology in the 21st Century: Contemporary Debates and Future Directions in the Study of Environmental Harm*, pp. 219–232, Surrey, UK: Ashgate.

Brisman, A. and South, N. 2018. 'Green cultural criminology,' in W. S. DeKeseredy and M. Dragiewicz (eds.) *Routledge Handbook of Critical Criminology* 2nd ed., pp. 132–142, London and New York: Routledge.

Brisman, A., McClanahan, B. and South, N. 2014. 'Toward a green-cultural criminology of "the Rural",' *Critical Criminology: An International Journal*, 22(4): 479–494.

Brisman, A., McClanahan, B., South, N. and Walters, R. 2018. *Water, Crime and Security in the Twenty-First Century: Too Dirty, Too Little, Too Much*. London: Palgrave Macmillan.

Brown, M. and Carrabine, E. (eds.) 2017. *Routledge International Handbook of Visual Criminology*. New York: Routledge.

Burns, R., Ferrell, J. and Orrick, E. 2005. 'False advertising, suggestive persuasion, and automobile safety: Assessing advertising practices in the automobile industry,' *Southwest Journal of Criminal Justice*, 2(2): 132–152.

Butler, C.T. and McHenry, K. 2000. *Food Not Bombs*. Tucson, AZ: See Sharp Press.

Carlsson, C. 2002. 'Cycling under the Radar: Assertive desertion,' in C. Carlsson (ed.) *Critical Mass: Bicycling's Defiant Celebration*, pp. 75–82, Oakland, CA: AK Press.

Carlsson, C. and Manning, F. 2010. 'Nowtopia: Strategic exodus?' *Antipode*, 42(4): 924–953.

Carrabine, E. 2018. 'Geographies of landscape: Representation, power and meaning. *Theoretical Criminology*, 22(3): 445–467.

Clark, D. 2004. 'The raw and the rotten: Punk cuisine,' *Ethnology*, 43(1): 19–31.

Coletto, D. and Bisschop, L. 2017. 'Waste pickers in the informal economy of the global South: Included or excluded?' *International Journal of Sociology and Social Policy*, 37(5/6):280–294. doi: 10.1108/IJSSP-01-2016-0006.

Croall, H. 2007. 'Food crime,' in P. Beirne and N. South (eds.) *Issues in Green Criminology: Confronting Harms against Environments, Humanity and Other Animals*, pp. 206–229, Cullompton, Devon, UK: Willan.

Croall, H. 2013. 'Food crime: A green criminology perspective,' in N. South and A. Brisman (eds.) *Routledge International Handbook of Green Criminology*, first edition. Abingdon, Oxon, UK: Routledge.

Davies, P., Francis, P. and Wyatt, T. (eds.) 2014. *Invisible Crimes and Social Harms*. Basingstoke, Hampshire, UK: Palgrave Macmillan.

de Freytas-Tamura, K. 2017. 'East Africa Curbs Imports on the West's Hand-Me-Downs,' *The New York Times*, (12 October): A4.

Donohoe, K. 2011. 'Food not bombs members arrested for feeding the hungry,' *The Nation* (27 June). Available at: www.thenation.com/article/food-not-bombs-members-arrested-feeding-hungry/.

Ferrell, J. 1996. *Crimes of Style: Urban Graffiti and the Politics of Criminality*. Boston, MA: Northeastern University Press.

Ferrell, J. 1999. 'Cultural criminology,' *Annual Review of Sociology*, 25: 395–418.

Ferrell, J. 2001. *Tearing Down the Streets: Adventures in Urban Anarchy*. New York: Palgrave/McMillan.

Ferrell, J. 2003. 'Speed kills,' *Critical Criminology: An International Journal*, 11(3): 185–198.

Ferrell, J. 2006. *Empire of Scrounge: Inside the Urban Underground of Dumpster Diving, Trash Picking, and Street Scavenging*. New York: New York University Press.

Ferrell, J. 2007. 'For a ruthless cultural criticism of everything existing,' *Crime Media Culture* 3(1): 91–100.

Ferrell, J. 2011. 'Interview with Jeff Ferrell', *MetalTheft.net*, 1(3), December. Available at: http://metaltheft.net/interviews.html.

Ferrell, J. 2018. *Drift: Illicit Motion and Uncertain Knowledge*. Berkeley, CA: University of California Press.

Ferrell, J., Hayward, K. and Young, J. 2015. *Cultural Criminology: An Invitation*, 2nd ed. London: Sage.

Ferrell, J. and Sanders, C. (eds.) 1995. *Cultural Criminology*. Boston, MA: Northeastern University Press.

Fincham, B. 2006. 'Bicycle messengers and the road to freedom,' in S. Bohm, C. Jones, C. Land and M. Paterson eds.) *Against Automobility*, pp. 208–222, Malden, MA: Blackwell.

Furness, Z. 2010. *One Less Car: Bicycling and the Politics of Automobility*. Philadelphia, PA: Temple.

Gill, K. 2010. *Of Poverty and Plastic*. New Delhi: Oxford.

Harvey, D. 2008. The Right to the City. *New Left Review* 53: 23–40.

Hayward, K. 2004. *City Limits: Crime, Consumer Culture and the Urban Experience*. London: Glasshouse.

Hayward, K. 2012. 'Five spaces of cultural criminology,' *The British Journal of Criminology* 52(3): 441–462.

Hayward, K. and Presdee, M. (eds.) 2010. *Framing Crime: Cultural Criminology and the Image*. London: Routledge/GlassHouse.

Industrial Workers of the World. 1973 [1908]. 'Preamble of the industrial workers of the world,' in *Songs of the Workers*, 34th ed. Chicago, IL: Industrial Workers of the World.

Jenkins, P. 1999. 'Fighting terrorism as if women mattered: Anti-abortion violence as unconstructed terrorism,' in J. Ferrell and N. Websdale (eds.) *Making Trouble: Cultural Constructions of Crime, Deviance, and Control*, pp. 319–346, New York: Aldine de Gruyter.

Jorgensen, F. A. 2011. *Making a Green Machine: The Infrastructure of Beverage Container Recycling*. Camden, NJ: Rutgers University Press.

Kane, S. 2009. 'Stencil graffiti in urban waterscapes of Buenos Aires and Rosario, Argentina,' *Crime Media Culture*, 5(1): 9–28.

Kane, S. 2012. *Where Rivers Meet the Sea: The Political Ecology of Water*. Philadelphia, PA: Temple University Press.

Lauer, J. 2005. 'Driven to extremes: Fear of crime and the rise of the sport utility vehicle in the United States,' *Crime Media Culture*, 1(2): 149–168.

Lutz, C. and A. L. Fernandez. 2010. *Carjacked*. New York: Palgrave Macmillan.

Markusen, A. and Schrock, G. 2009. 'Consumption-driven urban development,' *Urban Geography*, 30(4): 344–367.

McClanahan, B., Brisman, A. and N. South. 2015. 'Privatization, pollution and power: A green criminological analysis of present and future global water crises,' in G. Barak (ed.) *The Routledge International Handbook of the Crimes of the Powerful*, pp. 223–234, London and New York: Routledge.

Mills, C. W. 1959. *The Sociological Imagination*. London: Oxford University Press.

Mitchell, D. 2003. *The Right to the City*. New York: Guilford.

Muzzatti, S. 2010. '"Drive it like you stole it": A cultural criminology of car commercials,' in K. Hayward and M. Presdee (eds.) *Framing Crime: Cultural Criminology and the Image*, pp. 138–155. London: Routledge/GlassHouse.

Naegler, L. 2016. Resistance Post-Occupy. A Cultural Criminological Analysis of Resistance, Knowledge Production and Imagination in the Radical Movement in New York City. PhD Thesis, Universität Hamburg and University of Kent.

Packard, V. 1960. *The Waste Makers*. London: Penguin.

Pellow, D. N. 2004. *Garbage Wars: The Struggle for Environmental Justice in Chicago*. Cambridge, MA: MIT Press.

Presdee, M. 2000. *Cultural Criminology and the Carnival of Crime*. London: Routledge.

Presdee, M. 2004. 'The story of crime,' in J. Ferrell, K. Hayward, W. Morrison and M. Presdee (eds.) *Cultural Criminology Unleashed*, pp. 41–48. London: Routledge/GlassHouse.

Pritchett, L. 2009. *Going Green: True Tales from Gleaners, Scavengers, and Dumpster Divers*. Norman, OK: University of Oklahoma Press.

Redmon, D. 2005. *Mardi Gras: Made in China (documentary film)*. New York: Carnivalesque Films.

Rodríguez Goyes, D. and South, N. 2016. 'Land grabs, bio-piracy and the inversion of justice in Colombia,' *The British Journal of Criminology*, 56(3): 558–577.

Rosenthal, E. 2011. 'Used batteries from U.S. Expose Mexicans to risk,' *The New York Times*, 9 December: A1, A12.

Ruggiero, V. 2010. 'Dirty Collar Crime in Naples,' *Freedom from Fear Magazine 6*.

Ruggiero, V. 2013. 'Creative destruction and the economy of waste,' *Critica Penal y Poder* (4): 34–48.

Sabin, A. and Redmond, D. 2009. *Kamp Katrina (documentary film)*. New York: Carnivalesque Films.

Shuqin, Y. 2010. 'The polluting behaviour of the multinational corporations in China,' in R. White (ed.) *Criminological Perspectives*, pp. 150–158. Cullompton, Devon, UK: Willan.

Sollund, R. 2017. 'Doing green, critical criminology with an auto-ethnographic, feminist approach,' *Critical Criminology: An International Journal*, 25(2): 245–260.

South, N. 1998. 'A green field for criminology,' *Theoretical Criminology*, 2(2): 211–234.

South, N. 2007. 'The "Corporate colonization of nature": Bio-prospecting, bio-piracy and the development of green criminology,' in P. Beirne and N. South (eds.) *Issues in Green Criminology: Confronting Harms against Environments, Humanity and Other Animals*, pp. 230–247. Cullompton, Devon, UK: Willan.

South, N. 2010. 'The ecocidal tendencies of late modernity,' in R. White (ed.) *Global Environmental Harm: Criminological Perspectives*, pp. 228–247, Cullompton, Devon, UK: Willan.

Story, B., (dir). 2016. The Prison in Twelve Landscapes (documentary film). Oh Ratface Films.

Strasser, S. 1999. *Waste and Want: A Social History of Trash*. New York: Henry Holt and Company.

Takemura, N. 2010. 'The criticality of global environmental crime and the response of chaos criminology,' in R. White (ed.) *Global Environmental Harm: Criminological Perspectives*, pp. 210–227, Cullhompton, Devon, UK: Willan.

Tunnell, K. 2011. *Once Upon a Place: The Fading of Community in Rural Kentucky*. Bloomington, IN: Xlibris.

Turner, Allan. 2002. '"Civility" Push, Light Rail Tough on Panhandlers,' *Houston Chronicle* (16 June). Available at: www.HoustonChronicle.com.

Varul, M. Z. 2006. 'Waste, industry and romantic leisure: Veblen's theory of recognition,' *European Journal of Social Theory*, 9(1): 103–117.
Veblen, T. 1953 [1899]. *The Theory of the Leisure Class*. New York: Mentor.
Walker, L., Jardim, J. and Harley, K. (dir). 2010. *Waste Land [Lixo Extraordinario] (documentary film)*. London: Almega.
Walters, R. 2011. *Eco Crime and Genetically Modified Food*. Abingdon, Oxon, UK: Routledge.
Wender, J. 2004. 'Phenomenology, cultural criminology and the return to astonishment,' in J. Ferrell, K. Hayward, W. Morrison and M. Presdee (eds.) *Cultural Criminology Unleashed*, pp. 49–60. London: Routledge/GlassHouse.
White, R. 2002. 'Environmental harm and the political economy of consumption,' *Social Justice* 29(1–2): 82–102.
White, R. 2003. 'Environmental issues and the criminological imagination,' *Theoretical Criminology*, 7(4): 483–506.
White, R. 2008. *Crimes against Nature: Environmental Criminology and Ecological Justice*. Cullompton, Devon, UK: Willan.
White, R. 2009–2010. 'Environmental victims and resistance to state crime through transnational activism,' *Social Justice*, 36(3): 46–60.
Wilson, J. and G. Kelling. 1982. 'Broken windows,' *Atlantic Monthly* (March): 29–38.
Young, J. 2011. *The Criminological Imagination*. Cambridge, UK: Polity.
Zukin, S. 1997. 'Cultural strategies of economic development and the hegemony of vision,' in A. Merrifield and E. Swyngedouw (eds.) *The Urbanization of Injustice*, pp. 223–243, New York: New York University Press.
Zukin, S. 2010. *Naked City: The Death and Life of Authentic Urban Places*. New York: Oxford University Press.

38

Littering in the Northeast of England

A sign of social disorganisation?

Kelly Johnson, Tanya Wyatt, Sarah Coulthard and Cassandra O'Neill

Introduction

Environmental degradation and harm are often portrayed as global concerns and challenges. While this is clearly true, we should not overlook seemingly small environmental harms and crimes that affect individual people and local communities. One such pervasive environmental crime is littering. Littering has significant environmental impacts and creates public health risks (Eunomia Research and Consulting 2014). Furthermore, litter is an ongoing problem in public spaces, though this varies from place to place.

In the summer of 2016, we conducted a study in the Northeast of England to explore the nexus of personal wellbeing linked to the environment and to anti-social behaviour. In conducting the research, we found that it is not only wellbeing that is linked to littering and anti-social behaviour, but other factors are at play and we returned to the data using a grounded theory approach. This chapter describes the results of re-examining the data collected under the lens of social disorganisation. Stretesky and colleagues (2014) argue that there are clear links between ecological and social disorganisation in the area of green crime and that research is needed to unpack these links. The first section will distinguish between 'fly-tipping' and 'littering', and will offer background context as to ongoing conceptualisations and attempts to deal with litter. Next, the original research questions and methodology will be described. This will be followed by the findings and then an analysis of the data in relation to social disorganisation.

Definition and background

For the purposes of this research, there is a need to distinguish the differences between the acts of 'fly-tipping' and 'littering'. According to the Department for Environment, Food and Rural Affairs (DEFRA 2016), '[f]ly-tipping is [the] illegal dumping of liquid or solid waste on land or water', which is more than a black bag's worth and is 'usually dumped to avoid dispersal costs'. 'Litter', on the other hand, 'is "anything" that is left, thrown, dropped or deposited and causes defacement in a public place. The offence of littering relates to what is done with the litter, rather than what it is' (Woodland Trust 2002: 4). The locations of fly-tipping and littering are different: with respect to the former, individuals are usually attempting to hide their activities; the latter, in contrast, occurs in public space. The scale of the offences also differs. Fly-tipping is a more substantial dumping of waste, whereas littering could be a single item. Tjell (2010: 863) argues that litter can be 'waste materials such as containers, papers, and wrappers which have been disposed of without permission' of the landowner.

In terms of legislation in the United Kingdom (U.K.), Part IV Section 87 of the Environmental Protection Act 1990 (the '1990 Act') states that it is a criminal offence for a person to intentionally or unintentionally drop, leave or deposit litter in a public place, but the '1990 Act does not provide a comprehensive definition of litter' (DEFRA 2006: 11). The definition of litter used by the U.K. courts has been argued to be wide and is often associated with eating and drinking materials (DEFRA 2006; Priestley 2017). Section 27 of the Clean Neighbourhoods and Environment Act 2005, which updated the Environmental Protection Act and introduced a new Section 98(5A) to the 1990 Act, includes discarded cigarette/cigar ends (or 'butts,' in the United States) and chewing gum in the list of items considered to be litter. In our observations, as we describe in the methodology, we looked for such materials in various public places.

Globally, littering has become an environmental pollution issue (Ojedokun 2015). Not only does the presence and accumulation of litter in public spaces have a negative social effect on the environment and reduce the aesthetic appeal of such places, but it also has devastating impacts on local ecosystems, contributes to environmental disasters, such as flooding (Ojedokun 2015), and creates health risks and extra expense for tax payers (Eunomia Research and Consulting 2014). In 2017, the House of Commons argued that '[l]itter is perhaps the most significant low-level crime affecting the UK' (Priestley 2017: 3), and it has been found to have observable correlations with social deprivation and more serious criminal activity (Communities and Local Government Committee 2015). Yet, remarkably, as Groombridge (2013) pointed out in the first edition of this volume, criminology has had little to say about littering beyond its connection to anti-social behaviour and incivility. With such widespread negative impacts, there is a need for criminologists to explore the causes and consequences of littering. The next section examines how the act of littering has evolved throughout history from a consequence of consumerism and mobility to a global environmental concern.

The evolution of perspectives on littering

It has been suggested that littering is a twentieth-century invention (Cooper 2013). Yet, there has always been some form of littering plaguing streets. During the nineteenth century, in what was thought to be a useful approach to cleaning the streets, street rubbish was combined with horse manure, which was given to local farmers for fertiliser (Jack 2005). This ended when horses stopped being the primary source of transportation. The consequence was rubbish being left on the streets (Jack 2005). As a modern phenomenon, littering as a social problem emerged in the years following the Great War (World War I) and because of the changing patterns of consumerism during the early twentieth century (Cooper 2013; Jack 2005).

The early-twentieth-century rise of modern transportation opened up the countryside to urban residents, and picnicking became an 'integral and seemingly harmless part of the fun' (Jack 2005: 1). This led to a growing concern regarding the litter left in 'beauty spots and city parks, which was seen to be a consequence of growing working-class recreation that coincidently "spoilt" the countryside environment' (Jack 2005: 2). The Women's Institute (WI) became involved actively in anti-littering campaigns, which targeted people visiting green spaces in cars. Their campaign failed, however, as evidenced in 1930 when people visiting the New Forest, in the south of England, were observed throwing the anti-litter posters out of the windows of their cars and coaches. It is these actions that highlight the state of 'the anti-littering campaigns in the inter-war years' (Jack 2005: 2).

At the beginning of the twentieth century, littering was viewed less as a national or environmental issue than as a class problem. Litter in the countryside was associated with the newly found freedoms of the working classes (Cooper 2013)—a perspective that was supported by a correspondent to *The Times* who, in 1925, wrote that it seemed as if:

> a place dedicated to the people (parks) has not really passed into the possession and usufruct [right to enjoy other people's property] of the people unless they are allowed to do exactly as they please in it … to leave behind them any rubbish which they are too lazy to conceal or take home with them.
>
> *(in Cooper 2013)*

Thirty years later, a 1957 article in *The Times*, titled 'Litter by the Ton', reflected a new mood in which 'at last … the government intends to throw their weight behind the anti-litter campaign' (Jack 2005: 3). The result was the 1958 Litter Act, which criminalised littering and introduced £10 fines for offenders (Cooper 2013). Nevertheless, while there were a few successes 'upon passing the Act', any long-term success 'was limited because of the costly and complicated procedures involved in bringing prosecutions' (Jack 2005: 3).

Little change occurred until the 1970s, when the Keep Britain Tidy campaigns secured celebrity endorsements for their anti-littering messages (Jack 2005). At this time, the focus was on the role of industry with respect to non-biodegradable plastics and packaging that were blowing around the streets and overwhelming landfills (Jack 2005). Yet, by 1974, informed by academic research into 'attitudes of those who litter', governmental educational programmes were then directed towards 'perceived regular offenders', such as young men, smokers and children, instead of companies (Jack 2005: 3). Despite these efforts, entities like the Policy Exchange and Campaigns to Protect Rural England (CPRE) have argued that the rate of dropped litter has increased since the 1960s by 500 per cent (Lewis et al. 2009). In addition, the Policy Exchange and CPRE highlight that councils spend an estimated £500m per year on the cleanup of areas and that littering is now a concern not only for local governments, but also for central government (Lewis et al. 2009).

Over the past two decades, there has been a wave of environmental campaigns by Keep Britain Tidy to reduce the amount of litter. As Lewis and colleagues (2009) argue, despite the small decrease of litter between 2001 and 2004, the future is not promising. In October 2014, new legislation from the Anti-Social Behaviour, Crime and Policing Act authorised local authorities to enforce 'Community Protection Notices (CPNs) against people who drop litter' (Communities and Local Government Committee 2015: 18). The previous Conservative Government has argued these *civil* notices 'will direct the individual, business or organisation responsible to stop causing the problem' (Communities and Local Government Committee 2015: 18). Yet, Part IV of the Environmental Protection Act defines littering as a criminal offence and offenders can be fined a maximum of £2,500. The Communities and Local Government Committee (2015) has noted, however, that due to the administrative costs of taking an offender to court, littering in the UK is often dealt with as a civil matter. Local authorities issue the above-mentioned CPNs or impose fines under the guise of fixed penalty notices (FPN), a civil sanction. Despite both of these notices being in affect, in 2017 The House of Commons asserted that now, '[l]itter is perhaps the most significant low-level crime affecting the UK' (Priestley 2017: 4). In addition, in 2018, The National Rural Crime Network reported that residents of rural communities raised concerns regarding the increase of fly-tipping, which has lowered residents' confidence in police in dealing with such matters (Bodkin 2018; National Rural Crime Network 2018).

Northeast England

We noted earlier that at the beginning of the twentieth century, littering was viewed as a class problem rather than an environmental one (Cooper 2013). Historically, the Northeast of England—especially areas such as North Tyneside and Newcastle upon Tyne—has been associated with the working class (Kerley 2015; Robinson 2002), whereas places such as Northumberland have often been associated with upper-middle class and elite residents (Kerley 2015). Over the years, however, economic and social changes have created a more mixed picture of the region, with some areas becoming more affluent than others (Robinson 2002). It has now become a 'region of fragments, a region shaped by an industrial past, then fractured by the upheaval of deindustrialisation and, now, a patchwork of places of renewal and decay' (Robinson 2002: 317).

In Northeast England, the amount of litter, according to the Regional Results Summary 2013/14 for regional litter levels, was at an 'acceptable' standard (Priestley 2017). Yet, all regions in the country were at an acceptable standard for litter and the Northeast was third from the bottom when compared with other regions (Priestley 2017). The data came from a survey carried out by Keep Britain Tidy on behalf of DEFRA. They measured seven indicators—'litter, detritus, weed growth, recent leaf and blossom fall, staining, fly-posting and graffiti'. Each indicator was graded A, B, C or D for cleanliness with the possibility of an additional three intermediate grades (i.e., B+). Thus, each region was graded on each indicator from a score out of seven, which was then used to make 'comparisons between regions' (Priestley 2017: 6).

Another measure of the amount of litter—or, at least, an indicator of the local council's engagement with the problem—was the number of FPNs issued. In three major counties in the Northeast in the past few years, the number of FPNs each local authority handed out diverged. Between April 2014 and March 2017, Newcastle City Council had issued 8,525 FPNs for littering, with 2,981 being issued on Northumberland Street, the city's main shopping street (Fuller 2017). Northumberland County Council (2016) issued 455 FPNs in 2016, which was an increase of 47 per cent from 2014. North Tyneside Council (2017a) issued the lowest number of FPNs of the three: 245 FPNs between January 2014 and March 2017. The demographics of each county differ, along with the mobility of residents and non-residents, which raises questions regarding possible links between the problem of pervasive littering and social class, sense of ownership and attachment. A brief examination, therefore, is warranted.

Newcastle upon Tyne is the biggest shopping city in the Northeast, which attracts nearly two million visitors per year (NewcastleGateshead, n.d.). In 2016, the city had a population of 296,500 (NOMIS 2017a), which indicates that it is used by more people than just those who live there, especially when compared with the other areas in the region. Between July 2016 and June 2017, there were 74,200 employed men and 64,100 employed women; out of the economically active people residing in Newcastle upon

Tyne—people able to work and of working age—there were only 10,300 who were unemployed (NOMIS 2017a). Of people employed, 56,900 of them were found to hold positions in managerial, professional, or associate professional and technical areas, and 39,700 people in retail, machine and elementary occupations[1] (NOMIS 2017a). Nonetheless, even though Newcastle upon Tyne has a large economically active population, it also has 57,500 economically inactive people—people not able to or not of working age (NOMIS 2017a). This is comprised mostly of 24,900 students living in the city, 10,900 people on long-term sick leave, 9,800 residents looking after family and/or home, and 6,000 retired individuals.

Newcastle upon Tyne has 57,955 owner-occupied households and 57,168 rented households (Office for National Statistics 2016). It must be acknowledged, however, that in the case of household tenure, official figures do not often reflect all those living in temporary accommodation or those who are categorised as having no fixed abode (Rose and Davies 2014).

Bordering Scotland, the northernmost county in Northeast England is Northumberland. Home to stunning beaches and countryside, the county has a population of 316,000: 154,200 men and 161,800 women. Out of the 70,400 men and 67,200 women who are employed, 54,400 of people work in managerial, professional, or associate professional and technical occupations, whereas 40,800 hold jobs in retail, machine and elementary occupations (NOMIS 2017b). There is also a big difference in size regarding the economically active unemployed population. Northumberland only has 7,900 economically active unemployed people (NOMIS 2017b). The composition of the economically inactive also has stark differences with Newcastle upon Tyne. At a lower amount of 43,800 people, much of this population is made up of those who are retired; the remaining people, in order, comprise students, those that are on long-term sick leave and, finally, those looking after family or home (NOMIS 2017b). Another difference when comparing Newcastle upon Tyne's demographics and Northumberland's is tenancy. There are more owner-occupied properties and fewer rented-occupied households in Northumberland with 91,207 owner-occupied households compared with 44,258 rented households (NOMIS 2017b).

The market town of Hexham, situated 23 miles away from Newcastle upon Tyne and in the southwest corner of Northumberland, is home to 13,100 of the 316,000 inhabitants of the county (Hexham Town Council 2012). Hexham lies inside the Hadrian's Wall Corridor and overlooks the Tyne Valley; it is also situated between Northumberland National Park and The North Pennines Area—'two important areas of wild and high-value landscape and ecology' (Hexham Town Council 2012: 6). Economically speaking, many of Hexham's residents 'are very well represented in some of the top earning occupation areas—managers, directors, senior officials, professions and associate professionals' (Hexham Town Council 2012: 7). The Town Council has noted, however, that Hexham is facing an 'identity crisis' due to the increase in working families and lower-income families in the town's rental accommodations (Hexham Town Council 2012: 9).

Neighbouring Newcastle upon Tyne and Northumberland is the metropolitan borough of North Tyneside, which is divided into 20 wards. Like Northumberland, North Tyneside borders the North Sea and has beaches as well as a country park built on reclaimed colliery (coal mine) land (North Tyneside Council 2017b). With an overall population of 203,300, North Tyneside is the least populated area out of the three (NOMIS 2017c). Of the 52,700 men and 48,500 women in the workforce, 41,700 of them are employed in managerial, professional, or associate professional and technical occupations and 30,200 hold jobs in the retail, machine and elementary occupations (NOMIS 2017c). North Tyneside not only has the smallest population, but it also has the fewest economically active unemployed with

5,700 economically active people unemployed (NOMIS 2017c). The county also has more owner-occupied properties than Newcastle upon Tyne at 59,136, but fewer rental accommodations than both areas with 36,977 rented households.

Rich in history, North Tyneside is home to many diverse places, such as Battle Hill and Cullercoats. Cullercoats, the older of the two, was once home to the coal and salt industries; since the demise of these local industries, however, Cullercoats village is now a popular seaside destination (Tales of the Herring 2018). According to the 2011 Census for England, the ward of Cullercoats had a population of 9,202 (Office for National Statistics 2016), residing in 3,457 owner-occupied households and 724 rented households (Office for National Statistics 2016). In Cullercoats, the majority of residents (903) are employed in professional occupations with associate professional and technical occupations ranking second (592 residents) (Office for National Statistics 2016). In addition—and at the other end of the scale—the 2011 Census highlighted that the least number of residents are plant and machine operatives and in elementary occupations (Office for National Statistics 2016).

In contrast to Cullercoats, Battle Hill is one of the newest of the North Tyneside wards. Developed in the 1960s after the establishment of the main A road leading from the Northeast coast to Newcastle city centre, Battle Hill is located between Wallsend and the Rising Sun Country Park (Hutchinson 2015). The ward of Battle Hill, according to the 2011 Census, has a population of 10,717 (Office for National Statistics 2016). Like Cullercoats, Battle Hill has a higher number of owner-occupied households at 3,270, compared with 1,405 individuals or families that live in rented accommodation (Office for National Statistics 2016). Unlike Cullercoats, Battle Hill has a different economic make up. The majority of Battle Hill's economically active residents (870) are employed in administrative and secretarial occupations, followed by 720 economically active residents employed in skilled trade occupations, 681 residents in sales and customer service, 622 employed in professional occupations, 560 residents employed in elementary occupations and only 352 in managerial or senior positions (Office of National Statistics 2016).

Hopefully, it is clear that the areas where we conducted our study are mixed demographically, particularly in terms of employment/unemployment/retirement property, owners/renters and social class. It is worth noting as well the existence of easily accessible public transportation, such as the Tyne and Wear Metro, busses and National Rail, which connects the three areas to each other and other parts of the country. The demographics, along with the mobility of residents and non-residents, raise questions regarding possible links between the problem of pervasive littering and social class, sense of ownership and attachment, and transportation.

Causes and consequences of litter

As mentioned above, criminology has largely neglected littering, with Groombridge's (2013) chapter an exception. Our original theorising as to the causes of littering sought to link littering with people's understanding of their own personal or possibly environmental wellbeing. Whilst this approach yielded interesting results in relation to people's perspectives around wellbeing, we felt there were other approaches that might help to better understand why it is that people litter. With that in mind, we returned to the criminological literature.

Since the turn of the twentieth century, the notion of social disorganisation in urban environments has been researched extensively (e.g., Barnes 2006; Lynch and Boggess 2015; Sampson and Raudenbush 1999; Tunnell 2008). The concept of social disorganisation emerged from the Chicago School, which noted the influence of the urban ecology on the resource allocations that influence patterns of crime (Hallsworth and Young 2013; Lynch and Boggess

2015). Advanced by Shaw and McKay (1942), Kurbrin and Weitzer (2003: 374) state that social disorganisation refers to a community's inability to realise 'common goals and solve chronic problems'. Theorists have suggested that urban areas that are disorganised, physically depressed, stricken by poverty and are unstable, lack the formal and informal controls necessary to prevent crime, and encourage crime and delinquency, whereas areas that are organised, stable and have a settled residency promote law-abiding behaviours (Hallsworth and Young 2013; Kurbrin and Weitzer 2003; Shaw and McKay 1942). While there has been much research on urban environments, social disorganisation and crime, there has been limited research on social disorganisation, rural environments and environmental degradation and harm. An exception is the work of Donnermeyer and DeKeserdy, who have highlighted the research on rural crime and social disorganisation, and who have noted that 'much of what is defined as environmental crime occurs at rural localities and affects rural people' (2014: 93). Our study combined investigation of social disorganisation in urban and rural environments with littering as the crime (see 'Research design and methodology' below).

Social disorganisation theorists have noted littering and other physical incivilities as factors for crime and disorder (Sampson and Raudenbush 1999). Even though, as noted previously, littering has become a global issue, littering is experienced at the town- and city-level—and it is at these levels that littering's relationship to social disorganisation and weak social integration is experienced (Brandt 2017; Tunnell 2008). Sampson and Raudenbush (1999) observed high levels of litter, including cigarette ends, in public spaces in socially disorganised areas with low social control, and Nash and Christie (2003) noted that areas that are prone to high levels of litter are also likely to have residents with a low sense of attachment. Therefore, as suggested above, the question arises as to whether having a sense of attachment or ownership influences a person to litter.

Low economic status has been also argued to be a factor of social disorganisation (Shaw and McKay 1942). It is this low economic status of communities that can be a hindrance to the cleanup of litter and other environmental problems. In Scotland, the *Third Force News* has highlighted that the most deprived communities are suffering from increased litter and fly-tipping (Armour 2017). Poor communities, councils with limited budgets and poorly funded third sector agencies are unable to supply the resources needed to clean up litter (Jones 2017).

The financial aspect of rubbish was also evident in Tunnell's (2008) study, where he found that local government oversight of disorganised communities often face financial constraints and waste disposal services may suffer limitations. This could prevent residents from being able to dispose of their waste properly, and thus, instead, they dispose of it by any means necessary—littering or fly-tipping. If this is the case, then areas with low socio-economic status may have high levels of litter due in part to the inability to dispose of rubbish correctly or because the costs of clean up are too high. Conversely, then, areas populated with people of a higher socio-economic status may have lower levels of litter due to the ability to afford proper waste disposal and cleanup operations.

Several authors have noted that certain factors—crime levels, upkeep of neighbourhoods, levels of litter and graffiti—prevent the formation of social networks (Barnes 2006; Brandt 2017; Tunnell 2008). Social networks are crucial in the enforcement of informal social control. Tunnell (2008: 40) notes that '[w]ithin rural areas, manifestations of social disorganisation occur out of sight', due to there being fewer people to observe these manifestations, as well as more isolated spaces in which such activities/incivilities can occur. Even though Tunnell found high levels of litter and fly-tipping in rural residential communities that might not have observers watching their negative actions, this does not necessarily provide insight into why there is a large amount of litter in rural tourist areas where there might be potential observers who might observe the littering.

Wilson and Kelling (1982) argued that indicia of physical disorder, such as littering and unrepaired broken windows in buildings, signal that nobody is interested in the upkeep of the area and thus that the area may be more accommodating of crime and disorderly behaviour. Even though this perspective had much public support in its early days, it has been heavily criticised for neglecting the socio-economic circumstances of the residents affected by this physical disorder (Sampson and Raudenbush 1999). Furthermore, Brisman (2012: 381) has argued that in some areas physical disorder 'convey[s] a hip, urban grit, rather than ominous disorder and criminality'. Despite such criticisms of Wilson and Kelling's work, many have agreed that physical disorder in an area can lead to social disorganisation (e.g., Sampson and Raudenbush 1999). We now describe the research design and methodology. Factors that are linked to social disorganisation will be highlighted.

Research questions and methodology

In order to investigate the litter problem in the Northeast of England, we undertook a mixed-methods research project. Our project aimed to answer the following questions:

1 What is the nature and extent of litter at four observation sites (lone or group littering)?
2 What are the demographics of litterers (gender, estimated age)?
3 Does sense of ownership or space affect whether a person litters (resident or visitor)?

Our project consisted of non-participant covert observations and structured interviews at the four Northeast England locations described above: Hexham city centre in Northumberland, Newcastle city centre and Cullercoats Bay and the Rising Sun Country Park, which are both located in North Tyneside. These four locations were identified as areas with urban locals and tourists, and village/rural locals and tourists (see Table 38.1), thus providing a distinction in terms of size of the public space and the typical user. We recorded incidents of littering at the sites including: who littered (gender, estimated age, alone or in a group), what the rubbish was or consisted of, and any other qualitative information about the incident. Five hours of observation were undertaken at each of the four locations. The observations were recorded discreetly so as not to attract the attention of those being observed. In addition, ten interviewees over the age of 16 at each location (a total of 40 interviews) were randomly selected and asked to complete a survey and questionnaire, as well as to answer five questions. The interviewees were a convenience sample who may or may not have littered. All of the authors received University Ethical Approval prior to any fieldwork being conducted. The findings by research questions are below.

Table 38.1 People who thought litter was a problem in their area.

Area	*Yes*	*No*
Cullercoats	9	1
Hexham	7	3
Newcastle upon Tyne	9	1
Rising Sun	9	1

Findings

Nature and extent of littering

In relation to the first research question, when exploring the nature and extent of litter at four observation sites, we observed that on arrival to all destinations and on all occasions, there were noticeable amounts of litter already present on the streets and public spaces. We noted, however, that even though there was litter in the town centre, Hexham, in general, is a very tidy and clean place compared with the other areas and has many rubbish bins located around the town centre and recreational parks. On the first day of observation in Hexham, the local authority council workers (who are tasked with picking up rubbish and recycling) had not long before emptied the public bins. There was a council grass cutter in the main recreation park, which was one of the primary observation spots in the town. Even on the second observation visit, which occurred on a weekend in September 2016, Hexham still had a clean and tidy feel to it. On the other hand, Cullercoats Bay—a village in North Tyneside adjacent to the North Sea—had on both visits more litter dotted around the place than Hexham, ranging from beer cans and fizzy pop cans to random socks, broken glass bottles and cigarette ends peppered around by the shops, but also on the bay. Furthermore, like Hexham, Cullercoats has rubbish bins that are located around the village and bay.

Newcastle upon Tyne, which, as noted earlier, has more people circulating through the city than the other two boroughs, has, like the other two areas, many bins located around the city. Even though on both visits to Newcastle upon Tyne we observed that there were council workers picking up litter from the streets, we also noted that there was an abundance of litter dotted around the city, ranging from hot drinks cups and hot food wrappers to travel tickets and carrier bags. The Rising Sun Country Park, which is situated behind Battle Hill—a suburb of Wallsend in North Tyneside—is a main walkway from the suburb to the main Asda superstore. It is necessary to point out, however, that the Rising Sun Country Park is maintained not just by the local authority, but also by the Rising Sun Farm Trust, a private company with a charitable status (Rising Sun Farm 2015). The Rising Sun Country Park had more litter present on arrival than the other three locations combined. On entry to the southern entrance of the Rising Sun Country Park, we found the grounds covered with litter: plastic bottles and cans, broken glass bottles, various cardboard boxes, Asda carrier bags, McDonald's wrappers, broken garden or house bricks, cut grass in a black bag, builder's rubbish, dog faeces bags hung on trees or left by the side of walkways, cigarette packets, scratch cards and Asda trollies. We observed that there are not many bins situated around the country park.

The amount of litter found on the ground at the Rising Sun Country Park upon arrival was consistent with the amount of littering we observed from the country park users. For example, the most common objects dropped were sweet wrappers, followed by drinks cans, hot food wrappers and hot drinks cups. We also observed several incidents of dog fouling despite signs at the official entrance of the park stating the penalties of not cleaning up after one's dog. In addition, we noticed that after picking up the dog faeces with a bag, some people would then proceed to hang the filled bag on a nearby tree and walk away. Interviews revealed that this odd gesture was an expression of frustration to protest the lack of bins situated around the country park. We observed, however, that even though there were not as many bins around the country park as in the other observation sites, there are dog waste bins at every entrance.

Who is littering and what is the litter?

Due to the covert element to the observations, there were obstacles to gaining accurate demographic data on the people littering. Age was divided into six categories: 0–16; 17–21; 22–30; 31–40; 41–50; and over 50. Gender was broken down into male or female. The locality element was broken down into three categories: yes (resident/local); no (non-resident/visitor); or unsure. Even though gender was relatively easy to determine, accuracy about variables such as age and whether people were locals obviously faced some difficulties.

Age

In Hexham, the two categories of litter dropped the most—ice cream wrappers and crisp packets—were thrown on the ground by those under 16 years of age, some of whom were with an adult or a group of adults. The age range of those dropping the next three main types of litter in Hexham—drinks cans, drinks bottles and hot food wrappers—was mixed. It must be noted, however, that those littering the most in Hexham were all under the age of 21 with only two observed litterers being over the age 21 (see Figure 38.1). Furthermore, those observed littering the most in Hexham on one of the visits were also attending a local football match and were seated in social groups on the recreational field.

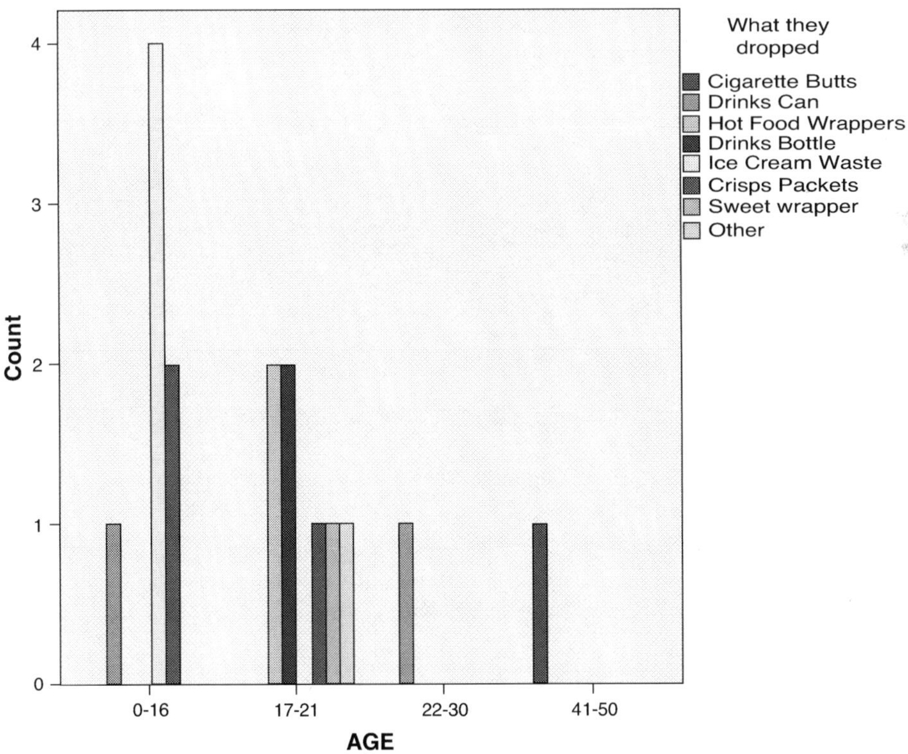

Figure 38.1 Graph showing what people dropped by age in Hexham.

In Newcastle upon Tyne, most of the observed litter dropped and the ages of those creating the litter were not the same as those in Hexham. For example, in Newcastle upon Tyne along the main shopping street—Northumberland Street—hot drinks cups were dropped by a wide variety of different people, all in different age ranges, followed closely by cigarette ends, which were discarded by those between the ages of 17 and 21, as well as by those in the 22–30 and 31–40 age ranges. This was followed by hot food wrappers, which were dropped by individuals in the 22–30, 31–40 and the 41–50 age brackets (see Figure 38.2). In addition, there was also only one observed instance of an individual under the age of 16 littering—a hot drinks cup, which was not the usual under-16 'type' of litter and which highlights how many different types of litter are discarded by a wide range of people. Even though there were many cold drinks bottles and cans already on the ground when the observations started in Newcastle upon Tyne, not many were observed being dropped. It was mainly hot drinks cups that were being dropped on the ground during the observation period. We did, however, observe a drink bottle dropped by a woman over the age of 50 who was on her own.

In Cullercoats, there were slightly different types of litter that we observed being dropped. The most common item was hot food wrappers, primarily fish and chips boxes, by those who were under 16 (see Figure 38.3), as well as other hot food/on-the-go food wrappers from establishments located away from Cullercoats. The second biggest observed dropped litter came from the category of 'other', which included cling film being thrown into the sea by

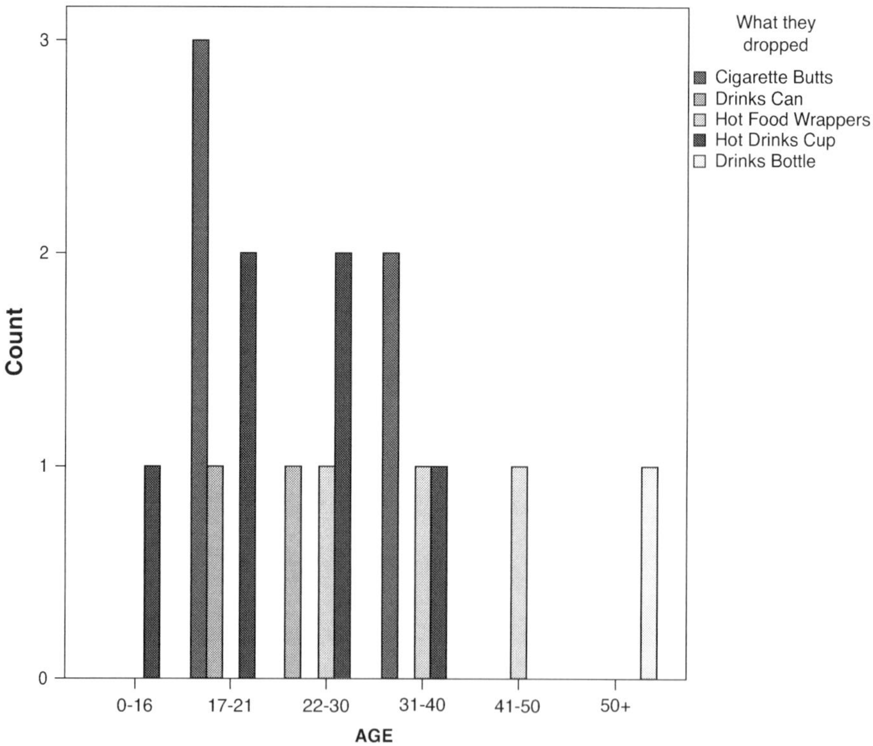

Figure 38.2 Graph showing what people dropped by age in Newcastle upon Tyne.

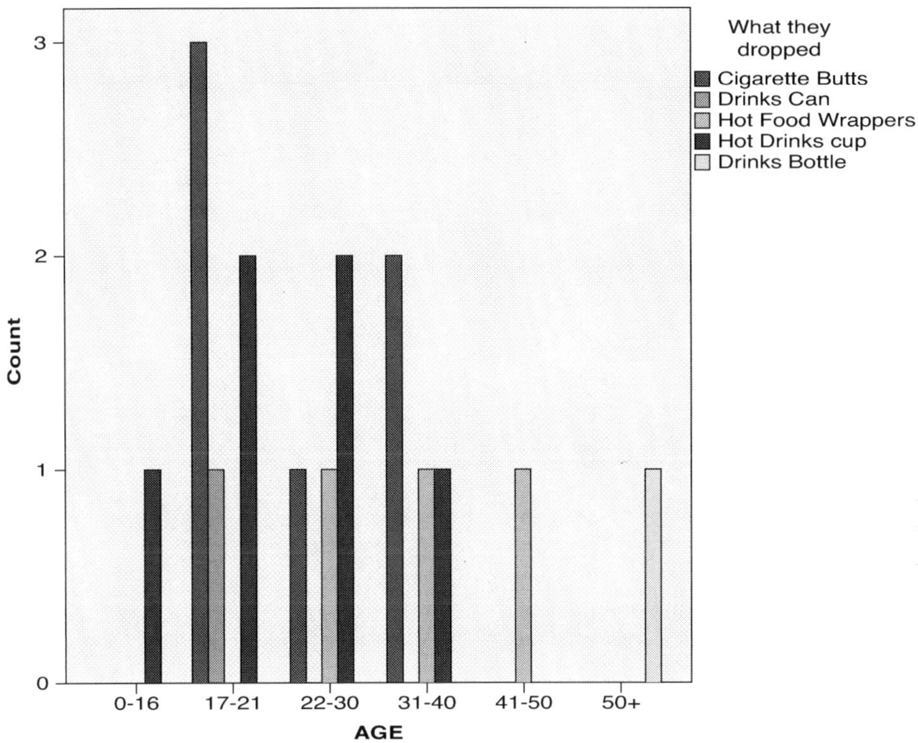

Figure 38.3 Graph showing what people dropped by age in Cullercoats.

a family, as well as a male in his 40s–50s cleaning out his wallet by throwing old receipts and travel cards on to the ground. Cigarette ends constituted the third most common item to be disposed of improperly—mostly by those over the age of 30. This was followed by sweet packets, which were dropped by someone in the 22–30 age bracket, as well as in the 40–50 age bracket. Finally, we observed the littering of ice cream wrappers and sticks, and crisp packets, which were both committed by children in the presence of their families.

There was a wide age range of observed litterers in the Rising Sun Country Park. Most observed litterers were under the age of 16 and were in the company of others, which was the same with Cullercoats and Hexham, and in contrast to Newcastle upon Tyne where, as noted previously, there was only one observed instance of an individual under the age of 16 dropping litter. The next age group dropping the second largest amount of litter was the 22–30 age group, of which there was a mixture of items dropped (see Figure 38.4). In addition, this was the only age group to be observed leaving dog foul, as well as the only area where people were observed not picking up their dogs' faeces.

Gender and groups

Interestingly, when examining littering and gender, we observed that in all places, bar the Rising Sun Country Park, men were observed dropping more litter than women (see Figure 38.5). On both observation days at the Rising Sun Country Park, there were, overall, more women at the

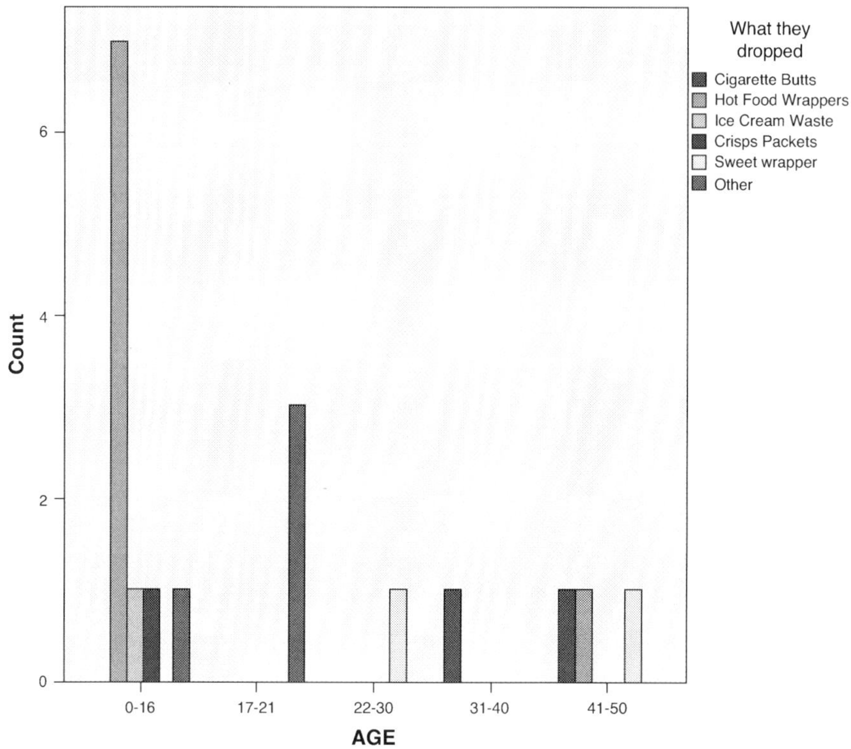

Figure 38.4 Graph showing what people dropped by age in the Rising Sun Country Park.

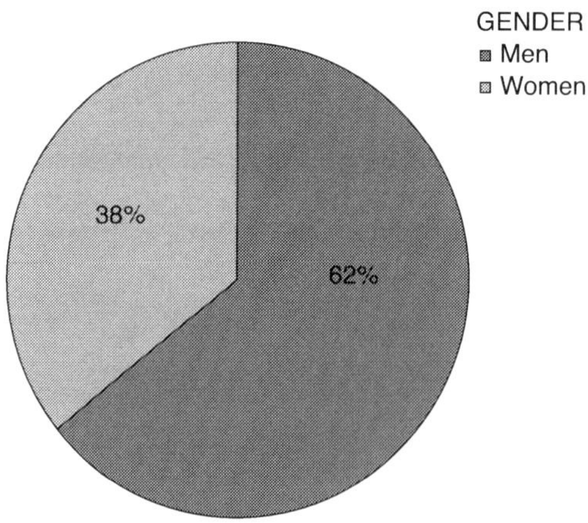

Figure 38.5 Overall gender of those littering from all sites.

site than men. Therefore, the observation at the Rising Sun Country Park site that there were more women littering could reflect the proportion of women there during the observations. We also observed in all areas that men in a peer group littered more than those on their own and it did not seem to matter whether they were near a bin or not. The women peer groups were slightly different, with some members opting to walk to a bin to discard their rubbish, while others simply put their rubbish in a bag and yet proceeded to leave the bag of rubbish where they had been sitting. This was the same with family groups, with some members seeking out a bin and others just leaving the rubbish and walking away.

We observed one incident of social shaming. When the younger children left their rubbish on the bench in the Rising Sun Country Park playground, an older couple, not part of but sitting near to the family, made a negative remark. This prompted the parents to send the children back to put the rubbish in the bins around the playground. This incident was not recorded as littering.

At all sites, we observed that littering behaviour happens more when in a peer or family group (see Figure 38.6). This did not seem to relate to the ages of the members in that group. As mentioned above, on only one occasion did anyone speak up about any group littering and that was at the Rising Sun Country Park. Even in Hexham and at Cullercoats, when the youths were observed littering, no adults confronted them or told them to stop. Not even when the children of the family group threw the cling film into the sea did any of the family members or onlookers reprimand the children for throwing plastic into the sea. In addition, we observed that once one member of the group had dropped litter without incident, it seemed to be an invitation for other members of the group to drop or leave litter behind.

Local or not?

The question of whether sense of ownership or place influences a person's littering was difficult to ascertain. Our hypothesis was that locals would not litter, as they would presumably feel attachment or ownership over their local space. With that in mind, during the covert observations, we tried to assess whether the person littering was a resident of the area. In

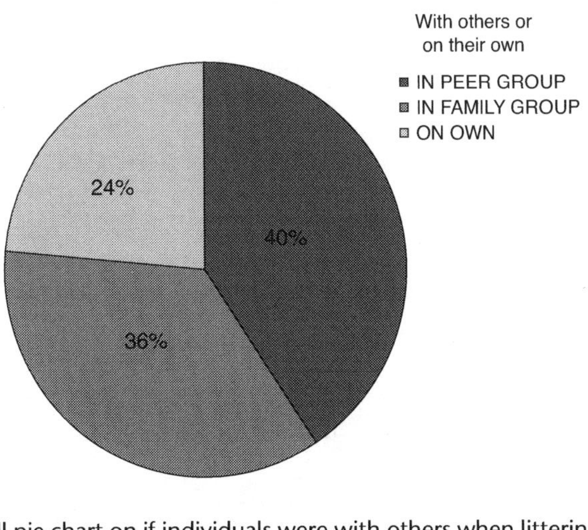

Figure 38.6 Overall pie chart on if individuals were with others when littering.

Hexham, out of the observed litterers, there were more people that could be identified as being local than visitors due to their cheering for the home team playing at the football match. It must be noted, however, that the away team was not observed dropping rubbish. The one person littering in Hexham who was identified as not being a local was a male tourist in a family group having a picnic in the park. In addition, it can be noted that this person was also within ten metres of a bin. When it came to the rest of the observed litterers, however, it was unknown if they were local or not.

The Rising Sun Country Park, as mentioned earlier, has a wide range of users—from dog walkers and bird enthusiasts to people walking to the local Asda. This made it a bit easier to determine who might be a resident of the surrounding area. Even though there was no one who was categorised as not being local, there were, however, a high number of users marked as 'unsure' compared with 'yes'. In Newcastle upon Tyne, it was also difficult to ascertain if litterers were local or not due to the number of visitors that visit the city each year. Therefore, the observation of whether the litterers were local or not ended in categorising many litterers into the 'unsure' category for Newcastle upon Tyne. In addition, this task was made particularly difficult due to the observations taking place during the summer holidays, which was also the same when observing Cullercoats because sunbathers and beach-goers from all over the region visit the bay due to its proximity to the metro station.

Nonetheless, in Cullercoats, most of the observed litterers were categorised as being local, with only five being marked as 'unsure' and two as a definite 'no'. Just opposite Cullercoats Bay is a stretch of eateries as well as a local 'members only' social club, which is where many locals drink and socialise. It is around this area that many people were observed dropping litter—from cigarette ends to receipts. For example, a smartly dressed local mother with a small child in a pushchair and a dog was observed dropping a sweet wrapper on the floor after giving the sweet to her child at the local play-park just off the bay. The mother was categorised as being local due to her presence with another group of mums that were congregated at the park for a playdate. Furthermore, the under-16 group throwing hot food waste into the North Sea was also classified as local due to the fact they had push bikes and a scooter with them, which are not allowed on public transport in the Northeast; therefore, they must have travelled only a short distance from Cullercoats.

The subjective nature of the local-versus-visitor categorisation makes it impossible to answer with certainty if this is a factor in whether a person litters or not. This is worth further exploration in order to unpack the link between attachment to an area and signs of social disorganisation, such as littering. In all four of the areas, interview participants who were local to the area were asked if they had dropped litter in the past year. Out of the 40 interviews, 24 of the participants stated they had not dropped litter in the past year. Thirteen participants were unsure, six replied in the affirmative, and one participant did not want to answer the question. It was in Hexham where the most participants stated that they had not littered in the past year, with eight out of the ten interviewees answering they had not littered in the past year. This is in contrast to the Rising Sun Country Park, with only two out of ten participants stating that they had not littered in the past year.

During the interviews, participants were also asked if litter was something that concerned them. Of the 40 interviews, 37 participants thought that litter was something that concerned them (see Table 38.1). Furthermore, 34 participants thought litter was a problem in the area in which they were interviewed, with only three participants in Hexham and one in each other area stating that they did not think litter was a problem in the area (see Table 38.2). It must be noted, however, that when asked earlier if the environment plays a part in their future and the ability to live well, most participants—except for two in all four areas—affirmed that the

Table 38.2 Number of people who stated that litter was something that concerned them.

Area	*Yes*	*No*
Cullercoats	9	1
Hexham	10	0
Newcastle upon Tyne	9	1
Rising Sun	9	1

environment plays an important role in their future. This highlights that even though people litter, the environment and the amount of litter is something that is a concern to many people.

Analysis

As noted above, littering has been reported to be prevalent in towns and cities that experience social disorganisation (Brandt 2017; Sampson and Raudenbush 1999; Tunnell 2008). Furthermore, low economic status is associated with social disorganisation (Shaw and McKay 1942). Upon examination of the household and economic data in our study, we found that most of the residents in all areas own their own home and, apart from Battle Hill/Rising Sun Country Park, hold a job in some type of professional or managerial occupation. Even though Hexham is a wealthy town, the town council noted that it has had a rise in lower-income families moving into the area, which would not be reflected in the census data. Nonetheless, during the observations, the least amount of observed littering took place in Hexham. This could be due to high social integration of the new residents or the fact that, overall, Hexham remains wealthy and can afford the cleanup costs. Some evidence for the latter is that Hexham was the only place where a council worker was out cleaning up the areas during the observation period.

Similarly, Newcastle upon Tyne has a large middle- to upper-income population and a majority of residents own their homes. Anton and Lawrence (2014) found that socio-demographic predictors such as home ownership helps secure place attachment. Newcastle upon Tyne attracts nearly two million visitors per year and this influx of visitors, with no actual attachment to the area and from various socio-economic backgrounds, may exacerbate the littering problem. In addition, this influx of visitors could contribute to an overall low level of social integration. Without further investigation into whether the litterers are local or not, however, it is not possible to determine the level of social integration and/or sense of attachment to an area. Moreover, further questions about the role of convenient transportation need to be asked because mobility appears to be linked to social integration and attachment. The connection may be that people who do litter only do so away from their own homes. Again, this will require further research to uncover the connection.

Even though Newcastle upon Tyne was the second lowest in observed littering, we noted earlier on that Newcastle City Council issued the highest number of FPNs to litterers. This again highlights the possibility that areas with higher economic status have more resources to address problems such as littering. In this case, the local authority seems to have the capacity to prioritise the enforcement of littering laws. In addition, even though it was not specifically observed, high numbers of people on the streets in Newcastle upon Tyne may provide informal social control, which may stop littering.

Like Hexham and Newcastle upon Tyne, Cullercoats has a relatively wealthy residential population. The area itself has no signs of social disorganisation apart from litter. The users of the area, like those of the city of Newcastle upon Tyne, are from various socio-economic backgrounds. Even though there are numerous people using the beach and promenades, litter was prevalent, which indicates that though there is the possibility for informal social control, it is not taking place. Again, due to the convenience of the local transport system to Cullercoats, the people littering the beaches may be those from outside Cullercoats. Therefore, further research should be undertaken in residential locations throughout the U.K. to unpack the connection to transportation. Research in residential locations would also potentially uncover whether people litter in their own neighbourhood.

The greatest amount of litter and the largest number of incidents of littering were observed at the Rising Sun Country Park. The adjacent residential population has a lower economic status than the rest of the areas, which, as noted earlier, has been found to be a factor contributing to social disorganisation. The area of Battle Hill exhibited other signs of social disorganisation (graffiti and vandalism), in addition to litter. The large amount of litter existed in spite of the fact that both North Tyneside Council and the country park charity oversee the area. The lack of upkeep may be due to the environmental priorities of the charity and local authority or a lack of resources. The area had the lowest possibility for informal social control, which presumably contributes to the social disorganisation in general, and litter in particular. Perhaps surprisingly, though, this was the one location where social shaming was observed. There is a need to better understand if the act of littering is seen as something that is harmful or even criminal by the wider society. It also raises questions about the effectiveness of social shaming with regard to littering.

Conclusion

Whilst we found that young men in groups appear to litter more than others, our attempt to link this to social disorganisation remains unresolved. Whereas the area with the lowest level of socio-economic development, which is linked to social disorganisation, was observed to have by far the greatest amount of litter, other factors may (also) be involved. Further research needs to be undertaken to discern the connection to transportation links and people's attachment to spaces. We speculate that the ease of mobility and the lack of attachment to places may be contributing to the noticeable litter problem in the Northeast of England. Furthermore, additional investigation into the lack of effective informal and formal social control is warranted as these also seem to play a role in littering. As one of Britain's biggest problems, it is research that could improve the daily lives of people around the country and the health of the environment.

Note

1 Elementary occupation refers to occupations that 'consist of simple and routine tasks which mainly require the use of hand-held tools and often some physical effort' (International Labour Organisation 2004).

References

Anton, C. and Lawrence, C. 2014. 'Home is where the heart is: The effect of place of residence on place attachment and community participation,' *Journal of Environmental Psychology*, 40(1): 451–461.

Robert, A. 2017. 'Poor areas more likely to be "dirty" communities,' *Third Force News*, Available at: http://thirdforcenews.org.uk/tfn-news/poor-areas-more-likely-to-be-dirty-communities.

Barnes, J. 2006. 'Networks, intervention and retaliation: Informal social control in four English neighbourhoods,' in K. Harris (ed.) *Respect in the Neighbourhood: Why Neighbourliness Matters*, pp. 19–33. Lyme Regis, Dorset, UK: Russell House Publishing.

Bodkin, H. 2018. 'Fly-tipping and speeding: Rural communities living in fear as confidence in police drops,' *The Telegraph*, 23 July. Available at: www.telegraph.co.uk/news/2018/07/22/fly-tipping-speeding-rural-communities-living-fear-confidence/ .

Brandt, A. 2017. 'Illegal dumping as an indicator for community social disorganisation and crime,' Master's Thesis and Graduate Research, San Jose State University.

Brisman, A. 2012. 'Coda: An elevated challenge to "broken windows": The high line (New York),' *Crime Media Culture*, 8(3): 381.

Communities and Local Government Committee. 2015. 'Litter and fly-tipping in England,' in *House of Commons Report*, London: The Stationery Office Limited.

Cooper, T. 2013. 'In defence of litter,' *The Conversation*, August 5, Available at: http://theconversation.com/in-defence-of-litter-15782.

Department for Environment, Food and Rural Affairs. 2006. *Code of Practice on Litter and Refuse*. London: Defra Publications.

Department for Environment, Food and Rural Affairs. 2016. 'Fly-tipping: Council responsibilities,' Available at: www.gov.uk/guidance/fly-tipping-council-responsibilities.

Donnermeyer, J. and DeKeseredy, W. 2014. *Rural Criminology*. London: Routledge.

Eunomia Research and Consulting. 2014. *Waste Crime: Tackling Britain's Dirty Secret*. London: Environmental Services Association Education Trust. Available at: www.esauk.org/application/files/4515/3589/6453/ESAET_Waste_Crime_Tackling_Britains_Dirty_Secret_LIVE.pdf?

Fuller, M. 2017. 'The amount of people fined for littering on this newcastle street will make you think twice,' *ChronicleLive*, 28 August, Available at: www.chroniclelive.co.uk/news/north-east-news/amount-people-fined-littering-newcastle-13538889.

Groombridge, N. 2013. 'Matter all over the place: Litter, criminology and criminal justice,' in N. South and A. Brisman (eds.) *The Routledge International Handbook of Green Criminology*, pp. 394–408. Abingdon, Oxon, UK: Routledge.

Hallsworth, S. and Young, T. 2013. 'Street collectives and group delinquency: Social disorganisation, subcultures and beyond,' in E. McLaughlin and T. Newburn (eds.) *The Sage Handbook of Criminological Theory*, pp. 72–95. London: Sage Publications.

Hexham Town Council. 2012. 'Hexham town plan 2013–2018,' Available at: www.hexhamtowncouncil.gov.uk/wp-content/uploads/2012HexhamTownPlanB.pdf.

Hutchinson, K. 2015. *Wallsend History Tour*. Stroud: Amberly Publishing.

International Labour Organisation. 2004. 'ISCO international standard classification of occupations,' Available at: www.ilo.org/public/english/bureau/stat/isco/isco88/9.htm.

Jack, C. 2005. *Blowin' in the Wind: A Short History of Litter in the Twentieth Century*. Stirling: AHRC Research Centre for Environmental History. Available at: http://139.153.105.44/resources/documents/jack-litter-web.pdf.

Jones, G. 2017. 'Third sector groups urged to cut cost of litter clear-up,' Available at: http://thirdforcenews.org.uk/tfn-news/third-sector-groups-urged-to-cut-cost-of-litter-clear-up.

Kerley, P. 2015. 'What is your 21st century social class,' *BBC NEWS*, Available at: www.bbc.co.uk/news/magazine-34766169.

Kurbrin, C. and Weitzer, R. 2003. 'New directions in social disorganisation theory,' *Journal of Research in Crime and Delinquency*, 40(4): 374–402.

Lewis, A., Turton, P. and Sweetman, T. 2009. 'Litterbugs: How to deal with the problem of littering,' in B. Caldecot (ed.) *Policy Exchange*. London: Policy Exchange. Available at: www.bl.uk/collection-items/litterbugs-how-to-deal-with-the-problem-of-littering.

Lynch, M. and Boggess, L. 2015. 'Ecocities, crime, and justice: Ecocity theory, social disorganisation, and green criminology,' *Sociological Spectrum*, 35(4): 309–328.

Nash, V. and Christie, I. 2003. *Making Sense of Community*. London: Institute for Public Policy Research.

National Rural Crime Network. 2018. 'Living on the edge: Why crime and anti-social behaviour is leaving rural communities and businesses frustrated, undervalued and isolated,' Available at: www.nationalruralcrimenetwork.net/content/uploads/2018/07/National-Rural-Crime-Survey-2018-Report-and-Recommendations.pdf.

NewcastleGateshead. (n.d.) 'Shopping centres and high street,' Available at: www.newcastlegateshead.com/shopping/shopping-centres-and-high-street.

NOMIS. 2017a. 'Labour market profile – Newcastle upon Tyne,' Available at: www.nomisweb.co.uk/reports/lmp/la/1946157065/report.aspx?town=newcastle.

NOMIS. 2017b. 'Labour market profile – Northumberland,' Available at: www.nomisweb.co.uk/reports/lmp/la/1946157061/report.aspx?town=northumberland.

NOMIS. 2017c. 'Labour market profile – North tyneside,' Available at: www.nomisweb.co.uk/reports/lmp/la/1946157066/report.aspx?town=north%20tyneside.

North Tyneside Council. 2017a. 'Fixed penalty notices for dog fouling and littering,' Available at: www.northtyneside.gov.uk/browsedisplay.shtml?p_ID=569190&p_subjectCategory=847.

North Tyneside Council. 2017b. 'History of the park,' Available at: www.northtyneside.gov.uk/browse-display.shtml?p_ID=523070&p_subjectCategory=.

Northumberland County Council. 2016. 'Crackdown continues to keep the county green,' Available at: www.northumberland.gov.uk/News/2016/Mar/Crackdown-continues-to-keep-the-county-green.aspx.

Office for National Statistics. 2016. '2011 census aggregate data,' *UK Data Service*, Available at: http://infuse.ukdataservice.ac.uk/.

Ojedokun, O. 2015. 'The littering attitude scale (LAS): Development and structural validation using data from an indigenous (Nigerian) sample,' *Management of Environmental Quality: An International Journal*, 26(4): 552–565.

Priestley, S. 2017. 'Litter,' in *House of Commons Briefing Paper*, London: The Stationery Office Limited.

Rising Sun Farm. 2015. 'About us: The North Tyneside community farm,' Available at: www.risingsunfarm.org.uk/aboutus.html.

Robinson, F. 2002. 'The North East: A journey through time,' *City*, 6(3): 317–334.

Rose, A. and Davies, B. 2014. 'Not home: The lives of hidden homeless households in unsupported temporary accommodation in England,' *Institute for Public Policy Research Report*, Available at: www.ippr.org/files/publications/pdf/not-home_Dec2014.pdf.

Sampson, R. and Raudenbush, S. 1999. 'Systematic social observation of public spaces: A new look at disorder in urban neighbourhoods,' *American Journal of Sociology*, 105(3): 603–651.

Shaw, C. and McKay, H. 1942. *Juvenile Delinquency in Urban Areas*. Chicago, IL: University Chicago Press.

Stretsesky, P., Long, M. and Lynch, M. 2014. *The Treadmill of Crime: Political Economy and Green Criminology*. Abingdon, Oxon, UK: Routledge.

Tales of the Herring. 2018. 'History of cullercoats,' Available at: www.taleoftheherring.com/cullercoats/history/.

Tjell, J. 2010. 'Littering – a persistent problem,' *Waste Management & Research*, 28(10): 863–864.

Woodland Trust. 2002. 'Urban woodland management guide 2: Litter and fly-tipping,' Available at: www.woodland-trust.org.uk.

Tunnell, K. 2008. 'Illegal dumping: Large and small scale littering in rural kentucky,' *Southern Rural Sociology*, 23(2): 29–42.

Wilson, J. and Kelling, G. 1982. 'Broken windows: The police and neighbourhood safety,' *Atlantic Monthly*, March, 29–38.

39

A short conclusion concerning a questionable future

Avi Brisman and Nigel South

Textbooks and readers often feature educational aids, such as tests and other resources, designed to enhance student understanding of the material in the preceding pages. Although we have envisioned this edition of the Handbook as a compendium rather than a manual of instruction in green criminology, we do hope that it will serve a pedagogical purpose for its readers. As such, we find it appropriate to conclude with a problem-exercise. The exercise differs from that of the first edition.

Name the figure(s) or person(s) who made the following statements:

1 'You know what I could go for? A global warming'.
2 'The concept of global warming was created by and for the Chinese in order to make U.S. manufacturing non-competitive'.
3 'The demonisation of carbon dioxide is just like the demonisation of the poor Jews under Hitler'.
4 'It's really cold outside, they are calling it a major freeze, weeks ahead of normal. Man, we could use a big fat dose of global warming!'
5 'Healthy debate is the lifeblood of American democracy, and global warming has inspired one of the major policy debates of our time. That debate is far from settled. Scientists continue to disagree about the degree and extent of global warming and its connection to the actions of mankind. That debate should be encouraged—in classrooms, public forums, and the halls of Congress. It should not be silenced with threats of prosecution. Dissent is not a crime'.
6 'Wouldn't be bad to have a little of that good old fashioned Global Warming right now!'

Need a hint?

A real, live human being spoke all but one of the above statements.

Need another hint?

The statements were issued in the following years:

1 2002
2 2012

3 2014
4 2015
5 2016
6 2019

Give up?

The first declaration was uttered by 'Sid', a talkative ground sloth, voiced by John Leguizamo, in the computer-animated comedy film, *Ice Age*, directed by Chris Wedge.[1] If you guessed that the other statements were issued by either Donald J. Trump or someone who would, has or is serving as a member of his administration, then, sadly, you are correct. More specifically, Donald Trump tweeted the second and fourth statements prior to and during his candidacy for President of the United States, and the sixth in January 2019 when a snowstorm froze much of the United States.[2] The third statement is attributable to Dr William Happer, a physicist without any formal training in climate science, who serves on the National Security Council as President Trump's deputy assistant for emerging technologies; although he said as much in an interview with CNBC in 2014,[3] his comments resurfaced in late May 2019 in a story by *The New York Times* on how the Trump Administration has hardened an attack on climate science (Davenport and Landler, 2019; see also Schroeder, 2019). Finally, Scott Pruitt (then the Attorney General of Oklahoma) and Luther Strange (then the Attorney General of Alabama) co-authored the fifth statement in a piece in the *National Review* in response to an announcement by a group of Democratic Attorneys General that it would open criminal investigations of oil and gas companies that have disputed the science behind anthropogenic climate change (Pruitt and Strange, 2016).[4]

Essentially, while *all* of the above statements should be the fantastical stuff of Blue Sky Studios, which has produced the *Ice Age* media franchise, and while each successive statement should be met with increasing scorn, we seem to be stuck in a rerun of *Groundhog Day*, the 1993 American comedy film. The difference, however, is that rather than repeatedly reliving the same day (as Bill Murray's character does) and eventually recognising the value of placing the needs of others above one's own selfish desires, we seem to be stuck in a denialist time loop in which we continue to act as if there are no consequences for our actions.

Because the recurrent refrain of those challenging the certainty of anthropogenic climate change is not innocuous (as Kramer and Bradshaw point out in Chapter 9)—because scientific fact is being treated as fairy-tale fiction, while cinematic dramas are unfolding as real-life horrors—because President Trump has 'turned the term "global warming" into a punch line rather than a prognosis' (Davenport and Landler, 2019)—maybe we need to engage in a different kind of exercise than the one offered at the outset of this conclusion. Maybe the message of *Groundhog Day*—an allegory of self-improvement—is too abstruse.

Consider the children's story, *Milo and the Magic Stones* (1997), by Marcus Pfister. The book begins by telling of Milo and other mice, who live on an island in the middle of the sea. The mice love their island, for it provides them with food, shelter and protection from rough storms and waves that pound against the cliffs of the island. During the summers, the mice work hard to collect food, and when winter arrives, the mice huddle in their 'dark, damp caves, dreaming of light and warmth'. One winter, one of the mice—Milo—creeps out of his cave and discovers a strange glowing stone. He brings the stone back to his cave and discovers that not only does it provide light, but also warmth. The stone attracts other mice, who, naturally, want stones of their own for their caves. Just as Milo is about to set off to show the other mice where he found his stone, Balthazar, the wisest of the mice, reminds them that 'The stones belong to the island. If you take something from the island, you must give something in return'.

At this juncture, the book's pages literally split in two, presenting readers with the choice between 'The Happy Ending', which appears on the pages on the top, and 'The Sad Ending', which appears below. In 'The Happy Ending', Milo carves a beautiful sun in a stone about the same size as the glowing one that he has taken and places it where he found the glowing stone. The other mice discover glowing stones like Milo and then, like Milo, each one locates an ordinary stone that he (all the mice appear to be male) decorates and places as a gift where he had taken his glowing stone. From here on out—and with the help of the glowing stones—the winters seem shorter, with the caves less damp and dark. And each year, the mice parade along the cliffs as a special tribute to their beloved island.

In 'The Sad Ending', by contrast, each mouse gathers more stones than he needs. Rather than enjoying the comfort and warmth from the stones, the mice argue and fight over who has the biggest stones, the brightest stones, the most stones. We learn that '[t]he mice were consumed with greed, and as they dug deeper and deeper, the walls of the mountain got thinner and thinner. Before long the mountain was hollowed out completely'. Eventually, the mountain collapses, burying the tunnels; waves flood most of the island. Only Milo and Balthazar remain with the one original stone lighting the one cave that remained. Balthazar laments how the stones could have brought so much happiness, while Milo continues to carve a stone to give to the island as thanks for its magical gift.

Hopefully, the message of *Milo and the Magic Stones* should be clear: either we act in a thoughtful, environmentally responsible manner, taking only what we need and expressing gratitude for what we receive *or* we proceed down the dangerous path of excessive consumption and materialism, and suffer the consequences of greed, envy and environmental pillaging. And while there is always a risk that some might dismiss *Milo and the Magic Stones* on the grounds that the story is simplistic and a little heavy-handed—and that the split pages mid-book are a little gimmicky—few can claim that the moral is recondite. And fewer still can argue that the choice between squabbling and destruction or stewardship and species survival is really much of a choice at all.

To be sure—and as Becktold (2019) reminds us—'[c]limate change isn't a binary—safe or unsafe, screwed or not screwed—but rather a spectrum'. Or, as Roberts (2019) puts it, '[i]n a sense, we're already screwed, at least to some extent. The climate is already changing and it's already taking a measurable toll'. But, as he continues, 'we have some choice in how screwed we are, and that choice will remain open to us no matter how hot it gets'. In other words, unlike Pfister's book, we have more than just two choices. But some of the choices that we make can result in 'sad endings'.

In April 2019, a church sign near where one of us lives (Brisman) offered the following: 'CHANGE IS MORE ABOUT TRUSTING THAN TRYING'. We would respectfully disagree. As *Milo and the Magic Stones* instructs and as many of the chapters in the second edition of this Handbook have attempted to describe—whether it is biodiversity loss, climate change, or pollution—we have choices and opportunities to change our relationships to the Earth. Those changes will require *trying* more than (just) trusting. But hopefully, this volume has demonstrated how and where we need to try (to change)—and why we should try to do so.

Notes

1 www.imdb.com/title/tt0268380/quotes/?tab=qt&ref_=tt_trv_qu.

2 The first tweet appeared on 6 October 2012; the second on 19 October 2015. See www.shortlist.com/news/most-ridiculous-trump-quotes-ever/54443. The third statement was tweeted on 20 January 2019 (see https://twitter.com/realDonaldTrump/status/1086971499725160448 and www.trumptwitterarchive.com/archive/global%20warming; see also Davenport and Landler, 2019; Grandoni, 2019; Plumer, 2019).

3 www.cnbc.com/video/2014/07/14/princeton-prof-shut-up-over-climate-change.html.

4 Scott Pruitt served as Administrator of the Environmental Protection Agency, despite his links to regulated industries and significant philosophical differences with the mission of the agency he was tasked to run (see, e.g., Krugman, 2017; Wittenberg, 2017; see generally Lipton and Ivory, 2017), before resigning in the face of mounting ethics controversies and scandals (Davenport and Landler, 2019); Strange, along with Pruitt, 'came to the defense of ExxonMobil when it fell under investigation by attorneys general from more liberal states seeking information about whether the oil giant failed to disclose material information about climate change' (Mooney, 2016).

References

Becktold, W. 2019. '10 reasons to feel hopeful about climate change in 2019,' *Sierra Magazine*. January 10. Available at: www.sierraclub.org/sierra/10-reasons-feel-hopeful-about-climate-change-2019.

Davenport, C. and Mark, L. 2019. 'In climate fight, trump will put science on trial,' May 28: A1. Published online as 'Trump Administration Hardens Its Attack on Climate Science' on May 27, 2019, at https://www.nytimes.com/2019/05/27/us/politics/trump-climate-science.html.

Grandoni, D. 2019. 'The energy 202: Another winter, another trump call for 'good old fashioned global warming',' *The Washington Post*. January 22. Available at:: www.washingtonpost.com/news/power post/paloma/the-energy-202/2019/01/22/the-energy-202-another-winter-another-trump-call-for-good-old-fashioned-global-warming/5c4640ac1b326b29c3778c59/?utm_term=.cedd0864259c.

Krugman, P. 2017. 'Making America polluted again,' *The New York Times*. August 25: A27. Published online as 'Trump and Pruitt, Making America Polluted Again' on August 25, 2017, at www.nytimes.com/2017/08/25/opinion/trump-pruitt-polluted-climate-.html.

Lipton, E. and Ivory, D. 2017. 'EPA slows enforcement against polluters under Trump,' *Lexington Herald-Leader*. December 11: 8A.

Mooney, C. 2016. 'Trump names Scott Pruitt, Oklahoma attorney general suing EPA on climate change, to head the EPA,' *The Washington Post*. December 8. Available at: www.washingtonpost.com/news/energy-environment/wp/2016/12/07/trump-names-scott-pruitt-oklahoma-attorney-general-suing-epa-on-climate-change-to-head-the-epa/?utm_term=.092decef7f4d.

Pfister, M. 1997. *Milo and the Magical Stones* [*Mats und die Felsmäuse*]. Marianne Martens, trans. New York and London: North-South Books (English translation copyright). [Nord-Süd Verlag AG, Gossau Zürich, Switzerland].

Plumer, B. 2019. 'Wildfires ignite climate debate,' *The New York Times*. March 3: A1. Published online as 'How the Weather Gets Weaponized in Climate Change Messaging' on March 1, 2019, at www.nytimes.com/2019/03/01/climate/weather-climate-change.html.

Pruitt, S. and Strange, L. 2016. 'The climate-change gang,' *National Review*. May 17. Available at: www.nationalreview.com/2016/05/climate-change-attorneys-general/.

Roberts, D. 2019. 'The case for 'conditional optimism' on climate change,' *Vox* January 29. Available at: www.vox.com/energy-and-environment/2018/12/28/18156094/conditional-optimism-climate-change.

Schroeder, R. 2019. 'Trump climate adviser compared 'demonization' of carbon dioxide to Jews' treatment under Hitler,' *MarketWatch*. May 28. Available at: www.marketwatch.com/story/trump-climate-advisor-compared-demonization-of-carbon-dioxide-to-jews-treatment-under-hitler-2019-05-28.

Wittenberg, A. 2017. 'Pruitt stars in industry video promoting WOTUS repeal,' *E&E*. August 21. Available at: www.eenews.net/stories/1060058985.

Index

Locators containing 'n' refer to notes

Made in the USA
Monee, IL
14 September 2026

62978590R00400